THE ROUGH GUIDE TO

Austria

D1347896

There are more than two hundred Rough Guide titles
covering destinations from Alaska to Zimbabwe
and subjects from Acoustic Guitar to Travel Health

Forthcoming travel guides include
The Algarve • The Bahamas • Cambodia • Caribbean Islands
Costa Brava • New York Restaurants • Bolivia • Zanzibar

Forthcoming Reference guides include
Elvis • Online Travel • Internet Radio • Cult TV

Rough Guides on the Internet
www.roughguides.com

ROUGH GUIDE CREDITS

Text editor: Lucy Ratcliffe
Series editor: Mark Ellingham
Editorial: Martin Dunford, Jonathan Buckley, Jo Mead, Kate Berens, Ann-Marie Shaw, Paul Gray, Helena Smith, Judith Bamber, Orla Duane, Olivia Eccleshall, Ruth Blackmore, Geoff Howard, Claire Saunders, Gavin Thomas, Alexander Mark Rogers, Polly Thomas, Joe Staines, Richard Lim, Duncan Clark, Peter Buckley, Sam Thorne, Clifton Wilkinson, David Glen, Alison Murchie, Matthew Teller (UK); Andrew Rosenberg, Stephen Timblin, Yuki Takagaki, Richard Koss (US)
Production: Susanne Hillen, Andy Hilliard, Link Hall, Helen Prior, Julia Bovis, Michelle Draycott, Katie Pringle, Mike Hancock, Zoë Nobes, Rachel Holmes, Andy Turner

Cartography: Melissa Baker, Maxine Repath, Ed Wright, Katie Lloyd-Jones
Picture research: Louise Boulton, Sharon Martins
Online: Kelly Cross, Anja Mutić-Blessing, Jennifer Gold, Audra Epstein, Suzanne Welles (US)
Finance: John Fisher, Gary Singh, Edward Downey, Mark Hall, Tim Bill
Marketing & Publicity: Richard Trillo, Niki Smith, David Wearn, Chloë Roberts, Birgit Hartmann, Claire Southern (UK); Simon Carloss, David Wechsler, Kathleen Rushforth (US)
Administration: Tania Hummel, Demelza Dallow, Julie Sanderson

ACKNOWLEDGEMENTS

Jonathan Bousfield: thanks also to Franca-Maria Kobenter and Claudia Krakolinig of Karntner Tourismus, Heiner Kolbe of the Salzburg State Tourist Board, Maria Altendorfer in Salzburg, Anton Bittner in Klagenfurt, Carmen Fender in Solden, Evy Halder in Bregenz, Karin Hauser in Spittal an der Drau, John and Helga Hinsby in Huntingdon, Marianne Hinterndorfer in Bregenz, Alexandra Kossler in Hall, Michael Kreissl in Lienz, Gerhard Kusternigg in Millstatt, Herbert Lackner in Launsdorf, Harald Londer in St Veit, Lauren Nadrag in Ossiachersee, Heinz Sillober in Innsbruck, Malcolm and Emma Wilkinson in Blackheath and Barbara Wille-Folie in Schwarz.

Rob Humphreys: Thanks to Val for book and Internet research, Gordon for book loans and a great Niederösterreich trip, and, to both for Burgenland. Lastly, thanks to Kate, Stan and Josh, who weathered the storms and the sunstroke in the Salzkammergut, all for the good of research.

Thanks also to Narrell Leffman and Nicky Agate for Basics research, The Map Studio, Romsey, Hants., for mapping; Katie Pringle for setting and David Price for proofreading.

PUBLISHING INFORMATION

This second edition published November 2001 by Rough Guides Ltd, 62–70 Shorts Gardens, London WC2H 9AH. Reprinted March 2002
Distributed by the Penguin Group:
Penguin Books Ltd, 80 Strand, London WC2R ORL
Penguin Putnam, Inc. 375 Hudson Street, NY 10014, USA
Penguin Books Australia Ltd, 487 Maroondah Highway, PO Box 257, Ringwood, Victoria 3134, Australia
Penguin Books Canada Ltd, 10 Alcorn Avenue, Toronto, Ontario, Canada M4V 1E4
Penguin Books (NZ) Ltd, 182–190 Wairau Road, Auckland 10, New Zealand
Typeset in Linotron Univers and Century Old Style to an original design by Andrew Oliver.
Printed in England, by Clays Ltd, St Ives PLC
Illustrations in Part One and Part Three by Edward Briant.

THE ROUGH GUIDE TO

Austria

written and researched by

Jonathan Bousfield and Rob Humphreys

with additional accounts by

Kev Reynolds and Christoph Wagner

ROUGH
GUIDES

We set out to do something different when the first Rough Guide was published in 1982. Mark Ellingham, just out of university, was travelling in Greece. He brought along the popular guides of the day, but found they were all lacking in some way. They were either strong on ruins and museums but went on for pages without mentioning a beach or taverna. Or they were so conscious of the need to save money that they lost sight of Greece's cultural and historical significance. Also, none of the books told him anything about Greece's contemporary life – its politics, its culture, its people, and how they lived.

So with no job in prospect, Mark decided to write his own guidebook, one which aimed to provide practical information that was second to none, detailing the best beaches and the hottest clubs and restaurants, while also giving hard-hitting accounts of every sight, both famous and obscure, and providing up-to-the-minute information on contemporary culture. It was a guide that encouraged independent travellers to find the best of Greece, and was a great success, getting shortlisted for the Thomas Cook travel guide award,

and encouraging Mark, along with three friends, to expand the series.

The Rough Guide list grew rapidly and the letters flooded in, indicating a much broader readership than had been anticipated, but one which uniformly appreciated the Rough Guide mix of practical detail and humour, irreverence and enthusiasm. Things haven't changed. The same four friends who began the series are still the caretakers of the Rough Guide mission today: to provide the most reliable, up-to-date and entertaining information to independent-minded travellers of all ages, on all budgets.

We now publish more than 150 titles and have offices in London and New York. The travel guides are written and researched by a dedicated team of more than 100 authors, based in Britain, Europe, the USA and Australia. We have also created a unique series of phrasebooks to accompany the travel series, along with an acclaimed series of music guides, and a best-selling pocket guide to the Internet and World Wide Web. We also publish comprehensive travel information on our Web site:

www.roughguides.com

HELP US UPDATE

We've gone to a lot of effort to ensure that the second edition of *The Rough Guide to Austria* is accurate and up to date. However, things change – places get "discovered", opening hours are notoriously fickle, restaurants and rooms raise prices or lower standards. If you feel we've got it wrong or left something out, we'd like to know, and if you can remember the address, the price, the time, the phone number, so much the better.

We'll credit all contributions, and send a copy of the next edition (or any other Rough Guide if you prefer) for the best letters. Please mark letters: "Rough Guide Austria Update" and send to:
Rough Guides, 62–70 Shorts Gardens, London WC2H 9AH, or Rough Guides, 4th Floor, 345 Hudson St, New York, NY 10014.
Or send email to: mail@roughguides.co.uk
Online updates about this book can be found on Rough Guides' Web site at www.roughguides.com

THE AUTHORS

Jonathan Bousfield was forced into his first pair of lederhosen at the age of 9 and has been a regular visitor to Austria ever since. In between times he has been the rock critic of the *European* newspaper and has worked on the (now defunct) *Rough Guide to Yugoslavia*, the *Rough Guide to Bulgaria*, written the *Rough Guide to Croatia* and is currently researching the *Rough Guide to the Baltic States*.

Rob Humphreys joined the Rough Guides in 1989, having worked as a failed actor, taxi driver and male model. He has travelled extensively in central and eastern Europe, writing guides to Prague, the Czech and Slovak Republics, and St Petersburg, as well as London. He has lived in London since 1988.

READERS' LETTERS

Thanks to the following people, whose letters and comments contributed to this edition: Mary Ann Daly, Niclas Davidsson, Carol James, Tomaz Jardim, Stewart Kemp, Peter de Leeuw, Ann & David Morton, Brian J. Picken, J.F. Routley, J.S. Clements, Rebecca Rainsford, John Walker, Helen Walton, & apologies to anyone else who wrote in, but, for some reason, has not been credited.

CONTENTS

Introduction x

PART THREE CONTEXTS   547

LIST OF MAPS

MAP SYMBOLS

– – – –	International border	▲	Mountain peak	⊠	Post office
– – ▪ – –	Länder border	⌇⌇	Gorge	✈	Airport
– – – ▪	Chapter division border	♜	Castle	★	Bus stop
══════	Major road	∴	Ruin	🅿	Parking
═════	Minor road	⸸	Church (regional maps)	Ⓤ	U-Bahn
══════	Unpaved road	⛪	Monastery	Ⓢ	S-Bahn
– – – –	Footpath	✡	Synagogue	⊥⊥	Fortifications
▬▬▬▬	Railway	♥	Museum	■	Building
▪▪▪▪▪▪▪	Funicular	⍦	Gardens	⊞	Church (town maps)
●– – –●	Cablecar	⚜	Vineyard	⊹	Cemetery
— —	Ferry route	⬯	Swimming pool	⬚	Jewish Cemetery
~~	River	⛺	Campsite	▦	Park
⚑	Waterfall	⊞	Hospital	▨	National Park
⌂	Cave	ⓘ	Information centre	⬚	Marsh

INTRODUCTION

I t's the spectacular, snowcapped mountains of regions like the Tyrol that provide the most familiar images of **Austria** – a landscape of jagged peaks and rampaging rivers, giving way to green pastures studded with onion-domed churches. Yet Austria is by no means all alpine vistas: the country stretches across central Europe for some 700km, from the shores of the Bodensee in the west to the edge of the flat Hungarian plain in the east. Far removed from the archetype are the wetlands and reed beds of Burgenland, and the dramatic sequence of stopes that carve their way up the Erzberg in Styria. In Upper and Lower Austria in particular, a predominantly low-key landscape of gentle rolling hills and vineyards can come as something of a surprise to first-time visitors. Yet this fertile, low-lying northern half of the country is, in fact, where the majority of Austrians live and work, many of them within commuting distance of the capital, **Vienna** – the country's chief tourist destination after the alpine regions.

For all its bucolic charm and fondness for the days of empire, when Vienna sat at the centre of the vast, multinational Habsburg dynasty, Austria today is thoroughly modern, clean, efficient and eminently civilized, with uniformly excellent tourist facilities. Like neighbouring Switzerland, it's also a supremely law-abiding nation, where no one jaywalks or drops litter, and the trains and trams run on time. Whether you're staying in one of the popular skiing, hiking or spa resorts, or in an out-of-the-way Gasthof, you're likely to experience "*Gemütlichkeit*" – a typically Austrian term expressing a mixture of cosiness and hospitality – at some point during your visit.

Looking at the country at the close of the twentieth century – stable, conservative and wealthy – you wouldn't think that Austria had spent the first half of the century struggling to find a national identity. After all, it was only in 1918, when the Habsburg Empire disintegrated, that the idea of a modern Austrian nation was born. The new republic, with a population of just eight million reluctant citizens, was riven by left- and right-wing political violence and, as a result, the majority of Austrians were wildly enthusiastic about the Anschluss with Nazi Germany in 1938. The price of Austria's participation, and ultimately defeat, in World War II, however, was Allied occupation. For ten years the country was split, like Germany, into Soviet, American, British and French zones. As a gesture of détente, the Soviets finally agreed to withdraw their troops, in return for Austria's "permanent neutrality". At this point, Austria turned over a new leaf, and recast itself as a model of consensus politics, with an almost Scandinavian emphasis on social policy as the guiding principle of national life. Postwar stability saw the growth of a genuine patriotism, while the end of the Cold War put the country, and its capital, back at the heart of Europe.

In 1995, Austria became a full member of the European Union, a move that for many was a sign that the country had finally entered the mainstream of European politics. From time to time, Austria's more reactionary elements have attracted widespread media attention, most notably during the Waldheim affair, when the wartime record of the president was called into question, and in the recent rise of the Far Right under the charismatic Jörg Haider. But the reality is that the Socialist party retains the strongest influence in government, as it has for much of the postwar period, and the country's political stability, for the most part, continues intact.

Where to go

There's a lot to be said for concentrating on just one or two regions, rather than trying to cover a bit of everything in one trip – you could happily spend a week or two in any one of the Austrian provinces, or *Länder*. Austria's unique combination of outdoor attractions and classic urban centres ensures that you can pack a lot of variety into your stay: take in some fresh air at a high altitude, linger over one of the country's world-class art collections, make the most of a musical heritage second to none, or select any number from the list of recommended highlights below.

Without a visit to **Vienna** you'll return home with only half the picture. Built on a grand scale as seat of the Habsburg Empire, it's a place that positively drips with imperial nostalgia. The pickings are rich, with the old palaces of the Hofburg and Schönbrunn high on the list, as are the cultural offerings from the gargantuan art collection at the Kunsthistorisches Museum and the hi-tech applied-arts displays of the MAK. Equally compelling, nowadays, are the ghosts of Vienna's golden age at the end of the nineteenth century, when the likes of Freud, Klimt, Schiele and Schönberg frequented the city's cafés. The city boasts some wonderful Jugendstil and early modernist buildings and a bevy of traditional fin-de-siècle cafés patrolled by waiters in tuxedos. Last, but by no means least, Vienna is by far the best place in the country for nightlife, and that means everything from top-class opera to techno.

Salzburg is no less intoxicating. Its Altstadt contains the country's most concentrated ensemble of Baroque architecture, and the Hohensalzburg fortress is arguably the country's most impressive medieval castle. A substantial musical pedigree is ensured by the city's status as the birthplace of Mozart and venue of the Salzburg Festival, one of the world's most renowned celebrations of classical music and theatre. Of Austria's other regional capitals, **Innsbruck** combines both a buzzing nightlife and close proximity to some of the Tyrol's highest peaks to make it one of Austria's most popular destinations. Its attractive and largely medieval city centre focuses on the Hofkirche, site of the memorial to sixteenth-century Habsburg strongman Emperor Maximilian I. In the Styrian capital, **Graz**, main attractions include the town centre, the fine-art collections of the Landesmuseum Joanneum and the Baroque Eggenberg Palace. Austria's second largest city is also a good base from which to venture out into the vineyards and pumpkin fields of the rural southeast.

Explorations down back streets of Austria's small **medieval towns**, many of which are still enclosed by their original walls, will reward you with hidden arcaded courtyards, tinkling fountains and overflowing flower boxes: Freistadt in Upper Austria, Hall in the Tyrol and Friesach in Carinthia present the pick of the bunch. Lower Austria has the country's highest concentration of **monasteries**, ranging from the Baroque excess of Melk, Altenburg and Zwettl to the likes of Heiligenkreuz, built on the cusp of the stylistic transition from Romanesque to Gothic. For unadulterated Romanesque architecture, head for Gurk in Carinthia; for Rococo floridity, Wilhering in Upper Austria is hard to beat. Austria also holds a bewildering variety of **castles and chateaux**, from fortified seats such as Forchtenstein in Burgenland to luxury aristocratic piles like Artstetten in Lower Austria. The two finest imperial palaces are the magnificent Baroque residence of Schönbrunn, on the outskirts of Vienna, and Schloss Ambras, the archduke Ferdinand of Tyrol's Renaissance treasure-trove near Innsbruck.

Musical pilgrimages are possible to the birthplaces or resting places of such luminaries as Beethoven, Bruckner, Haydn, Liszt, Mozart, Schönberg and Schubert. The country's top **music festivals**, among them the Salzburg Festival, the Haydn Festival in Eisenstadt and the chamber music festival in Lockenhaus, draw international performers and audiences alike. At both the Bregenz Festival and the operetta festival in Mörbisch, floating stages host top-class performances against a shimmering backdrop.

Austria's main **lakeland area** is the Salzkammergut, where the Wolfgangsee, Mondsee, Traunsee and Hallstättersee offer a combination of water-based pursuits and stunning scenery. To the south, the Carinthian lakes of the Wörthersee, Ossiachersee and Millstättersee boast good bathing, boating and windsurfing facilities. In the far east of the country, the reed-encircled Neusiedlersee, Austria's only steppe lake, provides a total contrast, and an opportunity to marry beach culture with a spot of bird-watching.

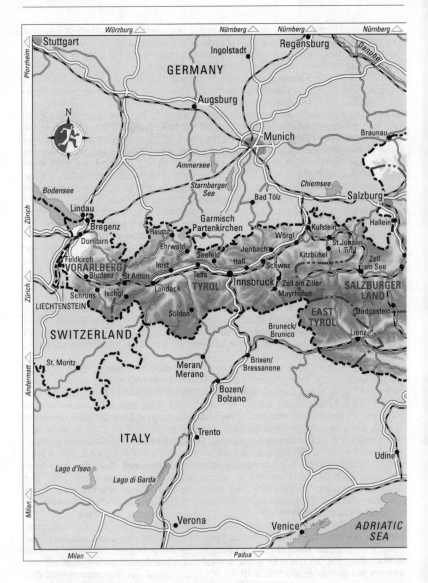

Austria forms one of Europe's most mountainous countries, yet an excellent network of transport links puts even the dizziest of heights within reach. Key summer **hiking** areas are the alpine regions of western Austria, stretching from northeastern Styria and eastern Carinthia through the Salzkammergut, Salzburger Land, Tyrol and Vorarlberg. For **snow sports**, the Salzburger Land, Tyrol and Vorarlberg boast the highest concentration and widest range of modern, fully equipped resorts.

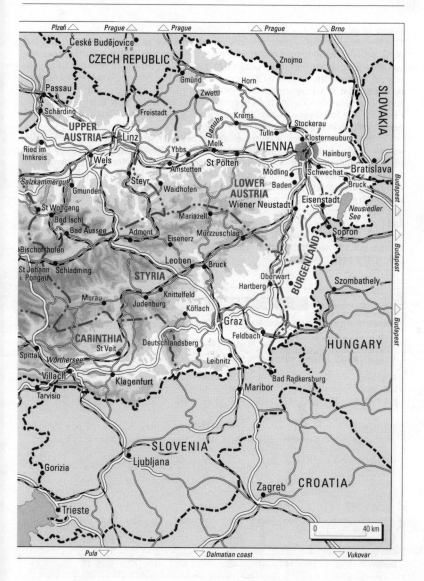

Finally, a great deal of Austria's industrial heritage has been put to good touristic effect, and many of the **show-mines** count among top attractions. If you have time to visit only one of them, pick from the following: the iron-ore workings at Eisenerz in Styria, the salt mine at Bad Dürrnberg in the Salzburger Land, the salt mine above Hallstatt in the Salzkammergut, the lead mine at Bad Bleiberg in Carinthia, and the silver mine at Schwaz in the Tyrol.

When to go

The best time to visit Austria depends on whether you're aiming for urban or rural parts. Most of the mountain resorts, for example, have **two distinct tourist seasons**, one for winter sports enthusiasts, the other for summer hikers. In between times, you may find many of the tourist facilities closed. More urban centres, however, act as **year-round tourist destinations**, with the number of visitors swelling during peak holidays and annual festivals – Vienna pulls in crowds over Christmas, New Year and, of course, Fasching (the ball season), while the Salzburg Festival ensures a steady stream of well-heeled visitors in July and August.

For the best of the warm weather, plan to go between **April and October** – Austrian summers, in particular, are reliably warm, but not overpoweringly so. If you're skiing, you can pretty much guarantee a good covering of snow from **November onwards to April**. Away from the ski resorts, winter travel can't really be recommended, since the weather can be pretty wet and miserable. Weather conditions vary only slightly across the country, with the alpine regions decidedly cooler, the lowland regions in the north and east enduring more continental conditions of colder winters and hotter summers, and the southeast of the country enjoying longer, warmer, almost Mediterranean summers. Be aware that whatever the season, if you're at a high altitude, the weather can change quickly and dramatically. The possibility of a thundery shower exists at any time of the year.

AUSTRIA'S CLIMATE

Average maximum/minimum daily temperatures in degrees Celsius/and monthly rainfall in millimetres.

Innsbruck

	Jan	Feb	March	April	May	June	July	Aug	Sept	Oct	Nov	Dec
Max Temp	1	4	11	16	20	24	25	24	21	15	8	2
Min Temp	-7	-5	0	4	8	11	13	12	10	5	0	-4
Rainfall	54	49	41	52	73	110	110	108	81	67	53	46

Klagenfurt

	Jan	Feb	March	April	May	June	July	Aug	Sept	Oct	Nov	Dec
Max Temp	-1	3	9	15	20	23	25	24	20	14	6	1
Min Temp	-9	-7	-2	3	7	11	13	12	10	5	0	-4
Rainfall	41	45	39	71	88	125	125	104	83	89	75	52

Vienna

	Jan	Feb	March	April	May	June	July	Aug	Sept	Oct	Nov	Dec
Max Temp	1	3	8	15	19	23	25	24	20	14	7	3
Min Temp	-4	-3	-1	6	10	14	15	15	11	7	3	-1
Rainfall	39	44	44	45	70	67	84	72	42	56	52	45

THE

BASICS

GETTING THERE FROM BRITAIN

The easiest way to get to Austria from Britain is by plane, with direct flights from London to Vienna, Salzburg or Innsbruck taking around two hours, and those from the rest of Britain, only a fraction longer. Trains represent a viable alternative if you're keen on overland travel and like the idea of being able to stop off en route; without stopping off, it takes around eighteen hours to get from London to Vienna, Salzburg or Innsbruck. Travelling by bus is the cheapest option, but also the most time-consuming, taking a full twenty-four hours.

FLIGHTS FROM BRITAIN

A **scheduled flight** is the most obvious way to go: Vienna is Austria's chief international gateway, with Salzburg and Innsbruck receiving mostly direct charter flights from Britain. Travellers bound for provincial capitals like Graz, Klagenfurt and Linz must first fly to Vienna and connect with an internal flight or take the train. If you're heading for Salzburg or western Austria, Munich and Zurich are better gateways to the country than Vienna.

The principal **carriers** are Austrian Airlines, British Airways, Lauda Air, and the ticketless air-

AIRLINES

Air France ☎0845/084 5111, *www.airfrance.fr*. Flights to Vienna and Innsbruck from London (and elsewhere in the UK) via Paris.

Austrian Airlines ☎0845/601 0948, *www.aua.com*. Nonstop flights from Heathrow to Vienna, with onward flights to all Austrian airports.

British Airways ☎0385/722 2111, *www.britishairways.com*. Daily nonstop flights from Heathrow to Vienna.

Buzz ☎0870/240 7070, *www.buzzaway.com*. Daily nonstop flights from Stansted to Vienna. Booking by phone and Internet only, ticketless travel, no free inflight meals.

Crossair ☎020/7434 7300, *www.crossair.ch*. A subsidiary of Swissair with daily nonstop flights to Zürich from London City and around the UK.

EasyJet ☎0870/600 0000, *www.easyjet.com*. Daily nonstop flights from Luton to Zürich. Booking by phone and Internet only, ticketless travel, no free inflight meals and unnumbered seating on the plane.

Go ☎0845/605 4321, *www.go-fly.com*. Daily nonstop flights from Stansted to Munich.

Booking by phone and Internet only, ticketless travel, no free inflight meals.

KLM Direct ☎0870/507 4074, *www.klmuk.com*. Flights from virtually all UK airports to Amsterdam, with easy connections to Vienna and Salzburg.

Lauda Air ☎020/7630 5924, *www.laudaair.com*. Daily nonstop flights from Gatwick and Manchester to Vienna, with connections to most Austrian airports.

Lufthansa ☎0845/773 7747, *www.lufthansa.co.uk*. Heathrow, London City, Stansted, Birmingham and Manchester to Frankfurt, with onward flights to Vienna and Salzburg.

Ryanair ☎0870/333 1231, *www.ryanair.co.uk*. Daily nonstop flights from Stansted to Salzburg. Ticketless travel, no free inflight meals and unnumbered seating on the plane.

Swissair ☎020/7434 7300, *www.swissair.com*. Nonstop flights into Zürich from London Heathrow, Stansted and around the UK, plus onward flights to Vienna, Salzburg, Innsbruck and Linz

line Buzz, all of which offer nonstop flights from London to Vienna. Lauda Air and Austrian Airlines also fly direct from Manchester. The discount airline Ryanair now flies direct from London to Salzburg, and two other ticketless airlines, EasyJet and Go fly to Zurich and Munich respectively, and are worth considering if you're heading for western Austria. Flights operated by KLM, Air France and Lufthansa require you to make at least one stop on the ground at their hubs, but can – along with BA – offer enormous flexibility of UK departure points.

The most competitive **fares** nowadays are almost always with the new discount airlines, which don't offer free inflight meals or other creature comforts. Buzz regularly offer fares of around £100 return from Stansted to **Vienna**, while Ryanair offer the same deal from Stansted to Salzburg. The more established airlines regularly try and compete with these fares, but at other times, a standard economy fare from London or Manchester to Vienna with British Airways, Austrian Airlines or Lauda Air can cost you more like £200 return. Fares can vary slightly according to season, tending to be highest from April to

October and around Christmas. However, price is determined more by the flexibility of the ticket and the time of the day and week in which you travel. The cheapest tickets tend to be non-changeable, non-refundable, midweek flights, valid for one month, and including a Saturday night away.

During the skiing season (roughly December to early April), and at the height of summer (July & August), package tour operators like Airtours and Crystal Holidays run frequent **charter** flights to **Salzburg** or **Innsbruck** from Gatwick, Manchester, and other British airports. These operators will happily sell you flight-only deals for around £100 return. If you can't find a suitable charter flight, you may well have to change planes, which can push the price to well over £200 return. However, this might still represent good value if you're flying from anywhere other than London, using an airline such as Air France, Lufthansa, KLM Direct or Swissair.

A cheaper alternative, if you're heading for Salzburg or the Tyrol is to take advantage of Go's £80 saver returns from Stansted to **Munich**, which is only around two hours away by bus or

---

DISCOUNT FLIGHT AGENTS

The following are sites worth checking out in your pursuit of a cheap deal: *www.cheaptickets.com*, *www.cheapflights.com*, *www.lastminute.com*, *www.deckchair.com*.

Flightbookers, 177–178 Tottenham Court Rd, London W1P 0LX (☎020/7757 2000, *www.ebookers.com*); Gatwick Airport, South Terminal inside the train station (daily 8am–10pm; ☎01293/568300). Low fares on an extensive offering of scheduled flights.
North South Travel, Moulsham Mill Centre, Parkway, Chelmsford, Essex CM2 7PX (☎01245/608291, *www.northsouthtravel.co.uk*). Friendly, competitive travel agency, offering discounted fares worldwide – profits are used to support projects in the developing world, especially the promotion of sustainable tourism.
STA Travel, 86 Old Brompton Rd, London SW7 3LH; 117 Euston Rd, London NW1 2SX; 38 Store St, London WC1E 7BZ; 11 Goodge St, London W1 (☎020/7361 6145, *www.statravel.co.uk*); 25 Queen's Rd, Bristol BS8 1QE (☎0117/929 4399); 38 Sidney St, Cambridge CB2 3HX (☎01223/366966); 75 Deansgate, Manchester M3 2BW (☎0161/834 0668); 88 Vicar Lane,

Leeds LS1 7JH (☎0113/244 9212); 36 George St, Oxford OX1 2OJ (☎01865/792800); and other branches in Aberdeen, Birmingham, Canterbury, Cardiff, Coventry, Durham, Glasgow, Liverpool, Loughborough, Newcastle-upon-Tyne, Nottingham, Sheffield and Warwick. Worldwide specialists in low-cost flights and tours for students and under-26s, though other customers also welcome. Also offices abroad.
Trailfinders, 215 Kensington High St, London W6 6BD (European ☎020/7937 1234, *www.trailfinders.com*); 58 Deansgate, Manchester M3 2FF (☎0161/839 6969); 254–284 Sauchiehall St, Glasgow G2 3EH (☎0141/353 2224); 22–24 The Priory Queensway, Birmingham B4 6BS (☎0121/236 1234); 48 Corn St, Bristol BS1 1HQ (☎0117/929 9000). One of the best-informed and most efficient agents for independent travellers; all branches open daily until 6pm. Student/youth travel specialists, with over fifty branches (some in YHA shops and on university campuses) all over Britain.

train from Innsbruck and Salzburg (and therefore much closer than Vienna). For Innsbruck, buses leave directly from the airport; for Salzburg, you must catch the S-Bahn to Munich train station and catch the train from there. For the Vorarlberg or the Tyrol, you could also fly EasyJet from Luton to **Zurich** for around £100 return. Direct trains to Innsbruck leave from the airport station itself and take around four hours. Bear in mind, however, the cost of a return ticket from Zurich or Munich to Austria, which will be around £50. Car journey times from Munich and Zurich are about the same as the bus and train, though car rental in Switzerland can be nastily expensive compared to EU countries.

Finding the best fare involves ringing round a few of the discount flight agents listed in the box opposite, comparing prices and routeings, or consulting Buzz, Go or EasyJet by phoning or via the Internet (they don't deal with agents, thus cutting out any commission). **Students and those under 26** can take advantage of discounted tickets – STA Travel and Usit Campus are your best bet for these, and they're worth calling even if you're not under 26, since they also offer highly competitive budget fares to all-comers.

PACKAGES AND CITY BREAKS

Package holiday deals can be worth considering, saving you the hassle of having to organize things for yourself. As a general rule, your accommodation will cost less when booked as a package, than when arranged independently. That said, you won't always get the most imaginative choice of hotel if you book through a travel agent.

SUMMER PACKAGES

Most high-street travel agents will have summer brochures that include "Lakes and Mountains" packages. Although the summer packages tend to focus on mountainous, western Austria, you can use your package resort as a jumping-off point for **side-trips** to destinations like Innsbruck, Salzburg, or even Vienna. Some of the bigger **alpine centres** (Kitzbühel, Zell am See and the like) are situated on major road and rail routes as well, and are therefore good bases from which to explore a large swath of western Austria.

Staying in less accessible **alpine valley resorts** – Alpbach, Söll, Pfunds and Galtür are among the most idyllic – means, if you want to roam further afield you'll be dependent on local

bus routes (which are adequate, but time-consuming), on coach tours offered by the local rep, or on self-organized car rental. It's also worth mentioning that the kind of après-ski **nightlife** that lightens up the alpine resorts in winter is usually conspicuous by its absence in summer, during which a fair proportion of bars and restaurants close down. Perhaps the best **rural/urban mix** is provided by the resorts of the **Salzkammergut** (St Wolfgang and St Gilgen are the most popular; Mondsee is a good alternative), which provide immediate access to a wide range of both lake and mountain scenery, and are within striking distance of Salzburg.

Many of the summer-package operators assume that their clients are interested in **walking** to some degree, and will either provide a range of free guided rambles as part of the package or point you in the direction of the short guided walks offered by local tourist offices over the summer. If you want to tackle a more demanding walking itinerary and prefer to do so in the company of a guided group, specialist operators like Ramblers Holidays and Waymark offer a selection of seven- and fourteen-day walking holidays, catering for a range of abilities. Most involve overnight accommodation in a hotel, with daily expeditions into the mountains, although some guided hut-to-hut walks are available (for more on which, see p.39). Some of the big tour operators (notably Thomson) also offer walking tours, such as a walk along a stretch of the Danube valley – these are usually easy-going affairs involving three to four hours' optional walking per day, with non-walkers and baggage transferred by bus to the next stop-off point.

The **season** for summer packages usually runs from mid-May to late September, with the cheapest deals falling in the first week or two of the season. The peak period, from late July to late August, is the most expensive time of the year to travel. **Prices** per person for seven days (assuming half-board in a double room in a three-star hotel) start at about £400 across the whole of Austria in mid-May, even in such traditionally expensive resorts as Kitzbühel and Seefeld. By contrast, peak-period prices for seven days in four-star hotels can rise to £700 or more.

Most summer packages involve travelling to Austria by plane, although the holidays offered by **coach travel** specialists (notably Shearings and Wallace Arnold) are worth considering – the range of destinations on offer is essentially the

PACKAGE AND SPECIALIST OPERATORS

Airtours, Wavell House, Holcombe Rd, Helmshore, Rossendale, Lancashire BB4 4NB (☎01706/260000, *www.airtours.co.uk*). Winter and summer packages in all major resort areas.

Anglo-Dutch Sports, 30a Foxgrove Rd, Beckenham BR3 5BD (☎0181/289 2808, *www.anglodutchsports.co.uk*). Seven-day cycling tours along the Danube from Passau to Vienna.

Austrian Holidays, Fifth Floor, Swiss Centre, 10 Wardour St, London W1 (☎020/7434 7399, *www.austrianholidays.co.uk*). Austrian package-tour specialist run by Austrian Airlines. City breaks in Vienna and Salzburg.

Crystal Holidays, King's Place, Wood St, Kingston-upon-Thames, Surrey KT1 1JY (☎0870/848 7000, *www.crstalski.co.uk* & *www.crystallakes.co.uk*). Impressive choice of winter and summer packages, and flight-only deals from all over the UK into Salzburg and Innsbruck. Also available are city breaks in Vienna and two-centre summer holidays combining a few days in Salzburg with an Austrian alpine resort.

Exodus, 9 Weir Rd, London SW12 0LT (☎020/8780 4444, *www.exodus.co.uk*). Experienced adventure tour operator running excellent small-group walking and cycling tours (or a combination of the two) in the Tyrolean Alps.

First Choice, First Choice House, Peel Cross Rd, Salford, Manchester M5 2AN (☎0870/750 0499 for flights; ☎0870/750 0001 for package holi-

days; *www.firstchoice.co.uk*). Flights-only deals to Salzburg and Innsbruck or a wide range of winter and summer packages, including mountain village resorts in the Tyrol and lakeside resorts in the Salzkammergut.

Interhome, 383 Richmond Rd, Twickenham TW1 2EF (☎020/8891 1294, *www.interhome.co.uk*). Specializes in ski-drive, fly-drive, accommodation-only and self-catering chalet/apartment packages to the Tyrol and Vorarlberg.

Habsburg Heritage Cultural Tours, 158 Rosendale Rd, London SE21 8LG (☎020/8761 0444). Highbrow cultural tours, including tailor-made visits to Eisenstadt for the International Haydn Festival (September) or to the Vorarlberg for the Schubertiade festival (June).

Inghams, 10–18 Putney Hill, London SW15 (☎020/8780 4444, *www.inghams.co.uk*). Major operator with a big range of skiing and Lakes & Mountains holidays, in the Tyrol, Vorarlberg, Salzburger Land and Salzkammergut, as well as flight-only deals and city breaks to Vienna.

Made to Measure, 57 East St, Chichester, West Sussex PO19 1HL (☎01243/533333, *www.madetomeasureholidays.com*). Luxury package-tour specialist with retail and "romantic escape" (off-the-peg) packages based in Vienna, Salzburg and Innsbruck, as well as more specialized "made-to-measure" tours.

Martin Randall Travel, 10 Barley Mow Passage, London W4 (☎020/8742 3355,

same. Most of the coach-based packages include a (free) pick-up service from the area of the UK in which you live, but the subsequent journey across Europe can be gruelling: you may have to spend one night on the coach on both your outward and return journeys, though some options allow for overnight stops in hotels. An advantage of a coach-based package is that they tend to be slightly cheaper, with a nine-day peak-season trip, staying in Kitzbühel or a Salzkammergut resort, weighing in at around £400.

CITY BREAKS

Several tour operators offer **city breaks** in Vienna, Salzburg and Innsbruck. Most of these are simple flight-and-accommodation deals, with prices depending on the grade of hotel you choose (most companies offer a choice). Three

nights' accommodation in a three-star hotel in Vienna, Salzburg or Innsbruck, plus return flights from London, can cost anything from £200 to £350 depending on the season. It's worth bearing in mind, too, that city breaks to Innsbruck and Salzburg often use Munich airport: your transfer from there to your hotel will be included in the price of the holiday, but it will add an extra couple of hours to your journey time. If you've more money to spend, it's worth checking agents specializing in **cultural or historical tours** (such as Martin Randall and Habsburg Heritage) who arrange such extras as opera and theatre tickets, visits to music festivals, as well as flight and accommodation – for which, of course, you pay a hefty (if all-inclusive) price. **Cruises** along the River Danube – which include a few leisurely days in Austria, and take in neighbouring coun-

www.martinrandall.com). Small-group cultural tours, led by experts on art, archeology or music. Tours include a cruise down the Danube, a Mozartian trip to Salzburg, the Haydn Festival in Eisenstadt and a Christmas visit to Vienna.

Mondial Travel, The Four Wents, Goudhurst Rd, Cranbrook, Kent TN17 2QD (☎01580/714714, www.mondialtravel.co.uk). Specialists in flights and accommodation for Central and Eastern Europe, with two-, three- and four-night city breaks to Vienna.

Neilson, 2–4 Godwin St Bradford BD1 2ST (☎0870/601 0425, www.neilson.com). Lots of skiing and snowboarding packages in the Tyrol and Salzburger Land.

New Millennium, Greville Court, 1665 High Street, Knowle, West Midlands B93 0LL (☎01564/776192, www.millennium-holidays .com). Very cheap package holidays to the Tyrol, travelling either by coach or plane (or both).

Ramblers Holidays, PO Box 43, Welwyn Garden City, Hertfordshire AL8 6PQ (☎01707/331133, info@ramblersholidays.co.uk). Long-established and reputable walking-holiday specialist offering organized trips to the Austrian Alps.

Shearings, Miry Lane, Wigan, Lancashire WN3 4AG (☎01942/824824, www.shearingsholidays.com). Coach, flight or train packages in spring and summer centred on Tyrolean and Salzkammergut resorts, plus packages to Vienna.

Tall Stories, 67a High St, Walton on Thames, Surrey KT12 1DJ (☎01932/252002, www .tallstories.co.uk). Summer adventure sports multi-activity packages based in Zell am See, involving mountain biking, paragliding, canyoning and white-water rafting, plus winter skiing and snowboarding packages on the Kitzsteinhorn Glacier.

Thomson, Greater London House, Hampstead Rd, London NW1 7SD (☎0870/606 1470 for skiing, lakes and mountains; ☎0870/606 1476 for city breaks; www.thomson.co.uk). Full range of skiing options, and probably the widest range of Lakes & Mountains-style packages, walking tours and a Danube cruise.

Travelscene, 11–15 St Ann's Rd, Harrow, Middlesex (☎020/8427 8800, www.travelscene.co.uk). City breaks to Vienna, Salzburg and Innsbruck.

Wallace Arnold, Gelderd Rd, Leeds LS12 6DH (☎0113/263 6456 or 020/8686 9833, www .wallacearnold.com). Coach holidays in summer to Salzburg, Vienna and the main Tyrolean and Salzkammergut resorts.

Waymark Holidays, 44 Windsor Rd, Slough SL1 2EJ (☎01753/516477). One and two-week walking holidays or cross-country skiing in the Tyrol.

Worldwide Journeys/Eurocity Breaks, 243 Stevenson Way, London NW1 2HD (☎020/7388 0888, www.j.uk.com). City breaks to Vienna.

---

tries as well – are offered by a couple of operators, notably Thomson and Habsburg Heritage.

WINTER PACKAGES

In the **alpine areas** of Austria (Vorarlberg, the Tyrol, the Salzburger Land, much of Carinthia and northwestern Styria), almost any settlement within chairlift distance of a serviceable slope has undergone tourist development to some degree, and the range of Austrian destinations offered by the large package-tour companies is huge. Even for non-skiers, a winter package presents a good way of enjoying alpine Austria at its snowy best.

The factors that will influence your choice of resort are covered in more detail under "Skiing and snowboarding" on p.56. Suffice it to say here that a winter package is usually cheaper than a ski trip organized independently, especially if any

extras (such as lift passes, boot and pole rental, lessons) are included in the price of the holiday. There's also a growing number of all-inclusive holidays on offer, in which you'll get full board as well as most of your drinks free. Accommodation is usually in a **hotel** or **pension**, although the number of **self-catering apartments** on offer is on the increase.

The **season** for winter packages runs from mid-December to early April, with the **peak** periods occurring between late December and early January, and early February to mid-March. Staying in a small two-star hotel, a week in one of the cheaper resorts (such as Alpbach, Mayrhofen or Söll) at the beginning or end of the season **costs** as little as £350, rising to £450 in mid-February. Prices in more fashionable resorts like Kitzbühel and St Anton aren't much higher, provided you stick to simple bed-and-breakfast accommodation, although rates rise steeply once you break into the three- and four-star hotel bracket, where rooms are also much more likely to be offered on a half-board basis. A free lift pass is included in some deals; otherwise, expect to spend an additional £100 per week on a lift pass, plus £50 per week on skis and boot hire and £100 per week on skiing lessons (depending on your requirements). Alternatively, you may find that you can get all the above in a package for around £200 for a week.

BY TRAIN

Travelling **by train** is a pleasantly old-fashioned, and extremely leisurely way to reach Austria. However, you're unlikely to save any money on the air fare; in fact, you may end up paying a bit more.

THE ROUTES

Which train route you choose really depends on which part of Austria you're visiting. From **London to Vienna** takes around eighteen hours by train if you go via the Channel Tunnel. By catching a train at around 2pm from London Waterloo International, you can arrive at Brussels Midi with an hour to spare before taking the Brussels–Vienna overnight service, which will get you into Vienna at around 9.45am.

Although you can simply crash out on the seats, you won't get much sleep as the ticket inspectors wake you up at regular intervals. To travel in more comfort, it's best to book a **couchette** (around £12–17 extra each way on top of the price of the ticket) before you leave. Couchettes are mixed sex and allow little privacy but you do get the chance of an unbroken night and free rolls and coffee in the morning. For your very own compartment, you'll need to book a berth in a **sleeper** (around £50 extra each way) – and take a friend to share it with. Sleeper compartments are either two-berth or three-berth (the latter being slightly cheaper). If you're travelling alone, however, you will not be required to share with passengers of the opposite sex. For sole occupancy of a sleeper, you must first purchase a first-class ticket.

If you're aiming for **Salzburg** you can catch the overnight train from Brussels to Munich, from where there are more or less hourly trains on to Salzburg; alternatively, you can change at Cologne and get a direct overnight train to Salzburg from there. For **Innsbruck**, you can also catch the overnight train from Brussels to Munich and change; however, you have another option of travelling via Paris and through Switzerland, though you have to cross Paris, and change two more times to complete your journey.

If you absolutely don't want to travel via Eurostar, it is still possible to travel from London to Brussels **via the ferry to Ostend**, though you may not save any money. Trains leave from Charing Cross for Dover Priory, and use the catamaran service Dover to Ostend. This leg of the journey takes roughly eight hours.

TRAIN INFORMATION & TICKETS

European Rail ☎020/7387 0444, *www.europeanrail.com*. Travel agency specializing in getting the best deal on international rail tickets.

Eurostar ☎0990/186186, *www.eurostar.com*. Latest fares and youth discounts (plus on-line booking) on the London–Paris and London–Brussels Eurostar service, but no bookings for through trains to Austria.

German Railways ☎0870/243 5363, *www.bahn.de*. Competitive discounted fares for any journey from London across Europe with very competitive prices for those journeys that pass through the German railway system.

Rail Europe ☎0870/584 8848, *www.raileurope.co.uk*. SNCF-owned information and ticket agent for all European passes and journeys from London or Ashford.

Thomas Cook Publishers of the famous red *Thomas Cook European Timetable* (£9.50), detailing schedules of over 50,000 trains in Europe, as well as timings of over 200 ferry routes and rail-connecting bus services. Updated monthly; main changes are in June and October editions. Available from P.O. Box 227, Peterborough PE3 6PU (☎01733/503571), or from high-street branches or main train stations across the UK.

USIT Campus ☎0870/240 1010, *www.usitcampus.co.uk*. Discounted fares on rail passes and Eurostar tickets only.

TICKETS AND PASSES

Fares for continental rail travel are much more flexible than they used to be, so it's worth shopping around for the best deal rather than taking the first offer you get. European Rail are adept at working out the cheapest deal available, which is usually with German Railways, who regularly offer a return ticket London–Vienna at around £200 (including couchettes). To qualify for the most heavily discounted fares, however, there are usually various restrictions: you may have to stay over a Saturday night, and your Eurostar ticket may well be non-exchangeable and non-refundable. If you're travelling with one or more companions, you may also be eligible for a further discount.

Virtually the only way **to buy** an international train ticket at the moment is via a travel agent or over the phone via European Rail, Rail Europe or German Railways, although the latter two can only book you a ticket from London or Ashford. For the journey within the UK, you must contact the relevant private train company or phone National Rail Enquiries (☎08457/484950). The only British train stations that can sell you an international train ticket over the counter are London's Euston and Charing Cross stations, though their prices are far from competitive. If you're travelling **via Ostend**, either of the above stations can sell you a return from London to Brussels (including the catamaran) for £65 return, as can Hoverspeed (☎0990/240241) and Network Leisure Travel (☎0870/001 0174).

Those **under 26** can purchase discounted tickets from Rail Europe or German Railways, thus saving up to 25 percent on the return fare. The above companies (and USIT Campus) also offer a range of **Euro Domino** passes, which allow unlimited travel within Austria. These range from £68 for three days (£53 for under 26s) to £108 for eight days (£83 for under 26s). Travellers over 60 also get small discounts on all tickets, and can get further discounts between, but not within, European countries by purchasing a **Rail Plus** card at a cost of £12. However, before you can buy this card, you must already possess a British Senior Card (£18); both are valid for a year.

If you're planning to visit Austria as part of a more extensive trip round Europe, it may be worth buying an **InterRail Pass**, which gives you unlimited rail travel within certain countries; you must, however, have been resident in Europe for at least six months. InterRail tickets are currently zonal: to

travel to Austria and back, you'll need at least a two-zone pass, costing £169 for one month for those under-26s, and £235 a month for those aged 26 and over. Passes are not valid in the UK (or whichever country you bought the pass in), though you're entitled to discounted fares at your country of origin, and on Eurostar and cross-Channel ferries. Either way, you're really only going to get your money's worth if you do a lot of travelling. For the latest information, visit the InterRail home page at *www.inter-rail.co.uk*.

If you haven't lived in the UK or Europe for six months, but are currently in the UK, you are eligible to a **Eurail** or Europass instead. Eurail is a simple unlimited rail travel pass, valid for 15 or 21 days, one, two or three months. The under-26 pass costs from £286 to £803; the adult pass is for first-class travel and costs from £409 to £1148. The **Eurail Flexipass** allows you 10/15 days' non-consecutive travel within a two-month period, and costs £338/£442 for under 26s, and £482/£635 for those who aren't (first class). Finally, the **Europass** gives you five to fifteen days' travel in a two-month period, does not cover travel within the UK and is zoned. For a pass to cover Austria, the cost ranges from £205 to £412 for under 26s and £330 to £636 for adults. There are further discounts if two or more people are travelling together, and a combination train/car rental pass. For more information on the above passes visit *www.raileurope.co.uk*.

BY BUS

The only Austrian destination served by a regular **bus** service from the UK is **Vienna**. There's a direct service run by **Eurolines** from London's Victoria Coach Station more or less daily. The bus sets off at around 10.30am, arriving in Wien-Mitte/Landstrasse roughly 22 hours later. The trip is bearable (just about), but only really worth it if you absolutely can't find the extra cash for the cheap flight. A flexible return (valid for six months) costs £111 return, whereas a non-

---

BUS INFORMATION

Busabout, ☎020/7950 1661, *www.busabout.com*. Busabout sell European bus passes.

Eurolines, ☎0870/514 3219, *www.gobycoach .com*. Tickets can also be purchased from any National Express agent.

exchangeable, non-refundable return bought fourteen days in advance and valid for one month costs just £79 return. Under 26s and over 60s get a ten percent discount. If you're heading for Salzburg or western Austria, it might be worth considering heading for **Munich** instead (£91 for a flexible return), or to **Zurich** (£96 for a flexible return and £69 for a fixed ticket).

Another option worth considering if you're heading for other parts of Europe as well as Austria is a **Eurolines pass**. The pass, which covers all the major cities in Europe (but only Vienna within Austria) is valid for either thirty days (low season Nov–March: £139 under 26/£175 26 & over; mid-season April, May, Sept & Oct: £153 under 26/£191 26 & over; high season June–Aug: £195 under 26/£245 26 & over) or 60 days (low season: £175/£219; middle season: £189/£237; high season: £227/£283). Alternatively, a **Euro Explorer** ticket allows you to travel on a Eurolines circuit comprising London–Vienna–Budapest–Prague–London for £116; tickets are valid for six months.

From April to October **Busabout** offer a hop-on, hop-off bus service, which calls in at Vienna, Salzburg and Innsbruck, as well numerous other cities in Western Europe (and Prague). The **Consecutive Pass** allows unlimited travel from two weeks (£169) to seven months (£699); the **Flexible Pass** gives you ten days travel in two months (£259) or thirty days travel in four months (£659). The buses travel along pre-determined circular routes in one direction only, so for instance you can only travel from Vienna to Venice and not vice versa. None of the Austrian cities are connected directly with one another, and buses depart only every two to four days. If you're travelling from London, you must add on the price of a London to Paris return, costing £30.

BY CAR

With two or more passengers **driving to Austria** can work out relatively inexpensive, however it is not the most relaxing option – unless you enjoy pounding along the motorway systems of Europe for the best part of a day and a night.

The quickest way of taking your car over to the continent is to drive to the Channel Tunnel, near Folkestone, where **Eurotunnel** operates a 24-hour service carrying cars, motorcycles, buses and their passengers to Coquelles, near Calais. At peak times, services run every fifteen minutes,

---

CROSS-CHANNEL INFORMATION

Hoverspeed ☎0870/524 0241, www.hoverspeed.co.uk. Dover–Calais and Dover–Ostend catamarans.

Eurotunnel, ☎0870/5353535, www.eurotunnel.com. Folkestone–Calais by car train through the Tunnel.

P&O Stena Line ☎0870/600 0600, www.posl.com. Dover–Calais ferry.

---

and the journey lasts about 35 minutes. It is possible to turn up unannounced and buy your ticket at the toll booths (after exiting the M20 at junction 11a), but you'll save yourself money and a possible wait if you book in advance. Rates depend on the time of year, time of day and length of stay; for example, in peak season (weekends in July and August), it can be cheaper to travel between 10pm and 6am. As an example, a standard period return at an off-peak time starts at around £180 (passengers included) in the low season and goes up to as much as £370 in the peak period. You can often save money buy buying in advance; such tickets are amendable up to a day before travel, but not refundable.

The alternative cross-Channel options for most travellers are the conventional **ferry and catamaran** links between Dover and Calais or Ostend. Fares are pretty similar to those via Eurotunnel, and vary enormously with the time of year, month and even day that you travel, and the size of your car. The standard off-peak fare on the Dover–Calais run, for example, is around £180 return for a carload (including passengers). On an August weekend, with no advance booking, you could pay £350 or more return. If you book far enough in advance (before March or April), you can reduce that fare by as much as fifty percent; tickets bought in advance are flexible, too, so you can change the timing of your crossing should you need to.

Once you've made it onto the continent, you've got something in the region of **1200km of driving** ahead of you. If you're heading for Salzburg, central Austria, eastern Austria and Vienna, the most direct route from Ostend or Calais is via Brussels, Cologne, Frankfurt and Nuremberg. For Innsbruck and the Tyrol, Brussels–Cologne–Stuttgart probably represents the fastest route. It costs nothing to drive on motorways in Belgium and Germany, but to go on an Austrian autobahn, you must buy and display a sticker or *Vignette* (available at border crossings and petrol stations); the cheapest version is valid for one week and costs öS70/€5.09. More information on-line at *www.vignette.at*.

If you're travelling by car, you'll need proof of ownership, or a letter from the owner giving you permission to drive the car. A British or other EU driving licence is fine; all other drivers must hold an International Driving Licence. You also need a country identification sticker, a red warning trian-

gle in case you break down, a first-aid kit (all these are compulsory in Austria), and a "Green Card" for third-party insurance cover at the very least. An even better idea is to sign up with one of the national motoring organizations like the AA or the RAC (see p.34), who offer continental breakdown assistance for an additional fee, and in extreme circumstances will get you and your vehicle brought back home if necessary.

GETTING THERE FROM IRELAND

The only direct flights from Ireland to Austria are the weekly charter flights from Dublin,

Cork and Belfast to Salzburg and Innsbruck in the skiing season (roughly December to early April), and at the height of summer (July & August). Flight-only deals hover around IR£250/€276 for Dublin to Salzburg, depending very much on availability.

There are no direct **scheduled flights** to Austria from Ireland, although a number of non-direct options are available. British Airways offer a Belfast–Vienna round trip for £300, and a Dublin–Vienna fare of IR£300/€236 return travelling via Heathrow. There's no guarantee, but low-cost flight agents such as Joe Walsh Tours and USIT can sometimes get you cheaper deals with other carriers (such as British Airways, Air France, KLM, Lufthansa or Aer Lingus).

The other option is to pick up a cheap flight to London for around £60 return, on one of the new

TRAVEL AGENTS AND TOUR OPERATORS IN IRELAND

Crystal Holidays, Northern Ireland ☎0870/848 7000, *www.crystalholidays.co.uk*; Irish Republic ☎01/670 8444. Impressive choice of winter and summer packages, and flight-only deals from Belfast, Cork and Dublin into Salzburg and Innsbruck. City breaks in Vienna also available.

Joe Walsh Tours, 69 Upper O'Connell St, Dublin 2 (☎01/872 2555); 8–11 Baggot St, Dublin 2 (☎01/676 3053); 117 Patrick St, Cork (☎021/277959); *www.joewalshtours.ie*. General budget-fares agent.

Liffey Travel, 12 Upper O'Connell St, Dublin (☎01/878 8322). Package tour specialists with city breaks to Vienna.

Neenan Travel, 12 South Leinster St, Dublin 2 (☎01/676 5181, *www.neenantrav.ie*). General travel agent.

Thomas Cook, 11 Donegal Place, Belfast (☎028/9088 3900, *www.thomascook.co.uk*); 118 Grafton St, Dublin 2 (☎01/677 1721). Package-holiday and flight agent, with occasional discount offers.

Trailfinders, 4–5 Dawson St, Dublin 2 (☎01/677 7888, *www.trailfinders.com*). Competitive fares out of all Irish airports, as well as deals on hotels, insurance, tours and car rental worldwide.

USIT Now, Fountain Centre, College St, Belfast BT1 6ET (☎028/9032 4073); 10–11 Market Parade, Patrick St, Cork (☎021/270 900); 33 Ferryquay St, Derry (☎01504/371 888); 19 Aston Quay, Dublin 2 (☎01/602 1600); Victoria Place, Eyre Square, Galway (☎091/565 177); Central Buildings, O'Connell St, Limerick (☎061/415 064); 36-37 Georges St, Waterford (☎051/872 601); *www.usitnow.ie*. Student and youth specialists for flights and trains.

discount airlines. Regular cheap flights are available from EasyJet, who fly from Belfast to Luton, Go, who fly Belfast to Stansted, or Ryanair, who fly from all over the Republic to London. You can book on-line with all the above airlines, and then pick up a similarly cheap deal on to Vienna, Munich or Zurich via the discount airlines listed on p.3.

Given the lack of direct scheduled flights from Ireland, **city breaks** can work out pretty good value. Liffey Travel offer three nights in a three-star hotel in Vienna for IR£400/€315. Flight and accommodation **packages** are another option, with Crystal offering ski packages for around IR£450/€354 for a week in a three-star hotel at half board, and starting at around IR£400/€315 for the same in the summer.

GETTING THERE FROM NORTH AMERICA

Austrian Airlines and United fly direct to Vienna from several US cities, and many other airlines have flights to Vienna via other major European cities. A direct flight from the East Coast of the States takes nine hours. Another option is to buy a cheap flight to London or Frankfurt and make your way overland from there (see p.3 for details of getting to Vienna from Britain).

Though in the account that follows we've quoted fares that are offered direct from the airlines, it's always worth checking out cheaper flight options by contacting discount travel agents or consolidators, who buy up blocks of tickets from the airlines and sell them at a discount.

The **high season** for travel is summer (for most airlines and tour operators June through to mid-September), and the weeks around Christmas and New Year, when fares are roughly $1200. **Low season**, when tickets can be as much as $800 cheaper, is generally from the beginning of November to mid-March (excluding Christmas and New Year). The **shoulder season**, which sees a rise in cost from low season by about $400, runs from mid-March to the end of May and from mid-September to the end of October.

SHOPPING FOR TICKETS

Barring special offers (advertised in newspapers and often with only a small window of time in which to make your bookings), the cheapest options available from the airlines are **Apex** fares. These generally need to be bought – and paid for – 21 days in advance and entail certain restrictions as to length of stay, such as a seven-night minimum and a three-month maximum. There are also winter **Super Apex** tickets, sometimes known as "Eurosavers", which are slightly cheaper than an ordinary Apex, but limit your stay to between seven and 21 days. Some airlines also issue **Special Apex** tickets to people younger than 24, often extending the maximum stay to a year. Many airlines offer youth or student fares to **under 26s**; a passport or driving licence are sufficient proof of age, though these tickets are subject to availability and can have eccentric booking conditions. It's worth remembering that most cheap return fares involve spending at least one Saturday night away and that many will only give a percentage refund if you need to cancel or alter your journey, so make sure you check the restrictions carefully before buying a ticket.

You can normally cut costs further by going through a **specialist flight agent** – either a consolidator, who buys up blocks of tickets from the airlines and sells them at a discount, or a discount agent, who in addition to dealing with discounted flights may also offer special student and youth fares and a range of other travel-related services such as travel insurance, rail passes, car rentals, tours and the like. Bear in mind, though, that penalties for changing your plans can be stiff. Remember too that these companies make their money by dealing in bulk – don't expect them to answer lots of questions. Some agents specialize in **charter flights**, which may be cheaper than anything available on a scheduled flight, but again departure dates are fixed and withdrawal penalties are high (check the refund policy). If you travel a lot, **discount travel clubs** are another option – the annual membership fee may be worth it for benefits such as cut-price air tickets and car rental.

Don't automatically assume that tickets purchased through a travel specialist will be cheapest – once you get a quote, check with the airlines and you may turn up an even better deal. Be advised also that the pool of travel companies is swimming with sharks – exercise caution and *never* deal with a company that demands cash up front or refuses to accept payment by credit card.

AIRLINES IN NORTH AMERICA

Air Canada ☎1-888/247 2262, *www.aircanada .ca*. One-stop flights from Toronto and Montreal via Frankfurt and from Montreal via Paris.

Air France US: ☎1-800/237 2747, *www .airfrance.com*; Canada: ☎1-800/667 2747, *www.airfrance.ca*. Good-value flights daily from Toronto, New York and other major North American hubs to Vienna via Paris.

Alitalia US: ☎1-800/223 5730, *www.alitaliausa .com*; Canada: ☎1-800/361 8336, *www.alitalia.ca*. Flights from New York (JFK or Newark), Boston, Miami, Chicago, Los Angeles and San Francisco to Vienna with stopovers in Rome and Milan.

Austrian Airlines ☎1-800/843 0002, *www .austrianair.com*. The most comprehensive service to Austria, with nonstop daily flights from New York, Washington DC and Chicago. From Vienna, you can fly onwards for free to Graz, Innsbruck, Klagenfurt or Salzburg.

British Airways ☎1-800/247 9297, *www.britishairways.com*. Offers a frequent, reasonable service from Toronto, New York and other major cities with a stopover in London.

Delta Airlines ☎1-800/2 41 4141, *www.delta.com*. Very reasonably priced flights from New York to Vienna via Paris and from New York to Munich (with onward connections).

KLM/Northwest US: ☎1-800/374 7747; Canada: ☎1-800/361 5073; *www.mwa.com*. Frequent but rather pricey flights from Toronto and Montreal to Vienna via Amsterdam.

Lufthansa US & Canada: ☎1-800/399 5838; US: *www.lufthansa-usa.com*; Canada: *www.lufthansa.ca.com*. Flies from Toronto, Montreal, New York and other major departure points to Vienna via Munich, Frankfurt and Dusseldorf.

SwissAir US: ☎1-800/221 4750; Canada: ☎1-800/563 5954; *www.swissair.com*. Daily direct flights from New York, Atlanta, Boston, Chicago, Cincinnati, Los Angeles, Miami, San Francisco and Washington DC and five times a week from Montreal to Zurich with onward connections.

United Airlines ☎1-800/241 6522, *www.ual.com*. Super-cheap and regular direct flights from New York and Washington DC to Vienna.

FLIGHTS FROM THE US

Prices quoted below assume midweek travel (count on $40–60 extra at weekends), exclude taxes and are subject to change. Austrian Airlines offers the most extensive service, with **nonstop daily flights** from New York, Washington DC and Chicago. From Vienna, you can fly onwards to Graz, Innsbruck, Klagenfurt or Salzburg at no extra cost. At the time of writing, their midweek Apex round-trip fares from New York or Washington range from $348 to $1860, depending on season, and from Chicago, $518 to $1902, with frequent special offers including a passport fee rebate scheme (contact ANTO for further details). United flies from Washington DC for $540 to $1325 and from Chicago for $590 to $1370. Lauda Air flies five times weekly from Miami to Vienna via Munich, starting at $388 (low season) up to $749 (high season).

Numerous European-based airlines – Lufthansa, KLM, Swissair, British Airways, Air France and Alitalia – fly from major US cities to Vienna with **stop-offs** at their gateway cities

(Frankfurt, Amsterdam, Zurich, London, Paris and Rome, respectively). The airlines are fiercely competitive, however, and you're not likely to find any difference between their fares and those of Austrian Airlines quoted above.

Another option, especially for hikers or skiers heading to western provinces, like the Tyrol (Innsbruck) or Vorarlberg (Bregenz and the Bodensee, the Bregenzerwald), is to take a round-trip flight to **Munich** and make your own way from there. Regular Apex fares to Munich are only in the region of $50–70 cheaper than those to the nearest Austrian city, but you might catch one of Lufthansa's or Delta's limited special offers and get a midweek round-trip ticket from New York or Atlanta to Munich for as little as $350.

FLIGHTS FROM CANADA

Though there are **no direct flights** from Canada to Austria, there are many competitively priced one-stop options. Flights take about eleven hours from Montreal, twelve from Toronto and fourteen from Vancouver. The best deals are usually on

DISCOUNT AGENTS, CONSOLIDATORS AND TRAVEL CLUBS IN THE US AND CANADA

Council Travel: *www.counciltravel.com*. National Reservation Center: ☎1-800/226 8624 or 617/528 2091. Other offices include: 205 E 42nd St, New York, NY 10017 (☎1-800/226 8624 or 212/822 2700); 530 Bush St, Suite 700, San Francisco, CA 94108 (☎415/421 3473); 931 Westwood Blvd, Los Angeles 90024 (☎310/208 3551); 1138 13th St, Boulder, CO 80302 (☎303/447 8101); 3301 M St NW, 2nd Floor, Washington, DC 20007 (☎202/337 6464); 1153 N Dearborn St, Chicago, IL 60610 (☎312/951 0585); 3606A Chestnut St, Philadelphia, PA 19104 (☎215/382 0343). Nationwide US organization that mostly, but by no means exclusively, specializes in student/budget travel.

New Frontiers/Nouvelles Frontières: *www.NewFrontiers.com*. Branches at 6 East 46th Street, New York, NY 10017 (☎1-800/677 0720 or 212/986 6006) and 1001 Sherbrook E, Suite 720, Montréal, PQ H2L 1L3 (☎514/526 8444). Other branches in LA, San Francisco and Québec City. French discount-travel firm.

STA Travel: *www.sta-travel.com*. Branches include: 7810 Hardy Drive, Suite 109, Tempe, AZ 8528410 (☎1-800/777 0112 or 1-800/781 4040); 10 Downing St, New York, NY 10014 (☎212/627 3111); 7202 Melrose Ave, Los Angeles, CA 90046 (☎323/934 8722); 36 Geary St, San Francisco, CA 94108 (☎415/391 8407); 297 Newbury St, Boston, MA 02115 (☎617/266 6014); 429 S Dearborn St, Chicago, IL 60605 (☎312/786 9050); 1905 Walnut St, Philadelphia, PA 19103 (☎215/568 7999); 317 14th Ave SE, Minneapolis, MN 55414 (☎612/615 1800). Worldwide specialists in independent travel; also student IDs, travel insurance, car rental, rail passes, etc.

Travac: *www.thetravelsite.com*. 989 6th Ave, New York NY 10018 (☎1-800/872 8800). Consolidator and charter broker, with another office in Orlando.

Travel Avenue: *www.travelavenue.com*. 10 S Riverside, Suite 1404, Chicago, IL 60606 (☎1-800/333 3335). Full-service travel agent that offers discounts in the form of rebates.

Travel Cuts: *www.travelcuts.com*. Branches include: 187 College St, Toronto, ON M5T 1P7 (☎1-800/667 2887; from US ☎416/979 2406); 180 MacEwan Student Centre, University of Calgary, Calgary, AB T2N 1N4 (☎403/282 7687); 10127a 124th Street, Edmonton, AB T5N 1P5 (☎708/488 8487); 1613 rue St Denis, Montréal, PQ H2X 3K3 (☎514/843 8511); Student Union Building, University of British Columbia, Vancouver, BC V6T 1Z (☎888/ FLY CUTS or 604/822 6890); University Centre, University of Manitoba, Winnipeg, MB R3T 2N2 (☎204/269 9530). Canadian student-travel organization.

European carriers such as Air France, Lufthansa, KLM or Swissair, which fly from major Canadian cities to **Vienna** via Paris, Frankfurt, Amsterdam and Zurich respectively. At the time of writing, KLM offer the best value, with a special low-season fare of CDN$775 (from Toronto or Montreal) or CDN$1040 (from Vancouver). In peak season, however, you'll pay around CDN$1430 (from Toronto/Montreal) or CDN$1810 (from Vancouver). Alternatively, you can fly from Toronto or Montreal with Air Canada for around CDN$1050 (low season) or CDN$1480 (high season), but you will have to switch planes and carriers in a European city, most likely London, Frankfurt or Zurich.

PACKAGE TOURS AND CITY BREAKS

It may be worth your while checking deals with **specialist agents**. Though specialist tours often don't include air fares, they do map your itinerary and activities, fix you up with experienced guides, and – essential if you're planning your trip around any of Austria's major music festivals – organize the purchase of opera and symphony tickets and the like.

Although we've given phone numbers of specialist operators (see box above), you're better off making tour reservations through your local travel agent. An agent will make all the phone calls, sort out the snafus and arrange flights and insurance – all at no extra cost to you.

RAIL AND BUS PASSES

If you're planning on doing a decent amount of travelling in Europe, you may want to look into getting a train pass to get you into Austria. A regular **Eurail Pass** can span from fifteen days (the two fares available are $388 for under 26s/$554

NORTH AMERICAN SPECIALIST TOUR OPERATORS

All prices quoted below exclude taxes and are subject to change. Where applicable, accommodation quoted is for double occupancy, and round-trip flights are from New York.

Adventures on Skis (☎1-800/628 9655 or 413/568 2855, *www.advonskis.com*). Customized tours and set packages to all the major ski resorts; seven nights in Innsbruck $930-1639 (flight included).

Blue Danube Tours (☎1-800/268 4155, *www.bluedanubeholidays.com*) Extensive range of customized tours operating out of Toronto. Offered excursions include an eight-day Austrian panoramic tour (CDN$1965), a twelve-day Eastern Europe tour, taking in Berlin, Prague, Budapest and Vienna (CDN $1499) and an eight-day Danube cruise (CDN $867–CDN $1900 land only).

Cross Culture (☎1-888/346 3220 or 413/256 6303, *www.crosscultureinc.com*). Offers nine-day "Mozart's Salzburg" ($2650) and eight-day "Salzburg Christmas" ($2690) tours. Also hiking and biking tours.

Delta Vacations (☎1-800/872 7786, *http://delta-air.deltavacations.com*). Fly-drives and city breaks to Vienna, Salzburg and Innsbruck.

Elderhostel (☎1-877/426 8056, *www .elderhostel.org*). Specialists in educational and activity programmes, cruises and homestays for senior travellers aged 55 and up (companions may be younger). Offer courses in Vienna and Salzburg, as well as a Danube study cruise, all under the auspices of UNESCO. Also a cycling tour along the Danube.

Eastern Europe Tours (☎1-800/641 3456 or 206/448 8400, *www.imp-world-tours.com/*). Most of their organized tours take in other countries as well as Austria, but they do offer a three-night city package to Vienna starting around $269 (land only) and an eight-day "Panorama of Austria" tour, which takes in Vienna, Graz, Klagenfurt, Innsbruck and Salzburg and costs from $1929 (flight included).

Europe Train Tours (☎1-800/551 2085 or 914/758 1777, *www.etttours.com*). Bus tours of

Austria, as well as packages centred around Vienna and Salzburg. Their speciality is customized tours.

Fugazy International (☎1-800/828 4488, *www.fugazytravel.com*). Group tours that include Vienna, or personalized packages to Vienna, with guided tours. The thirteen-day Central & Eastern Europe tour is $3650, based on double occupancy, all-inclusive.

Herzerl Tours (☎1-800/684 8488, *www .herzerltours.com*). Food, wine, spas and music are the focus of some of the many cultural tours on offer. A week-long Viennese cooking tour (including air fare, accommodation, classes, some meals, concert tickets and various other sundries) is $2295; an Austrian wine tour covers more of the country and costs $2545 for seven days.

Holidaze Ski Tours (☎1-800/526 2827 or 732/280 1120). Several ski packages, to six different Austrian destinations, including seven-night "Salzburg Ski Safari" from $721 (flight included).

International Gay and Lesbian Travel Association (☎1-800/448 8550 or 954/776 2626, *www.iglta.com*). Trade group that will provide lists of gay-owned or gay-friendly travel agents, accommodation and other organizations.

Smolka Tours (☎1-800/722 0057 or 732/576 8813, *www.smolkatours.com*). Specialists in Austrian group or fully independent travel, including cultural, hiking and biking itineraries, visits to the Salzburg Easter and summer music festivals, music packages and opera tours. Four-day River Danube cruises from $520; farmstays in the Salzburger Land from $30 a night.

Van Gogh Tours (☎1-800/435 6192 or 781/721-0850, *www.vangoghtours.com*). Nine-day guided bicycle tour taking in Vienna and Salzburg, at $1000 for bike rentals, meals, and accommodation in three- and four-star hotels.

for "first class" or over 26s) to three months ($1089/$1558). This covers seventeen countries: Austria, Belgium, Denmark, Finland, France, Germany, Greece, Hungary, Ireland (Republic), Italy, Luxembourg, Netherlands, Norway,

Portugal, Spain, Sweden and Switzerland. Probably the best value for your money is the **Flexipass**, which gives you any ten days ($458/$654) or fifteen days ($599/$862) of train travel over a two-month period in any of the sev-

---

RAIL CONTACTS IN NORTH AMERICA

CIT Tours: *www.cit-tours.com*. 15 West 44th St, 10th floor, NY 10036 (☎1-800/ CIT TOUR); 9501 W Devon Ave, Suite 502, Rosemont, IL 60018 (☎1-800/223 7987); 666 Sherbrooke St, Suite 910, Montréal H3A 1G7 (☎1-800/361 7799) and 80 Tiverton Court, Suite 401, Markham, ON L3 OG4 (☎1-800/387 0711). Specialists in travel to Italy and neighbouring countries; they are also agents for Eurail and Eurostar.

Online Travel: *www.eurorail.com*. 9501 W Devon Ave, Suite 1E, Rosemont, IL 60018 (☎1-800/660-5300). Eurail Pass, Europass, and individual country passes for Austria, Britain,

Bulgaria, Czech Republic, Germany, Greece, Holland, Italy, Norway and Spain.

Rail Europe: *www.raileurope.com/us*. 226 Westchester Ave, White Plains, NY 10604 (US: ☎1-800/438 7245; Canada: ☎1-800/361 7245). Provide Eurail, Europass and point-to-point tickets between any European destinations. They also have special deals on hotels, car hire and transatlantic flights.

ScanTours: *www.scantours*. 3439 Wade St, Los Angeles, CA 90066 (☎1-800/223 7226 or 310/636-4656). Specialists in Scandinavian travel, they also stock every conceivable kind of European rail pass.

---

enteen Eurail Pass countries. Also available are the **Austrian Railpass**, which grants any three days' unlimited train travel in a fifteen-day period ($102/$151) with up to five extra days at $16/$22 a day; and the **European East Pass**, for any five days in one month ($205) in Austria, Czech Republic, Hungary, Poland and Slovakia with the option of a maximum of five extra days at $23 a day. For details of train passes within Austria, see p.32.

Busabout Passes are another worthwhile option (see p.10). They're available from STA Travel and come in a number of configurations, from a 15-day consecutive pass for $229, to a three-month pass at $839. **Flexipasses** are also available, allowing a certain number of days' travel within a given time period. For travel within a two-month span, these rates are: $349 (ten days), $509 (fifteen days); for 21 days in a three-month period it's $669; for thirty days out of four months, $929 with additional days costing $29.

GETTING THERE FROM AUSTRALIA & NEW ZEALAND

There's a good selection of airlines that can get you to Austria from Australia and New Zealand; the most direct flights are with Lauda Air from Sydney to Vienna – all other airlines include either a transfer or stopover in the carrier's home city. Given the high cost of flights in general from Australasia, however, a "Round the World" fare is a good option. Destinations in western Austria are also served by flights to Munich, from where you can continue your journey by land. Several rail and bus passes are worth buying before you leave home should you intend to expand your trip into Europe.

BY PLANE

Air fares are seasonal, with low season from mid-January to the end of February and October to the end of November; high season is mid-May to the

AIRLINES IN AUSTRALIA AND NEW ZEALAND

Air France *www.airfrance.fr*; Australia ☎02/9244 2100; New Zealand ☎09/308 3352 Daily flights from Sydney, Brisbane, Melbourne, Perth and Auckland to Vienna via Paris (code-shares with Qantas).

Air New Zealand *www.airnz.com*; Australia ☎13/24 76; New Zealand ☎0800/737 000 or 09/357 3000 Code-shares with Lauda to provide a through service from Auckland, Wellington and Christchurch to Vienna.

Alitalia *www.alitalia.it*; Australia ☎02/9244 2400; New Zealand ☎09/ 302 1452 Three flights per week from Sydney to Vienna and Munich via Bangkok and Milan (code-share with Qantas).

Ansett Australia *www.ansett.com.au*; Australia ☎13/14 14, ☎02/9352 6707; New Zealand ☎09/336 2364 Code-shares with Swiss Air and Lauda to provide a through service from Sydney, Brisbane, Melbourne, Adelaide and Perth to Vienna.

Garuda Australia ☎1300/365 330; New Zealand ☎09/366 1862 or 1800/128 510 Three flights a week from Sydney, Brisbane, Cairns, Darwin, Melbourne, Adelaide, Perth and Auckland to Amsterdam and Frankfurt with a transfer/stopover in Jakarta/Denpasar.

KLM *www.klm.com*; Australia ☎1300/303 747; New Zealand ☎09/ 309 1782 Two flights a week from Sydney via either Singapore–Amsterdam or LA–Amsterdam from Auckland to Vienna, Innsbruck, Munich and Zurich, via Amsterdam and Singapore.

Lauda Air *www.laudaair.com*; Australia ☎1800/642 438 or 02/9251 6155; New Zealand ☎09/308 3368

Three flights a week to Vienna via Sydney from Sydney, Brisbane, Melbourne, Perth and Auckland with onward connections to Innsbruck and Graz (code-share with Ansett and Air New Zealand).

Malaysia Airlines *www.malaysiaair.com*; Australia ☎13/26 27; New Zealand ☎09/373 2741 or 008/657 472 Twice-weekly flights from Sydney, Brisbane, Darwin, Melbourne, Adelaide, Perth and Auckland to Vienna and Munich, with a transfer or overnight stop in Kuala Lumpur.

Qantas *www.qantas.com.au*; Australia ☎13/13 13; New Zealand ☎09/357 8900 or 0800/808 767 Daily flights from Sydney, Melbourne, Darwin, Cairns and Brisbane, and several flights a week from Adelaide to Vienna via London.

Singapore Airlines *www.singaporeair.com*; Australia ☎13/10 11 or 02/9350 0262; New Zealand ☎09/303 2129 or 0800/808 909 Several flights a week from Sydney, Brisbane, Melbourne, Perth and Auckland to Vienna and Munich with a transfer in Singapore.

Sri Lankan Airlines Australia ☎02/9244 2234; New Zealand ☎09/308 3353 Three flights a week from Sydney and Auckland to London, Rome, Frankfurt, Paris and Zurich with either a transfer or an overnight stop in Colombo.

Swissair *www.swissair.com*; Australia ☎02/9232 1744 or 1800/221 339; New Zealand ☎09/358 3216 Several flights a week from Sydney, Brisbane, Melbourne, Perth and Auckland to Vienna via Zurich. Code-shares with Ansett.

Thai Airways *www.thaiair.com*; Australia ☎1300/651 960; New Zealand ☎09/377 3886 Several flights a week from Sydney, Brisbane,

end of August, and December to mid-January. There is no price variation during the week. Flying time is long – between twenty and thirty hours – and can be physically and mentally taxing, so you may want to consider a **stopover** en route. Flights to Europe are generally cheaper and quicker via Asia than the USA.

Tickets purchased direct from the airlines tend to be expensive – travel agents offer better deals and have the latest information on special offers, such as free stopovers and fly-drive/accommodation packages. Flight Centres and STA (which offer fare reductions for ISIC card-holders and

under 26s) generally offer the lowest fares. You might also want to have a look on the **Internet**; *www.travel.com.au* and *www.sydneytravel.com* are two sites that have a good range of discounted fares. The information is intended to act as a general guide; be sure to shop around a bit when choosing your ticket.

Fares from all eastern Australian capitals are generally the same (with Ansett and Qantas providing a free connecting service between these cities), while from Perth and Darwin you'll pay between A\$100 and A\$200 less via Asia, or A\$200–400 more via Canada and the US. Fares

Cairns, Melbourne, Perth and Auckland to Vienna and Munich.

United Airlines *www.ual.com*; Australia; ☎13/17 77; New Zealand ☎09/379 3800 Several flights a week from Sydney and Auckland to Vienna or Munich via Los Angeles.

Anywhere Travel, 345 Anzac Parade, Kingsford, Sydney (☎02/9663 0411, *anywhere@ozemail.com.au*). Discount flight agent close to the airport offering discounted flights, as well as accommodation, tours and car rental.

DISCOUNT TRAVEL AGENTS

Budget Travel, 16 Fort St, Auckland, plus branches around the city (☎09/366 0061 or 0800/808 040). Long-established agent dealing with budget air fares and accommodation packages.

Destinations Unlimited, 220 Queen St, Auckland (☎09/373 4033). Discount fares plus a good selection of tours and holiday packages.

Flight Centre *www.flightcentre.com.au*; Australia: 82 Elizabeth St, Sydney (☎02/9235 3522), plus branches nationwide (nearest branch ☎13/16 00). New Zealand: 350 Queen St, Auckland (☎09/358 4310), plus branches nationwide. Competitive discounts on air fares, and a wide range of package holidays and adventure tours as well as rail passes.

Northern Gateway, 22 Cavenagh St, Darwin (☎08/8941 1394, *oztravel@norgate.com.au*). Low cost flights from Darwin.

STA Travel, *www.statravel.com.au*; Australia: fastfare telesales ☎1300/360 960; 855 George St, Sydney; 256 Flinders St, Melbourne; other offices in state capitals and major universities (nearest branch ☎13/17 76). New Zealand: fastfare telesales ☎09/366 6673; 10 High St, Auckland (☎09/309 0458), plus branches in Wellington, Christchurch, Dunedin, Palmerston North, Hamilton and at major universities. Fare

discounts for students and those under 26, as well as visas, student cards and travel insurance.

Student Uni Travel, 92 Pitt St, Sydney (☎02/9232 8444, *sydney@backpackers.net*) plus branches in Brisbane, Cairns, Darwin, Melbourne and Perth. Student/youth discounts and travel advice.

Thomas Cook, *www.thomascook.com.au*; Australia: direct telesales ☎1800/801 002175; Pitt St, Sydney (☎02/9231 2877); 257 Collins St, Melbourne (03/9282 0222); plus branches in other state capitals (local branch ☎13/17 71); New Zealand: 191 Queen St, Auckland (☎09/379 3920) Low-cost flights, also tours, accommodation, travellers' cheques, and bus and rail passes.

Trailfinders, *www.trailfinder.com.au*; 8 Spring St, Sydney (☎02/9247 7666); 91 Elizabeth St, Brisbane (☎07/3229 0887); Hides corner, Shield St, Cairns (☎07/4041 1199). Independent travel and long-haul flight specialist.

Travel.com.au, *www.travel.com.au*, 76-80 Clarence St, Sydney (☎02/9249 5444 or 1800/000 447). On-line flight discounts.

USIT Beyond, cnr Shortland St and Jean Batten Place, Auckland (☎09/379 4224 or 0800/788 336) plus branches in Christchurch, Dunedin, Palmerston North, Hamilton and Wellington. Student/youth travel specialists.

from Christchurch and Wellington are between NZ$150 and NZ$300 more than from Auckland.

From Australia, Lauda Air team up with Ansett to provide a connecting service from state capitals via Sydney to Vienna for around A$1899 low season to A$2499 in the high season. In addition, several airlines can take you to Vienna or Munich via a transfer in their Asian hubs and home cities. Of these the best deals are with Alitalia for A$1500–2600 via Bangkok and Milan, and Qantas via Singapore and London and Malaysia Airlines via Kuala Lumpur, both for A$1799–2459. Air France, Swissair–Ansett, KLM, Thai Airways, Cathay Pacific, and Singapore Airlines all offer reasonable deals, for around A$1999–2499.

From New Zealand, Lauda Air, in conjunction with Air New Zealand, have a good through-service to Vienna from Auckland, Christchurch and Wellington for about NZ$2199 low season to NZ$2799 high season. Good deals on flights to either Vienna or Munich are also offered by KLM, Malaysia Airlines, Alitalia, Thai Airways, Cathay Pacific and Singapore Airlines, via their Asian hubs and home cities, for around NZ$2299–2999. Alternatively, United Airlines fly to Vienna or Munich via LA from Auckland starting at NZ$2599 in the low season and rising to NZ$3099 in the high season.

If you want to fly to another European gateway and then travel overland to Austria by road or rail, you'll find lowest fares are with Garuda via either Jakarta or Denpasar, to Frankfurt, and Sri Lankan Airlines via Colombo to either Frankfurt, Zurich, Paris or Rome from A$1500/NZ$1899 to A$1900/NZ$2400.

If you're planning to visit Vienna as part of an extended trip, a **Round-the-World** ticket, valid for a year, can be very good value, often working out just a little more than a standard return ticket. There are a number of airline combinations to choose from that include Vienna or Munich, offering a range of stopovers: for example, the cheapest is a straightforward fare (no backtracking and side trips) from Sydney or Auckland to Singapore/Bangkok/Hong Kong, Frankfurt/Milan /Zurich, Vienna/Munich, London, New York/Toronto, LA/Vancouver and back home, which starts at A$2199/NZ$2599 during the low season to A$2599/NZ$3099. More flexible mileage-based tickets such as the "Star Alliance 1" offered by Ansett Australia/Air New Zealand/United/Thai, starting at A$2499/NZ$2899, and "One World Explorer" by Qantas/British Airways/American

Airlines/Cathay which starts at A$2599/NZ$2999, allow side trips, backtracking and open jaw travel.

SPECIALIST TOURS

If you're interested in Austrian art and architecture, music, or activities like skiing or hiking, and prefer to have all the arrangements made for you before you leave, then seeking the help of a **specialist agent** is a good way to plan your trip. Unfortunately, there are few pre-packaged tours that include air fares from Australasia, but most specialist agents will be able to assist with flight arrangements as well. In turn, many of the tours we've listed (see box) can also be arranged through your local travel agent.

RAIL AND BUS PASSES

If you're planning to visit Austria as part of an extensive European trip it's worth looking into one of a variety of **Eurail** passes, which are valid in seventeen European countries.

The **Eurail Youthpass** (for under-26s) costs A$733/NZ$915 for 15 consecutive days, A$942/NZ$1175 for 21 days, A$1176/NZ$1470 for one month, A$1665/NZ$2080 for two months and A$2055/NZ$2570 for three months; if you're 26 or over you'll have to buy a first-class pass, available in 15-day (A$1046/NZ$1307), 21-day (A$1355/NZ$1695), one-month (A$1680/ NZ$2100), two-month (A$2378/NZ$2970) and three-month (A$2940/NZ$3675) increments.

The **Eurail Flexipass** is good for a certain number of travel days in a two-month period and also comes in youth or first-class versions: 10 days A$865/1234 or NZ$1080/1542, 15 days A$1131/1627 or NZ$1415/2033. A scaled-down version of the Flexipass, the Europass, allows travel in France, Germany, Italy, Spain and Switzerland for (youth/first class) A$440/657 or NZ$550/821 for 5 days in 2 months, on up to A$968/1374 or NZ$1210/1717 for 15 days in 2 months; there's also the option of adding adjacent "associate" countries (Austria, Hungary, Benelux, Portugal and Greece) for around A$85/NZ$110 per country (the respective cost shrinks with the number of associate countries added). There's also a **Eurail Saverpass**, **Saver Flexipass** and **Euro Saverpass**. These are first-class passes, valid for between 2 to 5 people who must be travelling together on all journeys. The cost is slightly less than the full first-class passes.

If you just want to explore Austria on its own, the **Austrian Railpass** allows for unlimited trav-

SPECIALIST AGENTS

Adventure World, *www.adventureworld.com.au*; Australia: 73 Walker St, North Sydney (☎02/9956 7766 or 1300/363 055), plus branches in Adelaide, Brisbane, Melbourne and Perth; New Zealand: 101 Great South Rd, Remuera, Auckland (☎09/524 5118).
Offer Vienna city packages from A$310/NZ$385 (twin share) including accommodation, city tour and concert tickets; also day tours from A$210/NZ$260 and the Vienna Woods from A$75/NZ$90, as well as hotel accommodation in Salzburg, Innsbruck, and Arlberg and the surrounding skifields from A$55/NZ$70 per night (twin share); ski passes and car rental. Also agents for Lauda Air and an array of international adventure companies that offer trips to Austria.

Australians Studying Abroad, 1st Floor, 970 Armadale, Victoria (☎03/9509 1955 or 1800/645 755, *www.asatravinfo.com.au*). Twenty-day all-inclusive tours delving into the art and culture of the Habsburg cities of Vienna, Prague and Budapest, for around A$6000/NZ$7690 (land only).

CIT, 263 Clarence St, Sydney (☎02/9267 1255, *www.cittravel.com.au*) plus offices in Melbourne, Brisbane, Adelaide and Perth. Hotel and tour packages, including round-trip coach tours from Vienna via Graz, Franz-Josefs-Hohe, Salzburg and Melk, from A$990/NZ$1230 (twin share); rail passes and car rental.

Danube Travel, 800 Glenhuntly Rd, Caulfield, Melbourne (☎03/9530 0888). Extensive range of tours and accommodation throughout Austria, from budget to first class, including Danube cruises from A$130/NZ$160 and hydrofoil trips from Vienna to Budapest for A$150/NZ$185.

European Travel Office, 122 Rosslyn St, West Melbourne (☎03/9329 8844); Suite 410/368 Sussex St, Sydney (☎02/9267 7714); 407 Great South Rd, Auckland (☎09/525 3074).

Two-night accommodation and concert packages from A$300/NZ$375 (twin share); half-day Vienna city tours from A$75/NZ$90; and day boat trips on the Danube from A$150/NZ$185.

Explore Holidays, 55 Blaxland Road, Ryde NSW (☎02/9857 6200, *www.exploreholidays.com.au*). Offer three-night city-stays in Vienna from A$470/NZ$585 (includes a sightseeing tour, an opera ticket and a concert ticket); Vienna, Salzberg, Innsbruck hotel accommodation from A$70/NZ$90 (twin share); B&B country stays in Alpbachin, from A$45/NZ$55 twin share); and car rental.

Intrepid Adventure Travel, 12 Spring St, Fitzroy, Melbourne (☎1300/360 667 or 03/9473 2626). Seven- and eight-day walking and cycling holidays following the Inn and Danube rivers, from A$1200/NZ$1500 (twin share; land only).

Snow Bookings Only, 1141 Toorak Rd, Camberwell, Melbourne (☎1800/623266). Pension and hotel accommodation packages in the Alberg, Salzberg, Innsbruck, Tyrol-Kitzbühel, Hopfgarten, Neustift and Alpbach regions from A$400/NZ$500 for seven nights (twin share; ski hire and passes extra); and guided ski tours.

Travel Plan, 118 Edinburgh Rd, Castlecrag, Sydney (☎02/9438 1333 or 1300/130 754). All-inclusive skiing holidays in the Arlberg, Zell am See and Salzburger Land. Hotel accommodation packages from A$550/NZ$685 (twin share; ski hire and passes extra).

The Ski and Snowboard Travel Company, 343 Pacific Highway, Crows Nest, Sydney (☎02/9955 5201 or 1800/251 934). Customized ski holidays in St Anton, Lech, Kitzbühel and surroundings.

Walkabout Gourmet Adventures, PO Box 52, Dinner Plain, Melbourne (☎03/5159 5556). Leisurely, food-and-wine-focused walking tours from Munich through Bavaria, the Austrian Alps and the Dolomites from A$3525/NZ$4400.

el for four days in fifteen for (second/first class) A$230/A$336 or NZ$289/420.

All of the above rail passes can be obtained from CIT World Travel, Flight Centres (see box, p.19), or from **Rail Plus**: Australia Level 3, 459 Little Collins St, Melbourne VIC 3000, (☎1300/555 003 or 03/9642 8644, *info@railplus.com.au*); New Zealand Level 2, 6 Parnell Road, Auckland 1 (☎09/303 2484).

Bus passes are also available from **Trailfinders**, 8 Spring St, Sydney (☎02/9247 7666, *www.trailfinders.com.au*) and **Busabout Europe**, 27 Belgrave St, Manly NSW (☎1300/301 776). Busabout's hop-on hop-off bus passes cost around (youth/adult) A$359/399 or NZ$449/495 for fifteen days, A$669/749 or NZ$835/935 for one month and A$1029/1159 or NZ$1285/1449 for two months, see p.10 for more details.

RED TAPE AND VISAS

Citizens of EU countries need only a valid national identity card to enter Austria. Since Britain has no identity card, however, British citizens do have to take a passport. EU citizens can stay for as long as they want, but if they're planning on staying permanently they should register with the local police. Citizens of the US, Canada, New Zealand and Australia require a passport, but no visa, and can stay up to three months.

Visa requirements do change, however, and it is always advisable to check the current situation before leaving home. A list of Austrian embassies abroad is given below; addresses of foreign embassies and consulates in Vienna and other major cities are also given in the Guide.

CUSTOMS

Customs and duty-free restrictions vary throughout Europe, with subtle differences even within the European Union. British and Irish travellers returning home directly from another EU country do not have to make a declaration to customs at their place of entry. In other words, British and Irish citizens can effectively take back as much **duty-paid** wine or beer as they can carry, the guideline limits being 90 litres of wine (of which no more than 60 litres should be sparkling), 110 litres of beer, 800 cigarettes or 1kg of tobacco.

Residents of the US and Canada can take up to 200 cigarettes or 50 cigars and one litre of spirits (or 2.25 litres of wine, or three litres of beer) back home. **Australian** citizens must limit themselves to 200 cigarettes or 250g of tobacco and just one litre of wine or spirits, while **New Zealanders** are allowed 200 cigarettes or 250g of tobacco, 4.5 litres of beer or wine, and one litre of spirits. Again, if in doubt consult the relevant embassy.

AUSTRIAN EMBASSIES/CONSULATES ABROAD

Australia 12 Talbot St, Forrest, Canberra ACT 2603 (☎02/6295 1533, www.austriaemb.org.au). Consulates in Adelaide, Brisbane, Cairns, Melbourne, Perth & Sydney.

Canada 445 Wilbrod St, Ottawa, Ontario KIN 6M7 (☎613/789 1444, www.austro.org). Consulates in Calgary, Halifax, Montreal, Regina, Toronto, Vancouver & Winnipeg.

Ireland 15 Ailesbury Court, 93 Ailesbury Rd, Dublin 4 (☎01/269 4577, austroam@iol.ie).

New Zealand Consular General: Level 2, Willbank House, 57 Willis St, Wellington (☎04/499 6393). Consulate: 98 Kirtchner Road, Milford, Auckland 1 (☎09/489 8249)

South Africa 1109 Duncan St, Momentum Office Park, 0011 Brooklyn, Pretoria (☎460 3361). Consulates in Durban, Johannesburg & Cape Town.

UK 18 Belgrave Mews West, London SW1 8HU (☎020/7235 3731, www.austria.org.uk).

USA 3524 International Court NW, Washington, DC 20008 (☎202/895 6700, www.austria.org). Consulates in many US cities including Boston, Chicago, Houston, Honolulu, Los Angeles, Miami, New York & San Francisco.

HEALTH

No specific inoculations or health precautions are necessary for a trip to Austria. Minor complaints can be dealt with at any pharmacy (*Apotheke*); pharmacy hours are usually Monday to Friday 8am to noon and 2 to 6pm and Saturday 8am to noon. Pharmacies take turns in staying open at lunchtimes, weekends and overnight. Details of which pharmacies are open at these times are posted in all pharmacy windows, outside the police station and in local newspapers.

For serious complaints, head for the casualty department of the nearest hospital (*Krankenhaus*), or call an ambulance (☎144). As members of the EU, **citizens of the UK and Ireland** receive free emergency hospital treatment in Austria on production of their passport, though there may be a charge for any medication. Nationals of other countries should check whether their government has a reciprocal health agreement with Austria, or whether they are covered by their personal medical insurance.

The best readily accessible source of **information** about travel health matters is *www.cdc.gov* operated by the US government's Centers for Disease Control. In Britain, pick up the Department of Health's free booklet *Health Advice for Travellers*, available at post offices, by phone on ☎0800/555777, or at *www.open.gov.uk/doh/hat*. The booklet includes an application for Form E111, which entitles all EU citizens to free medical care across the EU.

WATER

Water is safe to drink all over Austria, whether from taps or from the ubiquitous public street-fountains. These fountains may look dodgy, but almost always gush with pure spring water. Exceptions to this rule are always clearly marked *"kein Trinkwasser"*, usually accompanied by a pictogram of a crossed-out drinking glass.

Take care, however, with **mountain streams**, which might look fresh, but may well have cows

> The **ambulance emergency number** for anywhere in Austria is ☎144. The word for ambulance in German is *Rettung*.

grazing further upstream. Contaminated water can bring on a list of diseases as long as your arm – raging diarrhoea is the best of the bunch. If you're thinking of heading off the beaten track, you should consider taking a **water purifier** with you. Boiling water for ten minutes should see off most micro-organisms, but it's not the most convenient method, especially as water boils at a lower temperature the higher the altitude, which may mean some of the bugs survive. Sterilization with iodine tablets renders the water unpalatable and is unsafe for pregnant women, babies and those with thyroid complaints. Portable water purifiers, which sterilize and filter the water, give the most complete treatment. A low-cost and highly recommended range made by Pre-Mac is available in the UK from British Airways Travel Clinics (for details of your nearest branch call ☎01276/685040 or visit *www.british-airways.com*) and specialist outdoor equipment retailers.

SUNBURN AND HYPOTHERMIA

The sun and the cold are probably your worst enemies in Austria. You can get **sunburnt** very quickly in the mountains, due to the combination of a thin atmosphere and reflection off snow, ice and/or water. High-factor sunscreen, a hat and total block (factor 25 or more) are essential. Reflection of the sun's glare can also damage your eyes after a time, so UV-protective sunglasses or ski visors are a must.

Hypothermia, when the body loses heat faster than it can conserve it, is usually brought on by a combination of cold, wind and driving rain, with hunger and fatigue often playing their part. Symptoms include exhaustion, lethargy or dizziness, shivering, numbness in the extremities and slurring of speech. In these initial stages, you must get the sufferer out of the elements and under cover, replace any clothing of theirs that is wet (with your own dry garments if necessary), give them hot liquids, and high-calorie, sugary food such as chocolate, and talk to and encourage them. Alcohol is generally not a good idea.

Virtually all high-altitude walks in Austria stay below 3000m, the rough cut-off point above which **altitude sickness** can rear its head. Headaches, dizziness and breathlessness are the

You can buy good pre-packed **travellers' first-aid kits** from ordinary pharmacies or travel shops. Particularly useful if you're planning to go hiking are: antiseptic cream, insect repellent, plasters/band aids, water purifier, lint and sealed bandages, knee supports, a course of flagyl antibiotics, paracetamol/aspirin (useful for combating the effects of altitude), hypodermic needles and sterilized skin wipes (more for the security of knowing you have them, than any fear that an Austrian hospital would fail to observe basic sanitary precautions).

main symptoms, all of which should pass after a day or two at altitude. If they don't, the only treatment is to head down.

TICKS

If you're anywhere near woodland, below 1200m, there's a possibility you may receive attention from **ticks**, tiny little parasites no bigger than a pin head, which bury themselves into your skin. Removing ticks by dabbing them with alcohol, butter or oil is now discouraged; the medically favoured way of extracting them is to pull them out carefully with small tweezers. There is a very slight risk of picking up some very nasty diseases from ticks such as encephalitis. Symptoms for the latter are initially flu-like, and if they persist, you should see a doctor immediately.

INSURANCE

A typical travel insurance policy usually provides cover for the loss of baggage, tickets and – up to a certain limit – cash or cheques, as well as medical emergencies and cancellation or curtailment of your journey. Many companies will also tailor policies for you if you plan on going skiing, or if you want to take part in other "dangerous" sports or adventure activities.

Read the small print and benefits tables of prospective policies carefully; **coverage** can vary wildly for roughly similar premiums. Many policies can be chopped and changed to exclude coverage you don't need – for example, sickness and accident benefits can often be excluded or included at will. If you do take medical coverage, ascertain whether benefits will be paid as treatment proceeds, or only after you return home, and whether there is a 24-hour medical emergency number. When securing baggage cover, make sure that the per-article limit – typically under £500 equivalent – will cover your most valuable possession.

If you need to make a **claim**, you should keep receipts for medicines and medical treatment, and in the event you have anything stolen, you *must* obtain an official statement from the police. Few insurers will arrange on-the-spot payments in the event of a major expense; you will usually be reimbursed only after going home (see p.30 for what to do if you lose your credit cards, travellers' cheques or money). Note that debit, credit and charge cards often have certain levels of medical or other insurance included, and you may automatically get travel insurance if you use the card to pay for your trip.

US and Canadian travellers may well already be covered and so should check their insurance policy before buying anything extra. Canadian provincial health plans typically provide

ROUGH GUIDE TRAVEL INSURANCE

Rough Guides now offers its own **travel insurance**, customized for our readers by a leading UK broker and backed by a Lloyds underwriter. It's available for anyone, of any nationality, travelling anywhere in the world.

There are two main Rough Guide insurance plans: **Essential**, for basic, no-frills cover, starting at £11.75 for two weeks; and **Premier** – with more generous and extensive benefits – starting at £12.50. Unlike many policies, the Rough Guides schemes are calculated by the day, so if you're travelling for 27 days rather than a month, that's all you pay for. Alternatively, you can take out annual **multi-trip insurance**, which covers you for any number of trips throughout the year (with

a maximum of 60 days for any one trip), starting at £47.26 (European) and £83.99 (worldwide). If you intend to be away for the whole year, the **Adventurer** policy will cover you for 365 days from £90. Each plan can be supplemented with a "Hazardous Activities Premium" if you plan to indulge in sports considered dangerous, such as skiing, scuba-diving or trekking. Rough Guides also does good deals for older travellers, and will insure you up to any age.

For a **policy quote**, call the Rough Guide Insurance Line on UK freefone ☎0800/015 0906, US freefone ☎1-866/220 5588 or, if you're calling from elsewhere ☎0044/1243 621 046. Alternatively, get an on-line quote at *www.roughguides.com /insurance.*

some overseas medical coverage, although they are unlikely to pick up the full tab in the event of a mishap. Holders of official student/teacher/youth cards are entitled to accident coverage and hospital in-patient benefits. Students may also find that their student health coverage extends during the vacations and for one term beyond the date of last enrolment. Homeowners' or renters' insurance often covers theft or loss of documents, money and valuables while overseas.

In **Australia and New Zealand** comprehensive travel insurance policies are generally put together by the airlines, major travel agents and some banks in conjunction with insurance companies. All are fairly similar in premium and coverage that includes medical expenses, loss of personal property and travellers' cheques, cancellations and delays, as well as most adventure sports.

INFORMATION AND MAPS

There are branches of the Austrian National Tourist Office in most large foreign countries

(for some current addresses, see p.28), although many only deal with the public by telephone rather than admit personal callers – ring ahead and check before trying to visit them in person. The staff are, as a rule, very helpful, and can usually supply brochures, accommodation lists and maps covering specific towns and resorts, providing you're focused about your interests.

Within Austria itself, most settlements of any size have a **tourist office**, although they come under an assortment of names: *Information, Tourismusverband, Verkehrsamt* and *Fremdenverkehrsverein* are just some of the titles you'll come across. All are helpful and well organized, and staff usually speak English. They will supply a

TRAVEL BOOKS AND MAPS

ENGLAND

Blackwell's Map and Travel Shop, 53 Broad St, Oxford OX1 3BQ (☎01865/792792, *www.blackwell.bookshop.co.uk*).

Daunt Books, 83 Marylebone High St, London W1M 3DE (☎020/7224 2295); 193 Haverstock Hill, NW3 4QL (☎020/7794 4006).

Heffers Map and Travel, 20 Trinity Street, Cambridge, CB2 1TJ (☎01223/568568, *www.heffers.co.uk*).

The Map Shop, 30a Belvoir St, Leicester LE1 6QH (☎0116/2471400, *www.mapshopleicester.co.uk*).

National Map Centre, 22–24 Caxton St, London SW1H 0QU (☎020/7222 2466, *www.mapsnmc.co.uk*).

Stanfords, 12–14 Long Acre, London WC2E 9LP (☎020/7836 1321, *www.stanfords.co.uk*); phone or on-line orders taken. Other branches are located within the British Airways offices at 156 Regent St, W1R 5TA (☎020/7434 4744), and at 29 Corn St, Bristol BS1 1HT (☎0117/929 9966).

The Travel Bookshop, 13–15 Blenheim Crescent, London W11 2EE (☎020/7229 5260, *www.thetravelbookshop.co.uk*).

Newcastle Map Centre, 55 Grey St, Newcastle upon Tyne NE1 6EF (☎0191/261 5622, *www.newtraveller.com*).

Waterstone's, 91 Deansgate, Manchester M3 2BW (☎0161/832 1992, *www.waterstones.co.uk*).

SCOTLAND

James Thin Melven's Bookshop, 29 Union St, Inverness, IV1 1QA (☎01463/233500, *www.jthin.co.uk*).

John Smith and Sons, 26 Colquhoun Ave, Glasgow, G52 4PJ (☎0141/221 7472, *www.johnsmith.co.uk*).

WALES

Blackwells, 13–17 Royal Arcade, Cardiff CF10 1AE (☎029/2039 5036, *http://bookshop.blackwell .co.uk*).

Uplands Bookshop, 27 Uplands Crescent, Swansea SA2 0NX (☎01792/470195, *wwwuplands/books.co.uk*).

IRELAND

Easons Bookshop, 40 O'Connell St, Dublin 1 (☎01/873 3811, *www.eason.ie*).

Hodges Figgis Bookshop, 56–58 Dawson St, Dublin 2 (☎01/677 4754, *www.hodgesfiggis.com*).

Waterstones Queens Building, 8 Royal Ave, Belfast BT1 1DA (☎028/9024 7355, *www.waterstones.co.uk*); 7 Dawson St, Dublin 2 (☎01/679 1415); and 69 Patrick St, Cork (☎021/276522).

USA

Book Passage, 51 Tamal Vista Blvd, Corte Madera, CA 94925 (☎415/927 0960, *www.bookpassage.com*).

The Complete Traveler Bookstore, 199 Madison Ave, New York, NY 10016 (☎212/685 9007).

surfeit of brochures covering local attractions and activities, and free maps are often available.

Local tourist offices almost **always book accommodation** for personal callers, sometimes for a small fee, a deposit, or both. **Opening hours** can be long, as late as 9pm in the larger cities during the summer and in alpine resorts during winter; outside this period, and in smaller towns and less touristy areas, times are likely to be more limited, often including a long lunch break (typically Mon–Fri 8am–noon & 2–5pm). It's worth visiting tourist offices even outside the advertised opening hours, as many of them leave a stock of leaflets and maps in a rack outside. Others have touch-screen computer information points in a lobby (often accessible 24hr, or at least from 6am or 7am until midnight), and sometimes even a free phone and map showing accommodation vacancies.

Elliot Bay Book Company, 101 S Main St, Seattle, WA 98104 (☎206/624 6600 or ☎1-800/962 5311, *www.elliotbaybook.com*).

Forsyth Travel Library, 226 Westchester Ave, White Plains, NY 10604 (☎1-800/367 7984, *www.forsyth.com*).

Globe Corner Bookstore, 28 Church St, Cambridge, MA 02138 (☎1800/358 6013, *www.globecorner.com*).

GORP Adventure Library, ☎1-800/754 8229, *www2.gorp.com*.

Map Link Inc., 30 S La Patera Lane, Unit 5, Santa Barbara, CA 93117 (☎805/692 6777, *www.maplink.com*).

The Map Store Inc.,1636 I St NW, Washington, DC 20006 (☎202/628 2608).

Phileas Fogg's Travel Center, #87 Stanford Shopping Center, Palo Alto, CA 94304 (☎1-800/533 3644, *www.foggs.com*).

Rand McNally, 444 N Michigan Ave, Chicago, IL 60611 (☎312/321 1751, *www.randmcnally.com*). Rand McNally now has almost thirty stores across the US; call ☎1-800/333 0136 ext 2111 for the address of your nearest store, or for direct-mail maps.

Sierra Club Bookstore, 6014 College Ave, Oakland, CA 94618 (☎510/658 7470).

Travel Books & Language Center, 4437 Wisconsin Ave, Washington, DC 20016 (☎1-800/220 2665, *www.bookweb.org/bookstore/travellers*).

CANADA

Novack's Travel Books, 211 King St, London, Ontario N6A 1C9 (☎519/434 2882).

Open Air Books and Maps, 25 Toronto St, Toronto M5R 2C1 (☎416/363 0719 or 1-800/748 9171).

The Travel Bug Bookstore, 2667 West Broadway, Vancouver V6K 2G2 (☎604/737 1122, *www.swifty.com/tbug*).

Ulysses Travel Bookshop, 4176 St-Denis, Montréal H2W 2M5 (☎514/843 9882, *www.ulysees.ca*).

World of Maps, 118 Holland Ave, Ottawa, Ontario K1Y 0X6 (☎613/724 6776, *www.itmb.com*).

World Wide Books and Maps, 1247 Granville St, Vancouver V6Z 1G3 (☎604/687 3320, *www.worldofmaps.com*).

AUSTRALIA

The Map Shop, 6 Peel St, Adelaide (☎08/8231 2033, *www.mapshop.net.au*)

Mapland, 372 Little Bourke St, Melbourne (☎03/9670 4383, *www.mapland.com.au*)

Perth Map Centre, 1/884 Hay St, Perth (☎08/9322 5733, *www.perthmap.com.au*)

Travel Bookshop, Shop 3, 175 Liverpool St, Sydney (☎02/9261 8200)

Walkers Bookshop, 96 Lake Street, Cairns (☎07/4051 2410).

Worldwide Maps and Guides, 187 George St, Brisbane (☎07/3221 4330)

NEW ZEALAND

Mapworld, 173 Gloucester Street, Christchurch (☎03/374 5399, *www.mapworld.co.nz*)

Specialty Maps, 46 Albert St, Auckland (☎09/307 2217, *www.ubd-online.co.nz/maps*)

MAPS

The **maps** in this Guide, together with the free plans you can pick up from tourist offices and hotels, should be sufficient to help you find your way around the towns and regions. Otherwise, the best maps are by Freytag & Berndt, who produce a 1:500,000 map of the whole country; or by Generalkarte, whose series of eight 1:200,000 regional maps are useful for lengthier touring.

Both Freytag & Berndt and rival firm Kompass produce numerous **walking maps**, or *Wanderkarten* (ranging in scale from 1:50,000 to 1:30,000 depending on the area), which cover most areas of western, alpine Austria and many rural parts of the east as well. The best walking maps of Austria's mountain areas, however, are those belonging to the 1:25,000 *Alpenvereinskarte* series, produced by the Austrian Alpine Association. In addition, many bookshops and

AUSTRIA ON THE NET

Specific Web sites for each of the regions, towns, sights, hotels and restaurants mentioned in the Guide are listed within the text at the relevant point. In addition, a few useful, quite general Web sites are reviewed below.

Austrian Encyclopaedia
www.aeiou.at
Web site based on the Austrian Encyclopaedia, so should give the answer to any Austrian query you have. You can navigate in English, though occasionally source material is in German only. Exhaustive links.

Austria – general information
www.tiscover.com.
An excellent site for tourist information, with almost everything in English and German. TIS stands for *Tourismus Informations Systeme* and it's based in Austria. Very detailed info about regions, towns and villages all over the country; can book accommodation, including self-catering and camp-sites, flights and car rental on-line. Detailed route planner by car/plane/railway. Updated regularly so it can tell what's happening in the next few weeks/months in all the various towns.

Austrian National Tourist Board
www.anto.com and *www.austro-tourism.at*
The official tourist board Web sites. Not much better than looking at the brochures.

Austrian Search Engine
www.austrosearch.at

The best Austrian-specific search engine on the Net. Not only can you get three-day weather forecasts and up-to-date Austrian news, you can join chat groups, and find links for all sorts of Austro-nonsense.

Austrian Today
www.austriatoday.at
Excellent Web site for the monthly English-language newspaper, with all the latest news and listings as well as lots of useful general tourist information on Austria.

Vienna Tourist Board
www.info.wien.at
The official Vienna tourist board's English/German Web site is very good indeed and leads to other useful sites. Information on everything from second-hand bookshops to late-night eating options and art exhibitions. Can book hotel accommodation on-line.

Wiener Zeitung
www.wienerzeitung.at
Web site of the official Vienna city authorities newspaper. The English version gives you lots of tourist information and has plenty of useful links.

tourist offices in Austria sell local walking and cycling maps produced by smaller publishers.

Both the Austrian National Tourist Office and relevant local tourist offices should be able to provide plans of the larger **towns and cities**, though they may occasionally charge for them. Kompass also produce good maps of Graz, Innsbruck, Salzburg, Vienna and other regional centres in their Kompass-Stadtplan series, each marked with public transport routes; Freytag & Berndt's plans of Innsbruck, Salzburg and Vienna are similarly serviceable. The latter's 1:20,000 spiral-bound *Buchplan Wien* map is the most comprehensive map of the Austrian capital, while Falkplan's fold-out map, with a good large-scale section of the city centre, is a worthy alternative.

AUSTRIAN NATIONAL TOURIST OFFICES ABROAD

Australia 1st Floor, 36 Carrington St, Sydney NSW 2000 (☎02/9299 3621, *www.austria-tourism.at*).

Britain 14 Cork St, London W1 (☎020/7629 0461).

Canada 2 Bloor St E, Suite 3330, Toronto, ON M4W 1A8 (☎416/967 3381, *anto-tor@sympatico.ca*).

Ireland Merrion Centre, Nutley Lane, Dublin 4 (☎01/283 0488).

New Zealand Agent: Adventure World,101 Great South Rd, Remuera, Auckland (☎09/524 5118).

USA PO Box 1142, New York, NY 10108-1142 (☎212/944 6880, *gabriele.wolf@oewnyc.com*) and 11601 Wilshire Blvd, Suite 2480, Los Angeles CA 90025 (☎310/477 2038, *michael.gigi@oewlax.com*).

COSTS, MONEY AND BANKS

Although Austria is by no means a budget destination, it is not quite as expensive as people imagine. It's true to say that there are few bargain deals around, and even though the cheapest coffee and cake at a traditional café will cost you dearly, restaurants on the whole are moderately priced, as are rooms in most pensions and hotels. That said, Austria is one of the wealthiest countries in the world, and if you have the money, it has plenty of luxury shops, hotels and restaurants ready to relieve you of it.

MONEY

Until it is superseded by the euro in 2002, the **currency** in Austria remains the Austrian Schilling (*österreichische Schilling*). It is abbreviated to öS within Austria (and within this book), but is also often written as ATS or AS. Each Schilling is divided into one hundred *Groschen*. Coins come in the denominations öS20, öS10, öS5 and öS1, plus 50 and 10 Groschen; notes are öS5000, öS1000, öS500, öS100, öS50 and öS20.

AVERAGE COSTS

Accommodation will be your biggest single expense, with hostel beds going for around öS200/€14.54 (£10/US$15) the cheapest reasonable double rooms in a pension going for about öS500–750/€36.34–54.50 (£25–38/US$38–57). A double in a more comfortable pension or hotel is more likely to be between öS750–1000/€54.50–72.67 (£38–50/US$57–75).

After you've paid for your room, count on a **minimum** of £20/US$30 a day, to buy your breakfast, a takeaway lunch, a budget dinner and a beer or coffee, but not much else. Eating sit-down meals twice a day, visiting museums and drinking more beer and coffee (especially coffee) will mean allowing something in the range of £40/$60 a day; if you want to go to the opera or a nightclub, then you could easily double that figure.

Tipping is expected in the more upmarket hotels, taxis and in most cafés, bars and restau-

THE EURO

Austria is one of twelve European Union countries who have changed over to a single currency, the **euro** (€). The transition period, which began on January 1, 1999, is, however, lengthy: euro notes and coins are not scheduled to be issued until January 1, 2002, with Schillings remaining in place for cash transactions, at a fixed rate of öS13.7603 to 1 euro, until they are scrapped entirely at the end of February, 2002.

Even before euro cash appears in 2002, you can opt to pay in euros by credit card and you can get travellers' cheques in euros – you should not be charged commission for changing them in any of the twelve countries in the euro zone (also known as "Euroland"), nor for changing from any of the

old Euroland currencies to any other (French francs to Schillings, for example).

Euro notes will be issued in **denominations** of 5, 10, 20, 50, 100, 200 and 500 euros, and coins in denominations of 1, 2, 5, 10, 20 and 50 cents and 1 and 2 euros.

All prices in this book are given in Schillings and the exact equivalent in euros. When the new currency takes over completely, prices are likely to be rounded off – and if decimalization in the UK is anything to go by, rounded up.

For information on the British government's current line on the euro visit *www.euro.gov.uk*; for the Irish view see *www.emuaware.forfas.ie*; and for the Austrian position go to *www.oenb.at*.

rants, usually up to the nearest öS5/€0.36 or öS10/€0.73 depending on how much you've spent and how good the service. In more expensive restaurants, you'll find the bill arrives with a fifteen percent service charge already tacked onto the total.

BANKS AND CHANGING MONEY

Out in the Austrian countryside, in small pensions, restaurants and shops, you'll find that **cash** is often the sole method of payment. In fact, there are plenty of relatively large towns where cash is still very much preferred. Make sure you always have a supply of cash on you, otherwise it's perfectly possible to carry your money in the form of debit/credit cards and withdraw money from cashpoints. Although not as convenient, travellers' cheques are still a good, safe option. Most banks in the West keep Austrian Schillings on hand for over-the-counter exchange, and it's a good idea to bring a small supply with you in case you can't find an exchange outlet on the first night.

Banking hours vary, but are generally Monday to Friday 8am to 12.30pm and 1.30 or 2pm to 3 or 4pm. Banks stay open until 5.30pm on Thursdays. Outside these hours, you will have to rely on the **Wechselstube**, or exchange booths. Those with the longest hours (typically daily 8am–8pm) are usually found at big-city train stations and at airports. There are also 24-hour automatic exchange machines dotted around the bigger towns, accepting notes of most major currencies, although commission rates may be more punitive than those charged in a bank.

PLASTIC MONEY

Plastic is by far the most convenient way to carry your money. You can pay with plastic in more upmarket hotels, shops and restaurants, but more usefully you can draw cash out on your card. Most towns in Austria have banks with English-language **ATMs** (cash machines or bankomats) which accept foreign debit and credit cards. Look out for branches of Bank Austria, Creditanstalt or Die erste Bank, and make sure you have a PIN number for your card. The daily limit for taking cash out of a bankomat is öS5000/€363.36. As usual, **charge cards** such as Amex and Diners are not as widely accepted as debit/credit cards, and tend to be restricted to top-end purchases.

If you have an Australian or New Zealand key or debit card, arrange for Cirrus, Plus or Maestro withdrawal facilities to be added before you leave home. You will be charged for withdrawing cash but the rates compare favourably.

CHEQUES

Travellers' cheques are still the safest way to carry money, and are accepted pretty much everywhere. They're available for a small commission (usually one percent of the amount ordered) from any bank and some building societies, whether or not you have an account, and from branches of American Express and Thomas Cook.

EMERGENCIES

When you buy your **travellers' cheques**, make a note of the emergency phone number given. On your trip, keep a record of all cheque serial numbers and note which ones you spend – and report any loss or theft immediately. All being well, you should get the missing cheques reissued within a couple of days. Things can be trickier if you lose your credit card: your bank should be able to give you details of the number to call if this happens, but you won't be provided with a replacement card until you get home.

Assuming you know someone who is prepared to send you the money, the quickest way to have funds sent out to you in an emergency is **wiring money** (see box opposite). If you have a few days' leeway, you can simply get your bank to wire your money to an Austrian bank, a process that shouldn't take more than a couple of days. If you can last out for a week, then an **international money order**, exchangeable at any post office, is by far the cheapest way of sending money.

If you're in really dire straits, you can get in touch with your consulate in Vienna (some countries also maintain consulates in regional capitals like Salzburg, Innsbruck, Graz and Bregenz – details are given in the relevant sections of this book), who will usually let you make one phone call home free of charge, and will – in worst cases only – repatriate you, but will never, under any circumstances, lend money.

WIRING MONEY FROM ABROAD

Wiring money is a fast but expensive way to send and receive money abroad, and should be considered in emergency situations. The sum wired should be available for collection in Austrian Schillings/euros, from the company's local agent within a few minutes of being sent via Western Union or Moneygram; both charge on a sliding scale, so sending larger amounts of cash is better value. Thomas Cook have a much cheaper flat rate but it takes 1–2 days for the money to arrive. You should always check with your bank before travelling to see if they have reciprocal arrangements with any banks in Austria.

Agents vary country to country; in Britain, for instance, Western Union is at Going Places travel agents and some newsagents and chemists, while Moneygram is at Thomas Cook offices, Eurochange and all post offices. Rates for both are broadly similar: £12–14 to send £100, or £33–37 for £500, for example, while from the US, wiring US$500 will cost about US$40. Thomas Cook's Telegraphic Transfer service from the UK costs £15 plus one percent of the amount to be sent (with a minimum charge of £25). Thomas Cook can also credit foreign bank accounts for the same fee (2–3 days).

Western Union
www.westernunion.com
UK: ☎0800/833 833
Eire: ☎1800/395 395
AUS: ☎1800/649 565
NZ: ☎09/270 0050
US & CAN: ☎1-800/325 6000

Moneygram
www.moneygram.com
UK: ☎0800/018 0104
Eire: ☎00800/8971 8971
AUS: ☎1800/230 100
NZ: ☎0800/262 263
US & CAN: ☎1-800/926 9400

Thomas Cook
www.thomascook.com
UK: ☎01733/318922
Eire: ☎01/677 1721
AUS: ☎02/9231/287
CAN: ☎1-888/8234 7328
NZ: ☎09/379 3920
US: ☎1-800/287 7362

GETTING AROUND

Austria's public transport system is fast, efficient and, all things considered, relatively cheap. Train and bus routes tend to be fully integrated, complementing each other rather than competing. You can reach most areas of the country by public transport, although rural villages may only be served by one bus per day, or just a couple per week. Getting around on Sundays and public holidays can be problematic: train services are reduced and many rural bus services cease altogether.

Most parts of Austria – including the big cities – operate a zonal **travelcard** (*Zeitkarte* or *Netzkarte*) system covering all forms of public transport in that particular area. Ticket durations and prices vary considerably from one place to another, and depend on how many zones in a particular region they cover, but it's safe to assume that, if you're staying in one area and are planning to explore the outlying region by a combination of rail and bus, then it will be much cheaper to buy a 24-hour ticket (*Tageskarte*) or seven-day ticket (*Wochenkarte*) for the relevant zone than to buy tickets for each individual journey. Travelcards of longer duration (a month-long season ticket is a *Monatskarte*) are also available in most regions. Travelcards can be bought from both train and bus stations, and often from tourist offices, too. A 24-hour pass for the whole of the Vorarlberg, for example, costs öS160/€11.68), and a seven-day pass öS310/€22.63. There are also (cheaper) passes for specific regions within the Vorarlberg, and reductions for children and over-60s.

TRAINS

Austrian Federal Railways or **ÖBB** (*Österreichische Bundesbahnen, www.oebb.at*) run a punctual, clean and comfortable rail network, which includes most towns of any size. Trains marked "EC" or "EN" (EuroCity and EuroNight international expresses), "ICE" or "IC" (Austrian InterCity expresses) are the fastest. Those designated "D" (*Schnellzug*) or "E" (*Eilzug*) are the next fastest, stopping at most intermediate points, while the *Regionalzug* is the slowest form of service, stopping at all stations. Both InterRail and Eurail passes are valid for the ÖBB network, as well as for the majority of small, privately owned railways that augment it – the three that you're most likely to come across are the Zillertalbahn (from Jenbach to Mayrhofen), the Murtalbahn (from Unzmarkt to Tamsweg via Murau) and the Graz–Köflacher-Bahn (from Graz to Köflach and from Graz to Wies-Ebiswald). Passes are less likely to be valid for the tourist-oriented mountain railways, such as the Schafbergbahn (see p.429) or the Achenseebahn (see p.491), although they may secure a reduction – be sure to ask about this, as regulations change.

Fares are calculated according to distance, with the first 100km costing öS178/€12.94; 200km costing öS320/€23.26; 500km, about öS590/€42.88. **Tickets** (*Fahrschein*) are bought either from the ticket office in the train station (*Bahnhof* or *Hauptbahnhof* if it's the main station in the big city) or on the train itself (usually on payment of a small supplement; around öS30/€2.18). If travelling from a small, unstaffed halt, however, tickets can be bought on the train without paying the extra supplement. When buying tickets from a ticket office, credit cards are only accepted on purchases exceeding öS200/€14.54. Return tickets are rarely cheaper than two singles, but are valid for two months and allow for unlimited stop-offs en route. Single tickets are only valid for four days. InterCity and EuroCity trains can get crowded at weekends, especially over the summer, when making a reservation is a good idea; reserving a seat costs öS30/€2.18 extra.

If you're travelling with another person (or child), ask about the **1-Plus-Ticket**, which gives discounts on journeys up to 100km. If you're a long-term resident, you might want to get a **Vorteilscard**, which for öS1290/€93.75 a year entitles the bearer to fifty percent reductions on all rail travel.

Two other services offered by the ÖBB are also worth considering: the **Von Haus-zu-Haus-Service** will take two pieces of your luggage (up to a total weight of 40kg) from your current hotel or pension to your next accommodation, for a fee of öS180/€13.08. Even more incredibly, the ÖBB, in association with the national tourist office, offers a free pick-up/transfer or **Abholservice** in over 100 towns across Austria. A taxi or hotel representative will pick you up from your hotel, take you to the station, and do the same at the other end.

Train **times** are displayed in the ticket halls and on the platforms of all stations. Yellow *Abfahrt* posters list departures, and white *Ankunft* posters list arrivals. A train **timetable** (*Kursbuch*, or *Fahrpläne*) covering the whole country comes in compact paperback form and is available from station ticket offices at a cost of öS100/€7.27. Some smaller regional timetables are available for around öS15/€1.09 each, though leaflets detailing specific routes are free from some stations and tourist offices. Note that domestic timetables change at the end of May each year. For **telephone information** on train times and prices, call ☎05/1717. With just a little German you can also look up specific train times on-line at *www.oebb.at*.

Most Austrian **train stations** are kept spotlessly clean, and offer a number of useful services. In towns and cities, they often harbour the only shops open after 6pm (or at all on a Sunday). Virtually every station also has a staffed left-luggage office and/or luggage lockers, see p.61, as well as decent toilets and, more often than not, offers bike rental, see p.36.

BUSES

Austria's *Bahnbus* and *Postbus* system fills most of the gaps left by the rail network. As a general rule, *Bahnbus* services (run by the ÖBB) depart from train stations, and *Postbus* services (run by the post office) stop outside the post office, though often either service calls in at both.

Bus **fares** work out slightly cheaper than train fares, costing around öS130/€9.45 per 100km; along routes served by both forms of transport, however, you'll find that trains are almost invariably quicker. Buses come into their own on routes serving out-of-the-way, alpine villages, where they constitute a valuable lifeline for the local community, carrying mail as well as ferrying the local kids to and from school. Indeed, bus timetables often reflect the needs of the school day, with a flurry of departures in the early morning and early afternoon, compared to fewer services later in the day. Generally, bus services are less frequent on Sundays and public holidays, and in some areas cease altogether on these days.

Bus **schedules** (*Fahrpläne*) for a particular route are usually displayed at bus stops (*Bushaltestelle*); larger towns will have a bus station (*Busbahnhof*, usually next to either the post office or the main train station), where a complete range of arrivals and departures is listed. A full timetable (*Kursbuch*) covering the whole of Austria is available for öS250/€18.17 from the ticket windows at bus stations, but it's divided into five volumes (each covering a separate geographical region) and weighs a ton; individual volumes are sold for öS75/€5.45 or less, depending on the region covered. Happily, free booklets containing local timetables are often available from both bus stations and tourist offices.

Tickets are usually bought from the bus driver, although it's possible to buy them in advance from the ticket window at a bus station. Twenty-four-hour travelcards (*Tageskarten*) for a particular route or zone are often cheaper than buying individual return tickets. A *Tageskarte* can usually be bought from the bus driver, though travelcards of longer duration (*Netzkarten*) must be purchased from the ticket office of a bus or train station.

BOATS

Passenger **boats** (*Schiffahrt*) ply many of Austria's lakes and waterways, notably the Salzkammergut and Carinthian lakes and the stretch of the Danube between Vienna and Linz. Operating times may well be seasonal (most lake steamers tend to run from April or May to Sept), and ships are invariably pleasure-oriented, duplicating routes which can be covered more cheaply and quickly by road or rail. However, if you have the time, a leisurely cruise across the Wolfgangsee, the trip over to Hallstatt, or down a stretch of the Danube, can be one of the most memorable and relaxed ways of sightseeing. Most ship services are run by private companies,

though the ÖBB runs the ones on Lake Cons and the Wolfgangsee. Public transport pass (InterRail and Eurail passes, Austrian regional travelcards) are valid (or give discounts) on some but by no means all of the services.

MOUNTAIN TRANSPORT

It's highly likely that at some point during your stay, you'll use transport to help you get to the top of a mountain quickly. A remarkable number of Austrian summits can be accessed by public transport, and the view from the top is invariably superb. You'll come across the *Standseilbahn*, or **funicular railway** and *Zahnradbahn* or **cog railway** in some resorts. In addition, there are various types of lift: *Seilbahn*, or single-cabin **cable car**, the *Gondelbahn*, or **gondola** (a succession of smaller cabins suspended from the same cable), and the *Sesselbahn*, or **chairlift**. The rudimentary *Schlepplift* or **T-bar lift** is only used during the ski season.

Fares on these journeys vary enormously depending on the height to which you're climbing. Discounts are sometimes available if you hold a Gästepass or some kind of travel pass. Invariably, the **ascent** (*Bergfahrt*) is more expensive than the descent (*Talfahrt*), and a return is cheaper than the sum of the two. If you're here in the ski season, you'll need to buy a **ski pass** to get the best value (for more on which see p.57).

DRIVING

Travelling by **car** (*Auto* or *PKW*) is very straightforward in Austria. The roads are in general impeccably maintained, and there's an extensive system of **autobahns** linking all main cities and providing onward routes to neighbouring countries. Autobahns are sometimes designated by name (the Salzburg–Villach *Tauern Autobahn*, for example), but more often by number. Note that the Austrian **numbering system**, in which autobahns are prefixed by the letter A, conflicts with the European numbering system, whereby all main continental routes are prefixed with the letter E – you'll therefore find that the main A1 Salzburg–Vienna autobahn is also marked on most maps as the E60. Main roads (*Bundesstrasse*) are usually marked in red on maps and designated by number; minor roads are usually marked in yellow and have no number.

All Austria's autobahns are subject to a single **toll**, which involves buying a *Vignette* (windscreen sticker) from the petrol stations or shops found at border posts when entering the country. You can also buy them from post offices and *Tabak* shops once inside the country. A ten-day *Vignette* costs öS105/€7.63 (and you'll need to buy a ten-day one even if you're merely passing straight through the country); a two-month *Vignette* öS300/€21.80. Motorbikers get a discount on all *Vignettes*. You don't need a *Vignette* at all, of course, if you intend to stick to normal main roads; however, those caught driving on Austria's autobahns without displaying a valid *Vignette* will be subject to a maximum of a öS3000/€218.02 fine.

Speed limits are 50kph in built-up areas, 100kph on normal roads and 130kph on motorways. You have to be eighteen to drive in Austria, but most **driving rules** are otherwise fairly standard. Yellow diamond signs indicate who has priority at junctions, rather than road markings. **Seatbelts** must be worn (in the back seats as well, if you're in a car that has them fitted). The wearing of crash helmets is compulsory for motorbike riders. The permissible alcohol limit is 0.8 percent – roughly two glasses of wine or two pints of beer. Watch out for **trams** in Austrian cities; it's forbidden to overtake them if they're at a stop without a pedestrian island. Another thing that can catch you out is that if you're turning right or left at **traffic lights**, you have to give way to pedestrians, who also have a "green man" encouraging them to cross.

As far as **parking** is concerned, most urban areas have time-limited parking zones (*Kurzparkzone*), allowing a parking time of ninety minutes to three hours. If the parking is free of charge, all you need to do is get hold of a cardboard clock (*Tolle Zeit* or *Zeitkarte*) on which you should then indicate your arrival time. If you have to pay up, there will either be a machine close by, or you'll need to purchase a sticker (*Parkschein*) from a *Tabak* shop or petrol station, which you must fill in and then display on the windscreen.

Many UK car insurance policies cover taking your car to Europe; check with your insurer while planning your trip. However, you're advised to take out extra cover for motoring assistance in case your car breaks down. If you are driving a car abroad and you are already a member of the AA (☎0800/444500, *www.theaa.co.uk*), RAC (☎0800/550055, *www.rac.co.uk*) or equivalent body, you can make use of the **breakdown ser-**vices offered by both the main Austrian motoring organizations, the Österreichischer Automobile, Motorrad und Touring Club (ÖAMTC, ☎120, *www.oemtc.at*), and the Auto-, Motor- und Radfahrerbund Österreichs (ARBÖ, ☎123, *www.arboe.or.at*). Call-out charges hover around the öS1000/€72.67 mark.

As regards **documentation**, if you're bringing your own car you need a valid driving licence plus an international green card of insurance, and an **international driving permit** if you're a non-EU licence holder. In Australia these are available from state motoring organization offices in major towns and cities (*www.aaa.asn.au*); in New Zealand contact your local Automoblie Association office (*www.aa.co.nz*). In North America get in touch with the American Automobile Association (*www.aaa.com*), the Canadian Automobile Association (*www.caa.ca*), or your local branch for details of the procedure.

ALPINE ROUTES

Most of the major **alpine routes** are kept open year-round, whatever the weather, but it's a good idea to carry **snow chains** in winter months if you're traversing alpine areas not served by autobahns. Road signs showing a white tyre on a blue background indicate that snow chains are compulsory. Several scenic, high-altitude mountain roads, usually marked as *Mautstrasse* on maps,

---

PRINCIPAL ALPINE ROAD ROUTES CLOSED TO TRAILERS

Enns Gorge (Weyer Markt–Hieflau)

Flexen Pass (Rauzalpe–Zürs–Lech–Warth)

Gerlos Pass (Zell am Ziller–Krimml)

Grossglockner Hochalpenstrasse (Zell am See–Heiligenblut)

Hochtannberg Pass (Au–Warth)

Holzleiten Sattel (Nassereith–Telfs)

Loibl Pass (Klagenfurt–Slovenia)

Plöcken Pass (Kötschach–Italy)

Pötschenhöhe (Bad Ischl–Bad Aussee)

Seeberg Sattel, Carinthia (Eisenkappel– Slovenia)

Seeberg Sattel, Styria (Bruck an der Mur–Mariazell)

Silvretta Hochalpenstrasse (Partenen–Galtür)

Timmelsjoch Pass (Obergurgl–Italy)

Würzen Pass (Villach–Slovenia)

are only open during snow-free months, and **tolls** (*Mäute*) are levied for their use. The Grossglockner Hochalpenstrasse, which links the Salzburger Land with Carinthia and passes Austria's highest mountain along the way, is one of the most popular; opening times and prices for this and other scenic toll roads are detailed throughout this book.

Many of Austria's steep, winding transalpine roads are unsuitable for **caravans** or other **trailers**. The box below details the major routes on which trailers are banned; you should refer to a good motoring map for details of the many minor roads in the Alps that are closed to trailers. Alternatively, contact your home motoring organization for details of which routes are recommended for trailers, or simply stick to the autobahns.

CAR RENTAL

All of the big international **car rental** (*Mietwagen*) companies have offices in most Austrian towns and at airports, and it's fairly easy

to book a car in your home country before you travel (see box below) – it's almost always cheaper to book from home and pick the car up at the airport. Holiday Autos are usually the cheapest of the big companies; typical charges range from öS1000/€72.67 per day or öS3200/€232.55 per week for a small car with unlimited mileage, to öS3000/€218.02 per day or öS9000/€654.06 for something at the top of the range. Ask about any special deals, too, as it's often cheaper to rent over the weekend.

Cars rented within Austria should come with a valid *Vignette* (a windscreen sticker showing that autobahn tax has been paid, see pp.33–34) – it's a good idea to check that this is in order before driving off. You need to be at least, and often over, 25 to rent a car, and have a clean driving licence. If you're thinking of popping over the border into one of the former Eastern Bloc countries, you need to say so when you collect the car; some companies have restrictions on this, and most will slap a daily surcharge on top of the normal rental fee.

CAR RENTAL AGENCIES

UK
Autos abroad ☎0870/0667788, www.autosabroad.co.uk
Avis ☎0870/606 0100, www.avis.com
Budget ☎0800/181181, www.budgetrentacar.com
Europcar ☎0345/222525, www.europcar.com
National Car Rental ☎01895/233300, www.nationalcar.com
Hertz ☎0870/844 8844, www.hertz.com
Holiday Autos ☎0870/400 0011, www.kemwel.com
Thrifty ☎01494/442 110, www.thrifty.com

REPUBLIC OF IRELAND
Avis ☎01/874 5844, www.avis.com.
Budget Rent-A-Car ☎0800/973159, www.budgetrentacar.com
Europcar ☎01/874 5844, www.europcar.com
Hertz ☎01/676 7476, www.hertz.com
Holiday Autos ☎01/872 9366, www.kemwel.com

USA AND CANADA
Alamo ☎1-800/522 9696, www.alamo.com
Auto Europe US ☎1-800/223 5555; Canada ☎1-888/223 5555; www.autoeurope.com

Avis US ☎1-800/331 1084; Canada ☎1-800/272 5871; www.avis.com
Budget ☎1-800/527 0700, www.budgetrentacar.com
Dollar ☎1-800/800 6000, www.dollar.com
Enterprise Rent-a-Car ☎1-800/325 8007, www.enterprise.com
Europe by Car ☎1-800/223 1516, www.europebycar.com
Hertz US ☎1-800/654 3001; Canada ☎1-800/263 0600; www.hertz.com
National US ☎1-800/227 7368, www.nationalcar.com
Thrifty US ☎1-800/367 2277, www.thrifty.com

AUSTRALIA AND NEW ZEALAND
Avis Australia ☎13/6333; New Zealand ☎0800/655111 or 09/526 5231; www.avis.com
Budget Australia ☎1300/362848; New Zealand ☎0800/652227 or 09/3752270; www.budget.com
Hertz Australia ☎1800/550067; New Zealand ☎0800/655955 or 09/309 0989; www.hertz.com

CYCLING

Austria is a bicycle-friendly country, with **cycling** lanes in all major towns. There are also a large number of designated cycle routes out in the countryside; these include stretches of pedestrian- and cycle-only pathway, but more often consist of a separate lane by the roadside.

Most well-touristed places in Austria boast a couple of **bike rental** (*Fahrradverlieh*) outlets – usually requiring production of a passport or other photo-accompanied ID. Over fifty train stations rent out bikes for öS180/€13.08 per day or öS900/€65.41 per week, öS120/€8.72 and öS600/€43.60 if you have a valid rail ticket or Vorteilscard. Children's bikes, and children's seats are also available. The bikes can be returned to a different station to the one you set out from for an extra fee of öS90/€6.54 (oS45/€3.27 if you have a ticket). Train stations don't always have the widest choice of bikes, however, and for something more specialized, like a **mountain bike**, it's often better to go to another bike rental operator, where prices may be up to öS50/€3.63 per day higher. Details of where to rent bikes in the larger towns and resorts are given throughout this book.

ACCOMMODATION

Despite profiteering in main tourist centres like Vienna and Salzburg, accommodation need not be expensive in Austria. Finding a room shouldn't present too many problems, either, although it can be a scramble in July and August, and in skiing areas between late December and April.

The majority of **tourist offices** will book accommodation on behalf of personal callers (most refuse to do so for those enquiring by phone, fax or email); other offices will supply you with an accommodation list and point you in the direction of a public telephone. Of the tourist offices who do book accommodation for you, some charge a small fee (usually not more than öS30–40/€2.18–2.91) and/or a deposit – in general, it's in the large urban centres (Vienna, Salzburg and Innsbruck, for example) that this extra charge is levied. The bigger tourist offices have accommodation lists on an information board (or touch-screen computer), either in the lobby or on the wall outside, for those who arrive during closing hours; these are often accompanied by a courtesy phone so you can call up whichever hotel or pension takes your fancy.

Inevitably, accommodation **prices** are subject to seasonal variations. In most areas rates are highest in July and August, with a shoulder season comprising April to June and September; in ski resorts, prices peak from December to March. Some areas (notably alpine resorts that remain popular throughout the year) have a peak season in both summer and winter, and offer cheaper prices in spring and autumn. Throughout this Guide, we've quoted **peak summer prices**, though an indication of what you might expect to pay in winter has been provided in alpine resorts where relevant. Whatever time of year you're here, you should always ask for a **Gästekarte** (guest card), as this perk for overnight visitors can give substantial discounts for local attractions and transport.

HOTELS AND PENSIONS

A high standard of cleanliness and comfort can be taken for granted in most Austrian hotels. **Hotels** call themselves either a Hotel or **Gasthof** (plural Gasthöfe) – there's little difference between the two terms, although use of the word Gasthof (originally used to describe a country inn offering both refreshment and lodging) is intended these days to connote a traditional, cosy feel. Most hotels and Gasthöfe have restaurants offering food and drink throughout the day; a **Hotel-Garni** is a hotel that offers breakfast but no other meals. A **Gästehaus** is usually a small B&B hotel, not to be confused with a **Gasthaus**, which is merely a restaurant – unless, of course, it's followed by the words "*mit Unterkunft*" (with lodging).

The label **Pension** or **Frühstückspension** denotes a bed-and-breakfast hotel that, although self-contained, occupies one or more floors, but not the whole, of a larger building. Pensions tend to be small, family-run affairs, but there are no hard-and-fast rules as to what they look like or what they offer: those in the big cities tend to occupy large apartment blocks, while those in country areas may well be in traditional, rustic houses.

A few other pieces of **terminology** you'll come across in accommodation brochures are worth explaining. *Komfortzimmer* ("comfort room"), is used to describe rooms that have both en-suite bath/shower (*Bad/Dusche*) facilities and TV. ÜF (*Übernachtung mit Frühstuck*) means "bed-and-breakfast"; HP (*Halbpension*) means "half board"; VP (*Vollpension*) means "full board"; EZ (*Einzelbettzimmer*) means "single room" and DZ (*Doppelbettzimmer*) means "double room".

COSTS AND STANDARDS

Hotels and pensions are graded on a **five-star scale**. The most basic, one-star places, offering simple rooms with shared toilets and bathrooms, are in very short supply, and rarely quoted in Austrian tourist-office literature. Most budget accommodation falls into the two-star category, offering rooms usually with en-suite shower and toilet (although some have en-suite toilet but shared shower) and a simple continental breakfast – typically a pot of coffee, bread rolls and jam. Generally speaking, pensions tend to fall into this category; some of Vienna's inner-city pensions, however, are luxury hotels in all but name. Outside of Vienna, in two-star hotels and most pensions, you can expect to pay öS500–800/€36.34–58.14 for a double with bathroom; slightly less for rooms with shared facilities.

Once beyond the two-star bracket, prices rise rapidly. Rooms in three-star places usually come with en-suite shower, telephone and TV (often with a range of satellite programmes, including a couple of English-language channels like CNN or the BBC), together with a larger range of breakfast food, often an as-much-as-you-can-eat buffet comprising cereals, cold meats and pastries. You should expect to pay öS800–1200/€58.14–87.21 for a double in this category. Once you break into the four- and five-star brackets, you can expect bigger rooms, an expanded range of creature comforts, like more luxurious furnishings and large baths to wallow in, and additional facilities like swimming pool, gym and sauna. Anything between öS1200/€87.21 and öS2500/€181.68 for a double is not unusual, with prestigious luxury hotels in Vienna and other big cities exceeding even this.

Note that **credit cards** are not accepted in many small hotels and pensions.

PRIVATE ROOMS AND FARMHOUSES

Staying in a **private room** (*Privatzimmer*), in the house of a local family, is another good option in most parts of Austria. While in many cases you'll be sharing a bathroom and eating your breakfast with the family, in others it's not that different from staying in a pension – you might be in a reasonably self-contained part of the house, and

ACCOMMODATION PRICE CODES

All **hotels and pensions** in this book have been coded according to the following price categories. All the codes are based on the rate for the least expensive double room during the **summer season**. In those places where winter is the high season, we've indicated both summer and winter room rates in the text.

① under öS400/€29.07
② öS400–600/€29.07–43.60
③ öS600–800/€43.60–58.14
④ öS800–1000/€58.14–72.67
⑤ öS1000–1200/€72.67–87.21

⑥ öS1200–1400/€87.21–101.74
⑦ öS1400–1600/€101.74–116.28
⑧ öS1600–1800/€116.28–130.81
⑨ over öS1800/€130.81

rooms can come with en-suite shower and toilet (and perhaps even a TV). Most tourist offices keep extensive lists of all the private rooms offered locally, and tourist office staff will usually book one on your behalf; in well-travelled, rural areas where the locals depend a great deal on tourism, roadside signs offering *Zimmer frei* (vacancies) are fairly common. Most private rooms are let on a bed-and-breakfast basis, with a continental breakfast often served in your host's kitchen, but do check to make sure that the price you're quoted includes breakfast. Prices for a double room are between öS400/€29.07 and öS600/€43.60. Single travellers shouldn't have difficulty in finding a room, although they may have to pay sixty to seventy percent of the price of a double.

Most tourist offices in small-town and rural Austria also book bed-and-breakfast rooms in local **farmhouses**. Promoted nationally under the rubric *Urlaub am Bauernhof* (farmhouse holidays), this kind of tourism is little different to staying in a private room, save for the fact that you'll be on a working farm and may be able to observe – or help out – as the animals are fed or cheese is made in an alpine dairy. Most farmhouses offer either double rooms, family-size apartments (typically sleeping four to six) or a mixture of both. Double rooms in farmhouses cost no more than comparable private rooms, while apartments usually offer even better value, often working out at öS150/€10.90 or less per person per night. Prices usually include breakfast, but not always; some of the farmhouse apartments have self-catering facilities.

Many farms offering rooms prefer guests to stay for about a week; you may get away with a stay of three or four days, especially if you're travelling outside the peak season, but anything less than this tends to be discouraged. Farmhouse accommodation is increasingly popular, and if you're travelling in July or August it's a good idea to book in advance before you travel: most tourist offices (addresses, phone numbers and Web sites of which are included throughout this book) will gladly send you a list or an illustrated brochure covering local options. Most farms are in quite remote areas, so you're likely to need your own transport if you want to enjoy a farmhouse holiday to the full.

HOSTELS

Youth hostels (*Jugendherberge* or *Jugendgästehaus*) are fairly widespread in Austria – around a hundred in all. They're run by two separate national organizations, the Österreichischer Jugendherbergsverband (ÖJHV) and the Österreichischer Jugendherbergswerk (ÖJHW), although both are HI (Hostelling International) affiliated. Hostels run by church organizations or private individuals can also be found in big cities like Vienna, Salzburg and Innsbruck. High standards of cleanliness and organization can be taken for granted, but such factors as number of people per room and range of facilities vary widely. Rural hostels tend towards the hearty and basic, with large numbers of bunk beds crammed into a small number of rooms; that said, many large resorts and cities have almost hotel-like hostels, which contain a mixture of both multibed dorms and well-appointed double rooms with en-suite facilities. Overcrowding, however, can be a problem – especially during school holidays, when hostels everywhere are besieged by kids – so book in advance whenever possible.

Rates hover between öS150/€10.90 and öS250/€18.17 depending on how plush the hostel. Expect to pay something nearer the lower rate for a rural hostel with dorm accommodation; the higher rate for a city hostel with lower person-per-dorm ratios or accommodation in double rooms. Prices for double rooms are indicated in the text, as are dorm beds when the cost varies considerably from those quoted above. If you're not already a member of an HI-affiliated youth hostel organization, an extra öS40/€2.91 or so will be charged, which will go towards paying for your guest membership card (*Gästekarte*) – after six visits you should then be a full guest member.

Sheet sleeping bags are obligatory, and the cost of hiring one is often included in the overnight charge. A very simple breakfast – two rolls, jam and coffee – is also usually included in the price. In addition to breakfast, many hostels serve meals and snacks throughout the day in cafeteria-like surroundings, often at very competitive prices. Most hostels close during the day, and you're expected to check in either in the morning (before 10am) or in the evening (typically between 5 and 10pm); you may also be expected to vacate the premises at 9am on the dot, so be prepared. Outside the big cities, most hostels also operate a curfew at around 11pm, although in many cases you'll be given a key (often on payment of a small deposit) enabling you to come and go as you please.

For a full list of HI-affiliated hostels in Austria, buy the **HI Europe handbook**, which costs

HOSTELLING ASSOCIATIONS

AUSTRIA

Österreichischer Jugendherbergsverband (ÖJHV), Schottenring 28, 1010 Wien (☎01/533 5353, *www.oejhv.or.at*).
Österreichisches Jugendherbergswerk (ÖJHW), Helferstorferstrasse 4, 1010 Wien (☎01/533 1833, *www.oejhw.or.at*).

ENGLAND AND WALES

Youth Hostel Association (YHA), Trevelyan House, 8 St Stephen's Hill, St Alban's, Hertfordshire AL1 2DY (☎0870/8708 808, *www.yha.org.uk*). International Booking Network ☎01629/581418.

IRELAND

Youth Hostel Association of Northern Ireland, 22 Donegal Rd, Belfast BT12 5JN (☎028/9031 5435, *www.hini.org.uk*).
An Oige, 61 Mountjoy St, Dublin 7 (☎01/830 4555, *www.irelandyha.org*).

SCOTLAND

Scottish Youth Hostel Association (SYHA), 7 Glebe Crescent, Stirling FK8 2JA (☎0870/1553 255, *www.syha.org.uk*).

USA

Hostelling International-American Youth Hostels (HI-AYH), 733 15th St NW, Suite 840, PO Box 37613, Washington, DC 20005 (☎202/783 6161, *www.hiyaha.org*).

CANADA

Hostelling International/Canadian Hostelling Association, Room 400, 205 Catherine St, Ottawa, ON K2P 1C3 (☎1-800/663 5777 or 613/237 7884, *www.hiyaha.org*).

AUSTRALIA

Australian Youth Hostels Association, 422 Kent St, Sydney (☎02/9261 1111, *www.yha.com.au*)

NEW ZEALAND

Youth Hostels Association of New Zealand, 173 Gloucester St, Christchurch (☎03/379 9970, *www.yha.co.nz*).

£8.00, or write to both the Austrian youth hostel organizations in Austria (note that neither organization will give out information on hostels run by the other). Beds at all the big city hostels, and some of the more popular small ones, can be booked up to six months in advance via the **International Booking Network** (IBN), which you can phone via your national hostelling association back home. You can also book hostels on the IBN via the Internet on *www.iyhf.org*. For all other hostels, you'll have to phone, email or fax the individual hostels concerned; details are given in the Guide.

MOUNTAIN HUTS

Highland areas of Austria are equipped with an extensive network of **mountain huts**, known as *Schutzhütte* or simply *Hütte*, catering for hikers and mountaineers. More than 500 of these are run by the Austrian Alpine Club (Österreichischer Alpenverein, or ÖAV; see p.55), and an addi-

tional 500 are either privately owned or belong to smaller mountain clubs. Originally intended as simple refuges, most huts these days are rather like mountain inns, offering a range of accommodation. Mixed-sex dormitories (bring your own sheet sleeping bag) are the norm, although two-bed rooms or family rooms are often available. The hut warden provides meals and sells assorted drinks – tea, coffee, hot chocolate, beer, wine and schnapps – but prices are likely to be higher than those charged down in the valley.

Most huts are open from the beginning of July to mid-September; a few open in late May or June, and some may be open for longer periods to provide accommodation during the spring ski-touring season. Huts are at their busiest from mid-July to mid-August, but booking in advance is rarely necessary. If you arrive to find that all the beds are taken, you'll be allocated an emergency bed (*Notlager*) – a mattress on the floor. Expect to **pay** around öS100/€7.27 for a *Notlager* bed;

öS100–300/€7.27–21.80 for a dorm bed; öS300–500/€21.80–36.34 for a bed in a two-person room. A rudimentary breakfast (comprising bread, jam and tea or coffee) is usually available for an extra öS100/€7.27 or so. Members of the ÖAV (they have a branch in Britain; see p.55) receive a fifty percent reduction on the price of a bed in all ÖAV-administered huts. A list (in German) of all huts, their opening dates, facilities and the like, can be found in the book *Der Alpenvereinshütten* (8th edition £15 for members, £18 for non-members), available from the UK branch of the Austrian Alpine Club.

CAMPING

Austria's high standards of accommodation are reflected in the country's **campsites**, the vast majority of which are clean, well-run affairs offering laundry facilities, shops and snack bars, as well as toilet and shower facilities. The only drawback is their tendency towards over-regimentation, with a plethora of rules and regulations – it's usually forbidden to light fires, make noise between certain hours, and some sites lock the gates for a couple of hours at lunchtime ensuring that no vehicle can get in or out. The larger sites often provide a wealth of activities and sports facilities – especially the lakeside sites of the Salzkammergut and Carinthia – and are good places to enjoy a family break; if you

want to avoid a holiday-camp atmosphere, however, opt for a smaller, rural site. While most places cater just for tents and caravans, some sites offer four- to six-person bungalows. Sites usually open May to September only, although a great many in the winter resorts of western Austria never close. Prices vary enormously depending on the facilities available and the season. In general, you can expect to pay about öS60–80/€4.36–5.81 per person, öS40–120 /€2.91–8.72 per pitch, plus öS20–50 /€1.45–3.63 per vehicle. Use of electricity is usually öS30–50/€2.18–3.63 extra.

If you're planning to do a lot of camping, an international camping carnet (Camping Card International or CCI; £4.50) is a good investment, available from the AA or the RAC, or from the Camping and Caravanning Club, Greenfields House, Westwood Way, Coventry, CV4 8JH (☎024/7669 4995, *www.campingandcaravanningclub.co.uk*). The carnet serves as useful identification, and many campsites will take it instead of making you surrender your passport during your stay. It covers you for third-party insurance when camping, and sometimes helps you get ten percent reductions or other incentives at camp sites listed in the CCI Information booklet which comes with your carnet.

Caravanners should note that some transalpine roads are considered unsafe for caravans. The principal routes to avoid are listed on p.34.

EATING AND DRINKING

Austrian cuisine revolves around a solid pork- and veal-based repertoire, of which *Wiener Schnitzel* is the most famous example. Main meals tend to be meat-heavy affairs, however, and don't reflect the variety offered by Austria's main contribution to global gastronomic culture – the consumption of endless varieties of coffee, cakes and sweets. Partaking of the calorific delights in the cake-filled cafés and coffeehouses is an essential part of the Austrian experience – whatever consequences this might have for your waistline.

The kinds of venues where you will do your eating and drinking tend to overlap, making precise definitions difficult. Many cafés and coffeehouses offer breakfast and lunchtime menus alongside the expected range of drinks and sweets, while bars and other night-time drinking venues often have a wide choice of hot evening food. Similarly, many of the less grand restaurants are good places in which to simply sit and enjoy a beer.

BREAKFASTS AND SNACKS

Breakfast (*Frühstuck*) in Austria usually comprises a pot of tea or coffee, together with a couple of rolls with butter and jam – this is what you'll get if you're staying in a youth hostel, private room, pension or inexpensive hotel. One step up, a "full continental breakfast" means you should get a bit of choice, perhaps cold meats and cheeses and, if you're really lucky, a hot egg-based snack. Most hotels at mid-range and above offer a buffet breakfast, which means you can gorge yourself on as much cereal, muesli, eggs, bread, rolls, cheese and meats as you can eat. Most cafés will have a set breakfast menu (again, usually a pot of coffee and a couple of bread rolls and/or pastries) for around öS50–80/€3.63–5.81, and you can of course order extra bits and pieces separately.

If you're self-catering, then fresh round bread rolls (*Semmeln*) or finger rolls (*Stangerl*) bought from a supermarket or bakery (*Bäckerei*) are delicious, as are *Kipferl*, croissant-style pastries, or the slightly sweeter *Kolatschen*. Bread (*Brot*) is taken very seriously in Austria, and there is usually a wide variety of lovely crusty loaves on display in most bakeries. The standard loaf is *Hausbrot*, a mixture of wheat (*Weizen*) and rye (*Roggen*), often with caraway (*Kümmel*) or sunflower seeds (*Sonnenblumen*).

Austrian **snacks** centre on the ubiquitous *Würstelstand*, or sausage stand, which sells hot sausage (*Wurst*) as well as a few other things – usually French fries, soft drinks, canned beer and occasionally burgers. Numerous varieties of Wurst are available: *Frankfurter*, *Bratwurst* (fried sausage) or *Burenwurst* (boiled sausage) are the most common, but you could also try a *Debreziner*, a spicy Hungarian sausage, a *Currywurst*, which speaks for itself, a *Käsekrainer*, a sausage filled with blobs of molten cheese, or a *Bosna*, a thin and spicy Balkan sausage. To accompany your sausage, you usually get a roll (*Semmel*) and some mustard (*Senf*), which can be either *scharf* (hot) or *süss* (sweet).

MAIN MEALS

The main meals of the day can often be taken in a **Kaffeehaus** or **café** (see p.45), although a larger choice of dishes will be offered by a **restaurant** or a **Gasthof** – the latter traditionally

---

CHEAP EATS

For a cheap sit-down meal, budget travellers shouldn't overlook the cheap two-course set menus (*Mittagsmenü*) offered by many cafés at lunchtime, usually priced at under öS100/€7.27. Otherwise, you could try one of the **self-service restaurants** (*Selbstbedienung*) chains like Wienerwald (an upmarket fried chicken joint) and Nordsee (serving fish- and seafood-based snacks), which you'll find in most major towns, and which offer a slightly more central European alternative to the international burger chains. *Prima* is the biggest chain of self-service restaurants, with branches throughout Austria, and big town-centre department stores often have a self-service restaurant of their own. They're a good place to get a cheap meal, although surroundings are pretty uninspiring, and they're usually only open in the daytime, closing at around 6pm. Train station buffets usually offer reasonably inexpensive meals of the schnitzel and chips variety, although they're not always the kind of place that you'd want to sit down in for long.

Billa is the largest national chain of **supermarket**, with outlets in most towns. However, Austria has yet to become a fully paid-up member of the supermarket society, and most stores are relatively modest in size, even in large towns. Nevertheless, since individually owned specialist food shops can be pretty thin on the ground, you'll probably find yourself relying on supermarkets if you're self-catering, or gathering **picnic supplies**. If you can, though, it's worth seeking out the weekly local market, often known as a *Bauernmarkt* (farmers' market), the best source of fresh local produce, and usually a good place for street snacks. Anker, the national bakery chain, is ubiquitous, but its bread and pastries are reliably good.

AUSTRIAN FOOD AND DRINK GLOSSARY

BASICS

Abendessen	supper/dinner	*Käse*	cheese	*Salz*	salt
Auflauf	omelette	*Knödel*	dumplings	*Semmel*	bread roll
Beilagen	side dishes	*Kren*	horseradish	*Senf*	mustard
Brot	bread	*Löffel*	spoon	*Spätzle* or	pasta/noodles
Butter	butter	*Messer*	knife	*Nocker*	
Ei	egg	*Mittagessen*	lunch	*Speisekarte*	menu
Frühstuck	breakfast	*Nachspeise*	dessert	*Suppe*	soup
Gabel	fork	*Öl*	oil	*Tasse*	cup
Gebäck	pastries	*Pfeffer*	pepper	*Teller*	plate
Hauptgericht	main course	*Reis*	rice	*Vorspeise*	starter
Honig	honey	*Salat*	salad	*Zucker*	sugar

VEGETABLES (*GEMÜSE*)

Blaukraut	red cabbage	*Maiskolben*	corn on the cob
Bohnen	beans		
Champignons	button mushrooms	*Paprika*	green or red peppers
Erbsen	peas	*Paradeiser*	tomatoes
Erdäpfel	potatoes	*Kohlsprossen*	Brussels sprouts
Fisolen	green beans	*Rote Rübe*	beetroot
G'röste	fried grated potatoes	*Pilze*	mushrooms
Gurke	gerkhin /cucumber	*Pommes Frites*	chips/French fries
Karfiol	cauliflower	*Sauerkraut*	pickled cabbage
Karotten	carrots		
Knoblauch	garlic	*Spargel*	asparagus
Kohl	cabbage	*Spinat*	spinach
Lauch	leek	*Zwiebeln*	onions

MEAT (*FLEISCH*) AND POULTRY (*GEFLÜGEL*)

Eisbein	pig's trotters	*Hirsch*	venison	*Puter*	turkey
Ente	duck	*Huhn*	chicken	*Rindfleisch*	beef
Fasan	pheasant	*Innereien*	innards	*Schinken*	ham
Gans	goose	*Kalbfleisch*	veal	*Schweinefleisch*	pork
Hackfleisch	mincemeat	*Kuttelfleck*	tripe	*Speck*	bacon
Hammelfleisch	mutton	*Lamm*	lamb	*Taube*	pigeon
Hase	hare	*Leber*	liver	*Zunge*	tongue
Hirn	brains	*Nieren*	kidneys		

FISH (*FISCH*)

Aal	eel	*Krabben*	prawns	*Scholle*	plaice
Fogosch	pikeperch	*Krebs*	crab	*Seezunge*	sole
Forelle	trout	*Lachs*	salmon	*Thunfisch*	tuna
Hecht	pike	*Makrele*	mackerel	*Tintenfisch*	squid
Hummer	lobster	*Matjes*	herring		
Karpfen	carp	*Muscheln*	mussels		

COMMON TERMS

Am Spiess	on the spit	*Gebraten*	roasted	*Heiss*	hot
Blau	rare	*Gedämpft*	steamed	*Kalt*	cold
Eingelegte	pickled	*Gefüllt*	stuffed	*Kümmelbraten*	roasted with
Frisch	fresh	*Gegrillt*	grilled		caraway seeds
Gebacken	fried in	*Gekocht*	cooked	*Powidl*	plum sauce
	breadcrumbs	*Hausgemacht*	homemade	*Geräucht*	smoked

FRUIT (*OBST*)

Ananas	pineapple	*Grapefruit*	grapefruit	*Ribisel*	redcurrants
Apfel	apple	*Heidelbeeren*	bilberries	*Rosinen*	raisins
Banane	banana	*Himbeeren*	raspberries	*Trauben*	grapes
Birne	pear	*Kirschen*	cherries	*Zwetschgen*	plums
Brombeeren	blackberries	*Marillen*	apricots		
Erdbeeren	strawberries	*Pflaumen*	plums		

DESSERTS (see also "Coffee and cakes" box on p.46)

Baiser	meringue	*Marillenknödel*	sweet apricot dumplings
Bienenstich	honey and almond tart	*Mohr im Hemd*	chocolate steamed pudding
Buchteln	sweet dumplings		with cream
Käsekuchen	cheesecake	*Palatschinken*	pancakes

AUSTRIAN SPECIALITIES

Backhendl	chicken fried in breadcrumbs	*Schweinshaxe*	pork knuckle
Bauernschmaus	platter of cold sausage, pork and ham	*Stelze*	leg of veal or pork
		Tafelspitz	boiled beef, potatoes and horseradish sauce
Beuschel	chopped lung		
Brettljause	platter of cold meats and bread	*Tiroler Gröstl*	potatoes, onions and flecks of meat fried in a pan
Debreziner	paprika-spiced sausage		
Grammelknödel	pork dumplings	*Tiroler Knödel*	dumplings with pieces of ham, often eaten in a soup
Kärntner Käsnudl	large parcel of pasta dough filled with cheese		
Kasspätzln	pasta noodles with cheese	*Wiener Schnitzel*	breaded veal
Schinkenfleckern	ham with noodles	*Zwiebelrostbraten*	slices of roast beef topped with fried onions
Schlipfkrapfen	ravioli-like pasta parcels with a meat and/or potato filling		

DRINKS (*GETRÄNKE*)

Apfelsaft	apple juice	*Kir*	white wine with blackcurrant	*Sauermilch*	sour milk
Bier	beer			*Schnapps*	spirit
Flasche	bottle			*Sekt*	sparkling wine
Gespritzer	white wine with soda	*Korn*	rye spirit	*Sturm*	new wine
		Kräutertee	herbal tea	*Tee*	tea
Glühwein	mulled wine	*Milch*	milk	*Traubensaft*	grape juice
Grog	hot water with rum and sugar	*Mineralwasser*	mineral water	*Trocken*	dry
		Obstler	fruit schnapps	*Wasser*	water
Kaffee	coffee	*Orangensaft*	orange juice	*Weisswein*	white wine
Kakao	cocoa	*Roséwein*	rosé wine	*Zitronentee*	tea with lemon
		Rotwein	red wine		

describing an inn, though nowadays use of the word merely implies that the establishment has a homely, traditional feel. A **Stübe**, or **Stüberl** ("small room" or "parlour"), also denotes an eating venue with a traditional or cosy atmosphere. Other words for restaurant to look out for are **Gasthaus** and **Gastwirtschaft**. In mountain areas you can eat in an atmospheric, pine-clad **Hütte**, or **Almhütte** (literally "meadow-hut"), which will offer a modest range of food and drink to skiers in winter and walkers in summer.

For many Austrians, lunch (*Mittagessen*) rather than dinner (*Nachtmahl*) is the day's principal repast, although this doesn't usually affect the choice of food that you'll be offered in the evening. As a general rule, restaurants and Gasthöfe are open for lunch between noon and 2pm, and for dinner between 6pm and 9.30pm, although in cities and tourist resorts many establishments remain open until 11pm or midnight.

Eating out need not be expensive. Standards are generally high wherever you choose to eat, and **price** differences from one establishment to the next are usually reflected in the decor, the choice of items on the menu, and the way in which the food is presented, rather than in the quality of ingredients. A hearty soup will set you back something in the region of öS30–50/€2.18–3.63, wherever you choose to eat. A main course of the schnitzel variety (with accompanying veg or salad) will cost öS90–130/€6.54–9.45 in the more unassuming restaurants, and will rarely rise above a ceiling of öS200/€14.54 in plush establishments. The cheapest main courses on offer are often the combinations of cheese and pasta-style noodles (such as *Kasspätzln* or *Käsnudl*; see "What to eat" below) so characteristic of Austrian rural cuisine. They're usually priced somewhere in the öS80–100/€5.81–7.27 bracket, and even the most upmarket restaurants will have at least one basic, inexpensive dish of this kind on the menu.

Most places will have a full menu (*Speisekarte*) of individually priced dishes, as well as a two- or three-course **set menu** (often chalked up on a board outside), which is often much better value. A *Mittagsmenü* is a lunchtime set menu, and a *Tagesmenü* is a set menu that's available all day. Note that you should make a mental note of any **bread or rolls** (*Gepäck*) you consume with your meal, as the waiter will ask you how many you've had before totting up the bill at the end.

WHAT TO EAT

The basis of Austrian cooking is what is known as *gute bürgerliche Küche* – literally "good burghers' cuisine", so called in order to distinguish it from the noodles-and-cheese dishes that once formed the diet of the peasantry. As a result, the kind of food you'll find on restaurant menus today is often rather uniform, revolving as it does around a set repertoire of solid, meat-based dishes.

The most common starters (*Vorspeise*) are **soups**, such as *Frittatensuppe*, a clear soup containing small strips of pancake, *Leberknödelsuppe*, a clear beef broth with liver dumplings, *Gulaschsuppe*, a much more substantial, paprika-rich beef-and-vegetable soup, the sweet smelling *Knoblauchsuppe* or garlic soup, and *Serbische Bohnensuppe* (Serbian bean soup), a spicy affair that makes a good lunchtime meal on its own. Another common lunchtime light snack is *Bauernschmaus*, a platter of cold meats, slices of sausage and bread.

Most common of the **main dishes** (*Hauptspeise*) are the schnitzel dishes (pan-fried cutlet), based on veal (*Kalb*) and pork (*Schwein*): *Wiener Schnitzel*, a veal or pork cutlet fried in breadcrumbs, is the most famous, although *Pariser Schnitzel* (fried in batter) and *Natur Schnitzel* (schnitzel fried on its own or with a creamy sauce) are also ubiquitous. The other classic Austrian dishes you'll find almost anywhere are *Backhendl*, chicken fried in breadcrumbs, *Schweinsbraten*, slices of roast pork, *Zwiebelrostbraten*, slices of roast beef liberally covered with fried onions, and *Tafelspitz*, a quintessentially Viennese dish of boiled beef, potatoes and horseradish sauce. Main courses like these usually come served with potatoes and either vegetables or a small salad. Look out for the following traditional side dishes: *G'röste* (*rösti* or fried grated potato), *Knödel* (dumplings) and *Erdäpfelsalat*, boiled potatoes in a watery sweet and sour dressing.

In addition, most restaurants offer one or two **regional dishes** reflecting local rustic cuisine. The most common of these is the combination of pasta noodles and alpine cheese that goes under the name of either *Kasspätzln* or *Käsnockn*. In Carinthia, *Käsnudl* (large pieces of ravioli-like dough filled with cheese) almost enjoys the status of a national dish. Styrian cuisine, meanwhile, is characterized by liberal use of the delicious, nutty, dark *Kürbisöl* (pumpkin oil). Specialities to look out for in the Tyrol include *Schlipfkrapfen* (ravioli-like parcels with meat and/or potato filling), *Tiroler Knödel* (dumplings with small pieces of ham) and *Tiroler G'röstl* (grated onion, meat and potato fried in a pan). Traditional Austrian working-class dishes that sometimes appear on menus include *Schweinshaxe* (pork knuckle), *Stelze* (leg of veal or pork) and *Beuschel* (minced offal). The prevalence of *Gulasch* or *Gulyas* (goulash) is a Hungarian legacy, while the Italians make their presence known with dishes featuring *Nockerl*, the Austrians' heavy version of pasta – *Schinkenfleckerl*, flecks of ham baked in pasta, is especially popular.

You'll find **fish** featured all over Austria, but especially in areas near lakes or mountain streams. Trout (*Forelle*) is by far the most common dish, although native pike (*Hecht*), carp (*Karpfen*) and pikeperch (*Fogosch*) are also popular. **Game** (*Wild*) is popular throughout the year, but especially in autumn when the bulk of the hunting takes place. Most restaurants in rural Austria will offer a special game menu in the second half of October, although many establishments (especially top-of-the-range ones) will offer game dishes outside this period. The most common dishes are venison (*Hirsch*), chamois (*Gems*) and roe deer (*Reh*), and sometimes *Wildschwein* (wild boar) crops up. **Seasonal menus** are also worth looking out for in May, when dishes featuring freshly harvested asparagus (*Spargel*) appear almost everywhere, and in November, when the period around St Martin's Day (November 11) is marked by the serving of roast goose (*Gans*).

Austria is hardly a paradise for **vegetarians**. In small restaurants and Gasthöfe, you might have to rely on omelettes, or dishes such as *Knödel mit Ei* (dumplings with scrambled egg) or *Gebackener Käse*, a slab of cheese covered in breadcrumbs and deep fried. Trendier, or more upmarket establishments usually have a couple of more imaginative vegetarian choices on the menu: *Strudel* containing vegetables, spinach or cheese feature fairly often. Note, however, that most soups are based on meat stock. Regional dishes like *Kärntner Käsnudl* and *Kasspätzln* (see opposite) are usually completely meat-free, although some traditional noodles-and-cheese combinations include small pieces of ham – again, it's a good idea to ask before ordering. On a more positive note, look out for *Eierschwammerl*, chanterelle mushrooms that appear in various guises on menus in the late summer and autumn.

The main alternative to Austria's stolid meat-and-potatoes cuisine is provided by **pizzerias**, which crop up in most settlements of any size – largely good-quality, inexpensive, authentic affairs producing pizzas on traditional Italian lines, and usually offering a wide range of pasta dishes as well. Most medium-to-large-sized towns will have a Chinese restaurant, while other cuisines – notably Mexican and Indian – are increasingly represented in the big cities. Chinese restaurants in particular are often good places to look for a cheap *Mittagsmenü*, or set lunchtime menu.

Obviously in a country with such a famous sweet tooth, there's no shortage of rich **desserts** (*Mehlspeisen*) on most menus. Apart from the omnipresent *Apfelstrudel*, *Palatschinken* (pancakes) filled with jam and/or curd cheese are a regular feature. Look out, too, for *Salzburger Nockerl*, stodgy, incredibly filling egg dumplings sprinkled with icing sugar, *Marillenknödel*, sweet apricot dumplings, and the politically incorrect *Mohr im Hemd* – literally "Moor in a shirt" – a chocolate pudding with hot chocolate sauce and whipped cream. See also "Coffee and cakes" overleaf.

CAFÉS

For urban Austrians, daytime drinking traditionally centres around the **café** or the **Kaffeehaus**. There's no real difference between the two: the name "*Kaffeehaus*" suggests some historical pedigree – a relaxing, urban café, furnished with a stock of the day's newspapers, in the vein of the grand, atmospheric Viennese cafés – but cafés, too, offer essentially the same range of food and drink. Both serve alcoholic and soft drinks, cakes and a wide range of different coffees (see "Coffee and cakes" overleaf). Places where cakes and pastries are baked on the premises often call themselves a *Café-Konditorei*, or Kaffee-Konditorei. Many places also serve substantial lunches and main evening meals, although the choice is usually more limited than in restaurants. Cafés and coffeehouses often open as early as 7am and continue until early evening; those in big cities remain open until 11pm or later.

BARS AND HEURIGEN

Although some cafés stay open quite late in the evening, most night-time drinking centres on a growing number of **bars** and late-night **cafés**,

COFFEE AND CAKES

COFFEE

On average, the Austrians drink almost twice as much coffee as beer (over a pint a day per head of the population). Austrian coffee culture is at its most developed in Vienna and the east of the country, where the varieties of coffee on offer are legion – when ordering, few Austrians ever ask for a straight *Kaffee* (if you do order a "Kaffee", you'll get a *Verlängerten* – see below). Cities like Salzburg, Graz and Innsbruck possess coffeehouses as grand and dripping in atmosphere as those of the capital, but outside these urban centres you mustn't expect the full range of beverages to be offered.

Once you've selected the type of coffee you want, you may be asked whether you want it *kleiner* (small) or *grosser* (large). The grander the coffeehouse, the more likely your infusion will come served on a little silver tray with a glass of water.

Brauner	Black coffee with a small amount of milk	*Mélange*	Equal measures of frothed milk and coffee – in other words more of a cappuccino than an Austrian *Cappuccino*
Einspänner	A small black coffee, served in a tall glass and topped with whipped cream (*Schlagobers*).	*Milch Kaffee*	Large hot, frothy, milky coffee.
Eiskaffee	Iced coffee with ice cream and whipped cream	*Pharisäer*	Coffee in a glass topped with whipped cream, served with a small glass of rum on the side
Fiaker	A coffee with a shot of rum and whipped cream.	*Schwarzer* or *Mokka*	Black coffee
Kaffee Crème	Coffee served with a little jug of milk	*Türkische*	Coffee grains and sugar boiled up together in individual copper pots to create a strong, sweet brew
Cappuccino	Austrian version of a cappuccino, with whipped cream.		
Konsul	Black coffee with a spot of cream	*Verlängerter*	Slightly weaker than normal coffee, served with optional milk
Kurz	Viennese version of an espresso		
Mazagran	Coffee served with an ice cube and laced with rum, drunk in one gulp.		

CAKES

Many cafés will have *Torten* piled high in a display cabinet, in which case you can simply point to the one that takes your fancy. The best cafés still bake their own cakes, and all can be served with a helping of *Schlagobers*. The following are some of the more common choices.

Apfelstrudel	Apple and raisins wrapped in pastry and sprinkled with icing sugar	*Mohnstrudel*	A bread-like pudding rather like an Apfelstrudel, but with a poppyseed and raisin filling
Dobostorte	A rich Hungarian cake made up of alternate layers of biscuit sponge and chocolate cream	*Sachertorte*	The most famous of the Viennese cakes, and in some ways the least interesting – a chocolate sponge cake coated in chocolate, most often with a layer of apricot jam beneath the chocolate coating
Esterházytorte	Several layers of cream and sponge coated in white icing with a feather design on top		
Guglhupf	Sigmund Freud's favourite, at its most basic a simple marbled sponge cake baked in a fluted ring mould and cut into slices	*Topfenstrudel*	Like an *Apfelstrudel*, but with a sweet curd cheese filling
Linzertorte	Essentially a jam tart made with almond pastry		

where there might be a live DJ though not necessarily any dancing. Most stay open until 1–2am; in cities and alpine resorts opening hours may extend further, especially on Friday and Saturday nights. An alternative place to do your drinking is in one of Austria's many **Heurigen**, the wine taverns found predominantly in the former villages of Vienna's outer suburbs, on the slopes of the Wienerwald, and in the many wine regions of Lower Austria, Burgenland and Styria. The word *heurig* means "this year's", as it was here that the vintner would encourage tastings in order to try and sell a few bottles of his (exclusively white) wine. In the good old days, people used to bring their own picnics to consume and sat on wooden benches in the vintner's garden whilst sampling the wine, but nowadays most *Heurigen* provide a self-service (usually, but not exclusively, cold) buffet of traditional peasant fare. Traditionally, a visit to a *Heuriger* is accompanied by *Schrammelmusik*, sentimental fiddle, guitar and accordion music, though today such music only features at the more touristy ventures in Vienna. Real *Heurigen* are only permitted to open for 300 days in any one year, and may only sell wine and food produced on the premises. If the *Heuriger* is open, the custom is to display a *Buschen*, or bunch of evergreen boughs, over the entrance, with a sign telling you it's *ausg'stekt* ("hung out"). Those that still abide by the strict *Heurigen* laws generally have a sign saying *Buschenschank*, though it has to be said that some have now attained restaurant licences in order to open all year round. A display board at the centre of the smaller villages lists those *Heurigen* that are currently open; otherwise the local tourist office will have the details.

WHAT TO DRINK

Most Austrian **beer** is a high-quality brew of the light, continental-lager or pilsner type. Beers that you'll encounter throughout Austria, not just in their home region, are *Ottakringer* and *Gold Fassl* from Vienna, *Gösser* from Leoben in Styria, *Stiegl* from Salzburg, *Villacher* from Villach and *Puntigamer* from Graz. Smaller breweries still have big influence locally: *Weitrabräu* from

Weitra in Lower Austria, *Murauer*, from Murau in Styria, and *Fohrenburg*, from Bludenz in Vorarlberg, are well worth looking out for. Many Austrian breweries produce speciality beers alongside their regular brews, such as *Märzen*, a slightly stronger, maltier concoction than the norm, and *dunkeles Bier* (dark beer), a sweeter, porter-like beer. In addition, many Austrian bars serve foreign beer on draught, especially the excellent Czech brands *Budvar* and *Pilsener Urquell*, as well as international favourites like *Guinness*. Beer is generally drunk by the half-litre, known as a *Grosser Bier* or *Krügerl*, but you can also ask for a third of a litre, a *Kleiner Bier* or *Seidl*, a fifth of a litre, *Pfiff*, and occasionally a *Mass*, or litre jug. Draught beer is *Bier vom Fass*, and is cheaper than buying either Austrian or imported bottled beers – of which most bars offer an impressive selection. Bottled *Weissbier* (wheat beer) is worth trying: it's extremely fizzy, and you must pour it painfully slowly to avoid creating a vast head.

Wine runs beer a close second as Austria's favourite alcoholic tipple. A wide range is available in bars, restaurants and cafés everywhere, but in the main wine-producing areas, the best place to try the local vintage is in a *Heuriger* or a *Buschenshenk* (wine tavern; see above). Wine is drunk by the *Viertel* (a 25cl mug) or the *Achterl* (a 12.5cl glass). The majority of wine produced in Austria is white, the dry, fruity *Grüner Veltliner* being the most popular. Look out, too, for *Sturm*, the half-fermented young wine that hits the streets and bars in autumn. Most red wine hails from Burgenland, where the most sought-after is *Blaufränkisch*.

Common to the **apple**-growing areas of Austria – mostly Styria and Carinthia – is a drink called *Most*, drier than cider and slightly less alcoholic. Austrians are also extraordinarily fond of **spirits**, particularly *Schnapps*, made in a variety of delicate fruit flavours and occasionally known as *Obstler*. Many towns and villages produce their own brand of *Obstler* – especially in the south, where fruit orchards abound – and it's a good idea when you're drinking or dining out to ask which local variety the staff recommend.

COMMUNICATIONS

Most post offices – identified by a yellow sign saying *Postamt* – are open Monday to Friday 8am to noon and 2 to 6pm; those in larger towns often stay open during lunchtime, in addition to a couple of hours on Saturday morning (8–10am). Vienna, and cities like Graz, Salzburg and Innsbruck, have at least one post office that is open 24 hours a day, seven days a week. Addresses of these are given in the relevant parts of the Guide.

Air mail (*Flugpost*) between Austria and the UK usually takes three or four days, about a week to reach the US, and ten days to Australia and New Zealand. For stamps (*Briefmarken*) for postcards within the EU, you may be able to go to a tobacconist (*Tabak*), though for anything more complicated or further afield, you'll probably have

to go to a post office in order to have your letter or parcel weighed.

Poste restante (*Postlagernd*) letters can be sent to any post office, if you know the address. To collect mail, go to the counter marked *Postlagernde Sendungen* – mail should be addressed using this term rather than "poste restante". It will be held for thirty days (remember to take your passport when going to collect it).

TELEPHONES

Austrian **phone booths**, usually dark green with a bright-yellow roof and logo, are easy enough to spot and to use, some even having instructions in four languages (including English). The dialling tone is a short and then a long pulse; the ringing tone is long and regular; engaged is short and rapid. Although the minimum charge is öS2, at the time of going to press, you're likely to need much more than that in order to make even a **local call**, since telephone calls are still quite expensive despite the recent deregulation.

You can make an **international call** from any phone; it's easiest to do so with a **phone card** (*Telefonkarte*) rather than fumbling for change. *Telefonkarten* are available from all post offices, tobacconists and some other shops, currently in öS50, öS100 and öS200 denominations. The other option is to go to one of the larger post offices and use their **direct phone service** facility: a booth will be allocated to you from the counter marked *Fremdgespräche*, which is where you pay once you've finished. The post office is also the

---

DIALLING CODES

TO AUSTRIA

From Australia and New Zealand ☎0011 43
From Britain and Ireland ☎00 43
From North America ☎011 43

The dialling codes for individual Austrian towns and cities are provided throughout the Guide. (When dialling from abroad, don't include the 0 that precedes each regional code.) Note that the Vienna city code is 1 when phoning from abroad; but 0222 when phoning from elsewhere in Austria.

FROM AUSTRIA

Australia ☎0061
Ireland ☎00353
New Zealand ☎0064
North America ☎001
UK ☎0044

INFORMATION

Local directory enquiries ☎1611
International operator ☎1616

place to go if you want to make a collect call (*Rückgespräch*).

Mobile phones work on the GSM European standard. Young Austrians are very keen on mobiles (known as a *Handy* in German), but outside the big cities, they're not yet that common – the mountains can make things awkward. If you're taking your mobile, make sure you have made the necessary "roaming" arrangements before you leave home – which may involve paying a hefty (refundable) deposit.

The number of digits in **telephone numbers** in Austria can vary wildly from region to region. Often, a telephone number is followed by a hyphen and a couple of additional digits – this merely denotes that it's an extension number that can be dialled direct.

EMAIL AND THE INTERNET

Use of the **Internet** by organizations and individuals is highly developed in Austria. However, facilities for those wishing to send or receive **emails** whilst away are pretty limited. Most large towns will have a café or bookshop with Internet access, but cybercafés themselves are by no means commonplace. We've listed the more interesting or useful Internet cafés in the relevant sections in the Guide. As for Web sites, we've listed them throughout the text, and gathered together a few useful general sites on Austria on p.28.

THE MEDIA

Newspaper stands in city centres, large train stations and well-touristed resorts stock a variety of **English-language newspapers**. You can usually get the European edition of the British broadsheet *The Guardian* (*www.guardian.co.uk*), printed in Frankfurt, by mid-morning the same day. Similarly, the *International Herald Tribune* (*www.iht.com*) is widely available the same day, and contains a useful distilled English version of the *Frankfurter Allgemeine*, also available on-line at *www.faz.de*. Other papers tend to be a day or so old. The weekly English-language newspaper *Austria Today* is occasionally available in the big cities, and a fairly dull rundown of Austrian news.

Heavily subsidized by the state, the **Austrian press** is for the most part conservative and pretty uninspiring. Nearly half the population reads the reactionary *Neue Kronen Zeitung* tabloid, while plenty of the rest read another right-wing tabloid, *Kurier*. Of the qualities, *Der Standard*, printed on pink paper, tends to support the Social Democrats (SPÖ) while the rather strait-laced *Die Presse* backs the conservative People's Party (ÖVP). The latter two are considered to be Vienna-centric by folk outside the capital, hence the popularity in western Austria of two major regional dailies, the Salzburg-based *Salzburger Nachrichten*, and Innsbruck's *Tiroler Tageszeitung*, both of which are again fairly conservative. One peculiarly Austrian phenomenon is the bags of newspapers you'll find hung from lampposts. Law-abiding Austrians take one and put their money in the slot.

Vienna boasts a good weekly **listings** tabloid, *Falter* (*www.falter.at*), which is lively, politicized and critical, and comes out on a Friday. Although it's entirely in German, it's easy enough to decipher the listings. The national and regional dailies will also have limited listings of what's on in their particular area. Nearly all cafés and bars, and the traditional Viennese coffeehouses, have a wide selection of newspapers and magazines for patrons to browse through, occasionally even English-language ones.

Austrian **television** is unlikely to win any international awards for cutting-edge programming or presentation. There are just two state-run channels: ORF 1 and ORF 2, with no independent competition at all as yet. As a result, Austrians tend to tune into German channels such as ARD and ZDF for a bit of variety. Many hotels and pensions have satellite TV, bringing the joys of CNN and MTV straight to your room.

The state-run **radio** channels all feature a lot of chattering, though Ö1 (87.8/92FM) offers some decent classical music, in addition to news in English and French at 8am. The state-run English-language Blue Danube Radio was axed in 2000 after over twenty years of service, to be replaced with FM4 (103.8FM), an anodyne AOR music station with hourly news and weather in English. The BBC World Service (*www.bbc.co.uk/worldservice*) broadcasts in English on 100.8FM in Vienna, though you'll have to revert to short wave in order to receive it anywhere else in the country. If you do have short wave, look out, too, for Radio Austria International, which broadcasts Austrian news in English, Spanish and Russian.

OPENING HOURS, PUBLIC HOLIDAYS AND SIGHTSEEING

Opening hours in Austria are currently in the process of being liberalized. However, after decades of strict control, old habits die hard, and it can still be very difficult to obtain even the most basic provisions in the evening or at weekends.

Until very recently, all shops had to conform to the following **opening hours**: Monday to Friday 9am to noon and 2 to 6pm, with late shopping on Thursdays, and Saturday 8am to noon – except on the first Saturday of the month (known as the *Langersamstag*, or "long Saturday"), when hours are 8am to 5pm. Shops may now open all day on every Saturday, but many shops still stick to the old *Langersamstag* routine; some shops in the larger towns and cities also stay open at lunchtimes. The only shops you're likely to find open after hours and on Sundays and public holidays, however, are the small general stores at the main train stations and airports. Those in search of cigarettes after hours will find cigarette machines outside most state-run tobacconists.

Cafés either keep normal shopping hours or open even earlier and close at midnight or later. Formal **restaurants** tend to open at lunch and dinner, but close between times. Most places where you can drink and eat have a weekly **closing day** or *Ruhetag*, which you'll find listed throughout the text.

PUBLIC HOLIDAYS

On national **public holidays** (see box), banks and shops will be closed all day. Museums and galleries will, somewhat confusingly, either be closed or open for free; for example, the vast majority are open for free on October 26, whereas most are closed on December 25 & 26. During the school summer holidays – July and August – you'll find that many theatres and other businesses in Vienna and some provincial centres close for all or some of the period.

MUSEUMS, GALLERIES, CASTLES AND CHURCHES

There are no hard-and-fast rules governing opening times for **museums and galleries** in Austria. More often than not, they're closed on Mondays, especially in Vienna, but check opening times within the text of this Guide and/or with the local tourist office before setting out.

Museums and galleries in Austria go under a number of different names. Designations like *Historischesmuseum* and *Archäologischesmuseum* are fairly self-explanatory, although in the major provincial capitals you'll also come across *Landesmuseum* (provincial museum; also *Landesgalerie*), which deals more specifically with the history of a whole province (*Land*). Those at Graz (Styria), Innsbruck (the Tyrol) and Bregenz (Vorarlberg) provide a comprehensive introduction to the art and culture of the surrounding region. A *Stadtmuseum* (town museum) is usually more localized in its focus, while a *Heimatmuseum* (literally "homeland museum") is likely to include material on regional customs and crafts – as is a *Volkskunstmuseum*

PUBLIC HOLIDAYS

January 1 (Neues Jahr)
January 6 (Epiphany/Dreikönigsfest)
Easter Monday (Ostermontag)
May 1 (Labour Day/Tag des Arbeits)
Ascension Day (6th Thursday after Easter/ Christi Himmelfahrt)
Whit Monday (6th Monday after Easter/ Pfingstmontag)
Corpus Christi (Fronleichnam)

August 15 (Assumption Day/Maria Himmel-fahrt)
October 26 (National Day/Nationalfeiertag)
November 1 (All Saints' Day/Allerheiligen)
December 8 (Immaculate Conception/Maria Empfängnis)
December 25 (Weihnachtstag)
December 26 (Boxing Day/Zweite Weihnachtsfeiertag)

(folklore museum). One of the best introductions to traditional Austrian culture is a *Freilichtmuseum*, or open-air museum, in which wooden farmhouses and other rustic buildings have been assembled and frozen in time – the best of these are at Stübing just outside Graz, Grossgmain near Salzburg, and Maria Saal in Carinthia.

Many of Austria's **castles and palaces** now hold local museums or displays relating to their erstwhile princely owners – *Schloss* is a loose term that can mean either castle or palace, while *Burg* tends to describe a hilltop fortress. **Churches** (*Kirche*) in city centres and well-touristed areas usually stay open daily from 7am to 7pm or later, but many of those in suburbs or rural areas only allow you to peep in from the foyer, except just before and after Mass. Again, if a church has set opening times, we've said so in the text of the Guide. The churches and chapels of Austria's many historic **monasteries** and **abbeys** (*Stift*) are usually (but not always) accessible to all-comers. Abbeys like those at Melk (Lower Austria), St Florian (Upper Austria) and Admont (Styria) house some of the best of Austria's Gothic and Baroque religious art, as well as sumptuous libraries and *Prunkräume* (state rooms), although almost invariably you must pay an entrance fee and often join an obligatory guided tour too.

Finally, Austria's industrial heritage is often dramatically showcased in a *Schaubergwerk*, or **show-mine**. Those that deserve special mention are the former iron-ore workings at Eisenerz in Styria, the Terra Mystica lead-mine near Villach in Carinthia, and the silver-mine at Schwaz in the Tyrol.

Labelling in English and other languages other than German is fairly patchy, even in the big city museums, though it's always worth asking if there's any information in English, as you may be handed a free translated text to take round with you. Otherwise, you may have to buy a small **English-language brochure** (typically öS40/€2.91) in order to get the best out of the attraction. Some sights, especially castles, former palaces, monasteries and show-mines, are only accessible by **guided tour** (*Führung*). Tours usually depart on the hour (opening times are given throughout the *Guide* where relevant), although some establishments only go ahead with the tour if a sufficient number of people have turned up (usually around five). By the same token, you may be turned away from a tour if it's already over-subscribed. Big attractions may offer tours in English, but in most cases you'll have to tag along with a German-speaking guide and hope that he or she is prepared to give an English summary at intervals.

When quoting **entrance fees**, throughout this Guide we've given the full adult rate (*Erwachsene*). Bear in mind, however, that museums, and other attractions, often give a **reduction** of about fifty percent to students (*Studenten*), children (*Kinder*) under the age of sixteen, and pensioners (*Pensionisten* or *Senioren*). Very young children, usually under 6s, are often admitted free, although the cut-off age for this varies from place to place. Nearly all museums throughout Austria are open free of charge on May 17 (International Museum Day).

FESTIVALS

Vienna and Salzburg tend to hog the lime-light as far as cultural festivals are concerned, but many provincial centres also host festivals of music and theatre that attract top international performers and enjoy a global reputation. There is also a full calendar of local religious festivals, many of which have their roots in rural folk customs that pre-date Christianity.

Annual **cultural festivals** occupy an important place in the Austrian calendar. The Salzburger Festspiele (Salzburg Festival) is perhaps the most renowned – and least accessible – of a long list of festivals, ranging from classical music to operetta, from jazz to film. We've listed the most important of these (see box, opposite), while further information on how to obtain tickets is included in the relevant sections of the main text.

FOLK AND RELIGIOUS FESTIVALS

Austria retains a surprising number of rural festivals, which, despite their pagan origins, were taken over by the Catholic Church and vigorously promoted during the Counter-Reformation, in order to wean the populace away from Protestantism.

The year kicks off on the night of January 5–6 with one of the oddest of Austria's folk practices, the **Perchtenlaufen**, when folk dressed as *Perchten* – kindly spirits wearing elaborate head-dresses – parade through the streets in the hope of ensuring good fortune and good harvests in the coming year. It's celebrated in various locations in the Salzburger Land and western Austria: the Pongauer Perchtenlauf (whose venue changes every year; see p.406) is the most renowned *Fest.* The same night sees the **Glöcklerlaufen** in the Salzkammergut town of Ebensee, a related ritual in which the men of the community don giant tissue-paper head-dresses illuminated from within by lanterns. Both *Perchten* and *Glöckler* costumes are a common sight in regional museums.

January and early February sees the height of **Fasching**, or the carnival season, which officially starts on November 11 and comes to an end on Shrove Tuesday (*Faschingsdienstag*). The weeks in the run up to Shrove Tuesday are marked by lavish society balls in Vienna, Salzburg and other major cities and towns. On Ash Wednesday, families greet the arrival of Lent by eating *Heringschmaus*, a platter of various dried, salted and pickled fish. Also in February, but only at four-year intervals, are two Tyrolean New Year fertility rituals, which echo the costumed parades of the *Perchtenlaufen*: the *Schemenlaufen* in the town of Imst and the *Schellerlaufen* in nearby Nassereith.

The three great moveable feasts of spring and early summer, **Easter** (*Oster*), **Whitsun** (*Pfingsten*) and **Corpus Christi** (*Fronleichnam*), all provide the excuse for long-weekend holidays and family outings. Corpus Christi is marked by religious processions in the Salzkammergut towns of Traunkirchen and Hallstatt – in both cases, celebrants take to the waters of nearby lakes in flotillas of tiny boats. The summer solstice is the occasion for the lighting of bonfires on high mountains in some areas on the night of June 21–22 (known as the *Bergfeuer* in Ehrwald, see p.519; or the *Sonnwendfeier* in the Gasteinertal, see p.408). In alpine parts of Austria, September and October see the **descent of the cattle herds** from the high mountain pastures where they spend the summer. Festivals marking the event – usually called *Alpabtrieb* or *Almabtrieb* – are held in many areas, notably Zell am Ziller (see p.486) on the first weekend in October, and Mayrhofen (see p.488) on the second weekend of the same month. October is the pumpkin month, with a **pumpkin festival** (*Kürbisfest*) in just about every town in the agri-

ANNUAL CULTURAL FESTIVALS

BREGENZ

Bregenzer Festspiele (late July to late Aug). Opera performed outdoors on a floating stage on the Bodensee. See p.526.

EISENSTADT

Haydntage (Sept). Festival featuring large-scale orchestral works and smaller chamber pieces by Haydn, and involving top international performers. See p.251.

FELDKIRCH

Schubertiade (June). Orchestral and chamber music with a strong Schubert bias. See p.534.

GRAZ

Styriarte (mid-June to mid-July). Classical music. See p.285. **Steirischer Herbst** (late Sept to late Oct). Avant-garde music, theatre, film and art. See p.285.

LINZ

Ars Electronica (Sept). Electronic, avant-garde music, installations and virtual art. See p.230.

Brucknerfest (early Sept to early Oct). Orchestral music by Bruckner and contemporary composers. Opens with a big laser and fireworks display. See p.233.

MILLSTATT

Internationale Musikwoche (July–Aug). Classical chamber music. See p.354.

MÖRBISCH

Seefestspiele (mid-June to Aug). Operetta performed on an open-air stage on the shores of the Neusiedler See. See p.260.

SALZBURG

Mozartwoche (Jan). Mozart-penned classical music. See p.398.

Sommer Szene (June & July). Experimental theatre, dance and rock. See p.399.

Salzburger Festspiele (July & Aug). Theatre, opera and symphonic music, usually featuring some Mozart. See p.396.

Salzburger Jazz Herbst (Nov). International jazz festival. See p.399.

VIENNA

Wiener Festwochen (May to mid-June). Opera, music and theatre. See p.152.

Klangbogen Wien (July to early Sept). The city's big summer music festival, which includes a two-week Jazzfest in July. See p.152.

Viennale (late Oct). The trendy Vienna film festival. See p.152.

Wien Modern (late Oct to early Nov). Contemporary classical music. See p.152.

WIESEN

Festglände (June–Sept). Series of open-air music festivals at the "Austrian Woodstock", 15km southwest of Eisenstadt. See p.256.

---

cultural heartlands of Lower Austria, Burgenland and Styria. **All Saints' Day** (*Allerheiligen*) on November 1 is taken seriously across the country, with hordes heading out to the cemeteries to pay their respects to the dead.

The feast of **St Barbara**, patron of miners and tunnellers, is celebrated in mining areas (such as at the Styrian towns of Leoben and Eisenerz) with parades and special church services, either on the day itself (December 4) or on the nearest Sunday. Also at the beginning of December, Christmas preparations get under way with a **Christmas market** (*Christkindlmarkt*) of some sort taking place in most towns and cities. The biggest of these is in front of the Rathaus in Vienna, although big markets also take place in the

Domplatz in Salzburg and in Innsbruck's old town. **St Nicholas' Day** on December 5 sees a procession in Innsbruck and, on the night of December 5–6, St Nicholas, accompanied by the devil (Krampus) and sometimes an angel, goes round handing out gifts for children. Meanwhile the **Krampuslaufen** (when demonically masked males run through the streets to symbolize the evil spirits chased away by the goodly St Nicholas himself) takes place all over Austria, and most notably in Zell am See (see p.414). **Christmas** (*Weihnacht*) is usually a private, family affair, with the highlight (for kids at least) coming on Christmas Eve when Baby Jesus (*Christkindl*) finally hands out the presents. In some areas carol singers also go from house to house in order to symbolize the visit of the three Wise Men to Bethlehem; a record of their visit is chalked above the door of each household, using the letters K, M and B to denote Kaspar, Melchior and Balthazar –

you're bound to encounter some of these strange chalk marks as you travel around Austria, because it's considered unlucky to wipe them off until the following year's visit.

SPORTS AND OUTDOOR ACTIVITIES

Whatever the season, if you're looking for an active outdoor holiday you'll be spoilt for choice in Austria. In summer, well-maintained footpaths and expansive mountain scenery make it something of a paradise for walkers. Fast-flowing alpine rivers and tranquil lakes offer a great range of water-based pursuits, and most holiday resorts of any size cater to tennis, swimming and golf enthusiasts. In winter, wherever you are in alpine parts, you'll be in striking distance of a winter sports centre of one sort or another. Winter sports have deep roots in Austria, and locals will ski or snowboard anywhere there's a serviceable slope. The season generally lasts from early December to early April, though skiing and snowboarding are possible all the year round on a small number of high-mountain glaciers.

WALKING

Austria offers some of the finest **walking** (*Wandern*) terrain in Europe. Variety is the order

of the day, with lowland walks in the east of the country, and gently rolling hills in southern Styria, Upper Austria and Lower Austria, contrasting sharply with the more challenging, alpine regions of central and western Austria. Tracks are for the most part well marked and well maintained, and numerous, well-positioned signposts often include an estimation of how long a particular route will take.

In alpine Austria, much of the tourist infrastructure developed for the winter sports crowd is available for ramblers and hikers in the summer, and the basic forms of mountain lift (cable cars, gondolas and chairlifts; see "Skiing and Snowboarding", p.56) are often pressed into service from late spring until early autumn in order to convey sightseers and walkers to higher altitudes. Walks that require spending a night or more on the mountain utilize the network of mountain huts (*Hütte*), which provide rudimentary dorm accommodation in mountain areas (see p.39). Some huts are privately owned, but most are run by the Österreichischer Alpenverein or their affiliates. Details of some all-day mountain walks and more ambitious hut-to-hut walks are included in this Guide.

PLANNING YOUR WALK

Whatever level of walking you intend to do, a good **map** is essential. There's usually a wide choice of maps on sale in tourist offices, bookshops and souvenir shops once you arrive; details of map-buying options outside Austria are given on pp.26–27. If you buy a 1:50,000 map, or one even more detailed, walking routes are usually marked in red and numbered (as they are on the ground). Some maps differentiate between well-marked paths and insufficiently marked paths; others differentiate according to the level of difficulty, dividing the paths into Wanderweg (hiking

THE AUSTRIAN ALPINE CLUB
Österreichischer Alpenverein, Wilhelm-Griel-Strasse 15, Innsbruck (☎0512/59547, *www.alpenverein.at*).

UK branch: Austrian Alpine Club, PO Box 43, Welwyn Garden City, Hertfordshire Al8 6PQ (☎01707/324835, *www.aacuk.co.uk*).
Members are entitled to a fifty percent reduction on accommodation in all alpine huts run by the ÖAV. Membership costs £30 per year (£23 for under 26s and over 60s; £9 for under 18s).

trail), Wanderpfad (steep hiking trail) and Steig (climbing trail). In the Tyrol, and other alpine areas, paths are marked according to a **colour scheme**: tracks marked in blue designate easy routes, while red ones are intermediate, and black ones difficult. Tracks marked in blue are usually on the flat, or involve an ascent gentle enough to be accessible to most people with average mobility. Those in red usually involve steeper gradients, but they shouldn't pose too many problems to people of reasonable fitness. Those in black may have been designated as such for a number of reasons: they might be high-altitude tracks prone to year-round snow and ice; involve a sheer drop on one or both sides of the track, therefore requiring a good head for heights; or include stretches where a certain amount of scrambling or climbing is necessary (such stretches are usually protected with cables). On no account should you set off to tackle a black route unless you're an experienced walker, or you're in the company of someone who is. One good way of getting an introduction to walking in the Alps – especially black routes, or walks on glaciers, neither of which you should attempt on your own – is to join one of the many **guided walks** organized by tourist offices throughout Austria in the summer. Sometimes these are free, but you can usually expect to pay öS80–120/€5.81– 8.72 per person for a half-day walk.

Always check the **weather** forecast before setting out, as mountain weather can change rapidly. Even if you're merely going on a cable-car ride to the summit of some local peak in order to enjoy the view and embark on a brief amble, it's worth taking a pullover and a waterproof jacket at the very least. For anything more ambitious than this, windproof and waterproof clothing is essential. Choosing the right footwear is of prime importance, too: trainers are only really adequate

for a short walk on the flat, and you'd be foolish to attempt walks of any duration in alpine regions without a good pair of walking boots.

Numerous paths have sections which feature rudimentary or even built-in **safety features** such as steps (*Klettersteig*) and/or ropes or cables to hang on to. Signs announcing *nur für Geübte* warn that the route is for experienced walkers only. Be extra vigilant when crossing mountain streams, patches of snow or exposed rocks. Avoid straying onto glaciers and snowfields unless accompanied by a mountaineer who is experienced in glacier travel and has the necessary equipment to deal with crevasse rescue. You should never embark on a walk that can't reasonably be completed well before dusk. Gauging distance that can be covered depends on many variables, including terrain, fitness levels, weight being carried and so on. Reasonably fit people carrying a light rucksack should be able to manage 4.5km per hour on the flat, plus an additional hour for every 350m of ascent. Don't be too proud to turn back should the weather deteriorate or the route become difficult or dangerous. If you do make it to the top of a summit, you'll probably find a little wooden box containing a stamp and/or visitors' book, so you can record your feat for posterity.

For those on all-day or **hut-to-hut walks**, the list of what to take with you increases. Although signposts and waymarks are frequent in most areas, it is prudent to carry a good map and compass – and know how to use them. A first-aid kit, whistle and torch should also be taken in case of emergencies. Carry food for the day, including emergency rations and at least one litre of liquid per person. Leave a note of your itinerary and expected time of return with a responsible person, and when using mountain huts enter the route details in the book provided. If unable to reach the destination at which you're expected, try to send a message to prevent the mountain rescue team being called out. If you do get into trouble, the **International Distress Signal** is six quick blasts on a whistle (or flashes with a torch) followed by a minute's pause. Then repeat. The response is three signals followed by a minute's silence. Mountain rescue can be very expensive, and it won't be covered by most regular travel **insurance** policies. If you're devoting all or most of your holiday to serious walking in the Alps, it's a good idea to ask a travel agent or insurance company about getting specific cover for what you're doing. Membership of the Austrian Alpine

Club includes worldwide mountain accident rescue cover.

LAKE AND RIVER ACTIVITIES

Austria's many lakes serve as centres of warm-weather sporting action – predominantly the lakes of the Salzkammergut, the Wörthersee, Ossiachersee and Millstättersee in Carinthia, and the Neusiedler See in Burgenland. All of the above are well equipped with **windsurfing** and **sailing** schools, the latter usually offering a range of courses in a variety of craft. Courses in all disciplines tend to last a week, although shorter, two-day crash courses are often available. Expect to pay around öS2500/€181.68 for a seven-day course. Courses will be in German and, although not all instructors speak English, most schools will make an effort to tailor their courses to suit your needs. Most sailing and windsurfing schools will also rent out surfboards and boats to those who already have experience. On the larger lakes, **waterskiing** and **paraskiing** are usually on offer.

Scuba diving is a popular activity in the lakes of the Salzkammergut, although each lake only allows diving in designated areas, and at certain times of the year (transgressors will be fined). A one-day course should cost around öS500/€36.33, a seven-day marathon öS50,000/€363.36.

RAFTING

Rafting is an increasingly popular activity on the fast-flowing rivers of the Tyrol, and involves sharing a large dinghy with a ten- to fifteen-strong group of people and hurtling downstream. The dinghy will be captained by a local guide, and safety equipment (such as lifejackets) will be provided. A trip usually costs around öS600/€43.60 per person depending on duration, and you can often choose between travelling a mild stretch of the river, or a more fast-flowing one – children under a certain age may be excluded from the latter.

The main centres for rafting are the towns of Imst and Landeck on the River Inn, Taxenbach near Zell am See, and the village of Sölden in the Ötztal. (Most tourist resorts in western Austria run regular trips to these centres, so you don't have to stay in the Inn Valley or the Ötztal in order to take part. These areas are also popular for **canoeing** and **kayaking**, and it's fairly easy

to rent equipment and obtain advice on which stretches of the river you can use once you arrive – local tourist offices are the obvious starting point for enquiries, although other contact addresses are given in the *Guide* where relevant.

FISHING

It's relatively easy to indulge in a spot of **fishing** on Austria's lakes and rivers, even if you're only spending a day or two in a particular area. Tourist offices should be your first point of contact when enquiring about where to fish and where to hire equipment. You'll have to buy a fishing **licence** (*Amtliche Fischerkarte*) – the tourist office will sell you one, or at least point you in the direction of a local sports shop where they're available. The cost of a licence often depends on whether you're intending to fish from dry land or from a boat: for the former, expect to pay öS250/€18.17 per day, öS1000/€72.67 per week.

SKIING AND SNOWBOARDING

Almost all Austrians know how to **ski** (*Schifahren*), and for those living in alpine areas skiing represents (for much of the year at least) the major recreational activity. The emphasis is very much on **downhill** skiing, although **nordic** (cross-country) skiing is practised almost anywhere there's enough snow to make it practicable. The increasing popularity of **snowboarding** is injecting the Austrian skiing scene – and the après-ski scene – with a new vigour. Most resort areas have a mixture of terrain suitable for different ability levels, with runs coded by colour: blue runs are for beginners, red runs for intermediates, and black for advanced skiers only.

GLOBAL WARMING

It's not a subject that many in the ski industry like to talk about, but if **global warming** continues, according to the latest forecasts, the prospects for skiing could be bleak. No industrial country in the world is as dependent on skiing as Austria, where the industry generates 4.5 percent of the country's GNP. Worse still, three quarters of the country's ski lifts are situated below 1000m, where the snow is most vulnerable to rising global temperatures. To find out whether there's any snow on your piste, log on to *www.skihotline.com*.

PLANNING YOUR TRIP

Most places in alpine Austria will have nursery slopes and a ski school of sorts, and if you're a **beginner** (or you're travelling with children who are new to skiing) you can learn to ski or snowboard almost anywhere. However, it's a good idea to pick a resort where the nursery slopes are in the valley floor near the hotels, rather than some distance away, and where easy runs (which a beginner might progress onto after a few days) are within good striking distance. It may also be worth avoiding resorts (notably in the Arlberg region) that are traditionally popular with advanced skiers and where beginners may feel out of place. The relatively laid-back, small-scale village resorts like Alpbach, Niederau and Obergürgl in the Tyrol, and Neukirchen in the Salzburger Land, are enduringly popular with first-time skiers; that said, glitzy, fashionable and traditionally more expensive Lech in the Vorarlberg is just as good a place to learn. All of the above feature regularly in the package-holiday brochures. If you're travelling independently, Kals in the East Tyrol is a good place for young families and children learning to ski – it's not a destination offered by package companies.

Intermediate skiers have a much wider choice, with most Austrian resorts of any size offering extensive intermediate areas linked together by interconnecting lift networks. You'll find a wide and varied skiing terrain at your disposal at Söll, Ischgl, Mayrhofen and Kitzbühel in the Tyrol; and at St Johann and Saalbach–Hinteglemm in the Salzburger Land. Saalbach–Hinterglemm also boasts several runs for the **advanced** skier, and the Badgastein region is worth investigating, although the most challenging terrain is to be found in the Arlberg region, Austria's top destination for off-piste skiing. St Anton provides the best access to the Arlberg slopes, although St Christoph, Lech and Zürs are sufficiently nearby to be serviceable bases.

All-year skiing is possible on a number of high-mountain **glaciers**, except during particularly hot summers when conditions can get too slushy. The main glacier areas are the Dachstein, accessible from Schladming in Styria; the Kitzsteinhorn, accessible from Zell am See–Kaprun in the Salzburger Land; Sölden in the Ötztal; and Stubai, accessible from Fulpmes or Innsbruck in the Tyrol.

Your choice of resort will also depend on whether you're looking for a lively place with lots of nightlife or a more laid-back, traditional village. As a general rule, a resort that is at the same time a sizeable town (Zell am See, Badgastein, Kitzbühel) is going to see more night-time action than a small village. Village resorts like Alpbach, Niederau and Wagrain have preserved their unspoilt, rural character, and in places such as these après-ski tends to be confined to your hotel-bar. Villages like Söll, Sölden and Ischgl, on the other hand, have experienced much more indiscriminate tourist development, and bars and discos are correspondingly thick on the ground. Some of these places (notably Söll) have earned a largely undeserved reputation as lager-lout resorts in the past, and such alarmist reports shouldn't dissuade you from spending a family holiday there. The swishest nightlife is to be found in high-society resorts like Kitzbühel and Lech–Zürs – bear in mind that food and drink prices will be correspondingly high.

LIFTS, PASSES AND BASIC COSTS

Access to the slopes is provided by a variety of **lifts**. Single journeys can be quite expensive, so you should buy a **ski pass**, which entitles you to unlimited use of all the various lifts in your area over a certain period of time. A variety of passes are usually available, ranging in duration from one-day to six-day, thirteen-day, one-month and occasionally longer.

Prices of ski passes vary wildly from one area to the next, and are usually dependent on how fashionable the resort is, and how wide an area the pass covers. Wherever you are in Austria, one-day ski pass prices rarely fall below the öS350/€25.55 mark, and most are in the öS400–450/€29.20–32.85 range (although the cost of a one-day pass is often graded according to how early in the day you buy it). A six-day ski pass for the low-key resorts of western Carinthia and the East Tyrol, covering the slopes above Lienz as well as Heiligenblut, Kals and Matrei, costs around öS1800/€131.40, whereas a six-day ski pass for more trendy St Anton covers the whole of the Arlberg region (embracing nearby resorts Zürs and Lech) and weighs in at a hefty öS2410/€175.14 – wide-ranging passes such as these are undoubtedly worth it if you're an experienced skier keen to cover a lot of ground.

Assuming you're not already kitted out, **rental** of skis (or snowboard) and boots for six days will probably set you back öS1500/€109.50 or more. If you're a beginner, you'll also have to budget for **tuition**, with six days' worth of lessons (usually about 4hr of tuition a day) costing something in the region of öS1500–1900/€109.50–138.70. Beginners' snowboarding courses usually last about three days and cost upwards of öS1400/€102.20.

SNOWBOARDING

Snowboarding is becoming the dominant winter activity for increasing numbers of younger Austrians, and an increasing number of resorts are geared up with the kind of facilities – a funpark featuring obstacles and jumps, or a half-pipe (a kind of cross between a ski piste and a bobsleigh run) – specifically designed with snowboarding in mind. A well-equipped resort favoured by Austrian snowboarders but rarely featured in holiday brochures is Axamer Lizum, just southwest of Innsbruck; if you're staying in the Tyrolean capital, it's relatively easy to pop out there for the day. Schladming is a good place to learn how to snowboard, while St Anton and Zell am See are both well equipped to deal with the demands of the more experienced. The glacier above Zell am See's sister resort Kaprun is a good spot for all-year snowboarding. It's easy to rent snowboard gear and sign up for some lessons in all the above-mentioned resorts, and Schladming, St Anton and Zell am See–Kaprun all feature regularly in the package-holiday brochures.

NORDIC SKIING

Most alpine resorts will offer the chance to sample *Langlauf*, or **nordic** (cross-country) skiing, utilizing prepared trails (known as *Loipe*) down in the valley floor below the main alpine ski slopes. Both Ramsau above Schladming and Ehrwald-Lermoos

in the Tyrol offer the most challenging network of trails, although other resorts shouldn't be discounted if all you want to do is take a few lessons and try the sport out. Few companies offer specific nordic packages in Austria – save for Waymark Holidays (see "Package and specialist operators", p.6) – but you can always book a standard skiing package to a mainstream resort like Ischgl, Kitzbühel or Schladming, and then register for a nordic skiing course once you arrive.

SKIING AS A SPECTATOR SPORT

The main venues for **international skiing competitions** in Austria are Schladming, St Anton and Kitzbühel, each of which hosts World Cup downhill and slalom races in January (contact local tourist offices for precise dates). The most famous of these is the Hahnenkamm downhill in Kitzbühel, which usually takes place mid-January for women and the end of January for men – the latter is an important date in the society calendar. Austria's most important ski-jumping sites are Bischofshofen in the Salzburger Land and the Bergisel just outside Innsbruck; again the big international World Cup meetings are usually scheduled for January, and you should check with local tourist offices for details.

EISSTOCKSCHIESSEN

One popular sport that you'll see a lot of in alpine areas over the winter is **Eisstockschiessen**, which (rather like curling) involves sliding heavy objects down a sheet of ice. Most towns and villages will have an area set aside for this – enquire at local tourist offices if you're interested in either watching or taking part.

POLICE, TROUBLE AND SEXUAL HARASSMENT

The Austrians are a law-abiding lot, almost obsessively so. Few people drop litter, and no one jaywalks. That said, crime does, of course, exist and is on the rise, so it's as well to take the usual precautions.

Almost all problems encountered by tourists in Austria are to do with **petty crime**. Reporting thefts to the **police** is straightforward enough, though it'll take some time to wade through the bureaucracy. The Austrian police (*Polizei*, known in some areas as *Gendarmerie*) – distinguishable by their dark-green uniforms and army-style offi-

cers' caps – are armed, and are not renowned for their friendliness especially towards other races. It's important to carry ID with you at all times (ideally your passport, or at least a driving licence). Making photocopies of your passport and tickets is a very sensible precaution.

There are a few specific areas in which **women** might feel uncomfortable. In Vienna, large sections of the Gürtel ring road double as a red-light district, and as such are best avoided. The area just southwest of the main train station in Graz has a similar reputation. Big-city train stations (particularly the Südbahnhof in Vienna) can be unsavoury after dark. Even so, none of these places are strictly speaking no-go areas. ÖBB (Austrian railways) have introduced *Damenabteilen* (women-only sections) on some InterCity and EuroCity expresses, especially those that involve travel late at night. You'll have to ask about these at station ticket offices when buying your ticket.

EMERGENCY PHONE NUMBERS
Fire ☎122.
Police ☎133.
Ambulance ☎144.

TRAVELLERS WITH DISABILITIES

As in most European countries, there are now regulations in force in Austria which mean that all public buildings must provide wheelchair access. As a result, the country is becoming gradually more accessible for travellers with special needs.

Wheelchair access to **hotels** is by no means universal, however, and is more likely to be a feature of upmarket establishments than the more inexpensive places. Unfortunately, there's no list currently available of Austria-wide hotels that are geared up for wheelchairs, so you'll have to ring up local tourist offices and ask them which estab-

lishments are *Rollstuhlfreundlich* (wheelchair-friendly). Access to the **public transport** system is quite good providing you plan your trip and contact the relevant train station several days in advance.

Nationwide, an increasing number of ÖBB **rail** services (marked by a wheelchair symbol in timetables) are equipped for wheelchair-bound travellers, and you'll be seated in a place with plenty of room and a wheelchair-accessible WC close at hand. The main drawback is that you have to book your trip at least three days in advance. Wheelchair access to trains is provided

CONTACTS FOR TRAVELLERS WITH DISABILITIES

AUSTRALIA

ACROD (Australian Council for Rehabilitation of the Disabled), PO Box 60, Curtin, ACT 2605 (☎02/6282 4333).

BRITAIN

Access Travel, 6 The Hillock, Astley, Lancashire M29 7GW (☎01942/888844, *www.access.co.uk*). *Small tour operator that can arrange flights, transfer and accommodation.*

Holiday Care, 2nd Floor, Imperial Building, Victoria Rd, Horley, Surrey RH6 9HW (☎01293/774535, Minicom ☎01293/776943, *www.holidaycare.org.uk*). *Information on all aspects of travel.*

RADAR, 12 City Forum, 250 City Rd, London EC1V 8AS (☎020/7250 3222; Minicom ☎020/7250 4119, *www.radar.org.uk*). *A good source of advice on holidays and travel abroad.*

IRELAND

Irish Wheelchair Association, Blackheath Drive, Clontarf, Dublin 3 (☎01/833 8241, *www.iwa.ie*). *National voluntary organization working with people with disabilities with related services for holidaymakers.*

NEW ZEALAND

Disabled Persons Assembly, 173–175 Victoria St, Wellington (☎04/801 9100).

NORTH AMERICA

Access-Able, (*www.access-able.com*). *An online resource for travellers with disabilities.*

Directions Unlimited, 123 Green Lane, Bedford Hills, NY 10507 (☎1-800/533 5343 or 914/241 1700). *Tour operator specializing in custom tours for people with disabilities.*

Mobility International USA, 451 Broadway, Eugene, OR 97401 (Voice and TDD ☎541/343 1284, *www.miusa.org*). *Information and referral services, access guides, tours and exchange programmes. Annual membership $35 (includes quarterly newsletter).*

Society for the Advancement of Travelers with Handicaps (SATH), 347 5th Ave, New York, NY 10016 (☎212/447 7284, *www.sath.org*). *Non-profit educational organization that has actively represented travelers with disabilities since 1976.*

Travel Information Service, (☎215/456 9600). *Telephone-only information and referral service.*

Twin Peaks Press, Box 129, Vancouver, WA 98661 (☎360/694 2462 or 1-800/637 2256, *www.twinpeak.virtualave.net*). *Publisher of the Directory of Travel Agencies for the Disabled ($19.95), listing more than 370 agencies worldwide; Travel for the Disabled ($19.95); the Directory of Accessible Van Rentals ($12.95); and Wheelchair Vagabond ($19.95), loaded with personal tips.*

Wheels Up!, (☎1-888/389-4335; *www.wheelsup.com*). *Provides discounted air fare, tour and cruise prices for disabled travellers; also publishes a free monthly newsletter and has a comprehensive Web site.*

by all manned stations – the service isn't available from unstaffed wayside halts. People who aren't wheelchair-bound but who lack full mobility will be helped onto the train by station staff – although you're expected to register with staff at least thirty minutes before the time of departure.

Access to **urban transport** in the big cities is more patchy – only Vienna is in any way geared up for disabled travellers. In the capital, only the new U3 and U6 subway lines are fully equipped with lifts, escalators and a guidance system for the blind. The old trams are not at all user-friendly, but the newer ones are, and buses in Vienna "kneel" to let people on and off. For a clearer picture, phone for the leaflet (in English) *Vienna for Guests with Handicaps* from the Austrian tourist board before you set off. This describes the level of access to U-Bahn stations, hotels and many tourist sights, and contains lots of other useful pieces of information. Leaflets covering other cities are sadly lacking.

DIRECTORY

ADDRESSES The name of the street always comes before the number of the building. If there are two numbers after the street name, separated by a forward slash, the first denotes the house number, the second the flat number. In Vienna, an additional number (denoting the district within the city) precedes the name of the street.

BEACHES Austria's many lakes usually have bathing beaches, and some rivers – notably the Danube in and around Vienna – provide popular bathing areas as well. You can't just swim anywhere, though, and bathing is usually restricted to a specific area known as a *Strandbad* (plural *Strandbäder*), where you'll find a stretch of waterfront, a grassy area on which to lay your towel, changing cubicles and a snack stall or café. Some *Strandbäder* are free, but most charge about öS20–40/€1.45–2.91 per day.

CIGARETTES are rarely sold in restaurants or bars, and you might have trouble stocking up late at night. Your best bet is to buy them from tobacconists (*Tabak*) during normal shop opening hours, or from the vending machines that are to be found outside the *Tabak*s.

ELECTRIC POWER 220 volts, out of round, two-pin plugs. Equip yourself with an adapter before leaving home if you want to use your hairdryer, laptop, etc. while travelling.

LAUNDRY Launderettes (*Schnellwäscherei*) are fairly easy to find in most towns, and addresses of big-city launderettes are included under "Listings" in this Guide.

LEFT LUGGAGE The bigger train stations have coin-operated lockers (*Schliessfächer*) costing from öS30–60/€2.18–4.36 for 24 hours. Most train stations (although not the small ones) have a left-luggage counter (*Gepäckaufbewahrung*) costing between öS30–60/€2.18–4.36 per item.

LOST PROPERTY Lost-property offices (*Fundämte*) are usually located at the local police station.

NATURISM Austrians are very keen naturists, and you'll find a nudist section at most outdoor swimming spots; just follow (or steer clear of) the signs saying FKK (*Freikörperkultur*).

SWIMMING Most Austrian towns of any size will have somewhere where you can swim (*Schwimmbad*). A *Freibad* is an open-air pool; a *Hallenbad*, an indoor pool; and an *Erlebnis-Hallenbad*, an adventure pool, which will probably feature water slides, whirlpool effects and so on. Spa resorts will have public swimming pools filled with mineral-rich waters from the local thermal springs. Entrance fees are rarely steep, ranging from about öS50/€3.63 for a small-town *Freibad* to about öS80/€5.81 for a big-city *Erlebnis-Hallenbad*.

TIME Normally one hour ahead of the UK and Ireland, six hours ahead of Eastern Standard Time and nine hours ahead of Pacific Standard Time. Austrian Summer Time lasts from late March to late October.

TIPPING When paying in restaurants, cafés and bars it's customary to add a tip of around five to ten percent – even for a single drink at the bar.

TOILETS As a general rule, free (and invariably spotless) public toilets are found in all town centres in Austria, and are usually located somewhere near the main square. However, they do tend to close relatively early in the evenings, in which case head for the nearest train station.

CHAPTER ONE

VIENNA

M ost people visit **Vienna** with a vivid image of the city in their minds: a monumental vision of Habsburg palaces, trotting white horses, old ladies in fur coats and mountains of fat cream cakes. And they're unlikely to be disappointed, for the city positively feeds off imperial nostalgia – High Baroque churches and aristocratic mansions pepper the Innere Stadt, monumental projects from the late nineteenth century line the Ringstrasse, and postcards of the Emperor Franz-Josef and his beautiful wife Elisabeth still sell by the sackful. Just as compelling as the old Habsburg stand-bys are the wonderful Jugendstil and early Modernist buildings, products of the era of Freud, Klimt, Schiele, Mahler and Schönberg, when the city's famous coffeehouses were filled with intellectuals from every corner of the empire. Without doubt, this was Vienna's golden age, after which all has been decline: with the end of the empire in 1918, the city was reduced from a metropolis of over two million, capital of a vast empire of fifty million, to one of barely more than 1.5 million and federal capital of a small country of just eight million souls.

Given the city's twentieth-century history (for more on which, see below), it's hardly surprising that the Viennese are as keen as anyone to continue plugging the good old days. The visual scars from this turbulent history are comparatively light – even Hitler's sinister wartime *Flacktürme* (anti-aircraft towers) are confined to the suburbs – though the destruction of the city's enormous Jewish community, the driving force behind the city's fin-de-siècle culture, is a wound that has proved harder to heal. The city has struggled since to live up to the glorious achievements of its past, and has failed to shake off a reputation for xenophobia. Yet for all its problems, Vienna is still an inspiring city to visit, with one of the world's greatest art collections in the **Kunsthistorisches Museum**, world-class orchestras and a superb architectual heritage. It's also an eminently civilized place, clean, safe (for the most part) and peopled by citizens who do their best to live up to their reputation for *Gemütlichkeit*, or "cosiness". And despite its ageing population, it's also a city with a lively nightlife, with plenty of late-opening *Musikcafés* and drinking holes. Even Vienna's restaurants, long famous for quantity over quality, have discovered more innovative ways of cooking and are now supplemented by a wide range of ethnic restaurants.

Most first-time visitors spend the majority of their time in Vienna's central district, the **Innere Stadt**. Retaining much of its labyrinthine street layout, it's the city's main commercial district, packed with shops, cafés and restaurants. The chief sight here is the **Stephansdom**, Vienna's finest Gothic edifice, standing at the district's pedestrianized centre. Tucked into the southwest corner of the Innere Stadt is the **Hofburg**, the former imperial palace and seat of the Habsburgs, now housing a whole host of museums, the best of which is the Schatzkammer, home to the crown jewels.

The old fortifications enclosing the Innere Stadt were torn down in 1857, and over the next three decades gradually replaced by a showpiece boulevard called the **Ringstrasse**. Nowadays, the Ringstrasse is used and abused by cars and buses as a ring road, though it's still punctuated with the most grandiose public buildings of late-imperial Vienna, one of which is home to the city's new cultural centre, the **Museumsquartier**, and another of which houses the famous **Kunsthistorisches Museum**. Beyond the Ringstrasse lie Vienna's seven **Vorstädte**, or inner suburbs,

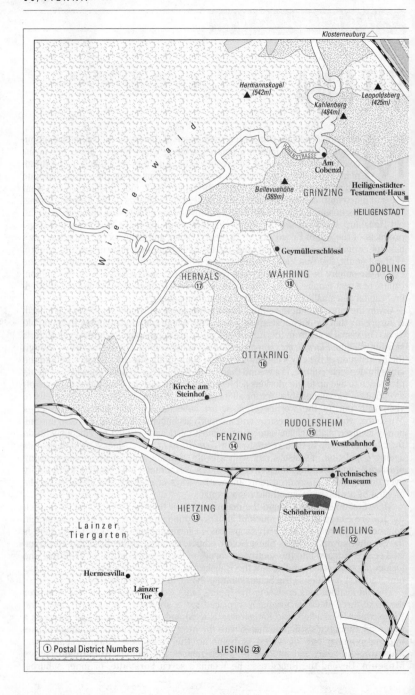

Klosterneuburg △

Hermannskogel
(542m) ▲

Leopoldsberg
(425m) ▲

Kahlenberg
(484m) ▲

HÖHENSTRASSE

Am
Cobenzl ●

Bellevuehöhe
(388m) ▲

GRINZING

Heiligenstädter-
Testament-Haus

HEILIGENSTADT

● Geymüllerschlössl

HERNALS
⑰

WÄHRING
⑱

DÖBLING
⑲

W i e n e r w a l d

OTTAKRING
⑯

Kirche am
Steinhof ●

THE GÜRTEL

RUDOLFSHEIM
⑮

PENZING
⑭

Westbahnhof ●

● Technisches
Museum

HIETZING
⑬

Schönbrunn

MEIDLING
⑫

Lainzer
Tiergarten

Hermesvilla ●

Lainzer
Tor ●

① Postal District Numbers

LIESING ㉓

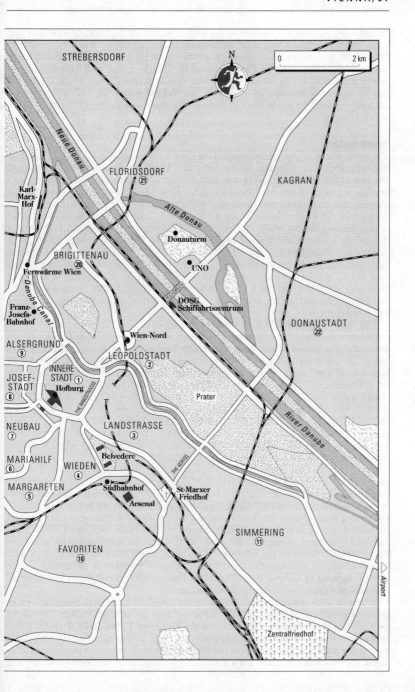

whose outer boundary is marked by the traffic-clogged *Gürtel* (literally "belt"), or ring road. The highlight out here is the **Belvedere**, where you can see a wealth of paintings by Austria's pre-eminent trio of modern artists – Egon Schiele, Gustav Klimt and Oskar Kokoschka – followed by the **Prater**, east of the Danube Canal, with its famous Ferris wheel and funfair. On the whole, there's little reason to venture beyond the *Gürtel* into the *Vororte*, or outer suburbs, except to visit **Schönbrunn**, the Habsburgs' former summer residence, a masterpiece of Rococo excess and an absolute must if only for the wonderful gardens.

Some history

Vienna's history as showpiece imperial capital is a comparatively brief one. From having been a not very important Roman fort called **Vindobona** on the military border of the River Danube, Vienna had to wait until the rise of the Babenberg dynasty before it became a capital of any sort. In 1156, under Heinrich II Jasomirgott (1141–72), the Babenbergs' margravate was elevated to a duchy, with the ducal palace situated somewhere near Am Hof in Vienna. When the Babenberg male line came to an end in 1246, a long-running dispute broke out over who should rule over the region. In the end, it was a little-known count, **Rudolf of Habsburg**, who proved victorious, much to the annoyance of the Viennese, who had backed the loser, King Otakar II of Bohemia. Although the Habsburgs were to rule over the city for the next 640 years, Vienna only sporadically served as the dynastic capital. **Rudolf IV** (1356–65) was one of the few to treat it as such, and was given the nickname "The Founder" after he established the city's university and laid the foundation stone of the future cathedral during the course of his short reign.

The main stumbling block to Vienna's development was the threat posed by the Turks, who besieged the city twice. Although it is the later siege of 1683 that has captured the imagination of historians, the **1529 Turkish siege** was a much closer-run thing. The Ottoman empire was at the zenith of its power, and Vienna was defended by only a small garrison under Count Salm. Having shelled the city and killed some 1500 of its citizens, the Turks suddenly withdrew – quite why, no one knows. During the **1683 siege**, the city garrison of 10,000 men faced an Ottoman army of over 200,000. That the city was saved was no thanks to its emperor, Leopold I (1658–1701), who fled for the safety of Upper Austria. This time the Turks' defeat was assured by a combination of the sultan's greed – he tried to force the city to surrender by besieging it for over two months, rather than storming it and sharing the booty with his soldiers – and the arrival of a relief force under Polish King Jan Sobieski.

It was only after the Turks had been beaten back from the gates of Vienna a second time that the city finally established itself as the Habsburgs' permanent *Residenzstadt,* or *Kaiserstadt*. Over the next hundred years, an outpouring of **Baroque art and architecture** transformed the city, which could now safely spread out beyond the walls of the Innere Stadt. During the Napoleonic era, Vienna was besieged twice more in short succession by the French – in 1805, and again in 1809. Emperor Franz I (1792–1835) followed tradition by fleeing to safety, but this time the city surrendered on both occasions, and had to suffer the ignominy of occupation by French troops. In 1815, with Napoleon almost defeated, the city regained some of its pride as the setting for the great **Congress of Vienna**, at which the new European balance of power was thrashed out, amidst a great deal of dancing and feasting.

In March 1848, **revolution** broke out on the streets of the capital, and wasn't extinguished until imperial troops brutally suppressed the uprising in October. The upshot of it all was the accession of the 18-year-old **Emperor Franz-Josef I** (1848–1916), whose immensely long reign encompassed the city's golden age. The old walls were torn down and the great edifices of the **Ringstrasse** built: the court museums, parliament, the university, to name but a few. The city's population swelled to over two million, some ten percent of whom were Jewish immigrants, giving Vienna the largest Jewish community in the German-speaking world. At the same time, anti-Semitism as a viable modern political force was invented here, in front of the young Hitler's very eyes, in the first decade of the twentieth century.

In the 1920s and early 1930s, Vienna became renowned for its enlightened municipal socialism, during a period that has since gone down in history as *Rotes Wien*, or **Red Vienna**. However, for much of the century the city, rather like Berlin, had the misfortune of serving as a weather vane of European history. The political battles between Left and Right fought out on the streets of Vienna mirrored those in Berlin, and the weekend Hitler enjoyed his greatest electoral victory in the Reichstag, Austro-fascism was declared in Vienna. In 1938, Vienna was the first foreign capital to fall "victim" to the Nazis, greeting the Führer with delirious enthusiasm, and sounding the death knell on the city's 200,000 Jews. For a decade after the war, Vienna, like Berlin, was under **Allied occupation**, divided into French, American, British and Soviet sectors, with the Innere Stadt as an international zone, in which the Allies patrolled the streets together "four in a jeep", as the period became known.

Since the withdrawal of the four Allied powers in 1955, Vienna has lived a fairly peaceful existence, best known as one of the three cities that serve as UN headquarters and as host to international conferences. However, the opening up of Eastern Europe and the break-up of Yugoslavia have had a profound effect on the city, with an estimated ten percent of the population now made up of recently arrived immigrants. Although most Viennese can trace their ancestry back to the far corners of the old empire, many locals are fearful of the newcomers. The impact on voting patterns has been marked, with 1996 proving something of a watershed: the Socialists lost overall control of the city council for the first time in its democratic history, while the far right Freedom Party (FPÖ) gained a staggering 27 percent of the vote, becoming the main opposition in the city council.

Arrival, information and city transport

For all its grandiosity, Vienna is surprisingly compact: the centre is just a kilometre across at its broadest point, and you can travel from one side of the city to the other by public transport in less than thirty minutes. Although the **Danube** is crucial to Vienna's identity, most visitors see very little of the river, whose main arm flows through the outer suburbs to the northeast of the centre.

Arrival

The city's **international airport**, Flughafen Wien-Schwechat (*www.viennaairport .com*), lies around 20km southeast of the city. It's connected to the centre by S-Bahn line S7; **trains** leave every thirty minutes between 5am and 10pm, taking thirty minutes to reach Wien-Mitte, where most people alight, and terminating at Wien-Nord. This is the cheapest way of getting into town, costing just öS38/€2.76 for a single ticket, or öS19/€1.38 plus the price of a travel pass for the central zone (see p.71), which you can buy at the same time. **Buses** from the airport to the City Air Terminal bus station underneath the *Hilton Hotel* (adjacent to Wien-Mitte), are faster and more frequent, leaving every twenty minutes from 6.30am until 11.30pm, and every thirty minutes throughout the night; they take around twenty minutes to reach the city centre, and cost öS70/€5.09 one way. There are also hourly buses to the Südbahnhof and Westbahnhof (see below). For more information on the buses and trains to and from the airport, visit the Web site *www.oebb.at/regional/wien/wien4.html*. **Taxis** to the centre take twenty minutes or so and charge around öS400/€29.07.

Arriving in Vienna by train from the west, you'll end up at the **Westbahnhof**, just west of Stephansplatz in the city centre. Trains from the east, Italy and the Balkans terminate at the **Südbahnhof**, to the south of the city centre; you can either walk five minutes west to Südtiroler Platz U-Bahn station, or hop on tram #D into town. Of Vienna's other stations, **Franz-Josefs-Bahnhof**, in the northern suburb of Alsergrund, serves as arrival point for services from Lower Austria and the odd train from Prague (take tram #D into town), while Wien-Nord (U-Bahn Praterstern), in Leopoldstadt, is used exclusively by local and regional trains, including the S-Bahn to the airport (see above).

International, long-distance buses arrive at Vienna's **main bus terminal** beside Wien-Mitte, on the eastern edge of the city centre (U-Bahn Landstrasse). If you arrive on one of the **DDSG boat** services (*www.ddsg-blue-danube.at*) from further up the Danube, or from Bratislava or Budapest, you'll find yourself disembarking at the Reichsbrücke, some way northeast of the city centre; the nearest station (U-Bahn Vorgartenstrasse) is five minutes' walk away, one block west of Mexicoplatz.

The **telephone code** for Vienna is ☎0222 from the rest of Austria and ☎01 from outside the country.

Information

The main **tourist office** of the Vienna Tourist Board or *Wiener Tourismusverband* is behind the opera house on Albertinaplatz (daily 9am–7pm; ☎21114-222; phone enquiries Mon–Fri 8am–4pm only; *www.info.wien.at*). There are only a few leaflets on open display, but if you have a specific enquiry the staff will happily help out. It's worth asking for the latest *Museums* leaflet, listing all the current opening times. Other leaflets include the tourist board's monthly *Programm* for opera, concert and theatre schedules, and upcoming exhibitions and events. Depending on your age, you might prefer to try the youth-oriented tourist office, *Jugendinfo*, at Babenbergerstrasse 1 (Mon–Sat noon–7pm; *www.jugendinfowien.at*), on the corner of the Ringstrasse. There are also **information desks** at the airport (daily 8.30am–9pm) and at the Westbahnhof (daily 7am–10pm).

For the most comprehensive and critical **listings**, you need the weekly tabloid *Falter* (öS28/€2.03; *www.falter.at*), which comes out on Wednesdays. Even if your German isn't great, you should be able to decipher the pull-out *Wienprogramm & Lexicon* section, which contains the week's listings. A cheaper alternative is the free weekly, *Winside* (*www.winside.cc*), which comes out every Thursday, or the monthly *Wien Magazin* (öS28/€2.03; *www.wienmagazin.at*), which gives you a whole month's listings.

City transport

Vienna's Innere Stadt is best explored on foot, but for covering larger distances you'll need to use the enviable **public transport system**, known as the *Wiener Linien* (*www.wienerlinien.co.at*). Predictably enough, the trams and buses are punctual and the ever-expanding U-Bahn clean and very quick. The whole system runs from between 5 and 6am to between midnight and 1am. The only way of getting home in the small hours is to catch one of the NightLine **night buses**. These run every thirty minutes from 12.30am to 4am, and all 22 routes pass through Schwedenplatz at some point. **Taxis** are plentiful and fairly reliable too, with the minimum charge around öS25/€1.82, followed by an extra öS10/€0.73 or so per kilometre or couple of minutes. You can't flag down a taxi, but you can catch a cab at one of the taxi ranks around town, or phone ☎31330, 40100 or 60160. The most expensive way to get about, of course, is by **Fiaker**, one of the horse-drawn carriages driven by bowler-hatted, multilingual coachmen. There are *Fiaker* ranks at Stephansplatz, Heldenplatz, Michaelerplatz and Albertinaplatz. It's best to settle on the price and duration of your ride beforehand; the going rate is öS500/€36.34 for twenty minutes, or öS800/€58.14 for forty minutes.

Tickets

A single-journey **ticket** (*Fahrschein*), standard for all forms of public transport (excluding night buses, see below), costs öS19/€1.38 from machines and ticket booths (*Vorverkauf*) at U-Bahn stations, and also from tobacconists (*Tabak-Trafik*). When you enter the U-Bahn, or board a tram or bus, you must punch (*entwerten*) your ticket in one of the blue machines. You can then make one journey, during which you can change buses, trams or U-Bahn lines as many times as you like, as long as you proceed in a logical direction without any "breaks".

If you're planning on making more than two journeys a day, you should invest in a **travel pass**, or *Netzkarte*, which allows travel on all trams, buses, U- and S-Bahn trains within the city. You can buy a 24-hour ticket (öS60/€4.36) or a 72-hour ticket (öS150/€10.90) from machines and booths at all U-Bahn stations; when buying your ticket from a machine, select the central zone, or *Kernzone* (*Zone 100*), which covers the whole of Vienna. You must punch your single *Netzkarte* at the beginning of your first journey – your 24 or 72 hours starts from that point.

The much-touted **Wien-Karte** or Vienna Card (öS210/€15.26; *www.wienkarte.at*) gives various minor discounts at local attractions, as well as being a 72-hour *Netzkarte*. In addition, you get small discounts at such sights as the Hofburg and Schönbrunn, plus selected restaurants and shops. If you're in Vienna for a long weekend and intend to do quite a bit of sightseeing, the ticket will probably pay for itself.

Another option is the **8-day ticket**, or *8-Tage-Karte* (öS300/€21.80), which is valid for eight (not necessarily consecutive) days' unlimited travel, calculated in 24-hour blocks from the hour of punching. It can be used by one or more people – one person for eight days, two people for four, and so on – simply punch one strip on the card for

---

GUIDED TOURS

Vienna Sightseeing Tours (*www.viennasightseeingtours.com*) run a variety of **bus tours** around the city and surrounding districts. Their standard city tour (daily 9.30am, 10.30am & 2.30pm; öS400/€29.07) takes around three and a half hours; pick up a leaflet at the tourist office or any hotel or pension. They also run a **hop-on hop-off bus** hourly (daily 9.30am–4.30pm), with running commentary in English and German; tickets cost öS250/€18.17 and are valid for two days. Alternatively, you can save yourself the relentless commentary by hopping on **tram #1 or #2**, which circumnavigate the Ringstrasse clockwise and anticlockwise respectively. Every Saturday (11.30am and 1.30pm) and Sunday (9.30am, 11.30am & 1.30pm) from early May to early October, you can also leap aboard a beautiful 1920s tram outside the Otto-Wagner-Pavillon on Karlsplatz and go on an hour-long **tram tour**, run by *Wiener Linien*; tickets cost öS200/€14.54 and are available from Karlsplatz U-Bahn.

Even more appealing are the **walking tours** organized by Vienna's official tourist guides – you'll find details, such as whether the tours are in German or English, in the monthly *Wiener Spaziergänge* leaflet from the tourist office (*www.wienguide.at*). These cover a relatively small area in much greater detail, mixing historical facts with juicy anecdotes in the company of a local specialist. Subjects covered range from Jugendstil architecture to Jewish Vienna – the weekly Third Man tour takes you round the locations associated with the eponymous 1948 film (☎774 8901). Tours cost around öS140/€10.17 and last between one and a half and two hours. Simply turn up at the meeting point specified.

each person in the group. To do this you must fold the card over before inserting it in the blue machines, starting with strip 1.

If you're staying in Vienna longer than three days, it might be worth buying a **weekly card**, or *Wochenkarte* (öS155/€11.26), available only from the ticket offices at U-Bahn stations. The pass runs from 9am Monday to Monday, so there's no need to punch the ticket. The **monthly ticket**, or *Monatskarte* (öS560/€40.70), which runs for a calendar month, works in much the same way. Note that none of the passes are valid on **night buses**, for which you must buy a separate ticket on the bus costing öS15/€1.09.

The Viennese being a law-abiding bunch, there are few **ticket inspectors**, but if you are caught without a valid ticket or pass, you'll be handed an on-the-spot fine of öS560/€40.70 (on top of the appropriate fare).

The U- and S-Bahn

Vienna's **U-Bahn**, currently boasting five lines (U1–4 and U6), is by far the fastest way of getting around the city. Not all U-Bahn lines are underground: the U4 and U6 lines run partly on the old overground Stadtbahn created in the 1890s, and both lines retain some of their original stations and bridges designed by Otto Wagner.

The **S-Bahn**, or *Schnellbahn* in full, is of most use to Viennese commuters, though it's also the cheapest way of getting to and from the airport (see p.69) and is useful for

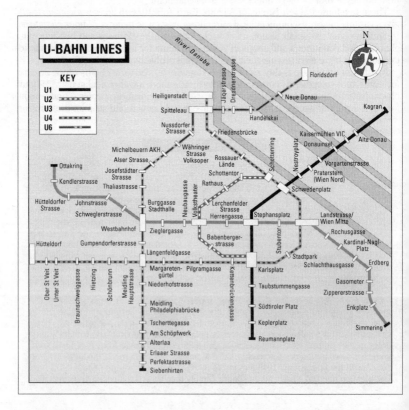

day-trips to places in Lower Austria (see p.157). S-Bahn trains are less frequent than U-Bahn trains – running every fifteen to thirty minutes – and are strictly timetabled.

Trams and buses

Vienna has one of the world's largest networks of **trams** – the *Strassenbahn* or *"Bim"* (after the noise of the bell), as they're known colloquially – with more than thirty routes crisscrossing the capital. After the U-Bahn, trams are the fastest and most efficient way of getting around, running every five to ten minutes. They're fairly punctual, though some lines don't run at weekends or late at night so be sure to check the timetables posted at every stop (*Haltestelle*).

Buses (*Autobusse*) mostly ply the narrow backstreets and outer suburbs and, despite having to battle with the traffic, are equally punctual. In the heart of the Innere Stadt, where there are no trams and only two U-Bahn stations, there are several very useful bus services: #1A, which winds its way from Schottentor to Stubentor; #2A from Schwedenplatz through the Hofburg to Burgring; and #3A from Schottenring to Schwarzenbergplatz.

Accommodation

As you might expect, Vienna has some of the most opulent, historic **hotels** in Europe, with mesospheric prices to match. However, reasonably priced central accommodation can be found, especially in the numerous **pensions**. These are not necessarily inferior in quality to hotels – in fact some are a whole lot better. Vienna also has plenty of space in official HI and independent **hostels**, although these can be booked up months in advance, so try and ring or email ahead to make a reservation before you leave. The city's tourist offices (see p.70) have a limited number of **private rooms** for upwards of öS300/€21.80 per person per night (with a minimum of three nights' stay) for a small commission. Inveterate **campers** have a wide choice of peripheral sites. If you arrive without a booking, any of the tourist offices can make a reservation for you, for which they charge around öS40/€2.91. Our recommendations are divided by district, and listed alphabetically.

Hotels and pensions

Hotels and pensions in Vienna as a rule adhere to the standards of efficiency, modernity and cleanliness you'd expect in Austria. It's perfectly possible to stay right in the Innere Stadt without breaking an arm and a leg, although the cheapest places tend to be in the districts beyond the Ringstrasse. This is no great hardship, especially

---

ACCOMMODATION PRICE CODES

All **hotels and pensions** in this book have been coded according to the following price categories. All the codes are based on the rate for the least expensive double room during the **summer season**. In those places where winter is the high season, we've indicated both summer and winter room rates in the text.

① under öS400/€29.07
② öS400–600/€29.07–43.60
③ öS600–800/€43.60–58.14
④ öS800–1000/€58.14–72.67
⑤ öS1000–1200/€72.67–87.21

⑥ öS1200–1400/€87.21–101.74
⑦ öS1400–1600/€101.74–116.28
⑧ öS1600–1800/€116.28–130.81
⑨ over öS1800/€130.81

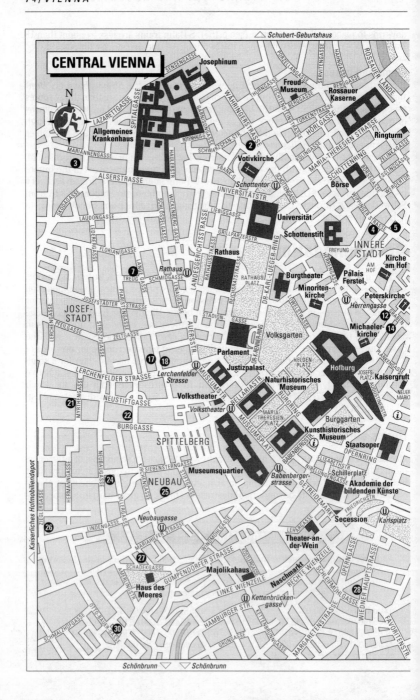

△ Schubert-Geburtshaus

CENTRAL VIENNA

N

Josephinum

Freud Museum

Rossauer Kaserne

Allgemeines Krankenhaus

❸

Ringturm

❷

Votivkirche

Schottentor Ⓤ

Börse

Universität

Schottenstift

INNERE STADT

❹ ❺

Kirche am Hof

Rathaus

Freyung

AM HOF

❼

Rathaus Ⓤ

RATHAUS PLATZ

Burgtheater

Palais Ferstel

Minoriten-kirche

Peterskirche

Herrengasse

❶❷

JOSEF-STADT

Volksgarten

Michaeler-kirche

❶❹

Parlament

Hofburg

JOSEFS-PLATZ

Kaisergruft

❶❼ ❶❽

Justizpalast

Naturhistorisches Museum

NEUER MARKT

❷❶

HELDEN PLATZ

Volkstheater

Volkstheater Ⓤ

MARIA-THERESIEN-PLATZ

Burggarten

ⓘ

❷❷

BURGGASSE

SPITTELBERG

Kunsthistorisches Museum

ⓘ

Staatsoper

❷❹

NEUBAU

❷❺

Museumsquartier

Babenberger-strasse

Schillerplatz

Akademie der bildenden Künste

❷❻

Neubaugasse Ⓤ

Secession

Karlsplatz

Theater-an-der-Wein

❷❼

Majolikahaus

Naschmarkt

❷❽

Haus des Meeres

Kettenbrücken-gasse Ⓤ

❸❶

Schönbrunn ▽   ▽ Schönbrunn

Kaiserliches Hofmobiliendepot △

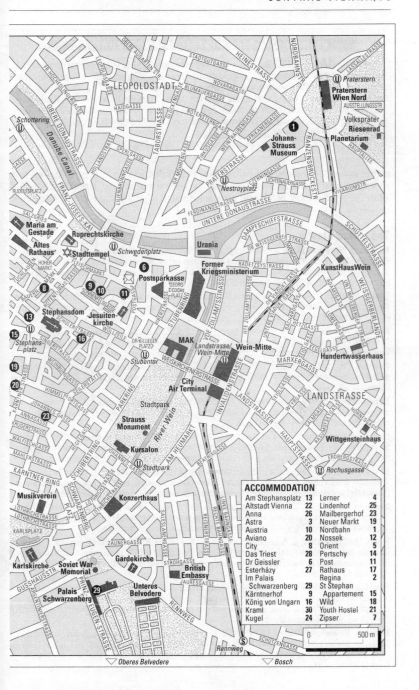

LEOPOLDSTADT

Praterstern
Praterstern
Wien Nord
AUSSTELLUNGSSTR

Volksprater
Riesenrad
Planetarium

Johann-
Strauss
Museum

Schottering

Danube Canal

Nestroyplatz

RUDOLFSPLATZ

SALZGRIES

Maria am,
Gestade
Ruprechtskirche

Urania

Altes
Rathaus'
Stadttempel
Schwedenplatz

Former
Kriegsministerium

KunstHausWien

HOHER
MARKT
Postsparkasse

Stephansdom
Jesuiten-
kirche

MAK
Landstrasse/
Wein-Mitte

Wein-Mitte

Hundertwasserhaus

Stephans-
platz

Stubentor

City
Air Terminal

LANDSTRASSE

Stadtpark

Strauss
Monument

River Wein

Kursalon

Stadtpark

Wittgensteinhaus

Rochusgasse

Musikverein

Konzerthaus

Karlskirche
Soviet War
Memorial
Gardekirche

British
Embassy

Palais
Schwarzenberg

Unteres
Belvedere

0   500 m

ACCOMMODATION			
Am Stephansplatz	13	Lerner	4
Altstadt Vienna	22	Lindenhof	25
Anna	26	Mailbergerhof	23
Astra	3	Neuer Markt	19
Austria	10	Nordbahn	1
Aviano	20	Nossek	12
City	8	Orient	5
Das Triest	28	Pertschy	14
Dr Geissler	6	Post	11
Esterházy	27	Rathaus	17
Im Palais		Regina	2
Schwarzenberg	29	St Stephan	
Kärntnerhof	9	Appartement	15
König von Ungarn	16	Wild	18
Kraml	30	Youth Hostel	21
Kugel	24	Zipser	7

Rennweg

Oberes Belvedere   Bosch

VIENNA'S POSTAL DISTRICTS AND ADDRESSES

Vienna is divided into 23 *Bezirke*, or **postal districts**, which spiral outwards from the first district (the Innere Stadt), in a clockwise direction, with only the odd geographical hiccup. When writing **addresses**, the Viennese write the number of the district first, followed by the name of the street, and then the house number; most residential addresses also include an apartment number, separated from the house number by a slash. For example: 9, Löblichgasse 11/14, denotes apartment no. 14 at no. 11 Löblichgasse in the ninth district.

---

as the seventh (Neubau) and eighth (Josefstadt) districts have, if anything, an even wider choice of restaurants and bars than the central tourist zone. **Breakfast** is included in the price at most hotels and pensions, though what it comprises can differ enormously.

The Innere Stadt

Hotel am Stephansplatz, 1, Stephansplatz 9 (☎53405, *www.nethotels.com/am-stephansplatz*); U-Bahn Stephansplatz. Just about as central as you can get, with lots of rooms overlooking the west door of the Stephansdom. The decor is pretty dated, but perfectly comfortable and spacious, and all rooms are en suite, with cable/satellite TV. ⑨.

Hotel Austria, 1, Wolfengasse 3 (☎51523, *members.eunet.at/hotelaus*); U-Bahn Schwedenplatz. Plush family-run hotel, pleasantly located in a quiet cul-de-sac off Fleischmarkt, with some cheap rooms without en-suite facilities. ⑤.

Pension Aviano, 1, Marco d'Avianogasse 1 (☎512 8330, *www.pertschy.com*); U-Bahn Karlsplatz. Part of Pertschy pension chain. Squeezed onto the top floor of a building just off Kärntnerstrasse. Low ceilings, but roomy rooms, all en suite, with TV and fluffy, floral decor. ⑥.

Pension City, 1, Bauernmarkt 10 (☎533 9521); U-Bahn Stephansplatz. On the second floor of a wonderful late-nineteenth-century building and run by a friendly woman proprietor. Tastefully decorated rooms, all en-suite. ⑤.

Pension Dr Geissler, 1, Postgasse 14 (☎533 2803); U-Bahn Schwedenplatz. Anonymous modern pension on the eighth floor; all rooms with cable/satellite TV, and those with shared facilities are among the cheapest in the Innere Stadt. ③.

Hotel Kärntnerhof, 1, Grashofgasse 4 (☎512 1923, *www.karntnerhof.com*); U-Bahn Schwedenplatz/Stephansplatz. Located in a cul-de-sac off Köllnerhofgasse, with pleasant, characterful rooms. Make sure you see your room first, however, as some can be a bit dingy. ⑥.

Hotel König von Ungarn, 1, Schulerstrasse 10 (☎51584, *www.kvu.at*); U-Bahn Stephansplatz. Tastefully modernized hotel with a remarkable wooden-panelled, covered courtyard bar/lounge. Pleasantly decorated rooms equipped throughout with air-conditioning, TV and en-suite facilities. ⑨.

Pension Lerner, 1, Wipplingerstrasse 23 (☎533 5219, *www.pensionlerner.com*); U-Bahn Schottentor/Herrengasse. Small pension with just seven bright, simple rooms with shower, toilet, TV, plus nice high ceilings and fans. Big buffet breakfasts served until 11am. ④.

Hotel Mailbergerhof, 1, Annagasse 7 (☎512 0641); U-Bahn Karlsplatz/Stephansplatz. Converted Baroque palace on a delightfully discreet, narrow side street off Kärntnerstrasse, with attractively furnished rooms. The hotel is smart, but the ambience is relaxed, and the staff are supremely efficient and friendly. ⑨.

Pension Neuer Markt, 1, Seilergasse 9 (☎512 2316); U-Bahn Stephansplatz. Very popular central pension on the second floor of a lovely old patrician building. Rooms are clean, comfortable and modern; those without shower, and those without en-suite toilet are a relative bargain – only a few have views over Neuermarkt. ④.

Pension Nossek, 1, Graben 17 (☎533 7041, *pensions.nossek@faxvia.net*); U-Bahn Stephansplatz. Large family-run pension on three floors of an old building on the pedestrianized Graben, with en-suite doubles of varying sizes, and some real bargain singles with shared facilities. It's popular, so book in advance. ⑥.

Hotel Orient, 1, Tiefer Graben 30 (☎533 7307); U-Bahn Herrengasse. Vienna's equivalent of a Tokyo "love hotel", with rooms rented by the hour and per night. Couples come for the mind-boggling exotic decor, and the wide range of themed rooms from inexpensive to more than öS2000/€145.35. ④–⑨.

Pension Pertschy, 1, Habsburgergasse 5 (☎53449, *www.pertschy.com*); U-Bahn Stephansplatz. Flagship of the Pertschy pension chain, with rooms off a series of plant-strewn balconies looking onto a lovely old courtyard. The rooms have lots of character, high ceilings, tasteful furnishings and TV. ⑥.

Hotel Post, 1, Fleischmarkt 24 (☎51583, *www.hotel-post-wien.at*); U-Bahn Schwedenplatz. Civilized, central hotel with over a hundred mostly large, old rooms with modern furnishings. The ones without shower and toilet are the real bargains. ④.

St Stephan Appartement-Pension, 1, Spiegelgasse 1 (☎512 2990); U-Bahn Stephansplatz. Incredible location in the Braun building overlooking Graben. A beautiful antique lift takes you up to the fourth floor, where there are just six doubles, with creaky parquet flooring and furnishings in keeping with the period. All have TV, shower, toilet, fridge and cooking facilities, and some have views out on to the Graben and Stephansdom. No breakfast. ⑥.

The Vorstädte

Altstadt Vienna, 7, Kirchengasse 41 (☎526 3399, *www.altstadt.at*); U-Bahn Volkstheater. A cut above most other pensions, with laid-back, well-informed staff, relaxing lounge and full-on buffet breakfast. Tastefully decorated en-suite rooms with high ceilings, and a great location, near Spittelberg and within easy walking distance of the U-Bahn and Ring. ⑦.

Pension Anna, 7, Zieglergasse 18 (☎523 0160, *pension.anna@chello.at*); U-Bahn Zieglergasse. First-floor pension run by a friendly couple. The startling light-blue decor doesn't extend into the fourteen bedrooms, all of which have en-suite shower and toilet. ⑤.

Pension Astra, 8, Alserstrasse 32 (☎402 4354, *hotelpensionastra@aon.at*); U-Bahn Alserstrasse. Mid-sized pension on the mezzanine of an old patrician building. Friendly staff and a range of modernized rooms, from simple doubles without toilet to roomy apartments. ③.

Pension Bosch, 3, Keilgasse 13 (☎798 6179); S-Bahn Rennweg. Attractive old-fashioned rooms, some of which are en suite, situated near the Südbahnhof, in a quiet residential backstreet behind the Belvedere, and an easy tram ride into town. ③.

Das Triest, 4, Wiedner Hauptstrasse 12 (☎58918, *www.designhotels.com*); U-Bahn Karlsplatz. Vienna's only truly hip designer hotel is hidden away in a nondescript building a short stroll from Karlsplatz. The super-smooth, minimalist interior comes courtesy of Terence Conran, and is quirky in an understated way. Rooms, which start at around öS3000/€218.02, are immaculate, of course, and those on the top floor have great views across the city skyline. ⑨.

Pension Esterhazy, 6, Nelkengasse 3 (☎587 5159); U-Bahn Neubaugasse. Basic rooms, with shared facilities, close to Mariahilferstrasse. There's no reception as such (it's run by the old lady on the floor below), and no breakfast, but it's clean and just about the cheapest place to stay short of a hostel. ②.

Hotel im Palais Schwarzenberg, 3, Schwarzenbergplatz 9 (☎798 4515, *www.palais-schwarzenberg .co.at*); U-Bahn Karlsplatz or tram #D. Hidden behind the Soviet War Memorial, this is *the* hotel to go for if money's no object – doubles start at over öS3500/€254.35. A family-owned Baroque palace designed by Hildebrandt and Fischer von Erlach, with period furnishings courtesy of, among others, Rubens, Meissen and Gobelins. ⑨.

Pension Kraml, 6, Brauergasse 5 (☎587 8588); U-Bahn Zieglergasse/Neubaugasse. Probably the friendliest and most reliable of the cheap pensions in the quiet streets off Mariahilferstrasse. Smart, clean, modern rooms, some with en-suite facilities, some without. ③.

Hotel Kugel, 7, Siebensterngasse 43 (☎523 3355, *www.hotelkugel.at*); U-Bahn Neubaugasse. Good location within spitting distance of Spittelberg's numerous restaurants and bars. Plain but clean rooms, some with shared facilities, some en suite; continental breakfast is served in the *gemütlich* peasant-style breakfast room. ③.

Pension Lindenhof, 7, Lindengasse 4 (☎523 0498); U-Bahn Neubaugasse. On the first floor of a lugubrious fin-de-siècle building at the Spittelberg end of this long street. Lovely, up-only lift (öS1), plant-strewn communal area and appealing rooms (some of which are en suite), with creaky parquet flooring. ③.

Hotel Nordbahn, 2, Praterstrasse 72 (☎21130, *www.hotel-nordbahn.at*); U-Bahn Nestroyplatz/Praterstern. If you need to stay in the second district, then the birthplace of Max Steiner, composer of film music to *Gone with the Wind* and *Casablanca*, is probably your best bet. It's now a large, pleasantly modernized hotel with shower, toilet and TVs in all rooms. ⑥.

Hotel Rathaus, 8, Lange Gasse 13 (☎406 0123, *www.nethotels.com/rathaus*); U-Bahn Lerchenfelder Strasse. Clean, comfortable and quiet hotel in an old patrician building a few blocks west of the Rathaus, with some cheap singles without en-suite bathroom. ⑤.

Hotel Regina, 9, Rooseveltplatz 15 (☎40446, *www.kremslehner.hotels.or.at/regina*); U-Bahn Schottentor. Huge Ringstrasse hotel next door to the Votivkirche, with gloriously heavy Viennese decor in the public areas and some of the rooms. ⑨.

Pension Wild, 8, Lange Gasse 10 (☎406 5174, *www.pension-wild.com*); U-Bahn Lerchenfelder Strasse. Friendly, laid-back pension, a short walk from the Ring in a student district behind the university, and especially popular with backpackers and gay travellers. Booking essential. ③.

Pension Zipser, 8, Lange Gasse 49 (☎404540, *www.notehotels.com/zipser*); U-Bahn Rathaus. Well-equipped, modern pension, offering a buffet breakfast – a reliable choice, just a short walk from the Ring behind the Rathaus. ⑤.

Hostels, student halls and camping

Vienna's official **Hostelling International** *Jugendherbergen* are efficient, clean and, occasionally, even friendly. However, with just one exception, they're all a long way from the centre. Most of the beds are in segregated dorms, but some do have bunk-bed doubles. Prices vary slightly, but are usually around öS200/€14.54 a night, including a simple continental breakfast. There are also **curfews**, though several HI hostels have 24hr receptions and will give you a night key on request. If possible, you should make an advance **reservation** as soon as you know when you might be arriving, as places can be booked out months in advance; at the very least, you should ring before turning up. The biggest practical drawback to the official hostels is that they throw you out each day at 9am in order to clean, and won't let you back in until 3 or 4pm. The lure of the **independent hostel** then, is that while the prices are much the same as the HI hostels, the atmospherre is a bit less institutional, there's generally no curfew, and either no lockout or a more generous one allowing a longer lie-in.

From July to September, there are singles and doubles, plus a few triples and quads, available in *Studentenheime* or **student halls** of residence. The rooms rarely have much character, and kitchen facilities are not always available, but the location is usually fairly central and you definitely get more privacy than in a hostel. Prices tend to be a little higher (and breakfast is often not included), but there's no curfew, no lockout, and no limit to how long you wish to stay.

Finally, Vienna's **campsites** are all quite far out from the centre, on the perimeters of the city, and so for committed campers only. Pitches cost around öS40–60/€2.91–4.36, plus a fee of around öS60–80/€4.36–5.81 per person.

Hostels

Jugendgästehaus Brigittenau, 20, Friedrich-Engels-Platz 24 (☎332 8294, *oejhv-wien-jgh-brigittenau @oejhv.or.at*); tram #N from U-Bahn Schwedenplatz or Dresdner Strasse. Huge modern hostel in a dour working-class suburb, with dorms and en-suite bunk-bed doubles. No curfew; 24hr reception.

Jugendgästehaus Hütteldorf-Hacking, 13, Schlossberggasse 8 (☎877 0263, *jgh@wigast.com*); S- and U-Bahn Hütteldorf. A 220-bed dorm-only hostel way out in the sticks, but convenient for those who wish to explore the wilds of the Lainzer Tiergarten and Schönbrunn. 11.45pm curfew, but night key available for a small fee.

Kolpingfamilie Wien-Meidling, 12, Bendlgasse 10–12 (☎813 5487); U-Bahn Niederhofstrasse. Modern hostel easily reached by U-Bahn from the centre. Beds in the big dorms go for as little as öS130/€9.45 (without breakfast). Curfew midnight; 24hr reception.

Jugendherberge Myrthengasse/Neustiftgasse, 7, Myrthengasse 7/Neustiftgasse 85 (☎523 6316, *hostel@chello.at*); bus #48A or 10min walk from U-Bahn Volkstheater. The most central of all the official hostels, with 200-plus dorm beds divided between two addresses, round the corner from each other. Book well in advance and go to the Myrthengasse reception on arrival. Curfew 1am.

Hostel Ruthensteiner, 15, Robert-Hamerling-Gasse 24 (☎893 4202, *hostel.ruthensteiner @telecom.at*); U-Bahn Westbahnhof. Excellent hostel, with a nice courtyard to hang out in, within easy walking distance of the Westbahnhof, with dorm beds, doubles and triples (discounts for HI members). Open all year. No curfew.

Schlossherberge am Wilhelminenberg, 16, Savoyenstrasse 2 (☎458503-700); bus #146B or #46B from S- and U-Bahn Ottakring or tram #J terminus. Offering 164 beds in a beautiful location next to a Neoclassical mansion in the Vienna Woods, but not a great base from which to sample the nightlife. Curfew 11.45pm. Dorm beds and doubles available.

Turmherberge "Don Bosco", 3, Lechnerstrasse 12 (☎713 1494); U-Bahn Kardinal-Nagl-Platz. Don't go with high expectations, but these are probably the cheapest beds in town (öS80/€5.81 without breakfast), in a church tower in the back end of Landstrasse. Curfew 11.45pm. Open March–Nov.

Wombat's, 15, Grangasse 6 (☎897 2336, *wombats@chello.at*); U-Bahn Westbahnhof. Plain dorm beds and bunk-bed doubles, but a party atmosphere at this friendly, laid-back hostel, within easy walking distance of Westbahnhof. 24hr reception.

Hostel Zöhrer, 8, Skodagasse 26 (☎406 0730, *info@zoehrer.com*); U-Bahn Josefstädter Strasse or trams #5 and #33. Small private hostel centrally located in the inner suburbs with dorms and bunk-bed doubles. No curfew and no lockout. Open all year.

Student halls

Auersperg, 8, Auerspergstrasse 9 (☎406 2340); U-Bahn Lerchenfelder Strasse. Excellent, central location, just off the Ring. Singles and doubles with or without shower and toilet. ②.

Haus Döbling, 19, Gymnasiumstrasse 85 (☎347631); tram #38. Huge place where prices vary according to whether you want "hotel service" or not. ①.

Porzellaneum, 9, Porzellangasse 30 (☎317 7282); tram #D. Functional singles, doubles and quads for öS175/€12.72 per head, popular with backpackers. No breakfast, but showers, courtyard and lounge with TV. ①.

Campsites

Camping Neue Donau, 22, Am Kaisermühlendamm 119 (☎202 4010, *west2@vie.at*); S-Bahn Lobau or bus #91A from U-Bahn Kaisermühlen-VIC. Not a first choice, but easy to get to by car as it's squeezed between the autobahn and the railway lines on the east bank of the Danube. Open mid-May to mid-Sept.

Camping Rodaun, 23, An der Au 2 (☎888 4154); tram #60 from U-Bahn Hietzing to its terminus, then 5min walk. Nice location by a stream in the very southwestern outskirts of Vienna, near the Wienerwald. Open April to mid-Nov.

Wien West, 14, Hüttelbergstrasse 80 (☎914 2314); bus #151 from U-Bahn Hütteldorf, or a 15min walk from tram #49 terminus. In the plush, far-western suburbs of Vienna, close to the Wienerwald, with 4-people bungalows to rent between April and October (öS400/€29.07). Closed Feb.

The Innere Stadt

The **Innere Stadt** (Inner City), Vienna's first district, has been the very heart of the place since the Romans founded Vindobona here in 15 BC. It was here, too, that the Babenburg dukes built their powerbase in the twelfth century, and from 1533 the Habsburgs established the **Hofburg**, their imperial residence (dealt with in detail under a separate section on p.96). In fact, the city occupied pretty much the same space until the zigzag fortifications, which had protected the city on two occasions against the Turks, were finally taken down in the mid-nineteenth century.

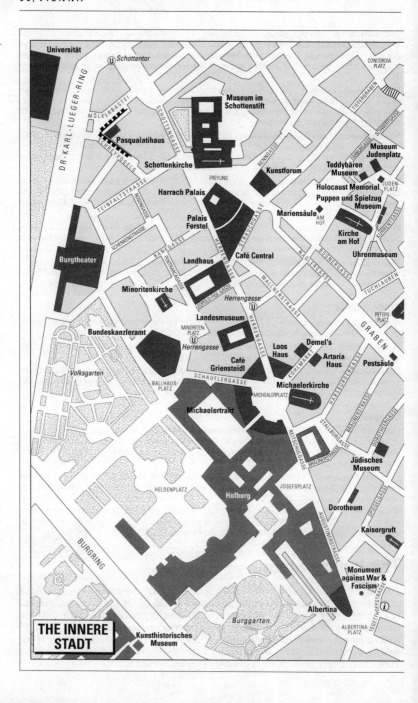

Universität

Schottentor

CONCORDIA PLATZ

MÖLKERBASTEI

Museum im Schottenstift

TIEFERGRABEN

Pasqualatihaus

SCHOTTENGASSE

RENNGASSE

Museum Judenplatz

Schottenkirche

FREYUNG

Kunstforum

Teddybären Museum

Holocaust Memorial

JUDEN-PLATZ

DR.-KARL-LUEGER-RING

SCHREYVOGELG

Harrach Palais

STRAUCHGASSE

Puppen und Spielzug Museum

TEINFALTSTRASSE

ROSSMGASSE

Palais Ferstel

Mariensäule
AM HOF

Kirche am Hof

KURRENTGASSE

SCHENKENSTRASSE

HERRENGASSE

Burgtheater

BANKGASSE

Landhaus

Café Central

NAGLERGASSE

BOGNERGASSE

Uhrenmuseum

TUCHLAUBEN

Minoritenkirche

PENTHARGASSE

LEOPOLD HOF-GASSE

WALLNERSTRASSE

Herrengasse

Volksgarten

Bundeskanzleramt

MINORITEN-PLATZ

Landesmuseum

Herrengasse

HERRENGASSE

Loos Haus

Demel's

PETERS-PLATZ

GRABEN

BALLHAUS-PLATZ

Café Griensteidl

SCHAUFLERGASSE

KOHLMARKT

Artaria Haus

Pestsäule

HABSBURGERGASSE

BRAUNERSTRASSE

Michaelerkirche

MICHAELERPLATZ

Michaelertrakt

STALLBURGGASSE

DOROTHEERGASSE

REITSCHULGASSE

BRAUNERSTRASSE

Jüdisches Museum

HELDENPLATZ

JOSEFSPLATZ

Hofburg

Dorotheum

SPIEGELGASSE

Kaisergruft

AUGUSTINERSTRASSE

BURGRING

Monument against War & Fascism

TEGETTHOFFSTRASSE

Albertina

THE INNERE STADT

Kunsthistorisches Museum

Burggarten

ALBERTINA PLATZ

ⓘ

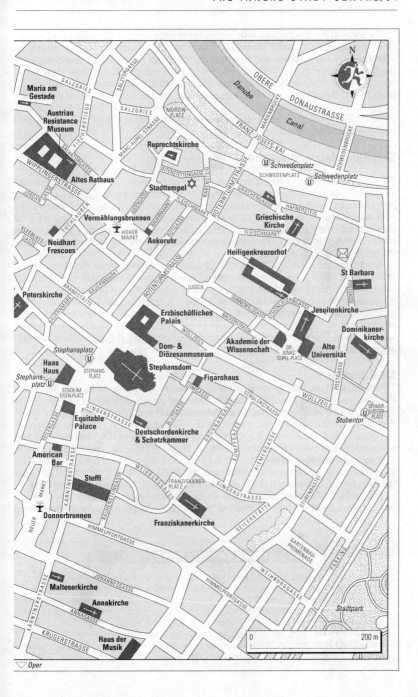

OBERE
DONAUSTRASSE
Danube
Canal
FRANZ-JOSEFS-KAI
MARIENBRÜCKE
SCHWEDENBRÜCKE

N

SALZGRIES

Maria am
Gestade

Austrian
Resistance
Museum

FISCHERSTIEGE

SALVATORGASSE

MARC-AUREL-STRASSE

SALZGRIES

SALZGRIES

MÖRZIN-
PLATZ

Ruprechtskirche

Schwedenplatz

SCHWEDENPLATZ

Schwedenplatz

WIPPLINGERSTRASSE

Altes Rathaus

JORDAN
GASSE

TUCHLAUBEN

SEITENSTETTENGASSE

Stadttempel

JUDENGASSE

RABENSTEIG

ROTENTURMSTRASSE

GRIECHENGASSE

HAFNERSTEIG

KLEEBLATT-
GASSE

Neidhart
Frescoes

Vermählungsbrunnen

BAUERNMARKT

FLEISCHMARKT

BAUERNMARKT

HOHER
MARKT

Ankeruhr

ROTGASSE

Griechische
Kirche

FLEISCHMARKT

Peterskirche

BRANDSTÄTTE

ROTENTURMSTRASSE

LUGECK

Heiligenkreuzhof

SONNENFELSGASSE

KÖLLNERHOFGASSE

St Barbara

POSTGASSE

Erzbischöfliches
Palais

BÄCKERSTRASSE

Jesuitenkirche

Dominikaner-
kirche

Dom- &
Diözesanmuseum

WOLLZEILE

Akademie der
Wissenschaft

DR-
IGNAZ-
SEIPEL-
PLATZ

Alte
Universität

POSTGASSE

Stephansplatz

Haas
Haus

Stephans-
platz

STEPHANS-
PLATZ

STOCK-IM-
EISEN-PLATZ

Stephansdom

Figarohaus

DOMGASSE

BLUTGASSE

GRÜNANGERGASSE

SCHULERSTRASSE

WOLLZEILE

RIEMERGASSE

DR-KARL-
LUEGER-
PLATZ

Stubentor

Equitable
Palace

SEILERGASSE

SINGERSTRASSE

Deutschordenkirche
& Schatzkammer

KUMPFGASSE

American
Bar

KÄRNTNERSTRASSE

Steffl

RAUHENSTEINGASSE

WEIHBURGGASSE

FRANZISKANER-
PLATZ

SINGERSTRASSE

SEILERSTÄTTE

STUBENBASTEI

NEUER
MARKT

Donnerbrunnen

HIMMELPFORTGASSE

Franziskanerkirche

GARTENBAU-
PROMENADE

PARKING

KÄRNTNER STRASSE

JOHANNESGASSE

HIMMELPFORTGASSE

WEIHBURGGASSE

Malteserkirche

Annakirche

ANNAGASSE

Stadtpark

KRUGERSTRASSE

Haus der
Musik

0   200 m

Oper

The focus of the Innere Stadt is the magnificent cathedral, the **Stephansdom**, whose spire also acts as a useful landmark. Close by are the chief shopping streets of **Kärntnerstrasse**, **Graben** and **Kohlmarkt**, which get progressively more exclusive the nearer you get to the Hofburg. There's a steady ebb and flow of folk along these streets at most times of the day, but the cathedral and the **Kaisergruft**, the last resting place of the Habsburgs, just off Kärntnerstrasse, are the only sights that get heavily clogged up with tour groups. Head off into the rest of the Innere Stadt, with its baffling medieval lanes, hidden courtyards and *Durchhäuser* (literally, "through-houses"), and you'll soon lose the crowds.

Stephansplatz and around

The geographical heart of the Innere Stadt is **Stephansplatz**, the lively, pedestrianized square that surrounds the hoary Gothic bulk of **Stephansdom**. As such, it's one of the best places for watching Viennese streetlife, from the benign young flame-haired punks who lounge around on the benches by the U-Bahn escalators to the beleaguered folk in eighteenth-century costumes wearily flogging tickets for up-and-coming classical concerts. The smell of horse dung wafts across the square from the fiacres lined up along the north wall of the cathedral.

Apart from the cathedral, the dominant feature of the square is the **Haas Haus**, probably the single most inappropriate building in the Innere Stadt and one which, not surprisingly, caused something of a furore when it was first unveiled in 1990. The real disappointment is that the architect, Hans Hollein, is capable of much better – his equally uncompromising jewellery stores along Graben and Kohlmarkt are minor masterpieces. Here, though, the metal-coated glass and polished stone facade lacks subtlety, and the protruding turret is a veritable carbuncle; to cap it all, the interior is an unimaginative mini-shopping centre.

Stephansdom

The **Stephansdom**, distinguished by the multicoloured chevrons on its roof, dominates the Viennese skyline as it has done for centuries. An obvious military target, it has endured two Turkish sieges, Napoleonic bombardment and, in the later stages of World War II, the attentions of American bombers and Russian artillery. That it survived at all is a miracle, and has ensured it a special place in the hearts of the Viennese. The first church on this site was a Romanesque basilica, begun in 1137, but replaced after a fire in 1193 by an early-Gothic variant, which was itself reduced to rubble in the fire of 1258. The foundation stone of the current building was laid in 1359 by Rudolf IV, but it wasn't until the early twentieth century that the choir and several of the chapels were completed.

The cathedral's most magnificent feature is the sublime south tower (daily 9am–5.30pm; öS30/€2.18) – nicknamed "**Steffl**" (Little Stephen) by the locals – which

---

VISITING THE STEPHANSDOM

Although the cathedral **opening hours** are daily 6am to 10pm, tourists are discouraged from sightseeing during the religious services. In practice, this means visiting times are restricted to Monday to Saturday 9am to noon and 1pm to 5pm and Sunday 12.30pm to 5pm. Entrance is free, though to have a proper look at anything beyond the transept, you really need to join a **guided tour** (*Domführung*). These run Monday to Saturday 10.30am and 3pm, Sunday 3pm, with English tours daily at 3.45pm (April–Oct only), and cost öS40/€2.91; you meet just inside the cathedral by the main door. Additional charges are made for the catacombs, the Pummerin and the Steffl.

soars to a not-so-little height of around 137m. The north tower, or Eagle Tower (daily: April, June, Sept & Oct 9am–6pm; July & Aug 9am–6.30pm; Nov–March 8.30am–5pm; öS40/€2.91), was to have been built along similar lines, but fell victim to cost-cutting during the build-up to the first Turkish siege of 1529, its half-finished stump eventually receiving a copper cupola in 1556. You can take the lift up the north tower to see the cathedral's great bell, known as the **Pummerin** (Boomer), though the Steffl, a blind scramble up 343 steps, has better views.

THE INTERIOR

The first thing that strikes you as you enter the gloomy, high-vaulted interior of the cathedral is that, despite the tourists, Stephansdom is still very much a place of worship. At peak times of worship, it can be difficult to get a seat in the area immediately to your right, facing the **Pötscher Madonna**, which sits below a delicate late-Gothic baldachin. Legend has it that the Madonna, an object of great veneration even today, wept tears from her unusually large eyes during the Battle of Zenta against the Turks in 1697, and in so doing miraculously secured victory against the infidels. Another saviour of the city, Prince Eugène of Savoy, hero of the campaigns against the Turks in the early eighteenth century, is buried in the **Tirna Chapel**, on the other side of the cathedral, off the north aisle – he's mostly here, that is, for his heart lies in Turin. Sadly, the chapel is usually shut behind heavy iron gates, which prevent even the slightest glimpse of the prince's tomb on the south wall.

The highlight of the cathedral, though, is without doubt the early sixteenth-century carved stone **pulpit**, with portraits of the four Church fathers, sculpted by an unknown artist who "signed" his work by showing himself peering from a window below the pulpit stairs. The filigree work above and below the staircase is masterly, as are the salamanders and toads (sadly now under protective perspex), symbolizing good and evil, pursuing one another up the banister towards a barking dog who keeps them all at bay. The Moravian sculptor, Anton Pilgram, who was until recently thought to be responsible for the pulpit, can be spotted peeping out of the wall of the north aisle, in polychrome, below one of his works, the now defunct organ case.

Beyond the transepts, the **choir** is roped off, and only visitable by guided tour (see box opposite). At the far end of the north choir aisle, however, you should just be able to make out the winged **Wiener Neustädter Altar**, a richly gilded masterpiece of late-Gothic art, whose central panels, sculpted from wood, are closed from view during Advent and Lent. Below the altar to the left lies the **Donor's Tomb**, adorned with sandstone effigies of Rudolf IV and his wife Catherine of Bohemia (they're actually buried in the catacombs), once richly gilded and peppered with precious stones. In the Apostles' Choir to the south stands the glorious red-marble **Tomb of Emperor Friedrich III**. In amongst the 240 statues, 32 coats of arms and numerous scaly creatures that decorate the tomb is the emperor's mysterious acronym AIEOU (for more on which, see p.216).

THE CATACOMBS

A stairway in the north transept leads down into the **catacombs** (guided tours every 30min Mon–Sat 10–11.30am & 1.30–4.30pm, Sun 1.30–4.30pm; öS40/€2.91), which, initially at least, are a bit disappointing, having been over-restored in the 1960s. It's here that Rudolf IV and his wife rest with other early Habsburg rulers, sundry priests, bishops and archbishops. Beyond a small chamber filled with bronze caskets holding the entrails of the later Habsburgs is the entry to the damp, dimly lit labyrinth of eighteenth-century catacombs, which were closed in 1783 after the stench became too overpowering. Around 16,000 locals are buried here, their bones piled high in more than thirty rooms; in the final chamber, there's a particularly macabre pile left over from a medieval plague pit. You exit from the catacombs via a secret staircase, which deposits you outside the cathedral beside the place where Mozart's body was blessed before being buried in St Marxer Friedhof (see p.126).

Around Stephansplatz

Stephansplatz was badly bombed in the war, and few of the other buildings are worthy of mention, though you might want to visit the **Dom-** and **Diözesanmuseum** (Tues–Sat 10am–5pm; öS70/€5.09) on the first floor of the Zwettlhof; access is via Stephansplatz 6 on the north side of Stephansplatz. This is basically the dumping ground for a mishmash of the cathedral's most valuable treasures, church plate and artwork. There are some arresting medieval sculptures in wood and some kitsch Baroque pieces, like the Madonna shrine, whose cloak opens up to reveal God (forming her body), surrounded by a host of worshippers' faces. The highlight, though, is the dimly lit treasury of monstrances and macabre reliquaries, including Saint Leopold's hipbone, a piece of the Virgin Mary's belt and the cranium of Saint Stephen.

A much more intriguing ecclesiastical treasure trove can be seen at the **Schatzkammer des Deutschen Ordens** (Treasury of the Order of Teutonic Knights; May–Oct Mon, Thurs & Sun 10am–noon, Wed 3–5pm, Fri & Sat 10am–noon & 3–5pm; Nov–April closed Fri am & Sun; öS50/€3.63), spread over five rooms on the second floor of the Deutschordenshaus; enter from Singerstrasse 7, one block south of Stephansplatz. The treasury's varied collection, assembled by seven centuries of Grand Masters, ranges from the mundane – seals, coins and crosses – to the bizarre: an adder's tongue used for testing food for poison, and a red coral salt-cellar tree hung with the fossils of sharks' teeth. The Order's military past is represented by a collection of exotic arms and armour, including a wiggly sixteenth-century Malaysian sword and scabbard, and a poisoned dagger with a handle carved out of rhino horn into the shape of the Buddha, with sapphire eyes and ruby eyebrows. Before you leave, be sure to pop inside the *sala terrena* on the ground floor, at the bottom of the staircase, to admire the Baroque trompe l'oeil decor.

To get to the **Figarohaus** (Tues–Sun 9am–6pm; öS25/€1.82), Vienna's chief Mozart memorial, immediately east of the cathedral, pass through the Durchhaus at Stephansplatz 5a, and enter at Domgasse 5. Here, on the first floor, Mozart, Constanze and their son, Karl Thomas, lived for three years, during which the composer enjoyed his greatest success. It was Mozart's swankiest accommodation in Vienna, where he even had his own billiards room. The composer Johann Nepomuk Hummel stayed here as Mozart's live-in pupil for two and a half years, and Josef Haydn – who opined that Mozart was "the greatest composer that I know in person or by name" – was a regular visitor. Sadly, however, there's not a lot to see inside, and only one of the rooms retains the original decor of marble and stucco (the Camesina family, who owned the property, were stucco artists). There are none of Mozart's personal effects, no period furniture, no atmosphere; just a few facsimiles of his scores and reproductions of the composer and his circle of friends. Nevertheless, it's worth a visit, if only for the building's lovely courtyard, the views along Blutgasse, and the chance to hear some of Mozart's music on the headphones provided.

Kärntnerstrasse and around

As its name suggests, **Kärntnerstrasse** lies along the old road from Vienna to the southern Austrian province of Carinthia (Kärntner), and beyond to the Adriatic. Widened in the nineteenth century, badly bombed in World War II and pedestrianized in the 1970s, it retains only a few reminders of the days when it was home to the city's luxury retail trade. Nevertheless, it's still a favourite street for promenading, and for window-shopping.

MOZART IN VIENNA

It's almost as difficult to avoid images of **Wolfgang Amadeus Mozart** (1756–91) in Vienna as it is in his home town of Salzburg (see p.384). For it was in Vienna that Mozart spent the last decade of his life, during which he composed nearly all his most famous works. Mozart moved to Vienna in March 1781 after a summons from his employer, the irascible Archbishop of Salzburg, Count Colloredo, who was visiting his sick father in the city. Within three months Mozart had resigned from his post as court organist to the archbishop, or "arch-oaf" (*Erzlümmel*) as he called him in his letters, causing a rift with his overbearing father, who was assistant *Kapellmeister* in Salzburg. The relationship was further strained when Mozart, against his father's wishes, moved in with the all-female Weber family, and grew particularly attached to one of the daughters, Constanze. In August 1782 Mozart eventually married the 19-year-old Constanze in the Stephansdom. Their union appears to have been happy, despite most biographers' misogynist attacks on Constanze as unworthy of his genius. Mozart himself hated to be parted from her, if his letters – "I kiss and squeeze you 1,095,060,437,082 times" – and the fact that he rarely left her side, are anything to go by.

After giving many concerts as conductor and pianist, Mozart turned his hand again to opera, enjoying his greatest success in July 1782 with what is now the least known of his major operatic works, *Die Entführung aus dem Serail* (The Escape from the Harem). It was after hearing *Die Entführung* for the first time that the Emperor Josef II is alleged to have said: "Too beautiful for our ears, and an awful lot of notes, dear Mozart"; to which Mozart replied, "No more notes than necessary, Your Majesty!" Such tales have led to a popular belief that Mozart and Josef were constantly feuding over artistic issues: in his letters, however, Mozart's criticisms of the notoriously stingy emperor were on purely financial matters.

Mozart's next opera, *Le Nozze di Figaro* (The Marriage of Figaro), was premiered in May 1786 to a decidedly mixed reception, running for just nine performances. This was partly because its subject matter, in which a lecherous count is prevented from seducing a servant girl by an alliance between the serving classes and his own long-suffering wife, was controversial – as a play it had already been banned in Paris and Vienna. Josef II obviously liked it, however, inviting the cast to give a special performance at his summer residence at Laxenburg. And Figaro's subversive overtones went down a storm in Prague, where Mozart premiered two later operas, *Don Giovanni* and *La Clemenza di Tito* (The Clemency of Tito), both of which were written in Vienna. Mozart's final work was his *Requiem*, which was commissioned anonymously by an "unknown messenger" in the last year of Mozart's life. Only after Mozart's death did the patron's identity become known: it was the recently widowed Count Franz Walsegg-Stuppach, who wished to pass the composition off as his own. In the end it became Mozart's own *Requiem*, still unfinished when he died during the night of December 4–5, 1791, after two weeks of rheumatic fever. Few biographers have forgiven Constanze for not attending the funeral service at the Stephansdom; others assert that she was too distraught to attend. She has also been criticized for having the *Requiem* completed by one of Mozart's pupils, Sussmayr, so as to get the final payment – though this seems fair enough for a widow left with two children to raise (and apparently it was Mozart's suggestion on his deathbed).

Yet more anecdotes surround the generally accepted rivalry with the *Kapellmeister* Antonio Salieri, though this, too, has been overplayed. Salieri was primarily an opera composer, while Mozart, at least until 1786, was known chiefly as an instrumental composer and virtuoso pianist. Some went as far as to suggest that Salieri himself poisoned Mozart, an allegation strenuously denied by Salieri on his deathbed years later, but to no avail: Alexander Pushkin dramatized it, Nicolai Rimsky-Korsakov made it into an opera, and most famously, *Amadeus*, Peter Shaffer's play on the subject, was made into an Oscar-winning film by Milos Forman. For the story of how Mozart was condemned to a pauper's grave, see p.126.

As a whole the street has gone downmarket. One exception, however, is **J. & L. Lobmeyr** (Mon–Fri 9am–6pm, Sat 10am–4pm), at no. 26, which, as well as flogging expensive glass and crystal, also houses an informal glass museum. The assistants are quite happy for you to wander through to the back of the shop, where you'll find the stairs that lead to the second-floor balcony. The wonderful, mostly antique, exhibits here include an incredible range of chandeliers, culminating in a copy of the 1960s chandelier that graces the New York Metropolitan Opera. Downstairs, in the shop itself, you'll see glassware sets still made to designs by Adolf Loos and Josef Hoffmann for the Wiener Werkstätte (see p.117).

Neuer Markt and the Kaisergruft

Kärntnerstrasse's most interesting sights lie off the street itself, most conspicuously in the **Neuer Markt** to the west, formerly the city's medieval flour market. The centre-piece of the square is the **Donnerbrunnen**, a Baroque fountain designed by Georg Raphael Donner. The nudity of the figures perched on the edge of the fountain – they represent the four Austrian tributaries of the Danube – was deemed too risqué by the Empress Maria Theresia, who had the lead statues removed in 1770 to be melted down into cannon. They were returned unharmed in 1801, and in 1873 replaced by bronze copies: the young male figure of Traun, in particular, depicted dipping his triton into the waters, clearly showed rather too much buttock for contemporary tastes, hence the judiciously placed fig leaf.

The square's grim-looking Kapuzinerkirche hides one of the premier sights in Vienna: its crypt, the **Kaisergruft** (daily 9.30am–4pm; öS40/€2.91), which has been the unlikely resting place of the Habsburgs (with just a few notable exceptions) since 1633. The crypt is entered from a doorway to the left of the church. While a monk relieves you of your money, notices demand a respectful "*Silentium!*" – but don't let them kid you, this place is a tourist attraction above all else. Inside, though the crypt isn't gloomy, it is, nevertheless, an intriguing insight into the Habsburgs' fascination with death. As you enter the burial vault, you're confronted with the monster Baroque sarcophagi of Leopold I and Josef I, both designed by Johann Lucas von Hildebrandt, and the latter sporting ghoulish skulls in full head armour below and with bat wings above. Those of Karl VI and his wife are his'n'hers designs by Rococo artist Balthasar Ferdinand Moll: his sits on lions, with toothy skulls sporting crowns at each corner; hers sits on eagles, with women in mourning veils at each corner. The main focus and highlight of the crypt is Moll's obscenely large double tomb for the Empress Maria Theresia and her husband, Franz Stephan, immediately to the left as you enter. Over 3m high and wide, 6m long, and smothered in Rococo decorations, the imperial couple are depicted sitting up in bed, as if indignantly accusing one another of snoring. Immediately below their feet lies the simple copper coffin of their son, Josef II, to whom such pomposity was anathema. It was he who instigated the idea of a reusable coffin, and issued a decree enforcing its use in all funerals – not surprisingly, given the Viennese obsession with elaborate sendoffs, the emperor was eventually forced to back down. Several more of Maria Theresia's sixteen children lie in the shadow of their mother, in ornate Rococo coffins, as does the only non-Habsburg among the crypt's 143 occupants, Karoline Fuchs-Mollard, the empress's governess.

It's all downhill aesthetically after Maria Theresia, though the gloomy postwar bunker of the New Vault features some jazzy concrete vaulting. Star corpses here include Maximilian I, Emperor of Mexico, who was executed in 1867, and Marie Louise, Napoleon's second wife. Their son, the Duke of Reichstadt – or "L'Aiglon" – who died of tuberculosis at the age of 21, was also buried here until 1940, when Hitler had his remains transferred to Paris as a gesture of goodwill. Finally, there's **Franz-Josef I**'s sarcophagus, permanently strewn with fresh flowers. Even more revered, though, is his wife, Empress Elisabeth, who was assassinated in 1898, her tomb draped in Hungarian wreaths and colours. On the other side of the emperor is the coffin of their eldest son, Crown Prince Rudolf, who committed suicide in 1889 (see p.209). The **chapel** beyond contains the Kaisergruft's most recent arrival, Empress Zita, who died in 1989 in exile and was buried here with imperial pomp and circumstance.

Haus der Musik

Signposts on Kärntnerstrasse point east to the **Haus der Musik** (daily 10am–10pm; *www.haus-der-musik-wien.at*; öS110/€7.99), a hugely enjoyable new attraction down Annagasse in the newly revamped headquarters of the Wiener Philharmoniker (Vienna Philharmonic). On the first floor is a museum dedicated to this world-famous orchestra, which only allowed women to join its ranks in 1996. It comes as something of a surprise, then, to find, on the second floor, a startling, state-of-the-art exhibition on the nature of sound, filled with high-tech installations. To get you into the mood, the walls of the first, bare room you enter, vibrate with synthesized prenatal sounds. After a brief rundown on the biology of the ear, you enter the "laboratory of perception", where a bank of beautifully designed touch-screen computers explore human responses to frequency, volume and so on. Elsewhere on this floor, you can watch and stretch the sound waves created by your own voice and play around with prerecorded sounds in the dimly-lit "sea of voices" room.

On the third floor, the subject is more conventional, with a room to each of the big three classical composers – Haydn, Mozart and Beethoven – as well as one each dedicated to Schubert, Strauss, Mahler and Schönberg's modernist posse. The displays are a whole lot more imaginative than all the city's other musical memorials put together. There's plenty of hands-on fun and games: you can isolate each of the parts to Mozart's *Eine kleine Nachtmusik*, have a virtual tour of musically significant parts of Vienna, and do some virtual conducting. There's yet more musical tomfoolery upstairs in the Brain Opera, where you can create your own music on the Gesture Wall, the Rhythm Tree, and finally via a sophisticated visual computer bank of sounds.

Graben and Kohlmarkt

The prime shopping streets of **Graben** and **Kohlmarkt** retain an air of exclusivity that Kärntnerstrasse has lost. Their shops, many of which are preserved in aspic, as if the empire lives on, advertise branches in places such as Karlsbad, Leipzig and Prague. Others still sport the *K.K.* or *k.u.k* emblem – *kaiserlich und königlich* (Imperial and Royal) – the Austrian equivalent of "By Appointment to Her Majesty the Queen". In between these old-fashioned stores are several Art-Nouveau edifices and designer jewellers produced by the old man of modern Austrian architecture, Hans Hollein.

Graben

Graben – its name translates as "ditches" – was once a moat that lay outside the Roman camp. It was filled in sometime in the thirteenth century and, like Kärntnerstrasse, was widened at the beginning of the nineteenth century, from which era most of its buildings date. The most conspicuous monument on Graben is the **Pestsäule**, or plague column, a towering, amorphous mass of swirling clouds, saints and cherubs, covered in a cobweb of netting to keep the pigeons off. Ostensibly erected to commemorate the end of the 1679 plague, this monument – like similar ones throughout the empire – was raised on the initiative of the Jesuits, to celebrate deliverance from the Protestant or Turkish "plague". The Pestsäule, in addition to the Hildebrandt-designed Bartolotti-Partenfeld palace, at no. 11 on the corner of Dorotheergasse, are the only survivors of the Baroque era on Graben. More arresting, though, are the shop fronts by Hans Hollein from the 1960s and 1970s, in particular the Schullin (now Deutsch) **jewellers**,

Graben 26, a polished marble facade spliced by a seam of gold which trickles down into the doorframe.

Set back slightly from Graben, occupying a little square of its own, is the **Peterskirche**, completed by Hildebrandt in 1733, and without doubt the finest Baroque church in the Innere Stadt. From the outside, the great green oval dome overwhelms the church's twin towers; inside, the dome's fresco by Johann Michael Rottmayr is difficult to discern, leaving the High Baroque side altars and the trompe l'oeil ceiling painting in the choir to create a sense of theatrics. The lavish gilded pulpit is truly magnificent, but the most dramatic work of art is the monument opposite, designed by Lorenzo Matielli and depicting St John of Nepomuk being thrown off Prague's Charles Bridge by some nasty-looking Czech bullyboys, with Václav IV in Roman garb directing the proceedings.

The Jüdisches Museum

Just off Graben, up Dorotheergasse, is the city's intriguing **Jüdisches Museum** (daily except Sat 10am–6pm, Thurs until 9pm; öS70/€5.00; *www.jmw.at*), halfway up in the Palais Eskeles at no. 11. Vienna was home to the first Jewish Museum in the world, founded in 1896 but forcibly closed by the Nazis in 1938; it wasn't until 1989 that it was finally re-established in these state-of-the-art premises.

On the ground floor, beyond the swanky café and bookshop, the covered courtyard is dominated by a giant glass cabinet of Judaica etched with quotations from the Torah and other sources, whose prophetic nature is revealed on the walls, over which are scattered photographic images from the Holocaust. On the whole, though, the curators have rejected the usual static display cabinets and newsreel photos of past atrocities. Instead, the emphasis of the museum's excellent temporary exhibitions on the first floor is on contemporary Jewish life.

Special exhibitions also occupy part of the second floor, which contains the museum's permanent displays. Taking the Marxist Jewish critic Walter Benjamin's contention that "the past can only be seized as an image which flashes up at the instant when it can be recognized and is never seen again", the museum employs a series of freestanding glass panels imprinted with holograms – ranging from the knob of Theodor Herzl's walking stick to a short clip capturing an everyday instance of anti-Semitism from 1911. These ghostly images, accompanied by judiciously selected soundbites (in German and English) on Zionism, assimilation and other key issues, pithily trace the history of Vienna's Jewry, juxtaposing the enormous achievements of the city's Jews – from Gustav Mahler to Billy Wilder – with its justified reputation as a hotbed of anti-Semitism.

Taking something of a different tack, the third floor contains the museum's *Schaudepot*, or storage depot. The displays of Hanukkah candelabra and other ritual objects in large moveable glass cabinets, are deliberately haphazard – they constitute all that is left of the pre-1938 Jewish Museum and the community it served, and include many items pulled from the burnt embers of the city's synagogues, torched in *Kristallnacht*.

Kohlmarkt

Even more than Graben, **Kohlmarkt** is the last bastion of luxury retailing, and kicks off, appropriately enough, with the flagship store of **Julius Meinl** (*www.meinl.com*), the Harrods food store of Vienna. Further up, at no. 14, is the very *k.u.k.* establishment of **Demel**, which still advertises itself as an imperial and royal confectioners. Established in 1786 as *Zuckerbäckerei* to the Habsburgs, its very famous and opulent Kaffee-Konditorei, dates from 1888. Another Viennese institution is the **Artaria Haus**, a Jugendstil building set back from the street at no. 9, and faced in marble by Max

Fabiani in 1901, the bolted slabs on the first floor anticipating Otto Wagner's Postsparkasse (see p.121). The bookshop of the master mapmakers, Freytag & Berndt, occupies the ground floor, while Artaria & Co themselves, publishers of music by the likes of Haydn, Mozart and Beethoven, live on the first floor.

Michaelerplatz

At the far end of Kohlmarkt lies **Michaelerplatz**, dominated on one side by the exuberant arc and green dome of the neo-Baroque **Michaelertrakt**, the southern gateway into the Hofburg (see p.96), begun in the 1720s by Fischer von Erlach's son, but only completed in the 1890s. Its curving balustrade bears a lively parade of eagles, giant urns and trophies, while the gate's archways are framed by gargantuan statues of Hercules and, at either end, fountains overburdened with yet more ungainly statuary. The centre of the square is now occupied by a collection of archeological remains uncovered during work on the nearby U-Bahn station of Herrengasse. LED texts in several languages explain the significance of the rubble that lies exposed in a designer concrete trench (another of Hollein's works); most of what you see are nineteenth-century heating ducts – hardly heart-stopping stuff.

Much more significant is the **Loos Haus**, on the corner of Kohlmarkt and Herrengasse, which caused an uproar when it was built in 1910–11 by Adolf Loos. Franz-Josef despised this "house without eyebrows" – in other words, without the sculpted pediments that sit above the windows of most Viennese buildings. Work on the building was temporarily halted due to the protests, and only allowed to continue after Loos had acquiesced to adding bronze flower boxes. Today, with its rich Cippolin marble columns that frame the main entrance, it's difficult to see what all the fuss was about. If you want to take a closer look, the bank holds regular exhibitions on the first floor of the building, so feel free to walk in.

Michaelerkirche

The oldest building on Michaelerplatz, and the inspiration for its name, is the **Michaelerkirche**, built in the thirteenth century, though the Neoclassical facade, added in 1792, somewhat obscures this fact. Inside, the church retains its plain Gothic origins, but it's the later additions that are of more interest, in particular the *Fall of Angels*, a Rococo cloudburst of cherubs and angels rendered in alabaster, tumbling from the ceiling above the high altar.

From November to April you can get a closer look at this by simply walking in via the west door; from May to October, however, you can only do so by entering from the *Durchgang* via the south door and paying a small fee (Mon–Sat 10.30am–4.30pm, Sun 1–5pm; öS25/€1.82). After picking up a confusing information sheet in English, you may then explore the church and the interesting exhibition that spreads out into the adjoining monastery. From a doorway in the north choir aisle, you can also descend into the church's labyrinthine **crypt**, which stretches the length and breadth of the building. A brief guided tour in German (Mon–Fri 11am and 3pm; öS25/€1.82) reveals piles of paupers' bones and numerous musty coffins taken from the now defunct graveyard, many with their lids off revealing desiccated bodies, still clothed and locked in a deathly grimace.

Herrengasse

Herrengasse was the preferred address of the nobility from the time the Habsburgs moved into the Hofburg until the fall of the dynasty in 1918. Its name dates from the sixteenth century, when the Diet of Lower Austria built its **Landhaus**, which still stands at no. 13. Vienna was for centuries the capital of Lower Austria – the region surrounding the city – but in 1986 the small provincial town of St Pölten took over the mantle (see p.184), making the Vienna Landhaus redundant.

Opposite the Landhaus is the grandiose Italianate **Palais Ferstel**, built in the Ringstrasse style by Heinrich Ferstel in 1860 and home to Vienna's most famous *Kaffeehaus*, **Café Central**, restored in 1986 primarily as a tourist attraction (though a very beautiful one at that). At the turn of the twentieth century, the café was *the* meeting place of the city's intellectuals, including the first generation of Austrian Socialists – Karl Renner, Viktor Adler and Otto Bauer – occasional chess adversaries of Leon Trotsky, who also whiled away several years here before World War I. At the entrance to the café is a life-size papier-mâché model of the moustachioed poet Peter Altenberg, another of the café's fin-de-siècle regulars.

Further up Herrengasse, past the café, is the entrance to the **Freyung Passage** – built in the 1860s as part of the Palais Ferstel – an eminently civilized, lovingly restored shopping arcade, which links Herrengasse with Freyung. The focus of this elegant marble passage is a glass-roofed, hexagonal atrium, with a fountain, crowned by a statue of the Donaunixen (Danube Mermaid), whose trickling water echoes down the arcade.

Minoritenplatz

On the opposite side of Herrengasse, hidden away round the back of the Hofburg, **Minoritenplatz** is a peaceful, cobbled square entirely surrounded by Baroque palaces, now transformed into ministries and embassies. At its centre is the fourteenth-century **Minoritenkirche**, whose stunted octagonal tower is one of the landmarks of the Innere Stadt (the top was knocked off by the Turks during the 1529 siege). Inside, the church is impressively lofty, but it's the kitsch copy of Leonardo da Vinci's *Last Supper*, on the north wall, that steals the show – only close inspection reveals it to be a mosaic. The work was commissioned in 1806 by Napoleon, who planned to substitute it for the original in Milan, taking the latter back to Paris. By the time it was finished, however, Napoleon had fallen from power and the Emperor Franz I bought it instead, though it wasn't until 1847 that it arrived back in Vienna.

On the south side of the square stands a magnificent palace built for the Emperor Karl VI by Hildebrandt as the Court Chancery, and now the **Bundeskanzleramt** (Federal Chancery), home of the Austrian chancellor and the Foreign Ministry, whose main entrance opens onto Ballhausplatz. It was in this palace that Prince Metternich presided over the numerous meetings of the Congress of Vienna in 1814–15, and here, in the chancellor's office, that the Austro-fascist leader, Engelbert Dollfuss, was assassinated during the abortive Nazi putsch of July 25, 1934.

Freyung and the Mölker Bastei

The Freyung Passage from Herrengasse brings you out onto **Freyung** (meaning "Sanctuary") itself, a misshapen square centred on the Austria-Brunnen. Unveiled in 1846, the fountain bears bronze nymphs representing Austria and the key rivers in the Habsburg Empire at the time: the Danube, Po, Elbe and Vistula. Freyung boasts two major art galleries: the **Harrach Palais** (*www.khm.at*), adjacent to the Freyung Passage, which hosts temporary exhibitions put on by the Kunsthistorisches Museum; and the **Kunstforum** (*www.kunstforum-wien.at*), a major venue for visiting exhibitions of fine art.

To the north stands the **Schottenstift**, a former Benedictine monastery, which contains an impressive art collection in its **museum** (Thurs–Sat 10am–5pm, Sun

11am–5pm; öS50/€3.63). To view the paintings, you must buy a ticket from the *Klosterladen* (shop) beside the church, and take the stairs to the first floor of the monastery. The prize exhibit is the fifteenth-century winged altarpiece that used to reside in the Schottenkirche. Thirteen out of the original sixteen panels survive: one side depicts scenes from the life of the Virgin; the reverse side (originally shown only at Easter) features the Passion. The vivid use of colour, the plasticity of the faces and the daring stab at perspective single this out as a masterpiece of late-Gothic art.

The **Mölker Bastei**, one of the few remaining sections of the old zigzag fortifications that once surrounded the Innere Stadt, can be found on Schreyvogelgasse, to the west of Freyung. The sloping cobbled lane below the fortifications should be familiar to fans of the movie *The Third Man*, for it's in the doorway of no. 8 that Harry Lime (played by Orson Welles) appears for the first time. High up on the Bastei itself, at no. 8, is the **Pasqualatihaus** (Tues–Sun 9am–12.15pm & 1–4.30pm; öS25/€1.82), where Beethoven lived on and off from 1804 onwards (he moved 68 times during his 35 years in Vienna). The composer's apartment is now a museum (for more on Beethoven, see p.137), though there's no indication of how the place might have looked at the time he lived there. Perhaps this is just as well – according to one visitor it was "the darkest, most disorderly place imaginable . . . under the piano (I do not exaggerate) an unemptied chamber pot . . . chairs . . . covered with plates bearing the remains of last night's supper". Instead, you're left to admire Ludwig's gilded salt and pepper pots and battered tin sugar container, or sit down and listen to some of his music through headphones.

Am Hof and around

Am Hof is the largest square in the Innere Stadt, an attractive, tranquil spot, marred only by the surface protrusions of its underground car park. The name – *Hof* means both "royal court" and "courtyard" – dates from medieval times, when this was the headquarters of the Babenbergs, who lorded it over Vienna until the Habsburgs took the reins in 1273. The centrepiece of the square is the rather forbidding, matt-black **Mariensäule** (Marian column), erected by the Emperor Ferdinand III as a thank-you to the Virgin for deliverance from the Protestant Swedish forces in the Thirty Years' War. At the base of the column, blackened cherubs in full armour wrestle with a dragon, lion, serpent and basilisk.

Dominating the square is the **Kirche am Hof**, from whose balcony the Austrian Emperor Franz I proclaimed the end of the Holy Roman Empire in 1806, on the orders of Napoleon. The church's vast Baroque facade, topped by a host of angels, belies the fact that this is, for the most part, a fourteenth-century structure. Inside, it's quite frankly a stylistic mess, with the old Gothic church struggling to get out from under some crude later additions.

Pass under the archway by the Kirche am Hof, head down Schulhof, and you'll come to the **Uhrenmuseum** (Tues–Sun 9am–4.30pm; öS50/€3.63), a clock museum ranged over three floors at Schulhof 2. Founded in 1917, this is the world's oldest museum of its kind, but, sadly, it lacks the crucial information in either German or English to bring the collection alive. Nevertheless, you'll find every kind of time-measuring device from sophisticated seventeenth-century grandfather clocks to primitive wax candles containing tiny lead balls, which drop onto a metal dish as the candle melts. Other exhibits include the smallest pendulum clock in the world, which fits inside a thimble, and a wide selection of eighteenth-century *Zwiebeluhren*, literally "onion clocks", set within cases shaped like fruit, musical instruments and the like.

"Nine tenths of what the world celebrated as Viennese culture of the nineteenth century was a culture promoted, nurtured or in some cases even created by Viennese Jewry."

Stefan Zweig, *The World of Yesterday*, 1942

Most Jews have mixed feelings about Vienna: the city that nurtured the talents of such Jewish geniuses as Sigmund Freud, Gustav Mahler and Ludwig Wittgenstein also has a justifiable reputation as a hotbed of anti-Semitism. The city where the father of Zionism, Theodor Herzl, spent much of his adult life, is also seen by many as the cradle of the Holocaust, where Hitler spent five years honing his hatred; where in 1986, Kurt Waldheim was elected president, despite rumours that he had participated in Nazi atrocities in the Balkans; and where, in 2000, Jörg Haider's extreme right-wing FPÖ became a partner in a new coalition government.

Jews have lived in Vienna intermittently for something like a thousand years, yet like most of the Diaspora they have been tolerated only when it suited the powers that be. They have been formally expelled twice, first in 1420, when the community was accused of supporting the Czech Hussite heretics (the real incentive for the expulsion was to boost the royal coffers by appropriating the Jews' property). The following year, those that remained – around 200 of them – were burnt at the stake. Apart from a few individual exceptions, Jewish resettlement only took off again at the beginning of the seventeenth century, when Ferdinand II established a walled ghetto east of the Danube (now Leopoldstadt). For around fifty years Jewish life flourished in the ghetto, but as the Counter-Reformation gathered pace, there was increasing pressure from Catholics to banish the Jews altogether. Finally in 1670, Emperor Leopold I once more expelled the community.

The city suffered financially from the expulsion, and with the Turks at the gates a small number of Jewish financiers and merchants were hastily granted the status of *Hofjuden*, or "Court Jews", and permitted to resettle. The most famous of the Court Jews was Samuel Oppenheimer, who was appointed chief supplier to the imperial army by Leopold I in 1677. Despite the elevated status of the Court Jews, their posi-

For most people, the **Puppen und Spielzeug Museum** (Doll and Toy Museum; Tues–Sun 10am–6pm; öS60/€4.36), next door on the first floor of Schulhof 4, holds more appeal, further enhanced by the building's well-preserved Baroque interior. It's an old-fashioned kind of a place, with ranks of glass cabinets and no buttons to press for younger kids. The majority of the exhibits are dolls, with just a small selection of teddies, toys and trains. Also on show are a toy marionette stage, a Punch and Judy booth, a shadow screen and a dolls' toy shop, grocer's and house, complete with miniature Jugendstil coffee set. Off Am Hof, a short way down Drahtgasse, another toy museum, this time the **Teddybären Museum** (Mon–Sat 10am–6pm, Sun 2–6pm; öS45/€3.27), holds a private collection of antique teddy bears from all over the world. As well as the cuddly variety, there are china bears, bears on carousels and one of the very earliest battery-operated bears from before World War I, whose eyes light up in a way that would give most kids nightmares.

Judenplatz and around

Taking either of the two alleyways that lead north from Schulhof brings you to **Judenplatz**, one of the prettiest little squares in Vienna, now totally dominated by a

tion was precarious, and it wasn't until Josef II's 1781 *Toleranzpatent* that they were allowed to take up posts in the civil service and other professions and to build their own synagogue. At the same time, the *Toleranzpatent* began the process of assimilation, compelling Jews to take German names and restricting the use of Yiddish and Hebrew.

After the 1848 revolution, all official restrictions on Jews were finally abolished. At this point, there were only around 2000 Jews living in Vienna. In the next sixty years, thousands arrived in the city from the Habsburg provinces of Bohemia, Moravia (now the Czech Republic) and Galicia (now in Poland and Ukraine), the majority of them settling, initially at least, in Leopoldstadt. By 1910, there were approximately 180,000 Jews – almost ten percent of the total population and more than in any other German-speaking city. Though the majority of them were far from well off, a visible minority formed a disproportionately large contingent in high-profile professions like banking, medicine, journalism and the arts. The Rothschilds were one of the richest families in the empire; virtually the entire staff on the liberal newspapers, *Neue Freie Presse* and the *Wiener Tagblatt*, were Jewish; the majority of the city's doctors were Jews, as were most of the leading figures in the Austrian Socialist Party. Other prominent Viennese Jews were the writers Arthur Schnitzler, Robert Musil, Stefan Zweig and Josef Roth, and the composer Arnold Schönberg, and the Strauss family.

Those Gentiles who found themselves sinking into poverty after the stock market crash of 1873 desperately needed a scapegoat. They eagerly latched onto anti-Semitism, which began to be promoted by the Christian Social Party under Karl Lueger, the city's populist mayor from 1897 to 1910. Perversely, however, this virulent anti-Semitism helped to save more Jews than in other more tolerant places, causing thousands to flee the country even before the 1938 Anschluss; by 1941, a total of 120,000 Viennese Jews had escaped. Nevertheless, some 65,000 died in the Holocaust, and are now commemorated by the Judenplatz memorial (see below). Currently, the community numbers around 7000 – many of them immigrants from the former Eastern Bloc – and is enjoying something of a renaissance, much of it centred once again in Leopoldstadt, maintaining a dozen synagogues and several schools across the city.

bleak concrete mausoleum designed by British sculptor Rachel Whiteread as a **Holocaust Memorial**, and unveiled in 2000. Smothered in row upon row of concrete casts of books like an inside-out library, the bunker-like memorial deliberately jars with its surroundings; a chilling A to Z of Nazi death camps is inscribed into its low plinth. Ironically, Judenplatz already has a much older memorial commemorating the pogrom of 1421, and clearly visible on the oldest house on the square, **Zum grossen Jordan** (The Great Jordan), at no. 2. However, in this case, the inscription, beside a sixteenth-century relief of the Baptism of Christ, celebrates the slaughter, when the Jews were driven out of Vienna. The lucky ones fled to Hungary, the rest were burnt at the stake, or – to avoid that fate – killed by the chief rabbi, who then committed suicide.

Judenplatz was originally the site of the city's medieval Jewish ghetto, dating as far back as the twelfth century, and during the building of the Holocaust memorial, excavations revealed the smoke-blackened remains of the ghetto's chief synagogue, which was burnt to the ground in 1421. The foundations, and a few modest finds, can now be viewed in the **Museum Judenplatz** (Mon–Thurs & Sun 10am–6pm, Fri 10am–2pm; öS42/€3.00), whose entrance is at no. 8. In addition, there's a short video with an English audio guide, and an interactive multimedia exhibition, both on medieval Jewish life in Vienna.

One block north of Judenplatz, on the other side of busy Wipplingerstrasse, lies the **Altes Rathaus**, a dour-looking Baroque palace that served as the city's town hall until 1885. The main courtyard is undistinguished but for Donner's wonderful **Andromeda Brunnen** from 1741, which depicts the Greek myth in lead relief. The reason to come here, though, is to visit the highly informative **Austrian Resistance Museum** (Mon, Wed & Thurs 9am–5pm; free), which has a permanent exhibition on the Austrian anti-Fascist resistance, with labelling in German and English throughout. The bulk of the displays cover resistance to the Nazi regime, but there's also a brief summary of the political upheavals of the interwar republic, including a detailed section on the rise of Austro-fascism in the 1930s. Despite the high level of popular support for the Nazis, the Austrian resistance remained extremely active throughout the war, as a result of which 2700 of its members were executed and thousands more were murdered by the Gestapo.

One block north of the Altes Rathaus on Salvatorgasse stands one of Vienna's finest Gothic churches, **Maria am Gestade**, up Salvatorgasse, topped by an elaborate filigree spire depicting the Virgin's heavenly crown, a stunning sight after dark when lit from within. With its drooping, beast-infested pendants and gilded mosaics, the stone canopy of the slender west facade is also worth admiring, best viewed from the steps leading up from Tiefergraben. The unusual interior – the nave is darker and narrower than the choir and set slightly askew – is a product of the church's cramped site, lying as it does on the very edge of the old medieval town. Much of what you see, both inside and out, is the result of nineteenth-century over-restoration, as the church caught fire in 1809 when it was used by the Napoleonic forces as an arms depot.

Hoher Markt and around

It's difficult to believe that the **Hoher Markt**, now surrounded by dour, postwar buildings and packed with parked cars, is Vienna's oldest square. Yet this was the heart of the Roman camp, Vindobona, a conduit of which you can see beneath the shopping arcade on the south side of the square (Tues–Sun 9am–12.15pm & 1–4.30pm; öS25/€1.82). The square's centrepiece is Fischer von Erlach's **Vermählungsbrunnen**, or Marriage Fountain, depicting the union of Mary and Joseph by the high priest, for which there is no biblical evidence and few iconographical precedents. Even more remarkable is the ornate bronze baldachin and gilded sunburst, held aloft by Corinthian columns with matching ram's-head urns, under which the trio shelter.

The real reason folk crowd into Hoher Markt, however, is to see the glorious Jugendstil **Ankeruhr**, a heavily gilded clock designed by Franz Matsch in 1914, which spans two buildings owned by the Anker insurance company on the north side of the square. Each hour, a gilded cut-out figure, representing a key player in Vienna's history, shuffles across the dial of the clock, and at noon tour groups gather to watch the entire set of twelve figures slowly stagger across to a ten-minute medley of slightly mournful organ music. The identities of the figures, which range from Marcus Aurelius to Josef Haydn, are revealed on the clock's street-level plaque. Before you leave, check out the brackets on the underside of the clock bridge, which feature Adam, Eve, the Devil and an angel.

There's one other sight worth seeking out in the streets around Hoher Markt: the secular medieval **Neidhart Frescoes** (Tues–Sun 9am–12.15pm; öS25/€1.82), at Tuchlauben 19, discovered in 1979 during rebuilding works. Executed around 1400, the wall paintings are patchy but jolly, some of them illustrating the stories of the *Minnesinger* (aristocratic minstrel) Neidhart von Reuenthal, others depicting a snowball fight, a ball game, dancing and general medieval merriment.

The Bermuda Triangle

Since the 1980s, the area around the Ruprechtskirche has been known as the **Bermuda Triangle** (Bermuda Dreieck), the idea being that there are so many bars in these few narrow streets that you could get lost for ever. It's certainly true that a staggering number of designer bars, late-night drinking holes and music venues are literally piled on top of one another, particularly along Seitenstettengasse and Rabensteig, but you'd have to do some serious drinking to actually lose your way. The night-time clientele tends to be young(ish) and well turned out but not that trendy. During the day, however, the scene is pretty muted, and you're more likely to rub shoulders with tourists who've come to appreciate the area's narrow cobbled streets and the two main sights: the Ruprechtskirche, the city's oldest church, and its oldest surviving synagogue, the Stadttempel.

Ironically, it was the building restrictions in force at the time the **Stadttempel** (guided tours Mon–Thurs 11.30am & 3pm; öS30/€2.00) was built in 1826 that enabled it to be the only synagogue (out of 24) to survive *Kristallnacht*. According to the laws enacted under Josef II, synagogues had to be concealed from the street – hence you get no hint of what lies behind Seitenstettengasse 2–4 until you've gone through the security procedures (take your passport) and passed through several anterooms to the glass doors of the temple itself. Despite its hidden location, it suffered some damage in 1938 when this predominantly Jewish area was torched, and it has since been lavishly restored. Designed from top to bottom by Biedermeier architect Josef Kornhäusel, it's a perfect example of the restrained architecture of the period, its top-lit, sky-blue oval dome delicately dotted with golden stars, and its two-tiered curving women's gallery supported by yellow Ionic pillars. The slightly sinister presence of police with dogs and machine guns outside on Seitenstettengasse is a sad consequence of the terrorist attack on the Stadttempel in 1983, which killed three people, and the continuing vandalism of Jewish property that takes place in Austria.

Round the corner from the Stadttempel on Ruprechtsplatz stands the ivy-covered **Ruprechtskirche**, its plain, stout architecture attesting to its venerable age. Founded as long ago as the eighth century, the current building dates partly from the twelfth century and has been much altered and expanded since. Inside, the vivid reds and blues of the modern stained glass are a bit overwhelming, detracting from the church's uniquely intimate ambience. Mass is still said here, and the space is also frequently used for art exhibitions.

Fleischmarkt to Dr-Ignaz-Seipel-Platz

One block south of the Bermuda Triangle, **Fleischmarkt**, the old meat market, straddles Rotenturmstrasse and extends east as far as Postgasse. Greek merchants settled here in the eighteenth century, and following the 1781 *Toleranzpatent* built their own Greek Orthodox church on Griechengasse. On Fleischmarkt itself, there's another, more imposing **Griechische Kirche**, a stripy red-brick affair redesigned in mock-Byzantine style in 1861 by Ringstrasse architect Theophil Hansen, its decorative castellations glistening with gilt. Opening hours are erratic, and you may not be able to get past the gloomy, arcaded vestibule – the best time to try is on a Sunday – to see the candlelit interior, pungent with incense and decorated with icons and gilded frescoes. Next door to the church is the popular inn, *GriechenBeisl*, a Viennese institution for over five centuries, and now firmly on the tour group itinerary.

At the end of Fleischmarkt, turn right into Postgasse past another neo-Byzantine edifice, the Greek-Catholic church of **St Barbara**, and the Italianate **Dominikanerkirche**, and you'll come to Bäckerstrasse. One block west lies **Dr-Ignaz-Seipel-Platz**, named after the anti-Semitic leader of the Christian Socials, who became the country's chancellor in 1922. The east side is taken up by the **Alte Universität**, founded by Rudolf IV in 1365, and thus the second oldest university (after Prague) in the German-speaking world. By the eighteenth century, the university had outgrown its original premises, and a more fanciful Baroque extension – now the **Akademie der Wissenschaften** (Academy of Sciences) – was built on the opposite side of the square. The building's barrel-vaulted Freskenraum, decorated with frescoes by Franz Maulbertsch, is occasionally open to the public for exhibitions (Mon–Fri 10.30am–5.30pm).

Next door is the **Jesuitenkirche** (also known as the Universitätskirche), whose flat facade rises up in giant tiers that tower over the square. Begun in 1627 at the peak of the Jesuits' power, this church smacks of the Counter-Reformation and is by far the most awesome High Baroque church in Vienna. Inside, the most striking features are the red and green barley-sugar spiral columns, the exquisitely carved pews and the clever trompe l'oeil dome – the illusion only works from the back of the church: walk towards the altar and the painting is revealed as a sham.

The Hofburg

His gaze wandered up high walls and he saw an island – gray, self-contained, and armed – lying there while the city's speed rushed blindly past it.

Robert Musil, *The Man Without Qualities*

Enmeshed in the southwest corner of the Innere Stadt, the **Hofburg** (Court Palace) is a real hotchpotch of a place, with no natural centre, no symmetry and no obvious main entrance. Its name is synonymous with the Habsburgs, the dynasty which, at its zenith, ruled a vast multinational empire, stretching the length and breadth of Europe. Nowadays, apart from the tiny proportion that has been retained as the seat of the Austrian president, the palace has been taken over by various state organizations, museums and, more prosaically, a conference centre.

Two of Vienna's most famous attractions keep the Hofburg at the top of most visitors' agendas: the **Wiener Sängerknaben** (Vienna Boys' Choir), who perform regularly in the Burgkapelle, and the **Spanische Reitschule** (Spanish Riding School), who trot their stuff in the Winter Reitschule. Getting to see either of them takes time and money, however, which you might well decide you'd be better off spending elsewhere. The tourist office leaflet, *Spanische Reitschule/Wiener Sängerknaben*, explains the intricate schedules of both institutions. The other chief sights are the dull **Kaiserappartements**, where the Emperor Franz-Josef I (1848–1916) and his wife Elisabeth lived and worked, the **Schatzkammer**, with its superb collection of crown jewels, and the **Prunksaal**, Fischer von Erlach's richly decorated Baroque library. The palace also boasts several excellent museums and galleries: the **Albertina**, home to one of the world's great graphics collections; several departments of the Kunsthistorisches Museum – the **Hofjagd- und Rüstkammer** (Court Hunting and Arms Collection), the **Sammlung alte Musikinstrumente** (Collection of Early Musical Instruments) and the **Ephesos Museum** (Ephesus Museum); and the **Museum für Völkerkunde** (Museum of Ethnology).

Kaiserappartements

Of all the sights within the Hofburg, it is the **Kaiserappartements** (daily 9am–4.30pm; öS80/€5.81; combined ticket with Hofsilber- und Tafelkammer öS95/€6.90) that are the most disappointing. Virtually every room is decorated in the same style: creamy-white walls and ceiling with gilded detailing, parquet flooring and red furnishings. There aren't any guided tours in English to bring these mundane surroundings to life, nor is there any information or labelling in the rooms themselves, forcing you to fork

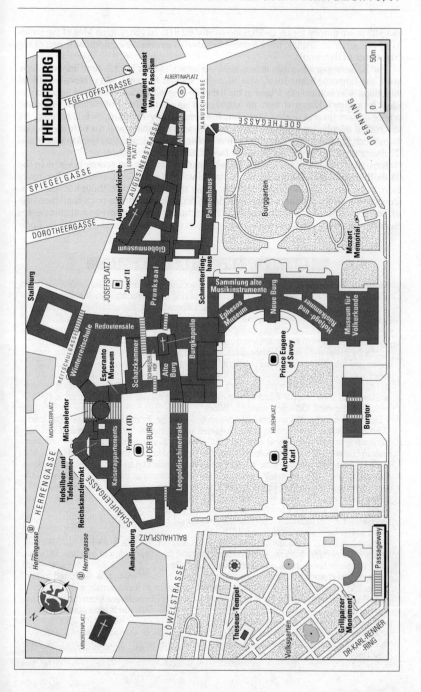

out still more money for an audioguide (öS40/€2.91). To give you an idea of the paucity of treasures on display, the Empress Elisabeth's gymnastic equipment is one of the highlights of the rooms.

The Kaiserappartements' current state is a legacy of their last full-time imperial occupant, the Emperor Franz-Josef, who, though a stickler for pomp and protocol at official functions, was notoriously frugal in his daily life (the simple iron bedstead on which he slept is on view). Rising at 4am, he would eat a simple breakfast of coffee, *Semmel* and a slice of ham (except during Lent); lunch was invariably *Tafelspitz*, or boiled rump. He distrusted telephones, cars, electricity and modern plumbing, and his only concession to modern life was the telegraph. If you're looking for opulence, you need to visit Maria Theresia's apartments at Schönbrunn (see p.130).

Beyond the ticket office for the Kaiserappartements are six rooms devoted to the **Hofsilber- und Tafelkammer**, the "Court Silver and Porcelain Collection". You really have to be seriously into dinner services to get the most out of it, though if you're visiting the Kaiserappartements anyway it doesn't cost much more to get a combined ticket, see above. Among the star exhibits is the eighteenth-century, green and gold Sèvres Service, originally made up of 290 separate pieces, given to Maria Theresia by Louis

---

EMPEROR FRANZ JOSEF I (1848–1916)

Emperor Franz-Josef I was Europe's longest-serving monarch, and Austria's most popular. His 68-year reign was the most sustained period of relative stability the country had ever known, and a stark contrast with what followed. Like his grandfather, Franz I – "Franz the Good" – he was a legend in his own lifetime, and, thanks to the Viennese love of nostalgia, the myth continues today. As historian William Johnston wrote, "Franz-Josef I symbolized more than he achieved". His aversion to innovation was legendary, epitomized by his addiction to the Spanish Court Ceremonial. According to the latter, every guest had to cease eating at the moment the emperor finished each course. Since Franz-Josef was served first and was a very fast eater, his guests rarely got more than a few mouthfuls. Such dinners were also very silent, as no one was permitted to speak unless spoken to by the emperor – and he was more intent on eating. "Lord, this court is stuffy" remarked Edward VII, when prince of Wales.

Despite the pomp and protocol which surrounded him, Franz-Josef was a simple man. When the first official census was conducted in Austria, he famously wrote down his occupation as "self-employed civil servant". Indeed, his dedication to his job was legendary: he woke at 4am (occasionally 3.30am), washed in cold water and would be at his desk by 5am. Twice a week he would give general audience to any of his citizens who wished to see him – as many as one hundred in a morning (the supplicants were, of course, vetted first). After finishing work around 5.30pm, he would tidy his desk and, towards the end of his life, be in bed by 8.30pm. He had no great love of the arts – "I go to the opera as a sacrifice to my country" he once wrote to his mistress. His only passions were hunting and mountain climbing, and his annual holiday was invariably taken in Bad Ischl, in the Salzkammergut (see p.433).

Franz-Josef's personal life was something of a disaster. He was in awe of his powerful mother, the Archduchess Sophie, who arranged and then proceeded to sabotage his marriage to one of his cousins, Elisabeth (see p.135). Despite Elisabeth's indifference – she spent as little time as possible in his company – Franz-Josef remained dedicated to her all his life. Meanwhile, for over thirty years, he conducted a passionate affair with the Burgtheater actress Katharina Schratt. Matters outside the bedroom were no better. His brother Maximilian was executed in Mexico in 1867, his only son Rudolf committed suicide in 1887, and his wife was assassinated in 1898.

On the morning of November 20, 1916, at the age of 86, Franz-Josef rose at 3.30am for the very last time. His last words to his valet that night were: "tomorrow morning, half past three".

XV, and the monster Milanese centrepiece in gilded bronze, which stretches for 3.
along a table strewn with classical figures and (more) gilded bronze and crystal urns.
For the sake of variety, check out the stone jugs and salvers, with which the emperor
and empress used to wash the feet of twelve ordinary men and women every year on
Maundy Thursday.

Schatzkammer

By far the most rewarding of all the Hofburg museums (daily except Tues
10am–6pm; öS100/€7.27), is the imperial **Schatzkammer** or Treasury. Here you can
see some of the finest medieval craftsmanship and jewellery in Europe, including the
imperial regalia and relics of the Holy Roman Empire, not to mention the Habsburgs'
own crown jewels, countless reliquaries and robes, gold work and silverware. You
can wander at will around the twenty or so rooms, but, since the labelling is in
German only, it's worth picking up one of the portable computer guides available free
of charge.

Centre stage in room 2, you'll find the stunning golden **Crown of Rudolf II** (later to
become the Austrian imperial crown), studded with diamonds, rubies, pearls and, at
the very top, a huge sapphire. The mother of all cots resides in room 5, an over-
wrought, silver-gilt cradle with silk and velvet trimmings, made in 1811 for the short-
lived **Duke of Reichstadt**, or King of Rome, son of Napoleon and his second wife,
Marie Louise, daughter of the Emperor Franz I. The poor boy must have had nightmares from the golden eagle that hovers over the cot.

Among the remnants of the **Habsburgs' private jewellery**, in room 7, there are
some serious stones on display, like the 2680-carat Colombian emerald the size of your
fist, carved into a salt cellar in Prague in 1641, and the huge garnet, "La Bella", which
forms the centre of a double-headed eagle, along with an amethyst and an opal, set in
enamel. Another notable treasure is the solid gold Turkish crown of the rebel King of
Hungary, István Bocskai, from 1605, inlaid with pearls and precious stones. Room 8
contains the so-called **"inalienable heirlooms"**, two pieces collected by Ferdinand I,
which the Habsburgs were very keen to hold onto: a fourth-century agate dish, stolen
from Constantinople in 1204 and thought at the time to be the Holy Grail, and a 2.43
metre-long narwhal's horn, which was originally believed to have come from a unicorn.

The highlights of the whole collection, however, are the **crown jewels of the Holy
Roman Empire** in room 11. The focal point is the octagonal imperial crown itself, a
superb piece of Byzantine jewellery, smothered with pearls, large precious stones and
enamel plaques. Legend has it that the crown was used in the coronation of
Charlemagne, the first Holy Roman Emperor, in 800, but it now seems likely that it
dates back only to that of Otto I, in 962. Also on display here is the legendary **Holy
Lance**, with which the Roman soldier pierced the side of Christ. The lance – which
actually dates from the eighth century – was alleged to have magic powers, so that who-
ever possessed it held the destiny of the world in their hands. It was in front of this
exhibit that the young Hitler is supposed to have had a mystical revelation, which
changed the course of his life (and therefore of twentieth-century history), though the
story is probably apocryphal.

The last four rooms (13–16) of the Schatzkammer house the substantial dowry that
came into Habsburg hands in 1477, when the Emperor Maximilian I married the only
daughter and heiress of the duke of Burgundy. By so doing Maximilian also became
Grand Master of the **Order of the Golden Fleece**, the exclusive Burgundian order of
chivalry founded in 1430, whose insignia are displayed here: heavy mantles embroidered with gold thread, a collar of golden links, from which the "fleece" would hang,
and the ram emblem, worn by the 24 knights of the order at all times.

Burgkapelle

The **Burgkapelle** (guided tours Jan–June & mid-Sept to Dec Mon–Thurs 11am–3pm, Fri 11am–1pm; öS15/€1.09), up the stairs above the entrance to the Schatzkammer, was built in the late 1440s by the Emperor Friedrich III. Despite numerous alterations over the centuries, the interior retains its Gothic vaulting, carved ceiling pendants, and much of its fifteenth-century wooden statuary protected by richly carved baldachins. It's a favourite venue for society weddings, but the public only get to see it on guided tours. In any case, the real point of going there is to hear the *Hofmusikkapelle*, made up of members of the *Wiener Sängerknaben*, or **Vienna Boys' Choir**, supplemented by musicians from the Staatsoper, sing Mass for the tourists on Sunday mornings (and on religious holidays) at 9.15am. To find out about how to get tickets, see p.152.

Founded back in 1498 by the Emperor Maximilian I, the choir was closely linked to the imperial family, for whom they used to perform (famous *Sängerknaben* include Schubert and Haydn). In 1918, the choir went under with the dynasty, but was revived in 1924 and, dressed in ludicrous sailors' uniforms and caps, has since become a major Austrian export. There are, in fact, four choirs, who take it in turns to work, rest, play and tour the world.

Spanische Reitschule (Spanish Riding School)

The Habsburgs' world-famous **Spanische Reitschule** (*www.spanische-reitschule.com*) originated with the Archduke Karl, brother of Maximilian II, who established several studs at Lipizza, northeast of Trieste (now the Slovene town of Lipica) in the 1570s. By cross-breeding Spanish, Arab and Berber horses, the Lipizzaner strain was born, and subsequently supplied the Habsburgs with all their cavalry and show horses. However, it was only properly expanded by the Spanish-bred Emperor Karl VI, who gave the riding school a permanent home in the Hofburg. After World War I, the stud was moved to Piber, near Graz (see p.286), though the silver-white stallions are now bred at both places.

The Spanish Riding School is such an intrinsic part of Vienna's Habsburg heritage industry, it's difficult not to feel a certain revulsion for the whole charade. That said, to witness the Lipizzaners' equestrian ballet is an unforgettable experience; certainly those with any interest in horses will feel compelled to see at least a rehearsal. Performances take place regularly in the splendidly Baroque **Winterreitschule** (Winter Riding School), on the west side of Reitschulgasse, purpose-built by Josef Emanuel Fischer von Erlach in 1735.

Access to the Winterreitschule is from the north side of Josefsplatz. The complicated public schedule of training sessions and performances is written up outside the entrance. There are one or two **performances** (*Vorführungen*) a week (usually Sun 10.45am and, less frequently, Wed 7pm) between March and June and September and December, though for at least a month of the latter period the school is usually on tour. Seats **cost** öS300–900/€21.80–65.41, and standing room is öS200/€14.54. Even at those prices, the performances are booked solid months in advance; to be sure of a place, you must **check the Web site** and then email *tickets@srs.at*. From mid-February to June and from late August until early November, the school also holds **training sessions** (*Morgenarbeit;* Tues–Sat 10am–noon), which are open to the public. Seats cost öS100/€7.27 and are sold at the Josefsplatz entrance box office; the queue for tickets is at its worst early on, but by 11am it's usually easy enough to get in.

The cheapest option of all is to visit the **Lipizzaner Museum** (daily 9am–5pm; öS70/€5.09; combined ticket with a training session öS140/€10.17; *www.lipizzaner.at*), which is housed in part of the *Stallburg* (stables). Along with various equestrian bits (literally) and bobs, you can watch videos of the several set pieces of equestrian ballet, look at the horses snoozing in their stables through a two-way mirror, and catch a clip from the Disney film of the riding school's liberation by the US Army under General Patton in 1945.

Prunksaal

If the Karlskirche (see p.116) is Johann Bernhard Fischer von Erlach's sacred master-piece, then the **Prunksaal** (mid-May to Oct Mon–Wed, Fri & Sat 10am–4pm, Thurs 10am–7pm, Sun 10am–1pm; Nov to mid-May Mon–Sat 10am–2pm; closed for the first three weeks of Sept; öS60/€4.36; *www.onb.ac.at*) is his most stunning secular work. The library was begun in 1723, the year of his death, and, like so many of his projects, had to be finished off by his son, Josef Emanuel. It's by far the largest Baroque library in Europe, stretching the full eighty-metre length of the first floor of the central wing of the Hofburg facing onto Josefsplatz. Now part of the Nationalbibliothek, access to the Prunksaal is via the monumental staircase in the southwest corner of the square.

Not an architect to be accused of understatement, Fischer von Erlach achieves his desired effect by an overdose of elements: massive marble pillars and pilasters, topped by gilded capitals, gilded wood-panelled bookcases, carved balconies accessed by spiral staircases, and from floor to ceiling, more than 200,000 leather-bound books, including the 15,000-volume personal library of Prince Eugène of Savoy. The space is divided by a transverse oval dome, which is decorated with Daniel Gran's magnificent fresco of the winged figure of Fame holding a rather misshapen pyramid. Among the many celestial groups there's a model of the library, to which the woman depicted as Austrian magnanimity is pointing. At the lowest level, Gran has painted trompe l'oeil balconies, on which groups of figures hold scholarly discussions. If you're really keen to work out what's going on, there's an inexpensive guide to the dome fresco available (in English) at the ticket desk.

There are several antique globes in the Prunksaal itself, but if that has only whetted your appetite, you can view lots more in the two rooms of the **Globenmuseum** (Mon–Wed & Fri 11am–noon, Thurs 2–3pm; öS15/€1.09), situated on the third floor. The museum also displays a selection of the library's map collection. Check out the upside-down map of the world from 1154, and the sixteenth-century charts, one of which features a magnificent sea dragon happily swimming in the South Atlantic, while another depicts a bevy of parrots in the *terra incognita*, now known to us as South America.

Augustinerkirche

Masked by Picassi's bland facade, the **Augustinerkirche**, to the south of Josefsplatz, is one of the oldest parts of the Hofburg, dating back as far as the 1330s. Inside, the church has taken a beating over the years, though it retains its lofty Gothic vaulting. The chief attraction is Antonio Canova's Neoclassical **Christinendenkmal**, in the right-hand aisle, a lavish memorial to Maria Christina, favourite daughter of Maria Theresia, erected in 1805 by her husband, Albrecht, Duke of Saxony-Tetschen. A motley procession of marble mourners heads up the steps for the open door of the pyramidal tomb, while a winged spirit and a sad lion embrace on the other side, and another genius holds aloft the duchess's medallion. They'd be disappointed if they ever got inside, for she's actually buried in the Kaisergruft. Canova's pupils were so taken with the mausoleum that they adapted the design for Canova's own mausoleum in Venice's Frari.

Several more monumental tombs can be found in the **Georgskapelle**, a self-contained, two-aisled chapel, built in the fourteenth century to the right of the chancel, and only infrequently open. In the centre of the chapel lies the empty marble tomb of the

Emperor Leopold II, whose brief reign of less than two years ended in 1792. Balthasar Ferdinand Moll's gilded wall tomb to Count Leopold Daun, on the far wall, is significantly more extravagant, and includes a relief of the 1757 Battle of Kolín in which Daun trounced the Prussians. To get to the Georgskapelle, you must pass through the Lorettokapelle, at the far end of which lies the **Herzgrüftel** (Little Heart Crypt), where, arranged neatly on two semicircular shelves, are 54 silver urns containing the hearts of the later Habsburgs. Guided tours in German take place on Mondays and Fridays at 11am & 3pm, or by phoning ☎533 7099.

Albertina and around

Beyond the Augustinerkirche lies the **Albertina** (*www.albertina.at*), a mishmash of a building, incorporating parts of the former Augustinian monastery, the late eighteenth-century Taroucca Palace and the southernmost bastion of the Hofburg. There are steps up to the bastion, which overlooks the back of the Staatsoper and is surmounted by a grand equestrian statue of the Archduke Albrecht, who vanquished the Italians at the Battle of Custozza, one of the few bright moments in the otherwise disastrous Austro-Prussian War of 1866. Founded in 1768 by Albrecht, Duke of Saxony-Teschen (after whom the gallery is named), the Albertina boasts one of the largest collections of **graphic arts** in the world, with approximately 50,000 drawings, etchings and water-colours, and more than 1.5 million printed works. Within its catalogue, it has some 43 drawings by Raphael, 70 by Rembrandt, 145 by Dürer – more than any other gallery in the world – and 150 by Schiele, plus many more by the likes of Leonardo da Vinci, Michelangelo, Rubens, Bosch, Pieter Bruegel the Elder, Cézanne, Picasso, Matisse, Klimt and Kokoschka. With such a vast archive, the gallery can only hope to show a tiny fraction at any one time, and in any case, graphics are notoriously sensitive to light. As a result, the Albertina only ever stages temporary exhibitions, devoted to one artist, period or theme, as well as showing a few facsimiles giving some idea of the range of the collection. After more than a decade's worth of refurbishment, the Albertina is due to open once more in 2002, with newly expanded exhibition halls, an international study centre, a winter garden, and a restaurant on the terrace, and whatever the exhibition, it'll be worth a look.

The Philipphof, a typically ornate Ringstrasse-style building that was home to the exclusive Jockey Club, originally stood to the northeast of the Albertina. However, during the air raid of March 12, 1945, the building received two direct hits, killing several hundred people sheltering in the basement. The lot remained vacant until the 1980s, when the city council commissioned Alfred Hrdlicka to erect a **Monument Against War and Fascism**, a controversial move given the site's history and its extreme prominence. The monument includes a crouching Jew scrubbing the pavement, recalling the days following the Anschluss, when some of the city's Jews were forced to clean up anti-Nazi slogans with scrubbing brushes dipped in acid. Many Jews found the image degrading, among them Simon Wiesenthal, who successfully campaigned for a proper Holocaust memorial to be erected in Vienna, which can now be seen in Judenplatz (see p.93).

Neue Burg

The last wing of the Hofburg to be built – completed in 1913 – was the **Neue Burg**, a piece of pure bombast designed in heavy neo-Renaissance style by Gottfried Semper and Karl von Hasenauer half a century earlier. Semper planned another new palatial wing to mirror the Neue Burg and enclose Heldenplatz (Heroes' Square). In the end, time (and money) ran out, leaving Heldenplatz as a wide, slightly meaningless, expanse, which nonetheless affords a great view across to the Rathaus and Parlament

---

VISITING THE NEUE BURG MUSEUMS

A single ticket (öS60/€4.36) covers the **Hofjagd- und Rüstkammer**, the **Sammlung alter Musikinstrumente** and the **Ephesos Museum**. The museums have the same opening times: daily except Tuesday 10am–6pm. Very little information is available in English, unless you buy a guide, but a free audioguide commentary (in German) is available for the first two collections. Access to all three collections is via the main entrance. The **Museum für Völkerkunde** (daily except Tues: Jan–March 10am–6pm; April–Dec 10am–4pm; öS60/€4.36), which houses the country's chief ethnographical collection, has its own separate entrance, and requires a separate ticket.

---

buildings on the Ringstrasse. The Neue Burg is now home to the Nationalbibliothek's main reading room, an offshoot of the Naturhistorisches Museum and three departments of the Kunsthistorisches Museum (*www.khm.at*). For the Viennese, though, it's forever etched in the memory as the scene of Hitler's victorious return to Vienna on March 15, 1938, when thousands gathered here to celebrate the Anschluss. Hitler appeared on the central balcony of the Neue Burg and declared: "As Führer and Chancellor of the German nation and the German Reich I hereby announce to German history that my homeland has entered the German Reich."

Hofjagd- und Rüstkammer (Court Hunting and Arms Collection)

The **Hofjagd- und Rüstkammer** boasts one of the world's finest assemblages of armour, mostly dating from the fifteenth to the seventeenth century. Chronologically, the collection begins on the stairs, where you can view two dog-snout-shaped visors – devised to replace the closed helmet, in which it was extraordinarily difficult to breathe – from the estate of Duke Ernst of Austria (1377–1424), who was responsible for starting the weaponry collection. There's a splendid array of jousting equipment, to the right of Saal I, made for the knights of Emperor Maximilian I, and a display of High Renaissance **costume armour** (Saal III), which was meant only for show, its design deliberately imitating the fashionable clothes of the time: puffy sleeves, decorative bands inlaid with gilded silver, and slightly comical pleated skirts.

The museum's other great weaponry freak was the manic collector Archduke Ferdinand of Tyrol (1525–95), who ordered the bank-breaking **Adlergarnitur** (eagle armour) in Saal V, with its exquisite gilded garniture. Saal VI features some great Turkish arms and armour, while yet more richly decorated suits of armour fill Saal VII, including the "rose-petal" garniture ordered by Maximilian II for the tournament held in Vienna in 1571 to celebrate his brother Karl's wedding; equally fancy suits were created for his two sons, Rudolf and Ernst. Last of all, there's some truly exquisite Milanese craftsmanship in Saal VIII, including a rapier whose hilt features numerous Moors' heads.

Sammlung alter Musikinstrumente (Collection of Early Musical Instruments)

If you've absolutely no interest in instruments of death, however beautifully crafted, you can skip the entire collection and head straight for the **Sammlung alter Musikinstrumente**. The Archduke Ferdinand of Tyrol is again responsible for many of the rare pieces, such as the unique set of six sixteenth-century **dragon-shaped shawms**, in Saal X. The vertically strung **clavicytherium**, in Saal XI, richly inlaid with ivory, ebony, tortoiseshell and mother-of-pearl, was actually played by the Emperor Leopold I, who was a musician and composer in his own right. Saal XII is loosely based around Josef Haydn, featuring instruments from his day, plus a quadruple music stand for a string quartet; the extraordinarily lifelike beeswax bust of the composer sports a wig of real human hair. The **tortoiseshell violin**, decorated with gold and ivory, in room XIII, was bought by Maria Theresia for the Schatzkammer, and, like many such showpieces, is totally unsuitable for playing. Also in this room is an early nineteenth-century **glass harmonica** of the variety invented by the American statesman Benjamin Franklin. Beyond the ornate **Marmorsaal** (Saal XIV) – still occasionally used as a concert venue – there are eye-catching exhibits in Saal XV that include a **crystal flute**, and a string instrument that doubles as a walking stick. An aluminium violin and a "**dummy keyboard**" – stringless, for silent practice – can be found in Saal XVI, and in the final room there's an entire late-nineteenth-century orchestra, as well as a grand piano designed by Theophil Hansen and given to the Emperor Franz-Josef for his wife, Elisabeth, to play.

Ephesos (Ephesus) Museum

From 1866, until a ban on the export of antiquities from Turkey stopped the flow early this century, Austrian archeologists made off with a lot of first-class relics from the ancient city of Ephesus. It wasn't until 1978 that the loot was finally publicly displayed in the **Ephesos Museum**, occupying one half of the Neue Burg's monumental staircase. The most significant find of the lot is the forty-metre-long **Parthian Frieze**, sculpted in high relief around the second century AD, shortly after the Roman victory in the Parthian Wars. The relief formed the outer walls of a pantheon in honour of the commander of the Roman forces, Lucius Verus, who was joint emperor of the Roman Empire, along with his adoptive brother, Marcus Aurelius. The adoption of the two brothers by Antoninus Pius (himself adopted by the Emperor Hadrian) is depicted at the end of the corridor on the right.

Museum für Völkerkunde (Museum of Ethnology)

In the section of the Neue Burg nearest the Ring, the **Museum für Völkerkunde** (*www.ethno-museum.ac.at*) houses a bewildering array of secular and religious artefacts from around the world. Unfortunately, large sections of the museum are likely to be closed for renovation over the next few years as it drags itself into the 21st century. The ground-floor galleries, despite being badly in need of modernization, contain some interesting pieces from the **Far East**: check out the cheek-whipping device from China, dried frog from Korea, and Japanese reed raincoat with complementary rice straw boots. The new displays upstairs are a great deal more enticing to look at, beginning with the **Polynesia** section, much of it brought back from Captain Cook's expeditions, and then snapped up at auction in 1806 by the Emperor Franz I – who could resist the Hawaiian firelighter shaped like a giant penis? The highlight of the Americas section is undoubtedly the stunning sixteenth-century gilded **Aztec feather head-dress** of the Emperor Montezuma II, who was stoned to death by his own people for his passivity in the face of Cortés, the Spanish imperialist.

The gardens

The **Volksgarten**, which forms a large triangular wedge to the northwest of the Neue Burg and Heldenplatz, was opened in 1820 on the site of the old Burgbastei, blown up by Napoleon's troops in 1809. Appropriately enough, given its origins, it was laid out as a formal French garden and now features a Neoclassical temple, and a memorial to the ever-popular Empress Elisabeth. The more informal **Burggarten** likewise came into being fortuitously after Napoleon blew up the bastions around the Hofburg. It was retained as a private garden for the Habsburgs until 1918, and now lies hidden behind the giant Neue Burg. On the northeast side of the garden stands the elegant glass **Palmenhaus** (Palm House), designed by Friedrich Ohmann in Jugendstil around

1900. The left-hand section provides a suitably steamy environment for the colourful tropical butterflies and moths of the **Schmetterlinghaus** (Butterfly House; daily: April–Oct 10am–5pm; Nov–March 10am–4pm; öS50/€3.63), which until recently lived out in Schönbrunn. The much larger, middle section of the Palmenhaus has been converted into a very swish, palmy café (see p.144).

The Ringstrasse

On Christmas Eve 1857, the Emperor Franz-Josef I announced the demolition of the zigzag fortifications around the old town and the building of a **Ringstrasse**, a horse-shoe of imperial boulevards to be laid out on the former glacis (the sloping ground between the walls and the suburbs). Twelve major public buildings were set down along its course between 1860 and 1890 – among them the court opera house and theatre, two court museums, the imperial parliament, the city university and town hall – all at no cost to the taxpayer. By the end of World War I, though, the Habsburgs were no more: as Edward Crankshaw wrote, the Ringstrasse "was designed as the crown of the Empire, but it turned out to be a tomb".

Today Vienna's Ringstrasse looks pretty much as it did in last days of the Habsburgs, studded with key landmarks. The monumental public institutions remain the chief sights: heading anticlockwise, they include the **Votivkirche**, **Rathaus**, **Burgtheater** and **Parlament** buildings, the two monster museums – the **Naturhistorisches** and **Kunsthistorisches** – the new cultural centre of the **Museumsquartier**, and the **Staatsoper**. Countless other cultural institutions occupy prime positions on the Ring and neighbouring Karlsplatz, most notably, the **Musikverein**, the city's premier concert venue, the glorious Jugendstil **Secession** building, and three more excellent museums: the **Akademie der bildenden Künste**, the **Historisches Museum der Stadt Wien**, and the **MAK** (Museum of Applied Art). Last, but not least, Karlsplatz also boasts Vienna's most imposing Baroque church, the **Karlskirche**.

Votivkirche

The first public building on the Ringstrasse – begun in 1854, even before the emperor had ordered the demolition of the city ramparts – was the **Votivkirche**, a monumental church built by the Vienna-born architect Heinrich Ferstel in the style of the great Gothic cathedrals of Cologne and Chartres. Built opposite the spot where a Hungarian tailor, János Libényi, had tried to stab the Emperor Franz-Josef the previous year – he was thwarted only by the emperor's collar and cap – the church was to be "a monument of patriotism and of devotion of the people to the Imperial House". For all its size, there is something spiritually lacking in the Votivkirche. Built partly to serve the large influx of soldiers to the capital following the 1848 revolution, the church has no natural parishioners, and the gloomy interior, badly damaged in World War II, remains underused and little-visited. The one monument worth a look is the sixteenth-century marble tomb of Count Salm, who commanded Vienna during the Turkish siege of 1529.

Rathausplatz

Rathausplatz is the Ringstrasse's showpiece square, framed by no fewer than four monumental public buildings – the Rathaus, the Burgtheater, parliament and the university – all completed in the 1880s. The most imposing building of the four is the cathedralesque **Rathaus** – strictly speaking the Neues Rathaus – a powerful symbol of the city's late-nineteenth-century political clout, designed by the German architect Friedrich Schmidt in imitation of Brussels' town hall. To get a look at the ornate interior, you must join a 45-minute guided tour in German (Mon, Wed & Fri 1pm; ☎52550). Concerts are occasionally held in the main Arkadenhof and, in July and August, free opera and classical concerts are beamed onto a giant screen on the main facade. Restaurants set up stalls selling food and beer, though these are as nothing compared to the number of stalls set up during the famous **Christkindlmarkt** (mid-Nov to Christmas; *www.christkindlmarkt.at*). In the month before Christmas, the area in front of the Rathaus is crowded with stalls selling candy, decorations, traditional wooden toys, and just about every kitsch Christmas present you can think of. Families come to admire the luminous tree decorations, play on the rides, and participate in the workshops for kids within the town hall, while even more folk flock here after work to drink *Glühwein* and *Punsch* to ward off the cold. For the New Year, the area in front of the Rathaus is turned into a giant outdoor ice-skating rink.

Directly opposite the Rathaus, the **Burgtheater** (*www.burgtheater.at*) seems modest by comparison – until you realize that the sole function of the theatre's two vast wings was to house monumental staircases leading to the grand boxes. In practical terms, though, the design by Gottfried Semper and Karl Hasenauer was none too successful. Less than a decade after the opening night in 1888 the theatre had to close in order to revamp the acoustics, which were dreadful, and to modify the seating, some of which allowed no view of the stage at all. The auditorium was gutted by fire during the liberation of Vienna in April 1945, and has since been totally modernized. Thankfully, the staircase wings survived, and still boast their sumptuous decor, including ceiling paintings by Franz Matsch and Gustav Klimt. The easiest way to get to see the Burgtheater is to go to a performance (see p.153); alternatively, you can sign up for one of the daily guided tours in German (Tues, Thurs & Fri 9am & 3pm, Sat 3pm, Sun 11am & 3pm; öS50/€3.63).

The **Universität** (university; *www.univie.ac.at*) – strictly speaking the Neue Universität – is the most unassuming of the four public buildings on Rathausplatz, built in neo-Renaissance style by Heinrich Ferstel in the 1870s. Sadly, it's no longer possible to view the paintings, commissioned for the university's Festsaal, which caused possibly the biggest scandal in the institution's history. When the first picture, *Philosophy* by Gustav Klimt, was unveiled in March 1900, its tangled mass of naked, confused humanity prompted 87 professors to sign a petition of protest. The scandal drew 34,000 onlookers to see the painting in just two months. In the end, Klimt returned his fee and claimed back the paintings. All three were placed in Schloss Immendorf for safekeeping during World War II, but were destroyed in a fire started by retreating SS troops on May 5, 1945.

On the south side of Rathausplatz stands the Neoclassical **Parlament** (parliament; *www.parlament.gv.at*), one of five major Ringstrasse buildings by the Danish architect Theophil Hansen. From street level, it's difficult to see past the giant Corinthian portico and its accompanying wings and pavilions. Stand back, though, and it becomes clear

---

EXPLORING THE RINGSTRASSE

Blighted by heavy traffic, the **Ringstrasse** is not much fun to stroll along nowadays. In addition, the boulevard's sheer size – 5km from end to end – and its uneven distribution of sights precludes exploration on foot. You're better off adopting a hit-and-run approach, making forays from the nearest U-Bahn or tram stop. The best way to circumnavigate and appreciate the scale of the Ring is by **tram** – #1 goes round in a clockwise direction, and #2 runs anticlockwise. From the trams, only Karlsplatz lies entirely hidden from view. Each section of the Ring is **individually named** (eg Schottenring, Dr-Karl-Lueger-Ring, etc); the account beginning on p.105 works **anticlockwise** starting with the Votivkirche.

that the huge main body of the building is mostly hidden behind the projecting facade. The main pediment frieze shows the Emperor Franz-Josef I reluctantly granting the seventeen peoples of the empire a deeply undemocratic constitution. In front of the building, a gargantuan statue of Athena, goddess of wisdom, sporting a natty gilded plume in her helmet, presides over a fountain served by four writhing mermen. The attic of the main building, meanwhile, is peppered with 76 classical statues, 66 reliefs and 4 bronze chariot groups – these are best viewed from the sides of the building, where you'll find porticoes held up by caryatids modelled on the Erechtheion on the Acropolis. If you want to see inside the building, you can simply turn up for one of the free guided tours in German, provided there's no parliamentary session taking place (mid-Sept to June Mon–Thurs 11am and 3pm, Fri 11am, 1, 2 & 3pm; July to mid-Sept Mon–Fri 9, 10 & 11am and 1, 2 & 3pm).

Naturhistorisches Museum

The **Naturhistorisches Museum** (daily except Tues 9am–6pm, Wed until 9pm; öS30/€2.18; *www.nhm.at*) is the first of the pompous neo-Renaissance museums that stand on the other side of the Ringstrasse from the Hofburg. Whereas most European cities have tried to pep up their natural history collections with automated dinosaurs, ecological concerns and the like, the hard sell has, so far, passed Vienna by, and little has changed here since the museum opened in 1889. The display cabinets are over a century old, as is the exclusively German labelling – places as distant as Illyria (the eastern Adriatic coast) and Galicia (part of present-day Ukraine) are still described as if part of Austria – the dim panes of glass are almost preindustrial, and the stuffed animals have all succumbed to a uniform, musty, grey hue.

The ground floor kicks off with five rooms of minerals (I–V), of little interest to non-specialists, except perhaps room IV, which displays some incredible objects made from precious and semiprecious stones – including an ostrich made with 761 precious stones and 2102 diamonds, given as a (morning-after) wedding gift from Maria Theresia to Franz Stephan – and room V, which has an impressive collection of meteorites. The adjacent paleontology section is currently under wraps, with the exception of room X – a huge hall decorated with caryatids struggling with weird, prehistoric beasts – where you can find the skeleton of a diplodocus and various fossils. The prehistoric civilizations section begins in room XI with the **Venus of Willendorf**, by far the most famous exhibit in the entire museum. This tiny fertility symbol – a stout, limestone figure with drooping breasts – stands just a few centimetres high, but is something like 25,000 years old, and as such is an object of some fascination.

The west wing includes finds from the prehistoric Beaker folk and various implements, jewellery and arms from Iron Age burial tombs at Hallstatt in the Salzkammergut (see p.447). There's some impressive Thracian silver jewellery, a reconstructed funereal chariot from the Iron Age, and a staggering collection of human skulls. The *Kindersaal*, beyond, is the museum's one concession to modernization, though this tired children's playroom, built in the 1970s, isn't going to impress kids brought up on interactive, hands-on displays. The zoological displays, on the top floor, progress from starfish, corals and seashells in the east wing to a bevy of bears, cats and monkeys in the west. More interesting is room XXI, which contains a panopticon and several 3D viewfinders.

Kunsthistorisches Museum

In a city somewhat overloaded with museums, the **Kunsthistorisches Museum** (*www.khm.at*) stands head and shoulders above the rest. Thanks to the wealth and artistic pretensions of successive Habsburg rulers, it contains not only the fourth

VISITING THE KUNSTHISTORISCHES MUSEUM

The museum's opening times are Tuesday to Sunday 10am to 6pm; the picture gallery is also open until 9pm on Thursdays, while some of the ground-floor galleries close at dusk in winter. Tickets cost öS100/€7.27, a lot of money for what is supposed to be a public institution, though it does include entry into the museum's temporary exhibitions. There's no readmission, and even if you spend the whole day here you'll be pushed to see everything, so it's best to concentrate on just one or two areas. You'll also be extremely hungry, since the only place to eat is the architecturally superb, but over-priced café in the upper foyer, which has only a limited menu. Guided tours of the museum in English set off daily at 3pm and cost öS30/€2.18.

The paintings of the first-floor Gemäldegalerie are arranged in parallel rooms around two courtyards: the Italians, plus a few French and Spanish, lie to one side; the Germans, Dutch and Flemish, to the other. The larger rooms, which face onto the courtyards, sport Roman numerals (I–XV), while the smaller outer rooms use the standard form (1–24), though the latter are often unmarked. It would be difficult to concoct a more confusing numerical system, but at least both wings are laid out (vaguely) chronologically. The ground floor galleries are laid out entirely chronologically using only Roman numerals.

largest collection of paintings in the world, but also Egyptian, Greek and Roman antiquities, plus sundry *objets d'art*. So numerous are the exhibits that several of the museum's departments are now housed in the Neue Burg wing of the Hofburg (see p.102).

Most people come here to see the sixteenth- and seventeenth-century art in the Gemäldegalerie, in particular the collection of **Bruegels** – the largest in the world – which forms part of a superlative early Dutch and Flemish section. Thanks to the Habsburgs' territorial acquisitions, the museum is also loaded with **Venetian** works, by the likes of **Tintoretto**, **Veronese** and **Titian**, and a goodly selection of **Velázquez** portraits. In addition, there are numerous works by **Rembrandt**, **Cranach** and **Dürer**, and whole rooms devoted to **Van Dyck** and **Rubens**. Lastly, don't miss the unrivalled collection of Mannerist works from the court of Rudolf II, especially the surrealist court painter, **Giuseppe Arcimboldo**.

The Gemäldegalerie

The **Gemäldegalerie** (Picture Gallery), on the first floor, has around eight hundred paintings on display at any one time, a mere tenth of the museum's total catalogue. It's easy to become overwhelmed by the sheer volume of art. Unlike most big galleries, the Kunsthistorisches makes no attempt to cover a broad span of art history – the collection has changed very little since the Habsburgs bequeathed it. Consequently, British and French artists, and the early Italian Renaissance, are all underrepresented, and the collection stops at the late eighteenth century.

BRUEGEL

The great thing about the museum's Bruegels is the breadth and range of the collection, from innovative interpretations of religious stories to allegorical peasant scenes. Though well connected in court circles in Antwerp and, later, Brussels, **Pieter Bruegel the Elder** (*c.*1525–69) excelled in these country scenes, earning himself the soubriquet "Peasant Bruegel" – the story goes that he used to disguise himself in order to move freely among the peasantry. A classic example of the genre is his *Children's Games*, an incredibly detailed picture with more than 230 children playing 90 different games. Perhaps the most beguiling of all Bruegel's works within the peasant genre are the cycle of seasons, commissioned by a rich Flemish banker. Three (out of six) hang in this room: *The Gloomy Day, The Return of the Herd* and, the most famous of the lot,

Hunters in the Snow, in which Bruegel perfectly captures a monochrome wintry land-scape.

Several of Bruegel's peasant works clearly have a somewhat high-handed moral message, too, as in the *Peasant Dance*, where the locals revel irreverently, oblivious to the image of the Madonna concealed in the top right-hand corner. Similarly, the *Peasant Wedding* comes over less as a religious occasion than as another excuse for gluttony.

Even in Bruegel's overtly religious paintings, the biblical events are often subordi-nated to the whole. In *The Procession to Calvary*, the typically vigorous Bruegelian crowd seem utterly unmoved by the tragedy quietly unfolding in their midst. Gruesome characters, revealing the influence of Bosch, inhabit *The Fight Between Carnival and Lent*, a complex painting in which the orgy of Shrove Tuesday is contrasted with the piety of Ash Wednesday. *The Tower of Babel* (inspired, it's thought, by the Colosseum in Rome) is more straightforward, illustrating the vanity of King Nimrod – the detail on both the tower and the city below it is staggering.

DÜRER, CRANACH AND HOLBEIN

If you head off into the smaller side rooms, you come to the excellent German collec-tion, in particular the so-called "Danube School", an extremely loose title used to group together various sixteenth-century German-speaking painters inspired by the land-scape around the Danube. Room 16 shelters a colourful *Adoration of the Trinity* by **Albrecht Dürer** (1471–1528). Amidst his gilded throng are the donor, Matthäus Landauer (lower row, to the left), his son-in-law (lower row, to the right) and, with his feet firmly on the ground, Dürer himself (bottom right). The frame (a modern copy of the original) bears closer inspection, too, with those not heading for heaven being chained up and devoured by the Devil. Dürer also appears, somewhat incongruously dressed in black, in the centre of his *Martyrdom of the Ten Thousand*: amid scenes of mass murder, he strolls deep in conversation with his recently deceased friend, the humanist Conrad Celtes.

A prime example of the Danube School of painting is *The Crucifixion* by **Lucas Cranach the Elder** (1472–1553), in room 17 – one of his earliest works, with its gory depiction of Christ, spattered with, and vomiting up, blood, set against a rugged Danubian landscape. His depiction of the *Stag Hunt of Elector Frederick the Wise*, in which numerous stags are driven into the water so the royals can pick them off with crossbows, is almost playful, and his son, Lucas Cranach the Younger (1515–86), con-tributes an equally jolly scene of slaughter in *Stag Hunt of the Elector John Frederick*, which hangs close by.

The portraits in room 18 by **Hans Holbein the Younger** (1497–1543) date from his period as court painter to the English King Henry VIII. One of his first royal commis-sions was a portrait of *Jane Seymour*, lady-in-waiting to Henry VIII's second wife, Anne Boleyn, who, after the latter's execution, became his third wife (she died giving birth to Henry's one and only son, the future Edward VI).

ARCIMBOLDO, BRUEGHEL AND VAN DYCK

In room 19, you enter the court of Rudolf II (1576–1612), the deeply melancholic emperor who shut himself up in Prague Castle surrounded by astrologers, alchemists and artists. It is Rudolf, whose portrait by **Hans von Aachen** (*c.*1551–1615) hangs in the room, we have to thank for the Bruegels and Dürers in the museum. One of Rudolf's favourite court artists was **Giuseppe Arcimboldo** (1527–93), whose "com-posite heads" – surrealist, often disturbing, profile portraits created out of inanimate objects – so tickled the emperor that he had portraits made of every member of his entourage, right down to the cook. Among the four in the Kunsthistorisches, all of which are allegorical, are *Water*, in which the whole head is made of sea creatures, and *Fire*, where it's a hotchpotch of burning faggots, an oil lamp and various firearms.

Room 19 also contains several works by the son of "Peasant Bruegel", **Jan Brueghel the Elder** (1568–1625), whose detailed still lifes of flowers were highly prized, his luminous paintwork earning him the nickname "Velvet Brueghel". One of his most famous, non-flowery paintings is his reverential *Adoration of the Kings*, a beautifully detailed work that's a firm favourite on Christmas cards. **Anthony van Dyck** (1599–1641) predominates in the adjacent room (XII): some pieces, like *The Apostle Philip*, date from the time when van Dyck was working closely with Rubens, hence the characteristic, "ruffled" brushstrokes; others – mostly portraits – from after van Dyck's appointment as court painter to the English King Charles I.

RUBENS, REMBRANDT AND VERMEER

Thanks to the Habsburgs' long-term control of the southern Netherlands, the Kunsthistorisches Museum boasts one of the largest collections of paintings by **Peter Paul Rubens** (1577–1640), spread over three rooms (rooms 20, XIII and XIV). Perhaps the best known of all his works here is *The Fur*, in room XIII, a frank, erotic testament to the artist's second wife, Hélène Fourment, who was 37 years his junior. Rubens was clearly taken with his 16-year-old wife, who appears as an angel, saint or deity, in two other of his late works: the *Ildefonso Altar* and the *Meeting Near Nördlingen*. The loose brushwork and painterly style in these two bear comparison with Titian's late work in room I, and Rubens pays tribute to the Italian in his *The Worship of Venus*, a veritable cherub-fest set in a classical landscape.

Rubens' Baroque excess is a million miles from the sparse, simple portraits of **Rembrandt van Rijn** (1606–69), several of which hang in room XV. There's a sympathetic early portrait of his mother, the year before she died, depicted in all the fragility and dignity of old age, and a dreamlike later study of his son, Titus, reading. There are also three self-portraits from the 1650s, when Rembrandt was beginning to experience financial difficulties. Next door, in room 24, is the museum's one and only painting by **Jan Vermeer** (1632–75), *Allegory of the Art of Painting*. The bright light from the onlooker's left, the yellow, blue and grey, the simple poses, are all classic Vermeer trademarks, though the symbolic meaning, and even the title, of the work have provoked fierce debate.

NORTHERN ITALIAN PAINTINGS

Over in the west wing, the museum boasts an impressive selection of Venetian paintings, especially works by **Titian** (*c.*1490–1576), which span all sixty years of his artistic life. Very early works like *The Gypsy Madonna* in room I reveal Titian's debt to Giovanni Bellini, in whose studio he spent his apprenticeship. The colours are richer, the contours softer, but the essentially static composition is reminiscent of Bellini's own *Young Woman with a Mirror* (see below). The largest canvas in room I is Titian's *Ecce Homo*, from his middle period, in which, amidst all the action and colour, Christ is relegated to the top left-hand corner.

In *Girl in a Fur* and the portrait of Benedetto Varchi, Titian shows himself equally capable of sparing use of colour, allowing the sitter's individual features maximum effect. By contrast, Titian's very last portrait, of the art dealer Jacopo Strada, whom the painter disliked, is full of incidental detail, colour and movement. Towards the end of his life, Titian achieved a freedom of technique in his own personal works (as opposed to those produced for commission by his studio), in which "he used his fingers more than his brush" according to fellow painter Palma il Giovane. A masterpiece of this period is the *Nymph and Shepherd*, painted without a commission, using an autumnal palette and very loose brushwork.

Young Woman with a Mirror and *Presentation of Christ in the Temple*, both by **Giovanni Bellini** (1460–1516), hang in the adjacent room 1, along with a sculptural *St Sebastian* by his brother-in-law, **Andrea Mantegna** (*c.*1431–1506), and three fragments of an altarpiece by Antonello da Messina, who is credited with introducing oil painting to northern Italy. Next door, in room 2, the subject matter of the *Three Philosophers* is almost as mysterious as its painter, **Giorgione** (*c.*1478–1511), about whom we know little other than that he was tall, handsome and died young, possibly of the plague; as for the painting, no one's sure if it depicts the Magi, the three stages of man's life or some other subject. Giorgione's sensuous portrait *Laura* – fur and naked breasts are a recurring theme in the gallery – is one of his few works to be certified and dated on the back.

Colourful, carefully constructed, monumental canvases by **Paolo Veronese** (1528–88) fill the walls of room II – the *Anointing of David* is a classic example, with the subject matter subordinated to the overall effect. In room III, there are several impressive portraits by **Tintoretto** (1518–94), and a voluptuous *Susanna and the Elders*, full of contrasts of light and shade, old age and youthfulness, clothing and bare flesh. Another work that draws your attention is the series of horizontal panels depicting scenes from the Old and New Testaments with refreshing immediacy and improvised brushstrokes.

RAPHAEL, THE MANNERISTS AND CARAVAGGIO

In room 3, the scene shifts across northern Italy to the Mannerist school of Emilia. **Antonio Correggio** (*c.*1494–1534) puts his bid in for the gallery's most erotic painting with *Jupiter and Io*, in which the latter is brought to the verge of ecstasy by Jupiter in the form of a cloud. *Self-Portrait in a Convex Mirror* by **Parmigianino** (1503–40) was just the sort of tricksy art that appealed to Rudolf II, in whose collection it appeared in 1608. There's a masterly study in Renaissance harmony and proportion in room 4, with the *Madonna in the Meadow*, painted by **Raphael** (1483–1520) at the tender age of 22. (Further on, a typically icy *Holy Family* by **Agnolo Bronzino** (1503–72) hangs in room 7.)

Caravaggio (1573–1610), several of whose works hang in room V, was nothing if not controversial. His chief artistic sin, in the eyes of the establishment, was his refusal to idealize his biblical characters, frequently using street urchins as his models, as in his *David with the Head of Goliath*; he also painted his own self-portrait as the severed head of Goliath. He may have managed to outrage more than a few of his religious patrons, but his works had a profound effect on seventeenth-century artists like Rubens and Bruegel, both of whom at one time or another owned the *Madonna of the Rosary*.

VELÁZQUEZ, BELLOTTO AND CANALETTO

If the Italians start to get you down – and there is a lot of less-than-fantastic seventeenth-century art out there – head for the Spaniards in rooms 9 and 10. The museum's smattering of works by **Diego Velázquez** (1599–1660), most of them gifts from the Spanish Habsburgs to the Austrian side of the family, include one of Queen Maria-Anna of Spain, whose hairdo is twice the size of her face, and two of Charles II of Spain, though neither is as grotesque as the early portrait by Juan Carreño de Miranda – it's scary to think that he probably looked even worse in real life. The most famous of Velázquez's works are those of the Infanta Margarita Teresa, who was betrothed to her uncle, the future Emperor Leopold I, from the age of three.

Lastly, you might want to take a look at the eighteenth-century views of Vienna in room VII, commissioned by the court from **Bernardo Bellotto**, to see how little the view from the Upper Belvedere has changed over the centuries. The Viennese insisted on calling Bellotto "Canaletto", though he was in fact the latter's nephew and pupil. For real **Canalettos** (1697–1768), you must go next door, to room 13, where his views of Venice hang alongside those of his compatriot Francesco Guardi.

The ground-floor galleries

The **ground-floor galleries** kick off with the Egyptian and Near Eastern Collection (I–VIII), pass through Greek and Roman Antiquities (IX–XVIII) and head off into

Sculpture and Decorative Arts (XIX–XXVII). However, for what seems like an eternity now, rooms XXVIII onwards, and the Coin Cabinet, have been closed for renovations, with eight rooms from this collection remaining open.

EGYPTIAN AND NEAR EASTERN COLLECTION

Immediately to the right as you enter the museum are the purpose-built galleries of the **Egyptian and Near Eastern Collection**, beginning in room I, which is devoted to the **Egyptian death cult**. The entrance to the room is guarded by two statues of the fearsome, lion-headed goddess, Sekhmet; the museum owns just four out of the six hundred that once formed a colossal monument to the deity erected at Thebes by Amenophis III. In the room itself, there's only one actual mummy, wrapped in papyrus leaves, but there are numerous wooden inner coffins in the shape of mummies, smothered with polychrome symbols and hieroglyphs. Below the mummy cases are the tiny canopic jars, used for storing the entrails removed during mummification, with lids carved in the shape of animal deities. Another display cabinet to make for, in room III, contains the mummies of various animals, including cats, falcons, snakes, crocodiles and a bull's head, alongside figurines evincing the strength of Egyptian animal cults.

The Kunsthistorisches Museum owns some superb examples of **Egyptian sculpture**, beginning in room V with an unusual depiction of a lion tucking into a bull, and Isis, sporting cow's horns, a solar disc and a vulture head-dress, breastfeeding Horus. Horus appears in his adult, falcon-headed form in a rather wonderful duo in room VII, seated alongside King Horemheb, who was the power behind the throne of Tutankhamen. Also in this room is a winsome blue pottery hippo, whose body is tattooed with papyrus leaves, lotus flowers and a bird. Room VIII contains one of the collection's most prized possessions, the so-called **Reserve Head** from around 2450 BC, a smooth, stylized head carved in limestone, which exudes an extraordinary serenity.

GREEK AND ROMAN ANTIQUITIES

The **Greek and Roman Antiquities** begin in room X, though one of the most prominent statues here – the **Youth of Magdalensberg** – is in fact a sixteenth-century bronze copy of the Roman original, something that was only discovered in 1983 when research was being conducted into the methods used in the casting. At the centre of the large, arcaded room XI, is the magnificent fourth-century AD **Theseus Mosaic**, discovered in a Roman villa near Salzburg. Theseus and the Minotaur are depicted in the middle of a complex geometric labyrinth, out of which the hero escapes with the help of the red thread given to him by Ariadne, who is pictured abandoned to the right.

Those in search of **Greek vases** need look no further than room XIV, which contains an excellent selection from early Geometric vases from the eighth century BC to the sophisticated black- and red-figure vases of the Classical period. Among the many onyx cameos in the adjoining room XV is one of the finest in the world, the **Gemma Augusta**, a mere 19cm in height. The upper scene depicts the Emperor Augustus in the guise of Jupiter, seated on a bench alongside Roma, with the emperor's star sign, Capricorn, floating between them.

The last three small rooms (XVI–XVIII) contain **gold work**, much of which, strictly speaking, postdates the collapse of the Roman Empire. The chain of honour with 52 pendants is an excellent example of early Germanic gold, its centrepiece a bead of smoky topaz, mounted with two tiny pouncing panthers. The most impressive haul is the treasure from Nagyszentmiklós (Sînicolaul Mare) in Romania, 23 pure gold vessels, weighing a total of 20kg, with runic inscriptions that continue to fox the experts.

SCULPTURE AND DECORATIVE ARTS

The **Sculpture and Decorative Arts** collection occupies more than half of the ground floor galleries. It's a patchy collection, with some real gems, and a lot of objects of great

MUSEUMSQUARTIER

If you stand between the two big museums with your back to the Hofburg, you will find yourself confronted with Vienna's new **MuseumsQuartier** (*www.mqw.at*), which was due to open as this book went to print. Housed in the former Messepalast (Trade Fair Palace), originally built in the eighteenth century as the imperial stables by Johann Bernhard Fischer von Erlach, the MuseumsQuartier hopes to do for Vienna what the Tate Modern has done for London. Designed by Ortner & Ortner, the MuseumsQuartier is now the home of, among other things, the city's chief permanent collection of modern art, previously on show at the Palais Liechtenstein and the 20er Haus. Here, you should get to see early-twentieth-century works by home-grown talents such as Kokoschka, as well as the likes of Picasso, Miró, Magritte, Kupka, Klee, Kandinsky and Kirchner, a smattering of Pop Art and a fair cross-section of pieces by the Wiener Aktionismus group, Austria's very own violent performance art movement. In addition, you'll find several other museums and galleries here, the Kunsthalle (*www.kunsthallewien.at*), which stages contemporary art exhibitions, and the Leopold Museum (*www.leopoldmuseum.org*), containing the world's biggest collection of works by Egon Schiele, as well as smaller concerns such as the Kinder Museum (Children's Museum), and the state-sponsored Tabakmuseum (Tobacco Museum), To service the needs of the MuseumsQuartier's visitors, numerous restaurants and bars will stay open until the early hours.

craftsmanship, but dubious artistic taste. Most of the exhibits were collected or specially commissioned for the various *Kunstkammern* (Chambers of Marvels), which became *de rigueur* among German-speaking rulers during the Renaissance – the most avid collectors were the Archduke Ferdinand II of Tyrol (see p.472) and the Emperor Rudolf II.

Room XIX contains objects made from precious and semiprecious stones, and sets the tone – slightly vulgar, exquisitely executed kitsch – of much of the collection. Prime examples are the gold vase holding tulips made from agate, jasper, chalcedony and rock crystal, or the gold chain, inset with rubies and made up of 49 portraits of the Habsburgs carved in shell. Most of the exhibits have no function, but the rock-crystal dragon-lions were something of a party piece: liquid poured into their tails would gush into a shell through nozzles in the beast's breasts.

In room XXV you can see an elaborate piggy bank belonging to the Archduke Ferdinand II of Tyrol, but the most famous exhibit in the entire collection is Benvenuto Cellini's **Saliera**, in room XXVII, a slightly ludicrous sixteenth-century salt cellar, in which the gold figures of Neptune and Earth appear to be engaged in some sort of erotic seesaw.

Staatsoper

That the **Staatsoper** (State Opera House; *www.wiener-staatsoper.at*) was the first public building to be completed on the Ringstrasse – opening in May 1869 with a performance of Mozart's *Don Giovanni* – is an indication of its importance in Viennese society. Prestigious past directors include Gustav Mahler, Richard Strauss, Herbert von Karajan and Claudio Abbado, though each one had notoriously difficult relationships with the opera house. The building itself was designed in heavy Italian Renaissance style – even the Viennese deferred to Italy as the home of opera – and has a suitably grandiose exterior, with a fine loggia beneath which carriages could draw up. There are English 35-minute guided tours (öS60/€4.36) of the interior, schedules for which are listed beneath the arcade on the east side of the building, though the main auditorium

GUSTAV MAHLER (1860-1911)

Mahler's symphonies are now firmly established in the concert repertoire, but it wasn't that long ago that his music was only rarely performed. In his lifetime Mahler was much better known as a conductor. Born to a Jewish family in provincial Bohemia, he studied at the Vienna Conservatory, before spending the best part of a decade as a jobbing Kapellmeister at various provincial theatres in the Prussian and Habsburg empires. At the age of just 28, the ambitious Mahler got his big break when he landed the job at the Royal Hungarian Opera in Budapest. Ten years later, in 1897, following a judicious (and entirely mercenary) conversion to Roman Catholicism, he reached his "final goal" and became director of the Hofoper, Vienna's imperial opera house (now the Staatsoper).

Mahler's ten years in charge of the Opera (including a couple as chief conductor of the Vienna Philharmonic as well), were stormy to say the least. He instituted a totally new regime in the house, banning claques (opera stars' paid supporters), insisting that the lights of the auditorium were dimmed during performances, and allowing latecomers entry only after the overture or between acts. Among his performers he was also something of a tyrant, hiring and firing with abandon and earning himself the nickname of *Korporal vom Tag* (Duty Corporal) for his demanding work schedules and his bluntness. "Is music meant to be so serious?" the emperor is alleged to have said when hearing of these innovations, "I thought it was meant to make people happy."

The music critics were evenly divided, many praising his painstaking attention to detail, others lambasting him for constantly reworking other composers' scores. Needless to say, the anti-Semitic press had a field day, subjecting Mahler to racist jibes, and caricaturing his eccentric appearance. The gossip columnists were also kept busy, especially when in 1902, Mahler married Alma Schindler, the strikingly beautiful stepdaughter of Carl Moll, the Secession artist, and, at 22, a woman almost half his age. Mahler's views on marriage were rigidly bourgeois: she was to give up her music (she was a fledgling composer in her own right); "you must become 'what I need' if we are to be happy together, ie my wife, not my colleague", he wrote to her. Not surprisingly, the marriage was to prove an extremely difficult one for both parties.

Towards the end of 1907, Mahler pinned a farewell note to the opera house notice board, saying "I was honest in my intentions, and I set my sights high... In the heat of the moment, neither you nor I have been spared wounds, or errors." The previous summer, at the Mahlers' private villa by the Wörthersee in Carinthia (see p.325), their elder daughter, Maria (Putzi), had died of scarlet fever, and Mahler himself had been diagnosed as having a heart valve defect. It was time to move on. By signing up with the New York Metropolitan Opera, Mahler simultaneously doubled his income and drastically reduced his workload. However, the increased travelling, and the strain it put his marriage and health under, proved too much.

By 1910 Alma was more or less openly conducting an affair with the Modernist architect Walter Gropius, and Mahler, in desperation, travelled all the way to Holland to consult Freud. Mahler blamed himself (probably rightly so) for selfishness, and attempted to make amends, showering Alma with affection and encouraging her to compose again. As it turned out, Mahler didn't have long to live. In New York he was diagnosed as having subacute bacterial endocarditis, and the family travelled back to Vienna for the last time. Crowds gathered outside the sanatorium, the press issued daily bulletins from the bedside of "der Mahler". He died during a thunderstorm (just like Beethoven), and his last words are alleged to have been "Mozartl". According to his wishes, his tombstone in Grinzinger Friedhof, designed by Josef Hoffmann, has nothing but "Mahler" written on it. "Any who come to look for me will know who I was", he explained, "and the rest do not need to know."

is pretty undistinguished, having been destroyed in an air raid in 1945. In any case, for less than the price of the tour, you can buy one of the hundreds of standing-room tickets (*Stehplätze*) that are sold each day on a first-come, first-served basis (and limited to one ticket per person).

Akademie der bildenden Künste

Set back from the Ring, on Schillerplatz to the southwest of the Staatsoper, the **Akademie der bildenden Künste** (Academy of Fine Arts; Tues–Sun 10am–4pm; öS50/€3.63; *www.akbild.at*) occupies an imposing neo-Renaissance structure built by Theophil von Hansen in 1876. The Academy itself was founded in 1692, and its main purpose continues to be teaching, but the school also houses a small, much-overlooked study collection. To see the paintings, follow the signs to the **Gemäldegalerie**: turn right after the porter's lodge, head up the stairs to the second floor, then right again to the end of the corridor. The **Aula** – straight ahead as you pass through the main entrance – is also worth a glimpse, both for its decor and for the regular wacky student installations.

Badly lit and indifferently hung, the Academy's collection is tiny compared with the Kunsthistorisches Museum. Nevertheless, it does have one star attraction: *The Last Judgement* by **Hieronymus Bosch** (*c*.1450–1516), the only Bosch triptych outside Spain. The action in the left panel, *Paradise*, is a taster for the central panel, the *Last Judgement* itself, most of which is taken up with strange, half-animal diabolic figures busy torturing sinners in imaginatively horrible ways; the right panel, *Hell*, looks even less fun. Overall, the possibility of salvation seems painfully slim, with only a lucky few having made it to the small corner of the painting given over to heaven.

Displayed in the same room as the Bosch are two works by Lucas Cranach the Elder: *Lucretia*, a classic Cranach nude, and his moralistic-erotic *Ill-Matched Couple*. The Academy's Italian works are fairly disappointing, with the exception of a Botticelli rondel of the Madonna and Child, and Titian's *Tarquin and Lucretia*, a late work replete with loose brushwork and brooding, autumnal colours. In the same room as the last two, look out for Murillo's sentimental *Two Boys Playing Dice*.

It's Flemish and Dutch paintings that make up the core of the Academy's collection, however, with an early Rembrandt portrait of a young woman in a black dress, a self-portrait by Van Dyck aged just fourteen, preparatory studies for the Jesuit Church frescoes in Antwerp (and lots of nudes) by Rubens, plus works by Jordaens, Ruisdael, Hoogstraten and David Teniers the Younger. After Bosch, though, the other outstanding masterpiece is the *Family Group in a Courtyard* by **Pieter de Hooch** (1629–84), with its sublime tranquillity and clever play on perspective.

Karlsplatz

Overlooked by the city's most awesome Baroque church, several key Ringstrasse institutions, the gilded **Secession** building and Otto Wagner's wonderful Art Nouveau pavilions, **Karlsplatz** should be one of Vienna's showpiece squares. Instead, the western half is little more than a vast traffic interchange, with pedestrians relegated to a set of seedy subways that stretch north as far as Oper. The problem is there has never been any grand, overall plan at Karlsplatz – the **Naschmarkt** was held here until the 1890s, but when it moved to the nearby **Wienzeile** the heart was ripped out of the square. The city council provided a site for the Secession, but the avenue that should have connected it with the **Karlskirche** never materialized. As a result, it's actually impossible to stand back and admire the Secession building without seriously endangering your life. The latest abomination is Adolf Krischanitz's Kunsthalle, a mustard-yellow and blue pre-fab steel box built for contemporary art exhibitions.

Secession

In 1898, Joseph Maria Olbrich completed one of the most original Jugendstil works of art in Vienna: **Secession** (*www.secession.at*), headquarters for the artistic movement of the same name (see box, p.117). The dome of gilded bronze laurel leaves is the most startling feature – the Viennese dubbed it the "golden cabbage" – though all the building's decorative details are unusual. On the sides, three wise owls suddenly emerge from the rendering, while the main entrance is adorned with a trio of Medusas, a pair of salamanders and copious gilded foliage; above is the group's credo "For every age its art; for art its freedom", replaced after being removed by the Nazis. Don't miss the tortoises at the feet of the ornamental bowls, Georg Klimt's bronze doors with snake handles, and Arthur Strasser's nearby bronze statue of an overweight Mark Antony on a chariot drawn by panthers.

The main hall upstairs stages provocative contemporary art installations, while downstairs in the basement Gustav Klimt's **Beethoven Frieze** is on permanent display (Tues–Sun 10am–6pm, Thurs until 8pm; öS60/€4.36). The frieze was intended to last only for the duration of the fourteenth exhibition held in 1902 – in the end it was preserved but not shown to the public again until 1986. With much of the mural consisting of huge blank spaces framed by floating maidens, the frieze looks strangely half-finished. In between the blank spaces are three painted sections: *Longing for Happiness*, where the weak, represented by three naked emaciated figures, appeal to a knight in golden armour; *Hostile Forces*, which features a slightly comical giant ape, with a serpent's tail and wings, and his three daughters, the Gorgons, backed up by the figures of Disease, Madness and Death, and surrounded by decorative sperm and ovaries; and finally *Ode to Joy*, which culminates in an embracing couple, offering, in Schiller's words, "this kiss to all the world". There's an excellent English commentary available, which explains in greater detail the symbolism behind the frieze; also on display are Klimt's preparatory sketches.

The Karlsplatz pavilions, Künstlerhaus and Musikverein

Another Jugendstil masterpiece in Karlsplatz is Otto Wagner's duo of entrance pavilions for the now defunct **Station Karlsplatz**, erected in 1899. Wagner broke with his usual design here, partly in deference to the presence of the nearby Karlskirche, adding gold trimmings and a sunflower motif. The green, wrought-iron framework, which was a feature of all his Stadtbahn stations, forms an essential part of the overall design, framing a series of thin marble slabs and creating a lovely, curving, central canopy. Today, one of the pavilions has been converted into a café (daily 10am–7pm), while the other holds exhibition space for the Historisches Museum (April–Oct Tues–Sun 1–4.30pm; öS25/€1.82).

From the terrace between the pavilions, you can also admire two key institutions on the north side of Karlsplatz, both executed in Ringstrasse style. The neo-Baroque **Künstlerhaus** was built in 1881 as the exhibition hall of Austria's leading artists' association (from which the Secession group split in 1897, see opposite); its diminutive extension was converted into a mid-scale theatre in the 1970s. Next door stands the **Musikverein**, Vienna's number-one concert hall, designed by the ubiquitous Theophil Hansen in the 1860s. The classical terracotta exterior apes the opera house with its front loggia, but you need to attend a concert in the Grosser Saal to appreciate the unbeatable acoustics and the sumptuous decor with its parade of gilded caryatids. Home to the world-famous Vienna Philharmonic, the Musikverein's most prestigious event is the annual New Year's Day concert, which is transmitted live around the world to an estimated 1.3 billion viewers.

Karlskirche

Rising majestically above everything around it, the **Karlskirche** (Mon–Sat 9–11.30am & 1–5pm, Sun 1–5pm; öS40/€2.90), designed by Johann Bernhard Fischer von Erlach and completed by his son Johann Michael in 1737, is, without doubt, the city's finest Baroque church. A huge Italianate dome with a Neoclassical portico, flanked by two

A BRIEF GUIDE TO THE VIENNESE SECESSION

In 1897, a number of artists broke away from the Künstlerhaus, Austria's leading independent artists' association, and set up their own organization, which they named the **Secession**. The second half of the nineteenth century had seen the ossification of the arts in Vienna, exemplified in architecture by the heavy-handed historicism of the Ringstrasse, and in painting by the flattery of Hans Makart. Broadly speaking, the aims of the new group were to regenerate the arts in Vienna, and to promote "art for art's sake", in particular the latest style, Art Nouveau, known in German as Jugendstil ("youth-style"). "We want to declare war on sterile routine, on rigid Byzantinism, on all forms of bad taste," declared the critic Hermann Bahr, one of the literary champions of the movement. The other major thrust, which sat less happily with the Secession's other commitments, was to strip off the mask of historicism and, as Otto Wagner put it, "to show modern man his true face".

The first president of the Secession was the artist **Gustav Klimt** (1862–1918), who became the group's driving force over the next eight years. Klimt had begun his career as a promising young master of the old ideology. In the movement's striking, purpose-built headquarters, in full view of the Künstlerhaus, he now helped put on a series of exhibitions of new work. Initially, the reception among Viennese critics and the public was good, but the movement ran into trouble when Klimt exhibited *Medicine* here, part of his controversial mural intended for the university. The ensuing public scandal, and the mixed reception given to the group's fourteenth exhibition in 1902, eventually prompted Klimt, along with a number of his followers, to secede from the Secession and retreat from public life for several years.

Between 1898 and 1903, the Secession group published *Ver Sacrum*, a successful arts journal employing lavish Jugendstil typography and layout. Instrumental in its production and design were two of the Secession's co-founders, **Josef Hoffmann** (1870–1956) and **Kolo Moser** (1868–1918), who went on to pursue their interest in applied art, forming the craft-based Wiener Werkstätte in 1902. Hoffmann and Moser left the Secession in 1905 with Klimt, and, although the trio helped organize the Kunstschau exhibitions of 1908 and 1909, these two shows marked a fundamental shift in the art scene. The decorative art of the Secession was left behind in favour of Expressionism, and the two leading artists to emerge from the Kunstschau were Oskar Kokoschka and Egon Schiele.

Though only a peripheral character in the Secession, the architect **Otto Wagner** (1841–1918) was a seminal figure in the Viennese art world throughout the period – as Hermann Bahr wrote, "without Wagner, there would be no Secession, no Klimt group, no applied art". Wagner not only completed more buildings than any other Secession architect, he also designed the entire Stadtbahn system from 1894 to 1901 – many of his stations are extant on the U4 and U6 metro lines. As such, he remains the most high-profile exponent of the Secession style, though his works in fact range from nineteenth-century historicism to twentieth-century Modernism.

Last, but certainly not least, it's worth mentioning the Modernist architect **Adolf Loos** (1870–1933), who published two articles in *Ver Sacrum*, one of which was a stinging attack on Ringstrasse architecture. Loos's relationship with the Secession was brief, however, and in 1908 he published a thinly veiled criticism of the movement in an article entitled "Ornament is Crime".

giant pillars modelled on Trajan's Column, and, just for good measure, a couple of hefty Baroque side towers, it's an eclectic and rather self-conscious mixture of styles, built to impress. Even surrounded by the mess that is now Karlsplatz, the church is an awesome sight – and must have been even more so when there was nothing between it and the Hofburg except the open space of the glacis.

The church is dedicated to the sixteenth-century saint, Carlo Borromeo, though the fact that the emperor and saint shared the same name no doubt played a part in

Emperor Karl VI's choice, conveniently glorifying both of them at the same time. The Karlskirche's dual nature – votive and imperial – is nowhere more evident than with the columns, imperial symbols whose reliefs illustrate the life of Borromeo. The interior is surprisingly sparse and light, allowing a much better appreciation of Johann Michael Rottmayr's vast fresco than you get of the artist's work in the Peterskirche. The subject is the apotheosis of Carlo Borromeo, along with a bit of Counter-Reformation Luther-bashing – see the angel setting fire to the German's Bible. Everything else in the church finds it rather hard to compete with the sublime beauty of the dome, though Fischer von Erlach's sunburst above the main altar is definitely worth a closer look.

Historisches Museum der Stadt Wien

Housed in an unprepossessing Modernist block to the side of the Karlskirche, the **Historisches Museum der Stadt Wien** (Tues–Sun 9am–6pm; öS50/€3.63) is an uneven collection, but it does contain, among other things, a pretty good fin-de-siècle section – which alone more than justifies a visit – and excellent temporary exhibitions are often held on the ground floor.

The permanent display begins on the first floor where you can view a smattering of spoils from the city's two Turkish sieges in 1529 and 1683: a vast red silk banner, Turkish horse plumes sporting crescent moons, several swashbuckling sabres, and an ornate tent lantern. The museum also owns a welter of paintings, including minor works by all the key artists of Austrian **Baroque**. Before you head upstairs, take a look at the model of Vienna shortly before the old zigzag fortifications were torn down in 1857.

On the top floor, by far the most interesting section in the whole museum, the centrepiece is another model of Vienna, this time after the construction of the great Ringstrasse buildings of the late nineteenth century, accompanied by "before" and "after" photos. To the side is an entire living/dining room designed in 1903 by the Modernist architect **Adolf Loos** for his first marital home on nearby Bösendorferstrasse. Despite his diatribes against ornament of any kind, Loos loved rich materials – marble, mahogany and brass – and created for himself a typically plush interior. Nearby hangs **Gustav Klimt**'s *Pallas Athene* from 1898, marking his first use of gold, which was to become a hallmark of his work.

Dotted around the next two rooms are various other works of art from Vienna's artistic golden age. The copy of Max Klinger's nude statue of Beethoven, which formed the centrepiece of the Secession exhibition of 1902, is displayed here, albeit without its coloured marble drapery and seat. There are several glass cabinets – including one designed by Kolo Moser – stuffed with Wiener Werkstätte produce, but it's the collection of works by **Egon Schiele** that really stand out. A typically distraught study of sunflowers from 1909 and the harrowing *Blind Mother II* hang beside a fondly painted view of the artist's bedroom in Neulengbach, a clear homage to Van Gogh, executed shortly before his brief imprisonment on a charge of "displaying an erotic drawing in a room open to children". The characteristically angular portraits of the art critic and collector Arthur Roessler and his wife Ida – loyal friends and patrons throughout Schiele's life – are among the artist's earliest commissioned portraits in oils.

Naschmarkt and Linke Wienzeile

The **Naschmarkt** (Mon–Sat 9am–6pm), which stretches away to the southwest of Karlsplatz, is now the city's premier source of fruit and vegetables, and one of the few places where you get a real sense of the city's multicultural make-up: Turks, Arabs, Slavs and Chinese stallholders vie for customers all the way to the Kettenbrückengasse metro station. On Saturdays, the market extends even further west as the weekly flea market joins in. The Linke and Rechte Wienzeile, which run parallel to each other on either side of the market, now function as a six-lane motorway, but there are a couple of sights along the Linke Wienzeile to make a stroll through the market doubly rewarding.

At the far end of the Naschmarkt, near Kettenbrückengasse U-Bahn, are two of Otto Wagner's most appealing Secession buildings from 1899: the apartment blocks of **Linke Wienzeile 38** and **40**. The right-hand building (no. 38) is richly embossed with gold palm leaves and medallions, but the other is more unusual, its pollution-resistant cladding of majolica tiles giving rise to the nickname **Majolikahaus**. To contemporary eyes, the facade looks highly decorative, but what mattered to the Viennese was that – as with the Looshaus – there was virtually no sculptural decoration, and no mouldings or pediments above the windows. Instead, Wagner weaves an elaborate floral motif – a giant, spreading rose tree or a vine of sunflowers – on the tiles themselves.

Schwarzenbergplatz and the Stadtpark

Faced with the din of cars and trams whizzing across its cobbles, it's difficult to believe that the large rectangular traffic intersection of **Schwarzenbergplatz**, one block east of Karlsplatz, was once a fashionable address. At the southern end of the square, dramatically floodlit at night and spurting water high into the air, stands the **Hochstrahlbrunnen** (High Jet Fountain), erected in 1873 as a celebration of the city's nascent modern water-supply system. Once the focal point of the square, it now acts as a kind of screen to hide the bombastic **Russen Heldendenkmal** (Russian Heroes' Monument), behind. A giant curving colonnade acts as the backdrop to the central column, crowned by the Unknown (Soviet) Soldier in heroic stance, flag aloft, sporting a gilded shield and helmet; on the red granite plinth are the names of the fallen and a quote from Stalin (after whom the square was briefly renamed in 1945). For the Viennese, though, it's more a grim reminder of the brutality of the liberators and the privations suffered by those in the city's postwar Russian zones.

To the east of the monument, on the corner of Zaunergasse and Daffingerstrasse is the **Arnold Schönberg Center** (Mon–Fri 10am–5pm; öS70/€5.09; *www.schoenberg.at*), which puts on temporary exhibitions about the composer, on the second floor of the building, whose entrance is on Zaunergasse. Schönberg is considered the father of atonal music, and was the leading figure in what has become known as the Second Viennese School. He was an accomplished artist, too, and one or two of his drawings are usually on display as part of the exhibitions. There's also a reconstruction of Schönberg's study from Los Angeles (to which he fled in the 1930s), containing original furniture and objects, many of which he himself designed from recycled materials.

Opened in 1862 as the city council's first public park, the **Stadtpark**, to the northeast of Schwarzenbergplatz, is best known for Edmund Hellmer's eye-catching **Strauss Monument** from 1925, with its statue of the "Waltz King", Johann Strauss the Younger, violin in hand. Gilded from head to toe and dramatically floodlit at night, the composer stands framed by a stone arch of naked, swirling naiads. Tour groups turn up at regular intervals to admire the monument, while the benches close by are a favourite spot for Vienna's elderly population. Vienna's younger generation hangs out here, too, smoking, drinking on the grass and selling dope; the authorities occasionally move the scene on a few hundred metres or so, but without any great enthusiasm.

MAK

One of the most enjoyable museums in Vienna is the **Österreichisches Museum für angewandte Kunst** (Austrian Museum of Applied Art), better known simply as the

MAK (Tues 10am–midnight, Wed–Sun 10am–6pm; öS90/€6.54; *www.mak.at*), north of the Stadtpark. The highlights of its superlative, highly eclectic selection of *objets d'art*, stretching from the Romanesque period to the twentieth century, are Klimt's *Stoclet Frieze* and the unrivalled collection of Wiener Werkstätte products. But what really sets it apart is the museum's interior design, for which the MAK gave some of Austria's leading designers free rein to create a unique series of rooms. At the ticket office in the beautiful, glass-roofed courtyard, with its double-decker loggia, you'll be given a plan of the museum in German and English. On the wall of each room there's a slightly pretentious, bilingual introduction by the designer, and a leaflet in English cataloguing and explaining each exhibit. Temporary exhibitions are held, for the most part, in the museum's Ausstellungshalle, whose main entrance is on Weiskirchnerstrasse. If you've got the time and energy, don't neglect the museum's crowded, off-beat **Studiensammlung** (Study Collection) in the basement.

The ground floor

To follow the collection chronologically, you should begin with the **Romanik, Gotik, Renaissance** room, on the ground floor, where the minimalist display cabinets are beautifully offset by deep cobalt-blue walls. Aside from a few pieces of furniture and some very early thirteenth-century ecclesiastical garments, most of the exhibits are items of Italian sixteenth-century majolica, decorated with mythological scenes and grotesque faces. The main focus of the room next door – **Barock, Rokoko, Klassizismus** – is a room within a room. Acquired by the museum in 1912, the mid-eighteenth-century Porcelain Room was removed piece by piece from the Palais Dubsky in Brno and reassembled here. It derives its name from the ceramics that have been used to decorate everything right down to the wall panelling, candelabra, chandeliers and table-tops.

As you cross the main courtyard to the next set of rooms, the designers begin to impose themselves more emphatically. **Barock, Rokoko** consists of two long, central glass cabinets hung from the ceiling displaying Bohemian, Silesian and Venetian glass, with examples of Italian, French and Flemish lacework set against a black background all along the walls. The **Empire, Biedermeier** room is much quirkier: a parade of early nineteenth-century Viennese chairs, arranged as if for a game of musical chairs, occupies the central space, while, up above, the cornice is broken by fast-moving, multilingual LED text. To take it all in, sit down on the aluminium mock-Biedermeier sofa.

The museum's pièce de résistance, though, in terms of design, comes in the **Historismus, Jugendstil** room. Two parallel shadow screens, running the length of the room, create a corridor down which you can stroll, whilst admiring the changing geometry of chair design over the last hundred years in silhouette. If you want a 3D look at the chairs, you can simply go round the back of the screens. Next door, the final ground-floor room is devoted to tiles and carpets from the **Orient**, covering the walls and floors to create a peaceful, mosque-like atmosphere.

The first floor

Three rooms on the **first floor** are given over to the permanent collection. One room is devoted to the **Wiener Werkstätte** (Vienna Workshops), founded in 1903 by the architect Josef Hoffmann, the designer Kolo Moser and the rich Jewish textile merchant Fritz Waerndorfer. The range and scope of the WW is staggering, and just about every field in which they were active is represented here from jewellery and metalwork, primarily by Dagobert Peche and Hoffmann, to an upper gallery containing the WW's prolific fashion offshoot. One of the finest works is Kolo Moser's wood-inlaid writing desk, which includes a retractable armchair that can be slotted into place to make the whole thing appear like a chest of drawers.

The **Jugendstil**, **Art Deco** room is dominated by Gustav Klimt's working designs for his *Stoclet Frieze*, a series of mosaics commissioned in 1904 for the dining room of the Palais Stoclet in Brussels. Predominantly gold, with Byzantine and Egyptian overtones, the frieze marks the climax of Klimt's highly ornamental phase (the finished product was inlaid with semiprecious stones). Aside from the Klimt, there's furniture by the likes of Otto Wagner and Kolo Moser, along with contemporaries Charles Rennie Mackintosh and Margaret Macdonald, and an amazing selection of Bohemian glass. A staircase leads up to an entire room of contemporary applied art. More recent work is displayed in the adjacent **20. Jahrhundert, Architektur, Design**, including a monochrome room installation by Jasper Morrison, architectural models by the Austrian deconstructionists Coop Himmelblau, and Frank Gehry's wonderful cardboard armchair.

Postsparkasse

The final segment of the Ringstrasse, from Stubentor to Urania, was the last to be laid out, erected mostly in the decade before World War I, and contains one of Vienna's most celebrated pieces of modern architecture, the **Postsparkasse** (Mon–Wed & Fri 8am–3pm, Thurs 8am–5.30pm; free), completed in 1912 by Otto Wagner. The building still functions as a savings bank, and from the outside it looks something like a giant safety deposit box, its otherwise smooth facade studded with aluminium rivets, used to hold the thin grey marble slabs in place. Aluminium – a new and expensive material at the time – is also used for the delicate glazed canopy over the entrance and, most famously, for the heating cowls, which rise up into the main banking hall like giant curling tongs. Sadly, some of the interior furnishings have been carelessly modified, but the curved glass ceiling and the thick glass tiles in the floor survive intact. There's also a model of the building and regular exhibitions on modern architecture on display in the main banking hall.

The Vorstädte (inner suburbs)

A horseshoe of seven districts – the third to the ninth – form the inner suburbs known as the **Vorstädte**. Neatly confined between the Ringstrasse and the Gürtel, they have remained predominantly residential, though each one is cut through with a busy commercial thoroughfare, the largest of which is the city's main shopping drag, **Mariahilferstrasse**, which divides the sixth and seventh districts. Sights in the Vorstädte are widely dispersed, so it pays to be selective. The one sight that no visitor should miss is the **Belvedere**, in the third district, with its formal gardens and twin-set of Baroque palaces, which house some wonderful works of art. Two other sights that positively heave with visitors in summer are the wacky **Hundertwasserhaus**, also in the third district, and the **Freud Museum** in the ninth. Even for those not keen on military paraphernalia, the **Arsenal** is worth visiting for its quasi-Moorish architecture alone.

Hundertwasserhaus and KunstHausWien

In 1983 the ageing hippie artist **Friedensreich Hundertwasser** (1928–2000) was commissioned to redesign some council housing on the corner of Löwengasse and Kegelgasse, in an unassuming residential area of Landstrasse, Vienna's third district. Following his philosophy that "the straight line is godless", he transformed the dour apartment block into **Hundertwasserhaus** (tram N to Hetzgasse from Schwedenplatz U-Bahn), a higgledy-piggledy, childlike jumble of brightly coloured textures that caught the popular imagination, while enraging the architectural establishment. It certainly runs the gamut of styles: a frenzy of oriel windows, loggias, ceramic pillars, glass embellishments, a gilded onion dome, roof gardens and even a slice of the pre-1983 building.

Understandably, the residents were none too happy when hordes of pilgrims began ringing on their doorbells, asking to be shown round, so Hundertwasser obliged with an even tackier shopping arcade opposite, called **Kalke Village**, providing a café (with a stream running along the bar) and information centre to draw the crowds away from the apartments (which are closed to the public), while simultaneously increasing the sales outlets for his artwork. Here, you can get the full Hundertwasser experience, the most disconcerting aspect of which is his penchant for uneven floors.

There's another of Hundertwasser's Gaudiesque conversions, **KunstHausWien** (daily 10am–7pm; öS95/€6.90; Mon half-price; *www.kunsthauswien.com*), three blocks north up Untere Weissgerberstrasse, though it has been less successful at attracting visitors; it features another shop and café, and a gallery devoted to Hundertwasser's own life and works. The gallery also hosts temporary exhibitions by other headline-grabbing contemporary artists. Another Hundertwasser project, the rebuilding of a rubbish incineration plant, Fernwärme Wien, is visible from the U-Bahn to Heligenstadt.

The Belvedere

The **Belvedere** (*www.belvedere.at*) is the finest palace complex in the whole of Vienna, at least from the outside. Two magnificent Baroque mansions, designed in the early eighteenth century by Lukas von Hildebrandt, face each other across a sloping formal garden, commanding a superb view over central Vienna. The man for whom all this was built was **Prince Eugène of Savoy**, Austria's greatest military leader, whose campaigns against the Turks helped push them back from the gates of the city. Today, the loftier of the two palaces, the **Oberes Belvedere**, houses one of the most popular art galleries in Vienna, with an unrivalled collection of paintings by Gustav Klimt, plus a few choice works by Egon Schiele and Oskar Kokoschka. A single ticket (öS120/€8.72) lets you into both parts of the Belvedere (Tues–Sun 10am–6pm); take tram #71 one stop from Schwarzenbergplatz – or just walk – to get to the **Unteres Belvedere**, from where you can either walk through the garden or jump on tram #D from the Ringstrasse to get to the Oberes Belvedere.

Unteres Belvedere

Completed in 1716, at the bottom of the formal gardens, the **Unteres Belvedere** (Lower Belvedere) is a relatively simple, one-storey garden palace, built for Prince Eugène's personal use, rather than for affairs of state or entertainment. Inside, however, it preserves more of its original, lavish decor than the Oberes Belvedere, and for that reason alone it's worth exploring the **Barock-Museum** now installed in its rooms.

The highlight of the palace is the richly decorated **Marmorsaal** (Marble Hall), which extends over two floors at the central axis of the building. The whole hall is a hymn to Prince Eugène's military prowess, white stucco trophies and reliefs contrasting with the rich red marbling. Extra depth is given to the walls through trompe l'oeil niches and balconies, and to the ceiling by illusory moulding, leading up to Martino Altomonte's fresco featuring Prince Eugène himself enjoying his apotheosis in the guise of Apollo. At ground level, you can admire the original lead statues from the Donnerbrunnen on Neuermarkt, sculpted by Georg Raphael Donner (1693–1741).

At the far end of the wing lies the **Groteskensaal**, with a decor of "grotesque" birds and beasts, and fanciful floral murals. Displayed here is a series of bizarre, hyperrealist "character heads", carved by the eccentric sculptor Franz Xaver Messerschmidt

(1732–83), each depicting a different grimace. Next comes the **Marmorgalerie**, a richly stuccoed white-and-red reception room built by Prince Eugène to house his trio of classical statues from Herculaneum (now in Dresden). By far the most mind-blowing room, though, is the adjacent **Goldkabinett**, a cabinet of mirrors, dotted with oriental vases and adorned with yet more grotesques painted onto a vast expanse of gaudy, 23-carat-gold panelling. Dominating this small room is the *Apotheosis of Prince Eugène*, an explosion of marble by Balthasar Permoser, in which a tangle of figures struggles to stay on the plinth.

The Goldkabinett marks the end of the Barock-Museum, but there are further artistic treasures in the former orangery, down the steps from the palace. Converted into stables by Maria Theresia, the orangery now houses the **Museum mittelalterlicher Kunst** (Museum of Medieval Art), housing a collection of sculptures and paintings, the greater part of which dates from the fifteenth century, and includes works by Tyrolean artist Michael Pacher (c1430–c1490).

Oberes Belvedere

Purpose-built for the lavish masked balls, receptions and firework displays organized by the prince, the **Oberes Belvedere** (Upper Belvedere), completed in 1724, is at least twice as big and twice as grand as the Unteres Belvedere from the outside. Guests would pull up in their coaches underneath the central *sala terrena*, which was glassed in during the nineteenth century and now serves as the ticket office and entrance area of the museum. To the right is the trompe l'oeil-frescoed **Gartensaal**, occasionally used for temporary exhibitions; to the left lies the bookshop and the café. The permanent galleries, displaying nineteenth- and twentieth-century art, are located on the first and second floors. The exact position of the paintings on the first floor changes from year to year, and you may find a handful of the paintings described below are on tour elsewhere.

If you're here for the Klimts, then head straight upstairs to the **Marmorsaal**, a lighter and loftier concoction than the one in the Unteres Belvedere; it was here that the Austrian State Treaty of 1955 was signed, guaranteeing the Allied withdrawal in return for Austria's neutrality. The permanent collection usually begins in the room to the right of the Marmorsaal with works by Van Gogh, Richard Gerstl, Egon Schiele and Auguste Rodin.

GUSTAV KLIMT

The gallery's works by **Gustav Klimt** (1862–1918) are displayed along with works by his contemporaries, Kolo Moser, Carl Moll and Max Kurzweil. Klimt's ethereal, slightly aloof *Portrait of Sonja Knips*, from 1898, marked his breakthrough as an independent artist, and was the first of several portrait commissions of the wives of the city's wealthy Jewish businessmen. Two later examples are the *Portrait of Fritza Riedler*, from 1906, in which Klimt's love of ornamentation comes to the fore, and the *Portrait of Adele Bloch-Bauer I*, painted at the height of his "golden phase" in 1908, with the subject almost engulfed in gilded Mycenaean spirals and Egyptian eyes.

The culmination of Klimt's golden age is his monumental work *The Kiss*, depicting Klimt himself embracing his long-term partner, Emilie Flöge. Klimt's use of gilding – derived partly from his father, who was an engraver – proved extremely popular, and the painting was bought for the Austrian state during the *Kunstschau* of 1908, a rare seal of official approval for an artist whose work was mostly frowned upon by the establishment. The gallery also owns eight landscapes on square canvases painted at the Flöge family house on the Attersee in the Salzkammergut. As a way of relaxing, Klimt liked to paint landscapes alfresco straight onto canvas, without preliminary sketches. The results are rich, almost flat, one-dimensional tapestries of colour – some almost pointillist – which are easy on the eye and sold extremely well in the salons.

During Klimt's late period, he dispensed with gold, and became more influenced by Japanese art and the primary colours of Fauvists such as Matisse. The results can be seen in the doll-like *Portrait of Adele Bloch-Bauer II*, painted in 1912. Klimt regularly worked on several canvases at once, often painting his models in the nude before clothing them, as is clearly demonstrated in *The Bride*, discovered unfinished in his studio at his death.

EGON SCHIELE

Klimt actively supported younger artists like **Egon Schiele** (1890–1918), introducing them to his patrons, allowing them to exhibit in shows he organized, and even, in the case of Schiele, passing on his young models after he'd finished with them. Such was the case with the 17-year-old Wally Neuzil, with whom Schiele enjoyed a four-year affair. *Death and the Maiden* is a disturbingly dispassionate farewell portrait to Wally, painted in 1915, the year they split up. In it, Wally clings to Schiele, who is depicted in deathly, detached decay. The gallery also owns one of Schiele's most famous erotic oil paintings, *The Embrace*, a double nude portrait of the artist and his model.

Schiele went on to marry Edith Harms, who came from a respectable middle-class family, and is depicted in *The Artist's Wife*. Edith's pregnancy in spring 1918 was the inspiration for *The Family*, Schiele's last great painting, which remained unfinished at the time of his death from the influenza epidemic that had claimed Edith's life, and that of their unborn child, just three days earlier (and Klimt's eight months before that). Schiele is the father figure, the child is Schiele's nephew, Toni, but Edith had reservations about posing nude and is clearly not the model for the mother.

Often displayed alongside Schiele's works is **Richard Gerstl**'s manic *Laughing Self-Portrait* from 1908, a deeply disturbing image given that its subject was deeply depressed at the time – his lover, Mathilde, had gone back to her husband, the composer Arnold Schönberg. Gerstl committed suicide the very same year at the age of 28.

OSKAR KOKOSCHKA AND OTHERS

The works by **Oskar Kokoschka** (1886–1980) mostly date from his first ten creative years when he lived in Vienna. After 1915, Kokoschka only occasionally returned, usually staying with his mother, an affectionate portrait of whom hangs in the gallery. Kokoschka's several portraits displayed here contrast sharply with those of Schiele: "A person is not a *still* life", Kokoschka insisted, and he encouraged his sitters to move about and talk, so as to make his portrayals more animated. Kokoschka's *Still-Life with Dead Mutton* from 1909, was painted in the kitchen of the art collector Dr Oskar Reichel, who had commissioned him to paint a portrait of his son. There's a smattering of other artists' works here, too, among them a characteristically dark, intense work by **Emil Nolde**, a Cubist offering from **Fernand Léger** and **Max Oppenheimer**'s evocative *Klingier Quartet*.

HISTORICISM, REALISM, IMPRESSIONISM

The seven rooms in the west wing, on the other side of the Marmorsaal, are given over to late nineteenth-century paintings. The first few rooms are crowded with works by French Impressionists, among them Manet and Monet, and their immediate predecessors, like Camille Corot. Less well known, and less well thought of now, is the Austrian artist **Hans Makart** (1840–84), whose influence went far beyond painting. He was a high-society figure and, appropriately enough, the room devoted to his works has been decked out with sumptuous furnishings much as Makart's own studio was. On one side hangs the gigantic, triumphant flesh-fest of *Bacchus and Ariadne*; on the opposite wall in long vertical panels are four of the *Five Senses*, featuring typically sensuous Makart nudes.

In the adjacent room, you can admire more work by Makart, whose fame eclipsed several of his more innovative contemporaries, among them **Anton Romako** (1832–89), so much so that the latter's death was rumoured to be suicide. Compared with Makart's studied flattery, it's easy to see why Romako's uncomfortably perceptive psychological portraits were less popular. Romako's most famous work, *Tegetthoff at the Naval Battle of Lissa*, hangs in the final room, and again reveals his unconventional approach; there's no hint of heroics, but simply fear and foreboding in the expressions of the crew.

Arsenal (Heeresgeschichtliches Museum)

Further south still, down Arsenalstrasse, lies the city's former **Arsenal**, a huge complex of barracks and munitions factories, built on strategic heights above the city in the wake of the 1848 revolution. At the same time, the Emperor Franz-Josef I ordered the construction of the city's first purpose-built museum, the **Heeresgeschichtliches Museum** (Museum of Military History; daily except Fri 9am–5pm; öS70/€5.09; *www.bmlv.gv.at/hgm*), designed to glorify the imperial army. All Vienna's leading architects were invited to compete for the commission, and the winning design, a wonderful red-brick edifice by the Ringstrasse architect Theophil Hansen was completed in neo-Byzantine style in 1856. The ticket office is in the vaulted foyer, or **Feldherrnhalle** (Hall of the Generals), which is crowded with life-size marble statues of pre-1848 Austrian military leaders. Pick up the museum's excellent audioguide and head upstairs to the **Ruhmshalle** (Hall of Fame) on the first floor, a huge domed hall of polished marble, gilded, arcaded and decorated with worthy frescoes depicting Austrian military victories over the centuries.

The museum kicks off with the **Thirty Years' War** and an informative video showing how hellish it was to try and fire a musket. The rich pickings to be had during the **Turkish Wars** proved a useful incentive to the imperial troops fighting the Ottomans, and a fine selection of trophies is displayed in the **west wing**, including the vast audience tent of the Grand Vizier. To continue chronologically, you need to retrace your steps and walk to the far room of the **east wing**, which deals with the **Napoleonic Wars**, splendid early nineteenth-century military uniforms, and concludes with paintings of the disastrous **Austro-Prussian War**, which the Habsburgs lost at Königgrätz in 1866.

A large section of the ground-floor west wing is taken up with the glorious **uniforms of the imperial army**, and their opponents, but by far the most famous exhibits in this wing relate to the **Archduke Franz Ferdinand**. In particular, you can view the splendid Gräf & Stift convertible in which the archduke and his wife, Sophie, were shot dead on June 28, 1914. Even more macabre is the archduke's reverentially preserved blood-stained light-blue tunic and his unblemished, slightly comical hat with green feathers. The final rooms of the wing are devoted to **World War I** memorabilia. There are some great posters and paintings, including Albin Egger Lienz's chilling tribute *To the Unknown Soldier*, whose repetitive image of advancing infantry perfectly captures the mechanical slaughter of modern warfare.

Beyond the café on the ground floor, the **Republic and Dictatorship** section takes you through the heady, violent interwar years that ended with the Anschluss. You can view the couch on which Dollfuss died during the abortive Nazi coup of 1934, and the bust of Hitler that used to stand in the Hall of Fame during the Nazi period. The last room in the east wing is concerned with Austria's **Naval Power**, not something you associate with a land-locked country, though, of course, under the Habsburgs, the empire had access to the Adriatic.

St Marxer Friedhof

In the 1780s, the Emperor Josef II closed all the inner-city cemeteries and decreed that all burials, for health reasons, should take place outside the city walls. The first of these out-of-town graveyards, founded in 1784, was the **St Marxer Friedhof** (St Mark's Cemetery; daily 7am–dusk), by the Landstrasser Gürtel (tram #18 or #71). Planted with a rather lovely selection of trees, the cemetery today gives little indication of the bleak and forbidding place it must have been when, on a rainy night in December 1791, **Mozart** was given a pauper's burial, in an unmarked mass grave with no one present but the grave-diggers.

Though to contemporary minds the bare facts of Mozart's final journey seem a particularly cruel end for someone considered by many to have been the greatest composer ever, the reality is less tragic. In the immediate period after Josef II's reforms, mass burials were the rule; only the very wealthy could afford to have a family vault, and the tending of individual graves was virtually unknown. Funeral services took place in churches (Mozart's in the Stephansdom), and it was not customary for mourners to accompany the funeral cortege to cemeteries. In fact, bodies were only allowed to be taken to the cemetery after nightfall, where they were left in the mortuary overnight for burial the next day. By the mid-nineteenth century, however, the Viennese had adopted the lavish tastes for funerals and monuments for which they remain famous to this day. It was in this context that it became a scandal that no one knew where Mozart was buried. In 1844, his wife Constanze returned to try and locate the grave, but to little avail as graves were usually emptied every eight years to make way for more corpses. The most Constanze could find out was that he had probably been buried three or four rows down from the cemetery's central monumental cross. In 1859, the Mozartgrab was raised around this area, featuring a pillar, broken in half to symbolize his untimely death.

To get to the Mozartgrab, head up the main avenue and bear left. You'll also find the graves of several other eighteenth-century artists here – a plan at the entrance to the cemetery locates the most famous graves.

Kaiserliches Hofmobiliendepot (Imperial Furniture Collection)

Set back from Mariahilferstrasse, the city's busy, mainstream shopping street which separates Vienna's sixth and seventh districts, is the expensively revamped **Kaiserliches Hofmobiliendepot** (daily 9am–5pm; oS90/€6.54), at Andreasgasse 7, which, despite its uninviting title, is a surprisingly interesting museum – something like a cross between a junk warehouse and an applied arts study collection. Established by Maria Theresia in 1747, the Hofmobiliendepot basically supplied all the furniture needed by the Habsburgs for their various palaces, which, as a rule, were only furnished when members of the family stayed there. It was also a dumping ground for those items of furniture which had gone out of fashion. After 1918, the depot found itself with over 650,000 items, and no imperial family to serve, so it became a museum.

The first room, **Das Erbe** (The Heritage), gives you some idea of the sheer scale of the collection, with its forests of candelabra and coatstands, not to mention the bevy of Biedermeier spittoons. The **Habsburgersaal** panders to imperial nostalgia with Crown Prince Rudolf's ebony high-chair, scallop-shell cot, and, later on, funeral crown, while Maximilian of Mexico's serpent-wrapped walking stick and vastly oversized sombrero have to be seen to be believed. What follows is a whole series of reconstructed **period interiors** ranging from one of Prince Eugène's wonderful chinoiserie rooms to the aforementioned Rudolf's Turkish boudoir. More fun, however, is the **Hygienemöbel**

(Sanitary Furniture), which displays imperial commodes, bed-pans and more spittoons through the ages.

Alsergrund

Alsergrund – Vienna's large, roughly triangular ninth district to the north of the Innere Stadt – is dominated by its medical institutions and associations. A vast swath of land is taken up with the **Allgemeines Krankenhaus** (General Hospital), established by Josef II in 1784, and now more than double its original size. The following year, Josef founded the **Josephinum**, an academy for training military surgeons, next door. Since then, various university science faculties have relocated here, and the area remains popular with doctors and medical students, as it has done since **Freud**'s day – his museum is now Alsergrund's chief tourist attraction.

Josephinum
Founded in 1785 to the northeast of the Allgemeines Krankenhaus, the **Josephinum** (Mon–Fri 9am–3pm; öS20/€1.45) is housed in an austere silver-grey palace, set back from Währinger Strasse behind a set of imposing wrought-iron railings (take any tram heading up Währinger Strasse from U-Bahn Schottentor). Having observed at first hand the primitive techniques used by army surgeons during his military campaigns, the Emperor Josef II decided to set up an Institute for Military Surgery. The institute was closed in 1872, and now houses, among other things, a museum containing a remarkable collection of anatomical wax models, the Wachspräparate Sammlung, commissioned by Josef II from a group of Florentine sculptors in 1780. The serene, life-size human figures are for the most part presented as if partially dissected, revealing the body's nerves, muscles and veins in full technicolour. Equally beautiful are the original display cases, fashioned from rosewood and fitted with huge, bobbly, hand-blown panes of Venetian glass.

Sigmund Freud-Museum
Sigmund Freud moved to the second floor of Berggasse 19 in 1891 and stayed here until June 4, 1938, when he and his family fled to London. His apartment, now the **Sigmund Freud-Museum** (daily: July–Sept 9am–6pm; Oct–June 9am–5pm; öS60/€5.09; *www.freud-museum.at*), is a place of pilgrimage, even though Freud took almost all his possessions – bar his library, which he sold – with him into exile. His hat, coat and walking stick are still here, and there's home movie footage from the 1930s, but the only room with any original decor – and consequently any atmosphere – is the waiting room, which contains the odd oriental rug, a cabinet of antiquities, and some burgundy-upholstered furniture, sent back from London by his daughter Anna after the war. The rest of the flat is taken up with a couple of rooms of photographs, a library, with a CD-ROM on Freud, and a shop. There's a file available with English translations of the museum's captions, or an audioguide in English (for an extra öS20/€1.45).

Schuberts Geburthaus
Further north, at Nussdorfer Strasse 54, stands **Schuberts Geburthaus** (Tues–Sun 9am–12.15pm & 1–4.30pm; öS25/€1.82), the unassuming, two-storey house where the composer was born in 1797. Inside, the charming courtyard has been lovingly restored, with wooden balconies festooned with geranium-filled flower boxes. As so often with Vienna's musical memorials, however, there has been no attempt to reconstruct Schubert's family home, which would have consisted of just one room and a kitchen (the latter survives). In any case, Schubert would have had very little recollection of the

SIGMUND FREUD (1856–1939)

Few people are so intimately associated with one place as **Sigmund Freud** is with Vienna. He may have been born to a Jewish wool merchant in Freiberg in Moravia in 1856, and died in 1939 in exile in London, but in the intervening 83 years, he spent most of his life in Vienna. The family moved to the capital when Freud was just four years old, and in 1873 he entered the university's medical faculty determined to be a scientist. He took three years longer than usual to complete his degree, and then decided to switch tack and train as a medic at the Allgemeines Krankenhaus. In 1887 Freud began practising as a neuropathologist, experimenting with cocaine, electrotherapy and hypnosis, before eventually coming up with the "pressure technique", using a couch for the first time and asking questions, while pressing his hand on the patient's forehead. He later switched to the method of "free association", during which the patient says whatever comes into their mind. "The aim is modest," Freud said when describing his new science: "to turn neurotic misery into common unhappiness."

In 1896, Freud coined the term "psychoanalysis", and four years later published the book which established his originality, *The Interpretation of Dreams*. In it, Freud argued that "all dreams represent the fulfilment of wishes", and that these wishes are often (but not always) sexual. Freud's impact on twentieth-century thought has been profound, and several of his discoveries – the death wish, the Oedipus complex, transference, the Freudian slip, penis envy, the oral, anal and phallic stages of childhood, and so on – have become common parlance.

In 1902, Freud founded the Psychoanalytical Society, which met every Wednesday evening in his apartment, his wife serving *Guglhupf* and coffee, while academic papers were read and discussed. Freud ruled his disciples with an iron hand, ejecting anyone who disagreed with him, most famously Carl Jung, the Swiss psychoanalyst, in 1913.

Though Jung accused Freud of having slept with his wife's attractive younger sister, Minna, who lived with the family in Berggasse, Freud was in fact a disappointingly conventional Viennese paterfamilias. "What a terrible man! I am sure he has never been unfaithful to his wife. It is quite abnormal and scandalous," reported one of his fans, the French poet Countess Anna de Noailles, after meeting him. He was happily married all his life to Martha Bernays, a good Jewish *Hausfrau*, who gave birth to and brought up six healthy children. He saw patients without appointment daily from three to four in the afternoon, using the proceeds to buy the (occasionally erotic) antiquities that filled his study; afterwards he would write until as late as three in the morning. Every afternoon, he would walk the entire circuit of the Ringstrasse at a brisk pace; every Saturday evening he played the card game Tarock; every Sunday in summer, the family would dress up in traditional Austrian peasant gear, right down to their leather underpants, and go mushroom picking in the Wienerwald.

In 1923, he was diagnosed as having cancer of the jaw (he was an inveterate cigar-smoker) and given just five years to live. In the end, he lived another sixteen years in some considerable pain. Shortly after the Anschluss in March 1938, the SS raided Freud's flat and confiscated the family's passports and money. Only through the efforts of his friends was Freud able to escape to Britain on June 3, 1938. Four of his sisters were not allowed to join him and died in the Holocaust. Finally, just over a year after having arrived in London, Freud's doctor fulfilled their eleven-year-old pact, and, when the pain became too much, gave him a lethal dose of morphine.

place as the family moved down the road, to Säulengasse 3, when he was four years old. So, beyond admiring the composer's broken spectacles and his half-brother's piano, there's little to do here but listen to the excerpts from his music on the headphones provided.

To reach the museum, take tram #38 or #39 five stops from U-Bahn Schottentor. Schubert's brother's house – 4, Kettenbrückengasse 6, near the Naschmarkt – in which

FRANZ SCHUBERT

Of all the composers associated with Vienna, **Franz Schubert** (1797–1828) fulfils more Romantic criteria than most. He died of syphilis at the age of just 31 (younger even than Mozart), he really was penniless (unlike Mozart, who was just careless with his money), and he never lived to hear any of his symphonies performed (the first one wasn't published until fifty years after his death). The picture would be complete had he died whilst writing his *Eighth (Unfinished) Symphony* – in fact, he abandoned it before he died, and went on, instead, to complete a *Ninth Symphony*.

Schubert was born the eleventh child of an impoverished teacher. At the age of nine or ten, he was sent to study with the organist at the local church on Marktgasse, where he had been baptized. He went on to become the church organist, and composed his first mass for the church at the age of 17. In between times, he served as a chorister at the Burgkapelle, where he studied under Antonio Salieri, Mozart's famous court rival, before working as an assistant teacher at his father's school for three years. At the end of this period, he became a freelance musician, thanks to financial help from his friends, and spent two summers as music tutor for the Esterházy family. His intensely lyrical chamber music, copious songs – in one particularly productive year he wrote 145 of them – and piano works were popular amongst the Viennese bourgeoisie, and he performed at numerous informal social gatherings, which became known as "*Schubertiaden*".

In his personal life, he was fairly dissolute: a heavy drinker, who frequented "revolutionary" circles, he remained unmarried, his sexual appetite confined to prostitutes. Towards the end of his short life, he fulfilled a lifetime's ambition and met up with his hero Beethoven, though there are no reliable details of the encounter. He was one of the torchbearers at the great composer's funeral, and was buried, according to his wishes, three graves away from him in Währinger Friedhof the following year (he now lies with Beethoven in the Zentralfriedhof; see p.139).

the composer died, has been made into a similarly unenthralling museum; Tues–Sun 9am–12.15pm & 1–4.30pm; öS25/€1.82.

The Vororte (outer suburbs)

Vienna's vast outer suburbs, or **Vororte**, have a scattering of interesting sights, many of them outdoor attractions, that call for a targeted approach, relying on the transport system to get you around. Top of the list, and one of Vienna's most popular tourist attractions, is the Habsburgs' former summer residence, **Schönbrunn**, to the west of the city centre. The palace boasts some of the best Rococo interiors in central Europe, while the surrounding **Schlosspark** is home to the **Tiergarten**, Vienna's zoo. Nearby is the newly revamped **Technisches Museum**, and further west is the much wilder parkland of the **Lainzer Tiergarten**, a former royal hunting ground that's now a haven for wildlife.

After Schönbrunn, the most popular attraction in the suburbs is the **Prater**, the vast city park and funfair on the east bank of the Danube Canal, famous, above all, for its giant Ferris wheel, or Riesenrad. Another possible day-trip can be made to the **Wienerwald** (Vienna Woods), the forested hills that stretch from the alpine foothills to the southwest of Vienna right up to the doorstep of the capital and offer glorious views over the entire city. Finally, there's the **Zentralfriedhof**, Vienna's awesome Central Cemetery, featuring copious quantities of artistic corpses, including those of Beethoven, Schubert, Brahms, Schönberg and the Strauss family.

Schönbrunn

Compared with the hotchpotch that is the Hofburg, the Habsburgs' summer residence of **Schönbrunn** (*www.schoenbrunn.at*) is everything an imperial palace should be: grandiose, symmetrical and thoroughly intimidating. Built over the course of the eighteenth century to a design by Johann Bernhard Fischer von Erlach, it contains nearly 1500 rooms and, in its day, would have housed more than a thousand servants.

The exterior is plain, but inside, there's a superb array of Baroque and Rococo **Prunkräume** (State Rooms), dating from the time of the Empress Maria Theresia, the first of the Habsburgs to make Schönbrunn the official imperial summer residence. There's also a fine collection of imperial carriages in the outbuilding of the **Wagenburg**, plus temporary exhibitions in the **Orangerie**. In the **Schlosspark**, you'll find the **Tiergarten** far more uplifting than most inner-city zoos, which combines easily with visits to the nearby **Palmenhaus** and **Irrgarten** (Maze).

Prunkräume

Compared to the sterility of the Hofburg's state apartments, Schönbrunn's **Prunkräume** are a positive visual feast. That said, not every room is worthy of close attention, so don't feel bad about walking briskly through some of them. Whichever tour you're on (see box below), the entrance is via the **Blauerstiege** (Blue Staircase) on the ground floor of the west wing. If you're on the "Imperial Tour", you'll miss the nine private apartments of Franz-Josef – no great loss – entering at **Elisabeth's Salon**, which smack even less of her personality than those in the Hofburg. The decor, in fact, mostly dates from the time of the Empress **Maria Theresia**, a century or so earlier, and the walls of the next three rooms are lined with portraits of the empress's numerous offspring. Two of her sons went on to become emperors, Josef II and Leopold II, but the most famous of the lot was her youngest daughter, **Marie Antoinette**, who married Louis XVI and followed him to the guillotine in 1793. Under her portrait in the nursery is the only piece of furniture sent back to Vienna by the French after her execution.

The first of the more elaborate state apartments is the **Spiegelsaal** (Mirror Hall), where, in 1762, the seven-year-old Mozart performed a duet with his older sister, Nannerl, in the presence of the Empress Maria Theresia and family, and famously

---

VISITING SCHÖNBRUNN

Approaches to the palace suffer from the roar of traffic from the nearby Linke Wienzeile and Schönbrunner Schloss Strasse. Consequently, the best way to **get there** is to head straight for the Meidlinger Tor on Grünbergstrasse from U-Bahn Schönbrunn, rather than struggle along the multilane freeway to the main gates. You could also continue one stop further on the U-Bahn to Hietzing, and dive into the park via the Hietzinger Tor on Hietzinger Hauptstrasse. This enables you to peek at the nearby Hofpavillon Hietzing, the imperial family's private U-Bahn station (Tues–Sun 1–4.30pm; öS25/€1.82), built in extravagant Jugendstil by Otto Wagner in 1899 (and only used twice).

To visit the Prunkräume (daily: April–Oct 8.30am–5pm; Nov–March 8.30am–4.30pm), head for the ticket office on the ground floor of the east wing immediately, as visits are carefully choreographed. Here, you'll be allocated a visiting time; if the palace is busy, you may have to wait several hours, in which case you should head off into the gardens or visit one of Schönbrunn's other sights. There's a choice of two tours: the "Imperial Tour" (öS95/€6.90), which takes in 22 state rooms (skipping the palace's most magnificent Rococo delights), and the "Grand Tour" (öS125/€9.08), which includes all 40 rooms. For both tours, you're given a hand-held audioguide in English. There are also guided visits of the "Grand Tour" in English; these take an hour and cost öS150/€10.90.

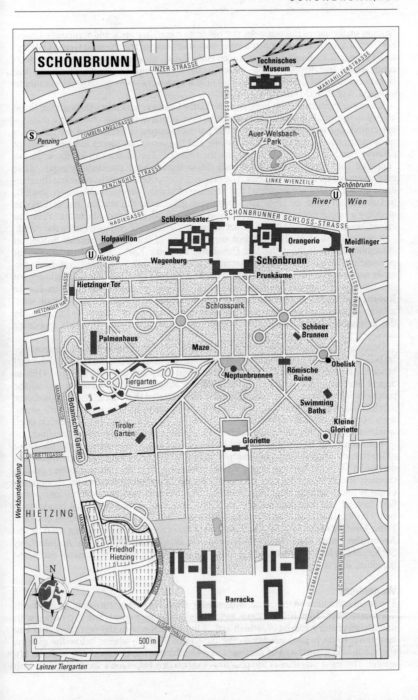

SCHÖNBRUNN

LINZER STRASSE

Technisches Museum

MARIAHILFERSTRASSE

SCHLOSSALLEE

CUMBERLANDSTRASSE

S Penzing

Auer-Welsbach-Park

PENZINGHER STRASS

LINKE WIENZEILE

HADIKGASSE

SCHÖNBRUNNER SCHLOSS-STRASSE

Schönbrunn U

River Wien

Schlosstheater

Hofpavillon

U Hietzing

Wagenburg

Orangerie

Schönbrunn

Meidlinger Tor

Prunkäume

GRÜNBERGSTRASSE

Hietzinger Tor

HIETZINGER HAUPTSTRASSE

Schlosspark

Palmenhaus

Schöner Brunnen

Maze

Obelisk

Neptunbrunnen

Römische Ruine

Tiergarten

MAXINGSTRASSE

Botanischer Garten

Tiroler Garten

Swimming Baths

Kleine Gloriette

Gloriette

GLORIETTEGASSE

Werkbundsiedlung

HIETZING

MAXINGSTRASSE

Friedhof Hietzing

N

GASSMANNSTRASSE

SCHÖNBRUNNER ALLEE

Barracks

ELISABETHALLEE

0   500 m

▽ Lainzer Tiergarten

"sprang on the lap of the empress, put his arms round her neck and vigorously kissed her", according to his father. From here, both tours take in the splendid **Great Gallery**, a vast long hall, heavy with gilded stucco embellishments and originally lit by over 4000 candles. Of the three ceiling frescoes by Guglielmo Guglielmi glorifying the Habsburgs, the last – depicting Austria's military prowess – was destroyed by bombing in World War II, and is therefore a copy.

It's worth venturing from here into the **Little Gallery**, which lies through the three arches to the south of the Great Gallery, to take a peek at the two chinoiserie rooms – one round, one oval – to either side. The parquet flooring is sublime, as are the oriental lacquer panels set into the wainscoting, and the numerous pieces of blue-and-white Chinese porcelain, that give the rooms their names. The final room for those on the "Imperial Tour" is the **Ceremonial Hall**, displaying five large paintings by pupils of the court painter Martin van Meytens. The majority are concerned with recording the elaborate festivities that accompanied the wedding of Maria Theresia's eldest son, Josef II, to Isabella of Parma, in 1760. The magnifying glass, over the section that depicts the wedding's opera performance, helps you pick out Mozart and his father from the crowd, though the family didn't in fact arrive in Vienna until two years after the event.

It was next door in the beautiful surroundings of the **Blue Chinese Salon**, on November 11, 1918, that the last Habsburg, Emperor Karl I, signed the document renouncing "all participation in the affairs of state" – though he refused to abdicate formally and would later attempt to regain the Hungarian half of his title. The lightness of this room is in complete contrast to the next, the oppressively opulent **Vieux-Laque Room**, with its black-and-gold lacquer panels, exquisite parquetry and walnut wainscoting. During his two sojourns at Schönbrunn, Napoleon is thought to have slept in the neighbouring walnut-panelled **Napoleon Room**, lined with Brussels tapestries depicting the Austrian army in Italy.

Despite its name, only three items in the remarkable **Porcelain Room**, designed by Isabella of Parma, are genuine Meissen porcelain: the chandeliers, the clock and the wall bracket. The rest of the decor is carved from wood and painted over in blue and white to appear like porcelain. Further on, the **Millions Room** – the most precious of all the rooms in Schönbrunn – is so called because it's estimated that Maria Theresia paid over a million silver florins to have it decorated. Unfortunately, the priceless miniature seventeenth-century Persian watercolours of life in the Moghul court are somewhat overwhelmed by the richly gilded cartouches set into the Caribbean rosewood panelling.

The **Memorial Room** is dedicated to Napoleon's son, known variously as the Duke of Reichstadt, King of Rome, or simply "L'Aiglon" ("The Little Eagle"). After Napoleon's demise in 1815, the boy was kept a virtual prisoner here in the palace. Passing quickly through the next few rooms, you reach **Maria Theresia's Bedroom**, though the empress never actually slept in the room's red velvet and gold-embroidered four-poster bed. Instead, the room was used exclusively for *levées* – a kind of official breakfast in bed – during her frequent pregnancies. This was also the modest little room in which Franz-Josef was born in 1830. The last few rooms of the "Grand Tour", last used by the **Archduke Franz Karl** (Franz-Josef's epileptic father), and his wife, the Archduchess Sophie, are of little interest, decked out as they are in the usual red damask and white panelling, and stuffed full of Habsburg portraits.

Wagenburg

The main exhibition space of the **Wagenburg** (April–Oct daily 9am–6pm; Nov–March Tues–Sun 10am–4pm; öS30/€2.00), to the west of the main courtyard, is crowded with nineteenth-century carriages, which are of limited interest to the non-specialist. The best thing to do is pass quickly to the far end of the hall, where, below the gallery, there's an odd assortment of carriages and sleighs used to transport the imperial offspring. The most poignant is the phaeton designed for Napoleon's son "L'Aiglon", with mudguards in the shape of eagle's wings; the bees that decorate the sides of the carriage were the Bonaparte family symbol. The highlights of the collection, though, lie beyond the gallery, where you'll find the Baroque and Rococo carriages of the Habsburgs. The most outrageous is the **coronation carriage of Franz Stephan**, enormously long, dripping with gold plate, and fitted with windows of Venetian glass. The ornate carriage opposite, painted entirely in black, was used during oath ceremonies for the new emperor, which coincided with periods of official mourning for the previous incumbent. Somewhat incredibly, the relatively modest **red-leather litter,** studded with over 11,000 gold-plated nails and buckles, was used solely for transporting the Archduke of Austria's hat from Klosterneuburg to Vienna and back for the aforementioned ceremonies. The richly carved, gold-plated carousel or **racing sleigh of Maria Theresia** is the sole survivor of a whole set built in the shape of giant scallops for the special ladies' tournament held in the Winter Reitschule in 1743.

Schlosspark

Even if you've no interest at all in visiting the interior of Schönbrunn, it's worth coming out here to enjoy the glorious **Schlosspark** (daily 6am–dusk; free) concealed behind the palace. The lower section is laid out in the formal French style, with closely cropped trees and yew hedges forming an intricate network of gravel paths. The first thing that strikes you, however, is the central axis of the **parterre**, decorated with carefully regimented flowerbeds, leading to the **Neptunbrunnen** (Neptune Fountain), and, beyond, to the triumphal arch of the Gloriette, the focal point of the park. If you do nothing else in the Schlosspark, you should make the effort to climb up the zigzag paths to the **Gloriette**, built to celebrate the victory of the Habsburgs over the Prussians at the 1757 Battle of Kolín, and now housing a swanky café (daily 9am–dusk), from which – if you can get a window table – you can enjoy the view down to the palace.

Hidden amongst the foliage to the east of the Neptunbrunnen are various architectural follies, sprinkled throughout the park in the late eighteenth century. Particularly fine are the **Römische Ruine** (Roman Ruins), built as a stage set for open-air concerts and theatre, a tradition that continues to this day in August and September. Close by the ruins is the outlet of the original **Schöner Brunnen**, a small grotto pavilion in which the nymph, Egeria, dispenses mineral water from a stone pitcher into a giant scallop basin. Further east stands an obelisk, topped by an eagle and an orb, and supported at the base by four, originally gilded, long-suffering turtles.

A substantial segment of the palace gardens is taken up by the **Tiergarten** (daily: Feb 9am–5pm; March & Oct 9am–5.30pm; April 9am–6pm; May–Sept 9am–6.30pm; Nov–Jan 9am–4.30pm; öS95/€6.90), which, originating in the royal menagerie founded by Franz Stephan back in 1752, is the world's oldest zoo. Here, the imperial couple would breakfast among the animals, in the octagonal pavilion designed for them by Jean-Nicholas Jadot, and decorated with frescoes by Guglielmi depicting Ovid's *Metamorphoses*. The pavilion is now a very good restaurant and, along with several of the original Baroque animal houses, makes this one of the most aesthetically pleasing zoos any captive animal could hope for.

If you're thinking of admiring the tropical plants of the **Palmenhaus** (daily: May–Sept 9.30am–6pm; Oct–April 9.30am–5pm; öS45/€3.27), then it's worth forking out for a "KombiKarte" (öS120/€8.72), covering entry to the zoo and the palm house. Last of all, don't miss out on the new hedge maze or **Irrgarten** (daily: April–Sept 9am–5.30pm; Oct 9am–4.30pm), close by the Neptunbrunnen.

Technisches Museum

The **Technisches Museum** (Mon–Wed, Fri & Sat 10am–6pm, Thurs 9am–8pm, Sun 10am–6pm; öS120/€8.72; *www.tmw.ac.at*) lies on the opposite side of Auer-

Welsbach-Park from the main gates of Schönbrunn, and is accessible from the Westbahnhof via tram #52 or #58. Having been closed for many years, the museum has recently undergone a massive transformation and emerged as a truly innovative, hands-on museum, with just about enough English information to enable non-German speakers to enjoy the exhibits. Leave yourself at least half a day to give the museum justice, and relax in the knowledge that the café on the ground floor is relatively good and inexpensive.

The museum's main entrance is now down in the basement, where you'll also find the **Concepts and Consequences** section, which should teach you some basic scientific concepts from gravity to electromagnetics, while entertaining you at the same time. Also on this level is the interactive **Phenomena and Experiments** gallery, where you can play at animation and doodle with a giant Spirograph. Upstairs is the hangar-like main hall, with the Heavy Industry gallery on one side, and the **Energy** gallery on the other. The latter is more fun, especially the giant, wind-up energy contraption by the entrance. At the time of going to press, few of the upstairs galleries had been fully refurbished, although the temporary exhibitions on the first floor are definitely worth investigating. So too is the **Transport** section on the second floor, which boasts the oldest car in working order, dating back to 1875, along with a load of old bicycles, motorbikes, model ships, trams and trains.

Vienna's **IMAX cinema** (*www.imax-wien.at*) stands next door to the Technisches Museum, and has daily showings of the usual less-than-brilliant IMAX films, specially shot to show off the 180-degree projection system; tickets currently start at a hefty öS115/€8.36 for a forty-minute long film.

Lainzer Tiergarten

In the far west of Vienna, some 3km beyond Schönbrunn, lies the former imperial hunting reserve of **Lainzer Tiergarten**, enclosed within a 25-kilometre-long wall by the Emperor Josef II in the late eighteenth century. Since 1923, however, the reserve has been the wildest of Vienna's public parks – with virtually no traffic allowed inside its boundaries and no formal gardens – and serves as the place in summer to escape the urban sprawl. It may not boast the views of Wienerwald, but you're more likely to spot wildlife here, including wild boar, wolves and, most easily, deer; in addition, the famous Lipizzaner horses of the Spanische Reitschule spend their summer holidays in the park.

The park's chief sight, the **Hermesvilla** (April–Sept Tues–Sun 10am–6pm; Oct–March Tues–Sun 9am–4.30pm; öS50/€3.63), built in 1882 by the Emperor Franz-Josef in an effort to ingratiate himself with his estranged wife (see box, opposite), is just ten minutes' walk from the main gates of Lainzer Tor, at the end of Hermesstrasse. Carl Hasenauer was employed to design the building, and Gustav Klimt and Hans Makart among those commissioned to decorate the interior; there was even a purpose-built exercise room in which the empress could indulge in her daily gymnastics. In the end, though, the villa failed to entice Elisabeth back to Vienna, and she stayed there only very occasionally. The house is now used to host exhibitions put on by the Historisches Museum der Stadt Wien. Even if the particular show doesn't grab you, the well-preserved interior is rewarding, though there's no information on the Hermesvilla's imperial days, nor anything specific on the Empress Elisabeth herself.

This section of the Lainzer Tiergarten is open year-round; the rest of the park is only open from Easter to October (Wed–Sun 8am–dusk); the St-Veiter Tor and the Adolfstor entrances, to the north of Lainzer Tor, are only open on Sundays and public holidays. To get to the Lainzer Tor, take tram #60 or #61 from Hietzing U-Bahn to Hofwiesengasse, then it's fifteen minutes' walk or bus #60B down Hermesstrasse.

EMPRESS ELISABETH

The **Empress Elisabeth** (1837–98) was born into the eccentric Wittelsbach dynasty that produced the likes of "Mad" King Ludwig II of Bavaria, one of Elisabeth's cousins. She enjoyed a carefree, if sheltered upbringing, only to find herself engaged to the Habsburg **Emperor Franz-Josef I** – another cousin – at the age of 16, after an entirely public, two-day courtship. Franz-Josef was undoubtedly devoted to his new bride, but he was also in thrall to his mother, the Archduchess Sophie, who was a control freak obsessed with court ceremonial. She prevented Elisabeth from fulfilling her role either as empress or as mother to her children, by hand-picking her ladies-in-waiting and having the children removed from her care as soon as they were born. Later, Elisabeth was to advise her daughter "marriage is an absurd institution. At the age of fifteen you are sold, you make a vow you do not understand, and you regret for thirty years or more that you cannot break it."

By 1860, having dutifully produced a male heir, Elisabeth developed a pathological aversion to the Viennese court, abandoning her children and husband and fleeing to Madeira for six months. She spent much of the rest of her lonely life travelling around Europe, under the pseudonym of the Countess Hohenembs. She crisscrossed the continent, never staying in one place for long, and went on interminable cruises – she had an anchor tattooed on her shoulder – alarming her companions by asking to be tied down on deck during storms. She sought solace in fencing, hiking, riding – she was reckoned to be one of the finest horsewomen in Europe – and in the preservation of her beauty. When her cousin, King Ludwig, and then her only son Rudolf, committed suicide within a few years of each other, she became convinced that she too was mentally unstable. From then on, she dressed only in black, and carried a black fan that she used to hide the wrinkles that were beginning to appear on her face. As she herself put it, "When we cannot be happy in the way that we desire there is nothing for it but to fall in love with our sorrows."

The similarities between Elisabeth's life and that of Princess Diana are difficult to ignore. Her marriage to Franz-Josef was the wedding of the century. The emperor was marrying a "fairytale princess", whom he hardly knew, and, despite public appearances, the marriage was a disaster. Like Diana, Elisabeth – or Sisi as she was and still is affectionately known – won over people's hearts with her beauty. Yet many Viennese resented her frequent absences from the capital, and were appalled at her pro-Hungarian sentiments. The issue of Franz-Josef and Elisabeth, like that of Charles and Diana, divided folk then, as it does historians and biographers now: either Franz-Josef was a boorish, unimaginative prig, who visited brothels during their honeymoon, or Elisabeth was a frigid, neurotic, narcissistic brat, obsessed with her looks. After a brief reconciliation between the imperial couple, which resulted in the birth of Marie Valerie, the only child Elisabeth took any great notice of, Sisi and Franz-Josef remained irrevocably estranged. She even encouraged Franz-Josef to get a mistress, introducing him to the actress Katharina Schratt, "very much as a woman might put flowers into a room she felt to be dreary", as Rebecca West put it.

By 1897, Elisabeth's health began to deteriorate rapidly – a condition partly brought on by anorexia – to the extent that she could barely walk. Despite her poor health, and her obsession with madness and death, few would have predicted her final demise. On September 10, 1898, the empress was assassinated by an Italian anarchist, Luigi Lucheni, on Lake Geneva. A local newspaper had unwisely announced the arrival of the empress, who was attempting to travel incognito. As she was about to board a steamer to go to tea with Baroness Rothschild, Lucheni rushed up and stabbed her in the heart. Like the empress, Lucheni had also been wandering aimlessly around Europe, in his case looking for someone famous to kill. He was fixed on assassinating the Duke of Orléans, but when he failed to turn up in Geneva as planned, resolved to attack the Austrian empress instead. Naturally enough, thousands turned out for Sisi's funeral in Vienna. Over the years, her martyrdom has ensured that the myth and intrigue around her life remain as compelling as ever.

Kirche am Steinhof

Despite its limited opening hours, anyone with even a passing interest in Jugendstil architecture should make the effort to visit the **Kirche am Steinhof** (guided tours in German Sat 3pm; öS40/€2.91), completed in 1907 by Otto Wagner as a chapel for the city's main psychiatric hospital. The church occupies a fantastic site on the commanding heights of the Baumgartner Höhe; to get there, take bus #47A from Unter-St-Veit U-Bahn. Like the Karlskirche (see p.116), the church is topped by a giant copper dome and lantern, both of which were originally gilded, and features two belfries capped with copper statues of seated saints. Inside, the church is deliberately organized on a north–south axis, rather than the usual east–west configuration, in order to allow more light through the glorious mosaic windows, designed by Kolo Moser. The focus of the interior is very much on the main altar, with its eye-catching, cage-like gilt baldachin, against a backdrop mosaic featuring St Leopold and sundry other saints. Sadly, the church is little used nowadays; it's too cold for services during the winter, and even in summer there are few takers amongst the patients.

Geymüllerschlössl

In the first decade of the nineteenth century, the wealthy banker Johann Heinrich Geymüller had a luxury summerhouse – known today as the **Geymüllerschlössl** (March–Nov Thurs–Sun 10am–5pm; öS30/€2.18; *www.mak.at*) – built in the sleepy village (now suburb) of Pötzleinsdorf. The house is no standard Biedermeier residence, but is, in fact, an exotic mixture of Gothic and Moorish elements executed by an unknown architect. It now houses the MAK's (see p.119) collection of early nineteenth-century furniture, as well as temporary Biedermeier exhibitions, which are staged on the ground floor. The first-floor rooms house the collection of clocks bequeathed, along with the house in 1965, by Dr Franz Sobek. The clocks – fascinating though they are – are a sideshow to the overall effect of the painstakingly restored Biedermeier decor, the most startling of which is the Salon mit Panoramatapete, a drawing room equipped with period furniture made from ebony and gold and upholstered in deep blue, and dominated by the panoramic murals of idealized, Oriental landscapes. To get to the Geymüllerschlössl, take tram #41 to its terminus from Volksoper U-Bahn.

Karl-Marx-Hof

If there is one housing complex that has come to symbolize the interwar municipal socialism of "Red Vienna", it is the **Karl-Marx-Hof**, the kilometre-long, peach-and-salmon-coloured "people's palace", whose distinctive giant archways greet you as you exit from Heiligenstadt U-Bahn, in the city's northern suburbs. Though right-wing critics charged that these housing complexes were built as fortresses by the socialists to protect their workers in case of civil war, their fragility was proved on February 12, 1934, when the World War I artillery of the Austro-fascist government reduced much of the Karl-Marx-Hof to rubble in a few hours. It took another four days for the government forces to flush the last defenders out, however. This is only the most famous of the battles of the civil war, which began in Linz, and was fought just as keenly and bloodily in numerous other working-class housing estates in Vienna and other Austrian cities.

Heiligenstädter-Testament-Haus

Beethoven moved out to the **Heiligenstädter-Testament-Haus**, Probusgasse 6 (Tues–Sun 9am–12.15pm & 1–4.30pm; öS25/€1.82), in 1802 on the advice of his doctor, who hoped the country air would improve his hearing. It was here he wrote his "Heiligenstadt Testament" – a facsimile of which is at the museum – addressed but never sent to his brothers. In it he apologizes for appearing "unfriendly, peevish, or even misanthropic", talks honestly about his deafness – "a sense which in me should be more perfectly developed than in other people" – and the pain and embarrassment it brought him: "I was on the point of putting an end to my life – the only thing that held me back was my art." It reads like a will, though it was more of a confession, the cathartic soliloquy of someone who's reached rock bottom. Despite his personal distress, while resident at Probusgasse Beethoven completed his joyful *Second Symphony*, "brought home right from the meadows of Heiligenstadt, so full is it of summer air and summer flowers".

Beethoven changed addresses more times even than Mozart (see p.85), and spent a further four summers at various addresses in Heiligenstadt. The house in Probusgasse, however, is one of the best preserved of all his residences, and probably the most rewarding of the city's three memorial museums to the composer. Confusingly, there are, in fact, two museums situated here. The official municipal one, on the far side of

---

LUDWIG VAN BEETHOVEN

Born in 1770 in Bonn, **Ludwig van Beethoven** came to Vienna in 1787, but remained for just a few months due to his mother's illness. Her death, and his father's subsequent death from alcoholism in 1792, freed Beethoven to return to the Austrian capital, where he lived until his own demise in 1827. Like Mozart, who was fourteen years his senior, he was taught by his father, a singer in the Hofkapelle, and played piano in public at a very early age (though his father used to pretend he was two years younger than he actually was). Again like Mozart, Beethoven was a virtuoso pianist, yet their techniques couldn't have been more different: Mozart gliding over the keys with smooth fluency, Beethoven raising his hands above his head, and smashing the keys with such force that he regularly broke the strings. Unlike both Haydn and Mozart, Beethoven was never a slave to the aristocracy, but an independent artist, whose patrons clubbed together to pay him an annuity just to keep him in Vienna, and prevent him having to take up the post of *Kapellmeister* at Westphalia which was offered him in 1809.

Though recognized as a genius by Viennese high society, he was also regarded as something of a freak: unprepossessing, scruffily dressed, reeking of body odour and swearing like a trooper. Despite such shortcomings, he was clearly attractive to women, and was, in his own words, "generally involved in one entanglement or the other". However, while the names of the women he was involved with are well known, no one can be sure that his love was ever consummated or even fully reciprocated. The objects of his affections were almost invariably young, beautiful, educated, aristocratic, and occasionally even married – in other words, unobtainable. One theory put forward as to why Beethoven never married is that he had syphilis, hence why he frequently changed doctors, and talked in his letters of "a malady which I cannot change and which brings me gradually nearer to death" – some suggest it may even have been the cause of his deafness.

In 1815, Beethoven's brother, Karl, died at the age of just forty-one. Beethoven then made the fateful decision to adopt his nephew, also named Karl, no doubt hoping that Karl would be the son he never had. After a long drawn-out custody battle with his sister-in-law, Beethoven succeeded in removing the boy from his mother in 1820, only to send him to boarding school. Beethoven proved totally unsuitable as a father, and Karl's misery reached such a pitch that in 1826, the fifteen-year-old tried unsuccessfully to shoot himself. He was immediately removed from Beethoven's care, at which the composer fell into despair, eventually dying of pneumonia in March 1827. His funeral, in contrast to Mozart's, attracted a crowd of 20,000 to the Trinity Church of the Minorites on Alserstrasse, with Austria's chief poet, Franz Grillparzer, composing the funeral oration. He was buried in Währinger Friedhof, but now rests in the Zentralfriedhof (see p.139).

the shady, cobbled courtyard, occupies the rooms rented by Beethoven, and contains a lock of the composer's hair and his death mask. On the opposite side of the courtyard is the rival **Beethoven Ausstellung** (Tues, Thurs & Sat 10am–noon & 1–4.30pm; öS10/€0.73), run by the elderly lady who lives at no. 5, on behalf of the Beethoven Society. There's more of an attempt at recreating some period atmosphere here, and there's an information sheet in English detailing the exhibits. To reach the museum, take bus #38A to Armbrustergasse from U-Bahn Heiligenstadt, or walk five minutes from the tram #37 terminus.

Wienerwald

The forested hills of the **Wienerwald** (Vienna Woods) stretch from the northern tip of the city limits to the foothills of the Alps, away to the southwest – few other capitals can boast such an impressive green belt on their doorstep. In the eighteenth century, the wealthier folk used to move out into the villages on the vine-clad slopes of the Wienerwald for the duration of the summer. With the arrival of public transport, even those without such means could just hop on a tram to the end of the line, and enjoy a day in the countryside. Still today, the Wienerwald remains a popular weekend jaunt, and throughout the summer, the wine gardens of the local *Heurigen* (for more on which, see p.148) are filled not only with tour groups, but also with the Viennese themselves, who come here to sample the new wine.

The most popular place from which to admire the view over Vienna is **Kahlenberg** (484m), the higher of the two hills that rise to the north of the city. There's a café, with a magnificent terrace and a viewing platform, though the whole place is mobbed at weekends. According to tradition, this was where Polish King Jan Sobieski celebrated Mass in 1683, before leading the army down the mountain to relieve the city from the Turks. The Baroque Josefskirche nearby, in which the event is supposed to have taken place, is now run by the Poles, and the church's Sobieski Chapel is a Polish national shrine. The most striking thing about the plain interior is the hundreds of rosaries, pendants and lucky Madonna and Child talismans, which hang on the walls from floor to ceiling.

Tradition notwithstanding, it has been proved fairly conclusively that the aforementioned Mass actually took place on the neighbouring peak of **Leopoldsberg** (425m), just over 1km by road east of Kahlenberg. To confuse matters further, the two hills swapped names after the Leopoldskirche was built on what is now Leopoldsberg in 1693. This is certainly a more beguiling spot in which to relax and enjoy the view. There's a much more pleasant courtyard and café, shaded by pine trees, and a more dramatic view from the restored ramparts, built by the Babenbergs in 1135. The church itself is also better looking than the one on Kahlenberg, and has a historical display of prints and documents relating to the Turkish siege.

There are several ways of **approaching the Wienerwald**. Tram #38 deposits you in the centre of Grinzing. If you walk up Cobenzlgasse, turn right up Krapfenwaldgasse and then straight on at the crossroads, up Mukenthalerweg, you'll find yourself on the right path to Kahlenberg. To avoid the worst of the crowds and the traffic, though, it's probably better to start walking from the terminus of tram D in Nussdorf, following Beethovengang past the Beethoven memorial, then up Kahlenberger Strasse. Either way, it's a good 3km uphill to Kahlenberg itself. Alternatively, bus #38A from Heiligenstadt U-Bahn will take you all the way to Kahlenberg, Cobenzl and (less frequently) Leopoldsberg.

Prater

The only good reason to venture onto the eastern bank of the Danube Canal is to visit the **Prater** (derived from the Spanish *prado*). This large, flat tract of land, taking up almost half of the island formed by the various arms of the Danube, first opened to the public in 1766 by Josef II, includes vast acres of mixed woodland, sports stadiums, racecourses, a miniature railway, allotments, a trade-fair centre, a planetarium, a football museum, an amusement park and, most famously of all, Vienna's giant Ferris wheel, or Riesenrad. In sum, the Prater is vast, and its backbone is the chestnut-lined Hauptallee, which runs dead straight for 5km.

By far the busiest section of the Prater is the northwest end, where you'll find the park's permanent funfair, known as the **Volksprater** (Easter–Oct daily 8am–midnight). Tourists flock here for the Riesenrad, but the Viennese come here for the other rides, a strange mixture ranging from hi-tech helter-skelters and white-knuckle affairs to more traditional fairground rides like ghost trains and dodgems. Taking a ride on the **Riesenrad** (daily: March & April 10am–10pm; May–Sept 9am–midnight; Oct 10am–10pm; Nov to early Jan 10am–6pm; öS45/€3.27), built in 1898 by the British military engineer Walter Basset, is one of those things you simply have to do if you go to Vienna; it's also a must for fans of the film *The Third Man* (see box below), as the place in front of which Orson Welles does his famous "cuckoo clock" speech. Be prepared for the fact that the wheel doesn't so much spin as stagger slowly round, as each gondola fills up with passengers; once you've done a complete circuit, you've had your twenty-minute ride.

The easiest way of approaching the Prater is from the northwest, from Wien-Nord station (U-Bahn Praterstern), the terminus for tram #5 and #O, and a stop on tram #21. Alternatively, tram #N from U-Bahn Schwedenplatz has its terminus right by the Hauptallee, a third of the way down from the Ferris wheel. Getting around the Prater, you can walk, jog, rollerblade, cycle, take a fiacre, or rent one of the pedal carriages, which seat two adults (plus two kids if you wish). Another possibility is to buy a one-way ticket on the miniature railway or *Liliputbahn*, which will get you almost halfway down the Hauptallee.

Johann-Strauss-Museum

Fans of the "Waltz King" might like to head for the **Johann-Strauss-Museum** (Tues–Sun 9am–12.15pm & 1–4.30pm; öS25/€1.82), on the first floor of Praterstrasse 54 (U-Bahn Nestroyplatz), where the composer lived from 1863 until the death of his first wife, the singer Jetty Treffz, in 1878. In contrast to most of the city's musical museums, some attempt has been made here to recreate a period interior: one room, decorated with ceiling panels of cherubs, contains his grand piano, house organ and standing desk at which he used to compose. There's also a fascinating collection of ephemera from the balls of the day, with various gimmicky dance cards – one laid out in the form of a staircase – and quirky ball pendants, which were kept as a sort of memento of the evening. Strauss is of course best known for having written the city's signature tune, *An der schönen blauen Donau* (known to the English-speaking world as *The Blue Danube*). Originally scored for male chorus, not orchestra, complete with ludicrous lyrics, it wasn't at all well received after its inept first performance. Only when Strauss took it to Paris, and performed it with an orchestra, did it become a stratospheric success.

Vienna's cemeteries

In a city where some people still keep a separate savings account in order to ensure an appropriately lavish funeral, it comes as little surprise that Vienna's chief cemetery, the **Zentralfriedhof** (March, April, Sept & Oct 7am–6pm; May–Aug 7am–7pm; Nov–Feb 8am–5pm), is one of the biggest in Europe. Larger than the entire Innere Stadt, and with a much greater population – 2.5 million – than the whole of the city, it even has its

THE STRAUSS FAMILY

Of all the many tunes associated with Vienna, perhaps the best known are the waltzes composed by the Strausses. Born in Vienna to a Jewish innkeeper in Leopoldstadt, **Johann Strauss the Elder** (1804–49) kept quiet about his origins, though it was the Nazis themselves who felt the need to falsify the parish register of Vienna's Stephansdom, in order to make the Strauss family appear as true Aryans (a similar leniency was shown towards Hitler's much-loved composer Franz Lehár, whose wife was Jewish, see p.436). Strauss began his career serenading diners in Viennese restaurants, along with the likes of Josef Lanner, who was to become his chief musical rival. However, it was in the dance hall of *Zum Sperl* in Leopoldstadt that Strauss the Elder made his name as a band leader, conducting a mixture of dances, orchestral phantasies and more serious music. His gypsy-like features, and wild, vigorous conducting style soon became very popular in Vienna. Later, he and his orchestra achieved a modicum of fame touring Europe, and he was eventually appointed k.k. Hofballmusikdirektor (Imperial-Royal Director of Music for Balls). Strauss's touring took its toll on domestic life, and he created a public scandal in 1842 when he left the family home and moved in with a young seamstress, who bore him several illegitimate children.

His eldest son, **Johann Strauss the Younger** (1825–99), followed in his footsteps, writing his first waltz at the age of six, though much against the latter's wishes (he wanted him to be a banker). It was, in fact, Johann's long-suffering mother, Anna, who directed her sons into musical careers. Father and son soon became rivals, both musically and politically. In 1848, while the Elder was busy conducting his famous *Radetzky March*, the signature tune of the *ancien régime*, the Younger was composing stirring tunes such as the *Revolution March* and the *Song of the Barricades*. Fourteen years after his father's death, Strauss the Younger was appointed k.k. Hofballmusikdirektor in 1863, rapidly surpassing even his father's enormous fame. He was one of the world's first international celebrities, feted on both sides of the Atlantic. On one memorable occasion in Boston in the US, he conducted *The Blue Danube* with 20,000 singers, an orchestra of over 1000 and 20 assistant conductors, to an audience of more than 100,000. Johann's operetta, *Die Fledermaus*, written to take Viennese minds off the economic crash of 1873, was another huge success – by the end of the decade, it was playing in some 170 theatres.

Despite his success, Johann, a difficult character like his father, was something of an outsider. He was also constantly irked by his lack of acclaim among serious musical critics, and his several attempts at straight opera flopped. Again like his father, he too caused a scandal, divorcing his second wife, Lili, in order to marry his mistress Adele. As the Vatican would not annul his marriage, he was forced to convert to Lutheranism and become a citizen of Saxony, though he continued to live in Vienna until his death in 1899.

As for the remaining Strauss sons, Johann's two younger brothers, **Josef** – "the romantic-looking, chaotically pale" Strauss as he was dubbed by one Viennese critic – and **Eduard**, were also musicians (again against their absent father's wishes). Josef was a successful composer in his own right, but died at the age of forty-three, while Eduard became k.k. Hofballmusikdirektor after Johann in 1872 and was left in charge of the Strauss orchestra.

own bus service to help mourners get about. Opened in 1874, at the height of Viennese funereal fetishism – when having *eine schöne Leich* ("a beautiful corpse") was something to aspire to – it's still very much a working graveyard. It's particularly busy on Sundays and on religious holidays, most notably All Saints' Day (November 1), when up to a million Viennese make the trip out here and leave candles burning in remembrance on virtually every grave. To get there, take tram #71 or #72 from U-Bahn Simmering and get out at the monumental Jugendstil Zweite Tor.

Most of the so-called **Ehrengräber** (Tombs of Honour) are in Gruppe 32A, to the left, as you approach the central Jugendstil church. Centre stage is a memorial to

Mozart, though he was buried in St Marxer Friedhof (see p.126). At a respectful distance lie the graves of Beethoven and Schubert, who were disinterred from Währinger Friedhof in 1889 and reburied here. Other composers to look out for include **Christoph Willibald Gluck**, **Johannes Brahms**, **Hugo Wolf** and the entire **Strauss** clan. The sunken roundabout in front of the main church is the illustrious **Prezidentsgruft**, containing the remains of the presidents of the Second Republic. Close by, in Gruppe 32C, you'll find more intriguing incumbents like the composer **Arnold Schönberg**, and his mentor **Alexander Zemlinsky**, both of whom died in exile in the USA.

A majority of Vienna's most famous personages are to be found in the Zentralfriedhof, but there are a few notable exceptions. Gustav Klimt, for example, is buried in the **Friedhof Hietzing** (March, April, Sept & Oct daily 8am–5pm; May–Aug until 6pm; Nov–Feb 9am–4pm), ten minutes' walk from Hietzing U-Bahn up Maxingstrasse, in the western suburbs. Other notables buried here include Klimt's friend the artist Kolo Moser, Engelbert Dollfuss, the Austro-fascist leader murdered by the Nazis in 1934, Katharina Schratt, the Emperor Franz-Josef's mistress, the composer Alban Berg, and Otto Wagner, whose rather pompous tomb was designed by the architect himself, but is devoid of even a hint of Jugendstil motifs. Egon Schiele is buried in the nearby **Friedhof Ober-St-Veit**; take bus #54B or #55B from Ober-St-Veit U-Bahn. Devotees of Gustav Mahler need to head for **Grinzinger Friedhof**, where the composer was buried in 1911, having converted to Catholicism earlier in his career in order to make himself more acceptable to the anti-Semitic Viennese music establishment. His modernist tombstone, designed by Josef Hoffmann, was commissioned by his widow, Alma Mahler-Werfel, who lies close by. Other notable corpses here include the one-armed pianist Paul Wittgenstein (brother of philosopher Ludwig). To get to the Grinzinger Friedhof, take tram #38 to its terminus.

Eating and drinking

More so than anywhere else in Austria, Vienna has a huge variety of places to **eat and drink**, from *Beisln*, the Viennese version of a local pub, to upmarket restaurants, as well as a wide range of cuisines, from Balkan to South American. Even the country's ubiquitous protein-heavy food is given a new lift in the capital thanks to the popularity of *Neu Wiener Küche*, the Viennese version of *nouvelle cuisine*, which uses fresh produce to give a slightly Mediterranean bent to traditional dishes.

Vienna is, of course, also home of the *Kaffeehaus*, and has by far the largest selection in the country. While the rest of the world queues up for fast food, the Viennese *Kaffeehaus* implores you to slow down; as the sign in one such café says, "sorry, we do not cater for people in a hurry." For the price of a small coffee, you can sit for as long as you like without being asked to move on or buy another drink. Understandably, then, the price of this first drink is astronomical and will regularly set you back around öS35/€2.54.

Eating and drinking establishments are divided into **Kaffeehäuser**, incorporating snack bars and Kaffee-Konditorei, and **restaurants**, which includes some of the city's *Beisln*. Phone numbers have been given only for those restaurants where it's advisable to **book a table**. Don't get too excited by those places that boast a *Schanigarten*, as this is rarely much of a garden; simply a few tables alfresco. For more pleasant, atmospheric alfresco eating and drinking, you need to head off to one of the simple **Heurigen** in the wine-making suburbs.

Cafés

The Viennese take their cafés seriously – on average they drink twice as much coffee as beer – and the capital's *Kaffeehäuser* are by no means a uniform bunch. As well as

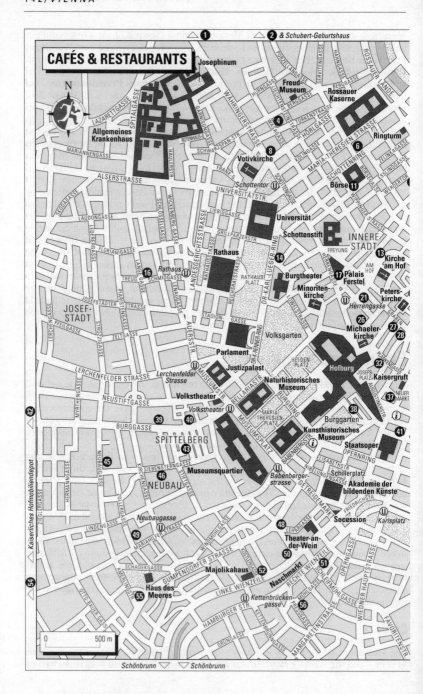

CAFÉS & RESTAURANTS

N

❶

❷ & Schubert-Geburtshaus

Josephinum

PORZELLANGASSE

SERVITENGASSE

HAHNGASSE

ROSSAUER LÄNDE

BERGGASSE

Freud-Museum

Rossauer Kaserne

LAZARETTGASSE

SPITALGASSE

WÄHRINGERSTRASSE

THURNGASSE

BERGGASSE

TÜRKENSTRASSE

HÖRLGASSE

MARIA-THERESIEN STRASSE

SCHOTTENRING

Ringturm

❹

ROTENHAUS-G.

Allgemeines Krankenhaus

HALLERSTR.

SCHWA

SPAN-STR.

FRANK-G.

COLLINGASSE

ZELINKAG.

SCHLICKG.

Börse

❻

Votivkirche

❽

MARIANNENGASSE

ALSERSTRASSE

SKODAGASSE

LAUDONGASSE

SCHLÖSSELGASSE

WICKENBURGGASSE

LANGE

Schottentor Ⓤ

SCHOTTENGASSE

WIPPLINGER STRASSE

WERDERTOR

❶❶

MÖLKERBASTEI

LEDERERGASSE

FLORIANIGASSE

UNIVERSITÄTSTR.

LIEBIGGASSE

Universität

INNERE STADT

GRILLPARZERSTR.

Schottenstift

FREYUNG

❶❸ Kirche am Hof

LANDESGERICHTSSTRASSE

RATHAUSSTRASSE

Rathaus

❶❹

AM HOF

Palais Ferstel

Peters-kirche

❶❻ *Rathaus*

SCHMIDGASSE

LENAUGASSE

TREUG.

Burgtheater

❶❼

❷❶ *Herrengasse*

Minoriten-kirche

Ⓤ

JOSEF-STADT

JOSEFSTÄDTER STRASSE

PIARISTENGASSE

STROZZIGASSE

ZELTGASSE

LERCHENGASSE

PFEILGASSE

STADION-GASSE

AUERSPSTR.

Volksgarten

Michaeler-kirche

❷❻

❷❼

❷❽

DR.-KARL-LUEGER-RING

DR.-KARL-RENNER-RING

RATHAUS PLATZ

Parlament

HELDEN-PLATZ

Hofburg

❸❷

Kaisergruft

JOSEFS-PLATZ

Justizpalast

LERCHENFELDER STRASSE

Lerchenfelder Strasse

MUSEUMSTR.

BELLARIASTR.

NEUER MARKT

❸❼

MYRTHENGASSE

NEUSTIFTGASSE

Volkstheater

Naturhistorisches Museum

AUGUSTINERSTR.

ⓘ

MARIA-THERESIEN-PLATZ

❸❽

❹❷

❸❾

Volkstheater Ⓤ

❹❶

❹❸

MUSEUMSPLATZ

BURGGASSE

SPITTELBERG

Kunsthistorisches Museum

ⓘ

Staatsoper

SIEBENSTERNGASSE

KIRCHENGASSE

STIFTG.

BABENBERGERSTR.

OPERNRING

NEUBAUGASSE

❹❺

NEUBAU

HERMANNGASSE

ZIEGLERGASSE

Museumsquartier

Babenberger-strasse

GETREIDEMARKT

ELISABETHSTR.

NIBELUNGENG.

Schillerplatz

Akademie der bildenden Künste

❹❻

LINDENGASSE

Neubaugasse Ⓤ

MARIAHILFER STRASSE

WINDMÜHLGASSE

KÖSTLERG.

Secession

FRIEDRICHSTR.

Karlsplatz

❹❽

LEHARGASSE

❹❾

Theater-an-der-Wein

❺❶

OPERNGASSE

SCHADEKGASSE

GUMPENDORFER STRASSE

Majolikahaus

❺❷

❺❶

WIENER HAUPTSTRASSE

AMRUFER

Haus des Meeres

❺❺

LINKE WIENZEILE

Naschmarkt

RECHTE WIENZEILE

SCHLEIFMÜHLGASSE

❺❻

OTTAKRINGER GASSE

Kettenbrücken-gasse Ⓤ

MARGARETENSTRASSE

HAMBURGER STR.

GRÜNGASSE

KETTENBRÜCKENGASSE

FAVORITENSTR.

❺❹

Kaiserliches Hofmobiliendepot

0 |————| 500 m

Schönbrunn ▽   ▽ Schönbrunn

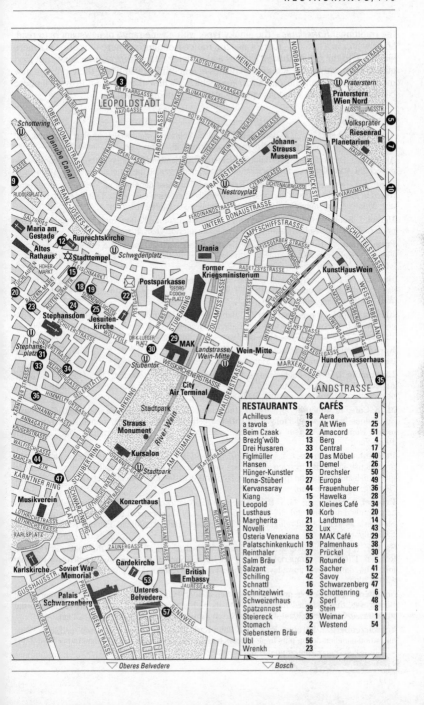

RESTAURANTS		CAFÉS	
Achilleus	18	Aera	9
a tavola	31	Alt Wien	25
Beim Czaak	22	Amacord	51
Brezlg'wölb	13	Berg	4
Drei Husaren	33	Central	17
Figlmüller	24	Das Möbel	40
Hansen	11	Demel	26
Hünger-Kunstler	55	Drechsler	50
Ilona-Stüberl	27	Europa	49
Kervansaray	44	Frauenhuber	36
Kiang	15	Hawelka	28
Leopold	3	Kleines Café	34
Lusthaus	10	Korb	20
Margherita	21	Landtmann	14
Novelli	32	Lux	43
Osteria Venexiana	53	MAK Café	29
Palatschinkenkuchl	19	Palmenhaus	38
Reinthaler	37	Prückel	30
Salm Bräu	57	Rotunde	5
Salzant	12	Sacher	41
Schilling	42	Savoy	52
Schnattl	16	Schwarzenberg	47
Schnitzelwirt	45	Schottenring	6
Schweizerhaus	7	Sperl	48
Spatzennest	39	Stein	8
Steiereck	35	Weimar	1
Stomach	2	Westend	54
Siebenstern Bräu	46		
Ubl	56		
Wrenkh	23		

▽ *Oberes Belvedere*   ▽ *Bosch*

the traditional *Kaffeehaus* – the smoky type, with a wide range of newspapers to read, and a waiter in a tuxedo – there's also the Kaffee-Konditorei, where the coffee is a mere sideshow to the establishment's cakes and pastries. Many *Kaffeehäuser* serve hot food all day long, with the best choice of dishes at lunchtime. In addition, there are also new modern variants on the old *Kaffeehaus* which eschew the tuxedos, heavy Viennese cooking and *Torten*, and consequently attract a younger crowd.

The Innere Stadt

Aera, 1, Gonzagagasse 11; U-Bahn Schwedenplatz. Relaxing café upstairs serving tasty food, and dimly lit cellar downstairs where live bands perform. Daily 10am–2am.

Alt Wien, 1, Bäckerstrasse 9; U-Bahn Stephansplatz. Bohemian *Kaffeehaus* with *Beisl* decor, posters on nicotine-stained walls, and a dark, smoky atmosphere even on the sunniest day. Daily 10am–2am.

Central, 1, Herrengasse 14; U-Bahn Herrengasse. The most famous of all Viennese cafés, resurrected in the 1980s and still the most architecturally interesting (see p.90). Trotsky was once a regular. Mon–Sat 8am–8pm, Sun 10am–6.30pm. Piano music Mon–Fri 4–7pm.

Demel, 1, Kohlmarkt 14; U-Bahn Herrengasse. The king of the Kaffee-Konditorei – and one of the priciest. The cake display is a work of art, as is the interior. Daily 10am–7pm.

Frauenhuber, 1, Himmelpfortgasse 6; U-Bahn Stephansplatz. One of the oldest *Kaffeehäuser* in Vienna – Beethoven was a regular – with vaulted ceiling, deep burgundy upholstery and an excellent menu. Mon–Sat 8am–11.30pm.

Hawelka, 1, Dorotheergasse 6; U-Bahn Stephansplatz. Small, smoky bohemian café run by the same couple since it opened shortly after World War II; you may have to fight for a table. Mon & Wed–Sat 8am–2am, Sun 4pm–2am.

Kleines Café, 1, Franziskanerplatz 3; U-Bahn Stephansplatz. Cosy little café, one of the first of the crossovers between the new and the traditional *Kaffeehaus,* designed by the Viennese architect Hermann Czech in the 1970s. Mon–Sat 10am–2am, Sun 1pm–2am.

Korb, 1, Brandstätte 9; U-Bahn Stephansplatz. Traditional 1950s-style *Kaffeehaus* tucked in the backstreets of the Innere Stadt. Mon–Sat 8am–midnight, Sun noon–9pm.

Landtmann, 1, Dr-Karl-Lueger-Ring 4; U-Bahn Herrengasse/Schottentor. One of the poshest of the *Kaffeehäuser* – and a favourite with Freud – with impeccably attired waiters, and a high quota of politicians and Burgtheater actors. Daily 8am–midnight.

MAK Café, 1, Stubenring 5; U-Bahn Stubentor. Not strictly speaking a traditional *Kaffeehaus*, but it does have a wonderfully high coffered ceiling. This is a trendy hangout, as you might expect from the MAK (see p.119). The food is pricey, with a Mediterranean edge. Tues–Sun 10am–2am.

Palmenhaus, 1, Burggarten; U-Bahn Karlsplatz. Stylish modern café set amidst the palms of the greenhouse in the Burggarten. Breakfasts are great, the inexpensive, daily menu specializes in grilled fish and meats, and there are even DJ nights occasionally. A wonderful treat after visiting the Hofburg. Daily 10am–2am

Prückel, 1, Stubenring 24; U-Bahn Stubentor. The *Prückel*'s dowdy 1950s refurbishment looks appealingly dated now, and still draws in lots of elderly shoppers and dog-owners from the nearby Stadtpark, as well the odd refugee from MAK opposite. Daily 9am–10pm. Piano music Mon, Wed & Fri 7–10pm.

Sacher, 1, Philharmonikerstrasse 4; U-Bahn Karlsplatz. For all its fame, the *Sacher* is a bit of a letdown. The decor is imperial red and gold, but the *Sachertorte* overrated – practically the only folk who come here nowadays are tourists. Daily 6.30am–11.30pm. Piano music Mon–Sat 4.30–6.30pm.

Schottenring, 1, Schottenring; U-Bahn Schottentor/Schottenring. Situated on the corner of Börsegasse, this L-shaped *Kaffeehaus*, with its high stuccoed ceiling, is an oasis of calm on the Ringstrasse. Mon–Fri 6.30am–11pm, Sat & Sun 8am–9pm. Live piano daily 3.30–6.30pm.

Schwarzenberg, 1, Kärntner Ring 17; U-Bahn Karlsplatz. Opulent café with rich marble, ceramic and wood-panelled decor, plus huge mirrors and a great cake cabinet. Live piano music Wed & Fri 7–9pm, Sat & Sun 5–7pm. Mon–Fri & Sun 7am–midnight, Sat 9am–midnight.

The Vorstädte

Amacord, 5, Rechte Wienzeile 15; U-Bahn Karlsplatz. Laid-back *Kaffeehaus* by the Naschmarkt, with trendy (occasionally live) music playing, lots of papers and inexpensive food on the menu. Daily 10am–2am.

Berg, 9, Berggasse 8; U-Bahn Schottentor. Relaxed modern mixed gay/straight café with an attractive assortment of chairs and great *Neu Wiener Küche*. Daily 10am–1am.

Drechsler, 6, Linke Wienzeile 22; U-Bahn Kettenbrückengasse. Laid-back, scruffy Mariahilf *Kaffeehaus*, by the Naschmarkt; popular with the younger generation of Viennese, especially clubbers attracted by the early opening hours. Mon–Sat 3.30am–8pm.

Das Möbel, 7, Burggasse 10; U-Bahn Volkstheater. Café-bar on the edge of Spittelberg, packed with minimalist furniture (which you can buy), a youngish crowd, weird toilets and reasonable sustinence on offer. Daily noon–1am.

Europa, 7, Zollergasse 8; U-Bahn Neubaugasse. Lively, spacious café that attracts a trendy crowd, who love the posey window booths. Food is tasty mixture of Viennese and Italian; DJ nights in the back room. Daily 9am–5am.

Lux, 7, Spittelberggasse 6; U-Bahn Volkstheater. Pared-down modern version of a *Kaffeehaus*, with a friendly bistro feel and an eclectic menu featuring tofu-based dishes, pizzas and pancakes. Daily 10.30am–2am.

Rotunde, 2, Ausstellungstrasse/Mölkereistrasse; tram #21. Real neighbourhood *Kaffeehaus*, deeply untrendy but a great escape from the nearby Volksprater, two stops from Praterstern. Mon–Sat 7.30am–2am.

Savoy, 6, Linke Wienzeile 36; U-Bahn Kettenbrückengasse. Wonderfully scruffy, but ornate fin-de-siècle decor, packed with bohemian bargain-hunters during Mariahilf's Saturday flea market. Mon–Fri 5pm–2am, Sat 9am–2am.

Sperl, 6, Gumpendorfer Strasse 11; U-Bahn Karlsplatz/Babenbergerstrasse. One of the classics of the *Kaffeehaus* scene, just off Mariahilferstrasse, L-shaped, with billiard tables and a hint of elegant, bohemian shabbiness. Mon–Sat 7am–11pm, Sun 3–11pm (July & Aug closed Sun).

Stein, 9, Währingerstrasse 6; *www.café-stein.com*; U-Bahn Schottentor. Posey, studenty designer café, on the corner of Kolingasse, with minimalist decor, funky music, trendy loos, on-line facilities, baguettes, veggie food and breakfasts served until 8pm. Mon–Sat 7am–1am, Sun 9am–1am.

CHEAP EATS

The best place to grab a quick bite and **eat cheaply** at the same time is the Naschmarkt, Vienna's premier fruit and vegetable market (Mon–Sat), where you can feast on seafood, kebabs, felafel, burek, noodles and much more besides, or, if you prefer assemble a king-sized picnic. As well as the student *Mensa* (see p.146), there are plenty of other self-service places, such as *Rosenberger*, Mayserdergasse 2 (U-Bahn Karlsplatz), and *Naschmarkt*, Schottengasse 1 (U-Bahn Schottentor), with branches all over the city. More specialized, but equally reliable self-service chains include the fish and seafoody *Nordsee*, Kärntnerstrasse 25 (U-Bahn Stephansplatz), and the Middle Eastern *Levante*, Wollzeile 19 (U-Bahn Stephansplatz), again, each with numerous other branches.

Smarter, more congenial stand-up options include *Trzśniewski*, the minimalist *Brötchen* bar, at Dorotheergasse 1 (U-Bahn Stephansplatz), that is a veritable Viennese institution. *Zum schwarzen Kameel*, Bognergasse 5 (U-Bahn Herrengasse), is a terribly smart, convivial deli with stand-up tables only. The veggie restaurant, *Wrenkh*, has a small weekday-only snack bar at Rauhensteingasse 12 (U-Bahn Stephansplatz), round the back of the Steffl department store on Kärntnerstrasse, while the newly refurbished *Julius Meinl*, on the corner of Kohlmarkt and Graben (U-Bahn Stephansplatz), has an excellent stand-up buffet at the rear of the ground floor, where you can eat traditional hot dishes and lighter snacks, and a seafood bar upstairs. Lastly, there's a conveniently central Billa supermarket just down Singerstrasse from Stephansplatz.

Weimar, 9, Währinger Strasse 68; tram #40, #41 or #42. L-shaped *Kaffeehaus* with a high ceiling, chandeliers, tuxedoed waiters and snug booths. Good-value öS85/€6.18 lunchtime menu. Mon–Thurs 8am–midnight, Fri & Sat 8am–4am, Sun 10am–midnight. Live piano daily 7.30–11.30pm.

Westend, 7, Mariahilferstrasse 128; U-Bahn Westbahnhof. Conveniently located directly opposite Westbahnhof, this traditional *Kaffeehaus* is the best possible introduction to Vienna for those who've just arrived by train. Daily 7am–11pm.

Inexpensive and mid-range restaurants

Vienna has plenty of **affordable restaurants**, although prices overall, particularly in the Innere Stadt, are slightly higher than in the rest of Austria. Outside the centre, the **Spittelberg** area, behind the Messepalast (MuseumsQuartier), has the highest concentration of cafés and restaurants, though there are further options dispersed more widely throughout the surrounding district of **Neubau** (seventh district), and in neighbouring **Josefstadt** (eighth district). Prices are slightly lower in a *Beisl*, or city pub: these places serve standard Austrian dishes and there's often a lunchtime special offer for under öS100/€7.27. In more formal restaurants, you can still eat very reasonably, with prices for most main dishes hovering between öS100–150/€7.27–10.90.

The Innere Stadt

A Tavola, 1, Weihburggasse 3–5 (☎512 7955); U-Bahn Stephansplatz. Relaxed and very popular Italian *osteria* with a stylish, cave-like interior and some excellent innovative cuisine. Daily noon–3pm & 6pm–midnight.

Achilleus, 1, Köllnerhofgasse 3; U-Bahn Schwedenplatz. Strangely Austrian-looking, but excellent Greek restaurant. Daily 11.30am–3pm & 5.30pm–12.30am.

Beim Czaak, 1, Postgasse 15; U-Bahn Schwedenplatz. Lovely dark-green wood panelling and low-lighting give this well-established *Beisl* a cosy, yet smart feel. Mon–Fri 8.30am–midnight, Sat 11am–midnight.

MENSA

If you're on a tight budget, then it's worth considering using the city's numerous university canteens, or **Mensa**, which are open to the general public (you get an extra discount with student ID). It might not be cordon bleu, but the food is generally perfectly decent traditional Viennese fare, and you usually get a couple of courses for under öS50/€3.63 – about half what you'd pay in a restaurant.

Afro-Asiatisches Institut, 9, Türkenstrasse 3; U-Bahn Schottentor. Vienna's most multiethnic clientele, but not great for veggies; situated on the ground floor through the archway. Mon–Fri 11.30am–2.30pm.

Katholische Hochschulgemeinde, 1, Ebendorferstrasse 8. Two choices of set menu (occasionally veggie). Mon–Fri 11.30am–2pm. Closed Easter & Aug to mid-Sept.

Musikakademie, 1, Johannesgasse 8. Small central, musical *Mensa* with a pleasant summer courtyard; good for breakfast, but not great for veggies. Mon–Fri 7.30am–2pm.

Neues Instituts Gebäude, 1, Universitätsstrasse 7; U-Bahn Schottentor. This is the main university *Mensa*; take the dumb-waiter lift to floor 6 and then walk up flight of stairs – there's a nice view over to the Votivkirche. Mon–Fri 11am–2pm.

Technische Universität, 4, Wiedner Hauptstrasse 8–10; U-Bahn Karlsplatz. Big *Mensa* on the first floor (follow the yellow B signs) of the building behind the main university block on Karlsplatz, with regular veggie options. Mon–Fri 11am–2.30pm.

Wirtschaftsuniversität, 9, Augasse 2–6; U-Bahn Spittelau. Unusually this *Mensa* is open for breakfast as well as lunch; some veggie options. Mon–Thurs 7.30am–7.30pm, Fri 7.30am–6.30pm. July & Aug closes 3.30pm.

Brezlg'wölb, 1, Ledererhof 9; U-Bahn Herrengasse. Wonderful candlelit cave-like restaurant with deliberately olde worlde decor. Hidden in a cobbled street off Drahtgasse, it serves the usual Austrian favourites. Daily 11.30am–1am.

Figlmüller, 1, Wollzeile 5; U-Bahn Stephansplatz. It's in every guide to the city there is, and, as a result, doesn't need to make any effort to make folk welcome. Wash your humungous *Wiener Schnitzel*, down with wine (there's no beer). Daily 11am–10.30pm.

Hansen, 1, Wipplingerstrasse 34 (☎532 0542); U-Bahn Schottentor. Attractive, smart restaurant located in the flower and gardening shop in the vaulted basement of the city's splendid stock exchange – good for brunch. Mon–Fri 9am–8pm, Sat 9am–5pm.

Ilona-Stüberl, 1, Bräunerstrasse 2; U-Bahn Stephansplatz. Gypsy-music-free Hungarian restaurant with lashings of goulash on offer. Mon–Sat noon–3pm & 6–11pm.

Kiang, 1, Rotgasse 8; U-Bahn Schwedenplatz. Vienna's best-known designer Chinese restaurant (with a sushi bar attached) decked out in loud primary colours with huge fish-bowl windows. The food is prepared right in front of your nose. Mon–Sat 11.30am–3pm & 6–11.30pm. (Branches at 6, Joanelligasse 3; U-Bahn Kettenbrückengasse; 8, Lederegasse 14; tram #5.)

Margherita, 1, Wallnerstrasse 4 (☎533 0812); U-Bahn Herrengasse. Smart, bustling Neapolitan pizza and pasta joint in the inner court of the Palais Esterházy. Pizzas are cooked in a stupendous lava oven, and you can eat alfresco in the summer. Mon–Sat noon–3pm, 6pm–midnight.

Novelli, 1, Bräunerstrasse 11 (☎513 4200); U-Bahn Stephansplatz. Elegant new Italian restaurant, with a popular posey bar, and top-notch modern Italian cuisine at above average prices. Mon–Sat noon–3pm & 6–11pm.

Palatschinkenkuchl, 1, Köllnerhofgasse 4; U-Bahn Schwedenplatz. Informal restaurant popular with kids and adults alike for its savoury and sweet pancakes and milkshakes. Mon–Sat 10am–midnight, Sun 5pm–midnight.

Reinthaler, 1, Gluckgasse 5; U-bahn Karlsplatz. Dive down the steps to this genuine, no nonsense busy Viennese *Beisl*. No concessions to modern cooking and certainly none to veggies. Mon–Fri 9am–11pm.

Salzamt, 1, Ruprechtsplatz 1; U-Bahn Schwedenplatz. Typical of Vienna's trendy modern *Beisln*: popular, minimalist and serving up excellent traditonal Viennese food in a *nouveau* way. Tables outside in summer. Daily 6pm–2am.

Wrenkh, 1, Bauernmarkt 10 (☎533 1526); U-Bahn Stephansplatz. The fashionable decor and ambience are a cut above the average vegetarian restaurant, the food is OK, too, though not always as imaginative as it sounds. Mon–Sat 11am–1am.

Landstrasse & around Naschmarkt

Osteria Venexiana, 3, Rennweg 11/corner of Marokkanergasse; tram #71. Genuinely delicious Venetian menu in this small, attractive restaurant, just round the corner from the Unteres Belvedere. Mon–Sat 10am–11pm, Sun 6–11pm.

Ubl, 4, Pressgasse 26; U-Bahn Kettenbrückengasse. Lovely, long-established *Beisl* near the Naschmarkt serving inexpensive, traditional food, plus a few Italian dishes. Daily noon–2.30pm & 6pm–midnight.

Mariahilf, Neubau, Josefstadt & Alsergrund

Hunger-Künstler, 6, Gumpfendorferstrasse 48 (☎587 9210); U-Bahn Kettenbrückengasse. Candlelit but unpretentious Mariahilf restaurant serving Vorarlberg specialities and plenty of veggie options. Daily 11am–2am.

Schilling, 7, Burggasse 103; tram #5 or bus #48A. A modish crowd frequent this *nouveau* strippeddown *Beisl* on the corner of Halbgasse; the food is traditional but imaginatively presented and freshly prepared. Daily 11am–1am.

Schnattl, 8, Lange Gasse 40 (☎405 3400); U-Bahn Rathaus. Innovative, *Neu Wiener Küche* cooked with a Styrian bent by Herr Schnattl himself; call to reserve a table in the courtyard. Mon–Fri 11.30am–2.30pm & 6pm–midnight, Sat 6pm–midnight.

Schnitzelwirt, 7, Neubaugasse 52; tram #49. Aside from Figlmüller (see above), this is the place to eat Wiener Schnitzel – they're just as humungous and cheaper, too. Mon–Sat 10am–11pm.

Siebenstern Bräu, 7, Siebensterngasse 19; tram #49. Popular modern micro-brewery, serving solid Viennese pub food, with lots of pan-fried dishes served with dark rye bread. Tues–Sat 10am–1am, Mon & Sun 10am–midnight.

Spatzennest, 7, Ulrichsplatz 1; bus #13A and #48A. Traditional Viennese *Beisl* with a good "salad and vegetable lovers' menu". Sun–Thurs 10am–midnight.

Stomach, 9, Seegasse 26; tram #D. A *Beisl* specializing in creative beef dishes, but also offering enough *Neu Wiener Küche* for veggies, too. Wed–Sat 4pm–midnight, Sun 10am–10pm.

Leopoldstadt

Leopold, 2, Grosser Pfarrgasse 11; tram #N or #21. Chic modern designer *Beisl*, with high ceiling, pine furniture, imaginative *Neu Wiener Küche*; a real oasis in Leopoldstadt. Daily Mon–Sat 6pm–2am, Sun 10am–1am.

Lusthaus, 2, Hauptallee (☎728 9565); bus #77A. Eighteenth-century rotunda at the far end of Hauptallee that makes a perfect food halt whilst exploring the Prater. May–Sept Mon, Tues, Thurs & Fri noon–11pm, Sat & Sun noon–6pm; shorter hours in winter.

Salm Bräu, 3, Rennweg 8. Conveniently located beer hall, which brews its own beer, and serves filling pub food, right outside the Unteres Belvedere. Daily 11am–midnight.

Schweizerhaus, 2, Strasse des 1 Mai 116; U-Bahn Praterstern. Czech-owned restaurant in the Prater; known for its draught beer and Czech specialities such as tripe soup and grilled pigs' trotters (*Steltzen*). March–Oct daily 10am–midnight.

Expensive restaurants

With the United Nations on its doorstep, and a good year-round calendar of conferences to cater for, it comes as no surprise that Vienna has plenty of top-drawer **expensive** restaurants, where you can find cuisine to match the best in the world. Dining within Vienna's top hotels is nearly always superb: the *Korso* in the *Hotel Bristo*, Kärntner Ring 1 and the restaurant in the *Palais Schwarzenberg*, Schwarzenbergplatz 9, are both particularly good, with the latter also offering a beautiful Baroque interior and garden as well as top-quality food. The following is a tiny selection of non-hotel places; each one will set you back around öS800–1000/€58.14–72.67 a head.

Drei Husaren, 1 Weihburggasse 4 (☎512 1092); U-Bahn Stephansplatz. Although only opened in 1933, this place plays heavily on nostalgia for the days of the Empire, with a menu packed full of Austro-Hungarian specialities. Daily noon–3pm & 6pm–1am.

Kervansaray, 1, Mahlerstrasse 9 (☎512 8843); U-Bahn Karlsplatz. This is the city's top fish and seafood restaurant, which specializes in lobster (*Hummer*), though a few meat dishes are also served up. On the ground floor, in the *Hummerbar*, there's a slightly cheaper array of dishes available.

Steiereck, 3, Rasumofskygasse 2 (☎713 3168); tram #N to Löwengasse. The *Steiereck* is considered by many Viennese to be the best restaurant in the city (if not the entire country). It serves up international and Austrian dishes with an emphasis on Styrian cuisine, has an impressive wine list, superb cheeses, and a bargain set brunch for around öS100/€7.27. Mon–Fri noon–3pm & 7pm–midnight.

Vienna's Heurigen

The city's traditional **Heurigen** are located out in the wine-producing villages, at the foot of the Wienerwald, that now form the outer suburbs of Vienna. These are good places to go in fine weather, preferably during late summer and autumn, and the areas to head for are listed in the box below. In addition, however, Vienna boasts a handful of centrally located wine-taverns known as **Stadtheurigen**, often housed in the cellars of the city's former monasteries. These are not real Heurigen at all, but are still great places to drink wine and eat the simple food on offer.

SELECTED HEURIGEN

Grinzing is the most famous of Vienna's *Heuriger* village-suburbs, and consequently the most touristy. There are numerous *Heurigen* on the main street of Sandgasse, but to avoid the worst of the crowds head further up Cobenzlgasse. Next most popular are the nearby areas of **Heiligenstadt** and **Nussdorf**. Less touristy alternatives include Sievering and Neustift am Walde, or you can cross over the Danube and head for the village of Stammersdorf. There are no specific listings for the villages, as the opening times of most *Heurigen* are unpredictable (most don't open until mid-afternoon). Part of the fun of visiting a *Heuriger* is to simply set off to one of the districts and take pot luck.

   Below are single recommendations intended to serve as starting points for each district:

Grinzing *Weingut am Riesenberg*, 19, Oberer Riesenbergweg 15; bus #38A tram #38 to the terminus.

Heiligenstadt *Mayer am Pfarrplatz*, 19, Pfarrplatz 2: bus #38A from U-Bahn Heiligenstadt.

Neustift am Walde *Schreiberhaus*, 19, Rathstrasse 54: bus #35A from U-Bahn Nussdorfer Strasse.

Nussdorf *Schübel-Auer*, 19, Kahlenberger Strasse 22; tram #D to the terminus.

Sievering *Haslinger*, 19, Agnesgasse 3; bus #39A from U-Bahn Heiligenstadt to the end stop.

Stammersdorf *Wieninger*, 21, Stammersdorfer Strasse 78; tram #31 to the terminus.

Stadtheurigen

Augustinerkeller, 1, Augustinerstrasse 1; U-Bahn Karlsplatz. Vast array of green-and-black-striped booths in the cellars underneath the Albertina. Fast service and hearty Viennese food; a tad touristy, but fun – prices are cheaper in the day. Schrammelmusik from 6.30pm. Mon–Fri & Sun 11am–midnight, Sat 11am–1am.

Esterházykeller, 1, Haarhof 1; U-Bahn Herrengasse. Snug, brick-vaulted wine-cellar with a limited range of hot and cold snacks. Situated off Naglergasse. Inexpensive. Mon–Fri 11am–11pm, Sat & Sun 4–11pm.

Göttweiger Stiftskeller, 1, Spiegelgasse 9; U-Bahn Stephansplatz. Ground floor monastic wine cellars that feel more like a family *Beisl*. Utterly traditional food and a mixed clientele – very popular, especially at lunchtime. Mon–Fri 11am–11pm.

Melker Stiftskeller, 1, Schottengasse 3; U-Bahn Schottentor. Vast, high-ceilinged wine-cellar owned by the famous Melk monks. Mon–Sat 5pm–midnight.

Zwölf-Apostelkeller, 1, Sonnenfelsgasse 3; U-Bahn Stephansplatz. An attractive seventeenth-century building with bars housed in three levels of cellars. *The* place to drink wine, but often difficult to find a space; cold food only. Daily 4.30pm–midnight. Closed July.

Bars, clubs and live venues

Surveys have shown that a vast majority of the Viennese are safely tucked up in bed by as early as 10pm. Meanwhile, however, a hard core stay up until very early in the morning – in fact it's quite possible to keep drinking round the clock. Vienna's late-night **bars** are concentrated in three main areas, the most famous of which is the so-called **Bermuda Triangle**, or *Bermuda Dreieck*, which focuses on Rabensteig, Seitenstettengasse, Ruprechtsplatz and the streets around. The emergence of the Triangle in the 1980s helped kick-start Vienna's nightlife out of its stupor, though the area has become a victim of its own success. That said, such is the variety packed into these few streets that you're bound to find somewhere that appeals.

The two other areas worth exploring are the **Naschmarkt**, where late-night licences abound, and Neubau's **Spittelberg** area – the narrow streets between Burggasse and Siebensterngasse, behind Messepalast – which has the highest concentration of late-night drinking holes, many of which double as restaurants and cafés.

Vienna's **club** scene is very small indeed for a city of 1.5 million. Dance culture, such as one would find in, say, London, is restricted to just a few venues. Aside from discos, the majority of Vienna's clubs are, in fact, bars, which either occasionally, or regularly, have live bands, or, more often than not, resident DJs spinning discs (both danceable and non-danceable). As it's so difficult to differentiate between what is a bar, what's a club and what's a live venue, we've simply organized the listings by area. To find out what's on at Vienna's clubs, check out the numerous flyers as well as the "Musik-U" section and "Party-Timer" calendar in the weekly listings tabloid *Falter*. Drink prices are relatively high – bars in the Bermuda Triangle tend to charge öS40/€2.91 and upwards for a *Krügerl* (half-litre) – but in those clubs where there is an admission charge, it's rarely more than öS100/€7.27.

The Bermuda Triangle

First Floor, 1, Seitenstettengasse 1; U-Bahn Schwedenplatz. As the name suggests, an upstairs bar, with a vast array of aquariums and packed with a more sophisticated crowd than your average BT hangout. Daily 8pm–3am.

LESBIAN AND GAY NIGHTLIFE

Vienna's **lesbian and gay scene** is pretty limited for your average Western European capital. However, in the 1990s, it enjoyed something of a blossoming, best symbolized by the establishment of an annual pride event, Regenbodenparade (Rainbow Parade; *www.pride.at*), held in June. Nevertheless, there are only the merest handful of gay bars and clubs, scattered across the city, with a cluster in the "gay district" around Naschmarkt. The social and political heart of the gay community is focused on the **Rosa-Lila Villa**, 6, Linke Wienzeile 102 (U-Bahn Pilgramgasse), which proudly flies the rainbow flag and proclaims itself as a Lesben und Schwulen Haus.

The best gay clubs are often the one-nighters like the mixed gay/lesbian Heaven, every Thursday at *U4*, 12, Schönbrunner Strasse 222. In addition, check out the following:

Café Berg, 9, Berggasse 8; U-Bahn Schottentor (also reviewed on p.145). Cool café with mixed gay/straight clientele, especially during the day. The food's good, and you can pick up flyers about up-and-coming gay events. Daily 10am–1am.

Café Savoy, 6, Linke Wienzeile 36; U-Bahn Kettenbrückengasse (also reviewed on p.145). Even more than the Berg, this scruffy fin-de-siècle café is by no means exclusively gay, but things pick up in the evening (for men at least). Mon–Fri 5pm–2am, Sat 9am–2am.

Café Willendorf, 6, Linke Wienzeile 102; U-Bahn Pilgramgasse. Café-restaurant inside the Rosa-Lila Villa, with a nice leafy courtyard. Another good place to pick up information about events. Daily 6pm–2am.

Frauencafé, 8, Lange Gasse 11; U-Bahn Lerchenfelderstrasse. Vienna's only permanent women-only space is a small, but friendly café next door to a feminist bookshop. Tues–Sat 5pm–2am.

Santo Spirito, 1, Kumpfgasse 7; U-Bahn Stephansplatz. Friendly Mediterranean bistro run by a gay couple, with an arty mixed straight/gay clientele and great Sunday brunches to loud classical music. Mon–Thurs & Sun 11am–2am, Fri & Sat 11am–3am.

Why Not?, 1, Tiefergraben 22. Late-night gay/lesbian bar and disco, popular with (but not exclusively patronized by) young gay men. Thurs–Sat 10pm–4am.

Jazzland, 1, Franz-Josefs-Kai 29; U-Bahn Schwedenplatz. Vienna's main trad-jazz venue, just below the Ruprechtskirche. Mon–Sat 7pm–2am.

Krah Krah, 1, Rabensteig 8; U-Bahn Schwedenplatz. Crowded bar known for its excellent selection of draught and bottled beers; decent snacks also on offer, and occasional live music. Mon–Sat 11am–2am, Sun 11am–1am.

Roter Engel, 1, Rabensteig 5; U-Bahn Schwedenplatz. Stylish café-bar designed by deconstructionist mob, Coop Himmelblau, in 1979. Live music most nights; sets at 9.30pm (Fri & Sat at midnight, too). Daily 5pm–4am.

The rest of the Innere Stadt

American Bar (*Kärntner Bar*), 1, Kärntner Durchgang; U-Bahn Stephansplatz. Small, dark late-night bar off Kärntnerstrasse with a rich interior by Adolf Loos. Shame about the strip club next door. Daily noon–4am.

Flex, 1, Donaukanal/Augartenbrücke; *www.flex.at*; U-Bahn Schottenring. Serious dance music bar by the canal, overlooking Wagner's Schützenhaus attracting the city's best DJs and a very young crowd. Daily 8pm–4am.

Flanagan's, 1, Schwarzenbergerstrasse 1–3; U-Bahn Karlsplatz. The most central, and probably the best of Vienna's rash of Irish pubs, with Guinness and Kilkenny, Irish/British food and big-screen sports. Daily 1pm–late.

Meierei, 3, Am Heumarkt 2a; U-Bahn Stadtpark. Staid Stadtpark café by day, but throbbing, sweaty DJ nights take place more or less every Fri & Sat, and occasionally on other days. From 10pm to 4am.

Roxy, 4, Operngasse 24; U-Bahn Karlsplatz. Central nightclub with an eclectic mix of DJ tunes, located underneath Wagner's Karlsplatz pavilions. Mon–Sat 5.30pm–2am, Mon–Sat 10am–2am.

Porgy & Bess, 1, Riemergasse 11; *www.porgy.or.at*; U-Bahn Stubentor. Converted porn cinema provides the new home for this, Vienna's top jazz venue that attracts serious jazz acts from all over the world.

Volksgarten, 1, Burgring 1; *www.volksgarten.at*; U-Bahn Volkstheater. Situated in the park of the same name, Vienna's longest-running club and a firm favourite with the dance crowd; the outdoor dance floor is a summertime treat, as is the *Pavillon* garden café upstairs. May–Sept daily 10pm–5am.

The Vorstädte and beyond

Arena, 3, Baumgasse 80; U-Bahn Erdberg. It's a long trek out to this former slaughterhouse on the corner of Französengraben, but there's a real variety of stuff that goes on here – all-night raves, outdoor concerts, open-air cinema – so check the listings before setting out. Daily 4pm–2am.

Blue Box, 7, Richtergasse 8. Café with resident DJs and a good snack menu, including excellent brunch buffet. Live music from 8pm. Mon 6pm–2am, Tues–Thurs & Sun 10am–2am, Fri & Sat 10am–4am.

Chelsea, 8, U-Bahnbögen 29–31, Lerchenfelder Gürtel; U-Bahn Thaliastrasse. Favourite venue with up-and-coming Brit guitar bands; situated underneath the U-Bahn. Mon–Sat 7pm–4am, Sun 4pm–4am.

Fischerbräu, 19, Billrothstrasse 17; U-Bahn Nussdorferstrasse. Very civilized micro-brewery pub, which produces a great, lemony, misty beer. Lots of tasty snacks and more substantial pub fare to be consumed in the bare-boards interior or the shady courtyard. A short walk from the U-Bahn, but worth the trek. Mon–Sat 4pm–1am, Sun 11am–1am.

Rhiz, 8, Stadtbahnbögen 37–38, Lerchenfelder Gürtel; *www.rhiz.org*; U-Bahn Lerchenfelder Strasse. A modish cross between a bar, a café and a club, with several DJs spinning everything from dance to trance. Daily 6pm–4am.

U4, 12, Schönbrunnerstrasse 222; *www.u4club.com*; U-Bahn Meidling-Hauptstrasse. Dark, cavernous disco, mostly rock/indie, with frequent gigs; a mecca of the alternative crowd. Gay/lesbian night Thursday. Daily 10pm–4am.

w.u.k., 9, Währinger Strasse 59; *www.wuk.at*; tram #40, #41 or #42. Formerly squatted old red-brick school, now legitimate arts venue with a great café and a wide programme of events, including live music; check the *Falter* listings. Daily 11am–2am.

The performing arts

Vienna prides itself on its musical associations, and classical music and opera, in particular, are heavily subsidized by the Austrian state. The chief cultural festival – featuring opera, music and theatre – is the **Wiener Festwochen** (*www.festwochen.or.at*), which lasts from early May until mid-June. In July and August, when the Vienna Philharmonic go on tour, the **Klangbogen** (Summer Music Festival) pulls in guest orchestras and more opera, while on the Donauinsel, on one weekend in August, there's a huge free pop festival, known as the **Donauinselfest** organized by the SPÖ. The city's film festival, or **Viennale** (*www.viennale.or.at*), runs for two weeks from mid-October, followed shortly afterwards by the **Wien Modern** festival of contemporary classical music in early November. But by far the busiest time of the year is **Fasching**, Vienna's ball season, which begins on November 11, and continues until Ash Wednesday the following year. To find out what's on in Fasching, pick up a *Wiener Ballkalender* (*www.ball.at*) from the tourist office in the months leading up to and during the season.

Information and tickets

To find out **what's on** in general, pick up the tourist board's free monthly listings booklet *Programm*, which gives the programmes of the big opera and concert houses, plus a day-by-day concert guide, ball calendar and details of the current art exhibitions. The weekly listings tabloid *Falter* also lists classical concerts under its *Musik-E* section.

Ticket **prices** vary enormously in Vienna: the Staatsoper is a case in point, with seats ranging from öS70/€5.09 to öS3500/€254.35. For some events – most notably the Vienna Boys' Choir and the New Year's Day Concert – it's not so much the price as the availability that's a problem. However, the big state venues offer cheap *Stehplätze*, or **standing-room tickets**, which can cost as little as öS30/€2.18 each and usually go on sale one hour before the performance; some venues also offer unsold tickets at a discount to students, around an hour or thirty minutes before the show starts.

The cheapest way of **buying tickets** is to go to the venue's own box office. With the big four state theatres – Staatsoper, Volksoper, Burgtheater and Akademietheater – you can either buy direct or from their shared central box office, the *Bundestheaterkassen*, not far from the Staatsoper at 1, Hanuschgasse 3 (☎51444-2960; Mon–Fri 8am–6pm, Sat & Sun 9am–noon; U-Bahn Karlsplatz; *www.oebthv.gv.at*). There's also a ticket booth which sells tickets for all venues next to the Staatsoper (daily 10am–7pm).

Opera and classical music

Vienna has a musical pedigree second to none, boasting one of Europe's top opera houses in the **Staatsoper**, served by one of its finest orchestras, the **Wiener Philharmoniker**, whose New Year's Day Concert (*Silvesterkonzert*) in the Musikverein is broadcast across the globe. When the big state theatres are closed in July and August, opera and classical music concerts captured on film are also shown for free every evening outside the Rathaus.

The most famous musical institution in the city is the **Wiener Sängerknaben** (*www.wsk.at*), or Vienna Boys' Choir, who perform Mass at the Burgkapelle in the Hofburg every Sunday from mid-September to June at 9.15am. Tickets for the Mass (öS70–380/€5.09–27.62) are sold out weeks in advance, though some are held over each week and go on sale on Fridays (11am–1pm & 3–5pm) – you need to be there at least half an hour before the box office opens. To book in advance, write to Hofburgkapelle, Hofburg, A-1010 Wien, Austria, stating which Sunday Mass you wish to attend. The other option is to settle for one of the free *Stehplätze*, which are distributed before Mass; get there for 8.30am to be sure of a place (although some people leave early having got bored). Be warned, however, that most of the choir remain out of sight up in the organ loft for the whole of Mass.

Opera and operetta

Kammeroper, 1, Fleischmarkt 24 (☎513 6072, http://*members.magnet.at/wienerkammeroper*); U-Bahn Schwedenplatz. Vienna's smallest opera house, hidden in the backstreets of the Innere Stadt and performing a variety of works from Rossini to Britten. In July and August, when the theatre is closed, the Kammeroper stages open-air Mozart operas in the Roman ruins in Schönbrunn's Schlosspark.

Staatsoper, 1, Opernring 2 (☎51444-2250, *www.wiener-staatsoper.at*); U-Bahn Karlsplatz. Vienna's largest opera house stages around forty operas a season played in rep. It's a conservative place, but attracts the top names, and has the benefit of the Wiener Philharmoniker in the pit. Ticket prices range from öS70/€5.09 to öS2500/€181.68, but with over 500 *Stehplätze* (öS50/3.63) going on sale every night, an hour before the curtain goes up, it is one of the most accessible opera houses in the world.

Volksoper, 9, Währinger Strasse 78 (☎51444-3670, *www.volksoper.at*); U-Bahn Volksoper or tram #40, #41 or #42. Vienna's number-two opera house, which specializes in operetta, but also branches out into Janáček, Shostakovich and the late Romantics; over 100 *Stehplätze* a night.

Classical music

Bösendorfer Saal, 4, Graf Starhemberg-Gasse 14 (☎504 6651); U-Bahn Taubstummengasse. Chamber-music concert hall belonging to the famous Austrian piano manufacturers.

Konzerthaus, 3, Lothringerstrasse 20 (☎712 1211, *www.konzerthaus.at*); U-Bahn Karlsplatz. Early twentieth-century concert hall designed by Viennese duo Helmer & Fellner. Three separate halls: the Grosser Saal, Mozart-Saal and Schubert-Saal.

Musikverein, 1, Bösendorferstrasse 12 (☎505 8190, *www.musikverein-wien.at*); U-Bahn Karlsplatz. Two ornate concert halls in one building, gilded from top to bottom inside. The larger of the two, the Grosser Saal, has the best acoustics in the country, while the smaller hall, the Brahms-Saal, is used mainly for chamber concerts; *Stehplätze* available for the Grosser Saal.

Theatre and musicals

Obviously for the non-German speaker, most of Vienna's theatres and satirical cabarets have limited appeal. However, there are a couple of English-speaking theatre groups: International Theatre, 9, Porzellangasse 8 (☎319 6272; tram #D), and the more professional Vienna's English Theatre, 8, Josefsgasse 12 (☎402 1260, *www.englishtheatre.at*; U-Bahn Lerchenfelderstrasse). There are also a few theatres that specialize in musicals, several puppet theatres, where language is less of a problem, and, of course, the Burgtheater, whose interior alone is worth the price of a ticket.

Straight theatre and musicals

Burgtheater, 1, Dr-Karl-Lueger-Ring 2 (☎51444-4140, *www.burgtheater.at*); U-Bahn Herrengasse. Vienna's most prestigious theatrical stage puts on serious drama in rep. The foyer and staircases are spectacular; the auditorium was modernized after bomb damage in 1945. Tickets cost from öS50/€3.63 to öS600/€43.60, with 150 *Stehplätze* (öS25/€1.82) going on sale every night, an hour before the curtain goes up.

Raimund Theater, 6, Wallgasse 18 (☎59977); U-Bahn Westbahnhof. Late-nineteenth-century theatre, which puts on Broadway musicals and other popular productions.

Ronacher, 1 Seilerstätte 9 (☎5141 1207); U-Bahn Stephansplatz. Beautifully refurbished turn-of-the-twentieth-century music hall that puts on a variety of dance shows and musicals.

Theater-an-der-Wien, 6, Linke Wienzeile 6 (☎58830); U-Bahn Karlsplatz/Kettenbrückengasse. Historic, early-nineteenth-century theatre, specializing in musicals.

Volkstheater, 7, Neustiftgasse 1 (☎524 7263, *www.volkstheater.at*); U-Bahn Volkstheater. Modern plays and classics and even the odd operetta.

Puppet theatre

Lilarum Figurentheater, 3, Göllnergasse 8 (☎710 2666); U-Bahn Kardinal-Nagl-Platz. Puppet theatre out in Landstrasse, with several performances a day Wed & Fri–Sun.

Märchenbühne der Apfelbaum, 7, Kirchengasse 41 (☎523 1729-20). Puppet theatre specializing in classic fairy tales, so even without any German, you can at least follow the plot. Sat & Sun.

Schönbrunner Schloss-Marionettentheater, 13, Schloss Schönbrunn, Hofratstrakt (☎817 3247, *www.merionettentheater.at*). String-puppet theatre in Schönbrunn specializing in Mozart operas – try and catch a different show if you can. Performances Wednesday–Sunday 4 & 8pm.

Cinema

Austrian cinema is not really up there with the greats, and unless your German is up to scratch you're best off sticking to British and American films. One film that's fun to see, and is shown here every weekend at the *Burg-Kino* (see below), is *The Third Man* – **Der Dritte Mann** – made in 1949, set amidst the rubble of postwar Vienna and starring Orson Welles. The best place to check out the week's cinema listings is either *Der Standard* or *Falter*, the city's weekly tabloid. *OF* means it's in the original (without subtitles); *Omengu* means it's in original with English subtitles; *OmU* means it's in the original with German subtitles, but should not be confused with *OmÜ*, which means it's in the original, but has a live voiceover German translation; and *dF* means it's dubbed into German.

Artis International, 1, Schultergasse/Jordangasse; U-Bahn Stephansplatz. Central multiplex cinema showing films in English in six different salons.

Burg-Kino, 1, Opernring 19; U-Bahn Babenbergerstrasse. Cinema on the Ringstrasse that only shows films in the original language.

Filmmuseum, 1, Augustinerstrasse 1; U-Bahn Karlsplatz. Vienna's main art-house cinema, on the ground floor of the Albertina, with a very esoteric programme.

Imax Filmtheater, 14, Mariahilferstrasse 212 (*www.imax-wien.at*); U-Bahn Schönbrunn or tram #52 and #58. Specially made forty-minute films to show off the 400-square-metre wraparound screen's awesome scope.

Kino unter Sternen, 2, Augarten; tram #31 from Schottenring. Open-air cinema showing classics in their original versions from mid-July to August.

Listings

Airlines Air France, 1, Kärntnerstrasse 49 (☎51419, *www.airfrance.fr*); Alitalia, 1, Kärntner Ring 2 (☎505 1707, *www.alitalia.it*); Austrian Airlines, 1, Kärntner Ring 18 (☎517 66, *www.aua.com*); British Airways, 1, Kärntner Ring 10 (☎505 7691, *www.britishairways.com*); Canadian Airlines, 1, Krugerstrasse 4 (☎515 55-40, *www.cdnair.ca*); Delta, 1, Kärntner Ring 17 (☎512 6646, *www.delta-air.com*); Lauda Air, 1, Opernring 6 (☎51477, *www.laudaair.com*); Qantas 1, Opernring 1 (☎587 7771, *www.qantas.com.au*); TWA, 1, Opernring 1 (☎586 6868, *www.twa.com*). The nearest U-Bahn for all the above airlines is Karlsplatz.

American Express 1, Kärntnerstrasse 21–23 (☎515 4077, *www.americanexpress.com*); U-Bahn Stephansplatz.

Books Shakespeare & Co, 1 Sterngasse 2; U-Bahn Schwedenplatz. Tiny, friendly English-language bookstore packed to the rafters with a great selection of novels, art books and magazines.

Boats DDSG, 1, Friedrichstrasse 7 (☎58880, *www.ddsg-blue-danube.at*); U-Bahn Karlsplatz.

Embassies and consulates Australia, 4, Mattiellistrasse 2–4 (☎512 8580); Canada, 1, Laurenzerberg 2 (☎531 3830); Czech Republic, 14, Penzinger Strasse 11–13 (☎894 1200); Hungary,

1, Bankgasse 4–6 (☎533 2631); Ireland, 3, *Hilton Centre*, Landstrasse Hauptstrasse 2 (☎715 4246); Slovakia, 19, Armbrustergasse 24 (☎318 9055); Slovenia, 1, Niebelungengasse 13 (☎586 1304); South Africa, 19, Sandgasse 33 (☎320 6493); UK, 3, Jauresgasse 12 (☎716130); USA, 9, Bolzmanngasse 16 (☎31339).

Exchange Outside normal banking hours, the exchange booths at the airport (daily 6am–11pm), Westbahnhof (daily 7am–10pm) and Südbahnhof (Mon–Fri 7am–7pm; July & Aug also Sat & Sun 6.15am–9pm) are open. Banks with 24hr automatic exchange machines include Bank Austria, Stephansplatz 2; Creditanstalt, Kärntnerstrasse 7; Die Erste Banke, Graben 21.

Hospital Allgemeines Krankenhaus, 9, Währinger Gürtel 18–20; U-Bahn Michelbeuern-AKH.

Internet Free Internet access at Amadeus, fourth floor of Steffl department store, 1, Kärntnerstrasse 19 and in the basement of their flagship store at Mariahilferstrasse 99; *www.amadeusbuch.co.at.*

Laundry 8, Josefstädter Strasse 59; tram #J. Mon–Fri 7.30am–7.30pm.

Lost property Zentrales Fundamt, 9, Wasagasse 22 (Mon–Fri 8am–noon); if lost on public transport phone ☎7909 43500; lost on Austrian Railways phone ☎5800 35656.

Maps Freytag & Berndt, 1, Kohlmarkt 9; U-Bahn Stephansplatz. Flagship store of Austria's most prestigious map-makers, with loads of maps, as well as guides on Vienna and the rest of the world in English, including a large selection of *Rough Guides*.

Markets Naschmarkt, 6 & 7, Linke & Rechte Wienzeile (Mon–Sat); U-Bahn Karlsplatz/Kettenbrückengasse: Vienna's most exotic fruit and veg market, with Turkish, Balkan, Chinese, Middle Eastern and Austrian produce, takeaway stalls plus clothes and sundries. On Saturday mornings, there's a flea market (*Flohmarkt*) extension west of Kettenbrückengasse U-Bahn. Spittelberg, 7, Spittelberggasse (April–June, Sept & Oct every third weekend; Aug & Dec daily); U-Bahn Volkstheater: artsy, crafty market in the narrow streets of the Spittelberg area.

Police The main police station in the first district is at Deutschmeisterplatz 3; U-Bahn Schottenring.

Post office The main post office is at Fleischmarkt 19 (U-Bahn Schwedenplatz). It's open 24hr, seven days a week.

Soccer Vienna's top soccer team, SK Rapid, play at the Gerhard Hanappi Stadion on Keisslergasse in Hütteldorf (U-Bahn Hütteldorf); FK Austria, their main rivals, play at the Franz Horr Stadion in Favoriten; big international games are played at the Prater (aka Wiener) Stadion in the Prater (U-Bahn Praterstern).

Swimming The Amalienbad, 10, Reumannplatz 23 (U-Bahn Reumannplatz) has a wonderful Art-Deco interior, particularly the sauna; the Jörgerbad, 17, Jörgerstrasse 42–44 (tram #43), is also very beautiful inside. The Krapfenwaldbad, 19, Krapfenwaldlgasse 65–73 (bus #38A), is an outdoor pool up in the foothills of the Wienerwald (May–Sept) with great views; so too is the Schafbergbad, 18, Josef-Redl-Gasse (bus #42B).

travel details

Trains

(*www.oebb.at*)

Vienna (Franz-Josefs Bahnhof) to: Eggenburg (hourly; 1hr–1hr 20min); Gmünd NÖ (every 2hr; 2hr–2hr 20min); Klosterneuburg-Kierling (every 30min; 15min); Krems an der Donau (hourly; 1hr–1hr 15min); Tulln (every 30min; 30–45min).

Vienna (Südbahnhof) to: Baden (every 30min; 30min); Bruck an der Leitha (every 30min; 25–35min); Bruck an der Mur (hourly; 1hr 55min); Graz (every 2hr; 2hr 40min); Klagenfurt (every 2hr; 2hr 5min–2hr 25min); Laa an der Thaya (hourly;

2hr); Leoben (every 2hr; 2hr 15min); Marchegg (7–12 daily; 45min); Mödling (every 15min; 25min); Neusiedl am See (every 2hr; 50min); Semmering (hourly; 2hr); Villach (every 2hr; 4hr 25min–4hr 50min); Wiener Neustadt (every 30min; 50min).

Vienna (Westbahnhof) to: Attnang-Puchheim (hourly; 2hr 35min); Bregenz (8 daily; 10hr); Feldkirch (8 daily; 7hr 40min); Innsbruck (every 2hr; 5hr 20min); Kufstein (every 2hr; 3hr 15min–3hr 35min); Linz (1–2 hourly; 1hr 50min–2hr); Melk (every 1–2hr; 1hr); Pöchlarn (every 1–2hr; 1hr 15min); St Anton (8 daily; 6hr

45min); St Pölten (1–2 hourly; 40min); Salzburg (1–2 hourly; 3hr–3hr 20min); Wels (hourly; 2hr 10min).

Vienna (Wien-Nord) to: Bad Deutsch Altenburg (hourly; 1hr 10min); Flughafen Wien-Schwechat (every 30min; 30min); Petronell-Carnuntum/Hainburg Ungartor (hourly; 1hr 5min–1hr 15min); Retz (every 2hr; 1hr 5min).

International trains

Vienna (Südbahnhof) to: Berlin Zoo (2 daily; 9hr 30min); Bratislava (3 daily; 1hr 20min); Brno (3–4 daily; 1hr 40min); Florence (2–3 daily; 11hr 30min); Ljubljana (3 daily; 6hr); Prague (3–4 daily; 6hr 30min); Rome (2 daily; 13hr 30min); Venice (4–6 daily; 8hr); Warsaw (3 daily; 8hr 30min); Zagreb (2 daily; 7hr).

Vienna (Westbahnhof) to: Amsterdam (4 daily; 12 hr 30min); Belgrade (2 daily; 10hr); Berlin Ost (2 daily; 11hr 30min); Brussels (3 daily; 13hr); Bucharest (4 daily; 5hr); Budapest (7 daily; 3hr); Cologne (6 daily; 9hr 30min); Copenhagen (1–2 daily; 20hr 30min); Munich (10 daily; 6hr); Paris Est (3 daily; 14hr); Zurich (3 daily; 9hr).

CHAPTER TWO

LOWER AUSTRIA

Lower Austria (Niederösterreich; *www.noe.co.at*) is by far the largest and most populous of all the Austrian Länder, yet it is also the least explored by tourists. One problem is that, apart from the foothills that form the border with Styria, the landscape doesn't conform to the alpine image of Austria. Most visitors don't come all the way to Austria to roam the gently rolling countryside that characterizes much of Lower Austria, or the unrelenting flat plain of the Marchfeld that extends east of Vienna. Only the famously un-blue Danube (Donau), which splits the region in two, attracts tourists in any great number, particularly along the most scenic stretch known as the Wachau, justifiably the most popular destination in the Land.

Lower Austria's other big problem is that it has something of an identity crisis. Along with Upper Austria (Oberösterreich), it forms the country's historic heartland – together these regions give their name to the entire country. But while Upper Austria has Linz as its regional capital, Lower Austria's natural capital is Vienna. Indeed, Vienna doubled as the regional capital until 1986, when its place was taken by the small provincial town of St Pölten. Vienna still dominates the region, however, and serves as the main transport hub, which means that much of Lower Austria can be easily visited on day-trips from Vienna. To do so, though, would be to skim the surface, and to miss out on the slow pace of life that makes the region so appealing.

The **Wachau** is definitely better visited over a couple of days than as a rushed day-trip from Vienna. You could easily spend a whole day just exploring **Krems**, the remarkable medieval town that marks the entrance to the valley. From Krems, the river cuts its way through steep, vine-clad hills, emerging some 40km later at **Melk**, whose cliff-top monastery gets more visitors than any other in the country. Both the above places are less than an hour by train from the capital, but to explore the valley's smaller wine-producing villages – something that's possible by road, rail or river – or the cliff-top castles in between, it's worth setting aside a day or two.

Some of the more remote areas are, in any case, simply too far away to be reached comfortably in a day. This is particularly true of the alpine foothills around the mountain spa-resort of **Semmering**, and along the **Ybbstal**, which lies along the southern border with Styria. It's also true of the **Waldviertel**, the little-visited agricultural region in the northwest that's considered something of a rural backwater by most Austrians.

ACCOMMODATION PRICE CODES

All **hotels and pensions** in this book have been coded according to the following price categories. All the codes are based on the rate for the least expensive double room during the **summer season**. In those places where winter is the high season, we've indicated both summer and winter room rates in the text.

① under öS400/€29.07
② öS400–600/€29.07–43.60
③ öS600–800/€43.60–58.14
④ öS800–1000/€58.14–72.67
⑤ öS1000–1200/€72.67–87.21

⑥ öS1200–1400/€87.21–101.74
⑦ öS1400–1600/€101.74–116.28
⑧ öS1600–1800/€116.28–130.81
⑨ over öS1800/€130.81

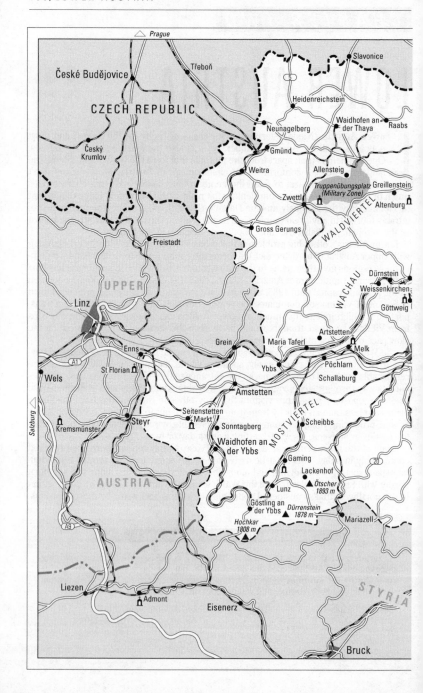

△ *Brno*

N

Vratěnín
Vranov
Znojmo
Mikulov
Břeclav
Drosendorf
Hardegg
Geras
Retz
45
Laa an der Thaya
Poysdorf
Horn
WEINVIERTEL
Hohenau
Rosenburg
Eggenburg
Mistelbach
Gars
4
Hollabrunn
SLOVAKIA
6
Krems
Grafenegg
Stockerau
River Danube
3
Traismauer
Tulln
Klosterneuburg
Gänserndorf
Herzogenburg
VIENNA
Marchegg
St. Pölten
WIENERWALD
MARCHFELD
A1
Bratislava
Eckartsau
Hainburg
Orth
Petronell
Bad Deutsch
Rohrau
Altenburg
Mödling
Laxenburg
Mayerling
Heiligenkreuz
Bruck
A4
Lilienfeld
Baden
A3
Neusiedl
am See
Wiener
Neustadt
Eisenstadt
Schneeberg
2075 m
Rax
2069 m
Neunkirchen
Neusiedler See
Payerbach
Sopron
Reichenau
Gloggnitz
BURGENLAND
Mürzzuschlag
Semmering
Aspang Markt
HUNGARY

Bratislava ▷
Budapest ▷

0   50 km

A2

▽ *Graz*

The proximity of the Iron Curtain helped to keep it that way for over forty years, and tourists who do make it here appreciate the region precisely for its soporific qualities and gentle, rural charms. It takes a day or two to get used to the relaxed pace of life in the region's numerous tiny, walled towns, like **Drosendorf** or **Zwettl**, which have changed surprisingly little over the last two hundred years.

The **Wienerwald**, which stretches away southwest of Vienna, is another area that needs to be taken at a leisurely pace, allowing time for a walk in the densely wooded hills: the spa-town of **Baden** or neighbouring **Mödling** are the perfect launching pads. There are, of course, one or two places that can be happily visited on a day-trip, **Wiener Neustadt** being a case in point. Less than an hour by train from Vienna, its attractions are easily covered in a day and its appeal as an overnight stop is limited. With a population of just 50,000, the young capital of **St Pölten** is never going to compete on equal terms with Vienna, though it's worth a day-trip if only to look at the innovative, new Landhausviertel, built to house the new regional administrative headquarters.

Up the Danube: Klosterneuburg and Tulln

The first place of interest up the Danube from Vienna is the glorious monastery of **Klosterneuburg**, separated from the capital only by the thin northeasternmost wedge of the Wienerwald. Beyond Klosterneuburg, you reach the wide plain of the Tullnerfeld, a patchwork of vineyards and fields of maize and sunflowers, with the hills of Wienerwald becoming ever more distant to the south. **Tulln**, the birthplace of celebrated artist Egon Schiele, is the first stop for boats heading upriver (see box below). Thanks to Austria's efficient public transport system, both the above places make for day-trips from Vienna.

Klosterneuburg

Just north of Vienna's city limits, hidden from the capital by the hills of the Wienerwald, the village of **KLOSTERNEUBURG** is one of the quickest and easiest day-trips from Vienna. Its chief attraction is its imposing Augustinian monastery, the oldest and richest in Austria, whose Baroque domes and neo-Gothic spires soar above the right bank of the Danube. However, Klosterneuburg also has a spanking-new private modern art museum hidden in its suburbs and filled with postwar Austrian art.

Stift Klosterneuburg

The **Stift Klosterneuburg** (*www.stift-klosterneuburg.at*) was founded in the twelfth century by the Babenberg Duke Leopold III, who, so the story goes, vowed to build an

---

BOATS UP THE DANUBE

On Saturdays and Sundays, from mid-May to October, the Donaudampfschiffahrtsgesellschaft (DDSG; *www.ddsg-blue-danube.at*) run a daily boat up the Danube from Vienna to Dürnstein. The boat leaves from Vienna's Reichsbrücke at 8.45am, calling at Tulln at 11.20am and Krems at 1.55pm. The DDSG boat from Dürnstein calls in at Krems on the way back downstream at 4.50pm, reaching Tulln at 6.45pm, and arriving two hours later in Vienna. These times were correct when going to print, however, you should check with the local tourist office before setting out. DDSG, and several other companies, also run more frequent daily sailings along the most picturesque section of the river known as the Wachau (see p.171), which lies between Krems and Melk. Note that a boat launch in German is a *Schiffsstation*.

abbey on the spot where he found his wife's veil, which had been carried off by the wind from a nearby castle. Leopold himself was canonized in 1485, and later became the patron saint of Austria, making Klosterneuburg a popular place of pilgrimage. Having withstood the Turkish siege of 1683, the monastery enjoyed a second golden age under the Emperor Karl VI (1711–40), who planned a vast imperial palace here, along the lines of El Escorial in Spain. The project was never fully realized, but the one wing that was completed gives some idea of Karl's grandiose plans.

To visit the monastery, you must sign up for a **guided tour** (Mon–Sat hourly 9–11am & 1.30–4.30pm, Sun 11am & 1.30–4.30pm; Nov–March no 9am tour; öS70/€5.09); the ticket office is right by the entrance to the monastery at Rathausplatz 20. The tour starts with the **Stiftskirche**, which still hints at its origins as a Romanesque basilica, despite overzealous nineteenth-century restoration. Neo-Gothic finials and other details obscure the west front of the church, but the south door, with its blind arcading, is still much as it would have been in the Babenbergs' day. Inside, the church is a riot of seventeenth-century early Baroque, replete with frescoes and mountains of stucco-work. The most impressive craftsmanship is in the chancel: the richly gilded choir stalls, the exuberant high altar and, above all, Johann Michael Rottmayr's *Assumption*, without doubt the pick of the frescoes.

To the north of the church are the **medieval cloisters**, built in the late thirteenth century. The central courtyard is encroached upon, in the southwest corner, by the little L-shaped Freisingerkapelle, containing the episcopal tomb of its namesake, who died in 1410. More intriguing is the polygonal wellhouse, which juts out into the courtyard from the eastern cloister, and boasts some fine tracery over the portal; the highlight, though, is the magnificent, giant bronze candelabra, crafted in Verona in the twelfth century.

The monastery's outstanding treasure, however, is the **Verduner Altar**, in the Leopoldskapelle to the east of the cloisters. This stunning winged altar, completed in 1181 by Nicholas of Verdun, comprises more than fifty gilded enamel plaques depicting biblical scenes from both Testaments. Sadly, you can't get close enough to appreciate the detail, but the overall effect is dazzling. The top half of St Leopold is buried in the Wiener Werkstätte casket underneath the altar; his legs are buried beneath the nearby wrought-iron grille.

You can get some idea of the Spanish-bred Emperor Karl VI's big plans for Klosterneuburg from the **Residenztrakt**, to the east of the medieval buildings. Plans were drawn up in 1730 for a vast imperial edifice, enclosing four inner courtyards, in deliberate imitation of El Escorial in Spain, which the Habsburgs had recently lost to the Bourbons. The building was intended to sprout numerous domes, each to be capped by a crown representing one of the Habsburg lands. In the end, the money ran out even before the completion of the first courtyard, and the roof sports just two domes, one capped with the imperial crown, the other with the archducal hat of Niederösterreich. The showpiece of the Baroque wing is the **Marmorsaal** (Marble Hall), with its giant oval dome, supported by coupled composite columns, and decorated with frescoes by Daniel Gran glorifying the Habsburg dynasty.

After the tour, it's worth taking a stroll round the outlying monastic buildings, particularly those surrounding the **Leopoldhof**, a secluded little cobbled courtyard to the northwest of the monastery church, with an attractive, late-Gothic oriel window on one side. The main courtyard, Stiftsplatz, to the south of the church, centres on a lovely Gothic **Lichtssäule** (Lighted Column), once a common sight in Austrian towns, now a rare, surviving example. If you're keen to see more of the monastery, there are also occasional guided tours of the **Orangery** and **Stiftsgarten**, and of the wine cellars (Mon–Sat only). In addition, the monastery's **Stiftsmuseum** (May to mid-Nov Tues–Sun 10am–5pm) is worth a visit for the four painted panels, originally attached to the Verduner Altar in 1331, as well as several Renaissance bronzes, ivory work and nineteenth and twentieth-century paintings, including an early work by Schiele.

KAFKA IN KIERLING

While you're in the vicinity of Klosterneuburg, you might be interested to know that the Prague-born writer Franz Kafka died of tuberculosis in Sanatorium Hoffmann (now converted into flats), in the nearby village of **Kierling** on June 3, 1924, at the age of forty. Die-hard devotees can catch a bus from outside the train station to Hauptstrasse 187, and visit the place in which he spent the last few weeks of his life, correcting proofs of his collection of short stories, later published as *The Hunger Artist*. The **Kafka-Gedenkraum** (Mon–Sat 8am–noon & 1–5pm; free), on the second floor, is not, in fact, the very one in which he died, as that overlooked the garden and is currently occupied. To gain entry to the Gedenkraum, you must retrieve the key from flat D along the corridor. Inside there are photos of Dora Dyment, who nursed him in his sickness, and whom he intended to marry, and of the old sanatorium, plus lots of books about (and by) Kafka.

Sammlung Essl

Klosterneuburg is also home to Austria's largest private art collection, the **Sammlung Essl** (Tues–Sun 10am–7pm, Wed until 9pm; öS80/€5.81; *www.sammlung-essl.at*), which is displayed in a purpose-built gallery down by the Danube, to the south of the monastery. Featuring just about every renowned postwar Austrian artist, the collection was accumulated over the last fifty years by Karlheinz and Agnes Essl, who inherited the bauMax chain of DIY stores, which has its corporate headquarters in Klosterneuburg. Originally destined for the new MuseumsQuartier in the heart of Vienna (see p.113), the collection found itself without a home after Ortner & Ortner's competiton-winning entry for the complex ran into controversy in the mid-1990s, and was eventually scaled down. The Essls responded by opening their own museum in a sort of concrete, modernist factory designed by Heinz Tesar.

The big white rooms on the first floor are used to display a sort of overview of the collection, which is characterized by large abstract canvases, but ranges from Surrealist works by Maria Lassnig and "kaleidoscopic landscapes" by Friedrich Hundertwasser to works by the leading lights of Aktionismus, Vienna's very own extremely violent version of 1960s performance art. In addition to the Austrian art, there are works by international contemporary artists such as Britain's Sean Scully and the American Nam June Paik. Half the gallery space is given over to temporary exhibitions drawn from the collection. On the second floor, you'll find the Grosser Saal, with its distinctive floating, curved ceiling, and a café and bookshop, the latter currently the only place where you can get any information in English about the collection.

Practicalities

The easiest way to get to Klosterneuburg from Vienna is on **S-Bahn line S40**; trains depart from Franz-Josefs Bahnhof every half-hour, taking just eight minutes to get to Klosterneuburg-Weidling (for the Sammlung Essl), and twelve minutes to get to Klosterneuburg-Kierling (for the monastery). To reach the Sammlung Essl, walk under the railway tracks and turn left, following the signs to the gallery. For the monastery, which is clearly visible from the train station, head up Hundskehle, and then take the steps to your left. To get to the monastery from the gallery, cross back over the railway tracks and head up Leopoldstrasse.

If you want a bite **to eat**, or have time to kill before your tour departs, the *Stiftscafé*, next door to the monastery, offers reasonable food, and a chance to sample the local wine. The upper floor of the pricier *Stiftskeller* restaurant, next door, is open all day, though the *Keller* itself is only open in the evenings. A much more congenial place to have an evening meal, though, is the *Römerhof*, up the Stadtplatz, at the beginning of

Kierlinger Strasse, which offers a range of beers on tap, all the usual pub snacks and a range of *Spätzle* dishes.

It's easy enough to find **accommodation** in Klosterneuburg itself. *Hotel Schrannenhof* (☎02243/32072; ④), on Niedermarkt, opposite the train station, is a nicely modernized hotel that has retained plenty of original features; the hotel also runs the marginally cheaper, but equally good *Pension Alte Mühle*, Mühlengasse 36 (☎02243/37788; ④), ten minutes' walk up Stadtmarkt and Kierlinger Strasse. For a cheaper option, head for the family-run *Hotel-Pension Höhenstrasse*, Kollersteig 6 (☎02243/52757; ③), which enjoys a quiet location a kilometre or so south of the town centre (and closer to the Klosterneuburg-Weidling train station). The local **HI hostel** (☎02243/83501; May–Sept) is about 3km west of Klosterneuburg, beyond Kierling in Gugging; frequent local buses ply the route. The *Donaupark* **campsite** (☎02243/52757; Feb–Nov) is located by the Danube, on the other side of the railway from the town; it's efficiently run, and handy for the Klosterneuburg-Kierling train station. If you have any queries, there's a **tourist office** (summer daily 9am–7pm; winter Mon–Fri 9am–noon; ☎02243/32038, *www.klosterneuburg.net*) in the train station.

Tulln an der Donau

TULLN, a quiet provincial town situated in the fertile Danube plain roughly 25km northwest of Vienna, has an ancient history dating back to its foundation as the Roman naval fort of Comagena. Its main claim to fame today, however, is as the birthplace of the painter Egon Schiele (1890–1918), who was born above Tulln's main train station, where his father was stationmaster.

The Town
On the hundredth anniversary of the artist's birth, Tulln finally honoured its most famous son by opening an **Egon Schiele-Museum** (Tues–Sun 9am–noon & 2–6pm; öS40/€2.90) in the town's former prison by the banks of the River Danube. Before you set off round the exhibition, be sure to pick up the free booklet in English from the ticket desk. The ground floor is filled with reproductions of his works, and photographs from his brief life. One of the original cells has been transformed to represent the Neulengbach prison cell in which Schiele was incarcerated for 24 days in 1912. He was charged with displaying erotic drawings in a room open to children, and sentenced to three days in prison (by a judge who was himself a collector of pornography); since he had already served more than that in the course of his remand, he was immediately released. On the walls are reproductions of the watercolours he executed whilst a prisoner, mostly angst-ridden self-portraits and simple interiors of his tiny cell.

The museum's modest collection of Schiele originals is displayed on the first floor. There's a goodly selection of pencil sketches, among them numerous nudes, a ghostly *Madonna and Child* in chalk and an early oil painting from 1908 of Trieste harbour, a favourite destination of the artist, who, as the offspring of an employee of the railways, benefited from cheap train tickets. In the attic, you'll find one of the artist's sketchbooks and the powerfully energetic *Ruined Mill at Mühling*, painted in oil in 1916, when Schiele was employed as a clerk in a POW camp for Russian officers.

The town's brand-new museum complex, the **Tullner Museen** (Wed–Fri 3–6pm, Sat 2–6pm, Sun 10am–6pm; öS30/€2.18), housed in the former Minorite (Franciscan) monastery, three blocks west down Albrechtsgasse, is a bit of a disappointment, despite its stylish new premises. The main courtyard, sporting an elegant glass roof, houses the town's collection of historic fire engines from the horse-drawn carts of the eighteenth century to the diesel monsters of the 1970s. Other displays tell the story of

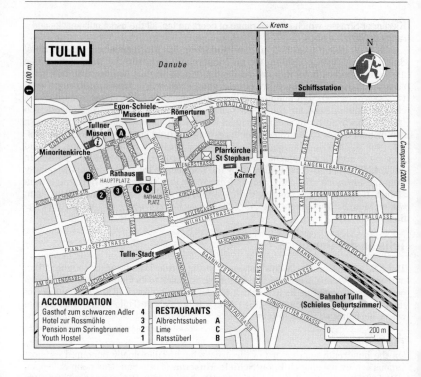

the town's uneventful history, while the basement is given over to the less-than-impressive archeological finds dug up during the renovation of the cloisters.

You're better off taking a quick peek inside the adjacent Baroque **Minoritenkirche**, which has been lovingly restored and is positively gleaming with white Rococo stuccowork and colourful frescoes depicting, among other things, St John of Nepomuk being thrown to his death off Prague's Charles Bridge (also featured in gold relief on the pulpit). Be sure to peek through the glass door at the church's sacristy, with its cabinets of exquisite inlaid wood and Rococo ceiling decoration. At the west end of the church, is the brick-built Loretokapelle, a mock-up of Mary's house in Nazareth, complete with obligatory Black Madonna and Child, surrounded by silver clouds, gold sunbeams and cherubs.

The town's most impressive Roman remain is the bulky **Römerturm**, an old bastion later used to store the town's precious salt supplies (and sometimes still referred to as the Salzturm), originally built under the Emperor Diocletian (284–305 AD), on the riverfront beyond the Schiele Museum. Also worth a once-over is the **Pfarrkirche St Stephan**, two blocks east of the main square of Hauptplatz. Underneath this bulky Baroque church, the original Romanesque basilica can still be seen at ground level. Particularly fine is the west portal, which boasts thirteenth-century mug shots of the apostles. Best of all, though, is the **Karner** (Charnel House) to the east of the church, one of the best-preserved Romanesque buildings in Austria, dating to 1250. The hexagonal rib vaulting looks clumsily restored, but the series of weird and wonderful animals and beasts that decorate the walls, above the blind arcading, are fantastic, as are the devilish characters with outsized ears and noses that accompany them.

Finally, if you've time to kill while waiting for the next train back to Vienna, you might as well visit **Schieles Geburtszimmer** (June–Sept Tues–Sun 10am–noon & 3–5pm; öS20/€1.45), occupying two rooms on the first floor of the main train station (Bahnhof Tulln), which has changed very little since Schiele's childhood. However, there's not a great deal to see beyond a reconstruction of the bedroom in which the artist was born in 1890, and a small model railway – understandably, trains were a major feature of Schiele's childhood, and a few of his early drawings of trains are reproduced here.

Practicalities

Fast trains from Vienna's Franz-Josefs Bahnhof take just 25 minutes to reach Bahnhof Tulln, the **main station**, some fifteen minutes' walk southeast of the town centre. S-Bahn trains take 45 minutes, but depart more frequently and terminate at Tulln-Stadt, less than five minutes' walk south of the centre. Tulln's **tourist office** (May–Oct Mon–Fri 9am–noon & 2–6pm, Sat & Sun 1–6pm; Nov–April Mon–Fri 9am–noon; ☎02272/65836, *www.tulln.at*), on the east side of Minoritenplatz, will furnish you with a free map and can organize **private rooms**. By the river to the west of the Tullner Museen, you'll find the town's simple **hostel**, the *Alpenvereinsherberge* (☎02272/62692; May–Oct). Other **accommodation** options include the *Hotel zur Rossmühle*, Hauptplatz 12 (☎02272/62411; ⑤), a spacious hotel, with an attractive plant-strewn interior complete with caged birds; the much plainer *Pension zum Springbrunnen*, a few doors up at no. 14a, (☎02272/63115; ④); or the friendly *Gasthof zum schwarzen Adler*, near the Rathaus at no. 7 (☎02272/62676; ③). The town's *Donaupark* **campsite** (☎02272/652000, *www.tiscover.com/donaupark-camping.tulln*) is set amidst the leisure facilities 1.5km east of the town centre.

The best place for a bit of no-nonsense Austrian **food** is the *Albrechtsstuben*, Albrechtsgasse 24 (closed Sun eve & Mon), east of Minoritenplatz, or the down-to-earth *Ratsstüberl*, Hauptplatz 19 (closed Sun), with tables looking over the main square. If you're looking for food on a Sunday, you may well find the *Lime* restaurant, on Hauptplatz, which offers crepes and baguettes as well as the usual fare, the only place open. For **late-night drinking**, head for *Mythos*, on the north side of Hauptplatz, which has a disco (Wed–Sat).

Krems an der Donau and around

Some 75km northwest of Vienna, **KREMS AN DER DONAU** sits prettily on the terraced, vine-clad slopes of the left bank of the Danube. Site of a twelfth-century Babenberg mint, in the course of the thirteenth century Krems became a wealthy provincial wine-growing town. The architectural fruits of this boom period, which lasted until the seventeenth century, are clearly visible in the narrow streets of the Altstadt. Devastation in the Thirty Years' War, a shift in the trade routes, and a decline in traffic on the Danube led to comparatively little building work during the Baroque period. Krems remains an important Danube port, but the foundation of a postgraduate university, and a swanky new arts centre, have added a much-needed dose of youthful culture to what is essentially a sedate, prosperous town.

Arrival, information and accommodation

The town's **tourist office** is situated in the former Und monastery, halfway between Krems and Stein at Undstrasse 6 (May–Oct Mon–Fri 9am–6pm, Sat 10am–noon & 1–6pm, Sun 10am–2pm; Nov–April Mon–Fri 8.30am–noon & 1.30–5pm; ☎02732/85620, *www.tiscover.com/krems*). If you want to stay in the centre of Krems, then it's worth considering the **private rooms** on offer through the tourist office. Situated one block

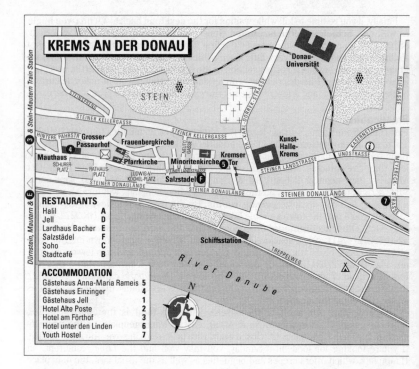

KREMS AN DER DONAU

RESTAURANTS

Halil	A
Jell	D
Lardhaus Bacher	E
Salzstädel	F
Soho	C
Stadtcafé	B

ACCOMMODATION

Gästehaus Anna-Maria Rameis	5
Gästehaus Einzinger	4
Gästehaus Jell	1
Hotel Alte Poste	2
Hotel am Förthof	3
Hotel unter den Linden	6
Youth Hostel	7

south is the town's **HI hostel**, Ringstrasse 77 (☎02732/83452, *oejhv-noe@oejhv.or.at;* April–Oct), a favourite with passing cyclists. The nearest **campsite** is close by, overlooking the Danube (☎02732/84455; April–Oct), though if you have your own transport the tiny campsite in Senftenberg (☎02719/2319; March–Oct), 7km northwest of Krems, is much quieter. Wherever you stay the night, you should ask your hosts for a **Gästepass**, which costs nothing but allows you small discounts at various places – from swimming pools to museums – in Krems and elsewhere in the Wachau–Niebelungengau area of the Danube Valley.

Hotels and pensions

Gästehaus Anna-Maria Rameis, Steiner Landstrasse 16 (☎02732/85169). Modernized sixteenth-century house in Stein, with a pleasant inner courtard; rooms with or without en-suite facilities. ②.

Gästehaus Einzinger, Steiner Landstrasse 82 (☎02732/82316). Reasonably priced option, situated in a converted Renaissance house in Stein, with a beautiful arcaded courtyard. ③.

Gästehaus Jell, Schiessstattgasse 1 (☎02732/82345). The very comfortable rooms at *Jell* are not above the restaurant on Hoher Markt (see p.169), but above the wine cellars in amongst the vineyards themselves, up Wachtertorgasse. ③.

Hotel Alte Poste, Obere Landstrasse 32 (☎02732/82276). Krems' premier Altstadt hotel, a 500-year-old building with a spacious cobbled and arcaded Renaissance courtyard, offering reasonably priced and very tastefully rustic en-suite rooms. Lots of character. Closed Jan & Feb. ④.

Hotel am Förthof, Förthofer Donaulände 8 (☎02732/83345). Biedermeier-style hotel, to the west of Stein on the banks of the Danube, with a justly famous gourmet restaurant. Traffic noise can be a problem, so choose your room carefully. ⑤.

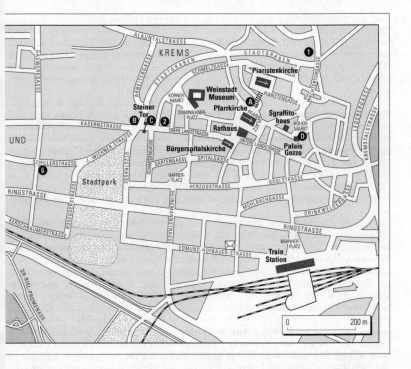

Hotel unter den Linden, Schillerstrasse 5 (☎02732/82115, *www.udl.at*). Perfectly located, large family-run hotel in the quiet neighbourhood of Und, with a lovely shady *Gastgarten*; cheaper rooms have shared facilities. ④.

Krems

Present-day Krems is actually made up of three previously separate settlements, Krems, Und and Stein, giving rise to the side-splitting local joke, "Krems Und Stein sind drei Städte" ("Krems and Stein are three towns"). Most people tend to restrict their wandering to Krems proper, though it's worth taking the time to explore Stein, too, since, in many ways, it's Stein that has most successfully retained its medieval character.

Krems' main thoroughfare, **Landstrasse**, three blocks north of the train station, is a busy, pedestrianized shopping street studded with old buildings. The finest of these is the **Bürgerspitalskirche**, originally built in 1470 on the site of the old Jewish ghetto as the town's hospital chapel. Over the doorway is the AEIOU motto of the Emperor Friedrich III (see p.216), while the inside boasts some attractive lierne vaulting. On the opposite side of the street stands the sixteenth-century **Rathaus**, whose Renaissance origins are glimpsed in the corner oriel window facing onto Kirchengasse. Further west along the main street, at Oberer Landstrasse 10, it's worth peeping into the exquisite arcaded courtyard of **Fellnerhof**.

To the north of Landstrasse, the quieter, hilly cobbled streets and squares boast some of Krems' finest late-medieval buildings. The largest of the squares, Pfarrplatz, is dominated by the **Pfarrkirche**, originally a late-Romanesque church, enlarged at the end of the seventeenth century – you can see this most clearly in the tower. The interior is a perfect example of High Baroque drama, with trompe l'oeil masonry and gold covering just about everything, including the entire pulpit and the high altar: an explosion of gilded saints and cherubs set against the background of an enormous sunburst. The ceiling frescoes are by local-born Baroque artist Johann Martin Schmidt, known as "Kremser Schmidt", whose works can be found in churches and museums all over town.

A covered stairway known as the "Piaristen Stiege", on the far side of Pfarrplatz, leads up to the imposing late-Gothic **Piaristenkirche**. The church boasts some fine stellar vaulting, and several Baroque altarpieces by Kremser Schmidt, but it's worth the climb up the stairs, above all, for the stupendous view across town. From here, you can descend via **Hoher Markt**, perhaps the prettiest of Krems' cobbled squares, which slopes down to the wonderfully scruffy-looking **Palais Gozzo**, a honey-coloured medieval palace with a loggia on the ground floor. Round the corner, at Margarethenstrasse 5, is the **Sgraffitohaus**, which, as its name suggests, is smothered in sixteenth-century sgraffito decoration depicting medieval folk frolicking and feasting.

West of Pfarrplatz lies the town's recently overhauled **Weinstadt Museum** (March–Nov Tues 9am–6pm, Wed–Sun 1–6pm; öS40/€2.90), atmospherically located in the former Dominican monastery on Körnermarkt. Most of the museum amounts to little more than a mildly diverting trot through the history of the town and, in particular, its viticulture. However, you do get the chance to look around the thirteenth-century monastery, whose cloisters feature unusual zigzag trefoil arcading, and whose church – now used for temporary exhibitions – is refreshingly free of Baroque clutter and boasts the remnants of its original medieval frescoes. The museum also allows you the opportunity to take a closer look at some of **Kremser Schmidt**'s artworks and sculptures. There's something dark and tortured about Schmidt's work that makes it compulsive viewing. Born in nearby Grafenwörth in 1718, he trained under local artisans and set up his own workshop in Krems, eschewing the cosmopolitan art scene of the capital, and it's this attachment to his provincial roots that sets his work apart from the more academic painters of the Austrian Baroque.

Landstrasse, and the old medieval town of Krems, officially terminate at the strangely hybrid **Steiner Tor**, a monstrously belfried fifteenth-century town gate, flanked by two cone-capped bastions. Appropriately enough, the district of **UND** links Krems, in the east, with Stein, to the west. There's no reason to pause in Und, unless you wish to visit the town's tourist office (see p.165), housed in the former Capuchin monastery. And if you're keen to sample some of the region's wines, you can sign up for a **wine-tasting** tour of the monastery's cellars.

Stein

The **Kremsor Tor**, ten minutes' walk west of the Steiner Tor, confusingly, signals the beginning of **STEIN**. As you approach the gateway, it's difficult to miss the **Kunst-Halle-Krems** (daily 10am–6pm; entrance fee varies; *www.kunsthalle.at*), the town's vast new arts venue, which hosts major modern art exhibitions, stages shows in the nearby Minoritenkirche (see below) and puts out a series of events on Friday and Saturday evenings.

Stein is much quieter than Krems, and really does feel like a separate town, its narrow main street, **Steiner Landstrasse**, a sequence of crumbling old Renaissance facades with beautiful, often arcaded, courtyards, and every 100m or so, small cobbled squares that face onto the Danube. The first church you come to is the impressive thirteenth-century shell of the **Minoritenkirche**, whose high-vaulted, late-Romanesque interior was used as a tobacco warehouse, and now stages art exhibitions, organized by the Kunst-Halle-Krems. At the southern end of Minoritenplatz stand two sixteenth-century **Salzstädel** (salt barns), sporting the distinctive red-and-white quoins, or cornerstones, that are characteristic of many of Stein's old buildings.

Further along Landstrasse, the Pfarrhof stands out due to its rich Rococo stuccowork, followed shortly afterwards by the Gothic **Pfarrkirche**, which sports a classic Baroque onion dome, and some finely carved choir stalls, but is otherwise fairly undistinguished. Steps round the east end of the church climb sharply to the fourteenth-century **Frauenbergkirche**, now a chapel to Austrian war dead. From here, you get a great view across Stein and the Danube to the domes of the hilltop monastery of Göttweig to the south. It's worth continuing a little further along Steiner Landstrasse to appreciate Stein's two other winsome squares, Rathausplatz and Schürerplatz, and its remarkable parade of Renaissance houses: in particular, the **Grosser Passauerhof**, with its half-moon battlements, and the **Mauthaus**, which boasts faded trompe l'oeil frescoes.

Kremser Schmidt lived in the prettily gabled Baroque house close by the squat **Linzer Tor**, which marks the western limit of the old town of Stein. If you're heading back to Krems, the backstreet of Hintere Fahrstrasse provides an interesting alternative to Steiner Landstrasse.

Eating and drinking

Without doubt, one of the best places to **eat** is at *Jell*, Hoher Markt 8–9 (closed Sat & Sun lunch & Mon), a seriously *gemütlich* rustic place, with imaginatively prepared food, and exellent wine from their own nearby vineyards. The Turkish-run *Halil*, Pfarrplatz 8 (closed Tues), serves decent pizza and pasta, and the sushi sets and bento boxes at the stylish, minimalist *Soho*, Obere Landstrasse 36, make for a pleasant change from Austrian cuisine. If you're in Stein, the simple *Salzstädl* in the house of the same name, is a convenient fuelling point; *Hotel am Förthof* is the more formal and expensive alternative. The most celebrated gourmet restaurant in the vicinity is *Landhaus Bacher* (☎02732/82937; closed Mon & Tues) just over the river in Mautern.

The *Stadtcafé*, on Südtirolerplatz, overlooking the Steiner Tor, is the town's most Viennese of **cafés**. For local wine, and traditional lunchtime food, head for *Metternich Stube*, Schlüsselamtsgasse. On a warm, summer's evening, it's worth heading out of town to one of the numerous *Heurigen* in the backstreets of Stein: one of the more central is *Erich Hamböck*, Kellergasse 31. Several new **drinking** holes have opened recently in Krems: try the minimalist cellar bar, *Hendrik*, just down from the Palais Gozzo, *Fredo* (closed Sun), on the same street, at the corner of Pfarrplatz, which serves the excellent *Weitra Bräu*, or *Amadeus*, Pfarrplatz 11, where you can play pool until the early hours.

Stift Göttweig

As you walk around the upper reaches of Krems and Stein, you're repeatedly treated to tantalizing glimpses of **Stift Göttweig**, the palatial hilltop Benedictine monastery some 5km south of the Danube. The original monastery, founded by the Bishop of Passau in the eleventh century, was destroyed by fire in 1718; the imposing Baroque complex you see today is the partial realization of an even more grandiose plan by Johann Lukas von Hildebrandt. To get to see the interior of the monastery, you must join a guided tour (mid-March to mid–Nov daily 10 & 11am, 2, 3, 4 & 5pm; öS60/€4.36; *www.stiftgoettweig .or.at*), in German only, lasting 45 minutes.

Even if you don't fancy the guided tour, you're free to visit the pastel-pink **Stiftskirche** (daily 6am–noon & 1.15–6.15pm), which overlooks the manicured lawns of the main courtyard. The church's Tuscan loggia, flanked by two symmetrical square towers, adds a Palladian touch to the unfinished exterior. Inside, the church is a bit of a mess: Gothic in scale, clumsily converted to Baroque, and then given a dubious pink-and-blue colour scheme in the nineteenth century. The richly gilded Baroque furnishings are the most attractive feature, particularly the inlaid choir stalls, topped by gilded filigree work, and the main altarpiece, flanked by turquoise and gold barley-sugar columns. Note, too, the thoroughly upstaged, but surviving medieval stained-glass windows above the main altar.

Guided tours begin with Göttweig's most celebrated Baroque masterpiece, Hildebrandt's light and airy **Kaiserstiege** (Imperial Staircase), which boasts spectacular views north to Krems. The staircase – up which Napoleon is alleged to have ridden his horse – is lined with pilasters featuring wonderful atlantes, wrestling with their togas, in the place of capitals, and niches containing urns, symbolizing the twelve months, and statues representing the four seasons, all by Kremser Schmidt. Completed in just four months, the ceiling fresco by Paul Troger glorifies the Emperor Karl VI, who looks slightly ludicrous in the guise of the sun-god Apollo in his heavenly chariot. The best of the rest of the state rooms, which host changing exhibitions taken from the abbey's treasury and art collection, is the **Altmannsaal**, the former banqueting hall, in which feasting guests would have been observed in turn by the guests partying on the trompe l'oeil balcony of the *Wedding at Cana* ceiling fresco.

To get to the monastery, you can either catch one of the infrequent buses from Krems, or take the train to Klein-Wien (every 2hr; 10min), from which it's a stiff, but pretty, kilometre-hike through the woods. The *Stiftsrestaurant*, in the grounds of the monastery, serves traditional fare and has a terrace looking north to the Danube; down in Klein-Wien, the *Landgasthof Schickh* (☎02736/7218; ④), next to the train station, has a rather more adventurous (and expensive) menu, featuring lobster and crayfish, and an old train carriage for a café.

Schloss Grafenegg

Situated 10km away in the fertile plain east of Krems, is **Schloss Grafenegg** (Tues–Sun 10am–5pm; öS60/€4.36; *www.grafenegg.at*), a neo-Gothic fantasy castle set in a mature, wooded English-style park. The current building was designed by Leopold Ernst in the mid-nineteenth century, with a single tower, the Schwedenturm, and the basic lay-out of the castle, with its dry moat, the only reminders of the old medieval seat. The new Schloss is all pristine cream-coloured mock-crenellations, stepped gables and fiendish-looking gargoyles. The interior is currently used as a venue for frequently engaging exhibitions, which also allow you the opportunity to take a look inside this slightly vulgar, but immaculately constructed aristocratic pile.

The first place to head for, once you've bought your tickets, is the **Schlosskapelle**, a perfectly restored neo-Gothic fancy vibrantly decorated in cobalt blue, its stalls, bristling with pinnacles and filigree work (The winged altar is actually an original late fifteenth-century work, as are the painted panels on the walls). In the state rooms of the **Prunkräume**, it's all decadent and expensive fun, with heavy wood furnishings, incredible strapwork ceilings and awesome fireplaces. Don't miss the ceramic and marble bathroom, or the wonderful glassed-in gallery, overlooking the grounds, with its incredible painted ceiling, with artichoke-like pendants and mischevous elvish creatures below the brackets. The Herrensalon – a favourite for weddings and functions – features lots of heavy-handed gilded wood furnishings, and an underlit ceiling with angels and armoured figures leaping from the beams brandishing lances.

The extensive grounds are informally laid out, feature some fairly exotic trees and are perfect for a **picnic**. Alternatively, you can pay up and eat in some style at the *Zur Taube* **restaurant** in the old riding school. Several other outbuildings have been converted into a hotel, *Schloss Grafenegg* (☎02738/2616, *www.moerwald.at*; ⑤), where you can stay in some considerable style and comfort. To reach Grafenegg, you need to either catch one of the infrequent buses, or catch one of the frequent **trains** from Krems to Wagram-Grafenegg, whose train station is 2km northeast of the Schloss.

The Wachau

Krems marks the beginning of the most picturesque, tortuously winding stretch of the Danube, known as the **Wachau** (*www.wachau.com*). Vine-bearing, ruin-encrusted hills roll down to the river on both sides, and in springtime the banks are a mass of apricot blossom. Marking the upstream end of the Wachau is **Melk**, arguably Austria's most spectacular monastery, a stunning Baroque confection that towers over the town and river below, and which, like Krems, merits its own separate section (see p.175). Inevitably, given the above attractions, the Wachau – less than 40km in length – is by

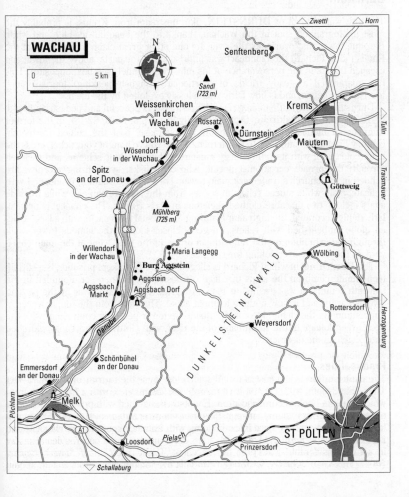

far the most popular section of the river, and, indeed, the most heavily touristed bit of Lower Austria.

To really appreciate the joys of the Wachau, you need to travel slowly, preferably by bike, boat or train, rather than by car. Bike is by far the most popular mode of transport for visitors of all ages, with a well-marked **cycle path**, the *Donauradweg*, linking all the villages north of the river. A single-track rail line also hugs the northern bank, stopping at every village along the way. Finally, there are frequent sailings along this stretch of the **Danube**; for more details pick up a leaflet from one of the tourist offices. Although there are no bridges over the river between Mautern and Melk, there are numerous little boats, known as *Rollfähre*, attached to high wires stretched across the Danube, which carry cars, bicycles and pedestrians from one side of the river to the other.

Dürnstein

The tiny, walled town of **DÜRNSTEIN**, 9km upstream from Krems, is probably the most photographed spot in the Wachau, thanks to the beautiful ice-blue and white Baroque tower that overlooks the river. Its one other great claim to fame is that the English king Richard the Lionheart was imprisoned in the castle above the town, and escaped thanks to the perseverance of his minstrel, Blondel (see box, opposite). This has guaranteed a steady trickle of (particularly English-speaking) tourists since tourism first began, and is now fairly shamelessly exploited by the town.

Dürnstein's pretty little main street, Hauptstrasse, is peaceful and pedestrian-friendly. To get to the **Stiftskirche** (April–Oct daily 9am–6pm; öS30/€2.18), in the former Augustinian monastery, head south off Hauptstrasse, past the ruined thirteenth-century Franciscan nunnery, to Klosterplatz. Once you've bought your ticket, cross the main courtyard, with its rather nasty mustard-and-grey colour scheme, and turn left through the ornate ceremonial portal, whose obelisks, symbolizing eternity, are echoed in the church's trademark main tower. The church's vaulting is adorned with delicate, plain white stucco reliefs of scenes from the New Testament, while the side altars include two macabre clothed skeletons in glass coffins. The chancel is particularly richly decorated, the high altar featuring an unusual tabernacle, with a large golden globe embellished with reliefs. To get a closer look at the famous tower, walk through the exhibition on the Augustinian order, in the west wing of the main courtyard, to the terrace overlooking the river.

The **Burgruine**, in which Richard is alleged to have been kept prisoner, is a stiff fifteen-minute climb up the steps that lead off beside the Steiner Tor. Founded in the eleventh century, it was trashed in 1645 during the Thirty Years' War by the passing Swedish army, and is now nothing to shout about. The view from the top, however, is quite stunning: the richly decorated Stiftskirche tower perfectly contrasting with the deep green foliage of the south bank of the river, with Göttweig and Weissenkirchen both visible in the distance.

Practicalities

The **train station** is just east of the Altstadt; close by is the **tourist office** (April–Oct Thurs–Sat 2–6pm; ☎02711/219, *www.tiscover.com/duernstein*), with a free phone from which you can book **accommodation**. Hauptstrasse is lined with private rooms (look out for "Zimmer frei" signs) and pensions. *Pension Altes Rathaus* (☎02711/252; ③) is a lovely sixteenth-century sgraffitoed building with an inner courtyard at Hauptstrasse 26; *Pension Böhmer*, (☎02711/239; ③), at no. 22, is another good bet. You can also stay in some considerable luxury at the excellent, family-run *Gasthof Sänger Blondel* (☎02711/253, ⑤), a pretty, wisteria-strewn villa overlooking Klosterplatz, and, at con-

THE KIDNAPPING OF RICHARD THE LIONHEART

After the successful recapture of Acre in 1191, during the Third Crusade, the English **King Richard I** and the French King Philip II upset several of their fellow crusaders by sharing the spoils between them, leaving nothing to those who had been fighting outside the city for up to two years before the kings' arrival. And when the Babenberg Duke Leopold V tried to raise his own standard and lay a claim to some of the booty, Richard uprooted the Austrian flag and threw it into a ditch. It was an action he lived to regret, for on his way home, the following year, he was shipwrecked in the Adriatic, and forced to travel incognito across Babenberg territory. Despite growing a beard and travelling under a false name, Richard attracted attention to himself on several occasions: either due to his good looks, by throwing his money around carelessly, or because of the splendour of his gloves. He was eventually arrested at an inn in Erdberg (now a suburb of Vienna), imprisoned in Dürnstein and ransomed by Leopold.

Here the tale falters and legend takes over, as Richard's loyal French minstrel, Blondel, wanders through the land looking for his master. Having made it to Dürnstein, Blondel, according to one version of the tale, "called to mind a song which they had made between them two and which no one knew save the king". On hearing the tune, Richard joined in, and Blondel returned to England to break the news. Two English knights then arrived, paid the ransom and delivered Richard back to England, where he got a distinctly cool reception from his brother John, who had already announced his death. Some chroniclers even suggest that it was at Dürnstein that Richard got his nickname "Lionheart". So the story goes, a hungry lion was set loose on the king after it was discovered that he had seduced the daughter of the jailer. Undaunted, Richard wrapped his cloak around his arm and thrust it down the lion's throat, tore out its heart and ate it.

In the end, though, it was Richard who had the last laugh in his feud with Leopold. He got his revenge by complaining to the pope, who promptly excommunicated Leopold for harming a "Soldier of Christ". As if that weren't enough, poor Leopold fell off his horse a few days later and broke his leg in such a way that it needed amputating. No surgeon was willing to do the job, so Leopold himself took an axe to it and chopped it off in three blows. Unfortunately, it was too late, and Leopold died before he could make it up with the Vatican.

siderable cost, at the town's seventeenth-century riverside *Schloss Dürnstein* (☎02711/212, *www.schless.at*; ⑨), which has its own sauna and pool.

Food at the *Sänger Blondel* (closed Sun lunch & Mon), where main dishes are öS150/€10.90 or more, is superb; *Goldener Strauss*, Hauptstrasse 18, offers simpler dishes for öS90/€6.54 and upwards. The *Alter Klosterkeller* (closed Tues), set in the vineyards on Anzuggasse, just east of the Altstadt, is the town's most popular *Heuriger*.

Weissenkirchen in der Wachau

Nowhere else in the Wachau enjoys quite the same idyllic situation as Dürnstein, but the wine-producing village of **WEISSENKIRCHEN**, 6km upstream, has even more charm and character. Set back slightly from the river amidst sloping vineyards, its narrow matrix of streets is centred on a small cobbled square, overlooked by the eye-catching, pink sixteenth-century Teisenhoferhof, whose pretty little arcaded courtyard, hung with vines and corn on the cob, is home to an eighteenth-century winepress and the **Wachaumuseum** (April–Oct Tues–Sun 10am–5pm; öS30/€2.18). Amidst folk artefacts from the region and Romantic nineteenth-century landscape paintings of the Wachau, there are several works by Kremser Schmidt, including some Bacchanalian etchings and a rare self-portrait of the artist and his family. A covered stairway leads up from the square to the Gothic **Pfarrkirche**, which rises up above the town's terracotta jumble of rooftops, and was fortified against the Turks in 1531. A couple of superb Gothic statues, in particular an artless fifteenth-century *Pietà*, adorn the interior, and there's a tiny modern statue, *Schmerzensmann* (Grieving Man), in a niche on the south side of the church's smaller tower, sculpted in 1990 by a Bavarian priest.

There are some picturesque places to **stay overnight** in Weissenkirchen, most notably the *Raffelsbergerhof* (☎02715/2201, *www.schlosshotels.co.at*; ⑥; May–Oct only), an old arcaded sixteenth-century shipmaster's house filled with antiques, and with a lovely garden out the back. The **tourist office** (April–Oct Mon–Sat 10am–noon & 3–6pm; ☎02715/2600, *www.gem.weissenkirchen/wvnet.at*), in the Teisenhoferhof, can give you the full rundown, and book private rooms. The Teisenhoferhof is also part of the *Ludwig Stüberl*, an unpretentious inn where you can eat and drink for very little.

Spitz an der Donau

Another six kilometres brings you to **SPITZ AN DER DONAU**, a larger and more disparate village. Like most in the region, it makes its money nowadays from a combination of viticulture and tourism. Less than a century ago, however, the river would have played a much more important part in local life, through fishing and as a means of transport, a story told in more detail by the **Schifffahrtsmuseum** (April–Oct Mon–Sat 10am–noon & 2–4pm, Sun 10am–noon & 1–5pm; öS60/€4.36), housed in Schloss Erlahof, an old Baroque mansion, up the road to Ottenschlag, and once owned by a wine-producing monastic order. Amidst the old oars, winches and boats, there's an instructive model showing how, before the advent of steam, three large barges needed a team of more than forty horses to pull them upriver. The building itself is quite something, too, retaining several fancy stone doorways and fine stucco ceilings. The real centre of Spitz lies northwest of the train station up the tree-lined Marktstrasse which leads to Kirchenplatz, the meeting point of several cobbled streets. The nearby Gothic **Pfarrkirche**, with its lovely dappled roof tiles, is remarkable primarily for its outstanding parade of fourteenth-century sculptures of Christ and the apostles, set in niches along the organ loft.

Spitz's **train station** lies between the Schiffsstation and the village centre, and rents out bikes. The local **tourist office** (April–Oct Mon–Sat 11am–noon & 3–8pm, Sun 3–7pm; *www.tiscover.com/spitz*), just off the main road, opposite the Schiffsstation, can book **private rooms** for you. A good **hotel** to go for in the centre is the pretty *Barock-Landhof Burkhardt* (☎02713/2356; ③), on the corner of Kremserstrasse and Marktstrasse. Other possible choices include the family-run *Wachauerhof* (☎02713/2303; ④), an old-fashioned three-storey hotel on Hauptstrasse, or the smart *Weinhotel* (☎02713/2254; ③), opposite the museum on Ottenschlägerstrasse.

Burg Aggstein and around

By far the most awesome of the numerous ruined castles that crown the hills of the Wachau is **Burg Aggstein** (daily dawn to dusk; öS25/€1.82), perched some 300m above the right bank of the Danube, 5km south of Spitz (where you need to cross the river). Built literally into the rock, in the twelfth century, and sacked by (among others) the Turks, the castle was, as Patrick Leigh Fermor calls it, a "gap-toothed hold of the Künringers", a family of medieval robber-barons who were notorious highwaymen in this area. The place is not entirely in ruins, retaining large parts of the outer defences intact and a keep, up which you can climb for an incredible view down to the Danube. The old castle kitchens now serve as a simple summertime café-restaurant, with tables outside in the main courtyard.

If you're up for it, it's only 3km by foot (and about 7km by road) inland from Aggstein to the Baroque **Wallfahrtskirche** of **Maria Langegg**, nothing special to look at from the outside, but a feast of trompe l'oeil painting inside. Not only do the ceiling frescoes play tricks on the eye with their perspective, but the paintings along the north and south walls are framed by illusionistic side altars; ditto the impressive high altar, whose medieval *Madonna and Child* is set within a putti- and cloud-spattered sunburst. As you leave, note the delightful Rococo organ, with its delicate gold filigree and giant clock suspended between the organ pipes.

If you do decide to head off for Maria Langegg by road, you need to get back down to river level, go 2km south to the village of **AGGSBACH-DORF**, and head inland. En route, it's worth taking a closer look at the intriguing set of buildings, at the east end of the village, that used to belong to an old Carthusian monastery, heralded by a startlingly tall partial set of fortifications. The Gothic **Kartäuserkirche** itself is worth a peek inside for its decorated ceiling bosses (take some binoculars for a good look), and its unusual Jugendstil main altar relief.

Melk and around

Strategically situated at the western entrance to the Wachau, some 40km upstream from Krems, the town of **MELK** boasts by far the most spectacular Baroque monastery in Austria. Dramatically perched on a high granite bluff overlooking the Danube, the palatial mustard-yellow abbey dominates the landscape from whichever direction you approach, dwarfing the town into insignificance. Initially a Roman border post and later a tenth-century Babenberg fortress, the site was handed to the Benedictines in 1089. Very little of the medieval structure survives; what draws in a staggering half a million tourists a year is the flamboyant Baroque pile built in its place in the first half of the eighteenth century.

Stift Melk

Melk's early renown was based on its medieval scholarship (discussed in some detail in Umberto Eco's monastic detective story *The Name of the Rose*), and its possession of some very valuable relics, including the body of the Irish missionary St Koloman, who was revered for his powers of healing. The abbey was gutted by fire during the Turkish invasion of 1683, and lay in ruins until Melk's ambitious abbot Berthold Dietmayer commissioned local architect Jakob Prandtauer to design a new showpiece **monastery**. The project was so overblown that Dietmayer initially faced a rebellion by his own monks, dismayed by the affront to their asceticism, and the abbot had to prove that the monastery could afford the work before building could recommence. The abbey continues to function today, and its monastery school, containing some 700 boys and girls, remains one of Austria's most prestigious academic institutions.

Access to the **Stift** (mid-April to mid-Nov daily 9am–6pm; mid-Nov to mid-April guided tours only 11am & 2pm; *www.stiftmelk.at*) is via the main gates to the east. You can walk through several of the courtyards and take a peek at the abbey church without paying, but to see inside the monastery, you must buy a ticket (öS100/€7.27; öS30/€2.18 extra with a guided tour; Kombi-Karte (öS120/€8.72 covering entry to Schloss Schallaburg, see below, and the monastery) from the monastery's information point on the south side of the Torwartlhof (the first courtyard).

The Kaisergang, Marmorsaal and Bibliothek

The **Kaisergang**, at the top of the Kaiserstiege, is a vast gallery – over 190m in length – designed to provide access to the 88 imperial chambers, some of which now house

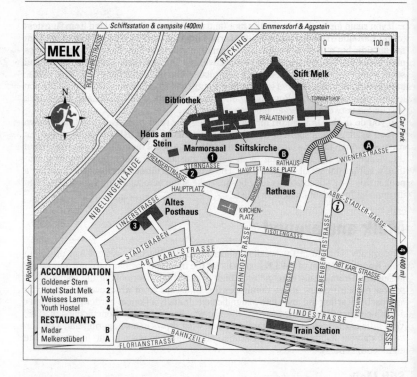

the abbey museum. Unfortunately, the abbey's most precious trio of exhibits are kept in the treasury, and only come out on public display on October 13 (St Koloman's Day): the Melker Kreuz, a fourteenth-century cross, containing a piece of Christ's cross and studded with aquamarines, pearls and gems; the eleventh-century portable altar of Swanhild, portraying the life of Christ in walrus horn; and a thirteenth-century reliquary of the lower jaw and tooth of St Koloman. Nevertheless, the museum owns a good crop of medieval reliquaries on permanent display, including a striking example that once held St Agnes's head. Another work of art that you can be sure of seeing is the winged altarpiece from around 1502 by Jörg Breu the Elder, one of the "Danube School" of artists that included Lucas Cranach the Elder and Albrecht Dürer. The altar panels tell the story of Christ, employing the exaggerated facial expressions that were one of the hallmarks of the Danube School.

The rest of the abbey museum, which is basically a propaganda exercise by the monastery and its school, can be happily passed over in order to reach the two rooms by Prandtauer that make the visit to Melk worth the effort. The first is the red-and-grey **Marmorsaal** (Marble Hall), featuring Paul Troger's superb fresco depicting the Enlightenment. Troger specialized in fresco paintings, and his masterly handling of perspective makes the ceiling appear much higher than it really is. Despite its name, the only furnishings in the hall made from real marble are the doorframes. To get to Prandtauer's **Bibliothek** (Library), you must first take a stroll outside across the curvaceous terrace, from whose balcony you can admire the town below and the Danube in the distance. The library's ancient tomes – rebound in matching eighteenth-century leather and gold leaf – are stacked up to the ceiling on beautifully carved shelves of aspen, walnut and oak. Despite never having been restored, Troger's colourful fresco – a cherub-infested allegory of Faith – has kept its original hue thanks to the library's lack of lighting and heating. From the library, you descend a cantilevered spiral staircase to the Stiftskirche.

Stiftskirche

The **Stiftskirche**, designed by Jakob Prandtauer in 1702 and completed in 1738 after his death, occupies centre stage at Melk, dominating the monastery complex with its fanciful symmetrical towers and octagonal dome. From the balconies above the side altars to the acanthus-leaf capitals of the church's fluted pilasters, the red stucco interior drips with gold paint. The Galli da Bibiena family of Italian theatrical designers is responsible for the stunning all-gold pulpit, and the design of the awesome high altar with its gilded papal crown suspended above the church's patron saints, Peter and Paul. The airy frescoes and side-altar paintings are mostly by Johann Michael Rottmayr, who, along with Troger, was responsible for importing High Baroque art to Austria from Italy.

It's impossible not to notice the grisly reliquaries that lie in the church's side altars, some of them featuring full-scale skeletons reposing in glittering garments. However, the most hallowed bones, those of St Koloman (presumably not including his jaw), are hidden away from the public gaze inside the sarcophagus in the north transept. Beyond this lies the entrance to the **Babenbergergruft**, where the remains of the long line of Babenberg rulers were traditionally thought to have been buried. In 1969, however, the remains were exhumed and examined, after which it was concluded that only Adalbert (1018–55), Ernst (1055–75) and possibly Heinrich I (994–1018) were actually interred here.

The Altstadt

Melk's **Altstadt** is hardly much bigger than the monastery, and, inevitably, with such enormous numbers of tourists passing through, it suffers from overcrowding in the summer. However, there are a few good-looking buildings that repay a stroll around the town. Pretty painted shutters adorn the pharmacy's, next door to the **Rathaus**, and there are a couple of dinky turrets on the old bakery at the corner of Sterngasse, but the single most attractive structure is the **Altes Posthaus**, built in 1792, at Linzerstrasse 3–5. The facade features stucco reliefs of horses' heads, agricultural tools, an eagle holding a post horn in its beak and so on, while the roof balustrade is dotted with urns spouting golden cacti and, as its centrepiece, a double-headed crowned eagle. For a glimpse of old Melk that few tourists get to see, seek out the vine-covered **Haus am Stein**, set back in its own courtyard behind Kremser Strasse.

Practicalities

Melk's **train station** is at the head of Bahnhofstrasse, which leads directly into the Altstadt. If you're travelling by train along the other bank of the Danube, the nearest station is Emmersdorf an der Donau, a walk of 3km from Melk. The **tourist office**, on Abbe-Stadler-Gasse (April–Oct Mon–Sat 9am–7pm, Sun 10am–2pm; Nov–March Mon–Fri 9am–noon & 1–4pm; ☎02752/52307, *www.tiscover.com/melk*), can book **private rooms** for you, though most are out of the centre. Melk's **HI hostel** is just ten minutes' walk east of the tourist office, at Abt Karl-Strasse 42 (☎02752/52681, *oejhw-wien-noe@telecom.at*; March–Oct). A similar distance in the opposite direction is the town's **campsite**, *Melker Camping* (☎02752/53291; March–Nov), adjacent to the Schiffsstation on the Danube.

Most folk come to Melk on a day-trip, so **hotel** prices, even in the Altstadt, are surprisingly reasonable. The *Goldener Stern*, Sterngasse 17 (☎02752/52214; ②), offers clean doubles with shared facilities, and serves reliable pub food on a pleasant terrace, while the *Weisses Lamm*, Linzerstrasse 7 (☎02752/54085; ②), has simple rooms with shower and toilet. Rooms at the back of the plush *Hotel Stadt Melk*, Hauptplatz 1 (☎02752/52475, *www.tiscover.com/hotel-stadt-melk*; ④), have views onto the abbey, and all are fully en suite; the hotel also has the town's finest **restaurant**, and a sauna. Other places to eat include *Gasthaus Melkerstüberl*, which is a good local for lunch, with a three-course Tagesmenü for öS100/€7.27, slightly off the tourist track at Wienerstrasse 7, or the family-run *Madar* café-restaurant (closed Wed) on Rathausplatz.

Schloss Schallaburg

Schloss Schallaburg (May–Oct Mon–Fri 9am–5pm, Sat & Sun 9am–6pm; öS80/€5.81), 4km south of Melk, is a popular day-trip: you can even get a discount **Kombi-Karte** (öS120/€8.72) covering entry to the castle and the monastery at Melk. Part ruined medieval keep, part Renaissance chateau, the building is a strange hybrid. Its most celebrated (and much-photographed) treasure is the unusual, and strikingly beautiful, terracotta arcading in the **Grosser Arkadenhof**. Each pillar is richly decorated with atlantes and caryatids, each spandrel with cartouches, and each keystone with grotesques, while slightly comical busts emerge from along the entablature. Unfortunately, nothing else in the Schloss can quite compete with this sixteenth-century Italianate masterpiece, though the exhibitions staged within the castle are usually excellent. Buses to Schallaburg are pretty infrequent, however; hiring a bike from Melk station is a more sensible idea.

The Danube beyond Melk

The **Danube Valley west of Melk** can't hope to compete scenically with the magic of the Wachau, though the hillier north bank tries hard enough, boasting the spectacularly sited pilgrimage church of **Maria Taferl**, and numerous other riverside castles along the way. The noble seat that receives the greatest number of tourists is **Artstetten**, resting place of the ill-fated Archduke Franz Ferdinand and his wife, Sophie Chotek, who were assassinated at Sarajevo in 1914. The only other truly compelling sight along the river is **Pöchlarn**, the pretty little town where Oskar Kokoschka (1886–1980) was born.

Schloss Artstetten

While the rest of the Habsburg dynasty lie in Vienna's Kaisergruft, the **Archduke Franz Ferdinand** (1863–1914) is buried in a private chapel beneath the majestic, multi-onion-domed **Schloss Artstetten** (April–Oct daily 9am–5.30pm; öS70/€5.09), 10km west of Melk, on the opposite bank of the river. The reason for this lies in the archduke's morganatic marriage to Sophie Chotek, which he embarked upon in 1900 against the wishes of his uncle, the Emperor Franz-Josef I. As crown prince, and heir to the imperial throne, Franz Ferdinand was expected to marry a princess of royal blood, not a mere countess, like Sophie, who ranked lower than more than thirty archduchesses (she had even been lady-in-waiting to one of them). As a result, Sophie was forbidden to accompany her husband to any official court function, including the court opera and theatre; at official banquets, her place was laid, but remained unoccupied. As a result of this rigid and humiliating court protocol, the archduke and his family spent

Riesenrad, Vienna

Belvedere Palace, Vienna

Melk abbey

Tram car, Vienna

View of Vienna and Stephansdom roof

Logs in the Waldviertel

Storks' nest, Burgenland

Open-cast mine workings, Erzberg

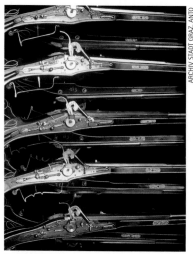

Guns in the Zeughaus, Graz

Detail in the library at Admont

Heiligenblut and the Grossglockner

NIBELUNGENLIED

The stretch of the Danube between Melk and Persenbeug is known as the Nibelungengau, after the **Nibelungenlied**, the great epic German poem, written around the end of the twelfth century, and based on Scandinavian legends about the destruction of the Burgundian kingdom by the Huns in the fifth century AD.

Nibelung himself was the mythical king of Nibelungenland (Norway), who, along with his twelve paladins, all giants, guarded a mythical hoard of treasure. Siegfried, prince of the Netherlands and hero of the first part of the poem, kills Nibelung and the giants and gains possession of the hoard, which he gives as a dowry to his new wife Kriemhild of Burgundy. Siegfried then helps Kriemhild's brother, Gunther, King of Burgundy, to gain the hand of Brunhild of Iceland. This is no simple task as Brunhild has announced that she will only marry a man who can beat her at the javelin, shot put and long jump. Siegfried, who rather handily possesses a cloak of invisibility, helps Gunther to cheat and therefore marry Brunhild. After the marriage, Kriemhild tells Brunhild how Siegfried aided Gunther. Brunhild, furious, gets Gunther's retainer (and the big baddy of the poem), Hagan, to murder Siegfried, grab the treasure, and bury it in the Rhine. The plan is to recover it later, but by the end of the poem everyone's dead, so the treasure is lost for ever. The second part of the poem tells of Kriemhild's subsequent marriage to Attila the Hun (known as Etzel in the poem). She invites the Burgundians en masse to the Hunnic court, where Hagan, rather rudely, kills Etzel's son. Kriemhild then decapitates Gunther and Hagan with her own hands, but is herself killed by Old Hildebrand of Bern, who is horrified by her behaviour.

Thanks to Wagner, whose *Ring* cycle is based on a version of the tale, most people associate the myths with the Rhine Valley, though much of the action, in the second part of the poem, takes place along the Danube, as first Kriemhild, and then Gunther, Hagan and the rest of the Burgundians, travel en route to meet Etzel. (Most people also think of the Nibelungen as dwarfs, although in the myths the term is used for whomever possesses the treasure). The topography in the poem is pretty vague, but Pöchlarn (dubbed Nibelungenstadt by the local tourist authorities) features as the residence of Margrave Rüdiger, who puts on a four-day feast for Kriemhild and her entourage "in colored tents all over the meadows", and escorts her to her meeting with Etzel, downriver at Tulln, where he "allowed not the king to caress his bride in secret".

as little time as possible in Vienna, preferring instead to hole up in their Bohemian properties and, to a lesser extent, in Schloss Artstetten.

Apart from the wonderful majolica-clad bathroom (*c*.1869), very little of the chateau's original decor remains. Instead, the rooms now house the exhaustive and hagiographical **Franz Ferdinand-Museum**, which includes the archduke's *Schussliste*, cataloguing the more than 270,000 wild animals he bagged – everything from pigeons to tigers – during his globe-trotting hunting expeditions (in 1911 alone, he clocked up 18,709 kills). Naturally enough, the museum carefully documents the archduke's final hours in Sarajevo in 1914, when he and his wife, who was allowed to accompany her husband on an official visit for the first time as a special favour, were assassinated by the Bosnian Serb Gavrilo Princip. In the main courtyard, there's a replica of the Gräf & Stift convertible in which they were killed (the original is in Vienna; see p.125). On hearing of the tragedy, the Emperor Franz-Josef is alleged to have said: "God will not be mocked. A higher power has put back the order I couldn't maintain." Franz Ferdinand and his wife were refused burial in the Kaisergruft, alongside the rest of the Habsburgs, and now lie in Artstetten's subterranean crypt; every half-hour, visitors are permitted a brief glimpse of the modest marble sarcophagi.

Artstetten is hard to get to without your own set of wheels. The nearest **train station** is 3km away in Klein Pöchlarn, which is linked by ferry to Pöchlarn, on the south bank (see opposite). You can picnic happily in the chateau's English-style gardens, or enjoy a reasonably priced **meal** at the excellent local *Schlossgasthof* (☎07413/8303; ③), which also has large en-suite rooms above it, should you need a **bed** for the night.

Maria Taferl

It's impossible to miss the Baroque **Wallfahrtskirche** (pilgrimage church) of **Maria Taferl**, which occupies a magnificently ostentatious position high above the Danube, 5km upstream of Klein Pöchlarn. The church gets its name from the *Taferl* (board), containing a crucifix, that was attached to an oak tree that once stood on this spot. In 1633, so the story goes, a local farmer tried to fell the oak with an axe, but succeeded only in hacking both his legs to bits. At this point, he spotted the crucifix, fell to his knees and prayed for forgiveness. His legs were immediately healed and, after several further miracles and apparitions over the course of the next thirty years, the foundation stone of Maria Taferl was eventually laid in 1660. Today, just about every tour group heading along the Danube Valley pauses here at some point, so you're unlikely to have the spot to yourself; but the effort of getting here is amply rewarded both by the stupendous views, and by the church's glorious interior.

Although the original cruciform plan survives, the **interior** was finished off in High-Baroque style by Carlo Lurago and Jakob Prandtauer. The latter is responsible for the central cupola, whose fresco, though not of the highest quality, creates a pleasing overall effect with its trompe l'oeil masonry. There's plenty of gold throughout the church, from the acanthus-leaf capitals to the filigree work on the organ and the particularly fine pulpit. There's also a **Schatzkammer** (May–Oct daily 9am–5pm; öS20/€1.45) inside the church, containing a copy of the miraculous *Pietà* carved from the original oak tree, not to mention a rain gauge made from the wedding dress of the Empress Elisabeth, while the nearby **Mechanische Krippe** (April–Oct daily 9am–5pm; öS10/€0.73) contains a mechanized Bethlehem scene set beneath a copy of the church.

The nearest train station to the village of Maria Taferl is 3km below the church, in the village of **Marbach an der Donau**. There are numerous places to stay in the village, but you're really much better off back in Artstetten, or across the river in Pöchlarn.

Pöchlarn

PÖCHLARN, 10km upstream from Melk, is a pretty little walled town of winding, narrow streets, which features in the *Nibelungenlied* (see box, p.179), though its chief claim to fame nowadays is as the birthplace of **Oskar Kokoschka**. At Regenburgerstrasse 29, to the west of the Altstadt, stands the house in which the artist was born in 1886 – it was not, in fact, the family home, but a sawmill belonging to one of his uncles – now the **OK-Dokumentation** (May–Sept Tues–Sun 9am–noon & 2–5pm; öS30/€2.18). The courtyard displays reproductions of the artist's most famous works, many of which are scattered around the art museums of the world, but some of which can be seen in the Belvedere in Vienna (see p.122). On the ground floor, the museum puts on temporary exhibitions from its own collection, mostly little-known drawings, sketches and watercolours, but interesting nonetheless. In the attic of the old house, there's also an exhibition (in German only) on Kokoschka's very long, prolific life. Perhaps the most startling exhibit is the bullet that had to be removed from the artist's skull by military surgeons during World War I. Kokoschka left Austria before the end of the war, and from there on led a peripatetic existence, returning only sporadically to his homeland. During the 1930s, he lived in exile in Prague, and later London, eventually becoming a British citizen in 1947. He died at the age of 94 in Montreux, Switzerland.

With regular boats connecting the town with Klein Pöchlarn on the north bank, Pöchlarn makes a good base for exploring the surrounding district. The town's **tourist office** (April–Oct Mon–Sat 9am–5pm; ☎02757/2310), in the Rathaus at Regensburgerstrasse 11, can book **private rooms**. Alternatively, you can **stay** in a simple room, with en-suite shower and toilet, above the pleasant *Futtertrögl* restaurant on Kirchenplatz (☎02757/2395; ②); or opt for the modernized, family-run *Hotel Moser* (☎02757/2448, *www.hotelmoser.at*; ④), opposite the train station, whose rooms are fully en suite. There's a **campsite** (May–Oct), by the Schiffsstation, north of the Altstadt.

Mostviertel

The southwest corner of Lower Austria – known as the **Mostviertel**, after the local cider – hides the Land's most spectacular, unspoilt scenery, dominated by the region's largest peak, the colossal **Ötscher** (1893m), which provides an impressive snowcapped backdrop as you approach from the north. The chief summer and winter resort here is **Lackenhof**, situated just below the Ötscher. To the west is the peaceful meandering **Ybbstal**, once home to numerous forges, powered by the River Ybbs, and supplied with iron ore from the Styrian town of Eisenerz (see p.299). Nowadays, the Ybbstal's economy relies solely on agriculture, supplemented by a modicum of tourism. The pilgrimage church of **Sonntagberg** is an impressive landmark, and the monastery of **Seitenstettenmarkt** definitely worth a visit, but the most obvious base for the region is the attractive walled town of **Waidhofen an der Ybbs**.

Sonntagberg

If you're approaching the region from the main line or autobahn around Amstetten, 40km west of Melk, you can't fail to notice the pale pink and white **Wallfahrtskirche** (pilgrimage church), 18km or so to the south, which enjoys a heavenly position atop the highest hill for miles around, **Sonntagberg** (704m). Begun in 1706 by Jakob Prandtauer, and completed by Josef Munggenast, there's something about the basilica that sets its apart from its rivals, whether it's the panoramic views from the terrace, the dizzying impact of its High Baroque interior, or the church's strange gargantuan emptiness outside the pilgrimage season. Grey pilasters, crowned with gilded acanthus leaves, line the nave, while every square centimetre of the ceiling vaults and central cupola is taken up with trompe l'oeil plasterwork and frescoes by Daniel Gran. The pulpit is a sculptural symphony in gold and the high altar is crowned by an equally ornate gilded baldachin. Be sure to have a look at the glass coffins on either side of the nave, in which two saintly female skeletons publicly repose, in bejewelled costumes, with veils over their skull faces and quills in their bony hands. Incidentally, there's a restaurant and the fairly luxurious *Hospiz Sonntagberg* (☎07448/339, *www.sonntagberg.at*; ⑤) up here if you want food or a bed for the night.

Seitenstetten Markt

If you're on a tour of Austrian monasteries, it's definitely worth taking a detour to **SEITENSTETTEN MARKT**, roughly 10km to the west of Sonntagberg, where you'll find the Benedictine **Stift Seitenstetten** (May–Oct daily 10am–3pm; *www.stift-seitenstetten.at*). Refreshingly, you're free to walk round the complex, much of which is now given over to the monastery's busy Gymnasium. The **Stiftskirche**'s Baroque makeover, with its slightly stomach-churning pink and grey colour scheme, is not altogether successful, though the painted biblical "wallpaper" (after sketches by Kremser Schmidt) that lines the chancel is interesting enough. Behind the church is the oldest part of the complex, the **Ritterkapelle**, dating back to medieval times, but currently smothered in foliaceous white stucco. Much more impressive than either of the above, however, is the **Abteistiege**, on the north side of the courtyard, a monumental staircase desigend by Josef Muggenast, and decorated with playful vanilla yellow, silver grey and white stucco-work, and a vast luminous fresco by Altomonte, depicting St Benedict being led to heaven in a chariot, with allegories of the four continents looking on.

All the above sections of the monastery are open to the public without charge, but to get to see the rest of the complex, including the spectacular **Marmorsaal**, with its trompe l'oeil decor and colourful fresco by Paul Troger, you must get here in time for one of the **guided tours** (May–Oct daily 10am & 3pm; öS50/€3.63). Seitenstetten also boasts a vast **Stiftsgalerie** (Sat & Sun 2–5pm; öS70/€5.09), ranging from medieval altarpieces, to modern works by the likes of Fritz Wotruba and Peter Pichl, and including paintings by Gran, Maulpertsch, Altdorfer, Dürer, and no fewer than ten pieces by Troger and 38 by Kremser Schmidt. Opposite the main entrance to the monastery, the **Hofgarten** (April–Oct dawn to dusk), with its rambling rose and clematis-strewn arbours and fountain, makes the perfect picnic spot.

Waidhofen an der Ybbs

By far the prettiest town in the Ybbstal is **WAIDHOFEN AN DER YBBS**, situated at the northwestern head of the valley, just 5km south of Sonntagberg. Waidhofen's compact Altstadt is picturesquely perched high above the rushing river, and its distinctive forest of assorted towers create a striking impression when approaching from the north. It makes by far the best base for exploring the region, and is also somewhere worth a visit in its own right.

The Altstadt

The **Altstadt** is basically made up of two large parallel squares – Oberer and Unterer Stadtplatz – between which stands the onion-domed medieval **Stadtturm** (May–Oct Tues–Sun 10am–5pm; öS30/€2.18), erected in honour of the victory over the Turks in the early sixteenth century. You can climb the tower to the tiny room, where the local watchman lived until 1907, from which there's a great view over the neighbouring spires and rooftops. Round the corner, on Obere Stadtplatz, is the **Heimatmuseum** (Tues–Sun 10am–5pm; öS35/€2.54), which has an above-average collection, including a model of the medieval town, showing just how well fortified it was. There's a great sixteenth-century *Plagenbild*, depicting the various plagues that hit the town from finches and grasshoppers to the Turks themselves. Other oil paintings graphically depict the tribulations of the town during the Napoleonic era, when Waidhofen was occupied by French troops on three separate occasions. Elsewhere, there's an interesting section on the town's interwar, Nazi and postwar periods, as well as the usual flora and fauna. If you've children in tow, make sure you visit the top floor, where the kids can play with replicas of some of the traditional wooden toys on display.

At the far end of the Obere Stadtplatz, the **Stadtpfarrkirche** reveals its fifteenth-century origins in its Gothic lierne vaulting. The winged high altar also dates from this time, and has gilded relief sculptures of the Madonna and Child, flanked by St Barbara and St Katherine. The top left panel scene celebrates the happy marriage of St Elisabeth of Hungary with Ludwig of Thüringen, but the other three detail the gruesome martyrdoms of St Agatha, who had her breasts cut off, St Katharine who was beheaded, and St Ursula, who drowned in a ship, along with innumerable virgins. The church's other treasure is hidden away in the southwest corner, in the befrescoed Marienkapelle, where a high-kitsch sixteenth-century wax copy of the famous **Praguer Jesukind** (*Bambino di Praga*) poses in expensive swaddling clothes. Beyond the church is the striking machicolated tower of the town's **Schloss**, originally built around

1407, and only saved from dereliction in the 1880s by the Rothschild family, who employed the German Friedrich von Schmidt, architect of the Vienna Rathaus (see p.105), to create the current mock-medieval fantasy. It's now home to the local college of forestry and closed to the public.

Practicalities

Waidhofen's main **train station** is a fifteen-minute walk north of the Altstadt (bus #1 covers the distance roughly every hour). You'll find the **tourist office** (Mon–Fri 8.30am–noon & 2.30–5pm, Sat 8.30am–noon; ☎07442/511-255, *www.waidhofen.at*) on the ground floor of the Stadtturm. The choicest **accommodation** in town is the *Hotel Moshammer* (☎07480/54018; ④), which is situated on Kirchenplatz, on the other side of the Ybbs in the suburb of Zell – five minutes' walk south from the Altstadt via the Ybbstor. The central *Gasthof zum goldenen Hirschen* (☎07480/52132; ②), on Unterer Stadtplatz, is less remarkable, but has a nice atmospheric *Stube* in which you eat your breakfast. The best places for **food** are all outside the Altstadt: the cosy *Ybbsturm Stube*, just outside the Ybbstor, has a menu guided by the seasons, with lots of local specialities and veggie options; the *Zeller Weinstube* (closed Mon) in the *Hotel Moshammer* (see above*)* is another good choice.

Ybbstal to the Ötscher

Waidhofen is the starting point for the narrow-gauge **Ybbstalbahn**, which winds its way through the beech- and pine-forested valley to the south. Some 30km along the circuitous Ybbstal, is the pretty little village of **GÖSTLING**, where you can stay in the highly recommended rustic vine-clad *Hotel zum goldenen Hirschen* (☎07484/2225; ③) by the church.

Another 11km further along the railway line, **LUNZ AM SEE** (*www.lunz.at*) is a leisurely little village, with a superb sgraffitoed sixteenth-century Rathaus, better known as the **Amonhaus**, decorated with a frieze featuring Jonah cheerily waving as he's swallowed by the whale. Ten minutes' walk east of the village is the **Lunzer See**, in whose calm waters the wooded mountainsides are perfectly reflected; the main activities here are swimming, rowing and sunbathing. The nearby *Gasthof Kirchenwirt* (☎07486/8203; ②), on Kirchenplatz, is a decent place to **stay**, as is *Seebach* (☎07486/8307; ②), a simple pension overlooking the lake on the Seepromenade, and there's a **campsite** (☎07486/8413) beside the lake. The *Seerestaurant* at the western end of the lake has a terrace overlooking the water.

Over a small pass, another 11km northeast of Lunz, lies the town of **GAMING**, worth a brief visit, if you're passing that way, for its former Carthusian monastery or **Kartäuserkloster** (now a very active international theological school). Founded in 1330, the sheer size of the complex gives you an idea of the importance of Gaming in its heyday. The main courtyard or Prälatenhof is stupendously large and has Renaissance arcading on two sides. The church is a relatively simple Gothic structure, as befits the order, but has since been given a Baroque makeover. Cream-coloured compound pilasters line the single-aisled nave, while the ceiling is a mass of frivolous Rococo stucco-work and late Baroque frescoes featuring the reclusive monks. At the far end, the church ends in a raised cupola, held up by angelic atlantes. To get to see any more of the monastery, including the befrescoed library, you must join a **guided tour** (May–Oct daily 11am & 3pm; öS50/€3.63).

Lackenhof

LACKENHOF, nestling amongst meadows, 12km east of Lunz, on the west side of the Ötscher, is the region's busiest resort. It's by no means an unattractive or overdeveloped village, but the chief reason for being here is either to go walking or skiing in the surrounding mountains. The longest and most frequent of the various chairlifts is the **Ötscherlift** (daily: summer 8–11.30am & 1–4.30pm; winter 9am–4pm; öS110/€7.99 return), to the east of the tourist office, which takes you as far as the *Ötscherschutzhaus* (1420m), from which it's about an hour's hike to the summit, or back down to Lackenhof.

The **tourist office** (daily 9am–5pm; ☎07480/5286), near the Ötscherlift at Käferbichlstrasse 14, can help you find a **private room**. Alternatively, you can choose **to stay** in the simple *Ötscherschutzhaus* (☎07480/5249; closed Nov; ①), at the top of the chairlift; or, near the bottom of the chairlift, the *Gasthof Schützenwirt* (☎07480/5202; ③) is a comfortable but relatively inexpensive option. For a real treat, head for the *Bio-Hotel Jagdhof* (☎07480/5300, *jagdhof@netway.at*; ⑧), a mini health farm where you'll be treated to delicious organic, wholefood cooking. There's also a **campsite** (☎07480/5276; open all year), behind the *Gasthof zur Ötscherwiese*, beyond the chairlift, and a typically efficient and clean **HI hostel** (☎07480/5251, *oejhw-wien-noe@telecom.at*) a short walk north of the tourist office, on Ötscherweg.

St Pölten and around

It's only forty minutes by train west from Vienna to **ST PÖLTEN**, but most visitors simply pass through on their way to or from the capital. The biggest town in Lower Austria, with a population of over 50,000, St Pölten is small and provincial at heart – it only really began to expand with the arrival of the railway in 1860. Today, as the new regional capital, or *Landeshauptstadt*, St Pölten is enjoying another period of growth, with a whole administrative quarter, known as the *Landhausviertel*, recently constructed on the banks of the Traisen, in order to accommodate the new regional government offices, which have now moved here from Vienna. As well as being an easy day-trip from Vienna, St Pölten is a useful base for exploring the nearby monasteries of Herzogenburg and Lilienfeld, not to mention Melk (see p.175), or for taking a trip on the spectacular railway to Mariazell (see p.296).

The Town

Kremser Gasse, across the road from the train station, is the main pedestrianized street leading into town, and is lined with shops whose upper storeys boast pretty pastel-shaded Baroque facades. However, the street's most noteworthy piece of architecture is the little-heralded Jugendstil **Stöhr Haus**, at no. 41, a startlingly beautiful building dominated by a grand curvaceous gable. The relief on the gable depicts a snake drinking from a golden bowl held by a Greek goddess with golden hair, while the rest of the exterior decoration is predominantly vegetal: mini cabbages, gilded berries and green and gold foliage. The house was designed in 1899 by Joseph Maria Olbrich, architect of the Secession building in Vienna (see p.115), for Ernst Stöhr, a local artist, poet and musician who was one of the chief ideologues of the Secession movement.

The town's chief claim to Baroque fame rests with the spectacular interior of its **Dom**, on Domplatz, originally built in the middle of the thirteenth century as the abbey church of the neighbouring Augustinian monastery. The rather dour exterior gives no indication of the exuberant Baroque makeover that took place inside under the supervision of Jakob Prandtauer, the architect responsible for Melk (see p.175), in the first half of the eighteenth century. There's a rich autumnal flavour to the interior, the red, orange, brown and fawn marbling combining with the gilded stucco-work to great effect. The ceiling frescoes in the nave, mainly by Daniel Gran and Bartolomeo

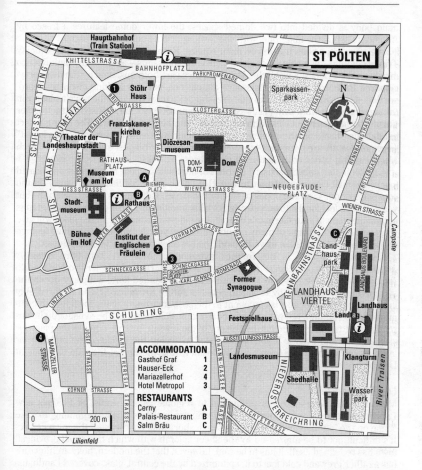

Altomonte, are dramatically framed by trompe l'oeil masonry; the best fresco of the lot is the one above the main altar depicting the archangel and a mob of cherubs smiting the sinful with a bolt of lightning. It takes time to take in the full extent of the rich decoration: the pulpit, smothered in gilded drapery, reliefs and cherubs, is crowned by an entire Crucifixion scene; more frescoes hide in the cupolas of the side aisles; and the organ features a splendid turbaned and gilded statue of David with his harp. The only bit of the medieval cathedral to have survived is the rib-vaulted **Rosenkranzkapelle**, whose capitals are carved with mischievous grimacing faces and strange creatures; the chapel can be reached by an entrance in the middle of the choir stalls.

St Pölten's other Baroque masterpiece is the **Institut der Englischen Fräulein** (aka the Institute of the Blessed Virgin Mary), on Linzer Strasse, which is part of the religious order founded by the English Catholic nun, and pioneer in women's education, Mary Ward). The institute's light pink palatial facade, thought to be by Prandtauer, is punctuated with fluted white pilasters and scalloped niches filled with gesticulating statuary and crowned by gilded sunbursts. Inside, the tiny Institutskirche has been beautifully restored, from its magnolia stucco-work to its gilded, life-size apostles. The main body is divided into two domed spaces: the lower dome features a fresco by Altomonte, while the taller one, with windows, sports a Paul Troger fresco.

The town's spacious traffic-free main square, **Rathausplatz**, features a top-quality Trinity column – an amalgam of clouds, cherubs and saints – and a frothy pink Rococo facade on the Franziskanerkirche. However, these are both upstaged by the raspberry-coloured **Rathaus**, built to Renaissance dimensions, but now looking distinctly ill-proportioned in its more recent Baroque dressing. The trawl through the town's history in the nearby **Stadtmuseum** (Tues–Sat 9am–5pm; öS20/€1.45), housed in the former Carmelite monastery on Hess Strasse, is also something of a letdown. The changing art exhibitions staged in the museum's "Dokumentationszentrum für moderne Kunst" (*www.noedok.at*) are occasionally worth a look, but the biggest surprise is the Czech MiG-21 sitting in one of the museum courtyards.

A much better (albeit partisan) account of the town's recent history can be gleaned from the small two-room **Museum am Hof** (Wed, Fri & Sat 9am–noon; free), in the courtyard of no. 4, on the opposite side of the street. Labelling is in German only, but you can get a feel for the town's strong Socialist tradition from the copious photographs and mementoes. If your German's up to it, the old Socialists who run the place will give you eyewitness accounts of many events, and show you the museum's archive footage of the Führer's triumphant drive through the town following the 1938 Anschluss.

Also worth a look is the **former synagogue** (Mon–Fri 9am–4pm; *members .magnet.at/injoest*), southeast of the town centre at Dr-Karl-Renner-Promenade 22. Built in late-Jugendstil style in 1912, with beautifully painted floral wallpaper decor, the synagogue was damaged by local anti-Semites during *Kristallnacht*, and restored only in the 1980s. Its sheer size is testament to the prewar strength of the local Jewish community, which numbered over four hundred in St Pölten alone. The synagogue is currently home to the Institute for the History of the Jews in Austria, who use the place for various talks and events. If you're interested in seeing the inside of the building, or learning more about the town's Jewish history, ring the bell at the side entrance at Lederergasse 12.

Landhausviertel

More than ten years after its promotion to regional capital status, St Pölten's new **Landhausviertel** (also known as "Regierungsviertel") is finally beginning to take shape on the left bank of the River Traisen, a short walk southeast of the town centre. It's difficult not to be impressed by the sheer aplomb with which this small provincial town has redefined itself. It has to be said, however, that the modern, boxy architecture has a rather grey and cold feel to it, epitomized by the central, glass-covered Landhaus-Boulevard. This is the quarter's commercial zone; though, as with most shopping precincts, it's a soulless place dominated by franchises, with a Billa supermarket slap bang in the middle of the boulevard, as if to underline the point.

All large projects must have their phallic symbol, and the Landhausviertel is no exception. So, for an overview of the whole administrative district, you can ride by glass lift to the top of the 67-metre-tall **Klangturm** (March–Nov Mon–Fri 9am–6pm, Sat & Sun 2–6pm; öS20/€1.45), a see-through iron, steel and glass "sound tower", designed by Ernst Hoffmann, that transforms itself into a red- and blue-lighted beacon at night; "sound events" and other happenings regularly take place here. The shiny stainless-steel- and glass-encased **FestSpielHaus**, designed by Klaus Kada, and resembling a giant ice cube, is another building that looks at its best when lit up at night.

By far the funkiest building in the whole complex, however, is Hans Hollein's **Shedhalle** (Tues–Sun 9am–5pm; öS60/€4.36), with its distinctive wavy glass canopy held up by giant coloured biros, and its zigzag roof. Eventually, the Shedhalle will be joined by the new Landesmuseum (still in the process of being built; *www.landesmuseum.net*), but in the meantime its warehouse-style main gallery puts on temporary exhibitions that give a taster of what's to come.

Practicalities

Staff at the **tourist office** (Easter–Sept Mon–Fri 8am–6pm, Sat 9.30am–6.30pm, Sun 1.30–6.30pm; Oct–Easter Mon–Fri 8am–6pm; ☎02742/353354, *www.st-poelten.at*), in the Rathaus, are very helpful, and there are free telephones outside the office and the train station for booking accommodation.

Given the general absence of tourists in St Pölten, you should have few problems getting a **room**, though there's not a great deal of choice if you want to stay close to the centre. *Gasthof Graf* (☎02742/352757; ④), opposite the train station, is convenient and comfortable enough, but the one to head for is the Jugendstil *Hauser-Eck*, Schulgasse 2 (☎02742/73336, *www.tiscover.com/stadthotel-hauser*; ④), which has bright and cheerful rooms, a few period features in the public areas, and a cosy restaurant. The same family also run the *Mariazellerhof*, Mariazellerstrasse 6 (☎02742/76995; ③), which has decent enough en-suite rooms. There's also the new business-oriented *Metropol* (☎02742/70700, *www.austria-trend.at*; ⑧), in a modern shopping mall on Schillerplatz. The nearest **campsite** is the *Freizeitzentrum Megafun* (☎02742/251510), 3km northeast of the centre by a lake, on the banks of the Traisen.

The best place for a drink and some traditional pub **food** is *Salm Bräu*, on Rennbahnstrasse, a purpose-built micro-brewery near the Landhausviertel. *Cerny* (closed Sun), a daytime-only self-service cafeteria on Kremser Strasse, specializes in tasty fish dishes, but lacks atmosphere. For that and excellent Austrian food, head for the *Palais-Restaurant*, situated on the first floor of the Renaissance palace on Riemerplatz, which has main dishes for öS100–200/€7.27–14.54.

St Pölten has a fairly busy **cultural calendar**, especially now that it boasts a state-of-the-art theatre in the FestSpielHaus (*www.festspielhaus.at*). The latter's programme is adventurous compared with many Austrian theatres, but is still almost entirely composed of classical concerts, operas and ballets, with only an infrequent foray into contemporary dance. Operettas, musicals, new theatre and children's shows are put on in the Theater der Landeshauptstadt, on Rathausplatz (closed July & Aug), while more youth and child-oriented performances are staged at the Bühne im Hof, on Linzerstrasse (*www.bih.at*). For **nightlife**, it's easy enough to hop on a train to Vienna, though occasionally one-off raves prompt the human traffic into flowing in the opposite direction (look out for flyers in the tourist office).

Around St Pölten

Given that St Pölten's distractions are limited, there's a lot to be said for spending the afternoon visiting one of the nearby monasteries, **Herzogenburg** and **Lilienfeld** (or Melk, see p.175), which are a short train ride away. St Pölten is also the starting point for the **Mariazellerbahn**, the spectacular narrow-gauge railway that takes two and a half hours to wind its way south to the Styrian pilgrimage centre of Mariazell (see p.296). Trains run regularly throughout the year, and are occasionally pulled by steam locomotive (pick up a leaflet from the train station to get the current schedule).

Herzogenburg

The remarkable copper-crowned tower of the Augustinian monastery at **HERZO-GENBURG** rises majestically out of the flat landscape, 4km north of Pottenbrunn. The bishop of Passau founded the monastery in the thirteenth century, though the current, scruffy-looking, pinky-brown buildings date from the early eighteenth century, when the monastery was completely rebuilt by three of Austria's greatest Baroque architects: Johann Bernhard Fischer von Erlach, Jakob Prandtauer and his cousin Josef Munggenast. To get to see Fischer von Erlach's magnificent **Festsaal**, which contains a vast celestial fresco by Altomonte glorifying the prince-bishops of Passau, the richly stuccoed library and the outstanding Gothic art collection, you must sign up for one of the hour-long guided tours (April–Oct daily 9–11am & 1–5pm; öS70/€5.09; *www.herzogenburg.at/stift*), in German only.

The **Stiftskirche**, by contrast, is open to all-comers, and is, in many ways, the highlight of the monastery. The rich, playful, pink, grey and gold interior is lined with Corinthian columns and pilasters wrapped in spiralling painted garlands, and decorated from top to bottom in trompe l'oeil frescoes, mostly by Altomonte. The nave gradually narrows, forcing your eye to focus on Daniel Gran's main altarpiece, which is crowned by a copper ducal cap and gilded sunburst. As you leave, look up at the wonderful, richly gilded, pastel-green Baroque organ case, within which you should just be able to make out a trompe l'oeil statue of David with his harp.

Saurierpark

If you're looking to entertain your children with something other than Baroque monasteries, visit the **Saurierpark** (mid-March to Oct daily 9am–6pm; öS50/€3.63), or dinosaur park, 20km or so northeast of St Pölten. Set in shady woodland on the left bank of the River Traisen, the park lies roughly 1.5km from the train station in **TRAISMAUER**; walk through town, cross the river, and head right up Ing. Toder-Gasse. Jurassic Park it's not, but with numerous life-sized fibreglass models of dinosaurs concealed in the undergrowth, it's unlikely to disappoint younger children, who can happily explore the maze of pathways looking for their favourite prehistoric friend.

Lilienfeld

With its beautiful setting amidst forested alpine foothills, the Cistercian monastery in the village of **LILIENFELD**, 20km south of St Pölten, makes for a fine day-trip (you may need to change trains in Traisen). Although from a distance you wouldn't guess it, the abbey retains much of its Romanesque and Gothic architecture, dating back to its foundation in 1202 by Duke Leopold VI. The striking main portal of the **Stiftskirche** is a perfect example of this transitional style; sixteen slender marble columns form what the Austrians call a *Trichterportal* ("funnel portal"), whose arches are very slightly pointed, heralding the beginning of the Gothic style. Inside, the three-aisled basilica features simple quadripartite vaulting and crocket capitals typical of the transitional phase. The matching black-and-gold Baroque furnishings provide a striking contrast to the church's pinkish-white stone; the wooden inlay of the choir stalls is particularly fine, topped by a parade of gilded cherubs and angels. You're free to take a look at the church's interior through iron railings, and explore the monastery's thirteenth-century cloisters, but in order to walk round the church or visit the rest of the monastery – including the Baroque library and the groin-vaulted medieval dormitory – you must sign up for one of the hourly, hour-long guided tours in German (Mon–Sat 8–11am & 2–4.30pm, Sun 2–4.30pm; öS50/€3.63; *www.stift-lilienfeld.at*).

Weinviertel and Waldviertel

The huge swath of Lower Austria that lies between the Danube and the Czech border is probably the least-visited area in the whole country. The northeastern half, the so-called **Weinviertel**, may be the country's agricultural heartland and chief wine-producing region, but its flat, featureless landscape holds little of any great interest to the tourist. The only conceivable reason to find yourself here is if you happen to be heading for the Czech Republic.

The rolling countryside of the **Waldviertel**, to the west, however, has much more to offer. Less forested than its name would suggest, it's a pleasantly undulating region of prettily meandering river valleys harbouring sleepy, but picturesque walled towns. **Retz** and **Drosendorf** are probably two of the most attractive destinations in the Thayatal hard by the Czech border, while **Eggenburg**, on the edge of the Weinviertel and Waldviertel, is a possible base for the more central **Kamptal**, a valley punctuated by two exceptionally fine monasteries, **Altenburg** and **Zwettl**.

Poysdorf and Laa an der Thaya

The road from Vienna to Brno (Brünn) is a particularly miserable one, with **POYS-DORF** (*www.tiscover.com/poysdorf*) the only place of any size – in many ways, you'd be far better off continuing for 15km to Mikulov (Nikolsburg), a much more interesting town on the Czech side of the border. Poysdorf's local cemetery contains a passionate memorial to 120 victims of the **Brno Death March** of May 1945, when the city's 23,000 German-speakers were forced to walk across the border, taking only what they could carry (and no money or jewellery).

The violent expulsion of ethnic Germans from the border regions of Czechoslovakia that took place after World War II is more thoroughly explored in the fascinating **Südmährer Heimatsmuseum** (April–Oct Sun 2–5pm; free), housed on the top floor of the Altes Rathaus, on the main square in **LAA AN DER THAYA**, 22km west of Poysdorf, flush with the Czech border. Laa is also home to Austria's ubiquitous Hubertus Bräu, and the inspiration behind the small **Biermuseum** (May–Oct Sat & Sun 2–4pm; free), located in one wing of the scruffy Schloss, in the northeastern corner of the town. With two giant duty-free shops, situated in no-man's-land within walking distance of the town centre, it's a miracle that there are any shops left at all in Laa. If you need to **stay the night**, there's just the fully en-suite *Hotel zum Brüdertor* (☎02522/8286; ④), on Raiffeisenplatz, or the simple rooms with shared facilities in the *Gasthof Helmut Koffler* (☎02522/2386, *klaus.koffler@netway.at*; ③), on Stadtplatz.

Retz

Another 30km or so west of Laa lies the walled town of **RETZ**, a place of considerable charm, on the border between the Weinviertel and the Waldviertel. The town's showpiece **Hauptplatz** is a beautifully proportioned, sloping, cobbled rectangle, lined with pastel-coloured buildings, among them the salmon-hued sixteenth-century **Verderberhaus**, whose castellated bulk acts as a sort of gateway to the square. The town's one **Sgraffitohaus**, on the south side of the square at no. 15, is worth a closer look, with Greek mythology scenes, from Narcissus to Medea, on the main facade, and, down the side in Kremser Strasse, the ages of woman in decades from zero to a hundred. At the western end of this vast space is the town's freestanding, ochre-coloured sixteenth-century **Rathaus**, a suitably imposing building with a strikingly tall Renaissance tower. Access is granted twice a day to the **Rathauskapelle** (May–Oct daily 10.15am & 3.45pm; free), which is decorated from floor to (very low) ceiling in vibrant trompe l'oeil Rococo stucco-work and frescoes. The Rathaus is also the meeting point for guided tours of the town's labyrinthine underground **Weinkeller** (May–Oct daily 10.30am, 2 & 4pm; öS80/€5.81), which last an hour and a half and include a tasting.

Wandering the backstreets of Retz, you should head for the **Dominikanerkirche**, in the southwest corner of the Altstadt, which sports an exquisite early Gothic stone tympanum over the north door, featuring Mary, Jesus and a fine collection of lions. Inside, particularly fine Baroque and Rococo furnishings include the richly gilded pulpit, replete with cherubim, and the organ loft, from which gold flames appear to be escaping. Retz has a Schloss in two corners of its Altstadt: the *Althof* being a hotel-restaurant complex, while the picturesquely peeling ivy-covered Schloss Gatterburg, in the southeastern corner is in private hands, with a small **Fahrradmuseum** (May–Oct daily 2–5pm; öS40/€2.91), filled with old bicycles in the north wing. Retz's most famous monument, however, is its recently restored eighteenth-century **Windmühle** (Easter to All Saints Sat & Sun 10.30am–4.30pm; öS15/€1.09), one of the country's few remaining windmills. To reach it, pass under the Verderberhaus and the medieval Znaimer Tor, turn left up Windmühlgasse, and follow the signs up through the vineyards for ten minutes. There's a *Buschenschank* up by the windmill, where you can enjoy a glass of the local wine while taking in the view, and beyond, a Baroque Calvary and a World War II cemetery.

Practicalities

The **tourist office** (April to mid-Nov Mon–Sat 9am–noon & 1.30–6pm, Sun 9am–noon & 1.30–4pm; mid-Nov to March Mon–Sat 9am–noon; ☎02942/2700, *www.tiscover.com /retz*), at no. 30 in the northeastern corner of the square, can book **private rooms**, though none are actually in the Altstadt. The two other **accommodation** possibilities in Retz are the *Althof Retz* (☎02942/3711, *www.tiscover.com/hotel-althof-retz*; ⑤), a nicely converted castle hotel in the northwest corner of town, and the more modest en-suite rooms above the *Gasthof zum weissen Löwen* (☎02942/2418; ④), on Hauptplatz. The nearest **campsite** is *Waldcamping Hubertus* (☎02942/3238; open all year), 4km towards the Czech border in the village of Oberretzbach.

If you want to sit outside and admire the square, head for the stylish *Cyrill Blei* **café**, a few doors down from the tourist office, with an old established bakery at the back. A good place to sample the **local wines** is at the *Vincenz Liebl* bar on Klostergasse, while for inexpensive Austrian **food**, you'll find most main dishes well under öS100/€7.27 at *Gasthaus Brand* on Windmühlgasse (closed Tues & Sun evening). Don't overlook the *Althof Retz* (see above), which has a restaurant with dishes around öS150/€10.90, and a Heuriger, with tables outside in the courtyard. Lastly, for a daytime or night-time meal or drink, it's worth checking out the *Schlossgasthaus* (closed Mon), beside Schloss Gatterburg.

Retz is only 5km from the Czech border, and twenty minutes by train from Znojmo (Znaim); the **train station** is ten minutes' walk southeast of Hauptplatz. If you're **driving into the Czech Republic**, bear in mind that the Kleinhaugsdorf–Hatě crossing is 24-hour, whereas the Mitterretzbach–Hnanice crossing (for Czech, Slovak and EU citizens only) has limited opening hours (daily 6am–10pm).

Hardegg and around

To the northwest of Retz, the wiggling River Thaya briefly marks the Czech–Austrian border. At the heart of this wonderful, woody gorge studded with rocky outcrops is the peaceful little town of **HARDEGG**, hard by the Czech border. It's a landscape full of drama, made all the more so by the forbidding presence of the town's medieval **Burg** (daily: April to mid-Nov 9am–5pm; July & Aug 9am–6pm; öS72/€5.23; Kombi-Karte with Schloss Riegersburg öS150/€10.90), which occupies the highest bluff of all, splitting the town in two. Built in the eleventh century, the castle was partially restored in the late nineteenth century by Johann-Carl von Khevenhüller-Metsch, loyal companion of the **Emperor Maximilian of Mexico** (1832–67), who is the subject of the castle museum. Younger brother of Franz-Josef, Maximilian foolishly accepted the offer of the throne of Mexico in 1864. Even more unwisely, he proceeded to alienate his conservative supporters by refusing to repeal the liberal reforms passed by Juárez, and was eventually executed by firing squad some three years later. There's a model of the *Novara*, in which he set sail for Mexico, a copy of Max's heavy, gilded imperial crown, and photos of Khevenhüller's funeral, which took place in Hardegg in 1905 (he's buried in the family vault underneath the castle's lovely stellar-vaulted chapel).

During the Cold War, Hardegg had to endure an uncomfortable proximity with the Iron Curtain. Nowadays, pedestrians and cyclists can cross the reopened **Thayabrücke** (mid-April to Oct daily 8am–8pm) and enjoy a day exploring the Podyjí National Park on the Czech side. If you set out early enough, you could make it all the way to Vranov nad Dyjí (Frain) and back, a journey of about 16km. There are one or two weekday buses from Retz to Hardegg, though you might be better off hiring a bike or walking. There are a few **private rooms** available in Hardegg, and one simple pension, *Gasthof Hammerschmiede* (☎02949/8263; ③).

Just 8km west of Hardegg, close by the Czech border, there's an entirely different kind of aristocratic pile, the **Schloss Riegersburg** (April to mid-Nov 9am–5pm; July & Aug 9am–7pm; öS90/€6.54); guided tours set off every half-hour, and you can buy a *Kombi-Karte* with Hardegg's Burg (öS150/€10.90). This classic cream-coloured Baroque chateau makes quite an impression, with its symmetrical, south-facing facade, flanked by two domes, the apex of its pediment occupied by Atlas holding up the world. Special exhibitions are staged within the Schloss, whose best-looking room is probably the **Chinesisches Zimmer**, with its Chinoiserie wall decorations.

Geras

GERAS, 20km southwest of Hardegg, is a small town dominated by its palatial, magnolia-painted Premonstratensian abbey, which was founded around 1150 but entirely rebuilt in the Baroque period by Josef Munggenast. Unfortunately, to visit the interior, the highlight of which is the showpiece **Marmorsaal**, with its ceiling fresco by Paul Troger, you must sign up for a guided tour (Easter–Oct Tues–Sat 10 & 11am, 2 & 3pm, Sun no 10am tour; öS70/€5.09), in German only. However, without going on a tour you can still visit the **Stiftskirche**, arguably the finest work by Munggenast in the entire complex. The interior, though by no means large, is lavishly decorated in faux pink and grey marble, and trompe l'oeil ceiling frescoes. Oval paintings, interspersed with windows crowned by open-topped pediments, line both walls of the church, but the most striking feature of all is the Rococo ornamental icing, composed mostly of gilded acanthus leaves strewn over the choir stalls, the organ and even the pews.

Geras is on the branch line from Retz to Drosendorf; from the **train station**, it's a fifteen-minute walk south into town. The **tourist office** (Mon–Thurs 8am–4pm, Fri 8am–noon; ☎02912/7050) is on the main street, in the *Stadtgemeinde*, Haupstrasse 16, and can arrange **private rooms**. The most unusual **place to stay**, however, is in the *Alter Schüttkasten* (☎02912/332; ④), a converted seventeenth-century monastic granary on the northern fringe of the village, with a good restaurant, and comfortable rooms with lots of exposed beams. You can also stay, more cheaply, in the monastery's *Meierhof* (☎02912/332; ②; March–Sept), a converted dairy, off the road to Kottaun. Another reliable option is the simple hotel-pension *Elite*, Hauptstrasse 18 (☎02912/221, *www.members.aon/elitehotel*; ③). If you've children in tow, you might like to visit the **Naturpark** (Easter–Oct daily 9am–7pm; Nov–Easter Sun 9am–4pm; öS30/€2.18), where you can see some rare woolly pigs, goats, sheep and rabbits, and feed some (fairly tame) wild boars and red deer. Beyond the Naturpark is the tiny *Edlersee* **campsite** (☎02912/266; open all year), with an adjacent open-air swimming pool and bikes for hire.

Drosendorf

Geras makes a good base for exploring the area, but, without doubt the prettiest place in which to hole up is the tiny walled town of **DROSENDORF**, perched above one of the Thaya's numerous S-bends, 10km to the northwest, by the Czech border. Confusingly, it's Drosendorf Stadt (not Drosendorf Altstadt) that's the walled town, made up of little more than the long, leafy **Hauptplatz**; at the eastern end stands the town's sixteenth-century **Rathaus**, with its shapely gable and richly sgraffitoed facade; to the south lies the pinkish Renaissance **Schloss**, which now functions as a hotel (see below). In the sixteenth-century Bürgerspital, in the backstreet east of the main square, you'll find the small **Stadtmuseum** (July & Aug daily 3–6pm; free), housing a moderately interesting collection of artefacts, including the old night watchman's horn, pike and uniform from the turn of the nineteenth century.

Buses arrive at Hauptplatz, while the **train station** is ten minutes' walk to the southeast, off the road to Geras. As for **accommodation**, *the* place to stay is the town's wonderful *Schloss Drosendorf* (☎02915/2321, *schloss-drosendorf@wvnet.at*; ③), in the southeastern corner of the town, where the huge bedrooms boasting stucco ceilings and Baroque stoves are surprisingly affordable. Failing that, you've a choice between the two excellent family-run Gasthöfe on the main square: the *Goldenes Lamm* (☎02915/2327; ④) or *Die Traube* (☎02915/2227; ③). If you leave the town via the Raabser Tor, and follow the signposts, you'll quickly come to the town's **HI hostel**, at Badstrasse 25 (☎02915/2257, *oejhw-wien-noe@telecom.at*; mid-April to mid-Oct), and, beyond to the pleasant riverside **campsite** (☎02915/2285; open all year). Note that the Oberthürnau–Vratěnín border crossing, 4km northwest of Drosendorf, is only open from 8am to 8pm.

Raabs an der Thaya

Public transport west of Drosendorf is pretty thin on the ground, so if you want to continue along the Thayatal, you're best off walking or cycling the 13km upstream to **RAABS AN DER THAYA**. The medieval **Schloss Raabs** (Wed, Sat & Sun 10am–5pm; öS50/€3.63), which hovers above the town, makes quite an impression as you approach from the west, but is only really worth visiting if the current exhibition takes your fancy. The footpath from Drosendorf to Raabs along the Thaya takes you past the vast, sprawling **Ruine Kollmitz**, some 4km southeast of Raabs itself. With two towers and its huge main gate and drawbridge still intact, the ruin is well worth a visit. There's a small exhibition in one room, with press cuttings from the 1920s when the Hungarian Bolshevik Béla Kun was exiled close by. The castle can also be reached from the main road via Kollmitzdörfl and the Böhmische Mauer gateway.

Raabs **train station** is on the south bank of the Thaya, to the southeast of Hauptplatz. **Private rooms** can be arranged through Raabs **tourist office** (June–Sept Mon–Fri 9am–noon & 1–5pm, Sat 9am–noon; ☎02846/365), in the Rathaus, at the eastern end of the triangular Hauptplatz. The late-nineteenth-century *Hotel Thaya* (☎02846/202; ③), opposite the Rathaus, has **rooms** in a modern wing overlooking the castle and the river, and there are two other very inexpensive Gasthöfe to choose from on Hauptplatz, most of whose rooms have shared facilities only. Raabs has better connections with the rest of the Waldviertel, with regular buses and trains to Göpfritz an der Wild, on the main line from Vienna to Gmünd, and to Horn.

Eggenburg

Despite its convenient location halfway between the Danube and the Czech border on the main line from Vienna to Gmünd, the walled town of **EGGENBURG** is too far from the likes of Altenburg to act as a base unless you have your own vehicle. Nevertheless, there are plenty of good reasons for visiting Eggenburg itself, not least because it's home to the **Österreichische Motorradmuseum** (Mon–Fri 8am–4pm, Sat & Sun 10am–5pm; öS60/€4.36; *www.motorradmuseum.at*), at the top of Museumgasse, one block east of the train station. The forecourt, littered with scores of old bikes and even a vintage Viennese tram, gives a fair indication of the scale of the enterprise – there are more than three hundred pristinely restored motorbikes inside. The museum kicks off with a parade of sleek, black interwar BMWs and ends with a posse of great British bikes, including classic 1950s café racers like the BSA Gold Star. In between, there's every conceivable type of bike, from a couple of Laurin & Klements from before World War I to the fabulous three-seater Böhmerland 600, built in 1929 and the longest motorbike ever in production.

At the bottom of Museumgasse is the **Krahuletz-Museum** (April–Dec daily 9am–5pm; öS40/€2.91), purpose-built in 1902 to house the mineral and fossil collection of local-born geology professor, Johann Krahuletz (1848–1928). The subject matter might not immediately grab you, but this is a well-laid-out museum that succeeds in making what could be a deathly subject as interesting as possible. You can look into a microscope and inspect fifteen different types of crystal at close quarters, and there are plenty of other hands-on exhibits aimed to appeal to children in particular. The local museum, occupying the first floor, is less interesting, though it does contain an exceptionally fine collection of (mostly eighteenth- and nineteenth-century) clocks and watches. Special exhibitions are staged on the top floor, along with a permanent display on the Iron Age.

Museums aside, Eggenburg has a very attractive **Altstadt**, to the north of the Krahuletz-Museum up Kremserstrasse, centred on the spacious **Hauptplatz**, with its dazzling plague column. The most remarkable single building on the square is the sixteenth-century **Gemaltes Haus**, smothered with sgraffito scenes: Old Testament scenes on the Kremserstrasse, and a moralist tale on the main facade, with some very nasty devils walking over the flames of hell towards the sinner. Unfortunately, the town's Gothic **Pfarrkirche**, west of the main square up Kirchengasse, is usually kept closed, but you can retrieve the key from the Pfarrhof, Pfarrgasse 6 (Mon–Fri 8am–noon & 3–6pm), or outside these hours from *Gasthaus Seher* on the main square, in order to admire the church's fine lierne vaulting, and the gilded figures peeping out from amidst the Gothic tracery of the pulpit. Outside the church, follow the signs to the **Beinhaus**, by the foundations of the old Karner, and switch the light on to see the gruesome wall of bones and skulls illuminated within. To view Eggenburg's fortifications at their most impressive, head up Judengasse from the church, where the walls stand 10m high on either side of the **Kanzlerturm** (May–Sept Sun 10am–noon & 2–6pm; öS20/€1.45), which houses a museum to the local *Bürgerkorps*, and allows you access up onto the walls.

Practicalities

Eggenburg **train station**, ten minutes' walk south of the Altstadt, has frequent connections to Gmünd and Vienna, but to get here from Horn you must change at Sigmundsherberg. There are a couple of **private rooms** available through the **tourist office** (daily 9am–5pm; ☎02984/3400, *www.tiscover.com/eggenburg*), housed within the Krahuletz-Museum, situated halfway between the station and Hauptplatz. Otherwise, **accommodation** is limited to the large, comfortable *Stadthotel*, Kremserstrasse 8 (☎02984/3532, *www.tiscover.com/stadthotel.eggenburg*; ④). Take-away pizza (and delicious Yugoslav *burek*) can be had from *Imbiss Ingrid*, next door to the hotel on Kremserstrasse, and standard Austrian **food** from *Gasthaus zum goldenen Kreuz*, on Hauptplatz (closed Wed & Thurs out of season), which serves up filling, inexpensive meals. Eggenburg lies on the edge of the Weinviertel, so if you fancy visiting one of the

Heurigen in the neighbouring villages of Stoizendorf or Röschitz, to the east, pick up a timetable from the tourist office to see which ones are currently open.

Horn and around

With a host of attractions all within spitting distance, **HORN**, 14km west of Eggenburg, is the obvious place from which to explore the central Waldviertel. Aesthetically, however, it can't really compete with the nearby towns of Gars am Kamp or Eggenburg, though it is a tad livelier. Apart from the obligatory Renaissance **Sgraffitohaus**, at Hauptplatz 3, depicting, among other things, Joseph with Potiphar's wife tugging at his monochrome dreamcoat, there's the pale-yellow sixteenth-century **Schloss Horn**, off Wienerstrasse, closed to the public but worth a peek. Close to the Schloss, the former Bürgerspital has been tastefully converted into the **Höbarth- and Madermuseum** (Palm Sunday–Oct daily 9am–noon & 2–5pm; öS35/€2.54). Among the Roman finds, Greek vases, local history and folk art, there's a cabinet of curiosities belonging to a Herr Höbarth, the local post office clerk, amateur scholar, collector and all-round eccentric, after whom the museum is named. The adjacent Madermuseum, meanwhile, is even more of an acquired taste: despite its name (*Mader* means "worm"), it is, in fact, a collection of agricultural machinery assembled by a local farmer called Dr Mader. More memorable than either of the above is Paul Troger's light and feathery fresco decorating the main dome of the powder-pink Baroque **Wallfahrtskirche** (pilgrimage church) of **Maria Dreieichen**, 4km southeast of Horn, on the road to Eggenburg (even this is no match for Troger's work in nearby Altenburg).

Horn doesn't have a **tourist office** but it does have a small cubicle by the museum, where you can pick up information (open until 10pm; ☎02982/2372) and they can help arrange **private rooms** in the vicinity. The nicer of the town's two **Gasthöfe** is the family-run *Gasthof zum weissen Rössl* (☎02982/2398; ③) on Hauptplatz itself. A **bar and café** crawl in Horn should begin either at the cosy *Café Florian*, Florianigasse 8, or at *The Corner*, further up Florianigasse (closed Mon), followed by a game of pool or billiards and some Zwettler Bier at the *Carambol*, Thurnhofgasse 14, finishing up at *Brooklyn* (Fri–Sun only), the only disco for miles around, southwest of the town off Mühlfelder Strasse. Horn's **train station**, ten minutes' walk east of the town centre off the Vienna road, is not in fact on the main line from Gmünd to Vienna, but there are frequent connections to the nearest station that is: Sigmundsherberg, 7km to the northeast.

Stift Altenburg

The chief reason for staying in Horn is to visit the Benedictine **Stift Altenburg**, 5km to the southwest. Founded in 1144, but trashed by the Swedes in 1645, Altenburg was transformed in the 1730s by Josef Munggenast into one of the finest Baroque monasteries in the entire country, on a par with Melk, yet it receives a fraction of the visitors. It's certainly more difficult to get to without your own transport, with buses between Horn and Altenburg restricted to schoolboys only. Given the riches within, however, it really is worth getting to, even by foot or bike, try *Jump & Bike*, Wienerstrasse 3, in Horn, and signing up for the guided tour (Easter–Oct Tues–Sun 10 & 11am, 1, 2, 3 & 4pm; öS80/€5.81), in German only. Without the tour you'll only be able to view the **Stiftskirche**, whose tower rises to the west of the main Prälatenhof. The church's phalanx of red marble pilasters, turquoise pendentives and generous sprinkling of light-giving lunettes create a splendid overall impression, but it's Paul Troger's apocalyptic fresco, adorning the main cupola, that steals the show, with its rich colouring and pin-sharp detailing. God is depicted commandeering his archangels in the final battle against the forces of evil, represented here by a very nasty-looking bunch of devils, a huge fire-breathing dragon and the many-headed beast from Revelation.

The guided tour begins with the **Alter Kloster**, in which archeologists have discovered patches of frescoes, a sixteenth-century oven decorated with biblical tiles, and other sections of the medieval monastery. Most folk come here, though, to admire the combined artistry of Munggenast and Troger, as revealed in the **Kaiserstiege**, in the marble-clad **Festsaal** and, above all, in the magnificent **Bibliothek**, whose trio of domes sport three superbly vibrant Troger frescoes, their subject matter ranging from Jesus arguing with the rabbis in the synagogue to Solomon receiving the Queen of Sheba. The library's most startling feature, however, is the sea-blue Corinthian columns, topped by gilded capitals and dramatically set off against the heavy red marble plinth and cornice. Perhaps the most remarkable chamber in the whole complex, however, is the barrel-vaulted **Krypta**, where Troger's students practised the art of "grotesque" painting, decorating the walls and ceilings in fanciful arabesques and fabulous images based around the theme of death. Considering the subject matter, the murals are full of action: there's Death as Neptune, Death as Mercury, and a wonderful scene featuring skeletons picking off cherubs with their bows and arrows.

Schloss Greillenstein

Five kilometres west of Altenburg, and no easier to reach by public transport, **Schloss Greillenstein** (daily: April–Oct 9.30am–5pm; July & Aug until 6pm; öS65/€4.72; *www.greillenstein.at*) makes for another memorable day-trip from Horn. Built in the late sixteenth century by the parvenu Hans Georg III von Küfstein, Greillenstein is still owned by the family, one of whom conducts guided tours if there are enough visitors; if not, you'll be free to explore the place on your own, and will be given some explanatory notes in English. The chateau was once famous for its hi-tech **Wasserspielanlage** (Watergames Park), built in 1720, employing some 1.5km of pipes to pump water down a seventy-step waterfall at the bottom of which was a fearsome dragon fountain. The Wasserspielanlage has long since gone, but the Baroque statues that adorned it can still be seen on the ground floor of the chateau. The dragon fountain now stands in the courtyard, which has a three-tiered loggia along one side, along with two grotesque huntsmen statues who used to lurk in the woods, while a collection of nine dwarfs shelter in a nearby room. Several more exotic Baroque sculptures dot the balustrade in front of the chateau, including a series of sphinxes, tussling cherubs and shaggy lions, while a pair of African servants flank the main entrance, naked except for their crowns, fig leaves and swords. The main rooms of the chateau harbour a few fine Renaissance ceilings, some wonderful seventeenth-century portraits of Turks, and the occasional modern art exhibition, but little else of note. Look out for the *Geistertouren* (ghost tours) that take place on occasional Friday evenings, and the costumed *Kinderführung* (kids' tours) that take place on occasional Sunday afternoons.

Schloss Rosenburg and Gars am Kamp

Medieval **Schloss Rosenburg** (April–Oct daily 9am–5pm; *www.rosenburg.at*), situated high above the River Kamp, 5km south of Horn, has one distinct advantage over Greillenstein, and that is accessibility. It's also a much more commercial enterprise. It's not the architecture but the **displays of falconry** (*Flugvorführung*; daily 11am & 3pm; öS100/€7.27, or öS130/€9.45 if performed to music by horse-riders), held in the castle's wonderful seventeenth-century arcaded tiltyard, that pull in the crowds. That said, it's not a bad-looking pile, if a mite over-restored in the nineteenth century. The entry fee allows you to wander round the tiltyard, see a dull exhibition on the Hoyos family (who own the place), and visit the *Burgtaverne* in the second courtyard, which does a decent öS100/€7.27 Tagesmenü. There's not an awful lot to see inside the castle – the highlight is probably the Mannerist strap-work ceiling in the library – but to do so you must join a guided tour. From the **train station** to the castle, it's a one-kilometre hike across the railway bridge over the Kamp and up through the woods of the Graslhöhle.

The modest *Landsgasthof Mann* (☎02982/2915; ③) is the better of the two Gasthöfe in Rosenburg. Alternatively, you could head 5km down the verdant Kamptal to the spa-town of **GARS AM KAMP**, which specializes in treatments using peat. The town's land-mark *Hotel Gars* (☎02985/2666, *www.dungl.at*; ⑧) is a handsome imperial yellow build-ing, with an excellent KaffeeKonditorei and a top-class restaurant (three-course menus start at öS250/€18.17), but **rooms** don't come cheap. Less formal and a third of the price is the nearby *Gästehaus Winglhofer* (☎02985/2294, *www.gars.at/gastro/winglhofer*, ②), or the secluded *Waldpension* (☎02985/2365, *www.gars.at/gastro/mueck*; ③), a grand turn-of-the-twentieth-century villa on Wozniczakgasse, off the road to Krems. The *Café-Konditorei Ehrenberger*, on Dreifaltigkeitsplatz, offers a filling two-course Tagesmenü for around öS100/€7.27. If you're around for a few days, ask at the **tourist office** (Sat 10am–noon & 2–4pm, Sun 10am–noon; ☎02985/2276, *www.gars.at*), in the Rathaus, about the open-air opera performances that take place in the medieval Burgruine over-looking the town from the opposite bank.

Zwettl

Deep in the heart of the rolling, forested hills of the Waldviertel, 50km west of Horn, **ZWETTL** boasts the region's second finest monastery after Altenburg. The town itself is also very appealing, with a well-preserved, partially walled **Altstadt**, tucked into a U-bend of the River Zwettl, and centred on a series of interconnecting squares, lined with prettily painted and gabled sixteenth- and seventeenth-century houses. The most dis-tinguished edifice is the sgraffitoed **Altes Rathaus** (May–Oct Fri 2–6pm, Sat & Sun 10am–noon & 2–6pm; July & Aug also Tues–Thurs 2–6pm; öS30/€2.18), worth explor-ing more for its architecture than the Stadtmuseum within; the town hall's carillon belts out a ditty from Beethoven's *Ninth Symphony* on the hour. A more recent addition to the main square is the **Hundertwasserbrunnen**, by the eponymous maverick (see p.121). All his usual trademark touches are evident – ceramic tiles, baubles and wonky paving, and even a roof garden – though for a notorious self-publicist it's remarkably under-stated.

Stift Zwettl

Stift Zwettl, the Cistercian monastery for which the town is most famous, is actually situated a good 3km downstream (east) from Zwettl. Founded in 1159 by Hadmar I von Kuenring, the abbey retains much of its original twelfth-century architecture, though it was greatly enlarged and embellished during the Baroque period by the likes of Josef Munggenast and Paul Troger, the pair responsible for Altenburg. Unfortunately, the monastery's spendid **Bibliothek**, by the aforementioned duo, is closed to the public, but by signing up for a 45-minute **guided tour** (May–Oct Mon–Sat 10 & 11am, 2 & 3pm, Sun 11am, 2 & 3pm; July & Aug also daily at 4pm; öS65/€4.72; *www .stift-zwettl.co.at*), at the door marked *Pforte*, you can get to see a reconstructed innova-tive Cistercian latrine, the medieval dormitory, and the **Kreuzgang** (cloisters), which span the stylistic shift from Romanesque to Gothic, and retain their original chapter-house and wash house.

The abbey's real jewel, however, is the **Stiftskirche**, which you can peek at without a guided tour. The church's landmark 93-metre-high tower, built in grey granite, cuts a striking figure amidst the uniform imperial yellow of the surrounding conventual com-plex, its undulating facade peppered with urns, obelisks and statuary in a lighter stone – particularly fine are the cherubs holding giant burning hearts, and the archangel dealing a death blow to a winged devil. Inside, the architectural bare bones of the orig-inal Gothic hall church remain more or less unchanged. The furnishings, however, are predominantly High Baroque, reaching their climax in the choir, whose entrance is flanked by matching pulpit and choir organ, both heavily gilded and littered with putti and angels. Beyond lie the **choir stalls**, richly inlaid with exquisite marquetry, their entablatures occupied by a parade of gilded saints. Finally, your eye is drawn to the extraordinary **high altar**, an explosion of red, brown and orange stucco marbling, white statuary and gilded sunburst and crown. The unusual central statue of Christ crucified on an oak tree in full foliage, itself carved from oak, is a reference to Hadmar's New Year's Eve dream, in which the Virgin told him to found his abbey wherever he might find an oak tree in full bloom. The church does have one piece of late-Gothic art that's worth a glance: the **winged altar of St Bernhard**, in the second chapel in the north aisle, centred on a statue of Christ standing up on the Virgin's lap, with eight scenes from the life of Bernhard, founder of the Cistercian order, by Jörg Breu of the Danube School. Also worthy of note are the exceptionally ornate confessionals that line the nave, each one topped by pediment statues depicting contrite sinners. The church's fine Baroque **organ**, which is decorated with an orchestra of angels and cherubs, is put to good use every year at the monastery's annual Orgelfest, from late June to late July.

Practicalities

Zwettl's **train station** is half a kilometre or so north of the Altstadt, and there are frequent trains to and from Schwarzenau, on the main Vienna–Gmünd line. Transport to and from Stift Zwettl is limited to one or two buses a day, so you might be better off hiring a bike or walking. A small number of **private rooms** are available through the **tourist office** (Mon–Fri 8am–noon & 1–5pm; ☎02822/52233, *www.zwettl.at*), in the Altes Rathaus. Other **accommodation** possibilities include a parade of fairly modest Gasthöfe or pensions on the main street of Landstrasse: try *Schwarzer Kater* (☎02822/52410, *sbeisl.todt@wvnet.at*; ②) at no. 15, or *Zum goldenen Hirschen* (☎02822/52373; ③), at no. 49. For **luxury hotels**, you need to head out of town, either to the modern *Schwarz-Alm* hotel, restaurant and conference centre (☎02822/53173, *www.tiscover.com/schwarzalm*; ⑥), in the village of Gschwendt, 5km to the southwest, or to *Schloss Rosenau* (☎02822/58221, *www.tiscover.com/schloss.rosenau*; ⑤), a pretty

---

TRUPPENÜBUNGSPLATZ ALLENSTEIG

If you're travelling from Horn to Zwettl, it's impossible to miss the vast military zone of the **Truppenübungsplatz Allentsteig**, which stretches more than 30km at its widest point. The area was handed over to the military by Hitler shortly after the Anschluss, since it contained the village of Döllersheim, where Hitler's paternal grandmother, Maria Anna Schicklgruber, was buried. Hitler was very keen to destroy all evidence of his ancestry, so Döllersheim was used for target practice, and by the end of the war it had been totally destroyed.

Hitler's paranoia dated back to 1930, when he received a letter from the son of his half-brother, Alois Junior, attempting to blackmail him by hinting at dark secrets in his family history. Hitler immediately dispatched his lawyer, Hans Frank (later to become Nazi governor of Poland), to investigate. The rumour was that Maria Anna had become pregnant after sleeping with a 19-year-old Jewish lad named Frankenberger while she was working as a maid in the Frankenberger house in Graz. The illegitimate product of this union was Hitler's father, Alois Schicklgruber, born in Döllersheim parish in 1837. Money was sent to Maria Anna from Graz even after she had married Georg Hitler and moved to the Waldviertel. Even though Hans Frank could find no conclusive proof either way, Hitler was clearly rattled by the story; hence his determination to wipe Döllersheim and its parish records off the face of the earth in 1938, and his decision to instruct the Gestapo to make further enquiries in 1942.

Baroque chateau 8km west of Zwettl, that's also home to several museums devoted to freemasonry, dolls and fairy tales. There are also several **campsites** to the east of Zwettl, along the banks of the River Kamp, the nearest one being *Camping Lichtenfels* (☎02826/7492; May–Sept), 9km east.

You can **eat** heartily and quaff some of the local *Zwettler Bier* at the *Gasthof zur goldenen Rose*, a late-sixteenth-century inn overlooking the town's plague column. If you're visiting Stift Zwettl, and haven't brought a picnic, the *Stiftstaverne* outside the monastery is perfectly decent.

Gmünd

Hard by the Czech border, on the main line from Prague to Vienna, **GMÜND** – often written "Gmünd (NÖ)" to distinguish it from Gmünd in Carinthia – is an obvious place to halt your journey, whichever direction you're heading. The main square, **Stadtplatz**, makes for a pretty introduction (or farewell) to the Waldviertel, with its dinky Renaissance **Altes Rathaus** sporting a shapely Baroque gable and tall onion-domed steeple, and now housing a florist's and the **Stadtmuseum** (May–Sept Sun 9am–noon; öS20/€1.45). Stadtplatz also has two exceptionally lovely adjacent **Sgraffitohäuser**, from the same period as the Rathaus, which understandably tend to feature on almost every picture of the town produced by the local tourist board. Both houses are castellated, but only the right-hand house features lively mythological scenes: Actaeon (top right) has been transformed into a stag by Diana, as a punishment for stumbling upon the goddess and her nymphs bathing naked; below, Medea is nonchalantly slaughtering one of her children (appropriately enough, the building itself is now a butcher's). On the south side of the square, the **Glas- und Steinmuseum** (Glass and Rock Museum; May–Sept Mon–Fri 9am–noon & 1–5pm, Sat & Sun 9am–noon; öS20/€1.45) is mildly diverting. Skip the rocks and the snakes in formaldehyde that occupy the ground floor, and head instead for the history of the local glass industry, as revealed on the top two floors, where there's a decent selection of fin-de-siècle glassware and jewellery.

A good place to picnic and explore is the **Naturpark Blockheide**, where a series of strangely shaped sandstone protrusions are dotted about the woods to the northeast of the town centre. It's roughly ten minutes' walk from Stadtplatz to the park: cross the river from Braunauplatz, east of the main square, and follow the signs. At the centre of the park is a look-out tower (öS10/€0.73) and a few refreshment outlets. Another popular activity in summer is to ride on the narrow-gauge **Waldviertler Schmalspurbahn**, which winds its way through the forests via Weitra (see below) to Gross Gerungs, 43km to the south. Eight normal trains a day make the journey throughout the year; steam trains run along the line most weekends from June until October.

Practicalities

From Gmünd **train station**, it's about ten minutes' walk north up Bahnhofstrasse to Stadtplatz, where you'll find the **tourist office** in the Glas- und Steinmuseum (May–Sept Mon–Fri 9am–noon & 1–5pm, Sat & Sun 9am–noon; ☎02852/500261, *www.gmuend.at*). The latter can arrange private rooms, which are a good option given that **accommodation** in Gmünd can be expensive. Choose between the very comfortable *Goldener Stern* (☎02852/54545, *www.goldener-stern.co.at*; ⑤) at Stadtplatz 15, or the excellent *Gasthof Werner Pauser*, Bahnhofstrasse 44 (☎02852/53860, *gasthofpauser @wvnet.at*; ③), whose **restaurant** does tasty local carp dishes. For a choice of pizzas, and the usual Austrian fare, washed down with local Schrems beer, head for the *Kupferkandl* (closed Mon & Tues), opposite the *Goldener Stern* at Stadtplatz 10.

The **Czech border crossing** is about 200m northwest of Stadtplatz, up Litschauerstrasse. You can walk into the neighbouring town of České Velenice (which was merely a suburb of Gmünd until the border split the town in two in 1920), in around fifteen to twenty minutes, though there's not a lot to see there. The main road from Prague to Vienna passes 6km to the north of Gmünd, at Neunagelberg, where there's an **HI hostel** (☎02859/7476, *oejhv-noe@oejhv.or.at*; closed mid-Dec to mid-Jan), by the lake to the north of the main road. Gmünd's lakeside **campsite**, *Camping Assangteich* (☎02852/51552; May–Sept), is ten minutes' walk south of the train station on Albrechtserstrasse.

Weitra

The walled town of **WEITRA**, 16km to the southwest, is an easy day-trip from Gmünd and a much more peaceful place to spend the night. The sloping main square, **Rathausplatz**, is prettier, too, and is entered from the east via a lovely little crenellated Renaissance gateway, the **Obere Tor**. As in Gmünd, the most eye-catching building is the **Sgraffitohaus**, its lowest allegorical cartoon depicting the stages of a man's life in decades from birth to one hundred years of age. On the opposite side of the square, another sgraffitoed house features a gloriously wild dragon being done in by St George.

From Rathausplatz, take a stroll up Schlossgasse to the Fürstenberg-owned **Schloss** (May–Oct daily except Tues 10am–12.30pm & 2–5.30pm; öS85/€6.18), a bulky, slightly ugly affair from the outside, but boasting a gabled, triple-decker Renaissance loggia in its main courtyard. The local museum inside is unremarkable, but the view from the main tower is impressive, and the pretty little Schlosstheater (still in use) is worth a glance, built in the eighteenth century but enlarged in twiddly, gilded neo-Rococo style in 1885. Weitra is home to Austria's oldest brewery, Weitra Bräu, founded in 1321, and the cellars of the chateau now house an exhibition on the Fürstenbergs' brewing concerns, and a staggering array of beer mats and glasses from all over Europe.

The much-heralded **Museum Alte Textilfabrik** (May, June & mid-Sept to Oct Thurs & Fri 2–5pm, Sat & Sun 10am–noon & 2–5pm; July to mid-Sept daily except Mon 10am–noon & 2–5pm; öS35/€2.54), in an old textile factory fifteen minutes' walk northeast of the Altstadt in the suburb of Brühl, is fairly low-key compared with the Schloss, though the temporary exhibitions on the top floor are occasionally worth catching.

The **train station** is five minutes' walk southeast of the Altstadt, with eight regular trains a day from Gmünd, and steam trains at weekends between June and October. Weitra is an easy day-trip from Gmünd, though you may prefer to **stay** overnight at *Gasthof Karl Waschka* (☎02856/2296; ③), one of two Gasthöfe to be found on Rathausplatz, or at the comfortable and cosy *Brauhotel Weitra*, also on Rathausplatz (☎02856/2936, *www.brauhotel.at*; ④). **Private rooms** can be organized through the **tourist office** (May–Oct Mon–Fri 8am–noon & 1.30–5.30pm; ☎02856/2998, *www.wvnet.at/gemeinden/weitra*), in the Rathaus. The best place to accompany your meal with the delicious local beer is at the aforementioned *Brauhotel*, which serves very good (mostly organic) food even in its informal *Bierstube*.

Donau-Auen and Marchfeld

The Danube flows across the flat lands east from Vienna for 50km or so before going on to form the border between Slovakia and Hungary. In contrast to Vienna, where the river has been ruthlessly canalized, here in the **Donau-Auen**, the Danube is still allowed to flood the surrounding woods and meadows, thus providing an important natural habitat for beavers, and numerous other flora and fauna. To the north lies the featureless plain of the **Marchfeld**, whose name is derived from the River March (Morava), which marks the border between Slovakia and Austria. Chateaux are dotted across this prime hunting, shooting and fishing region, though as many folk come here nowadays to watch the wildlife as to kill it. In Roman times, of course, it was the **Danube** that formed the empire's natural eastern border or *Limes*, strengthened by a series of forts along its banks. The main camp along this stretch of the Danube was **Carnuntum**, 40km or so east of Vienna, which now boasts the best Roman remains in the country, and is by far the most popular sight in the district.

Nationalpark Donau-Auen

The narrow strip of flood meadows on either side of the Danube comprises the **Nationalpark Donau-Auen**, which stretches from the very edge of Vienna to the Slovak border. The vast majority of the national park is on the north bank, where a cycle track runs along the top of the flood barrier embankment or Marchfelddamm, which passes through the area's characteristic birch, poplar and willow trees. Several marked footpaths explore the arms of the Danube and for a time run alongside the river itself.

Orth an der Donau

The easiest point of access, east of Vienna, is via the village of **ORTH AN DER DONAU** (*www.orth.at*), 24km east of the capital. Orth is not, in fact, on the Danube, but set back 2km from it, though there is a road leading down to the river, where the popular *Uferhaus* **restaurant** (closed Wed out of season; *www.uferhaus.at*) serves up delicious carp, pike and other local fish dishes. From May to October, the *Uferhaus* is also one of the meeting points for **guided walks** (Auwanderung) and rigid inflatable (Schlauchboot) **boat excursions** up the quiet arms of the Danube. These are organized by the national park, and need to be booked through the information office in Eckartsau (see below).

Back in Orth itself, the scruffy local Schloss is home to a **Fischereimuseum** (mid-March to mid-Nov Tues–Fri 9am–noon & 1–5pm, Sat & Sun 9am–5pm; öS40/€2.91). The displays are all in German, though there are one or two live carp and eel in tanks in amongst the stuffed and model fish. Surprisingly there's also a modest piscatorial ethnographic collection including a giant reed boat and a fish cult mask from Melanesia. Your ticket also covers the **Donaumuseum**, on the second floor, which contains stuffed birds and animals of the region, models of famous Austrian bridges over the Danube, and lots of model boats. The largest model of all, though, is devoted to Prince Eugène of Savoy's siege of Belgrade against the Turks in 1717 when he blockaded the Danube with ships. Amateur apiarists will also want to have a look round the **Bienenmuseum** (öS20/€1.45), housed in the northwest tower of the castle, with colourful hives in the grounds.

Orth proper has another good **fish restaurant**, the *Binder* (☎02212/2252; ②), with a lovely shady garden by the side of the castle. The *Binder* also offers simple **rooms** for the night, or you could try the more hotel-like *Danubius* (☎02212/2400; ③), on the main road.

Schloss Eckartsau

Set in a patch of mature woodland to the south of the village of Eckartsau, 5km east of Orth, **Schloss Eckartsau** (April–Oct Sat & Sun 11am & 2pm; öS60/€4.36) was built in the 1720s as a convenient hunting lodge within easy reach of the capital by the powerful Kinsky family. The impressive Baroque west portal, with its pediment frieze of Diana and cherubs restraining hounds and stags, dates from this time. After a brief period of use by the Habsburgs, who acquired it in 1760, the chateau was mothballed for over a hundred years until the Archduke Franz Ferdinand decided to restore it (and

THE LAST EMPEROR

Emperor Karl I was born in 1887 at Schloss Persenbeug in Lower Austria, and spent the carefree, privileged childhood typical of a Habsburg archduke. As the Emperor Franz-Josef I's great nephew, Karl hardly expected to become emperor himself. However, Franz-Josef's only son, Rudolf committed suicide in 1889 (see p.209), and the emperor's brother, Karl Ludwig died unexpectedly in 1896 after drinking contaminated water whilst on a pilgrimage to the Holy Land. Karl Ludwig's eldest son, the Archduke Franz Ferdinand, became heir to the throne, but he had to agree to cut his children out of the royal inheritance in order to marry the lowly Countess Chotek (see p.178). As a result, when Franz Ferdinand was assassinated in Sarajevo in 1914, it was his nephew, Karl, who was unexpectedly elevated to the status of crown prince. Two years later, in the midst of World War I, Franz-Josef died at the age of 86, and Karl somewhat reluctantly took up the reins of power.

The Emperor Karl's brief reign is best known for his bungled attempt at negotiating a separate peace for the empire in March 1917, using as an intermediary Sixtus of Bourbon-Parma, brother of his wife, Zita, and a soldier in the Belgian army. When the whole affair became public knowledge in the spring of 1918, it caused a great deal of embarrassment all round, particularly in view of the fact that the young emperor had agreed that Alsace-Lorraine should be returned to the French (without asking the Germans). In the end, on Armistice Day, ensconced in Schönbrunn with the empire crumbling around him, Karl agreed to sign a document relinquishing "all participation in the affairs of state", a compromise formula which avoided an official abdication. The very same day, the family left for the imperial hunting lodge at Eckartsau in the Marchfeld, where, two days later, Karl was forced to agree to withdraw from Hungarian state affairs, though again he refused to abdicate outright.

When the Austrian republic's first parliament convened in March 1919, Karl was given an ultimatum: abdication, exile or prison. He chose exile, and he and his family left Eckartsau for Switzerland, under British escort. Shortly afterwards, the Austrian government passed a law confiscating the family's property and banishing them from the country, unless they renounced their rights to the throne. Restoration in Austria was out of the question, but the situation in Hungary was much more hopeful. The communist regime of Béla Kun had fled, and Karl's former naval chief, Admiral Horthy, had seized power and declared himself regent. However, when Karl travelled incognito overland across Austria to meet Horthy face to face in Budapest, in March 1920, the admiral refused to hand over power. The "Easter Bid" was a resounding failure, but in October the same year Karl made a last, desperate attempt to regain the Hungarian half of his empire, flying secretly into Sopron, in western Hungary, accompanied by his pregnant wife. After a brief skirmish with Horthy's forces in the suburbs of Budapest, Karl was forced to admit defeat for a second time, and sailed, once more under British escort, into permanent exile on the island of Madeira, where he died of pneumonia less than six months later at the age of 35. The irrepressible Zita outlived her husband by 77 years, dying in her late nineties in 1989.

Of course, monarchists are eager to point out that Karl was, in fact, by no means the last Habsburg. In the 1930s, Karl's eldest son, Otto, kept the dynastic cause going from the family's refuge outside Brussels. An apocryphal story has it that when asked if he would be watching the Austria–Hungary football match, Otto replied, "Who are we playing?" Eventually, in the 1960s, he renounced his claim to the throne (though his brothers still refused), handing it onto his son, Karl, and was therefore able to pay a few brief visits to his homeland. In the 1980s, Otto became a Euro MP for Bavaria, where he continues to live in exile. Austria has recently rescinded the law banning the Habsburgs from the country unless they abdicate their claims to the throne, but a return of the monarchy looks as unlikely as ever.

install electricity), inviting Kaiser Wilhelm II over for a shooting party in 1908. Eckartsau is best known, however, as the final refuge of the Emperor Karl I and the imperial family, who lived here for five months between the end of World War I and their journey into exile from the local train station on March 23, 1919.

Despite the restricted opening times, a visit to Eckartsau is well worth the effort. Access to the royal apartments is via the frescoed **Grosses Stiegenhaus**, designed by Fischer von Erlach, with its enormous gilded lamps, and stucco hunting panoplies. The **Festsaal**, with a Daniel Gran ceiling fresco of Olympian gods lounging around in the clouds, is probably the single most impressive room. Like all the chateaux in the Marchfeld, Eckartsau suffered in the aftermath of World War II from looting by locals, and by Russian soldiers, who even stole the gold thread from the silk wall hangings. It was in the Grandsalon on November 13, 1918, that the Emperor Karl suspended his claim to the throne of Hungary. After some wonderful bird-themed silk wall hangings and Chinoiserie shutters, you finally enter Franz Ferdinand's living quarters, decked out in the usual heavy wood furnishings, though equipped with a tiled bathroom and sunken bath and shower that were clearly the height of modernity at the time.

Schloss Eckartsau is also home to the **Nationalpark information office** (April–Oct daily 9am–4pm; ☎02214/2335, *wwwdonauen.at*), where you can pick up information and book yourself a place on one of the regular guided walks or boat excursions.

Marchfeld

The flatness of the **Marchfeld** is pretty relentless, but it does boast a handsome bevy of chateaux worth visiting. However, getting around with public transport can be tricky: Marchegg is on the Vienna–Bratislava train line, and Niederweiden is a short walk from Engelhartstetten train station, but buses are few and far between. As a border region, the Marchfeld has seen more than its fair share of battles over the centuries. It was at the **Battle of Marchfeld** in 1278 that Rudolf of Habsburg defeated King Otakar II of Bohemia, and thus secured the Austrian lands – roughly Upper and Lower Austria – and Styria for the dynasty. And in 1809 the Marchfeld was the scene of two of the bloodiest battles in the Napoleonic Wars. In May, at the **Battle of Aspern** (now within Vienna's city limits), Napoleon suffered his first ever defeat at the hands of the Habsburg Archduke Karl: Austrian losses amounted to an unhealthy 23,000, but the French lost nearly half of their entire army, with 43,000 being killed or taken prisoner. Austrian victory was short-lived, and two months later at the **Battle of Deutsch-Wagram**, despite losing another 34,000 soldiers, Napoleon reversed the result and defeated the Austrians, whose casualties exceeded 50,000.

Schloss Niederweiden and Schlosshof

Some 10km northeast of Eckartsau and visible for miles around across the flat Marchfeld, is the French chateau-style hunting lodge of **Schloss Niederweiden** (May–Oct Tues–Sun 10am–5pm; öS25/€1.82), designed in 1693 by Fischer von Erlach for Count Starhemberg. Once surrounded by ornate formal gardens, this ochre chateau, with its natty black shutters, now looks slightly forlorn amidst the intensive agriculture of the Marchfeld, with a busy main road passing right past its front gates. The chateau's bare interior is now used for special art exhibitions, though there are a few permanent displays telling a little of the history of the place. In addition, the central, oval **Kuppelsaal** – added by Nicolo Pacassi – retains its original floor-to-ceiling trompe l'oeil frescoes featuring foliage, swallows and Chinese figures.

Just 3km northeast of Niederweiden, is Prince Eugène of Savoy's much more palatial country seat of **Schlosshof** (April–Oct Tues–Sun 10am–5pm; öS70/€5.09; *www.schlosshof.at*), a severe, three-winged, imperial yellow colossus designed by Johann Lukas von Hildebrandt in the late 1720s. Once again, the chateau's interior is given over to temporary exhibitions. However, a couple of rooms from Eugène's day survive, and are worth the entry fee alone: the original Baroque chapel, with its red and grey marbling and frescoed cupola, and the **Grosse Saal**, whose magnolia and white stucco-work includes a cast ceiling relief of a mythological hunt. The gardens at Schlosshof, which used to stretch down in terraces to the east of the chateau, were clearly quite something in their day. The views – over to the factories and high-rise housing of Devínská Nová Ves, on the Slovak side of the River March – are not what they once were, and only a few of the original sphinxes and fountains survive, but the idea is to restore the gardens to their former glory over the next few years.

Marchegg

The small, walled town of **MARCHEGG**, 8km north of Schlosshof, sits right on the banks of the River March and Slovak border, and boasts a modest little ochre-coloured Schloss of its own, to the north of the main square. The main part of the chateau contains a predictable **Jagdmuseum** (mid-March to Nov Tues–Sun 9am–noon & 1–5pm; öS30/€2.18), filled with the stags' heads, crossbows, guns, hunting horns, and falconry equipment. The same ticket covers the much more unusual **Afrikamuseum** in the outbuildings, which displays the booty of various imperial African explorers – masks, Ashanti statues and stuffed birds and animals – mostly from West Africa. Behind the chateau, you can gain access to a network of paths and viewing platforms in the neighbouring Marchauen **WWF nature reserve**, which is home to, among other creatures, Europe's largest colony of white storks, who nest here from March to August. The *Gasthof Marcheck*, on the town's Hauptplatz, serves decent **food** for weary travellers. It's also worth noting that Marchegg's **train station** is a good 2km south of the town itself.

Gänserndorf Safaripark

Strategically situated within easy driving distance of the Czech Republic, Slovakia, Hungary and, of course, Vienna, **Gänserndorf Safaripark** (April–Oct daily 9.30am–5.30 or 6.30pm; öS200/€14.54; *www.safaripark.at*), 4km south of Gänserndorf itself, is really only of any interest if you've got children to entertain. You need your own car to drive round the safari area, where a collection of listless lions and hyperactive monkeys, among other animals, have a modicum of room in which to roam free. In addition to the Safaripark, there are a conventional zoo, or Arbenteuer Park, and various "shows", featuring circus acts, parrots, snakes, tigers, sea lions, panthers and leopards. Kids are unlikely to leave disappointed, but the experience is less edifying for adults.

Archäologischer Park Carnuntum

Carnuntum was founded as a permanent military camp for the XV Legion around 40 AD, and in the course of the next century became the military and civil capital of the Roman province of Upper Pannonia, with a population of over 50,000. The Emperor Marcus Aurelius used it as his chief military base during his campaign against the Marcomanni and Quadi tribes (171–173 AD), and wrote his second book of Meditations here. In 198 AD the local commander Septimius Severus was declared emperor by the Pannonian legions. Carnuntum's other moment of glory was in 307 AD when Emperor Diocletian came out of retirement and staged a conference in order to try and reconcile the emperors of the East and West Roman Empires. Around 400 AD the town was abandoned by the Romans and soon afterwards sacked by the Goths.

Today, its Roman remains spread across 5km between the villages of **Petronell** and **Bad Deutsch Altenburg**. In order to impose some logic on the disparate sites, the whole area has been dubbed the **Archäologischer Park Carnuntum** (*www .carnuntum.co.at*), and divided into three zones (from east to west): Kernzone I, cen-tred on Bad Deutsch Altenburg, where the most important finds are now displayed in the Archäologisches Museum Carnuntinum; Kernzone II, centred on the military camp, or Legionslager-Lagerstadt; and Kernzone III around Petronell-Carnuntum (as the village is now known), where the civilian town (Zivilstadt Carnuntum) was situated. In the account below we've reversed the order of the zones to reflect the fact that most visitors approach the park from Vienna. If you don't have your own car, the best way to visit the sights is on foot, or by bike, which you can hire from Petronell or Bad Deutsch Altenburg train stations.

Petronell-Carnuntum

To get your bearings in **PETRONELL-CARNUNTUM**, it's best to head straight for the main excavation site and **information centre** (April–Oct Mon–Fri 9am–5pm, Sat & Sun 9am–6pm; öS49/€3.56; *Carnuntum Pass* öS100/€7.27 includes entry to the muse-um in Bad Deutsch Altenburg), at the west of Hauptstrasse, opposite the rather attrac-tive Romanesque Rundkapelle; here, you can pick up a map of the sites and lots of other useful info. Your ticket allows you entry to the nearby excavation site of the **Antikes Wohnstadtviertel** (ancient civil town) of Carnuntum, but unless you buy a guidebook or pay the extra öS45/€3.30 for an audioguide (in English) you won't get much out of the ruins, which rarely rise above foundation level. At the far end of the site's sloping field, you can, however, view an excellent example of Roman engineering, where a sub-stantial slice of the *Limes* road and accompanying drainage system have been pre-served, not to mention a full-scale reconstruction of the classical facade of the town's Temple of Diana. Beyond the excavation site lie the slightly more intriguing founda-tions of the **Grosse Therme** (public baths), a vast complex thought to have been sig-nificantly embellished in preparation for the 307 AD conference.

If you're pushed for time, though, you're probably best off skipping the excavation site altogether and heading off to the more substantial ruins in Kernzone III. The most impressive of these, is the **Heidentor**, a gargantuan gateway that stands in the fields a kilometre or so to the southwest of the village, beyond the railway tracks and route 9. Signs from the Heidentor will lead you to the nearby **Amphitheater II**, an out-of-town theatre even in Roman times, which was capable of seating 13,000 on its grassy banks. A lot more impressive, however, is the smaller **Amphitheater I**, in the military camp (Kernzone II), situated off the road to Bad Deutsch Altenburg, to the east of Petronell, where much more of the Roman stonework has been preserved, including the entrance tunnels.

Bad Deutsch Altenburg

The chief sight in the spa-town of **BAD DEUTSCH ALTENBURG** is the **Archäologisches Museum Carnuntinum** (mid-Jan to mid-Dec Tues–Sun 10am–5pm; öS60/€4.36; *Carnuntum Pass* öS100/€7.27 includes entry to the other sites and information center), overlooking the Kurpark at the far eastern end of the main street, Badgasse. The museum is a pleasure to visit, thanks in part to the lovely building in which it's housed, purpose-built by Friedrich Ohmann in 1904 to look some-thing like a giant Roman villa. All the museum's labelling is in German, but luckily, if your German isn't up to it, some of the finds are impressive enough without any addi-tional information. The museum's finest individual piece is the marble *Dancing Maenad* (*"Tanzende Mänade"*), whose finely carved drapery reveals her beautifully formed (and much-photographed) buttocks. In the foyer, there's also an interesting (mostly recon-structed) Mithraic relief, from the male-only cult popular among Roman legions before the advent of Christianity. The relief depicts the Persian deity Mithras slaying a cosmic bull, while a scorpion grasps its genitals and a dog licks its wounds (the bull's blood was seen as life-giving, and initiates to the cult had to bathe in the stuff in subterranean tombs).

While you're in Bad Deutsch Altenburg, it's worth strolling up the nearby hill, known as the Kirchenberg, to take a closer look at the town's landmark **Marienkirche** (aka Stephanskirche), a bizarre Gothic edifice made up of three elements that look like they belong to separate churches. The octagonal west tower is remarkably small and features a series of grimacing gargoyles, while at the opposite end of the church is a fanciful presbytery, prickling with delicately carved finials, which looks like it should form part of a much larger church. Between the two is the older Romanesque nave, which is much plainer and sits much lower than either the tower or the chancel.

Practicalities

The **train station** in Petronell is a short walk south of the village centre, while the one in Bad Deutsch Altenburg is a similar distance southwest of the spa. It takes about an hour to reach either station on S-Bahn line 7 from Wien-Mitte or Wien-Nord, making the whole area an easy day-trip from Vienna. There's a **tourist office** (April–Oct daily 9am–5pm; ☎02163/2228, *www.tiscover.com/petronell-carnuntum*) in Petronell, opposite the main excavation site; there's another (Mon–Fri 8am–noon & 12.30–4pm; ☎02165/62459, *www.tiscover.com/baddeutschaltenburg*) in the *Kurhotel* on Badgasse in Bad Deutsch Altenburg.

As for **accommodation**, the *Gasthof zum Heidentor* (☎02163/2201; ②), in Petronell, has rooms, each with en-suite facilities and TV; the *Hotel Marc Aurel* (☎02163/2285, *hotel.marc-aurel@contact.at*; ③) offers plusher rooms, though no TV. A better bet, however, is Bad Deutsch Altenburg, with a nice leafy Kurpark and, being a spa town, a much wider choice of places. A good bet is the family-run *Pension Madle* (☎02165/62763; ②), which has a nice outside terrace, and en-suite facilities in all rooms. All the above places have restaurants attached, where you can get decent, reasonably priced Austrian food.

Hainburg an der Donau

Squeezed between two hills that signal the end of Austrian territory, the little walled town of **HAINBURG**, 3km east of Bad Deutsch Altenburg, is another good base for exploring the area. As befits a border town that is still every bit the gateway into Austria from Slovakia and northern Hungary, Hainburg boasts extensive fortifications, including three substantial gateways, the largest of which is the colossal thirteenth-century **Wiener Tor**.

The *Hotel zur goldenen Krone* (☎02165/62105; ③), on the main square, is a bit dowdy but very friendly; alternatively, there's the more homely *Gasthof zu drei Raben* (☎02165/62407; ②), on Ungarstrasse. The best place to eat out is *Zur alten Bampress*, an excellent *Stadtheuriger* on Ungarstrasse (closed Tues), with a lovely courtyard. Hainburg has two **train stations**: Hainburg-Donau Frachtenbahnhof, to the west of town, and Hainburg Ungartor, closer to the centre, east of the Altstadt.

Rohrau

The composer Josef Haydn was born in **ROHRAU**, a one-street village 4km south of Petronell, on the banks of the River Leitha. The **Haydn-Geburtshaus** (Tues–Sun 10am–5pm; öS20/€1.45) is a lovely thatched cottage, with a delightful arcaded courtyard covered with vines and a cosy, folksy feel to it. This creates something of a false impression, as it was clearly a hovel when Haydn was born here in 1732 (the original building, built by Haydn's father in 1728, burnt down in 1899). By all accounts, Haydn had a pretty miserable childhood – with "more floggings than food", according to one of his letters – and was no doubt relieved when he was sent off to nearby Hainburg at the tender age of five, eventually becoming a choirboy at the Stephansdom in Vienna (for more on Haydn's life, see p.254). Few of his personal belongings have made their way here, apart from a baptismal bowl and a rather attractive tortoiseshell snuff box.

In order to make ends meet, Haydn's mother was for a while employed as a cook at the nearby **Schloss Harrach** (Easter–Oct Tues–Sun 10am–5pm; öS60/€4.36; *www.volkskulturnoe.at/museen/0026.htm*). The present, rather plain, late-Baroque moated chateau is still occupied, in part, by the Harrachs, though the public are allowed in to admire their extensive private art collection displayed on the first floor, along with the family's Meissen porcelain and Chinese vases. The bulk of the art collection came into the family thanks to a couple of illustrious ancestors: Ferdinand Bonaventura (1636–1706), who served as imperial ambassador in Madrid, and Aloys Thomas (1669–1742), who served as Viceroy of Naples. However, despite the smattering of big-name painters – there are some minor works and sketches by the likes of Van Dyck, Rubens, Teniers and Jan Breughel the Elder – there are few masterpieces here.

Bruck an der Leitha

When the River Leitha formed the historical border between Austria and Hungary under the Habsburgs, the walled town of **BRUCK AN DER LEITHA**, 9km southwest of Rohrau, served as the main border post. Now most folk simply pass through the town en route to the Neusiedler See, but it's a more promising place to stay than Rohrau if you're in the area. The town walls are particularly impressive as you approach from Vienna, and the spacious central **Hauptplatz** boasts a parade of monuments – a Marian column, a Trinity column, punctuated by two fountains – overlooked by a handsome silver-white Pfarrkirche. The Pompeiian-red **Schloss Harrach**, east of the main square at the end of Stefaniegasse, though closed to the public, has a nice park for a picnic.

The town's **tourist office** (Mon 9am–noon & 1–5pm, Tues & Wed 9am–noon, Fri 9am–6pm; May–Oct also Sat 10am–noon; ☎02162/62221, *www.tiscover.com/bruck .leitha*) is by the church on Hauptplatz, and can furnish you with a map of the town and help with other enquiries. **Accommodation** options include the *Ungarische Krone* (☎02162/62777; ③), a three-star hotel on the other side of the Leitha off Parndorferstrasse, or the excellent *Pension Eitler* (☎02162/63206; ②), further down at no. 173. *Café Haas*, on the east side of Hauptplatz, is a really nice, classy café-restaurant and pizzeria with tables outside overlooking the square. The best place to sample the local wine is in the lovely ivy-strewn *Schanigarten* of the secluded *Harrachkeller*, on Schlossgasse.

The Wienerwald area

The gentle wooded hills of the **Wienerwald** (Vienna Woods) stretch from the suburbs of Vienna itself southwest to the alpine foothills that form the border between Lower Austria and Styria. As such, they have been a favourite weekend destination for the Viennese, who can simply hop on a tram to get there (see p.210 for details). In many ways, this accessibility is the woods' chief virtue. Compared to the country's sublime alpine peaks, the Wienerwald's scenery is pretty low-key. The main resorts, such as **Mödling** and the spa-town of **Baden**, cling to the eastern edge of the Wienerwald, where the hills dip down into the vineyards of the plain, and make for easy day-trips from the capital; if you want to spend a day or two walking in the woods themselves, you're best off overnighting at either of the above places.

Mödling bei Wien

Like Baden (see below), **MÖDLING**, 15km south of Vienna, makes great play of its associations with Beethoven, who stayed here in the summer of 1819. Even if you've no interest in the composer, Mödling is a very pretty little town, which has preserved a remarkable number of sixteenth- and seventeenth-century houses in its minuscule Altstadt.

From the **train station**, to the east of town, it's a ten-minute walk along **Hauptstrasse** to Freiheitsplatz on the northeastern edge of the old town. Beethoven rented three rooms nearby at the Hafnerhaus, Hauptstrasse 79, now the **Beethoven-Haus** (Sat & Sun 10am–noon & 1–4pm; öS15/€1.09), whilst he worked on, among other things, the *Diabelli Variations* and the *Missa Solemnis*. "From behind the closed door of one of the parlours we could hear the master working on the fugue of the *Credo*, singing, yelling, stamping his feet", some friends, who dropped in on him, recalled; "when we had heard enough of this almost frightening performance and were about to depart, the door opened and Beethoven stood before us, his features distorted to the point of inspiring terror. He looked as though he had just engaged in a life and death struggle with the whole army of contrapuntists, his everlasting enemies." The following year Beethoven intended to stay in Mödling again, but was refused lodgings "on account of his strange behaviour".

From Freiheitsplatz, head up Herzoggasse, which is flanked by attractive houses bearing frescoes and sgraffiti, into the pedestrianized main square, **Schrannenplatz**, with its distinctive fountain decorated with ornamental pineapples, and, beyond, the town's dinky little sixteenth-century **Rathaus**, sporting a tiny loggia at one corner. A short hike up Pfarrgasse will bring you to the town's huge **Pfarrkirche St Othmar**, built in the fifteenth century to double as a defensive stronghold. Close by stands a distinctive circular tower-like charnel house, featuring a superb knotted Romanesque portal, and sporting a Baroque onion dome.

A network of paths crisscrosses the adjacent Wienerwald: from the other side of the town's river, to the south, you can explore the woods of the **Naturpark Föhrenberge**, which is punctuated with numerous monuments, the most famous of which is the Neoclassical Husarentempel. An easy two-kilometre walk west along the river from Mödling is the popular tourist attraction of the **Seegrotte Hinterbrühl** (daily; April–Oct 8.30am–noon & 1–5pm; Nov–March 9am–noon & 1–3.30pm; öS60/€4.36; *www.tourist-net.co.at/seegr1.htm*), a former gypsum mine, which fell into disuse when it was flooded in 1912. Later, the caves were used by the Nazis as a work camp for building fuselages for jet fighters. Guided tours (in a variety of languages including English) are quite fun – but cold, so wrap up before you enter – and finish with an atmospheric boat ride through the flooded mineshafts.

You can pick up **tourist information** from either the Stadtmuseum (Mon–Fri 9am–noon, Sat & Sun 10am–noon & 2–6pm), or the post office (Mon–Fri 8am–4pm), on the main square. There's a wide range of **accommodation**, from intimate pensions such as *Haus Monika* (☎02236/257359; ③), Badstrasse 53, in the villa quarter to the south of the Altstadt, to the plush *Babenbergerhof* (☎02236/22246; ⑥), in the heart of the Altstadt at Babenbergergasse 6. If you're staying the night in Mödling, be sure to check out what's on at the town's stylish theatre/cinema, Mödlinger Bühne, on Babenbergerstrasse.

Laxenburg

Though not strictly speaking in the Wienerwald, the former imperial residence of **LAXENBURG** is within striking distance of the woods, 5km or so east of Mödling. The town's links with the Habsburgs go back to the fourteenth century, when Duke

Albrecht III built the **Altes Schloss**, but the place really came into its own four hundred years later under the reign of Maria Theresia, who built the **Neues Schloss** (also known as the Blauer Hof and now headquarters of the suspicious-sounding International Institute of Applied Systems Analyses), overlooking the town's Schlossplatz. Laxenburg quickly became the family's favourite country retreat, a place in which the stifling court formalities of Vienna could be abandoned. According to one of Josef II's numerous decrees, each guest was "free to do as he will, to ride, to drive, to join in the hunt or to stay at home". Not surprisingly, it was also much frequented by the reclusive Empress Elisabeth, who gave birth to her only son, Rudolf, in the Blauer Hof in 1858 (for more on Rudolf, see opposite).

The chief attraction nowadays is the beautifully landscaped and extensive grounds of the **Schlosspark** (dawn–dusk; öS15/€1.09), whose woods are dotted with various follies: a Neoclassical temple, a grotto, a jousting arena and, at the centre of a wooded *étoile*, the Grünes Lusthaus, a summer pavilion decorated with frescoes, where Maria Theresia's husband, Franz Stephan, used to play cards. The largest folly of the lot is the **Franzensburg** (guided tours Easter–Oct at 11am, 2 & 3pm; öS50/€3.63), a mock Gothic castle, described in 1814 by an English visitor as "an imperial toy . . . a little building provided with numerous turrets and watch-towers, loop-holes, irongates, and portcullises". Built in the park's artificial lake, on one of the islands linked by bridges and a little raft on a chain, the castle was conceived by the Emperor Franz I as a sort of romantic retreat, based loosely on the dynasty's original seat in Switzerland. There's a café in the castle courtyard, and regular open-air theatre performances on summer weekends. Alternatively, you can go on a guided tour of the interior, which features lots of arms and armour, portraits and busts of the Habsburgs, quasi-medieval furnishings and even a faux dungeon, complete with fake prisoner.

If you're not picnicking in the park, the *Laxenburgerhof* does bargain three-course lunches for under öS100/€7.27, or else there's a pizzeria in the former Kaiserbahnhof, built in neo-Gothic style in 1845. If you're camping, Laxenburg makes for a good base, especially as a convenient launching pad for day-trips to Vienna. The **campsite** (☎02236/71333; April–Oct), situated ten minutes' walk out of town along the road to Münchendorf, has an adjacent outdoor pool and a gate into the Schlosspark. There are hourly **buses** to Wien-Mitte, and regular trains to the Südbahnhof, though the Laxenburg-Biedermannsdorf **train station** is a good two-kilometre walk from the campsite.

Heiligenkreuz

The majority of monasteries in Austria enjoy spectacular, cliff-top locations, but the Cistercians always preferred well-watered, wooded spots for their abbeys, and **HEILIGENKREUZ**, which nestles unassumingly in the undulating landscape of the Wienerwald, 14km west of Mödling, is no exception. Don't let that put you off, however, for Heiligenkreuz is easily one of the finest examples of Romanesque-Gothic architecture in the country, and boasts, in addition, some very fine Baroque furnishings, courtesy of Italian sculptor Giovanni Giuliani.

Though the monastery was founded in the twelfth century by Duke Leopold III, who planned to establish a burial place for the Babenberg dynasty, the whole complex looks thoroughly Baroque from the outside, having been extensively rebuilt after being looted by the Turks in 1683. The main courtyard features a bevy of fantastically bushy beech trees and a splendidly animated Baroque Trinity column and fountain sculpted by Giuliani. Only on the eastern side of the courtyard do you get the first hint of the monastery's medieval origins, in the plain Romanesque facade of the **Stiftskirche**. To gain full access to the church, you must join one of the guided tours, which set off hourly (in German only; Mon–Sat 10am, 11am & 2–4pm, Sun 11am & 2–4pm;

THE MAYERLING TRAGEDY

Numerous theories continue to be put forward as to why the Crown Prince Rudolf, only son of Franz-Josef I and heir to the throne, chose to take his own life. The Viennese, who love to sentimentalize the tragedy, tend to claim it was all for love, yet Rudolf was a notoriously fickle womanizer, and Maria Vetsera just one in a long line of pretty mistresses. The plot thickens when you consider that the previous summer Rudolf had proposed a suicide pact to his long-term mistress Mizzi Caspar, but was turned down. On the very night before his suicide, Rudolf spent the evening with Mizzi Caspar, before leaving to meet Maria at Mayerling. It's true that his marriage to Princess Stephanie of Belgium – arranged by his father for political reasons – was a dismal failure, but it wasn't enough to drive him to suicide, and certainly didn't prevent him from keeping bachelor digs at the Hofburg where he could receive his numerous mistresses. One plausible theory is that, in 1887, he contracted a venereal disease, which he believed to be incurable. Worse still, it's thought that he had infected Stephanie, causing her to become infertile (having failed to produce a male heir to the throne).

Others contend that it was a political act, born of frustration with his lack of any part in the decision-making process of government. Franz-Josef allowed his son little real power and, in any case, disagreed with him on most issues. Rudolf, who was never close to his father, tended to mix with liberals opposed to his father's ministers' policies, and even wrote anonymous, critical articles to the liberal *Neues Wiener Tagblatt*. There were rumours at the time that Rudolf had been assassinated by his political opponents or French secret agents, a version of events upheld by the late Empress Zita as recently as 1982. Another possible explanation is that Rudolf, having written to the pope to seek an annulment of his marriage, had been snubbed by the pontiff, who had returned the petition directly to Franz-Josef. Finally, on January 26, 1889, Rudolf and his father are known to have had a fierce argument – what it was about we shall never know.

Four days later, Rudolf and Maria's bodies were discovered by Rudolf's hunting partner, Count Hoyos, who had got no answer when he called in at Mayerling. The first official version of events was that Rudolf had died of apoplexy, but after the post-mortem it was admitted that he had shot himself. As suicides were denied a Christian burial, the pathologists in charge were wise enough to suggest that "the act was committed in a moment of psychological unbalance", thus allowing the Catholic authorities an escape clause. Rudolf's request to be buried in the nearby village of Alland alongside his mistress was denied, and he was buried in the Kaisergruft amid much pomp and circumstance. Maria Vetsera's presence at Mayerling was never acknowledged by the Habsburgs, though rumours abounded. Some 36 hours after the incident, her fully clothed corpse, in the first stages of rigor mortis, was wedged upright between her two uncles in a carriage, transported to Heiligenkreuz and secretly buried in the cemetery there.

öS65/€4.72; *www.stift-heiligenkreuz.at*). Inside, the church is the product of two distinct building periods: the plain round arches of the nave are Romanesque, while the lofty, vaulted presbytery is Gothic. The Baroque choir stalls, by Giuliani again, are outstanding, each one decorated with a lime-wood relief from the Life of Christ, and crowned by cherubs and busts of eminent aristocrats, priests and bishops. They're put to good use by the brothers, who come here to sing five times a day.

The guided tours begin with the monastery's beautifully preserved thirteenth-century **cloisters**, lined with more than three hundred slender pink marble columns, which, like the church itself, perfectly illustrate the transition from the rounded arches of the Romanesque style to the pointed arches of the Gothic. Several chapels are connected to the cloisters, among them the **Kapitalkapelle**, where many of the Babenberg dynasty are buried, and the polygonal Brunnenkapelle, which echoes noisily to the sound of its fountain. Best of the lot is the ghoulish **Totenkapelle**, decked out with black and gold furnishings by Giuliani, including a macabre set of four candelabra, supported by skeletons in shrouds. The guided tours end with a stroll round the **sacristy**, an extraordinarily rich Baroque concoction, furnished with stunning inlaid wooden cabinets and decorated with frescoes framed by pink and white stucco-work.

Mayerling

Mystery still surrounds the motives behind the suspected double suicide of **Crown Prince Rudolf** (1858–89), eldest son of the Emperor Franz-Josef I and heir to the throne, and his half-Greek, 17-year-old mistress, Baroness Maria Vetsera, which took place in the early hours of the morning on January 29, 1889, at Rudolf's hunting lodge at **MAYERLING**, 2.5km southwest of Heiligenkreuz. Subject of a ballet, several films and countless books, the event has captured the popular imagination for over a hundred years – as recently as 1988, an Austrian businessman confessed to having stolen Maria's coffin after becoming obsessed with Mayerling.

Although the site of the lodge is only half an hour's walk from Heiligenkreuz, it's hardly worth the effort. Franz-Josef had the building demolished shortly after the incident, and a neo-Gothic chapel (April–Sept Mon–Sat 9am–12.30pm & 1.30–6pm; Oct–March closes 5pm), run by Carmelite nuns, erected in its place. Despite the fact that there's very little to see, folk still flock to the chapel, where they're relieved of a few Schillings, and ushered into the two side rooms that contain furniture and a bit of carpet from the old hunting lodge, plus photos and portraits of the tragedy's, protagonists.

Baden bei Wien

Just 25km south of Vienna, the spa town of **BADEN** is an easy day-trip from the capital, accessible either by train or via its very own tram link. This compact little town, peppered with attractive Neoclassical buildings in varying shades of magnolia and ochre, comes across as deeply provincial, a haven of peace for its elderly spa patients. But back in the eighteenth and nineteenth centuries, Baden was *the* most fashionable spa town in the Habsburg Empire, the favourite summer holiday retreat of none other than the Emperor Franz II (1792–1835). Baden's distinctive uniform Biedermeier appearance is largely the result of a building frenzy – much of it under the direction of the architect Josef Kornhäusel – prompted by a devastating fire in 1812. A swim in Baden's hot thermal baths is highly recommended and, as the town lies on the very edge of the Wienerwald, the walking and picnicking possibilities are a further enticement.

The Town

The small, triangular **Hauptplatz**, at the centre of Baden's pedestrian zone, gives you an idea of the modest scale of things in Baden. Almost dwarfing the surrounding buildings, including Kornhäusel's Neoclassical **Rathaus** from 1815, is the central plague column, erected a hundred years earlier, and crowned with a gilded sunburst. Even the last of the Holy Roman Emperors, Franz II, chose an unassuming three-storey building – now the **Kaiserhaus**, on the east side of the square – as his summer residence. The last of the Habsburgs, Emperor Karl I, also stayed here, during World War I, when Baden became the Austrian army headquarters. (Baden later reached its nadir in the decade after World War II, when it was used as the Soviet army headquarters.)

From 1804 onwards, Baden became a favourite retreat of Beethoven, too; he made a total of fifteen visits, staying at various addresses, one of which, at nearby Rathausgasse 10, has been turned into the **Beethoven Schauräume** (Tues–Fri 4–6pm, Sat & Sun 9–11am & 4–6pm; öS20/€1.45). In the 1820s, Beethoven was well

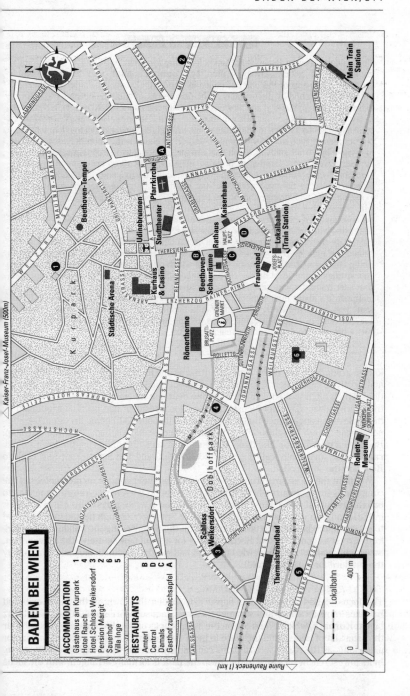

BADEN BEI WIEN

ACCOMMODATION
Gästehaus am Kurpark 1
Hotel Rauch 4
Hotel Schloss Weikersdorf 3
Pension Margit 2
Sauerhof 6
Villa Inge 5

RESTAURANTS
Amterl B
Central D
Demals C
Gasthof zum Reichsapfel A

S&M IN BADEN

The staid spa-town of Baden is the unlikely setting for *Venus im Pelze* ("Venus in Furs"), an account of sexual slavery written by **Count Leopold von Sacher-Masoch** (1835–95). The son of the chief of police in Lemberg (Lvov), the count was allegedly influenced as a child by the brutality of the prisons. As an adult, he became professor of history at Graz University, and wrote several historical and folkloric novels. His renown today, however, rests on his affair in the 1860s with "Baroness Bogdanoff", or "Wanda" (real name Fanny Pistor), to whom the count willingly signed away his freedom – becoming her manservant, taking the name of Gregor, and embarking upon "a liaison, marked materially by a prodigality in which furs and foreign travel were to be conspicuous". She agreed to wear furs "as often as possible, especially when in a cruel mood", while he agreed to "comply unreservedly with every one of her desires and commands". After six months of slavery, the two parted company, but the affair had inspired the count to write *Venus im Pelze*, which was published in 1870. In 1873 the count married Aurore Rümelin, who changed her name to Wanda in honour of the book's heroine. "Gregor" and Wanda became involved in a weird *ménage à trois* with a fake Polish countess, Anna von Kottowitz, who turned out to be a chemist's assistant.

We have the count to thank for the term "sadomasochism", though he himself never coined the phrase. That was left to one of Freud's early mentors, Richard von Krafft-Ebing (1840–1902), who first used the term – with reference to Sacher-Masoch's numerous writings on the S&M theme – in his *Psychopathia Sexualis*, published in Latin in 1886 (but later translated into seven languages), about which the Emperor Franz-Josef I once quipped, "it's about time someone brought out a decent book on Latin grammar". The same year, Sacher-Masoch split from Wanda, and he married his children's governess in 1887. He died in 1895, depressed by the decline of his reputation and by Krafft-Ebing's use of his name to designate a sexual perversion.

known around the spa as the local eccentric; as one friend recalls, "his hair was coarse and bristly . . . and when he put his hand through it, it remained standing in all directions which often looked comical". On one occasion he even got himself arrested, in the nearby town of Wiener Neustadt, after a local resident had been so frightened by his dishevelled appearance that she had called the police. On being arrested, the composer said "I am Beethoven", to which the constable replied, "You are a tramp, Beethoven doesn't look like that." It wasn't until later that night that the town's musical director was finally called out to identify him, and the mayor sent him back to Baden in the state coach.

Woefully, the three small rooms Beethoven rented out contain no mementoes of the composer's three sojourns here (there's a section on later, lesser-known Badenites to pad things out). It was in these rooms that Beethoven wrote parts of his *Missa Solemnis* in 1821, and, two years later, finished his *Ninth Symphony*, though he had to get a friend to persuade the landlord to take him back on the promise of good conduct. The landlord agreed on condition that Beethoven pay for a set of new shutters (the previous set, on which Beethoven had scrawled financial and musical calculations, had been sold by the landlord for a piece of gold).

THE KURPARK AND LONGER WALKS

The focus of Baden the spa, as opposed to Baden the town, is the ochre-coloured Kurhaus (now a casino) and summer theatre (Städtische Arena), north of Hauptplatz by the **Kurpark**, which is laid out on the steep slopes of the Wienerwald. This is by far the nicest bit of Baden, and the place to head for if you're intent on a spot of walking or picnicking, as the park's web of paths can quickly transport you high above the town. In its lowest reaches, closest to the town, the park is formally arranged, with the focus on the bandstand and the **Udinebrunnen**, an eye-catching fountain featuring a gilded water sprite emerging from a vast rockery replete with oversized frogs, serpents, fish and the sprite's giant stepfather. In fine weather, concerts take place in the nearby bandstand (May–Sept Tues–Sun 4.30pm). Higher up the park, various monuments emerge from the foliage: statues of Johann Strauss and his chief rival Josef Lanner, a temple to Mozart, and, biggest of the bunch, the vine-garlanded **Beethoven-Tempel**, a Neoclassical rotunda sporting some dubious underlit 1920s frescoes, but the best of all views across the spa.

For a more physically taxing walk, follow the signs to the offbeat **Kaiser-Franz-Josef-Museum** (April–Oct Tues–Sun 1–7pm; öS30/€2.18), roughly half an hour's walk through the woods from the bandstand, in a northwesterly direction. Although it advertises itself as a museum of folk art and craftwork, the collection is a lot more eclectic than you might imagine. The reconstructed smithy is par for the course, but the mousetrap from the room in which the commander in chief of the imperial forces during the Thirty Years' War, Albrecht von Waldstein, was murdered in 1634 is rather more unusual. In addition, there's a whole collection of arms and uniforms from the seventeenth to the twentieth century, banknotes, Habsburg memorabilia, a paper theatre, cake moulds, two penny farthings, and more.

Baden is also a perfect starting point for a full day's **hiking** in the Wienerwald. From the western end of Weilburgstrasse, a path leads up to the twelfth-century rubble of the Ruine Rauheneck. Beyond here lies the Kalternberger Forst, whose main peak is the Hoher Lindkogel (834m), 6km across the forested hills to the west; the hike there and back is relatively easy and takes about six hours nonstop.

THE ROLLETT-MUSEUM AND DOBLHOFFPARK

A bizarre collection of exhibits fills the **Rollett-Museum** (daily except Tues 3–6pm; öS20/€1.45), ten minutes' walk southwest of Hauptplatz on Weikersdorfer Platz. It's worth trekking out here for the building alone, designed in extravagant neo-Renaissance style in 1905 as the town hall for Weikersdorf, only to become redundant seven years later when Weikersdorf was subsumed into Baden. The most fascinating section of the collection within is the array of skulls, busts, brains and death masks – plus a wax model of Marie Antoinette's hand, and a plaster cast of Goethe's – amassed by Franz-Josef Gall (1758–1828), the founder of phrenology, a pseudo-science that claimed a person's talents or criminal traits could be traced to the size of certain areas of the brain. The rest of the museum is a hotchpotch: some crystals, an Egyptian sarcophagus and a cabinet of curios from the world tour of local nineteenth-century bigwig Josef von Doblhoff.

If you'd prefer something less mentally taxing, head for the vast hot thermal **open-air swimming pool** complex, which hides behind the 1920s facade of the *Thermalstrandbad* on Helenenstrasse, or the ultramodern, stylish *Römertherme* (*www.roemertherme.at*), on Brusattiplatz, which is open daily until 10pm. After your dip, you can relax in the nearby **Doblhoffpark**, a lovely mix of formal gardens and English park, with a large rosarium, a pergola and a huge, bushy plane tree at the centre. To the north is the Schloss Weikersdorf, built in the sixteenth century – you should be able to sneak a look at the arcaded courtyard – and seat of the Doblhoff family from 1741 until 1966 (it's now a hotel; see below). Finally, if you've time to spare, check out the latest contemporary art exhibitions in the low-slung Neoclassical **Frauenbad** (Tues–Sun 10am–noon & 3–7pm), on Josefplatz.

Practicalities

S-Bahn and regular trains from Vienna's Südbahnhof arrive at Baden's **main train station**, ten minutes' walk southeast of the town centre. Lokalbahn trams, distinguishable by their Prussian blue-and-cream livery, depart from Vienna's Staatsoper and arrive at the **station on Josefsplatz**. Baden's **tourist office** (May–Oct Mon–Sat 9am–6pm, Sun 9am–noon; Nov–April Mon–Fri 9am–5pm; ☎02252/41833-59, *www.baden-bei-wien.at*) is attractively ensconced in the Leopoldsbad, a magnolia-coloured Biedermeier building on Brusattiplatz.

There's a wide choice of **accommodation** in Baden, though much of it is in the higher price categories, with the handful of **private rooms** on offer through the tourist office the only truly inexpensive option. The rooms at *Hotel Rauch*, Pelzgasse 3 (☎02252/44561; ④), have nice high ceilings and en-suite facilities; *Pension Margit*, Mühlgasse 15–17 (☎02252/89718; ③), though slightly further from the centre, is another typical Baden building, and has some cheaper rooms with shared facilities; *Gästehaus am Kurpark* (☎02252/89104, *members.eunet.at.dirkg*; ②), as the name suggests, is a modern villa on the edge of the Kurpark; and there are several pleasant garden villas along the leafy boulevard of Weilburgstrasse, such as *Villa Inge*, at nos. 24–26 (☎02252/43171; ③). More upmarket accommodation can be had at the *Hotel Schloss Weikersdorf* (☎02252/48301; ⑤–⑨), a converted Renaissance castle in the Doblhoffpark (see p.213). The cheaper rooms here are in the modern annexe, *Dependance*, though all guests get free use of the sauna and pool. Another grandiose option is the palatial Biedermeier *Grandhotel Sauerhof* (☎02252/41251, *www.sauerhof.at*; ⑥), where the composer Salieri used to stay.

The *Café Central*, on Hauptplatz, is a big traditional *Kaffeehaus* in the Viennese style, and a great place for watching life go by. *Café Damals*, Rathausgasse 3 (closed Sat eve & Sun), offers reasonably priced **food**, but if the weather's fine you could easily pack a picnic and head off into the woods. The *Gasthaus zum Reichsapfel* is a homely inn just east of the Pfarrkirche, down Spiegelgasse, offering a range of beers, traditional pub fare and good veggie options; the *Amterl*, at the top of Hauptplatz (closed Sun), serves up nicely presented dishes, and has tables on the street. Baden is a sedate place at the best of times, and by nightfall spa patients are tucked up in bed, while everyone else heads for the town's **casino** (daily 3pm–3am; öS260 minimum) in the Kurhaus – you'll need jacket and tie to get in.

Wiener Neustadt

Considering that an estimated 52,000 bombs fell on the industrial town of **WIENER NEUSTADT**, 50km south of Vienna, during the latter stages of World War II, killing 790 civilians and destroying some 88 percent of the town's buildings, the place doesn't look that bad – in fact, the pedestrianized Altstadt is even quite attractive in places. Sections of the ancient walls, erected by Babenberg Duke Leopold V in 1194 when he founded the town as a fortress on the Hungarian frontier, have survived, and there are reminders, too, of the town's fifteenth-century heyday, when it served briefly as the Habsburgs' chief residence under Emperor Friedrich III (1440–93). Later, Friedrich's old seat was turned into the Theresianische Militärakademie, where none other than the "Desert Fox", General Rommel, was once in command, and it remains a prestigious military academy to the present day. However, the reason Wiener Neustadt attracted the attentions of the Anglo-American bombers was the town's heavy industrial base, which made, among other things, locomotives and armaments, and included a Daimler factory where the young Tito worked for a time.

The Town

Despite being the largest town in Lower Austria after St Pölten, Wiener Neustadt has a surprisingly compact Altstadt, centred on the spacious **Hauptplatz**, which has kept its original arcading on two sides, and is enlivened by a small morning market (Mon–Sat)

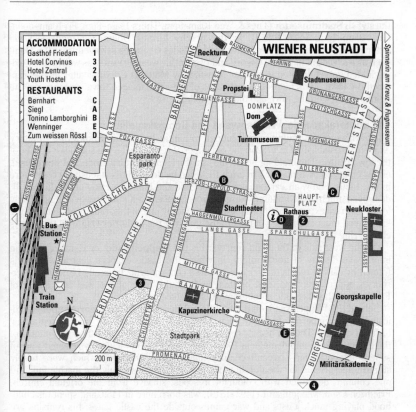

ACCOMMODATION
Gasthof Friedam   1
Hotel Corvinus   3
Hotel Zentral   2
Youth Hostel   4
RESTAURANTS
Bernhart   C
Siegl   A
Tonino Lamborghini   B
Wenninger   E
Zum weissen Rössl   D

WIENER NEUSTADT

that gathers round the Mariensäule. The prettiest building on the square is the salmon-pink **Rathaus**, featuring Ionic pilasters, a clock pediment flanked by balustrades, and a lovely little wrought-iron balcony held up by oversized brackets.

Dominating the skyline, a couple of blocks north of Hauptplatz, is the town's Romanesque **Dom**. Heavily restored in the late nineteenth century, the church's west front, with its tall twin broach spires and arch friezes, still makes a powerful impression. The west front also has an unusual miniature freestanding tower to one side, about which you can find more from the **Turmmuseum** (May–Oct Tues & Wed 10am–5pm, Thurs 10am–8pm, Fri 10am–noon), though first you must retrieve the key from the Stadtmuseum (see below). Like the exterior, the Gothic interior of the Dom, with its chancel set slightly askew, is equally awesome in scale. The furnishings are mostly Baroque, but patches of medieval fresco survive, the red marble pulpit dates back to 1609, and there's a wonderful set of colourful and expressive fifteenth-century wooden statues of the twelve apostles adorning the pillars of the central aisle.

One of the best-preserved sections of the old town walls – paid for, incidentally, by the ransom money extracted from England for the release of Richard the Lionheart (see p.173) – lies to the northwest of the Dom, around the **Reckturm** (May–Oct Tues–Thurs 10am–noon & 2–4pm; Sat & Sun 10am–noon; free), a corner tower now housing a small collection of medieval arms and armour. The collection of exhibits at the stylish **Stadtmuseum** (Tues & Wed 10am–5pm, Thurs 10am–8pm, Fri 10am–noon, Sun 10am–4pm; öS30/€2.18), in the nearby former Dominican monastery on Petersgasse, is a lot more interesting, and includes treasures salvaged from the Dom, such as a silver-gilt medieval gospel, and two Gothic weathervanes, as well as the golden, lidded goblet donated to Wiener Neustadt by Matthias Corvinus after he had captured the town. Look out, too, for pictures of the war-damaged town, and three of the bombs that fell on the town and didn't explode.

The Militärakademie, Wappenwand and Georgskapelle

The town's most intriguing sight is hidden within the local **Militärakademie** (Military Academy), established in 1752 in the old imperial residence on the southeast corner of the town centre. The building began life as a thirteenth-century castle, but was considerably enlarged by Emperor Friedrich III, when he decided to establish his court here in the 1450s. Sadly, an earthquake in 1768, and the bombing raids of World War II, destroyed much of the building's original appearance, but it's still worth visiting, if only for the surreal experience of being guided round by one of the soldiers on duty. To get inside, you must announce yourself to the guard at the Südtor or Osttor (if the gate is closed, ring the bell).

On the west side of the main courtyard is the **Wappenwand**, or Heraldic Wall, an impressive display of noble might, in which the castle chapel's central window is framed by carved reliefs of over one hundred coats of arms from all of Friedrich's territories and connections, real or imagined. At the base of the wall is a statue of Friedrich, with his cryptic monogram, **AEIOU** (see box).

Behind the Wappenwand, on the first floor, Friedrich built the **Georgskapelle**, dedicated to the emperor's favourite saint, George, in whose honour he founded a new order of chivalry. Though heavily restored inside – the soldier will show you photos of the extent of the bomb damage in 1945 – the chapel has miraculously retained a set of superb fifteenth- and sixteenth-century stained-glass windows, which were wisely stored underground for the duration of the war. Otherwise, only the marble font and one column, decorated with colourful frescoes, survive from the original church. Friedrich's son, Maximilian I (1493–1519), was born here in 1459, and spent his childhood playing mock jousts and war games outside the castle gates; his remains are buried beneath a modern graveslab behind the main altar, though his splendid mausoleum lies in Innsbruck (see p.468).

AEIOU

The mysterious acronym **AEIOU**, which became the Emperor Friedrich III's personal logo, was emblazoned on everything from library books to new buildings, and can still be seen at several locations across Austria, most notably on his tomb in Vienna's Stephansdom, and his mausoleum in Graz's Domkirche. Composed of all the vowels of the Roman alphabet (in which the letters "u" and "v" are both rendered as "V"), it is open to various interpretations, ranging from the obvious A*ustria* E*rit* I*n* O*rbe* U*ltima* (Austria will be last in the world), to the ingenious A*quila* E*lecta* I*ovis* O*mnia* V*incit* (The chosen eagle conquers all things). Friedrich himself revealed the German version to be A*lles* E*rdreich* I*st* Ö*sterreich* U*ntertan* (The whole world is subject to Austria), though some wags put forward the more appropriate A*ller* E*rst* I*st* Ö*sterreich* V*erloren* (In the first place, Austria is lost), since Friedrich had great difficulty in keeping hold of his Austrian lands, losing Vienna to the Hungarian king Matthias Corvinus in 1485 and his beloved Wiener Neustadt the following year.

The Neukloster, Spinnerin am Kreuz and Flugmuseum

One other work of art from Friedrich's day that's worth seeking out is the beautiful red-marble tombstone of the emperor's beloved Portuguese wife, Eleonore, which lies in the lugubrious Gothic church of **Neukloster**, a short walk north of the Militärakademie. To get to see the tombstone, stroll out into the vine-clad cloister to the south and back into the church behind the main altar. Opposite her finely carved tombstone are the graveslabs of the three of her five children who died in infancy.

Another exceptional work of Gothic art that predates even Friedrich's reign, the **Spinnerin am Kreuz** (Spinner at the Cross), stands 1km north of the Altstadt, set back from the busy Wiener Strasse. Donated by the local judge in the late fourteenth century, it is a highly ornate wayside column decorated with blind arcading and pinnacles.

Another 2km north, in a godforsaken industrial estate off the Wiener Strasse is a new **Flugmuseum** (Tues–Thurs 10am–5pm, Fri–Sun 10am–7pm; öS60/€4.36), housed in a hangar alongside an airfield busy with light aircraft. The majority of planes on display are, in fact, gliders, though there are plenty of parachutes, ripcords, altometers, balloon baskets, model planes and uniforms to keep most plane-spotters happy. To get to the museum, there's a half-hourly bus from Hauptplatz (Mon–Sat).

Practicalities

The **train** and **bus station** are next door to each other ten minutes' walk west of the Hauptplatz, where you'll find the **tourist office**, housed next door to the Rathaus (Mon–Fri 8am–noon & 1–4pm, Sat 8am–noon; ☎02622/29551, *www.tiscover.com /noe-sued*). Wiener Neustadt sees few tourists, so the choice of **accommodation** is fairly limited; it's the sort of place that's best visited on a day-trip from Baden or Vienna. The cheapest place **to stay** is the simple, family-run *Gasthof Friedam* (☎02622/23081; ②), a local pub with rooms, located in the backstreets, fifteen minutes' walk west of the train station at Schneeberggasse 18. Of the town's two hotels, *Hotel Zentral* (☎02622/23169, *www.hotel-zentral.tos.at*; ④), on the main square at Hauptplatz 27, has greater character than the more modern eyesore, *Hotel Corvinus* (☎02622/24134, *www.hotel-corvinus.at*; ⑦), on Ferdinand Porsche-Ring; both offer en-suite facilities, but only the *Corvinus* has a sauna and steam bath. The town also has a high-season-only **HI hostel**, *Europahaus* (☎02622/29695, *oejhv-noe @oejhv.or.at*; July & Aug), situated in the park near the distinctive chalice-shaped water tower, south of the Militärakademie. Reception is open from 7am to 10am, and from 5pm to 8pm, but you'd be well advised to ring ahead before tipping up as the place is often full.

Several **cafés** spill out onto Hauptplatz in the warmer weather. The *Bernhart*, on the east side, is the most venerable *Kaffeehaus*, but you're better off snacking on *crostini* at the stylish *Siegl*, on the opposite side. For the real *Kaffeehaus* experience, head for the smoke-filled booths of *Café Wenninger*, Neunkirchnerstrasse 36, near the Militärakademie, a sepia-coloured place with lots of newspapers, and a chance to play backgammon and billiards. *Zum weissen Rössl*, by the Rathaus, is a traditional pub serving inexpensive and filling **food**, though it closes around 8pm. Another possibility is *Tonino Lamborghini*, Herzog-Leopold-Strasse 18, an *alimentari* and small *caffé* serving delicious filled fresh pasta and salads.

Despite the fact that the local tourist office stocks a bilingual German-English "young generation guide" to the town's **nightlife**, most folk looking for nightlife take the train into Vienna. Currently late-night drinkers under 25 gather at *GMBH*, Herrengasse 5, while the over 25s mellow out at *Hemingway*, Hauptplatz 24.

Beyond Wiener Neustadt: Schneeberg, Semmering Pass and Raxalpe

South and west of Wiener Neustadt, you begin to enter the alpine foothills that form the border between Lower Austria and Styria. The main autobahn to Graz heads south through the undulating countryside of the Bucklige Welt (literally "Bumpy World"), but the more spectacular route by road and rail is via the Semmering Pass. As the nearest alpine resort to the capital, **Semmering** has long been a popular holiday destination with the Viennese, though it's really the rail journey there that is the main attraction. In addition, the two highest mountain ranges in the vicinity, the evil-sounding **Raxalpe** and the more benevolent **Schneeberg**, can be ascended via chairlift and cog railway respectively.

Puchberg-am-Schneeberg

The **steam cog railway**, which climbs Lower Austria's highest mountain range of Schneeberg, has been a popular day-trip since its completion in 1897. The **Schneebergbahn** (late April to early Nov 10–11 trains daily; öS290/€21.08 return; *www.schneebergbahn.at*) departs from the village of **PUCHBERG-AM-SCHNEE-BERG** (*www.puchberg.at*), itself accessible by regular train from Wiener Neustadt 30km to the west. The cog railway (*Zahnradbahn*) then wiggles its way along 9km of track ascending over 1200m to the top station of Hochschneeberg (1796m). Two types of train take the strain: the original steam engine (*Nostalgie-Dampfzug*) takes just under one and a half hours of huffing and puffing, while the grotesque salamander diesel takes just 45 minutes. The view from the top is pretty impressive, but if the weather's clear it's worth walking onwards to one of the nearby viewpoints: the highest peak of the **Schneeberg** range, **Klosterwappen** (2076m), is an hour's hike from the top of the railway, and gives views over to the Raxalpe (see below); the right-hand fork is less strenuous, and will take you to the *Fischerhütte* restaurant, just over two kilometres away, and beyond, to the Kaiserstein (2061m).

If you're planning a **day-trip** from either Wiener Neustadt or Vienna, it's worth picking up the Schneebergbahn leaflet, which lists train connections. If you want to do some hiking from the top station, or simply want to take it easy, it's probably best to stay the night somewhere near Puchberg. En-suite **rooms** at the traditional *Gasthof-Pension Hausmann* (☎02636/2231; ③) are good value, while *Pension Bruckerhof* (☎02636/2315; ③) has comfortable rooms with geranium-festooned balconies.

Semmering

The rail line over the 985-metre **Semmering Pass** to the Styrian town of Mürzzuschlag is another spectacular feat of engineering. Completed in 1854, it was one of the first railways to forge its way across an alpine pass, employing seventeen tunnels and numerous switchbacks and viaducts; the most scenic stretch of track is the final section between Payerbach and **SEMMERING**. A pleasant, if somewhat amorphous resort, Semmering lies strung out along the northern slopes of the pass, and is dotted with attractive turn-of-the-twentieth-century villas. Hovering at around 1000m, and famed for its clean air, it has also been a very popular spa with the Viennese for nearly 150 years.

There are two **tourist offices** in Semmering: one concerned mostly with the resort's spa facilities (Mon–Thurs 8am–noon & 1–4pm, Fri 8am–noon; ☎02664/20025), twenty minutes' walk along Hochstrasse by the vast *Jugendstilhotel Panhans*, and a more general one at the Passhöhe (Mon–Fri 9am–4pm; *www.semmering.or.at*), by the main road at the top of the pass. There's an enormous choice of **accommodation** along Hochstrasse. *Pension Daheim* (☎02664/2381; ②) is a characteristic wooden villa, set amidst pine trees. A couple of notches up in the luxury stakes, is the highly recommended *Hotel Belvedere* (☎02664/2270; ④), where guests have free use of the hotel's sauna and pool, and the hotel restaurant is excellent. Further still up the star ratings are the luxurious *Panhans* itself (☎02664/8181, *Hotel@panhans.at*; ⑤), or the smaller no-smoking *Panoramahotel Wagner* (☎02664/2512, *www.semmering.cc*; ⑥).

Höllental and Raxalpe

The River Schwarza cuts a very narrow and dramatic defile, known as the **Höllental** (Valley of Hell), between the limestone massifs of Schneeberg, to the north, and the **Raxalpe**, to the south. The twenty-kilometre section between Reichenau and Schwarzau is popular with cyclists (and car drivers), but most folk only make it as far as the **Raxseilbahn** (daily 9am–4.30pm; öS200/€14.54 return), Austria's first ever cable car, which opened in 1926, and sets off from just beyond the village of Hirschwang, 3km west of Reichenau. The cable car climbs just over 1000m, leaving you half an hour's hike from the Jakobskogel (1737m), and around two hours from the highest peak of the range, **Heukuppe** (2007m), on the Styrian side of the Raxalpe. If you want to ascend Schneeberg from the Höllental, you'll have to rely on your legs: a marked path sets off from *Naturfreundhaus Weichtal*, 6km beyond the Raxseilbahn; it takes roughly two hours to reach the summit of Klosterwappen (see opposite).

As buses along the Höllental are infrequent, your best bet if you want to explore the valley is to hire a **bike** from the train station at Payerbach (Semmering train station doesn't offer bike rental). Just south of Payerbach, in the hamlet of Kreuzberg, you can **stay** at the *Alpenhof* (☎02666/52911, *steiner@looshaus.at*; ②), a surprisingly rustic villa designed by the Austrian father of modernism, Adolf Loos, in the 1930s, with good views over the surrounding countryside.

travel details

Trains

Gmünd (NÖ) to: Weitra (3–6 daily; 20min).

Horn to: Gars-Thurnau (every 1–2hr; 15min); Krems an der Donau (every 2hr; 1hr); Rosenburg (every 1–2hr; 10min).

Krems an der Donau to: Emmersdorf (every 1–2hr; 50min); Dürnstein (every 1–2hr; 10min); Gars-Thurnau (every 2hr; 55min); Marbach-Maria Taferl (1–4 daily; 1hr 25min); Rosenburg (every 1–2hr; 1hr); St Pölten (every 40min–1hr; 35–45min); Spitz an der Donau (every 1–2hr; 25min); Tulln (hourly; 40min); Wagram-Grafenegg (every 2hr; 20min); Weissenkirchen (every 1–2hr; 20min).

Retz to: Drosendorf (up to every 2hr; 1hr); Geras-Kottaun (up to every 2hr; 45min); Znojmo (3–5 daily; 25min).

St Pölten to: Herzogenburg (1–2 hourly; 12min); Melk (1–2 hourly; 15–20min); Mariazell (6–7 daily; 2hr 40min); Pöchlarn (1–2 hourly; 20–25min); Tulln (every 2hr; 1hr).

Vienna (Franz-Josefs Bahnhof) to: Eggenburg (hourly; 1hr–1hr 20min); Gmünd (NÖ) (every 2hr; 2hr–2hr 20min); Klosterneuburg-Kierling (every 30min; 15min); Krems an der Donau (hourly; 1hr–1hr 15min); Tulln (every 30min; 30–45min).

Vienna (Südbahnhof) to: Baden (every 30min; 30min); Bruck an der Leitha (every 30min; 25–35min); Laa an der Thaya (hourly; 2hr); Marchegg (7–12 daily; 45min); Mödling (every 15min; 25min); Payerbach-Reichenau (hourly; 1hr 30min/2hr); Semmering (hourly; 2 hr) Wiener Neustadt (every 30min; 50min).

Vienna (Westbahnhof) to: Melk (every 1–2hr; 1hr); Pöchlarn (every 1–2hr; 1hr 15min); St Pölten (1–2 hourly; 40min);

Vienna (Wien-Nord) to: Bad Deutsch Altenburg (hourly; 1hr 10min); Hainburg Ungartor (hourly; 1hr 15min); Petronell-Carnuntum (hourly; 1hr 5min); Retz (every 2hr; 1hr 5min).

Waidhofen an der Ybbs to: Lunz am See (5–8 daily; 1hr 25min).

Wiener Neustadt to: Payerbach-Reichenau (every 30min; 30min); Puchberg-am-Schneeberg (hourly; 45min); Semmering (hourly; 1hr).

Buses

Horn to: Drosendorf (Mon–Sat 1–2 daily; 1hr); Laa an der Thaya (Mon–Fri 3 daily; 1hr 20min); Raabs an der Thaya (1–2 daily; 1hr 15min); Vienna (1–4 daily; 2hr 30min).

Krems an der Donau to: Melk (3–4 daily; 1hr).

Mödling to: Heiligenkreuz (Mon–Fri 10 daily, Sat 5 daily, Sun 7 daily; 15min); Laxenburg (Mon–Fri every 30min, Sat & Sun hourly; 20min).

Orth an der Donau to: Bad Deutsch Altenburg (1–2 daily; 45min); Eckartsau (1–2 daily; 15min); Hainburg (1–2 daily; 55min).

CHAPTER THREE

UPPER AUSTRIA

Upper Austria (Oberösterreich; *www.tiscover.com/upperaustria*) shares a great deal, both politically and geographically, with neighbouring Lower Austria. Although fought over for centuries by the Bavarians and Habsburgs, it has remained, for the most part, in Habsburg hands since the thirteenth century. Stretching from the Czech border in the north to the alpine foothills of Styria in the south, the landscape is characterized by rich, rolling farmland, which is generally overlooked by tourists, who are drawn more towards Austria's craggy mountainscapes. The few visitors who do find their way here are concentrated in the very south of the province, in the lakeland area known as the **Salzkammergut**, which is divided between several Länder, and covered separately in Chapter 8. To the Austrians themselves, Upper Austria is seen as something of a rural backwater, with the most provincial of all Austrian cities, **Linz**, as its capital. Despite being much maligned because of its all-too-visible industrial baggage, the city is full of surprises. It preserves a very attractive Altstadt in the centre, and also boasts one of the country's most **innovative museums**, the Ars Electronica.

Like Lower Austria, Upper Austria is also a region replete with spectacular monasteries, which were transformed into Baroque showpieces during the Counter-Reformation. **St Florian** is the best known thanks to its associations with the composer Anton Bruckner, but the Rococo masterpiece of **Wilhering**, and **Kremsmünster**, with its remarkable fish basins, art collection and observatory, are both equally stunning architecturally – and all three lie within an easy train ride of Linz. Austria's most notorious concentration camp, based in the granite quarries of **Mauthausen**, is also a short journey from the regional capital. The camp was housed in a purpose-built granite fortress, which even the retreating SS couldn't demolish, and it stands today as a salutary reminder of the atrocities committed by the Nazis.

After Linz, Upper Austria has just two other towns of any great size: **Wels**, which has a handsome enough Altstadt and some impressive Roman remains, and **Steyr**, the more compelling of the two, a place of considerable charm, which enjoys a splendid location at the confluence of the Enns and Steyr rivers. Again, you could comfortably see either town on a day-trip from Linz, but Steyr, in particular, makes a pleasant overnight halt, too. There are plenty of picturesque walled towns dotted about the

---

ACCOMMODATION PRICE CODES

All **hotels and pensions** in this book have been coded according to the following price categories. All the codes are based on the rate for the least expensive double room during the **summer season**. In those places where winter is the high season, we've indicated both summer and winter room rates in the text.

① under öS400/€29.07

② öS400–600/€29.07–43.60

③ öS600–800/€43.60–58.14

④ öS800–1000/€58.14–72.67

⑤ öS1000–1200/€72.67–87.21

⑥ öS1200–1400/€87.21–101.74

⑦ öS1400–1600/€101.74–116.28

⑧ öS1600–1800/€116.28–130.81

⑨ over öS1800/€130.81

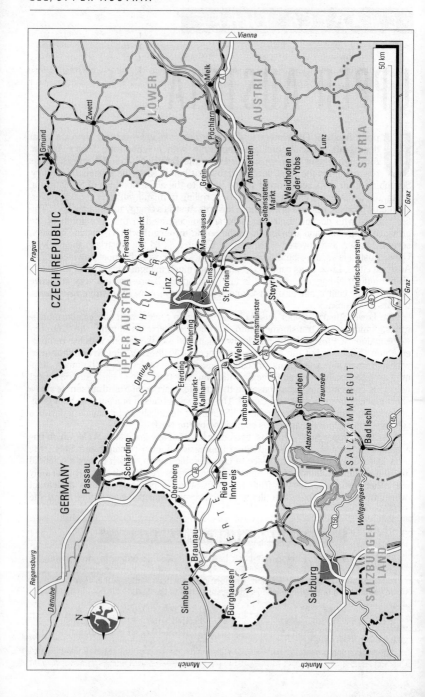

province, none very large but each a minor architectural gem. If you're heading in or out of the Czech Republic, the perfectly preserved fortified town of **Freistadt** is a worthwhile stop-off. Likewise, if you're travelling to or from Germany, you've a choice of picture-perfect towns along the banks of the Inn, from **Braunau-am-Inn**, Hitler's unreasonably pretty birthplace, to **Schärding**, a short hop across the Inn from the German town of Passau.

Linz

LINZ is definitely the underdog when it comes to Austrian cities. It receives the smallest number of tourists, and is looked down on, even by fellow Austrians, as both deeply provincial and, at the same time, predominantly industrial. By whatever means you approach the city, it's impossible to ignore the chemical plants, steelworks and dockyards ranged along the banks of the Danube. However, in the well-preserved and attractive **Altstadt** you can still see the core of the much smaller, preindustrial provincial town. Linz may not bowl you over with its beauty, but it's a place that grows on you – and it does have one remarkable museum, the **Ars Electronica**, dedicated to the "virtual" arts, that alone justifies a visit here. Finally, as if the city didn't have a big enough PR problem, Linz is also famous for being "Hitler's home town" (see p.229), the place where he spent his "happiest days", and to which he eventually planned to retire.

Some history

Linz began life as the Roman port of Lentia, later becoming a major medieval trading centre, controlled first by the bishops of Passau, and later by the Babenbergs. Apart from its brief stint as imperial capital under the Emperor Friedrich III from 1489 to 1493, however, the city was better known for its peasant revolts than anything else. Along with much of Upper Austria, Linz became a bastion of Protestantism following the Reformation, hosting an important Protestant confederation in 1614, and attracting the Lutheran astronomer Johannes Kepler to work in the city. In 1626, an estimated 16,000 local peasants revolted against the Catholicizing policies of Maximilian of Bavaria and besieged Linz. In the end, the Bavarians relieved the city, though at some considerable cost. More than two hundred buildings were destroyed, and the majority of the city's merchant families fled, leaving Linz to languish as a provincial backwater for the next two centuries, and the Counter-Reformation kicked in with a vengeance.

It was the city's strategic position as a bridge over the Danube that ensured its resurgence in the nineteenth century. In 1832, the first horse-drawn railway on the continent was built between Linz and the Bohemian town of Budweis (České Budějovice), and by the end of the century the city had developed into the largest railway junction in the empire. At the same time, Linz became something of a musical centre, thanks to the presence of Anton Bruckner, who took the post of cathedral organist. Like the rest of Austria during the 1920s and 1930s, Linz was torn between paramilitary wings of Left and Right, with violent skirmishes frequently played out on the city's streets. On February 12, 1934, the country was plunged into civil war when a dawn raid by the right-wing *Heimwehr* on a socialist weapons cache in the *Hotel Schiff*, on the corner of Landstrasse and Mozartstrasse, was met with armed resistance. Although widespread, the fighting in Linz was over in a day, ending in defeat for the *Schutzbund*, the paramilitary wing of the socialists.

Despite the delirious reception given to Hitler when he arrived in Linz after the Nazi invasion of March 1938 (it's estimated that five-sixths of the population came out to greet him), Linz had not been a Nazi stronghold during the 1930s. It was, however, a keenly anti-Semitic town, whose persecution of its Jewish population was so thorough that the local stormtroopers found no Jewish property left to destroy on *Kristallnacht*.

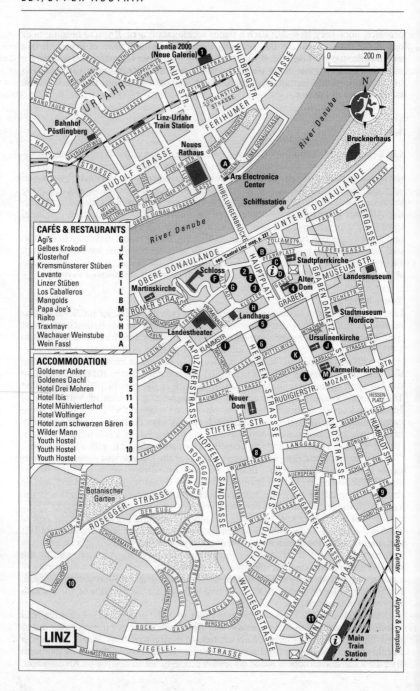

Lentia 2000
(Neue Galerie)

Bahnhof
Pöstlingberg

URFAHR

Linz-Urfahr
Train Station

Neues
Rathaus

Ars Electronica
Center

Schiffsstation

Brucknerhaus

River Danube

CAFÉS & RESTAURANTS

Agi's	G
Gelbes Krokodil	J
Klosterhof	K
Kremsmünsterer Stüben	F
Levante	E
Linzer Stüben	I
Los Caballeros	L
Mangolds	B
Papa Joe's	M
Rialto	C
Traxlmayr	H
Wachauer Weinstube	D
Wein Fassl	A

ACCOMMODATION

Goldener Anker	2
Goldenes Dachl	8
Hotel Drei Mohren	5
Hotel Ibis	11
Hotel Mühlviertlerhof	4
Hotel Wolfinger	3
Hotel zum schwarzen Bären	6
Wilder Mann	9
Youth Hostel	7
Youth Hostel	10
Youth Hostel	1

River Danube

OBERE DONAULÄNDE

see 'Central Linz' map, p. 227

UNTERE DONAULÄNDE

Zollamtstr

Stadtpfarrkirche

Pfarrplatz

Landesmuseum

Schloss

Martinskirche

Alter
Dom

Stadtmuseum
Nordico

Landhaus

Landestheater

Ursulinenkirche

Neuer
Dom

Karmeliterkirche

Botanischer
Garten

ROSEGGER-STRASSE

LINZ

Main
Train
Station

Design Center

Airport & Campsite

0   200 m

N

(The only local-born Jew to survive the war was Hitler's childhood family doctor, Eduard Bloch, who was left unmolested on the Führer's own orders.) Economically, Linz benefited enormously under the Nazis. Hermann Göring himself founded the giant iron and steelworks by the Danube, which to this day provides employment for the local population. After the war, Linz found itself on the very border of the Soviet and American sectors, with Urfahr, north of the river, occupied by the Russians, and Linz proper controlled by the US. In 1955, the occupation forces withdrew, and since then Linz, like the rest of Austria, has enjoyed a fairly peaceful and increasingly prosperous existence.

Arrival, information and transport

Linz's **airport** is just over 10km southwest of the city in Hörsching. There's only one daily bus into the centre and a taxi all the way to Linz will set you back around öS300/€21.90. Alternatively you can take a short taxi ride to Hörsching station about 3km from the airport, from which there are hourly trains into Linz. Virtually all trains arrive at Linz's **main train station**, 2km south of the city centre (buses pull up on the Bahnhofplatz outside). The only exception are slow trains from the Mühlviertel region to the northwest of Linz, which arrive at Linz-Urfahr station, on the north bank of the river. Passenger **boats** chugging along the Danube from Passau (daily services from May to October) or Krems (three weekly from May to October) dock at the *Schiffsstation* to the east of the Nibelungenbrücke, a short walk from Hauptplatz.

The **tourist office**, in the Altes Rathaus on Hauptplatz (May–Oct Mon–Fri 8am–7pm, Sat 9am–7pm, Sun 10am–7pm; Nov–April Mon–Fri 8am–6pm, Sat 9am–6pm, Sun 10am–6pm; ☎0732/7070-1777, *www.linz.at* or *www.tiscover.com/linz*), has a wealth of bumf on the city and Upper Austria in general. It's a long walk into town (and to most of the city's accommodation) from the train station, so you might prefer to make use of the city's ultra-efficient **public transport**. To get into town, take tram #3, which heads up Landstrasse, through Hauptplatz and across the river into Urfahr. For a single ride (öS20/€1.46), simply press the *"Midi"* button on the ticket machine by the tram stop. If you're planning on going on more than one tram or bus, it's best to buy a 24-hour *Netzkarte* (öS40/€2.92) by pressing the *"Maxi"* button; the *"Mini"* button is for children's tickets. All tickets need validating in the machines on board. If you're planning on staying in Linz for a couple of days, it might be worthwhile investing in a *Linz City Ticket* (öS399/€29.13; available from the tourist office), which gives you a two-day *Netzkarte*, a return ride on the Pöstlingbergbahn, entry to one museum and the botanical gardens, and a voucher for öS300/€21.90 which can be used in a selection of the city's restaurants.

Accommodation

Although Linz probably sees more business travellers than out-and-out tourists, **accommodation** is, on the whole, very reasonably priced for a major city. That said, there are no private rooms on offer through the tourist office, and only a limited selection of places to stay close to the centre.

Linz has three **youth hostels**. The one at Kapuzinerstrasse 14 (☎0732/782720; March to mid-Nov) is small, friendly and conveniently located five minutes' walk from the centre, with 4- and 6-bed dorms. If it's full, head for the youth hostel at Stanglhofweg 3 (☎0732/664434; mid-Jan to mid-Dec), off Roseggerstrasse, 2km southwest of the centre (bus #27 from the train station), which has en-suite doubles (②) as well as some singles. Your last choice should be the high-rise hostel (☎0732/737078) over the river in Urfahr above the Lentia 2000 shopping centre on Blütenstrasse (tram #3), which has dorms as well as doubles (①) but is often booked up with school groups.

The city's main **campsite** (☎0732/305314; March–Nov) is by the Pichlinger See in the suburb of Pichling, 5km southeast of the city centre (on the train bound for Asten), but it's too close to the autobahn for comfort. For a more peaceful site, for tents only, head to the *Pleschinger See* (☎0732/247870; May–Sept), 3km northeast of the centre, on the north bank of the Danube (bus #33 or #33a from Reindlstrasse in Urfahr).

Hotels and pensions

Goldener Anker, Hofgasse 5 (☎0732/771088). Old, family-run Gasthof in the Altstadt. A choice of bargain rooms with shared facilities (②), or cosier en suites with TV and breakfast (③).

Goldenes Dachl, Hafnerstrasse 27 (☎0732/775897). Plain but clean rooms over a simple Gasthaus, at bargain prices. Conveniently located midway between train station and Hauptplatz. ②.

Hotel Drei Mohren, Promenade 17 (☎0732/72626, *www.drei-mohren.at*). Great location and pleasantly modernized interior; all rooms are fully en suite, and the lounge has a nice balcony overlooking the Promenade. ⑧.

Hotel Ibis, Kärntnerstrasse 18–20 (☎0732/9401, *hotel-ibis.linz@netway.at*). Modern hotel right next to the train station. A comfortable mid-range business choice. ⑤.

Hotel Mühlviertlerhof, Graben 24 (☎0732/772268). Tastefully modernized, fairly swish hotel right in the centre, with en-suite facilities and TV in all rooms. ④.

Hotel Wolfinger, Hauptplatz 19 (☎0732/7732910, *wolfinger@austria-classic-hotels.at*). Wonderful old converted nunnery, with creaking parquet floors and a lovely balcony at the back. A couple of doubles come with shared facilities (③); most are en suite with TV and a tasteful mix of antique and repro furniture (⑤).

Hotel zum Schwarzen Bären, Herrenstrasse 9–11 (☎0732/772477, *hotel.zum.schwarzen.baeren @aon.at*). Simply furnished hotel with a bit more character than most in town. Conveniently central, and all rooms with en-suite facilities. ④.

Wilder Mann, Goethestrasse 14 (☎0732/656078). Simple no-frills Gasthof, 5min walk from the train station, and only one block east of Landstrasse. Some rooms have a shower but none have en-suite WC. ③.

The City Centre

Linz's main thoroughfare is the kilometre-long **Landstrasse**, traffic-free for the most part, except for trams, and lined on both sides by shops, cafés and department stores. For such a large city, Linz's **Altstadt**, at the far northern end of Landstrasse, is remarkably small: Graben and Promenade now lie along the line of the old city walls. Just about everything of interest on this side of the river lies within easy walking distance of the showpiece main square, **Hauptplatz**.

The Altstadt

Linz's rectangular **Hauptplatz** is one of the finest squares of any Austrian city, with its tall, pastel-coloured facades, and a vast, marble Trinity column, crowned by a gilded sunburst, as the perfect centrepiece. There is, however, something a bit cool and aloof about the whole ensemble – it looks a bit softer and more welcoming when lit up at night. Few of the buildings on the square stand out individually, with the possible exception of the salmon-coloured **Altes Rathaus**, on whose ridiculously small balcony Hitler appeared after his triumphant homecoming in March 1938 (see box on p.229) to greet the delirious crowds. As well as housing the tourist office, the Rathaus is also home to **Linz Genesis** (Mon–Fri 9am–1pm & 2–6pm; free), a brand-new museum which traces the history of the city in snazzy style, its imaginatively lit exhibits accompanied by audio effects and short films.

Rising above the houses in the southeast corner of Hauptplatz are the twin towers of the pea-green Jesuit church, or **Alter Dom** (daily 7am–noon & 3–7pm), where the composer Anton Bruckner was organist from 1855 to 1868. Built by the Jesuits at the zenith

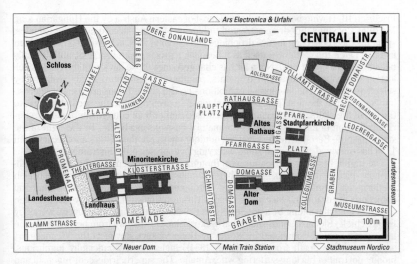

of their power in the 1670s, it was taken off them in 1773, and given cathedral status in the following decade, only to be returned to them in 1909 when the cathedral was superseded by the Neuer Dom. The white stucco-work on the barrel-vaulted ceiling of the nave is outstanding, as are the finely carved choir stalls, peppered with grotesques and grimacing cherubs, and the magnificent black and gold pulpit.

Round the corner from the Alter Dom is the much smaller **Stadtpfarrkirche**, a Gothic–Baroque church that's a bit gloomy inside. Its chief claim to fame is the red marble slab stuck into the wall to the right of the high altar, behind which the heart of Emperor Friedrich III is buried (he died in Linz in 1493, but the rest of him was buried in Vienna's Stephansdom). More memorable, though, is the marble-clad chapel in the southwest corner of the church, with its trompe l'oeil dome and statue of St John of Nepomuk by Georg Raphael Donner.

No Austrian city would be complete without its own Mozart plaque, and Linz's is at Klostergasse 20, west off Hauptplatz, now known as the **Mozarthaus**, where the composer stayed with his wife in 1783. He was due to give a concert in the city and, having no other symphony with, him, knocked out his 36th (now known as the *Linz*) at breakneck speed – in about four days. On the opposite side of the street is the **Minoritenkirche** (daily 8–11am), its small Rococo interior lined with pinkish side altars culminating in a high altar that positively froths with gilded clouds, cherubs and angels.

Next door stands the regional parliament, or **Landhaus**, a vast complex intended as a Minorite monastery, but bought by the locals in 1564. Very little remains from that period, save for the splendid red-marble entrance portal, on Klostergasse, with its triumphal-arch motif and Dutch gable. The courtyard immediately to the right preserves its triple-decker Renaissance loggia on two sides, and has at its centre the *Planetenbrunnen*, from 1582, a fountain whose figures each represent one of the seven planets then known.

The Schloss and Martinskirche

From the Landhaus, it's a short stroll north through the most picturesque of the Altstadt's narrow streets to the city's dour, fortress-like **Schloss** (Tues–Fri 9am–5pm, Sat & Sun 10am–4pm; öS50/€3.65), built on high ground above the city by Emperor

Friedrich III. Having been kicked out of most of eastern Austria by the Hungarian king Matthias Corvinus, Friedrich retreated to Linz in 1489 and, according to the enemies, spent his days collecting mouse droppings and catching flies, before dying here of gout in 1493. Later, the castle was used as a hospital, a prison and a barracks, until it finally became a museum in 1960. Not a lot has changed since those days, and the castle's collection of weapons, musical instruments, paintings and sculptures only really repay selective viewing. The temporary exhibitions on the ground floor are usually interesting enough, but the first floor is better skipped in preference to the second, where, to the left of the stairs, there's a prettily decorated timber-built cottage interior, plus a terrific collection of folk costumes and miniature Passions-in-a-bottle. To the right of the stairs, past the Baroque heaters and the outdoor chess set, the castle's apothecary from 1700 has survived, along with some worrying bygone scientific instruments.

The highlight of the entire museum, though, is the nineteenth- and early twentieth-century picture collection, which begins inauspiciously with a load of mawkish Biedermeier paintings, epitomized by Ferdinand Georg Waldmüller's sentimental depictions of rural folk. Once you've waded through this stuff, though, you'll get to an early, allegorical painting by a pre-Secession Gustav Klimt, along with several works by Egon Schiele, Richard Gerstl and Oskar Kokoschka. Downstairs from here, there's one last room to enjoy, dominated by works by Hans Makart, doyen of the Viennese art scene (until his death from syphilis in 1884), including a wonderfully lugubrious, moody portrait of his long-suffering wife, Amalie. The superb, iridescent Jugenstil and Art-Deco glassware on display here comes mostly from nearby Bohemia, but the samovar, cigarette cases and brooches by Kolo Moser and Josef Hoffmann are pure Wiener Werkstätte.

A short walk west up Römerstrasse from the Schloss is Austria's oldest church, the diminutive **Martinskirche**. Originally a much larger, eighth-century Carolingian construction, built using the ruins of an ancient Roman wall, it's a touch over-restored and really not that impressive. Inside, the bare stone nave features patchy frescoes contemporary with the fifteenth-century choir, and modern stained-glass windows. Unless you either sign up for one of the guided tours of the city organized by the tourist office, or attend a service here, however, you can only peek through the glass doors at the interior.

The Neuer Dom, Stadtmuseum Nordico and Landesmuseum

Away from the Altstadt and the Schloss, there's not much to quicken the heart. The awesome presence of the neo-Gothic **Neuer Dom** is impossible to ignore as you walk around the city. Situated a couple of blocks west of Landstrasse, and topped by a steeple that soars to 134m – just short of Vienna's Stephansdom, as stipulated by the authorities – this massive building is Austria's largest cathedral. It was begun in 1855 under Bishop Franz-Josef Rudigier, a tireless patron of Anton Bruckner, whom he commissioned to write a choral piece to celebrate the laying of the foundation stone. Yet, for all its size, the Neuer Dom is a graceless, academic exercise from the outside; inside, it's slightly more appealing, particularly in the ambulatory, where the sun scatters multicoloured lights through the modern stained-glass windows.

The **Stadtmuseum Nordico** (Mon–Fri 9am–6pm, Sat & Sun 2–5pm; öS50/€3.65), a couple of blocks east of Landstrasse down Bethlehemstrasse, houses a model of Linz from 1740 and hosts modern art exhibitions, but that's about it. The building itself was used until 1786 by the Jesuits to train young students from Scandinavia, hence the "Nordico" suffix. The nearby **Landesmuseum** (Mon, Tues & Thurs 9am–noon & 2–5pm, Wed & Fri 9am–noon; öS50/€3.65) sometimes known as the Francisco-Carolinum Museum, occupies a splendid mustard-coloured building, built in 1887 with red-brick infill, a Neoclassical frieze, and cherub-guarded obelisks on its roof. The interior is equally ornate, but there's no permanent collection, just a series of temporary art and natural history exhibitions.

Urfahr

Urfahr, once a separate town, now a workaday suburb of Linz, lies on the north bank of the River Danube, clearly visible (and just a short walk) across the Nibelungen Brücke from Hauptplatz. Dominated by the supremely ugly Neues Rathaus by the

---

HITLER'S HEIMATSTADT

Although **Adolf Hitler** (1889–1945) was born in Braunau-am-Inn (see p.246), he considered Linz to be his *Heimatstadt* or home town, something about which today's tourist authorities are understandably coy. To begin with, the family lived just outside Linz, in the village of Leonding, 5km to the southwest. Hitler commuted to the Linz Realschule from 1900, but was forced to leave in 1904 (the year that philosopher Ludwig Wittgenstein entered the school), after failing his exams twice. Hitler fared little better at the Steyr Realschule, where his first report card was so bad he got drunk and used the document as toilet paper, forcing him to ask for a duplicate to be issued. His father died shortly afterwards, and Hitler left school without graduating, before moving with the rest of the family to Humboldtstrasse 31, in the heart of Linz. The future Führer spent the next couple of years going to the local opera house, sketching and daydreaming.

Hitler left Linz in an unsuccessful attempt to enter art school in Vienna, beginning a period of rootless drifting which only ended with the outbreak of World War I. Hitler was in Germany at the time, and enthusiastically joined the German army in the hope that the coming conflict would give his life meaning and purpose. After the war, Hitler opted to stay on in Germany rather than return to the Austrian Republic – most German-speaking subjects of the former Habsburg Empire regarded the German Reich as their natural motherland after the Empire's collapse, and Hitler was no exception. Now based in Munich, Hitler exploited the discontents of Germany's demobbed war veterans to mould the populist movement which subsequently became the Nazi Party.

Some thirty years after leaving his home town, Hitler returned in triumph on March 12, 1938. Driving into the Hauptplatz in his open-top Mercedes, the dictator was greeted by such wildly jubilant crowds that he decided, there and then, to go for a full Anschluss, in other words, the incorporation of Austria into the Third Reich; "the cares and troubles of this city are over because I have assumed its personal protection," he declared over dinner at the city's *Hotel Weinzinger*. Two days later, after paying his respects to the graves of his parents in Leonding, Hitler continued on his triumphal journey to Vienna.

Though he rarely returned to his home town as Führer, Hitler had elaborate plans for Linz, which he was going to transform into a "Second Budapest", with a new opera house, theatre, concert hall, university, art gallery, museum, park, boulevard – the lot. Within days of the Anschluss, engineers arrived to draw up plans for a new Nibelungen Brücke (designed years before by Hitler himself). Among the Führer's more fanciful proposals were the construction of a gigantic statue of Siegfried on the Freinberg, a hill to the west of the city centre, where Hitler also planned to build his retirement home. The Altstadt was to be left intact, but the riverfront was to be totally transformed with bombastic Neoclassical architecture, and a 160-metre-high tower erected in Urfahr, containing a vaulted crypt for the remains of Hitler's parents, and, in the bell tower where Hitler wished to be buried, a carillon capable of playing passages from Bruckner's *Fourth Symphony*.

An illuminated model of the planned improvements to Linz occupied pride of place in Hitler's Berlin bunker, but very few projects were ever actually realized. Apart from the Nibelungen Brücke, and a few minor buildings, the most significant progress was made in buying, borrowing and appropriating over 5000 priceless artworks ready for the city's new art gallery. Initially, these were stored in Munich, but towards the end of the war the cache was shipped to the salt mines of Alt Aussee in the Salzkammergut, where they were saved in the final days of the war by a group of partisans who blocked the entrance and prevented the local Nazis from carrying out their orders to destroy them.

riverfront, Urfahr in fact boasts three of the finest sights in Linz: the remarkable **Ars Electronica Center**, the city's top art gallery, the **Neue Galerie**, in the unprepossessing Lentia 2000 shopping centre, and the **Pöstlingbergbahn**, whose cream-coloured trams will lift you high above the city.

Ars Electronica

Before you've even reached the end of the Nibelungenbrücke, the starkly Modernist building housing the **Ars Electronica Center** (Wed–Sun 10am–6pm; öS80/€5.84; *www.aec.at*) appears on your right, advertising its *"Museum der Zukunft"* (Museum of the Future). This is a truly remarkable place: a museum dedicated to new technology, in particular to its artistic possibilities. The biggest single attraction is the museum's "CAVE" (Cave Automatic Virtual Environment, and a reference to Plato's "Simile of the Cave"), situated in the basement. A virtual-reality room with 3-D projections on three walls and the floor, this is one of only a handful of such installations in Europe, and the only one open to the public. By standing in the centre of the room, wearing a special 3-D viewfinder, you can navigate your way through a series of virtual spaces, from the solar system to rooms and landscapes.

The other floors of the museum feature a wide range of exhibits, all of which are fun to experiment with, from riding a bicycle across an imaginary landscape, to flying over a computer-generated virtual image of Upper Austria. Even the museum's lift, drolly dubbed Apollo 13, has rear-projected graphics to make you think you're taking off from Linz into outer space, like Charlie in Roald Dahl's *Charlie and the Great Glass Elevator*. Short English-language texts are provided, and most of the staff speak excellent English, and will happily explain and demonstrate any of the exhibits for you. The biggest problem is the museum's popularity, which means it's a good idea to get here early (or late) to avoid the crowds. Also, if you want to see the cave, you need to book a place in advance from the ticket desk as you enter. When you're virtually exhausted, you can visit the 1960s-sci-fi-style rooftop cybercafé and enjoy a surf on the Net, or just enjoy views out over the Danube and the Altstadt.

Neue Galerie

It comes as little surprise that the city's **Neue Galerie** (daily 10am–6pm, Thurs till 10pm; öS60/€4.38; *http://neuegalerie.linz.at*) gets so few visitors, given its location on the first floor of the supremely unattractive shopping centre called Lentia 2000 on Blütenstrasse. Thankfully, the whole collection is due to move to a purpose-built site on the southern bank of the Danube some time in 2002, when it will be relaunched as a high-profile modern art museum under the name of *Kunstmuseum Linz*. In the meantime, the Neue Galerie is still well worth a visit, since, in addition to hosting temporary exhibitions by contemporary artists, it boasts a high-quality permanent collection of nineteenth- and twentieth-century Austrian art. Pride of place goes to **Oskar Kokoschka**'s typically agitated rendition of Linz, painted in 1955 and emphasizing the city's industrial character, while his portrait of the Austrian president Theodor Körner, from the same year, employs an exuberant Fauvist palette. There are several much earlier portraits, too, including the darkly drawn *Die Freunde*, depicting a malevolent-looking bunch of friends, whom you wouldn't wish on your worst enemy. **Egon Schiele**, whose life was as short as Kokoschka's was long, pitches in with two oil paintings: a joyful *Krumau Landscape*, inspired by his brief sojourn in the south Bohemian birthplace of his mother, known today as Český Krumlov; and a striking, almost monochrome double portrait, *Heinrich and Otto Benesch*. Heinrich Benesch (the older of the two) was something of a father figure for Schiele, and a keen collector of the artist's work, pleading with Schiele not to "put any of your sketches, no matter what they are, even the most trivial things, on the fire. Please write on your stove in chalk the following equation:

'Stove equals Benesch'." Completing the country's most famous trio of artists, there are a couple of unfinished works by **Gustav Klimt**, one of which, the *Portrait of Maria Munk*, is a typical Japanese-influenced late work, in which the gold ornament for which he made his name has been entirely replaced by bright colours and a profusion of plants. The rest of the collection can't quite compete with these works, though the demure, but unfinished *Lady in Red* by Hans Makart, Klimt's teacher, and the Tyrolean Albin Egger-Lienz's touching portrait of the artist's daughter, Ila, manage to hold their own.

Pöstlingberg

With an afternoon of fine weather in prospect (or a child or two to entertain), one of the best things to do is take a ride on the narrow-gauge **Pöstlingbergbahn** (daily 6am–7pm; öS44/€3.21 return), which departs from the timber and red-brick *Talstation*, just beyond Linz-Urfahr train station. The electrified trains depart every twenty minutes, wind their way up the world's steepest "adhesion" railway, past some swanky villas, to the top of the **Pöstlingberg** (539m), nearly 300m above the Danube.

The views over Linz are pretty spectacular, as is the Baroque **Wallfahrtskirche**, which occupies the crest of the hill. The interior is decorated with an outstanding set of frescoes, and copious rich Rococo stucco-work bristling with gold, but the church's object of greatest veneration is the eighteenth-century carved *Pietà*, which occupies centre stage in the stupendously ornate high altar.

If you have small children, you might consider it necessary to pay a visit to the miniature **Märchenfeld** (Fairy World) and its attendant **Grottenbahn** (March, April & mid-Sept to Oct daily 10am–5pm; May–Aug daily 9am–6pm; Dec Sat & Sun 10am–4pm; öS45), a subterranean railway pulled by a dragon. Everyone else should give the place a wide berth, however, unless they've a penchant for technicolour garden gnomes.

Eating and drinking

Linz's **restaurants** are concentrated in the Altstadt and on and off Landstrasse. The range of cuisines may be modest, though it's a significant improvement on most Austrian towns. The city itself is famous for just one culinary invention, the *Linzertorte*, a raspberry jam tart made with almond pastry, which is available from just about every café and restaurant in Linz, and as a souvenir from the much-esteemed Philipp Wrann, Landstrasse 70. Of the **cafés**, the most famous is *Café Traxlmayr*, which has changed very little over the last century; the *Gelbes Krokodil* is the best of the modern ones. If you need to cut costs and assemble a picnic, the city's main Billa **supermarket** is on the corner of Landstrasse and Mozartstrasse, and there's a smaller Spar store on Steingasse.

Restaurants

Agi's Restaurant, Altstadt 9. Decent Greek restaurant that doesn't try too hard to look Greek; in fact, it looks more like a traditional vaulted *Gasthaus*, which no doubt contributes to its popularity.

Klosterhof, Landstrasse 30. This place serves standard Austrian fare in the labyrinthine rooms of the former monastery: the *Bierstuben* is a smoky beer hall; the designer *Stieglitz* bar is flashier, with occasional live music; upstairs, there's a traditional wood-panelled and arcaded restaurant; outside is Linz's largest beer garden.

Kremsmünsterer Stuben, Altstadt 10 (☎0732/782111). Imaginative takes on standard Austrian dishes, served up in a lovely Renaissance-era monks' dormitory. More expensive than most places, with main dishes öS200/€14.60 and over. Closed Mon & Sun.

Levante, Hauptplatz 13. Smart, vaulted Turkish restaurant with a tasty selection of inexpensive *pide* dishes and kebabs. Takeaway snacks available too.

Linzer Stuben, Klammstrasse 7 (☎0732/779028). Eminently *gemütlich* place with capacious armchairs and soft furnishings, specializing in Hungarian food. Closed Mon.

Los Caballeros, Landstrasse 32. Passable Tex-Mex food, including meat or veggie enchiladas and burritos, plus ribs, steaks and tequila cocktails. In an arcade just off the street.

Mangolds, Hauptplatz 6. Despite the sanitized atmosphere, this self-service veggie cafeteria is a popular spot to grab one of the bargain daily hot dishes (öS45–65/€3.30–4.75), or fill up at the giant salad bar. Closed Sun.

Papa Joe's, Landstrasse 31. Lively Tex-Mex and Creole eatery done out in brash, bright colours, with a lively bar.

Rialto, Rathausgasse 7. Standard Italian job, with bargain weekday, lunchtime two-course menu for öS70/€5.15, and lots of pizzas for under öS100/€7.30.

Wachauer Weinstube, Pfarrgasse 20. Typical wood-panelled local *Stube* situated just off Hauptplatz, serving hearty Austrian food for under öS100/€7.30. Closed Sun.

Wein Fassl, Kirchengasse 6. Traditional Urfahr wine-tavern next door to the Ars Electronica, with cheap lunchtime menus from öS65/€4.75 and outdoor seating. Closed Sat & Sun.

Cafés and bars

The so-called "Bermuda Triangle", one block west of Hauptplatz, is *the* place to go of an evening (the triangle is formed by the streets Hofgasse, Hahnengasse and Altstadt). Quiet and quaint enough by day, these narrow medieval streets provide the most concentrated selection of **late-night bars** in the city, and are usually full of youthful drinkers on a summer evening. It doesn't make a huge difference which place you go for, but as a basic pointer *Kistl*, Altstadt 17, serves a range of beers and tasty munchies, while *Smaragd*, nearby, is usually good for a spot of live music. In the summer, a similar drinking crowd homes in on the **cafés and wine bars** by the Danube in Urfahr. Again, virtually any one will do, though *Biergartl*, west of the bridge, probably has the nicest beer garden. The cafés and bars listed below are more widely dispersed around town, and attract a slightly more discerning crowd.

1. Akt, Klammstrasse 20a. Buzzy, funky wine bar set back from the street in its own cobbled courtyard, and popular with a thirty-something professional crowd.

Alte Welt, Hauptplatz 4. Sweaty, late-night, cellar wine bar that puts on regular live jazz, folk and world music, plus two upstairs rooms and a nice courtyard, offering a decent range of food. Closed Sun.

Café Ex-Blatt, Waltherstrasse 15. Popular and studenty, evenings-only café-bar decked out in nostalgic posters and adverts, with just a few snacks and mini-pizzas on offer.

Café Landgraf, Hauptstrasse 12 (*www.landgraf.at*). A cross between a stylish *Kaffeehaus* and a modernistic chrome-and-glass cocktail bar, one of the few fashionable drinking haunts in Urfahr. Packed with young, glamorous Linzers on Friday and Saturday nights, many of whom descend into *Zizas* disco-bar, in the basement below, in the early hours.

Café Traxlmayr, Promenade 16. A Linz institution, and the city's only real *Kaffeehaus* (in the Viennese tradition), *Traxlmayr* is still very popular with Linz folk of all ages. Coffee, cakes, newspapers, backgammon, chess, cigarette smoke, crystal chandeliers and tuxedoed waiters all guaranteed.

Joseph, Landstrasse 49. Gargantuan beer garden with numerous bars doling out ales brewed by the local city brewery. One counter offers sausage snacks, and there's a sit-down restaurant with Schnitzel-fare off to the side.

Gelbes Krokodil, Dametzstrasse 30. Superb, stylish café inside the city's Moviemento arts cinema (see opposite). Good spot to spend an evening, and with an excellent selection of Med-influenced food. Tucked away behind a multistorey car park one block east of the Landstrasse. Closed Sat & Sun lunchtime.

Kitty Kiernan's, Hessenplatz 19. Every city in the world appears to need an Irish theme pub, and Linz is no exception – so far, it's proved very popular. Expensive range of Irish beers on tap. Home-from-home pub-food menu includes fish and chips and cottage pie.

Strom, Kirchengasse. Relaxed, friendly hangout for a wide range of alternative music fans and other nonconformists. Resident DJs spin an eclectic, eccentric mix of cutting-edge sounds, and themed dance nights are held in the neighbouring *Stadtwerk* club. On the Urfahr side of the Nibelungenbrücke, down the steps behind Ars Electronica.

Entertainment

Linz is big enough to accommodate a wide variety of tastes, but **highbrow culture** still predominates. Full-scale opera goes on at the Grosses Haus in the city's Landestheater, on the Promenade (☎0732/7611, *http://linz.info.at/landestheater*), with straight drama on the theatre's two smaller stages. Children's theatre and puppet shows are staged at *Kuddelmuddel*, Langgasse 13. There are regular concerts at the converted convent of the Ursulinenhof on Landstrasse, but the modern Brucknerhaus, by the river, at Untere Donaulände 7 (☎0732/775230, *www .brucknerhaus.linz.at*), is the main concert hall, and the focus of the annual **Brucknerfest**, which takes place from mid-September to early October. The festival begins with the *Klangwolken-Weekend*, with live transmissions of a Bruckner symphony, a laser show and open-air party by the Danube. The city's most offbeat festival is undoubtedly the **Ars Electronica Festival**, which takes place in early September, and features avant-garde music, installations and a competition for the most innovative piece of art using virtual reality.

The best programme of **gigs** is that put on at *Posthof*, an alternative arts centre at Posthofgasse 43, over by the docks (☎0732/781800, *www.posthof.at*; bus #21 to the Zollfreizone); events range from modern dance to discos and raves. Themed DJ-driven nights also take place at *Zizas*, underneath the *Café Landgraf* (see opposite), or *Stadtwerk*, next door to *Strom* (see opposite); otherwise the best **clubbing** venue is *Cembranikeller*, an old wine cellar hosting weekend raves and party events 500m northwest of the train station at Kellergasse 4. The local first-division **soccer** team, LASK, are in action every other Saturday during the football season (and occasionally on Wednesday evenings) at the Stadion der Stadt Linz, up by the botanical gardens (bus #27 to Roseggerstrasse). A wide selection of films are shown in their original languages at Moviemento, the city's main **arts cinema**, at Dametzstrasse 30. For a rundown of the month's events, pick up the *Linz ist los* **listings** leaflet from the tourist office.

Listings

Bike hire At the train station.

Boats Passenger services to Passau and Krems are operated by Wurm & Köck, Untere Donaulände 1 (☎0732/783609), between May and October.

Car hire Avis, Europaplatz 7 (☎0732/662881); Europcar, Wienerstrasse 91 (☎0732/600091); Hertz, Bürgerstrasse 19 (☎0732/784841).

Hospital Krankenhausgasse 9 (☎0732/7806-0).

Internet access Ars Electronica (Wed–Sun 10am–6pm; entrance ticket to the museum includes unlimited surfing).

Pharmacy Central pharmacies are open Mon–Fri 8am–noon & 2–6pm, Sat 8am–noon; Central Apotheke, Mozartstrasse 1 is one of the most convenient.

Post Office The main post office is at Bahnhofplatz 11 (daily 6am–midnight).

Around Linz

Linz lies within easy reach of two of Upper Austria's finest monasteries, **St Florian**, where Anton Bruckner is buried, and the lesser-known abbey of **Wilhering**, both of which are primarily of interest for their outstanding Baroque and Rococo architecture. Austria's most infamous concentration camp, **Mauthausen**, downriver from Linz, is a chilling reminder of the country's wartime experience, and could be combined with a more light-hearted trip to the small town of **Enns**.

Stift St Florian

The Augustinian **Stift St Florian**, 12km southeast of Linz, is Upper Austria's most illustrious abbey, renowned not simply for its Baroque architecture, but also for its close associations with Anton Bruckner (see box below). The composer joined the abbey choir at the age of 11, eventually went on to become organist here, and is buried, according to his wishes, beneath the ornate, and extraordinarily loud, 7000-pipe organ in the **Stiftskirche**, which stands at the northern end of the vast ochre-coloured monastic complex. Begun in 1686 by Carlo Carlone, the church boasts a gleaming-white interior flanked by imposing Corinthian half-columns, crowned with a heavy, stuccoed cornice. Decorated with a continuous band of predominantly golden-brown trompe l'oeil frescoes, the nave's vaulting creates a somewhat lighter atmosphere. Of all the furnishings, the choir stalls are the most playful, with gold-winged cherubs making music, frolicking amongst the carved foliage of the balustrade, and acting as apprentice Atlantes. From mid-May to mid-October you can hear the organ being put through its paces for half an hour, at 2.30pm every day except Saturday.

To visit the rest of the abbey complex, you must join one of the hourly **guided tours** (April–Oct daily 10 & 11am, 1, 2 & 3pm; öS60/€4.38), which begin with the **Bibliothek**, lined with undulating bookshelves and balconies and sporting a ceiling

---

ANTON BRUCKNER

As a composer, **Anton Bruckner** (1824–95) was a figure of towering stature, his nine symphonies held up with those of Brahms and Mahler as the greatest since Beethoven; but as a person he was seen as figure of fun. In Vienna, he was mocked for his provincial appearance – he liked to wear baggy, black, homespun clothes and a wide-brimmed hat – and caricatured as a country bumpkin because of his regional accent and disingenuousness. The anecdotes attesting to his naivety are legion. After Hans Richter had conducted the première of the *Eighth Symphony* in 1892, Bruckner is alleged to have waited at the artists' entrance with 48 piping-hot doughnuts and presented them to Richter in gratitude. He was also famous for his lack of success in love: his pursuit of young women in their late teens, and his rejection by them, was a constant theme of his life-long bachelorhood.

The details of his life are relatively mundane. Born in the village of Ansfelden, 10km south of Linz, where his father was a schoolteacher and organist, Bruckner followed in his father's footsteps until 1855, when he took up the post of cathedral organist in Linz. It was there, in 1862, while studying under Otto Kitzler, a teacher ten years his junior, that Bruckner heard Wagner's *Tannhäuser* for the first time, a revelatory moment that sparked his first compositional masterpieces. In 1868, he became a teacher at the Vienna conservatory, and later a lecturer at the university. It was in the capital that he wrote the bulk of his work, and that he eventually died, though he chose to be buried back at the monastery of St Florian, where he had been a choirboy and, later, teacher.

He was, without doubt, an obsessive man. He took his work very seriously, practising ten hours at the piano, three hours at the organ, then studying into the night. He constantly revised his work, especially towards the end of his life, and suffered from bouts of numeromania (an obsession with counting), keeping a tally of the number of prayers he had said each day, insisting on numbering all the bars in his scores, and, when his condition worsened, even counting the leaves on trees and the stars in the night sky. His other major obsession was with death. He made sure he was present at the exhumation of both Beethoven and Schubert, and apparently visited the mortuary to see for himself the charred remains of the victims of Vienna's Ringtheater fire of 1881. He was buried, according to his own very specific wishes, in the suitably macabre necropolis below the organ in St Florian's Stiftskirche.

fresco by Bartolomeo Altomonte. Next, you get to see Jakob Prandtauer's **Marmorsaal**, a marble extravaganza in patriotic red-and-white Babenberg colours, with a Martino Bartolomeo fresco celebrating the victory over the Turks, who sit around above the cornice dejected, chained and exhausted. A stroll up Prandtauer's monumental staircase, which takes up almost the entire west facade of the main courtyard, brings you to the 200-metre-long corridor, off which are the **imperial apartments**. With their red damask walls, and richly stuccoed ceilings, these VIP guest rooms have remained pretty much unaltered since they fell into disuse in 1782. Prince Eugène of Savoy's four-poster bed (in which the diminutive general never actually slept) is the star attraction: an over-the-top Rococo contraption built in imitation of a Turkish tent, featuring technicolour Turks tied to its corner posts. At the end of the corridor, there's the **Bruckner Gedenkraum**, with yet another bed, this time a special, bouncy, English-sprung brass bedstead bought for the composer by his students, of which Bruckner was especially proud, and in which he died.

Lastly, the abbey owns the world's largest single collection of works by **Albrecht Altdorfer** (1480–1538) of Regensburg, namely fourteen panels from the *Altar of St Sebastian*, painted in 1518 for the old Gothic church of St Florian. Along with Albrecht Dürer and Lucas Cranach the Elder, Altdorfer was a leading figure in the group of painters loosely known as the "Danube School". Danubian scenery features prominently in many of the school's works, particularly in the case of Altdorfer, whose scenes from the Passion are played against luxuriant Upper Austrian landscapes; in the Crown of Thorns scene, the old St Florian church can even be seen in the background. Altdorfer also makes ambitious and unorthodox use of perspective, most noticeably in the Crucifixion scene, where the three crosses are placed at right angles to one another. The tour ends in the Stiftskirche (see opposite), where you get a chance to see Bruckner's tomb in the crypt, set against a mountain of over 6000 bones.

In honour of the town and abbey's namesake, Florian, who is also the patron saint of firefighters, there is a **Feuerwehrmuseum** (May–Oct Tues–Sun 9am–noon & 2–4pm; öS30/€2.19) in one of the monastic outbuildings, housing a collection of ancient and modern fire engines and equipment, as well as one of the trams that used to run to the village from Linz. Florian was the chief Roman official at the nearby town of Lauriacum (Enns), but when he converted to Christianity he was imprisoned, tortured and eventually martyred in 304 AD by being thrown into the River Enns with a millstone around his neck. The story goes that he was washed up and buried at the spot where the abbey was later built. An easy two-kilometre walk west of St Florian, the engaging **Jagdmuseum** (April–Oct Tues–Sun 10am–noon & 1–5pm; öS30/€2.19) is dedicated to hunting, shooting and fishing. It's housed in the **Schloss Hohenbrunn**, another work by Prandtauer.

If you're in need of **food**, the *Stiftsrestaurant*, off the main courtyard in St Florian, offers simple lunchtime soups, main schnitzel courses from just öS90/€6.60, as well as some fancier freshwater fish dishes.

Wilhering

The Cistercian monastery at **WILHERING**, 8km upriver from Linz, may not have the associations with Bruckner that St Florian has – and therefore receives a fraction of the visitors – but it's an equally alluring prospect. Although founded in the twelfth century, the current abbey was mostly designed by local craftsman Johann Haslinger, after an arson attack by a 12-year-old girl in 1733 destroyed the old monastery. The chief attraction is the remarkable Rococo **Stiftskirche**, which dominates the apricot-coloured complex and overlooks the grassy main courtyard with its circle of conical yew trees and potted palms. Austrian Baroque architecture may be flamboyant, but it only rarely spills over into full-blown Rococo excess – Wilhering is one such occasion. Such is the wealth of decoration of the stunning interior, designed by Martino Altomonte and his nephew Bartolomeo, it takes a while simply to take in the whole bombastic creation. The visual drama is at its most intoxicating in the ceiling, where the rich colouring of Bartolomeo Altomonte's frescoes is matched in its exceptional detail by the surrounding stucco-work, presided over by acrobatic angels and cherubs in colour-co-ordinated robes. The organ is also a perfectly executed piece of Rococo art, with its gilded filigree, its music-making putti and, above all, its clock suspended between the organ pipes, which boldly chimes in unison with the church clock every quarter of an hour. You're free to walk round the remaining sections of the old medieval monastery, too, including the **cloisters**, which shelter eighteen more paintings by Altomonte on the life of St Bernhard, one of the founders of the Cistercian order.

Mauthausen

By the end of the war, Hitler's home district of Upper Austria had been endowed with more concentration camps than any other region in the Third Reich. The most notorious of the lot was **KZ Mauthausen** (daily: Feb, March & Oct to mid-Dec 8am–4pm; April–Sept 8am–6pm; öS25/€1.83. Price includes English-language leaflet and audiotape guide), some 20km downriver from Linz, built in August 1938 by prisoners transferred from the concentration camp in Dachau outside Munich. Theoretically, Mauthausen was intended as a slave labour camp, not an extermination camp, its inmates forced to work in the adjacent granite quarries. However, the death toll was such that economic considerations were clearly secondary: of the 200,000 inmates who passed through the camp, around half perished. The life expectancy of the Jewish inmates was shortest of all, but an equal number of those who died were Soviet POWs and Poles.

The most striking thing about Mauthausen is its solidity and its sheer visibility: this is no ad hoc camp, but a huge, granite fortress, and it occupies a commanding position overlooking the Danube. Only a few of the 25 flimsy wooden barracks that housed the prisoners have survived. The former **Sick Quarters** now contain a museum detailing life inside the camp. More poignant and affecting, though, are the numerous personal memorials scattered throughout the camp, erected by family and friends of the camp's victims, who hail from countries as far apart as Greece and Great Britain. Underneath the Sick Quarters were the camp's gas chambers, disguised as showers, as at Auschwitz. The cyanide gas Zyklon B was in fact given its first test run in Schloss Hartheim, near Linz, where the Nazis transformed a school for children with special needs into a euthanasia centre. Here, under the guidance of Linz doctor Rudolf Lonauer, 12,000 sick and mentally ill patients, transported there from all over Austria, were gassed and burnt in the castle's crematorium.

The granite quarries themselves lie to the northwest of the camp, beyond the field filled with a vast array of official national memorials. Thousands were literally worked to death on the infamous **Todestiege** (Stairway of Death), the 189 steps that lead out of the granite quarry. En route, you pass what the SS jokingly referred to as the "Parachutists' Jump", a sheer cliff overlooking the quarry, where prisoners were pushed to their deaths. One of the best-known survivors of Mauthausen is **Simon Wiesenthal**, who has since spent his life trying to bring those responsible for Nazi war crimes to justice.

Getting to the camp by **public transport** is not easy. By train from Linz, you must change at St Valentin, and from Mauthausen train station it's a steep five-kilometre hike up to the camp, although the station does hire out bikes. Alternatively, you can catch the bus from Linz and get off at the bottom of the hill, cutting the walk in half. The village of Mauthausen itself is extremely pretty, but it's difficult to relax there after having been to the camp. The best advice is to hop on a train to Enns.

Enns

The winsome little walled town of **ENNS**, 6km southeast of Mauthausen, makes for an easy day-trip from Linz by train. Situated close to the confluence of the Enns and the Danube, it has been a strategically important site for more than two millennia. Under the Romans, the town was known as Lauriacum, and served as the civil capital of Noricum and military base of the Second Legion, who guarded this section of the imperial frontier. As recently as 1945–55, Enns served as the key entry/exit point between the Soviet and American occupation zones; today, it lies along the border between Lower and Upper Austria.

The town's **Hauptplatz** is very attractive, each side lined with a parade of pastel-coloured Baroque facades, many of which conceal much older, arcaded courtyards. Numerous examples can be clearly seen from the top of the colossal sixteenth-century **Stadtturm**, a lookout tower and belfry which rises to a height of 60m from the centre of the rectangular main square. To examine one of the arcaded courtyards at close quarters, check out the **Alte Burg**, on Wienerstrasse, or no. 4a Bräunerstrasse, which runs parallel with Linzerstrasse, a street that itself boasts a couple of very fine Renaissance houses – one sporting turrets, the other crenellations – facing each other halfway down.

Back on Hauptplatz, the pink, sixteenth-century Altes Rathaus now serves as the **Museum Lauriacum** (April–Oct Tues–Sun 10am–noon & 2–4pm; Nov–March Sun only; öS30/€2.19), housing an exhaustive display of pottery, ironware and funerary sculpture unearthed from the Roman settlement. Undoubted showpiece is the second-century ceiling fresco which has been reassembled in one of the upstairs rooms, depicting a ruddy-skinned Cupid whispering sweet nothings to a young woman. An adjacent alcove displays a set of silver tableware from the same period, notably a beaker decorated with animated hunting scenes. Further archeological remains can be viewed in the Gothic **St Laurenz-Basilika**, situated 1km northwest of the Altstadt, off the road to Linz, on the site of the old Roman civilian town. Here, the high altar has been moved forward, and the chancel floor ripped away to reveal the foundations of a Romano-Celtic temple (180 AD), an early Christian church (370 AD), perhaps founded by St Severin, and a later Carolingian church (740 AD). Roman fresco-fragments and the remains of a hypocaust heating system can be seen in the church crypt (guided tour only; mid–April to mid–Oct daily at 4pm; öS30/€2.19).

Practicalities

Enns **train station** is 1500m northwest of the Hauptplatz, beyond the St Laurenz-Basilika; buses from Linz and Steyr drop you off on the main square. If you want to stay the night, you can get private **rooms** (①–②) in the Altstadt through the **tourist office**, just downhill from the Hauptplatz at Mauthausnerstrasse 7 (May–Sept Mon–Fri 9am–6.30pm; Oct–April Mon–Fri 9am–3pm; ☎07223/82777, *www.tiscover.com/enns*). The *Hotel Lauriacum*, Wienerstrasse 5–7 (☎07223/82315, *www.austria-classic-hotels.at/lauriacum*; ⑤), is the top place to stay in town, offering tastefully decorated en suites. However, *Gasthof zum Goldenen Schiff* (☎07223/86086, *www.tiscover.com/hotel.brunner*; ④), at Hauptplatz 23, offers similar levels of comfort for a slightly cheaper price. For no-nonsense Austrian **food**, try the specials and fixed-price menus on offer for around öS80/€5.84 at the *Gasthaus zur Stadt Linz*, at Hauptplatz 4.

Mühlviertel

The **Mühlviertel**, to the north of Linz, between the Danube and the Czech border, is a lost corner of Austria, where few tourists venture. The wonderful sweep and roll of the wooded countryside is more Bohemia than Austria, and holds just two places of compelling interest: **Kefermarkt**, with its remarkable carved altarpiece, and the walled town of **Freistadt**, both reached by the main road and rail line heading north into the Czech Republic.

Kefermarkt

The sole reason for making it out to **KEFERMARKT**, 30km or so northeast of Linz, is to visit the fifteenth-century **Wallfahrtskirche**, clearly visible, and a ten-minute walk up the hill, from the village train station. The church has some attractive lierne vaulting, but it's the enormous winged **altarpiece**, carved entirely out of limewood by an unknown artist around 1490, that is the chief draw. The depth of expression in the faces of the three life-size saints at centre stage is startling, as is the thicket of finials and tracery that reaches to a height of 13m above the main section. Note, too, the two beautifully carved saints in full armour flanking the altarpiece: Florian, casually dousing a tiny fire, and George, nonchalantly dealing with a minuscule dragon.

If you're looking for a bite to eat, walk up the road to **Schloss Weinberg**, a lovely little, double-moated castle with a Baroque keep, which now serves as an art and music school; you can eat hearty fare for under öS100/€7.30 for a main dish at the *Gasthausbrauerei* in the castle's former brewery by the gates.

Freistadt

Surrounded by one of best-preserved sets of town fortifications in the country, **FREIS-TADT**, 17km short of the Czech frontier, is your archetypal medieval border town. The town's moat may be grassed over, but it's clearly visible and still overlooked by several of the original bastions, as well as two imposing gateways, the finest of which is the wedge-shaped Linzer Tor. The current defence system was thrown up around the town during the fourteenth century, as Freistadt grew rich on the salt trade that passed through, and on the privileges heaped upon it by successive Babenberg and Habsburg rulers in order to keep it as a loyal bulwark in the Bohemian borderlands. With both sides of the border in Habsburg hands after 1526, however, Freistadt's strategic significance waned, and not a lot has changed since those days – the town even has a night watchman.

On the central square of **Hauptplatz**, the pale-coloured facades are mostly Baroque, but they hide much older buildings. The most unusual is the pea-green house, two doors down from the Rathaus, which sports an onion dome on one of its two projecting bays. In one corner of the square, the town's fourteenth-century **Schloss** is clearly visible, in its coat of flaking ochre. The castle now houses the local **Heimatmuseum** (tours daily at 9am, 10.30am, 2pm and 3.30pm; öS30/€2.19), unremarkable except for its collection of *Hinterglasbilder*, pictures painted on the backs of panes of glass, in a technique perfected in the nineteenth century by artists from the nearby village of Sandl. In the opposite corner of the square stands the **Katharinenmünster**, its ostentatious pink and white Baroque tower totally out of keeping with the calm Gothic interior, whose vaulting retains patches of medieval mural. More than any specific sight, though, the back streets of Freistadt are rewarding simply to stroll down, particularly Waaggasse, and along the eastern border of the old town walls.

Practicalities

Regular **buses from Linz** stop just below the entrance to Freistadt's Altstadt and are much more convenient than **trains**, which arrive some 3km southwest of the centre, connected to the centre by infrequent municipal bus. You can pick up a plan of the Altstadt from the **tourist office** at Hauptplatz 14 (Mon–Fri 9am–5pm; also May–Sept

Sat 9am–noon; ☎07942/75700, *www.tiscover.com/kernland*). Freistadt is an atmospheric and peaceful town in which to spend the night, with several excellent **hotels** in the heart of the Altstadt, starting with the venerable *Gasthof Deim zum goldenen Hirschen*, Böhmergasse 8–10 (☎07942/72258, *deim@upperaustria.or.at*; ④), an old-fashioned family-run inn dating to the fifteenth century and still full of character, followed by *Gasthof zum goldenen Adler*, Salzgasse 1 (☎07942/72112; ④), not quite as special but a decent second choice. Other, cheaper possibilities include the simple en-suite rooms at *Pension Pirklbauer*, Höllgasse 2/4 (☎07942/72440; ②), and *Gasthof Tröls*, Eisengasse 16 (☎07942/72297; ③). The town's **youth hostel** (☎07942/74365; June–Sept) is right by the Schloss, and the nearest **campsite** (☎07942/72624; April–Sept) is a short walk east of the Altstadt, beyond the River Feldaist.

The popular *Lubinger* café by the Schloss is good for a coffee and cake, and *Vis à Vis*, Salzgasse 13 (closed Sun), does hot snacks and a daily two-course lunch for öS90/€6.60; but for the full monty, you can't beat the aforementioned *Gasthof Deim zum goldenen Hirschen*, where you can dine in lovely wood-panelled rooms or a plant-filled conservatory; or the slightly cheaper *Goldener Adler*. Wherever you decide to eat, be sure to try some of the town's excellent Freistädter Bier, which has been communally owned since 1777.

Steyr

Franz Schubert considered **STEYR** "inconceivably lovely", when he stayed here in 1819 and wrote the famous *Trout Quintet*, and although he was hardly the world's most travelled man he wasn't far wrong. Strategically and dramatically situated at the fast-flowing confluence of two alpine rivers, Steyr is characterized by its picturesque zigzag riverfront of red rooftops. It's a town that grew rich on the trade in iron ore from the Eisenerzer Alps, and then, in the nineteenth century, became one of the most important arms-manufacturing towns in Austria. Even today, it remains a primarily industrial town, though you'd never know it from the beautifully preserved Altstadt.

The Town

The best way to approach the Altstadt from the train station is from the south, through the town's last remaining gateway, Neutor, and past the sgraffitoed Innerberger Stadel, a seventeenth-century granary that now houses the **Heimatmuseum** (April–Oct Tues–Sun 10am–4pm; Nov–March Wed–Sun 10am–4pm; free), the usual local history collection, enlivened by a nativity scene in the form of a mechanical rod puppet theatre, with more than four hundred moving figures, though the latter only works during Advent and New Year. Steps by the side of the Innerberger Stadel lead up to the **Stadtpfarrkirche**, built in the late fifteenth century by the architect of Vienna's Stephansdom, but rather crudely re-Gothicized in the 1880s. A more rewarding church interior, decked out with Rococo adornments, can be found in the **Marienkirche**, set back from Grünmarkt.

Steyr's elongated main square, **Stadtplatz**, creates a grand impression, with handsome town houses, three or four storeys high, facing each other across the cobbles. The most famous building on the square is the emblematic **Bummerlhaus**, built in 1497 as an inn and sporting a distinctive triangular gable and first-floor overhang, decorated with intricate tracery and blind arcading. The building now serves as a bank, and during opening hours you're free to wander through to the inner courtyard – one of several hidden behind the houses on the main square – and upstairs to admire the finely painted ceiling from 1543. The **Rathaus**, on the opposite side of the square, is a

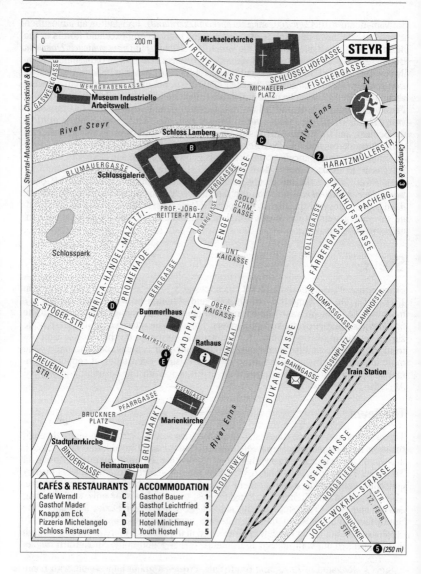

CAFÉS & RESTAURANTS		ACCOMMODATION	
Café Werndl	C	Gasthof Bauer	1
Gasthof Mader	E	Gasthof Leichtfried	3
Knapp am Eck	A	Hotel Mader	4
Pizzeria Michelangelo	D	Hotel Minichmayr	2
Schloss Restaurant	B	Youth Hostel	5

suitably imposing edifice, designed by the town mayor with a pink Rococo facade and flamboyant belfry topped with a pile of copper onion domes and a barley-sugar column. There are several more superb Rococo facades at the north end of Stadtplatz, in particular the **Sternhaus**, from 1768, with its garish sky-blue and yellow colour scheme, fancy stucco-work and posing cherubs in high relief. Stadtplatz eventually funnels into the narrow defile of Engegasse, a busy shopping street lined with yet more brightly painted, overhanging houses.

As you cross the bridge over the River Steyr, to the equally ancient suburb of Steyrdorf, the spectacular facade of the **Michaelerkirche** rises up directly ahead of you. Built by the Jesuits in 1635, its twin towers flank a wonderfully dramatic and colourful gable fresco featuring the Archangel Michael. The picturesque cobbled streets off to the west, up Kirchengasse, are beautifully peaceful and repay a casual wander, or else you can cross over a narrow arm of the Steyr and visit the excellent **Museum Industrielle Arbeitswelt** (Tues–Sun 9am–5pm; öS65/€4.75), housed in a converted factory on Wehrgrabengasse. This state-of-the-art museum explains the history of the town's industrialization and analyses its social impact. Departing from the patriotic tone adopted by many Austrian museums, it's a display that often sides with the underdog: there are sympathetic references to seventeenth-century Protestant artisans who were persecuted by a Counter-Reforming Habsburg regime, generous dollops of working-class history, and unflinching coverage of the forced labour used by Steyr's factories during World War II. The town's importance to the Austrian armaments industry is highlighted in the coverage of the nineteenth-century entrepreneur Josef Werndl, whose factory supplied modern rifles to an imperial army which, defeated by the Prussians at Königgratz in 1866, was desperate for up-to-date equipment. Werndl was a benevolent capitalist who built houses (and a swimming pool) for his workers, but he forbade union agitation, and the next part of the exhibition is devoted to the rise of socialism in Steyr, and the town's interwar transformation into the so-called Rote Insel ("Red Island"), in which the Austrian Socialist Party oversaw most aspects of political and cultural life.

The nearby pedestrian-only bridge over the Steyr will bring you back to just below the **Schloss Lamberg**, whose two towers – one castellated, one Baroque – barely rise above the castle's barracks-like blank wall. Lying beyond a moat in which captive ibex frolic, much of the complex is now used for the town council and police headquarters, but you can wander through the tranquil, triangular courtyard, surrounded by Baroque statues of dwarfs in various poses. On the northwest side of the Schloss lies the **Schlossgalerie** (Tues–Sun 10am–noon & 2–5pm; free), site of changing exhibitions usually devoted to contemporary art. To the southwest lies the leafy **Schlosspark**, which culminates in a set-piece and rather overblown statue of Josef Werndl, seen here brandishing one of his mass-produced rifles, and surrounded by heroic-looking smiths earnestly banging away at lumps of iron. Werndl's ostentatious town house, the turreted, neo-Gothic Schloss Voglsang, can be glimpsed at the end of Preuenhuberstrasse, a side street 20m beyond the statue.

From June to September, steam trains run at the weekend along the narrow-gauge **Steyrtal-Museumsbahn** (Sat & Sun 2–3; öS120/€8.76 return) to Grünberg, 17km to the southwest. The Lokalbahnhof from which they depart is ten minutes' walk west of Schloss Lamberg, down Blumauergasse. If you continue for another 1.5km upriver, past the train station, you'll come to the Baroque church of **Christkindl**, set high above the river. It was built in the seventeenth century to house a wax figure of Jesus (still the centrepiece of the church's altar), which had been attracting a steady stream of pilgrims because of its supposed healing powers. It's still a major draw, though for rather different reasons. At Christmas time, more than a million and a half Christmas cards are sent from the church's special post office to philatelists across the globe. Thousands more are sent to the church – each getting a reply – from Austrian kids asking for a present from *Christkind* (Baby Jesus), the traditional giver of Christmas presents in Austria.

Practicalities

The **tourist office** (mid-Jan to Nov Mon–Fri 8.30am–6pm, Sat 9am–noon; Dec to mid-Jan Mon–Fri 8.30am–6pm, Sat 9am–4pm, Sun 10am–3pm; ☎07252/53229, *www.tourism-steyr.at*) is in the Rathaus, and can help organize **private rooms** (②). Steyr's finest **hotel** is the *Hotel Mader* (☎07252/53358, *www.mader.at*; ⑤), a splendid Renaissance building on Stadtplatz, with an arcaded inner courtyard, and modern en-suite rooms. For spectacular views overlooking the confluence of the Enns and Steyr rivers, head for *Hotel Minichmayr*, Haratzmüllerstrasse 1–3 (☎07252/53410, *minichmayr@austria-classic-hotels.at*; ⑤), which has satisfyingly plush en suites, or the more modest *Gasthof Leichtfried*, at no. 25 (☎07252/52438, *g.leichtfried@aon.at*; ③). All other inexpensive options are well out of the centre, the most convenient being *Gasthof Bauer*, Josefgasse 7 (bus #2b or #5 from the train station to Schwimmschulstrasse; ☎07252/54441; ③), a cosy pension-style place on one of the river islands offering en suites with TV. The town's **youth hostel**, with especially cheap accommodation in multi-bed dorms (öS110/€8.03 per person), is at Hafnerstrasse 14 (☎07252/45580; mid-Jan to mid-Dec; reception 5–10pm), a fifteen-minute walk from the train station; turn right out of the station, then right down Damberggasse, under the railway tracks, right again at Arbeiterstrasse, and fourth right down Otto-Glockel-Strasse. The nearest **campsite** is *Campingplatz Forelle* (☎07252/78008; May–Sept), by the River Enns in the woody suburb of Münichholz, 2.5km north (bus #1 from the train station).

For full **meals**, *Gasthof Mader* (closed Sun), at the hotel of the same name (see above), does a very good two-course Tagesmenü for under öS100/€7.30, and the *Schloss-Restaurant* in Schloss Lamberg is pretty reasonable. *Knapp am Eck*, 50m west of Arbeitswelt on the corner of Wehrgrabengasse and Gaswerkgasse, is an intimate and cosy restaurant which is also a decent place for a drink. If the weather's fine, a table outside at *Pizzeria Michelangelo*, in the Schlosspark, is an enticing option. For **drinking**, *Café Werndl*, beside the bridge over the Steyr, enjoys fabulous riverside views, while *Café Treffpunkt*, an engaging cross between a Habsburg-era café and a modern bar, down on the Ennskai, is better for an evening drink. Fly-posters around town advertise gigs and club nights at *Röd@*, a cultural centre just west of Museum Arbeitswelt at Gaswerkgasse 2.

Kremsmünster

The Benedictine monastery of **Kremsmünster** is one of the most unusual and reward-ing of all Austria's abbeys. It's a huge complex, built on raised ground above the River Krems, its skyline punctuated not simply by the obligatory twin spires of the monastery church, but by the strange silo-like bulk of the abbey's observatory, or Sternwarte. In addition, Kremsmünster boasts a uniquely preserved set of seventeenth-century fish ponds, as well as the usual feast of Baroque interiors. Below the monastery, the village of Kremsmünster itself is an unassuming, frumpy little place which offers little incen-tive to stick around. The monastery is an easily accessible day-trip by train from Linz, or by bus from either Wels or Steyr.

The Fischkalter and Stiftskirche

The abbey's most remarkable architectural set piece, its unique Baroque series of **Fischkalter** (Fish Basins), is accessible via the abbey's ticket office/shop (daily 9am–noon & 1–5pm; öS15/€1.10), in the first courtyard. Designed in 1690 by Carlo Carlone, and expanded by Jakob Prandtauer some thirty years later, the Fischkalter consist of five perfectly symmetrical ponds surrounded by a set of Italianate arcades held up by slender Tuscan columns, and originally decorated with frescoes, only patch-es of which now survive. Each basin has a mythological or biblical fountain at the centre, and the cumulative noise of the water echoing round the arcades is quite deafening. If you want to watch the carp go crazy, you can buy some fish food from the abbey shop. You can also eat some of the previous inhabitants of the Fischkalter at the *Stiftsschenke* (closed Mon), across the courtyard.

The **Stiftskirche**, across the moat in the second courtyard, is also the work of Carlo Carlone, who redesigned much of the abbey in Baroque style from the 1670s onwards. The interior is coated with a staggering quantity of thick, white stucco, which totally upstages the ceiling frescoes. The other unusual decoration in the church is the set of eight seventeenth-century Flemish tapestries wrapped round the pillars of the nave, depicting the story of Joseph in Egypt. The side altars are refreshingly cherub-free, their oil paintings flanked only by pairs of finely carved angels by Michael Zürn. The sole reminder of the original Gothic Stiftskirche is the exquisitely serene, thirteenth-century tomb of Gunther, which lies in the chapel beneath the south tower. Gunther's death in the woods hereabouts, at the trotters of a wild boar, prompted his father, Duke Tassilo III of Bavaria, to found a monastery here in 777. The figure of Gunther lies on his sepulchre beside the aforementioned boar, with a hunting horn in his hand and his dog by his feet.

The Kunstsammlung and Sternwarte

To see the interior of the monastery, you must sign up for an hour-long guided tour (in German only) of the **Kunstsammlung** (daily: Easter–Oct 10 & 11am, 2, 3 & 4pm; Oct–Easter 11am & 2pm; öS55/€4.02). After a quick visit to the Fischkalter, you get a chance to wander through the **Kaisersaal**, designed by Carlone in the 1690s as a summer dining room, and so called because of Martino Altomonte's series of imperial portraits set into the wall, framed by ornate stucco-work. The whitewashed walls contrast sharply with the colourful and energetic trompe l'oeil ceiling fresco, depicting the triumph of light over darkness (for which read Habsburgs over Turks). The most precious medieval *objet d'art* in the monastery's tapestry-lined treasury is the eighth-century Carolingian **Tassilo-Kelch**, a remarkable gilded copper chalice decorated with portraits of Christ and his disciples, surrounded by what looks remarkably like Celtic interlacing. The decor in the monastery's enormously long **Bibliothek**, again by Carlone, is reminiscent of the Stiftskirche, with heavy stucco-work framing richly coloured frescoes. A bewilderingly large art collection is crammed into several more rooms of the monastery, with works ranging from unknown fifteenth-century Bohemian artists to the likes of Bartolomeo Altomonte and Kremser Schmidt. Finally, there's a small **Kunstkammer**, whose most renowned artefact is the chair made from the bones of the first elephant brought to Austria (in 1552 by crown prince Maximilian II) and a collection of arms and armour.

Without doubt the most unusual building in the entire complex is the **Sternwarte** (May–Oct daily 10am & 2pm; July & Aug extra tour at 4pm; öS60/€4.38), a fifty-metre-high, eight-storey tower block completed in 1759. The tower was purpose-built to house a museum that would take visitors from the inanimate world of minerals and fossils on the lower floors, through the animal and plant kingdom, to the human arts and sciences and beyond to the observatory, finishing up with contemplation of God in the rooftop chapel. The collections within the Sternwarte are still arranged pretty much in the above order, with paleontology exhibits down below, and astrology up top. Unfortunately, in order to visit the tower you have to endure an hour-and-a-half-long guided tour in German. If you persevere, however, you'll be rewarded with a fabulous view over the monastery and the surrounding countryside from the rooftop terrace.

Wels

Despite a history stretching back to Roman times, when it was known as Ovilava, **WELS** lacks the drama of Steyr. Situated on the banks of the River Traun, amid the flat landscape to the southwest of Linz, it is, however, the second largest town in Upper Austria, and a place you're almost bound to find yourself passing through. It also has the advantage of being situated on one of the region's most important railway junctions, making it an easy place in which to stop off for an hour or two – just long enough to explore the town's small, but handsome Altstadt.

The Town

The showpiece of the **Altstadt** is the central **Stadtplatz**, a long, relatively narrow space, closed off at one end by the town's last surviving gateway, or **Ledererturm**, erected in 1376. The square's parade of attractive, mostly Baroque facades features some very fine plasterwork, particularly on the square bulk of the imperial-yellow **Rathaus** from 1748; but by far the most exotic and distinctive single building is the Renaissance **Haus der Salome Alt**, with its rich trompe l'oeil brickwork, patterned with red-and-white diapers and ornate, stone window surrounds. The house was at one time home to Hans Sachs – the most famous of Nuremberg's medieval *Meistersänger*,

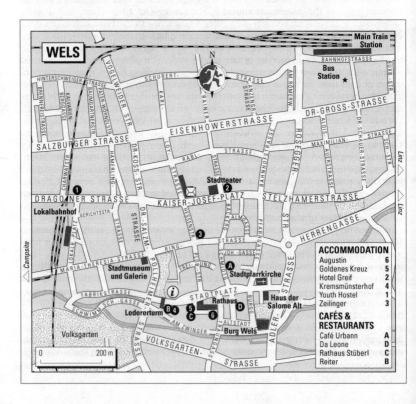

who wrote his first poems at the school in Wels – but it gets its name from Salome Alt, mistress of Wolf Dietrich, Prince-Archbishop of Salzburg, who moved here after Dietrich fell from power and was imprisoned in 1612. Directly opposite the Haus der Salome Alt stands the **Stadtpfarrkirche**, Gothic and fairly undistinguished for the most part, but with a finely preserved Romanesque west door and some excellent medieval stained glass hidden away in the chancel.

On the other side of Salome Alt's house is the imperial **Burg Wels** (daily 10am–6pm; öS40/€2.92), where the Emperor Maximilian I died in 1519, having been refused bed and board by the folk of Innsbruck, who were fearful that he wouldn't pay his bills. Maximilian was eventually buried in Wiener Neustadt (see p.216), though his tomb remains in Innsbruck (see p.468). In the 1980s, Burg Wels's interior was converted into a cultural centre and local history museum, the latter with a particular emphasis on agriculture and bread-making. The town's best Roman remains are to be found in the **Stadtmuseum und Galerie** (same times as above; free), housed in a fanciful turn-of-the-twentieth-century former bank on Pollheimerstrasse. Temporary art exhibitions are held on the ground floor, while the first floor is given over to the museum's permanent collection. Among the Roman finds are the tiny second-century AD bronze *Venus of Wels*, several graves sporting sphinxes and lions, a conical milestone, hoards of coins, and patches of mosaic.

Practicalities

Wels **tourist office,** at Hauptplatz 55 (July & Aug Mon–Fri 9am–7pm, Sat 9am–noon; Sept–June Mon–Fri 9am–6pm; ☎07242/43495, *www.tiscover.at/wels*), publishes a useful series of leaflets, including a bimonthly listings booklet, and can help you find somewhere to stay. Many of the **hotels** in Wels, like comfortable *Hotel Greif*, Kaiser-Josef-Platz 50/51 (☎07242/45361, *avalon.hotel.greif@telecom.at*; ⑧), are efficiently run by big hotel chains and cater for the business crowd, but there are less expensive options, such as the excellent *Kremsmünsterhof* (☎07242/46623; ④), a converted monastic lodge on Stadtplatz itself, with a fine arcaded courtyard, and the nearby *Goldenes Kreuz* (☎07242/46453; ④), a more traditional and characterful inn. Of the town's Gasthöfe, the no-frills *Zeilinger*, Ringstrasse 29 (☎07242/47440; ②), and the similarly basic *Augustin*, Traungasse 8 (☎07242/46305; ② without breakfast), enjoy the most central locations. Wels' **youth hostel** (☎07242/235757; mid-Jan to mid-Dec) is centrally located, at Dragonerstrasse 22, while the nearest **campsite**, *Campingplatz Rosenau* (☎07242/44195; June–Sept), is a fifteen-minute walk southwest of the Altstadt (bus #16 from outside the Stadtpfarrkirche).

The *Café Urbann*, Schmidtgasse 20 (closed Sat eve & Sun), is the longest-established *Kaffeehaus* in Wels, and a reliable place for a coffee and cake. Another town institution is the old-fashioned self-service café/butcher's *Reiter*, Stadtplatz 62 (Mon–Thurs 9am–2pm, Fri & Sat 9am–5pm, Sun closed), which offers a whole range of cheap soups, sausages and schnitzels. For a more imaginative take on standard Austrian **food**, head further up Stadtplatz to the traditional *Rathaus-Stüberl* (closed Sun) in the *Goldenes Kreuz* hotel. *Da Leone* (closed Sun) is an upmarket pizzeria and Italian restaurant with a pleasant, arcaded *Schanigarten* in narrow Hafnergasse, just off the southern side of the Stadtplatz. The same street boasts several decent places to linger over a **drink**, such as *Café Rewü*, which also offers good-value lunchtime menus.

Wels is Upper Austria's main cultural centre after Linz, so there's usually a fair selection of **live entertainment** to enjoy. The main stage at the Stadttheater, on the corner of Kaiser-Josef-Platz and Rainerstrasse, plays host to everything from full-scale opera to comedy, while the programme at *Im Kornspeicher*, Freiung 15, is less mainstream, ranging from cabaret and dance to jazz. For more details of what's on, pick up the latest **listings** information from the tourist office.

The Innviertel

The River Inn forms the western border between Bavaria and Upper Austria, from just below Braunau to its confluence with the Danube at Passau. The region between the Inn and the Danube, known as the **Innviertel**, is rich, rolling farming country reminiscent of much of Bavaria – indeed, until 1779, and briefly again during the Napoleonic period, the region belonged to the duchy of Bavaria. Inevitably, this gentle landscape can't compete with the alpine scenery further south around Salzburg and the Salzkammergut, and most people tend simply to pass through the region, but there are three picturesque border towns that make for a more interesting introduction to Austria, from south to north: **Braunau-am-Inn**, **Obernberg-am-Inn** and, above all, **Schärding**.

The region is relatively easy to get to by public transport, with frequent **trains** from Linz and Wels to Schärding and Braunau (sometimes involving a change at the uninspiring junction town of Neumarkt-Kallham). Travelling between Schärding, Obernberg and Braunau is more problematic, with only one daily **bus** linking the three of them.

Braunau-am-Inn

BRAUNAU-AM-INN, in the western corner of Upper Austria, is saddled with an unfortunate legacy, as the birthplace of Adolf Hitler. This rather overshadows the fact that Braunau is also a very handsome border town, worth a quick stop-off whether you're on your way in or out of the country. Lined with pretty, pastel-coloured houses, the town's **Stadtplatz** is stretched out along a north–south axis, its northern end abutting the bridge over the Inn to Germany, while its southern end is closed by the imposing medieval **Torturm**, crowned with a tiny carillon. The town's chief landmark, though, is the spectacularly tall stone tower of the fifteenth-century **Stephanskirche**, to the west of the main square, a hybrid affair decorated with blind Gothic tracery and topped by a giant onion dome, which reaches to a height of nearly 100m. The exterior is plastered with finely carved grave slabs, including that of Hans Staininger, whose curly beard reaches down to his toes, while the interior features net vaulting and a series of fine Baroque side chapels, one of which is flanked by a superb pair of grimly reaping skeletons.

Outside **Hitler's birthplace** at Salzburger Vorstadt 15, on the far side of the Torturm, stands a large slab of granite from Mauthausen (see p.236), inscribed with the words "For peace, freedom and democracy/never again fascism/in memory of the millions who died." Hitler's father, Alois, had been a customs inspector in Braunau for eighteen years, and was onto his third marriage (to his niece, and former maid, 23 years his junior) when the future Führer was born in 1889. He was actually born Adolf Schicklgruber, his paternal grandmother's maiden name (see p.197), and only became Adolf Hitler when his father changed his own surname in 1893, shortly after the family had moved to the nearby German border town of Passau. The family eventually settled in Leonding, just outside Linz.

Braunau's **train station** is about 1km east of the Stadtplatz, where you'll find the **tourist office** (Mon–Fri 8.30am–noon & 1.30–6pm, Sat 9am–noon; ☎07722/2644) within the *Volksbank* at no. 9. Two **hotels** enjoy the perfect location on Stadtplatz itself: *Hotel Post* (☎07722/63492; ③) is the plusher of the two, with all rooms en suite; *Hotel Gann* (☎07722/3206; ②) is simpler, and has some cheaper rooms with shared facilities. Braunau also has a **youth hostel** (☎07722/81638; mid-Jan to mid-Dec), 1km southwest of the Altstadt, at Osternbergerstrasse 57, and a **campsite** (☎07722/7357;

April–Sept) a similar distance to the southeast, on the other side of the River Enknach. *Bogner* is a great little place on Stadtplatz that brews its own **beer**, and serves pizzas, toast, coffee and cakes. Both the *Post* and *Gann* hotels have restaurants offering the standard repertoire of Austrian food at reasonable prices. For something slightly different, try the Tex-Mex on offer at *Cantina Mexicana* on Kirchenplatz, which also features live music at the weekend, and a regular tequila happy hour in the early evening.

Obernberg-am-Inn

OBERNBERG-AM-INN, 25km downstream from Braunau, is the smallest of the trio of pretty towns that dot the banks of the Inn. The wide expanse of its central **Marktplatz**, lined with boldly coloured Baroque houses sporting beautifully shaped gables, is, if anything, even more attractive than the one at Braunau. Two houses in particular stand out for their exceptional Rococo stucco-work: the bile-green *Café Woerndle*, and the adjacent pastel-pink apothecary, with a statue of the Virgin clad in pink occupying centre stage. Once you've soaked in the prettiness of the town square, there's nothing specific to keep you in Obernberg unless you want to grab a bite to **eat** at the excellent *Braugasthof zur Post*, on Marktplatz, which has main dishes from öS100/€7.30 and serves Keller Bräu from the nearby town of Ried. You can also **stay** the night on Marktplatz at the *Goldenes Kreuz* (☎07758/2202; ②), which has rooms with or without en-suite facilities. There's also the *Panorama* **campsite** (☎07758/2601; open all year), 1km southwest of the Altstadt, off Salzburgerstrasse.

Schärding

SCHÄRDING, 20km downstream of Obernberg, is more picturesque still, with a large and well-preserved Altstadt, surrounded by large swaths of its original fortifications. The sprawling, sloping, central **Stadtplatz** is broken up by two clusters of houses at the centre, but its most distinguished feature is the much-photographed **Silberzeile** – "Silver Row", so called because of its wealthy inhabitants – an uninterrupted, multi-coloured parade of identically shaped gables that form a wave-like roofscape on the north side of the square. The cobbled backstreets of the Altstadt are fun to explore, and the town retains several of its original gate towers, one of which, Burgtor, up Schlossgasse, allows access to the **Schlosspark**, laid out on the site of the town's old moated castle, and from which you get fine views across the Inn over to the German town of Neuhaus-am-Inn.

From Schärding, trains, buses and boats run north to Passau. Boats on the Linz-Passau run (May to Oct) leave from the Schiffahrtsstation at the northern tip of the Altstadt; trains and buses from Schärding's **train station**, 1.5km northeast of the Altstadt, beyond the River Pram. There are several **private rooms** (①) in the Altstadt, which you can book through the **tourist office** at Unterer Stadtplatz 19 (Mon–Fri 8am–noon & 1–5pm, ☎07712/4300). Without doubt the finest place to **stay** is the family-run *Förstingers Wirtshaus*, at Unterer Stadtplatz 3 (☎07712/2302; ⑥), though there's at least one less expensive option in the Altstadt in the shape of the comfortable *Hotel Scheurecker*, Innsbruckstrasse 6–8 (☎07712/4404; ④). The best place to feast on some typical Austrian **food**, washed down with the local Baumgartner Bier, is at the *Wirthaus zur Bums'n*, a traditional pub in the backstreet of Denisgasse.

travel details

Trains

Linz to: Braunau-am-Inn (hourly; 2hr 15min); Freistadt (every 2hr; 1hr 10min); Kefermarkt (every 2hr; 55min); Kremsmünster (every 2hr; 25min); Schärding (every 2hr; 1hr 15min); Steyr (every 1–2hr; 40min); Wels (2–3 hourly; 15–25min).

Wels to: Braunau-am-Inn (every 2hr; 1hr 30min–2hr); Passau (every 1–2hr; 1hr–1hr 30min); Schärding (every 1–2hr; 50min–1hr 15min).

Buses

Braunau to: Obernberg-am-Inn (Mon–Fri 1 daily; 45 min); Schärding (Mon–Fri 1 daily; 1hr 35min).

Enns to: Mauthausen (Mon–Fri 1 daily; 25min).

Linz to: Freistadt (Mon–Fri 20, Sat 8, Sun 6; 1hr 10min); St Florian (Mon–Fri 17, Sat 8, Sun 2; 35min); Wilhering (Mon–Sat 5 daily; 20min).

Steyr to: Kremsmünster (Mon–Sat 4 daily; 1hr); Wels (Mon–Sat 4 daily; 1 hr 40min).

Wels to: Kremsmünster (8 daily; 40min).

Boats

Linz to: Krems (May–Oct three times weekly; 4–6hr); Passau (May–Oct daily; 5–7hr).

CHAPTER FOUR

BURGENLAND

The diminutive province of **Burgenland** (*www.burgenland.at*) is the easternmost and the least Austrian Land of all. An integral part of Hungary from the seventeenth century, it was only handed over to Austria at the end of World War I, after a controversial plebiscite (see box on p.251) left the region's natural capital, Ödenburg (Sopron), in Hungary. Naturally enough, with an awkward salient virtually squeezing Burgenland in two, the province faced enormous problems, not just in terms of communications but in forging any sense of collective identity. Add to these the Russian occupation and the imposition of the Iron Curtain after World War II, and it's easy to see why the last decade or so has been by far the best yet in the region's history. Burgenland has long been a predominantly German-speaking region – hence why it was handed over to Austria in the first place – and the residual **Hungarian**-speaking community now makes up less than three percent of the total population. In fact, the Hungarians are outnumbered by the region's ten percent **Croatian** minority, whose ancestors were encouraged by the local Hungarian lords to settle here in the sixteenth century, to revitalize an area devastated by the Turkish army. However, apart from the odd bilingual sign, and the names of some of the border villages, you'd hardly even notice the presence of the Croatians, whose assimilation continues apace.

In the absence of Ödenburg, the small provincial town of **Eisenstadt** took over the regional administrative role. What brings most people to the town nowadays, however, is its affiliation with **Josef Haydn**, who spent some thirty years here in the second half of the eighteenth century, under the patronage of the powerful Hungarian **Esterházy family**. After Eisenstadt, the most popular destination in Burgenland is the nearby reed-fringed **Neusiedler See**, the country's largest inland lake and the only one in Europe with no natural outlet. For the Austrians, this is the closest the country gets to a coastline, and many come here purely and simply for a fix of beach culture. The **wine-growing** villages around the See have a distinctly Hungarian feel to them, as does the flat *puszta* (steppe) landscape and the consistently warm summer weather. The rest of Burgenland, south of the region's 5km-thin "waist", receives a tiny fraction of the tourists that pack the resorts of the Neusiedler See – and with some justification. The rolling, forested countryside is attractive enough, but there are very few places you'd go out of your way to visit.

ACCOMMODATION PRICE CODES

All **hotels and pensions** in this book have been coded according to the following price categories. All the codes are based on the rate for the least expensive double room during the **summer season**. In those places where winter is the high season, we've indicated both summer and winter room rates in the text.

① under öS400/€29.07
② öS400–600/€29.07–43.60
③ öS600–800/€43.60–58.14
④ öS800–1000/€58.14–72.67
⑤ öS1000–1200/€72.67–87.21

⑥ öS1200–1400/€87.21–101.74
⑦ öS1400–1600/€101.74–116.28
⑧ öS1600–1800/€116.28–130.81
⑨ over öS1800/€130.81

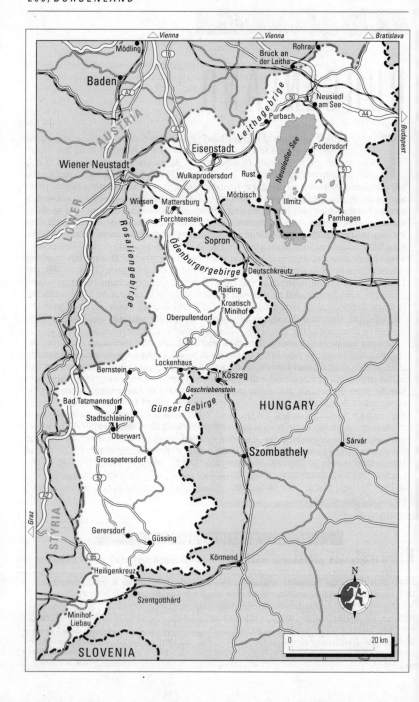

THE FIGHT FOR BURGENLAND

They may have shared an empire, but when the ruling dynasty fell in 1918, Austria and Hungary were at each other's throats in no time, arguing over their mutual border. The disputed territory comprised the four predominantly German-speaking border districts of western Hungary: **Pressburg** (Bratislava), **Wieselburg** (Moson), **Ödenburg** (Sopron) and **Eisenburg** (Vasvár). With no historical collective term for this area to hand, the Austrians, in the process of staking their claim, had to invent a name for the proposed province. They eventually decided on "Vierburgenland" (eventually reduced to Burgenland) not because of the number of castles in the region, but because of the endings of the four provinces.

Pressburg, however, was already occupied by the Czechs, and with only a forty percent German population, was soon disregarded; in addition, the rail line running through Wieselburg was deemed too strategically important to Hungary, and the district was taken out of the equation. In September 1919, therefore, just Eisenburg and Ödenburg provinces were added to the Austrian Republic as part of the Treaty of St Germain. At this point, however, the Allies wavered in their support of the treaty. Initially, they had strongly supported the Austrian claim, preferring the Social Democrat government in Vienna to Béla Kun's Bolsheviks in Budapest. However, when Béla Kun and his Communists fell from power and were replaced in November 1919 by the authoritarian regime of Admiral Horthy, the Allies' support for the left-wing government in Vienna weakened. Matters were complicated by the fact that the Austrians, who had been deemed an "enemy state" by the Allies, had been disarmed. Not so the Hungarians, who had been dubbed a "successor state" and who promptly refused to withdraw their troops, saying they were not a party to the treaty.

Eventually, in July 1921, the Hungarians themselves were forced to sign the Treaty of Trianon, agreeing to secede Burgenland. Once more, however, the Hungarians resisted and, under the noses of the Allied troops supposedly overseeing the transfer, drove the Austrians back out of the area. Yielding to the Hungarian military pressure, the Allies advised the Austrians to give up Ödenburg in exchange for the rest of the district. To add a little spice to the course of events, the exiled Habsburg Emperor Karl I turned up in Ödenburg on October 20, 1921, in the vain hope of resuscitating the Hungarian monarchy (see p.201). A plebiscite was finally agreed upon, whereby Ödenburg and eight surrounding rural communes would vote. The Austrians wanted the Hungarians to withdraw their troops before the plebiscite took place, and for the area to be occupied by Allied troops, but the Hungarians refused, in the end withdrawing less than a week before the December vote. Voting lists were therefore drawn up by, and the administration remained in the hands of, the Hungarians. In Ödenburg, the Hungarians got over seventy percent of the vote, but in the rural districts they narrowly lost. As a result, Burgenland lost both its natural centre and its capital. On January 1, 1922, the last border change resulting from World War I was completed, as Hungary formally accepted Ödenburg, now Sopron.

Eisenstadt and around

For a provincial capital – albeit of Austria's second smallest Land – **EISENSTADT** is a tiny little place, with a population of just 11,000. Situated some 50km southeast of Vienna, where the Leithagebirge fuse gently with the Hungarian *puszta*, it became the regional capital only by default in 1921 (see box above). The town is known, above all, for its associations with the composer **Josef Haydn**, who was in the employ of the local bigwigs, the Esterházys, for most of his adult life. Haydn may be the main draw nowadays, but the town also has a well-preserved **Jewish ghetto** and an excellent Jewish **museum**.

The Town

Eisenstadt's Altstadt comprises a mere three streets. **Domplatz**, the southernmost of the three, is open to traffic and used primarily as the local bus station; its fifteenth-century Domkirche was only given cathedral status in 1960 and, apart from its gilded pulpit and organ, is nothing special. **Hauptstrasse**, the pedestrianized main street, is prettier; among its striking facades is that of the Rathaus, with shapely Baroque gables, three oriel windows and lively folk paintings of the seven virtues.

Schloss Esterházy

Nothing prepares you for the sheer scale of the **Schloss Esterházy** (guided tours May–Oct Tues–Sun 9am–5pm; Nov–April Tues–Fri 9am–5pm; öS50/€3.63; *www.schloss-esterhazy.at*), which presides over Esterházy-Platz, at the western end of Hauptstrasse. The Schloss was built as a medieval fortress with bulky corner towers, later received a Baroque conversion, and was finally redesigned in Neoclassical style (though you can't actually see the fancy, colonnaded north facade overlooking the gardens). The result is a strange building, a sort of oversized French chateau, daubed in a fresh coat of imperial ochre-yellow paint set off by smart green shutters. Most of the rooms are now used as offices by the provincial government, but a few are open for an hour-long guided tour, which sets off on the hour and is usually in German, so ask for the English notes.

To be perfectly frank, the only room worth seeing is the one that kicks off the tour, the **Haydnsaal**, its coved ceiling smothered with more than thirty colourful frescoes,

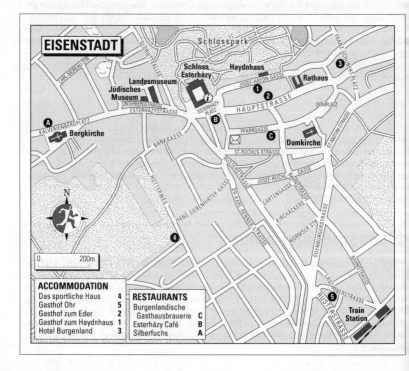

ACCOMMODATION

Das sportliche Haus	4
Gasthof Ohr	5
Gasthof zum Eder	2
Gasthof zum Haydnhaus	1
Hotel Burgenland	3

RESTAURANTS

Burgenlandische Gasthausbrauerie	C
Esterházy Café	B
Silberfuchs	A

s walls lined with painted roundels of Hungarian heroes. The acoustics are tremen-
ous, and Haydn himself conducted numerous performances of his own music here.
f you can catch a live concert, do (May–Oct weekly; *www.haydnfestival.at*) – it'll also
ave you having to endure the second half of the guided tour. This takes you round the
isterházy **Museum**, which contains Esterházy family treasures, and traces the his-
ory of the clan, who still own the Schloss and remain among the wealthiest landown-
rs in the country. At the end of this endurance test, you emerge in another fine con-
ert hall, the **Empiresaal**, which takes its name from the Neoclassical pastel green,
lue and brown trompe l'oeil decor. To get to the shady greenery of the **Schlosspark**,
ead down Glorietteallee; as well as the Neoclassical folly of the Leopoldinentempel,
here's a vast orangery, currently being restored to its former glory, and set to house
café.

Unterberg: the Jewish quarter

A hundred metres or so west of the Schloss lies the old Jewish quarter of **Unterberg**,
stablished as a walled ghetto back in medieval times, and for centuries home to a rel-
tively large Jewish population. All 446 of the town's Jews were deported to the camps
hortly after the Anschluss in 1938, and today there are just two Jewish families left in
isenstadt, though Unterberg has since been repopulated. The remarkable thing about
he district, however, is that despite the human destruction wrought on the communi-
y, the ghetto itself – comprised of five streets and two cemeteries to the north of
isterházystrasse – remains more or less physically intact. As you enter the ghetto's
nain street of Unterbergstrasse, you can even see one of the two stone piers between
vhich a chain was placed on the Jewish Sabbath (a practice that was continued right up
ntil 1938).

Further up Unterbergstrasse on the right, at no. 6, is the **Österreichisches
üdisches Museum** (Austrian Jewish Museum; May–Oct Tues–Sun 10am–5pm;
S50/€3.63), in the house that once belonged to Samson Wertheimer. Wertheimer was
hief administrator of financial affairs to three successive Habsburg emperors, became
irst rabbi of Eisenstadt, and was appointed Landesrabbiner (Chief Rabbi) of the
Iungarian Jewry in 1693 by Emperor Karl VI. The museum stages temporary exhibi-
ions on the ground floor, while the permanent exhibition on the first floor is a fairly
tandard rundown on Judaism, plus models of a few of Vienna's now demolished syna-
cogues and of Eisenstadt's old ghetto. Captions are exclusively in German, with the
nly English-language information in the museum's overpriced catalogue. On the first
loor is the **Wertheimer'sche Schul**, Wertheimer's private synagogue, built in the
arly eighteenth century, but whose trompe l'oeil decor dates from the early nine-
eenth. It was one of the few in the Third Reich to survive *Kristallnacht*, perhaps
ecause by then Eisenstadt had already been cleared of Jews, and was used in the
lecade after World War II by Jewish soldiers of the Red Army.

Another wealthy Jewish burgher's former home – the rather attractive house with
he corner oriel at the junction of Unterbergstrasse and Museumgasse – has been converted into the **Landesmuseum** (Tues–Sun 9am–noon & 1–5pm; öS30/€2.18). As
usual, there's no information in English, but the building itself is a lovely, rambling
nansion, with a plant-filled rooftop loggia, and, in the cellar, a whole series of impres-
ive Roman mosaics, the largest of which features Bellerophon killing the hybrid mon-
ter Chimera. The local history section on the first floor is particularly strong on the
erritorial dispute after World War I, with propaganda posters from the period, such as
)eath in Hungarian costume playing the fiddle over Ödenburg. Finally, you shouldn't
niss Franz Liszt's plushly furnished Blauer Salon, transferred here in its entirety from
he Schottenhof in Vienna, where the local-born composer stayed when in the capital
rom 1869 to 1886.

JOSEF HAYDN

"Well, here I sit in my wilderness, forsaken like a poor waif, almost without any human society, melancholy, full of the memories of glorious days gone by – alas, long gone! And who knows when these days shall return? Those wonderful parties . . . . Here at Estoras [Esterháza], no one asks me: 'Would you like some chocolate, with or without milk? Will you take some coffee, black or café Liègois? What may I offer you, my dear Haydn? Would you like a vanilla or pineapple ice?'"

Letter to Maria Anna von Genzinger, February 9, 1790,
from Josef Haydn

Of the big three classical composers, **Josef Haydn** (1732–1809) is seen as coming a poor third to Mozart and Beethoven, despite the fact that his music was in many ways just as radical – not only did he entrench the symphony, the string quartet and the sonata in the cultural landscape, he also experimented with the rigid Baroque symmetry of classical music, often developing a single theme in a way that prefigured much nineteenth-century music. Part of the problem undoubtedly lies in the ordinariness of both Haydn's character and his life – during his lifetime, he acquired the nickname "Papa Jo" for his generally amiable personality (notwithstanding his boorish behaviour towards his wife).

Haydn was born in the Lower Austrian village of Rohrau (see p.205). His father, a master wheelwright who played the harp, recognized his son's musical talents, and at the age of five Josef joined the choir of the Stephansdom in Vienna, where he was a pupil for the next nine years. At this point, in 1749 Haydn's voice broke, and he was kicked out of the choir, his little brother Michael becoming the new star pupil. Haydn then endured a difficult, poverty-stricken decade as a freelance musician, which finally ended with his appointment in 1758 as music director for Count von Morzin, a rich Bohemian nobleman. Two years later, Haydn made the biggest mistake of his life, as he later saw it, and married Maria Keller, the daughter of a hairdresser, with whom he could neither get on nor conceive children. She showed virtually no interest in his work, and is alleged to have used his manuscripts as pastry-pan linings and curl papers.

More auspiciously, in 1761 Haydn was appointed assistant Kapellmeister to the Esterházy family at Eisenstadt. Haydn's patron, Prince Paul Anton Esterházy, was a keen music lover – he even published his own songbook, *Harmonia Celestis* – but he died the following year. Luckily, he was succeeded by Prince Nikolaus (Miklós) "the Ostentatious", another music fan and a lavish entertainer. After a visit to Versailles in 1764, Prince Nikolaus decided to establish his own version of the French chateau, on the other side of the Neusiedler See from Eisenstadt. Although equipped with a theatre, opera house and a marionette theatre, the palace – named Esterháza (Fertöd) – was intended only as a summer residence. In the end, however, it became a more or less permanent home for Prince Nikolaus and for Haydn, now the family's chief Kapellmeister, who was, in any case, glad of the chance to escape his wife and sleep with his mistress, the young Italian mezzo-soprano, Luigia Polzelli.

In 1790, Prince Nikolaus died; his successor, Anton, was less interested in music (and had less money). The family's court orchestra was disbanded, but as a sign of respect for his loyalty the Esterházys continued to pay Haydn's salary and allowed him to keep his title. He immediately moved to Vienna, embarked on two long tours of England, and enjoyed late, but great acclaim, letting his hair down and earning himself a great deal of money at the same time. His final years were plagued by illness, and he died during the second French occupation of Vienna. Such was his renown that – so the story goes – Napoleon placed a guard of honour outside his house, and a French Hussars officer came and sang an aria from *The Creation* at his deathbed.

Haydn's Eisenstadt: the Haydnhaus and Bergkirche

The house that Haydn bought in Eisenstadt, where he kept chickens, two horses and probably a cow, is now the **Haydnhaus** (Easter–Oct daily 9am–noon & 1–5pm; öS20/€1.45), on Josef-Haydn-Gasse. This was Haydn's home on and off from 1766 to 1788, though there's no attempt here to re-create his abode in any way. With no information at all in English (unless you buy the pricey catalogue) and only a few battered sections of one of the composer's own organs to look at, this is one for all but the most fanatical to skip.

A better way of paying your respects to Haydn is to head for the squat, Baroque **Bergkirche** (April–Oct daily 9am–noon & 1–5pm; Nov–Feb by appointment only; öS20/€1.45; ☎02682/62638), which, as its name suggests, is located on raised ground 400m west of the Schloss, on the other side of Unterberg. The church interior is a trompe l'oeil fantasy in pinks and greys, but the reason most folk come here is to visit the purpose-built **Haydn-Mausoleum**, erected by the Esterházys at the west end of the church in 1932 in order to receive Haydn's decapitated corpse. At the time his head was still in Vienna's Gesellschaft der Musikfreunde, to which it had been bequeathed in 1895, having been stolen by one of Haydn's friends, a keen phrenologist, shortly after the composer's burial in Vienna in 1809. Finally, in 1954, Haydn's head was reunited with his body, and the whole of Haydn now lies in the marble tomb under the mournful gaze of four lounging cherubs.

The Bergkirche's other star attraction (covered by the same ticket) is the **Kalvarienberg** (Calvary Hill), accessible from the outside on the eastern side of the church. Here, steps lead up to a small chapel, beside which a turnstile lets you into a labyrinth of mini-chapels begun in 1701, recounting the story of the Passion through a series of theatrical tableaux of full-size statues. First, you enter a subterranean grotto, then you wind your way round the outside up to the Crucifixion tableau on top of the church (with great views over Burgenland), and finally back down to the Entombment on the other side.

Practicalities

Eisenstadt's **train station** is just ten minutes' walk southeast of the town centre; **buses** arrive and depart from Domplatz. You'll find the **tourist office** (May–Oct daily 9am–5pm; Nov–April Mon–Fri 9am–noon & 2–5pm; ☎02682/67390, *www.tiscover.com/eisenstadt*) in the east wing of the Schloss, and the regional Burgenland tourist office next door (times as above; ☎02682/63384-16, *www.burgenland-tourism.at*). The tourist office can help with **accommodation**, but they only have a handful of **private rooms** to offer at the height of the summer season. For hostel-style lodgings, try *Das sportliche Haus*, Hotterweg 67 (☎02682/62326-12; ②), a functional place aimed at visiting sports teams. There's nothing to choose between the two clean and unpretentious Gasthöfe in the centre, *Gasthof zum Haydnhaus*, Josef-Haydn-Gasse 24 (☎02682/64636; ③), and *Gasthof zum Eder*, Hauptstrasse 25 (☎02682/62645; ③), both of which have en-suite facilities. The excellent cooking of the *Gasthof Ohr*, Rusterstrasse 51 (☎02682/62460; closed Feb; ④), is a major part of its appeal; all rooms also have en-suite facilities and TV. Top-notch accommodation is available at the *Hotel Burgenland*, on Franz-Schubert-Platz (☎02682/696; ⑦), which boasts an indoor swimming pool and sauna. If you're **camping**, it's probably best to pitch your tent at one of the sites on the western shores of the Neusiedler See, and come to Eisenstadt on a day-trip.

A nice place to **eat and drink** alfresco, and enjoy a view of the Schloss, is the smart, but reasonably priced *Esterházy Café*, directly opposite in the former stables and winter riding school, on Esterházy-Platz. Alternatively, *Silberfuchs*, near the Bergkirche on Kalvarienbergplatz, offers a good range of Austrian dishes and daily specials for around öS75/€5.45. Another good bet is the *Burgenländische Gasthausbrauerei*, Pfarrgasse 22 where you can wash down your food with the new micro-brew, Haydnbräu. You can also eat well at the aforementioned *Gasthof zum Eder*, which has a sushi bar and a restaurant with a decent vegetarian menu.

Concerts are held in the Haydnsaal of the Schloss Esterházy from May to October and there are regular Haydn chamber music recitals performed in period costume (Thurs–Sat 11am). The big annual event, however, is the ten-day festival of Haydn's music called the **Internationale Haydntage**, held in the first half of September. The festival attracts top-class international performers, and the programme varies from large-scale orchestral works and operas to smaller chamber pieces. Tickets start at around öS200/€14.54, though you enjoy open-air screenings of past festival highlights for free in the Schlosspark. For more information, contact the tourist office, the festival box office (☎02682/61866) or visit the Web site *www.haydnfestival.at*.

Burg Forchtenstein and Wiesen

Even in a border region renowned for its castles, the fourteenth-century **Burg Forchtenstein** (April–Oct daily 9am–4pm; Schatzkammer öS70/€5.09; Waffenkammer öS70/€5.09; Kombi-Karte öS120/€8.72; *www.burg-forchtenstein.at*) 20km southwest of Eisenstadt, stands head and shoulders above the rest. On the one hand, it occupies an absolutely unassailable position on the eastern slopes of the Rosaliengebirge, with the most stupendous views across the *puszta*. On the other, it contains one of the finest arms collections in the country, courtesy of the Esterházy family, who have owned the property since 1622. It was the only fortress in what was formerly western Hungary not to be captured by the Turks in the 1680s. When the Turkish threat receded, however, Forchtenstein was deemed too uncomfortable for regular use, and became the family arms depot, and as early as 1815, a museum. You're free to walk round the **Schatzkammer**, with its dazzling jewelled armour, intriguing automata and Meissen porcelain, on your own. To visit the **Waffenkammer**, however you must join a guided tour (in German or English). The weapons remain *in situ*, as if the family's private troops might rush in at any moment and gird themselves up, and are displayed along with Turkish spoils and numerous family portraits. Forchtenstein makes a rewarding **day-trip** from Eisenstadt (or Wiener Neustadt), but public transport connections are pretty dire, and would need careful planning. The *Burgstüberl*, outside the castle gates, cooks up simple, inexpensive fish and meat dishes.

Burgenland's (and the country's) biggest open-air music events take place in the Festgelände, near the village of **WIESEN**, 5km north of Burg Forchtenstein. Begun in 1976 by Franz Bogner, the "Austrian Woodstock" is now big business, staging a whole series of summer festivals, ranging from a reggae *Sunsplash* to a *Jazz Fest*, and attracting thousands of punters. For more information drop into the *Jazz-Pub*, Hauptstrasse 140 in Wiesen (☎02626/81648), or visit the Web site at *www.wiesen.at*.

Neusiedler See

Eisenstadt is close enough to the **Neusiedler See** (Fertö to the Hungarians) to make a day-trip to its western shores perfectly possible, though you'll get more out of the area by staying over for a night or two. It's quite unlike anywhere else in Austria. Fringed by giant reed beds and vineyards, and set amidst the flat steppe landscape of the *puszta*, the area feels more Hungarian than any other part of Burgenland. The lake itself is a strange ecological phenomenon: it has no major water source feeding into it – the water just sits on the surface of the land, with a slightly saline quality to it. The water is never much more than one or two metres deep – it has been known to dry up

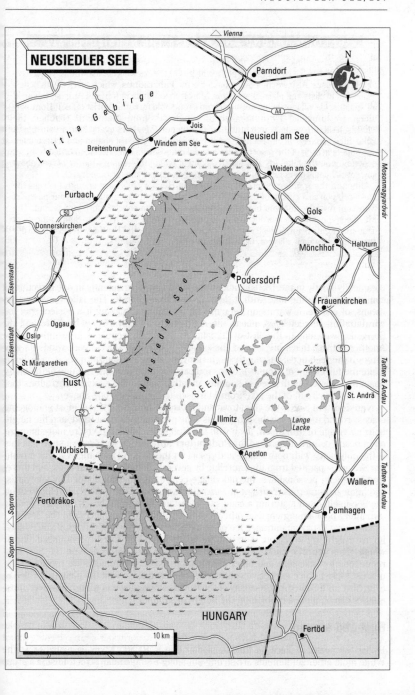

GETTING AROUND AND ACROSS THE NEUSIEDLER SEE

Train services link a few of the villages on the western shore with Eisenstadt and Neusiedl am See, as well as some of the villages of the Seewinkel. Elsewhere, you'll have to rely on buses. Also worth looking out for is the **Fahrradbus**, which carries both pedestrians and cyclists and plies its way from Mörbisch to Illmitz in July and August, calling at all the lakeside villages in between (pick up a timetable from the tourist office). **Boat services** are provided by a number of companies from May until October; the Mörbisch–Illmitz route is one of the most frequent (May–Oct every 30min 9am–6pm). **Bike hire** (*Radverleih*) is available from Neusiedl am See train station and from numerous outlets in each of the resorts; a day's rental ranges from öS75/€5.45 to öS150/€10.90, depending on the bike. It's also worth asking at one of the region's tourist offices about any special deals on combined tickets covering boat, bus and/or train travel.

Although the southern shore of the lake is in Hungary, it's easy enough to cross the border: if you're a citizen of the EU, USA or Canada, you can simply take your passport with you; if you're not, you may need to obtain a visa, so check before you set out. The Mörbisch–Fertörákos border point (daily: April, May & Oct 8am–8pm; June–Sept 6am–midnight) is for pedestrians and cyclists only, while the Pamhagen–Fertöd border crossing (open daily all year; 6am–midnight) is for cars, too.

completely (lastly in the 1860s) – and, if the wind blows persistently in one direction, it can literally take the lake with it, leaving one shore bereft. The lake's shallowness means, of course, it warms up very quickly in summer, making it a perfect spot for **windsurfing**. Its reed beds, meanwhile, are home to a wide variety of **bird life**, and the Seewinkel wetlands to the east of the lake are especially popular with ornithologists. Another activity that's big around these parts is **cycling**: a cycle path winds its way through the reed beds, passing through Hungary along the southern shore in order to make the full circuit of around 100km. You can also take your bike on one of the many boats that crisscross the See in summer months, and on the special Fahrradbus that does a partial circuit of the lake from Mörbisch to Illmitz (see box above).

Neusiedl am See is the chief town and transport hub, but the two most photogenic places around the See are the prosperous wine-producing town of **Rust**, and the neighbouring village of **Mörbisch**, flush with the Hungarian border. If you're more interested in beach culture, then head for **Podersdorf am See**, on the eastern shore, as this is the only place with both village and resort on the lake. All the other villages around the See are separated from the shoreline by several kilometres of reed beds, and therefore have split personalities: the old village centre, usually surrounded by vineyards, and home to numerous *Heurigen* or *Buschenschänken*, and the modern development on the See itself, often featuring a campsite, a restaurant, a small beach, and an open-air swimming pool among copious other leisure facilities. To gain access to the See, you usually have to pay an entrance fee of up to öS50/€3.63 per day, though if you're staying overnight in the region, then you are entitled to a **VIP-Card** (pronounced "Vip"), which gives you free parking and entry to most of the resorts around the See, plus reductions for bike hire and other charges; take your accommodation receipt to the nearest tourist office to receive your card. The best time to visit the Neusiedler See is from May until September, as many of the facilities close down in winter; however, mosquitoes can be quite a problem in the height of summer.

Rust and around

By far the prettiest place on the Neusiedler See is **RUST**, 13km east of Eisenstadt. While most other settlements are strung out along a single main street, Rust is a proper town, albeit a very small one, built from the profits of the local wine trade, and with a well-preserved Altstadt centred on the lovely cobbled square of **Rathausplatz**. The Rathaus itself, a seventeenth-century building decked out in Pompeiian red, is just one of the square's many perkily painted houses, each of which features big barn doors, and geraniums spilling out from windows flanked by French shutters. Above all, though, Rust is famous for its **storks**, whose nests perch permanently on the chimneys of just about every house in the Altstadt. Each year towards the end of March, these huge birds return to the very same chimney top, lay their eggs and rear their young, leaving around late August for warmer climes.

Overlooking the main square is the venerable **Fischerkirche** (Easter, April & Oct Mon–Sat 11am–noon & 2–3pm, Sun 11am–noon & 2–4pm; May–Sept Mon–Sat 10am–noon & 2.30–5pm, Sun 11am–noon & 2–5pm; öS10/€0.73), a tiny Gothic church set into the old town walls, and dating, in parts, to the thirteenth century. The interior is richly painted with medieval patterning and frescoes depicting the Crucifixion, and the cute little Baroque organ of 1705 is the oldest in Burgenland. The Fischerkirche tower is a great place from which to view the town's storks' nests; the rather handsome Baroque tower beyond the Fischerkirche belongs to the local Protestant church, testifying to the historic strength of Hungarian Calvinism in the area.

Practicalities

Rust's **tourist office** (May–Sept Mon–Fri 8am–noon & 3–6pm, Sat 9am–noon, Sun 10am–noon; Oct–April Mon–Fri 8am–noon & 1–4pm; ☎02685/502, *www.tiscover com/rust*), housed in the Rathaus, can organize private rooms – if it's closed, there's a free phone for booking **accommodation** outside the office underneath the archway. Budget recommendations include *Stadt Rust* (☎02685/268; ②), on Rathausplatz, with some rooms en suite, and *Arkadenhof* (☎02685/246, *arkadenhof@aon.at*; ③), on Franz-Josef-Platz, just outside the Altstadt. One of the choicest places to stay in the Altstadt is the sixteenth-century *Rusterhof* (☎02685/6416; ⑥; May–Dec only), also on Rathausplatz; the rooms all have self-catering facilities, the restaurant is excellent and booking ahead is pretty much essential. Another option is the modern *Hotel Sifkovits* (☎02685/276, *www.bnet.at/rust/tohotel.htm*; closed Jan & Feb; ⑤), just outside the Altstadt on the road to the lake, which also boasts an excellent restaurant. Like all the settlements around the See, Rust has a small lakeside development, 2km away through the reed beds. Here, you'll find Rust's new **HI hostel** (☎02685/591) and **campsite** (☎02685/595; April–Oct), plus a marina, beach and all the usual facilities for bike hire, windsurfing and so forth.

Apart from the excellent restaurants in the *Rusterhof* and *Sifkovits*, the nicest **places to eat** cheaply, and enjoy a taste of the local wine, are the various *Buschenschänken* in the Altstadt. A good one, with a typical vine-clad, cobbled courtyard is *Kicker*, on Haydngasse. The atmospheric cellars of the *Rathauskeller* (closed Wed), underneath the Rathaus, are also a pleasant place to while away the evening.

St Margarethen and Oslip

A handful of very disparate attractions lie immediately to the west of Rust: the **Märchenpark and Zoo** (March–Oct daily 9am–6pm; öS115/€8.36), a kilometre or so west of Rust on the road to St Margarethen. Along with the kangaroos, wild boar, deer and the like, there are various "animal shows", and rides of all kinds from waterboat slides to ghost trains.

The vast **St Margarethen limestone quarry**, a kilometre or so further along the road between Rust and St Margarethen, has something for everyone. Stone from the quarry was used to build the Roman town of Carnuntum (see p.203), and Vienna's Stephansdom. Nowadays, it's used primarily as a venue for an annual summer symposium of sculptors, and for open-air opera (*www.ofs.at*); every five years – 2001, 2006 and so on – it's also used for a Passion play to rival Oberammergau (*www.passion.at*). There's a tacky gift shop and a small exhibition of fossils, finds and sculptures from the quarry (öS35/€2.54), a café and organized fossil hunts for kids.

A few kilometres to the north of St Margarethen, just beyond the Croatian-speaking village of **OSLIP**, lies the enormously popular **Cselley-Mühle** (Thurs–Sat 5pm–midnight, Sun 11am–10pm; ☎02684/2812, *www.cselley-muehle.at*), a lovely old complex of farm buildings with a dovecote. Serious gigs take place here, accompanied by copious drinking. For a quieter venue head for the *Storchmühle* in Oslip itself, an attractive restaurant with a courtyard and terrace, famed for its Croatian and Hungarian specialities, and its live music in summer.

Mörbisch am See

MÖRBISCH, 5km south of Rust, is a classic one-street village, its whitewashed houses strung out like a ribbon along Hauptstrasse. Off the main street, beautifully scented cobbled courtyards, filled with potted plants and hung with vines and dried corn cobs, lead down to back lanes on the edge of the vineyards that press in on the village from all sides. You can visit one of these traditional houses (and its wine cellars) by following the signs to the **Heimathaus** (Easter–Oct daily 9am–noon & 1–5pm; öS10/€0.73) at Hauptstrasse 53; to get the key (and a guided tour in German), you must call in at the house across the courtyard.

Mörbisch is best known for its **Seefestspiele**, the annual open-air operetta festival that takes place on the See at the **Seebühne**, or floating stage, 2km east of centre, from the middle of July to the end of August. For information or tickets, you can book on-line or contact either the festival box office in Eisenstadt (☎02682/66210, *www.seefestspiele-moerbisch.at*) or, after the middle of June, the box office in Mörbisch (☎02685/81810). Sharing the lakeside with the Seebühne are all the usual waterfront facilities, including an especially good children's swimming pool. Cyclists and pedestrians can **cross into Hungary** at Mörbisch (daily: April, May & Oct 8am–8pm; June–Sept 6am–midnight), but car drivers must use the 24-hour border crossing at Klingenbach, more than 20km away by road.

Mörbisch **tourist office**, Hauptstrasse 27 (March to mid-June & mid-Sept to Oct Mon–Fri 9am–5pm; mid-June to mid-Sept daily 9am–6pm; Nov–Feb Mon–Thurs 9am–3pm; ☎02685/8420, *www.tiscover.com/moerbisch*), can assist with the bewildering array of **accommodation** on offer; it also has a free phone and vacancy information board. Try *Das Schmidt* (☎02685/8294, *www.tiscover.com/das.schmidt*; ④; Easter–Oct only), the large hotel on Raiffeisenstrasse, parallel to Hauptstrasse, which sports a nice arcaded balcony round the back; its rooms have en-suite facilities and views over to the See. The lakeside *Seehotel* (☎02685/8217; ③) is in the thick of the beach resort, while *Mörbischer Hof*, on Seestrasse (☎02685/8011; ④), has rooms facing the See, and its own swimming area in an adjacent inlet. *Seepension Stephanie* (☎02685/13815; ②) is hidden away in the thick of the reed beds, off the Seestrasse. The *Gemeindegasthaus*, Hauptstrasse 22, opposite the tourist office, serves good local **food**, with a pleasant *Gastgarten* out the back, and there are numerous other *Buschenschänken* to choose from.

Purbach am Neusiedler See

PURBACH, the most appealing of the villages to the north of Rust, also has the advantage of a **train station** and frequent **bus** services to Eisenstadt and Neusiedler See. The town's emblem is a stone statue of a bearded, turbaned Turk, known as the **Purbacher Türke**, to be found on the town's northern battlements (you'll need to ask a local for directions). It's by no means the only reminder of the Turkish threat: the double gateway of the **Türkentor** now protects the village from the main road, while two Turkish cannonballs can be seen within a glass-fronted niche (inscribed with the jokey warning "Türkennot") set into the wall of the picturesque old inn, *Purbachhof*, on Schulgasse.

The town's **tourist office** (May–Sept Mon–Sat 9am–noon & 3–6pm; July & Aug also Sun 4–6pm; Oct–April Mon–Fri 9am–noon; ☎02683/5920, *www.tiscover.com/purbach*) is at Hauptgasse 38. You can enjoy a memorable night's **accommodation** at the afore-mentioned *Purbachhof* (☎02683/5564; ④), or in *Am Spitz* (☎02683/5519, *amspitz@aon.at*; ③), set amidst its own vineyards above the village, a kilometre or so to the west, with a gourmet restaurant in a tastefully converted monastery (Thurs–Sun), and wonderful views over to the See. At Purbach's outlet to the See, 4km southeast through the reeds, there's a **campsite** (☎02683/5170; April–Oct), with a **hostel** attached, as well as all the usual leisure facilities. The village's numerous *Buschenschänken* offer the best **food and drink** options, with perhaps the prettiest of the lot, the thatched *Martinschenke*, Bodenzeile 16; *Turkenkeller*, Schulgasse 9, is another good option (Fri–Sun only out of season). Considerably more expensive is the high-class gourmet *Nikolauszeche* (☎02683/5514; mid-March to Nov only; closed Wed), housed in another beautiful old building at Bodenzeile 3–5, with a typical cobbled court-yard.

Neusiedl am See

NEUSIEDL AM SEE, the tacky, one-street town at the northern tip of the lake, is the only place with a frequent train service to and from Vienna; it's also a good place to get your bearings and pick up some information about the area – otherwise, its attractions are distinctly limited. If you've time to kill, you could do worse than check out the stag-geringly large private collection of bygone farming equipment at the **Pannonisches Heimatmuseum** (May–Sept Tues–Sat 2.30–6.30pm, Sun 10am–noon & 2.30–6.30pm; free), at Kalvarienbergstrasse 40, off Untere Hauptstrasse.

Neusiedl's **tourist office** (June & Sept Mon–Fri 8am–noon & 1–4.30pm; July & Aug Mon–Fri 8am–7pm, Sat 10am–noon & 2–6pm, Sun 4–7pm; Oct–May Mon–Thurs 7.30am–noon & 1–4.30pm, Fri 7.30am–1pm; ☎02167/2229) is conveniently located in the Rathaus on the main street. **Trains** from Vienna, and most buses, arrive at the main train station, some 2km northwest of the town centre (your train ticket covers the bus into town); the Bad Neusiedl-am-See station, three blocks south of the main street, is served only by slow Raaberbahn trains.

THE NEUSIEDLERSEEBAHN

The single-track railway to the east of the lake, known as the **Neusiedlerseebahn**, runs from Neusiedl am See to the Hungarian village of Fertöszentmiklós, and is a subsidiary of the Raab-Ödenburg-Ebenfurther Eisenbahn (RoeEE or GYSEV), established in the 1870s. The company is also known as the Raaberbahn as it also runs trains from Ebenfurth in Austria to the Hungarian city of Györ (Raab). This private line, whose trains sport a smart green and yellow livery, miraculously survived both the redrawing of the borders after World War I and the imposition of the Iron Curtain in 1945. The engines only changed over from steam to diesel in 1980, and the line was only electrified in 1986. It continues to be 61 percent owned by the Hungarian state, 33 percent owned by the Austrian state, and 6 percent owned by small shareholders, primarily the Port of Hamburg. Rail passes are valid, and the ticketing is fully integrated into the Austrian and Hungarian state-run railway systems.

If you need to grab a bite to **eat**, or **stay** the night, the *Rathausstüberl* (☎02167/2883; ③), situated directly behind the Rathaus, is hard to beat: it serves up a fresh fish of the day, has a shady, vine-covered courtyard and clean en-suite rooms. An alternative is *Hotel Leiner*, Seestrasse 15 (☎02167/2489; ④), which is quiet, but near enough to the centre. Neusiedl has the only official **HI hostel** in the area (☎02167/2252; March–Nov), fifteen minutes' walk from the station and the centre, at Herberggasse 1, off Wienerstrasse.

Podersdorf am See

PODERSDORF, 12km south of Neusiedl, is the only town that can really claim to be "am See". Don't come here expecting the charms of Rust, however; Podersdorf is basically a convenient and serviceable place with a pebbly beach, allowing easy, reed-free access to the water. It also happens to be the most popular destination in the whole of Burgenland, and the best spot from which to watch the sun set over the See. Swimming, boating, windsurfing, cycling, horse-riding and bird-watching are the chief attractions, though the village does boast a **Windmühle** (July & Aug; daily 6–7pm; öS25/€1.82), on the southern edge of town, off the road to Illmitz.

Podersdorf has two **tourist offices**: the main one is on the main street at Hauptstrasse 2 (July & Aug Mon–Fri 7.30am–noon & 1–6pm, Sat 8am–noon & 1–6pm, Sun 8am–noon; Sept–June Mon–Fri 7.30am–noon & 1–4.30pm, Sat 9am–noon & 2–4pm, Sun 9am–noon; ☎02177/2227, *www.tiscover.com/podersdorf*); the summer-only office (July & Aug, times as above; ☎02177/3400-20) is by the See, next door to the *Tauber* restaurant. Either office can book **private rooms**, and the main one has a computer screen outside showing the current state of room vacancies. In the especially busy months of July and August, you're best off getting the tourist office to book **hotel** accommodation for you, as vacancies can be thin on the ground. Most places are fairly simple, modern and functional, though some have pleasant inner courtyards and balconies: two such B&Bs are *Pension Steiner*, Seestrasse 33 (☎02177/2790; ②), which doubles as a *Heuriger*, and *Arkadenhof*, at no. 13 (☎02177/2402; ②). If you want a room overlooking the See, book in at the modern *Gästehaus Preiner*, on Seeweingärten (☎02177/2346; ②), or the nearby *Gasthof Seewirt* and its adjacent annexe, *Haus Attila*, on Strandplatz (☎02177/2415; ④). Podersdorf's **campsite** (☎02177/2279; April–Oct) is a vast, efficiently run site spread out along the shore to the southwest.

Undoubtedly, one of the best places to eat out is *Zur Dankbarkeit*, Hauptstrasse 39, which serves excellent Austrian dishes and is a real favourite with the locals. Seasonal fish, especially carp, zander and eel, feature strongly on the menu, served "in the pan" at *Pfandlwirt*, by the campsite, (hence the name), and served *gebacken* (in batter), *Serbisch* (spicy) or *blau* (natural) at *Gasthof Kummer*, near the seasonal tourist office. The cheapest and most convivial places to spend the evening, though, are the town's numerous *Heurigen*: try the *Heuriger zum 18er*, Seestrasse 40, a typical wine tavern with check tablecloths and a vine-strewn courtyard.

Frauenkirchen and Halbturn

If you're looking for a bit of cultural distraction around Podersdorf, pay a visit to the outstandingly beautiful **Basilika** in **FRAUENKIRCHEN**, 8km to the east. Built in the fourteenth century, and subsequently destroyed by the Turks on several occasions, the pilgrimage church was redesigned in High-Baroque style in 1702 by Francesco Martielli with Esterházy money. Inside, it's the cross-vaulted ceiling that makes the greatest initial impression, its frescoes framed by rich white and gold stucco-work. The richly carved pulpit, crowded out with polychrome angels and cherubs of varying sizes, also features an almost comical, disembodied gilded arm bursting out of the side and brandishing a crucifix. If you're hungry, drop into the *Altes Brauhaus* (closed Jan & Feb), on the other side of Kirchenplatz, which offers good regional specialities., and has a lovely shady garden surrounded by arcades, out the back.

The pretty, pale-blue Baroque **Schloss** (May–Oct daily 9am–6pm; öS60/€4.36) in **HALBTURN**, 5km northeast of Frauenkirchen, provides another welcome distraction. Designed in 1710 by Johann Lukas von Hildebrandt as a palatial hunting lodge for the Harrach family, and boasting a fresco by Franz Anton Maultbertsch, it now hosts temporary exhibitions taken from the imperial collections of the Österreichische Galerie. The chateau's formal gardens are perfect for a picnic, and there's a *Schlosstaverne* for those without provisions.

The Seewinkel

Podersdorf is also a good base for exploring the nearby **Seewinkel**, the marshy grasslands to the south, dotted with tiny, saltwater lakes, which provide a haven for a wide variety of flora and fauna. Much of the area has been granted protected national park status, and there's a solar-powered **Nationalparkhaus** (April & Oct Mon–Fri 9am–5pm, Sat & Sun noon–5pm; May–Sept Mon–Fri 9am–6pm, Sat & Sun 10am–5pm; Nov–March Mon–Fri 8am–4pm; ☎02175/3442), just outside **ILLMITZ**, 11km south of Podersdorf. Here, you can buy expensive binoculars, cheap local apple juice and head up the viewing tower to try and spot one of the estimated 250 different species of bird that live in the marshlands. Exhibitions, videos and talks are held in the centre, and, though most information is in German, there are folk who speak English on hand to advise on where to go and what to see. If you prefer, you can sign up for one of the centre's organized excursions, which cost öS100/€7.30 per person and usually last around three and a half hours. Note that there's a small entrance charge to each of the inland lakes.

One of the easiest places to spot some birdlife is around the **Lange Lacke**, 4km east of Illmitz, home to avocets, great white egrets and spoonbills. However, you'll need binoculars to get a good look at the birds, as the path keeps you some distance from the water. The Lange Lacke tends to dry up completely in high summer, but not so the **Zicksee**, a soda lake to the northeast, which is deeper than most of the other lakes, and, consequently, a popular place to swim, and yet still manages to be home to bitterns and black-necked grebes. The grassy beach on the eastern shore is more sheltered, much shadier and generally a lot more laid-back than the one at Podersdorf. The lake is a short walk from the nearby **train station** at **St Andrä am Zicksee**, and has a **campsite** (☎02175/2144; April–Sept). If you've come to the Seewinkel in search of the elusive **great bustard**, Europe's heaviest bird, head south out of the village of Tadten, 8km southeast of St Andrä, towards the Einser Canal, to the watchtower where, with a telescope (and a lot of luck), you might catch a glimpse of one in the swampy lands towards the Hungarian border; at the very least, you're very likely to see a raptor or two.

Southern Burgenland

Burgenland is very nearly split in two by the Sopron salient given to Hungary in 1922 (see p.251). At the region's "waist" there's barely 5km of Burgenland between the Hungarian border and Lower Austria. Add to this the thickly forested Rosaliengebirge and Ödenburgergebirge that form a continuous arc of hills from Sopron to Wiener Neustadt, and southern Burgenland starts to feel like a separate province. While Eisenstadt and the Neusiedler See feel as if they're teetering on the edge of the Great Plain of Hungary, southern Burgenland is a patchwork of gently rolling hills, forests, vineyards and rich farmland. There are very few places here that you'd go out of your way to visit, but if you're heading south to Slovenia or Styria the road that winds its way down the length of Burgenland is a pretty enough route to take. **Raiding**, the birthplace of Franz Liszt, receives a trickle of pilgrims, while **Lockenhaus**, hard by the Hungarian border, hosts a world-famous festival of chamber music. The museum in **Bernstein** dedicated to serpentine is of more general interest, as is the landmark castle at **Güssing**, in the far south of the province.

Raiding

The Hungarian composer Franz Liszt (1811–86) was born in the village of **RAIDING**, some 40km south of Eisenstadt, where his father was steward of the Meier estate. The family home, now the **Liszt Geburthaus** (Easter–Oct daily 9am–noon & 1–5pm; öS20/€1.45), like the Meier estate itself, belonged to the Esterházy family. Over the entrance to the lovely sixteenth-century whitewashed cottage, set in its own beautiful walled garden, is an old Hungarian inscription commemorating Liszt Ferenc, unveiled in the composer's presence (there's a picture of the ceremony in the museum), and a more recent one in German. Liszt spent the first eleven years of his life here, before the family moved to Vienna (where he studied under Czerny and Salieri), and eventually to Paris, to further the Wunderkind's promising musical career as "one of the great renovators of nineteenth-century music" – as the English notes say. As usual, there's very little attempt to re-create the interior as it would have been in Liszt's day, but, to the strains of his *Piano Concerto No. 1*, you get to see a lot of photographs of the wild-looking Liszt, who spent much of his life as a roaming virtuoso.

Buses to Raiding are pretty infrequent, but the nearest **train station**, Raiding-Lackendorf, is 2km north of the village; alternatively, you could hire a bike from the station at Deutschkreuz, 10km northeast of Raiding.

Lockenhaus and around

LOCKENHAUS (*lockenhaus.at*), at the foot of the Günsergebirge, 25km southwest of Raiding, is as good a place as any to stop off if you're passing this way. The town's focal point is its gargantuan Baroque **Pfarrkirche**, overlooking the main square, whose interior features a wild, technicolour high relief of winged cherubs clinging to giant acanthus leaves on the north wall of the nave and, on the opposite wall, a gruesome, full-scale Crucifixion scene, played out against a mural of Jerusalem. Check out the church's crypt, too, which contains several ornate red marble tombs belonging to the local Hungarian bigwigs, the Nádasdy family, into which the notorious "Blood Countess", Elizabeth Báthory, married (see box opposite).

The medieval fortress of **Burg Lockenhaus** (daily: April–Sept 7.30am–6pm; Oct & Nov 8am–5pm; Dec–March 8am–4pm; öS50/€3.63), which rises up out of the woods high above the town, is Burgenland's oldest, built around 1200 to defend the region against the Mongols. One wing has been converted into a hotel (see p.266), including the high-vaulted Rittersaal, formerly used for mass eating and drinking. It has two courtyards, the lower one having a pleasant *Burgtaverne*. Amid the hotchpotch of rooms on the first floor, the most intriguing is the double-apsed **Kultraum** in the exact centre of the castle, originally entered and lit only by a hole in the ceiling. It appears to have been connected with the ritual of the Knights Templar whose robed descendants still meet at the round table in the Burgherrenzimmer, off the upper courtyard. The castle also boasts a gruesome torture chamber with the original instruments and handy directions on how to use them – check out the hole in the "Iron Maiden" for the blood to run out. The Festsaal is used for concerts and forms the centrepiece of the town's world-famous *Kammermusikfest*, established by the Latvian-born violinist Gidon

THE BLOOD COUNTESS

Born in 1560, **Countess Elizabeth** was the offspring of two branches of the noble Báthory family. She shared a tendency towards fainting spells and fits of uncontrollable rage with other **Báthory** family members, like her uncle, Prince "Crazy" Gábor. As a child Elizabeth was intelligent and well educated, being fluent in Latin, Hungarian and German at a time when many nobles, including the ruling prince of Transylvania, were barely literate. Brought up in the family seat at Nagyecsed, a humble town near the Hungarian-Romanian border, she witnessed at the age of just nine the rape and murder of her sisters by the local peasantry, and absorbed from her surviving relatives the notion that peasants were little more than cattle – to be harshly punished for any act of insubordination.

As was customary in the sixteenth century, Elizabeth's marriage was arranged for dynastic reasons, and an illegitimate pregnancy hushed up. Betrothed in 1571 – the same year that her cousin István became prince of Transylvania – she was married four years later, at the age of 15, to 21-year-old Ferenc Nádasdy. In the course of the next decade, Ferenc was usually away fighting Turks, earning his reputation as the "Black Knight", while Elizabeth grew bored at the family's castles in Sárvár, Kereshtur and Lockenhaus. She began to torture serving women, an "entertainment" that gradually became an obsession. With the assistance of her maids Dorothea Szentes and Anna Darvulia (who was also her lover), Elizabeth cudgelled and stuck pins into servants to "discipline" them; even worse, she forced them to lie naked in the snowy courtyard and then doused them with cold water until they froze to death. Ferenc balked at this on his return (although he, too, enjoyed brutalizing servants), so it wasn't until after his death in 1604 that Elizabeth started torturing and murdering without restraint.

Her victims were invariably women or girls, and – most importantly – always peasants. Killing peasants could be done with impunity. Poor women could always be enticed into service and, should word of their deaths leak out, the authorities would hardly believe the accusations of the victims' parents against the countess. With the assistance of Szentes, Darvulia, Elizabeth's son's former wet-nurse Helena Jo, and one man, the diminutive Fizcko, the countess allowed her sadistic fantasies full rein. On occasion she bit chunks of flesh from servants' breasts and necks – probably the origin of the legend that she bathed in the blood of virgins to keep her own skin white and translucent.

In this fashion Elizabeth murdered over six hundred women and might well have continued undetected had Darvulia not died. Grief-stricken, the countess formed an attachment to a local widow, Erzsi Majorová, who encouraged her to seek aristocratic girls for her victims. Enquiries by their parents could not be so easily ignored by the authorities, who in any case by now had their own motives for investigating *die Blutgräfin*: Ferenc Nádasdy had loaned the Habsburg crown 17,000 gulden, which Elizabeth had persistently, and vainly, demanded back – if she were to be found guilty of serious crimes, this debt would be forfeited. Among Elizabeth's other adversaries were her son Paul, who had grown up apart from her at Sárvár, and one Count Thurzo, both of whom were anxious to prevent the confiscation of the Báthory estates and so gathered evidence against her.

On December 29, 1610, Thurzo's men raided Aachtice Castle, another family seat (now in Slovakia), and on entry almost tripped over the corpse of a servant whom Elizabeth had just bludgeoned for stealing a pear. Thurzo secretly imprisoned the "damned woman" in her own castle immediately, so that (in his words) "the families which have won such high honours on the battlefield shall not be disgraced . . . by the murky shadow of this bestial female". Due to his cover-up, knowledge of the scandal was mainly confined to court circles, although when Elizabeth died in 1614 the locals protested at her burial in Aachtice cemetery. She was later reburied at Nagyecsed in the precincts of the family vault. Due to her sex (then considered incapable of such deeds) and rank, records of her trial were hidden and mention of her name subsequently prohibited by royal command.

Kremer in 1981, and held annually in late June/early July. Last, but not least, the castle has a **Griefvogelstation** (April–Sept daily 10am–5pm, Oct Sat & Sun only; öS50/€3.63), home to numerous well-trained birds of prey, who put on regular demonstrations of their talons.

The **Hungarian border** is just 2km east of Lockenhaus, and, if you want to visit the nearby Hungarian town of Köszeg (Güns), which can justifiably claim to have the prettiest town centre in Hungary, there's a border crossing 8km further east at Rattersburg. If you just want to look over into Hungary, you could enjoy a full day's hike along the marked path to **Geschriebenstein** (884m), 10km south of Lockenhaus, the highest peak in the Günsergebirge, with a lookout tower from which there are glorious views over the Great Plain of Hungary.

Lockenhaus has a good **tourist office** (April–Oct Mon–Fri 8am–noon & 1–4.30pm; ☎02616/2247, *www.lockenhaus.at*), at Hauptstrasse 21, with a smattering of private rooms to offer. The most memorable **place to stay** is, of course, in the *Burghotel Lockenhaus* (☎02616/2394; ④), though make sure you get one of the atmospheric medieval rooms, and not one in the modern annexe. If the Burg is full, or your budget's not up to it, *Gasthof Schlögl* (☎02616/2225; ②), on Hauptplatz, is a good fall-back.

Bernstein and around

BERNSTEIN, 15km west of Lockenhaus, means "amber" in German, and most likely got its name from the ancient "Amber Road" that linked the Baltic to the Adriatic, and passed through the town. Confusingly, the gemstone for which Bernstein is best known, however, and the subject of the town's **Felsenmuseum** (March–Dec daily 9–11.30am & 1.30–5.30pm; öS50/€3.63), is **serpentine**, which was first commercially mined here in the mid-nineteenth century. Despite the lack of information in English, this is an intriguing museum, decked out like a dimly lit mineshaft, and glistening with all sorts of startling crystals and gemstones. On the first floor, you get to see what the local serpentine, which turns spinach-green when polished, can be made into at the hands of Otto Potsch, the sculptor who set up the museum. Potsch's slightly kitsch carved animals might not be everyone's cup of tea, but the craftsmanship is first class.

The main road runs right through Bernstein, so you're better off spending the night back in Lockenhaus, or continuing further south – unless, that is, you're up for staying in the medieval *Burg Bernstein* (☎03354/6382; ⑥; May–Oct), which sits above the village. This family-owned castle is the real thing, a wonderfully rambling place, complete with dungeon, ghosts and a candlelit dining hall with an Italian stucco-work ceiling; rooms have real fires, lots of antiques and few mod cons.

Most people seem to go to the walled town of **STADTSCHLAINING**, 12km south of Bernstein, to attend some conference at the UNESCO-funded Austrian Study Centre for Peace and Conflict-Resolution, which resides in the town's little medieval **Burg Schlaining**. You can also visit the castle on a thirty-minute guided tour (Easter–Oct Tues–Sun 9am–noon & 1–5pm; öS30/€2.18), which takes you up the round tower and past a bit of folk art and the odd leftover from the days of the Batthyány family, who sold it off to a local railway magnate in 1849. After the tour, you can eat, drink and relax in the dry moat, now part of the castle's *Burgtaverne*. Stadtschlaining does have one other, rather more intriguing sight: the **Friedensbibliothek** (Mon–Thurs 8am–5pm, Fri 8am–noon; free), housed in the town's former synagogue, across the Hauptplatz from the Burg through an archway at no. 3. The building has been lovingly restored, and its barrel-vaulted ceiling is richly decorated with trompe l'oeil plasterwork, so settle down with a book (there are plenty in English) and take some time out.

Some 10km south of Bernstein, the main road bypasses the smart spa town of **BAD TATZMANNSDORF**. Other than to take the waters, there are two main reasons you night want to pause here: to have a swim in the lovely open-air pool, on Josef-Holzel-Allee, off Bahnhofstrasse, or to visit the neighbouring **Burgenlandisches Freilichtmuseum** (daily 9am–5pm; öS10/€0.73). Neatly laid out in an orchard, with a few sheep, hens and goats for added authenticity, this laid-back open-air folk museum holds around fifteen, mostly thatched buildings that were commonplace in the nineteenth century. If your appetite is whetted, there's an even better selection of folk buildings near Güssing (see below).

Güssing and around

At the very foot of Burgenland (though not quite the toe), more than 50km south of Bad Tatzmannsdorf, the little town of **GÜSSING** (Németújvár) lies wrapped round the base of a medieval castle – a striking sight as you approach from the north. The rambling interior of **Burg Güssing** (May–Oct daily 9am–5pm; öS75/€5.45) contains a half-decent art collection, including one or two gems by Dürer and Cranach, plus an array of Turkish and Hungarian arms and armour; it also hosts special exhibitions, stages open-air events in its main courtyard, and has an inexpensive *Burgtaverne* with great views over the surrounding countryside. In summer, you can reach the castle via a state-of-the-art funicular (öS20/€1.45). The **Franziskanerkirche**, on Hauptplatz in the town centre below, is filled with gilded Baroque altarpieces, but the church's fame rests on its **Batthyánysche Gruft**, the Batthyány family mausoleum, which has a separate entrance set into the south wall of the church. Access to the ornate, eighteenth-century lead sarcophagus, commissioned by one of the Batthyány from eminent sculptor Balthasar Ferdinand Moll, has to be arranged through the priest. If you're here at the weekend, call in at the **Auswanderer Museum**, Stremtalstrasse 2 (May–Oct Sat & Sun 2–6pm; öS20/€1.45), which tells the story of the thousands of Burgenländer who emigrated to North America in the half-century leading up to World War I (Fred Astaire's father among them).

Güssing **tourist office** (Mon–Thurs & Sat 9am–noon, Fri 9am–noon & 3–6pm; ☎03322/42311-23) is at Hauptplatz 7, and can book private rooms for you. Other **accommodation** is limited, but *Hotel Josef Fabiankovits*, Hauptstrasse 49 (☎03322/42341; ②), and *Gasthof-Pension Kedl*, 3km north of Güssin, in Urbersdorf (☎03322/42403; ②), both have decent en-suite facilities. If you want something **to eat** or are just breaking your journey in Güssing, the *Stadt Café* is a stylish *Kaffeehaus* on the main street, and you can get full Austrian cuisine and pizzas at the *Gasthof zur Burg*, further down the street on Marktplatz. Alternatively, you could continue 10km south to Heiligenkreuz, where the warmly welcoming *Gasthof Gibiser* (☎03325/4216, g.gibiser@aon.at; ④) offers excellent food, and accommodation in lovely thatched buildings in the grounds.

Gerersdorf and Naturpark Güssing

It's only a six-kilometre drive from Güssing through the cornfields and vineyards to the privately run **Freilichtmuseum** (Mon & Wed–Fri 8am–3pm, Sat & Sun 10am–noon & 3–6pm; öS40/€2.91), in the village of **GERERSDORF**, to the northwest. This is an excellent open-air folk museum, where around twenty, mostly thatched farm buildings – from beehives and dovecotes to fruit presses and pigsties – have been reassembled. There's no information in English, but the German explanations are easy enough to follow.

Five kilometres to the northeast of Güssing, a large section of forest has been turned into a sort of open-air zoo – what the Austrians like to call a *Wildpark* – for rare and endangered species. Wild horses, red deer, water buffalo, European bison and several other unusual types of cattle have considerable space in which to roam, and can be easily spotted from the park's network of paths. The best time to see the animals at the **Naturpark Güssing** (free) is towards dusk, when they come out to feed. To reach the park, you'll need your own car: take the road east to Urbersdorf, and skirt the Stausee to the north.

travel details

Trains

Eisenstadt to: Neusiedl am See (hourly; 35min); Purbach am Neusiedler See (hourly; 20min); Vienna Meidling (Mon–Fri hourly; 1hr 10min).

Neusiedl am See to: Frauenkirchen (Mon–Fri 10 daily, Sat & Sun 6 daily; 25min); Pamhagen (Mon–Fri 10 daily, Sat & Sun 6 daily; 40min); Purbach am Neusiedler See (Mon–Fri hourly, Sat & Sun 9 daily; 15min); St Andrä am Zicksee (Mon–Fri 10 daily, Sat & Sun 6 daily; 30min); Vienna Südbahnhof (every 2hr; 50min).

Buses

Bernstein to: Bad Tatzmannsdorf (Mon–Fri 3–5 daily; 15min).

Eisenstadt to: Forchtenstein (3–4 daily; 30min); Rust (hourly; 1hr); Vienna (8 daily; 1hr 10min).

Neusiedl am See to: Podersdorf am See (Mon–Fri hourly, Sat & Sun every 2–3hr; 20min).

Rust to: Vienna (7 daily; 2hr).

CHAPTER FIVE

STYRIA

Styria (Steiermark; *www.steiermark.com*) reaches up from Austria's southeastern corner deep into the centre, across some of the most varied terrain the country has to offer. A gently undulating landscape to the south, rich in vineyards, orchards and fertile, arable land, gives way to the industrialized ribbon of the middle **Mur Valley** further north. Beyond here, in the increasingly alpine west and far north, a lack of classic skiing terrain ensures that imposing mountain ranges like the **Tauern** and the **Hochswab** preserve their laid-back, rural atmosphere.

Marketed today, reasonably enough, as the "green heart of Austria" by the local tourist board, Styria was historically the **industrial** powerhouse of the nation, with the rich iron-ore deposits of the **Erzberg** fuelling the iron and steel workshops of the Mur Valley. During the seventeenth- and eighteenth-century heyday of Habsburg expansion, this iron-based industrial might ensured a constant supply of weaponry to armies engaged in the struggle against the Ottoman Empire. Due to its position on the fringes of the Hungarian plain, Styria was, like Vienna, exposed to Turkish attacks from the fifteenth century onwards. The provincial capital, **Graz**, became the key military stronghold in a line of defences that kept the Turks out of central Europe, and for a while it rivalled Vienna, Innsbruck and Prague as a centre of political, cultural and religious influence.

Still the main target for most visitors to the province, Graz is one of Austria's most promising urban centres, an elegant and prosperous city with a rich choice of cultural diversions and a buzzing nightlife. It's also an ideal base for exploring the relatively little-visited region of **southern Styria**, whose agricultural villages and rural market towns have little in common with the alpine Austria of the tourist brochures. Wine-producing communities are scattered throughout the region, most notably in the villages towards the Slovene border, while apple growing sustains the settlements northeast of Graz. Undisputed king of the south Styrian farming scene, however, is the pumpkin, whose seeds are milled to produce the province's most characteristic culinary product, pumpkin oil (*Kürbisöl*). This dark, nutty-flavoured liquid, not unlike sesame oil, is as ubiquitous as salt and pepper in the region's restaurants.

The abundance of local rail links means that for those dependent on public transport many of the south's outlying attractions can be reached on day-trips from the Styrian

---

ACCOMMODATION PRICE CODES

All **hotels and pensions** in this book have been coded according to the following price categories. All the codes are based on the rate for the least expensive double room during the **summer season**. In those places where winter is the high season, we've indicated both summer and winter room rates in the text.

① under öS400/€29.07
② öS400–600/€29.07–43.60
③ öS600–800/€43.60–58.14
④ öS800–1000/€58.14–72.67
⑤ öS1000–1200/€72.67–87.21

⑥ öS1200–1400/€87.21–101.74
⑦ öS1400–1600/€101.74–116.28
⑧ öS1600–1800/€116.28–130.81
⑨ over öS1800/€130.81

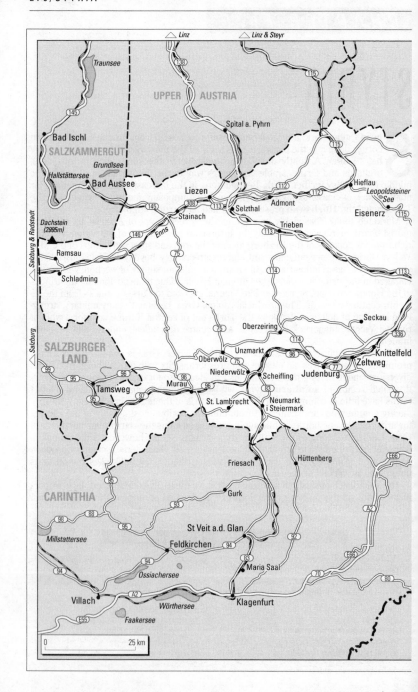

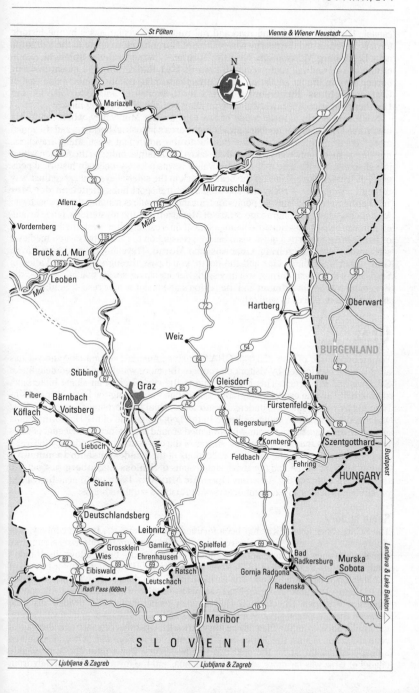

capital. The main southbound road and rail route to Slovenia passes by the historic town of **Leibnitz** and the nearby wine village of **Ehrenhausen**, home to the extraordinary **Eggenberg Mausoleum**. Near the Austrian–Slovene border at **Spielfeld**, another minor road and rail route veers off towards **Bad Radkersburg**, a quaint if sleepy border town in the far southeast. Main attractions in the rolling farmland due east of Graz are **Schloss Riegersburg**, Styria's most impressive medieval fortress, and **Hartberg**, an attractive historical town nestling beneath vine-bearing hills.

Northern Styria is really a tale of two regions: the Mur Valley, where workaday towns like Leoben and Judenburg proclaim the area's industrial heritage, and the much more appetizing mountain regions that lie to the north and west. Many travellers, hurtling at speed between Vienna and the lakes of Carinthia, only see the former, which is a shame: while it's true that the Mur Valley towns possess a certain historical pedigree, the real excitment lies off the beaten track in the side-valleys that carve their way through a sequence of rocky massifs. Important transport hubs, **Bruck an der Mur** and **Leoben** are good starting points for trips into the valleys fringing the Hochschwab Mountains, where the pilgrimage centre of **Mariazell** and the mysterious, pine-shrouded mining town of **Eisenerz** are main points of interest. Further west, the hilltop town of **Judenburg** is worth a quick visit, before pressing on to relatively isolated medieval settlements like **Oberzeiring**, **Oberwölz** and **Murau**. Travelling by road or rail from Graz towards Salzburg, Linz and the north, you'll pass through the **Enns Valley** in Styria's northwestern corner, worth visiting for its alpine scenery alone – here, the Benedictine abbey at **Admont** and the region's one major winter resort, **Schladming**, are the obvious places to stop off.

Graz

With a population of over 250,000, **GRAZ** ranks as Austria's second city, and yet has always been overlooked by visitors en route to the more widely publicized delights of Salzburg and Innsbruck. This is partly due to the city's lack of an alpine hinterland, although the Styrian capital's geographical situation – straddling the River Mur and surrounded by rolling hills – is undeniably attractive. Until the seventeenth century, Graz was a genuine rival to Vienna, as home to the Leopoldine line of the Habsburg family and an assemblage of aristocrats who swarmed around their court. The elegant palaces and town houses that line the narrow streets of the city centre bear testimony to Graz's Baroque heyday, as do the museum collections of the **Landesmuseum Joanneum** – among Austria's best – and the lavish state rooms of **Schloss Eggenberg**, just outside the town. In addition, the **Austrian Open-Air Museum**, 18km north near the village of Stübing, provides an excellent overview of Austria's rural traditions.

Some history

The Schlossberg above Graz has been fortified since at least the twelfth century, possibly earlier – the name "Graz", derived from the Slav word *gradec*, or fortress, suggests that the Slovenes were here several centuries beforehand – but the town itself didn't really come into its own until 1379, when Duke Leopold III, head of a junior branch of the Habsburg family, adopted Graz as his capital. The dukes of Styria subsequently based themselves here, ensuring Graz's status as a centre of imperial power – Leopold's grandson Friedrich III, crowned Holy Roman emperor in 1452, divided his time between three capitals: Graz, Wiener Neustadt and Linz. The town gained vital strategic significance: from the fifteenth century onwards, Graz was crucial to the defence of central Europe against the Turks, who first ventured into Styria in 1478 and remained a near-constant threat for the next two hundred years. For a time, the impregnable citadel of Graz was far more secure than Vienna, and the town benefited greatly from the influx of military architects, freebooters and warrior-aristocrats grown fat on the profits of the Turkish wars. Painters and craftsmen flocked here from northern Italy to decorate the palaces and town houses of Graz's sixteenth-century elite, and Baroque styles were adopted here a generation earlier than elsewhere in Austria.

Intellectuals, too, were drawn to Graz in the sixteenth century: as traditional Catholicism all but ebbed away in **post-Reformation Styria**, Graz became an important local centre for Protestant theologians and liberal-leaning academics. The astronomer Johann Kepler taught mathematics in one of Graz's Protestant schools in the 1590s, although a change in the religious climate eventually forced him, along with many others, to seek sanctuary in the more tolerant court of Emperor Rudolf II in Prague. The man who pulled the curtain down on Styrian Protestantism was Archduke Ferdinand (who, as Emperor Ferdinand II, was to become the principal architect of the re-Catholicized Habsburg monarchy), a fanatically pious, Jesuit-educated 18-year-old when he became governor of Styria in 1595. By expelling preachers, demolishing churches, burning books and harrying Protestant-leaning magnates, Ferdinand soon dragged Styria back into the **Catholic** fold. Lorded over by the Jesuits who had been introduced to the city by Ferdinand's father Karl, Graz was to become a major seat of Catholic learning during the seventeenth century.

On becoming emperor in 1619, Ferdinand moved his court to Vienna, and after the defeat of the Turks outside Vienna in 1683, the city on the Danube began to replace Graz as Austria's main political, cultural and commercial centre. Graz has loitered on the fringes of history ever since, although stout defence in the face of **Napoleon's armies** in 1809 endowed the place with a modicum of civic pride.

By the late nineteenth century, Graz's mild climate had made it a popular retirement choice for ageing army officers and civil servants, and its reputation as a conservative town swarming with pensioners has since proved hard to shake off. Nowadays, however, partly due to the presence of a 37,000-strong student population, it's a rich and culturally varied city, with plenty of night-time diversions. There's a distinct and internationally respected local school of **architecture**, which specializes in producing audaciously modern buildings on a human scale; although few of its products are tourist attractions in themselves, they certainly give the town a contemporary feel. Further evidence of the town's commitment to modern culture is provided by the *Steirische Herbst*, or **Styrian Autumn**, a festival of avant-garde music, theatre, art and film, which takes place every October.

Arrival, information and transport

Graz's **train station** is on the western edge of town, a fifteen-minute walk or short tram ride (#1, 3, 6 or 7) from the central Hauptplatz. **Buses** arrive either at the train station or at the bus station at Andreas-Hofer-Platz, a couple of blocks west of the Hauptplatz. Graz airport, 9km south of the centre, is served by about six buses a day from the train station, between 6am and 6pm (öS20/€1.46). A taxi doing the same trip will cost about öS200/€14.60.

There's a **tourist office** on platform one of the train station (Mon–Fri 9am–6pm, Sat 9am–3pm), and a bigger one a couple of hundred metres southeast of the Hauptplatz at Herrengasse 16 (Mon–Fri 9am–6pm, Sat 9am–3pm, Sun 10am–3pm; ☎0316/835241-11, *www.graztourismus.at*), either of which can provide free town plans and a wealth of brochures and advice.

Graz is served by an integrated network of local **buses** and **trams**. A single ticket costs öS20/€1.46 and is valid for one hour, including any number of changes. A 24-hour ticket costs öS42/€3.07, and a seven-day ticket, öS100/€7.30. Tickets can be bought from *Tabak* shops, the tourist offices, or from ticket machines at the main tram stops.

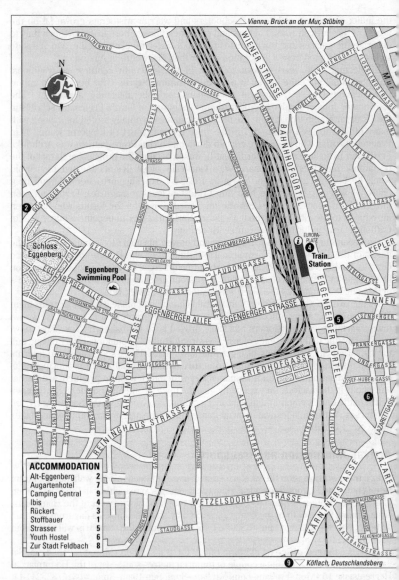

△ Vienna, Bruck an der Mur, Stübing

Schloss Eggenberg

Eggenberg Swimming Pool

EUROPA-PLATZ

ⓘ

④ Train Station

ACCOMMODATION

Alt-Eggenberg	2
Augartenhotel	7
Camping Central	9
Ibis	4
Rückert	3
Stoffbauer	1
Strasser	5
Youth Hostel	6
Zur Stadt Feldbach	8

⑨ ▽ Köflach, Deutschlandsberg

Accommodation

Budget accommodation is hard to come by in what is a prosperous, business-oriented town, although both branches of the tourist office will book private **rooms** (②); beware that almost all of these are a lengthy bus ride from the centre. The town's **youth hostel**, four blocks south of the station at Idlhofgasse 74 (☎0316/714876), is a pristine mod-

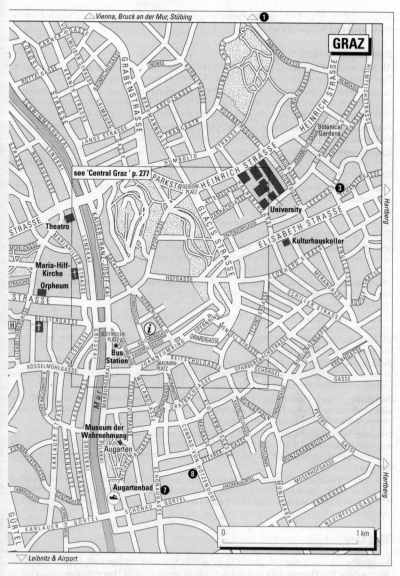

see 'Central Graz' p. 277

ern building with 4-bed dorms (öS230/€16.79 per person) or natty en-suite doubles (②; single occupancy is also available for öS390/€28.47). Reception is open 7am–11pm, with a longish midday break at weekends. It's an easy-going and justifiably popular place; book ahead if at all possible.

There are two **campsites** about 6km southwest of town, of which *Camping Central*, Martinhofstrasse 3 (☎0316/3785102, *www.tiscover.com/campingcentral*; bus #32 from

Jakominiplatz; May–Oct), is the easier to get to by public transport. There's a swimming pool and restaurant on site.

HOTELS AND PENSIONS

Alt Eggenberg Wagenhofer, Baiernstrasse 3 (☎0316/586615). Comfortable pension near Schloss Eggenberg offering good-value en suites with TV. Tram #1 from the train station. ③.

Augartenhotel, Schönaugasse 53 (☎0316/20800, *www.augartenhotel.at*). Ultramodern glass-and-steel palace in the quiet Augarten area just south of the centre. Ultra-cool minimalist rooms with big bathrooms, plus an indoor pool, and contemporary artworks in the reception and hallways. ⑨.

Erzherzog Johann, Sackstrasse 3–5 (☎0316/811616, *www.erzherzog-johann.com*). Atmospheric, old-fashioned city-centre hotel, with high standards of service and comfort. ⑨.

Grand Hotel Wiesler, Grieskai 4–8 (☎0316/7066-0, *www.gcongress.com/wiesler1.htm*). Graz's best (and most expensive) hotel, decorated in fin-de-siècle styles and just across the river from the Hauptplatz. ⑨.

Grazerhof, Stubenberggasse 10 (☎0316/824358). Good mid-range choice in the heart of town, although some of the rooms are on the poky side. ④.

Ibis, Europaplatz 12 (☎0316/778-0, *www.ibishotel.com*). Modern concrete wedge rising up out of the square in front of the train station. Good mid-range option, with en-suite facilities, air-con, satellite TV and telephone in all rooms. ⑤.

Iris, Bergmanngasse 10 (☎0316/322081). Pleasant pension in nineteenth-century apartment block within walking distance of both the city centre and the university district. It's on a noisy road, but the relative calm of the Stadtpark is nearby. ④.

Mariahilf, Mariahilferstrasse 9 (☎0316/713163-0). Nice old hotel just across the river from the centre, with a range of widely differing rooms. Those without en-suite facilities (④) can seem a bit threadbare; others are quite roomy and atmospheric. ⑤.

Rückert, Rückertgasse 4 (☎0316/323031). Pension housed in a suburban villa amid quiet, leafy streets 2km east of the centre. Handy for the university district. Good buffet breakfast. Take tram #1 from the train station, Hauptplatz or Jakominiplatz to Teggethofplatz, then walk down Hartenaugasse to Rückertgasse. ③.

Schlossberg, Kaiser Franz Josef Kai 30 (☎0316/8070-0, *www.schlossberg-hotel.at*). Bastion of luxury at the foot of Schlossberg hill, a few steps north of the city centre. Sumptuous rooms with antique furnishings, rooftop swimming pool. ⑨.

Stoffbauer, Oberer Plattenweg 21 (☎0316/685300, *stoffbauer@styria.com*). Smart but homely pension on the green fringes of the city, 3km north of the centre. Nowhere near any public transport routes, but worth considering if you have a car. ④

Strasser, Eggenburger Gürtel 11 (☎0316/713977, *hotel.strasser@noten.com*). Drab apartment building 5min walk south of the station, and therefore handiest of the budget places for a quick departure. Rooms with en-suite facilities (④) can be quite comfortable; those without (③), a bit cramped and gloomy.

Zur Stadt Feldbach, Conrad-von-Hötzendorf-Strasse 58 (☎0316/829468). Nineteenth-century apartment block 1km south of the centre. Uninspiring but habitable rooms with shared facilities (③) or with en-suite showers (④). Take tram #4 or #5 from Hauptplatz or from Jakominiplatz to Jakominigürtel.

The City

Most of what you'll want to see in Graz is concentrated on the east side of the River Mur, where the **Hauptplatz** and the neighbouring streets of **Herrengasse**, Sporgasse and Sackstrasse provide the core of a busy downtown area. Immediately above hangs the **Schlossberg**, site of Graz's medieval fortress, while the **Stadtpark**, to the east, provides the town with an attractive promenading ground. The main public transport hubs are on the east bank of the river, too: the Hauptplatz itself, as key crossroads for various tramlines; and Jakominiplatz, 500m southeast, where tramlines and local bus routes converge. There's little to see on the west bank of the river, save for a couple of

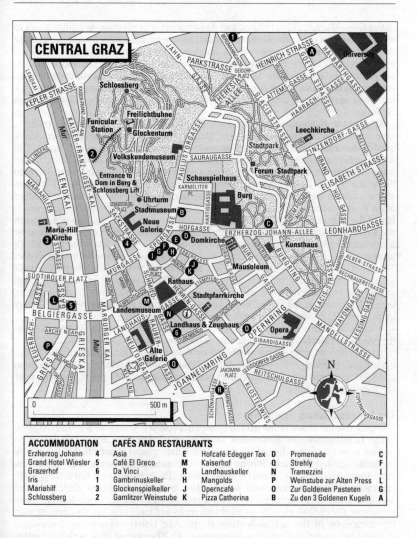

CENTRAL GRAZ

ACCOMMODATION		CAFÉS AND RESTAURANTS					
Erzherzog Johann	4	Asia	E	Hofcafé Edegger Tax	D	Promenade	C
Grand Hotel Wiesler	5	Café El Greco	M	Kaiserhof	Q	Strehly	F
Grazerhof	6	Da Vinci	R	Landhauskeller	N	Tramezzini	I
Iris	1	Gambrinuskeller	H	Mangolds	P	Weinstube zur Alten Press	L
Mariahilf	3	Glockenspielkeller	J	Operncafé	O	Zur Goldenen Pasteten	G
Schlossberg	2	Gamlitzer Weinstube	K	Pizza Catherina	B	Zu den 3 Goldenen Kugeln	A

Baroque churches and the princely residence of Schloss Eggenberg, some 4km from the centre.

The Hauptplatz and Herrengasse

Everything in Graz revolves around the **Hauptplatz**, a triangular market square bordered by seventeenth- and eighteenth-century facades. It also serves as the city's biggest tram stop, and is consequently alive with the bustle of shoppers and commuters most hours of the day. In the middle of the square stands a statue of Emperor Franz-Josef's uncle Archduke Johann, who did much to modernize Graz in the early nineteenth century, founding a Technisches Universität, sponsoring the construction of the Graz–Mürzzuschlag railway, and donating his art collection and other items to form the basis of the Landesmuseum, which now bears his name. Despite disgracing the family by marrying a postmaster's daughter from Bad Aussee, he was one of the few nineteenth-century Habsburgs to enjoy true mass popularity (for more on him, see p.452). The statue of the Archduke is accompanied by a quartet of nymphs symbolizing Styria's main rivers, the Enns, Mur, Drau and Sann – although the latter, rising in the south Styrian mountains was lost to Austria in 1918, and now flows through Slovenia.

Most of the Hauptplatz's buildings are dignified without being attention-grabbing, save perhaps for the Baroque **Luegg** on the northeastern corner, an apartment block gaudily decorated with orangey-yellow swirls of stucco. At the southern end of the square, where the nineteenth-century, neo-Renaissance **Rathaus** looms, Herrengasse leads towards the much more interesting **Landhaus** at no. 16, built in the 1550s to house the Styrian Diet. Designed by the military architect Domenico dell'Allio, who also worked on the fortification of the Schlossberg, it's quite an unassuming building when viewed from outside, although the Italianate arcading of the inner courtyard is one of the best examples of Renaissance architecture in Austria. You can pop through the archway to admire the courtyard's three storeys of balustraded galleries, linked by an elevated walkway – topped by pyramid-like bollards – which spans the courtyard's southern side. Next door to the Landhaus, the **Zeughaus**, or armoury (March–Oct Tues–Sun 9am–5pm; Nov–Jan 6 Tues–Sun 10am–3pm; öS60/€4.36), was built in 1642 to provide the citizenry with a readily available stock of weapons in case of Turkish attack, and is preserved very much in its original form. With over 30,000 helmets, breastplates, swords, pikes and other items on show, it's an impressive, if ultimately quite numbing, display of the town's erstwhile military might.

A little way further along Herrengasse, a fine eighteenth-century bell tower sits atop the **Stadtpfarrkirche**, an elegant jumble of Baroque and neo-Gothic styles that's home to an *Assumption of the Virgin* attributed to Tintoretto on the right-hand side of the nave. Equally striking is the postwar stained glass by Albert Birkle behind the altar: one panel (in the window to the left) clearly portrays Hitler and Mussolini watching over the flagellation of Christ.

The Landesmuseum Joanneum

The only real attraction in the grid of nineteenth-century streets west of Herrengasse is the **Landesmuseum Joanneum** (*www.museum-johanneum.at*), a vast collection housed in two separate, though neighbouring, buildings and bequeathed to the city by the public-spirited Archduke Johann in 1811. The **natural history** section (Tues–Sun 9am–4pm; öS60/€4.36), entered from either Raubergasse or Kalchberggasse, embraces geology, zoology and botany. The attractively-mounted display of the (stuffed) fauna of Styria culminates with a stag killed by Kaiser Franz-Jozef in 1890; elsewhere, the endless glass cases filled with rocks and fossils can't really compete with the attractions of the **art collection** in the Alte Galerie (Tues–Sun 10am–5pm; öS60/€4.36), round the corner at Neutorgasse 45. The ground floor is rich in Gothic devotional work, much of it rescued from decay in the village churches of Styria, and credited to anonymous artists known only by the name of the place where their work was found. The "Master of St Lambrecht" is a good example; his *Cavalry Battle of St Louis of Hungary*, depicting the saintly monarch's victory over the Turks in 1377 (a victory attributed to the miraculous powers of the Virgin of Mariazell; see p.296), is a vivid evocation of the horrors of medieval warfare. The prolific fifteenth-century Tyrolean master, Michael Pacher (see p.429), is represented by the two-panel *Scenes from the Life of Thomas à Becket*, showing his martyrdom and funeral. Sixteenth- and seventeenth-century works on the first floor include a *Judgement of Paris* by Lucas Cranach the Elder, and a grippingly macabre *Triumph of Death* by Pieter Breughel the Younger. The rest of the collection focuses on the Austrian Baroque, with a representative selection of work by the "big four" – Rottmayr, Maulbertsch, Tröger and Kremser Schmidt – together with sculptures by the Graz-born J.T. Stammel.

The Mausoleum of Ferdinand II and the Domkirche

On the northern side of Herrengasse, Stempfergasse leads into a neighbourhood of narrow alleyways that dogleg their way up the hill towards the **Mausoleum of Ferdinand II** (May–Oct Mon–Sat 11am–noon & 2–3pm; Nov–April Mon–Sat 11am only; öS10/€0.72), a dome-encrusted structure that was begun in 1614 when the intended incumbent was a healthy 36 years old. Designed by the Italian Pietro de Pomis, who spent most of his life working for a Styrian aristocracy greedy for Italian style, the mausoleum skilfully blends a variety of styles, coming over as a cross between Classical temple and Baroque church. Prominent among the statues which seem poised to topple from the pediment is a graceful figure of St Catherine, resting against the wheel on which she was tortured, and flanked by two angels. Inside, Ferdinand is entombed alongside a sarcophagus intended for both his parents, Emperor Karl II and Maria of Bavaria, although only Maria is actually buried here (her husband lies in the Abbey of Seckau; see p.302). The fine stucco-work on the ceiling and some of the frescoes were added by Fischer von Erlach in the 1690s.

Next door is the **Domkirche**, or cathedral, which has preserved much of its late-fifteenth-century Gothic character. It was built by Emperor Friedrich III, whose coat of arms and whose motto, AEIOU (usually taken to stand for *Austria Erit In Orbe Ultima*, or "Austria will be last in the world", although see p.216 for other possible versions), adorn the west portal. Inside, there's a fifteenth-century Crucifixion on the right-hand side of the nave, but most of the other decorations are Baroque. The elaborate side altars are largely the work of local Jesuit craftsmen; the Jesuits were also responsible for gaining possession of the two fifteenth-century reliquary chests, each bearing ivory reliefs depicting allegories of Love, Death and Time among other moralizing subjects, which now stand at the entrance to the choir. Made to contain the dowry of Paola di Gonzaga, Duchess of Mantua, in advance of her wedding to Leonhard of Görz (a big cheese in Lienz; see p.361) in 1470, the chests ended up in the abbey at Millstatt (see p.354) – an abbey that was comprehensively asset-stripped by the Graz Jesuits when they took it over in the seventeenth century.

The Burg, Sporgasse and the Steirisches Volkskundenmuseum

Immediately north of the cathedral lies the **Burg**, once the residence of Friedrich III, who briefly made Graz one of three imperial capitals in the mid-fifteenth century (he also maintained courts at Wiener Neustadt and Linz). Now much rebuilt and given over to local government offices, there's nothing specific to visit here save for the double spiral of a fifteenth-century Gothic staircase, found in the archway at the end of the first courtyard. Another archway leads eastwards through the wall of the Burg directly into the Stadtpark (see overleaf), while Hofgasse heads west from the Burg towards Sporgasse, a busy shopping street that winds its way along the flanks of the Schlossberg. Among the many historic town houses that also line the **Sporgasse**, the **Palais Saurau** at no. 25 features an elegant seventeenth-century portal, and a Turkish figure throwing himself from a small upper window.

In its upper reaches Sporgasse becomes Paulustorgasse, where the **Steirisches Volkskundenmuseum**, or "Styrian Folklore Museum", at no. 13 (April–Oct Mon–Sat 9am–4pm, Sun 9am–noon; öS30/€2.19) houses the usual collection of traditional costumes and reconstructed house interiors, alongside a curious Baroque sculpture of the bearded woman St Kümmernis. According to a legend of Portuguese origin, the young woman in question prayed for facial hair in an attempt to repel the advances of a husband forced upon her by her heathen father. Crucified by way of punishment, she went on to become an important symbol of piety during the Catholic upsurge of the Counter-Reformation.

Sackstrasse and the Schlossberg

Leading out of the northern end of the Hauptplatz, **Sackstrasse** is one of Graz's most attractive streets, where former town houses of the nobility preside over the bustle of shoppers and rumble of trams. The plain exterior of the seventeenth-century **Palais Herberstein** at no. 16, built as a pied-à-terre for the Eggenberg family (see p.282), hides a marvellous staircase, which ascends towards ceiling frescoes depicting mythological scenes, as well as the luxurious Rococo interiors of the second floor, which now provide an absorbing backdrop to the paintings of the **Neue Galerie** (Tues–Sun 10am–6pm, Thur till 8pm; öS60/€4.36; *www.neuegalerie.at*), a municipal collection of nineteenth- and twentieth-century works that includes a sprinkling of Klimts and Schieles. The Palais Khuenberg next door at no. 18 was the birthplace of ill-starred Archduke Franz-Ferdinand in 1863, and currently houses the **Stadtmuseum** (Tues 10am–9pm, Wed–Sat 10am–6pm, Sun 10am–1pm; öS50/€3.63), notable largely for the excellent model of Graz as it looked in 1800. From here it's worth popping over the road to peep inside the portals of **Palais Attems** (now the offices of Graz's principal cultural festivals, *Styriarte* and the *Steirische Herbst,* see box p.285) at no. 17, where intricately patterned stucco mouldings overlook an imposing Baroque staircase.

From Schlossbergplatz, halfway down Sackstrasse, a balustraded stone staircase zigzags up to the **Schlossberg**, a wooded hill overlooking the town. Immediately underneath the staircase a tunnel leads to the **Dom im Berg** or "Cathedral in the mountain"; an atmospheric, barrel-vaulted space hosting state-of-the-art multimedia cultural exhibitions (times and prices depend on what's on) occupying one of the cavernous chambers used as bomb shelters during World War II. The tunnel continues past the Dom, climbing a gentle gradient before emerging on the eastern side of the Schlossberg – from where you can follow paths up towards the summit of the hill itself. Easier ways of scaling the Schlossberg include the Schlossberg lift (entrance right beside the Dom im Berg; daily 8am–9pm; öS20/€1.46 one way), or the Schlossbergbahn funicular, which departs from Sackstrasse's northern end (every 15min 9am–10pm; öS30/€2.19 one way). However you arrive, the top of the Schlossberg is one of the most popular strolling venues in the whole of Graz, a concentrated patch of wooded parkland from which you can savour panoramic views of the city. The Schloss from which the hill derives its name was the key point in the city's defences from the Middle Ages onwards, and held out stoutly against Napoleon's armies in 1809, although its destruction was made a condition of the subsequent Treaty of Vienna. Now only two main features survive, the first of which is the sixteenth-century **Uhrturm**, or clock tower, near the top of the staircase from Sackstrasse, whose steep overhanging roof figures prominently in the town's tourist literature – unusually, the clock's big hand is the hour hand. Uphill to the north, near the summit of the funicular, is the **Glockenturm,** or bell tower, set amidst parklands that are ideal for a picnic or a ramble.

The Stadtpark, the university district and the Augarten

Paths descend southwards from the Schlossberg towards Sporgasse, whence you can soon get back to the Hauptplatz; or eastwards to the **Stadtpark**, a leafy barrier that divides the city centre from the residential suburbs beyond. Laid out on the site of the town fortifications after their demolition in 1784, it's a popular area for a daytime stroll, and a smattering of cafés ensures it remains lively well into the evening. An unassum-

ing pavilion in the middle of the park houses the **Forum Stadtpark**, an important centre for avant-garde artists in the 1960s. The temporary exhibitions held here (Mon–Sat
2–6pm, Sun 11am–3pm; free) are always worth checking out – the tourist office should
have details of what's on. Continuing southwards, you'll soon come across the popular
and sumptuous *Promenade Café*, just outside the Burgtor, the medieval gate where
Hofgasse leads back into the city centre. Across the road from the café is the
Kunsthaus (daily 11am–6pm; prices vary), a modern venue for more top-notch seasonal contemporary art exhibitions.

Immediately east of the Stadtpark lies the **university district**, an initially unwel-
coming grid of nineteenth-century apartment blocks around Graz University, which
only really comes to life in the evenings – largely thanks to the numerous bars and
eateries catering for a youngish clientele. The imposing, nineteenth-century bulk of
the main university building itself lies just off Halbärthgasse, but the surrounding
area is short on real sights. Worth a brief visit, however, is the **Leechkirche**, a few
steps east of the park on Rittergasse, a delicate Gothic church with a delightful thirteenth-century relief of the Madonna and Child above the main portal. Before
becoming the parish church for Graz University, the Leechkirche belonged to the
Teutonic Order of Knights, and there's a fine grave relief of one of their number
inside. From here, Zinzendorfstrasse (subsequently Schubertstrasse) leads northeast towards the **Botanic gardens**, about fifteen minutes' walk beyond (April–Oct
Mon–Fri 8am–5pm, Sat & Sun 8am–1pm; free), site of one of the more well-known
examples of contemporary Graz architecture in the shape of Volker Giencke's stately greenhouses, which appear to rise naturally out of the ground like glass-and-steel
hillocks.

Returning to the Stadtpark, the broad sweep of the Burgring (later the Opernring)
heads downhill towards the southern fringes of the city centre, passing the nineteenth-
century **opera house** before arriving at **Jakominiplatz**, an important public transport
interchange. There's little of interest beyond here save for the **Augarten**, a stretch of
riverside park patrolled by pram-wielding parents and strolling pensioners. Lurking at
the park's northwestern end at Friedrichgasse 41 is the Oktagon, a turn-of-the-
twentieth-century building that originally served as a bathhouse and is now the
Museum der Wahrnemung (Museum of Perception; Mon & Wed–Sun 2–6.30pm;
öS40/€2.90; *www.muwa.at*). This entertaining but ultimately rather pointless museum
aims to demonstrate the fallibility of human senses through a small selection of installations and visual tricks, including the "mixed-identity mirror", in which the viewer's
features appear to blend with the face of the person sitting opposite.

West of the river

Graz west of the River Mur attracts few tourists, although the area around
Annenstrasse and Südtirolerplatz is a popular shopping area for the locals. Beyond
here, the grid of streets between the river and the train station becomes increasingly
drab and unappealing. There's one worthwhile church just across the river from the
town centre: the **Maria-Hilf-Kirche**, a popular pilgrimage church on
Mariahilferstrasse, whose exterior is best viewed from Kaiser-Franz-Josef-Kai on the
east bank of the river – from here you can fully appreciate the stupendous twin towers
of its facade, each bearing an elegantly tapering onion dome topped by a dazzling gold-
en sunburst. Slightly lower down, the pediment is crowned by a dramatic sculptural
ensemble, in which the Archangel Michael hurls a snarling demon towards the street.
Inside, the altar picture of the Virgin (hovering above the sick and destitute, accompanied by saints Francis, Anne and Clara) was painted by Pietro de Pomis, the artist and
architect employed by both Emperor Ferdinand II and Johann Ulrich von Eggenberg
to bring Italian style to Graz. De Pomis's final resting place is marked by a plaque on a
pillar to the left of the high altar. Hiding in cloisters behind the church is Graz's

Diözesianmuseum (Tues–Sun 10am–5pm; free except for special exhibitions), with Baroque statuary, and a wealth of late Gothic art including a fifteenth-century altarpiece from Bad Aussee in the Salzkammergut, in which a severely-tonsed St Leonhard is pictured performing various pious deeds, including releasing minor miscreants from the stocks, and overseeing the construction of an abbey.

Schloss Eggenberg

Situated some 4km west of the town centre at the end of Eggenberger Allee (you can reach it by tram #1 from the Hauptplatz or the train station – get off at Schloss Strasse), the Baroque **Schloss Eggenberg** was built for one of the region's most important families. Hailing from Bad Radkersburg in southeast Styria, the Eggenbergs became leading financiers in Graz before using their wealth to fund military careers. Ruprecht von Eggenberg led Austrian armies against the Turks in the late sixteenth century, and his son Hans Ulrich became Ferdinand II's chief minister. Accorded the title of prince in 1623 and appointed governer of Inner Austria (Styria, Carinthia and present-day Slovenia) two years later, Hans Ulrich was desperate for a residence that would match his status. Pietro de Pomis, already working on Ferdinand II's mausoleum in Graz, was the man for the job. Recognizing the post-Renaissance pretensions of Ferdinand II's new generation of courtly followers, de Pomis came up with a building that served as an allegory of universal order. Among the Schloss's more obvious symbols are the four towers marking the points of the compass, the 365 windows, and the 24 state rooms.

A ticket to the grounds (April–Oct daily 8am–7pm; Nov–March 8am–5pm; öS2/€ 0.14) allows you to amble around the landscaped **park** that boasts deer and peacock, and take a peek at the palace's elegant galleried courtyard. A ticket to the Schloss itself (May–Oct daily 9am–5pm; öS80/€5.81) includes entrance to the palace's three **museum collections** as well as a **guided tour** in German, but English summaries provided on request, (Mon–Fri hourly from 10am; Sat & Sun hourly from 9am) of the **Prunkräume**, or state rooms.

The museums

Of the three, the **Collection of Pre- and Early History** is probably the most interesting. There's a wealth of local finds from Hallstatt-period Celtic settlements, notably the metre-high bronze *situlae* (big ceremonial jars) decorated with either abstract patterns or rows of grazing animals. Pride of place goes to the eighth-century BC Strettweg chariot, a small but impressively ornamented bronze wheeled platform unearthed in a burial mound near the Styrian town of Judenburg. In the centre of the platform, a female deity holds up a bowl, while hunters, mounted warriors and impressively endowed male fertility figures cavort around her. Less gripping are the Roman-era domestic implements that make up the rest of the collection, most of which were culled by Habsburg-era archeologists from the towns of Ptuj and Celje, both now in Slovenia.

Aside from a couple of Egyptian mummies and a range of ancient Greek vases, the **Münz- und Antiken Kabinett** (Coin and Antiquity Room), the second of the three collections, is given over to a bewildering array of golden ducats and silver talers adorned with the heads of leading Austrian aristocrats – many of whom had the right to mint their own coins up until the nineteenth century. Worth looking out for are seventeenth-century pieces stamped with the imposing profile of Hans Ulrich von Eggenberg himself. Finally, a modest **Jagdmuseum** (Hunting Museum; the third collection) displays stuffed examples of a variety of alpine beasts, and didactic posters from the interwar years showing, among other things, the best parts of a stag's body to aim for when shooting.

The state rooms

Lasting almost one hour and conducted in German (a few explanatory words in English will be provided on request), the guided tour of the state rooms provides useful insights into the princely world of the Eggenbergs, although ultimately there's a limit to the number of Bohemian glass chandeliers and Baroque velvety wall-coverings that the human eye can assimilate. Visitors troop round a series of bedrooms, reception rooms and themed rooms (such as the Porcelain Room, with Chinese plates set into the wall, or the Romulus and Remus Room decorated with scenes from Roman mythology), but the highlight is the **Planetensaal**, or room of the planets, with paintings depicting signs of the zodiac and a figure of the sun-god Helios symbolizing Emperor Leopold I.

Eating and drinking

As befits a city of Graz's size, there are plenty of city-centre **restaurants** catering for a variety of tastes, none of which needs break the bank – although real bargains are more usually found in the university district to the east. As usual in Austria, the distinction between eating and drinking venues is quite a hazy one: many of Graz's cafés and bars serve good food (from snacks to full meals) at reasonable prices.

There are several classic coffeehouses in the centre, while night-time **drinking** revolves around two specific areas: the so-called **Bermudadreieck**, or "Bermuda Triangle", which comprises the streets of Prokopigasse, Färbergasse and Engegasse immediately east of the Hauptplatz; and the university district, east of the city centre beyond the Stadtpark. The Stadtpark itself harbours a couple of cafés and bars that shouldn't be ignored, especially on summer evenings when it's pleasant to sit outside.

For eating **snack food** on the move, there's usually at least one Würstelstand open 24 hours a day on the Hauptplatz. Just outside the train station, the *Annenpassage* subterranean shopping mall holds various fast-food joints offering sandwiches and French-bread pizzas during the daytime.

Cafés

Hofcafé Edegger Tax, Hofgasse 8. Venerable *Konditorei* whose origins are said to go back to the sixteenth century, selling a range of own-brand chocolates and fancy biscuits. The attached sit-down café is the favoured refuge of the city's more sedate citizens. Not cheap.

Kaiserhof, Kaiserfeldgasse 1. Another long-established upmarket café dripping with fin-de-siècle atmosphere. The nearest thing that Graz has to the classic Viennese coffeehouse.

Operncafé, Opernring 22. Popular city-centre café, mixing old-fashioned elegance with modernist decor. Attracts a mixed, young and old, crowd during the day, plus a smattering of affluent posers at night.

Promenade, Erzherzog-Johann-Allee. Neoclassical pavilion in the Stadtpark with an attractive, hi-tech interior. Good range of lunches and snacks – including the typically Styrian *Kürbiscremesuppe* (cream of pumpkin soup). Usually open after midnight.

Strehly, Sporgasse 12. A *Kaffee-Konditorei* serving excellent sweets and cakes. A large outdoor seating area makes it popular with city-centre shoppers.

Tramezzini, Sporgasse 2. Simple daytime coffee bar/night-time wine bar, with a tempting range of dainty sandwiches and more filling baguettes.

Restaurants

Asia, Färbergasse 7. Popular Bermuda Triangle joint serving reliable range of Chinese food, with cheap lunchtime menus.

Café El Greco, Schmiedgasse 18. Although hardly a budget choice, with typical entrées weighing in at around öS160/€11.68, the Greek menu is varied and excellent and there's live bouzouki music most nights. Closed Sun.

Da Vinci, Jakominiplatz 19. Big downtown café-pizzeria with a good range of inexpensive thin-crust *poes* and a wide range of pasta dishes too. Food available until 1am.

Gambrinuskeller, Farbergasse 6–8. Looks and feels like a traditional Austrian Gasthof, although it's actually a well-regarded Balkan grill restaurant. Wide choice of cuts of pork or beef, as well as cheaper Serbian staples like *pasulj* (pork and beans) or *sarma* (stuffed cabbage leaves). Closed Sun.

Gamlitzer Weinstube, Mehlplatz 4. Old-fashioned wine cellar in the centre of the Bermuda Triangle offering traditional Styrian snacks (such as *Bauernschmaus* and other cold-meat platters) as well as full Austrian meals.

Glockenspielkeller, Mehlplatz 3. Hearty, mid-priced Austrian staples popular with city-centre sightseers. Outdoor seating on a pleasant pedestrianized square.

Landhauskeller, Schmiedgasse 9 (☎0316/830276). Top-quality Austrian and Styrian fare in atmospheric medieval surroundings. Outdoor seating in courtyard during summer. Closed Sun.

Mangolds, Griesgasse 11. A self-service health-food restaurant a couple of blocks west of the river, but with limited opening hours: Mon–Fri closes 8pm, Sat closes 4pm; closed Sun.

Pizza Catherina, Sporgasse. Bright and breezy pizzeria with thin-crust pies in the öS90/€6.57 to öS110/€8.03 range.

Weinstube zur Alten Press, Griesgasse 8. Cosy place one block west of the river, offering a small range of cheapish Austrian and Styrian dishes.

Zur Goldenen Pasteten, Sporgasse. Traditional Styrian food on several floors of a late-medieval town house. Slightly more expensive than other central restaurants, this is a popular venue for a business lunch or a special family meal.

Zu den 3 goldenen Kugeln, corner of Goethestrasse and Heinrichstrasse. Student pub-restaurant decorated in the style of a cosy Gasthof, offering dirt-cheap Schnitzel-and-chips menus (from öS50/€3.65) to penny-pinching scholars. Good place to start a nocturnal tour of the University district.

Bars

Admiral Sportwetten Café, corner of Europaplatz and Eggenburgergürtel. A cross between bar, betting shop and amusement arcade, with TV screens carrying sporting events and results. Not much atmosphere as a bar, but a good place to catch midweek European soccer on the big screen.

Baltimore, Mariahilferplatz 5. Best place for a drink on the west bank of the Mur. Tasteful cross between pub and café-bar, with 1960s rock memorabilia (including an entire drumkit) on the walls and ceiling. A variety of soups, salads and sandwiches on the menu.

Bier Baron, Heinrichstrasse 56. 10 minute's walk east of the Stadtpark, but worth the effort. A large beer-hall-style venue with over twenty varieties of German, Austrian and Czech beer on tap. Food menu includes grills, pasta, and a small vegetarian selection.

Café Harrach, Harrachgasse 24. An enduringly popular student hangout one block away from the university, offering a bohemian pub atmosphere and simple snacks.

Der Kleine Elefant, Franziskanerplatz. Cool bar minimalist decor and jazzy background music, popular with a stylish upwardly mobile crowd.

Don Camillo, Franziskanerplatz. Stylish but homely Italian-themed bar drawing a varied clientele, ranging from the posey to the studenty. Big choice of wines and grappas, plus mouthwatering hams, cheeses and crostini. Closed Sun.

Flann O'Brien's, Paradiesgasse. Liveliest of the city's growing number of Irish pubs, attracting a cross-section of Graz society from students to suits. Large place with lots of seating and minimal barstool space; spills onto the Paradiesgasse in the warmer months.

Music House, Mondscheingasse 9. Cellar bar catering for a young, grungey crowd, in an alley just southeast of Jakominiplatz. Not on an established bar-crawl route, but worth heading out to if you need a fix of indie rock.

M1, Färberplatz. Smart drinking venue in the heart of the Bermuda Triangle area, on the third floor of a tastefully designed example of contemporary Graz architecture. Roof terrace in summer.

O'Carolan's, Badgasse 2. Nicest of Graz's Irish pubs if you want a quiet drink: intimate barrel-vaulted space with unobtrusive music, in a cobbled alleyway off Murgasse.

Park House, Stadtpark. A pavilion in the park usually open until 2am. DJs provide rock and dance music most nights, and live bands often play on Sundays. There's a snack menu featuring tasty salads.

Stern, Sporgasse 38. Medieval vaulted cellar with ascetic nineties' decor, three separate bar areas, and a relaxed, youngish crowd.

Stockwerk, Jakominiplatz 18. Funky bar above *Mcdonald's* with jazz on the sound system or live – big names sometimes appear here.

Three Monkeys, Elizabethstrasse 31. Stylish, dimly-lit cellar in the heart of the university district, with late-night drinkers crowding around a giant-sized oblong bar. Dancing at weekends; occasional live music.

Wartburg, Halbarthgasse 14. A favourite student hangout of long standing, hardly surprising given its location diagonally opposite the main university building. Primarily a large and raucous drinking venue, although cheap meals are available.

Entertainment

Graz's two main cultural institutions are the **Opera**, Kaiser-Josef-Platz 10 (☎0316/8008), for classical music, opera and ballet, and the **Schauspielhaus**, Hofgasse 11 (☎0316/8005), for theatre; both are closed in August. Tickets and programme information for both venues are available from the *Tageskasse*, Kaiser-Josef-Platz (Mon–Fri 8am–8pm; ☎0316/8000).

Touring rock or world music acts play at either the *Orpheum*, Orpheumgasse 8 (☎0316/913478), or *Theatro*, Neubaugasse 6 (☎0316/916027), which is also a jazz and fringe theatre venue. Other jazz venues include *Miles*, Mariahilferstrasse 24, a cramped and intimate bar hosting regular jam sessions by local musicians; and *Stockwerk*, Jakominiplatz 18 (see "bars" above), which attracts bigger touring acts.

For **clubbing**, best place for a drink and a bop is the *Kulturhauskeller*, Elizabethstrasse 31 (Tues–Sat from 10pm until the early hours; *www .kulturhauskeller.com*), a cavernous bar-cum-disco in the university district with a relaxed, and hedonistic clientele. Those in search of alternative-oriented clubbing should head for the west side of the river: *Screenbar*, on the same premises as *Theatro* (see rock and world music above) hosts cutting-edge dance music events at weekends; while *Arcadium*, Griesgasse 25 (*www.arcadium.at*), organizes a regular programme of techno, reggae and alternative rock nights. *Explosiv*, fifteen minutes' south of the centre at Schützgasse 16, is the venue for less frequent club nights (anything from ambient techno to hardcore punk) but is a little bit out of the way: best to check what's on before heading out. The best way to find out what's going on in Graz is to leaf through the local edition of the *Kleiner Zeitung* daily newspaper – or enquire at the tourist office.

FESTIVALS IN GRAZ

Graz's most important annual event involving high culture is **Styriarte**, a festival of top-quality opera and orchestral music that takes place from mid-June to mid-July. A variety of venues are used, including the Freilichtbuhne (open-air stage) on the Schlossberg. Information is available from the Styriarte Kartenbüro, Sackstrasse 17 (☎0316/812941-22).

The **Steirischer Herbst**, or "Styrian Autumn", takes place in October and focuses on the avant-garde in art, contemporary classical music, jazz, film and theatre. A great opportunity to catch up on experimental and ground-breaking work in all fields of culture, it is nevertheless a pretty cerebral affair. Exhibitions and performances take place in venues all over town, and programmes and booking forms can be obtained in advance from the Steirischer Herbst Informationsbüro, Sackstrasse 17 (☎0316/823007, *www.steirischerbst.at*).

Listings

Airport information ☎0316/2902-0.

Bike rental At the train station.

Books The English Bookshop, Tummelplatz, has a good selection of English-language paperbacks.

Car rental Avis, Schlögelgasse 10 (☎0316/812920); Budget, Europaplatz 12 (☎0316/716966); Europcar, at the airport (☎0316/296757); Hertz, Andreas-Hofer-Platz 1 (☎0316/825007).

Cinemas Kino Geidorf, Geidorfplatz, offers first-run international movies, as well as art-house films in the adjoining studio cinema.

Consulates UK, Schmiedgasse 10 (☎0316/826105). The nearest consulates for other nationalities are in Vienna.

Exchange Banks are open Mon–Fri 8am–noon & 2–4pm. Outside those hours try the main post office at Neutorgasse 46.

Football Graz has two top-flight football teams, Sturm and GAK. Both play at the Arnold-Schwarzenegger-Stadion, a stylishly modern 15,000-capacity arena in the suburb of Liebenau, 3km south of the centre (tram #4 from the Hauptplatz). Sturm have made successive appearances in the UEFA Champions' League and have a Styria-wide following: they have club shops both at the stadium itself and just outside the train station on the corner of Eggenberger Gürtel and Eggenberger Strasse.

Hospital Krankenhaus der Elisabethinen, Elisabethinergasse 14 (☎0316/7063). In emergencies, call ☎144.

Laundry Coin-operated machines and service washes at Putzerei Rupp, Jakoministrasse 34 (Mon–Fri 8am–5pm, Sat 8am–noon).

Motoring organizations ARBÖ, Kappelenstrasse 45 (☎0316/271 6000); ÖAMTC, Conrad-von-Hötzendorf-Strasse 127 (☎0316/504).

Pharmacy Bärenapotheker, Herrengasse 11 (☎0316/830267). Names and addresses of duty pharmacies are posted in the windows of all pharmacies.

Police Paulustorgasse 8 (☎0316/888-0). In emergencies, call ☎133.

Post office Neutorgasse 46 (Mon–Fri 7am–9pm, Sat 8am–2pm).

Swimming pools There's a large open-air pool at the Augartenbad, 1.5km south of the centre on the Schönaugürtel (tram #5 from Hauptplatz to Schönaugürtel); and there are both open-air and indoor pools at Bad Eggenberg, 3km west of centre near Schloss Eggenberg (tram #1 from Hauptplatz or the train station).

Taxis ☎0316/2801; ☎0316/1718.

Train information ☎0316/1717.

Travel agents ÖKISTA, Brandhofgasse 8 (Mon–Fri 9am–5pm).

Around Graz

The **Österreichisches Freilichtmuseum**, or Austrian Open-Air Museum, is a one-of-a-kind collection of vernacular architecture in an extremely attractive setting some 18km north of Graz. About eight trains a day make the twenty-minute journey from the Styrian capital to **Stübing**, the nearest settlement to the museum. Two other possible day-trips from Graz are the **Lipizzaner stud farm** at Piber and the Hundertwasser-decorated parish church at **Bärnbach**. Both small villages lie just north of the town of Köflach, about 40km west of Graz, which is served by regular trains on the privately owned Graz-Köflacher-Bahn (all rail passes valid).

The Austrian Open-Air Museum

Strung out along a pine-fringed vale, the **Österreichisches Freilichtmuseum** (April–Oct daily 9am–5pm; öS75/€5.48) preserves more than ninety outstanding examples of **village**

architecture. The whole thing is about 2km long, so you'll need a couple of hours in order to take everything in. Indeed there's such a bewildering array that the English-language guidebook sold at the entrance (öS30/€2.19) is a worthwhile investment.

Beginning with the easternmost provinces, the museum tackles Austrian architecture by region, so it's the thatched-roofed farmhouses of **Burgenland** that command initial attention. Encrusted with vines, and with verandahs running along their south-facing sides, these single-storey buildings have more in common with the architecture of Hungary and the Pannonian Plain than with the alpine, timber-built farmhouses that follow. Of these, there are numerous examples of **Rauchstubenhäuser**, farmhouses in which the living room was built around an open hearth, and which were once widespread across eastern Styria, Carinthia and Salzburg province. The most curious variation on this theme is the **Rauchhaus** from Siezenheim near Salzburg, a chimneyless dwelling in which smoke from the hearth was allowed to escape through slats in the ceiling. Grain was stored in the loft to be dried by the ascending smoke. Further along, the characteristic Tyrolean farmstead familiar from picture-postcard views of the Alps is represented by the **Hansler Farm** from Alpbach, a large square-shaped structure embracing both animal stalls and living quarters, with a wide gabled front and flower-decked balconies outside, and intricate wood panelling inside. At the far end of the complex stands the **Bregenzerwald Alphütte**, or alpine dairy, where cheese was made and stored during the summer before being taken down into the valley in the autumn.

You can go inside the houses, where traditional **crafts** such as bread-making, spinning and weaving are demonstrated by volunteers over the weekends, weather permitting. An **Erlebnistag**, or activity day, takes place on the last Sunday in September, featuring traditional food, folk dancing and displays of traditional agricultural machinery.

It's a twenty-minute walk to the museum from Stübing train station: turn left out of the station and bear right at the southern end of the village. There's a café-restaurant at the entrance to the museum, and a couple of Gasthöfe serve decent lunch fare back in the village.

Piber and Bärnbach

The **Gestüt**, or stud farm, at **PIBER** has provided Lipizzaner horses for the Spanish Riding School in Vienna (see p.100) since 1920, when it was moved here from the village of Lipizza (now Lipica in Slovenia). The farm can only be visited by signing up for one of the 75-minute guided tours in German with English-language summaries provided on request (Easter–Oct daily departing between 9–10am and 2–3pm; öS100/€7.30; ☎03144/3323). After watching a video providing a brief introduction to the farm's history, you can linger in the stables, and observe the horses grazing on the pastures above the village. Although the horses are renowned for their pure white coats, they are born almost black, gradually lightening as they get older.

A further 2km northeast, the village of **BÄRNBACH** huddles around the **Pfarrkirche St Barbara**, a church of postwar construction, which was extensively renovated in 1987 by Hundertwasser. The church displays several of Hundertwasser's playful, decorative trademarks, notably the use of multicoloured ceramic surfaces to jazz up the exterior. From a distance, the church's irregular, bent-looking roof, sporting red tiles covered in green spots, looks like the skin of a friendly cartoon dinosaur. Equally eye-catching is the series of gates in the small park surrounding the church; there are twelve of them in all, each of which ostensibly represents one of the world's major faiths or cultures. Those symbolizing Islam and Judaism are relatively easy to pick out, although there are some typically Hundertwasseresque eccentricities on display – notably the Urtor ("Ur-gate"), decorated with three round stones, inspired by the spiritual beliefs of prehistoric man (whatever they were), and an undecorated gate which represents the faithless. The church interior is restrained in comparison, but is

WINE ROUTES IN STYRIA

The best-known **wines** to come out of Styria are the dry white **Gewürztraminers** of the southeast, cultivated around Klöch, a village north of Bad Radkersburg, and the towns of Riegersburg and Hartberg. A variety of other whites are grown around Leibnitz and Ehrenhausen, and **Schilcher**, a medium dry rosé, is produced in the countryside near Deutschlandsberg and Stainz.

All this has encouraged local tourist authorities to promote the idea of the **Weinstrasse**, or wine-road, a suggested touring itinerary that links together the main vine-growing villages of a particular area. The most travelled of these routes in Styria are the **Schilcherstrasse**, which runs from Stainz southwards to Deutschlandsberg and on to Ebiswald near the Slovene border; the **Sausaler Weinstrasse**, which covers a small group of hilltop villages in the Sausal Gebirge just west of Leibnitz; the **Südsteirische Weinstrasse**, starting in Ehrenhausen and zigzagging its way west along the Austrian–Slovene border; and the **Klöcher Weinstrasse**, which heads from Bad Radkersburg northwards to Fehring. Local wine-makers sell their produce from a **Buschenschank** (the local equivalent of the Viennese *Heuriger*; see p.149), often no more than a converted garage with a few chairs and tables set out. There you can buy wine by the glass or the bottle, and enjoy a bite to eat, although food may amount to a simple platter of bread and cold meats.

Autumn is a good time to visit, when new wine is offered for tasting alongside a part-femented, lightly alcoholic grape derivative known as *Sturm*, which is best quaffed accompanied by another seasonal delicacy, *Maroni* (roast chestnuts). **Wine festivals** take place in Leutschach on the last weekend of September, Gamlitz on the first weekend of October, and Leibnitz on the second weekend of October (contact Leibnitz tourist office, see opposite, for details of these).

not without its attention-grabbing set-pieces: Hundertwasser's Lifespiral stained-glass window, a snail-shell swirl of colour to the left as you enter; and Erwin Talker's glass altar, a gargantuan fish tank of a thing filled with twelve different layers of soil (taken from the Vatican and Bethlehem among other places) to symbolize the twelve tribes of Israel.

Piber is 3km out of Köflach, while Bärnbach is a further 2km out along the same road. From Köflach train station, there are about seven buses a day (fewer Sat & Sun) to Bärnbach, passing through Piber on the way. Should you miss any of the buses, it's easy enough to walk to Piber from the station: head down Bahnhofstrasse to the town's Hauptplatz, turn right, then left onto Piberstrasse, which takes you to the village and the stud farm after thirty to forty minutes. Once you've looked round the farm, you can walk to Bärnbach in about 35 minutes. If you're visiting Bärnbach on its own, it's possible to get off the train at Bärnbach station (one stop before Köflach) and walk the 2km north into the village.

South of Graz

South of Graz, both the A9 motorway and the railway line speed towards the Slovene border, some 40km distant, passing Styria's prime pumpkin- and wine-producing areas en route. Despite being the main market centre for this rolling agricultural landscape, **LEIBNITZ**, 30km out of Graz, is more of a gateway to the countryside than a tourist town in itself, and it may be better to base yourself somewhere like Ehrenhausen just beyond (see p.290) if you're looking for a taste of the rural south. The Leibnitz tourist office is a good source of information on the villages to the south and east, and the town is also a useful launching pad for trips to the village of Grossklein, home to a small but rewarding museum of Celtic culture.

Leibnitz centres on the **Hauptplatz**, a bustling shopping area with a church at each end, neither of which really merits a visit. The town's main attractions lie further afield; Rudolf-Hans-Bartsch-Gasse heads west from the Hauptplatz towards the **Seggauberg**, a wooded hill on the other side of the river Sulm. Fifteen minutes' walk up the hill is **Schloss Seggau**, built by the archbishops of Salzburg in the thirteenth century. The Renaissance touches added by the region's subsequent rulers, the bishops of Seckau, can be appreciated by venturing into the elegant, galleried courtyard. Numerous Roman stone reliefs, many of them family gravestones, have been built into the walls of the Schloss, giving the courtyard the appearance of an outdoor sculpture gallery. Visits to the state rooms, including the bishopric of Seckau's picture gallery, are possible only by prior arrangement (☎03452/82435).

Immediately south of Seggauberg rises another hill, the **Frauenberg**, site of a Baroque pilgrimage church and the **Tempelmuseum** (April–Oct daily 10am–noon & 2–4pm; öS20/€1.46), built above a Roman-period temple of Isis. Associated with religious cults ever since the Celts first settled the hill a thousand years before Christ, the Frauenberg became a temple district in Roman times serving the people of Flavia Solva down in the valley. There's not much to see here save for the temple foundations and a few sculptural fragments, but the hillside setting is evocative.

Three kilometres southeast of Leibnitz, just beyond the suburb of Wagna, lie the remains of **Flavia Solva**, a once-thriving Roman garrison town established some time around 70AD. There's little left of the place save for a small grid of excavated streets, although the surrounding park will host a sizeable exhibition on the Romans in Styria during summer 2002, which will feature a reconstruction of a small Roman town, complete with craft shops, and an amphitheatre. In the meantime however, the archeological museum occupying a neighbouring pavilion is facing an uncertain future – best to make enquiries at the tourist office before setting out.

Leibnitz's **tourist office**, in a courtyard behind the town hall at Hauptplatz 24 (Mon, Tues, Thurs & Fri 9am–noon & 1–4.30pm, Wed & Sat 9am–noon; ☎03452/82620), has a wealth of bumf on the locality and can book **private rooms** (①) in town or in surrounding villages, including Ehrenhausen. Best of the central **hotels** is the *Römerhof*, just southeast of the Hauptplatz at Marburgerstrasse 1 (☎03452/82419; ③), which offers en suites with TV and telephone, and also has a good **restaurant**.

The Celtic museum at Grossklein

Twelve kilometres southwest of Leibnitz, just off the Leibnitz–Deutschlandsberg road, the village of **GROSSKLEIN** is home to the small but well-laid out Museum der Hallstattzeit (Museum of the Hallstatt Period; Tues–Sun 10am–noon & 2–4.30pm; öS35/€2.56). Recalling the Celtic culture of the Late Bronze Age (a period named after the village of Hallstatt; see p.447), the museum assembles a host of ornaments, weapons and implements retrieved from extensive eighth-century BC burial grounds located north and west of the village. Four of the graves are believed to be those of local princelings, and it's in one of these that the museum's star exhibits were found: an exquisite ceremonial bronze face mask, and a bronze pair of hands engraved with geometric patterns. Elsewhere in the museum, there are a series of tableaux re-creating scenes from Hallstatt-era daily life, and an impressive collection of *Zisten* – large, lidded bronze containers decorated with animal and bird shapes.

The eight daily **buses** plying the Leibnitz–Arnfels–Leutschach route pass through Grossklein.

Ehrenhausen and around

Ten kilometres south of Leibnitz, the small village of **EHRENHAUSEN** lurks beneath a wooded crag chosen by the Eggenbergs as the site of the sixteenth-century fortress that served as a base for their campaigns against the Turks. The Eggenberg coat of arms hangs over Ehrenhausen's **Pfarrkirche**, centrepiece of an attractive village Hauptplatz. Most of the cherub-laden interior is the result of an eighteenth-century remodelling, although the high altar features a moving Pietà sculpted in the 1430s. On the right side of the nave, a stone relief marks the tomb of Christoph von Eggenberg, shown here kneeling in prayer and flanked by wife Helena and six children.

Christoph's son Ruprecht lies in the **mausoleum**, which dominates the village from a hilltop to the south and is accessible by a stairway from the southern end of the village square. A key to the mausoleum should be collected from the parsonage next door to the church before embarking on the climb. Having made his name by leading the Austrian army against the Turks at the Battle of Sisak in 1593, Ruprecht von Eggenberg engaged Italian architect Pietro de Pomis (whose masterpiece is the Mausoleum of Ferdinand II in Graz; see p.279) to design a suitably imposing funerary monument shortly before his death in 1611. The results are certainly impressive, with an elegant pastel blue facade flanked by towering, fancifully clad warriors, who appear to be sitting on vanquished lions. Austrian master builder Fischer von Erlach was drafted in by Ruprecht's descendants some eighty years later to plan an interior rich in late-Baroque imagery. Held aloft by Corinthian columns wreathed in vines, the cupola shelters roof angels brandishing, respectively, a skull, an hourglass, a burning torch and an extinguished torch – all serving as reminders of mortality. The Eggenbergs' castle, a short distance above the mausoleum, though still imposing, is private property and not open to the public.

Practicalities

There are plenty of private **rooms** (①) in the environs of both Ehrenhausen and neighbouring Gamlitz, 3km to the east, although you'll have to book them through the tourist office in Leibnitz (see p.289), or simply look for *Zimmer frei* signs. As for **hotels**, there's little to choose between the two nice old inns on Ehrenhausen's main square, both offering good-value, comfortable rooms: *Zum goldenen Löwen*, Hauptplatz 28 (☎03453/2312; ②), and *Zur goldenen Krone*, Hauptplatz 24 (☎03453/2640; ②). Either of these is also a good place to have a main meal or a quick snack and a drink.

Around Ehrenhausen

West of Ehrenhausen, Bundesstrasse 69 offers a scenic drive through a succession of villages sheltering beneath steeply banked vineyards. **GAMLITZ**, 3km away, is one of the most picturesque: it has a tourist office at Marktplatz 41 (☎03453/3922) as well as its own Schloss, which now holds a museum of the wine industry. Eleven kilometres further on, **LEUTSCHACH**, with a tourist office at Hauptplatz 8 (☎03454/6311), is another rustic wine-producing centre with a sprinkling of private rooms and *Buschenschänken*, or wine-taverns. From here, you can continue onwards to **EBISWALD** 20km to the west, where a right fork heads for the Radlpass and the Slovene frontier; alternatively, you can follow a minor road that meanders back towards Ehrenhausen through the extremely picturesque vineyard communities of Sulztal and Ratsch.

Bad Radkersburg

Nestling in flatlands of the far southeastern corner of Styria, where corn and pumpkins proliferate, **BAD RADKERSBURG** was once an important market centre for goods brought down the River Mur, and a crucial strongpoint in the Habsburgs' defences against the Ottoman Turks. Now that the main trade routes have shifted 35km to the west, the town has drifted into a provincial torpor, somewhat cut off from the main currents of Austrian life. The remains of sixteenth-century fortifications offer some reminder of the town's past glories, but today it's best enjoyed for its rural, market-town feel, and it's growing importance as a spa centre – the spanking new swimming pool just west of the centre is worth a dip, even if you're not here to take the waters.

On the opposite side of the River Mur is the Slovene town of Gornja Radgona, easily reached by a bridge immediately to the south of the town centre. You can walk over without any problem, providing you have a passport handy.

The Town

Bad Radkersburg's main point of reference is **Langgasse**, a bustling shopping street that bisects the town from north to south. A few steps east of here in the former armoury is the **Heimatmuseum**, at Emmenstrasse 9 (Mon–Fri 9am–noon & 2–6pm; öS40/€2.92), a fairly standard collection of local crafts and old farm tools, enlivened by a few oddities, as well as exquisitely painted targets used by nineteenth-century rifle associations, and the Negau helmet, an impressive bronze headpiece crafted by local Celts in the first century BC.

Further south along Langgasse, Kirchgasse leads through to the fifteenth-century **Pfarrkirche**, surrounded by the tombs of the knights who once defended this area against the Ottomans. Inside, a Gothic altarpiece shows Christ the Shepherd cradling a lamb. Just beyond is the **Hauptplatz**, ringed by elegant sixteenth-century mansions, many of which harbour leafy courtyards. More old houses, groaning under red-tiled roofs, are to be found along Murgasse to the south, beyond which you'll emerge onto the remains of the town's seventeenth-century **fortifications**. Remaining town walls girdle the town centre on the southern, eastern and northern sides, although there's little to savour apart from the sight of several protruding bastions, and a certain sense of crumbling grandeur.

Practicalities

Bad Radkersburg's **train station** is 1km north of town. Some trains are met by a local bus, which goes direct to the Hauptplatz (which is also the place to catch regional buses), otherwise it's quite easy to walk: turn left outside the station and then take a right into Bahnhofstrasse. The **tourist office**, at Hauptplatz 14 (April–Oct Mon–Fri 9am–6pm, Sat 10am–3pm; Nov–March Mon–Fri 9am–noon & 1–5pm, Sat 10am–noon; ☎03476/2545, *www.bad-radkersburg-online.at*), has information on private **rooms** (①). Some of these are central, but many are in the suburb of Altneudörfl, 1km west of town and handy for the spa facilities.

Among the numerous **pensions** available are the *Altneudörflerhof*, Altneudörfl 172 (☎03476/2253; ②), with comfortable, balconied rooms, 1km west of town; and *Gästehaus Ferk*, Murgasse 11 (☎03476/2584; ②), offering en-suite rooms in an old house in the town centre. Top spa **hotels** include the 4-star *Radkersburger Hof*, bang in the middle of the spa area just west of the town centre (☎03476/3560-0, *www.radkersburgerhof.at*; ⑥), offering swanky rooms and a range of spa treatments on site; or the smaller family-run *Hotel Garni Birkenhof*, Thermenstrasse 8 (☎03476/2461; ③), which has smart en suites and is near to the swimming pools. A **campsite** (☎03467/267725) lies at the western end of the town park, about 800m from the centre; it is well signposted from the southern end of town.

As far as **eating and drinking** are concerned, plenty of daytime cafés cluster around the Hauptplatz. *Bistro*, opposite the tourist office, offers pizzas, pasta dishes and traditional Austrian schnitzels, as well as performing the function of a daytime coffee-and-cakes venue. *Murstüberl*, just south of the main square at Murgasse 12, is a traditional Gasthof-restaurant offering good-value local food and wines, with outdoor seating in the courtyard.

East of Graz

East of Graz, road and rail routes head through arable farmland and orchard-bearing hills towards the southernmost finger of Burgenland and the Hungarian frontier at Szentgotthard. **Feldbach**, forty kilometres out of Graz, is a convenient point at which to take a breather, not least because it's the obvious jumping-off point for the nearby castle of **Riegersburg**, eastern Styria's most imposing attraction. Just beyond Feldbach, the branch rail line from Fehring to Wiener Neustadt winds through the hills of the Styria-Burgenland border to **Hartberg** (buses from Graz are quicker and more direct, but not quite so scenic), a bucolic wine-producing town that boasts a sprinkling of worthwhile historic sights.

Feldbach

Most people only stop in **FELDBACH** for as long as it takes to catch a bus to Riegersburg, and it shows. Tourist facilities in this humdrum town are minimal, and there's little to hold the visitor's attention save perhaps for the Tabor, a fortified quadrant of buildings erected around the parish church in the early 1500s. Built to provide the local populace with a safe haven in case of attack, the Tabor proved its worth during raids by the *haiduks*, Hungarian peasant bandits who raided the prosperous towns of eastern Austria in the early seventeenth century. The Tabor now houses a decidedly odd array of local **museums** (May–Oct Mon–Fri 9–11am & 2–5pm, Sat & Sun 9am–noon; combined entrance fee öS30/€2.19). These include an old smithy, a Styrian fishery museum featuring a variety of historic nets, a fire brigade museum, a geology museum, and an ethnographic collection showcasing antique agricultural implements, local costumes and a reconstructed eighteenth-century school room.

To find the Tabor, simply head down the single road into town from the train station, and you'll find it on your right after about five minutes. Regular **buses** to Riegersburg depart from Feldbach's train station, but if you get stuck here, the **tourist office** just beyond the Tabor on the Hauptplatz (Mon–Fri 9am–noon & 1–5pm, Sat 9am–noon; ☎03152/3079-0, *www.feldbach.tourismus.at*) will have a list of local **private rooms** (①).

Two kilometres north of the town on the Riegersburg road (Feldbach–Riegersburg buses pass by) is **Schloss Kornberg** (March to mid–Dec daily 10am–6pm; price varies according to exhibition), a Renaissance chateau that boasts a pentagonal galleried courtyard. It's now the venue for themed historical exhibitions and art shows: the tourist offices in Graz or Feldbach will have details.

Schloss Riegersburg

Ten kilometres north of Feldbach, **Schloss Riegersburg** is a breathtaking sight, dominating a landscape of rolling cornfields and pasturelands from a sheer crag of volcanic basalt some 200m above the valley floor. The original fortress was built in 1122 by

Rüdiger von Hohenberg to keep the Magyars at bay, although its current extent, including over 3km of walls and numerous gateways and bastions, dates from the seventeenth century, when the Turks were the major threat. It was acquired in 1822 by the Liechtenstein family, who still use parts of the building as a residence.

Pathways lead up from Riegersburg village through a succession of gates and outer fortifications, passing vine-bearing terraces and a memorial to the World War I dead, before arriving at the **Wenzelstor**, the entrance to the inner fortress. The **museum** (April–Oct 9am–5pm; öS90/€6.57) doesn't differ a great deal from any of Austria's other castle museums with its array of weapons, suits of armour and the odd cannon, but it's an excellently presented collection nevertheless. There's an understandable emphasis on the history of the **Liechtensteins** themselves: originally from Mödling near Vienna, they were influential in Habsburg court circles throughout the Middle Ages. However, their subsequent rise to princely status owed a lot to **Karl I** (1569–1627), whose statesman-like visage peers from many of the display cabinets in the museum. Despite being brought up as a Protestant, Karl chose to support the ultra-Catholic Ferdinand II in the religious disputes that foreshadowed the outbreak of the **Thirty Years' War**, and was responsible for rounding up and prosecuting rebellious Protestant nobles in Bohemia after 1620. Rewarded with vast tracts of land (often land confiscated from the rebels), Karl was made a prince for his efforts, although it was the family's acquisition of the crown lands of Vaduz and Schellenberg (the present-day Principality of Liechtenstein) in 1712 that secured their hereditary monarchical status. The museum exhibition ends with a tour of some of the castle's state rooms, most sumptuous of which is the fifteenth-century **Rittersaal**, whose ceiling and portals display stunningly intricate wood panelling.

Practicalities

Riegersburg is 13km south of the Graz–Wiener Neustadt motorway, although there are no direct buses from either of these two towns. For those dependent on public transport, the best way to get here is to take one of the eight daily trains from Graz to Feldbach, where there are six bus departures a day to Riegersburg. There's a small **tourist office** just outside the lowest of the castle's many gates (☎03153/8670, *www.riegersburg.com*), which will direct you to the growing number of pensions in the village (②). There are several Gasthöfe offering solid Austrian **food** and good-value **accommodation**: *Bio-pension Knapp ober'm See*, Riegersburg 165 (☎03153/8282, *pension-knapp@ccf.net*), at the edge of the village overlooking a small lake, has simple en suites (②), some with balconies; while those at the *Gasthof Fink*, Riegersburg 29 (☎03153/8216, *fink@surfen.at*; ④) are a shade more luxurious, and come with TVs. The former has a café with homemade cakes, while the latter has a superb Austrian-food **restaurant**.

Blumau

A minor road heads northeast of Riegersburg towards the provincial town of Fürstenfeld, 20km distant, and the village of **BLUMAU**, 10km beyond, a small spa-resort which can also be reached via the branch rail line that leaves the main Graz–Szentgotthard line at Fehring and heads north towards Hartberg (see overleaf). Blumau was a pretty unremarkable place until the opening in 1997 of the ambitious resort complex of the *Rogner Bad Blumau* just north of the village (and about 20min walk from the train station; ☎03383/5100; ⑦), designed by the eccentric architect **Friedensreich Hundertwasser**, whose unorthodox but enduringly popular creations can also be seen in Vienna (p.121) and Bärnbach (p.287). More of a self-contained village than a hotel, the resort draws a regular stream of Hundertwasser-inspired day-trippers, as well as those who want to take the waters. Indeed it's an impressive sight, with an irregular jumble of rainbow-coloured accommodation blocks linked by winding, crazily paved pathways to the swimming and spa facilities. Some of the hotel's roofs have been grassed over, mirroring the contours of the surrounding low hills.

Hartberg

Sprawling at the foot of the vine-covered Ringkogel hill, **HARTBERG**, near the Burgenland border, is one of the most pleasant small towns in Styria, combining a well-preserved historic town centre and an overwhelming sense of rural calm. It's little visited, which is surprising given its location just 4km west of the A2 autobahn from Graz to Wiener Neustadt (it's also accessible by train from either city, although the buses are quicker), and the relative wealth of tourist facilities on offer here.

At the southern end of a dainty Hauptplatz, the **Pfarrkirche St Martin** contains an impressive array of Baroque altars, notable for the striking contrast between the dark-grey pillars and pediments of their frames and their fussy gilt embellishments. Lurking behind the church is a squat round tower known as the **Karner**, or Charnel House, a Romanesque baptistry originally used to house the bones of the local dead. Inside are some fine thirteenth-century frescoes, if garishly painted over by nineteenth-century restorers. An *Apocalypse* near the ceiling portrays sinners being driven into the mouth of hell by a demon, while just below four princes riding fanciful beasts symbolize the worldly pursuit of wealth and power.

Just west of the main square, the **Stadtmuseum** on Herrengasse (Wed & Sat 9–11am) displays a few prehistoric implements and everyday utensils from the Roman settlement at Löffelbach 3km west of town. Just up the road from here is **Schloss Hartberg**, a largely modernized Renaissance building that now hosts art exhibitions. A pathway leads from the forecourt of the Schloss to the **Stadtpark**, which runs alongside crumbling remnants of the town's fortifications.

Practicalities

Hartberg's **train station** is some twenty minutes' walk east of town; head down Bahnhofstrasse and turn left in order to reach the centre. Buses use the forecourt of the post office, 300m east of the main square along Wienerstrasse.

The **tourist office** (Mon–Fri 9am–noon & 2–5.30pm, ☎03332/66505, *tourismusverband @htb.at*) is at Ressavarstrasse 23, just behind the Schölbingerturm, a medieval tower easily spotted if you're approaching the town centre from the east. They can provide a list of **private rooms** (①–②), although you may have to phone the places yourself to check on vacancies. Most of the rooms are to be found above town on the slopes of the Ringkogel, a lovely spot, although the walk uphill can be tough if you're heavily laden with baggage. Worth recommending is Theresia Oswald, Ring 272 (☎03332/63772; ②), who has a large house with excellent self-contained rooms, most of which have fine views of the valley below.

With such a wealth of good private rooms you may not need to fall back on Hartberg's **hotels**. Among them, *Zur Sonne*, Hauptplatz 9 (☎03332/62342; ③), and the nearby *Zum Brauhaus* (☎03332/62210; ③), are both nice old inns on the main square boasting cosy en suites with TV. There's a municipal **campsite** (May–Sept) just south of the centre and well signposted from the main road through town, with open-air and indoor swimming pools a stone's throw away.

Best place for a daytime bite to **eat** is *Café-Pub s'Eck* on Hauptplatz, which does ham-and-eggs-style brunches, tasty savoury pancakes, and is also a decent place for an evening drink. *Zum Brauhaus*, on the corner of Hauptplatz and Wienerstrasse, has the best range of stolid Austrian veal and pork dishes; while *Casa Mulino*, Hauptplatz 5, is an inexpensive and reliable pizzeria. For **drinking**, *Stadtheurige*, uphill from the main square along Presslgasse, is the place to sample local wines accompanied by cold meat snacks; while *Noarnkastl*, Wienerstrasse 10, is a friendly bar on the main street that also serves food.

Northeastern Styria

North of Graz, the gently rolling landscape of the Styrian south gradually gives way to a much more dramatic mixture of deep fir-lined valleys and craggy alpine peaks. Despite its undeniable natural beauty, the area is relatively untouristed in comparison with the more ski-friendly mountain regions of western Austria. The one long-established focus for travellers is the pretty pilgrimage centre of **Mariazell**, nestling deep in the northeastern corner of the province, although the ore-mining town of **Eisenerz** – where a combination of industrial heritage and alpine beauty seems ripe for discovery – has a mystique all of its own. The populous Mur valley is the area's main transport corridor, and harbours a couple of towns which are worth a quick peek before moving on. **Bruck an der Mur** is an important transport hub where you'll probably have to change buses for Mariazell; **Leoben** is the starting point for routes over the hills to Eisenerz.

Bruck an der Mur

Despite **BRUCK AN DER MUR**'s importance as a road and rail junction straddling major north–south and east–west routes, the town itself is an unassuming place that betrays few signs of its role as northeastern Styria's main business and shopping centre. From the train station at the southern end of town, Bahnhofstrasse leads down towards the foot of the **Schlossberg**, where a couple of pathways ascend towards the meagre remains of Schloss Landskron and an excellent view across the red roofs of the town centre. A five-minute walk down Herzog-Ernst-Strasse brings you to the main square, Koloman-Wallisch-Platz, lined by an attractive ensemble of ochre-hued town houses, and centring on a municipal well which sports an intricate seventeenth-century wrought-iron canopy. The square's most impressive feature is the flowery arcading of the **Kornmesserhaus** on the southeast corner, an incongruous slice of Venetian Gothic built for wealthy ironmonger Pankraz Kornmess in the final years of the fifteenth century. Providing something of a contrast are the caryatids and geometric designs adorning the Secessionist facade of the Antauer house, diagonally opposite at Koloman-Wallisch-Platz 10.

Bruck's star historical attraction is the **Ruprechtskirche**, a dainty Romanesque church nestling in the town graveyard fifteen minutes' walk west of the square (to get there, cross the river Mur and follow the main Leoben road until you see the graveyard on your left). The church's pride and joy is the fifteenth-century *Last Judgement* fresco occupying the arch above the high altar. A feast of vivid imagery, it portrays white-robed righteous folk trooping off to be met by a key-brandishing St Peter at the gates of paradise, while over to the right, sinners are roped together and led away by demons. The various forms of punishment that await them evidently allowed the artist's imagination to run riot; one particular torment involves having to stand in barrels of hot water while being bitten by frog-like amphibians.

Practicalities

Bruck's **tourist office** at Koloman-Wallisch-Platz 1 (Mon–Fri 10am–noon & 2–5pm, Sat 10am–1pm; ☎03862/890120, *www.bruckmur.at*), will help you find a **private room** (①), although most of these are in outlying villages and you may need your own transport to get there. Although billed as a **hostel**, the HI-affiliated *Jugend und Familiengästedorf,*

Stadtwaldstrasse 1 (☎03862/58448, *jgh.bruck@jgh.at*; ①–②), fifteen minutes' walk south of the centre, offers simple but smart double rooms in a woodland setting. Best of the **hotels** are *Schwarzer Adler*, Minoritenplatz 8 (☎03862/56768; ④), a traditional down-town Gasthof with comfy en suites midway between the train station and the main square; and *Arcotel Landskron* (☎03862/58458, *www.arcotel.co.at*; ⑤), a modern place by the river just west of the square.

There are plenty of **eating and drinking** opportunities on and around the Koloman-Wallisch-Platz. *Gasthof zur Post Riegler* on the corner of the Platz and Schiffgasse is a good mid-range restaurant serving local dishes, such as *Steirergröstl* (small pieces of pan-fried potato, onion and ham), with main courses starting at around öS90/€6.57; while *Da Vinci*, Burggasse 6, is a snazzy pizzeria which doubles up as bar/nightclub at weekends. There are some nice café-bars on the streets leading off the main square, notably *Seinerzeit*, Roseggerstrasse 28, filled with nostalgic nick-nacks, including one half of a VW minivan which now forms the bar; and the nearby *Kaktus* at Roseggerstrasse 27, a cosy pub nestling in an off-the-street courtyard.

Towards Mariazell

There are two ways of getting from **Bruck** to **Mariazell**, 50km to the north, both of which involve a fairly scenic ride through the eastern spur of the Hochschwab Mountains. The most direct (and the one served by regular buses) takes the A20 Bundesstrasse north towards the small ski resort of Aflenz 16km away, before gradu-ally climbing into the high pasturelands of northeastern Styria. The other route (not possible by public transport) involves heading for Mürzzuschlag, 40km northeast of Bruck, before turning north onto the A23, an attractive drive up the increasingly nar-row Mürz Valley, which passes through the village of Neuberg an der Mürz, grouped around the evocative ruins of a fourteenth-century Cistercian abbey.

Mariazell

Ranged on a hillside and encircled by pine-covered mountains, **MARIAZELL** would be worth a visit even without the religious associations that have made it Austria's most important place of pilgrimage. The local population of 2000 welcomes more than a hun-dred times that number of visitors every year; although most come to visit the miracu-lous statue of the Madonna and Child inside the Basilica that dominates the town, Mariazell's alpine charms are also a powerful draw. The town is far from comparable with the big package resorts of the Tyrol as a winter sports centre, but the presence of the 1266-metre Bürgeralpe immediately to the east and the 1626-metre Gemeindealpe to the northwest ensure good skiing in winter and excellent walking conditions for the rest of the year.

The town has been a religious centre ever since the Benedictine monks from St Lambrecht (see p.308) established a priory here in 1157, although it's not known when, or exactly why, the site became associated with the miraculous healing powers of the Virgin Mary. The town was certainly on the pilgrimage circuit by 1377, when King Louis of Hungary attributed his victory over the Turks to the intervention of the Virgin of Mariazell. The cult was subsequently adopted by the Habsburgs as a symbol of the supranational, Catholic unity of the empire, and it remains popular with believers from all over central Europe. Crowds throng the town centre on Saturdays and Sundays throughout the summer, with special ceremonies taking place on August 15 (Assumption) and September 8 (Birth of the Virgin).

About five buses a day run up to Mariazell from Bruck via Aflenz, and there are a couple of direct buses from Graz at weekends. For those approaching Mariazell from the north, a branch line (served by about five trains a day) connects Mariazell train station – actually 1.5km away in the village of St Sebastian – with St Pölten on the main Vienna–Salzburg line.

The Town
Girdled at a discreet distance by a ring of souvenir stalls, the **Basilica** looms over all else in Mariazell from its lofty position at the top of the Hauptplatz. Outwardly, it's not immediately attractive: begun in the thirteenth century and enlarged in the seventeenth to accommodate ever-increasing numbers of visitors, it sports a single Gothic spire squeezed awkwardly between later Baroque domes. Once inside, pilgrims congregate around the Gnadenkapelle, or Chapel of Mercy, halfway down the nave, where a twelfth-century statue of the Virgin and Child stands behind a silver grille. With the Virgin herself a curiously doll-like figure dressed in billowing silver skirts, the pair's image has become a trademark for the village as a whole, repeated endlessly on souvenirs and devotional prints. More sumptuous still is the high altar, designed by leading Baroque architect Fischer von Erlach and featuring a serpent crawling across a silver-plated globe, overlooked by a cherub-encircled Crucifixion. Elsewhere the Basilica is stuffed with tombs and relics, the most macabre of which are the glass caskets on either side of the nave holding the remains of third-century saints Paulilus and Modestus, their fragile skeletons shrouded in bejewelled robes. Stairways on either side of the porch are decorated with nineteenth-century devotional paintings commissioned from local artisans by the grateful recipients of the Virgin's miraculous healing powers. Most of them follow a set formula, depicting the Virgin of Mariazell hovering benignly above the sickbeds of the faithful. The church **treasury** (daily except Mon 10am–5pm; öS50/€3.65), approached from the southeastern side of the basilica, houses a treasure trove of ecclesiastical silverware, and a painting of the Virgin given to the church by Louis of Hungary in thanks for his deliverance from the Turks.

THE BÜRGERALPE AND ERLAUFSEE
There's not much else to Mariazell save for Wienerstrasse, the main shopping street which leads north from the Hauptplatz, passing the terminal for the cable car (May–Oct & Dec–Easter; öS105/€7.67 return) to the **Bürgeralpe**, which commands superb views towards the Hochschwab range to the southwest. Continuing along Wienerstrasse, the road eventually descends into the neighbouring village of **St Sebastian**, site of Mariazell's train station and starting point for the forty-minute walk to **Erlaufsee**, along a well-signed path that starts just behind the station. On summer weekends an antique tram-locomotive makes the trip from the train station to the lake six times a day (öS50/€3.65 one way, öS80/€5.84 return). The lake itself is a charming spot, fringed by a shingle beach where you can rent pedalos and rowing boats.

Practicalities
Mariazell's **bus station** is on Dr-Leber-Strasse just below the Hauptplatz, while **trains** terminate in St Sebastian, fifteen minutes' walk away to the north. The **tourist office**, Hauptplatz 13 (May–Sept Mon–Sat 9am–12.30pm & 1.30–5.30pm, Sun 9am–noon; Oct–April Mon–Fri 9am–12.30pm & 1.30–5pm, Sat 9am–noon; ☎03882/2366, *www.mariazell.at* & *www.mariazellerland-hochschwab.at*), will arrange **private rooms** (①) in Mariazell or St Sebastian. There's a modern, well-appointed HI youth **hostel** in St Sebastian at Erlaufseestrasse 49 (☎03882/2669-0), offering smart doubles (②) and singles for öS330/€24.10. Other good-value sources of **accommodation** include *Marienheim*, Abelplatz 3 (☎03882/2545; ②), a simple, centrally located place managed by nuns which offers basic rooms with shared facilities (②) or en suites (③); and *Zum Heiligen Brunnen*, a comfortable pension just northeast of the main square at Dr-

Lueger-Gasse 10 (☎03882/2131), which again has a choice of rooms with shared facilities (②) or en suites (③). Of the several traditional Gasthöfe in the centre, both the *Goldene Krone*, Grazerstrasse 1 (☎03882/2583, rooms with en-suite shower ③; with WC and shower ④), and the *Wirtshausbrauerei*, Wienerstrasse 5 (☎03882/2523-0, *brauhaus@mariazell.org*, ④), manage to combine modern comforts with a bit of olde-worlde atmosphere.

There are plenty of **eating** establishments surround the basilica, none of them charging too exploitative prices. You might try *Gasthof zum Jägerwirt*, Hauptplatz 2, a good place for schnitzel-based meals or a hearty bowl of goulash; or *Goldene Krone*, Hauptplatz, which has an affordable range of typical Austrian main courses as well as salad-based snacks. *Wirtshausbrauerei*, Wienerstrasse 5, is a good place to sample Styrian food, and is also one of the best places to **drink** in town, serving the excellent local Girrer beer on tap.

Leoben and around

Nineteen kilometres west of Bruck, **LEOBEN** has been a centre of the Styrian iron industry since the Middle Ages, processing the ore brought down from the hills of Eisenerz 25km to the north. The steelworks in the suburb of Donawitz still blights the northern approaches to the town, but central Leoben, enclosed by a curve of the River Mur, remains surprisingly industry-free. There are few essential sights here, save perhaps for the Gothic murals of the **Stiftskirche** in the nearby suburb of Göss, but the town does serve as a useful introduction to the iron-dominated heritage of central Styria. Industrial archeology figures prominently in the **Steirische Eisenstrasse** (Styrian Iron Road), an itinerary contrived by the local tourist authorities to breathe new life into Styria's decaying industrial heartland, which heads northwards from Leoben through Vordenberg to Eisenerz, before heading down to the Enns Valley towns of Hieflau, Grossreifling and Altenmarkt.

The Town

Leoben's **train station** is fifteen minutes' walk north of town; cross the River Mur and head down Franz-Josef-Strasse to reach the pedestrianized **Hauptplatz**, lined with elegant seventeenth-century facades. Most imposing of these is the **Hacklhaus**, at Hauptplatz 9, a stately maroon-and-cream edifice, whose stucco adornments, executed in 1660, include four female figures as allegories of the seasons. Immediately to the west stands the **Stadtpfarrkirche St Xaver**, an imposing monument to the Jesuits who once held sway here, whose interior is very much an ensemble piece: an impressive series of black-framed Baroque altars, each enshrouded in gilded tendrils and leaves. The painting on the high altar, by seventeenth-century Augsburg master Johann Heinrich Schönfeld, shows St Francis-Xaver ascending to heaven above a crowd of writhing plague sufferers, a reference to the saint's status as patron of the seriously ill. Behind the church in a former Jesuit college lies the **Stadtmuseum** (Mon–Thurs 10am–noon & 2–5pm; öS30/€2.19), strong on local mining history, although there's also a room devoted to Leoben's brief flirtation with world history, the Treaty of Leoben, signed here by Napoleon in 1797. After a whirlwind campaign in northern Italy, the wily Corsican marched into Styria in spring 1797 and, having set up camp in Leoben, looked set to advance on Vienna. After negotiations in the Benedictine nunnery in Göss (see below), the Austrians secured Napoleon's withdrawal by ceding their possessions in the Low Countries to the French.

Leoben's most venerable attraction is the Romanesque **Stiftskirche** in the southern suburb of **Göss**, ensconced among the outbuildings of an erstwhile Benedictine nunnery. Late-fourteenth-century frescoes fill the arch above the entrance; there's an animated Calvary scene, below which a Madonna shelters believers under her cloak. The nearby **Bischofskapelle** contains older paintings but is rarely accessible (Mon–Fri 8am–noon, advance reservation essential; ☎03842/22148). Behind the nunnery lies the brewery responsible for Styria's most ubiquitous ale, Gösserbrau, although the chance to look around the display of brewing techniques through the ages at the Gösser **Braumuseum** is limited to weekends (Sat & Sun 9am–6pm). *Brauhaus Göss*, opposite the nunnery at Turmgasse 3, is a convenient place to stop off, have a bite to eat and sample the local brew. To get to Göss, turn right at the southern end of the Hauptplatz and then left into Gösserstrasse, which runs along the banks of the River Mur – a walk of about 25 minutes. Otherwise, take bus #G from Leoben train station.

Practicalities

Leoben's **tourist office**, Hauptplatz 12 (Mon 7am–5pm, Tues–Thur 7am–6.30pm, Fri 7am–1pm & 3–6.30pm, Sat 9am–12.30pm; ☎03842/48148, *www.leoben.at*), has a very limited selection of **private rooms** (①). Cheapest of the downtown **hotels** is *Zum Möhren*, just off the Hauptplatz at Hormanngasse 7/9 (☎03842/42207; ③), which has a number of plain but comfortable rooms with shared bathrooms; those with en-suite facilities are more expensive. The similarly central *Hotel Kindler*, Straussgasse 7–11 (☎03842/43202-0, *www.kindler.at*; ④), is a good mid-range choice; all rooms come with en-suite facilities, TV and telephone.

Best of the downtown **cafés** is the *Steinscherer* in the Hacklhaus, which does a good line in cakes, pastries and daytime nibbles, with outdoor seating that spills out onto the square in summer. For more substantial **food**, the nearby *Arkadenhof-Restaurant schwarzer Adler*, Hauptplatz 11, has some reasonably priced Austrian staples in a vaulted inner courtyard; while *Da Vinci*, a block east of the Hauptplatz on the corner of Josef-Graf-Gasse and Langgasse, is a smart and snazzy café-pizzeria with plenty of veggie pasta options.

Towards Eisenerz: Vordenberg and the Erzbergbahn

Regular trains, as well as buses, make their way from Leoben train station towards **VORDENBERG**, a settlement that straggles along either side of the Vordenbergerbach. There's a **tourist office** at Hauptstrasse 85 (☎03849/9119, *www.vordernberg.steiermark.at*) which has a smattering of private rooms (①); and two nice old guesthouses along the sinuous main street: *Zur Post*, Hauptstrasse 86 (☎03849/274; ②), and the *Schwarzer Adler*, at no. 98 (☎03849/264; ②). The town used to be a mining settlement, and the area around the village is dotted with the winching towers of abandoned mine workings. It's also the start of the **Erzbergbahn**, a narrow-gauge railway originally built to carry ore from Eisenerz (see below) down the valley towards Leoben. A tourist-oriented rail service runs between Vordernberg and Eisenerz on Sundays between June and September (single ticket öS120/€8.76; return öS180/€13.14); otherwise regular Leoben–Eisenerz buses are the best means of embarking on the journey. Five kilometres above Vordenberg, the road crosses the 1232-metre **Präbichl Pass**, beyond which fleeting glimpses of the extraordinary ore-bearing Erzberg herald the descent into Eisenerz.

Eisenerz

It's not often that a landscape scarred by industry proves strikingly attractive, and yet the Erzberg ("ore mountain"), rising above **EISENERZ**, is perversely beautiful, carved into a ziggurat shape by decades of open-cast mining, its colour shifting from ochre to red to purple as the sunlight flits across its slopes. First mined by the Celts, iron ore from Eisenerz went on to feed an armaments industry that helped push Habsburg power southwards and eastwards against the retreating Turks. It continued to provide Austria's iron and steel industry with almost all of its requirements until the 1980s, when under-ground mining here ceased, priced out of the market by imports from the Developing World. A limited amount of open-cast mining on the Erzberg still goes on, but today's Eisenerz – blighted by high unemployment – has a tired and world-weary feel. However the town is beginning to turn its industrial heritage to good touristic effect: the Erzberg is now a show-mine, while the presence of one of Austria's few remaining fortified churches and an absorbing town museum, combined with some excellent alpine scenery all around, ensures that there are plenty of other things to do too.

The Town

Surveying the attractive town houses of downtown Eisenerz from a hillock to the south is the walled **Pfarrkirche St Oswald**, fortified in the sixteenth century against the advancing Ottoman Turks. The Turks never got this far, but the fortifications proved their worth in 1599 when the Protestant townsfolk warded off an attack led by the Catholic bishop of Seckau. The church itself dates from the thirteenth century, but it gained its current late-Gothic character from an extensive face-lift in the 1470s. It's full of reminders of Eisenerz's mining history: the relief of Adam and Eve above the door as you enter shows Adam dressed in medieval mining gear, while inside a wooden sculpture of a miner high up in the roof strikes a bell every hour. The church's most impressive feature is the organ loft, an ornate piece of late-Gothic stonework carved with interweaving patterns (reminiscent of intricate wickerwork) across which wild beasts frolic.

Below the church lies an attractive main square, **Bergmannsplatz**, grouped around a sixteenth-century **Rathaus** decorated with abstract sgraffito motifs. Beside the Rathaus is the **Krippenhaus** (literally the "crib-house"), where exhibitions of the typi-cally Austrian craft of constructing *Krippen*, or Nativity scenes are held during Advent and at other times of the year (ask at the tourist office for details – see opposite).

THE MUSEUM

Two hundred metres north of Bergmannsplatz on Schulstrasse, the **Stadtmuseum** (May–Oct Mon–Fri 9am–5pm, Sat & Sun 10am–noon & 2–5pm; Nov–April Mon–Fri 9am–noon; öS45/€3.29) is situated in the Kammerhof, once the seat of the imperial officials sent to oversee the iron trade, and taken over as a hunting lodge by Franz-Josef in 1880. There's an imaginative display of local crafts and costumes inside, but it's the section on Eisenerz's mining history that is most interesting. Miners originally belonged to a highly respected medieval guild, whose uniform, the *Maximilianische Tracht*, is modelled by a life-size mannequin chipping away at a rock face. A white, hooded tunic with leather rear flaps (the so-called *Arschleder*, or "arse-leather", neces-sary for negotiating the wooden slides that linked one mine gallery to another), this garment served as the miners' uniform from the late Middle Ages until the mid-nine-teenth century, when it was replaced by more military-style black outfits, still in use today on ceremonial occasions. There are numerous photographs of miners past and present, an imposing scale model of the Erzberg that dominates an entire room, and a cut-away model of a late-nineteenth-century smelting furnace, one of many that used to litter the valley. In a bizarre variation on the *Krippen* theme, there's a glass case hold-ing a model of the mine workings with a carved figure of St Barbara in the middle. Barbara is the patron saint of miners, and her feast day on December 4 (the *Brauchtumfest*) is still marked in Eisenerz with parades in traditional uniforms.

THE ERZBERG

One kilometre east of the centre along the road to Leoben (if you're walking, follow the path which begins opposite the Bipa/Libro supermarket just uphill from

Bergmannplatz), the ticket office of the **Schaubergwerk** (show-mine) marks the starting point for visits to the Iron Mountain itself. The **tour** (May–Oct daily at 10am,
12.30pm and 3pm; öS160/€11.68) involves a ninety-minute trip through the former
mine workings with a German-speaking guide; ask for an English-language leaflet at
the ticket counter. The trip begins with a bus ride to a midway point up the Berg, where
visitors disembark to admire a vast iron ore crusher – a man-made pit that gobbles up
rocks thrown at it from the rear of a dumper truck before grinding them down into
more manageable morsels. A short trip by underground train then delivers passengers
into the heart of the mountain, where the tour continues on foot through a maze of galleries, including the Wendel – a tunnel which corkscrews its way down through the
Erzberg, linking one level of the mine to the next. A short video film tells the story of
how iron deposits were originally formed; while in another chamber a bearded spirit
known as the Wassermann, looking rather like an out-of-place garden gnome, emerges
from a pool to relate how he promised the Eizenerzers an unending supply of ore in
return for being allowed his freedom – a well-known local folk tale. Elsewhere, drilling
machines are noisily demonstrated, and, in a masterful piece of stagecraft, a section of
the rock face appears to be dynamited, creating a tumble of ore-bearing stone.
Claustrophobic types might prefer a bumpy though scenic one-hour ride around the
terraces of the Erzberg in the "Hauly," an enormous truck originally designed to transport prodigious amounts of ore (ask at the ticket desk about departures; öS160/€11.68,
combined ticket for mine tour and Hauly öS250/€18.25).

Practicalities

Buses terminate on the main Hieflau–Leoben road, 200m uphill from Bergmannplatz.
Five minutes' walk to the west is the **tourist office** at Schulstrasse 1 (May–Oct
Mon–Fri 9am–1pm & 3–5pm; Nov–Dec Mon–Fri 10am–noon & 3–4pm; ☎03848/3700,
www.erzbergland.at) which offers a wealth of local information and can help with private
rooms (①), although all but a few are in outlying villages. Among the **hotels**,
Frühstuckspension Krapf, Schlingerweg 3 (☎03848/3457; ①), has excellent-value rooms
(some with en-suite facilities) some fifteen minutes' walk south of the centre with views
towards the Erzberg; while the *Gasthof zur Post*, Lindmoserstrasse 10 (☎03848/2232;
②), is an attractive old inn in the town centre with TV and en-suite facilities in simply
furnished rooms. The *Eisenerzer Hof*, Hieflauerstrasse 17 (☎03848/2551; ②), just west
of the centre by the tourist office, offers the same comforts but in slightly less atmospheric surroundings. *Gästehaus Weninger*, just around the corner from the *zur Post* at
Krumpentalerstrasse 8 (☎03848/2258, *weninger@eisenerz.com;* ③), has neat en suites
as well as 2– to 4-person apartments with fridge and kitchenette.

Both the *Gasthof zur Post* and the *Eisenerzer Hof* have restaurants serving standard
Austrian **food**, both with good-value main courses from öS90/€6.57 upwards. *Il
Fornaio*, just south of Bergmannplatz at Lindmoserstrasse 1, offers a chic blend of rustic and modernist decor, quality thin-crust pizzas and salads; it's also a good spot just
for a drink. *Barbara Stub'n Tagescafé*, Bergmannplatz 2, is the place to sip coffee and
eat cakes; while for evening **drinking** you can try *Zeitensprung*, a rather chic bar in an
arcade off Karl-Renner-Strasse; or the *Café City Pub*, an unpretentious, friendly bar
behind the *Eisenerzer Hof*.

Eisenerzer Ramsau and the Leopoldsteinersee

Eisenerz is hardly a winter sports resort, but there's one of sorts at **Eisenerzer Ramsau**,
a side-valley that begins at the southern end of town (take Krumpentalerstrasse from the
centre) and stretches uphill for a couple of kilometres. There's a big chalet-style hotel, the
Pichlerhof, Schlingerweg 19a (☎03848/3414; ③), which can hire out gear for cross-country skiing in winter, or serve as a base for walking in summer.

Four kilometres north of town on the Hieflau road there's a turning for the **Leopoldsteinersee** (local buses stop beside the turn-off), a popular local beauty spot a further kilometre away, dramatically situated below the sheer rock face of the **Seemauer**. There are a couple of cafés at the northern end, and a bathing area with a shingle beach 1.5km away at the southern end, where several trails lead off to skirt round the forested slopes of the 1871-metre Pfaffenstein suitable for either a Sunday stroll or a more taxing hike – the tourist office back in Eisenerz sells regional walking maps.

The Mur valley

Beyond Leoben, the main road and rail route to western Styria and Carinthia continues to ascend the **Mur Valley**, passing a string of settlements which, despite their economic importance, harbour few attractions. The few tourist destinations in the area tend to be just off the main valley route: the Benedictine abbey at **Seckau** is reached by bus from the otherwise uninteresting town of Knittelfeld; while the historic highland towns of **Oberzeiring** and **Murau** can be easily accessed from **Judenburg**, arguably the area's most useful transport hub. The Mur valley's only other claim to fame is the **Österreichring** racing circuit, midway between Knittelfeld and Judenburg, just outside the town of Zeltweg. It's here that the Austrian grand prix is held – at which time all accommodation in the valley is booked solid.

Getting around the valley is reasonably straightforward, with Bruck–Klagenfurt expresses speeding through the Murtal towns every hour or so. **Buses** for Oberzeiring start out from Judenburg, while **trains** for Murau use a narrow-gauge branch line which leaves the main route at Unzmarkt, just west of Judenburg.

Seckau

The only reason to stop off in **KNITTELFELD**, a semi-industrialized market town 30km west of Leoben, is to catch buses (Mon–Sat only; 7 daily) to the Benedictine **Stift Seckau** some 16km to the north, an Augustinian foundation established in the mid-twelfth century. Set amid rippling fields patrolled by dairy herds, the abbey served as the ecclesiastical capital of Styria and the seat of its bishops until the modernizing Emperor Josef II closed the place down in 1782, moving the episcopal seat to Graz. It was refounded by the Benedictines in 1883, and has flourished ever since, operating a prestigious secondary school which draws in pupils from all over the Mur valley – those visiting Seckau on weekday mornings will find the din emanating from the abbey classrooms hard to avoid.

Buses from Knittelfeld train station pull up right outside the abbey gates. Inside, an arcaded Renaissance courtyard is watched over by a fine twin-towered Romanesque **Basilica**, a welcoming golden-brown structure that looks as if it could have been made from huge chunks of gingerbread. The basilica's west porch features a worn, but recognizably tender Madonna and Child of 1260 in the tympanum, and at ground level, a pair of snarling feline beasts of similar vintage standing guard at either side of the main doorway. The nave is lined with fat, bulging pillars, but is otherwise minimally decorated, focusing all attention on the mesmerizing wooden *Crucifixion*, made around 1140, which hangs above the main altar. The slender, graceful form of Jesus exudes a sense of spiritual calm typical of the art of the period – quite unlike the tortured and often harrowing Crucifixion scenes of later medieval art. Figures of the Virgin Mary and St John stand at either side, gazing up towards Christ in wonder rather than grief. To the left of the high altar lies the Mausoleum of Karl II (father of Ferdinand II), fashioned by Lugano artist Alessandro de Verda and completed in 1612. A relief of the

Emperor, clad in full armour, adorns the lid of the marble sarcophagus, surrounded by cherubs holding up heraldic symbols of the imperial house. Off one side of the nave to the north is the **Bischofskapelle**, remodelled in 1590 by the then bishop of Styria Martin Brenner, who had the chapel decorated with portraits of all Styria's bishops from the earliest times up to and including himself, who can be seen looking pleased with his labours on the back wall. The chapel's main focus, however, is a fifteenth-century altarpiece depicting the Coronation of the Virgin, which features Mary and three regal figures representing the Holy Trinity enclosed in a circular frame carved to look like a wreath of twigs, in which angels perch like birds in a tree. Next door in the **Sakramentskapelle**, stagey lighting accentuates the luminous qualities of a small twelfth-century alabaster image of the Virgin.

Seckau is usually visited as a day-trip, although the **tourist office** opposite the abbey gates (Mon, Tues, Wed & Fri 8am–noon; Thur 8am–5pm; ☎03514/5205, *gde@seckau.steiermark.at*) has a list of **private rooms** (①) in local farms. The rather smart *Hofwirt*, just along from the tourist office, doubles as a luxury **hotel** (☎03514/5645-0, *www.abtei-seckau.at*; ⑧) and top-notch **restaurant**. The rather more down-to-earth *Gasthof zur Post*, round the corner on Marktstrasse, serves up satisfying meat-and-potatoes fare from öS100/€7.30.

Judenburg

Dramatically situated on a ridge overlooking the Mur Valley, **JUDENBURG** was Styria's leading mercantile centre in the late Middle Ages, controlling the trade routes between Vienna, southern Germany and northern Italy. Like most other Mur Valley towns, Judenburg grew rich on the export of iron (and, oddly, the lavender trade), and was by the fifteenth century an important site for the manufacture of weaponry. The town's name is thought to derive from one of its early medieval rulers, Jutho, although popular tradition subsequently identified it with the large Jewish colony that settled here in the thirteenth century. A pogrom in 1496 forced them to flee the town, and there's little trace of their culture today.

The Town

The scene of lively markets on Saturdays and Mondays, Judenburg's Hauptplatz is dominated by the 75-metre-high **Stadtturm** (May & June Fri–Sun 10am–6pm; July–Sept daily 10am–6pm; Oct Fri–Sun 10am–5pm; öS20/€1.46), built in the fifteenth century as a symbol of the town's commercial wealth, although its appearance has drastically altered since then as a result of repeated fires and rebuildings. It's now the venue for temporary historical exhibitions, and there's a viewing gallery near the top offering a panorama of the local countryside. Beside it is the sixteenth-century **Pfarrkirche**, where the heavy-handed flourishes of the Baroque interior are lightened by a Gothic statue of the Madonna and Child, carved locally around 1420.

Kaserngasse heads eastwards from the Hauptplatz to the **Stadtmuseum** at no. 27 (July & Aug Mon–Fri 9am–noon & 3–5pm, Sat 9am–noon; Sept–June Mon–Fri 9am–noon; donation requested), a rather old-fashioned display of miners' uniforms, tools used by local ironmongers, and the intricate wooden moulds used by tilemakers. There's a reasonable collection of folk art on show, though, including a seventeenth-century wooden Christ figure, which was carried through the town on feast days.

A little further along Kaserngasse, Langganggasse descends to the banks of the Mur, from which the dainty, whitewashed **Magdalenakirche** is clearly visible on the other side of the river. Built around 1350, the church still preserves some of its original stained glass, together with exuberant fourteenth-century frescoes, beginning with a monumental St Christopher, carrying the Christ Child on his shoulder, on the southern exterior wall. Inside, the ceiling is held up by two central pillars, from which ribbed vaulting sprouts forth like the leaves of a palm tree. Attached to the second of the pillars is a fifteenth century statue of the Virgin and Child – the latter a lively-looking infant brandishing a bunch of grapes. Best of the interior frescoes are on the north wall of the choir, where a lively Crucifixion scene is busy with gossiping onlookers and Roman soldiers – three of whom squat round a table to play dice, oblivious to the spiritual drama going on above their heads.

Practicalities

Judenburg's **train station** is 500m north of the centre. Turn right into Gussstahlwerkstrasse, cross the river, and take one of the paths leading up into the old town to reach the Hauptplatz. The **bus station** is much nearer at hand, just off Burggasse, one block west of the Hauptplatz. The **tourist office** (Mon–Thur 9am–12.30pm & 2–5pm, Fri 9am–12.30pm, Sat 9am–noon; ☎03572/85000, *www .judenburg-online.at*), Hauptplatz 1, has a small list of private **rooms** (①), all within walking distance of the town centre. There's a youth **hostel** 200m east of the main square at Kaserngasse 22 (☎03572/87355), occupying one end of an arcaded former governmental palace. Two centrally located **pensions** are *Gasthof Reichsthaler*, Burggasse 22 (☎03572/82448; ②), with several budget-priced rooms with shared bathrooms, and more expensive ones with en-suite facilities; and *Pension Karlbauer*, Herrengasse 4 (☎03572/83415; ②), a smaller, more intimate place where all the rooms come with shower and WC. Also good value and handy for the train station is *Gasthof Murblick*, Sensenwerkgasse 11 (☎03572/83671; ②), near the Magdalenakirche on the north bank of the Mur, offering cosy en suites with TV – half of which come with excellent views of the old town.

For **food**, *Gasthof Gruber*, Hauptplatz, offers a broad range of standard Austrian dishes and is a good daytime café, too; *Pizzeria San Marco*, immediately south of the Hauptplatz down the narrow Weyergasse, is consistently the most enjoyable of several pizza outlets in the town centre. *Little Dublin*, on Herrengasse, is a cramped but friendly place for an evening **drink**.

North of Judenburg: Oberzeiring

Eight kilometres beyond Judenburg, a minor road leaves the main westbound route to head northwards towards Liezen in the Enns Valley, crossing the easternmost spur of the Tauern range. After about 10km, a left turn leads to the highland village of **OBERZEIRING**, an ancient silver-mining centre, which provided medieval Judenburg with much of its wealth. Silver extraction ceased in the seventeenth century, although iron ore extraction continued for another 300 years, leaving a network of galleries which can be explored in the **show-mine** (Schaubergwerk; May–Oct tours daily at 9.45am, 11am, 2pm, 3pm and 4pm; tours only take place if a minimum of 5 people have turned up; öS60/€4.38) situated just uphill from Oberzeiring's Hauptstrasse. Tours involve a 50-minute trip through some of the underground workings, passing narrow tunnels in which medieval miners worked on hands and knees, and the preserved skeleton of one of the dogs which dragged leather bags of rock through the galleries. The mine's cool, dry, calcium carbonate-rich air has also helped turn Oberzeiring into a minor health resort, with bronchitis and asthma sufferers flocking into the healing galleries or **Heilstollen** (☎03571/2811-0, *www.heilstollen.at*) next door to the show-mine. An hour-long session is relatively easy to arrange if you want to try it, costing around öS160/€11.63, although it's unlikely that anything less than a week-long course of treatment would have any appreciable impact on your health.

Getting to Oberzeiring is pretty straightforward, with hourly buses from Judenburg arriving at the village's tiny main square. The **tourist office**, a few steps away at

Hauptstrasse 16 (Mon–Fri 8am–noon; ☎03571/2255, *www.oberzering.at*), can arrange **private rooms** (①), and there are a couple of good **hotels**: *Gasthof zum grunen Specht* (☎03571/2238; ②) is a cosy guesthouse on the main square; while *Silberhof*, just to the west at Hauptstrasse 22 (☎03571/2811; ③), is an altogether more upmarket 4-star place specializing in rest cures. There's a **campsite** in a meadow on Bachstrasse (☎03571/2438; May–Oct), five minutes from the centre – head to the western end of the village to find the turn-off.

Unzmarkt and Oberwölz

Continuing westwards from Judenburg along the Mur Valley, the industrial character of much of central Styria is gradually left behind, with both road and railway winding their way up an increasingly narrow valley studded with farmsteads and rural villages. There's an important parting of the ways at **UNZMARKT**, where the main rail line begins to wheel south on its way towards Klagenfurt and Villach, and the privately owned Murtalbahn (see box) continues to follow the Mur Valley westwards to Murau and Tamsweg. If you're heading for Murau by public transport you'll have to change trains at Unzmarkt, and if you have time to kill between connections, consider walking to the **pilgrimage church of Frauenburg** on a hill north of town, an easy thirty-minute ascent from the train station. The church interior isn't always accessible outside mass times, but impressive views of the valley below make the climb worthwhile. Next to the church are the ruins of a thirteenth-century fortress once owned by warrior-aristocrat and minstrel Ulrich von Liechtenstein, an important figure in the history of Murau (see p.306), who died here in 1276.

At **Niederwölz**, 10km beyond Unzmarkt, a minor road heads northwards to the village of **OBERWÖLZ**, another 10km away up the valley of the Wölzer Bach. It's hard to imagine that this isolated settlement of a thousand souls was once a prosperous medieval mercantile centre that grew rich on the profits of the salt and silver trades. Much of the village's fourteenth-century fortifications, including three gates and two towers, still survive, enclosing an endearing jumble of old houses. At its centre stands the **Stadtpfarrkirche St Martin**, a Romanesque structure with Gothic additions embellished by a *Last Judgement* painted around 1500 on the south outer wall. The nearby **Sigmundskirche**, originally the chapel of a fourteenth-century hospital, has some intricate rib vaulting towards the back of the nave.

For those dependent on public transport, Oberwölz is difficult to get to, with only a couple of local buses leaving Niederwölz train station (on the Unzmarkt–Murau line) in the early morning and early afternoon. If you want to stay in Oberwölz, the **tourist**

THE MURTALBAHN

The **Murtalbahn** (*www.stlb.co.at*), the privately owned **narrow-gauge railway** that provides a public transport service between Unzmarkt and Tamsweg, also operates tourist-oriented, steam-hauled services in summer. Trains run between Murau and Tamsweg every Tuesday and Wednesday from late June to early September: return tickets cost öS200/€14.60. An extra service in August runs from Murau to Stadl, a picturesque village between Murau and Tamsweg, every Saturday for öS160/€11.68 return.

Committed enthusiasts will enjoy the **engine-driver training sessions**, which take place at Murau station every Monday morning between early July and late August, offering all-comers the chance to ride up and down for a few minutes in the driver's cab. However, it's not cheap, at öS800/€58.40 for fifteen minutes or öS2200/€160.60 for 45 minutes. Interested parties should contact Reisebüro Murau, just outside Murau train station (☎03532/2233, *reisebuero-murau@stlb.co.at*) a few days in advance.

office on the Hauptplatz (Mon–Fri 9am–noon & 2–5pm; ☎03581/8420, *oberwoelz @netway.at*) has details of numerous **private rooms** (①) in and around the village, and there are several good **hotels**: the *Graggober*, Stadt 56 (☎03581/315; ③), is an attractive chalet-style building, while *Zum Möhren*, Stadt 17 (☎03581/7389; ②), is an old Gasthof attractively modernized, with sauna and solarium on site.

Murau

Of all the provincial towns in Styria, **MURAU** is probably the most attractive, with a photogenic jumble of houses arranged alongside the clear, fast-flowing waters of the young River Mur. Despite the town's isolation from the main tourist routes, a sprinkling of historic churches set against an attractive alpine backdrop make a detour here worthwhile. Getting to Murau by public transport is relatively simple, with regular services on the Murtalbahn narrow-gauge railway running up to town from Unzmarkt on the main Bruck–Klagenfurt line.

Courtly poet and unruly magnate **Ulrich von Liechtenstein** built a castle here in 1250, establishing a market at the foot of the castle soon afterwards. The Murau branch of the Liechtenstein line came to an end when Christoph von Liechtenstein died childless in 1580, but the subsequent marriage of his widow **Anna Neumann** (see box below) to leading magnate Georg Ludwig zur Schwarzenberg ensured Murau's continuing prosperity. The town's importance as a trading post on the transalpine routes between Italy and Germany is now a thing of the past, and although traditional trades like wood-carving are still practised here, the town is now largely known as a beer-making centre. The local Murauer Bier is served in all the establishments, and the Murauer Doppelmaltz, a dark stout, is also well worth trying.

The Town

A compact town centre is grouped around the triangular **Schillerplatz**, bordered by the elegant town houses of late-medieval merchants. At the western end of the square, a covered walkway leads up to the thirteenth-century **Pfarrkirche St Matthäus**, whose southern face is decorated with a faded but still recognizable fresco of St Christopher holding aloft the boy Jesus. At ground level, plaques marking the graves of sixteenth-

---

ANNA NEUMANN

Daughter of a local merchant, **Anna Neumann** (1535–1623) had already been widowed once (she'd married local knight Johannes Jakobus von Thenhausen in 1557) before catching the eye of Christoph von Liechtenstein in 1566. When Liechtenstein died without an heir in 1580, Anna's combined inheritance – from both the Liechtenstein family and her own – made her one of the most powerful, and most eagerly courted, women in Styria. Three more childless marriages followed before the "Black Widow of Murau" eventually married, at the age of 88, the 29-year-old Georg Ludwig zur Schwarzenberg, signing over her property rights to him. The marriage was ordered by Archduke Ferdinand of Styria, the future Emperor Ferdinand II, who wanted to see the Schwarzenbergs (important allies in his campaigns against the Protestants) firmly established in the Murau area.

Widely resented for her ability to accumulate wealth from a succession of husbands without ever providing them with children, Anna Neumann was dubbed a witch by Catholic propagandists, who feared her influence as a supporter of local Protestantism. Neumann's marriage to Schwarzenberg, an enthusiastic supporter of the Counter-Reformation, suggests that she'd given up the cause towards the end of her life.

century burghers are built into the wall, and an iron grille offers glimpses of the charnel house, home to a chaos of skulls and bones. The frescoes that fill the interior are also faded, but on days when sunlight streams in through the windows the effect can be quite stunning. The oldest works, an *Entombment* and an *Annunciation* dating from the 1370s, are on the south side of the nave, although the faces of the holy ones depicted were rubbed out by iconoclastic Protestants in the sixteenth century. Much of the finest work is to be found in the north transept, where the medieval view of life and mortality is summed up by a picture of Eve standing beside the tree of life – a white mouse and a black mouse nibble at the tree's roots, while a figure of death approaches in the background. The east wall of the north transept is decorated with a memorial to the house of Liechtenstein, painted sometime in the 1570s: Christ's ascent to heaven from Mount Tabor is displayed at the top; just below, successive generations of the family are shown kneeling at the grave of Otto von Liechtenstein. Below this, a series of panels depicts different branches of the family. Christoph von Liechtenstein and Anna Neumann are shown in the top left panel.

A covered wooden stairway leads from the church to the **Schloss Obermurau** perched on the hill above. Originally built as a fortress by Ulrich von Liechtenstein in 1250, the Schloss was converted into a princely residence by Georg Ludwig zur Schwarzenberg in the 1630s. It's still owned by the Schwarzenberg family, and guided tours of the Schloss's state rooms are frustratingly infrequent (mid-June to mid-Sept Wed 3pm, Fri 10am; öS30/2.19). However, you might be able to get a glimpse inside the fine arcaded courtyard, where one wall is adorned with a seventeenth-century sundial incorporating a figure of Atlas shouldering a globe.

Heading east out of Schillerplatz along Grazerstrasse, an alley to the left leads down to the village graveyard and the **Annakirche**, a Gothic chapel that holds yet more excellent frescoes, most of which date from around 1400. An exhuberant *Tree of Jesse* fills the arch above the entrance to the choir. There's a fine *St George and Dragon* on the north side of the nave, alongside a series of scenes illustrating the *Stations of the Cross*, in which Christ is mocked and tormented by a characterful gallery of low-lifes. St Anne herself is depicted on the south wall of the choir hard up by the main altar, where she, together with the infant Jesus, is cradled by the Virgin Mary. Don't miss the seventeenth-century wooden pews, decorated with curious, griffin-like forms.

A little further out along Grazerstrasse is the **Kapuzinerkirche**, once serving a Capuchin monastery founded by Georg Ludwig zur Schwarzenberg in order to bolster the Counter-Reformation. His grave, alongside that of Anna Neumann, is inside on the left. Next door is the **Heimatmuseum** (irregular opening times; visits often restricted to two guided tours a day; enquire at the tourist office), which documents the contemporary woodcarving industry, and looks back in time at the merchants of the Middle Ages who exported felt and iron across the Alps to Italy and southern Germany.

The oldest church in Murau is the twelfth-century **Ägydikirche**, 1km from the centre on the main eastbound road. It's an endearingly simple, squat structure with a wooden steeple, and there are yet more frescoes inside, including a fifteenth-century picture of St Aegidius on the north wall of the choir, and some thirteenth-century scenes from the Life of the Virgin in the nave.

Practicalities

Murau's **tourist office** (Mon–Fri 9am–12.30pm & 2.30–6pm, Sat 8.30am–noon; ☎03532/2720, *www.murau.at*), immediately outside the **train station** on Bahnhofplatz, will provide a list of the town's numerous private **rooms** (①). Murau's youth hostel, near the train station at St-Leonhard-Platz 5 (☎03532/2395, *jgh.murau@jgh.at*), has beds in dorm rooms. One inexpensive, old-fashioned Gasthof in the centre of town is the *Bärenwirt*, at Schwarzenbergstrasse 4 (☎03532/2079), offering simple doubles with shared bathrooms (②) and some en suites (③). For something a little more comfortable, *Gasthof Ferner*, north of the centre at Roseggerstrasse 9 (☎03532/2318, *gasthof.ferner@murau.at*; ④), is a family-run hotel whose spacious rooms boast en-suite facilities, telephone and TV; while the *Hotel zum Brauhaus*, Raffaltplatz 17 (☎03532/2437, *www.murau.at/brauhaus*; ④), is a stylish, modern, business-standard hotel with balconied rooms overlooking the River Mur.

For **food**, *Fleischerei Imbissstube*, Schwarzenberggasse 1, offers solid sausage-salad-and-chips-type sit-down meals from öS70/€5.11, while the restaurant of the *Bärenwirt* (see above) is another inexpensive restaurant serving up Styrian staples from öS80/€5.84. *Gasthof Lercher*, Schwarzenbergstrasse 10, is a step up in style and quality, with a range of Austrian standards augmented by local fish such as *Forelle* (trout) and *Zander* (pike-perch). *Platzhirsch*, on Schillerplatz, harbours an excellent Italian restaurant/pizzeria and a café-bar which is one of the best places to **drink** in town, offering occasional live music and themed party nights at weekends. Similar events are on offer at the riverside *Indien Pub*, Grazerstrasse 10, which attracts a youngish crowd. *Konditorei Fragner*, just off Schillerplatz at Liechtensteinerstrasse 6, is the most civilized of the daytime coffee-and-cake venues.

St Lambrecht Abbey

Several daily buses (reduced service on Saturdays, none on Sundays) travel from Murau to the **Stift St Lambrecht**, a Benedictine foundation of eleventh-century vintage set in verdant uplands some 15km southeast of the town. The twin-towered Stiftskirche is largely Gothic, although the main portal displays surviving fragments of the original Romanesque structure. The Baroque interior is dominated by Valentin Khautt's high altar of 1632, a stuccoed, marble-effect ensemble of statues surrounding a painting of the *Assumption*, and crowned by a figure of St Michael. Also inside the abbey courtyard is the smaller Peterskirche, housing a winged altar bearing a *Crucifixion* and various saints by the fifteenth-century Master of St Lambrecht. The abbey buildings are only accessible by tour (mid-May to mid–Oct Mon–Fri at 10.45am & 2.30pm; Sun 2.30pm; öS25/€1.83), which takes in the abbey church, a collection of stuffed birds; and an optional visit to the monastic art collection, which is rich in Gothic wood sculpture.

The Ennstal

Rising in the Salzburger Land and emptying into the Danube just east of Linz, the River Enns cuts through the mountainous northwestern corner of Styria to create one of the more attractive subalpine itineraries in this part of Austria. Although the market town of **Liezen** is the valley's main commercial centre, there are few obvious tourist destinations save for the rustic village of **Admont**; and the sophisticated winter sports centre of **Schladming**, which provides access to the slopes of the region's most impressive peak, the **Dachstein**.

The mountains of central Styria render the Enns Valley slightly isolated from the rest of the province, but both the A9 autobahn and a main Linz- and Salzburg-bound rail route provide access to the region, leaving the Mur Valley at St Michael and heading northwest through the **Eisenerzer Alpen** before reaching the lower Enns Valley at the village of **Selzthal**, a transport hub that's otherwise pretty unremarkable. From here, the Salzburg-bound road and rail routes lead westwards to the upper Enns Valley and Schladming, while a secondary road and branch line lead to Admont, just east of Selzthal.

Approaching the area from Eisenerz to the southeast, you'll pass through the former iron-working town of **Hieflau** (where rail travellers must change trains) before proceeding to Admont through the **Gesäuse**, a fifteen-kilometre-long gorge where the River Enns forces its way between forested hillsides and rugged cliffs.

Admont

A sleepy agricultural community set against the backdrop of the **Haller Mauern** Mountains to the north, **ADMONT** owes its place on the tourist map to the library and museum collections of the Benedictine abbey that stands at the centre of the village. However, Admont's charm doesn't end there: surrounded by pasturelands and wooded hills, it's an excellent place for a rural breather.

Founded in the eleventh century by Hemma von Friesach, the same Carinthian noblewoman who established the monastery at Gurk (see p.337), **Admont abbey** (*www.stift-admont.at*) has gone through numerous reincarnations over the centuries. Remodelled in the Baroque style in the seventeenth century, it was almost completely destroyed by fire in 1865, and today you are greeted by a rather grim-looking neo-Gothic reconstruction. Happily, the sumptuous **library** (April–Oct daily 10am–1pm & 2–5pm; öS60/€4.38) was largely untouched by the conflagration, and it's this that most visitors come to see. Built in 1774, the library's interior decorations add up to a vast allegory of human learning: ceiling frescoes by Bartolomeo Altomonte, a sequence of heavenly skyscapes filled with pinkish clouds, show figures representing the arts, the natural sciences and theology, while the busts of famous intellectuals that hover above the ornate library shelves embrace the gamut of cultural endeavour from Socrates to Dürer. The focus of the library at ground level is the ensemble of four lime-wood figures by Josef Stammel, representing *Heaven*, *Hell*, *Justice* and *Death* – the skeletal, winged personification of the latter, glowering over the shoulder of a hurrying mortal, is the Graz-born sculptor's greatest masterpiece. Display cases contain some of the library's most valued possessions, including some beautifully illustrated medieval manuscripts.

The abbey's extensive **art** and **natural history collections** are currently undergoing reorganization, but are due to reopen sometime in 2002.

Practicalities

Admont's **tourist office**, Hauptplatz 4 (Mon 8am–noon, Tues–Fri 8am–5pm; ☎03613/2164), will direct you to private **rooms** (①) in both Admont and the neighbouring village of Hall (500m north). *Jugendherberge Röthelstein* (closed Oct & Nov; ☎03613/2432), Austria's most impressive youth **hostel**, is situated on a hill just south of the town in an elegant Renaissance Schloss commanding excellent views across the valley. It has en-suite doubles (②) as well as multi-bed dorms. Down in the village, *Gästehaus Mafalda*, Obere Bachgasse 75 (☎03613/2188; ②), is a pleasant 6-room bed and breakfast with cosy en suites; while the slightly grander *Gasthof Zeiser*, Hauptstrasse 6 (☎03613/2147, *gasthof.zeiser@aon.at*; ③), offers rooms with en-suite facilities and TV. The swishest place to stay in the village is *Landgasthof Buchner*, 200m west of the abbey (☎03613/2801; ③), where you'll find smart modern rooms with TV, minibar and telephone along with a good-value breakfast buffet. Admont's **campsite** (☎03613/2839) occupies a pleasant riverside location, 500m north of the village in Hall.

Most **eating and drinking** takes place along the Hauptstrasse: *Café Wagner*, Hauptstrasse 5, is a good place for a quick sandwich or sausage; *Gasthaus Kamper*, at no. 19, has good-value Austrian staples, cheap lunchtime choices and nice outdoor seating; while *Pizzeria Marktcafé*, at no. 20, has a wide range of pizzas from öS100/€7.30 and is probably the best place for an intimate evening drink. The *Stiftskeller*, a swish modern café-restaurant in the abbey grounds, offers top-notch local specialities (such as *Ennstaler Nock'n-Reindl* – noodles in ham and cream sauce) from about öS110/€8.03, although it tends to close by 8pm on weekdays. *Pub Gesäuse-Eingang*, Hauptstrasse 4, is a late-opening bar with snack food; *Café-Pub Pfiff*, Hauptstrasse 7, is rowdier and rockier in its musical tastes.

Schladming

Fifteen kilometres west of Admont at Selzthal, the route forks, with the A9 autobahn and a main rail route heading north into Upper Austria (see Chapter 3), and another route continuing westwards up the Enns Valley towards Salzburg and Innsbruck. After passing the uninteresting, semi-industrialized town of Liezen, the latter route arrives at another major junction 15km upstream, where a branch line and a secondary road leave the Enns Valley at Stainach to climb towards Bad Aussee and the Salzkammergut (see Chapter 7). Continuing west, the valley narrows as impressive mountain ranges – the Dachstein to the north and the Niedere Tauern to the south – make their presence felt.

The valley floor is dotted with attractive villages (each harbouring a Gasthof or two), any of which would make an excellent base for hikes into the surrounding highlands, but it's really only **SCHLADMING**, 35km beyond Stainach, that's fully geared up for alpine tourism. Cradled by the southern slopes of the Dachstein, this is Styria's leading winter sports centre and an excellent base for walking, with the 1894-metre-high **Planai** towering over the town to the south and the mountain village of **Rohrmoos** only 5km to the southwest. Both destinations are accessible via gondola from Schladming itself; indeed the downhill run from Planai (a regular venue for World Cup competitions since 1972) ends dramatically just outside the town centre. In addition, the nordic skiing resort of **Ramsau** and the cable-car ride up the **Dachstein** are both only a short bus ride away. From December to April Schladming is an important package holiday centre, and independent travellers will find that accommodation is both heavily booked in advance and more expensive than during the rest of the year.

Originally a silver-mining centre, Schladming was the focus of a miners' and peasants' rebellion in 1525, and the insurgents were punished by having their town razed to the ground. Thus, little of Schladming's medieval character remains, apart from a few surviving traces of the town wall.

The Town and the mountains

With its smart shops, flower-bedecked buildings and beautiful background scenery, Schladming is an attractive and relaxing base from which to explore the mountains, but there's not that much in the place that's worth seeing. Much of the town is modern, reflecting Schladming's rapid, tourism-inspired, postwar growth, although a jumble of narrow streets west of the Hauptplatz preserves a more village-like feel. One of the nicest houses in this area is the seventeenth-century **Bruderhaus** on Talbachgasse, a traditional wooden building that originally served as a municipal hostel for old miners and widows. It's now the **town musem** (daily 3–6pm; öS30/€2.19), with the customary display of local crafts and costumes. The Pfarrkirche, north of here on Salzburger Strasse, boasts a yellow-orange Romanesque tower, but little else to shout about.

The most direct route to higher altitudes is the two-section **Planaibahn** (late June–Sept & Dec–mid-April; one-section return öS90/€6.57, two-section return öS155/€11.32), a gondola that ascends from a terminal just east of the Hauptplatz to the Schladminger Hütte café-restaurant, just below the summit of the 1906m Planai. There's a good view of the Dachstein range to the north, and an array of marked paths descending leisurely back down the valley – or winding upwards to the top of the Planai. At the western end of town, the **Rohrmoos-Hochwurzen** gondola

---

SKIING IN SCHLADMING

Schladming's major **winter sports** asset is the 1894m Planai immediately southeast of town, which offers a myriad of beginners' and intermediate runs – as well as one down-hill route for advanced skiers, which finishes up at the grandly named Olympiastadion (a concreted-over semicircle where World Cup downhill races terminate) just outside the town centre. The nearby 1850m Hochwurzen is less prolific in terms of the number of pistes available, but is another good mountain for novices and intermediates. Two more mountains – the Hauser Kaibling to the east and the Reiteralm to the west – are linked to the Planai and Hochwurzen ski areas by a well-integrated network of lifts, making the number of intermediate runs available to the Schladming-based skier pretty limitless. Ramsau am Dachstein has a few downhill slopes for beginners, but is primarily known for cross-country skiing – which can be practised all year round on the Dachstein glacier. A ski pass covering the Schladming–Ramsau am Dachstein region costs öS805/€58.77 for 2 days; öS1925/€140.53 for 6 days; öS3560/€259.88 for 13 days.

(July–Sept & Dec–mid-April; return öS115/€8.40) provides access to pleasant alpine meadows (and ski slopes in winter) to the southwest. In summer, hikers' buses serve the three side valleys which lie below Planai and Hochwurzen – Obertal, Untertal and Preuneggtal – which, when combined with the gondolas, facilitate an endless array of walking possibilities. The tourist office (see below) has a leaflet detailing routes and schedules, and also sells the Kompas 1:50,000 Dachstein-Tauern hiking **map**. The Dachstein-Tauern Summer Pass (available from the Planai gondola station) costs öS590/€43.07 for 6 days, öS690/€50.37 for 10 days, and covers all local lifts and buses.

Practicalities

Schladming **train station** is 500m west of town; turn left out of the station building, cross the river and keep straight on to reach the **tourist office** (☎03687/22268-0, *www.schladming.com* or *www.dachstein-tauern.at*) on the corner of Erzherzog-Johann-Strasse and Langegasse, where you can get information on vacancies in private **rooms** (②) as well as local pensions and **hotels**. There's a youth **hostel** (☎03687/24531) just east of the main square at Coburgstrasse 253. *Zirngast*, Rechte Ennsau 633 (☎03687/23195, *www.zirngast.at*), is an all-year-round riverside campsite north of the centre: from the train station, head for the tourist office as above, turn left down Langegasse and cross the river a second time. The best source of cheap bed-and-break-fast accommodation in the centre is *Haus Fischbacher*, Schulgasse 590 (☎03687/23428, *fischbacher@maierkg.at*; ②), offering balconied en-suite rooms in a traditional house. Pensions offering neat en suites with TV and telephone include *Mayer*, just off the main square at Salzburgerstrasse 26 (☎03687/22128, *www.mayer-schladming.at*; ③); and *Pension Talbach*, Griesgasse 455 (☎03687/23321; summer ③; winter ⑤), a chalet-style building beside the Talbach stream just west of the centre. The atmospheric *Alte Post*, Hauptplatz 10 (☎03687/22571, *www.alte-post.at*; summer ⑦; winter ⑨), is an old coaching inn offering all the creature comforts.

For **snacks**, you could do much worse than head for the Anker bakery on Hauptplatz, an enduringly reliable source of takeaway or eat-in pastries and coffee. More substantial **eating** options are provided by *Kirchenwirt*, Salzburgerstrasse 27, offering no-nonsense meat-and-two-veg dishes augmented by a couple of fancy steaks; *Vorstadt Stüb'n*, Salzburgerstrasse, which serves standard Austrian fare alongside a wide selection of Styrian wines; *Taalbachschenk*, Hammerfeldweg, beside the Talbach, which concentrates on grills and stays open until 2am; and *Giovanni's* just off the Hauptplatz on Siedergasse, where there's a wide choice of inexpensive pizzas as well as a range of pasta dishes, served up in a split-level bar-restaurant which is also a good place for a drink.

Kaffee-Konditorei Landgraf, Hauptplatz 37, is both the town's main daytime café and a relaxed evening **drinking** venue. For more serious inbibing, *Gasthof Braustüb'n*, Siedergasse, serves beer brewed on the premises (*Schwalbenbräu*, a form of *Weizenbier*), as well as filling soups and stews from around öS70/€5.11. In winter, après-ski kicks off in the mountain huts on the Planai before moving down into the valley: *Onkel Willis Hütte*, west of the Planaibahn top station, is one of the most popular stop-offs on the slopes. Best of the all-year-round late-night venues are *Hanglbar*, Salzburgerstrasse 96, a tightly packed place with chunky wooden furniture and low wooden ceiling; and *La Porta*, Salzburgerstrasse 2, a stylish cellar with a lengthy list of snazzy cocktails. *Sonderbar*, just round the corner from Hauptplatz at the beginning of Salzburgerstrasse, is a frenetic disco-pub that gets going after midnight and stays open until the early hours.

Ramsau and the Dachstein

Immediately north of Schladming, a minor road climbs up towards **Ramsau am Dachstein** – really a string of small hamlets rather than a single village, occupying a south-facing terrace of pastureland suspended high above the Enns Valley. Dotted with wooden farmhouses and grazed by sheep, cows and goats, it's an idyllic, yet highly touristed area, offering an enticing vision of rural prettiness beneath the shadow of the 2995-metre-high **Dachstein**.

The road up from Schladming ends beneath the Dachstein itself, where a cable car conveys visitors to the **Hunerkogel**, some 300m beneath the summit. Eleven buses a day make the journey from Schladming to the hamlet of Ramsau-Ort, seven of which go all the way to the Dachstein cable-car terminal. The last bus back from the cable car is at 5.50pm, or 4.50pm between October and June.

The first place you reach after climbing out of Schladming is **RAMSAU-KULM**, a hamlet famous for its fifteenth-century **church** decorated with frescoes of the time. Pictures of St Christopher carrying the young Jesus, and St George killing the dragon, adorn the north wall of the nave, while in the choir both the *Martyrdom of St Sebastian* and the *Annunciation* are given lively treatment.

Further up the valley is **RAMSAU-ORT**, a major centre for nordic or cross-country skiing in winter, and gentle walks in spring and summer. The **Pfarrkirche** is Evangelical rather than Catholic, a reminder that Protestantism survived in these isolated upland regions from the sixteenth century onwards, despite the success of the Counter-Reformation elsewhere in Austria. Among the village communities north of Schladming, Protestantism is still the dominant faith. The **tourist office** (*www .ramsau.com*) in the village centre is the best place to enquire about local **private rooms** (②).

Three kilometres beyond Ramsau-Ort, a left fork continues to hug the mountainside, while the right fork ascends towards the **Dachstein** cable-car station. The cable car (daily: July & Aug 8am–5.50pm; Sept & Oct 8am–4.50pm; Nov–June 8.30am–4.50pm; öS260/€19 return) ascends to the 2700-metre-high Hunerkogel, where the inevitable café-restaurant sits dramatically atop a lump of rock. It's an excellent viewpoint, from which you can look across the Dachstein glacier – a strange sight, with the *loipe* (tracks) used by cross-country skiers running like zebra stripes across its surface – and the mountains of the Salzkammergut to the north, and the vast sweep of the Niedertauern range to the south.

travel details

Trains

Bruck an der Mur to: Graz (hourly; 40min); Judenburg (12 daily, 50min); Klagenfurt (10 daily; 2hr 10min); Leoben (hourly; 15min); Unzmarkt (8 daily; 1hr); Vienna (hourly; 2hr); Villach (10 daily; 2hr 40min).

Graz to: Bruck an der Mur (hourly; 40min); Deutschlandsberg (10 daily; 1hr); Ehrenhausen (14 daily; 55min); Feldbach (8 daily; 1hr); Hartberg (4 daily; 2hr 40min); Innsbruck (3 daily; 6hr 15min); Kitzbühel (3 daily; 5hr 5min); Köflach (10 daily; 1hr); Leibnitz (14 daily; 45min); Linz (2 daily; 3hr 30min); Salzburg (3 daily; 4hr 15min); Schladming (6 daily; 2hr 45min); Selzthal (9 daily; 2hr 5min); Spielfeld-Strass (14 daily; 1hr); Stainach-Irdning (8 daily; 2hr 10min–2hr 40min); Vienna (9 daily; 2hr 30min).

Hieflau to: Eisenerz (8 daily; 25min).

Leibnitz to: Ehrenhausen (14 daily; 10min); Graz (14 daily; 45min).

Mariazell to: St Pölten (5 daily; 2hr 40min).

Schladming to: Graz (6 daily; 2hr 45min); Salzburg (3 daily; 1hr 45min).

Selzthal to: Admont (7 daily; 20min); Hieflau (7 daily; 40min); Schladming (9 daily; 1hr 10min).

Spielfeld-Strass to: Bad Radkersburg (8 daily; 50min).

Unzmarkt to: Murau (Mon–Fri 7 daily; Sat 3 daily; Sun 1 daily; 45min).

Buses

Bruck to: Aflenz (hourly; 30min); Mariazell (5 daily; 1hr 40min).

Eisenerz to: Hieflau (Mon–Sat only; 8 daily; 25min); Leoben (10 daily; 1hr).

Feldbach to: Bad Radkersburg (1 daily; 1hr 10min); Riegersburg (8 daily; 25min).

Graz to: Feldbach (3 daily; 1hr 30min); Grossklein (Mon–Fri only; 2 daily; 1hr 30min); Hartberg (Mon–Sat 10 daily; Sun 5 daily; 1hr 15min); Köflach (10 daily; 1hr 30min); Mariazell (Sat & Sun only; 2 daily; 2hr 20min); Riegersburg (1 daily; 1hr 50min); Voitsberg (1 daily; 1hr 15min).

Hartberg to: Graz (8 daily; 1hr 15min); Stubenberg (8 daily; 40min); Weiz (7 daily; 1hr).

Judenburg to: Oberzeiring (10 daily; 55min).

Knittelfeld to: Oberzeiring (2 daily; 1hr); Seckau (7 daily; 30min).

Köflach to: Bärnbach (Mon–Fri 5 daily; Sat & Sun 2 daily; 25min); Piber (Mon–Fri 8 daily; Sat & Sun 2 daily; 15min).

Leibnitz to: Grossklein (8 daily; 25min).

Leoben to: Eisenerz (10 daily; 1hr); Vordenberg (hourly; 20min).

Mariazell to: Graz (2 daily; 2hr 20min); Mürzzuschlag (1 daily Sat & Sun; 2hr); St Sebastian (8 daily; 20min).

Murau to: St Lambrecht (Mon–Fri 6 daily; Sat 2 daily; 20min).

Niederwölz to: Oberwölz (2 daily; 30min).

Unzmarkt to: Murau (Mon–Fri 2 daily; Sat & Sun 6 daily; 45min).

CHAPTER SIX

CARINTHIA AND THE EAST TYROL

C arinthia (Kärnten; *www.tiscover.com/carinthia*) is regarded by the Austrians (and a great many Germans and Italians, too) as one of central Europe's most enticing vacation spots. Austria's southernmost province, it enjoys warm summers and exudes a relaxed, Mediterranean feel; this, together with an impressive combination of lake and mountain scenery, makes it the perfect place for an outdoor holiday.

Carinthia lacks a historic urban centre capable of competing with the likes of Vienna, Salzburg, Graz or Innsbruck, but the provincial capital **Klagenfurt** is a relaxed, unassuming city and provides a good base for exploring the surrounding area. The city's main claim to fame is its position on the eastern shores of the **Wörthersee**, an enduringly popular summer playground that annually attracts a fashionable, affluent crowd, together with hordes of attendant wannabes. Flashy lakeside settlements **Pörtschach** and **Velden** are the main resorts, offering all kinds of water-based activities and swollen with visitors from June onwards through the summer. To the north of Kagenfurt lie the broad, fertile valleys of the Glan and Gurk rivers, tracing an area liberally sprinkled with historical remains. Ruins on the **Magdalensberg** recall periods of Celtic and Roman settlement, while the pilgrimage church in the nearby village of **Maria Saal** stands as testament to the missionary energies of the archbishops of Salzburg, who began the process of converting Carinthia to Christianity in the eighth century. Close at hand are Carinthia's medieval capital **St Veit an der Glan**, now a picturesque market town, and the sixteenth-century stronghold of **Hochosterwitz**, a breathtakingly situated hilltop castle. Further north, but still within reach of day-trippers from Klagenfurt, lie the charming medieval town of **Friesach** and the important ecclesiastical centre of **Gurk**, famed for its splendid Romanesque cathedral.

Western Carinthia revolves around the province's second city, **Villach**, a lively and sophisticated place with an engaging historic centre. It's an important transport hub,

---

ACCOMMODATION PRICE CODES

All **hotels and pensions** in this book have been coded according to the following price categories. All the codes are based on the rate for the least expensive double room during the **summer season**. In those places where winter is the high season, we've indicated both summer and winter room rates in the text.

① under öS400/€29.07
② öS400–600/€29.07–43.60
③ öS600–800/€43.60–58.14
④ öS800–1000/€58.14–72.67
⑤ öS1000–1200/€72.67–87.21

⑥ öS1200–1400/€87.21–101.74
⑦ öS1400–1600/€101.74–116.28
⑧ öS1600–1800/€116.28–130.81
⑨ over öS1800/€130.81

commanding links to Salzburg, Italy and Slovenia, and also acts as the gateway to two more lakes, the **Faakersee** and the **Ossiachersee**. In contrast to the brash and upmarket Wörthersee, the lakes in this part of Carinthia are much more oriented towards family holidays, offering a wealth of campsites and apartment-style accommodation. North of Villach the main road and rail routes to Salzburg pass **Spittal an der Drau**, a small town built around the imposing Renaissance Schloss Portia, and the jumping-off point for two popular tourist targets – the lakeland paradise of the **Millstättersee** and the tiny medieval town of **Gmünd**. Both Spittal and Gmünd are within striking distance of the **Hohe Tauern**, Austria's highest mountain range, shared with the Salzburger Land and the Tyrol, although if you want to immerse yourself fully in the alpine experience you should continue northwestwards to the skiing and mountaineering centre of **Heiligenblut**, a village standing in the shadow of the most imposing Hohe Tauern peak of all, the **Grossglockner**.

The southern slopes of the Hohe Tauern are also accessible from the **East Tyrol** (Osttirol), which borders Carinthia to the west. Geographically isolated by the Tauern range from the rest of the Tyrol, this compact knot of alpine valleys and mountains remains surprisingly untouched by the winter package-holiday trade. Mountain-ringed **Lienz**, small and provincial though it is, serves as regional centre, and offers a good mixture of urban tourism and alpine pursuits, while in the highland villages to the north – notably **Matrei** and the captivatingly beautiful **Kals** – the character of this undervisited region shines through. The area's international atmosphere owes a great deal to the proximity of **Italy** and **Slovenia**.

CARINTHIA

Carinthia was an important centre of Celtic and Roman culture until the sixth-century arrival of the **Slavs**, who settled on the Zollfeld, the fertile valley north of present-day Klagenfurt. The area remained predominantly Slav until the eighth century, when local tribes asked the Bavarians for assistance in their struggles against the **Avars**, a race of Turkic interlopers from the east. The Bavarian presence – strengthened by the missionary zeal of priests sent by the bishops of Salzburg – increased over the next century, leading to the Christianization of the province and an influx of German-speaking settlers.

Still considered by the Slovenes to be a cradle of their civilization, there's no doubt that the Slav heritage has left its mark on Carinthia. Local place names (most names ending in -*ach* are of Slavic origin) and Slavic-sounding surnames bear testimony to the non-Germanic roots of a large part of the population. After World War I, the infant **Kingdom of Serbs, Croats and Slovenes** (the state which subsequently became Yugoslavia) laid claim to southern Carinthia, and a Serb-dominated Yugoslav army moved in to occupy Klagenfurt and the surrounding countryside. Some locals organized themselves into a resistance movement, beginning the so-called **Abwehrkampf** ("Defence-struggle"), memories of which have formed an important plank of the

---

THE KÄRNTEN CARD

A worthwhile investment for anyone spending a reasonable length of time in Carinthia in the summer is the **Kärnten Card** (available early May to early October only), which allows the bearer free use of all public transport (including lake steamers, chairlifts and cable cars) and free entry to the vast majority of museums and tourist attractions (Minimundus at Klagenfurt being one of the few major exceptions). Valid for a three-week period, it's available from all the region's tourist offices and costs öS385/€28.11.

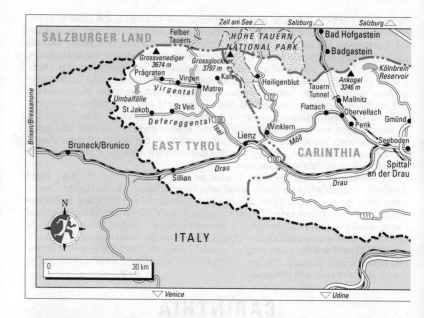

OUTDOOR ACTIVITIES IN THE CARINTHIAN LAKES

All of the lake resorts in Carinthia offer a wide choice of **outdoor activities**, ranging from messing around in a rowing boat or pedalo to waterskiing. A brief stroll along any lakefront will give you a good idea of who is offering what: otherwise, the local tourist office will be able to give you the relevant details.

Bike rental You can rent bikes from many of the larger train stations, which has the advantage of being convenient, and relatively cheap if you have a valid train ticket. However, you'll get a wider range from a specialist bike rental place. Ordinary bikes tend to cost öS120/€8.76 a day and upwards, whereas mountain bikes can cost as much as öS200/€14.53 or more.

Boat rental Each of the Carinthian lake resorts has numerous outfits that rent out rowing boats (*Ruderboote*) or pedalo-boats (*Tretboote*); electric boats (*Elektroboote*) are also fairly ubiquitous. Typical prices are around öS100/€7.30 for an hour, slightly more for the electric boats, slightly less for the rowing boats.

Golf There are two top-quality and undeniably scenic eighteen-hole courses in the region: the Millstättersee Golf Club, above Seeboden (☎04762/82548); and the Velden Golf Club at Oberdorf 70, Velden-Köstenberg (☎04274/7045). Both are open April–Nov, weather permitting. Expect to pay green fees in the region of öS600/€43.80.

Sailing Small sailing dinghies are available for hire on all the major lakes for öS100–150/€7.26–10.90 per hour. Places offering courses are almost everywhere on the Wörthersee, Ossiachersee and Millstättersee. The Segel- und Windsurfschule Seeboden at the *Sporthotel Royal* in Seeboden on the Millstättersee (☎04762/81715-704); or the Segelschule Wörthersee, Seecorso 40, Velden (☎04274/2691) are two of the best places to learn, although the sailing schools in the more laid-back village of Döbriach on the Millstättersee are worth considering if you want to stay in a quieter resort. Courses are usu-

ally tailored to suit all abilities and can last for anything from two days to two weeks; expect to pay around öS2200–2500/€160.60–182.50 for a couple of hours' tuition a day over a seven-day period.

Scuba diving You can hire scuba diving (*Tauchen*) equipment or go on a course for the uninitiated at the Millstättersee resorts of Millstatt (Tauchschule Millstatt, *Hotel Seewirt*, Kaiser-Franz-Josef-Strasse 49; ☎04766/2110) and Seeboden (Alpen-Adria Tauchcenter, *Hotel Pichler*, Seepromenade 46 (☎04762/81180); or the Ossiachersee resorts of Heiligengestade (Tauchschule Ing. Patterer; ☎04242/45663) or Annenheim (Diving Center Ossiachersee, *Hotel Aichelberghof*, Annenheim; ☎0664/130 1266). A one-day course should cost around öS500/€36.33.

Swimming Each of the towns and villages has a little stretch of grassy shoreline, known as the *Strandbad*, dedicated to sunbathing and watersports. Most have a jetty you can dive off, and most charge a small entrance fee (öS30/€2.19 in the smaller places, öS100/€7.30 in swanky Velden) in the summer season.

Tennis The more chic tennis clubs are in the Wörthersee resorts of Pörtschach and Velden, where court rental weighs in at öS125/€9.13–öS170/€12.41 per hour. Prices are slightly cheaper in the Millstättersee resorts of Seeboden and Döbriach, where it might also be easier to get a court.

Waterskiing The Wörthersee resorts of Pörtschach and Velden are the top venues for waterskiing, where most of the boat-rental places along the waterfront offer trips from around öS140/€10.22 per round. It is also very popular in Ossiachersee and Millstättersee.

Windsurfing Numerous places on the Wörthersee, Millstättersee and Ossiachersee rent out boards or offer courses. You'll pay around öS110/€8.03 for board rental; öS350/€25.55 for a day or afternoon introductory course; öS2100/€153.30 and upwards for seven days' tuition. The Segel- und Windsurfschule Seeboden on the Millstättersee (see under "Sailing") is situated on a sheltered inlet, and is an especially popular place for children to learn the ropes.

Carinthian patriotic tradition ever since. However southern Carinthia would probably have been awarded to Yugoslavia by the Versailles peace conference had it not been for the intervention of the Americans, who insisted that a plebiscite be held in order to ascertain the true feelings of the local population. Despite Yugoslav attempts at vote-rigging (the official turnout was over 100 percent), the resulting **Volksabstimmung** of October 10 1920 produced a majority in favour of the Austrian Republic, and the Yugoslavs were obliged to withdraw. October 10 became a sacred date for Carinthians, and is still celebrated by a wide cross-section of the population as a symbol of Carinthia's undying loyalty to Austrian values. Carinthian politicians have at times tended to portray the Volksabstimmung as a victory of Austrians over Slovenes, omitting to mention that most local Slovenes in fact voted to remain in Austria in 1920. Slovene loyalty to Carinthia was rewarded with forced Germanization under the first Austrian Republic, and outright expulsions during the Nazi period.

Today, locals who speak the **Slovene language** are hard to find – only 14,000 Carinthians considered it to be their mother tongue according to the 1991 census – although they still occupy a belt of territory in the south of the province stretching from Bleiburg westwards to the Faakersee. There are bilingual road signs in areas with a mixed population, and a Slovene-language high school in Klagenfurt, although the Slovene community is now too small to maintain a culture of great vibrance or visibility. The picture is complicated by the existence of the **Wends**, a group related to the Slovenes who nevertheless claim to be descended from a different group of Slav settlers originating from Dalmatia. Their language, Windisch, is still spoken in the Faakersee and Rosental areas southeast of Villach, and church services in the area are often bilingual.

Because of the patriotic traditions associated with the Abwehrkampf and the Volksabstimmung, unashamed right-wing nationalism is more common in Carinthia than anywhere else in Austria. The survival of conservative values has been aided by Carinthia's predominantly prosperous, semi-rural nature. Hardly surprising, therefore, that Carinthia has become the political powerbase of controversial FPÖ mainman **Jörg Haider**, whose mixture of right-wing populism and xenophobia has consistently won his party over 40 percent of the vote in a province which has few economic problems, and very few foreign immigrants.

Politics apart, the image of Carinthia that prevails elsewhere in Austria is largely a positive one: Carinthians are considered to be almost Mediterranean in character compared to the country's other inhabitants, with a pronounced sense of style, a taste for the good things in life, and a warm spontaneous nature.

Klagenfurt

Nestling among the low hills of southern Carinthia, sedate and prosperous **KLAGEN-FURT** may lack the historical and cultural pedigree of a Salzburg, Innsbruck or Graz, but it's an absorbing provincial capital nevertheless. It's a small, easily digestible city, whose appeal lies mostly in its proximity to the Wörthersee, just 3km west of the centre – the lakeside **Europapark**, site of the much-visited **Minimundus**, is a major tourist draw. In addition, a fairly absorbing provincial **museum** and a varied choice of restaurants and nightlife make this a good urban base for touring much of rural Carinthia.

Founded in the twelfth century by the Von Spannheims, a family of soldier-aristocrats from the Rhineland, Klagenfurt achieved regional pre-eminence after the intervention of Emperor Maximilian I, who ordered its redevelopment as provincial capital in 1518. Italian architect **Domenico dell'Allio** (who also worked on the Landhaus in Graz; see p.278) was responsible for the town's layout, creating the gridiron street plan

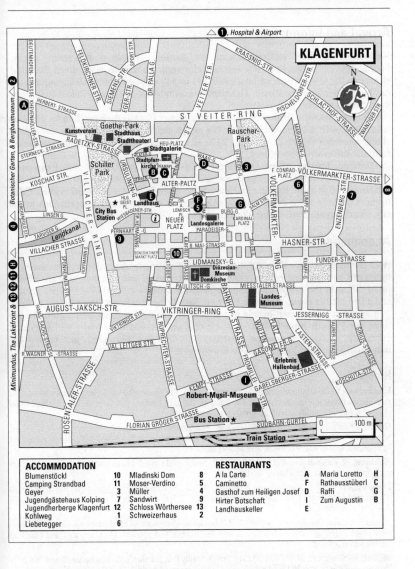

ACCOMMODATION

Blumenstöckl	10	Mladinski Dom	8	
Camping Strandbad	11	Moser-Verdino	5	
Geyer	3	Müller	4	
Jugendgästehaus Kolping	7	Sandwirt	9	
Jugendherberge Klagenfurt	12	Schloss Wörthersee	13	
Kohlweg	1	Schweizerhaus	2	
Liebetegger	6			

RESTAURANTS

A la Carte	**A**	Maria Loretto	**H**
Caminetto	**F**	Rathausstüberl	**C**
Gasthof zum Heiligen Josef	**D**	Raffi	**G**
Hirter Botschaft	**I**	Zum Augustin	**B**
Landhauskeller	**E**		

still very much in evidence today. The town was a Jesuit base in the seventeenth century, and became Carinthia's ecclesiastical capital in 1787, when Graf von Salm, Bishop of Gurk, moved the bishopric here in recognition of Klagenfurt's growing importance. As was the case with so many Austrian cities, the town walls were demolished in 1809 on the insistence of the victorious Napoleon – their outline is traced by a quadrangular ring road today. But, despite heavy damage in World War II, Klagenfurt's city-centre buildings retain many of their inner courtyards, now harbouring cafés and boutiques, which lend the place considerable charm.

Arrival and information

Both **train** and **bus stations** are on the southern fringes of the centre on the Südbahngürtel. From here it's a straightforward ten-minute walk down Bahnhof-strasse to the town centre, or buses #40, #41 or #42 will take you to Heiligengeistplatz on the centre's western fringe. The airport is 3km to the northeast, linked to the centre by buses #45 and #42.

Heiligengeistplatz, 100m west of the central Neuer Platz, is the main hub for **city bus transport**, with most municipal services either starting there or passing through. A single journey costs öS22/€1.61; a 24-hr ticket, öS55/€4.02. Tickets are purchased from the driver or *Tabak* stores.

The main **tourist office** (May–Sept Mon–Fri 8am–8pm, Sat & Sun 10am–5pm; Oct–April Mon–Fri 8am–6.30pm, Sat & Sun 10am–1pm; ☎0463/537223, *www.info .klagenfurt.at*) is in the Rathaus on Neuer Platz. There's also an information kiosk (May to mid-Oct daily 10am–8pm) outside Minimundus on the western approaches to the city, clearly signposted off the A2 autobahn from Villach.

Accommodation

Both the main tourist office and the kiosk outside Minimundus will check vacancies in hotels and book **private rooms**, although the latter are in short supply; there are a handful of rooms in the Klagenfurt suburbs for around öS200–250/€14.6–18.25 per person, and a few slightly cheaper ones in Viktring, 6km to the southwest (bus #80, #81 or #82).

Klagenfurt's downtown **hotels** include few real budget options, although there are three good **youth hostels** (two of which only open in summer) and a well-appointed **campsite**, *Camping Strandbad* (☎0463/21169; bus #12; May–Oct), just behind the municipal Strandbad in the lakeside Europapark.

Hotels

Blumenstöckl, 10-Oktober-Strasse 11 (☎0463/57793). For those who want comfortable rooms with en-suite facilities and multi-channel TV, bang in the city centre, this is probably the best-value choice. A fine old building with an arcaded courtyard. ⑤.

Geyer, Priesterhausgasse 5 (☎0463/57886, *hotelgeyer@carinthia.com*). Modern, medium-sized hotel a few steps away from the town centre. En suites modishly furnished with lots of varnished light-brown wood, warm colours and houseplants. ④.

Kohlweg, St Veiterstrasse 122 (☎0463/42418). Small, plain hotel 1.5km north of the centre, offering adequate rooms with shared facilities. ②.

Liebetegger, Völkermarkterstrasse 8 (☎0463/56935). An unspectacular family-run hotel, although it's conveniently located, just east of the town centre. There's a choice of rooms with en-suite facilities (④), or without (②).

Moser-Verdino, Domgasse 2 (☎0463/57878, *moser-verdino@arcotel.at*). Luxurious city-centre business hotel, offering comfortable rooms with bathrooms and satellite TV. Computer and emailing facilities available. ⑦.

Müller, Rankengasse 21 (☎0463/21254). Small, family-run pension with functional rooms. It's over 2km west of the centre, but is ideally located for the forested parklands of the Kreuzbergl – and you can just about walk to the lakefront from here, too. Rooms come with en-suite facilities (③), or without (②).

Sandwirt, Pernhartgasse 9 (☎0463/56209, *sandwirt@carinthia.com*). Central, upmarket hotel offering all the creature comforts. Nowadays holder of a *Best Western* franchise, it's strong on international uniformity rather than local colour. ⑦.

Sclosshotel Wörthersee, Villacherstrasse 338 (☎0463/21158, *www.schlosshotel-woerthersee.at*). Lakefront hotel in a fanciful nineteenth-century castellated building, with its own beach. All rooms have en-suite facilities and TV. Rooms come with a lake view (⑥), or without (③).

Schweizerhaus, Kreuzbergl 11 (☎0463/56721). Comfortable TV-equipped en suites in the "Swiss house", an alpine-style Gasthof on the shoulder of Kreuzbergl hill, 3km northwest of the centre. Good views of Klagenfurt from the terrace. Perfect for woodland walks. ③.

Hostels

Jugendgästehaus Kolping, Enzenberstrasse 26 (☎0463/56965). A large modern block only 10 minutes' walk east of the centre, with two- and three-bedded rooms with en-suite showers. Open July 10–Sept 10. ②.

Jugendherberge Klagenfurt, Neckheimgasse 6 (☎0463/230020, *jgh.klagenfurt@oejhv.or.at*). An attractively designed piece of contemporary architecture 3km west of the centre, within walking distance of the lakefront. It's in a modern, suburban area of town with a lot of student accommodation, so there are some good cheap bars and pizzerias in the immediate vicinity. Open all year round, it offers accommodation in four-bed dorms with en-suite showers for öS180/€13.14 per person. Double occupancy (①) and single occupancy (öS365/€26.25) are available. Reception is open 7–9am and 5–10pm. Take bus #12 from Heiligengeistplatz to Jugendherberge, or the more frequent #10 to the Neckheimgasse stop, which is only 200m north.

Mladinski Dom, Mikschallee 4 (☎0463/35651). Slovene-run student hostel (the name simply means "youth hostel"), 1.5km east of the centre, open from the first week in July to the first week in September. Doubles with breakfast (②); singles and triples also available. Bus #70 or #71 from Heiligengeistplatz to Windischkaserne.

The City

Klagenfurt centres on **Neuer Platz**, a broad flagstoned square whose focus is a statue of the curly-tailed **Lindwurm**, the mythical beast central to a local George-and-the-Dragon-style folk tale – and very much the city's trademark. Sixteenth-century sculptor Ulrich Vogelsang, who obviously intended his creation to look rather more fearsome than it does, based the head of the beast on a locally unearthed prehistoric rhino skull (now displayed in the Landesmuseum; see overleaf), which perhaps accounts for its hapless, gaping visage – from which a jet of water spurts into a basin. The Lindwurm is faced by a statue of a club-wielding, Hercules-like hero, added later by Michael Hönel – creator of the spectacular high altar at Gurk (see overleaf). This quaint sculptural ensemble is completed by a stout, greening statue of the Empress Maria Theresia several metres away to the east, who gazes out onto the square seemingly oblivious to the monster-slaying drama going on in front of her.

From here Kramergasse leads north to **Alter Platz**, heart of a pedestrianized shopping district where most of Klagenfurt's more historic town houses lie. Oldest of these, the **Haus zur goldenes Gans** stands at the western end of Alter Platz, a squat, medieval structure whose sloping buttresses were built to withstand the minor earthquakes that once shook the area. Behind it loom the twin towers of the **Landhaus**, seat of the Carinthian provincial government although built as an arsenal in the 1580s. Staircases lead from the galleried inner courtyard to the **Wappensaal**, or heraldic hall (April–Sept Mon–Fri 9am–1pm & 2–5pm; öS15/€1.09), the walls of which are covered with the coats of arms of the Carinthian nobility. The trompe l'oeil ceiling paintings by local artist **Josef-Ferdinand Fromiller** (1693–1760) portray nobles paying homage to Emperor Karl VI, father of Maria Theresia. There's more work by Fromiller adorning the ceilings of the **Stadtpfarrkirche St Egyd**, north of Alter Platz on Pfarrplatz, a fourteenth-century edifice studded with aristocratic grave plaques. The main attraction is, however, the church tower (May–Sept Mon–Fri 10am–5.30pm, Sat 10am–12.30pm; öS10/€0.73), which rewards a stiff climb with a fine view of Klagenfurt and surrounding hills.

The Landesgalerie, Domkirche and Diözesianmuseum

The **Landesgalerie**, just east of Neuer Platz on Burggasse (Mon–Fri 9am–6pm, Sat & Sun 10am–noon; öS20/€1.45; *www.landesgalerie.ktn.gv.at*), is the venue of high-profile temporary exhibitions, and also houses a permanent collection devoted to the history of Carinthian art – a fairly provincial backwater if the works on display here are anything to go by. The idealized nineteenth-century landscapes of Markus Pernhart, such as *Climbers Surveying the Grossglockner*, and the more expressionist rural views of locally born mid-twentieth-century painter Herbert Boeckl, provide some respite from the otherwise mediocre offerings on show.

Three blocks south of here, on Lidmanskygasse, Klagenfurt's unassuming **Domkirche** has been hemmed in by dreary grey office blocks since the 1970s, making the ebullient creams and pinks of its stuccoed interior all the more pleasantly suprising. This outwardly stern sixteenth-century structure was originally built at a time when most of Klagenfurt's nobles were Protestants; the colourful Baroque redecorating job carried out by the Jesuits, brought into Carinthia to help drive Protestantism out, was a deliberate slap in the face of Lutheran austerity. Just round the corner at Lidmanskygasse 10 is the **Diözesianmuseum** (1 to 14 June & mid-Sept to mid-Oct Mon–Sat 10am–noon; mid-June to mid-Sept 10am–noon & 3–5pm; öS30/€2.18), which harbours altarpieces and statuary retrieved from churches across the province. Pride of place belongs to Austria's oldest piece of stained glass, the twelfth-century *Magdalenscheibe*, a portrayal of Mary Magdalene which once adorned the Magdalenakirche in the village of Weitensfeld, near Gurk.

The Landesmuseum

A block south of Lidmanskygasse, the **Landesmuseum**, at Museumgasse 2 (Tues–Sat 9am–4pm, Sun 10am–1pm; öS40/€2.91; *www.landesmuseum-ktn.at*), provides a thorough and entertaining lesson in Carinthian history and culture. The overview begins in the entrance hall with the *Fürstenstein*, or prince's stone, a rudimentary throne made from the base of a Roman column and originally located in the village of Karnburg, 7km north of town. Rather like the *Herzogstuhl* (see p.334), the stone was used in ceremonies intended to confirm the authority of the German-speaking dukes of Carinthia over the Slav peasants of the Zollfeld. According to the chronicler Johann of Viktring, the ritual was still in use in the thirteenth century, was conducted in the Slovene language, and involved a local farmers' leader asking the duke whether he promised to be a just and Christian ruler before slapping him lightly on the cheek and inviting him to perch on the pillar.

The first floor has a rather pedestrian and unimaginatively presented geology and natural history collection, although it's worth looking out for the *Lindwurmschädel*, the fossilized rhino skull, unearthed near Klagenfurt in the fourteenth century, which served as a model for the Lindwurm statue in Neuer Platz. On the second floor, Hallstatt-era finds from Frög bei Rosegg (5km south of Velden) shed light on the thriving Celtic culture which once existed in Carinthia, including a display case full of exquisitely modelled, miniature lead horse-riding figures, rather like an army of toy soldiers. On a somewhat larger scale is the Roman-era Dionysus mosaic from Virunum (near present-day Maria Saal), first-century capital of the province of Noricum, depicting a youthful and near-naked Dionysus, his cloak slipping casually from a shoulder, surrounded by a colourful supporting cast of similarly *deshabillé* maenads and satyrs. Such a mosaic would have been used to decorate a room where feasting and entertaining took place – it's thought that the images of the Medusa at each corner of the design were intended as charms to ward off guilt- or shame-bearing spirits, thereby leaving house guests free to indulge in Dionysiac revelry unabashed. Elsewhere on the same floor, there's a fine collection of Gothic devotional paintings, including the anonymous *St Vitus Altarpiece* of 1470, in which the saint's various torments (beaten with clubs, bundled into an oven and thrown to the lions among other things) are pictured against a fanciful backdrop of fairy-tale turrets and spires. Look out too for a delightful wood-carved relief from sixteenth-century St Veit an der Glan, in which a princess plays with a unicorn in a garden enclosed by a wall, over which a knight – presumably her suitor – takes a discreet peek. Pride of place belongs to the two pictures relating to the Order of St George once based in Millstatt (see p.354), the first showing the swearing-in ceremony of Johann Siebenhirter as Grand Master of the Order by a boyish-looking Pope Paul II, assisted by Emperor Friedrich III, in 1469; the second showing Siebenhirter's successor Johan Geumann sheltering with his knights under the protective mantle of the Virgin Mary.

Further on, the **ethnographic section** sheds light on some fascinating Carinthian folk customs. Commanding immediate attention are the captivatingly demonic *Partl* masks – still made by craftsmen in rural Carinthia, such masks are donned on the eve of St Nicholas' Day to represent the bogeyman figure who, rather like Santa Claus in reverse, visits badly behaved children and takes them away in his bag. Nearby are the paper lanterns in the shape of churches used to celebrate the feast of Maria Lichtmess (Candlemass), on February 2, in the village of Eisenkappel in southeast Carinthia. Children process through the streets carrying the lanterns, which are then placed in the river and left to float downstream – a practice believed to protect children from mishaps.

The Robert-Musil-Museum

It's a short walk south from the Landesmuseum to the **Robert-Musil-Museum**, at Bahnhofstrasse 50 (Mon–Fri 10am–5pm, Sat 10am–2pm; öS40/€2.91; *www .musilmuseum.at*), housed on the lower floor of the building where Austria's leading twentieth-century novelist was born. Musil's connection with Klagenfurt is fairly tenuous – he only spent the first 11 months of his life here – but this is nevertheless an absorbing if stolid introduction to the man and his work, relying heavily on family photographs, German-language texts, and the Underwood Standard Portable typewriter on which he bashed out his manuscripts. There's also a section devoted to Klagenfurt-born writer Ingeborg Bachmann (1921–1973), whose short stories and essays confronted the suffocating conservatism of bourgeois postwar Austria – making her something of a heroine for the country's liberal-leaning artistic elite. There are gripping photographs of Hitler's triumphal visit to Klagenfurt in April 1938, an event witnessed by Bachmann herself. She later described this as the "specific point in time which destroyed my childhood. My memories begin on that day... that terrible, tangible brutality, those troops roaring, singing, marching up and down – and I was scared to death for the first time in my life".

Northwest of the centre

On the other side of the city centre, north of Alter Platz, the **Stadtgalerie**, at Theatergasse 4 (Mon–Fri 10am–7pm, Sat 10am–5pm, Sun 10am–3pm; öS70/€5.09; *www.galerie.klagenfurt.at*), is the town's principal venue for major touring art exhibitions. A few steps west, Theatergasse becomes Theaterplatz, opening out to reveal the striking Art-Nouveau **Stadttheater** (think bare-breasted muses brandishing lyres, and you're on the right track), Carinthia's main venue for serious drama, classical music and opera. From here Radetzkystrasse strikes northwestwards, with the verdant strolling areas of the **Goethepark** on the right and the **Schillerpark** on the left. Occupying stately villas in the Goethepark are two more venues for temporary art exhibitions: the **Stadthaus Galerie**, Theaterplatz 4 (Mon–Fri 10am–1pm & 4–7pm, Sat 10am–1pm; prices vary), and the **Kunstverein für Kärnten** (same hours; prices vary; *www.kunstvereinkaernten.at*).

Radetzkystrasse continues towards Prof-Dr-Kahler-Platz 1km further west, where pathways lead up to the **Kreuzbergl**, an area of partly wooded hilly parkland crisscrossed by paths. Sheltering at the base of the hills on the northern side of the square

ROBERT MUSIL 1880–1942

If one man could be said to personify the modern Austrian literary tradition it would be **Robert Musil**, whose ironic, cerebral dissections of Austrian society in the early twentieth century have exerted a profound influence over successive generations of novelists. Robert Edler von Musil, to give him his full name, had an unlikely background for a writer. Like many sons of well-to-do Austrian families – his father, Alfred, was professor of engineering at the University of Brünn (now Brno in the Czech republic) – Robert was sent away to a military academy at the age of 12, and looked set to become a promising young officer until he gave it all up and opted to study engineering at Brünn, where his father was still teaching. He spent the next ten years accumulating various degrees, finishing up with a PhD in philosophy at the University of Berlin. Unable to commit himself to an academic career, however, he subsequently worked as a librarian and civil servant before devoting himself entirely to writing in the mid-1920s.

Musil's first novel had been published while he was still a postgraduate student at Berlin. *The Confusions of Young Törless* (*Die Verwirrungen des Zöglings Törless*; 1906) explored the brutish and sadomasochistic undercurrents indulged in by pupils at an Austrian military boarding school – something of which Musil himself had personal experience. However he is primarily known for the vast, unfinished panorama of Viennese society on the eve of World War I *The Man Without Qualities* (*Der Mann ohne Eigenschaften*), the first book of which was published in 1930. Part of the second book appeared in 1933, but Musil laboured unsuccessfully over the conclusion: several more fragments were published in 1943, by which time the author was already dead. The book's main protagonist, Ulrich, is very much like Musil himself: a man of science who withdraws from the life of work and career (hence his supposed lack of "qualities"), all the better to contemplate the absurdities of the self-possessed, but doomed imperial capital in which he lives.

An intellectual feast brimming with ideas and essayistic digressions, *The Man* was never going to be a plot-driven populist read. Musil's publishing house, Rohwolt, was advised by its accountants not to publish the book for fear that it would drive the firm to bankruptcy, but went ahead all the same – convinced of the work's importance to European literature. The novel was indeed an instant critical success, but Musil had the misfortune to be writing at a time when the natural audience for his books – the sophisticated urban elite – was being squeezed out of Austrian and German life by the combined forces of Fascism and Nazism. With the Nazi annexation of Austria in 1938, Musil fled to Switzerland with his Jewish wife, where he lived in poverty until his death. Musil's works were banned in Austria and Germany by a Nazi state that considered them far too decadent and negative to contribute to the moral improvement of the Aryan race – making it impossible for the author to earn any royalties. His only source of income for much of his career came from the Musil societies: ad-hoc groups of friends and supporters who made collections on his behalf.

Despite such acts of generosity, Musil was bitter about the cultural elite's failure to accord him the appreciation which he felt to be his natural right. He had a low opinion of the succesful novelists of the day, and his diaries notoriously acccuse Nobel Prize-winning novelist Thomas Mann of cravenly pandering to a mediocre liberal intelligentsia. Musil never knew that Mann was a keen contributor to one of the Musil societies. Musil's international reputation grew slowly but steadily in the years following World War II, and he's nowadays recognized not only as Austria's greatest twentieth-century novelist, but also as a great European figure on a par with Proust.

is a small **Botanischer Garten** (May–Sept daily 9am–6pm; Oct–April Mon–Thurs 7am–4pm, Fri 7am–1pm; free), a cramped but beautifully laid out collection of native and exotic plants. Lurking at the back of the garden is the entrance to the **Bergbaumuseum** (April–Oct daily 9am–6pm; öS50/€3.63), a mining museum housed in tunnels that served as air-raid shelters in World War II. There are well-presented displays of local minerals and drilling equipment from the lead-mining centre of Bad Bleiberg (50km west of here in the hills above Villach), as well as a dinosaur egg from China, but the potted history of Carinthian mining on offer lacks the punch of Austria's several show-mines; a visit to Bad Bleiberg itself (see p.348) would be a better bet if you have the time.

Europapark, Minimundus and the lakefront

From central Klagenfurt, buses #10, #11 and #12 head due west along Villacherstrasse towards the lakefront 3km away. The street runs along the banks of the **Lendkanal**, built in the late Middle Ages to connect landlocked Klagenfurt to the lake. Between mid-May and late September, a **passenger trimaran** runs along the Lend (contact the tourist office for prices and times), leaving town from the eastern end of Villacherstrasse and arriving near the lakefront some twenty minutes later.

Stretching back from the lakefront for about one kilometre is the **Europapark**, a grassy expanse that harbours one of southern Austria's top tourist attractions, **Minimundus**, at Villacherstrasse 241 (daily: April & Oct 9am–5pm; May, June & Sept 9am–6pm; July & Aug 8am–7pm; öS130/€9.45; *www.minimundus.at*). With profits going to Rettet das Kind, the Austrian equivalent of Britain's Save the Children, it's a popular family-oriented attraction centred around 1:25 scale models of the world's famous buildings – with a smattering of model trains and boats. A large open-air garden dotted with flowerbeds contains more than 160 models, including many obvious international landmarks (the Eiffel Tower, Big Ben, the White House and the like), although there's a sufficient number of less instantly recognizable choices – such as Bulgaria's Rila Monastery and a Yemenite royal palace – to make the official English-language guide booklet (öS35/€2.56) a worthwhile investment.

Just north of Minimundus, **Happ's Reptilienzoo**, Villacherstrasse 237 (daily: May–Oct 8am–6pm; Sept–April 9am–5pm; öS110/€7.99; *www.reptilienzoo.at*), provides haven for snakes, lizards and crocs, together with an aquarium, home to some piranhas, and an outdoor model dinosaur garden.

The lakefront

The Europapark stretches westwards from Minimundus as far as the lakefront just under 1km away, where Klagenfurt's marvellously old-fashioned municipal **Strandbad** (öS35/€2.56) attracts bathers with its deckchair-covered lawns, long wooden piers and pedalos for rent. One incongruous concession to modernity is the nude sunbathing platform (open to men only on Tues, Thurs & Sat, women only on the other four days), separated from other bathers by a screen. Just north of the Strandbad is the ship station, where regular ferries depart for Velden, Pörtschach and other lakeside settlements between May and October. The whole area is understandably busy during the summer, but it's a nice place to stroll whatever the season, thanks to some satisfying views across the Wörthersee, and its hilly, forest-covered surrounds.

MAIERNIGG AND THE MAHLER HOUSE

Three kilometres away from Europapark, on the southeastern shoulder of the Wörthersee, lie the gently sloping lakeside lawns of **Strandbad Maiernigg** (öS35/€2.56), just outside the city limits, and a quieter alternative to the much larger Strandbad in the Europapark. From here, a well-signed path leads uphill for about 15 minutes in order to reach the **Gustav Mahlers Komponierhäuschen** (May–Oct daily 10am–4pm; öS10/€0.73), the idyllic garden-shed-like retreat built by the composer in 1900, along with his lakeside villa below. Mahler took a two-month break in Maiernigg each summer, rising at 6am and composing in solitude for five hours each day, before swimming in the lake and then heading off across the mountains. In the *Häuschen*, he worked on his Fourth, Fifth, Sixth, Seventh and Eighth symphonies, as well as finishing off the *Kindertotenlieder* (Songs for Dead Children), a song cycle which his wife Alma for one considered unduly morbid, seeing as the couple were starting a family at the time. In 1907 their elder daughter Maria (Putzi), who wasn't yet five, contracted scarlet fever at Maiernigg and died, drawing an end to the composer's eight-year love affair with the Wörthersee. Eager to distance themselves from painful memories, the Mahlers sold up and never returned. The *Komponierhäuschen* itself contains a few photographs, and there's a stack of Mahler CDs for sale, but the main attraction is the setting: high above the lake, and shrouded by woods, it's not difficult to see why Mahler found the environment so inspiring.

Maiernigg is difficult to combine with a visit to Europapark, unless you have a car or bike, as there is no direct footpath along the lakefront, driving potential walkers inland for long stretches. Best way to get here is to take one of the Klagenfurt–Maria Worth–Velden buses from the bus station, which pass right by the Strandbad.

Eating, drinking and nightlife

Klagenfurt is at first glance a relatively quiet place, as most of the best eating and drinking venues are hidden away from the main thoroughfares in charming alleyways and courtyards. The streets around Pfarrplatz – Herrengasse, Pfarrhofgasse and Osterwitzgasse – are the best places to look. In general Klagenfurt's **restaurants** provide a good introduction to Carinthian cuisine, with most places offering a mixture of local *Nud'l* dishes, Austrian staples, and fresh fish from the Wörthersee. For **snacks**, the one city-centre Würstelstand is in the bus station on Heiligengeistplatz, while *Cemal's Döner Kebab*, Lidmanskygasse 5, is a dependable source of good-quality Turkish fast food as well as offering sit-down meals.

There's a healthy sprinkling of **drinking** venues, a large proportion of which are concentrated in the area around Herrengasse and Pfarrplatz. Most of these keep buzzing until around 1 or 2am throughout the week, except on Sundays, when the city centre can seem eerily deserted. The town also quietens considerably during periods of good summer weather, when locals abandon Klagenfurt's bars in favour of trendier Wörthersee venues like Pörtschach and Velden.

Despite its status as the provincial capital, Klagenfurt is not a place in which to gorge yourself on **entertainment**, although the Stadttheater, Theaterplatz 4 (box office Tues–Sat: July & Aug 9am–noon & 5–7pm; Sept–June 9am–noon & 4–6pm; ☎0463/54064), has an all-year programme of opera, highbrow drama and ballet.

Restaurants

A la Carte, Khevenhüllerstrasse 2 (☎0463/516651). Northwest of the centre, an outwardly unspectacular restaurant that offers top-class French-Austrian cuisine and excellent fish. No official dress restrictions, but you'll feel out of place in jeans and T-shirt. Reservations advisable. Open until 9.30pm only. Closed Sun & Mon.

Caminetto, Rennplatz. Smart but cosy place in the pedestrianized alley behind the Hotel Moser-Verdino, with salads, sandwiches and cheap pasta dishes in one half of the building, and a slightly grander Italian restaurant in the other.

Gasthof zum heiligen Josef, Osterwitzgasse 7. Inexpensive mainstream Austrian food, including all the most popular schnitzel dishes, as well as Wörthersee fish. A good range of cheap soups and salads make this a lunchtime favourite.

Hirter Botschaft, Bahnhofstrasse 44. Smart subterranean beer hall/restaurant near the train station, with a trusty selection of inexpensive schnitzels and roast chicken dinners on offer, together with a cheap daily special.

Landhauskeller, Landhaushof. A popular daytime venue due to its plentiful outdoor seating in the Landhaus courtyard. Food is mid-priced Austrian. Closed Sun.

Maria Loretto, on the Wörthersee, just south of the main Strandbad (☎0463/24465). Mid-to-high-priced restaurant occupying an attractive lakeside villa, with plentiful outdoor seating facing the water. It's a good place for fresh trout and other Wörthersee fish, although the menu includes all the usual Austrian and Carinthian regulars as well. Closed Mon.

Rathausstüberl, Alte Rathausgasse. Cosy central place in an alleyway linking Alter Platz with the Pfarrplatz, providing cheap Carinthian *Nud'ln*, good-value schnitzel-based standards, and some good lunchtime choices, like salad platters and soups. Closed Sun.

Raffi, corner of Burggasse and Getreidegasse. Mid-price Austro-Italian restaurant with a cosy bistro feel and a meat-heavy menu, with choices ranging from *Tafelspitz* to *Saltimbocca*.

Zum Augustin, Pfarrhofgasse 2. Roomy and atmospheric eating and drinking venue with wooden bench seating a few steps west of the Pfarrkirche, offering hearty and inexpensive Carinthian *Nud'l* dishes. A good place for a beer, too.

Cafés and bars

In Vino Veritas, Burggasse. Relaxed, elegant bar with outdoor seating in one of central Klagenfurt's leafy courtyards, with occasional live music on summer weekends.

Kamot, Bahnhofstrasse 9. Cool jazz bar two blocks east of Neuer Platz in a cellar divided up into 4 rooms, with live music at weekends. Good place for a drink whether you're a member of the black turtleneck crowd or not.

Molly Malones, Theatergasse. Roomy pub which works well as both an animated boozing venue and a quiet place for an intimate drink, depending on where you decide to perch. Decent food, including fair-sized portions of ribs.

Pankraz, 8. Mai-Strasse 16. Largish café-bar chicly decorated in modern minimalist style. Vaguely alternative music. A magnet for trendy young things.

Segafredo, Alter Platz. Popular because of its location more so than anything else, a modern café-bar with plenty of outdoor seating on the pedestrianized central thoroughfare; a nice place for a drink by day or night – the cakes and ice creams are good, too.

Spektakel, Pfarrplatz 16. Cosy bar with cramped, pub-like indoor boozing area, and outdoor seating in a pleasant courtyard. Entrance also from Wienergasse 7. Open until 4am at weekends.

Ungekünstlt, Herrengasse 3. Busy but friendly place with a small area of outdoor seating, just off Herrengasse in an arcade that harbours a couple of other bars.

VIP, Domgasse. Chic bar with twenty-to-thirty-something, dressy clientele, and slightly higher prices than elsewhere. A good place to sip *prosecco* and enjoy piped cocktail-bar sounds.

Listings

Airport Flughafen Annabichl, 3km northeast of town, is served by buses #42 and #45 from Heiligengeistplatz. Information ☎0463/415000.

Bike rental At the train station.

Car rental Avis, Villacherstrasse 1c, and at the airport (☎0463/55938); Budget, at the airport (☎0463/46226); Hertz, St Ruprechtstrasse 12 (☎0463/56147).

Cinemas The Wulfenia, Luegerstrasse 5 (☎0463/22288), is a modern multi-screen cinema with first-run Hollywood films (usually dubbed in German), while the smaller Kammerlichtspiele, Adlergasse 1 (☎0463/54051), offers more art-house choices, sometimes in the original language.

Hospital Klagenfurter Krankenhaus, St-Veiter-Strasse 47 (☎0463/538).

Pharmacies Most central are the Adler Apotheke, Neuer Platz 9, and the Lendorf Apotheke, Seltenheimerstrasse 2. Signs in pharmacy windows give names and addresses of duty pharmacies, which open on a rota basis.

Post office The main post office (Mon–Fri 7.30am–6pm, Sat 7.30–11am) is at Pernhartgasse 7. The post office next to the train station at Bahnhofplatz 5 has longer hours (Mon–Fri 7am–10pm, Sat & Sun 8am–9pm).

Sailing Kärntner Yachtsportschule, Villacherstrasse 1a, on the lakefront (☎0463/511111). Offers boat hire and tuition.

Swimming pools Erlebnis Hallenbad, on the corner of Gabelsbergerstrasse and Lastenstrasse. Has water slides, whirlpools and children's areas. Open Sept–June. In summer, head for the Strandbad on the Wörthersee lakefront (see below).

Train information ☎0463/1717.

Travel agent Kärntner Reisebüro, Neuer Platz 2 (☎0463/56400).

Windsurfing Kärntner Yachtsportschule (see "Sailing" above). Board hire and a range of courses.

Around the Wörthersee

Both a high-energy summer playground and sedate retreat for affluent oldies, the **Wörthersee** stretches west from Klagenfurt for 20km, squeezed between low hills with the Karawanken Alps a distant backdrop to the south. The lake has long been regarded as a laid-back, small-scale Austrian version of the French Riviera, a status that dates back to the 1860s when the region was first linked to Vienna by rail. It soon became the favoured vacation spot for Vienna-based businessmen and industrialists, many of whom embarked on the construction of lakeside holiday homes in which to while away the *Sommerfrische*, or summer holiday. Although most are still in private hands and can't be visited, these villas – playfully embellished with details like little spires, balustrades and oriel windows – continue to give the region much of its elegant, nineteenth-century character. After World War II the Wörthersee resorts were frequently used as locations in the romantic comedies churned out by the Austrian and German film industries. Actors, playboys and hangers-on descended on the area in large numbers, giving the area a reputation for glamour and exclusivity that still lives on – in the minds of local Carinthians, if not always in real life. Today's Wörthersee offers a charming slice of sedate lakeside relaxation mixed with brash modern hedonism – a combination that few other waterside locations in Austria can match. The lake is at its best from spring through to early autumn: outside these times, visitor numbers dwindle to almost nothing, and many hotels and restaurants close their doors.

Klagenfurt commands the eastern approaches to the lake, but lacks the high-society reputation enjoyed by the Wörthersee's other main centres – **Velden** on the western shore, and **Pörtschach** to the north. Both of these have a better choice of daytime activities and night-time diversions, but they're also two of the most expensive lakeside resorts in the country. Standing in the shadow of the wooded **Pyramidenkogel**, settlements on the **southern shore** of the lake receive slightly less sun, and are that bit less fashionable as a result. **Maria Wörth**, with its attractive lakeside churches, is the most pleasing of the settlements on this part of the lake, while **Reifnitz** and **Dellach** offer plenty of accommodation and a sprinkling of lakeside activities, but not much else.

Each of the resorts along the lakeshore has an attractive waterside esplanade of one sort or another; elsewhere most of the shore is private property, so public rights of way enabling you to walk or cycle along the lakefront, or simply stop off for a spot of sunbathing, are few and far between. Many hotels have access to small stretches of the lakefront where guests are allowed to bathe, however, and there are numerous municipal or privately owned **Strandbäder** where you can loll around on the grass or swim in the lake on payment of a fee. As a general rule, **cycling** is best on the north side of the lake, where there are more opportunities for getting off the busy main road and onto specific cycle- and pedestrian-only paths. **Water-based activities** such as windsurfing and sailing are easily arranged.

Getting around the lake by boat is no problem in season, which usually runs from the first week in May to the beginning of October. **Boats** run from Klagenfurt to Velden and back, calling at intermediate points on both sides of the lake, five times a day at the beginning and the end of the season, rising to eight times a day in July and August. Compared to buses and trains, boat travel is pricey (for example, Klagenfurt–Velden costs öS140/€10.22 single, öS200/€14.60 return; Klagenfurt–Pörtschach costs öS80/€5.84 single, öS130/€9.49 return), but it can be the easiest way to get from one side of the lake to the other.

Pörtschach

Situated midway between Klagenfurt and Velden on the northern shore of the lake, **PÖRTSCHACH** is traditionally the Wörthersee's most exclusive resort. But while prices here are higher than anywhere else in Carinthia, the resort caters for a wide range of ages and tastes. Whether you're looking for a night of bar-hopping or a slow stroll along the lakefront, it's an invigorating place to be. There's not a lot to the town itself save for a main road, the shop- and café-lined Hauptstrasse, which runs through the town from east to west. Immediately south of here, a small peninsula juts out into the lake, where a promenade along the water's edge is lined with terrace cafés and kiosks offering boat hire and windsurfing. At the tip of the peninsula, beyond the high-rise *Hotel Park*, you'll find the landing stage for Wörthersee passenger boats, and a large Strandbad (daily: May, June & Sept 9am–7pm; July & Aug 9am–8pm; öS60/€4.38) occupying a partly wooded offshore island accessible by footbridge.

Arrival, information and accommodation

Pörtschach's **train station** is a few steps north of the Hauptstrasse: walk down the access road from the station and you'll see the **tourist office** diagonally opposite to the left at Hauptstrasse 153 (April–Oct Mon–Fri 8am–6pm, Sat & Sun 9am–5pm; Nov–March Mon–Thurs 8am–4pm, Fri 8am–1pm; ☎04272/4488-55, *www.tiscover.com/poertschach*), where you can pick up a town map and addresses of sporting facilities, and book **accommodation**. Bear in mind you don't come to Pörtschach to save money; as a general rule, any hotel near the water will be expensive, and a room with a lake view extortionate. There are plenty of comfortable mid-priced pensions, however, for around price code ③, in the residential streets north of the railway tracks, with prices falling to around öS250/€18.25 per head the further east you go. **Private rooms** start at about price code ②, although families and people travelling in groups will find **apartments** (stays of more than three days preferred) a cheaper option.

Of the **hotels**, *Haus Silvia*, Goritschacherweg 35 (☎04272/2996; ③; May–Sept only), on a hillside 1.5km east of town, has utilitarian en suites, most with balconies and TV, in a chalet-style house; while *Frühstückspension Iris*, ten minutes' walk east of the centre at Mühlweg 36 (☎04272/3498; ②), has adequate doubles with en-suite facilities, some with balconies facing the lake. *Hotel-Pension Auguste*, Augustenstrasse 12 (mid–May to mid–Oct; ☎04272/2272, *www.tiscover.com/villa-auguste*; ③), is a plain building bang in the centre of town, 100m from the lake, with functional but fully equipped rooms. *Strandhotel Prüller*, Annastrasse 33–35 (☎04272/2353-0, *www .strandhotel-prueller.at*; ⑦), is a standard well-appointed lakefront hotel with its own bathing area, and modern rooms with en-suite facilities and TV. There's a **campsite** on the lakefront at **Töschling**, a small settlement 2km west of Pörtschach. Klagenfurt–Pörtschach–Velden buses and local trains (not expresses) stop nearby.

Eating and drinking

Despite Pörtschach's stylish reputation, places to **eat** are on the whole fairly uniform. All the hotels along the lakefront have restaurants with outdoor terraces, most of which offer a range of standard Austrian cuisine, together with local fish, at a reasonable (though hardly budget) price. The restaurant of the *Strandhotel Prüller*, Annastrasse 33–35, is as reasonable as any. *Fallaloon*, at the western end of the Hauptstrasse, serves up Chinese meals and Japanese sushi dishes that won't break the bank, while the *Seerose*, Hauptstrasse 165, specializes in grilled meats at reasonable prices. The upmarket and undoubtedly atmospheric *Schloss Leonstain*, Hauptstrasse 228, is the place to splash out on fresh fish and fine wines. Konditorei Wieneroither, on the Hauptstrasse about 50m east of the tourist office, is the best place for buying pastries and cakes.

Most **nightlife** revolves around the smallish **Monte-Carlo-Platz**, halfway along the Hauptstrasse, which becomes one vast open-air bar at the height of summer. The busy *Rainer's Bar* has a reputation for attracting the dressed-up crowd, with *Montesol* just over the road offering a slightly funkier alternative. *Anna W*, just west of here at Hauptstrasse 218, has a slightly younger clientele, but still attracts the beautiful people. The biggest **clubbing** venue on the lake is *Fabrik*, a five-kilometre taxi ride west of Pörtschach in the tiny village of **Saag**.

Velden

Hugging the bay at the western end of the lake, brash and bustling **VELDEN** is larger and more crowded than Pörtschach, and less attractive as a result. It's another place where sybaritic youth mingle with strolling pensioners and sightseeing coach parties. Most visitors, coach or no coach, gravitate at some stage towards the central **Europaplatz**, where Velden's casino provides the fulcrum of the town's social life. The casino was opened in 1989, its attractive spire-like protrusions making it something of a landmark. From Europaplatz, Am Corso leads south towards the transport hub of Karawankenplatz, from where Seecorso leads round the lake. Overlooking Seecorso is the **Schloss**, a distinctive egg-yolk-coloured structure which is close to the hearts of many Austrians and Germans, having served as the backdrop to a popular 1990s television series, *Schloss am Wörthersee*. Armies of Teutonic soap fans continue to gravitate here, photographing each other outside the Schloss's portals. Built for leading Carinthian magnate Bartholomäus von Khevenhüller in 1590, it was largely destroyed by fire in 1762, and most of what you now see is the result of an 1891 rebuilding. Previously used as an exhibition venue and luxury hotel, it was bought by German millionaire Günther Sachs (erstwhile husband of Brigitte Bardot) in 1990, and it's not yet clear whether it will ever be reopened to the public. Sachs is best known in the non-German-speaking world for his walk-on role in a famous episode in pop history: it is thought that Sachs personally intervened to scotch the release of then-wife Bardot's steamy duet with Serge Gainsbourg, *Je t'aime... moi non plus*, forcing the Gallic lounge-pop genius to team up with Jane Birkin instead.

Arrival, information and accommodation

From Velden's **train station**, walk downhill along Bahnhofstrasse, turn right into Klagenfurterstrasse and keep going to reach the central ribbon of Europaplatz, Am Corso and Karawankenplatz. **Buses** from Klagenfurt and Villach pick up and drop off at Villacherstrasse, a five-minute walk west of Karawankenplatz. The **tourist office**, Villacherstrasse 5 (May, June & Sept Mon–Sat 8am–7pm, Sun 10am–6pm; July & Aug Mon–Sat 8am–8pm, Sun 10am–7pm; Oct–April Mon–Fri 8am–5pm, Sat 11am–5pm; ☎04272/4488-66, *www.tiscover.com/velden*), has lists of **private rooms** and holiday **apartments** (the latter only really open to those contemplating a stay of four or more days) in Velden and surrounding villages, but you might have to ring up the places yourself. The nearest **campsite** is the *Weisses Rössl* at Auen (see p.332), accessible on Velden–Maria Wörth–Klagenfurt buses.

Best of the local **pensions** are *Gästehaus Teppan*, Sternbergstrasse 7 (☎04274/3169, *pension.teppan@carinthia.com*; ②), a modern house with small balconied rooms just uphill from Villacherstrasse, the main road westwards out of town, and the *Frühstückspension Urania* at Mühlweg 2 (☎04274/2696; ③), a residential street southwest of the centre and only minutes from the lake. One of the best **hotel** deals on the lakefront is *Seehaus Ogris*, Seecorso 34 (☎04274/2079; ④), a simple family hotel with en-suite facilites and TVs in all rooms. Moving up slightly in price, the characterful *Mösslacherhaus*, Karawankenplatz 1 (☎04274/2020; ⑥), is a delightful cross between central European villa and English country house, offering rooms with en-suite facilities and TV, and use of a private Strandbad a few steps away.

Eating and drinking

Good, cheap Austrian **food** is thin on the ground in Velden, but there's a growing range of ethnic restaurants to fill the gap. Among the most popular are *Xjangiang-Hof*, Am Corso 2a, a passable Chinese restaurant with a large, reasonably priced menu and outdoor seating in a big courtyard, and two pizzerias: the cheap-and-cheerful *Pizzeria Domino*, Bahnhofstrasse 5, and the slightly more expensive *Pizzeria da Leopoldo*, Seecorso 18, a chic place that stays open beyond midnight. For something indigenous, *Mozartstuben*, uphill from the lakefront to the south at Augsdorferstrasse 36, knocks out no-nonsense schnitzel-and-chips dishes as well as traditional Austrian workingman's recipes like *Schweinshaxe* (pork knuckle). For good-quality Austrian fare and the best in Carinthian *Nud'l* dishes, there's little to choose between the two central Gasthof-restaurants *Alte Post*, Europaplatz 4–6, and the slightly more upmarket *Hubertushof*, Europaplatz 1.

Most **drinking** revolves around Europaplatz, where the outdoor tables of the Casino's own café vie for custom with three fashionable near-neighbours: the *American Bar* (also known as *Schinakel*), a society hangout of long standing, and relative newcomers *Krugerl* and *Café Gig*. The *Do & Ga Stehbar*, a little further west underneath the Volksbank, is a brasher, more youthful bar with regular live bands, while *Monkey Circus*, on the corner of Klagenfurterstrasse and Bahnhofstrasse, has Mexican beers alongside ribs- and wings-style nibbles. *Konzertkeller Kofler*, 1km east of town along Klagenfurter Strasse, hosts frequent blues and rock gigs. If you fancy trying your luck in the Casino, it is open from 3pm until the early hours and dress requirements are smart casual.

Schloss Rosegg and the Wildpark

You can walk, cycle or catch a bus (eight daily from Villacherstrasse) to the village of **ROSEGG**, 4km southwest of Velden, site of a Neoclassical **Schloss** (more of a country villa than a castle) built by Habsburg diplomat Graf Orsini-Rosenberg in 1770 for his Italian mistress Lucrezia – and currently owned by the Liechtenstein family. It's visited for the linden-lined avenues of its landscaped **park** (dawn–dusk; free), and the **Figurenkabinett Madame Lucrezia** (May–Oct Tues–Sun 9am–6pm; öS60/€4.38; *www.rosegg.at*), where the wax figures of Orsini-Rosenberg and his paramour mingle with other historical personages – including a portly Napoleon. But, if the weather's fine, your time would be better spent among the white wolves, deer and monkeys of **Wildpark Rosegg** (April–Nov daily 9am–5pm; July & Aug open till 6pm; öS70/€5.11), a short walk south of the Schloss.

The southern shore

Eight daily Klagenfurt–Velden buses speed along the Wörthersee Süduferstrasse, which runs from Klagenfurt to Velden along the **southern shore** of the lake, where a string of attractive if rather low-key settlements nestle beneath the wooded foothills of the Pyramidenkogel.

Ten kilometres west of Klagenfurt, **REIFNITZ** is the first place of any size, a quiet town with a municipal Strandbad and couple of café-restaurants on the lakefront. In recent years, it has gained notoriety for an annual meeting of Golf GTi fans, who assemble here from all across Europe over the *Pfingsten* (Whitsun) weekend. An unofficial affair conducted without the blessing of the local authorities, it basically involves a great deal of exuberant engine-revving, as enthusiasts trundle up and down the coast road in their vehicles. For the rest of the year, however, Reifnitz is a cheap and small-scale alternative to Pörtschach and Velden. The **tourist office**, on the main road through town (May–Oct Mon & Tues 8am–6pm, Wed–Fri 7.30am–6pm, Sat & Sun 9.30am–12.30pm & 1–6pm; ☎04273/2240), will fix you up with a **private room** or **pension**; alternatively, *Hotel-Pension Uschnig*, Seenstrasse 22 (☎04273/2294; ②–③), is a large B&B 500m from the lake with sparsely furnished but comfortable rooms, some with en-suite facilities. **Sailing** and **windsurfing** equipment rental and tuition can be organized at Segelschule Otto Stornig (☎04273/2371) on the lakefront.

From the centre of Reifnitz a road heads south then west towards the summit of the 850-metre **Pyramidenkogel**, 7km distant and topped by a futuristic **viewing tower** (daily: April & Oct 10am–6pm; May & Sept 9am–7pm; June 9am–8pm; July & Aug 9am–10pm; öS60/€4.38), where you can patronize the expensive café and savour a sweeping panorama of the Carinthian countryside. There are well-signposted **paths** up to the Pyramidenkogel from either Reifnitz or Maria Wörth (see below); the steep ascent through the forest takes a couple of hours. There's also one direct **bus** a day (April–Oct) from Klagenfurt to the Pyramidenkogel, passing through Reifnitz on the way.

Maria Wörth and beyond

Four kilometres west of Reifnitz, the hotels and holiday apartments of **MARIA WÖRTH** crowd onto a promontory jutting into the lake, presided over in picturesque fashion by the spires of two medieval chapels. The larger of the two, at the eastern end of the promontory, is the twelfth-century **Pfarrkirche SS Primus und Felician**. The two early Christian martyrs are portrayed on either side (Primus on the left) of the *Virgin and Child* which graces the Baroque high altar. On the south wall of the nave, a late-Gothic altar panel shows St Jerome (Hieronymus) in the company of the ape. On a knoll opposite, the **Winterkirche**, whose inside walls bear traces of twelfth-century frescoes depicting the Apostles, holds a striking stained-glass window showing the Madonna, behind the altar.

Maria Wörth's **tourist office** (May & Oct Mon–Fri 10am–noon & 1–4.30pm, Sat & Sun 10am–noon & 2–4.30pm; June & Sept Mon–Fri 10am–noon & 1–5pm, Sat & Sun 10am–noon & 2–5pm; July & Aug daily 9am–6pm; ☎04272/4488-33, *www.tiscover.com/maria-woerth*) is just inland from the churches at Am Corso 110, on the second floor of a block containing shops and restaurants. Maria Wörth is too small to have a stock of private rooms, but the village's **pensions** tend to offer better value than those in Pörtschach on the opposite side of the lake. *Gasthaus Erika*, St-Anna-Weg 14 (☎04273/2701; ②), attractively perched on the hillside, is a modern house in traditional style with simple balconied rooms, some with en-suite facilities, cheaper ones without. *Pension Martha*, Primusweg 6 (☎04273/2574; ②), at the western end of the village, is larger and more impersonal, but has a private Strandbad.

West of Maria Wörth, the Velden-bound road passes through the straggling settlements of **DELLACH** and **AUEN**. Dellach stands beside one of Carinthia's best eighteen-hole **golf courses** (it's a scenic course, too, on high ground with views back towards the lake), and most of the hotels in the village do a profitable line in golf packages from March to October – the Maria Wörth tourist office has details. Immediately beyond Dellach, Auen is the site of the southern shore's best **campsite**, *Camping Weisses Rössl* (☎04274/2898, *weisses.roessl@aon.at*), on a hillside above the lake and with free access to a water's-edge bathing area.

North of Klagenfurt

The area **north of Klagenfurt** is the historic heartland of Carinthia, for successive waves of immigrant cultures – Celtic, Roman, Slav and finally Bavarian – have moved in to stamp their identity on the fertile basin around the Glan and Gurk rivers. It's a territory laden with historic remains: the Celts settled the hummocks around the Zollfeld, where the remnants of a Celtic town lie on the slopes of the **Magdalensberg**. The Romans superseded, building the now-vanished city of **Virunum**, in the valley below. Stones from Virunum were used to build the pilgrimage church at **Maria Saal**, 10km north of Klagenfurt, once an important religious centre and now the site of the Carinthian Open-Air Museum. North of Maria Saal lies the rather more substantial market town of **St Veit an der Glan**, former capital of Carinthia, and a good base from which to visit **Hochosterwitz** castle, a startlingly attractive hilltop fortress, while the main northbound route continues onwards to **Friesach**, one of Austria's best-preserved small medieval towns. Lying slightly off the main north–south route are **Gurk** to the west, site of the province's most impressive cathedral, and **Hüttenberg** to the east, a former mining town that now harbours an intriguing ethnographic museum honouring local-born explorer Heinrich Harrer.

All of the above can be treated as day-trips from Klagenfurt. The main Vienna-bound rail line and Bundesstrasse 83 provide access to the area, striking north through the **Zollfeld** just beyond the Klagenfurt city limits, an area of rich corn-bearing farmland bordered by conifer-covered hills. If you're dependent on public transport, you'll find Maria Saal, St Veit, Hochosterwitz and Friesach fairly easy to get to, as they're all served by frequent **trains**. Less frequent **buses** run to Magdalensberg, Gurk and Hüttenberg.

Maria Saal

Back in the eighth century, when pagan Carinthia was a land of opportunity for any ambitious, evangelizing cleric, the great Bishop (and later St) Virgil of Salzburg dispatched the monk Modestus to the Zollfeld to lead the conversion – and Germanization – of the local Slavs. Modestus chose the hillock now occupied by the village of **MARIA SAAL** as his base, and this sleepy, rustic spot still revolves around the hilltop church he founded.

Arriving at Maria Saal's small **train station**, you can clearly see the famous **Wallfahrtskirche** on the high ground 500m to the east. A fifteenth-century structure built atop St Modestus's original foundation, the church is notable for the Roman gravestones pilfered from the ruins of nearby Virunum and built into its outer walls, especially around the south porch. Among the most expressive of these are one showing two horses pulling a wagon, and another showing a she-wolf suckling Romulus and Remus (the latter embedded inside the porch). Within the impressively lattice-vaulted interior, the high altar containing statuettes of the Madonna and Child serves as the main focus for pilgrims, although significantly more engaging is the Arndorfer altar in the northern apse, showing the Coronation of the Virgin, flanked by SS George and Florian. Outside the church, an octagonal charnel house features two storeys of arcading, the lower storey bearing medieval frescoes showing the Deposition.

Arndorferstrasse leads downhill northeast from the church towards a T-junction presided over by the **Pestkreuz**, a sixteenth-century wayside cross. A short walk west of here is the **Freilichtmuseum** (May–Oct Tues–Sun 10am–6pm; öS50/€3.65), occupying an attractive, partly wooded site on the edges of town and containing more than thirty farmsteads and other buildings collected from all over Carinthia. A German-language guidebook (öS50/€3.65) gives the full rundown, but an obvious highlight is the waterwheel-operated sawmill complex in a dell to the west. Above the sawmill is the humble *Holzknechthütte*, the improvised shelter with tree-bark roof in which the woodcutters dwelt while away working in the forest.

Enclosed by railings 1.5km north of Maria Saal, beside the old road to St Veit (which runs parallel to the modern Bundesstrasse), the **Herzogstuhl** is a granite throne about 2m high, assembled from bits of Roman-era masonry from much-plundered Virunum. Dating from the ninth century, it was used in ceremonies to confirm the authority of the dukes of Carinthia over the local populace. The venerable seat is not much to look at, but exudes a powerful whiff of history nevertheless. It's easily reached by car, and buses on the Klagenfurt–Maria Saal–St Veit run stop just next to it. If you're on foot, there's a path which leads from the Freilichtmuseum to the Herzogstuhl in about 15 minutes, passing underneath the railway line on the way; otherwise, simply turn right outside Maria Saal train station and keep going.

Practicalities

Local trains stop in Maria Saal, as well as a few of the expresses, and it's also on the Klagenfurt–St Veit bus route. The **tourist office**, just downhill from the church at Am Platzl 7 (May–Sept daily 9am–2pm; Oct–April Mon–Fri 9am–2pm; ☎04223/2214), can fix you up with one of a small number of **private rooms** (②). Two decent local **pensions** are *Haus Plieschnegger*, a large modern house just uphill from the village centre at Böcklstrasse 5 (☎04223/2293; ③); and *Haus Brenner*, on the northwestern fringes of the village at Schnerichweg 11 (☎04223/2483; ③). Both *Café zum Dom* and the more expensive *Gasthof Sandwirt*, on the Hauptplatz next to the church, offer good-quality Austrian **food**. For a quick lunch, *Jausenstazion Rauter*, just outside the entrance to the Freilichtmuseum, offers a range of Wurst and cold cuts.

The Magdalensberg

Ten kilometres north of Maria Saal, a minor road leaves the main northbound route near the village of **St Michael am Zollfeld** to snake its way up to the summit of the 1059-metre **Magdalensberg** to the east. The hilltop is now occupied by the **Wallfahrtskirche SS Helena and Magdalena**, a late-Gothic affair with some intricate stellar vaulting inside and a high altar whose panels tell the story of Helena's discovery of the Holy Cross and its re-erection by Emperor Heraclius. The church is the starting point of the annual *Vierbergelauf*, or "Four Mountains Walk", which takes place on the night of the first full moon after Easter. Up to 5000 people attend midnight Mass on the Magdalensberg before embarking on a torchlit hike that takes in three hills on the other side of the valley – the Ulrichsberg, Veitsberg and Lorenziberg.

Such rituals have their origins deep in the Celtic past, when spiritual life often centred on the area's hilltop shrines. The strength of Celtic culture in the area is evinced by the remains of a **Romano-Celtic town** 1.5km below the summit of the Magdalensberg, by the side of the road up to the summit. The site (May–Oct daily 9am–7pm; öS40/€2.92) is arranged on terraced slopes around a central grassy area that once served as a forum. The Celts who settled the area in the first century BC grew rich from the gold, amber and iron found in the nearby hills, and iron implements like axe heads and horse bits are proudly displayed in cabinets in the former trade and residential quarter, to the right of the forum. A Roman takeover took place early in the first century AD, and it's thought that the settlement here served as Roman regional capital before the city of Virunum was constructed in the valley below. Indeed, many of the finer remains here were built under Roman stewardship: the **painted house** to the right of the forum bears a cycle of pictures relating to Dionysus – the use of the "Pompeii red" pigment suggests that it was executed by a craftsman who learnt his trade in the Italian south. On the other side of the forum, the reconstructed **council chamber** (where leaders of local Celtic tribes were summoned to assemblies) now holds a display of both Celtic and Roman jewellery and the *Jungling von Magdalensberg* (Young Man of Magdalensberg), a copy of a statue unearthed by farmers here in the Middle Ages, which was sent to Spain in the sixteenth century, and promptly lost – our knowledge of the statue comes from a seventeenth-century replica now housed in the Kunsthistorisches Museum in Vienna.

Trips to the Magdalensberg are best accomplished by car: one daily bus (Mon–Sat only) heads up the hill from Klagenfurt, stopping some 500m below the Romano-Celtic site, but departs soon afterwards, leaving no real time to look around.

St Veit an der Glan

Standing at the northern end of the Zollfeld, the peaceful market town of **ST VEIT AN DER GLAN** bears little evidence that it served as the capital of Carinthia until 1518. Generously sprinkled with medieval and Baroque town houses, and preserving portions of its medieval town walls, it's riddled with picturesque corners and serves as a good place for a brief stop on your way to Magdalensberg or Hochosterwitz (see overleaf). The town comes to life during the last week of September, when the **Wiesenmarkt**, a medieval-styled fair featuring street entertainment and a bewildering array of stalls, pulls in as many as 500,000 visitors. Both the Wiesenmarkt and the *Pfingsten* (Whitsun) holiday are celebrated with marching displays by the **Trabanten**, a kind of honorary home guard comprised of local citizens who parade through town in antiquated uniforms.

Your best approach is to head for the elongated, rectangular **Hauptplatz** and indulge in a relaxed amble around the largely pedestrianized network of alleyways and courtyards around it. The **Pfarrkirche St Veit** at the northern end of the square is worth popping into for a glimpse of the colourful high altar (1752) by local master Johann Pacher, which features gilded figures of the Virgin flanked by SS Dominicus and Clara. The other end of the Hauptplatz is overlooked by the fine Baroque facade of the **Rathaus**, behind which lies an attractive arcaded courtyard (now covered with a modern glass roof), decorated with sgraffito dragon, snake and bird designs. Next door, with a collection of railway uniforms and antiquated ticket machines, the **Verkehrsmuseum**, or transport museum, Hauptplatz 29 (May to mid–Oct: daily 9am–noon & 2–6pm; öS40/€2.92), will primarily interest rail enthusiasts, though the model railway on the top floor might have broader appeal. It's certainly more fun than the **Stadtmuseum** in the Herzogsburg, or ducal palace, north of here on Burggasse (July–Sept Mon–Fri 10am–noon & 2–6pm, Sat 10am–noon; öS30/€2.19), offering a mundane collection of coins, traditional furnishings, old shooting targets and Trabanten uniforms. Finally, standing guard at the northern end of the town's main strip is the unabashedly garish **Hotel St Veit**, a feast of clashing colours designed by Ernst Fuchs, a painter and architect whose fondness for frivolous toy-town architecture makes Friedensreich Hundertwasser (see p.121) look like a dry minimalist in comparison. The hotel, finished in 1999, is considered to be Fuchs' masterpiece, although the neo-Egyptian facade has to been seen to be believed, and goodness knows what inspired the cluster of egg-like forms that appears to be blasting off into outer space just above the central lobby.

Practicalities

Buses and trains both stop at the **train station** at the northern end of town. From there, turn left onto the main road and walk straight for ten minutes before bearing right into the old town. The **tourist office**, in the Rathaus (Mon–Fri 9am–noon &

2–6pm, Sat 9am–noon; ☎04212/5555-668), has a limited list of private rooms (②) in town. Of the local **hotels**, *Gasthof Steirerhof*, Klagenfurterstrasse 38 (☎04212/2442; ②), is a basic but bearable place with rooms with shared toilet and shower facilities, while the *Weisses Lamm*, Unterer Platz 4 (☎04212/2362; ④), is a traditional town-centre Gasthof with cosy rooms with en-suite facilties and a nice restaurant in the courtyard. You'll be pleased to know that room interiors at the plush, 4-star *St Veit*, Ernst-Fuchs-Platz 1 (☎04212/4660-0, *hotel.st.veit@rogner.com*; ⑥) are much more tasteful and restrained than the hotel's wacky facade.

Those in search of **eating** and drinking venues shouldn't have to stray too far from the Hauptplatz and vicinity. The *Rathauscafé*, Hauptplatz 31, is a pleasant place for inexpensive pizza- or pasta-based lunches, while the nearby *Moser*, Spitalgasse 6, has a good range of mid-priced Carinthian *Nud'l* dishes. Top-quality Carinthian fare is the order of the day at the slightly more upmarket *Puckelsheim*, Erlgasse 11. *Cantina Toscana*, Klagenfurterstrasse, has a big garden, Sicilian staff and a good reputation for authentic Italian food.

For **drinking**, *Bieradies*, Hauptplatz 24, is a long, narrow bar with ten varieties of beer on tap, a youngish clientele and cheap lunchtime meals; while *Adele*, down an alleyway just next door, is a more stylish and laid-back watering hole offering a wide range of bar food both day and night.

Hochosterwitz and around

North of St Veit, Bundestrasse 83 cuts through low hills, climbing out of the Glantal before descending to trace the course of the River Gurk. The railway ultimately follows the same route after initially veering east to pass within striking range of the region's most awe-inspiring sight, the hilltop fortress of **Hochosterwitz**. Situated 10km east of St Veit, though clearly visible long before you arrive, the fortress sits fairy-tale-like on the rock (it's one of several European citadels claiming to be the inspiration behind the castle in Disney's *Snow White*), its turret-encrusted outer fortifications winding their way around the craggy slopes. This spot has been fortified since the early Middle Ages, but the current castle was largely the work of the governor of Carinthia, Georg von Khevenhüller, who purchased the site in 1571 and whose bust adorns the sixth gate on the approach to the fortress. Picturesque though the effect, his construction efforts had a serious purpose – the lowlands around St Veit and Klagenfurt were constantly under threat of Turkish raids at the time. Hochosterwitz still belongs to the Khevenhüllers, whose current head lives in a house in the valley below.

The **fortress** (daily: May–Sept 8am–6pm; April & Oct 9am–5pm; öS70/€5.11) is approached via a pathway that ascends through fourteen fortified **gates**, which once controlled access to Hochosterwitz's impregnable inner sanctum. Many of the gates are decorated with impressive busts and reliefs; the first, the **Fähnrichtor** (Ensign's Gate), bears the arms of the Khevenhüllers – featuring an acorn, symbol of the family's original fifteenth-century residence near Villach, Eichelberg (Acorn Hill) – together with the child Jesus with a lamb. The inner fortress at the top of the hill is a bit of a disappointment; there's not much, save for a café in the central courtyard and a patchy **museum**, inadequately labelled in German. Amongst the old weapons and family portraits lining the walls is a piece of paper bearing the signature of King James I of England – it's an entry taken from Hans von Khevenhüller's *Stammbuch*, the kind of diary-cum-album in which aristocrats of the day kept records of the dignitaries they'd met in the course of their travels.

There's a lift up to the fortress for those who don't fancy the climb, but be sure to take the path on the way down, otherwise you'll miss all the gates. Lift tokens (öS40/€2.92) are available from the castle ticket office beneath the first gate.

Practicalities

Hochosterwitz lies 2km south of the village of **Launsdorf**, on the Klagenfurt–Vienna rail route (all trains except intercity ones stop here): turn right outside the **train station** and keep going – you'll soon see the fortress. Those with their own transport should follow Bundesstrasse 82, which leaves Bundesstrasse 83 at St Veit and heads east towards Brückl; a well-signposted turn leads to the fortress, which is a further 1km off the road. St Veit–Brückl buses pick up and drop off at this turn-off.

There's nowhere to stay around the castle, so it's best to treat Hochosterwitz as a day-trip from Klagenfurt, St Veit or Friesach. As for **eating and drinking**, *Gasthaus Tatzer* next to the castle car park offers solid Austrian cuisine and good-value Tagesmenüs from around öS100/€7.30. Otherwise, it's best to eat in Launsdorf, where *Gasthof zur Post*, just opposite the train station on the Hauptstrasse, serves up serviceable if uninspiring Austrian and Carinthian dishes, while *Pizzeria Mama Mia*, a little further west at Hauptstrasse 1, is renowned for its fresh fish from the Adriatic, and has a range of authentic, inexpensive pizzas and Italian dishes too. For those who have a car, *Gasthof Prettner*, Zollfeldstrasse 3, in the village of **St Donat** (6km southwest of Hochosterwitz on the road back towards Klagenfurt), is one of the best local venues for good Carinthian cooking at a moderate price.

The Gurktal

Twenty kilometres north of St Veit, at **Pöckstein**, a secondary road (traversed by three daily Klagenfurt-Weitensfeld buses) leaves Bundesstrasse 83 to explore the **Gurktal** to the west, a narrow ribbon of pastureland squeezed between the pine-carpeted hills of the Gurktaler Alpen. The Gurktal's main attraction is the village of **Gurk** and its cathedral, although **STRASSBURG**, 10km up the valley, is worth a brief stop in order to explore its hilltop **Schloss**, which overlooks the town from the north. This largely Renaissance castle was home to the bishops of Gurk until the bishopric was moved south to Klagenfurt in 1787, and its arcaded courtyard now plays host to classical concerts over the summer. There's also a **folklore museum** (April–Oct Mon–Fri 9am–noon & 2–5pm; öS35/€2.56), showing the usual selection of craft implements and traditional wooden furniture, as well as some intriguing photographs of ritualistic Carinthian sports. These include *Kugelwerfen*, a quaintly pointless exercise in which a big wooden ball is thrown through village streets along a pre-agreed route at Easter time; and *Kranzelreiten*, a more straightforward horse race that takes place at Whitsun in the village of Weitensfeld, 15km west of Strassburg. Dating from the Middle Ages, the race recalls a time of plague when young men indulged in equine contests to decide who had first choice of the village's few surviving virgins. There's a fairly inessential hunting section (costing an additional öS10/€0.73) displaying the customary trophy animal heads, including those of stags Hansi and Mischko, who used to live in the castle grounds (they died peaceful deaths). The Schloss **café-restaurant** is a good place to enjoy a quality bite to eat before journeying further.

Gurk

Four kilometres beyond Strassburg, the dainty farming village of **GURK** is dominated by the imposing twin towers of its stately Romanesque cathedral. It's been an ecclesiastical focal point ever since Carinthian noblewoman Hemma of Gurk established a Benedictine convent here in 1043. Gurk was the last of a long line of churches and abbeys founded by this extraordinarily energetic and pious woman, and her tomb here quickly became an object of veneration for pilgrims. Hemma's convent was soon taken over by the archbishops of Salzburg, who were eager to consolidate their control over a region whose conversion to Christianity they had overseen. Gurk was upgraded to become a bishopric, necessitating the construction of a new cathedral to replace Hemma's church, and Bishop Roman I (1131–67) set about building a wondrous edifice that survives more or less intact today. Located in a side-valley some distance from the main north–south trade routes, however, Gurk's status as spiritual capital of Carinthia was something of an anomaly. In 1787 Bishop Salm relocated the episcopal court to Klagenfurt, and the village of Gurk settled back into rural slumber. Gurk is not really geared up for tourist accommodation, although the **tourist office** in the centre of the village (May–Oct Mon–Sat 8am–noon & 2–5pm; ☎04266/8520) might be able to find you a private room if you wish to stay. The *Kronenwirt*, just outside the cathedral's west gate, is a good place to pick up a hearty Austrian lunch.

THE CATHEDRAL

Despite later additions, notably the seventeenth-century onion domes that now grace the two towers, the **cathedral** is still essentially the same three-aisled basilica that was built by Bavarian masons between 1140 and 1200. Constructed from local iron-bearing limestone, the whole building exudes a curious, golden-yellow luminescence. Before venturing inside, it's worth wandering round to look at the tympanum above the south porch, which bears a figure of Christ, carved around 1150, holding aloft a book whose pages are inscribed with the words *ego sum hostium* – "I am the gate". On the east end of the cathedral, a small twelfth-century relief mounted high on the wall of the central apse shows a lion (symbolizing Christ) attacking a basilisk (representing the forces of darkness).

Entering the cathedral via the west door, you come face to face with thirteenth-century frescoes in the porch, showing scenes from Genesis on the left-hand side, and New Testament scenes on the right. From here an imposing Romanesque doorway, rich in abstract carving, leads through to the nave, where your eyes are drawn towards George Raphael Donner's **cross altar** of 1740, halfway up the nave, which features an expressive *Pietà* cast in lead. To the left of the altar, in the north aisle, the celebrated Romanesque **Samson tympanum** (1200) bears a relief of the biblical strongman breaking the jaws of a lion. At the east end of the cathedral, Michael Hönel's **high altar** (1626–32) shows the Ascension of the Virgin surrounded by an array of highly stylized statuettes – St Hemma kneels above the Virgin's head to the right. During Lent the high altar is covered by what amounts to an enormous painted curtain, the **Gurker Fastentuch**, or Gurk Lenten cloth, executed by Konrad von Friesach in 1458, and featuring 99 Bible scenes. Despite being one of the great masterpieces of Austrian late-Gothic art, the cloth remains in storage for the rest of the year, although pictures of it are always on display in the cathedral. In the **crypt**, a shrine to St Hemma, flanked by eighteenth-century statues, has been built above the eleventh-century sarcophagus. In the southeast corner of the crypt you'll find a rock shaped vaguely like a seat, traditionally sat upon by women who wish to conceive a child. One of the most impressive parts of the cathedral, the first-floor **bishop's chapel**, at the west end of the nave, is only accessible by guided tour (April–Oct daily at 1pm; öS40/€2.92). It's famous for its frescoes, painted in 1230 and restored in 1263 after a fire, depicting Old Testament scenes in vibrant turquoises, greens and ruddy browns.

Just north of the cathedral entrance is the infant-oriented **Zwergenpark**, or gnome park (daily: July & Aug 9am–6pm; May & June 10am–6pm; Sept & Oct 10am–5pm; öS60/€4.38), a tawdry display of garden gnomes with a tiny stretch of miniature railway on which the kids can ride.

Friesach

Back on the main northbound road and rail route, 10km north of Pöckstein, girdled by an impressive ensemble of ruins and enclosed within still-moated town walls,

FRIESACH hoves into view like something out of a fanciful medieval manuscript, its spindly towers and spires poking up from the various small hillocks on which the town is built. Like most places in this part of Austria, it was settled by Slavs in the sixth century, before their gradual displacement by Bavarians and Franks. Ninth-century Holy Roman Emperor Louis (Ludwig) the German gave the town to the archbishops of Salzburg, who established a thriving market here, and by the thirteenth century it was the most important urban centre in Carinthia. Richard the Lionheart passed through town on his way to the Crusades in 1192, although Friesach's main claim to fame in this period was the famous **Tourney** in 1224, when Duke Leopold VI of Austria invited the flower of central European chivalry to a gathering later immortalized in the poems of knight and minstrel Ulrich von Liechtenstein (lord of nearby Murau in Styria; see p.306). The event is nowadays remembered in the **Stadtfest** of May 30, when the locals dress up in medieval costumes and the streets fill with stalls selling food and drink. The exhibition of medieval culture held in Friesach in summer 2001, has meant the wholesale renovation of many of its historical buildings and their development as exhibition spaces.

The Town

Friesach's sleepy **Hauptplatz** is arranged around the **Stadtbrunnen**, an incongruously Italianate sixteenth-century fountain whose basin bears reliefs of Perseus and several other beast-slaying heroes. Over to the north, the Gothic bulk of the largely nineteenth-century **Stadtpfarrkirche** is probably worth missing in favour of the **Dominikanerkirche** further northeast, which looks equally plain on first inspection, but is much more rewarding inside. There's a harrowing fourteenth-century Crucifixion on the north side of the nave and, behind it, a seventeenth-century *Pietà*, the whole scene surrounded by brightly coloured, fruit-laden foliage. To the right of the altar stands another fine piece of medieval wood sculpture, the delicate *Friesacher Madonna* of 1320, while on the north side of the choir the Johannes altar of 1500 bears a central relief featuring Christ flanked by SS George and Florian, and wings showing scenes from the life of St John – including his exile on the island of Patmos and an attempt by Roman soldiers to boil him in oil.

West of the Hauptplatz, pathways lead up towards part-ruined stretches of the town's medieval fortifications. One of the better-kept bits, to the northwest, is the **Petersberg**, where the surviving keep of a thirteenth-century fortress now holds the **Stadtmuseum** (May–Oct daily 10am–5pm; öS40/€2.92), with archeological, art and craft exhibits on five floors. Most interesting are the Gothic altarpieces on the second floor – one of which was produced by the local workshop of Konrad von Friesach in 1435 (he of the *Gurker Fastentuch*; see opposite) – and the fifth-floor display of medieval copperware, featuring a fifteenth-century doctor's blood-letting beaker, decorated with an Adam-and-Eve motif. From the Petersberg's viewing terrace you can gaze out towards the Virgilienberg on the south side of town, where portions of a ruined thirteenth-century church stand silhouetted against the sky.

Practicalities

From the **train station** on the eastern fringes of town, it's a straightforward five-minute walk down Bahnhofstrasse to the Hauptplatz, where the **tourist office**, at no. 1 (May–Sept Mon–Fri 8am–noon & 2–6pm, Sat 9am–noon; Oct–April Mon–Fri 8am–noon & 2–4pm; ☎04268/4300), can point you in the direction of the very few **private rooms** (②) available. Alternatively, of the town's main **hotels**, grouped around the Hauptplatz, *Zum Goldenen Anker*, Bahnhofstrasse 3 (☎04268/2313) is the most basic, a traditional downtown Gasthof offering a couple of rooms with shower and TV (③), and a couple of cheaper ones with facilities in the hallway (②), while the *Friesacherhof*,

Hauptplatz 4 (☎04268/2123; ③), offers rooms with en-suite facilities together with satellite TV and phone. Best of the bunch is the 4-star *Metnitztalerhof*, Hauptplatz 11 (☎04268/2510, *metnitztalerhof@burgenstadt.at*; ⑤), which offers slightly more in terms of room size and plushness.

Cheapest place to **eat** is *Gasthof zum Mohren*, a few steps north of the Hauptplatz on Wienerstrasse 12, offering cheap Wurst and soups, and a range of schnitzels from öS80/€5.84. Otherwise, restaurants in the hotels lining the Hauptplatz have more style: both the *Friesacherhof* and *Metnitztalerhof* offer a tempting array of Carinthian specialities alongside some more expensive game and fish dishes, and both have plenty of outdoor seating in summer. There's not a great choice of spots for a **drink**, although the Hauptplatz hotels are good places to sit outside during the summer. For indoor drinking, try the *Craigher* on the corner of Hauptplatz and Herrengasse, a comfortable coffee-and-cakes venue which bakes its own sweets, or the thirteenth-century wine cellar of the *Metnitztalerhof*.

Hüttenberg

On arrival in **HÜTTENBERG**, a historic iron-ore-mining village in the hills 15km east of Friesach, it's difficult at first to believe you're still in Austria. A massive picture of the Buddha hangs from a cliff at the southern entrance to town, marking the starting point of the Tibetan-inspired **Lingkor**, a high-tech, cliffside-hugging stairway that is intended to aid meditation and prayer. That such Eastern esoterica should exist here at all is largely down to the local-born mountaineer and explorer **Heinrich Harrer** (see box, opposite), whose exploits – including the epic walk to Tibet from northern India that made him famous – are remembered in Hüttenberg's Heinrich Harrer **museum**. Hüttenberg's mining past also plays a role in the place's appeal, although it's difficult to imagine that this tranquil, rural environment of forest-fringed valleys was once a thriving centre of industry. A century ago, more than seven hundred people worked in the mines of **Knappenberg** – now the site of a **show-mine** – in the hills above Hüttenberg; and a further 800 worked in the blast furnaces of **Heft**, 2km up the valley to the east. By 1978 the whole mining and smelting operation had been wound down, the locally produced metal priced out of the market by cheap foreign imports. Mining traditions are celebrated, however, in the **Reiftanz**, which takes place on the first Sunday after Whitsun every three years (the next one is in spring 2004). In addition to a lot of processing around in traditional miners' uniforms and a good deal of alcohol-fuelled merrymaking, the *Reiftanz* centres on an age-old ceremony in which the social hierarchy is symbolically reversed – and local dignitaries have the honour of being lightly whipped on the backside by mining representatives.

Hüttenberg isn't accessible by train, but its position on Bundesstrasse 92 from Klagenfurt to Neumarkt in Steiermark ensures that it's not too difficult to reach. **Buses** from either Klagenfurt or St Veit pass through Hüttenberg village centre before heading uphill to Knappenberg.

The Town

Housed in a modern pavilion at the southern end of town, below the Lingkor, the **Heinrich-Harrer-Museum** (April–Oct daily 10am–5pm; öS100/€7.30, combined ticket with Knappenberg mine öS160/€11.68; *www.harrermuseum.at*) was blessed by the Dalai Lama himself when it first opened in 1992. The special throne that was built for the Dalai Lama, together with Tibetan costumes, prayer wheels and trumpets made from human bones (those made from the bones of young girls, holy men or murder victims are considered especially lucky) are displayed on the upper floor of the building. Downstairs, various totems associated with the Harrer cult are assembled, among

HEINRICH HARRER

Explorer, all-round sportsman, mountaineer and one of the great popularizers of Tibetan culture in the West, **Heinrich Harrer** (born 1912) is one of contemporary Austria's most compelling figures. He's best known for his book *Seven Years in Tibet*, a stirring account of his adventures in the 1940s, a story which was filmed for Hollywood in 1997 with Brad Pitt taking the role of Harrer. The release of the film looked set to put Harrer, and Hüttenberg, on the global map, but unfortunately things soured after revelations (courtesy of the German magazine *Stern*) that Harrer had been a member of the SS in the late 1930s.

That the Nazis were keen to recruit Harrer comes as no surprise: in the blue-eyed world of alpine sport, he was a demigod. Born in Obergossen near Knappenberg, he developed a passion for mountaineering and skiing early on, and represented Austria in both the downhill and slalom in the Winter Olympics of 1936. The young Harrer returned without any medals, but was crowned World Student Downhill champion the following year. Together with three colleagues, Harrer made the first successful assault on the north wall of the Eiger in 1938 (subsequently immortalized in his book, *The White Spider*), an exploit which made Harrer internationally famous and secured his place on an Austro-German Himalayan expedition the following year. By this time, he was a Party member and had become skiing instructor to the SS. He even got married (to Lotte Wenger, daughter of Greenland explorer Alfred Wenger) in an SS uniform. What's unclear is whether he was a committed believer, an ambitious careerist or merely the passive recipient of a status bestowed on him by a regime keen to associate itself with sporting heroes.

Fortuitously, Harrer was on the other side of the world scrambling around Himalayan foothills when World War II broke out. As a citizen of the German Reich, however, he was interned by the British at Dehra Dun in northwestern India, where he killed time learning Tibetan and Japanese. In April 1944 he escaped, intending to cross the Himalayas in search of Tibet, a country which had long exerted a fascination over right-wing German thinkers, who believed it to be the original home of the Aryan race. Together with colleague Peter Aufschneiter, Harrer finally reached the Tibetan capital Lhasa two years later, and immediately found a role for himself in this strange environment, becoming the Mr Fix-It that locals called for whenever some aspect of Western technology or culture needed explaining. He was in the process of teaching Buddhist monks how to skate when he was summoned by an intrigued Dalai Lama (then a child), and they've been friends ever since. Once back in Europe, the success of the book *Seven Years in Tibet* and the documentary film of the same name enabled Harrer to finance further expeditions, starting with a trip to the Amazon in 1953. For the next three decades, he was constantly on the road, visiting Africa, South America and the Far East, pausing only briefly in 1958 to become the Austrian golf champion. He now lives in semi-retirement in Liechtenstein, although he remains a regular visitor to Hüttenberg.

them his mountaineering boots, golf clubs and an old tennis racket – Harrer introduced tennis to Tibet, making a clay court out of dried yak droppings. A well-organized ethnographic collection follows, largely made up of the items collected by Harrer on his travels through South America, Borneo and Africa – odd, though eminently practical, are the wooden head supports used by the Turkana tribesmen of Kenya to prevent their extravagant hairstyles from becoming tousled during sleep. Labelling is in German and English.

From here, Hüttenberg's main street leads north to Reiftanzplatz, bordered by charming late-medieval houses, one of which shelters the mildly diverting **Helga Riedel Puppenmuseum**, or doll museum (May–Sept daily 10am–noon & 1–5pm; öS35/€2.56), a collection of exquisitely modelled figurines. Most are grouped together in scenes inspired by local author Dolores Vieser's rather whimsical novel of nine-teenth-century Carinthian life, *Der Bänderhut ("The Ribboned Hat")*.

Knappenberg and Heft

Ranged across the hillside 4km east of Hüttenberg, and served by local bus, **KNAP-PENBERG** (the name means "miners' hill") flourished as a centre of iron-ore mining from the days of the Celts until 1978. Some of the underground galleries have now been converted into a **Schaubergwerk** (May–Oct daily 10am–4pm tours depart hourly; öS100/€7.30, combined ticket with Harrer Museum öS160/€11.68), in which visitors are taken on a short walking tour and given several ear-splitting demonstrations of how different drilling tools worked. The ticket includes entry to the **museum** next door, a modest display that features miners' ceremonial uniforms, a model of the charcoal-fired smelting kilns once used by the Celts, and several cabinets full of crystals and miner-als.

Two kilometres east of Hüttenberg, the hamlet of **HEFT** is dominated by a semi-ruined nineteenth-century **blasting furnace**, an impressive piece of industrial heritage whose smelting towers bring to mind the fortifications of a medieval castle. Parts of the complex have been restored and modernized to house artists' studios, and high-profile **exhibitions** are held there over the summer (May–Oct Mon–Fri 2–5pm, Sat & Sun 10am–5pm). Hüttenberg's tourist office will provide details of what's on.

Practicalities

Most people visit Hüttenberg on a day-trip from elsewhere, though the town's **tourist office** (Mon–Fri 9am–5pm), in the Gemeindeamt on the main square, can offer **private rooms** (①) in either Hüttenberg or Knappenberg if you choose to stay overnight. *Zur Post*, Reiftanzplatz 14 (☎04263/212; ②), is the sole source of **hotel** accommodation in Hüttenberg itself, but only has four rooms, two of which have en-suite shower and WC. Up in Knappenberg, *Geo Centrum* (☎04263/720; ②) is a large modern place with sim-ple en-suite doubles, although it's popular with school groups and is often fully booked. Six kilometres south of Hüttenberg, a minor road heads east up into the hills to **LÖLLING-GRABEN**, another 6km distant, site of the best **hotel** in the area, *Landgasthof Neugebauer* (☎04263/407; ③), which has snazzy rooms, complete with TV and phone, as well as a highly regarded **restaurant** offering a mixture of Austrian stan-dards and Carinthian specialities.

Best places to **eat** in Hüttenberg are the *Gasthaus Zois*, Münichsdorferplatz 9, serv-ing all the usual schnitzels and, at lunchtime, an excellent *Bauernschmaus*, or cold meat platter, or the restaurant of *Zur Post*, which offers similarly hearty Austrian fare.

Villach and around

Sprawling across a lush plain near the confluence of the Drau and Gail, with the Karawanken Alps to the south, **VILLACH** ranks as Carinthia's most attractive provin-cial town. Local place names – like Villach itself, and suburbs of Vassach, Fellach and Pogöriach – are evidence of the area's Slavic origins, which gave way to German influ-ences in the late Middle Ages, when courtly families like the Diedrichsteins and the Khevenhüllers built town houses here to take advantage of its growing importance as a trade centre. While Villach's standing has since rested more on its role as a major rail and motorway junction, its core of medieval and Renaissance buildings present a convincing argument for a stay of a day or two. Nightlife in Villach is also generally better than that in its larger local rival Klagenfurt, and it's a good urban base from which to explore nearby mountains and lakes. **Schloss Landskron**, on the northern fringes of town, presents one obvious excursion, as do **Mount Dobratsch** and the

Terra Mystica show-mine at **Bad Bleiberg**, both to the west. **Warmbad Villach**, 3km south of town, is a modern spa-resort, which offers plenty of swimming pools and sporting activities. Although they're important resort areas in their own right, both the **Ossiachersee** and **Faakersee** are so close to Villach (and easily accessible by bus) that it's possible to stay in town and head out to a lakeside beach during the daytime.

Most important event on the folklore calendar is the **Villacher Kirchtag**, which falls on the first weekend in August, when people from all over Carinthia, Slovenia and northern Italy descend on the town to indulge in a weekend of folk music and outdoor drinking, culminating in a Saturday-night parade through town in traditional dress.

Arrival, information and accommodation

The **bus** and **train stations** are on Bahnhofplatz, just north of the centre. Walk south along Bahnhofstrasse, cross the river and proceed up the Hauptplatz to reach the **tourist office** on Rathausplatz (June–Sept Mon–Fri 8am–6pm, Sat 9am–noon; Oct–May Mon–Fri 8am–noon & 1–5pm; ☎04242/205-2900, *villach.tourismus @villach.at*). They will be able to book you into one of the few **private rooms** (②), though none are particularly convenient for the centre. Apart from a couple of inexpensive inner-city choices, most of the cheaper **hotels and pensions** are in Warmbad Villach (bus #1 from Bahnhofplatz), 3km away, or farther-flung suburbs. On the whole, the nearby **Faakersee** (see p.348) is better served with private rooms and traditional pensions.

There's a **youth hostel** some 1000m west of the centre at Dinzlweg 34 (☎04242/56368, *jgh.villach@oejhv.or.at*) with 5-person dorms and a limited number of doubles (①). Reception is open 5–10pm.

Hotels in central Villach

Fremdenheim Eppinger, Klagenfurter Strasse 6 (☎04242/24389). Old-fashioned lodging house just round the corner from the train station, slightly rough around the edges but perfectly adequate for a short stay. Most rooms have en-suite bath or shower, with shared toilet in the hall. Breakfast not included. ①.

Goldenes Lamm, Hauptplatz 1 (☎04242/24105, *www.tiscover.com/goldenes-lamm*). Ideally located main-square Gasthof offering rooms with en-suite shower and WC. ④.

Hotel City, Bahnhofplatz 3 (☎04242/27896, *www.hotelcity.at*). Modern business-oriented place directly opposite the train station, en-suite rooms with TV and minibar. ⑤.

Kasino, Kaiser-Josef-Platz 4 (☎04242/24449). Comfortable city-centre choice just west of the Hauptplatz on a quiet square. Smart en-suite rooms with all mod cons. ⑥.

Kramer, Italienerstrasse 14 (☎04242/24953, *www.hotelgasthofkramer.at*). Unpretentious, medium-sized downtown hotel a mere 5min walk south of the centre, offering standard en suites with TV. ④.

Romantik Hotel Post, Hauptplatz 26 (☎04242/26101-0, *romantik-hotel@magnet.at*). Classic central Gasthof occupying the sixteenth-century town house of the counts of Khevenhüller, which once hosted the likes of Emperor Karl V and Maria Theresia. Swish, modern and comfortable rooms. ⑥.

Zum Goldenen Löwen, Leinigengasse 4 (☎04242/24582). Simple en-suite rooms with TV, above a Gasthof-restaurant in an alley just off the Hauptplatz. ④.

Hotels in Warmbad Villach

Hotel Garni Wanker, Warmbader Strasse 42 (☎04242/33684, *www.tiscover.com/wanker*). Nice alpine-style house on the main street just north of the Warmbad Villach train station. All rooms have en-suite facilities and TV, and there's a pleasant garden. The hotel offers a couple of four- or five-person family apartments too. ③

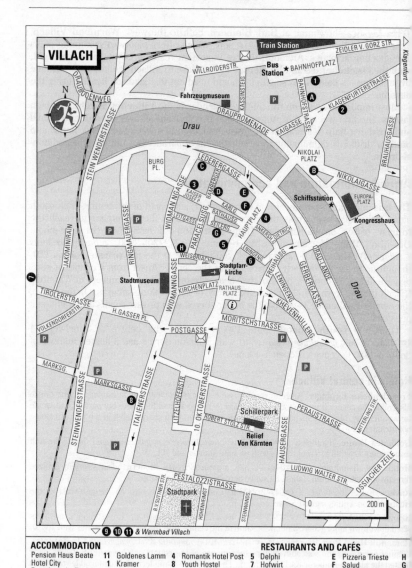

ACCOMMODATION

Pension Haus Beate	11	Goldenes Lamm	4	Romantik Hotel Post	5	
Hotel City	1	Kramer	8	Youth Hostel	7	
Fremdenheim Eppinger	2	Karawankenhof	10	Zum Goldenen Löwen	6	
Hotel Garni Wanker	9	Kasino	3			

RESTAURANTS AND CAFÉS

Delphi	E	Pizzeria Trieste	H
Hofwirt	F	Salud	G
Konditorei Draubrücke	B	Trattoria Adriatico	D
Malzamt	C	Villacher Brauhof	A

Karawankenhof, Kadischenallee 25–27 (☎04242/3002-0, *karawankenhof@warmbad.at*). Modern spa-hotel with spacious rooms, indoor and outdoor swimming pools, extensive grassy lawns, sauna and on-site doctors – everything you need in order to take the cure. ⑧.

Pension Haus Beate, Warmader Allee 64 (☎04242/35118, *www.tiscover.com/pension-beate*). Ten-room pension in a modern house some 10 minutes from the spa facilities, offering simple en suites with TV. ②.

The Town

Although lacking any individual star buildings, Villach's **Hauptplatz** is an extremely attractive affair, its lines of pastel-coloured town houses sloping gently upwards from the south bank of the Drau river. The largely pedestrianized warren of arcades and alleyways on either side of the square still holds an evocative, late-medieval atmosphere, making it an enticing area in which to wander. Raised on a terrace at the southern end of the Hauptplatz, the fourteenth-century **Stadtpfarrkirche Hl. Jakob** is home to a fine collection of sixteenth-century tombs. To the right of the high altar in the Diedrichstein chapel, Sigismund von Diedrichstein (lord of Finkenstein castle, south of Villach) is shown in full armour with his symbol, a snake, positioned above his head. To the left, the chapel and tomb of Christoph von Khevenhüller, master of Landskron castle, features a relief of the deceased together with wives Elizabeth and Anna-Maria. Along the south wall of the nave is an expressive relief of the tutor to Christoph's son, Dr Martin Siebenburger, who was allowed a last resting place here in the church by way of thanks. From the same era is the stone pulpit from 1555 carved in the form of the tree of Jesse, with the venerable Israelite himself shown lying at the base. Just outside the church, the **Stadtpfarrturm**, or bell tower, is worth scaling for an excellent panorama of the surrounding mountains (July & Aug Mon–Thurs & Sat 10am–6pm, Fri 10am–9pm, Sun noon–6pm; June & Sept Mon–Sat 10am–6pm, Sun noon–6pm; May & Oct Mon–Sat 10am–6pm; öS25/€1.83). A short distance to the west on Widmanngasse, the **Stadtmuseum** (May–Oct Mon–Sat 10am–4.30pm; öS30/€2.19) regales visitors with a well-presented if modest collection of local Bronze and Iron Age finds, together with some Gothic altar panels.

Tucked away in an area of attractive nineteenth-century villas southeast of the centre, the **Schillerpark**, on Peraustrasse, harbours a modern pavilion containing the **Relief von Kärnten** (May–Oct Mon–Sat 10am–4.30pm; öS20/€1.46), a vast 1:10,000-scale relief map of Carinthia – a rainy-day attraction, but hardly essential viewing other days.

The banks of the **Drau** just north of the centre are good for strolling or cycling along, with a sprinkling of cafés overlooking the river. On the northern side, the privately owned **Fahrzeugmuseum**, or motor museum, at Draupromenade 12 (mid-June to mid-Sept daily 9am–5pm; mid-Sept to mid-June Mon–Sat 10am–noon & 2–5pm; öS55/€4.02), contains an engaging jumble of vehicles. Early Vespas and Lambrettas rub shoulders with more eccentric machines like the Messerschmitt KR175, a half-bike/half-bubble car that somehow never made it as an icon of consumerism, while a couple of classic Porsches will satisfy the sports-car fetishists. But it's the less glamorous motors that are more compelling, such as the 1936 Fiat Topolino, which along with the German Volkswagen was an important step in bringing motoring to the masses.

Warmbad Villach

Three kilometres south of the city centre, **Warmbad Villach** is a chic, modern spa resort where the mild radioactivity of natural thermal springs serves to reinvigorate limbs and soothe away stress. It's also an important sport and recreation centre, offering the best of the city's parks, swimming pools and tennis courts (see "Listings" p.347). If you're serious about taking the cure, you can stay in one of the bigger, more expensive hotels, like the *Karawankenhof*, that offer swimming pools, a range of treatments, and in-house medical staff. Alternatively, stay in a more modest pension and use central spa facilities at the **Kurzentrum** (☎04242/37000) in the resort centre.

City buses (#1) and southbound local trains (not expresses) run from Villach train station to the Warmbad Villach halt in the centre of the resort. There's a **tourist office** across the way on Warmbaderstrasse (Mon–Fri 8am–1pm & 2–6pm, Sat 9am–1pm; (☎04242/37244, *therme.warmbad@villach.at*) which will advise on private rooms and pensions – though the main tourist office back in central Villach deals with these as well.

Eating, drinking and entertainment

Most of the central Gasthöfe offer reasonably good-value Austrian and Carinthian **food**, and it's well worth looking out for boards advertising set menus, especially at lunchtime. Fairly central **snacking** options include traditional Austrian sausage fare from the Würstelstand just north of the Hauptplatz by the bridge; or pizza slices, open sandwiches and filled rolls from *Panino* at the northern end of the Hauptplatz. *Ali Baba*, Ledergasse 13, does a good line in takeaway Turkish kebabs or more substantial sit-down grills.

The main **drinking** area, which remains animated well into the early hours at weekends, is the pedestrian zone, stretching westwards from the Hauptplatz, where a variety of bars lurk in the alleyways around Lederergasse and Paracelsusgasse.

Restaurants

Delphi, Lederergasse 5. Flashy Greek restaurant offering an appetizing and dependable mid-price range of souvlakia, *stifado* and moussaka.

Hofwirt, Hauptplatz 10. Traditional, homely Gasthof in an alleyway just off the main square. A good place to try Carinthian *Käsnudl*, although all the usual Austrian veal and pork dishes are also available. Not too expensive, and even cheaper daily specials are chalked up outside.

Hotel Post, Hauptplatz. Top-notch Austrian and modern European cuisine in the city centre's most evocative Gasthof. Expect to pay öS400–500/€29.20–36.50 per head for a meal with drinks.

Malzamt, Lederergasse 25. Restaurant and brewery offering excellent ale, traditional beer snacks (hunks of black bread with various porky toppings), and meaty main courses. The accompanying bar is a good place for a relaxed drink.

Pizzeria Trieste, Weissbriachgasse 14. One of several Italian places in the central pedestrianized area, a comfortable, traditional restaurant with a range of pizzas and spaghetti dishes for under öS100/€7.30.

Salud, Seilergasse. Mexican bar-restaurant in an alleyway just off the Hauptplatz, serving up a standardized range of Central American food. Bubbling atmosphere to a soundtrack of cool Latino-jazz sounds.

Trattoria Adriatico, Bambergergasse 5 (☎04242/26374). Highly regarded seafood restaurant just off Kaiser-Josef-Platz. An excellent place for oysters, lobster, and a variety of grilled fish, all in an atmosphere of starched-napkin elegance.

Villacher Brauhof, Bahnhofstrasse 8. Large restaurant and beer hall run by the local brewery, offering good-value Austrian food and a few Carinthian specialities.

Cafés and bars

Cabas, Lederergasse 26. Trendy, garishly decorated and cramped meeting point, regularly packed with beautiful young things listening to pumping techno music.

Filling Station, corner of Hausergasse and Peraustrasse. Cosy bar with arched brick ceiling and a vaguely Scottish theme. Ten minutes' southeast of the main square, just beyond the Schillerpark.

Konditorei Draubrücke, corner of Nikolaigasse and Bahnhofstrasse. Prime coffee-slurping and cake-nibbling venue on the first floor of a riverside building, with a terrace overlooking the Drau.

Martina, Lederergasse 21. Cosy café-bar in the heart of the pedestrian zone which soon gets crowded with a wide mixture of age groups.

Pelikan, Rathausgasse. Raw, unpretentious pub-style venue appealing to those with rock tastes and alternative leanings. Crowded and chaotic on occasions, but a diverting alternative to the smarter bars in town.

Rathauscafé, Rathausplatz. A good place to sit outside during the daytime, with busy indoor café-bar area on two levels for late-night drinking.

Viduli, Postgasse 6. Narrow, smart and self-consciously trendy designer bar just south of the pedestrian zone.

Entertainment

The modern Kongresshaus on Europaplatz (☎04242/23561), just behind the tourist office, is the main venue for **classical** concerts, big **theatrical productions** and **musicals**. Smaller-scale drama takes place in the Studiobühne im Kellertheater, Freihausplatz (☎04242/205205). Advance bookings for both of the above – as well as for other major cultural events in the region – can be made through Villacher Kartenbüro, Freihausgasse 3 (☎04242/27341). The Evangelical church in the Stadtpark sometimes holds concerts of religious music.

Venues for **pop-rock** concerts and rave-style happenings tend to change, although posters and flyers in the Kartenbüro will have details of anything going on during your stay. The main venue for **clubbing** is *Nightlife* (admission öS40–60/€2.92–4.38), fifteen minutes southeast of the centre at Ossiacherzeile 39, a large subterranean complex featuring an area for old-time dancing, an area for techno and house, and a couple of quieter bar areas.

Listings

Bike rental At the train station; also from Das Radl, Italienstrasse 22b (☎04242/26954), or Sports Unlimited, Gerbergasse 3 (☎04242/26998), both of which have a bigger choice of mountain bikes.

Car rental Avis, Ossiacher Zeile (☎04242/24737); Hertz, Hans-Gasser-Platz 1 (☎04242/26970).

Cinema Stadtkinocenter, Rathausplatz (☎04242/27000). Big multi-screen showing top international (dubbed) movies.

Hospital Landeskrankenhaus Villach, Nikolaigasse 43 (☎04242/208-0).

Motoring organization ÖAMTC, Kärntnerstrasse 25 (☎04242/34200, emergency breakdown service ☎120).

Pharmacy Kreis-Apotheke, Hauptplatz 9.

Police Bundespolizeidirektion Villach, Trattengasse 34 (☎04242/2033).

Post office Hauptpostamt, Willroiderstrasse, next to the train station (daily 7am–10pm).

Swimming Erlebnistherme, Kadischenallee 25–27, Warmbad Villach, is an indoor pool with water slides, whirlpools and other fun features (öS115/€8.40; bus #1 from Bahnhofplatz). For outdoor bathing, there are four small lakes strung out in the northern suburbs of Villach – the St Leonhardsee, Vassachersee, Magdalensee and Silbersee (all accessible by city buses from the Bahnhofplatz) – each of which has a small Strandbad. Otherwise, head for the nearby Faakersee or Ossiachersee.

Tennis Tenniscamp Warmbad Villach, Warmbachweg 16 (☎04242/32564); outdoor and indoor courts from öS120/€8.76 per hour.

Train information ☎04242/1717.

Travel agents Kärntner Reisebüro, Gerbergasse 12 (☎04242/29888); Alpe Adria Touristik, Bahnhofplatz 6 (☎04242/22536).

West of Villach: Dobratsch and Bad Bleiberg

A long, high ridge rising to the west of town, the 2166-metre **Dobratsch** is an easily identifiable landmark from whichever direction you approach Villach. Its upper reaches are accessible via a toll road, the **Villacher Alpenstrasse** (cars öS195/€14.24, motorbikes öS95/€6.94, bicycles free), which commences just southwest of town in the suburb of Möltschach and climbs steeply out of the valley before proceeding westwards along the ridge. About 8km out of Villach, the road passes the **Alpengarten** (mid-June to Aug daily 9am–6pm; öS20/€1.46), a large collection of alpine flowers and plants native to the region. Eight kilometres further on, the road terminates at **Rosstratten**, where a chairlift ascends to the 1957-metre **Höhenrain** (also accessible as an hour-long walk). Here, you can savour impressive views in all directions, or follow marked paths to the **Ludwig-Walter-Haus** (90min distant) just below the summit of Dobratsch itself.

Nestling below Dobratsch to the north, the erstwhile lead-mining settlement of **BAD BLEIBERG**, about 15km west of Villach, is reached by a minor road that leaves town from the suburb of Fellach. Mining stopped here in 1993, due to exhaustion of the ore deposits, and the galleries have now been transformed into one of Austria's most imaginative show-mines, **Terra Mystica** (daily: May–June & Sept–Oct tours at 11am, 1pm & 3pm; July–Aug tours depart regularly depending on visitor numbers 9.30am–4.30pm; Nov–April groups by appointment only ☎04244/2255; öS210/€15.33; *www.bleiberg.or.at*). A ninety-minute guided tour begins with a short video, in German, about the history of the mine, followed by a descent into the mine workings by wooden slide. Here, images are projected onto the cavern walls to create a highly effective underground son et lumière, with a German commentary (English leaflet available on request) on the creation of the earth and humans' relationship with the environment, plus an account of the cult of St Barbara, patron saint of miners, and jokey treatment of subterranean creatures like dwarfs and goblins.

There's a small museum in the show-mine's reception area displaying ceremonial mining uniforms and diagrams of the mine workings. Probably the most valuable item here is the banner presented to the Bleiberg miners by Prince Eugène of Savoy in 1717, after several of their number had served as sappers in the Habsburg armies – most memorably helping to blow up Turkish positions during the siege of Belgrade.

In addition to the regular show-mine tour, you can choose between two **guided walks** (3hr 30min or 5hr; öS500/€36.50 and öS600/€43.80 respectively) through deeper sections of the mine, in the company of a trained geologist (ring a day in advance to book a place; English-speaking guides are usually available; ☎04244/2255-10). The price includes a packed lunch, and the chance to indulge in *Bergmeditation* (mine meditation) – a few quiet moments spent in the depths of the mine is said to be an excellent cure for stress.

The Faakersee and around

Less than 10km southeast of Villach, the placid waters of the **Faakersee** offer a popular escape from the city on hot summer weekends. Despite its small size (its widest point is little more than 2km across), the Faakersee is far from being just a glorified daytime beach for the Villach-based hordes, functioning quite happily as a resort in its own right. A main selling point are the string of campsites that run along the southern and eastern shores, each with its own stretch of shingle beach and water sports facilities. It's fairly easy to get to the lake from Villach by **bus**, with some services going round the lake in a clockwise direction, others anticlockwise. **Trains** on the Villach–Rosenbach route stop at the lake's biggest town, Faak am See.

DROBOLLACH, nearest of the Faakersee communities to Villach, isn't much more than a strip of houses along the road set back slightly from the lake. It's from the lakeside walks around Drobollach, however, that you'll enjoy the Faakersee at its prettiest, with views south towards the Karawanken mountains, notably the 2143-metre Mittagskogel, which boldly marks the border with Slovenia. There's a **tourist office** (mid-June to mid-Sept Mon–Fri 9am–noon & 1.30–6.30pm, Sat 10am–noon & 3–6.30pm, Sun 3–6.30pm; mid-Sept to mid-June Mon–Fri 9am–noon & 1.30–4pm; ☎04254/2185, *drobollach@carinthia.com*) on the main street, in the Gemeindeamt. From here a path leads through meadows to the Strandbad (öS30/€2.19), where there's a small shingle beach, a couple of cafés and the opportunity to hire pedalos and rowing boats.

Four kilometres south of Drobollach, on the road that circumnavigates the lake, **FAAK AM SEE** is another small settlement set back by a kilometre or so from the waterfront, where you'll find a Strandbad and boat-rental facilities. It's the only Faakersee town that's accessible by rail from Villach: from the **train station** on the southern side of town turn left then bear right to get to the village centre, where the **tourist office**, in the Gemeindeamt (July & Aug Mon–Fri 9am–7pm, Sat 9am–noon & 1–4pm, Sun 10am–noon; June & Sept Mon–Fri 9am–6pm, Sat 10am–noon & 2–4pm; Oct–May Mon–Fri 9am–5pm; ☎04254/2110-0, *info-faak.am.see@net4you.co.at*), will fix you up with a **private room** (①). Besides the lake, the only attraction in town is the vast model railway at **Miniwelt**, just east of the train station (July & Aug daily 10am–noon, 1–6pm & 7–9pm; May, June & Sept daily 1–6pm; Dec 25–Jan 5 daily 1–5pm; Jan 6–April 30 Sat & Sun 1–5pm; öS20/1.46).

From Faak the lakeside road continues east then north, passing a series of big, family-oriented **campsites** ranged along the shoreline before arriving in **EGG**, 5km away. Another attractive if undramatic little resort, it's a popular centre for windsurfing, as well as being home to the best of the **restaurants** around the Faakersee – the *Gasthof Tschebull*, on the main road at Seeuferstrasse 26, is renowned for its fresh fish.

A road heads south out of Faak am See towards the partly ruined hilltop castle of **Finkenstein**, some 5km away. The spot was fortified by the Finkenstein family in the twelfth century, but with the death of the Finkenstein line the castle fell into the hands of the Habsburgs, after which Emperor Maximilian I sold it in 1512 to his finance minister Sigmund von Diedrichstein. The castle is now home to a café and restaurant, and the impressive view of the Drautal, taking in Villach, the Faakersee and the fortress of Landskron on the opposite side of the valley (see below), ensures a steady stream of sightseers. Built into the western hillside of the castle is the **Burgarena Finkenstein**, an open-air concert venue with terraced seating in the ancient Greek style. Big-name opera stars and a smattering of ageing rock has-beens perform here over the summer.

Schloss Landskron

Six kilometres northeast of Villach, just off the road to the Ossiachersee, **Schloss Landskron** dominates the northern side of the Drautal from its hilltop perch. The castle was a stronghold of Christoph von Khevenhüller in the sixteenth century. As a staunch Protestant, Christoph was to endure the confiscation of all his lands, however, and Landskron was handed over to the solidly Catholic Diedrichsteins. Though imposing from a distance, the castle is now largely ruined, the only habitable section housing a café and (fairly expensive) restaurant. Most people come here to sip coffee and admire the view towards the Karawanken mountains to the south, but there's also an **Adlerschau**, or eagle show (May–Sept daily 11am and 3pm; öS70/€5.11), which involves a falconer sending a domesticated hunting bird on several swooping errands down into the valley. Just below the castle gates, **Affenberg**, or Ape Mountain (April & Oct Fri, Sat & Sun 9.30am–5.30pm; May–Sept daily 9.30am–5.30pm; 20min tours depart at 30min intervals; öS70/€5.11; *www.affenberg.com*), is a small reserve containing a forty-strong community of Japanese macaques. **Buses** on the Villach–Ossiach route pass by the access road to the castle, whence it's a twenty-minute walk uphill. Private cars can be driven right up to the castle gates, although a **toll** (öS25/€1.83 per vehicle) is charged on the access road.

The Ossiachersee

Just beyond Landskron and only 8km from central Villach, the **Ossiachersee** has a completely different atmosphere from its near-neighbour the Wörthersee (see p.328). Squeezed between wooded hills, the settlements along the lake lack the hustle and bus-

tle of places like nearby Pörtschach and Velden, and generally cater for a quieter bunch
of tourists looking for family-oriented holidays. There's a wealth of campsites, small
pensions and outdoor, water-based activities; nightlife is meanwhile fairly low-key,
revolving around a few cosy restaurants and rustic bars.

The northern shore, served by Bundesstrasse 94 and the Villach–Feldkirchen–St
Veit rail route, can get traffic-clogged in summer, and resort towns like **Annenheim**,
Bodensdorf and **Sattendorf** lack any real character. However, the presence of the
Gerlitzen mountain immediately to the north – served by the Kanzelbahn gondola
from Annenheim – makes this a good spot for walking. The southern shore of the lake,
reached from Villach by bus, is an endless procession of lake-clinging campsites, punctuated by the villages of **St Andrä**, **Ostriach** and **Ossiach**. The last, site of a historic
abbey and a summer music festival, is probably the main destination in these parts for
visitors. There's a well-signposted cycle route all the way round the lake, although this
joins the main road for long stretches.

Boat transport links the main settlements on both shores from mid-May to early
October, with eight daily sailings in August – the high season – and three to four daily
at other times. A single ticket costs öS90/6.57, but a better option is the **Kreuzfahrt
ticket** at öS130/€9.49, which is valid for two and a half hours, during which time you
can hop off and on as many times as you wish.

The main **tourist offices** around the lake are in Bodensdorf and Sattendorf on the
northern shore, and in Ossiach on the southern shore. Each of them will book private
rooms or rooms in B&B-style **pensions** within their area. Tourist offices can also fix
you up with the many four- to six-person **apartments** (with per person prices working
out as cheaply as öS150/€10.95) on offer around the lake – for these you're expected
to stay a reasonable length of time, preferably a week.

The northern shore

Travelling westwards along the northern shore, the first settlement of any note is
ANNENHEIM, a small village whose houses creep up the sides of the **Kanzelhöhe**,
the wooded ridge to the north. The **Kanzelbahn** gondola (May–Sept & Dec–Easter;
öS180/€13.14 return) ascends the ridge, connecting with the **Gipfelbahn** chairlift,
which continues to the 1909-metre **Gerlitzen** – also accessible by a toll road from
Bodensdorf (see below). An attractive area of alpine meadow and the starting point for
a number of scenic walks, the Gerlitzen also commands one of the best views in
Carinthia, with Villach and the Faakersee laid out to the southwest, the Wörthersee to
the southeast, and the Karawanken and the Julian Alps (the triple-peaked Triglav,
Slovenia's highest mountain, is relatively easy to make out) running the length of the
southern horizon.

A **campsite**, the *Campingbad Ossiachersee* (☎04248/2757), edges the lake at the
western end of the village, though the site is largely unshaded. The *Aichelberghof*
restaurant, on the lakefront by the ship station, is a good place to dine on fresh trout
or simply to hang out and drink.

Another 5km east, the much larger **BODENSDORF** commands the lion's share of
the lakeside facilities along the northern shore, and serves as the departure point for a
panoramic **toll road** (cars öS60/€4.38, motorbikes öS25/€1.83), which winds its way
up to the summit of the Gerlitzen. There's a **tourist office** in the Gemeindeamt, midway through the village on the main road (June & Sept Mon–Fri 7am–6pm; July & Aug
Mon–Fri 7am–7pm; Oct–May Mon–Fri 9am–noon & 1–4pm; ☎04243/8383-23, *bodens-
dorf@ossiachersee.at*), which lists plenty of **private rooms** (①) in Bodensdorf itself and
also handles accommodation in Steindorf (see opposite). Among the **hotels** and **pensions** on offer are *Frühstückspension Fischer*, Burgweg 32 (☎04243/2748, *www.tiscover
.com/fp-fischer*, ②), a modern house with small but neat balconied rooms (most with en-
suite facilities, some cheaper ones without) at the western end of town; while

Sonnenhotel Garni, Helmut-Wobisch-Weg 4 (☎04243/616, *sonnenhotel.riegelbauer @aon.at*; ④), is a slightly more upmarket place on an attractive, reedy part of the lake-front 1km northeast of town, offering balconied rooms with en-suite facilities, satellite TV and phone.

At the head of the lake, **STEINDORF** has a small Strandbad, a small campsite and plenty of rooms (bookable through the tourist office in Bodensdorf). From here, a minor road veers southwards towards the southern shore, while both Bundesstrasse 94 and the rail line continue east towards the market town of **Feldkirchen** 7km distant, then proceed to **St Veit an der Glan** (see p.335).

The southern shore

In general, the southern shore is quieter and more characterful than the north. Heading east from Villach, the lakeside road passes through the hamlet of **HEILIGENGES-TADE**, site of *Camping Berghof* (☎04242/41133), the lake's most highly rated site and home to a tennis school and a large water activities centre. The next village along, **OSTRIACH**, is home to a further three enormous **campsites**: *Camping Kölbl* (☎04243/8223), *Terrassen Camping* (☎04243/8171) and *Camping Parth* (☎04243/2744), all visible from the main road and all enjoying a stretch of the lakeshore. There are a couple of other nice places to stay in the vicinity: *Frühstückspension Rosenheim*, Ostriach 73 (☎04243/438, *rosenheim@bigfoot.de*; ②), a part-wooden, balconied house with a small outdoor pool, about five minutes' walk from the lake, and *Strandhotel Fünfhaus*, Ostriach 85 (☎04243/432, *www.tiscover.com/fuenfhaus*; ③), a large lakeside hotel with its own waterside stretch of lawn and a waterskiing school.

Ostriach fades into **OSSIACH**, the lake's most popular settlement largely because the former Benedictine abbey adds distinction to its pretty, lakeside setting. The abbey **church** (mid-May to mid-Sept daily 9am–noon & 1.30–6pm; öS30/2.19) is renowned for the cake-icing stucco-work of its interior, and serves as a concert venue during the "Carinthian Summer" festival of chamber music, which runs from June to August – information and tickets are available from **Carinthischer Sommer**, A-9570 Ossiach, Stift (☎04243/2510). There's a windsurfing school at *Strandpension Prinz* (*www .tiscover.com/prinz*), just west of the abbey, and a large grassy Strandbad (öS35/€2.56) beyond. Ossiach's **tourist office**, in the Gemeindeamt on the main road in the village centre (mid-June to mid-Sept Mon–Fri 8am–7pm, Sat & Sun 9am–7pm; mid-Sept to mid-June Mon, Wed & Thurs 9am–noon & 1–5.30pm, Tues & Fri 9am–noon; ☎04243/8420, *osiach@ossiachersee.at*), will fix you up with a **private room** (①) in either Ossiach or Ostriach, and will also give advice on the numerous pensions (②). The most evocative place to stay in Ossiach is the *Gasthof Seewirt* (☎04243/2268, *www.tiscover.com/strandgasthof-seewirt*; ⑤), a sixteenth-century house down on the lakefront near the abbey. The **restaurant** of the *Gasthof zur Post*, on the main road, has a good selection of Austrian dishes, while *Pizzeria Mamma Mia*, on the lane from the main road towards the abbey and lakefront, offers good-value pizzas and pastas, in addition to a couple of fish dishes. Lower down the lane, *Naturgasthof Schlosswirt* offers organically reared meats as well as the best range of **vegetarian** food on the lake, with dishes like rice with spinach and tofu weighing in at around öS100/€7.30.

Spittal an der Drau and the Millstättersee

About 40km northwest of Villach, lying just off the main road and rail route to Salzburg, the **Millstättersee** lacks the nightlife, high-society reputation and high prices of the Wörthersee, but it holds the usual mixture of bathing, windsurfing, boating and other activities. The biggest of the three main settlements along the shore is **Seeboden**, at the western end of the lake, but by far the nicest is **Millstatt**, on the northern side, which boasts a historic abbey and a wealth of charming nineteenth-century villas, many now converted into hotels. **Döbriach**, at the eastern end, is a smaller version of Seeboden, offering accommodation and lakeside activities, but little else. There's little tourist development on the south side of the lake – only a few hotels and no real centres.

Four kilometres west of the lake, commanding the approaches to it, the historic town of **Spittal an der Drau** is an important provincial centre straddling the main Villach–Salzburg road and rail routes. The tourist office in Spittal can book **rooms** throughout the Spittal and Millstättersee area, making it a useful tourist gateway to the region; likewise, tourist offices on the lake can book rooms in Spittal.

Spittal an der Drau

SPITTAL AN DER DRAU owes its existence to the paternalism of twelfth-century aristocrats, the Ortenburgs, who established a *Spittal*, or hospice, here to care for the local poor and provide a waystation for travellers on their way across the mountain passes to the north. The hospice that gave the town its name no longer exists, and nowadays Spittal is instead largely visited for **Schloss Porcia**, a fine Renaissance chateau built by Gabriel von Salamanca, a Spanish nobleman who served as imperial treasurer in the sixteenth century. The Schloss was sold to the Austro-Italian Porcia family in 1662, although the Salamancas are still remembered by the annual **Salamancafest** in late June, when the townsfolk don sixteenth-century garb and street stalls dole out food and drink.

Spittal is the starting point of a cable car to the nearby **Goldeck** peak, and a good base from which to visit the Millstättersee. It's also the obvious place from which to catch buses to Gmünd (see p.356), 15km to the north.

The Town

Surrounded by a small park, the centrally located **Schloss Porcia** was built over seven decades from 1527 onwards. Its inner courtyard, with three storeys of balustraded galleries held up by finely carved Ionic and Corinthian columns, is now a venue for theatre performances and concerts over the summer. Occupying the upper two floors of the Schloss, the **Museum für Volkskultur** (daily 9am–6pm; öS50/€3.65) is divided up into thematically arranged rooms, devoted to such topics as education, religion, mining, village crafts and so on, each with explanatory texts in English. There's an intriguing section on winter sports, displaying the snowshoes with which locals used to get about in winter, together with the fanciful assertion that it was from footwear such as this that modern skis evolved (skis were in fact imported from Scandinavia at the end of the nineteenth century). Finally, the Fürstenzimmer contains the kind of Baroque and Rococo furnishings that might once have decorated the Porcia family home, as well as a portrait of the last of the Salamancas, Countess Catharina. According to popular myth, the miserly Catharina murdered a servant girl who had discovered the location of her secret horde of cash, and was condemned to wander the castle in ghostly form as a result. East of the Schloss, Spittal's **Hauptplatz** is a disappointingly plain shopping street, although the **Stadtpfarrkirche**, just off the Hauptplatz to the south, is worth a peek for the abstract purple patterns of its modern stained-glass windows.

About twenty minutes' walk south of the town centre, the **Goldeckbahn** cable car (usually operative mid-May to Oct and Dec–March; öS115/€8.40 one way; öS155/€11.32 return) provides access to the 2142-metre Goldeck, which rises above the valley floor to the southeast. The cable car runs first to a middle station, from where there's a chairlift to the Bergstation, starting point for numerous trails, including the walk to the Goldeck summit just above. There's also a toll road to a point just south of the summit, leaving the valley floor at the village of **Kamering**, 12km down the valley on the Villach road.

Practicalities

Spittal's **train** and **bus stations** are 500m southwest of the centre, on Südtirolerplatz. Walk down Bahnhofstrasse and head right across the Stadtpark to reach the **tourist office** (Mon–Fri 9am–6pm, Sat 9am–1pm; ☎04762/3420, *www.spittal-drau.at*), lurking on the far side of Schloss Porcia. You can book accommodation throughout the Millstättersee region here, as well as **private rooms** (①) in Spittal itself. There's a decent **youth hostel** (☎04762/3252) about 1km southwest of the train station, near the Goldeckbahn terminus.

Hotels include the family-run *Brückenwirt*, An der Wirtschaftsbrücke 2 (☎04762/2772; ②), on the banks of the Lieser stream just east of the centre, offering basic but comfy rooms with en-suite facilities. The modern, attractively designed *Edlingerwirt*, Villacherstrasse 88 (☎04762/5150; ④), 2km east of the centre, on the way into town from the Spittal-Ost exit of the autobahn, also has en-suite rooms with satellite TV. *Ertl*, Bahnhofstrasse 26 (☎04762/20480; ⑤), is a comfortable business-class hotel next to the train station, offering rooms with en-suite facilities, satellite TV, phone and minibar.

There's a moderately good choice of eateries in town and a healthy sprinkling of bars, making Spittal a better bet for evening diversions than the lakeside resorts of the nearby Millstättersee. For **food**, probably the best place to enjoy a good-value Carinthian *Nud'l* dish or a standard Austrian schnitzel is *Gösser Bräu*, a large brewery-owned restaurant with a sizeable beer garden about 500m east of the town centre on Villacherstrasse. The centrally located *Altdeutsche Weinstube*, just north of Schloss Porcia on Neuer Platz, has a pleasant garden out the back, and also serves a standard range of Carinthian *Nud'l* dishes, as well as much more expensive fish and steaks. *Formosa*, Kirchgasse 5 (entry from Hauptplatz), is the best of the Chinese restaurants, with cheap lunchtime menus (from öS60/€4.38) on weekdays. *Zellot*, in the far western corner of the Hauptplatz next to the *Hotel Post*, is a smart, top-quality, though not too pricey, restaurant with a wide range of traditional Austrian as well as Carinthian dishes.

For **drinking**, best and most convenient of the coffee-and-cakes venues is *Café Gabriel* on the Hauptplatz. An alleyway off the north side of Hauptplatz leads to *K & K Hofcafé*, a cosy and stylish bar which is good for an evening drink. Most of the nighttime action is centred on Bogengasse, which descends just beyond the western end of Hauptplatz towards the river Liesel, and contains a string of bars open until the early hours. Moving from west to east, *Bogo Music Pub* occasionally hosts local rock bands; *Petzl Bräu* has in-house DJs providing a techno-jungle-trip-hop soundtrack; and *Amigos*, right by the bridge over the Liesel, has Latin sounds and a lengthy cocktail menu.

Seeboden and around

A five-kilometre journey over the hill from Spittal, **SEEBODEN** is a bustling little resort town at the western end of the Millstättersee – even though the only attraction is the lakefront, and the hotels that serve it. There's a big municipal **Strandbad** at the northeast end of town, otherwise visitors tend to head for the village of **TREFFLING** in the hills to the north, where **Burg Sommeregg** provides a home for the popular **Foltermuseum**, or museum of torture (daily: May–June & Sept–Oct 10am–6pm; Jul–Aug 10am–9pm; öS70/5.11; *www.folter.at*), which is about a 45-minute walk from the centre of Seeboden – head out of town on the Spittal road and turn right when you see the sign for Treffling. With its flashy lighting and grisly tableaux, the museum goes for titillation rather than education, though a display detailing the good works of Amnesty International is prominently situated near the entrance, suggesting some moral purpose to the collection. Before Maria Theresia and her son Josef II (who appear here in wax form) began the slow process of reform, torture had been a standard means of extracting confessions in Austria as elsewhere; methods illustrated here include the Saw, popularized by the Spanish Inquisition, which sliced people in half from the rump upwards, and the Iron Maiden, a metal human-shaped cabinet with sharp spikes on the inside, into which suspected miscreants were placed. Smaller, more humiliating than painful punishments prove equally sobering, like the grotesque, animal-like *Schandmasken*, or "masks of shame", which petty criminals were forced to wear before being paraded through the streets, and the stocks and gags into which nagging wives were forced.

Treffling is also the starting point for walks up the 2088-metre **Tschernock** – also accessible by road as far as the **Hansbauer-Alm** just below the summit – a popular local beauty spot and vantage point.

Practicalities

Spittal–Millstatt **buses** drop off near the **tourist office**, at Hauptstrasse 93 (Mon–Fri 9am–5pm, Sat 9am–1pm; ☎04762/81210, *seeboden@netway.at*), where you can enquire about **private rooms** (①) in Seeboden, or rooms and **apartments** in the farmhouses of nearby Treffling. Of the local **hotels**, *Pension Elizabeth*, Steinerstrasse 43–47 (☎04762/81701; ③), is a mid-priced bargain occupying a traditional, balconied house near the lake, offering rooms with en-suite facilities and TV, and an owner who organizes mushroom-picking hikes. *Santners Sporthotel Royal*, Seehofstrasse 23 (☎04762/81714-0, *sporthotel@carinthia.com*; ⑤), is a large and well-appointed modern lakefront hotel, which also runs the best of the windsurfing schools and offers tennis packages in the summer. **Campsites** on the lakefront include *Strandcamping Winkler*, Seepromenade 33 (☎04762/81822 or 81927), a big grassy site with bathing area and plenty of sporting activities, while *Camping Lieseregg* (☎04762/2723, *ferienpark-lieseregg@carinthia.com*), 2km northwest of town along Liesereggerstrasse, is a family-oriented place with an outdoor swimming pool and entertainment laid on for kids.

Boats can be rented from numerous shacks along the Seepromenade; while Santners Sporthotel Royal offers a range of sailing and windsurfing courses, as well as renting out boards.

Millstatt

Four kilometres east of Seeboden, **MILLSTATT** is where Millstättersee tourism first took off in the mid-nineteenth century. The resulting building boom produced a spate of elegant lakeside holiday villas which, now transformed into hotels or family homes, lend the town a sedate, refined air. This, combined with an attractive lakeside promenade and a large municipal Strandbad, makes Millstatt the most enticing of the lake's resorts. The attractive hillside villages within reach above town help to broaden its appeal, while the historic **abbey** in the centre hosts an annual fix of high culture during the **Internationale Musikwochen** – from May to October, chamber music performances take place in the abbey, its courtyard and in the town's modern congress centre. Information and tickets can be obtained from Musikwochen Millstatt, Stiftgasse 1, A-9872 Millstatt (☎04766/2165), or from the tourist office.

Various places along the lakeside promenade rent out boats. Wassersport Strobl, Seemühlgasse 56a (☎04766/2263), is the main centre for hiring windsurfing, sailing and canoeing gear, and they also organize courses: expect to pay around öS1600/€116.80 for a short windsurfing course (15 hours over a 3– or 4–day period), öS2050/€149.65 for a basic sailing course (25 hours over 5 days), although other variants are available.

The abbey

Much the town's main feature, the **abbey**, just uphill from the lakefront, began life as an eleventh-century Benedictine foundation, but was handed over in 1469 to Emperor Friedrich III's **Order of the Knights of St George**. Friedrich had established the Order in 1462, largely in celebration of military successes in Vienna, where he'd been besieged in the Hofburg by the town's own citizens. The Order's golden age, however, was to come under Friedrich's son Maximilian I, who extracted enormous propaganda from his association with the cult of St George, who was regarded as a symbol of chivalry and courage. After Maximilian's death in 1511, the Order began to lose its importance, not least because its declared foe – the Ottoman Turks – rarely came within skirmishing distance of Millstatt anyway. Emperor Ferdinand II gave the abbey to the **Jesuits** in 1612, in preparation for the re-Catholicization of what had become a predominantly Protestant area. They used the abbey's revenue to fund Graz University, and high taxes imposed on the local community led to a peasant rebellion in 1737, which was brutally put down.

Framed by an eye-catching pair of onion-topped towers, the abbey **church** still preserves a few Romanesque touches, notably the tympanum above the west porch, which depicts a donor presenting Christ with a model of the church. Within the church's delicately rib-vaulted interior, the imposing grave of the Order's first grand master, Johann Siebenhirter, is marked by an imposing red granite relief in a side chapel over to the left as you enter. Though faded, Urban Görtschauer's sixteenth-century *Last Judgement* fresco, to the right of the high altar, is the best of the surviving Gothic paintings. Much of the abbey's art collection was dispersed after the abolition of the Jesuit order in 1773, which is why a number of Millstatt's treasures are now found in Graz or Klagenfurt rather than in the monastery's small **Stiftsmuseum** (May–Sept daily 9am–noon & 2–6pm; Oct–April Mon–Fri 9am–noon for groups of 5 or above; öS40/€2.92). Alongside pictures relating to the Order of St George, some copies of ecclesiastical manuscripts, and the red-marble tombs of medieval clerics, is one of the three ornately decorated wedding chests of Paola Gonzaga, which contained her dowry at her marriage in 1477 to Leonhard von Görz, master of Lienz Castle (see p.364). All three chests were presented to the Order of St George in Millstatt on Paola's death, but two were subsequently expropriated by the Jesuits, and are displayed in the Domkirche in Graz (see p.279). Beyond the museum lies the twelfth-century **cloister** (free access during daylight hours), whose arches are supported by pillars bearing delightful Romanesque details, including curious, peering faces and fanciful frolicking beasts.

Practicalities

Buses from Spittal stop near the lakeside promenade, just below the abbey. Walk up through the abbey complex to reach the **tourist office**, on Marktplatz (May–Sept Mon–Fri 7.30am–6pm, Sat & Sun 10am–noon & 4–6pm; Oct–April Mon–Thur 8am–noon & 1–5pm, Fri 8am–noon; ☎04766/2022-0, *millstatt@netway.at*), which will check vacancies in **private rooms** (①) in town or, if you have your own transport, in the rural suburb of **Obermillstatt**, which occupies a terrace of rich farmland above town to the north. The tourist office also has information on **apartments** by the lake or on hillside farms.

Other **accommodation** choices include *Haus Brigitte*, Grossdombra 18 (☎04766/3051; ①), a small, family-run place overlooking Millstatt from the village of Grossdombra, 1km uphill to the north; take Kalvarienberggasse (which becomes Laubendorferstrasse) out of the Marktplatz to get there. Set back slightly from the lake in a villa-crowded residential street east of the Marktplatz, *Villa Waldheim*, Mirnockstrasse 110 (☎04766/2061; ③), represents good value for a taste of nineteenth-century atmosphere; it's a friendly, family-run place with creaking floorboards and

Biedermeier furnishings. *Villa Margarethe*, Mirnockstrasse 72 (☎04766/2654; ③), is another pleasant pension in a suburban house just east of the centre, by the lake with its own stretch of shoreline (also offers a few big family apartments). Most evocative (and reasonably priced) of the nineteenth-century villas on the lake, *Seevilla*, Seestrasse 68 (☎04766/2102; ⑤), has traditionally furnished rooms, a private bathing area, sauna and tennis courts. The nearest **campsite** is *Terrassencamping Pesenthein* (☎04766/202122), on the lakefront 3km to the east.

There's little to choose between the generally excellent, and reasonably priced, hotel **restaurants** that line the lakeside promenade, most of which are also good places to sample the local freshwater fish. The *Hotel Forelle* has a particularly nice waterside terrace. Though many close in winter, the restaurant of the *Hotel Seewirt*, slightly inland at Kaiser-Franz-Josef-Strasse 49, stays open year-round. Elsewhere in the town centre, *Pizzeria Pepino*, just across the way from the Strandbad, is an inexpensive and lively place that stays open until 11pm – by which time most other places have closed – and *Hotel Post*, Mirnockstrasse 38, offers high-quality Austrian cuisine in comfortable surroundings, as well as a good-value lunchtime buffet.

Best of the **drinking** venues are *Café Columbia* on Georgsritterplatz, a good choice both day and night, which also serves cheap pizzas and wonderful ice creams, and the café of the *Hubertusschlössl* hotel on Seestrasse, a half-timbered gothic building which wouldn't look out of place in Transylvania, and has a nice lakeside terrace to boot. Late-night boozing takes place at the *Full House American Bar*, near the bus stop on Kaiser-Franz-Josef-Strasse.

Beyond Millstatt: Döbriach

Eight kilometres beyond Millstatt, **DÖBRIACH** marks the Millstättersee's eastern extent, a resort village full of modern apartment hotels that spreads over the flatlands where the Riegerbach enters the lake. There's a string of pay-to-enter bathing areas along the lakeshore, many of which also offer boat rental and other sporting activities. The **tourist office**, about 1km east of the lake on the Hauptplatz (☎04246/7878), has a list of **private rooms** (①) and **apartments**, though a stay of more than three days is expected in the latter; otherwise there are plenty of **pensions** in the ③ bracket. There's a wealth of **campsites** on or near the lakefront, all of which are well equipped, have access to bathing areas and lay on events for kids in summer: *Burgstaller* (☎04246/7774, *www.burgstaller.co.at/burgstaller*) is one of the biggest; *Ebner* (☎04246/7735-18, *camping@moessler.at*), is smaller and less animated. If you're into sailing, waterskiing or windsurfing, you'll find several places along the lakefront renting out gear or running courses.

Gmünd and around

The Salzburg-bound A10 autobahn heads north from Spittal up the Liesertal, continuing onwards to the **Katschberg tunnel**, which marks the border between Carinthia and the Salzburger Land. The obvious place to stop off en route is the medieval town-let of **Gmünd**, 15km north of Spittal and served by frequent local buses. An engaging destination in its own right, Gmünd is also a good base from which to visit the **Maltatal**, a highland valley nestling beneath an eastern spur of the Hohe Tauern range.

On leaving the Drautal, the autobahn advances up the Liesertal on concrete stilts, while the old Bundesstrasse (served by local buses) sticks to the valley floor, meandering along the forest-fringed course of the river. Twelve kilometres out of Spittal, the road passes through **TREBESING**, an important centre for family-oriented tourism dubbed "Austria's First Babydorf" by energetic local boosters. An unfashionable spa resort with an ageing clientele until the late eighties, the village is now packed with hotels and pensions offering facilities for infants and their respite-seeking parents. The "Bauer Point" **information bureau** is right on the main road (dawn–dusk; ☎04732/3000, *babydorf.trebesing@lieser-maltatal.at*), and can help allocate accommodation. Trebesing's bigger hotels offer on-site **baby-minding** facilities and a range of activities for children, while the smaller Gasthöfe and pensions make use of the central nursery facilities provided by the village. Something of a pioneer in the field, *Österreichs 1. Baby- und Kinderhotel*, Trebesing 1 (☎04372/2350-415; ④), is the biggest and best equipped of the establishments, although there are plenty of other alternatives. The resort's only drawback is its popularity – it's teeming with toddlers.

Gmünd

Founded by the archbishops of Salzburg in the eleventh century to protect the trade routes that gave them a firmer hold on Carinthian life, **GMÜND** preserves much of its medieval character. Small, compact and traversed by cobbled alleyways spanned by little arches, it shelters a profusion of small galleries and craft shops, together with a brace of idiosyncratic museums.

Lined with medieval houses colourwashed in pastel shades, Gmünd's pretty Hauptplatz stretches from north to south, with the old town gates standing guard at each end. Alleyways lead westwards from the Hauptplatz to the building known as "Im Loch", a former jailhouse, which now holds the **Eva Faschaunerin Ausstellung** (May–Oct daily 9am–noon & 2–6pm; öS40/€2.92), a collection recalling the local murderer who was the last person to be executed in the district. Eva allegedly killed her husband, Jakob Kary Hörlbauer, on a March day in 1770, by putting arsenic – mined locally for use in the dyeing industry – in his supper. She was executed in November 1773. Telling her story through a series of tableaux and (German-language) texts, the museum serves as a powerful evocation of eighteenth-century Carinthian life. There's a recreation of the kitchen where the dirty deed was done, and of the rack where she was tortured into confession.

A short distance south of the Eva Faschaunerin museum, the thirteenth-century **Pfarrkirche Maria Himmelfahrt** boasts the usual collection of gilded Baroque altarpieces; of greater interest, the **Karner**, or charnel house, outside is decorated with fourteenth-century frescoes depicting scenes of the New Testament, including a vibrant *Adoration of the Magi* in which Christ's manger is watched over by quaintly rendered farm animals. A few steps west of the church is the **Porsche-Automuseum** (daily: mid-May to mid-Oct 9am–6pm; mid-Oct to mid-May 10am–4pm; öS75/€5.48), a must for anyone who enthuses over cars, and an intriguing slice of history for anyone who doesn't. Assembled by local collector Helmut Pfeifhofer, the well-arranged exhibits document the output of the prolific Austrian-born designer Ferdinand Porsche. The oldest of the cars on show is the 1932 taxi built by the Austrian branch of Daimler, where Porsche worked as technical director after World War I. From 1934 he worked in Stuttgart on the development of the VW Beetle, but allied bombing forced Volkswagen to disperse their production facilities to more isolated locations in 1944, and Porsche and his design team relocated to the village of Karnerau, 2km north of Gmünd. They stayed here until 1950, though Porsche himself was imprisoned by the French for two years immediately after the war due to his work on military vehicles. It was in Karnerau that the classic Porsche 356 sports car was first built, several rare examples of which are on display.

Standing at the northern end of town on an easily scaled hillock are the remnants of the thirteenth-century **Alte Burg**, where representatives of the Salzburg archbishops once held sway. Habitable portions are occupied by a restaurant and café-bar, and rock and jazz concerts take place in the castle courtyard on summer weekends. Otherwise, it's a good place from which to enjoy views of Gmünd's tightly drawn web of streets below. Further north, 1km out of town beside the main Bundesstrasse, is the oddity known as the **Geteilte Kirche**, or divided church. Comprising two buildings divided by a country lane, the church began life as a small roadside chapel and became an increasingly popular shrine in the eighteenth century. Unfortunately, there was no space to enlarge it, so an additional building was constructed on the opposite roadside, allowing the priest to conduct services on one side while the congregation sat on the other.

Practicalities

Buses come to rest in the Hauptplatz, just opposite the **tourist office** at no. 20 (Mon–Fri 9am–5pm, Sat 9am–noon; ☎04732/2222, *www.lieser-maltatal.or.at*), which has a small number of **private rooms** (①) at its disposal. Best of the **hotels** is the *Kohlmayr*, Hauptplatz 7 (☎04732/2149, *gasthof.kohlmayr@netway.at*; ③), a lovely old Gasthof whose traditionally furnished rooms have en-suite facilities and TV; if it's full, *Gasthof Prunner*, Hauptplatz 15 (☎04732/2187; ③), is a comfortable alternative.

For **food**, the *Kohlmaier* is very much the focus of local life, offering a range of Austrian cuisine at medium prices, as well as being a good place to have a **drink**. The *Gasthof zur Post* immediately opposite has good food if slightly higher prices. *Café-Konditorei Nussbaumer*, also on Hauptplatz, is the town's main daytime coffee-and-cakes venue, while the *Café-pub* next door seems to take over in the evening.

The Maltatal

Heading northwest from Gmünd, a minor road ascends the **Maltatal** towards the **Kölnbrein reservoir**, 32km away at the head of the valley. It's a popular route, largely because it provides access to some desolate alpine uplands in the shadow of the 3246-metre Ankogel and its foothills, but also because the reservoir at the end boasts one of Austria's most impressive pieces of civil engineering, the **Kölnbreinsperre** (Kölnbrein Dam). Reaching the area is easy if you have your own transport, though the last 15km of the journey is via toll road, the **Malta-Hochalm-Strasse** (May to mid-Oct; öS120/€8.76 per vehicle). Public transport of a sort exists during the Hochalm-Strasse's period of operation, with a weekly bus running from Gmünd to the dam (currently Weds; check at the Gmünd tourist office for details). It's a highly scenic ride, as the narrow road negotiates tortuous switchbacks, passing through several tunnels along the way. Traffic lights control the flow of traffic by day in order to minimize the risk of collisions; they don't work after 6pm, when greater vigilance must be exercised.

The Hochalm-Strasse culminates beside the elegant curve of the dam, built in the 1970s to collect glacial waters from the ring of mountains that forms the Hohe Tauern range's easternmost spur. Above the dam sits the barrel-shaped **Panoramaturm**, a "panoramic tower" holding café, restaurant, 4-star hotel (☎04783/2504; ⑥) and the **Tauernschatzkammer**, a small exhibition of crystals (free), which includes a film about the Hohe Tauern National Park and a ten-minute video telling the story of the dam's construction. Guided **tours** of the dam interior are available throughout the summer (times are posted at the entrance of the Tauernschatzkammer; öS60/€4.38), worth considering for the eerie atmosphere that reigns within the dam wall, rather than the barrage of mind-boggling statistics about how many cubic metres of concrete were needed in order to build it. The tours last 45 minutes and are conducted in German, although guides might give an English summary if requested.

A broad track leads westwards around the reservoir from the dam, providing walkers with good views of the surrounding mountains. A popular walk suitable for the moderately fit day-tripper is the hike to the **Osnabrücker Hütte** (2hr one way), which lies just beyond the western end of the reservoir on the shoulder of the

Ankogel. A slightly more demanding itinerary, involving steeper ascents, is the walk from the dam to the **Katowitzer Hütte** (3hr 30min one way), which lies on the slopes of the Hafnergruppe to the southeast. To pick up this trail, walk back down the Hochalm-Strasse from the dam for about 1km until you see a sign leading uphill to the left.

Heiligenblut and the Grossglockner

Northwest of Spittal, both the main Salzburg-bound rail line and the A106 Bundesstrasse head up the Mölltal towards the imposing mountains of the **Hohe Tauern**. At **Obervellach**, a road splits off to the west and veers towards the Mölltal, climbing towards the chocolate-box alpine village of **Heiligenblut**, which shelters beneath Austria's highest peak, the **Grossglockner**. Both rail line and Bundesstrasse continue straight on from Obervellach towards the **Tauern tunnel**, emerging in the Gasteinertal and the Salzburger Land (see Chapter 7) on the other side. Car drivers must pay for their vehicle to be transported through the tunnel by rail; wagons carrying the cars operate from 6.40am to 9.40pm southbound, and from 6.10am to 9.10pm northbound (cars öS200/€14.60 one way, öS320/€23.36 return; motorbikes öS110/€8.03 one way, öS180/€13.14 return).

Heiligenblut

One of the most attractively situated villages in the Austrian Alps, **HEILIGENBLUT** is little more than a narrow strip of houses clinging to the western slopes of a dramatic, steep-sided valley, with the snow-clad summit of the 3798-metre **Grossglockner** in the distance to the north. It's a scene dominated by the cream-and-ochre **Pfarrkirche St Vinzenz**, whose tall, slender spire seems to mimic the peaks of the Glockner mountains behind it. Pictures of the church, with the snowy slopes of the Grossglockner glittering in the background, have featured on thousands of alpine calendars and postcards. The church was built by monks from Admont in Styria to hold a vial purported to contain the blood of Christ – hence the village's name, which translates as "holy blood". According to legend, the vial was brought to the area from Byzantium by St Briccius, who was consumed by an avalanche when attempting to cross the Alps, leaving the holy relic to be recovered by rescuers. It's now contained in a Gothic reliquary inside the church to the left of the high altar, an extravagantly pinnacled pillar of pale stone encrusted with statuettes of saints. The high altar itself, an early-sixteenth-century affair featuring the Virgin flanked by saints Barbara and Catherine, is thought to be the work of Wolfgang Asslinger, a member of Michael Pacher's studio. It's a simple attractive piece of work, its wooden statuary gaily painted to look like porcelain figurines, and harbours a wealth of delightfully idiosyncratic detail – in the bottom right-hand panel, the Ascension is depicted by a scene of two bare feet disappearing upwards into a cloud. The rib-vaulted ceiling above the altar is decorated with paintings of a slender Virgin holding a Child, and symbols of the Evangelists.

Slightly uphill from the church, round the back of the Gasthaus Schöber, the **Hohe Tauern National Park Centre** (daily 10am–4pm; *www.hohetauern.at*) gives away leaflets, sells maps and offers a small museum display on the park, including a series of short video films on the history of climbing on the park's most prominent peak, the Grossglockner. The mountain was first conquered in August 1800, when Count Salm, bishop of Gurk and an enthusiastic promoter of alpinism, led a 62-man expedition supported by 26 mules and horses up the mountain. Salm himself only went as far as his steed would carry him, although a local priest, Pfarrer Horasch, accompanied by

Heiligenblut farmers, carried on to the top. Early ascents tackled the gentler east slope of the mountain, and it wasn't until 1876 that the north face was conquered by Alfred Pallavicini, a Viennese army officer who ten years later lost his life on the Grossglockner while trying to pioneer yet more difficult routes.

The slopes east of the village provide ample **skiing** terrain suitable largely for intermediates; a one-day lift pass costs öS350/€25.55, seven-day öS1600/€116.80), and some of the lifts that serve them are open in July and August for summer walkers. A cable car leaves the village centre (just opposite the *Hotel Post*) for the 1750-metre **Rossbach**, from where you can take another cable car to the 2600-metre **Schareck**, or a funicular through a tunnel to the **Fleisalm**, an area of alpine meadow below the 2989-metre **Gjaidtroghöhe** – a marvellous place to savour the crisp mountain air and up-close views of the Glocknergruppe.

Practicalities

The best place from which to approach Heiligenblut by public transport is Lienz (see p.361), which offers two direct buses all year round. Spittal an der Drau is also a resonable jumping-off point, although you'll have to change at the village of Winklen. Buses stop just above the **tourist office** on the main street (Mon–Fri 9am–12.30pm & 2–5.30pm, Sat 9am–12.30pm & 2–4pm; ☎04824/2001-21), where you can enquire about vacancies in **private rooms** (summer ①; winter ②), pensions and apartments. Cheapest **pension** in the centre is probably the *Bergkristall*, near the Rossbach cable-car station at Hof 71 (☎04824/2005; ①), which has some rooms with shared facilities, as well as more expensive ones with en-suite shower and WC. There are plenty more good-value pensions down in the valley bottom: *Lagler*, Winkl 90 (☎04824/2280; ②), and *Edelweiss*, Hadergasse 17 (☎04824/2083; ②), are two comfy, family-run B&B places. If you want a central **hotel** with all the creature comforts, the most atmospheric is the *Villa Kaiser-Franz-Josef*, Hof 45 (☎04824/2084; ⑦), also featuring a sauna and gym, in a large, timber-balconied traditional house. There's a **youth hostel** just downhill from the centre, at Hof 36 (☎04824/2259; Jan–Sept), and a **campsite**, *Möllfluss* (☎04824/2129), lower down still in the valley bottom.

For **eating**, the *Dorfstube*, on the main street, features an inexpensive menu of Austrian regulars and pizzas, while the *Hotel Post* has a much wider range of local cuisine at only slightly higher prices. The *Laterndl* on Dorfplatz is a cosy wood-panelled café-bar which is open for daytime and night-time **drinking** all year round; while the *Eisbär*, a glass igloo plunked at the edge of a sun-catching terrace at the south entrance to the village, is a popular winter après-ski venue.

The local **mountain guide** association, Bergführerverein Heiligenblut, organizes guided ascents of the Grossglockner (contact them through the National Park centre; expect to pay in the region of öS3400/€248.20 for one person, öS5400/€394.20 for four people) as well as a range of other specialized ascents.

The Grossglockner Hochalpenstrasse

The main excursion from Heiligenblut is to drive or journey by bus along the **Grossglockner Hochalpenstrasse**, a scenic toll road (mid-May to late Oct; cars öS350/€22.55, motorbikes öS250/€18.25, bus passengers pay a small fee included in the price of their ticket) that heads northeast from the village, rising above the Möll Valley towards the **Grossglockner Pass** (just east of the mountain similarly named), which marks the border between Carinthia and the Salzburger Land. It's a tortuous but spectacular ascent, allowing glimpses of the Grossglockner itself, a lofty white mass which occasionally pokes its head above the surrounding crowd of peaks. Most sightseers turn left a few kilometres short of the top to enjoy a side-trip along the **Gletscherstrasse** to **Franz-Josefs-Höhe**, an itinerary more fully described on p.418.

One **bus** a day (three in July and Aug) serves the Franz-Josefs-Höhe, commencing in Lienz and passing through Heiligenblut on the way. Once there, you can pick up a connecting service to the lakeside resort of **Zell am See** (see Chapter 7) on the northern side of the pass.

EAST TYROL

Separated from the rest of the Tyrol by Italy, the **East Tyrol** (Osttirol) is most easily approached from Carinthia, the Land with which it has the best public transport links. Despite possessing some of the most dramatic mountain scenery in Austria, the East Tyrol has, strangely, never enjoyed the same level of tourist development as northern Tyrol or the Salzburger Land – and therein lies its appeal. Towns like the local administrative capital **Lienz** and villages like **Kals** and **Matrei** are perfectly equipped for skiing and walking, but are spared the large numbers of Eurotourists that regularly descend on places like Seefeld, Mayrhofen and St Anton. To outsiders, the East Tyrol seems marvellously unspoilt, though locals have sometimes felt a little left out of the main currents of Austrian life. The separation of East Tyrol from the rest of the province, following the award of the South Tyrol to Italy in 1919, was a big blow for the region, producing feelings of isolation only partially alleviated by the building of the Grossglockner Hochalpenstrasse in 1936 and the **Felber Tauern** tunnel in 1967.

Lienz can be reached by rail either from Innsbruck in the west (with trains running through a corner of Italy to get here) or from Spittal an der Drau to the east. The Felber Tauern tunnel presents the region's main road link with Austria north of the Alps, with two daily buses making the journey here from Kitzbühel and Kufstein in northeastern Tyrol. It's also possible to get here from Zell am See via the Grossglockner Hochalpenstrasse in summer, with bus passengers changing at the Franz-Josefs-Höhe.

Lienz

Standing at the confluence of the Drau and Isel, **LIENZ** sprawls beneath the ragged, hostile slopes of the **Lienzer Dolomiten**, strangely beautiful peaks that adopt a pinkish hue in the early morning sun. Located at the southern end of two important transalpine routes – the Felber Tauern and the Grossglockner Pass – the town has long

---

SKIING IN THE EAST TYROL

Few of the places in East Tyrol are featured in the package-holiday brochures, so travellers intent on tackling the pistes here will have to make arrangements independently. **Lienz** is probably the most versatile base, with the **Zettersfeld** east of town providing plenty of terrain suitable for beginners and intermediates – descents of the Hochstein to the northwest prove more demanding. Lienz is also a big enough town to possess a modicum of nightlife. The same can't be said of the three main resorts to the north – **Matrei**, **Prägraten** and **St Jakob** – small villages that are nonetheless good for beginners and intermediates. **Kals** is an emerging resort suitable for beginners and families, with nursery slopes just outside the village and several hotels catering for small children. **Ski passes** for the East Tyrol's winter resorts are slightly cheaper than those elsewhere in Austria: expect to pay öS300–330/€21.90–24.09 for one day (children about half as much). Combined Osttirol-Kärnten ski passes covering all the East Tyrolean resorts as well as Heiligenblut and a couple of other places in western Carinthia cost öS1800/€131.40 for 6 days (half as much for children).

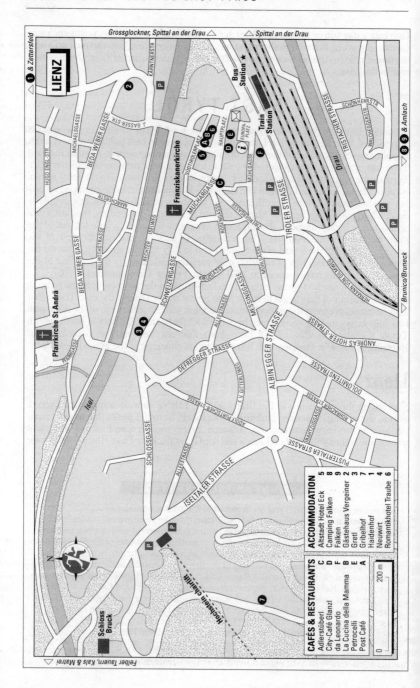

LIENZ

Grossglockner, Spittal an der Drau △ △ Spittal an der Drau

& Zettersfeld

Bus Station

Train Station

EUROPA PLATZ

HAUPTPLATZ

Franziskanerkirche

Pfarrkirche St Andrä

Schloss Bruck

Felber Tauern, Kals & Matrei △

Brunico/Bruneck ▽

& Amlach ▽

Isel

Hochstein chairlift

KÄRNTNERSTR

J. GASSER-STR

MICHAELSGASSE

BEDA WEBER GASSE

HUGO ENGL STR

MARCHERSTR

BEDA WEBER GASSE

BILROTHSTRASSE

RECHTER SELWEG

SCHWEIZERGASSE

SCHLOSSGASSE

ALLEESTRASSE

PFARRGASSE

SÜDTIROLERPLATZ

MÜHGASSE

MÜCHARGASSE

ROSENGASSE

KREUGASSE

MÜHLGASSE

MESSINGGASSE

ALLEESTRASSE

DEFREGGER STRASSE

ALBIN EGGER STRASSE

F.V. GÜTTLERWEG

ADOLF WURTSCHER STRASSE

ISELTALER STRASSE

PUSTERTALER STRASSE

ANDREAS HOFER STRASSE

DOLOMITENSTRASSE

A. ROHRACHER STRASSE

DRAHTZUGGASSE

TIROLER STRASSE

HERMANN VON GILMWEG

TRISTACHER STRASSE

SCHÖNHERRSTR

WALDNEGGERSTR

Drau

CAFÉS & RESTAURANTS

Adlerstüberl	C
City-Café Glanzl	D
da Leonardo	F
La Cucina della Mamma	B
Petrocelli	E
Post Café	A

ACCOMMODATION

Altstadt Hotel Eck	5
Camping Falken	8
Falken	9
Gästehaus Vergeiner	2
Gretl	3
Gribelhof	7
Haidenhof	1
Neuwirt	4
Romantikhotel Traube	6

N

0   200 m

been an important staging post for those travelling onwards to Italy. The Romans were the first to recognize this spot's potential, planting the settlement of **Aguntum** some 5km east of the modern town, near the village of Dölsach, where its scant remains can still be seen. Settled by German-speaking tribes in the ninth century, medieval Lienz enjoyed a brief period of importance as the seat of the powerful **counts of Görz**, from what is now Gorizia in Italy, until 1500, when the last of the counts, Leonhard, died without an heir. The territory then fell to Emperor Maximilian I, who incorporated Lienz and its environs into the Tyrol. Both **Schloss Bruck**, erstwhile residence of the counts of Görz, and the **Stadtpfarrkirche St Andrä**, where Leonhard was entombed, provide modern sightseers with a focus, although World War II air raids put an end to the town's other medieval remnants.

Arrival, information and accommodation

Both **bus** and **train stations** are on Tirolerstrasse, just southeast of the centre. Cross the street and head towards the modern flagstoned Europaplatz to your left in order to find the **tourist office**, at no. 1 (Mon–Fri 8am–6pm, Sat 9am–noon; ☎04852/65265, *www.tiscover.com/lienz*), which gives out free town maps and deals in a range of **private** rooms, both in town and in the neighbouring villages of **Thurn** and **Amlach** (suitable if you have your own transport). There's a **campsite**, *Komfort-Camping Falken*, Eichholz 7 (☎04852/64022), in the fields 1km south of town. To get there, turn left out of the station, take the next left, pass underneath the railway tracks and carry on until you see the sign.

Hotels

Altstadthotel Eck, Hauptplatz 20 (☎04852/64785). Cosy old-fashioned place right on the main square. Not quite as posh as the Traube (see below), but a worthy alternative. ④.

Falken, Eichholz 1 (☎04852/71022). In the fields south of town, next to the campsite of the same name (see above), offering comfortable rooms with en-suite bathroom, TV and a small balcony. Buffet breakfast included in the room price. ③.

Gästehaus Vergeiner, Kärntnerstrasse 19 (☎04852/62850). Simple place just over the river Isel from the centre, with en-suite rooms with TV. ③.

Gretl, Schweizergasse 32 (☎04852/62106). Cheapest centrally located source of B&B, offering simple rooms with en-suite facilities. ②.

Gribelhof, Schlossberg 10 (☎04852/62191, *www.gribelhof.web.com*). Overlooking the town from a hillside to the west, this is a wonderfully situated traditional Gasthof whose simple rooms have en-suite facilities and balconies. To get there, take the road to Schloss Bruck and keep on going past the castle. ②.

Haidenhof, Grafendorferstrasse 12 (☎04852/62440, *www.tirol.com/haidenhof*). A relaxing, comfortable hotel, whose rooms all have en-suite facilities, satellite TV and telephone. Attractively located amidst fields on the hillside in the northern part of town. ④.

Neuwirt, Schweizergasse 22 (☎04852/62101). Pleasant downtown Gasthof with plain, functional rooms, all of which have en-suite shower and TV. There's a good buffet breakfast included in the price, too. ④.

Romantikhotel Traube, Hauptplatz 14 (☎04852/64444, *www.hoteltraube.at*). Top hotel in town, with all the creature comforts including an indoor swimming pool. ⑧.

The Town

Lienz's attractive, café-filled **Hauptplatz** is a good introduction to the laid-back ambience of the Austrian south. The customary parade of handsome, pastel-coloured town houses is enhanced by the presence of the **Liebburg** on the southern side, a sixteenth-century courtly residence (now the town hall) which sports an attractive brace of towers, topped by onion domes which look like a pair of squashed meringues. A few steps west along Muchargasse, the **Franziskanerkirche** harbours a few garishly restored Gothic frescoes, but it's better to head for the town's two major sights on the fringes of the centre.

The first of these is the **Stadtpfarrkirche St Andrä**, a ten-minute walk northwest from the centre to the other side of the River Isel, its slender spire-topped form picturesquely ringed by an arcaded cemetery. Once through a main portal guarded by an age-battered pair of Romanesque lions, the church interior bears the heavy imprint of seventeenth- and eighteenth-century intervention, although impressive medieval paintings have survived, especially on the pillars lining the nave; one to the right as you enter shows a red-robed St Andrew on the cross, while another to the left carries a fourteenth-century cautionary image of Death trampling those who gorge themselves with meat during fasting periods. A red granite effigy of Graf Leonhard von Görz marks his burial place on the left side of the nave; above it, a late fifteenth-century *Journey of the Magi* in fresco form is filled with scenes of medieval pageantry. One of Leonhard's successors as lord of the local castle, Michael Freiherr von Wolkenstein, is honoured by a particularly touching piece of funerary sculpture on the opposite side of the church: Wolkenstein's head is inclined to one side to gaze fondly upon his wife, who is depicted beside him. An ebullient Baroque response to all this Gothic art can be found in the eighteenth-century choir, where Anton Zoller's melodramatic altarpiece showing St Andrew about to be set upon the cross is overlooked by Josef Adam Mölck's ceiling frescoes, in which the saint hovers ethereally above an alpine town vaguely recognizable as Lienz.

Set among the arcades outside the church, the **war memorial chapel** (key from Mrs Forcher, just across the square from the church at Pfarrplatz 13) contains starkly powerful frescoes executed shortly after World War I by local-born painter **Albin Egger-Lienz** (1868–1926), who is himself buried here. Born near Lienz (hence the adopted surname), Egger-Lienz was profoundly attached to his native Tyrol, portraying the sufferings of the region's peasantry in a hard, muscular style. He was also deeply affected by the Great War, having served on the Italian front, and his subsequent work was filled with spiritual pessimism. The mesmerizingly sombre cycle of paintings on display in the chapel is widely considered to be his masterpiece. The southern wall is dominated by a scene of Austrian infantrymen advancing under fire, their pale uniforms flapping around their limbs like shrouds, as if they're already dressed for the grave. On the opposite wall, a dead warrior lies atop a pile of grey coffins. This altogether bleak series is rounded off by the notoriously unsettling rendition of Jesus on the east wall: a sallow-skinned, emaciated figure whose skimpy loincloth leaves little to the imagination – a depiction which was considered so shocking that priests refused to celebrate Mass in the chapel until the 1980s. It's surprising that Egger-Lienz was commissioned at all given his status as an unfashionable outsider in Austrian art. His application for a teaching post at the Vienna Academy had been turned down in 1910 on the express instructions of Archduke Franz-Ferdinand, who fancied himself to be something of an arbiter of public taste. Egger-Lienz went to live in Italy after World War I, where his work was extremely influential, but his lack of a high profile elsewhere in Europe – especially in Austria – is hard to explain.

A fifteen-minute walk due west from the Hauptplatz along Schweizergasse, the formidable grey-brown bulk of **Schloss Bruck** (Easter–Oct Tues–Sun 10am–5pm; öS60/€4.38) overlooks the town from the partly wooded flanks of the Schlossberg. Outwardly, the tower, with its Romanesque windows, is the only sign of the castle's thirteenth-century origins; the rest of what you see was remodelled some two hundred years later. Inside, the jumble of domestic furnishings and agricultural implements that crowds the rooms of the **Heimatmuseum** is far outshone by the fifteenth-century frescoes in the Schloss's **chapel**, painted by Simon von Taisten for Count Leonhard. Leonhard and his wife, Paola von Gonzaga, feature prominently: they're shown kneeling in the depiction of the *Death of the Virgin*, on the left of the nave, as well as in the scene with St Elizabeth on the right, while also putting in an appearance with the *Madonna and Child* in the high altar. The castle's other main highlight is the **picture gallery**, which trots through a series of underachieving East Tyrolean artists before arriving at the canvases of **Franz von Deferegger** – an influential nineteenth-century realist whose paintings elevated the status of the Tyrolean peasant to that of a subject fit for art – and a rich selection of works by his spiritual successor, Albin Egger-Lienz.

Into the mountains

The jagged outline of the Dolomites provides an impressive backdrop to the town, but their upper reaches are inaccessible to all but the most experienced rock climbers. Most skiing and walking takes place on the more hospitable heights to the north, most notably the **Zettersfeld**, a large area of upland meadow served by cable car (mid-June to early Oct & Dec–Easter; öS140/€10.22 return; *www.lienzer.bergbahnen.at*) from the northern edge of town, at the end of Zettersfeldstrasse – a free minibus from the train station is sometimes laid on in summer: At the top, a chairlift continues to the 2214-metre **Steinermandl**, starting point for walks up to the **Neualpseen**, a group of small mountain lakes surrounded by desolate moorland. In **winter**, there's a range of light to intermediate descents down the southern slopes of the Steinermandl: you can register for ski and snowboard lessons and/or hire gear at the bottom of the Zettersfeldbahn.

At the western end of town, next to the access road to Schloss Bruck, the two-stage **Hochsteinbahn** chairlift (mid-June to mid-Sept & Dec–Easter; öS120/€8.76 return) rises to the 1016-metre **Moosalm**, site of the **Venedigerwarte** viewing tower and a farmyard zoo, for children, before continuing to the 1511-metre **Sternalm**, whence reasonably fit summer walkers can consider striking uphill towards the 2023-metre **Hochsteinhütte** above. As far as winter sports are concerned, the Hochstein boasts a couple of long unbroken descents which will appeal to intermediate and advanced skiers.

Eating and drinking

Notwithstanding a fair sprinkling of ethnic restaurants and typically Austrian Gasthöfe, **eating** out in Lienz is definitely a Tyrolean experience, with regional specialities like *Tiroler Gröstl* and *Schlipfkrapfen* dominating most menus. Proximity to Italy ensures a high standard of northern Italian cuisine, *haute* and otherwise: *Pizzadiele* on the Hauptplatz is a good place to pick up a pizza-slice **snack**. The outdoor cafés of the Hauptplatz help to turn **drinking** here into an almost Mediterranean experience in summer, and there's a wide choice of bars to boot.

Cafés

City-Café Glanzl, Hauptplatz. Lienz's classic daytime coffeehouse and patisserie, with a wide range of cakes, and cheap hot meals. The Glanzl annexe in the neighbouring shopping mall is a popular stop-off point for lunch.

Petrocelli, Hauptplatz. Funky upbeat daytime café with a tempting range of sandwiches, crostini, and succulent prosciutto platters on offer. A temple of laid-back trendiness at night.

Post Café, Südtirolerplatz 7. Quiet café down an alleyway just off the Hauptplatz, with a leafy garden courtyard. Cakes, pancakes, and a few main-course dishes, and a relaxing ambience for either a daytime or evening drink.

Restaurants

Adlerstüberl, Andrä-Kranz-Gasse 7. Lienz's oldest restaurant, a traditional Gasthof serving up a mid-priced range of Austrian and traditional Tyrolean food in plainly decorated, but rather atmospheric, medieval arched rooms.

da Leonardo, Tirolerstrasse 30. Providing you can get over the salmon pink decor this is an excellent pizzeria, with an impressive selection of thin-crust pizzas, good pasta dishes, and other Mediterranean odds and ends, notably grilled calamari.

Haidenhof, Grafendorferstrasse 12. Hotel restaurant north of town with mid-priced Tyrolean *Schlipfkrapfen* as well as the full range of Austrian dishes. The outdoor terrace provides a great view of the Dolomites on the opposite side of the valley.

La Cucina della Mamma/La Taverna, Südtirolerplatz. Best of the Italian places, with a not-too-pricey range of pizzas and pasta dishes served in wood-panelled, subterranean rooms.

Neuwirt, Schweizergasse 22. The best place to go for fish. Also offers the full repertoire of Tyrolean/Austrian dishes, and usually has at least one vegetarian special. Not too expensive, with plenty of outdoor seating.

Bars

Beckssound, alleyway off Rosengasse. Dark, minimally decorated bar which is a tight squeeze at weekends. Friendly place which favours vaguely alternative dance music and a laid-back crowd.

Deep Blue, Hauptplatz. Sizeable subterranean bar beneath the Hotel Traube, with ultramarine decor and a vaguely nautical theme. Long bar to sit/stand around and plenty of dark corners for an intimate drink.

Odin's, Schweizergasse 3. Popular, youthful hangout with alternative-rockish background music, a pool table in the back room, and a nice sideline in toasted sandwiches.

s'Eck, Hauptplatz 20. Best of the cafés with outdoor seating on the main square, plus a refined upstairs café and a pub-like beer cellar in a lovely medieval vaulted space downstairs.

s'Stöckl, Zwergergasse 2. Loud and friendly pub focused on a small circular bar. Fills up quickly on Friday nights.

Stadtkeller, Tirolerstrasse 30. Biggest of Lienz's discos, a predominantly techno-friendly venue in a cellar opposite the tourist office.

North of Lienz

North of Lienz, the main road ascends the Iseltal towards the **Felber Tauern**, an important route that tunnels from south to north through the Hohe Tauern and emerges near Mittersill in the Salzburger Land (see Chapter 7). **Matrei in Osttirol**, a small skiing and hiking resort, is the main centre along the way, although many of the side-valleys feeding the Isel are equally deserving of a visit. On the eastern side of Matrei, a road up the **Kalsertal** leads to the picturesque village of **Kals**, which lies in the southeastern shadows of the Grossglockner. To the west, both the **Defereggental** and the **Virgental** harbour a series of small ski villages worth a quick side-trip in summer.

The Defereggental

Twenty kilometres northwest of Lienz, the village of **Huben** stands at an important crossroads, as the main road continues north towards Matrei and the Virgental (see p.368), and a secondary road splits off to the northeast and Kals. A third road branches off due west into the **Defereggental**, a photogenic narrow valley slotted between two impressive mountain chains, the Defereggengebirge to the south and the Lasörlinggruppe to the north. Twenty-five kilometres out of Huben, the village of **ST**

JAKOB is a popular local skiing spot in winter. The two-stage **Mooserberg** gondola, 2km west of the village, provides access to an expanse of unspoilt alpine pastureland above the valley to the south. Six kilometres beyond St Jakob, the road splits: the left fork (served by twice-daily buses in summer) heads for the Italian border at the **Staller Sattel Pass**, 6km away, and a very steep descent towards Bruneck/Brunico; the right fork (May–Oct only) continues up the Defereggental as far as *Alpengasthof Oberhaus*, on the border of the Hohe Tauern National Park (see p.413) and the starting point for several walking trails.

Kals

From Huben, the road to **KALS** zigzags its way uphill from the Iseltal to the **Kalsertal**, an appealing subalpine vale strewn with wooden farmsteads and tumbledown barns. Properly speaking, Kals itself is the collective name for a grouping of three hamlets: Kals-Lesach, Kals-Ködnitz and Kals-Grossdorf. You encounter the rustic huddle of farms that calls itself **Lesach** 10km out of Huben – it's bypassed by the main road, but buses stop here. There's more in the way of facilities 2km further, in **Ködnitz**, site of the Kals tourist office, a couple of shops and the **Ruprechtskirche**, which boasts a sixteenth-century mural of the Crucifixion in a first-floor gallery. **Grossdorf**, barely 1km up the valley from Ködnitz, is where most tourist development has been concentrated, with a smattering of chalet-style hotels and plenty of farmhouses offering apartments. At the entrance to Grossdorf, the fourteenth-century **Georgikapelle**, a small whitewashed edifice dwarfed by its own spire, presides serenely over sheep-grazed pastures.

Into the mountains

It's Grossdorf that commands most of the routes into the mountains, with the **Glocknerblick** chairlift (June–Oct & Dec–Easter; öS190/€13.87 return; *www.tiscover .com/bergbahnenkals*) ascending to the *Bergrestaurant Blauspitz* on the heights west of the village, where views towards the Grossglockner to the northeast are the main draw. Eight kilometres north of Grossdorf up the Dorfertal, the café-restaurant at the **Kalser Tauernhaus** is another popular destination for both sightseers and walkers, where trails continue north up the Dabaklamm defile to the Dorfersee, with the Grossglockner to the right and the Granatspitze to the left. The road to the *Kalser Tauernhaus* lies within the Hohe Tauern National Park and is closed to private cars, but you can walk or take a bus from Kals-Ködnitz.

The **Kalserglocknerstrasse** toll road heads eastwards from Kals-Ködnitz up to the **Gasthof Lucknerhaus**, about 5km distant, whence several trails lead up onto the slopes of the Grossglockner. The most important, climbing to the 3454-metre *Erzherzog-Johann-Hütte* on the southeast shoulder, is one for experienced walkers or those accompanied by a local guide.

Kals as a whole is a good base for mounting supervised assaults on the peaks of the Hohe Tauern: **mountain guides** can be contacted through the tourist office or through the pension *Haus Zeiner*, Kals-Ködnitz 31 (mid-June to Sept Mon–Sat 8.30–10.30am & 5–7pm, Sun 5–7pm; ☎04876/263). Among the many trips offered, an ascent of Grossglockner in a four-person group would cost öS1400/€102.20 each.

Practicalities

The **tourist office** right by the church in Kals-Ködnitz (Mon–Fri 8.30am–noon & 2–6pm, Sat 8.30am–noon; ☎04876/211, *www.kals.at*) will sort out **private rooms** and apartments throughout the area; late arrivals should be able to find a place by heading straight for Kals-Grossdorf and looking for "*Zimmer Frei*" signs". Of the various **hotels and pensions** nearby, *Haus Oberlohr*, in Kals-Lesach (☎04876/266; ①), offers rooms with shared facilities in a nice wood-clad farmhouse, while the *Ködnitzhof*, Kals-Ködnitz (☎04876/201; ②), has adequate rooms, some en suite. The *Hotel Krone*, right by the Glocknerblick lift in Kals-Grossdorf (☎04876/241; ④), is a well-appointed modern building with its own dinky swimming pool, and the *Jenshof*, Kals-Grossdorf (☎04876/520; ⑤), is a "baby" hotel complete with playground, baby-listening devices and babysitting facilities. Five kilometres uphill to the east, the *Alpengasthof Lucknerhaus* (☎04867/291; ③) is an ideal base for walking; you might feel a bit cut off here, but it does have a reasonable restaurant.

Two places near the bus stop in Kals-Ködnitz function as combined **eating and drinking** venues: the *Ködnitzerhof*, which offers a respectable range of schnitzels, and *Café KK* nearby, which has acceptable pizzas.

Matrei and around

Thirty kilometres north of Lienz, just off the main road to the Felber Tauern, **MATREI** is a pleasantly sleepy, meadow-fringed resort, a good alternative to the skiing centres of the Salzburger Land and the Tyrol and equally satisfying in summer. The two-stage **Goldriedbahn** gondola one kilometre south of the village provides the main local excursion, although there are plenty of easy walks into the **Virgental**, which curves away to the east. Nearest of these is the walk to the historic **Nikolaikirche**, its whitewashed form clearly visible in a meadow 2km southwest of Matrei. The church is unusual in preserving a Romanesque choir on two levels, the upper, balustraded storey coloured by frescoes of the period. The Hohe Tauern National Park office, Rauterplatz 1 (☎04875/5161, *www.hohetauern.org*), has art and photography displays relating to the park, and is the best source of information on local hiking possibilities.

There's a **tourist office** on the village square (Mon–Fri 9am–noon & 3–6pm, Sat 9am–noon; ☎04875/6527), which will help with **private rooms** (summer ①; winter ②) and advise on vacancies in local ski-oriented hotels – note that many of these close in late spring and autumn. The *Hotel Goldried*, Goldriedstrasse 15 (☎04875/6113; ④), is an imaginatively laid-out cluster of buildings on a hillside, with outdoor pool. There's also a **campsite**, the *Edengarten*, at the southern end of the village. The **restaurant** of the *Hotel Rauter*, Rauterplatz, has a delicious and not-too-expensive range of top-quality Austrian food, and there are always a couple of vegetarian choices on the menu.

The Virgental

West of Matrei, a minor road runs up the verdant **Virgental** towards the village of **Virgen**, where the *Neuwirt* on the main road is a good place to stop off for some traditional Tyrolean food. Two kilometres further on, the village of **Obermauern** shelters below the small **Wallfahrtskirche unserer lieber Frau**, which is decorated with frescoes by Simon van Taisten – the man responsible for most of the work in the chapel at Schloss Bruck (see p.364). West of here, the road enters **Prägraten**, a small winter sports centre cowering beneath the Venedigergruppe massif to the north. Most buses from Lienz terminate here, although three daily services (summer only) proceed as far as **Ströden** at the head of the valley, where a three-kilometre walking trail leads to the **Umbalfälle**, a romantic spot popular with local daytrippers.

travel details

Trains

Klagenfurt to: Friesach (10 daily; 45min–1hr); Launsdorf-Hochosterwitz (6 daily; 35min); Maria Saal (8 daily; 10min); Salzburg (3 daily; 3hr 10min); St Veit an der Glan (22 daily; 15–20min); Vienna (8 daily; 4hr); Villach (30 daily; 25–40min).

Lienz to: Innsbruck (3 daily; 4hr 30min); Spittal an der Drau (10 daily; 1hr).

Spittal an der Drau to: Lienz (10 daily; 1hr); Villach (14 daily; 25–35min).

Villach to: Klagenfurt (30 daily; 25–40min); Pörtschach (16 daily; 20–25min); Salzburg (10 daily; 2hr 50min); Spittal an der Drau (14 daily; 25–35min); Velden (20 daily; 10–15min); Vienna (8 daily; 4hr 25min).

Buses

Gmünd to Spittal an der Drau (14 daily; 30min).

Klagenfurt to: Graz (2 daily; 3hr 30min); Gurk (3 daily; 1hr 30min); Hüttenberg (Mon–Fri 6 daily; Sat 3 daily; 1hr 15min); Magdalensberg (Mon–Sat 1 daily; 1hr); Maria Saal (16 daily; 25min); Maria Wörth (8 daily; 25min); Pyramidenkogel (1 daily; 30min); Reifnitz (10 daily; 20min); St Veit an der Glan (16 daily; 55min); Velden via Maria Wörth (Mon–Fri 6 daily; Sat 3 daily; 40min); Velden via Pörtschach (6 daily; 40min).

Lienz to: Franz-Josefs-Hohe (late June & Sept 1 daily; July & Aug 3 daily; 2hr 15min); Heiligenblut (summer 4 daily; winter 2 daily; 1hr 10min); Kals (6 daily; 55min); Kitzbühel (2 daily; 2hr 20min); Kufstein (2 daily; 3hr); Lucknerhaus (3 daily; 1hr 20min); Matrei (8 daily; 40min); Prägraten (8 daily; 1hr 10min); St Jakob (6 daily; 1hr 10min); Ströden (3 daily; 1hr 15min); Staller Sattel (2 daily; 1hr 40min).

St Veit an der Glan to Hüttenberg (Mon–Fri 5 daily; Sat 3 daily; 55min).

Spittal an der Drau to: Franz-Josefs-Hohe (July & Aug 2 daily; 3hr 30min); Gmünd (14 daily; 30min); Heiligenblut (change buses at Winklern; 3 daily; 2hr); Millstatt (20 daily; 30min); Seeboden (20 daily; 20min).

Velden to: Klagenfurt via Maria Wörth (8 daily; 40min); Klagenfurt via Pörtschach (6 daily; 40min); Rosegg (8 daily; 10min); Villach (6 daily; 30min).

Villach to: Drobollach (8 daily; 20min); Egg (8 daily; 25min); Faak am See (8 daily; 30min); Millstatt (4 daily; 1hr 20min); Ossiach (6 daily; 30min); Ostriach (6 daily; 25min); Pörtschach (6 daily; 50min); Velden (6 daily; 30min).

Ferries

Klagenfurt to: Maria Wörth/Pörtschach/Velden (May–Oct: 4 to 10 daily, depending on season; 45min/55min/1hr 45min).

Villach to St Niklas (end April to early Oct: 1 to 6 daily, depending on season; 45min).

CHAPTER SEVEN

SALZBURG AND THE SALZBURGER LAND

The borders of the modern **Salzburger Land** (*www.sagma.co.at/guide*) roughly correspond to the area ruled by the prince-archbishops of Salzburg (although the archbishopric was a typically feudal entity, comprising motley holdings dotted throughout central Austria and southern Germany), up until the Principality's incorporation into Austria in 1816. The **River Salzach**, which rises in the lofty heights of the Hohe Tauern range before flowing towards Salzburg, eventually joining the River Inn in Upper Austria, gives the area a measure of geographical cohesion; and it's the main transport routes along the Salzach Valley that link the provincial capital, **Salzburg**, with much of its hinterland. As a tourist destination, the Salzburger Land offers a good mixture of both the urban and the alpine, with its splendid Baroque capital proving the main focus for many visitors. Music is an important draw in a city that was the birthplace of **Mozart**, and the annual **Salzburg Festival**, held in July and August, is a world-renowned feast of classical music and theatre. South of Salzburg, the narrow confines of the Salzach Valley and a sequence of exhilarating mountainscapes provide a dramatic setting for historic towns like **Hallein** and **Werfen**, while further south, **Radstadt**, **St Johann im Pongau**, **Badgastein** and **Zell am See** serve as the best bases from which to explore the countryside – most notably the lofty heights of the **Hohe Tauern** range.

In **winter**, snow sports take hold in the south of the province, with Radstadt, St Johann im Pongau, Badgastein and the package resort of Saalbach-Hinterglemm providing a wealth of white slopes. Many of the Land's winter sports centres make equally good hiking bases in **summer**. A key destination for hikers is the Hohe Tauern National Park, which preserves the unspoilt highland areas above the towns of Badgastein and Zell am See. The most versatile area is around Zell am See, where a glacier above the neighbouring settlement of Kaprun provides **year-round skiing** and snowboarding.

ACCOMMODATION PRICE CODES

All **hotels and pensions** in this book have been coded according to the following price categories. All the codes are based on the rate for the least expensive double room during the **summer season**. In those places where winter is the high season, we've indicated both summer and winter room rates in the text.

① under öS400/€29.07
② öS400–600/€29.07–43.60
③ öS600–800/€43.60–58.14
④ öS800–1000/€58.14–72.67
⑤ öS1000–1200/€72.67–87.21

⑥ öS1200–1400/€87.21–101.74
⑦ öS1400–1600/€101.74–116.28
⑧ öS1600–1800/€116.28–130.81
⑨ over öS1800/€130.81

In the past, the Salzburger Land was divided into districts known as **Gaue** (*Gau* in the singular): the Flachgau north of Salzburg, the Tennengau to the south, the Pongau in the middle Salzach Valley, the Lungau in the far southeast, and the Pinzgau, which runs from Zell am See westwards along the Upper Salzach Valley. Each developed its own folkloric traditions, and regional differences still provide the people who live here with an important badge of regional identity. This is partly expressed in several surviving **folk festivals**, which include the **Pongauer Perchtenlauf**, when costumed figures rampage through the streets of one of four Pongau towns (see p.406), **Krampus** festivities in Zell am See (see p.414), and the **Samsonumzug** in the Lungau town of Tamsweg, in which an effigy of Samson is paraded through the streets on important summer feast days (see p.405).

SALZBURG

Up until 1816, **SALZBURG** led a separate life to the rest of Austria, existing as an independent city-state ruled by a sequence of powerful **prince-archbishops**. An ambitious and cultured bunch, they turned the city into the most Italianate city north of the Alps. Spread out below the brooding presence of the Hohensalzburg fortress, the churches, squares and alleyways of the compact Altstadt today recollect a long-disappeared Europe. For many, Salzburg is the quintessential Austria, offering the best of the country's Baroque architecture, subalpine scenery and a musical heritage largely provided by the city's most famous son, **Wolfgang Amadeus Mozart**, whose bright-eyed visage peers from every box of the ubiquitous chocolate delicacy, the *Mozartkügel*. Salzburg's captivation with Mozart is perhaps best reflected in the world-famous **Salzburg Festival**, a five-week celebration of opera, orchestral music and theatre that begins in late July, although there's a wide range of (not always Mozart-related) musical events on offer throughout the year. Souvenirs recalling the Salzburg-based musical *The Sound of Music* dangle round the city's neck like some bad-taste medallion, with coach tours and shows on the same theme providing an entertainingly lowbrow alternative to the more highbrow events.

Standing at the centre of a prosperous, economically booming region, Salzburg also represents Austria at its most **conservative**. Writer Thomas Bernhard, an acerbic critic of the postwar state who spent his formative years in Salzburg, called his home town "a fatal illness", whose Catholicism, conservatism and sheer snobbery drove its citizens to a state of terminal misery. The city certainly has a strong bourgeois ethos, easy to discern in the snooty cafés and refined restaurants of the city centre, and in a pre-Lent ball season that rivals that of Vienna. But if high culture and high society don't really turn you on, you can always take solace in the city's alternative nightlife or join the crowds at the football stadium – the local team, SV Salzburg, is one of the few outfits outside Vienna that enjoys a genuine mass following.

Salzburg is buzzing twelve months a year and there's not really a best time at which to come. Spring and summer bring a wealth of colour to the city's parks and the surrounding hills, and this period draws the biggest tourist crowds, although the **Advent season** (from the end of November through to Christmas) is an atmospheric and increasingly popular period. There's a Christkindlmarkt (Christmas market) in the square outside the cathedral, with stalls selling all kinds of handicrafts alongside irredeemable tat, and ad-hoc kiosks doling out sausage, Schmalzbrot (bread and dripping) and gallons of Glühwein, bringing an outdoor party atmosphere to the winter evenings.

Bearing in mind that there's no real low season here, **accommodation** tends to be constantly overpriced, oversubscribed or both. Once you've found yourself a place to stay, however, you'll find the city to be an easily manageable, hassle-free place to explore. The local bus and rail network makes Salzburg a convenient base from which

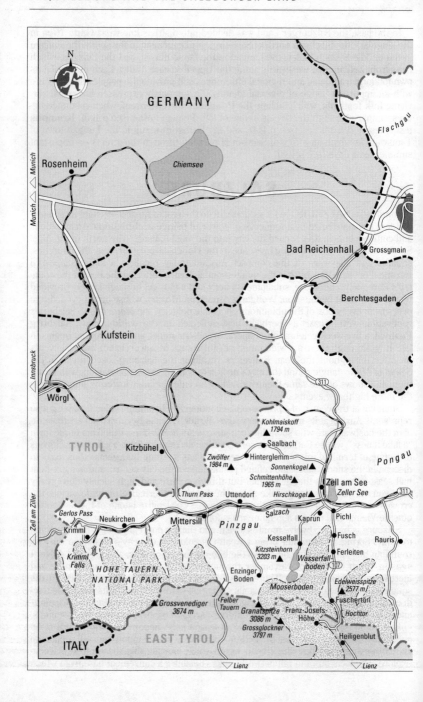

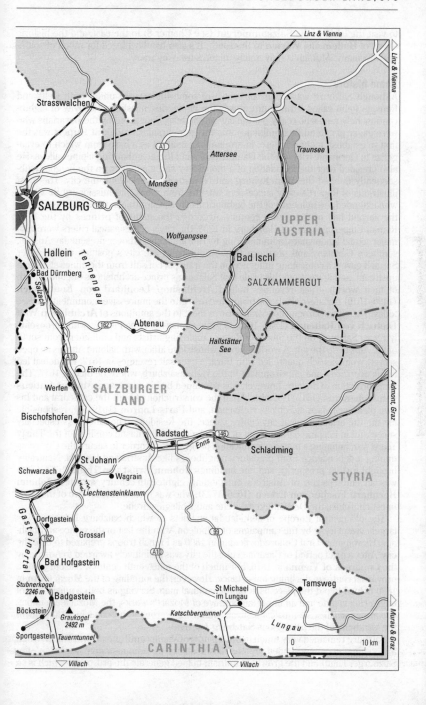

to visit the lakes of the **Salzkammergut** (see Chapter 8) to the east, and the historic towns of **Hallein** and **Werfen** to the south. It's also handily placed for much of southeast Germany: Munich is only ninety minutes away by train.

Some history

Although Salzburg was an urban centre of some importance under both Celts and Romans (who called it Juvavum), it was the pioneering missionary activity of eighth-century holy men who really put the city on the map. Sponsored by the Bavarians who were eager to extend their influence into the area, Frankish monk **St Rupert** was the first to establish a church here, in around 700, using it as a base from which to evangelize to Germanic tribes in the Danube basin and the neighbouring alpine valleys. He also presided over the foundation of a monastery and a nunnery on the heights (subsequently dubbed the **Mönchsberg** and **Nonnberg**) overlooking the city. The most illustrious of Rupert's early successors was the Irish monk and missionary **St Virgil**, who extended the influence of the bishopric as far as Carinthia in the southeast during the second half of the eighth century. Accorded the status of **princes** by the Holy Roman Emperor Rudolf of Habsburg in 1228, the city's ecclesiastical rulers were also major feudal landowners, administering territories scattered over present-day Austria, southern Germany and northern Italy. Additionally, the city's position on the River Salzach gave it a controlling influence on the transport of **salt** from the mines at Hallein upstream, and it was from this trade that Salzburg's prince-archbishops obtained much of their wealth – salt revenues helped **Archbishop Leonhard von Keutschach** (1495–1519) transform Hohensalzburg fortress into the impressive monument you see today. The city's Baroque appearance owes most to the ambitions of **Archbishop Wolf Dietrich von Raitenau** (1587–1612), a great-nephew of Pope Pius IV, who purposefully recast Salzburg on the model of Rome, employing artists and craftsmen from south of the Alps to do the job. A worldly figure whose love affair with Salome Alt was an open secret, Wolf Dietrich quarrelled with Bavaria over salt revenues in 1612. His defeat led to his overthrow and imprisonment in the Hohensalzburg, where he died in 1617. The transformation of the city, however, was continued by his successors **Marcus Sitticus von Hohenems** (1612–19), who began the construction of both the cathedral and his own pleasure-palace at Schloss Hellbrunn, and **Paris Lodron** (1619–53), responsible for the the archiepiscopal city-centre palace, the Residenz. The latter was especially successful in keeping Salzburg out of the religious and dynastic conflicts of the Thirty Years War, initiating a massive fortification programme in order to secure the city's continuing independence from predatory neighbours like Austria and Bavaria. Neutrality brought further prosperity, and fine buildings: **Johann Ernst von Thun** (1687–1709) was an early patron of Austria's outstanding eighteenth-century architect **Johann Bernhard Fischer von Erlach** (1656–1723), who was responsible for two of the city's finest churches, the Dreifaltigkeitskirche and Kollegienkirche.

The old central Europe of semi-feudal statelets to which Salzburg belonged was largely swept away by the campaigns of Napoleon, with the last of the prince-archbishops, Hieronymus Graf Colloredo, fleeing in 1800 as French troops prepared to take the city. After a brief period of Bavarian rule, the city was definitively awarded to Austria by the **Congress of Vienna** in 1816. For much of the nineteenth century, Salzburg was a provincial centre of declining importance. However, the founding of the **Mozarteum** in 1870 helped to put the place back on the cultural map. Serving as both a music school of growing repute and an important archive of Mozart's works, the Mozarteum initiated various small-scale musical festivals which were grouped together in 1920 to form the backbone of the prestigious **Salzburg Festival**.

Salzburg remained very much in the shadow of Vienna until after World War II, when a booming economy (aided by the city's status as administrative capital of the Salzburger Land) and the growth of tourism helped generate the prosperity which is so evident in the city today. The massive success of the 1964 film *The Sound of Music* served to reaffirm Salzburg's global profile, offering visions of a beautiful little town surrounded by wholesome alpine scenery to successive generations of would-be visitors. Nowadays the town receives an annual average of 36 tourists per inhabitant, putting it in the same league as Florence or Venice in the ratio of visitors to locals.

Arrival, information and transport

Salzburg is divided by the River Salzach into the **linkes Salzachufer** (left bank), on the western side of the river, and the **rechtes Salzachufer** (right bank), on the east. On the left bank, the **Altstadt** holds the concentration of historic sights, though most points of arrival are across the river. That said, central Salzburg is reasonably compact, and it's relatively easy to get around on foot.

The **Hauptbahnhof** is north of the centre on Südtirolerplatz, a 25-minute walk from the Altstadt (buses #1, #2, #5, #6, #51 and #55 run from the station to either F-Hanusch-Platz or Rudolfskai, both on the fringes of the Altstadt). The main **bus station** is in front of the train station, although most services also stop on Mirabellplatz, nearer the centre. Salzburg's **airport** is 3km west of the centre on the Innsbrücker Bundesstrasse (bus #77 runs in to Südtirolerplatz every 30min between 5.30am and 11pm).

Information

The main **tourist office** is in the heart of the Altstadt at Mozartplatz 5 (daily: May–Sept 9am–8pm; Oct–April 9am–6pm; ☎0662/88987-330, *www.salzburginfo.at*), but the first port of call for many new arrivals is the **information kiosk** on platform 2A of the train station (daily: May–Sept 8.30am–9pm; Oct–April 9am–8pm). Both are busy throughout the year, and staff – especially at the station branch – can sometimes appear overworked and short-tempered. Information **kiosks** at other likely points of arrival include: at the **airport**, outside the main terminal building in the car park (June–Oct daily 9am–7pm; Easter–May Mon–Sat 9am–6pm Nov–Easter Mon–Sat 9am–5pm); **Salzburg-Mitte**, Münchner Bundesstrasse 1, about 1km south of the Salzburg-Mitte exit from the A1 autobahn on the main road into town (May–Oct daily 9am–8pm; Nov–April Mon–Sat 11am–5pm); and **Salzburg-Süd**, Alpensiedlung-Süd, Alpenstrasse, about 5km north of the Salzburg-Süd exit of the A10 autobahn (same hours as Salzburg-Mitte).

All of the above provide a host of **free brochures** in English (although they charge öS10/€0.73 for a city map), and will book you into a hotel or pension (for a nominal fee, see below). They also sell a **Salzburg Card**, which gives free access to the majority of city museums and attractions, as well as unlimited use of city transport (öS230/€16.79 for 24hr, öS320/€23.36 for 48hr, öS410/€29.93 for 72hr) – it's worth the investment if you're visiting more than a couple of attractions a day.

City transport

Most of Salzburg's tourist sights are within walking distance of each other (and the Altstadt is in any case largely pedestrianized), but the municipal **bus network** is a good way of getting to far-flung attractions like Hellbrunn or the Untersberg.

The most important nodal points for public transport are **Südtirolerplatz**, in front of the train station, **Mirabellplatz**, just south of the station, and **F-Hanusch-Platz**, on the left bank on the fringes of the Altstadt. **Tickets** for single journeys cost öS20/€1.46, but it makes best sense to purchase a **Netzkarte** for 24 hours (öS42/€3.07) or seven days (öS110/€8.03), available from automatic vending machines next to major bus stops or from *Tabak* shops. The Salzburg Card, sold at the city's tourist offices (see above), is also worth considering if you're visiting lots of attractions.

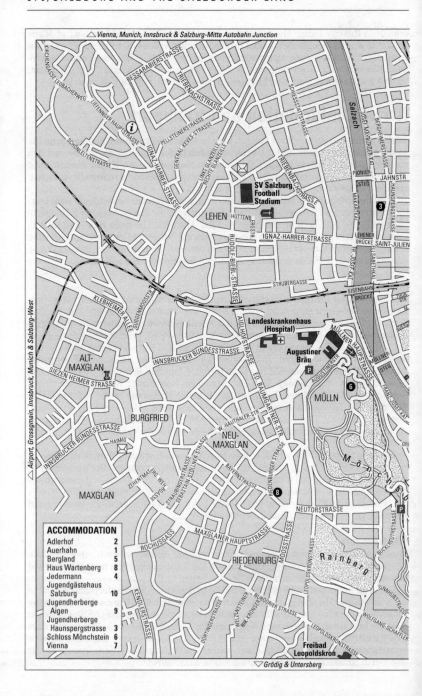

△Vienna, Munich, Innsbruck & Salzburg-Mitte Autobahn Junction

△ Airport, Grossgmain, Innsbruck, Munich & Salzburg-West

SV Salzburg
Football
Stadium

LEHEN

Landeskrankenhaus
(Hospital)

Augustiner
Bräu

ALT-
MAXGLAN

MÜLLN

BURGFRIED

NEU-
MAXGLAN

M—önch

MAXGLAN

RIEDENBURG

Rainberg

ACCOMMODATION

Adlerhof	2
Auerhahn	1
Bergland	5
Haus Wartenberg	8
Jedermann	4
Jugendgästehaus Salzburg	10
Jugendherberge Aigen	9
Jugendherberge Haunspergstrasse	3
Schloss Mönchstein	6
Vienna	7

Freibad
Leopoldskron

▽Grödig & Untersberg

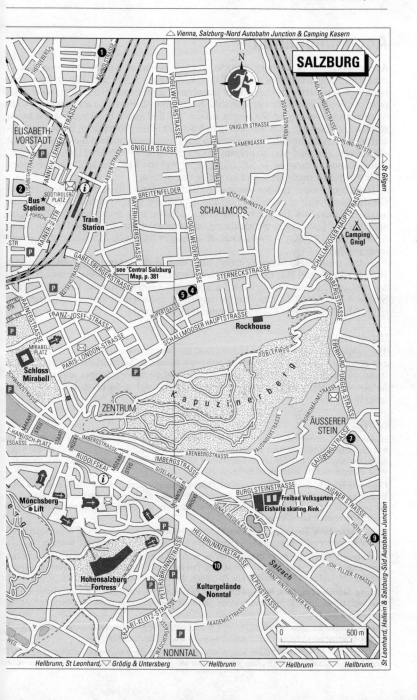

SALZBURG

△ Vienna, Salzburg-Nord Autobahn Junction & Camping Kasern

N

ELISABETH-
VORSTADT

❶

❷ Bus Station ★

i
SÜDTIROLER-
PLATZ

Train Station

GNIGLER STASSE

SAMERGASSE

GNIGLER STRASSE

BREITENFELDER

SCHALLMOOS

RÖCKLBRUNNSTRASSE

△ Camping Gnigl

see 'Central Salzburg'
Map, p. 381

STERNECKSTRASSE

❺ ❹

FRANZ-JOSEF-STRASSE

RUPERTGASSE

SCHALLMOOSER HAUPTSTRASSE

Rockhouse

PARIS-LONDON-STRASSE

DOBLERWEG

Schloss
Mirabell

MIRABELL
PLATZ

K a p u z i n e r b e r g

ZENTRUM

ÄUSSERER
STEIN

❼

F-HANUSCH-PLATZ

STEG

IMBERGSTRASSE

ARENBERGSTRASSE

IMBERGSTRASSE

RUDOLFSKAI

GISELAKAI

BURGLSTEINSTRASSE

i

Mönchsberg
Lift

Freibad Volksgarten
Eishalle skating Rink

❾

Hohensalzburg
Fortress

HELLBRUNNERSTRASSE

Salzach

❿

Kulturgelände
Nonntal

AKADEMIESTRASSE

0   500 m

NONNTAL

St Leonhard, Hallein & Salzburg-Süd Autobahn Junction

Hellbrunn, St Leonhard,▽ Grödig & Untersberg   ▽Hellbrunn   ▽ Hellbrunn   ▽ Hellbrunn,

Accommodation

Accommodation in Salzburg tends to be more expensive than elsewhere in Austria except for Vienna, and most places fill up fast, especially in July and August. It's best to book well in advance whether you're planning to stay in a top-of-the-range hotel, mid-price pension or one of the city's plentiful **hostel**-type places. If you arrive in town without a reservation, any of the tourist offices will find you a hotel room for a fee of öS35/€2.56 (plus a deposit amounting to 7 percent of the room price), but late arrivals will often find that the only remaining vacancies are a long way from the centre. Tourist offices can also find you a **private room** for around öS300/€21.90 per person, although most of these are in outlying suburbs, and you'd be wise to check their accessibility by public transport before accepting one of them.

There are cheaper **private rooms** (①) and **pensions** (③) in the village suburb of **Grödig**, 9km south of the city centre and not covered by the Salzburg tourist office's accommodation lists. Grödig **tourist office** is 100m away from the Untersbergbahn stop (bus #55 from Salzburg train station) at Gartenauerstrasse 8 (Mon–Fri: June–Sept 8.30am–5pm, Oct–May 8.30–11.15am & 2–5pm; ☎06246/73570, *www.salzburgerland .com/groedig*).

Of the **campsites**, *Camping Gnigl*, 2km east of the centre at Parscherstrasse 4 (☎0662/643060; mid-May to mid-Sept), is the easiest to get to by public transport – take bus #27 or #29 from Mirabellplatz to get there. *Camping Kasern*, Carl-Zuckmayer-Strasse 4 (☎0662/450576), is 4km north of town, just north of the Salzburg-Nord exit of the A1 autobahn. Bus #15 from Mirabellplatz passes by.

Hotels and pensions

The Altstadt and area around Linzergasse on the opposite side of the river contain any number of comfortable **hotels**, although rates can be exorbitant, especially for those establishments with any kind of historical pedigree. Budget and mid-priced hotels or pensions within walking distance of the sights do exist, but they fill up quickly.

LEFT BANK

Blaue Gans, Getreidegasse 43 (☎0662/841317, *www.blauegans.at*). A superbly located inn dating from the fifteenth century, with Gothic touches in some of the public rooms but modern and minimalist bedrooms. All doubles are well-appointed with en-suite WC and shower, although there are some cheaper singles with shared facilities. ⑦.

Goldener Hirsch, Getreidegasse 37 (☎0662/8084-0, *www.goldenerhirsch.com*). Very much the classic address in the Altstadt although you'll need to be feeling flush (prices start at öS2950/€215.35 per person in the high season, and breakfast is extra); an inn of medieval origin offering plush rooms with antique furnishings. ⑨.

Haus Wartenberg, Riedenburgerstrasse 2 (☎0662/848400). Good-value pension with a rustic feel, west of the centre on a suburban street behind the Mönchberg. All with en-suite facilities. ⑤.

Hinterbrühl, Schanzlgasse 12 (☎0662/846798, *hinterbruehl@kronline.at*). Situated at the eastern edge of the city centre just below the Nonnberg, this rather plain pension is nevertheless one of the best deals in Salzburg and therefore fills up quickly. Rooms are with shared facilities. ③.

Schloss Mönchstein, Mönchsberg-Park 26 (☎0662/848555-0, *www.monchstein.at*). Hilltop castle-hotel with small, intimate feel, and offering plush accommodation in idyllic surroundings. Room rates start at öS1700/€124.10 per person. ⑨.

Weisse Taube, Kaigasse 9 (☎0662/842404, *www.weissetaube.at*). City-centre hotel with medieval origins, offering plush rooms, just round the corner from Mozartplatz. ⑧.

Wolf, Kaigasse 7 (☎0662/843453-0, *www.hotelwolf.com*). Perfectly situated on an alleyway just off Mozartplatz, a small family-run place with smallish but characterful rooms. ⑤.

RIGHT BANK

Adlerhof, Elisabethstrasse 25 (☎0662/875236, *www.pension-adlerhof.at*). Comfortable if unexciting hotel near the train station, offering a mixed bag of rooms – some modern, some quaintly furnished in traditional wood. Most rooms with en-suite facilities (④), but some without (③).

Amadeus, Linzergasse 43–45 (☎0662/871401, *walkets@salzburg.co.at*). Popular sightseeing base on the right bank, with modern-furnished rooms in an otherwise historic house. Rooms have en-suite facilities and TV. ⑤.

Auerhahn, Bahnhofstrasse 15 (☎0662/451052, *auerhahn@eunet.at*). In an unfashionable area just north of the train station; therefore not the best sightseeing base, but a comfortable place. ⑤.

Bergland, Rupertgasse 15 (☎0662/872318-0, *pkuhn@sol.at*). Handy for the Linzergasse area on the right bank, a family-run pension offering generous breakfasts and a small English-language library. Most rooms come with en-suite shower but the shared toilet is in the hall (④), though there are some cheaper doubles without either (③).

Goldener Krone, Linzergasse 48 (☎0662/872300). Bills itself as a 3-star hotel but this is really more like an old-fashioned downtown pension: a friendly, family-run place on the right bank with smallish, plain but comfortable rooms. Most come with en-suite facilities, though there are some slightly cheaper rooms without. ④.

Jedermann, Rupertgasse 25 (☎0662/873241-0). Cosy, comfortable and friendly pension on the right bank of the Salzach in the Linzergasse area. ⑤.

Junger Fuchs, Linzergasse 54 (☎0662/875496). Right-bank pension in easy walking distance of the centre. A rare bargain if you can put up with austerely decorated rooms, bathrooms in the hallway, and low-power lightbulbs. Only 15 rooms, so ring in advance. ①.

Markus Sittikus, Markus-Sittikus-Strasse 20 (☎0662/871121-0, *markus-sittikus@austria.at*). Big downtown hotel on the right bank near the Mirabell gardens, with modern, functional but well-equipped rooms ⑥.

Sacher Salzburg Österreichische Hof, Schwarzstrasse 5–7 (☎0662/88977-0, *www.oehof.at*). This luxury right-bank establishment is the only surviving example of the big hotels built in the mid-nineteenth century to attract the social cream of Europe. Although much changed, some period details exist, and both rooms and service are top-notch. Rates from öS2100/€153.30 per person in high season. ⑨.

Schwarzes Rössl, Priesterhausgasse 6 (☎0662/874426, *www.academia-hotels.co.at*). Creaky old building in an excellent location on the right bank, serving as student accommodation during the academic year, but offering comfy, if plain, rooms in July and August. Some rooms with en-suite WC and shower (④), others with shared facilities (③).

Trumer Stube, Bergstrasse 6 (☎0662/874776, *hotel.trumer-stube.sbg@eunet.at*). Friendly pension on the right bank in the Linzergasse area, with bright, comfortable rooms. ⑥.

Vienna, Gaisbergstrasse 12 (☎0662/643657). Pleasant suburban pension with smallish but adequate rooms, 1.5km east of the centre on the right bank. Bus #6 from the train station or Mirabellplatz. ④.

Wolf Dietrich, Wolf-Dietrich-Strasse 7 (☎0662/871275, *www.salzburg-hotel.at*). If you're looking for a top-notch, reasonably central hotel that has indoor pool and sauna on site, then this, pricey though it is, is probably the cheapest. ⑨.

Hostels

Naturfreundhaus (aka Gasthaus Bürgerwehr), Mönchsberg 19c (☎0662/841729). Marvellously situated on the hill immediately above the Altstadt, this smallish place soon fills up – it's a good idea to reserve. Take buses #1 or #2 from the train station to the Mönchsbergaufzug stop, then take the Mönchsberg lift; or walk up the steps from behind the Toscaninihof (not recommended if you're heavily laden). A choice of accommodation in either dorms (öS150/€10.95 with breakfast) or double rooms (öS250/€18.25 per person). Open late May to late Sept.

Institut St Sebastian, Linzergasse 41 (☎0662/871386). A good sightseeing base on the right bank, with an evocative location next to St Sebastian's church. Dorm beds are available throughout the year to women only, and singles and doubles become available to travellers of both sexes in July and August when the local students move out. Reception open 8am–noon & 5–10pm. Dorm beds öS230/€16.79, single rooms from öS330/€24.09, doubles (②).

Jugendgästehaus Salzburg (HI), Josef-Preis-Allee 18 (☎0662/842670-0, *oejhv-sbg-jgh-nonntal @oejhv.or.at*). Large hostel popular with groups, less than 1km southeast of the Altstadt. Buses #5 or #55 from the train station. Midnight curfew. Dorms (öS170/€12.41) and some doubles (②).

Jugendherberge Aigen (HI), Aignerstrasse 34 (☎0662/623248). Swish and comfortable hostel in a quiet, suburban location 2km away from the sights. From the train station, take buses #5 or #55 to Rudolfskai then bus #49. Midnight curfew. Mostly 4-bed dorms (öS180/€13.14), but with a reasonable supply of doubles (②).

Jugendherberge Haunspergstrasse (HI), Haunspergstrasse 27 (☎0662/875030). Student place 5min west of the train station. Midnight curfew. Open July & Aug. Beds in 4- and 2-person dorms for öS180/€13.14 per person.

YO-HO, International Youth Hostel, Paracelsusstrasse 9 (☎0662/879649, *www.yoho.at*). Big place nicely poised between the train station and main sights, very popular with English-speaking backpackers. There's a bar on the premises, and it's probably worth coming here for the social life alone if you want to meet other travellers – but bear in mind that it can be noisy at night. *The Sound of Music* is shown daily in the bar on demand. No curfew. Bare bones 6- to 8-person dorms with bunks öS150/€10.95 per person, 4-person dorms öS170/€12.41 per person, doubles öS200/€14.60 per person, single occupancy of double room öS400/€29.20. Breakfast is extra: roll, butter and jam öS15/€1.10, eggs, bacon and sausage öS45/€3.29. Cheap evening meals also available.

The City

Salzburg's central ensemble of archiepiscopal buildings on the left bank of the river forms a tightly woven net of alleys and squares watched over by the sombre grey bastions of the medieval **Hohensalzburg** castle. The bulk of Salzburg's galleries and museums (including **Mozart**'s birthplace) are concentrated in this area, as are many of the city's **cafés**, ideal spots for observing the hordes of visitors that pulse through the streets. From here it's a short hop over the River Salzach to a narrow ribbon of essential sights on the right bank, where another of Mozart's residences, and the flowerbeds of the **Mirabell Gardens**, are the main draws. Both sides of the river add up to a surprisingly compact city centre, and you'll find you can cover a lot of ground in a single day, although you'll need much more time (probably two or three days) if you want to explore the city's sights in any great detail.

The left bank

Salzburg's **Altstadt** represents one of the best examples of Baroque town planning anywhere in Europe. Archbishop Wolf Dietrich was responsible for initiating the city's transformation, engaging Venetian Vincenzo Scamozzi to draft plans for an ensemble of fountains, squares and public buildings centred on a brand-new cathedral, the building of which was made neccessary by the destruction of the previous church by fire in 1598. Even though the archbishop never lived to see its completion (he was deposed in 1612), the cityscape that greets you is still very much Scamozzi's.

The Getreidegasse and Mozarts Geburtshaus

The Baroque Salzburg of Scamozzi and his successors was grafted onto an earlier, medieval city of narrow streets and squat town houses, and it's this that first hits tourists flowing into the Altstadt over the **Staatsbrücke**, main crossing point over the River Salzach. After passing under the archway of the fifteenth-century **Rathaus**, a right turn leads into the pedestrianized **Getreidegasse**, Salzburg's busiest thoroughfare, lined with opulent boutiques and characterized by overhanging wrought-iron shop signs. At no. 9 is **Mozarts Geburtshaus** (daily: July & Aug 9am–7pm; Sept–June 9am–5.30pm; öS70/€5.09), where the musical prodigy lived for the first seventeen years of his life. This crowded and rather sterile collection of musical manuscripts and

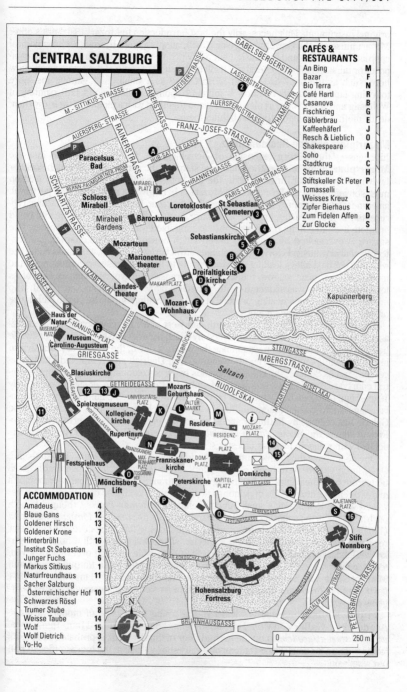

CENTRAL SALZBURG

CAFÉS & RESTAURANTS

An Bing	M
Bazar	F
Bio Terra	N
Café Hartl	R
Casanova	B
Fischkrieg	G
Gäblerbrau	E
Kaffeehäferl	J
Resch & Lieblich	O
Shakespeare	A
Soho	I
Stadtkrug	C
Sternbrau	H
Stiftskeller St Peter	P
Tomaselli	L
Weisses Kreuz	Q
Zipfer Bierhaus	K
Zum Fidelen Affen	D
Zur Glocke	S

ACCOMMODATION

Amadeus	4
Blaue Gans	12
Goldener Hirsch	13
Goldener Krone	7
Hinterbrühl	16
Institut St Sebastian	5
Junger Fuchs	6
Markus Sittikus	1
Naturfreundhaus	11
Sacher Salzburg Österreichischer Hof	10
Schwarzes Rössl	9
Trumer Stube	8
Weisse Taube	14
Wolf	15
Wolf Dietrich	3
Yo-Ho	2

Paracelsus Bad
Schloss Mirabell
Mirabell Platz
Mirabell Gardens
Barockmuseum
Loretokloster
St Sebastian Cemetery
Sebastianskirche
Mozarteum
Marionettentheater
Dreifaltigkeitskirche
Landestheater
MAKARTPLATZ
Mozart-Wohnhaus
PLATZL
Haus der Natur
MUSEUMS PLATZ
Museum Carolino-Augusteum
GRIESGASSE
Blasiuskirche
GETREIDEGASSE
Mozarts Geburtshaus
ALTER MARKT
Spielzeugmuseum
UNIVERSITÄTS PLATZ
Kollegienkirche
Rupertinum
Residenz
RESIDENZ PLATZ
MOZART-PLATZ
Festspielhaus
FRANZISKANERS
MAX-REINHARDT-PLATZ
TOSCANINI-HOF
Franziskanerkirche
DOM-PLATZ
Mönchsberg Lift
Domkirche
KAPITEL-PLATZ
Peterskirche
KAPITEL GASSE
KAJETANER PLATZ
Stift Nonnberg
Hohensalzburg Fortress
BRUNNHAUSGASSE

Kapuzinerberg
Salzach
RUDOLFSKAI
STEINGASSE
IMBERGSTRASSE
GISELAKAI

0   250 m

original instruments isn't necessarily the best introduction to Mozart (Salzburg's other Mozart museum, the Gewohnhaus (see p.389), adopts a more thorough, chronological approach to the man and his music), but many people with a strong interest in the composer or musicianship in general will thrill to the sight of some of the artefacts on show here, such as the baby-sized violin Mozart used as a small child. Among the more touching family portraits on show is Johann Nepomuk della Croce's 1781 painting of Wolfgang and sister Nannerl playing the piano together, with a picture of their (by then, dead) mother hanging on the wall behind them.

Mozartplatz and the Residenzplatz

Judengasse, the eastern extension of Getreidegasse, funnels crowds up into the **Mozartplatz**, home to a weathered bronze statue of the composer by Munich sculptor Ludwig Schwanthaler. In contrast to the the impish white-wigged youth pictured on most souvenirs and chocolate boxes, Mozart is here given a more dignified portrayal; an earnest adult visionary in flowing, toga-like overcoat. Erected in 1842, the statue represents the first occasion on which Salzburg's urban elite realized that the city could promote itself to potential visitors by associating itself with the famous composer. The square is overlooked by a pinkish tower which houses the **Glockenspiel**, a seventeenth-century musical clock whose chimes attract crowds at 7am, 11am and 6pm. The winding, cobbled alleys leading off Mozartplatz to the east preserve something of the medieval street plan: narrow, tunnel-like Pfeifergasse is a typical example. One of its former inhabitants was sixteenth-century medical pioneer Paracelsus (see p.388), who in 1524 briefly set up a healing practice at no.11, operating out of the public bathhouse owned by his friend Hans Rappl.

The complex of buildings to the south and west of Mozartplatz exudes the ecclesiastical and temporal power once wielded by Salzburg's archbishops, whose erstwhile living quarters, the **Residenz**, dominate the western side of the **Residenzplatz**. Begun in the sixteenth century during the reign of Wolf Dietrich and completed by his successor Marcus Sitticus, the complex spreads two vast colonnaded wings around a central courtyard. Inside lies a sequence of bombastic **Prunkräume**, or state rooms (daily 10am–5pm; öS91/€6.61), which can be viewed with the accompaniment of an English-language audio commentary. Highlights are relatively easy to pick out: the Schöne Galerie has ceilings by Rottmayr and a copy of the mysterious but overhyped Graeco-Roman statue, the *Young Man of Magdalensberg* (see p.334), while the Audienzsaal is decked with valuable Flemish tapestries.

One floor above the Prunkraüme, the **Residenzgalerie** (April–Sept daily 10am–5pm; Oct–March closed Wed; öS50/€3.63) offers a fine display of archiepiscopal acquisitions from over the centuries, beginning in the entrance hall with Caspar Memberger's mid-sixteenth-century cycle of paintings depicting the Flood. The collection's two most valued works, Rembrandt's small but compelling *Old Woman Praying*, thought to be a portrait of the artist's mother, and Rubens' *Allegory of Charles V as Master of the World* (1664), a blatant piece of Habsburg propaganda showing the (long-deceased) emperor receiving the gift of the globe from a cherub, share wall space with a host of lesser-known landscapes and still lifes that nonetheless provide a useful overview of seventeenth-century Flemish art. Of the Austrian works on display, a Rottmayr *Pietà* and Maulpertsch's *Last Supper* are full of sombre melodrama, while Hans Makart's 1871 portrait of his first wife, Amalie, presents a human side to this normally stuffy, bourgeois painter.

In case all these old masters leave you yearning for a taste of modern art, the **Academia Gallery** (Mon–Fri 11am–6pm, Sat & Sun 11am–1pm; free; *www.kunstnet.at/academia*) on the ground floor of the Residenz is probably Salzburg's leading venue for small-scale contemporary art shows – ask at the tourist office to find out what's on.

The Domkirche

Arches link the Residenzplatz with the **Domplatz** to the south, which is dominated by the pale marble facade of Salzburg's cathedral, the **Domkirche St Rupert**. Once the forum of Roman Juvavum, the site has held a succession of churches since Bishop Virgil first built a chapel here in the eighth century. Although initially conceived by Wolf Dietrich as a cathedral to outshine St Peter's in Rome, the current edifice, begun in 1614, reflects the more modest ambitions of his successor Marcus Sitticus and his favoured architect, Santino Solari. The crests of both Sitticus and Paris Lodron, who occupied the archiepiscopal throne on completion of the forty-year project, adorn the pediment of the cathedral's western facade; at ground level, modern bronze doors are flanked by monumental statues of ss Rupert, Virgil, Peter and Paul. The facade looks pretty stern and unadorned from this angle; to appreciate its delicate sense of proportion and balance step back a bit towards the western end of the square. The interior (donation requested) is impressively cavernous, although the overall effect is one of dark, cold spaciousness, only partially alleviated by the dizzying ceiling frescoes. They're at their best in and around the central dome, rebuilt after being destroyed by allied bombing on October 16 1944, where enough daylight filters through to bring out some of their colour. Best of the Dom's intricate stucco-work is in the sequence of small chapels, on each side of the nave, whose low ceilings are crowded with personable cherubs. Left of the entrance is the Romanesque font in which Mozart was baptized, a bronze affair resting on four feet in the shape of lions' paws and decorated with reliefs of saints. Below the dome, steps descend to a starkly modern crypt, where a succession of chambers house the graves of some illustrious prelates, Paris Lodron among them. The mixture of smooth concrete slabs and ancient lumps of stone exudes the spiritual calm sometimes lacking in the tourist-tramped main body of the church above.

The **Dommuseum**, immediately to your right as you enter the cathedral porch (mid-May to late Oct Mon–Sat 10am–5pm, Sun 1–6pm; öS60/€4.36), owes much to the acquisitive habits of mid-seventeenth-century Archbishop Guidobald von Thun, who keenly amassed a collection of wondrous artefacts on the model of the famous Wunderkammer established by Emperor Rudolf II in Prague. What's left of Guidobald's collection (much was moved to Vienna when Salzburg became part of Austria in 1816) is displayed in its original form, a series of cabinets arranged by category: rosaries, minerals, scientific instruments, ivory, things made from goat horn, crystals, seashells and globes. To the modern eye, it looks more like a sale of upmarket bric-a-brac than a serious museum, but contemporaries of Guidobald would have regarded the sheer variety of objects on display as a manifestation of God's creative genius. Recurring stylistic motifs such as hourglasses, half-empty goblets, mussel shells and skulls are reminders that mortality and transience were preoccupations of the time. The upper floor of the museum is more conventional, with an impressive array of altarpieces, notably a surreal Temptation of St Anthony by a follower of Hieronymus Bosch. Best of the few Baroque paintings is Rottmayr's fanciful portrayal of a cherubic St Vitus being boiled in a cauldron.

The damp and musty **Grabungen** beneath the cathedral (May to mid–Oct Wed–Sun 9am–5pm; öS20/€1.45), accessible via steps outside the cathedral's north wall, expose the modest remains of its predecessors, including St Virgil's eighth-century chapel and the Romanesque basilica that superseded it. Fans of classical archeology will probably benefit most from a visit here – the recently uncovered Roman mosaic fragments are indeed impressive, featuring abstract patterns in vivid colours – but there's little to captivate the nonspecialist.

Behind the cathedral to the south, **Kapitelplatz** centres on one of Salzburg's finest fountains, the **Kapitelschwemme**, an eighteenth-century horse-trough magnificently presided over by a trident-wielding statue of Neptune. At the southern end of the square, a steeply ascending pathway and the Festungsbahn funicular railway both provide access to the Hohensalzburg fortress above (see p.387).

MOZART: THE SALZBURG YEARS

It's ironic that such a large part of Salzburg's tourist industry revolves around a man who felt so stifled by his native city that he couldn't wait to leave. Born the son of Leopold Mozart, a member of the archbishop of Salzburg's chamber orchestra and a respected expert on violin technique, **Wolfgang Amadeus Mozart** (1756–91) was recognized early on as a prodigy, learning the piano at the age of 3, going on to teach himself the violin, and embarking on rudimentary compositions by the age of 5 (although these were heavily revised by his father, so we have no way of telling how good they actually were). Mozart's sister Maria-Anna ("Nannerl"), five years older, was equally precocious, providing *père* Leopold with a child-prodigy package with which he could tour the courts of Europe in search of financial reward. Between 1762 and 1771 the family was almost constantly on the road, visiting Munich, Vienna, Pressburg (now Bratislava in Slovakia), Frankfurt, Brussels, Paris and London to perform for princely houses and society figures. Stints back home in Salzburg were largely spent preparing for the next trip abroad. By the time the Mozarts embarked on the first of three trips to Italy in 1770 Wolfgang was developing a reputation as a composer as well as a performer, and was commissioned to write an opera by the ducal theatre in Milan at the age of 14 (*Mitridate, Re di Ponto*).

Initially, many people simply couldn't believe that Mozart was capable of all the feats attributed to him, and subjected him to various tests: both Daines Barrington (a fellow of the Royal Society) in London and Archbishop Sigismund von Schrattenbach in Salzburg shut him up in a room without his father to see whether he could transcribe pieces of music played to him without Leopold there to help. A Neapolitan audience forced him to play without a ring he customarily wore on his finger, which they believed to be a magic charm.

In August 1772, at the age of 16, Wolfgang was appointed Konzertmeister (leader of the court orchestra) by Hieronymous Graf von Colloredo, Schrattenbach's successor as archbishop of Salzburg. The young composer later became Colloredo's organ master, but the relationship between the archbishop and the Mozarts was never to be a satisfactory one. Wolfgang's father Leopold was eager to continue touring the courts of Europe, believing that his son would win further commissions, and perhaps be appointed to a top musical post by some foreign prince if only his talents could be showcased as widely as possible. Colloredo, understandably, had misgivings about allowing musicians who were supposedly in his employ to galavant around Europe and take on commissions from other patrons. Wolfgang himself found life at Colloredo's court dull and uninspiring – the archbishop didn't harbour any great passion for music, such that Mozart compared playing for him and his cronies to performing for an audience of table and chairs, and took to calling the archbishop the "arch-oaf" (*Erzlümmel*) in his letters. Court musicians were also treated in much the same way as any other servants – Mozart sat next to the kitchen staff at mealtimes – and this rankled with a young composer who had already tasted a degree of celebrity.

In an attempt to find another job, Mozart spent much of 1777 and 1778 in western Europe, but he re-entered the service of Colloredo on his return to Salzburg in 1779. Relations with the archbishop took a turn for the worse a year later, when Mozart sought six weeks' leave in order to supervise the production of *Idomeneo*, an opera he had been commissioned to write for the carnival season in Munich. He ended up staying in Munich for four months. In March 1781, Colloredo summoned Mozart to Vienna (where the prelate was visiting his sick father) in an effort to bring the errant composer back into line. By May, having spent several weeks of inactivity in the archbishop's household, Mozart was ready to cut himself loose: cosmopolitan Vienna not only seemed to offer wider opportunities for a freelance composer, it was also the home of Constanze Weber, with whom he was falling in love. When Mozart tried to give his notice to quit, he was literally kicked out of the building by the archbishop's steward. Mozart married Constanze in 1782 and visited Salzburg with her in 1783, but he was never to reside in the city of his birth again.

For more on Mozart's life in Vienna, see p.85.

The Franziskanerkirche

At the western end of Domplatz an archway leads through to Franziskanergasse and the **Franziskanerkirche**, a thirteenth-century reconstruction of an eighth-century edifice, noted for the high-roofed, semicircular choir held up by stately, slender columns. Set into the curve of the choir wall are nine chapels, the interior of each adorned with fussy stucco-work, statuettes and paintings – the result of an eighteenth-century Baroque face-lift courtesy of Fischer von Erlach. Erlach was also responsible for the high altar, although the Madonna that forms its centrepiece is a fine example of late-Gothic sculpture by Tyrolean master Michael Pacher (the Child is a later addition). It's easy to miss the church's oldest artwork, a twelfth-century marble lion guarding the stairway to the pulpit.

The building on the southern side of Franziskanergasse, opposite the church, boasts a fine piece of Renaissance portrait sculpture in a niche above the door, a relief of Wolf Dietrich in the (for him, unlikely) garb of a monk.

The Peterskirche

Opposite the Franziskanerkirche, arches on the south side of Franziskanergasse lead through to the **Peterskirche**, Salzburg's most dazzling Rococo statement. Although occupying a largely Romanesque shell, the church was extensively remodelled in the late eighteenth century, with Philip Hinterseer's elaborate wrought-iron gates separating the porch from a sumptuous visual feast of stucco mouldings in the nave. Among paintings crowding the walls are two dramatic renditions of the Crucifixion by Ignazio Solari and Kaspar Memberger – sombre, extravagantly staged affairs. Behind the church, the eighteenth- and nineteenth-century graves of Salzburg's middle class fill the arcades of the **Petersfriedhof**, lurking beneath the cliffs of the Hohensalzburg. Catacombs cut into the rock face by Christian inhabitants of third-century Juvavum are accessible by a brief guided tour (in German with English summary; May–Sept on the hour 10.30am–5pm; Oct–April Wed & Thur 10.30am–3.30pm, Fri–Sun 10.30am–4pm; öS12/€0.87), worth considering more for the atmosphere than any historic sights. Christianity died out after the Roman Empire abandoned the region to Germanic tribes in the fifth century, but was revived by ss Virgil and Rupert.

The Rupertinum

Continuing west along Franziskanergasse, it's not long before you hit Max-Reinhard-Platz and the **Rupertinum** on the corner of Wiener-Philharmoniker-Gasse (mid-July to Sept daily 9am–5pm, Wed until 9pm; Oct to mid-July Tues–Sun 10am–5pm, Wed until 9pm; öS40/€2.91), a picture gallery devoted to twentieth-century work and major touring exhibitions of contemporary art. Gustav Klimt's *Unterach am Attersee* is probably the most famous canvas here, a marvellous example of Post-Impressionist landscape painting from an artist more usually known for his florid Jugendstil excesses. Elsewhere are a couple of Kokoschkas, and a picture each by Emil Nolde and Ludwig Kirchner, after which the collection drifts into mediocrity, enlivened only by Robert Zepperl-Sperl's *Gastmahl*, a colourful evocation of Vienna's bohemian artistic elite in the 1960s.

Universitätsplatz and around

Immediately west of the Rupertinum, Fischer von Erlach's sizeable **Kollegienkirche** dominates the **Universitätsplatz**, an elongated square peppered with stalls selling local sausages and cheese. Squeezed between two chunky towers is the church's most idiosyncratic feature, a bowed facade which juts forth like a huge bay window. Anton Pfaffinger's high altar of 1740, with classical columns presenting a rather too literal allegory of the Seven Pillars of Wisdom, seems lost within Ehrlach's hangar-sized interior.

Behind the church, Hofstallgasse is dominated by the rather utilitarian facade of the 1930s **Festspielhaus**, built to provide the Salzburg Festival with a central concert venue. Guided tours daily: July–Aug at 9.30am, 2pm & 3.30pm; June & Sept at 2pm & 3.30pm; Oct–May at 2pm; öS70/€5.09) provide access to the two concert halls inside, as well as the courtyard in which outdoor performances are held – a curious quadrangle of rock-hewn niches which once served as the archiepiscopal riding school's stables. Beside the Festspielhaus, a staircase leads up onto the Mönchsberg hill (see opposite). The less energetic can take the nearby Mönchsberg lift (Mönchsbergaufzug; daily 9am–11pm; öS27/€1.96 return).

Northeast of the Festspielhaus, but still in the shadow of the Mönchsberg, is the **Pferdschwemme**, a horse-trough built in 1700 for the archbishop's riding school and embellished with a range of equine motifs. Murals of a range of different breeds form the backdrop to the fountain, which centres on a statue of a loincloth-clad youth grappling with an unruly horse – a clear reference to the story of Alexander the Great taming the wild horse Bucephalus. A couple of hundred metres down Bürgerspitalgasse, the **Bürgerspital** is a sixteenth-century almshouse now containing the **Spielzeugsmuseum** ("Toy Museum"; Tues–Sun 9am–5pm; öS30/€2.18), an unassuming and largely unlabelled collection of model railways, dolls houses, puppets and other playthings. It's a colourful display with enough to keep nostalgic adults amused, but there's little in the way of hands-on fun for younger kids.

Haus der Natur

Salzburg's natural history collection, in the **Haus der Natur** (daily 9am–5pm; öS55/€4.00), a few steps north of the Bürgerspital on Museumsplatz, has rather more to marvel at. Five excellently arranged exhibition floors make this one of the city's more fun-filled attractions, a welcome breather from the rather culture-heavy sights on offer elsewhere. Downstairs, the requisite moving dinosaur models (with accompanying sound effects) are joined by fascinating, if incongruous, dioramas detailing life in Tibet, and an aquarium inhabited by piranhas and Red Sea sharks, amongst others. Upstairs floors offer an endless parade of stuffed fauna of all kinds, including one section on "animal bastards" – rare cross-breeds such as a tiger-lion, and the cubs of mixed brown and polar bear parents – and one glass case labelled "yeti" which is filled with theatrical dry ice. The Reptilienzoo contains live snakes and alligators, and a section on space travel features the capsule of an American Mercury rocket.

Museum Carolino-Augusteum

Round the corner from the Haus der Natur, at Museumsplatz 1, is the city's main historical museum, the **Museum Carolino-Augusteum** (July–Sept Tues–Sun 10am–6pm, Thur until 8pm; Oct–June Tues–Sun 9am–5pm; öS40/€2.91), although it's due to move to new premises on the Mozartplatz some time in 2003. An excellent place to catch up on the history of Roman-era Salzburg, or Juvavum, its wide range of finds include a number of mosaics (the best, a third-century piece found just east of Mozartplatz depicting Europa's abduction) and the fragmentary remains of a Roman water clock decorated with figures of Andromeda and Perseus. Upstairs are a small folklore section and several dull paintings, and a room devoted to local-born Hans Makart, history painter and society portraitist whose works reflected the stuffy conventions of the late-nineteenth-century bourgeoisie. Considerably more interesting are the Gothic wood-sculptures and altar fragments nearby, with a winged altar from the Pinzgau village of Rauris (featuring a relief of the *Pietà*, flanked by panels depicting ss Margaret, Catharine, Dorothy and Barbara) the best of a generally stunning bunch. The next floor up concentrates on Baroque paintings, with the *Beheading of Saint*

Barbara (1727) the most notable of a grippingly dramatic trio of works by Paul Troger. Some reconstructed sixteenth-century interiors display a wealth of intricately inlaid wood surfaces, and there's also a delightfully odd eighteenth-century *Spottofen* (literally "oven of scorn"), a ceramic stove designed – no doubt with a pious Catholic household in mind – in the shape of a library filled with books fit for burning, the works of Luther, Calvin and Zwingli among them. Finally, Salzburg's musical heritage is reflected in a display of ancient musical instruments, and there's a nearby CD player (you can programme your own choices) on which you can listen to examples of them in action.

Hohensalzburg fortress and the Mönchsberg

Surveying the city from its hilltop perch to the south, the **Hohensalzburg fortress** originated in the eleventh century, when Archbishop Gebhard, an ally of the pope in the latter's quarrel with the Holy Roman Empire, needed a strongpoint from which to repel the attacks of the south German princes. Most of the present-day fortress is the result of rebuilding work carried out by Archbishop Leonhard von Keutschach in the early 1500s, who added some sumptuous state apartments.

The quicker of two routes up to the fortress is via the Festungsbahn funicular, from the southern end of Kapitelplatz (daily: May–Sept 9am–9pm; Oct–April 9am–5pm; öS65/€4.72 one way, öS76/€5.52 return; ticket includes entrance to the fortress), but the 15-minute journey on foot isn't as hard as it looks and offers some excellent views of the city along the way. A roam around the main courtyard of the **fortress** (daily 9am–5pm; öS42/€3.05), together with a few of the surrounding bastions and passageways, is enough to gain a feel for the place, though von Keutschach's **state rooms** can be visited as part of a forty-minute **guided tour** for an additional fee (departing on demand, in English if requested; 9.30am–4.30pm; öS42/€3.05). Starting with panoramic views from the castle watchtower, the tour takes in the **Fürstenzimmer**, whose ceiling and doorframes are masterpieces of late-Gothic woodcarving, and a glimpse of *Der Stier* ("The Bull"), a monstrous sixteenth-century organ whose sonorous tones can be heard all over the city centre on the rare occasions which it's played. The tour concludes with a chance to explore two small museums which can't be visited on their own: the **Rainer-Museum** (closed mid-Oct to April), displaying uniforms and weapons of the infantry regiment that was stationed in the castle until 1945; and the **Burgmuseum**, which includes Archbishop Wolf Dietrich's suit of armour, a small collection of Gothic statuary, and instruments of torture, among them grotesque *Schandmasken* ("masks of shame"), which petty criminals were forced to wear by way of punishment.

Paths lead east from the fortress to another example of pre-Baroque Salzburg architecture, the **Nonnberg convent**, whose church is a largely fifteenth-century rebuilding of a Romanesque structure. The convent was founded by St Rupert's niece St Erentrude, who is shown beside John the Baptist and the Virgin on the tympanum above the main doorway, and whose tomb lies in the church crypt. There's a fine collection of marble memorials to other, later abbesses along the north wall of the nave, and, on the right side of the chancel, a fine late-Gothic winged altar showing the Nativity.

Heading west from the Hohensalzburg, trails lead onto the neighbouring **Mönchsberg** hill, a partly wooded area which is a popular Sunday strolling arena. Also accessible from the staircase and lift beside the Festspielhaus (see opposite), the Mönchsberg offers superb views of Salzburg's Baroque monuments, especially from the viewing terrace beside the Naturfreundhaus hostel on the Mönchsberg's north-western tip. Beside the hostel runs a grizzled line of fortifications dating from Paris Lodron's seventeenth-century bastion-building craze, and a maze of leafy pathways leading down towards the suburb of Mülln to the north.

The right bank

Streets on the **right bank** of the Salzach zero in on **Platzl**, a small square at the eastern end of the Staatsbrücke. Entering Platzl to the north is Steingasse, originally the route by which the salt traders arrived in the city. Still preserving much of its character, it's a narrow, cobbled alley lined with buildings of medieval origin, many of which now house bars, restaurants and, in one case at least, a discreet high-class brothel.

PARACELSUS

The grandly named Philippus Aureolus Theophrastus Bombastus von Hohenheim (the self-styled "Paracelsus") was born in Einsiedeln, Switzerland, in 1493. He was a pupil of renowned alchemist Abbot Tritheim of Würzburg, and attended various European universities (later claiming, fraudulently, to have received a degree in medicine from the University of Ferrara), although much of his medical knowledge was obtained in the course of extensive wanderings as an itinerant healer. Crisscrossing Europe between 1517 and 1526, he came to believe that the medical establishment of his day was far too rooted in the ossified theories of ancient Greek and Roman writers, and argued that open-minded enquiry based on close observation of the effects of various medicines was far more important in the development of medical knowledge. However, he was also an arrogant and vain self-publicist, calling himself **Paracelsus** ("the equal of Celsus", a reference to the prodigious first-century compiler of medical encyclopedias), and treating his medical contemporaries with a contempt that was to ensure he remained, for much of his life, a distrusted outsider.

Indeed Paracelsus would probably have remained an unorthodox travelling healer had it not been for his adoption by the intellectual elite of Basel in 1526. It was here that he was engaged as the personal physician of Johannes Froben, a humanist and publisher of Europe-wide renown who went on to recommend Paracelsus to friends, notably among them the esteemed scholar Erasmus. The city fathers of Basel made Paracelsus their municipal doctor, and he was offered a chair in medicine by the local university. He began his university career by publicly burning the works of Galen, the third-century Greek physician who had remained the prime authority on all things medical ever since. Such iconoclasm seriously ruffled the feathers of the local medical elite, and Paracelsus was drummed out of office after two years.

Several parts of Austria boast Paracelsus connections. He lived in Villach as a young man (his father practised medicine here from 1502 to 1532), studied the respiratory ailments of Tyrolean silver-miners, and visited Badgastein, where he was impressed by the curative properties of the local spa waters. Not much is known of Paracelsus's two periods in Salzburg, the first in the 1520s when he briefly had a medical practice in Pfeifergasse, the second in 1541 when he died here, ostensibly as a result of a wound received in a brawl with one of his medical adversaries. He left behind a huge volume of published writings which, in typical sixteenth-century humanist fashion, tried to combine the discipline of scientific enquiry with a much more esoteric appreciation of the power of mysticism and magic. However many of his ideas were ahead of their time: he emphasized critical observation of the patient, and offered important insights into the psychological side of the healing process, believing that the patient's faith in the power of a particular medicine was often more important than the properties of the medicine itself. More importantly, he challenged the contemporary notion that the human body was governed by the four humours (and the four elements that made them up – choler, blood, phlegm and bile), and placed the role of pharmaceuticals in the treatment of illness on a sound scientific basis. Most peculiarly, he held that ailments should be treated with plants that resembled the afflicted parts of the body (and there are no prizes for guessing which organ he thought would benefit from contact with a cucumber). He was also responsible for introducing the word "gnome" to the lexicon, a creature that he believed dwelt beneath the earth's crust.

Ascending eastward from Platzl is the **Linzergasse**, a busy pedestrianized shopping street hung with the wrought-iron shop signs typical of the Getreidegasse. The street skirts the lower slopes of the **Kapuzinerberg**, which is named after the Capuchin monastery that crowns its summit. Fortified by Archbishop Paris Lodron during the Thirty Years' War, the hill still sports a brace of attractively pinnacled defensive towers, together with a stretch of wall, on its southern flanks. During World War II German planners earmarked the Kapuzinerberg as the site of the so-called Gauforum; a grandiose civic project featuring Party headquarters, a palace for the Gauleiter (regional governor), sports stadium and a brand new Festspielhaus. Envisioned as a Nazi acropolis that would help recast Salzburg as the Teutonic Athens, the Gauforum never got past the planning stage. Easily climbed in five minutes from Linzergasse, today's Kapuzinerberg is primarily known for its excellent view of Salzburg's domes and spires, a panorama which reveals skyline details not always visible at ground level, notably the high, broad roof of the Franziskanerkirche, billowing out like a circus big top; and the statues balancing precariously on the twin towers of Fischer von Erlach's Kollegienkirche.

Continuing along Linzergasse, the dour **Sebastianskirche** is less interesting than the **St Sebastian cemetery** (daily 7am–7pm) behind it, a colonnaded oasis of inner-city peace dominated by the **mausoleum of Archbishop Wolf Dietrich**. The tiled interior, with paintings by Elias Castello (whose own grave, in the arcade to the west, is one of the finest Renaissance monuments in the cemetery), adds delicacy to what is otherwise a pompous and self-regarding monument. The path leading from the cemetery entrance to the mausoleum passes the graves of Mozart's father Leopold and widow Constanze, the latter buried beside her second husband, Georg Nikolaus von Nissen, one of Mozart's first biographers. Elsewhere, innumerable family tombs attest to an Austrian love of the macabre: skulls abound and, on the von Goldenstein family tomb (under the arcade at the northern end), a fine, emaciated figure of Death holds an hourglass. In the southwestern corner of the cemetery is the **tomb of Paracelsus**, the Renaissance humanist and alchemist who was the founder of modern pharmacology (see box opposite).

Leaving the cemetery by the west entrance (just by the Paracelsus memorial) and turning right into a narrow alley soon brings you to the much rebuilt **Loretokloster** on Paris-Lodron-Strasse, infamous for the seventeenth-century gaol which occupied one corner of the monastery until it was destroyed by allied bombing in World War II. The **Hexenturm** or "witches' tower" was built to accommodate those accused of sorcery during one of the most notorious witch-crazes in Europe. Dubbed the **Zauberjackel Affair** after the nickname of one of its first defendants, the craze reached its height in 1678, when a total of 109 people were put on trial for a variety of devil-related offences. Two thirds of the suspects were under 21 years of age, and most were itinerant beggars or landless peasants looking for work – it's reasonable to assume that the witch hunt symbolized the discomfort felt by Salzburg cityfolk towards a potentially violent rural underclass. Those found guilty were rewarded with death by strangulation if they agreed to confess their sins, and public burning if they refused.

Makartplatz and Mozarts Gewohnhaus

Two blocks northwest of Platzl, the **Makartplatz** is presided over by Fischer von Erlach's **Dreifaltigkeitskirche**, or church of the Holy Trinity, notable for the graceful curve of its exterior and the oval plan of its dome, which boasts a crowd of vibrant paintings by Rottmayr. Much smaller than the same architect's Kollegienkirche, the church is a remarkably successful exercise in squeezing a structure of extreme delicacy and elegance into a restricted building space. Further along, the house at no. 8 is the site of **Mozart-Wohnhaus** (daily 9am–5.30pm; öS65/€4.72), where the Mozart family lived between 1773 and 1787. Though little of the original building survives, courtesy of allied bombing raids in World War II, the museum is a much better introduction to the composer's life and times than the Geburtshaus across the river, largely due to its modern, multimedia approach. Headsets deliver engrossing commentary together with well-chosen excerpts of music, a short video follows Mozart's journeys around Europe, and a small movie theatre screens documentaries on Mozart's career, to booming musical accompaniment. The well-labelled collection of period furniture, original manuscripts and eighteenth-century harpsichords won't disappoint the purists.

Schloss Mirabell and the Mirabell Gardens

From Makartplatz, Dreifaltigkeitsgasse leads northwest towards the broad flagstoned expanse of Mirabellplatz, where virtually every tour bus in the city seems to pick up and drop off its daily cargo of sightseers. Running along the western side of the square is the grey-brown facade of **Schloss Mirabell**, originally built by Archbishop Wolf Dietrich as a palatial home for Salome Alt, the mistress with whom the energetic prelate sired at least a dozen children. This relationship with the daughter of a respected local burgher actually endeared Wolf Dietrich to the Salzburgers, not least because it appeared to be a genuine love match. There's nothing to suggest that the archbishop was anything other than a loyal and devoted partner, and he did his utmost to secure a stable and dignified future for Salome and the kids – the Austrian Emperor Rudolf II graciously offered to provide them all with noble titles. After Dietrich's fall from power, the palace was requisitioned by Marcus Sitticus who, obviously far from satisfied with the Hohensalzburg and the Residenz, felt the need for a third official archiepiscopal home. Completely revamped by Lukas von Hildebrandt in the early eighteenth century, and further reconstructed after a fire in the nineteenth, the Schloss very much looks like the civic administration building it has now become – a rather unassuming office block centred on a plain courtyard. Its one truly outstanding feature is the marble **staircase** by Baroque master George Raphael Donner, located beside the west entrance (if you're approaching from Mirabellplatz, proceed straight through the courtyard to the arch on the far side, and go through the first door on your right). Given the utilitarian appearance of the rest of the Schloss, it's a deliciously extravagant and sensual piece of work. Plump cherubs lounge around on the balustrade, watched over by Graeco-Roman gods and goddesses who occupy wall niches in the stairwell, the whole ensemble sculpted out of smooth, pinkish stone.

The archway immediately west of the staircase leads through to the **Mirabell gardens** behind the building, laid out during the rule of Archbishop Johann Ernst von Thun according to plans provided by his favourite architect, Fischer von Erlach. The first thing that catches your eye is a greening copper statue of Pegasus, caught in mid-prance by sculptor Caspar Gras in 1661, and moved here on Erlach's instructions to provide a focus for this part of the garden. Just to the north, a staircase guarded by a brace of curiously goat-faced unicorns leads up to the rose-filled high ground of the adjoining **Kurgarten**, which offers a much-photographed view back across the city towards the Hohensalzburg. Immediately west of the Pegasus statue, steps followed by a small wooden bridge lead to the **Zwerglgarten** ("Dwarf Garden"), occupying the crown of an old defensive bastion, the only surviving portion of the massive system of fortifications built by Santino Solari between 1620 and 1646. It was laid out as a park and peopled with a series of grotesque statues of dwarfs a century later – proof that the Teutonic fascination for garden gnomes goes back a long way. The main body of the Mirabell gardens stretches south from the Pegasus statue, an avenue of trees running alongside ornamental flowerbeds which are seasonally replanted in order to provide year-round colour. A central pond is surrounded by four Baroque sculptures by Ottavio Muto, each of which purports to be an allegory of one of the four elements – earth, air, fire and water – although it's not easy to deduce this from the gratuitously writhing, semi-naked figures on display. Nestling on the eastern side of the gardens is the

Barockmuseum (Tues–Sat 9am–noon & 2–5pm, Sun 10am–noon; öS40/€2.91; www.barockmuseum.at), which focuses on Austrian art of that period, although it is primarily devoted to the preliminary sketches made by artists prior to the execution of a major work rather than the finished paintings themselves. While it's a useful insight into how the art of Troger, Donner and Maulpertsch developed, those with limited time should stick to the city's Baroque churches instead.

The outskirts of the city: Schloss Hellbrunn, the Untersberg and the Open-Air Museum

A clutch of worthwhile sights on the southern fringes of the city are easily reached on the municipal bus network. Most important of these are the palace, gardens and zoo at Schloss Hellbrunn, 5km south of the Altstadt and accessible via the #55 bus from the train station, Mirabellplatz or Rudolfskai. The Italianate palace was built by Santino Solari between 1613 and 1619 to serve as the suburban pleasure villa and hunting lodge of the urbane Archbishop Marcus Sitticus, who commissioned the job immediately on his accession to the archiepiscopal throne. Bus #55 continues to St Leonhard just beyond the city's southern suburbs, starting point for the cable-car ascent of the Untersberg, an impressively craggy height renowned for its expansive views.

On the road to the Bavarian town of Bad Reichenhall, Salzburger Land's excellent Open-Air Museum lies 12km to the southwest of Salzburg. You can escape to the museum by bus or cycle – there's a separate cycle path by the side of the road once leave suburban Salzburg.

Schloss Hellbrunn

For the worldly, Italian-educated Marcus Sitticus, Hellbrunn was a summer retreat where he could relax, enjoy the good things in life and entertain his guests. Foremost among the entertainments devised by the pleasure-loving prelate, the Wasserspiele (guided tours in English and German, April & Oct 9am–4.30pm; May, June & Sept 9am–5pm; July & Aug 9am–10pm; öS80/€5.81) is a themed pocket of the Schloss gardens featuring shell-encrusted grottoes, water-powered clockwork figures, and trick fountains that spurt unexpectedly into life – visitors should come prepared for a soaking. During the tour you'll pass the Stone Theatre, an outdoor stage built in order to satisfy Marcus Sitticus's love of opera and drama. Austrian Emperor Ferdinand II was treated to an operatic performance here during an official visit to Salzburg in 1619, five years after Marcus had staged the first ever opera in the city – Monteverdi's Orfeo, in the Residenz.

The Schloss itself (same times; obligatory 20min guided tours depart at regular intervals, in German but English translations on request; öS40/€2.91) is filled with reminders of Marcus Sitticus's passion for animals, both those he hunted and those he collected to stock his park: names of some rooms, like the Fish room, hint at the decor within. Disturbing to modern eyes, but relatively commonplace to the educated elite of Sitticus's time, are the paintings of the freaks of nature that once filled the archbishop's bizarre private zoo, notably various albino farm animals and an eight-legged horse. More refined tastes are revealed in the Chinese room, with hand-painted wallpaper depicting birds and cherry blossom, and in the Octagon room, where the archbishop's favoured musicians were invited to perform. The latter chamber features a series of wall paintings by Arsenio Mascagni in which the archbishop himself is portrayed in civilian clothes (a deliberate hint that he wished to be treated as a secular prince rather than Church leader when in the comfort of his own summer palace), together with his mistress, Katharine von Mabon. Despite issuing decrees against rowdy festivities and the keeping of brothels, Marcus Sitticus wore his own vow of celibacy rather lightly, conducting a well-known affair with officer's wife Frau von Mabon (for whom he constructed a country house on Hellbrunner Allee) as well as with her sister.

Behind the Schloss stretches an extensive **park** (dawn till dusk), with tree-lined avenues, ornamental flowerbeds and well-stocked fish ponds.

The Volksmuseum and Hellbrunn zoo

Tickets to the Wasserspiele also include entrance to the **Volksmuseum** (April–Oct daily 9am–5pm; öS20/€1.46 if visited on its own), in the **Monatsschlösschen**, or "month-castle" – so called because it was constructed in a single month. Set on a wooded hill at the far end of the park, it holds a respectable collection of folk costumes and painted wooden furniture, but it's the section on the Salzburger Land's rural festivals that commands most attention. Pride of place goes to the towering effigy of Samson the giant, one of many that used to be hauled through towns during the **Samsonumzug** processions that marked Corpus Christi. In a ritual of ancient origin whose precise meaning remains lost, Samson would have been accompanied by people dressed as the Zwerglmann and Zwerglfrau ("Mr and Mrs Dwarf"). A concerted effort was made to stamp out such practices throughout Austria during the reign of Josef II, and the custom nowadays survives in only a few towns to the southeast – Tamsweg (see p.405), Mauterndorf and St Michael im Lungau among them. Equally striking are the costumes donned during the **Perchtenlauf** processions, which take place on January 5 in the Pongau (see p.406), incorporating enormous head-dresses onto which mirrors, stuffed birds and other objects are mounted.

Adjoining the park, and stretching along the northern flanks of the hill, are the animal pens of **Hellbrunn Zoo** (daily: June–Sept 8.30am–6pm, Oct–May 8.30am–4pm; öS80/€5.81), a sizeable collection of worldwide fauna, which counts pumas, lions, jaguars, snow leopards and rhinos among its numerous inmates.

The Untersberg

From Hellbrunn, a few of the #55 buses continue to the village of **ST LEONHARD** 7km further south, where a cable car ascends the 1853-metre **Untersberg**. Local legend maintains that the Emperor Charlemagne is asleep under the mountain and will awaken when the ravens disappear from the skies around the summit. The cable car (9am–5pm; return öS215/€15.62; closed Nov) provides access to an impressive panorama of the surrounding countryside, with Salzburg laid out to the north and the high Alps to the south.

The Open-Air Museum

The **Salzburger Freilichtsmuseum**, the Salzburger Land's Open-Air Museum (Easter–Oct & Dec 25 to Jan 5 Tues–Sun 9am–6pm; öS70/€5.08), assembles over fifty historic farm buildings from all over the region in a large, partially wooded park. Buildings are grouped by area of origin within the Salzburger Land. The most visible distinction lies between the single-building farmsteads typical of the Flachgau and the Tennengau in the north and east, and the twin-building farmsteads (where animals and hay were kept in a separate building lying parallel to the farmer's house) that once predominated in the Pongau to the southwest. Pongau and Pinzgau farmhouses also tend to have a bell on the roof (with which wives called in their husbands from far-flung fields), usually mounted in a small, intricately carved belfry, and sometimes crowned by a cast-iron weathercock. Demonstrations of rural crafts such as embroidery, smithing and carpentry take place on summer Sundays.

The Open-Air Museum is 5km short of the village of **Grossgmain**, which stands on the Austrian–German border. Hourly buses on the Salzburg–Grossgmain–Bad Reichenhall route drop off at the museum. It's also just about practical to cycle the 12km to the museum from Salzburg (head out towards the airport on the Innsbrucker Bundesstrasse and keep going until you see signs for Grossgmain and Bad Reichenhall). There's little to see in Grossgmain itself, so it's best to avail yourself of the food-and-drink facilities inside the museum (a couple of café-restaurants are housed in some of the traditional wooden buildings) before heading back to the city.

Eating and drinking

There's no shortage of good **restaurants** in Salzburg, many of them dishing out traditional Austrian meat-based fare in atmospheric medieval town houses. Most of these are open for lunch and offer good-value two-course **Mittagsmenüs** as a way of attracting tourist custom – though, as is often the case in Austria, **ethnic restaurants** are best for an inexpensive midday meal. On the whole, prices are not unduly exploitative: an evening meal in Salzburg need not be any more expensive than in any of Austria's other urban centres. Phone numbers of restaurants where you may need to make a reservation are included in the listings below. Remember that good sit-down eating doesn't just take place in restaurants: many cafés and bars provide full meals. Restaurants and cafés tend to close at around 11pm–midnight, while bars often continue serving food until 2am or beyond, although there's no hard and fast rule.

For takeaway **snacks**, the best Würstelstand in town is bang in the centre on the Alter Platz, though there are others on F-Hanusch-Platz, and Platzl on the right bank of the river. *Trzesniewski*, Getreidegasse 9, has delicious, if dainty, open sandwiches, and is also the best place in town at which to pick up pastries; there's a small sit-down section at the back. *Nordsee*, with branches at Getreidegasse 11 and 27, is a reliable source of takeaway tuna sandwiches and other seafood. Billa, Griesgasse 21, is the handiest central supermarket.

Daytime drinkers and pastry nibblers are well catered for by Salzburg's many elegant **cafés**, which usually offer a sumptuous range of teas, coffees and alcoholic drinks, as well as snacks and full meals. They're often the best place at which to sample the two specialities for which Salzburg is famed – **Salzburger Nockerl**, a mound of sugary egg-whites and raspberries which has to be tried at least once, and the ubiquitous **Mozartkügeln**, the locally-made balls of chocolate-covered marzipan which are piled high in virtually every shop window in the town centre. Most of the Mozartkügeln sold in boxes and presentation packs are the gold-wrapped, mass-produced ones; connoisseurs prefer the silver-wrapped, handmade variety which are much richer in marzipan, and can be bought loose from Salzburg confectioners for around öS8–10/€0.58–0.73 each.

Night-time drinking venues are scattered throughout the town, although there are two well-travelled strips which traditionally attract sybaritic Salzburg youth. The Rudolfskai on the left bank is the main weekend boozing area for teen and twentysomething drinkers, with a string of bars pumping out loud techno music to a beer and tequila-sloshing crowd – great fun if you're in the mood for high-octane drinking and flirting. However bars here go out of fashion – and business – with alarming regularity. The area around Giselakai, Imbergstrasse and Steingasse, over on the right bank of the Salzach, has a clutch of designer bars attracting a slightly older clientele.

Cafés

Bazar, Schwarzstrasse 3. Classic daytime coffeehouse with an interior which looks as if it hasn't been touched since the late fifties, and a nice terrace overlooking the Salzach. Breakfast pastries, cakes and full meals, all served by notoriously superior waiters.

Bio Terra, Wiener-Philharmoniker-Gasse 9. Intimate, arty and informal café housed in the Rupertinum art gallery. Good range of main courses, salads and soups. One of the best places in Salzburg for a vegetarian nibble.

Fischkrieg, Ferdinand-Hanusch-Platz. Combined café and fishmongers in a bright pavilion right by the river, offering anything from dainty smoked-salmon canapés to full grilled-fish meals, including excellent grilled squid (Tintenfisch), all at reasonable prices. Mon–Fri 8.30am–6.30pm, Sat 8.30am–noon.

Kaffehäferl, Universitätsplatz 6. One of the nicer small daytime cafés, with tables set out in a courtyard, and a short menu of reasonably priced lunchtime snacks, including *Gefüllte Paprika* (stuffed red pepper), tortellini, and quiche. Mon–Sat 9am–7pm, Sun 9am–1pm.

Tomaselli, Alte Markt 9. Most renowned of the city's daytime cafés, serving a bewildering array of cakes and pastries. Can be deluged by tourists, but the elegant belle-époque interior is dripping with atmosphere.

Restaurants

An Bing, Goldgasse 13. Chinese cuisine on the first floor of a city-centre building (so no outdoor seating), one of the cheapest Mittagsmenüs around, from about öS75/€5.48.

Bürgerwehr, Mönchsberg 19c. Restaurant of the *Naturfreundhaus* hostel, offering cheap, no-nonsense Austrian home cooking. Marvellous view of town from the wooden benches on its outdoor terrace.

Café Hartl, Kaigasse 15. Tempting range of reasonably priced pizzas, pasta and crepes, conveniently located just round the corner from Mozartplatz.

Casanova, Linzergasse, 23. Bright, modern and dependable pizzeria with a big list of inexpensive thin-crust pies. In addition, cheap pasta specials chalked up outside.

Gäblerbrau, Linzergasse 9. Elegant without being wildly expensive, a big hotel-restaurant with a range of familiar Austrian standards like *Tafelspitz* and *Schweinsbraten* in the öS140–160/€10.22–11.68 range, and a couple of vegetarian pasta or noodle options.

Resch & Lieblich, Toscaninihof 1 (☎0662/843675). Good-value Austrian cuisine in a popular restaurant and wine bar next door to the Festspielhaus, its dining rooms carved out of the cliffs of the Mönchsberg. Despite plenty of outdoor seating, it still gets crowded here, especially during the Festival, when it's a popular haunt for musicians and concert-goers.

Shakespeare, Hubert-Sattler-Gasse 12. Laid-back, mildly bohemian place just off Mirabellplatz, that functions as café, bar and restaurant, serving a range of vegetarian and Chinese main courses, as well as cheap daily specials. There's usually a cool jazz soundtrack, and dance-music events are held in the back room at weekends.

Soho, Steingasse 61 (☎0662/878060). The menu is limited in this cosy, candlelit bar-restaurant, but the food – usually an Austrian-Modern European mix – is excellent. It's also a nice place for a drink.

Stadtkrug, Linzergasse 20. A popular barrel-vaulted, candlelit space offering trusty mid-priced favourites like *Wiener Schnitzel* and *Tafelspitz*. Daily set menus from öS130/€9.49. Always a few cheap *Gröstl* dishes (a Tyrolean staple made from grated potato fried in a pan together with onions and, usually, meat) on the menu, including one vegetarian option.

Sternbrau, Getreidegasse 34/Griesgasse 23 (☎0662/840717). Rambling establishment built around a courtyard in the heart of the Altstadt, featuring traditional Austrian restaurant, Italian trattoria, lots of outdoor seating in a beer-garden atmosphere, and there are a couple of vegetarian options on both menus.

Stiftskeller St Peter, St-Peter-Bezirk 4 (☎0662/841268). Medium-priced, traditional Austrian dishes in roomy, atmospheric surroundings, next to the Peterskirche. Abundant outdoor seating nonetheless tends to fill up quickly with tourist parties.

Weisses Kreuz, Bierjodlgasse 6 (☎0662/845641). Specializing in Balkan food, on a cobbled street below the fortress. Dishes range from cheap spicy *ćevapčići* (grilled mincemeat rissoles) to more expensive meat-heavy meals; there's usually also a three-course set menu from around öS150/€10.95. Closed Sun.

Zipfer Bierhaus, Universitätsplatz 19. Homely wood-furnished beer hall with the full range of Austrian staples and cheap lunchtime specials. A convenient bolthole from city-centre sightseeing.

Zum Fidelen Affen, Priesterhausgasse 8 (☎0662/877361). Small, wood-panelled, pub-like place on the right bank of the river, which also does a good line in traditional Austrian cooking. Cheap prices, informal atmosphere and good beer make this an enduringly popular choice for local students, so it's often very busy. Wooden bench seating outside in summer.

Zur Glocke, Schanzlgasse 2 (☎0662/845391). Homely Gasthof on the eastern fringe of the Altstadt, with inexpensive traditional food, plain decor, and an enthusiastic army of regular clients. Main courses in the öS150/€10.95 range include *Salzburger Bierfleisch* (beef cooked in beer) and trout. Closed Sun.

Bars

ARGE Nonntal (aka Kulturgelände Nonntal), Mühlbacherhofweg 5. Cultural centre fifteen minutes' walk from the centre, offering a largely alternative diet of music and theatre, and a popular café-bar – *Arge Beisl* – round the back. Relaxed atmosphere for an enjoyable evening's drinking, and veggie eats on the menu.

Augustiner Bräu, Augustinergasse 4–6. Although a 15min walk northwest of the centre, this is part of the Salzburg experience for many – a vast, open-air courtyard filled with students, local families and tourists. Beer (brewed on the premises) is served in archaic fashion: you collect a ceramic mug, rinse it under the tap provided, pay a cashier and present the receipt to the barman, who promptly fills your mug.

Bazillus, Imbergstrasse 2a. Bar on the right bank of the river which has proved enduringly popular with subsequent generations of twentysomething drinkers, although nobody really knows why. Small, dark, minimally decorated, and with a slightly more lived-in feel than some of its trendier neighbours. Outdoor bar in summer.

Bier Amt, Kaigasse 5. A smart, modern bar just off Mozartplatz with a wide range of ales on tap, and a small amount of outdoor seating. Well placed for a post-sightseeing drink.

O'Malley's, Rudolfskai. Homely Irish pub with unobtrusive music, cosy low-ceilinged rooms, and two bars. Liable to get crowded at weekends, a good place for a quiet pint midweek. Irish and Austrian beers on tap, international brews in bottles.

Pepe Gonzales, Steingasse 3. Bar serving Mexican beer and nibbles to a young and stylish crowd, with Latin American background music. Throbbing with life most nights; it's a real squeeze to find a place around the long, L-shaped bar.

Rockhouse Bar (aka Riff), Schallmooser Hauptstrasse 46 Narrow, tunnel-like and rather stylish bar hewn out of the rock of the Kapucinerberg hill. In-house DJs spin a range of rock and dance tracks to an open-minded crowd. Next to the Rockhouse music venue some 2km northeast of the centre – check local listings information (see below) to see what's on before heading out.

Rupertihof (aka Weissbrau), Rupertgasse. Beer hall a short walk northeast of the Linzergasse area serving locally brewed Weissbier in convivial surroundings. A popular place to eat, with a reasonably priced menu including all kinds of schnitzels, as well as fish. There's a large beer garden out the back. Closed Sun.

St Paul's Stub'n, Herrengasse 16. Unassuming, studentish bar hiding on the first floor of an old house below the castle, offering cheap beer and filling pizzas. You'll either find its down-to-earth atmosphere refreshing after Salzburg's other bars, or be turned off by its obstinate refusal to be anything other than plain.

Schnaitl Pub, Bergstrasse 5. Relaxed and tolerant studenty, grungey, sometimes gothy bar on the right bank with alternative rock on tape – and occasionally live.

Shamrock, Rudolfskai. Popular Irish pub with Guinness and Kilkenny on tap, and regular live music. The main bar area usually becomes a sea of people by 11pm on Friday.

Shrimps Bar, Steingasse 5. Youthful clientele frequent this classy bar-restaurant with Mediterranean decor and a range of prawn and salmon nibbles.

Stadtkino, Anton-Neumayr-Platz 2. Cool and trendy café-bar during the day, mecca for left-field DJ culture at night, with club nights (small admission charge) at weekends. Also a good place for food: breakfasts are served up until 1pm, sandwiches and other snacks thereafter.

Stieglkeller, Festungsgasse 10. Vast beer garden on the way up to the fortress, with outdoor terraces offering excellent views of the city. Was a main excursion spot for nineteenth-century Salzburgers but is now largely a tourist haunt.

Vis-à-vis, Rudolfskai. Smartish place with a long bar zigzagging its way down an attractive grotto-like interior, with a welcoming area of comfy seating down the bottom end. Attracts a slightly older and more civilized clientele than some of the rowdier Friday-night Rudolfskai venues nearby.

Zwettler's Gastwirtschaft, Kaigasse 3. One of the more relaxed, convivial and conveniently placed drinking venues in the Altstadt, featuring worn tables and wood-panelled snugs under low arched ceilings. Blues or jazz provide the musical background. Full range of standard Austrian soups and main meals, very reasonably priced.

Entertainment

As befits the city of Mozart, **music** is Salzburg's speciality. Most of this is of the classical variety, but a city of such size can't get away without at least a handful of rock venues and clubs. **Theatre** is also serious business here, although challenging German-language drama may not be everyone's cup of tea. The best sources of **listings** information are *Stadt Leben*, a free monthly available from the tourist office which, although printed in German, is pretty easy to decipher; the tourist office's own multilingual *Events* brochure, published every two months; or the *Salzburger Nachrichten* daily newspaper. The Salzburg Ticket Service, inside the tourist office (☎0662/840310, *www.salzburgticket.com*), has tickets for most of the performances going on in the city, including the Festspiele (see below).

Don't forget **sport**: addresses for activities like swimming and ice skating can be found in "Listings", p.400. The main spectator sport is without doubt **football**. Austrian champions in 1994, 1995 and 1997, local team **SV Salzburg** play at the Casino Stadion on Schumacherstrasse, 1.5km north of the Altstadt (☎0662/433332-0; buses #49 or #95 from F-Hanusch-Platz to Nelkenstrasse). Most matches are played on Saturday afternoons, and sometimes Saturday evenings.

Classical music

As one would expect from the birthplace of **Mozart**, a rich diet of classical music is available in Salzburg all year round. The Salzburg Festival is one of the most prestigious music festivals in the world, and Salzburg's music academy, the Mozarteum, Schwarzstrasse 36 (☎0662/873154), organizes a range of (both Mozart-related and other classical) concerts throughout the year. In addition, there are regular chamber music performances in Schloss Mirabell's Marmorsaal. The Salzburg tourist office will have details of what's on.

The Salzburg Festival and the Mozartwoche

The outstanding event in Salzburg's musical calendar is the **Salzburger Festspiele**, or Salzburg Festival, a five-week celebration of opera, orchestral music and theatre which runs from the last week of July to the end of August. First staged in 1920, the Festival grew out of discussions between the cinema, theatre and opera director Max Reinhardt, composer Richard Strauss, conductor Franz Schalk and playwright Hugo von Hoffmannstahl. Their aim was to gather the world's best musicians and performers for a celebration of all that was best in high culture, embracing both the traditional (set-piece performances of Mozart's works have always been a major feature of the festival) and the adventurously modern. This original conception of the Festival is still very much in place, and the main opera and theatre performances are often entrusted to ground-breaking directors.

Over the years the festival has provided Salzburg as a town with a sense of cultural mission, and its content is always a prime source of local debate. After Hitler's rise to power in Germany in 1933 the festival was widely considered to be a beacon of liberal,

THE SOUND OF MUSIC

Despite being the most successful advertisement for Austrian tourism ever produced, the Oscar-winning 1965 film **The Sound of Music** (*www.tcfhe.com/soundofmusic*) – dubbed into German and released under the distinctly unmemorable title of *Meine Lieder, meine Träume* ("My songs, my dreams") – flopped in Austria itself. Meanwhile, in the English-speaking world, the success of *Sing-Along-A-Sound-of-Music*, in which the audience are encouraged to dress up as nuns and carouse along with Maria and the kids, confirmed the film's status as a kitsch cult classic. By contrast, the film was only shown for the first time on Austrian television in January 2001, by which time the film's cult status was beginning to filter through to a younger generation of Austrians unlikely to be fazed by corny Hollywood portrayals of their homeland.

Notoriously dubbed "The Sound of Mucous" by its male lead, Christopher Plummer, the film tells the over-romanticized, but essentially true, story of the Von Trapp family, as related in Maria von Trapp's 1949 collection of reminiscences **The Story of the Trapp Family Singers.** What the film-makers did was to condense the entire story into one hectic summer. In reality, Maria and Captain von Trapp got married as early as 1927, and only started their singing career after the family lost everything in the Depression. By the time of the Anschluss in 1938 (the year in which the film is set), the family were already internationally famous – so much so that they were invited to sing at Hitler's birthday party. It was this, and the fact that Maria was pregnant with their second child, as much as the fact that the captain had received his call-up papers, that prompted them to take the train over the border into Italy. (And, for the record, it was the butler who was the Nazi, not poor old Rolf, the postboy, as in the film). Later that year, they set sail for America, and eventually settled in Stowe, Vermont, where they set up a music camp and lodge. The captain died in 1947, but the rest of the family enjoyed enormous success until they finally packed in the singing in 1956. Since Maria died in 1987, at the ripe old age of 82, the family have been involved in long-running legal disputes, but the lodge is still going strong.

Back in Austria, going on a **guided minibus tour** of the sights associated with the 1965 film *The Sound of Music* has become an essential part of the Salzburg experience for many visitors, even if only to wallow in kitsch in the company of other English-speaking tourists. There's little to choose between the two companies currently offering tours: Panorama Tours (☎0662/874029, *www.panoramatours.at*) and Salzburg Sightseeing Tours (☎0662/881616), both of which have offices on Mirabellplatz. Four-hour-long tours depart twice daily (although transfers from your hotel are usually included in the price), and both offer a similar itinerary, taking Salzburg's Nonnberg Nunnery (see p.387), where Maria was a novice, the Mirabell Gardens (see p.390), where they sing "Do-Re-Mi", the Rock Riding School of the Festspielhaus, where they performed their farewell show, Schloss Leopoldskron, the exterior of which was used to represent the back of the Von Trapp family home, the gardens of Schloss Hellbrunn (see p.391), 5km south of the city centre, where a summerhouse was used as the setting for the song "Sixteen Going on Seventeen", the area around the Fuschlsee, 30km east of Salzburg, where Maria does her "nun run", and the church at nearby Mondsee, (see p.431), used for the wedding scene. All the above places can, of course, be visited without going on a tour.

For those who can't get enough, there's a nightly *Sound of Music* show in the Sternbrau, Griesgasse 23 (☎0662/826617, *soundofmusic@aon.at*; öS520/€37.79 with dinner, öS360/€26.16 without), which basically involves a band performing songs from the film in perfunctory fashion.

cosmopolitan culture in a Europe increasingly dominated by nationalist ideologies, and the conductor Arturo Toscanini, a well-known antifascist, became the Salzburger Festspiele's trademark. After the Anschluss Hitler earmarked Salzburg as an important centre of spiritual and artistic life, and the festival became a propagandistic celebration of folksy Teutonic nationalism. The character of the postwar festival owes much to the energies of Herbert von Karajan, who was the Festspiele's director from 1956 until his death in 1989. Under Karajan's stewardship the festival attracted top performers and became a byword for high artistic standards, but lost some of its pioneering spirit. It also increasingly became a society event from which ordinary concertgoers felt excluded. In the last few years the programme has become more varied and attempts have been made to introduce a wider spread of admission prices, although tickets – especially those for the cheaper seats – sell out fast. Major productions take place in the purpose-built **Festspielhaus**, but other venues around town are pressed into service too. If you're interested in obtaining tickets you should write as far in advance as possible to *Kartenbüro der Salzburger Festspiele*, Postfach 140, A-5020 Salzburg (☎0662/804 5579), or log on to the Web site (*www.salzburgfestival.at*), for programme and booking details.

Salzburg's other major festival, the **Mozartwoche**, spotlights Mozart-penned opera, symphonic and chamber music and takes place every year at the end of January at the Mozarteum. For details, contact the Mozarteum direct at Postfach 34, A-5024 Salzburg (☎0662/873154).

Year-round events: church music and tourist-oriented shows

Sunday morning Mass in Salzburg's bigger churches often features Mozart's sacral compositions: services at the **Domkirche** (at 10am, featuring full choir and cathedral organ) and the **Franziskanerkirche** (at 9am, sometimes featuring full orchestra) are well worth trying. Many churches, including the Domkirche, also offer **organ recitals** throughout the year. Look out for posters or ask the tourist office if there's anything happening during your stay.

There's a whole host of year-round musical events and concerts aimed primarily at **tourists** drawn to the city by its reputation as musical centre, although this by no means indicates that they're some kind of rip-off – standards of musicianship are invariably high. We've listed a selection below.

TOURIST-ORIENTED SHOWS

Mozart Serenades (☎0662/436870, *www.austria.at/mozartserenaden*). In the Gothic Hall of the Blasiuskirche on Bürgerspitalgasse or in the Grosser Saal of the Mozarteum, performances of Mozart favourites and pieces by other eminent Austrians, on Fridays and Saturdays throughout the year.

Mozart Dinner Concerts Popular Mozart pieces performed by musicians in period costume, in the Stiftskeller, St Peter's opulent Baroque function room. Ticket price includes dinner. Daily in summer, 3–4 times weekly in winter. Contact Salzburger Konzertgesellschaft, Nonntaler Hauptstrasse 59/8 (☎0662/828695-0, *www.salzburg-concerts.com*). Tickets from from öS560/€40.88.

Salzburger Festungskonzerte (☎0662/825858, *festungskonz@salburg.co.at*). A small chamber orchestra plays a Mozart greatest-hits package in the Fürstenzimmer of the Hohensalzburg fortress. Performances all year round, and candlelit dinners with music (öS550/€40.15 per head) are sometimes on offer. Contact Direktion der Salzburger Festungskonzerte, A-Adlgasser-Weg 22. The same company organize Rezidenzkonzerte – popular works by Mozart and Johann Strauss performed in the former state rooms of Salzburg's archbishops' palace. Tickets from öS395/€28.84.

Salzburger Marionettentheater Schwarzstrasse 24 (☎0662/872406-0). Popular operas and operettas (usually works by Johann Strauss, Offenbach and Mozart) performed by puppets backed by a playback tape. It can be a bit hard going for younger children, but most adults will marvel at the imaginative set designs and dexterous puppeteering. Tickets from öS250/€18.25.

Schlosskonzerte in the Schloss Mirabell Chamber music with a strong, though not wholly, Mozartean content; performances a couple of times a week throughout the year. Contact Salzburger Schlosskonzerte, Mozarts Wohnhaus, Theatergasse 2 (☎0662/848586, *schlosskonzerte@esp.at*).

SILENT NIGHT

No account of Salzburg's musical heritage would be complete without some reference to **Josef Mohr**, assistant pastor in the nearby village of Oberndorf and author of the words to the hymn **Stille Nacht**, or *Silent Night*. The most-recorded song in musical history was penned on Christmas Eve 1818, when the Oberndorf church organ broke down just before the midnight service. Mohr decided to improvise a simple song that could be performed with a guitar, enlisting the help of the organist Franz-Xaver Gruber who came up with the chords, and *Stille Nacht* was the result.

Popular music, jazz and clubbing

For **rock and pop**, the *Rockhouse*, Schallmooser Hauptstrasse 46 (☎0662/884914, *www.rockhouse.at*; bus #29), is the main venue for medium-sized touring bands. *Kulturgelände Nonntal*, Mühlbacherhofweg 5 (☎0662/848784, *www.kulturgelaende.at*; bus #5 or #55), also features rock, **world music** and alternative theatre. The **alternative** end of the rock spectrum plays a significant part in the **Sommer Szene Festival** in June and July, which also features contemporary dance and experimental theatre. Advance information is available from *Szene*, Anton-Neumayr-Platz 2, A-5020 Salzburg (☎0662/843448-22).

For **jazz**, *The Club*, Anton-Neumayr-Platz 4, holds regular concerts and jam sessions – details on upcoming events are posted outside the door. It's one of the venues pressed into service during the **Salzburger Jazz Herbst** festival in November, which attracts top-ranking performers. Advance programme details are available from Viennaentertainment (☎0222/504 8500; *www.viennaentertainment.com*).

The **clubbing** scene in Salzburg is increasingly varied, with places like *Shakespeare* (see "Restaurants"), *Stadtkino*, *ARGE Nonntal*, and the *Rockhouse Bar* (see "bars") all offering club nights which may well range from off-the-wall avant-garde electronics to mainstream techno. In addition, *The Cave*, Leopoldskronstrasse 5–6 (*www.cave-club.at*), is the city's main specifically techno-trance club with events most Fridays and Saturdays. *Propaganda*, near the Salzburg-Nord exit of the A1 motorway at Hannakstrasse 17, is a large, pack-em-in-at-weekends techno venue, although it's a fair taxi ride from the centre. Expect to pay an entrance fee at all these venues: anything from öS40/€2.92 to öS140/€10.22 depending on what DJs are appearing.

To find out what's going on, scour the pages of *Stadt Leben*, look out for street posters, or pick up flyers from the Musikladen record shop at Linzergasse 58.

Theatre

Salzburg has one of Austria's most prestigious dramatic institutions in the shape of the Salzburger Landestheater, the city's main venue for top-quality, serious work. Drama also plays an important part in the **Salzburg Festival** (see "Classical music", p.396), most notably in the annual production of Hugo von Hoffmannsthal's *Jedermann* (an adaptation of the medieval English mystery play *Everyman*) on an outdoor stage in the Domplatz for the duration of the Festival. Seats are usually sold out weeks in advance, but tickets for standing places are sold on the day (see above for ticket outlets).

For non-German speakers, the drawback of most drama in Salzburg is the language, although some of the more avant-garde work can be visually interesting enough to make knowledge of the language irrelevant. Venues include: the **Kleines Theater**, Schallmooser Hauptstrasse 50 (☎0662/872154; bus #29), for cabaret and comedy; **Kulturgelände Nonntal**, Mühlbacherhofweg 5 (☎848784, *www.kulturgelaende.at*), for experimental theatre; **Elizabethbühne**, fifteen minutes' walk south of the Altstadt at Erzabt-Klotz-Strasse 22 (☎0662/8085-85, *www.ebuehne.at*), for a mixture of mainstream and experimental drama; and the **Salzburger Landestheater**, Schwarzstrasse 22 (☎0662/871512, *www.theater.co.at*), for classic German-language drama in its main auditorium, and smaller productions/fringe in its Kammerspiele studio theatre.

Listings

Adventure sports Crocodile Sports, Gaisbergerstrasse 34a (☎0662/642907, *office@crocodile-sports .com*), organize paragliding, canyoning, caving, mountain biking, ballooning.

Airlines Austrian Airlines (also serving Lauda Air and Tyrolean Airways), at the airport (☎0662/854511); British Airways, Griesgasse 29 (☎0662/842108); Lufthansa, Rainbergstrasse 3a (☎0662/800 900 800).

Airport information ☎0662/8580-251, *www.salzburg-airport.at*.

American Express Mozartplatz 5–7 (Mon–Fri 9am–5.30pm, Sat 9am–noon; ☎0662/8080-146, *www.amex.co.at*).

Bike rental At counter #3 in the main train station. Open 24hr.

Books Amadeus, Getreidegasse 5 (next door to Mozart's Geburtshaus), has English-language paperbacks on the 2nd floor, and loads of tourist-related titles on the ground floor.

Car rental Avis, Ferdinand-Porsche-Strasse 7 (☎0662/877278), and at the airport (☎0662/877278); Budget, at the airport (☎855038); Hertz, Rainerstrasse 17 (☎0662/873452), and at the airport (☎0662/852094).

Cinemas Current international films, usually dubbed into German, are shown at Central, Linzergasse 17–19 (☎0662/872283), and Mozartkino, Kaigasse 33 (☎0662/842222). Das Kino, Giselakai 11 (☎873100, *www.daskino.at*), is the place to go for art-house and cult films often in the original language.

Consulates UK, Alter Markt 4 (Mon–Fri 9am–noon; ☎0662/848133); USA, Alter Markt 1–3 (Mon, Wed & Fri 9am–noon; ☎0662/848776). Other nationals should contact their embassy in Vienna.

Dentists Dentistenkammer, Gstättengasse 21 (☎584377-7), will recommend a dentist.

Exchange Banks are open Mon–Fri 8.30am–12.30pm & 2–4.30pm. Outside these hours, you can try the exchange counter at the main train station (May–Sept 7am–9pm; Oct–April 7.30am–8.30pm); Salzburger Sparkasse at the airport (daily 8am–4pm); or the exchange counter on Alte Markt (July–Oct Mon–Fri 8.30am–4.30pm, Sat 9.30am–1pm; Nov–June Mon–Fri only).

Gay organizations HOSI (Homosexuelle Initiative), Müllner Hauptstrasse 11 (☎0662/435927, *www.hosi.or.at*).

Hospital St Johannsspital, north of the Altstadt at Müllner Hauptstrasse 48 (☎4482).

Ice skating Städtische Kunsteisbahn, on the right bank at Hermann-Bahr-Promenade 2 (open mid-Sept to March; buses #6 or #49 from Rudolfskai to Volksgartenbad). Entry öS45/€3.29, skate hire öS35/€2.56.

Internet access Internet Café, Mozartplatz (daily 10am–10pm; öS60/E4.38 per 30min); Piterfun, diagonally opposite the railway station at Ferdinand-Porsche-Strasse 7 (daily 11am–11pm; öS40/€2.91 per 30min).

Laundry Norge Exquisit, Paris-Lodron-Strasse 14 (Mon–Fri 7.30am–6pm, Sat 8am–noon).

Left luggage Lockers at the main train station (from öS20/€1.46).

Lost property Fundbüro, Alpenstrasse 90 (Mon–Fri 7.30am–12.30pm).

Motoring organizations ARBÖ ☎0662/433601, emergency service ☎123.

Police The main police station is 4km south of the centre, in the direction of the Salzburg-Süd autobahn junction, at Alpenstrasse 90 (☎0662/6383).

Post office The main post office is at Residenzplatz 9 (Mon–Fri 7am–7pm, Sat 8–10am); the branch at the train station is open daily (6am–11pm).

Pharmacies are open Mon–Fri 8am–12.30pm & 2.30–6pm, Sat 8am–noon. Elisabeth-Apotheke, Elisabethstrasse 1 (☎0662/871484), is near the train station. For emergencies, details of duty pharmacies are posted in all pharmacy windows.

Sightseeing tours Horse-drawn fiacres offer sightseeing tours of the Altstadt; a 25min ride should cost around öS400/€29.20 per four-person carriage. For coach tours, Panorama Tours, Mirabellplatz, by St Andrä church (☎874029, *www.panoramatours.at*), offer introductory city tours (hourly, lasting 1hr; öS200/€14.60), tours of the salt mines in Berchtesgaden, Germany (twice daily, lasting 4hr; öS480/€35.04), and Sound of Music tours (twice daily, lasting 4hr; öS400/€29.20); Salzburg Sightseeing Tours, Mirabellplatz 2 (☎881616, *sightseeing-tours@salzburg.co.at*), offer city tours (3 daily, lasting 2hr; öS300/€21.90), tours of the salt mines in Hallein (2 daily, lasting 4hr; öS500/€36.50) and Sound of Music tours (2 daily, lasting 4hr; öS400/€29.20). Bob's Special Tours, Kaigasse 10 (☎0662/8495-11, *bobs-special-tours@net4you.co.at*) also do Sound of Music tours (4hr; öS360/€26.28.

Swimming Paracelsus Bad, Auerspergstrasse 2, is a large, modern indoor pool complete with water jets, water slide and children's section; a solarium, mud baths and a nudist sunbathing terrace are also on the premises. Open-air pools (May–Sept) include Freibad Leopoldskron, 1km south of the centre at Leopoldskronstrasse 50 (bus #55 from Mirabellplatz) and Freibad Volksgarten, on the right bank at Hermann-Bahr-Promenade 2 (buses #6 or #49 from Rudolfskai).

Taxis There are taxi ranks at the main train station, F-Hanusch-Platz, Residenzplatz and Makartplatz. Or phone ☎8111 or 1715.

Train information ☎1717.

Travel agents ÖKISTA, Wolf-Dietrich-Strasse 31 (☎0662/883252, *www.oekista.co.at*); Young Austria, Alpenstrasse 108a (☎0662/625758-0, *www.youngaustria.at*).

Women's organizations Frauenkulturzentrum, Elisabethstrasse 11 (☎0662/871639).

THE SALZBURGER LAND

South of Salzburg, most of the attractions in the province that bears its name are of the outdoor variety, providing an alpine counterweight to the urban refinements of the Land capital. Many travellers heading for Innsbruck and the west miss out on this area altogether, following instead the direct route, which cuts through a corner of Germany before re-entering Austria at Kufstein in the Tyrol. An alternative, and worthwhile, road and rail route forges its way south, however, up the **Salzach Valley** through an area of increasingly rugged mountains. The salt mines and Celtic museum at **Hallein**, and the ice caves and castle at **Werfen** are the main destinations here, and both towns' sites can be treated as day-trips from Salzburg. At **Bischofshofen**, the main Salzach Valley route veers west towards **St Johann im Pongau**, an important skiing and hiking centre, before continuing to **Zell am See**, a classic lakes-and-mountains resort that provides the perfect base from which to strike south into the mountains of the **Hohe Tauern**, home to Austria's highest peak, the magisterial **Grossglockner**.

Bischofshofen also provides the gateway to the southeastern corner of the Salzburger Land: if you're en route to Styria, you might consider stopping off at the ski resort of **Radstadt** or the sleepy, folklore-rich village of **Tamsweg**. South of St Johann, the **Gasteinertal** centres on the evocative nineteenth-century spa resort of **Badgastein**, ideally placed for explorations of the eastern Hohe Tauern.

Accessing the region by **rail** couldn't be easier: four daily Salzburg–Innsbruck expresses stop at Hallein, St Johann and Zell am See, while an equal number of Salzburg–Villach trains run through the Gasteinertal (otherwise, get a train to Schwarzach-St Veit and change there), and Salzburg–Graz trains go through Radstadt (otherwise, change at Bischofshofen).

Hallein and around

Twenty kilometres south of Salzburg and served by regular bus and train services, the market town of **HALLEIN** has been synonymous with the **salt trade** since the sixth century BC. Celts from Hallstatt in the Salzkammergut opened up the salt mines in the hills around Bad Dürrnberg, immediately west of Hallein and, apart from a period of abandonment following the departure of the Romans from the region in the fifth century, the mines have been the dominant factor in the town's development ever since. While commercial salt extraction came to an end here in 1989, since then tours of the **Bad Dürrnberg show-mine** have constituted one of the biggest tourist attractions in the region. The historic centre of Hallein itself is picturesque enough to warrant a leisurely stroll, and the local museum has one of the country's richest collections of **Celtic artefacts**. Together Hallein and Bad Dürrnberg make a popular day-trip from Salzburg.

The Town

Hallein's historic importance as a salt-processing and distribution point is still in evidence in the centre's charming town houses, which once belonged to the wealthy merchants who controlled the trade. This clutch of tastefully restored seventeenth-century buildings, resplendent in shades of blue and salmon pink, line the compact, pedestrianized squares that form the core of the town – **Unterer Markt**, **Oberer Markt**, **Bayrhamerplatz** and **Kornsteinplatz**.

Hallein's **Celtic heritage** is the main attraction at the **Stadtmuseum** (May–Oct daily 9am–5pm; öS60/€4.38), a few steps north of Oberer Markt at Pflegerplatz 5. Housed in the former Saltzkammer, from which the salt trade was administered, the museum holds a well-presented collection of earthenware, daggers and bronze jewellery (labelled in German). The star exhibit is undoubtedly the *Schnabelkanne*, or beaked jug, of Dürrnberg, found in a princely grave near the salt mine, and decorated with a stylized leonine beast (a possible representation of the Celtic god Taranis) with a human head in its mouth. The next floor up concentrates on the history of the salt industry from the Middle Ages onwards, with models of the brine pipelines that brought the dissolved salt down from the mountain, the salt-panning workshops, which once stood on an island in the River Salzach, and the boats that ferried the stuff downstream. All stages of the production process feature in a cycle of eighteenth-century paintings, covering the walls of three rooms originally decorated for Sigismund III Graf von Schrattenbach, penultimate Prince-Archbishop of Salzburg.

Bad Dürrnberg

Eight buses a day (hourly in the morning, less frequently mid-afternoon) connect Hallein train station with **BAD DÜRRNBERG**, a hillside village immediately above town to the west. Providing a more direct route than the five-kilometre road journey, the **Salzbergbahn** cable car (öS130/€9.49 return, öS270/€219.71 including entry to the show-mine) is a five-minute walk to the southwest of Hallein town centre.

Tours of the local **salt mine** (daily April–Oct 9am–5pm; Nov–March 11am–3pm; öS100/€7.30) last about ninety minutes and begin with a ride on the **Grubenhunt**, or underground train, followed by a sound-and-light show introducing the history of the mine, and a descent to lower galleries via a wooden slide – a mode of transport characteristic of Austrian mines, rather akin to sitting astride a large banister and letting yourself go (and explaining why the *Arschleder* is such a common feature of traditional Austrian mining uniforms). Further highlights include a trip across an underground lake on a wooden raft, and a glimpse of the "Man in the Salt", the well-kept body of a medieval miner preserved on the spot where it was found.

It's thought that the **Celts** of Hallstatt (see p.447) opened up Dürrnberg as a centre of salt production some 2500 years ago, partly because their Hallstatt mines were increasingly liable to rock falls and floods, but also due to the excellent transport opportunities afforded by the River Salzach in the valley below. Up until the arrival of the

Romans, a Celtic community thrived beside the mine workings, now remembered in the open-air **Keltenmuseum** (April–Oct daily 9am–5pm; included in mine ticket; öS50/€3.65 on its own) outside the mine entrance. Alongside replicas of Iron Age huts and barns is the reconstruction of a princely grave, showing how the sumptuously clad body of the deceased would have been laid out on a chariot and surrounded by the weapons, drinking flasks and food necessary for a journey to the afterlife.

Surrounded by alpine meadows, Bad Dürrnberg is also a good spot for **walking** – a chairlift at the western end of the village ascends to a café-restaurant just below the summit of the 1337-metre-high Zinken, which marks the border between Austria and Bavaria.

Practicalities

The main north–south road and rail routes keep to the east bank of the River Salzach; Hallein's historic centre is over on the west bank. From the **train station**, it's a straightforward westward walk to the river, where the bridge leading across into the old town passes the **tourist office** on the Pernerinsel island (Mon–Fri 8.30am–5pm; ☎06245/85394, *www.hallein-tourism.at*). Here accommodation in **private rooms** (①) can be arranged, a few of which are in Hallein itself, though most are above the town in Bad Dürrnberg. There's a shortage of decent **hotels** in the centre, although *Bockwirt*, near the tourist office at Thunstrasse 12 (☎06245/80623; ③; closed Nov), has atmospheric rooms in a historic building in the old town; while *Hafnerwirt*, handily placed for the train station on the east side of the river at Bundesstrasse Süd 3 (☎06245/80319, *www.hafnerwirt.at*; ③), is a good-value three-star establishment, offering plain rooms with en-suite facilities, and more expensive ones with TV and phone. Up in Bad Dürrnberg near the salt mines, *Hochdürrnberg*, Rumpelgasse 14 (☎06245/75183; ②), is a small pension offering cosy rooms with shared facilities. There's a **youth hostel** at Schloss Wispach, a restored stately home fifteen minutes north of the train station (☎06245/80397; April–Sept only), with dorm beds from öS180/€13.14 per person, a few doubles (①), and cut-price entry to the open-air swimming pool next door.

Most conveniently central of the **eating** venues is *Unterholzerbräu*, Oberhofgasse 4, a traditional Gasthof offering a wide range of inexpensive *Knödel* and *Gröstl* dishes, together with slightly more costly schnitzels. *Café-Bistro Puppet*, two minutes' southeast of the centre at Griesplatz 8, is a funky, youngish restaurant offering a mixed Austrian–Italian menu; while *Tepito*, beside the *Hafnerwirt* hotel (you'll pass it on the way into town from the station), serves Mexican food and steaks in lively surroundings. The latter two are also good for evening **drinking**; otherwise try *Fallschirm* on Oberer Markt, an informal, friendly place that's usually open until 2am.

Werfen and around

Forty kilometres south of Salzburg, the village of **WERFEN** draws day-trippers from the provincial capital to see two very different attractions: the impressive, fanciful Hohenwerfen **fortress** presiding over the village itself, and the **Eisriesenwelt**, giant ice caves in the mountainside to the northeast. Werfen is fairly easy to get to, though not all southbound express trains from Salzburg stop here – check before you travel – and you do need to allow plenty of time to reach the caves if doing the trip by public transport. Provided you set off reasonably early, you should be able to see both the caves and the fortress in the space of a day.

Werfen itself comprises a single street and a clutch of *Gasthöfe* and shops, but its impressive geographical situation, in a valley wedged between sheer, rocky mountains, makes it an evocative place to stay for a night or two. There's a **tourist office** (Mon–Fri 8am–noon & 2–5pm, Sat 8am–noon; ☎06468/5388, *www.werfen.at*) on the main street with a small list of **private rooms** (①). The nearby *Gasthof Obauer*, Hauptstrasse 46 (☎06486/212-0; ④), is a medieval house that has modern rooms with en-suite shower and WC. Also on the main street, the *Goldener Hirsch*, Hauptstrasse 28 (☎06486/5342; ③) has simpler en suites. The **restaurant** at the *Obauer* is the place to go for Austrian/Modern European cuisine and has a nationwide reputation for gourmet excellence, while the cheaper *Goldener Hirsch* has all the usual schnitzels, and the *Alte Post*, also on the Hauptstrasse, offers an acceptable range of pizzas.

Hohenwerfen fortress

Immediately visible from all points of arrival, and a brisk fifteen-minute walk from Werfen train station, the **fortress** of Hohenwerfen (April & Oct 9am–4.30pm; May, June & Sept 9am–5pm; July & Aug 9am–6pm; öS110/€8.03) dominates the village from a rocky outcrop to the north. Subjected to a cycle of sackings, fires and rebuildings, the fortress has changed immeasurably since Salzburg's Archbishop Gebhard von Felsenstein first fortified the spot as insurance against Bavarian incursions in the eleventh century. The obligatory guided tour (in German with English summary, frequency depends on demand) takes you from an impressive inner courtyard to the chapel, where Gothic fresco fragments depicting the Apocalypse are preserved, before passing through state rooms and a torture chamber to the belfry, which offers impressive views of the Salzach Valley and the encroaching craggy peaks. The small **museum of falconry** at the fortress entrance anticipates the bird-of-prey flying displays that take place on the knoll above (mid-July to mid-Aug at 11am, 2pm & 4pm; mid-Aug to Oct & April to mid-July at 11am & 3pm).

The ice caves

Getting to the **Eisriesenwelt** is a scenic excursion in itself, involving a road and cable-car ascent to reach the cave entrance 1641m above the valley floor, and providing views back towards Werfen and the castle. A bus from Werfen train station (currently departing at 8.15am, 10.35am, 12.35pm & 2.35pm; öS70/€5.11 return; the driver sells a combined ticket covering bus, cable car and cave for öS270/€19.71) takes you uphill as far as the car park at the road's end (also accessible by private car) 5km above Werfen to the northeast; from there it's a ten-minute walk to the cable-car station (öS120/€8.76 return). The caves are only accessible by 75-minute guided tour (usually hourly, more frequently at peak periods; daily July & Aug 9.30am–4.30pm; May–June & Sept–Oct 9.30am–3.30pm; öS90/€6.57), which leads past some spectacular ice formations, diving through narrow passageways (involving some steep climbs) before emerging into breathtaking, imaginatively lit galleries. It's cold enough to warrant a sweater or jacket, so come prepared.

Central Salzburger Land

Eight kilometres south of Werfen, there's a parting of the ways at Bischofshofen, as one rail line heads westwards to **St Johann im Pongau**, Zell am See and the Tyrol, and the other turns eastwards towards Styria, running along the wide valley floor of the Ennstal with the magnificent ridge of the **Niedere Tauern** range rising to the south. Just short of the Styrian border lies **Radstadt**, an attractive historical town and skiing centre. The A10 autobahn also leaves the Salzach Valley near Bischofshofen, veering southeast across the western shoulder of the Niedere Tauern towards the **Tauerntunnel** and Carinthia. Minor roads just before the Carinthian border head into the upper Mur Valley in the far southeastern corner of the Salzburger Land, where pasture-covered hills shelter attractive villages such as **Tamsweg**, an alternative starting point for onward routes into Styria.

Radstadt

Midway between Bischofshofen and the Styrian ski resort of Schladming (see p.310), **RADSTADT** was fortified by the archbishops of Salzburg in the sixteenth century to provide a bulwark against the Turks (who, in fact, never got this far) – partly moated walls punctuated by a series of impressive towers still encompass the town centre. With the Tauern ranged imperiously to the south, it's an undeniably pretty spot, and a popular base for winter sports, but unless you're in this part of Austria to ski it probably merits only a brief stop.

The obvious thing to do on arrival is to take the fifteen-minute walk around the town walls. Marking the eastern gateway, the **Kapuzinerturm** (June–Sept Mon–Sat 9.30–11.30am & 2–4pm; öS35/€2.56) harbours a smallish display of medieval weaponry. West of here is the Romanesque **Pfarrkirche**, with wonderfully expressive postwar stained glass by Josef Wildmoser depicting scenes from the Life of the Virgin. Ten minutes' walk west of the centre, the **Heimatmuseum** in Schloss Lerchen (June to mid-Oct 10am–noon & 3–5pm; late Dec to April 10–11.30am & 3–4.30pm; öS50/€3.65) has the usual collection of local costumes and crafts, as well as an exhibition on local geology.

Practicalities

Radstadt's **train station** is five minutes' walk from the town centre: turn left out of the station and take the path that strikes off up the hill to the right. Another left turn at the top of the hill will bring you shortly to the Stadtplatz, where there's a **tourist office** (Mon–Sat 8am–noon & 2–6pm; ☎06452/7472, *www.radstadt.com*) next to the Rathaus, with touch-screen accommodation information in an outside lobby (7am–midnight). The tourist office also has a list of **private rooms** (①), though these don't feature among the touch-screen info. Of the local **hotels**, *Gasthof Torwirt*, Hoheneggstrasse 12 (☎06452/5541; ③), is an inexpensive central choice, offering bright, modern rooms with en-suite facilities and TV; a step up in price affords the comfort of the *Sporthotel Radstadt*, just north of the centre at Schlossstrasse 45 (☎06452/5590-0, *www .sporthotel-radstadt.com*; ④), which has an indoor pool and sauna.

A couple of *Gashöfe* on the Stadtplatz offer stolid Austrian lunches, otherwise the best **places to eat** are mostly found along the adjacent Schernbergstrasse, where *Gasthof Stegerbräu* at no. 14 has a wide range of inexpensive Austrian standards, and more costly freshwater fish.

Tamsweg

From Radstadt, the Bundesstrasse 99 (served by local buses) and the A10 autobahn follow roughly parallel routes across the **Radstädter Tauern** range towards the Upper Mur Valley, principal vale of the **Lungau**, an isolated corner of the Salzburger Land where archaic folk traditions have survived. The most spectacular of these is the **Samsonumzug**, or Samson procession, which takes place in **TAMSWEG**, 50km south of Radstadt, on several summer feast days, notably Corpus Christi (**Fronleichnam**, in late May), the last weekend in July and the first Sunday in August. An effigy of Samson, accompanied by two dwarfs and the town band, is paraded through the streets. One theory links the Samson effigy to giant figures constructed by sixteenth-century locals in order to frighten off the Turks, but the procession is more likely the Christianized version of some indecipherable pagan ritual.

The town of Tamsweg itself has a pleasant Marktplatz and a pilgrimage church above to the south. There's a **tourist office** (Mon–Fri 9am–noon & 2–5pm, Sat 9am–1pm; ☎06474/416, *www.tamsweg.at*) in the Rathaus, on the Marktplatz, which will find you a private room or hotel from among the limited options available, but be warned that things can get booked up during festival time. Tamsweg is at the westernmost end of the Murtalbahn, the railway that provides public transport downstream to Murau in Styria (see Chapter 5) and the main Vienna–Klagenfurt line beyond.

St Johann im Pongau

Main town of the **Pongau**, an area of lush alpine pastures that stretches from Bischofshofen in the north to the mouth of the Gasteinertal in the southwest, **ST JOHANN** has become one of Austria's most popular outdoor holiday centres. Together with **Alpendorf**, the hotel-filled village suburb 3km uphill to the southeast, it offers a wide range of sporting activities year-round, and it's these that constitute the main reason for being here. In wintertime, it's a much-favoured destination among European **skiers** (it features only intermittently in British package-holiday brochures). When the snow has melted, the slopes cater to an influx of **walkers**, while **swimming** and **tennis** are the summertime activities of choice in town.

The Town and around

Stretched along the eastern side of the River Salzach, St Johann is divided into two parts, **Obermarkt**, built on a bluff surmounted by the distinctive twin towers of the Domkirche, and **Untermarkt** on the river bank below it. You might think the place looks comparatively modern and charmless, and that's because it was largely destroyed by fire in 1855, so little of real vintage survives. People from all across the Habsburg monarchy raised money to rebuild the church, hence its current, neo-Gothic appearance.

For those who have come to ski, local passes (one-day öS390/€28.47; six-day öS1640/€119.72) cover a large area of interlinked pistes and lifts – known as the Sportwelt Amadé – which extends from St Johann, through the nearby villages of Wagrain and Flachau as far as Radstadt (see p.405) 25km to the east. Slopes are best suited to beginners and intermediates. For summer walkers, the most direct route to

---

THE PONGAUER PERCHTENLAUF

One of Austria's oddest midwinter folk rituals, the **Pongauer Perchtenlauf** takes place on the night of January 5–6. It's an annual event that is shared by the Pongau towns of Altenmarkt, Bischofshofen, Badgastein and St Johann, each of which takes a turn hosting the festival on a four-year cycle.

The Perchtenlauf revolves around a procession of young men dressed in the white costumes and masks of the *Schiachperchten*, kindly spirits who wave birch twigs and jangle cowbells in order to ward off demons and herald a year full of bumper harvests and good fortune. They're accompanied by *Schönperchten* who wear enormous head-dresses, some of which weigh up to 50kg, their finery designed to bring light to a world subsumed in midwinter darkness. Some head-dresses are decorated with mirrors, to scare away evil spirits afraid of seeing their own reflection. Performances of the Perchtenlauf are traditionally an all-male affair, which – seeing as the Schönperchten are supposed to be accompanied by young wenches – inevitably involves a certain amount of cross-dressing.

The Pongauer Perchtenlauf takes place in Badgastein in 2002, Altenmarkt in 2003, Bischofshofen in 2004 and St Johann in 2005.

the hills is from the village of **Alpendorf**, 3km to the south of St Johann (and accessible by hourly bus), where the Alpendorf Bergbahn gondola (June & July weekends only; Aug to mid–Sept daily; öS85/€6.21 return) leads up onto the pasture-covered slopes of the Gernkogel, from where a chairlift (same times; öS40/€2.92 return) continues to the 1787-metre summit.

Nestling in a wooded valley 5km south of St Johann, the **Liechtensteinklamm** (mid-May to Oct daily 8am–5pm; öS35/€2.56) is, by virtue of its extreme depth and narrowness, one of the most dramatic gorges in the Alps. The gorge is accessed by means of wooden walkways wedged against the sheer rock walls; with the torrent frothing energetically far below, it's an exhilarating trip. The gorge is easy to reach on foot in about an hour: from St Johann head south to the village of Plankenau, where signposted roads and paths bear off to the right; from Alpendorf, a footpath at the southern end of the village leads down to the gorge.

Practicalities

Both the main Bundesstrasse and the **train station** are on the west bank of the Salzach, on the opposite side of the river to the town itself. Turn left outside the train station and cross the river to reach the snaking Hauptstrasse, which curls round Untermarkt before climbing into Obermarkt, site of the **tourist office** (Mon–Fri 8.30am–noon & 2–6pm, Sat 9am–noon; ☎06412/6036, *www.stjohann.co.at*). The tourist office handles **private rooms** (summer ①; winter ②) in both St Johann and Alpendorf, as well as farmhouse accommodation (①) in neighbouring villages – although you'll probably need your own transport to get to the latter.

There are two **youth hostels** in the suburb of **Plankenau** 2km south of town on the way to the Liechtensteinklamm: *Plankenauer Hof*, Liechtensteinklammstrasse 126 (☎06412/8076); and *Schlosshof*, Liechtensteinklammstrasse 144 (☎06412/6394). St Johann's two well-appointed **campsites** are both open all year round: *Wieshof* (☎06412/8519) is nearest the train station, in Untermarkt just off the road to Plankenau, and *Hirschenwirt* (☎06412/6012) lies at the southern end of town, signposted off the Bundesstrasse.

Best value of the **hotels** are the *Lechner*, Kasernstrasse 26 (☎06412/4262; ③), a cosy downtown hotel in Untermarkt, all of whose rooms come with en-suite facilities, and *Sonnhof*, Alpendorf 16 (☎06412/7271, *www.hotel-sonnhof-at*; summer ③; winter ④), a smallish B&B-style place up the hill in Alpendorf offering buffet breakfast, plus sauna and solarium facilities, together with a range of four- and six-person apartments (①). *Sporthotel Prem*, Premweg 7 (☎06412/6315-0, *www.prem.at*; ⑤) is a top-of-the-range hotel in Obermarkt offering outdoor pool, indoor and outdoor tennis courts, and tennis courses run by an Australian coaching team.

Restaurants offering meat-and-two-veg Austrian dishes abound in St Johann: the *Braugasthof*, Hauptstrasse 22, is the best place in which to sample local cuisine at reasonable prices, with rustic wooden tables and chairs lending the place a homely, beer-hall atmosphere. *Bologna*, midway between Ober- and Untermarkt at Dr-Untersteiner-Weg 6, is an inexpensive Italian with a good selection of pasta dishes and pizzas; while *Lotus*, on Hauptstrasse in Untermarkt, is a bright and roomy Chinese with a good-value Mittagsmenü.

Tschecherl, Wagrainerstrasse 4, is a popular smart but relaxed **drinking** venue in Obermarkt which is usually busy all year round. The nearby *Titanik*, hidden away below the church at Spitalgasse 4, is a small and friendly place that fills up in winter. Up the hill in Alpendorf, *Oberforsthoferalm* is a year-round drinking and dancing venue, frequently featuring live music (usually folk), and attracting a youngish, partying crowd from all over the Salzburger Land.

The Gasteinertal

West of St Johann im Pongau, a main road and rail route splits off to head south up the **Gasteinertal**, before tunnelling under the **Hohe Tauern** mountains into Carinthia. Popular with skiers and a paradise for hikers, the Gasteinertal was developed as a centre for tourism early in the nineteenth century, when the **hot springs** of Badgastein attracted an influx of wealthy Central Europeans eager to take the cure. Still the valley's main centre, **Badgastein** remains one of Austria's most eccentric resorts, a stately cluster of nineteenth-century hotels catering to a strange mixture of mountain-bound outdoors enthusiasts and spa patients. Lower down the valley, the spa town of **Bad Hofgastein** has a more modern feel, while spa-free **Dorfgastein** is small, tranquil and rural by comparison. All three provide access to the surrounding mountains, although Badgastein and its two satellites, **Böckstein** and **Sportgastein**, nestling beneath the eastern spur of the Hohe Tauern, stand closest to the really spectacular alpine terrain. At the entrance to the valley, the cave at **Klammstein** makes for an interesting stop-off.

As far as **winter sports** are concerned, the slopes in the Gasteinertal offer a wider range of possibilities than anywhere else in the Salzburger Land save for Zell am See–Kaprun (see p.414). There's a variety of pistes suitable for beginners and intermediates above Dorfgastein, Bad Hofgastein, Badgastein and in the Angertal (a side-valley located between Bad Hofgastein and Badgastein), many of which are connected to each other by the chairlift network. There's enough to keep experienced skiers happy here too: Sportgastein offers off-piste skiing, and there are several black runs on the Graukogel just above Badgastein. Snowboarders are well catered for with half-pipes at Sportgastein, Badgastein and Dorfgastein, and there are snowboarding schools at all the valley's main centres. In addition, there are numerous cross-country skiing routes along the whole of the valley, notably around Hofgastein. The **Gastein Super Ski pass** (öS830/€60.59 for 2 days; öS2050/€149.65 for 6 days; öS3690/€269.37 for 13 days; other durations available) covers all lifts and buses in the Gasteinertal and is available from all lift stations.

Although the main Carinthia-bound **rail line** runs up the Gasteinertal, leaving the main Salzach Valley route at Schwarzach-St Veit, most express trains only stop at Badgastein itself, and **buses** present the best way of getting around once you're here.

Klammstein and Dorfgastein

Regional train services, as well as buses from Badgastein, stop at **KLAMMSTEIN** at the entrance to the valley, where the **Naturhöhle** (guided tours on the hour; Aug 10am–6pm; late March to July & Sept to mid-Oct 11am–3pm; closed Mon; öS110/€8.03) was once used by local Protestants for clandestine prayer. The chamber where they used to meet has been dubbed the **Fledermaus-Dom**, or bat cathedral. The cave entrance is off the main road to the east, about 45min by foot from the well-signposted car park. A visit to the hunting trophies and mineral display at the nearby sixteenth-century **Burg Klammstein** (45min tours at 2pm; Tues–Sun; öS45/€3.29) is less interesting, although kids might enjoy the **Gespensterschau**, or ghost show, a series of tableaux illustrating the spirits said to inhabit the nearby cave.

Ten kilometres up the valley, the attractive and quiet village of **DORFGASTEIN** lacks the thermal springs that supply the settlements to the south, and consequently tourism here is relatively low-key. Things liven up slightly in the winter, due to the village's nascent reputation as a good snowboarding area. Above the village to the east, there's a two-stage lift (chairlift to the mid-station, then gondola) to the 2033m Fulseck, and in the village centre are a number of small *Gasthöfe* and a **tourist office** (Mon–Fri 8am–noon & 2–6pm, Sat 8am–noon; ☎06433/7277) that has a list of **private rooms** (summer ②; winter ③).

Bad Hofgastein

Lacking both the rural charms of Dorfgastein and the post-imperial splendours of Badgastein, **BAD HOFGASTEIN** is a predominantly modern spa resort fed by the waters piped down from the head of the valley, its clinic-like hotels grouped around a pedestrianized centre bordered by leafy parks. There's nothing of any vintage save for the late-Gothic **Pfarrkirche** on the main square. Inside, the high altar features an early sixteenth-century Madonna and Child by a follower of Michael Pacher, flanked by contrasting eighteenth-century statuettes – featuring, from left to right, ss Rupert, Dominic, Catherine and Virgil. The whole thing is topped off by an allegory of the Holy Trinity after plans by **Fischer von Erlach** – the Father is on the right holding a globe, the Son on the left, and the Holy Spirit hovering between them in the form of a dove. Note, too, the cherub-bedecked pulpit featuring another traditional piece of symbolism common in areas once strongly Protestant – the outstretched arm holding a crucifix, depicting the triumph of the Catholic Church.

On the western side of the town centre, a direct route into the hills is provided by the **Schlossalmbahn** (June to mid-Oct & Dec–April 8am–4pm on the hour; ascent öS160/€11.68, return öS200/€14.60), which climbs in two stages: by funicular to the 1302-metre **Kitzstein Alm**, then by cable car to the 2051-metre **Kleine Scharte**, where there's a mountain café-restaurant and impressive views of the peaks over on the opposite side of the valley. About 1km south of the funicular station, roads ascend into the **Angertal**, an important skiing area in winter and attractive walking area in summer – but bear in mind the gondola and chairlifts here are only open during the winter season.

Practicalities

The main **train station** is 3km north of town, and most arrivals are met by a local bus which takes you into the centre. There's a smaller station, **Bad Hofgastein Haltestelle**, much nearer the town centre, but only regional trains stop here. The town's **bus station**, served by regular Badgastein–Zell am See and Badgastein–Schwarzach services, is just 1km west of the centre on the main road through the valley. The **tourist office** in the pedestrianized zone (Mon–Fri 8am–6pm, Sat 9am–noon; ☎06432/7110-0, *www.badhofgastein.com*) offers a deluge of information

---

TAKING THE CURE: BADGASTEIN

Badgastein owes its reputation as a health resort to an abundant supply of hot spring water rich in **radon**, a radioactive gas reputed to help the human body renew itself by stimulating cell growth. The medical establishment is far from united on the true efficacy of the spa water (it has been promoted as a cure for everything from diabetes to infertility over the years), although its beneficial effect on rheumatism and arthritis is incontrovertible – and, like any good bath, it's a great way to beat stress.

The easiest way to sample the soothing properties of the waters is to head for the town's main swimming pool, the Felsenbad on Bahnhofplatz (daily 9am–8pm; öS160/€11.68), which has both indoor and outdoor pools fed by spa water. The adjoining Kurhaus (Mon–Fri 8am–noon & 2–5pm) is probably the best place in which to try out some of the more obvious treatments, like a soak in a thermal bath (öS200/€14.60) or a massage (from öS220/€16.06).

Numerous other healing institutions exist offering a seemingly endless range of specific therapies involving the spa water – steam baths, radon mudpacks and mouthwash treatments being just a few, as well as exposure to radon in the underground Healing Galleries (see p.414). The Badgastein tourist office will happily supply details of these.

on local spa facilities. Bad Hofgastein isn't as characterful a place to stay as Badgastein up the valley, although the tourist office has innumerable **private rooms** (②), and there are a couple of top-notch spa **hotels**: the five-star *Grand Park*, Kurgartenstrasse 26 (☎06432/6356-0, *www.grandparkhotel-bad-hofgastein.co.at*; ⑨), is bang in the centre and has elegant, balconied rooms together with a thermal pool, massage, sauna and solarium facilities, while *Sporthotel Alpina*, Parkstrasse 13 (☎06432/8475-0, *www.alpina-hotel.com*; summer ⑦; winter ⑧), a good mid-price choice, offers the same facilities but without the fin-de-siècle pretensions.

For **eating**, *Café Röck*, on a small square just west of the church, is good for inexpensive daytime pasta dishes; *Kraut & Rüben*, Pirkerstrasse 3, is a mid-priced vegetarian restaurant; and *Gasthof zur Alten Post*, just outside the Pfarrkirche, serves traditional Austrian food including fish and game and at least one vegetarian choice.

To experience the soothing effect of the **spa waters**, head for the Thermentempel in the centre, a modern indoor pool complex with four thermal spring-fed pools – but it's expensive if all you want is a quick swim (daily 9am–8.30pm; öS160/€11.68).

Badgastein

Ranged across the head of the valley where the **Gasteiner Ache** descends in a series of cascades, the streets of **BADGASTEIN** gaze down on the Gasteinertal like rows of seating in some ancient amphitheatre. Although known as a **spa** since medieval times, Badgastein didn't really take off until the early nineteenth century, when a stream of society figures – led by Archduke Johann (see p.452), who built the *Meranhaus* here in 1828 – descended on the valley to take the cure. Emperor Franz-Josef, Kaiser Wilhelm I of Germany and Bismarck were among those who followed. The town has undergone numerous face-lifts since, although current attempts to turn it back into a chic society resort – complete with stylish hotels, modern congress centre and casino – are less than convincing. Despite the growing number of swanky four-star places, the sight of once-distinguished guesthouses falling into disrepair is a common feature of the Badgastein streets. The languorous, nineteenth-century ambience that still prevails is certainly unique in alpine Austria, however, and you'll find it either appealingly nostalgic or sombrely oppressive. The influx of ski tourists in winter invigorates this strangely ossified place, as do two events in summer that provide an excuse for general partying – the **Sonnwendfeier** on the night of June 21–22, when bonfires are lit on the hills above the valley to mark the summer solstice; and the annual **Strassenfest**, spread over the last weekend in July, featuring food, drink and live music in the streets.

Arrival, information and accommodation

Both **buses** and **trains** come to rest on Bahnhofplatz in the upper part of town; the centre is just downhill to the north. Turn left outside the train station and walk down the hill to reach the **tourist office**, at Kaiser-Franz-Josef-Strasse 1 (July–Sept Mon–Fri 8am–6pm, Sat 10am–noon & 4–6pm, Sun 10am–1pm; Oct–June Mon–Fri 8am–6pm; ☎06434/2531-0, *www.badgastein.at*), where you can buy a local **hiking map** and book into a **private room** (②) in either Badgastein, or **Böckstein** 3km up the valley. There's an HI **youth hostel** five minutes' south of the train station at Ederplatz 2 (signed off the main Böckstein-bound road; ☎06434/2080, *hostel@badgastein.salzburg.co.at*) with doubles (②) and dorm beds from öS190/€13.87.

Many of Badgastein's **hotels** have radon-rich spa waters on the premises (often piped direct to the bath in your room) free of charge, as well as a range of other spa-related services (massages, saunas, mud baths and so on), for which guests pay an extra fee.

HOTELS AND PENSIONS

Grüner Baum, Kötschachtal 25 (☎06434/2516-0, *www.grunerbaum.com*). In an idyllic side-valley 3km east of town, this is a luxurious complex of traditional, farmhouse-style buildings, complete with wooden balconies, grouped around a central hotel built to look like a historic Gasthof. Facilities include an open-air pool, tennis courts, a children's play area and spa waters on site. Summer ⑧; winter ⑨.

Haus Hirt, An der Kaiserpromenade (☎06434/2797, *www.haus-hirt.com*). A large villa that was once the favoured retreat of Thomas Mann, offering indoor pool, sauna, solarium. Spa waters on site. On the Kaiser-Wilhelm-Promenade, so a nice base for walks. Some rooms have excellent views of the valley. Summer ⑤; winter ⑦.

Krone, Bahnhofplatz 8 (☎06434/2330-0, *www.hotelkrone.at*). An old-fashioned cure-oriented hotel with long dark corridors, 1950s furnishings and en-suite facilities. Spa waters on site. Summer ④; winter ⑥.

Landhaus Gletschermühle, Gletschermühlstrasse 7 (☎06434/2097-0, *www.gletschermuehle.at*). Family-run chalet-style pension in a residential area just east of the train station. All rooms have en-suite facilities and TV. Spa waters on site. ④.

Pension Bader, Pyrkerhöhenstrasse 17 (☎06434/2031, *pension-bader@aon.at*). Small, family-run guesthouse in the residential streets east of the train station. All rooms have en-suite shower and WC. ③.

Pension Haussteiner, Schareckstrasse 7 (☎06434/2234). Small pension in residential streets south of the train station. Rooms have shared facilities. ②.

Around town

The main attraction of Badgastein is its situation, its streets zigzagging across the hillside and affording a new vista with every turn. **Kongressplatz** provides a focus of sorts, as the site of the modern Kongresshaus as well as a small museum in **Haus Austria** across the road (mid-May to Sept daily 10.30am–noon & 3.30–6pm; Oct to mid-May Wed 3.30–6pm; öS30/€2.19). The collection is limited to a few stuffed animals and an uninspiring account of gold-mining in Böckstein (see p.412). Immediately east of here the street bridges the Gasteiner Ache, a gushing torrent that cuts through the town. On the other side of the Ache, the main street leads northwards past two churches, the oldest and furthest of which is the fourteenth-century **Nikolaikirche**, where the roof of the short nave is supported by a single pillar. Many of the frescoes, painted in the late fifteenth century – including the image of St Nicholas on the north side of the choir – are badly faded, but look out for the vibrant *Day of Judgement* in the nave, with the dead rising from their tombs, and sinners being shepherded into hell by club-wielding demons.

Into the mountains

In summer you can scale two local peaks, which are also served by cable car. Just east of Badgastein train station, the Stubnerkogelbahn gondola (June to mid-Oct 9am–4pm leaving on the hour; öS180/€13.14 return), ascends to the 2230-metre **Stubnerkogel**, a superb vantage point providing vistas of the three main peaks in the area, with the Grossglockner to the west, the Ankogel to the southeast and the Dachstein to the east. It's also the starting point for numerous hiking trails. On the opposite side of the valley, the Graukogelbahn (July–Sept 9am–6pm leaving on the hour in good weather only; ascent öS155/€11.32, return öS180/€13.14) is a two-stage chairlift to the *Graukogelhütte*, on an alpine meadow some 500m below the 2492-metre-high peak of the **Graukogel** itself. It's an evocative place from which to look out over the wilds of the Hohe Tauern.

For walkers, one of two quick routes out of Badgastein and into the mountains is along the **Kaiser-Wilhelm-Promenade**, which leaves the northeastern end of town to work its way along the hillside, offering extensive views straight down the Gastein valley en route to the Kötschachtal, a side valley shrouded by dense pine forest. After about fifteen minutes the path emerges from the trees to head through the *Grüner Baum* hotel complex before continuing onwards into increasingly desolate alpine territory, with the mountains crowding in on either side. If you're looking for a drink and a snack before heading back into town, the **Himmelwand** hut, twenty minutes beyond the Grüner Baum, or the **Prossau** hut, a further two hours uphill, are reasonable targets to aim for. An alternative walk involves taking the **Erzherzog-Johann-Promenade**, which leaves the Bad Hofgastein road about 100m south of the Badgastein tourist office, and leads round the wooded flanks of the Stubnerkogel, opening up a sweeping panorama of the valley, including the sight of the hotels of Badgastein spilling down the hillside over to the right. After about an hour of gentle climbing the path arrives at the **Angeralm**, a bowl surrounded by mountains, where there's a café-restaurant.

Eating and drinking

Many of the hotels offer good-quality (if not always cheap) **food**, while the town's plentiful restaurants widen your choice of venues. There's a good range of bars for a nighttime **drink**, though some of them are only open in the winter season (early Dec to mid-April), and maybe for a couple of months in the summer (typically July & Aug).

RESTAURANTS

Fischerwirt, Karl-Heinz-Waggerl-Strasse 27. In an old wooden house at the southern end of town, specializing in fish and pizzas. Their Mittagsmenü (öS90/€6.57) is good value.

Jägerhäusl, Kaiser-Franz-Josef-Strasse. Brash city-centre place, serving a wide range of Austrian main dishes and lunchtime snacks in a lively atmosphere.

Kaiserstüberl, Kaiser-Wilhelm-Promenade. Unpretentious mountain-hut-style place, ten minutes out of town on the way up the Kötschachtal. Cheap and hearty snacks such as *Verhackertbrot* (bread and dripping), *Wurst* and *Gröstl*, and good views of the Gastein valley from the terrace.

Villa Solitude, Kaiser-Franz-Josef-Strasse 16. An excellent source of Austrian and Modern European cuisine, although the decor verges on kitsch – you can always escape to the outdoor terrace in summer.

Hofkeller at *Hotel Salzburger Hof*, Grillparzerstrasse 1. Hotel restaurant specializing in fondues and *raclette*, on the pricey side.

CAFÉS AND BARS

Bellevue Alm, on the hill above Kaiser-Franz-Josef-Strasse. A rustic mountain-hut-style venue with accordion-driven folk music and a limited menu of Austrian nibbles.

Eden Pub, Karl-Heinz-Waggerl-Strasse. Best of the central bars, with a convivial, pub atmosphere.

Filou Bier Kneipe, at the northern entrance to town on the main Bad Hofgastein road, near the tourist office. Smart but unpretentious café-bar. Usually open all year-round.

Schafflinger Schialm, at the south end of town on the Böckstein road. Old-time dancing and folk music, starting (in winter) with a tea dance at 5pm and becoming more rowdy as the evening progresses.

Schuh, Karl-Heinz-Waggerl-Strasse. Best of the places for a daytime coffee, with a tempting range of cakes, pastries and ice cream, and an outdoor terrace offering views down the valley.

Böckstein

Four kilometres south of Badgastein, and an easy walk if you follow the Kaiserin-Elisabeth-Promenade, which starts near the Stubnerkogel gondola station, the village of **BÖCKSTEIN** was once a mining settlement devoted to the extraction of gold from the Radhausberg to the southeast. Tucked away on the western side of the village, **Altböckstein** was founded by eighteenth-century Prince-Archbishop of Salzburg

Sigismund von Schrattenbach as a model community for the workers, complete with tenement-like living quarters, village green, and quaint chapel on a knoll. All the buildings have been tastefully restored, and there's a small **museum** in one of the old storehouses (☎06434/4253; mid-May to Sept daily except Mon 10am–noon & 3–6pm; Oct to mid-May by appointment only; öS30/€2.19) displaying old mining equipment, ceremonial uniforms and a model of the **Sackzug**, the rudimentary means by which ore was transported to the valley bottom – sacks of the stuff were tied together and then sent down a wooden chute, with a miner riding on the first sack rather like the pilot of a bobsleigh.

Böckstein's numerous **private rooms** can be booked through the tourist office in Badgastein. Of the handful of **hotels**, the *Rader*, Karl-Imhof-Ring 22 (☎06434/2405; ④), is well appointed, modern and near to the Altböckstein; and the *Achenhaus*, Böckstein 438 (☎06434/3212; ④), is a lovely, chalet-style pension with balconied rooms, a block west of the main road. The *Gasthaus Radhausberg* on the Altböckstein village green serves up excellent mid-priced Austrian **food**, and the *Forellenhof* is a good pizzeria on the road into the village from Badgastein. The *Mühlrad*, at the north end of Böckstein on the Badgastein road, is a wine and beer hall with substantial snack food and occasional live folk music.

Beyond Böckstein: the Heilstollen and Sportgastein

The main road and rail routes head southeast from Böckstein towards the twelve-kilometre-long **Tauern rail tunnel** 1km away, where road vehicles are loaded onto wagons and transported through the tunnel by train. Trains carrying private cars operate from 6.30am to 10.30pm southbound, and from 6am to 10pm northbound; a single journey costs öS190/€13.87, and a return is öS320/€23.36. On the other side of the tunnel, the road winds a scenic descent down the **Mölltal** towards Spittal an der Drau in Carinthia (see Chapter 6).

A toll road, the Gasteiner Alpenstrasse (öS50/€3.65 per person, öS20/€1.46 for bus passengers) heads southwest from Böckstein up the increasingly narrow valley of the **Nassfelder Ache**, whose steep sides are washed by numerous waterfalls, towards the winter sports area of Sportgastein. One kilometre out of Böckstein, you pass the access

---

THE HOHE TAUERN NATIONAL PARK

Established in 1971, the **Hohe Tauern National Park** was mapped out to protect the natural environment around the Hohe Tauern's highest peaks and to keep the building development below at bay. It embraces 1786 square kilometres and straddles the borders of the Salzburger Land, Carinthia and the Tyrol. Austria's highest mountain, the Grossglockner (see p.419) is within the park, as is the spectacular Krimml Falls (see p.421). The Grossglockner Hochalpenstrasse (see pp.418–419) forges a path straight through the area, but otherwise you're only likely to come across the park if you're out walking in the hills above the towns on its fringes – you'll usually encounter a small sign telling you that you're entering the park, accompanied by a short list of dos and don'ts, the most important of which are to stick to marked paths and take all your litter out with you. Among the wildlife encountered within the park are the elusive *Gemse* (chamois) and the ubiquitous *Mummeltier* (marmot). You're not supposed to feed these cute-looking beasts, although tourists invariably do. There are a few *Hütte* within the park boundaries catering for long-distance hikers.

Tourist offices in Badgastein (see p.410), Zell am See (p.414), Heiligenblut (p.359), Matrei (p.368), Kals (p.367) and other centres bordering the park usually have a stock of leaflets detailing hiking routes, flora and fauna.

road to the **Heilstollen**, or "Healing Galleries", 500m up the hill and hidden among the trees. Inside, an underground train ferries patients to radon-rich tunnels with high degrees of humidity in order to treat a variety of ailments, including respiratory diseases and arthritis. The shafts were first dug in the 1940s in an ultimately unsuccessful attempt to find gold and silver ore; those working on the project soon began to report that the atmosphere underground had a beneficial effect on their aches and pains. Nowadays the network of tunnels form a full-scale medical facility working in tandem with the spa hotels in Badgastein, although it's said that you need at least nine trips down (with at least a day's rest between each one) to reap the benefits – thereby discouraging casual visits. If you're interested in trying it, though, a single visit costs öS650/€47.45, and includes a medical check-up followed by an hour in the tunnels (phone at least a day in advance for an appointment: ☎06434/3753-0), but the humidity coupled with the exposure to radon tends to leave you exhausted. There's one daily **bus** from Badgastein train station to the Heilstollen, leaving around 10.30am and returning around 3.30pm. More frequent Badgastein–Sportgastein services pass by the end of the Heilstollen access road.

Five kilometres beyond the Heilstollen, **SPORTGASTEIN**, on the borders of the Hohe Tauern National Park, is a buzzing ski area in winter; in summer, it's little more than a car park, though facing a truly breathtaking amphitheatre of ravine-scarred mountains. Numerous enticing hiking trails radiate outwards from here, and there are a few *Hütte* which open their doors in summer to offer refreshments, including the **Nassfeld Alm** twenty minutes' walk south of the car park.

Zell am See and around

ZELL AM SEE is the quintessential Austrian resort, a compact town of picture-postcard perfection, with a lake on one side and an impressive mountain hinterland on the other. A skiing and hiking centre in its own right, Zell is also within easy striking distance of the Glemmtal resorts of **Saalbach** and **Hinterglemm** to the northwest, while the village of **Kaprun** to the south provides access to year-round glacier skiing below the **Kitzsteinhorn**. Other classic alpine excursions within reach are the two mountain

---

YEAR-ROUND ACTIVITIES IN ZELL AM SEE

The **winter** sports region served by Zell am See and Kaprun offers a wealth of opportunities for skiers of all abilities: the Kitzsteinhorn glacier above Kaprun is predominantly an area for beginners and intermediates, while the Schmittenhöhe (and its mountain neighbours) above Zell has plenty of pistes to keep novices happy, alongside some longish black runs for the advanced skier. There's a snowboard park in Zell and a half-pipe on the Kitzsteinhorn, and the presence of snowboarders making use of the snow-fields of the Kitzsteinhorn in the summer months helps to keep Zell's nightlife buzzing year-round. The season on the Schmittenhöhe runs from early December to mid-April, while the Kitzsteinhorn is skiable for all but the hottest summer months. A one-day ski pass for either Zell am See or the Kitzsteinhorn in the winter high season costs öS435/€31.61, while the *Europa Sportregion* pass covering both places costs öS810/€58.56 for 2 days, öS2050/€148.98 for 6 days and öS3450/€250.72 for 13 days.

The range of **summer** activities on offer is augmented by windsurfing and sailing on the lake, and the chance to try whitewater rafting in the Taxenbach Gorge, 20km to the east of town. Numerous local tour operators arrange trips to Taxenbach (enquire at the Zell am See tourist office for details); expect to pay around öS580/€42.34 (including transfer to the gorge and a 15km trip in a six- or eight-person dinghy).

reservoirs in the shadow of the Kitzsteinhorn, trips along the **Grossglockner Hochalpenstrasse**, which crosses the Hohe Tauern mountains to the south, and the magnificent **Krimml waterfalls** to the west. Two folk traditions with which Zell is associated are the **Krampusläufen** on December 5, when folk wearing demonic masks take to the streets (see below), and the Hogmoar wrestling competition, a 500-year-old trial of strength for local shepherds that takes place on midsummer's day near the summit of the 2117-metre Hundstein, which rises above the lake to the east.

Freytag & Berndt's 1:50,000 Zell am See & Kaprun **map** is the best aid for those eager to explore the region on foot or by bike.

Arrival, information and accommodation

From the **train station**, at the southern end of Zell's central pedestrian zone, it's a five-minute walk northeast to the **tourist office**, at Brucker Bundesstrasse 1 (Mon–Fri 8am–noon & 2–6pm, Sat 8am–noon; ☎06542/770, *www.zellamsee.com*), which is roughly opposite the small **bus station**. The tourist office will help book **private rooms**, either in Zell itself or in the nearby village of Schüttdorf, 2km away at the southern end of the lake. If the office is closed, there's an accommodation information board with courtesy phones outside. Schüttdorf holds the nearest **youth hostel**, the HI *Haus der Jugend*, at Seespitzstrasse 13 (☎06542/57185; to get there from the station, walk southwards along the lakeside path), which has dorm beds from öS180/€13.14 per person, and some doubles (①). Best of the **campsites** is *Seecamp*, 3km out of town at Thumersbacherstrasse 34, on the northern shore of the lake (☎06542/72115).

Hotels and pensions

Alpenrose, Schmittenstrasse 22 (☎06542/72570, *alpenrose.gruber@magnet.at*). Largish pension just uphill from the centre offering slightly cramped rooms, although all are en suite with TV, and there's a decent buffet breakfast. ③.

Gasthof Schmittental, Schmittenstrasse 60 (☎06542/72332, *www.schmittental.at*). Traditional alpine-style building 1km west of the town centre on the way to the Schmittenhöhebahn. There's a big garden, and all rooms have en-suite facilities and TV. Summer ③; winter ④.

Grand, Esplanade 4 (☎06542/788, *www.tiscover.com/grandhotel.zellamsee*). A stately nineteenth-century hotel whose ornate balconies and shuttered windows have French-Riviera pretensions, with its own private stretch of lakefront as well as an indoor pool. Summer ⑧; winter ⑨.

Herzog, Saalfeldnerstrasse 20 (☎06542/72503, *pension.herzog.tkh@aon.at*). One of the cheapest places near the lake, a rather anonymous but acceptable pension; some rooms with en-suite facilities. ②.

Hubertus, Gartenstrasse 4 (☎06542/72427, *www.hubertus-pension.at*). A large pension with adequate rooms on the western fringes of the centre. ③.

Lebzelter, Dreifaltigkeitsstrasse 7 (☎06542/776, *www.hotel-lebzelter.at*). Traditional, friendly downtown hotel with spacious rooms, all with en-suite bath or shower and TV. Summer ⑤; winter ⑥.

Zum Metzgerwirt, Sebastian-Hörl-Strasse 11 (☎06542/72520, *www.hotel-metzgerwirt.at*). Old-fashioned balconied Gasthof outside, luxurious within; all rooms have en-suite facilities and TV. Summer ⑥; winter ⑨.

The town and the mountains

The obvious focus of Zell am See is the **lake** itself, site of a pleasant 10 km-long promenade and cycle path which can be followed all the way round the shoreline, although it's occasionally forced inland by private plots of land. It's a scenic place for a stroll whatever the season, with the friendly-looking, relatively low-altitude Dientener Berge looming over the lake to the east, and the altogether more inhospitable peaks of the Tauern mountains forming a grey-white barrier far away to the south. At the southern end of the lake, fifteen minutes' walk from Zell, is a popular, grassy *Strandbad*, where rowing boats can be hired. At the height of winter the lake often freezes over, becoming a vast outdoor playground for skating or playing *Eisstockschiessen*, the Austrian version of curling.

Just inland from the lakefront in Zell's compact pedestrianized centre, the first thing you notice about the **Pfarrkirche** is the impressively sturdy tower, although its main claim to fame is the late-Gothic organ loft inside, supported by slender pillars chiselled into spiral shapes, and a delicately carved balustrade sporting floral designs. A few steps to the east of the church, the town's only other real historical sight is the **Vogturm**, a medieval tower that now houses the **Heimatmuseum** (Mon–Fri 1–5pm; öS25/€1.83), a cramped collection of stuffed animals, minerals, archaic skis and other local oddities – including the devilish, horned *Krampus* masks still made by local craftsmen and worn on the night of December 5 (the eve of St Nicholas' Day), when people run through Zell's streets in the guise of demons. According to folk belief, the *Krampus* is a shadowy counterpoint to St Nicholas, a hobgoblin figure who torments children who have behaved badly during the year and will therefore not be receiving any Christmas gifts.

A horseshoe of mountains immediately west of town is served by three main lift systems, catering for hikers and sightseers in summer, and skiers in winter, when they're augmented by a network of smaller chairlifts and drag lifts to form a sizeable integrated winter sports area. Nearest at hand is the **Zellerbergbahn** (June–Sept & early Dec–March; return öS145/€10.59) two minutes' walk uphill from the town centre, which involves a two-stage (gondola followed by chairlift) ascent of the Hirschkogel, a peak that can also be approached via the Areitbahn gondola (July–Aug & Dec to mid-April) from **Schüttdorf**, 3km south of Zell. Twenty-five minutes' walk further west of the Zeelerbergbahn (and served by a half-hourly bus), the **Schmittenhöhebahn** gondola (June–Sept & early Nov–late April; return öS120/€8.76), involves a ten-minute ride to the highland pastures of the 1965-metre Schmittenhöhe, where you'll find a café-restaurant and an impressive, all-encompassing panorama, with the lake down to the east and the ridge of the Hoher Tauern to the south. The **Sonnenalmbahn** (June–Sept & mid–Dec to March; return öS120/€8.76), which departs right next to the Schmittenhöhebahn, climbs in the opposite direction towards the alpine meadows of the Sonnalm, before connecting with a chairlift (included with the Sonnenalmbahn ticket) which rises to the 1850m Sonnkogel, from where you can gaze down on the Glemmtal to the north. Whichever way up you choose, you'll be greeted by wide-ranging views and an appetizing variety of walks – taking the gondola to the Schmittenhöhe and following the path northwards to the top station of the Sonnkogel chairlift (90min) is one of the more popular itineraries, and is often cleared of snow for winter walkers in the skiing season.

Eating and drinking

Innumerable **cafés and restaurants** crowd the streets of Zell's central pedestrianized zone. Most offer standard Austrian dishes at mid-range to expensive prices, although almost every establishment serves inexpensive traditional staples such as *Pinzgauer Käsnockn* (gnocchi-like noodles covered in cheese) and *Gröstl* (potato pieces, onion and meat fried in a pan) alongside the schnitzels and steaks. Fresh fish from the lake also features heavily on most menus. Given the town's favour as a winter resort, there's a reasonable **nightlife** on offer, much of which stays open for the bulk of the year.

For **snacks**, *Moby Dick*, on the corner of Kreuzgasse and Salzmannstrasse, is a fishmongers with a small sit-down section, selling cheap fishy sandwiches and more substantial servings of cod and chips. *Café Vanini*, a two-storey wooden pavilion on Bahnhofstrasse, is the best place to relax over cakes, ice cream and coffee.

Restaurants

Kupferkessel, Bruckner Bundesstrasse 18. Large place uphill from the train station which, despite a garish green interior, remains consistently popular for its reasonably priced pizzas, decent salad bar and late opening hours. Menu also includes a sizeable – if pricey – range of steaks.

Metzgerwirt, Sebastian-Hörl-Gasse. One of the best places to sample traditional Austrian and local Pinzgau food in comfortable surroundings. On the smart side, but *Käsnockn* and *Gröstl* rarely cost over öS100/€7.30; the other main courses start at around öS150/€10.95.

Schloss Prielau, Hoffmannsthalstrasse, Prielau (☎06542/72609). Located in a castle on the north side of the lake, 3km from the centre of Zell, this is one of the best gourmet restaurants in Austria. Main courses start at around öS300/€21.90. Reservations recommended.

Steinerwirt, Schlossplatz. A 500-year-old Gasthof offering the standard Austrian repertoire at affordable prices. Daily specials chalked up on a board outside.

Strandhotel Bellevue, Seeuferstrasse, Thumersbach (☎06542/73104). Pricey restaurant on the eastern side of the lake (a popular destination by ferry from the Zell am See waterfront) specializing in locally caught fresh fish. Reservations recommended.

Fünf Planeten, Loferer Bundestrasse 3. Handily placed Chinese with large selection of Oriental dishes – including some Indonesian choices – and Mittagsmenüs from öS75/€5.48.

Bars

B17, Salzmannstrasse. Corrugated tin hut which conceals a cosy and welcoming bar, crammed with US AirForce memorabilia. A few steps south of the *Grand* hotel.

Crazy Daisy, Bruckner Bundesstrasse. Garish, fun-pub popular with English-speakers. Irish-themed bar round one side, restaurant on the floor above.

Insider, Kirchengasse. Spacious bar in the centre of town with a good range of wines and cocktails. Plenty of outdoor seating in summer.

Hirschenkeller, Dreifaltigkeitsgasse. Friendly basement bar with rock/techno musical policy.

Lebzeltkeller, Dreifaltigkeitsgasse. Rustic, low-ceilinged cellar-bar beneath the *Lebzelter* hotel.

Pinzgauer Diele, Kirchengasse. Sizeable fun-pub with faux-rustic interior, expensive drinks (including wide range of international bottled beers) and pizzas. Turns into a disco after about 11pm (possible cover charge at weekends); a good-fun winter drinking-and-dancing venue when it gets going.

Kaprun and the Kitzsteinhorn

Sprawling across the plain where the Kapruner Ache joins the Salzach, **KAPRUN**, 5km southwest of Zell, is a modern resort village serving the ski slopes of the **Maiskogel** and the Kitzsteinhorn to the south. Predominantly a winter resort, it's an inoffensive if soulless place at any other time of the year, and anyone thinking of visiting the Kitzsteinhorn in summer (whether for the glacier skiing or the views) would probably do better to use Zell am See as a base. There's an efficient **tourist office** in Kaprun village centre (☎06547/86430) organizing **private room** rental (summer ②, winter ③). At the south end of the village at Kaprun 448, an HI **youth hostel** (☎06547/8507) offers dorm beds, and there's a **campsite** beside the Kapruner Ache, which flows along the western side of the village. Kaprun is only small and places to **eat and drink** are central and fairly easy to find: the *Dorfstadl* serves good Austrian and regional food in an old stable rustically furnished and decked with animal skins, while *Hielberger's Stadl* is a pub-like place with substantial snacks and good main meals. *Charly's*, a popular Brit-pub, and the *Baum Bar*, a more European-style drinking venue built around a tree, are the places to go if you need a drink.

Buses from Zell am See pass through Kaprun and then climb northwards for 5km to the station of the **Kitzsteinhornbahn gondola**, which serves the year-round skiing slopes below the **Kitzsteinhorn**. This 3203-metre mountain is the northernmost outpost of the **Glocknergruppe**, a cluster of high-altitude peaks that culminate with the

3798m Grossglockner (Austria's highest) 10km due south. The funicular railway which used to ascend the lower slopes of the Kitzsteinhorn, passing through a steep 4km-long tunnel on the way, was the pride and joy of the local tourist industry until November 2000, when it caught fire upon entering the tunnel, causing the deaths of 155 passengers – most of whom were on their way up the mountain to attend a snowboard festival intended to mark the beginning of the winter season. It remains uncertain whether the funicular will ever see service again. In the meantime the gondola remains the only way up. This ascends to the Häuslalm at the bottom of the ski area, from where a chairlift takes over to the Alpincenter café-restaurant. The final stage is undertaken by cable car, which finishes up at the 3029m Gipfelstation right beneath the conical summit of the Horn. There's an extensive panorama of neighbouring mountains, with the Hohe Tauern's second highest peak, the 3674-metre Grossvenediger, to the west, and (in clear conditions) unparalleled views northwest across the ridge of the Kitzbühler Alpen towards the Kaisergebirge 50km distant. Bear in mind that even in midsummer the summit can be icy underfoot and extremely cold – remember to take the appropriate clothing.

A road continues beyond the Gletscherbahn station towards two reservoirs, the **Wasserfallboden** and the **Mooserboden**, which shelter on the eastern flanks of the Kitzsteinhorn. Leading into an area of eerily desolate beauty, the route promises fine views down the valley at every turn. The full journey can only be made by public transport: the **Kesselfall Alpenhaus**, 2km above the Gletscherbahn station, is the end of the line for private cars. From Kesselfall, a first bus takes you to the **Lärchwand**, where a funicular climbs up from the valley floor to be met by a second bus, which dives through tunnels on the western side of the Wasserfallboden before reaching the **dam** at the northern end of the Mooserboden. Here you'll find a restaurant, trails leading off into the wilderness, and a chance to gaze at snow-clad peaks that crowd in on all sides. Weather permitting, you should also be able to pick out the ridge of the Salzburger Kalkalpen 40km to the northeast.

Saalbach and Hinterglemm

Hourly buses from Zell am See head up the **Glemmtal** immediately to the north, where the twin villages of **SAALBACH** and **HINTERGLEMM** entertain winter-package tourists from the Netherlands, Germany and Britain. Skiing is good for beginners and intermediates throughout the valley, and both villages have plenty of bars and pubs catering to a wide range of tastes, although Saalbach is the rowdier of the two. A **tourist office** (☎06541/7272, *www.saalbach.com*) on Saalbach's main street will point you in the direction of **private rooms** and **hotels** if you want to stay. The 1794-metre **Kohlmaiskopf** on the mountain ridge north of Saalbach can be reached by gondola; and further up the valley to the west there's a cable car to the 1984-metre **Zwölfer**, most prominent of the peaks south of Hinterglemm.

The Grossglockner Hochalpenstrasse

A deservedly popular excursion from Zell am See, the **Grossglockner Hochalpenstrasse** is one of the most spectacular routes across the Alps, running north–south over a high mountain pass just east of the **Grossglockner**, Austria's highest peak. A toll road for most of its length (cars öS350/€25.55, motorbikes öS250/€18.25; bus passengers pay a small toll as a proportion of their ticket price), the route is usually open from mid-May to late October – precise dates depend on weather conditions. **Buses** make the trip to the **Franz-Josefs-Höhe**, main vantage point for sightseers, once a day (three times a day mid-July to early Sept) from both Zell am See to the north and Lienz to the south. The buses stop long enough for you to enjoy the

Wrought-iron shop signs, Salzburg

Salzburger Land mountainscape

Pasterze Glacier, Grossglockner

Farmhouse near Gosau

Kitzbühel town houses

View from the fortress, Salzburg

Churchyard overlooking lake, Hallstatt

The Goldenes Dachl, Innsbruck

Tyrolean landscape

"Tales of Hoffman", Bregenz floating stage

Northeastern Tyrol

A HUT-TO-HUT TOUR OF THE GROSSGLOCKNER

While tens of thousands of tourists "do" the **Grossglockner** each year by car or bus, negotiating the innumerable hairpins of the environmentally insensitive Hochalpenstrasse, the most rewarding way to approach Austria's highest mountain is on foot. Beginning at **Kaprun**, a week's hut-to-hut tour will take you along a scenic route that wanders onto the south flank of the mountain before descending to **Kals am Grossglockner**, which has bus links with Matrei, Lienz and other East Tyrol destinations.

From Kaprun, take the Maiskogel cable car to reach a pleasant ridge-walk heading south to the *Krefelder Hütte* (☎06547/862 1361), set below the graceful Kitzsteinhorn. The ridge-walk is an uncomplicated one, albeit a little exposed in places, with the big snow peaks of the Hohe Tauern range, including a preview of Grossglockner, teasing ahead. Leaving the *Krefelder Hütte* on day 2, the route continues to the crowded Alpincenter, with its ski lifts and cableway to the Schmiedinger Grat, crosses the Kammerscharte on the Kitzsteinhorn's northeast ridge, slopes down to Fürthermoar Alm then rises over rough pastures to the big dam wall at the northern end of the Mooserboden. Overnight accommodation is available here in the drab-looking *Dr-Adolf-Schärf-Haus* (*Berghaus Mooserboden*; advanced booking advisable: ☎06547/827110), owned by the Touristenverein Naturfreunde. From here you look down the length of the reservoir towards a rim of snow- and ice-clad mountains effectively concealing the Grossglockner from view. On day 3, continue along the so-called Austriaweg, which follows the east shore before crossing glacier-fed streams at the far end. Here the trail climbs through the Wintergasse glen to gain the narrow cleft of the Kapruner Törl, giving access to a wild boulderscape through which a route is waymarked to the large, institutionalized *Rudolfs Hütte* (☎06563/8221), the Austrian Alpine Club's Alpinzentrum, equipped with sauna, fitness room and climbing wall. A more relaxing half-day's trek follows on day 4. Crossing the 2518-metre Kalser Tauern on the watershed crest, a descent (which could be tricky in poor visibility) leads to a junction of paths at Erdiges Eck, then drops down through the Dorfertal to the *Kalser Tauernhaus* (☎04876/283), set among larches almost due west of the Grossglockner. On day 5, the route continues down-valley, through the Dabaklamm to the hamlet of Taurer, then climbs steeply into the Teischnitztal draining from the northeast. As you gain height, the glaciers adorning the west and south faces of Grossglockner come into view. The busy *Stüdl Hütte* (☎04876/209) occupies the Fanatscharte at the foot of the Luisengrat, a ridge running south from Grossglockner itself. The final stage, on day 6, descends via the privately owned *Luckner Hütte* and *Lucknerhaus* (possible to hitch a lift on the road below the *Lucknerhaus*) through the Ködnitztal to Kals am Grossglockner, situated at a junction of green valleys and open pastures, and with plenty of good walks of its own.

Several other trails of varying degrees of difficulty cross the southern flanks of Grossglockner and link an assortment of huts, some privately owned, the rest belonging to member clubs of the Alpenverein. It's easy enough to cross from the Dorfertal in the west to the Mölltal in the east along visually spectacular routes, and continue northwestwards above the extensive icefield of the Pasterzenkees, the longest glacier in the Eastern Alps, thereby making a horseshoe round Austria's highest mountain (allow 2–3 days from Kals). But only those with experience of glacier-crossing and with the necessary equipment should attempt to make a full circle round the peak itself.

A recommended map is Freytag & Berndt's *Wanderkarte* 122 (Grossglockner, Kaprun, Zell am See; 1:50,000), covering the whole of the above area.

---

view for a while before embarking on the return journey. They're timed to connect with each other, so you can travel all the way from Zell to Lienz and vice versa.

Leaving the Salzach valley at **Pichl**, 5km southeast of Zell am See, the initial stages of the Hochalpenstrasse are leisurely enough, as the road heads up the verdant **Fuschertal**. There's a **campsite** at **Fusch**, 7km up the valley. A **Wildpark** (May–Oct daily 9am–5pm; öS75/€5.48) at **Ferleiten**, another 7km further, specializes in the chamois, deer and mouflon indigenous to the area. Beyond Ferleiten the toll gate marks the beginning of the road's first truly spectacular stretch, rising via a succession of steep hairpins to the **Fuschertörl**, a popular viewing point, and the start of a sideroad that leads to the **Edelweissspitze**, another spot offering panoramic views, 2km to the northeast.

After negotiating the 2575-metre summit of the pass via the **Hochtor** tunnel, the road descends for a few kilometres before arriving at a junction where the route's most popular side-trip – the **Gletscherstrasse** – forks right towards the Franz-Josefs-Höhe (the emperor made a much-publicized alpine excursion here in 1856, hence the name), a lookout point facing the 3798-metre peak of the Grossglockner itself. It's an odd juxtaposition of alpine wilderness and tourist development, with a multistorey car park, two **restaurants** and a **hotel**, the *Alpenhotel Kaiser Franz-Josef*, offering "nostalgia rooms" in nineteenth-century imperial style for öS600/€44 per person and upwards, overlooking the crevasse-riven wastes of the **Pasterze Glacier**. Somehow, the sheer desolate beauty of the place soon makes you forget the hundreds of other tourists who have come to mill around and enjoy the view. The glowering 3798m summit of the Grossglockner itself is due west of the Höhe, rising above the left-hand side of the glacier as you look along it. The landscape around the Franz-Jozefs-Höhe is too high up and too wild for it to be a hiking venue for the inexperienced, although you can take a few steps out on the ice if you have footwear with a solid grip. The Gletscherbahn funicular will take you down to the glacier surface (öS98/€7.15 return), although the price seems a bit stiff considering that you can make your own descent via (the admittedly rather slippery) footpath in 20–30 minutes.

From the Franz-Josefs-Höhe, it's back to the main road and a highly scenic descent towards Heiligenblut in Carinthia, and onwards to Lienz (see Chapter 5).

Along the Salzachtal to the Krimml Falls

Fifty kilometres west of Zell am See, situated at the head of the **Salzachtal** in the fertile, cow-strewn **Pinzgau**, the **Krimmler Wasserfälle** are justifiably one of the biggest attractions in this part of Austria – receiving 700,000 visitors a year at the last count. The sight of the Krimmler Ache cascading down from the Hohe Tauern, sending up clouds of spray, which hang suspended above the bottle-green pine forests, makes for a memorable experience. Hourly **buses** set out from Zell am See to the falls, but a more picturesque way to travel up the valley from Zell is to take one of the six daily trains along the **Pinzgaubahn**, an archetypal rural rail line that winds lazily across barn-dotted meadows.

The Salzachtal harbours a succession of pretty towns and villages, any number of which provide access to scenic alpine side-trips for those who have their own transport. Sixteen kilometres out of Zell, **Uttendorf** stands at the northern end of an attractive route up the tranquil **Stubachtal**, at the head of which a two-stage cable car ascends at **Enzinger Boden** to the **Weiss See**, a high-altitude beauty spot sheltering under the shadow of the 3086-metre **Granatspitze**. Ten kilometres further along the Salzachtal, **Mittersill**, the main tourist centre of the Pinzgau, provides access to the **Thurn Pass**, a panoramic road that heads north over the mountains to Kitzbühel (see p.499). Roughly halfway between Mittersill and Krimml, the small ski resort of **Neukirchen** offers a gondola trip (mid-June to Sept) up the slopes of the **Wildkogel** on the northern side of the valley, and several hiking routes run up the deep, ravine-like side-valleys, such as the Untersulzbach and Obersulzbach, which lead south towards the foot of the 3674-metre **Grossvenediger**, the Hohe Tauern's second highest peak.

Buses (and private cars) arrive at a car park a short distance away from the falls' **ticket booth**. Trains from Zell terminate at Krimml train station 4km short of the falls, entailing a well-signposted fifty-minute walk through woodland. From the ticket booth, a four-kilometre-long trail (April–Oct öS15/€1.10, Nov–March free) winds its way uphill passing three main sections of **waterfall** (which, starting with the lowest one, drop a distance of 65m, 35m and 60m respectively). The coach parties tend to thin out the further up you go, and it's worth persevering with the ascent until you reach the **Krimmlertal**, the starkly beautiful alpine valley from which the waters originate. The path is steep in places, and the full ascent should take about an hour and a half. Even if time is short, you should at least venture partway up the trail for a close-up look at the lower levels of the falls.

There are numerous Gasthöfe offering **food** and refreshment near the car park at the base of the falls, and a small **tourist office** (Mon–Sat 11am–4pm; ☎06564/7239, *www.salzburg.com/krimml-tourismus*), which has details of **rooms** in local farmhouses, although most visitors come here on a day-trip from Zell am See.

West of Krimml, the main road begins to climb towards the **Gerlos Pass** (a toll road: öS90/€6.57 per car, öS50/€3.65 per motorbike), before descending into the Tyrol and the Zillertal (see p.485).

travel details

Trains

Hallein to: Salzburg (16 daily; 25min).

Salzburg to: Attnang-Puchheim (24 daily; 45min–1hr 25min); Bad Hofgastein (10 daily; 1hr 25min); Badgastein (10 daily; 1hr 40min); Bischofshofen (30 daily; 50min–1hr); Graz (3 daily; 4hr 15min); Hallein (16 daily; 25min); Innsbruck via Bischofshofen (5 daily; 3hr 40min); Innsbruck via Kufstein (7 daily; 2hr); Klagenfurt (3 daily; 3hr 10min); Linz (hourly; 1hr 20min); Radstadt (3 daily; 1hr 15min); St Johann (20 daily; 1hr–1hr 20min); Schwarzach-St Veit (20 daily; 1hr 10min–1hr 30min); Vienna (hourly; 3hr 20min); Villach (10 daily; 2hr 50min); Werfen (12 daily; 55min); Zell am See (8 daily; 1hr 40min).

Zell am See to: Krimml (6 daily; 1hr 40min); Mittersill (6 daily; 1hr).

Buses

Badgastein to: Bad Hofgastein (hourly; 20min); Böckstein (6 daily; 10min); Heilstollen (1 daily; 20min); Sportgastein (6 daily; 30min).

Hallein to: Bad Dürrnberg (8 daily; 25min); Salzburg (8 daily; 35min).

Radstadt to: Tamsweg (4 daily; 1hr).

Salzburg to: Grossgmain (hourly; 30min); Hallein (8 daily; 35min).

Zell am See to: Franz-Josefs-Höhe (1 daily; 2hr 30min); Hinterglemm (hourly; 30min); Kaprun (hourly; 15min); Krimml (hourly; 1hr 30min); Mittersill (hourly; 50min); Rauris (5 daily; 40min); Saalbach (hourly; 25min); Taxenbach (8 daily; 25min).

International trains

Salzburg to: Amsterdam (1 daily; 12hr 30min); Berlin Zoo (5 daily; 8hr 30min); Cologne (7 daily; 7hr 30min); Ljubljana (3 daily; 4hr 30min); Munich (15 daily; 1hr 30min); Paris Est (3 daily; 10hr 30min); Rome (1 daily; 9hr); Venice (2 daily; 6hr 30min); Zagreb (3 daily; 7hr 30min); Zurich (5 daily; 6hr).

CHAPTER EIGHT

THE SALZKAMMERGUT

The **Salzkammergut** (*www.salzkammergut.at*) is Austria's premier and most spectacular lake district. Its peaks may not be as lofty as those further west, but they do have the added advantage of hovering above glacier-carved, lake-filled troughs, thus forming a landscape of unique beauty. The Salzkammergut offers relatively easy hiking (and mountain biking) possibilities, and, given that Austria has no coastline, the area's crystal clear lakes also attract anyone looking for water-based activities from yachting and windsurfing to sunbathing and swimming. Not a Land in its own right, the Salzkammergut is shared by Styria, the Salzburger Land and Upper Austria (by far the largest portion), though the tourist authority transcends the borders of the Länder.

The two most accessible lakes are the **Wolfgangsee** and **Mondsee**, each just an hour's journey from Salzburg. Watersports are popular on both – Mondsee, in particular, stands out as a good place for windsurfing – although there's plenty of historical interest here, too, with the pilgrimage church of **St Wolfgang**, and the abbey church in the town of **Mondsee**. Surprisingly, the largest of the lakes, **Attersee**, has many fewer points of specific sightseeing interest than, say, the **Traunsee**, which has several very fine churches along its western shoreline. Without doubt the most stunning of the region's innumerable stretches of water, however, is the **Hallstättersee**. Its tree-studded sides drop steeply into the lake, creating a spectacular backdrop for the prettiest of all the Salzkammergut villages, **Hallstatt**, whose Celtic finds are second to none.

Commercial and transport hub of the area is the nineteenth-century spa town of **Bad Ischl**, at the geographical centre of the region. It's not a big place by any means, but a modest menu of tourist sights combined with its proximity to three of the most scenic of the Salzkammergut lakes ensure that you're likely to pass through here at some stage during a tour of the area. Approaching the region from the north and east, you're more likely to pass through the handsome lakeside town of **Gmunden**, on the Traunsee, the only other place of any great size in the region. From the south you'll inevitably pass through **Bad Aussee**, another spa resort whose unassuming charm provides a good introduction to small-town Salzkammergut life.

The obvious gateway to the lake district is the city of Salzburg, whence regular **bus** services run to the Mondsee, Wolfgangsee and Bad Ischl – from the latter, you can then

---

ACCOMMODATION PRICE CODES

All **hotels and pensions** in this book have been coded according to the following price categories. All the codes are based on the rate for the least expensive double room during the **summer season**. In those places where winter is the high season, we've indicated both summer and winter room rates in the text.

① under öS400/€29.07
② öS400–600/€29.07–43.60
③ öS600–800/€43.60–58.14
④ öS800–1000/€58.14–72.67
⑤ öS1000–1200/€72.67–87.21

⑥ öS1200–1400/€87.21–101.74
⑦ öS1400–1600/€101.74–116.28
⑧ öS1600–1800/€116.28–130.81
⑨ over öS1800/€130.81

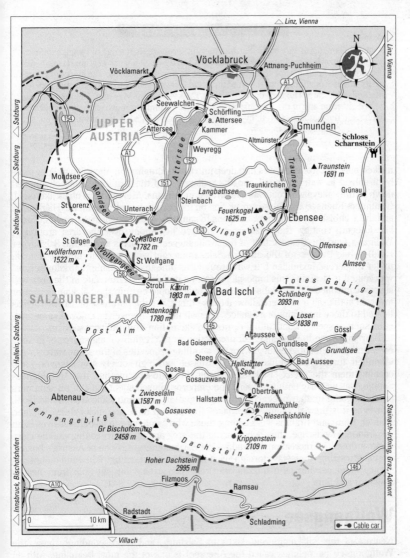

catch local buses to most of the places not served directly from Salzburg. In addition, a **rail** line runs through the region on a north–south axis, linking the Traunsee, Bad Ischl, the Hallstättersee and Bad Aussee on the way. To get on it, change at Attnang-Pucheim on the Vienna–Salzburg line or Stainach-Irdning on the Graz–Salzburg line.

Some history

The **salt** from which the area derives its name has been mined since at least 800 BC, when **Hallstatt** emerged as an important focus of **Iron Age culture**. Early miners

---

SALZKAMMERGUT CARD

If you're planning to stay in the Salzkammergut for more than a day or two, it's definitely worth your while buying a **Salzkammergut Card**, which gives you around twenty-five percent off the entrance charges to most of the region's attractions. The discount covers pretty much everything from the salt mines and local museums to tickets for the lake ferries and cable cars. The card costs öS65/€4.72, is valid from May until October, and can be bought from any of the region's tourist offices. To find out more, pick up a brochure, listing all the sights covered by the card; alternatively, visit the regional Web site *www.tiscover.com/salzkammergut*.

---

hacked pure salt from galleries dug deep into the mountains, but the salt was later slowly dissolved in water pumped into the galleries, and the resulting brine channelled down to the valleys where it was evaporated in saltpans. Mercantile centres like Ischl, Gmunden, Ebensee and Aussee grew rich on the resulting trade, giving the Habsburgs and the archbishops of Salzburg occasion to squabble over control of the profits. By the late fifteenth century the Salzburgers enjoyed hegemony over the area around St Wolfgang (and the western half of the Wolfgangsee still forms part of the Salzburger Land), while the rest of the modern Salzkammergut was made an imperial domain under Emperor Maximilian I. It was around this time that the name "Salzkammergut" was coined to describe this imperial territory's new-found status. Life in the area was strictly controlled by the Habsburg court: only people born in the Salzkammergut or involved in the salt trade were allowed to live there, and the purchase or sale of salt was limited to those in receipt of a licence. The salt miners themselves enjoyed some benefits, such as special woodcutting rights and exemption from military service.

Tourism began to challenge salt production as the region's main source of income early in the nineteenth century when the soothing properties of the saline waters were identified, turning places like Ischl and Aussee into high-society **spa resorts** – and earning them the prefix "Bad" as a result. Franz-Josef's mother, the Archduchess Sophie, was an early enthusiast, and the emperor himself spent most of his summers pursuing game (both two-legged and four-legged) in the countryside around Bad Ischl. However, it is the Salzkammergut's lakes that proved to be the major draw: Wagner, Mahler, Klimt and Brahms were among those who came here to lose themselves in an inspirational landscape, thus popularizing the area among a burgeoning middle class eager for outdoor recreation. Nowadays the Salzkammergut is one of Austria's busiest spots, attracting long-stay foreign visitors with its dazzling lakes-and-mountains scenery and serving as a buzzing weekend playground for city folk from nearby Salzburg and Linz.

Wolfgangsee

Nearest of the Salzkammergut lakes to Salzburg, and correspondingly busy, the **Wolfgangsee** (sometimes called the Abersee) is one of the most beguiling, with an impressive backdrop of craggy sandcastle-shaped mountains to the south, and the bleak bulk of Schafberg to the north. Despite its popularity, the Wolfgangsee manages to maintain a calm and relaxing air, its warm waters attracting plenty of watersports enthusiasts. The 15km-long lake is almost squeezed in two around the chief lakeside resort of **St Wolfgang**, a picturesque town with a fabulous Gothic altarpiece. Like the nearby Schafberg mountain railway, however, St Wolfgang is also a regular stop on the lakes-and-mountains package tourist circuit, and as such can get pretty crowded. **St Gilgen** is also attractive, and, as a low-key watersports resort and paragliding centre,

SALZKAMMERGUT OUTDOOR ACTIVITIES

Just about every one of the big lakes in the Salzkammergut offers a huge variety of **outdoor activities**, from the relatively simple pleasure of swimming to high-risk sports such as paragliding. The local tourist offices in each area will be able to give you the relevant details.

Bike rental You can rent bikes from many of the larger train stations, which has the advantage of being convenient, and relatively cheap if you have a valid train ticket. However, you'll get a wider range from a specialist bike rental place. Ordinary bikes tend to cost öS100/€7.30 a day, whereas mountain bikes can cost as much as öS200/€14.53 or more.

Boat rental Every lake in the Salzkammergut has numerous outfits that rent out rowing boats (*Ruderboote*) or pedalo-boats (*Tretboote*); electric boats (*Elektroboote*) are also fairly ubiquitous. Typical prices are around öS100/€7.30 for an hour, slightly more for the electric boats, slightly less for the rowing boats.

Paragliding On a fine day, there's an endless stream of folk launching themselves into the firmament off the top of mountains such as the Zwölferhorn or the Schafberg above the Wolfgangsee, or from the Loser above the Altaussee. The region's chief operators are *Flugschule Salzkammergut*, based at Weyregg am Attersee (*www.paragleiten.net*). One-day's course plus a flight costs around öS800/€58.14; a longer two to three-day course would be closer to öS2500/€181.68.

Sailing The region's best-known sailing school is the Segelschule Mondsee, with another in Gmunden on the Traunsee. Seven-day courses (mid-April to mid-Oct) cost around öS2500/€181.68. In addition, small sailing dinghies and catamarans are available for hire on all the major lakes for öS100–150/€7.30–10.90 per hour.

Scuba diving You can hire scuba diving (*Tauchen*) equipment or go on a course for the uninitiated at St Lorenz, just south of Mondsee, at the Strandbad at Ebensee, and at Hallstatt. A one-day course should cost around öS500/€36.33, a seven-day marathon öS5000/€363.36.

Skiing The area around the Wolfgangsee is a popular skiing destination, much favoured by weekend crowds from Salzburg, although it rarely features in the major package brochures. The main areas are the Postalm (where a popular ski school makes it a good place for beginners) above Strobl, the Zwölferhorn (with greater range for intermediate skiers) above St Gilgen, and the nearby Gosau (where advanced skiers should head – see p.450).The season is from late December to mid-March.

Swimming Each of the towns and villages has a little stretch of grassy shoreline, known as the *Strandbad*, dedicated to sunbathing and watersports. Most have a jetty you can dive off, and some charge a small entrance fee in the summer season. It's worth knowing that the temperature of the water is usually warmest in the Wolfgangsee and Mondsee, and can be freezing in some of the smaller, higher mountain lakes.

Waterskiing Waterskiing is very popular, particularly at Strobl and St Gilgen on the Wolfgangsee and at Mondsee town, and costs around öS130/€9.45 per round. Alternatively you can all pile onto an inflatable banana for öS90/€6.54, or cling on for dear life to a giant rubber ring for öS65/€4.72.

Windsurfing Windsurfing is often hard work in the Salzkammergut as there's rarely a particularly strong wind. If you know what you're doing, you can get board rental for öS100/€7.30, or sign up for a one-day crash course from öS500/€36.33, seven-day courses from öS2500/€181.68.

attracts a younger crowd, while laid-back **Strobl** at the eastern end of the lake is more focused purely on lakeside pursuits.

Salzburg is the obvious gateway to the region if you're approaching from the west. Hourly **buses** on the Salzburg–Bad Ischl route run along the southern shores of the

Wolfgangsee, calling at St Gilgen and Strobl en route. To get to St Wolfgang, you usually have to change at Strobl and pick up a connecting service there. Alternatively, **lake ferries**, run by the ÖBB, present a leisurely way of exploring the area between May and mid-October, when St Gilgen, St Wolfgang and Strobl (and various other points along the lake) are linked by frequent daytime services.

St Gilgen

In many ways **ST GILGEN** represents the perfect introduction to the Salzkammergut: a combination of quaint country town, modern lakeside resort and ideal base for refreshing walks. The town is centred on the twin focal points of the double-onion domed church and the attractive Rathaus, with its oriel window and porch, both of which are set back slightly from the lake. Between the church and the town hall, in what used to be a lace-weaver's house, is the picturesque **Heimatkundliches Museum**, on Pichlerplatz (June–Sept Tues–Sun 10am–noon & 2–6pm; öS40/€2.90), built in 1655. Inside, displays recall St Gilgen's role in the eighteenth century as an important lacemaking centre, aided by a decree of 1776 that forbade the import of foreign lace into Austria.

St Gilgen makes the most of its tenuous Mozart link with a **Mozart-Gedenkstätte**, (mid-June to mid-Sept Tues–Sun 10am–noon & 2–6pm; öS10/€0.72), in the Bezirksgericht (county court) at Ischlerstrasse 15, not far from the lake's edge, where the composer's mother, Anna Pertl, was born on December 25, 1720. There's a limited words-and-pictures display remembering Mozart's grandfather, Wolfgang Nikolaus Pertl, who worked as a magistrate in St Gilgen and dabbled in amateur dramatics, and Mozart's talented sister Nannerl, who, by coincidence, married one of Pertl's successors as magistrate (the impressively monikered Johann Baptist von Berchtold zu Sonnenberg) and ended up living in the house in which her mother grew up. The town's **Musikinstrument-Museum der Völker** (June to mid-Oct Tues–Sun 9–11am & 3–7pm; mid-Oct to Dec Mon–Fri 9–11am & 3–6pm; Jan–May Mon–Thurs 9–11am & 3–6pm, Fri 9–11am, Sun 3–6pm; öS45/€3.27), at Aberseestrasse 11, also has a video on Mozart, in amongst its collection of folk instruments from all over the globe.

Beyond the courthouse lies the Schiffsstation, where boats from St Wolfgang arrive and depart, and the pleasant waterfront **promenade** – a continuation of Ischlerstrasse – where most of the town's boat rental, waterskiing and windsurfing facilities are located. After they've wandered round the town, most visitors take a ride on the **Zwölferhorn Sielbahn** (June & Sept 9am–5pm; July & Aug 9am–6pm; Dec–May 9am–4pm; return öS180/€13.08), situated next to the bus station and main road, whose dinky yellow or red four-seater gondolas convey visitors to the summit of the 1522-metre **Zwölferhorn**. After watching the paragliders launch themselves off the top, you can walk back to town by a number of routes (allow 2hr–2hr 30min), two of the most popular of which stop off at either the Sausteig Alm or the Illingerberg Alm – both of which boast huts offering food and drink, with tables outside from which to enjoy the view.

Another popular three-hour **walk** heads round the peaceful, wooded northern end of the lake to St Wolfgang, one of the few stretches of lakeside in the Salzkammergut where there is no road for cars. En route, the path climbs up along the wooded flanks of the **Falkenstein** hill (795m), where, according to legend, St Wolfgang used to live as a hermit. To reach the path, leave St Gilgen via Mondseestrasse as far as the Hotel Fürberg, and from there follow the signs.

Practicalities

A right turn outside the **bus station**, and a second right, down Schwarzenbrunnerstrasse, lead to the Rathaus, home of the **tourist office** (Mon–Fri

9am–noon & 2–6pm, Sat 9am–noon; ☎06227/2348, *www.stgilgen.co.at*), which will advise on the availability of **private rooms** – prices depend on how near the lake you want to be. Two atmospheric village inns right in the centre offer the best **hotel** accommodation: *Kendler*, Kirchenplatz 3 (☎06227/2223, *www.salzburg.com /unterkuenfte/kendler*; closed Nov; ⑤), and the smaller, prettily frescoed *Hotel zur Post*, Mozartplatz 8 (☎06227/2157; ④). For the perfect lakeside location, however, head for the large, secluded *Gasthof Fürberg* (☎06227/2385, *www.fuerberg.at*; closed Nov–March; ⑤); to get there, you can either take the boat from St Gilgen, or walk, drive or cycle the 2km round the lake towards St Wolfgang, off Mondseestrasse. The town's luxurious **HI hostel**, *Jugendgästehaus Schafbergblick*, is a short walk down Mondseestrasse at no. 7 (☎06227/2365, *jgh.stgilgen@oejhv.or.at*), and has all types of rooms from single to large dorms. There are no **campsites** in St Gilgen itself, but a whole rash of them in the peaceful Abersee peninsula that juts out into the lake, 4km to the southeast.

For **eating**, the restaurant at the fifteenth-century *Hotel zur Post* (closed Mon except in July & Aug) serves up all the usual schnitzel dishes with some aplomb, and *Wirt am Gries*, Steinklüftstrasse 6, offers the familiar range of Austrian dishes and boasts a nice garden. *Fischerwirt* (closed Mon except in July & Aug; closed Nov & Jan; *www.fischerwirt.at*), near the Schiffstation, serves up local fish dishes on its large lakeside terrace, while *Pizzeria Papageno*, Ischlerstrasse 16, has a pleasant first-floor terrace. Establishments like *Frequenz* and *Podium* are among a string of lively **drinking** venues along Ischlerstrasse near the lake, while the boisterous *Grammophon*, further inland on Steinklüftstrasse, is also worth a try.

Strobl

Although a good deal less pretty than either St Gilgen or St Wolfgang (see below), **STROBL** also receives none of the tour groups that descend on the other two resorts. With plenty of places to hire boats and a couple of waterskiing schools along the lakefront, it's a great place in which to enjoy a quiet, relaxed beach-oriented lakeside holiday. The main bathing area, the **Seebad** (öS20/€1.45), is in a grassy lakeside park 1km to the northwest of the village centre.

Strobl is also a good base for touring the region, and offers access to some excellent **walks**. Best of the nearby walking destinations is the **Postalm** to the south, which is reached by a twelve-kilometre-long toll road that winds up a sequence of hairpin bends, and is served by a walkers' bus from Ströbl in season (late June to late Sept & late Dec to March; öS100/€7.30). A large expanse of alpine grazing land raised high above the valley floor, the Postalm offers some great high level walks, with excellent views of the surrounding mountains. Those with kids might like to have a go at the Sommerrodelbahn or **summer toboggan** (Easter to Oct daily 10am to dusk; öS70/€5.08), 2.5km west of Strobl off the main road to St Gilgen.

Turn left out of Strobl **bus station** and carry straight on for ten minutes to reach the village centre, huddled around a small church. The **tourist office** (Mon–Fri 9am–7pm, Sat 9am–noon & 4–7pm, Sun 10am–noon; ☎06137/7255, *www.salzkammergut.at /wolfgangsee*), on Dorfplatz, will check vacancies in **private rooms** for you. Moderately priced **accommodation** is available at the comfortable modern chalet-style *Pension Kasberger*, east of the village centre at Salzburgerstrasse 188 (☎06137/7249; ②). At the other end of the scale, the centrally located *Villa Brandauer*, Moosgasse 73 (☎06137/7205, *www.tiscover.com.villa-brandauer*; ⑦), is a lovely late-nineteenth-century villa with period furnishings and direct access to the lake. Somewhere between the two is the *Stroblerhof*, Ischlerstrasse 16 (☎06137/7308, *www.stroblerhof.at*; ⑤), which has a pool in its large garden. The nearest **campsites** are towards St Wolfgang (see below) or on the aforementioned Abersee peninsula, 3km west of town, off the St Gilgen road.

For **food**, the *Villa Brandauer's* restaurant has a good-value Tagesmenü, fish dishes aplenty, and attractive garden seating, while the *Lilly* restaurant at Seegasthof Jenisch (closed Tues) has a waterfront terrace and serves excellent fresh fish. Strobl **nightlife** centres on the *Stroblerhof*, which has a restaurant specializing in steaks, as well as a pub, a disco and an outdoor bar. The *Laimeralm* (☎06137/7262), in the hills 4km to the southeast and reached by courtesy buses from the centre of Strobl (check with the tourist office), is a well-known and enjoyably kitsch folk venue, with live shows on Friday evenings and Sunday afternoons (May to mid-Oct).

St Wolfgang

ST WOLFGANG, 4km west of Strobl, is by far the most ancient and picturesque place on the lake. With its handsome buildings, whose flower-bedecked balconies hang over narrow thoroughfares, the town is undeniably pretty, though it is also very touristy with more souvenir shops than anywhere else in the Salzkammergut. Part responsibility for the crowds, and the village's twee, Ruritanian image, goes to Ralph Benatzky and Robert Stolz's 1930 comic opera, *White Horse Inn*, inspired by the *Im Weissen Rössl* hotel on the lakefront. A stick of musical candy rarely heard outside Austria, it's regularly performed at St Wolfgang's cultural centre, the Michael-Pacher-Haus, on Michael-Pacher-Strasse, in summer. China effigies of the rearing white steed and other equine trinkets fill just about every shop window in town.

The town owes its existence – and its name – to the tenth-century Bishop of Regensburg, **St Wolfgang**, who came to this area to reorganize the Benedictine monastery at Mondsee while enjoying a spot of rural solitude on the shores of the lake that would later bear his name. He built a chapel on a small promontory jutting out into the lake, around which a settlement grew, soon to become a pilgrimage centre devoted to his cult. Wolfgang's original hermitage is now incorporated into the current **Pfarrkirche**, superbly situated above the shimmering lake at the centre of the town. Nowadays, tourists flock here primarily to admire the church's famous high altar by Tyrolean master **Michael Pacher** (see opposite), one of the high points of Austrian Gothic art (you'll need to feed the light meter in order to get a good look). An extravagantly pinnacled structure measuring some 12m high, the altar was probably built with the help of the artist's brother Friedrich, and was completed sometime between 1471 and 1481 in Pacher's home town of Bruneck before being carted over the Alps to St Wolfgang. Brightly gilded, sculpted scenes of the Coronation of the Virgin form the altar's centrepiece; St Wolfgang himself is the figure on the left holding a model of the church. The predella is devoted to a depiction of the Adoration, flanked by the Visitation and the Flight into Egypt. Most days only the outer panels of the altar wings are on display, depicting scenes from the life of St Wolfgang, but from Ash Wednesday to the day before Palm Sunday the wings are opened to allow a glimpse of the eight richly coloured paintings from the life of Christ. Providing a contrast to Pacher's work is the incredibly gaudy black and gold Baroque **Schwanthaler Altar** halfway up the nave. According to tradition (and such stories are common in places where Gothic altars like Pacher's survive), the artist commissioned to produce a replacement for the Pacher altar, which was due to be trashed, deliberately made his own work too big to fit into the space reserved for it. The equally ornate **pulpit**, is by Meinrad Guggenbichler (see p.431), and features a flock of sheep being hugged by various cherubs and the Good Shepherd. When you leave, be sure to have a drink from the delightful Renaissance **pilgrims' fountain** by the church.

There's nothing much to see in the rest of the town, though you can **hire boats** down by the traditional fishermen's huts near the St Wolfgang Markt Schiffsstation. It's here, too, that you'll find the last professional **fishmonger's** on the Wolfgangsee, Fischerei Höpflinger, whose shop doubles as a boathouse and smokehouse.

MICHAEL PACHER

Although nowadays recognized as the leading Austrian painter and sculptor of the fifteenth century, **Michael Pacher** remains a mysterious figure. He was a well-respected artist in his own time, but many of his works were destroyed or broken up during the eighteenth-century enthusiasm for all things Baroque, making it difficult for historians to piece together an accurate picture of Pacher's career. He was born sometime between 1430 and 1435 in or around the South Tyrolean town of Bruneck (now Brunico in Italy), the main settlement of an area known as the Pustertal. Having picked up the rudiments of painting and sculpture, probably as apprentice to a local artist, Pacher went to study in Padua, which was then the main cultural centre of northern Italy and the obvious place for a young artist to perfect his craft. Here, Pacher was able to absorb the artistic traditions of the Italian Renaissance – both from the fine paintings in Padua's churches, and from contact with the many other painters who congregated here at the time, among them Andrea Mantegna, with whom it is thought Pacher was acquainted. Most importantly, Pacher received a thorough grounding in contemporary experiments with perspective and light, giving his subsequent paintings a measure of depth and realism that was unique among the artists of the Austrian lands.

By the late 1460s Pacher had returned to Bruneck and established a workshop turning out altarpieces for local churches. Few of these survive, although individual pieces of sculpture and paintings from them have found their way into museums and galleries. It's unclear when exactly Pacher died, but his last-known works were completed in Salzburg (where a sculpture of the Virgin still survives in the Franziskanerkirche; see p.385) sometime in the early 1490s.

The altar at St Wolfgang is the only one of Pacher's altars to have remained completely intact. It was commissioned in 1471 by Benedict, Abbot of Mondsee, for a fee of 1200 Hungarian florins, 50 of which were paid in advance. There was no real deadline for completion of the work because Benedict was still in the process of building the choir of the church for which the altar was intended, and Pacher probably didn't make a start on it until 1478–79. It was a typical piece of workshop-made art, with Pacher himself planning the whole enterprise and executing the most demanding paintings and sculptures, while his assistants were charged with doing the rest. The *Adoration of the Magi*, on the predella – which hardly displays the same skill and expressiveness as the central *Coronation of the Virgin* – was probably the work of Pacher's son Hans. Many of the paintings on the altar wings were completed by Friedrich Pacher, another young artist apprenticed to Michael (the name "Pacher" was fairly common in the Pustertal, and he's not thought to be a relation). One of the panels known to be the work of Michael – and indeed one of the highlights of the piece as a whole – is the unsqueamishly graphic *Circumcision of Christ*, which you can see at the bottom of the wing to your left.

Elsewhere, the best collections of Michael Pacher's art are to be found in the Landesmuseum Ferdinandeum in Innsbruck (see p.469), the Museum mittelalterlicher Kunst in Vienna (see p.123) and the Alte Pinakothek in Munich.

Apart from the Pacher altar, the other thing that pulls in the tourists to St Wolfgang is the **Schafbergbahn**, a mountain rack railway operated by antique steam (and diesel) locomotives which ascends to the 1783-metre Schafberg, the bleak peak overlooking the lake to the north. To get there, either hop on one of the lake ferries to St Wolfgang Schafbergbahn, or walk the 1.5km west out of the town. There are between nine and twelve departures daily (May–Oct; return öS260/€18.89), but the trip is vastly (and deservingly) popular, so get there before 10am if you want to avoid queuing. For the full steam experience, make sure your train is a *Nostalgiezug* (for which a öS40/€2.90 supplement is payable). Alternatively, you can walk up the Schafbergweg that runs alongside the railway to the top in about three and a half hours. Once there, you can take in the awesome views over the Wolfgangsee, and towards the Mondsee and

Attersee to the north. The Schafbergspitze (☎06138/3542; ④) provides café, restaurant and accommodation should you get stranded at the top. If you're planning on walking down, the most exhilarating descent is via the Himmelspforte, to the west of the hotel, from which a precipitous zigzag path takes you under the sheer cliffs that characterize the northern face of the Schafberg. En route back to St Wolfgang, you can take a dip in the icy lake of the Mönichsee.

Practicalities

To keep traffic out of the centre, there is a road tunnel which bypasses St Wolfgang. **Buses** from Strobl will drop you off at the western end of the tunnel, a short stroll west of the town centre along Michael-Pacher-Strasse and right into Pilgerstrasse. Car drivers must use one of the numbered car parks before or after the tunnel. There are two **tourist offices**: the chief one is situated at the eastern entrance to the tunnel (Mon–Fri 9am–8pm, Sat 9am–noon & 2–8pm, Sun 2–8pm; ☎06138/2239, *www.salzkammergut.at /wolfgangsee*), with a subsidiary one at the eastern end of the tunnel in the Michael-Pacher-Haus (Mon–Fri 9am–noon & 2–5pm).

Either tourist office can fix you up with a **private room**, though there's no shortage of atmospheric and affordable Gasthöfe grouped around the church in the centre of town. The *Schwarzes Rössl*, Am Marktplatz 30 (☎06138/2373; closed Nov; ④), offers bright rooms with en-suite facilities, most with wrought-iron balconies. *Haus Erika*, Uferplatz 82 (☎06138/2387; ③), is another traditional building with window boxes, balconies and en-suite rooms overlooking the Schiffsstation. Set a little further back from the lakefront, *Pension Ellmauer*, Michael-Pacher-Strasse 183 (☎06138/2388, *sails@raudaschl.co.at*; ③), is a rather more functional, modern building, but most rooms come with south-facing balconies. Plush rooms with traditional wooden furnishings are the norm at the top-of-the-range, waterfront *Im Weissen Rössl*, Im Stöckl 74 (☎06138/2306, *www.weissesroessl.at*; ⑧), the hotel that inspired the operetta; another more secluded, and even more luxurious option is the venerable lakeside *Landhaus zu Appesbach* (☎06138/2209, *www.schlosshotels .co.at/appesbach*; closed Feb; ⑨), about 1km out of town along the road to Strobl, where the Duke of Windsor stayed following his abdication. There's a **campsite** right by the *Appesbach*, but you'll get better facilities, less traffic noise and more shade at the *Berau* (☎06138/2543, *www.berau.at*; open all year), another kilometre further along the road (and a short walk along the lake's shore from Strobl).

There's no end of hotel **restaurants** offering filling Austrian standards to the hordes of tourists prowling the streets, most of them charging fairly reasonable prices. *Andy's Stehbuffet*, on Markt in the village centre, is the place to go for Wurst-type **snacks**, while the nearby *Wolfgangstub'n* offers more substantial sit-down Austrian fare at low prices. *Pizzeria Mirabella*, Pilgerstrasse, serves inexpensive pizzas and pasta. Moving up in price, the *Hubertuskeller*, on Im Stöckl, has game dishes all the year round, while the *Weisses Rössl* (see above), offers top-quality grub (from öS150/€10.90 for main dishes; reservations advised) either on a lakefront terrace or in elegant dining rooms. *Seehotel Cortisen*, Schulgasse 9 (*www.cortisen.at*), west of the town centre, has a lakeside terrace, and often has wild mushrooms on its ambitious menu (main courses from öS150/€10.90; eves only), while the **bar** at *Disco Shooters*, opposite the Michael-Pacher-Haus, stays open until the early hours.

Mondsee

With the sheer rocky peaks of the Drachenwand and the Schafberg rising from its southern rim, the **Mondsee** lends itself equally to an all-out activity holiday or a spot of lazy waterside contemplation. If you want to loll by the lake, or have a quiet swim, head for one of the small settlements ranged along the southeastern half of the Mondsee. Most life on the lake, however, revolves around the town of the same name at the northwestern edge, an engaging place that grew up around a Benedictine **monastery** established by the Bavarians in the eighth century. It was here that St Wolfgang, Bishop of Regensburg, arrived in 976 to take a rest cure, embark on monastic reforms, and build a chapel in what is now St Wolfgang over the hills to the southeast. Mondsee town can be a quiet place, once the day-trippers drawn here by the monastery church pile back onto their coaches – but the proximity of Salzburg ensures a healthy influx of pleasure-seekers on summer weekends. The town is also the site of one of Austria's best **sailing and windsurfing** schools: the placid, warm waters of the lake make it ideal for children and novices, and there are boat- and board-rental facilities for those who no longer need tuition.

Getting to the lake presents few problems: the A1 Salzburg–Vienna autobahn sweeps past the lake and the resort to the north, and there are eight daily buses from Salzburg. There are no regular lake ferries on Mondsee.

The Town

MONDSEE's picturesque, café-strewn Marktplatz is set back from the lake, and lined with pretty pastel-coloured Baroque facades. On the east side of the Marktplatz is the broad expanse of Wrede Platz, presided over by the impressive vanilla-yellow bulk of the twin-towered **Pfarrkirche St Michael**, originally the church of the former Benedictine monastery, which retains its fifteenth-century net vaulting, and its distinctive red marble altar steps, familiar to many from the wedding scene of *The Sound of Music*. Other visitors are more likely to thrill to the name of **Meinrad Guggenbichler** (1649–1723), the Swiss-born sculptor who spent most of his life working at the monastery, producing seven of the thirteen black-and-gold Baroque side altars adorning the church. The harmonious combination of columns, arches and attendant statuary that form the altar-surrounds marks Guggenbichler as a master; the paintings that form the centrepieces of the altars were executed by other artists, and are for the most part less spectacular. The Corpus Christi Altar, the second one in the north aisle, is probably Guggenbichler's finest, its six spiralling, columns wreathed with gilded vines and supported by cherubic foursomes clutching grapes. To get a really good look at the altars, you may need to feed the light meter.

Next to the church, the former monastery buildings house the **Heimatmuseum** (May to mid-Sept Tues–Sun 10am–6pm; mid-Sept to mid-Oct Tues–Sun 10am–5pm; late Oct Sat & Sun 10am–5pm; öS40/€2.90), which features Baroque statuary from the monastery (including a few small-scale pieces by Guggenbichler) and an array of Neolithic finds. Nineteenth-century archeologists working at the eastern end of the Mondsee discovered lake dwellings that had been mounted on stilts (Pfahlen) dating from around 2500 BC, shedding light on a phase of Neolithic history that has subsequently been dubbed the "Mondsee culture". A selection of beakers and cups decorated with zigzags and circles steal the limelight in a collection otherwise dominated by fragments of functional, unadorned pottery.

A short stroll behind the church up Kirchengasse, on a grassy slope overlooking the town centre, is the small **Freilichtmuseum** (April Sat & Sun 10am–6pm; May to mid-Sept Tues–Sun 10am–6pm, mid-Sept to mid-Oct Tues–Sun 10am–5pm; late Oct Sat & Sun 10am–5pm; öS30/€2.18), comprised of a few outbuildings and one traditional farmhouse, the eighteenth-century **Rauchhaus** (literally "smoke-house"). One of two openhearth stoves on the ground floor is usually stoked up and smoking to give visitors an idea of what life might have been like – above it joints of meat would have been hung for home curing. The family living quarters are set to one side, away from the rising fumes, but farm labourers, servants and occasionally guests would have been expected to sleep in the malodorous bedrooms upstairs. Most of the furniture is unadorned and functional: the seeping smoke would have damaged anything more fancy.

A small promenading area and a public bathing beach, the Seebad (öS30/€2.18), extend along the **lakefront** 500m south of the centre. A couple of huts on the water's edge rent out rowing boats and pedalos, while windsurfing boards can be rented from the busy Segelschule beside the Seebad. Just inland, the **Lokalbahnmuseum** (mid-June to mid-Sept Sat & Sun 10am–noon & 2–5pm; July to mid-Sept also Fri 2–5pm; öS40/€2.90) recalls a now-disused narrow-gauge railway that once connected the Mondsee with Salzburg and Bad Ischl, displaying a couple of restored steam locomotives and a model railway.

Practicalities

Mondsee's **bus station** is a couple of blocks south of the town centre: head up Franz-Kreuzberger-Strasse, and then right down Rainerstrasse. The **tourist office** lies between the Marktplatz and the lake at Dr-Müller-Strasse 3 (July & Aug Mon–Fri 8am–7pm, Sat & Sun 9am–7pm; Sept–June Mon–Fri 9am–1pm & 2–5pm; ☎06232/2270, *www.mondsee.org*), and will fix you up with a **private room**. Mondsee is absolutely stuffed with a bewildering array of **accommodation** options, ranging from *Blaue Traube*, (☎06232/2237, *blaue.traube@magnet.at*; ④), an atmospheric old inn at Marktplatz 1, to *Pension Klimesch*, M.-Guggenbichler-Strasse 13 (☎06232/2563; ③), a roomier, more modern place near the lakefront. For a bit of lakeside luxury, head for the *Seehotel Lackner* (☎06232/23590, *www.seehotel-lackner.at*; ⑤), just west of the Seebad. The **HI hostel**, at Krankenhausstrasse 9 (☎06232/2418, *jgh.mondsee @oejhv.or.at*; closed mid-Dec to Jan), offers dorm beds together with a few double rooms, although it soon fills up. The most peaceful of the lake's campsites are those in St Lorenz, on the southern shore: try *Austria Camp Mondsee* (☎06232/2927; May–Sept).

If the weather's fine, it's nice to sit out at one of the **cafés** on the main square, the finest of which is the *Frauenschuh*, a venerable Kaffeehaus and Konditorei. Opposite, there's a choice between *Vini e Panini*, a more upmarket sandwich and pizza bar, and the next-door *La Cantina* which offers vaguely Mexican snacks on the ground floor, and pasta dishes upstairs. For a quick bite to eat, *Karl's Imbiss Stube*, M.-Guggenbichler-Strasse 5, is a good place for a stand-up sausage or sit-down chicken and chips, and there's fresh fish to be bought or served up for lunch from *Fischmarkt Seestern*, on Rainerstrasse (closed Sun). For more substantial fare, either the *Neue Post*, Rainerstrasse 9, or the restaurant of the *Blaue Traube* hotel, are the best places to sample traditional Austrian cooking. The restaurant of *Hotel Leitnerbräu*, Steinerbachstrasse 6 (out of season closed Wed), is a good (if pricey) place to sample fresh Mondsee fish.

For **drinking** near the waterfront, the *Lido Café*, Robert-Baum-Promenade, occupies a lakeside pavilion with plenty of outdoor seating. Further inland, there are several worthwhile bars along Herzog-Odilo-Strasse, the main street heading westwards from Marktplatz: *Café-Bar Tecini*, at no. 6, has a youngish clientele and relaxed feel, and *Mexaderros*, on the other side of the road, features kitsch decor and Mexican nibbles.

Attersee

Just a short hop east of the Mondsee lies the **Attersee** (or Kammersee), which, at 20km in length, is by far the largest of the Salzkammergut lakes. At its southern end, it is dominated by the Höllengebirge (Mountains of Hell), whose dramatic craggy outline can compete with that of any of the neighbouring lakes, but at its northern end, the hills fall away to reveal some fairly unsightly local industry. A hundred years ago, it was one of the region's most popular holiday spots, attracting thousands of pleasure-seekers, among them the likes of Mahler and Klimt. Even today, it has a steady flow of visitors, though what the lake really lacks is any truly compelling towns or sights. In short, if you've only got a small amount of time to spend in the lake region, the Attersee is not going to find its way to the top of your priority list, but if you're passing through, you could happily spend a lazy day or two here.

Fans of **Gustav Mahler** might like to pay a visit to **STEINBACH**, three-quarters of the way down the eastern shore, where the composer spent four successive summers from 1893 at the *Gasthof und Fleischhäuerei zum Höllengebirge* (now the *Gasthof Föttinger*) until they put up the prices. At the time the village was far from the hoi polloi, and Mahler spent most mornings cooped up in a little purpose-built *Komponierhäuschen*, where he worked on his second and third symphonies. Mahler was extremely sensitive to noise, and the rest of his entourage had to make sure they kept the children away and paid off organ-grinders before they started; in addition, the bells on the local cows were muffled and birds kept at bay by a scarecrow. A reconstructed version of Mahler's **Häuschen** now stands in the lakeside Seefeld campsite (to gain entry, pop into the Gasthof). Mahler was a keen walker, and Steinbach remains an excellent base for those wishing to explore the nearby peaks of the Höllengebirge. The tourist office (see below) can provide details.

Gustav Klimt was even more attached to the Attersee, whiling away every summer here from 1901 until his death in 1918. His mistress, the designer Emilie Flöge, owned a house in **UNTERACH**, a smart little village in the southwestern corner of the lake. Klimt spent the summers painting alfresco straight onto canvas, often rowing out into the lake to work. Unterach features in several of Klimt's paintings, as does nearby Weissenbach, the tree-lined avenue that leads to Schloss Kammer, and the small island near Litzlberg. Between Unterach and Weissenbach is probably the Attersee's most spectacular sight, the Burggraben Klamm or **Burgauklamm**, a thin 30ft waterfall in a dead-end rock amphitheatre suffused with spray. From the main road, it's not much more than a ten-minute walk up the ravine, along a dramatic (and often slippery) path.

Practicalities

Road and rail connections with the Attersee are best from the north, where the A1 Salzburg–Vienna autobahn skirts the lake, and there are two train stations. A narrow-gauge line runs from Vöcklamarkt on the main line to Attersee town, while another branch line runs from Vöcklabruck to Kammer-Schörfling. **Lake ferries** run only at the weekends: from Attersee station you have a choice of ferries, one serving the northern half of the lake, and another serving all points south; from Kammer-Schörfling you must change at either Weyregg or Attersee to continue south. There are **tourist offices** in the following resorts: Schörfling, Attersee, Weyregg, Nussdorf, Unterach and Steinbach, with the main one in the Gemeindeamt, west of Attersee train station (☎07666/7719, *www.attersee.at*), all of which can organize private rooms.

In Unterach, you can stay in one of small lakeside **pensions** like *Haus Stauber*, Jeritzastrasse 8 (☎07665/8273; ②), east of the village centre, or up in the hills to the north in some considerable luxury at the *Druckerhof*, Druckerstrasse 15 (☎07665/8295, *www.tiscover/druckerhof*; ④). The only **youth hostel** on the Attersee is just behind the main church in Weyregg, on the eastern shore (☎07664/2780; May–Oct). A good lakeside **campsite** is Unterach's own *Insel-Camping* (☎07665/7255, *camping@inselcamp.at*; Easter to mid-Oct) on an island just south of the town centre.

Bad Ischl

BAD ISCHL is without doubt Austria's most famous spa, primarily because the Emperor Franz-Josef I spent every summer here from his early childhood until his death at the age of 86 in 1916. Given that the town isn't actually on any of the region's cele-

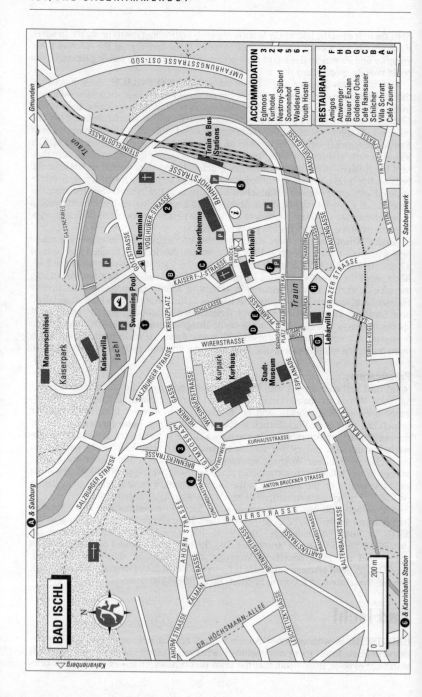

BAD ISCHL

ACCOMMODATION	
Eglmoos	3
Kurhotel	2
Nestroy-Stüberl	4
Sonnenhof	5
Waldesruh	6
Youth Hostel	1

RESTAURANTS	
Amigos	F
Attwenger	H
Blauer Enzian	D
Goldener Ochs	G
Café Ramsauer	C
Schilcher	B
Villa Schratt	A
Café Zauner	E

brated lakes, nor is it especially beautiful, it may seem an odd choice for your summer holidays when you've a whole empire to choose from. However, Franz-Josef was a man of simple tastes, and then as now, the town's main draw was probably its pivotal position within the Salzkammergut. All five of the major lakes (and their mountains) less than 20km away, have regular bus services to most places in the region and the region's north-south railway line runs through the town.

Bad Ischl started out as a centre for the region's salt-processing industry, only becoming a spa resort in the 1820s when Vienna's big-shot physicians discovered from local doctor, Josef Götz, that saltwater baths seemed to relieve the rheumatism suffered by the salt workers. Soon Bad Ischl had become one of central Europe's most important high society spas, attracting the likes of Strauss, Lehár, Bruckner and Brahms. The brother of Emperor Franz, Archduke Rudolph, Bishop of Olomouc (Olmütz), was an early visitor, and Metternich had Ischl saltwater delivered to him in Vienna. Archduchess Sophie ascribed prodigious powers to the Ischl waters after becoming pregnant with the future Emperor Franz-Josef here in 1829, and she proceeded to bring her brood (nicknamed the *Salzprinzen* (salt princes) due to Ischl's role in their conception) on holiday here every summer thereafter. It was here that Franz-Josef became engaged to the fifteen-year-old fellow spa guest and Bavarian princess, Elisabeth of Wittelsbach. The emperor eventually built himself the opulent hunting lodge of the **Kaiservilla**, from where he could walk upstream to the holiday home of his long-term mistress, Katharina Schratt, in time for breakfast.

Arrival, information and accommodation

Bad Ischl stands at the confluence of two rivers, with the compact town centre wedged between the Ischl to the north and the Traun to the south. Both the **bus** and **train station** are on the eastern fringe of the town centre, a few steps away from the **tourist office**, at Bahnhofstrasse 6 (Mon–Fri 9am–7pm, Sat 9am–3pm, Sun 10am–1pm; ☎06132/27757, *www.badischl.at*).

There are plenty of **private rooms**, and there's a modern, functional **HI hostel** near the swimming pool at Am Rechensteg 5 (☎06132/26577, *jgh.badischl@oejhv.or.at*), with a choice of beds in five-person dorms or in double rooms.

Hotels and pensions

Eglmoos, Eglmoosgasse 14 (☎06132/23154). An ivy-clad, balconied building with clean and comfy rooms, all with shared facilities. ②.

Kurhotel, Voglhuberstrasse 10 (☎06132/204, *www.tourism.co.at/badischl/kurhotel*). A modern, glass-and-concrete structure with all imaginable spa and health-cure facilities on site (aka the Kaisertherme). ⑨.

Nestroy-Stüberl, Brennerstrasse 16 (☎06132/23017, *www.nestroy-stueberl.atech.at*). A modern building in a residential area at the bottom of the Kalvarienberg, a wooded hill just west of the centre. All rooms have en-suite shower and TV. ③.

Sonnhof, Bahnhofstrasse 4 (☎06132/23078, *hotel@sonnhof.at*). One of the nicest (though not the cheapest) pensions in town, in an old villa near the town centre, offering rooms with en-suite facilities and elegant modern furnishings. ⑥.

Waldesruh, Kaltenbachstrasse 43 (☎06132/24558). Large, modern chalet-style pension 2km southwest of the centre, near the Katrin gondola station. All rooms have a balcony and en-suite facilities. ③.

The Town

For a spa resort, Bad Ischl is disappointingly urban, with traffic pounding round its one-way system and only a few leafy spaces in which to recuperate. The central **Kurpark**, west of Wirerstrasse, features the obligatory Kaisergelb (imperial yellow) **Kurhaus**, where the town's operetta season is staged, and there are occasional outdoor concerts given by the Kurorchester, but it's a fairly minuscule park. The largest green space is the **Kaiserpark**, north of the River Ischl, which has an admission charge and forbids visitors from walking on the grass (see below). The most obvious sign of spa life is at the **Trinkhalle** (Mon–Fri 8am–12.30pm & 1.30–5pm, Sat 9am–noon), the long, bare pump rooms on Auböckplatz, where old folk gather to quaff glasses of the local water (öS16/€1.16 a cup), read the free newspapers, and listen to a pianist or the Kurorchester play.

A few steps west of the Trinkhalle, the leafy **Esplanade** leads along the banks of the Traun past a sequence of elegant town houses. At no. 10, the **Stadtmuseum** (Tues & Thurs–Sun 10am–5pm, Wed 2–7pm; July & Aug also Mon 10am–5pm; öS50/€3.63) is housed in the former *Hotel Austria*, where the 24-year-old Emperor Franz-Josef became engaged in August 1853 to his cousin, the unfortunate future Empress Elisabeth (see p.135). Photographs and mementos of the imperial family understandably dominate the collection, but there's also a colourful section detailing Salzkammergut custom and costume. Among items on show are the enormous star-shaped hats worn by the Ebensee *Glöckler* (see p.440), as well as more local folk-costume essentials like the curious *Goldhaube*, an embroidered cap of gold-coloured material, gathered into a comb-like

---

FRANZ LEHÁR

Franz Lehár (1870–1948) was the Andrew Lloyd Webber of his day, writing popular music-theatre for a wide audience and making a great deal of money at it. He revitalized the world of Viennese operetta and made himself a dollar millionaire with *Die lustige Witwe* (*The Merry Widow*) in 1905, following it up with several scores which, if not repeating that astonishing success, were hugely popular all round the world.

Born in the Hungarian barracks town of Komárom (Komárno) where his father was a military bandmaster, Lehár was a true product of the Austro-Hungarian Empire. He spent his childhood stationed with his father's regiment in various towns across central Europe, and entered the Prague conservatory aged 12 to study the violin. Dvořák, no less, is reputed to have advised him: "Hang up your fiddle and start composing." When called up for military service he followed in his father's footsteps and served as a regimental bandmaster, then in 1902 settled in Vienna and started conducting at the Theater an der Wien, one of the city's principal operetta houses.

Featuring a plot charged with tingling emotional encounters, plenty of misunderstandings and a Ruritanian setting, *Die lustige Witwe* (with a libretto written by Oscar Léon and Leo Stein), became a Viennese sensation and went on to take audiences in Germany, London and New York by storm. The score inaugurated what was to become known as the Silver Age of Viennese operetta, which was epitomized by Lehár and fellow Hungarian Emmerich Kálmán.

After a couple of flops, Lehár scored another success with *Der Graf von Luxemburg* (1909) and *Zigeunerliebe* (*Gypsy Love*) in 1910, both of which won international acclaim. World War I served to dampen the worldwide popularity of Viennese music, but the subsequent downturn in Lehár's career was overcome by his association with the tenor Richard Tauber, who became the most celebrated performer of Lehár's music and gave his name to *Tauberlieder*, hugely popular songs which have become more famous than the operettas that spawned them. The most famous of these, *Dein ist mein ganzes Herz* (*You are my Heart's Delight*), comes from Lehár's last international triumph, *Das Land des Lächelns* (*The Land of Smiles*), 1929.

Despite having married a Jewish woman, Lehár chose to stay in Vienna during World War II. He was one of Adolf Hitler's favourite composers, and prepared a new overture to *Die lustige Witwe*, which he dedicated to the Führer in an attempt to protect himself and his wife. Lehár moved to Switzerland for a few years after the war, before taking up full-time residence in his villa in Bad Ischl, where he died in 1948.

protuberance at the back, and the *Schwammerlhut* (literally "spongy hat"), a white, wide-brimmed felt hat, at one time worn by peasants to keep the sun off while working in the fields, but subsequently adopted as a kind of Sunday best.

On the opposite bank of the Traun, across the Elisabethbrücke you can take a guided tour round the **Lehárvilla** (May–Sept daily 9am–noon & 2–5pm; öS55/€4.00), erstwhile summer home of **Franz Lehár** (see box), a handsome mansion with a lovely wooden balcony. The Hungarian-born military bandmaster, who achieved something of a career breakthrough with his 1905 comic opera *Die lustige Witwe (The Merry Widow)*, spent nearly every summer in the villa from 1910 to his death here in 1948. A few original manuscripts are on display, and the sumptuous furnishings (some belonging to Lehár, but most acquired later) provide an insight into how the opulent holiday retreats of the great and the good were arranged.

The Kaiserpark

Given that there's not much else to do in Bad Ischl, most visitors feel obliged to pay homage to the Emperor Franz-Josef's holiday home, which is situated in the **Kaiserpark**, on the wooded slopes of the north bank of the River Ischl. As you cross the bridge you must decide if you're going to visit just the park (öS40/€2.90), or go the whole hog and sign up for a guided tour of the Kaiservilla as well (öS130/€9.45). If, having paid to enter the park, you're expecting stunning floral displays and winsome herbaceous borders – think again. The (not particularly extensive) grounds are, in fact, laid in an informal "English" style, though you're still expected to keep to the paths.

The **Kaiservilla** (April Sat & Sun 9–11.15am & 1–4.45pm; May to mid-Oct daily 9–11.15am & 1–4.45pm) itself is a pompous Neoclassical mansion, complete with pedimental friezes on hunting themes, and was purchased from a Viennese lawyer by the Archduchess Sophie as an engagement present for Franz-Josef and Elisabeth of Bavaria. Anything less like a hunting lodge it would be difficult to imagine, and though Franz-Josef came here every summer for the next sixty years, it was never the happy love nest originally envisaged. In the 1880s, the Empress Elisabeth encouraged Franz-Josef to take the actress Katharina Schratt, as his mistress. Schratt was given her own Ischl retreat, the Villa Felicitas (now the Villa Schratt) at a discreet distance from the Kaiservilla, a couple of kilometres upstream – the key which enabled her to take a short cut through the Kaiserpark was presented to her by the empress herself. The emperor also liked to relax in the company of local serving girls, who were usually delivered to the mountain huts where he stopped off during hunting trips. Franz-Josef's passion for the hunt sent him roaming the hills around Ischl, Goisern and the Attersee in search of prey – the heads and antlers of his unfortunate victims now crowd the walls of the villa, and the Schussliste records that he personally shot over 50,000 creatures. The imperial apartments are otherwise suprisingly plain and functional, reflecting the disciplined, workaholic habits of this cold and austere Habsburg.

Beyond the villa lies the much more appealing **Marmorschlössel** (little marble castle), a neo-Gothic garden retreat built for the Empress Elisabeth, with a lovely vine-covered loggia. Today, the building houses a **Photomuseum** (April–Oct daily 9.30am–5pm; öS15/€1.08), containing archaic cameras, family albums from the turn of the twentieth century, and a section on the history of the Leica (with an English-language voice-over), the prototype for the compact cameras of today.

Walking and the Salzbergwerk

There are several small hillocks within easy reach of the centre of Ischl: **Siriouskogel** (599m), to the south, up Sirius-Kogel-Gasse; **Kalvarienberg** (606m), to the northwest; and **Jainzenberg** (834m), behind the Kaiserpark to the north. The most direct route to higher planes, however, is provided by the Katrinbahn gondola (mid-May to Oct &

early Dec to Easter; öS160/€11.62 return), which commences 2km southwest of the centre and rises to just below the peak of **Katrin** (1544m), the starting point for numerous walks. Bad Ischl–Lauffen buses pass by the gondola station, but they're far from frequent; to get there on foot, walk westwards along the Esplanade and keep going for 25 minutes.

Three kilometres south of the town, the Bad Ischl **Salzbergwerk**, or salt mine (daily: May & June 9am–3.45pm; July–Sept 10am–4.45pm; öS140/€10.17), is a showmine like the one at Hallein (see p.402). Guided tours are cold but fun, and involve a train ride into the mine and a chance to slide down the wooden slides that conveyed miners from one level of the galleries to another. Bad Ischl–Perneck buses stop nearby, but it's also possible to walk if you follow Grazerstrasse southwards from the Elisabethbrücke.

Eating, drinking and entertainment

There's a plethora of places to **eat**, with most central Gashöfe offering inexpensive Mittagsmenüs to pull in the milling crowds. For a real bargain lunch, head for the Schilcher deli, on Kaiser-Franz-Josef-Strasse (closed Sun), which serves up meaty dishes washed down with beer. *Goldener Ochs*, on Grazerstrasse, has outdoor garden seating, an emphasis on meat, especially veal, and a good-value Tagesmenü. *Blauer Enzian*, Wirerstrasse 2 (closed Sun), also serves inexpensive Austrian standards, in a courtyard or a cosy traditional dining room. *Weinhaus Attwenger*, Léharkai 12 (closed Mon), is an attractive, riverside chalet-style building with outdoor tables, offering the usual mid-priced Austrian staples. For a change from Austrian fare, the lively *Amigos*, Auböckplatz 9, serves up Tex-Mex food, at reasonable prices. For top-quality dining in period rooms stuffed with hunting trophies, try the *Villa Schratt*, 1.5km along the road to St Gilgen at Steinbruch 43 (reservations advised: ☎06132/27647; closed Tues & Wed), housed in the former villa of Franz-Josef's mistress – expect to pay more than öS500/€36.33 a head.

For daytime **drinking**, the *Café Zauner*, Pfarrgasse 7, is the classic Kaffee-Konditorei in which the cream of fin-de-siècle society whiled away the afternoons. There's also a branch of *Zauner* at Hasnerallee 2 (May–Sept only), in a nineteenth-century riverside pavilion with plenty of outdoor seating, and which is the more popular choice in summer. For a genuine smokey *Kaffeehaus*, however, you're better off heading for the *Café Ramsauer*, at Kaiser-Franz-Josef-Strasse 8. For night-time drinking, there's a string of bars in the narrow lanes behind the church on Auböckplatz: *Tapas* offers trendy imported beers and Spanish nibbles; *Heuriger zum Postgarten* is a good place to sample some Austrian wine and has a large area of outdoor seating; and *Rockcafé K3* features the kind of taped music suggested by its name.

Entertainment

Bad Ischl's impressive musical pedigree is remembered in the local operetta season, as well as in performances by the Kurorchester (Spa orchestra) around town throughout the summer. Bad Ischl's **Operetten Festspiele** (*www.operette.badischl.at*) runs from early July to early September, and its programme almost invariably centres around at least one major work by Johann Strauss the Younger. Tickets (starting at öS180/€13.08) are available from the Kartenbüro in the Kurhaus (Mon–Sat 9am–noon & 3–6pm; ☎06132/23839).

From late June to early September, waltz music and popular classics are performed by the **Kurorchester** two or three times a day, either in the Kurhaus, the Kurpark, the Trinkhalle or the *Café Zauner* on the Esplanade. Bad Ischl also has an annual country music festival over the Whitsun (Pfingsten) weekend, attracting top bands from Europe and medium-ranking acts from the USA. The tourist office (see p.435) will have details.

Traunsee

One of the Salzkammergut's busiest lakes in summer, the **Traunsee** owes much of its charm to the rugged grey mountains that dominate from the east – the Erlakogel, the Rötelspitze and, most majestic of all, the classically craggy peak of the **Traunstein** (1691m). In contrast to its immediate surroundings, **Ebensee**, at the southern end of the lake and the first town you come to from Bad Ischl, is a comparatively drab industrial town, with one of the Salzkammergut's best cable-car rides by way of compensation. The main road and the rail line hug the western shoreline, where **Traunkirchen** and **Altmünster** stand out amongst the numerous resorts. At the northern end of the lake lies **Gmunden**, the biggest lakeside resort in the area, and a place of some considerable charm despite the heavy traffic that ploughs through the centre. From Gmunden you can gain access to the peaceful, mountainous eastern shore of the lake.

All resorts along the western shore are accessible by short hops on the Attnang-Puchheim to Stainach-Irdning **railway**. Gmunden can also be reached on a privately operated narrow-gauge line from Vorchdorf-Eggenberg, which you can get to from Lambach on the main Vienna–Salzburg line. In fine weather, **lake ferries** (Easter–Oct Sat & Sun; mid-May to Sept also Tues; July & Aug daily; *www.tiscover.com /traunseeschiffahrt*) connect not only the western resorts, but also reach the more remote spots on the eastern shore.

Ebensee and around

EBENSEE straddles the River Traun at the point where it flows into the lake. The town has a perfectly serviceable lakefront, with a yachting marina on the west bank of the Traun and a Strandbad on the east, both of which are separated from the town itself by the main road and the railway line. First and foremost, though, Ebensee is an important centre for the salt industry, and as such looks incongruously workaday amidst such lovely scenery, with truck loads of the rock salt travelling across the main road on an overhead cable.

Ebensee concentration camp – KZ Ebensee

In November 1943, the Nazis established a **concentration camp** on the outskirts of Ebensee. In less than two years, around 27,000 prisoners passed through the camp, where more than 8000 died. One of the largest satellite camps serving Mauthausen (see p.236), the inmates of **KZ Ebensee** were put to work blasting a massive complex of tunnels into the nearby mountain of Seeberg (1143m). The idea was to relocate the Peenemünde missile testing centre on Germany's Baltic coast and make it safe from Allied air raids. In the end, the tunnels were simply used to store fuel and other equipment. Nothing remains of the camp, which held over 16,000 malnourished prisoners at the end of the war, except the original gateway, which stands incongruously surrounded by the well-to-do suburb of Finkerleiten. Signposts will lead you to the **KZ-Friedhof**, where a series of mass graves and multinational memorials, erected by relatives, commemorate the camp victims. Five minutes' walk away is the **KZ-Gedenkstollen** May, June & Oct Sat & Sun 10am–noon & 2–6pm; July–Sept Wed–Sun 10am–noon & 2–6pm; öS40/€2.90), housed in one of the vast underground galleries within the mountain, where a small, but harrowing exhibition (in English and German) recounts the grim history of the camp – the temperature is a constant eight degrees Celsius, so take warm clothing.

Feuerkogel, Offensee and Langbathsee

By far Ebensee's biggest crowd-puller is the **Feuerkogel-Seilbahn** (mid-May to Oct 8.30am–5pm; öS205/€14.90 return), the cable-car that departs from the western fringes of town, up the road to Langbathsee (see below). In summer, the cable car deposits passengers on a ski-run ravaged alpine meadow below the summit of the **Feuerkogel** (1625m), where there are several places to grab something to eat while enjoying the views. The descent to Ebensee takes about two hours, or you can continue west to the **Grosser Höllkogel** (1862m), the highest of the mountains in the Höllengebirge range, and about two and a half hours' walk from the Feuerkogel.

On a lazy, hot day, you might prefer to follow the steady stream of holiday-makers and head for one of the small lakes hidden in the nearby mountains. Seven kilometres west of Ebensee, the **Langbathsee** is, in fact, two lakes. The shoreline of the larger of the two, Vorderer Langbathsee is chock-a-block with bathers on a sunny summer's day, though the crowds thin the further you go away from the lakeside hotel. For a colder, quieter dip against the dramatic rocky backdrop of the Höllengebirge, continue on to the Hinterer Langbathsee, a gentle half-hour's walk through the woods. Alternatively, there are the slightly warmer waters of the **Offensee**, a lake 10km southeast of Ebensee, surrounded by a similarly impressive range of mountains, in this case, the Totes Gebirge. Neither lake is served by public transport, but both are an easy cycle ride from Ebensee.

Practicalities

Ebensee **train station** is 1km inland from the lake – it's better to get off at Ebensee-Landungsplatz, the station to the north, which is 200m away from the lakefront and virtually next door to the **tourist office** in the modern Rathaus on Hauptstrasse (Mon–Fri 8am–noon & 2–5pm; July & Aug Mon–Fri 8am–6pm, Sat 9am–noon & 2–6pm; ☎06133/8016, *www.tiscover.com/ebensee*), which can fix you up with a **private room**. Alternatively, try the *Seegasthof Rindbach*, at Strandbadstrasse 1 (☎06133/7187; Easter–Sept; ③), a lovely rustic-looking villa, which stands near the main lakeside bathing area, 1.5km east of the tourist office; the majority of the rooms have en-suite shower and a balcony. Nearby, at Rindbachstrasse 15, there's a good **youth hostel** (☎06133/6698, *ebensee@jutel.at*; May–Oct).

Ebensee is enlivened by a local **festival** on the night of January 5–6 by the **Glöcklerlaufen**, when the menfolk – clad in white, laden with cowbells and wearing enormous *Lichtkappen* (star-shaped hats made of tissue paper illuminated from within by lanterns) – rush about the town scaring away evil spirits.

Traunkirchen

To the north of Ebensee, the mountains plunge straight into the lake forcing both road and rail through a series of tunnels along the western shore. Before the advent of motorized transport, only boats could reach the tiny fishing village of **TRAUNKIRCHEN**, which perches prettily on a rocky promontory 5km up the lake. Traunkirchen's most photographed image is that of the little grey chapel on the wooded hill clearly visible when approaching the village from the south. However, it's the **Pfarrkirche**, to the north, with its tiny cemetery overlooking the lake, that actually merits closer inspection. Handed over to the Jesuits in the seventeenth century and rebuilt with a typically lavish Baroque interior, the church's star attraction is its **Fischerkanzel** (Fishermen's pulpit), which features a fabulous gilded fishing boat, with James and John at either end pulling in the miraculous draught of fishes (as described in Luke's Gospel), and giant sea monsters swimming around in the cascade of silver seawater beneath. The pulpit is topped by a statue of the Jesuit missionary St Francis-Xavier, accompanied by multiethnic cherubs in gilded head-dresses, and a lobster – the latter recalling the crustacean who retrieved a crucifix that the saint had lost at sea on the way to Japan. Also worthy of note are the unusual painted tapestries, depicting yet more Jesuit saints, that line the chancel. On the festival front,

Traunkirchen is the site of an annual **Corpus Christi procession**, when villagers take to the water in small boats festooned with banners, in similar fashion to the much larger affair in Hallstatt (see p.447).

To get to the village, alight at the Traunkirchen-Ort **train station**, rather than at Bahnhof Traunkirchen which is several kilometres north of the village. Here you're just uphill from the centre, where there's a **tourist office** in the Gemeindeamt (Mon–Fri 8am–noon & 2–4pm; ☎07617/2234, *www.tiscover.com/traunkirchen*) with a small list of **private rooms**. Two **pensions** just south of the tourist office, each occupying a chalet-style house with its own stretch of lakefront, are the *Zimmermann* (☎07617/2371; ②) and the smaller *Hüthmayr* (☎07617/3488; ③). The central *Hotel Post*, overlooking the main square (☎07617/2307, *www.tiscover.com/hotel.post*; ⑤), is the most characterful of a trio of big hotels. The **restaurant** at the *Post* is the place to go for top-notch Austrian cuisine, while the *Gasthof Goldener Hirsch* on the main road through town has some inexpensive lunchtime options and a traditional schnitzel-type repertoire, with dishes at around the öS100/€7.30 mark.

Altmünster

Heading north from Traunkirchen, the next settlement of any size is **ALTMÜNSTER**, an out-and-out recreational resort and where virtually every other house is a Gasthof, pension or holiday apartment. With the towering bulk of the Traunstein on the opposite shore, Altmünster boasts vistas as attractive as any the Salzkammergut has to offer, though the traffic that thunders along the main road is a definite turn-off. This noisy thoroughfare separates the lakeside promenade and public bathing area from the village centre up Marktstrasse, which nevertheless retains a quiet unspoilt atmosphere.

The village revolves around the Gothic **Pfarrkirche**, with its distinctive bare stone tower topped by a broach spire. Inside, the church is a strange mixture: modern entrances to the north and south, low, playful Gothic vaulting in the nave, and a taller, lighter Baroque chancel. Without prior knowledge, it would be easy to miss the church's most treasured object, the sixteenth-century **Allerheiligenaltar** (All Saints' Altar), hidden in a side chapel off the south porch. This lightly gilded sandstone altar features a lively melee of holy men carved in high relief, and set within a gloriously ornate Renaissance frame of decorated columns and entablature and crowned with a Crucifixion scene. The chapel also contains the tomb of Count Herberstorff, who, during the Upper Austrian peasant wars of the 1620s, forced Protestant rebels to play dice for their lives after capturing them near Frankenburg – the losers were hanged.

Altmünster also boasts a charming little **Zweiradmuseum** (Two-wheeled museum: May, June, Sept & Oct Sat & Sun 2–5pm, July & Aug daily 10am–noon & 2–6pm; öS45/€3.27), situated next to the Neoclassical Schloss Ebenzweier (now a boarding school for aspiring chefs), a short stroll west of Marktstrasse. Packed with rank upon rank of old bikes, plus a few scooters and motorcycles, and a lovely single-cylinder BMW Knutschkugel (Love Ball), built in 1959 – a bit of a cheat since it has three wheels. There's a four-in-a-row tandem from 1899, a Waffenrad (army bicycle), built in 1902 in Steyr, with a convenient holder for an officer's ceremonial sword and briefcase, and a wooden bicycle from 1813 with no pedals and no brakes.

Practicalities

Altmünster's **train station** is 1km south of the village centre down Bahnhofstrasse, which connects with Marktstrasse, where you'll find the **tourist office** (June–Sept Mon–Fri 8am–7pm, Sat 9am–noon & 4–7pm, Sun 3–6pm; Oct–May Mon–Fri 9am–noon & 2–5pm; ☎07612/8718, *www.tiscover.com/altmuenster*), next door to the Pfarrkirche. The office can fix you up with a **private room**, and there's also a free accommodation phone down by the main road. Good-value **hotels** include the balconied, family-run *Rittertal*, a few steps north of the Pfarrkirche at Lindenstrasse 7 (☎07612/87131; ③), and the pension, *Schlössl am See*, an attractive nineteenth-century villa along the lake south of the centre at Don-Alfonso-Weg 9 (☎07612/87136; open May–Sept; ③). Altmünster's **campsite** (☎07612/89313; May–Sept), on the lakeside promenade has good views of the Traunstein across the water, but suffers badly from traffic noise.

For **food**, the *Kirchenwirt*, just by the church on Marktstrasse, offers good-value traditional Austrian cuisine in unpretentious surroundings, while the *Gasthof Rieberstorfer*, Maximilianstrasse 2, is slightly more upmarket but without being prohibitively priced, and *Pizzeria Romantico*, Marktstrasse 1 (eves only), has a range of inexpensive pizzas and pasta dishes. The *Stau* next door is a lively, late place for a **drink**, as is *Bierwandl*, Ackerweg 2 (May–Oct only).

Gmunden

GMUNDEN is the only fully fledged lakeside town in the Salzkammergut. Self-confident nineteenth-century urban architecture sets the tone of the place, and reflects the wealth accrued by the town over the centuries through its key role in the local salt trade. During the nineteenth century, Gmunden also became one of the region's most popular resorts, boasting a guest list to rival that of Bad Ischl, including such august names as Kaiser Wilhelm II, Tsar Nicholas of Russia, Franz Schubert, Johannes Brahms, Arnold Schönberg and Béla Bartók. Nowadays, Gmunden has a well-established ceramic industry, and remains a popular resort, though the town's traffic-clogged streets can be oppressive on hot summer days. On wet weather days, or in the evening, however, the benefits of staying in or around Gmunden become apparent, with its decent range of eating options and choice of places to enjoy an alfresco lakeside drink.

Arrival, information and accommodation

Trains on the Attnang-Puchheim to Stainach-Irdning line stop at Gmunden's **main train station**, 2km northwest of the centre; a single **tram** line runs from here every thirty minutes to Franz-Josefs-Platz near the Theater (you buy your ticket from the driver); if you miss it, turn left out of the station, bear right, then carry on for about twenty minutes to reach the centre. Trains from Lambach, via Vorchdorf-Eggenberg, arrive at the **Seebahnhof** on the eastern bank of the Traun, whence it's a straightforward five-minute walk across the Traunbrücke to the centre.

The **tourist office** at Am Graben 2 (Mon–Thurs 8am–6pm, Fri 8am–7pm, Sat 9am–noon & 4–7pm, Sun 10am–noon & 3–6pm; ☎07612/64305, *www.tiscover.com /gmunden*) has a list of **private rooms** – a particularly enticing option here, since Gmunden's **hotels** are expensive by Salzkammergut standards.

Freisitz Roith, Traunsteinstrasse 87 (☎07612/64905, *www.tiscover.com/schlosshotel*). Full-on seventeenth-century chateau, with bags of atmosphere, very comfortable rooms, and its own lakeside terrace. Situated 1.5km southeast of the town centre. ⑨.

Goldener Brunnen, Traungasse 10 (☎07612/64431). Probably the best-value old-town option, a comfortable if unexciting place whose rooms come with en-suite facilities and TV. ④.

Hotel Schwan, Rathausplatz 8 (☎07612/63391, *www.bestwestern.com/at/seehoteschwan*). A town centre lakeside pile run by the *Best Western* chain offering all the usual creature comforts. ⑤.

Seepension Neuwirth, Traunsteinstrasse 149 (☎07612/63631). A modern chalet-style building 3km south of the town centre, along the quieter eastern shore of the lake. ②.

Zum Hois'n-Wirt, Traunsteinstrasse 277 (☎07612/77333, *www.hoisnwirt.at*; March–Oct). Excellent-value, small Gasthof some 5km down the eastern shore from Gmunden, though only a short walk from the lake ferry pier at Ramsau. ⑤.

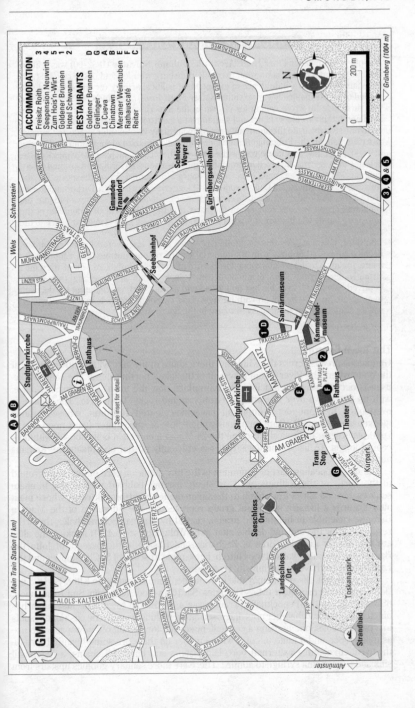

GMUNDEN

ACCOMMODATION
Freisitz Roith — 3
Seepension Neuwirth — 4
Zum Hois'n-Wirt — 5
Goldener Brunnen — 1
Hotel Schwann — 2

RESTAURANTS
Goldener Brunnen — D
Grellinger — G
La Cueva — A
Chinatown — B
Meraner Weinstuben — E
Rathauscafé — F
Reiter — C

◁ Main Train Station (1 km)
◁ Wels ◁ Scharnstein
◁ A & B
Altmünster ▽
Grünberg (1004 m) ▷
▷ 3, 4 & 5

Schloss Weyer
Gmunden Traundorf
Grünbergseilbahn
Seebahnhof
Stadtpfarrkirche
Rathaus
Seeschloss Ort
Landschloss Ort
Toskanapark
Strandbad

Sanitärmuseum
Kammerhof-museum
Stadtpfarrkirche
Rathaus
Theater
Kurpark
Tram Stop
Marktplatz
Rathaus-platz
Traungasse

See inset for detail

ARCHDUKE JOHANN SALVATOR

A nephew of Emperor Franz-Josef, **Archduke Johann Salvator** (1852–90) was a liberal-minded, romantic and somewhat excitable Habsburg who fell foul of the rule that forbade family members' indulgence in independent political activity (or any activity disapproved of by the manically conservative Kaiser Franz-Josef). Salvator's problems started with an article he wrote calling for reform in the imperial artillery. As a result he was sidelined by the Viennese court and sent to run a garrison in the virtual exile of Linz.

Eager to escape from the anonymity of provincial army life, Salvator suggested himself as a candidate for the Bulgarian throne following the abdication of Alexander Battenberg in 1886. After his candidacy was withdrawn on the orders of his exasperated uncle, Salvator then became involved in promoting the cause of vain German aristo (and future king of Bulgaria) Ferdinand von Saxe-Coburg. Consumed by enthusiasm for the Bulgarian cause (the small Balkan state was at loggerheads with both Turkey and Russia at the time, and under constant threat of invasion), Salvator next attempted to join the Bulgarian army, but was refused on the basis that the enlistment of a member of the Habsburg family would disrupt Austria's cautious diplomatic efforts to bring peace to the region.

Salvator, however, saw this as another personal slight engineered by the court, and decided to sever his links with the imperial family, renouncing his title, adopting the name Johann Orth and marrying low-born dancer Milly Stubel, of whom the court strongly disapproved. The death of Crown Prince Rudolf at Mayerling (see p.209) deprived Salvator-Orth of his last real friend and ally at court, precipitating his decision to emigrate. In 1890 he set off with his new bride for South America, in a self-captained sailing ship that went missing somewhere in the South Atlantic.

The Town Centre

Gmunden spreads across the whole northern shore of the lake with its town centre at the point where the River Traun flows out of the lake's northern end. The central lakefront is occupied by the spacious **Rathausplatz**, now the town's main market place, with its fine views over the wooded Grünberg and rocky Traunstein. The square is overlooked by Gmunden's imposing pistachio-coloured **Rathaus**, whose ceramic glockenspiel (summer 10am, then hourly noon–5pm & 7pm; winter 10am, noon, 2, 4 & 7pm) plays several classical ditties on the 24 Meissen porcelain bells housed within its central loggia. (A list of the day's tunes is efficiently posted up outside the Rathaus door.)

The most appealing part of Gmunden is the tiny medieval core on the high ground to the north of the Rathaus, with its steep, narrow, cobbled streets and intimate squares. Several alleys lead uphill to the onion-domed **Stadtpfarrkirche**, whose main altar features a life-size sculptural group representing the Adoration of the Magi, a Baroque ensemble of heightened drama, carved by Thomas Schwanthaler, the artist responsible for the unusual double altar at St Wolfgang (see p.428); flanking the altar are the heavily gilded figures of Zacharias and Elisabeth, the parents of John the Baptist. On the outer walls of the church, late-Gothic frescoes of St Christopher and the Last Judgement have been clumsily restored.

Without doubt, the most enjoyable of Gmunden's museums is the Klo & So (*Klo* is a "loo") or **Sanitärmuseum** (May–Oct Tues–Sat 10am–noon & 2–5pm, Sun 10am–noon; öS28/€2.03), in the Pepöckhaus, Traungasse 4, in the old town. The first room has nineteenth-century chamber pots disguised as everything from ruche cushioned stools to a pile of books, one housing a convenient section for storing old newspapers to use as toilet paper, and a knife to cut it with. Further on there are some beautiful turn-of-the-twentieth-century patterned porcelain *pissoirs* and hand-pull chains, a Jugendstil sink and a tin enema syringe to admire. There are more sanitary goodies upstairs from the post-flush era including the Empress Elisabeth's bidet from Corfu and Franz-Josef's stained water-closet from one of the local alpine huts he used. Also on this floor is a permanent display of local folk art and artefacts.

The **Kammerhofmuseum** (Mon–Sat 10am–noon & 2–5pm, Sun 10am–noon; öS28/€2.03), in the former medieval salt exchequer one block east of the Rathaus, is a much less distinguished local museum. The most interesting items here are the model of the town in 1650 – it was the only walled town in the Salzkammergut – and the model of the Traunsee's venerable paddle steamer, *Gisela*. Also worth seeking out is the small selection of predominantly turquoise local ceramics, versions of which you can see on sale in the town's shops.

Schloss Ort

The long leafy **Esplanade** runs southwest from the town centre along the lakefront, passing a yachting marina before eventually reaching the peninsula that juts out into the lake, and is home to the seventeenth-century quadrilateral **Landschloss Ort**, built by Count Herberstorff (instigator of the notorious Frankenburg dice game – see p.441) and subsequently owned by the endearingly flaky **Archduke Johann Salvator** (see box opposite). A Rococo fountain can be glimpsed in the courtyard of the Schloss (now a forestry training centre), but most visitors head straight for the wooden footbridge, which leads to the fifteenth-century **Seeschloss Ort** on an island just offshore.

This picturesque Schloss forms the centrepiece of the extremely successful German TV series, *Schlosshotel Orth*, which is shot at various locations around the Traunsee (each marked with special *Schlosshotel Orth* signs). You can admire the two-tier arcading in the triangular inner courtyard, and visit the small Gothic chapel and prison tower. Fans of the TV series can also relieve themselves of some money in the castle's souvenir shop, rather misleadingly called the "Filmmuseum", or sign up for a guided tour (Thurs & Sun 2.30pm; öS40/€2.90) – to enquire about one of the more extensive *Schlosshotel Orth* tours around the Traunsee, contact the Gmunden tourist office (see p.442). South of Schloss Ort, paths continue to Gmunden's main public **Strandbad**.

Schloss Weyer and the Grünberg

Anyone with a real passion for porcelain should head for **Schloss Weyer** (May–Sept Tues–Sat 10am–noon & 2–5pm, Sun 10am–noon; öS66/€4.80), a delightfully secluded little Renaissance chateau 1km east of the town centre and the River Traun, on Freygasse. The chateau basically has a gallery on the ground floor, which puts on exhibitions of porcelain which change annually – you can buy some of the pieces, too, at very serious prices.

The main draw on the eastern side of town, however, is the **Grünbergseilbahn** (daily: May, June, Sept & Oct 9am–5pm; July & Aug 9am–6pm; öS128/€9.30 return), a cable car which rises to the upper flanks of the rounded, wooded mountain of **Grünberg** (1084m). At the top you're treated to an expansive panorama of the Traunsee. A network of trails can lead you back down the mountain in an hour or so, or further south via the Laudachsee and back down to Hois'n or Ramsau on the lake's shore (3hr). If you're keen to climb the **Traunstein** (1691m) itself, bear in mind you have to approach the mountain from Mairalm to the south, from which it's a three-hour round trip.

Eating and drinking

As far as **food** is concerned, *Reiter*, Rinnholzplatz (closed Sun), is the place to pick up a cheap daytime snack. For more substantial fare, the restaurant at the *Goldener Brunnen* offers excellent-value Austrian food in a cosy, atmospheric dining room, with outdoor seating out the back, as does the *Meraner Weinstuben*, Kirchengasse 3 (eves only). *La Cueva*, Bahnhofstrasse 20 (closed Mon), serves Mexican food and sizeable steaks, and *Chinatown*, Bahnhofstrasse 16, offers reasonable Far Eastern food in a chic setting. Slightly further afield, the restaurant of *Zum Hois'n Wirt* (see p.442), is the place to eat fresh trout from local streams.

The most famous turn-of-the-twentieth-century **Kaffeehaus** is the small, old-fashioned *Café Grellinger*, right by the tram terminus at Franz-Josef-Platz 6; the *Rathauscafé*, on Rathausplatz, meanwhile, is a good place to observe the crowds along the lakefront and enjoy a daytime **drink**. Further along the Esplanade, the *Kulturcafé Villa Lehman* (aka *Spieleladen*), at number 27, is a stylish palm-filled café-bar playing jazzy, bluesy sounds. Two popular bars in the town centre are the *Blauer Affe*, Kirchengasse 8, and *Café-Bar Salzamt*, Am Graben 16 (closed Sun), a rustic cellar-bar open until 4am.

Schloss Scharnstein

Some 14km east of Gmunden lies **Schloss Scharnstein**, a late sixteenth-century castle, which sits above the River Alm, and is now home to a couple of museums and a reptile collection. Scharnstein is accessible by regular **bus** from Gmunden, and by **train** from Wels, to the north, on the main Vienna-Salzburg line.

The better of the castle museums is the **Museum der österreichischen Zeit-Geschichte** (Museum of Modern Austrian History; July to mid-Oct Tues–Sun 9am–noon & 1–5pm; öS50/€3.63), entered via the south door, which is a must for anyone with more than a passing interest in the history of modern Austria, and a little German (there's no English information at all). The museum kicks off with the end of the Empire and takes you as far as the postwar, post-occupation republic, though there's precious little on Austria's late-twentieth-century politics. What there is, however, is an unrivalled collection of memorabilia from the first half of the last century, from Karl Lueger mugs and badges, Austro-fascist Fatherland Front posters and Nazi ticker tape in the shape of swastikas from the Anschluss.

The **Kriminalmuseum** (May to mid-Oct Tues–Sun 9am–noon & 1–5pm; öS50/€3.63), which you enter from the west door, is far less compelling (once more there's no English info). The first half of the museum catalogues the tortures meted out on medieval miscreants from thumbscrews to head crushers. Much more disturbing, though, is the **Gendarmeriemuseum** upstairs (covered by the same ticket), which, aside from its collection of police uniforms, has extremely explicit, not to say prurient, displays on the crimes of just about every major Austrian murderer of the last hundred years. If you do decide to go to both museums, ask for a Kombi-Karte (öS60/€4.36).

Instead, you might prefer to inspect the murderous creatures in the **Reptilienzoo** (May–Oct Tues–Sun 9am–5pm; Nov–April Sat & Sun 1–4pm; öS60/€4.36), hidden in the basement of the north wing. For once, there's some information in English, telling you all about just how poisonous each of the snakes and spiders is, with graphic colour photos of victims' arms and legs.

Hallstättersee

If you only have time to visit one lake in the Salzkammergut, then the spectacular, fjord-like **Hallstättersee**, 12km south of Bad Ischl, would be a worthy choice. Mountains crowd around on all sides, with the Dachstein range to the south, the Sechserkogel to the east; a sheer rock wall to the west provides an eerily sculptural backdrop to the human settlements that cling to its base. The village of **Hallstatt** itself is one of the most appealing and rewarding destinations in the region. Equipped with a couple of worthwhile museums and a famous show-mine, it remains the obvious focus for tourists. **Obertraun** at the southern end of the lake provides access to the **Dachstein caves**, one of the most-visited attractions in the region, and is also a good spot for a swim.

About six daily **buses** from Bad Ischl follow the main road down the western side of the lake to Hallstatt (fewer on Sundays), while more frequent **trains** from Bad Ischl run along the eastern shore of the lake (where boats ferry passengers across to Hallstatt; see below), pausing at Obertraun before hurrying on to Bad Aussee to the east.

Hallstatt

One of Austria's most attractive villages and the real jewel of the Salzkammergut, **HALLSTATT** occupies a wonderfully dramatic position on the western shores of the Hallstättersee at the base of a precipitous hillside. Indeed the shoreline is so narrow that the rail line is confined to the opposite side of the lake, and disembarking the train at Hallstatt station and being ferried across to the town itself is one of the most atmospheric and evocative experiences that Austria has to offer. Hallstatt also has a historical pedigree second to none: salt has been mined in the mountains above the lake since at least the arrival of the Celts in the first millennium BC, and the wealth of finds is so great that the name "Hallstatt" has entered archeological terminology to denote the Celtic culture that blossomed in central Europe during the early Iron Age (800 to 500 BC).

Hallstatt's other main claim to fame is the **Fronleichnahm** (Corpus Christi) procession, which takes place every year at the end of May. The procession begins at the Pfarrkirche, moves down to the main square and then takes to the water as everyone boards boats bound for a small chapel on the eastern side of the lake. All available boats are pressed into service, including several of the traditional *Fuhr*, sharp-prowed boats propelled by a single paddle at the stern, rather like a punt. You can see a few of them still plying the waters (and available for hire) from the characteristic wooden boathouses along the village shoreline.

The Town

Though undeniably touristy, Halstatt is nevertheless a very pretty village, its houses, with their handsome wooden gables and flower-bedecked balconies, tumbling down steeply to the lake. Traffic is more or less excluded from the village centre, leaving visitors free to explore the tiny little triangular **Marktplatz**, and the surrounding network of narrow alleyways, in peace.

Hallstatt's most interesting church is the **Pfarrkirche** raised above the lake on a terrace to the north of the Marktplatz. The south portal is adorned with early sixteenth-century Calvary scenes, superbly executed by an artist from the "Danube School". Inside, the most interesting of the winged altars is the late-Gothic one on the right, with its heavily gilded statuettes of the Madonna and Child flanked by St Catherine (the patron of woodcutters, on the left) and St Barbara (the patron of miners); high-relief scenes from the lives of Mary and Christ are depicted on the wings. An adjoining chapel contains the central panel of an earlier, mid-fifteenth-century altar, with a stirring Crucifixion scene. In the graveyard outside stands a small stone structure known as the **Beinhaus** (daily 10am–6pm; öS10/€0.72). Due to limited space in the graveyard, the bones of the deceased are recovered from the earth once sufficient time has elapsed for complete decomposition of the body – usually ten years or so. The bones are then stored in the Beinhaus, with skulls arranged on the upper shelves and other bones stacked neatly below like firewood. The skulls are still painted by the town gravedigger: male skulls are decorated with oak or ivy leaves, female skulls adorned with floral motifs; sometimes the name of the deceased is added, and a symbol of the cause of death.

THE HALLSTATT CULTURE

It's not known precisely when the Celts came to **Hallstatt**, although a settled **salt-mining community** ruled over by a powerful warrior aristocracy certainly existed here by 800 BC, remaining for at least three hundred years. We owe much of our knowledge of the period to the efforts of Dr Johann Georg Ramsauer, an amateur archeologist (he was the works manager at the local salt mine), who began systematic exploration of the grave fields in the Salzbergtal above the town in 1846, uncovering more than a thousand graves in the ensuing eighteen years.

These finds indicated that accompanying the deceased on their journey to the afterlife were foodstuffs, elegantly fashioned pottery, exquisitely wrought bronze horse bits, and iron swords and daggers. Other discoveries in the Salzbergtal revealed that the salt-miners of the period were using iron picks.

Similar graves were subsequently unearthed throughout Austria, the Rhine Valley, France and northern Spain, demonstrating that an iron-bearing Celtic culture was spreading across much of Europe between the seventh and fifth centuries BC. It's not known what role the rulers of Iron Age Hallstatt played in this period of expansion – although they undoubtedly enjoyed the profits of a salt trade that stretched from the Baltic to the Mediterranean. It's thought that the Celts from Hallstatt relocated to Bad Dürrnberg (near Hallein in the Salzburger Land; see p.402) in the fifth century BC, probably because landslides in the Salzbergtal were making mining unsafe.

Indeed Austria's finest Hallstatt-era relics tend to have been found well outside the area that gave the period its name. The princely graves discovered at Bad Dürrnberg and at Grossgmain, where the bodies of tribal chieftains had been laid out on wagons and enclosed in wooden burial chambers covered with earth, have yielded a host of artefacts – the small archeological museums in both these places are well worth visiting.

Many of the Celtic finds that made the town famous can now be seen in the **Prähistorisches Museum** (April & Oct daily 10am–4pm; May–Sept daily 10am–6pm; Nov–March Wed 2–4pm; öS50/€3.63) opposite the tourist office in the centre of the village, where wooden mining implements, pit props and hide rucksacks used by Iron Age miners vie for attention with the delicate jewellery and ornate dagger handles retrieved from the richer graves. The same ticket is valid for the nearby **Heimatmuseum** (as above, but closed Nov–March), which houses the wide-ranging anthropological collection – African masks, Native American head-dresses – of the archeologist who worked on the Celtic sites in the 1930s, inveterate world traveller and hoarder, Friedrich Morton. There's also material on the history of salt mining, with tableaux illustrating working conditions across the centuries.

The Salzberg salt mines

Some 500m above the village is the wooded valley of the **Salzberg**, which you can reach via the Salzbergbahn funicular railway (daily: May to mid-Sept 9.30am–6pm; mid-Sept to mid-Oct 9.30am–4.30pm; öS105/€7.63 return). The cardiovascular alternative is either the zigzag Salzberg-Weg that sets off from near the Heimathaus, or the slightly gentler Gaiswand-Weg that begins behind the graveyard – either way it takes around an hour. The entrance to the Salzberg area is guarded by the **Rudolfsturm**, a tower built in 1284 by Rudolf I's son Duke Albrecht von Habsburg to defend the nearby **salt mines** that provided the area's prosperity.

Somewhat surprisingly, salt is still being mined here, and the brine pumped by pipe all the way to Ebensee on the Traunsee. About 800m beyond the tower, a section of eighteenth-century salt workings have now been opened as a show-mine. As at Hallein (see p.402), an hour-long tour (in German with an English summary) to the **Salzbergwerk** (daily: May to mid-Sept 9.30am–4.30pm; mid-Sept to Oct 9.30am–3pm;

öS140/€10.17 return) is a theatrical experience. First, you need to don coloured pyjamas, take a rail ride to an underground lake, where you get a son et lumière, followed by an exploration of the galleries on foot and the obligatory slither to lower levels of the mine via a wooden slide.

Practicalities

The **lake ferries** are timed to coincide with the trains. Ferries bearing passengers from the **train station** across the lake arrive just below the central Marktplatz, just north of Hallstatt's **tourist office** at Postfach 7 (July & Aug Mon–Fri 8am–6pm, Sat 10am–6pm, Sun 10am–2pm; Sept–June Mon–Fri 9am–noon & 1–5pm; ☎06134/8208, *www .hallstatt.net*). The main road bypasses Hallstatt via a long tunnel through the mountain; **buses** drop off at the southern end of the tunnel in the suburb of Lahn, from where it's a short walk into the village. The village centre is closed to **cars** (May–Oct daily 10am–5pm); if you're staying in the centre, you'll get a pass, but you won't be able to park, and you'll have to leave via a set of traffic lights which are on a seven-minute cycle. To park your car, use one of the **car parks**, halfway along, or at either end of, the tunnel; with a *Gästekarte* displayed on your dashboard, you can park for free.

The tourist office will check vacancies in **private rooms**, most of which are in the southern suburb of Lahn. The *Sarstein*, Gosaumühlestrasse 83 (☎06134/8271; ②), is a friendly lakeside **pension,** 200m north of the landing stage, the family-run *Seethaler*, Dr F. Mortonweg 22 (☎06134/8421; ②) is on a quiet backstreet with lake views from every room, while *Gasthof Bergfried*, Echerntalweg 3, (☎06134/8248; ③), offers comfy rooms with en-suite facilities and a gym and sauna on site, in Lahn. Classiest of the village's **hotels** is probably the *Gasthof Zauner-Seewirt*, Marktplatz 51 (☎06134/8246, *zauner@hallstatt.at*; ⑥), an evocative, old central inn, with the rooms equipped with all mod cons. The best hostel is the centrally located, independent *Gasthaus zur Mühle*, set back from the landing stage at Kirchenweg 36 (☎06134/8318; open all year), with dorm beds, as well as some doubles. The *Camping Höll* **campsite** (☎06134/8322; mid-April to mid-Oct). is beautifully situated at the beginning of the Echerntal, in Lahn, but if you want to be right by the lake, head for Obertraun (see below) or the site by *Gasthof Gosaumühle*, 4km north of Hallstatt (☎06134/8303; open all year).

The perfect picnic **food** – smoked fish fresh from the lake – can be bought from the fishmonger's round the corner from the tourist office. There's little to choose between the **restaurants** in the centre of the village – all offer a selection of Austrian regulars augmented by fresh fish, and you only need decide if you want a place with outdoor lakeside seating or not. *Bräugasthof*, Seestrasse 120, has a lakeside terrace and a competitively priced range of fresh fish, while the *Weisses Lamm*, behind the tourist office, has a tempting selection of Austrian standards, fish and game dishes. Best of the pizzerias is the *Gasthof zur Mühle*, just above the main square. Hallstatt's **drinking** opportunities revolve around the couple of café-bars on the main square, or the folksy *Gasthof Bergfried*.

Obertraun and around

Though set back slightly from the shore, the village of **OBERTRAUN**, at the southeastern tip of the lake, possesses better **beaches** than Hallstatt, with an extensive Strandbad ten minutes' walk west of the village centre (five minutes from the station), down Seestrasse. Obertraun also serves as the departure point for cable-car excursions to the **caves** – the Rieseneishöhle and the Mammuthölle – located high up on the flanks of the **Dachstein** (2995m), the snow-capped mountain that rises above the lake to the south.

There's little else going on in what is essentially a sleepy, rural place, although those in search of rustic tranquillity might fancy one of the **private rooms** offered by the local **tourist office** (Mon–Fri 8am–noon & 2–5pm; ☎06131/35, *www.demenet.com*) in the Gemeindeamt, 500m east of the station; most of these are in the farmhouses of Winkl, an attractive suburb ranged along the Hallstatt road to the west. There's also an HI **youth hostel** some way out of town at Winkl 26 (☎06134/360); follow the Hallstatt road, cross over the river and turn left onto the access road to the Dachstein cable car to reach it. Obertraun's shady Hinterer **campsite** (☎06134/265; May–Sept) is also in Winkl, by the lake, off the road to Hallstatt. Best places to **eat and drink** are the *Obertraunerhof* on the Hauptstrasse between the train station and the tourist office, and the *Haus am See* by the Strandbad, both offering tasty rustic Austrian dishes.

The Dachstein caves and the Krippenstein cable car

The **Dachstein caves** (*www.dachsteinregion.at*) above Obertraun are one of the most popular excursions in the Salzkammergut. There are, in fact, two groups of caves to explore: the awesome **Rieseneishöhle** (May to mid-Oct daily 8.30am–4pm; öS90/€6.54), or giant ice caves, whose galleries are adorned with dramatically lit ice formations, and the **Mammuthöhle** (mid-May to mid-Oct daily 9.30am–3pm; öS90/€6.54), or mammoth caves (the latter a reference to the system's size rather than the presence of any prehistoric animal), which lack the ice, but include the so-called "midnight cathedral", where abstract, psychedelic images are projected onto the cavern walls to dramatic effect. A wooden shingled building below the entrance to the caves houses a small **Höhlenmuseum**, which tells you a bit more about the history of the caves (if your German's up to it).

To get to either cave system, you must either walk all the way up from Obertraun (1hr 30min) or take the **Dachsteinbahn** (May–Oct), the modern cable car that begins just southeast of Obertraun village. To reach the cable car by car follow the signposts off the Hallstatt road; on foot, pass through the centre of the village from the train station until you see the signposted footpath (30min). The cable-car journey is itself a worthwhile excursion, offering stunning views of the Hallstättersee below. If you're heading for one or both of the caves, there are various combination tickets available from the ticket office; to reach the caves, get off at the middle station, **Schönbergalm** (öS170/€12.35 return), from which the caves are a fifteen-minute walk. A second cable car climbs from Schönbergalm as far as the 2109-metre peak of **Krippenstein** (öS260/€18.89), where you can grab a bite to eat, or spend the night in one of the dorm beds, at the *Schutzhaus Krippenstein* (☎06131/528). There are some excellent walks in the pastures below Krippenstein, under the watchful gaze of the forbidding Dachstein range, immediately to the south, and several more *Hütte* in which to spend the night.

Gosau

It's worth considering a side-trip along the minor road that heads west from Gosaumühle just north of Hallstatt towards **GOSAU**, 10km or so away. A pleasantly scattered settlement of alpine houses on a gently sloping pastureland, it's the jagged peaks of the Dachstein range to the south that make this region so spectacular. The village has a **tourist office** (Mon–Fri 8am–noon & 2–6pm, Sat 8am–noon; also Sun 8am–noon in high season; ☎06136/8295, *www.tiscover.com/gosau*) at the chief road junction, which can help with **accommodation**, from private **rooms** or **hostel** beds to a room in a comfortable **pension** like the *Kirchenwirt* (☎06136/8196, *www.kirchenwirt-peham.at*; ③), near the church. One or two **buses** go to Gosau from Bad Ischl and Hallstatt, and it's worth enquiring at the tourist office about the summer **Bummelzug** (mid-May to Oct) that does regular forays into the surrounding hills.

Five kilometres beyond Gosau, up the valley, is the **Vorderer Gosausee**, the first of two lakes with the Gosausee name. If the weather's fine, you can simply eat out on the terrace of the *Gasthof Gosausee* (☎06136/8514; ③) and drink in the views over the lake towards the mountains. Alternatively, you can take the **Gosaukammbahn** (daily: mid-May to mid-June & mid-Sept to mid-Oct 8.15am–4.50pm; öS90/€6.54; mid-June to mid-Sept 8.15am–5.20pm; öS135/€9.81) to the Zwieselalm (1587m), a peak to the west of the Gosausee, which gives an even better view of (and access to) the zigzag peaks of the Gosaukamm, which sit above the lake, and head southeast towards the glacier-pitted Dachstein range. It's also a pleasant and not too strenuous hour's stroll along the lake and up to the **Hinterer Gosausee**, a smaller green-blue lake enclosed within a whole host of stunning grey peaks. At the far end of the lake is another, more modest refreshment halt, the *Hohe Holzmeisteralm*.

Bad Aussee and around

Sprawling in a valley at the foot of lowland hills, **BAD AUSSEE** is the chief settlement in the southeastern, Styrian corner of the Salzkammergut. Another medieval salt-processing town that reinvented itself as a chic spa resort in the early nineteenth century, Bad Aussee owed much of its popularity to the regular visits of **Johann, Archduke of Styria**, whose love for the local postmaster's daughter Anna Plöchl (see box on p.452) was followed with intense interest by the Austrian public, adding a veneer of romance to the town's otherwise wholesome alpine image. The town today has very little of the spa about it, nor is there even a lake of its own. Nevertheless, it is within easy reach of the **Grundlsee** to the east, a five-kilometre-long lake overlooked by the disinctive humpbacked peak of the Loser, and beyond, the mountains of the Totes Gebirge.

Bad Aussee is deeply embedded in **folk culture** – you'll see more Lederhosen and Dirndl being worn here than anywhere else in the Salzkammergut – and is home to one of Austria's most colourful carnival customs. On **Faschingsdienstag** (Shrove Tuesday), the **Flinserln** don sequinned costumes and parade through the town to announce the coming spring. They're accompanied by the top-hatted **Zacherln**, whose job it is to keep the Flinsern in order by waving pigs' bladders on the ends of sticks. Also taking to the streets are the **Drum Women**, men in nightdresses who move from inn to inn banging drums and availing themselves of free food and drink – a misogynistic celebration of men's right to booze in peace without being pestered by their womenfolk. Bad Aussee's other big folk celebration is the **Narzissenfest**, a daffodil festival straddling a weekend at the end of May (check precise dates with the local tourist office), when floats bearing designs made from the flowers course the streets.

The Town

Traffic blights the narrow streets of Bad Aussee's small town centre, which is focused on the tiny, central **Kurpark**, whose manicured lawns overlook the babbling confluence of the Ausseer Traun and the Grundlseer Traun. A statue in the middle of the park honours the town's great popularizer, Archduke Johann, while the modern **Kurhaus** at the park's northern end houses the main downtown café and a concert hall, where the town's famous folk-dress band occasionally play.

To escape from the busy streets, cross over Hauptstrasse and head up to **Chlumeckyplatz**, centre of the old town and site of the **Kammerhofmuseum** (April to mid-June & Oct Tues 3.30–6pm, Fri 9.30am–noon, Sun 10am–noon; mid-June to Sept daily 10am–noon & 3–6pm; öS40/€2.90), occupying a Gothic building with Renaissance additions, which once housed the administration of the local salt industry. Inside, eclipsing the Flinserln and Zacherln costumes on display, the Kaisersaal boasts eighteenth-century frescoes showing vibrant local landscapes framed by floral designs.

ARCHDUKE JOHANN

It's impossible to visit Bad Aussee without coming across some reminder of **Archduke Johann** (1782–1859), one of the nineteenth century's more likeable Habsburgs, who scandalized the imperial family with his love for **Anna Plöchl**, daughter of Bad Aussee's postmaster. Although the archduke tends to be remembered nowadays as something akin to the romantic lead in a comic operetta, he was a powerful figure at court, whose reformist ideas were ultimately stymied by more cautious rivals. He was considered more capable than his brother the Emperor Franz II, who as a consequence had him spied upon and used as a scapegoat for Habsburg failures. Johann was thus blamed for Napoleon's victory at Deutsch-Wagram in 1809, because the troops he was commanding arrived late and missed the battle. Defeat at the hands of the French had a damaging effect on Habsburg prestige among German-speaking peoples, and Johann tried to reinvigorate the empire by encouraging a new, specifically Austrian identity that would unify all its subjects. However, the response to his ideas among ruling circles was less than positive, leaving him increasingly disillusioned. A keen mountaineer who loved nothing better than to hang out in the Styrian countryside in a pair of leather shorts and a huntsman's hat, the archduke preferred provincial life to the backbiting of the capital. His love for the low-born Anna, whom he met in 1818 and whose eyes he somewhat condescendingly described as of the type "which we highlanders compare to chamois", in any case ensured that he was increasingly given the cold shoulder by his fellow Habsburgs.

Johann's relatives didn't really know what to make of his sentimentality: in a family whose male children were expected to marry for dynastic reasons and quench whatever remaining lusts they had with the help of the local serving girls, romantic love was at best seen as a dereliction of duty; at worst, a sign of mental illness. Emperor Franz forbade the marriage on the advice of his chief minister Metternich (a staunch opponent of Johann's liberal-leaning politics), who warned that a wedding to a middle-class girl would only make Johann more popular with the lower orders. Johann himself refused any compromise, moving Anna into his house – his claim that they never shared the same bed seemed to placate a sceptical Catholic hierarchy. In 1829 an exasperated emperor finally gave in, and the couple were married at Brandhof, Johann's palatial hunting lodge near Mariazell.

The archduke continued to stay away from court if at all possible – though he played a key role in persuading Ferdinand I to abdicate in favour of the 18-year-old Franz-Josef (Johann's nephew) in 1848. In the same year, the German assembly in Frankfurt adopted Archduke Johann as its president in the hope that he would serve as a talismanic liberal figurehead, but Franz-Josef persuaded Johann to step down as soon as he felt strong enough to move against him. As a placatory gesture, Franz-Josef gave the hitherto shunned Anna the title of Duchess of Meran in 1850.

Haupstrasse heads east across the Grundlseer Traun to Meranplatz, site of the house, at no. 37, where **Anna Plöchl** grew up, and where she returned after Archduke Johann's death in 1859. Here, too stands the Gothic **Spitalkirche** (May–Oct daily 10am–noon & 2–5pm), which is stuffed full of top-notch Gothic art, reflecting the wealth of medieval Bad Aussee. The same is also true of the **Stadtpfarrkirche St Paul**, further east up Kirchengasse.

Practicalities

Bad Aussee's **train station** is southwest of the centre, a twenty-minute walk up Bahnhofstrasse. The **tourist office** (Mon–Fri 8am–7pm, Sat 9am–noon & 4–6pm; ☎03622/54040, *www.ausseerland.at*), at the southern end of the Kurpark, will fix you up with **private rooms** or a cheap pension, and offers touch-screen accommodation information and a free phone outside office hours. For all the creature comforts, try the stylish town-centre Gasthof, *Hotel Post*, on the corner of Kirchengasse and Meranplatz (☎03622/53555; ⑤), or the attractive alpine *Villa Kristina*, slightly northwest of town at Altausseerstrasse 54 (☎03622/52017, *www.aussee.com*; ⑤). There's a modern **HI hostel** about 400m southwest of the town centre at Jugendherbergsstrasse 148 (☎3622/52238; closed Nov to mid-Dec, *jgh.badaussee@jgh.at*), with beds in four-person dorms.

The best places to **eat** are the *Kirchenwirt* attached to the *Hotel Post*, which has good-quality Austrian food at medium prices, and the slightly more upmarket *Kupfer-Pfanne,* just west of the Kurpark at Ischlerstrasse 70, serving both Modern European and traditional Austrian cuisine. Meals are also served at the *Café Meran* on Meranplatz, a good place for a daytime or evening **drink**, which has an Art-Nouveau-influenced interior and a pleasant courtyard. The genteel, social centre of Bad Aussee, however, is the *Kurhaus Café*, with its smoke-filled, light wood-panelled interior, and waiting staff in traditional dress.

Grundlsee and the Drei-Seen-Tour

Four kilometres northeast of Bad Aussee, the peaceful **Grundlsee** can be reached by bus or by a signposted footpath, which starts at the eastern end of town uphill from Meranplatz and heads off through the woods. Stretching along the western shore of the lake, the village of **GRUNDLSEE** initially played host to nineteenth-century English fishing enthusiasts, though it didn't take long for urban Austrians to be seduced by its tranquil lakeside charm – Sigmund Freud, who loved to go mushroom-picking in the woods above the lake, was one famous Viennese intellectual who used to holiday here before World War I.

For over a hundred years the most popular excursion on the Grundlsee has been the **Drei-Seen-Tour** or "three-lake tour" (four daily in summer; the return trip takes about 3hr; öS150/€10.90), which takes in the Grundlsee and the two smaller lakes to the east. Embarking from a pier next to Gasthof Lindlbauer at the west end of Grundlsee village, you're shipped to **GÖSSL**, at the eastern edge of the lake, from where you walk through the woods a kilometre or so to the secluded **Toplitzsee**. There, another boat ferries you past impressive waterfalls on the northern side of the lake. An even shorter walk brings you to the **Kammersee**; source of the River Traun and too small for a boat trip, but where you have time to enjoy the view before turning back. Of course, you don't have to take the full three-lake option; you could simply have a one-hour tour of Grundlsee on its own, or bus it to Gössl, and walk to the Toplitzsee for that stretch of the tour.

The Grundlsee **tourist office** (April–Oct Mon–Fri 8am–7pm, Sat 9am–noon & 4–7pm, Sun 4–7pm; ☎03622/8666, *www.ausseerland.at*), on the main road through the village, will sort out **private rooms**. Just opposite the tourist office, *Gasthof Lindlbauer* is a good **restaurant** with a waterside terrace, serving fresh fish from the lake and the usual range of Austrian schnitzels. A similar menu is on offer at the more expensive *Restaurant Seeblick*, on a hill at the western end of the lake about a ten-minute walk from the waterfront.

Gössl squats beside a thin stretch of shingle beach, with the usual facilities. The **campsite** (☎03622/8689, *campingveit@campingplatz.at*; May–Sept) is just back from the lakefront at Gössl, where you'll find the usual pedalo- and rowing boat-rental facilities. Grundlsee **HI hostel** (☎03622/8629, *bookingcenter@jgh.at*; May–Oct) meanwhile, lies 1km southwest of Gössl, where the Bad Aussee–Gössl buses terminate.

Altausseer See and around

Regular buses also head 4km north from Bad Aussee to the **Altausseer See**, which is dominated, to the east, by the raw grey cliff face of the Trisselwand. At the western edge of the lake is the quiet and relatively pretty village of **ALTAUSSEE**, which manages to combine its role as a spa, summer lake resort and winter ski centre without losing its charm. There are several places where you can have a drink by the lake, and the odd spot amidst the pine trees on the north shore from which you can swim. A little boat does round-trips of the lake in the summer (*www.altaussee.at/moeve*).

There's a **tourist office** in Altaussee's Kur- und Amtshaus (Mon–Fri 8am–7pm, Sat 9am–noon & 4–6pm, Sun 9am–noon; ☎03622/71643, *www.altaussee.at*), where you can organize a **private room**. The two lakeside **hotels** are both luxurious and expensive: *Seevilla* (☎03622/71302, *www.seevilla.net*; ⑨) and *Hotel am See* (☎03622/71361, *hotel.am.see@aon.at*; ⑦). The nearest you'll get to the lake on a budget is about 300m from it at the excellent *Gasthof Loser* (☎03622/71373, *www.gasthof-loser.at*; ⑤) or the *Gästehaus Sochor* (☎03622/71320, *www.altaussee.at/haus-sochor*; ③).

To the north of the Altausseer See rises the bare-topped mountain of the **Loser** (1838m). There's a marked path which begins in Altaussee, though you might prefer to take the postbus (July–Sept twice daily), which wends its way up the fifteen hairpin bends of the Panoramastrasse to the car park outside the *Loser Bergrestaurant* – it's a toll road, so cars must pay öS100/€7.30 per passenger to reach the same point. From the restaurant, whose terrace enjoys fabulous views over the lake, it's an hour or so's walk, via the tiny Augstsee, to the top of Loser itself. There are, in fact, two summits, but head for the one with the cross on it, as it has by far the best views, as far as the Wolfgangsee and the Schafberg on a clear day.

The local **Salzbergwerk** (daily: April & Oct 10am–2pm; May–Sept 10am–4pm; öS150/€10.90), 3km northwest of Altaussee, is open to the public as a show-mine. Tours follow a similar pattern as at Hallstatt and Bad Ischl, with a short trip on the mining railway deep into the mountain, followed by a slide down to the lower galleries. The Altaussee mines' claim to fame over its rivals is that they were used by the Nazis in World War II to stash various artworks from all over occupied Europe.

---

travel details

Trains (*www.oebb.at*)

Attnang-Puchheim to: Altmünster (hourly; 20–25min); Bad Aussee (hourly; 1hr 40min); Bad Ischl (hourly; 1hr); Ebensee (hourly; 50min); Gmunden (hourly; 15min); Hallstatt (hourly; 1hr 25min); Obertraun (hourly; 1hr 30min); Salzburg (1–2 hourly; 45min); Stainach-Irdning (10 daily; 2hr–2hr 30min); Traunkirchen (hourly; 35min); Vienna (hourly; 2hr 35min).

Bad Ischl to: Altmünster (hourly; 35min); Attnang-Puchheim (hourly; 1hr); Bad Aussee (hourly; 40min); Ebensee (hourly; 10min); Gmunden (hourly; 45min); Hallstatt (hourly; 25min); Obertraun (hourly; 30min); Stainach-Irdning (10 daily; 1hr 30min); Traunkirchen (hourly; 25min).

Lambach to: Vorchdorf-Eggenberg (Mon–Fri 12–14 daily, Sat 8–10 daily, Sun 5 daily; 25min).

Salzburg to: Attnang-Puchheim (1–2 hourly; 45min); Lambach (8 daily; 1hr); Vöcklabruck (1–2 hourly; 1hr–1hr 25min); Vöcklamarkt (1–2 hourly; 45min–1hr).

Stainach-Irdning to: Altmünster (hourly; 2hr 10min); Attnang-Puchheim (10 daily; 2hr–2hr 30min); Bad Aussee (hourly; 40min); Bad Ischl (hourly; 1hr 30min); Ebensee (hourly; 1hr 40min); Gmunden (hourly; 2hr 15min); Graz (every 2hr; 2hr 15min); Hallstatt (hourly; 1hr); Obertraun (hourly; 50min); Traunkirchen (hourly; 2hr).

Vöcklabruck to: Kammer-Schörfling (Mon–Sat 10–12 daily, Sun 6 daily; 18min).

Vöcklamarkt to: Attersee (Mon–Sat 7–13 daily, Sun 3–6 daily; 30min).

Vorchdorf-Eggenberg to: Gmunden Seebahnhof (Mon–Fri 13–15 daily, Sat 9–11 daily, Sun 6 daily; 30min).

Wels to: Lambach (hourly; 10min) ; Scharnstein-Mühldorf 13 daily; 55min).

Buses

Bad Aussee to: Gössl (7 daily; 30min); Gründlsee (7 daily; 15min).

Bad Ischl to: Gosau (6 daily; 50min); Hallstatt (5–7 daily; 40min); Salzburg (hourly; 1hr 40min); St Wolfgang (hourly; 45min); Strobl (hourly 25min).

Gmunden to: Scharnstein (Mon–Sat 8–10 daily, Sun 5 daily; 35min).

Hallstatt to: Gosausee (4–5 daily; 45min); Obertraun (5 daily; 15min).

Mondsee to: St Gilgen (4 daily; 25min); Salzburg (8 daily; 55min); Unterach (Mon–Fri 9 daily; 25min).

St Gilgen to: Mondsee (Mon–Fri 3 daily; 25min); Salzburg (hourly; 45min); Strobl (hourly; 15min).

Salzburg to: Bad Ischl (hourly; 1hr 40min); Mondsee (8 daily; 55min); St Gilgen (hourly; 45min); Strobl (hourly; 1hr).

Strobl to: Postalm (2 daily; 40min); St Wolfgang (hourly; 15min).

Lake steamers

Attersee (*www.atterseeschiffahrt.at*)

Attersee to: Kammer (mid-April to June Sat & Sun 5 daily; July & Aug 6 daily; Sept Sat & Sun 3 daily; 40min); Steinbach (mid-May to mid-Sept 4 daily; 1hr 30min); Unterach (mid-May to mid-Sept 4 daily; 55min).

Hallstättersee

Hallstatt to: Obertraun (July to mid-Sept 3–5 daily; 25min).

Traunsee (*www.tiscover.com /traunseeschiffahrt*)

Gmunden to: Altmünster (mid-April to mid-May & Oct Sat & Sun 2 daily; mid-May to Sept 2–5 daily; 15min); Ebensee (mid-April to mid-May & Oct Sat & Sun 4 daily; mid-May to Sept 4 daily; 55min–1hr 20min); Ramsau (mid-April to mid-May & Oct Sat & Sun 2 daily; mid-May to Sept 4 daily; 20–35min); Traunkirchen (mid-April to mid-May & Oct Sat & Sun 3 daily; mid-May to Sept 6 daily; 30min–1hr).

Wolfgangsee (*www.oebb.at*)

St Gilgen to: Strobl (hourly; 1hr 15min); St Wolfgang (hourly; 30min).

St Wolfgang to: Strobl (1–2 hourly; 30min).

CHAPTER NINE

THE TYROL

A spectacular alpine playground filled with craggy peaks, verdant pastures, frothy mountain rivers and onion-domed hilltop chapels, the **Tyrol** (Tirol in German; *www.tis.co.at/tirol*) represents picture-postcard Austria at its most vivid. Apart from a few pockets of industrialization around Innsbruck and Wörgl, hardly a square centimetre of the province is anything but extremely attractive. Although the mountains naturally take centre stage, there's a surprising amount of urban tourism to be savoured here, too: the Tyrolean capital, **Innsbruck**, is a worthy focal point – a lively and attractive place that combines big-city thrills with a wide range of alpine pursuits. To the east, the historic Inn Valley towns of **Hall**, **Schwaz**, **Rattenberg** and **Kufstein** all reward a visit, however brief. An authentic taste of the Tyrolean great outdoors is best gained by a more leisurely approach – though the set-piece alpine valleys feeding into the River Inn are all perfectly accessible from the more urban centres. The deep, mountain-fringed **Zillertal** and **Ötztal** valleys provide the best of the grandiose scenery, and it's here that you'll find the densest concentration of summer **hiking** routes. Paths are well marked, maps are easy to come by, and many local tourist offices arrange guided walks – making the area ideal for the occasional rambler as well as the ambitious hut-to-hut enthusiast. Both summer and winter tourists are catered for in cosmopolitan mega-villages like **Kitzbühel**, **Seefeld**, **Mayrhofen** and **St Anton**, although the sheer variety of smaller resort villages and out-of-the-way alpine communities ensures that there's something here for everybody.

Much of the Tyrol's **skiing** scene is geared towards novices and intermediates, although St Anton has a worldwide reputation for its hair-raising downhill runs and generous off-piste opportunities, and attracts a sizeable crowd of serious winter sports freaks as a result. The Tyrol also offers more out-of-season skiing than anywhere else in Austria, with the **glaciers** above **Sölden** in the Ötztal, and in the **Tuxertal** near Mayrhofen, providing good snow conditions for much of the year. High-society big-spenders tend to congregate in St Anton, Seefeld, and most of all Kitzbühel, although there's little real social exclusivity about these places – you'll find that après-ski opportunities range from classy glitz to good-natured guzzling more or less wherever you go.

Wherever you are in the province, you'll see the imprint of a strong sense of Tyrolean identity. The Tyroleans are proud of their alpine surroundings, cherishing an unspoken

---

ACCOMMODATION PRICE CODES

All **hotels and pensions** in this book have been coded according to the following price categories. All the codes are based on the rate for the least expensive double room during the **summer season**. In those places where winter is the high season, we've indicated both summer and winter room rates in the text.

① under öS400/€29,07
② öS400–600/€29,07–43,60
③ öS600–800/€43,60–58,14
④ öS800–1000/€58,14–72,67
⑤ öS1000–1200/€72,67–87,21

⑥ öS1200–1400/€87,21–101,74
⑦ öS1400–1600/€101,74–116,28
⑧ öS1600–1800/€116,28–130,81
⑨ over öS1800/€130,81

belief that the best mountaineers and skiers in Austria come from here. You'll spot traditional dress – Lederhosen and feathered huntsmen's hats – in use more widely here
than elsewhere in the country, and uniquely Tyrolean dishes like *Gröstl*, *Schlipfkrapfen*
and *Tiroler Knödel* (see p.44) dominate local restaurant menus.

Getting around the Tyrol is simple enough: all the main Inn valley towns are connected by rail, while a pretty comprehensive bus system serves the side-valleys. The
system of integrated rail and bus passes operated by the Tyrolean transport authority
(*Verkehrsverbund Tirol* or *VVT*) presents an extremely good-value way of getting
around. If you're exploring a particular area, day tickets (öS165/€12.05) valid for one
of each of the 12 individual regions into which the Tyrol is divided are usually cheaper
than standard returns. A 7-day ticket covering the whole of the Tyrol (öS650/€47.45)
is a bargain if you're ranging far and wide.

Some history

After being settled by Bavarian tribes in the eighth century, the Tyrol began life as a
medieval dukedom centred on Meran (now Merano in Italy) on the south side of the
Alps. The political centre of gravity gradually shifted northwards, however, with the
strengthening of the economic power of Inn Valley towns such as Schwaz (a gold- and
silver-mining centre) and Hall (an important salt-producing town). The Tyrol fell into
the **Habsburg** orbit in 1363, when Duke Rudolf IV inherited it from his sister
Margareta, widow of Meinhard, last of the dukes of Görz-Tirol. For the next century
and a half, the Tyrol was home to a regional branch of the Habsburg house, and by
the time of **Sigismund the Rich** (1427–96; so named because he had better luck
than his father, Friedrich the Penniless), the area had gained a reputation for stability and prosperity, and was coveted by other members of the family as a result. In
1490, a coalition of Tyrolean nobles and Habsburg power-brokers persuaded
Sigismund to bequeath the Tyrol to his nephew **Maximilian I**, a Habsburg who
lacked a significant power base despite being in line for the imperial throne (he
became Holy Roman emperor in 1493). As it turned out, possession of the Tyrol was
crucial to Maximilian's fortunes. Using the silver mines of Schwaz as security, he bor-
rowed money from the financiers of Augsburg and set about paying off political opponents, establishing a modern army based on artillery, and assembling a glittering
court at his chosen capital, Innsbruck.

The development of the Habsburg state bureaucracy under Maximilian eroded the
traditional rights of the Tyrolean peasants, driving them into open **rebellion** in 1525.
Led by Michael Gaismair, the peasants were supported by the Schwaz miners, who –
solidly Protestant by this time – wanted to overturn the privileges of a grasping clergy
and their aristocratic backers. After initially offering compromises, the **archduke** (and
future Austrian emperor) **Ferdinand I** engaged mercenaries to put the uprising down.
Gaismair fled to Venice, while Ferdinand himself proceeded to cleanse the Tyrol of
Protestantism, helping to turn the province into one of the most devoutly Catholic areas
of Austria – or the **"Holy Land of Tyrol"** as it has since been named by regional
patriots.

Another important element of Tyrolean identity was provided by its defence forces.
During the reign of Maximilian, a piece of legislation known as the **Landlibell** of 1511
made the Tyroleans responsible for securing their own borders, while exempting them
from serving anywhere else in the Habsburg lands – an exemption that survived until
as late as 1918. As a result, the Tyroleans developed their own military institutions, with
the **Schützen**, or "riflemen", forming a local militia.

In the War of the Spanish Succession in 1703, the Land's defence forces defeated
invading Bavarians at Landeck, adding to the myth of the Tyrol's military might.
When the 1805 **Treaty of Pressburg** awarded the Tyrol to Bavaria, the *Schützen* provided patriotic local innkeeper **Andreas Hofer** with the core of a resistance move-

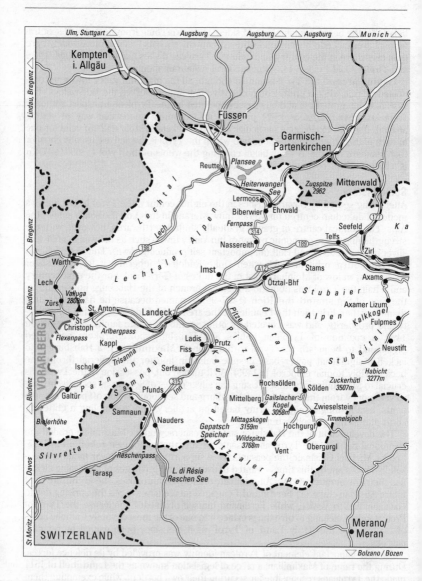

ment with which he could challenge the Bavarians and their French sponsors. Subsequently dubbed the **Tyrolean War of Independence**, this heroic but doomed escapade was launched with the encouragement of a Viennese court that had no real means of providing military support. After three times driving Franco-Bavarian forces out, the Tyroleans were finally overcome by superior odds, and Hofer himself was shot by the French in 1810. Franco-Bavarian control lasted until Napoleon's defeat in 1815, when the province was returned to the Austrian fold. Schützen rifle

associations still exist in an amateur capacity, their members turning out in tradition-al alpine regalia whenever there's a procession, wedding, or other excuse to mount a display of Tyrolean identity.

Tyrolean patriotism was given an added edge this century by a decision to award the **South Tyrol** (Südtirol) to Italy in the aftermath of World War I. It was a decision that paid scant regard to ethnic realities – and the South Tyrol (Alto Adige to the Italians), though within Italy's border, remains to this day a predominantly German-speaking area. The **East Tyrol** (Osttirol; see Chapter 6), meanwhile, was left geographically isolated from the rest of the province. Austrian membership of the European Union, and the phasing out of border controls along the Tyrolean-Italian frontier, have helped to bring the inhabitants of all the Tyrols closer together in the last decade, healing some of the wounds inflicted by enforced partition.

INNSBRUCK

Sprawling beneath the mountain ridge of the Nordkette, **INNSBRUCK** is the only major urban centre in Austria with an array of high Alps on its own doorstep. If you want to visit museums in the morning, walk up mountains in the afternoon and bar-hop well into the early hours, you'd be hard pushed to find a more convenient place in which to do it. With the Tyrol's largest concentration of mountain resorts in such close proximity, skiing is obviously big news here – and hosting the Winter Olympics in 1964 and 1976 provided the city with a wealth of sporting and tourist facilities to call its own. But for those who just want a taste of history, Innsbruck's compact centre – a classic Austrian hybrid of the Gothic and Baroque – invites aimless strolling. It's also a thriving commercial centre that depends on more than just tourism for its living, and has a down-to-earth, unpretentious air quite different to that of western Austria's other main urban centre, self-possessed Salzburg. Innsbruck is the nation's third biggest university city after Vienna and Graz, its sizeable student population helping to support a range of cultural and nightlife options wide enough to suit most tastes.

It's an amazingly easy city to explore, with many of its tourist attractions only a few paces apart, and a great deal of sightseeing can be achieved in the space of a day or two. However it's also a good base from which to explore the Tyrol as a whole, with regular trains whizzing you along the Inn valley to the province's main out-of-town attractions.

Some history

Although an important trading post on the River Inn since Celtic times, Innsbruck was in the shadow of wealthier Tyrolean centres like Hall, Schwaz and Meran until the 1380s, when **Duke Leopold III** began to hold court on the spot now occupied by the Hofburg. His great grandson **Maximilian I** made Innsbruck his imperial capital in the 1490s, catapulting a provincial alpine town into the heart of European politics and culture. Maximilian's affections for the place had been founded on material need – Innsbruck stood at the centre of an area whose mining wealth he wanted to exploit – but he soon came to love the city, largely because of the hunting opportunities in the neighbouring mountains. Innsbruck still bears the stamp of Maximilian's era: a fine ensemble of medieval buildings in the centre augmented by the **Goldenes Dachl** ("Golden Roof"), built to add splendour to Maximilian's court, as well as the imperial mausoleum in the **Hofkirche**, an ostentatious shrine to the Habsburg dynasty, and **Schloss Ambras**, home to the eccentric art collection of Maximilian's great-grandson, **Archduke Ferdinand II**, all attest to the Habsburgs' claim to the city. Although the ducal capital of the Tyrol remained at Meran until the 1860s, the dynasty's connection with Innsbruck remained strong. Empress **Maria Theresia** was a frequent visitor, adding a Baroque veneer to the city by rebuilding the **Hofburg**, and erecting the **Triumphpforte** in honour of her son, Archduke Leopold II. Pro-Habsburg patriotism made Innsbruck the obvious centre of Tyrolean resistance to Franco-Bavarian occupation during the Napoleonic wars, and it briefly served as resistance leader **Andreas Hofer**'s capital during his short-lived reign as regent of Tyrol in 1809. The city has played no more than a walk-on part in Austrian history ever since, quietly consolidating its position as a focus of regional business and culture. Modern-day Innsbruck is an

---

MOUNTAIN RESORTS AROUND INNSBRUCK

There are at least seven major **ski regions** within easy reach of Innsbruck, each of which can be treated as a very accessible day out from the Tyrolean capital. (One of them, **Seefeld**, is major enough to be dealt with separately on p.504.) Nearest to the city centre is the **Nordkette**, close enough for city dwellers to indulge in a spot of skiing during their lunch hour. South of the city and accessible by municipal transport, the villages of **Igls** and **Patsch** serve the slopes of the **Patscherkofel**, which is ascended via the Patscherkofelbahn cable car (daily 9am–4pm; one way öS110/€8.03, return öS180/€13.14). To the southwest, **Mutters** provides access to the popular **Mutterer Alm**, while **Axams** is the starting point for excursions to the varied skiing terrain of the **Axamer Lizum** 9km uphill to the south – also a booming snowboarding centre. Furthest from the city but most versatile is the **Stubai Glacier** 35km to the southwest, where skiing is possible all year round. The Innsbruck tourist office run day-trips for skiers to the glacier in summer for around öS599/€43.73 per person (including bus transfer, equipment rental and lift pass).

A range of **lift passes** is available, covering the above ski regions individually or in combination. A day on the Nordkette or the Patscherkofel will cost around öS300/€21.90. The Innsbruck Gletcher Ski Pass covers the whole of the Innsbruck area (it includes the Stubai Glacier but not Seefeld), includes ski buses, and costs bearers of the Innsbruck Club Card (see p.464) around öS1060/€77.03 for 3 days, öS1890/€137.34 for six days. The Innsbruck Super Ski Pass offers a variety of deals, combining some of the pistes in the Innsbruck region with those around the Arlberg and Kitzbühel, at around öS1790/€130.07 for four days. Passes are available from all lift stations or from the Innsbruck tourist office.

It's easy to rent equipment at lift stations, or in advance from Rental Ski Service, Leopoldstrasse 4 (☎0512/581742), or Schiverlieh Georg Moser, Universitätstrasse 1 (☎0512/589158).

---

engaging paradox: conservative and traditionalist in its attachment to Tyrolean values, it's also one of Austria's most cosmopolitan centres – largely due to its position on the increasingly busy transport routes between Germany and Italy.

Arrival, information and transport

Innsbruck's **airport** is at Kranebitten, 4km west of the centre. Bus F runs into town to the train station every twenty minutes (buy your ticket from the driver or a *Tabak* shop; öS22/€1.60). A taxi will set you back around öS140/€10.22. Buses serving **Munich airport** (six daily; öS460/€33.58 single, öS780/€56.94 return) arrive and depart from the Olympic Ice Stadium, 2km southeast of the centre on Burgenlandstrasse.

Innsbruck's main **train station** is on Südtirolerplatz on the eastern fringes of the centre, a mere ten minutes' walk from the **Altstadt**, at the city's core. The **bus station** is immediately south of the train station.

Information

The main **tourist office** is on the fringes of the Altstadt at Burggraben 3 (Mon–Sat 8am–7pm, Sun 9am–6pm; ☎0512/5356, *www.tiscover.com/innsbruck*). There's another branch on the train station forecourt (daily: June–Sept 8am–10pm, Oct–May 9am–9pm), and an information kiosk at the Innsbruck-Süd exit of the autobahn.

As well as booking rooms, changing money and selling concert tickets, the tourist offices have a wide choice of free **English-language brochures** covering the whole of the Tyrol. They also sell the **Innsbruck card**, a useful investment if you're planning a

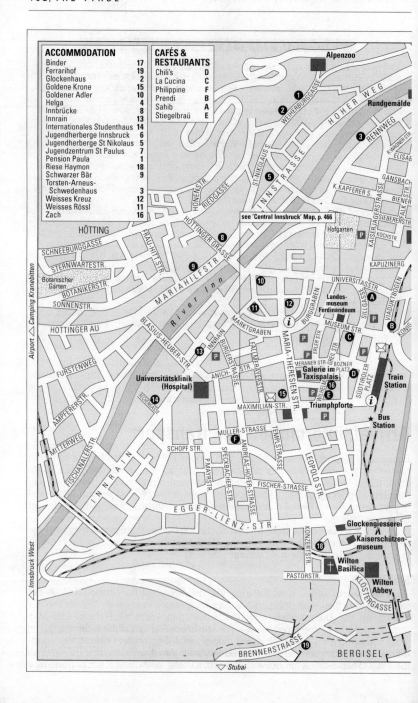

ACCOMMODATION

Binder	17
Ferrarihof	19
Glockenhaus	2
Goldene Krone	15
Goldener Adler	10
Helga	4
Innbrücke	8
Innrain	13
Internationales Studenthaus	14
Jugendherberge Innsbruck	6
Jugendherberge St Nikolaus	5
Jugendzentrum St Paulus	7
Pension Paula	1
Riese Haymon	18
Schwarzer Bär	9
Torsten-Arneus-Schwedenhaus	3
Weisses Kreuz	12
Weisses Rössl	11
Zach	16

CAFÉS & RESTAURANTS

Chili's	D
La Cucina	C
Philippine	F
Prendi	B
Sahib	A
Stiegelbraü	E

see 'Central Innsbruck' Map, p. 466

Alpenzoo

Rundgemälde

Hofgarten

HÖTTING

Botanischer Garten

Landesmuseum Ferdinandeum

Galerie im Taxispalais

Triumphpforte

Universitätsklinik (Hospital)

Train Station

Bus Station

Glockengiesserei

Kaiserschützenmuseum

Wilten Basilica

Wilten Abbey

BERGISEL

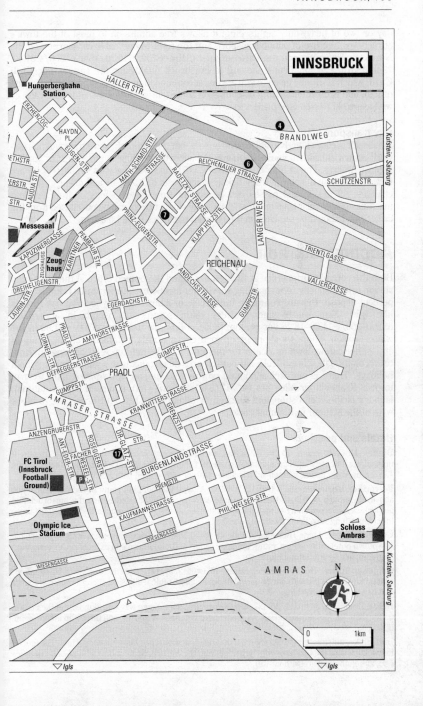

INNSBRUCK

Hungerbergbahn
Station

HALLER STR.

ERZHERZOG-

HAYDN
PL

EUGEN-STR.

RETHSTR.

CLAUDIA STR.

PERSTR.

STR.

MATH-SCHMID-STR.

STRASSE

RADETZKJ-STRASSE

REICHENAUER STRASSE

BRANDLWEG

④

⑥

SCHÜTZENSTR.

△ Kufstein, Salzburg

Messesaal

KAPUZINERGASSE

KARNTNER

PEMBAUR STR.

PRINZ-EUGENSTR.

KLAPPHOLZSTR.

LANGER WEG

⑦

Zeug-
haus

ZEUGHAUS

DREIHELIGENSTR.

LAURIN-STR.

REICHENAU

TRIENTLGASSE

VALIERGASSE

ANDECHSSTRASSE

EGERDACHSTR.

GUMPPSTR.

AMTHORSTRASSE

PRADLER-STR.

KORNER-STR.

DEFREGGERSTRASSE

GUMPPSTR.

PRADL

GUMPPSTR.

KRANWITTERSTRASSE

GRENZSTR.

ANZENGRUBERSTR

AMRASER STRASSE

ANT-EDER-STR.

FACHER

ROSEGGERSTR

⑰

DR-GLATZ-STR.

STR.

FRESE.E-STR.

BURGENLANDSTRASSE

FC Tirol
(Innsbruck
Football
Ground)

P

PREMSTR.

PHIL-WELSER-STR.

Olympic Ice
Stadium

KAUFMANNSTRASSE

WIESENGASSE

Schloss
Ambras

WIESENGASSE

AMRAS

N

△ Kufstein, Salzburg

0   1km

▽ Igls

▽ Igls

day or two of heavy-duty sightseeing: it allows free admission to most of the town's attractions, free use of public transport, and the right to one cable-car journey on the Nordkette-Hafelekar and the Patscherkofel (24hr öS230/€16.70, 48hr öS300/€21.80, 72hr öS370/€26.90). People staying in Innsbruck qualify for the **Innsbruck Club Card**, which is usually given to you at your accommodation (if not enquire at the tourist office), and is useful in getting discounts on some tourist attractions and cable cars, as well as on ski passes (see p.461).

City transport

Innsbruck is easy enough to get around on foot, but the comprehensive tram and bus network comes in handy if you're staying in the suburbs, heading to the airport or visiting Schloss Ambras. The 24-hour ticket (öS42/€3.07) and seven-day pass (öS130/€9.49) are better value than a single-journey ticket, which costs öS22/€1.61 and doesn't allow for changes. All tickets and passes can be bought from *Tabak* shops or from vending machines placed near tram and bus stops (only single tickets can be purchased from the driver), and should be punched in the relevant machines upon boarding.

Accommodation

Both the central tourist office at Burggraben 3 and the branch office at the main train station offer a speedy room-booking service for an öS40/€2.92 fee and a refundable 20 percent deposit. **Private rooms** in Innsbruck, or a bus ride away in suburban resorts like Igls (3km south) and Mutters (5km southwest), weigh in at around öS200–250/€14.60–18.25 per person; those in Igls rise to about öS300/€21.90 in the winter season. There's a shortage of good cheap **hotels** in Innsbruck, but plenty of atmospheric downtown inns cater for the middle of the market. A broad range of **hostel** accommodation is available, although spaces fill up quickly in summer and in school holidays. There is one well-appointed **campsite**, *Camping Kranebitten*, 5km west of town at Kranebittner Allee 214 (☎0512/284180; April–Oct), equipped with restaurant, laundry facilities and shop, and reached by taking bus LK from Boznerplatz (a block west of the station) to Klammstrasse.

Hotels and pensions

Binder, Dr-Glatz-Strasse 20 (☎0512/33436, *www.tiscover.com/hotel.binder*). Clean and friendly if uninspiring inner-city hotel in an unfashionable part of town some 25min walk from the centre (tram #3 runs nearby). Rooms with en-suite facilities (④), or with shared bath and WC (③).

Ferrarihof, Brennerstrasse 8 (☎0512/578898). A large Gasthof 3km south of the city centre just above the suburb of Wilten. Handy for those arriving by car, situated beside the Innsbruck-Süd autobahn exit, its proximity to the junction of the Inntal and Brenner autobahns may put off those intending a long stay. Rooms with en-suite facilities (③); without (②).

Goldene Krone, Maria-Theresien-Strasse 46 (☎0512/586160, *www.touringhotels.at*). Comfortable downtown hotel with modern, rather cramped rooms at the southern end of Innsbruck's main thoroughfare, just by the Triumphforte. ⑦.

Goldener Adler, Herzog-Friedrich-Strasse 6 (☎0512/571111, *www.tiscover.com/goldener-adler*). Classic city-centre inn with late-medieval pedigree and Gothic feel inside, though rooms are large and have modern furnishings. ⑧.

Helga, Brandlweg 3 (☎0512/261137, *hotel.helga@tirol.com*). Some way out, 3km east of the centre, on the main Bundesstrasse to Hall. All rooms have WC, shower and TV, and there's an indoor swimming pool. ④.

Innbrücke, Innstrasse 1 (☎0512/281934,*innbruecke@magnet.at*). Plain but comfortable Gasthof on the west bank of the Inn, just over the bridge from the Altstadt. Some rooms with en-suite facilities (④), although most are without (③).

Innrain, Innrain 38 (☎0512/588981) Small Gasthof within easy walking distance of the Altstadt. Rooms with en-suite facilities and TV (⑤); without (③).

Internationales Studenthaus, Rechengasse 7 (☎0512/501). A student hostel open to tourists July–Sept, in the university district 1km southwest of the Altstadt. Accommodation in single or double rooms with en-suite WC and shower, or with shared facilities. Bus C from the train station. ③.

Pension Paula, Weiherburggasse 15 (☎0512/292262, or 293016). A long-standing favourite with both Austrian and foreign visitors (so it's worth reserving well in advance), perched attractively on the hillside up towards the Alpenzoo. Rooms with en-suite facilities are slightly more expensive than those without. ③.

Schwarzer Bär, Mariahilfstrasse 16 (☎0512/294900). Plain but comfortable Gasthof just over the Inn river from the Altstadt; with ensuite WC and shower (④); without (③).

Weisses Kreuz, Herzog-Friedrich-Strasse 31 (☎0512/59479, *hotel.weisses.kreuz@eunet.at*). In the Altstadt, an attractive old inn with creaky wooden corridors yet bright, modern rooms; a good way of staying in a classic city-centre hotel without paying exhorbitant prices. Rooms with en-suite facilities (⑥); without (④).

Weisses Rössl, Kiebachgasse 8 (☎0512/583057, *www.tirol.com/weisses-roessl*). Cosy, family-run hotel in the Altstadt with fourteen modern, spacious bedrooms. ⑧.

Zach, Wilhelm-Griel-Strasse 11 (☎0512/589667, *www.hotel-zach.at*). Simple, convenient, mid-price downtown hotel only steps away from the sights. ⑥.

Hostels

Glockenhaus, Weiherburggasse 3 (☎0512/286515, *www.tirol.com/yhnikolaus*). Slightly uphill from the River Inn's west bank, within easy walking distance of the town centre. Bus K from the train station. A choice of dorm beds, or doubles (②).

Jugendherberge Innsbruck, Reichenauerstrasse 147 (☎0512/346179, *yhibk@tirol.com*). Large, modern and clean, and although it's 4km east of the Altstadt there are regular buses into town. Check-in time is 5–10pm, and there's an 11pm curfew (key available). Furthest from the centre, but bus O from Museumstrasse stops nearby. Dorm beds are complemented by single öS360/€26.28 and double rooms (②).

Jugendherberge St Nikolaus, Innstrasse 95 (☎0512/286515, *www.tirol.com/yhnikolaus*). Cheap, and therefore crowded, place on the west bank of the Inn, offering beds in dorm rooms. It's a pretty convenient base for exploring the centre, but not comfortable enough to merit a lengthy stay. Bus K from the train station.

Jugendzentrum St Paulus, Reichenauerstrasse 72 (☎0512/344291). Cheap and friendly church-run hostel, although it's over 2km from the Altstadt, and beds are in large dorms. Check-in time is 5–9pm, and there's an 11pm curfew (key available). Bus O from Museumstrasse. Open mid-June to mid-Aug only.

Torsten-Arneus-Schwedenhaus, Rennweg 17b (☎0512/585814). Large, conveniently central hostel about 1km north of the Altstadt by the River Inn. Beds in four-person dorms cost around öS130/€9.49. Check-in time is 5–10pm, and the 11pm curfew can be avoided by asking for a key. Open July & Aug only.

The City

Most of what you will want to see in Innsbruck is confined to the central precincts of the **Altstadt**. A small area of sturdy medieval houses, many attractively painted in pastel colours and supported by sloping earthquake buttresses, it's bounded by the River Inn and the Graben, a street following the course of the moat that once surrounded the town's medieval core. Leading up to the Altstadt from the south, Innsbruck's main artery is the **Maria-Theresien-Strasse**, famed for its view north towards the great rock wall of the Nordkette range. Outside this downtown area there's not a great deal to see, save for the former imperial arsenal or **Zeughaus**, in an anonymous area of

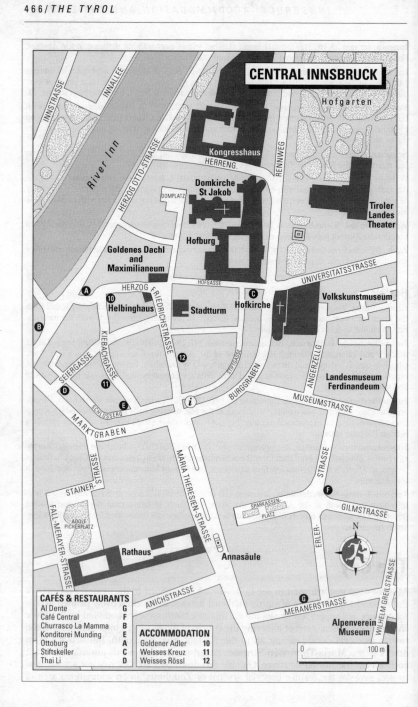

CENTRAL INNSBRUCK

Hofgarten

River Inn

INNSTRASSE

INNALLEE

HERZOG OTTO-STRASSE

Kongresshaus

HERRENG.

RENNWEG

DOMPLATZ

Domkirche
St Jakob

Tiroler
Landes
Theater

Hofburg

Goldenes Dachl
and
Maximilianeum

HOFGASSE

UNIVERSITATSSTRASSE

Ⓐ

HERZOG FRIEDRICHSTRASSE

Volkskunstmuseum

Ⓒ

🔟 Helbinghaus

Stadtturm

Hofkirche

Ⓑ

KIEBACHGASSE

STIFTGASSE

ANGERZELLG.

1️⃣2️⃣

Landesmuseum
Ferdinandeum

SEIERGASSE

BURGGRABEN

Ⓓ

1️⃣1️⃣

MUSEUMSTRASSE

SCHLOSSERG.

Ⓔ

ⓘ

MARKTGRABEN

STAINER-STRASSE

MARIA THERESIEN-STRASSE

STRASSE

Ⓕ

SPARKASSEN-PLATZ

GILMSTRASSE

FALLMERAYER-STRASSE

ADOLF
PICHERPLATZ

ERLER-

N

Rathaus

Annasäule

Ⓖ

MERANERSTRASSE

WILHELM GREILSTRASSE

ANICHSTRASSE

Alpenverein
Museum

0   100 m

CAFÉS & RESTAURANTS

Al Dente	G
Café Central	F
Churrasco La Mamma	F
Konditorei Munding	B
Ottoburg	E
Stiftskeller	A
Thai Li	C
	D

ACCOMMODATION

Goldener Adler	10
Weisses Kreuz	11
Weisses Rössl	12

apartment blocks and offices just east of the centre, and a cluster of Baroque churches and minor museums in the suburb of **Wilten** to the south.

The Altstadt

Main thoroughfare of the **Altstadt** is the broad, arcaded strip of **Herzog-Friedrich-Strasse**, which at its northern end opens out into a plaza lined with gift-shops and overlooked by the **Goldenes Dachl**, or "Golden Roof" (though the tiles that give the roof its name are actually copper), built in the 1490s to cover a balcony from which the imperial court could observe the square below. The balcony itself is adorned with a series of reliefs (these are replicas – the originals are in the Landesmuseum Ferdinandeum; see p.469), showing a troupe of Moorish dancers performing for Emperor Maximilian I and his second wife Bianca Maria Sforza – she's the one holding the apple, which would have been thrown to the dancers as a token of appreciation; the woman behind her is Max's beloved first wife, Maria of Burgundy. Part of the building behind the Goldenes Dachl now houses the **Maximilianeum** (May–Oct daily 10am–6pm; Nov–April Tues–Sun 10am–noon & 2–5pm; öS50/€3.65), a museum that puts a modern, show-biz gloss on the city's most famous resident. The collection's main drawback is its small size – there are a couple of original artworks by Maximilian's court painters (including a powerful deathbed portrait by an unknown master), but little else of real vintage. What you're really paying for is the headphone commentary (English available), and a chance to see a 20-minute documentary film about Maximilian's life.

A parade of Gothic-era town houses adds distinction to the western side of Herzog-Friedrich-Strasse, although most are outshone by the **Helblinghaus**, a medieval structure adorned with the swirling encrustations of icing-like Rococo stucco-work added in the 1730s. Across the road looms the fifteenth-century **Stadtturm** (daily: June–Aug 10am–6pm; March–May & Sept–Oct 10am–5pm; Nov–Feb 10am–4pm; öS30/€2.19); the viewing platform affords views across neighbouring rooftops towards the Nordkette rearing up to the north.

The Domkirche and the Hofburg

From the Goldenes Dachl, alleys lead north to the Domplatz and the **Domkirche St Jakob**, an unspectacular example of eighteenth-century architecture, which nevertheless conceals a couple of worthwhile artworks. Most renowned is the *Madonna and Child* by German master Lucas Cranach the Elder, buried amidst the fussy detail of the high altar. To the left is the funerary monument to Archduke Maximilian III (son of Emperor Maximilian II and nephew of Archduke Ferdinand II), whose statue kneels in prayer watched over by a paternal-looking St George, the latter accompanied by an expiring dragon. This sculptural ensemble shelters under a canopy embellished with carved birds, caterpillars and snails. Displayed on the walls behind the memorial are the arms of the Teutonic order of knights, of which Maximilian III was a member.

East of the Domkirche, the **Hofburg** marks the spot where Leopold III, the first Habsburg to wield power in Innsbruck, based his rudimentary court, though the whole complex was rebuilt in the eighteenth century on the instructions of Maria Theresia. Within the cavernous, and for the most part unremarkable, Rococo apartments (daily: May–Oct 9am–5pm; Nov–April 10am–5pm; öS70/€5.11), monumental wall paintings provide a pictorial guide to Habsburg family history – those in the state ballroom show Maria Theresia, Josef II and Francis I flanked by lesser members of the imperial family.

The Hofkirche and the Volkskunstmuseum

At the eastern entrance to the Altstadt, at the head of the Rennweg, the outwardly unassuming **Hofkirche** contains the most impressive of Innsbruck's imperial monuments, the **Cenotaph of Emperor Maximilian** (Mon–Sat: July–Aug 9am–5.30pm; Sept–June 9am–5pm; öS30/€2.19, combined ticket including the Tiroler Volkskunstmuseum öS60/€4.38). An extraordinary piece of imperial propaganda, masterminded by Maximilian himself, it was designed both to consummate Maximilian I's special relationship with Innsbruck and to bolster the prestige of the dynasty. Ambitious plans for the emperor's tomb to be flanked by a series of 40 larger-than-life statues, 100 statuettes and the busts of 32 Roman emperors, representing both the real and spiritual ancestors of Maximilian, were never realized, though the resulting ensemble is still impressive – its effect dulled only slightly by the knowledge that the emperor is actually buried at the other end of Austria. Maximilian died in Wels in January 1519 having been refused entry to Innsbruck by burghers fearful that his soldiers wouldn't pay their bills, and his body was interred in Wiener Neustadt (see p.214) far away to the east.

Twenty-eight statues line the emperor's empty **tomb**, including Maximilian's Habsburg ancestors Rudolf I, Albrecht II and Friedrich III, as well as more fanciful antecedents such as Clovis, fifth-century king of the Franks. Sculptor Peter Vischer was responsible for most of the figures, two of which were cast from designs by **Albrecht Dürer**: the quasi-mythical English King Arthur (he's recognizable from the three lions on his shield), and sixth-century leader of the Ostrogoths, Theoderic, the third statue to Arthur's left. The tomb itself is topped by a kneeling statue of Maximilian, and surrounded by marble reliefs depicting the emperor's great victories, all designed by Flemish artist Alexander Colin.

NATIVITY SCENES

Like so many other aspects of popular Catholicism in Austria, the practice of displaying **Nativity scenes** (*Krippen*, literally "cribs") in churches and homes goes back to the Counter-Reforming activities of the Jesuits, who considered the introduction of a little theatricality and colour at Christmastime to be an effective means of weaning the local population away from dour Protestantism. The history of the Nativity scene probably dates back to the fifteenth century, when freestanding wooden figures representing characters from the Gospels began to appear in European churches. However it wasn't until the early 1600s that the Jesuits began systematically encouraging their use in the run-up to Christmas. Nativity scenes were introduced all over south and central Europe, although Naples, Sicily and alpine Austria appear to be the places where they caught on most.

The two **main themes** depicted in Austrian cribs are the birth of Jesus, with statuettes of the Holy Family surrounded by model animals, and perhaps some shepherds; and the Journey of the Magi, with the three kings riding towards Bethlehem with a retinue of followers. In the heady Baroque atmosphere of seventeenth-century Austria, Christmas cribs became increasingly lavish and intricate, with vast crowds of delicately carved figures, model scenery and painted backdrops – investing the craft with the theatricality of the stage set. Some crib scenes were set in fanciful Oriental landscapes, while others were much more rooted in local culture, featuring figures clad in Austrian traditional costume, and recognizably alpine landscapes in the background.

Concerned by the Catholic church's excessive hold over Austrian society, the reform-minded **Emperor Josef II** banned cribs from churches in 1782. Paradoxically, this actually stimulated crib-making as a popular craft. With cribs now displayed in private houses instead of churches, the number of village craftsmen involved in their construction dramatically increased. Even now most places in Austria will have an association of crib-makers who produce new work every year, and some villages – notably Thaur in the Tyrol – are known for the crib exhibitions which take place either before or just after Christmas. If you're travelling outside the Christmas period, the **Tiroler Volkskunstmuseum** (see opposite) has the country's largest collection of cribs on permanent display.

Beside the church entrance, a more modern tomb, topped by a suitably heroic statue, holds the remains of **Andreas Hofer**, the Tyrolean patriot executed in Mantua on French orders in 1810 (see overleaf). Steps at the rear of the nave ascend towards the tomb of **Archduke Ferdinand II**, great-grandson of Maximilian I and regent of Tyrol (see p.472). It's located in the so-called **Silberkapelle**, or silver chapel – thus named because of the silver-plated Madonna that adorns the far wall. She is faced by Ferdinand's suit of armour, suspended in a kneeling position halfway up the wall. The bones of the man himself are housed in the tomb directly below, topped by a marble effigy that's also the work of Colin. The grave at the northern end of the chapel belongs to Ferdinand's beloved first wife, the commoner **Philippa Welser**, for whom the chapel was initially built.

Next door to the Hofkirche, the **Tiroler Volkskunstmuseum**, or Tyrolean Folklore Museum (Mon–Sat 9am–5pm, Sun 9am–noon; öS60/€4.38, ticket includes entrance to the Hofkirche), is replete with traditional woodcraft. There are instructive English-language texts, and an exhaustive collection of Tyrolean costumes on the second floor. Leading off the courtyard are a couple of rooms devoted to *Krippen*, or Nativity scenes, most of them nineteenth-century pieces from the village of Thaur (see p.481) near Hall, where the craft is still practised.

The Landesmuseum Ferdinandeum and the Zeughaus

A short walk south of the Volkskunstmuseum, at Museumstrasse 15, the **Tiroler Landesmuseum Ferdinandeum** (May–Sept daily 10am–5pm plus Thurs 7–9pm; Oct–April Tues–Sat 10am–noon & 2–5pm, Sun 9am–noon; öS60/€4.38) greets you with a motley collection of archeological fragments, but the unsurpassed range of paintings awaiting inspection upstairs should not be missed. Most space is devoted to the fifteenth-century "Pustertal Painters" based around Bruneck (Brunico) in the South Tyrol, pre-eminent among whom was Michael Pacher (see p.429), who introduced Italian Renaissance techniques into central European painting and sculpture. Pacher was in demand all over Austria in the late 1400s, and the gallery here is the best place to get a feel for the evolution of his, and his apprentice Friedrich Pacher's, art. Other highlights point to the unsqueamish nature of contemporary piety: Jakob von Seckau's *Martyrdom of St Ursula* (an entirely fictitious saint but no less popular) portrays the heroine standing in a boat and being shot at by bowmen, while an anonymous fifteenth-century *Martyrdom of St Erasmus* sees the saint being boiled, poked in the eye, disembowelled and having his fingernails torn out all at the same time. The Baroque collection on the upper storey is disappointing, although a few small eighteenth-century pieces are worth dwelling on, among them Simon Troger's sculpture of the Archangel Michael smiting Lucifer, and a house-altar by Stefan Föger – basically a miniature version of a church high altar, encased in a glass jar for the domestic mantelpiece. The odd Klimt and Kokoschka aside, twentieth-century Austrian art is best represented by a clutch of brooding canvases from the moody East Tyrolean painter Albin Egger-Lienz (see p.364).

The Zeughaus

Leaving the centre via Universitätstrasse, one block north of Museumstrasse, and passing under the railway viaduct, brings you in about ten minutes to Zeughausgasse and the former imperial arsenal, or **Zeughaus** (same times as the Landesmuseum Ferdinandeum; öS60/€4.38), built by Maximilian I to provide a secure base for the manufacture of gunpowder and cannon. The building now contains an attractively mounted chronological romp through the history of the Tyrol, beginning with a geological section on the various mineral deposits exploited by the medieval silver miners of Schwaz (see p.482). Engravings and pamphlets illustrate the religious struggles of the sixteenth century, and the church-supported campaigns against witches and devil-worshippers that followed. Most space, however, is devoted to Andreas Hofer, the innkeeper who led the struggle for Tyrolean independence from Napoleon and his Bavarian allies. A pile of crude staves and clubs graphically illustrates how poorly armed the Tyrolean insurgents were, rendering their initial military successes all the more impressive. Hofer's insurgents beat the Bavarians three times on the Bergisel hill just south of Innsbruck in 1809, and briefly set up a provisional government in Innsbruck's Hofburg, before being forced out by superior odds. The importance of Hofer to the Tyrol's sense of identity is evident – you'll see his bearded visage peering from political posters, playing cards, and even a tin of Andreas Hofer coffee. A TV screen shows a 25-minute feature film made about Hofer in 1929 – not one of the classics of silent cinema by any means, but worth watching for the extravagantly mounted battle scenes, in which Hofer's rag-tag army routs Napoleonic troops. Elsewhere in the museum, there's a music room in which you can listen to CDs of chamber music composed by Tyrolean court composers, and a colourful selection of early-twentieth-century tourism posters showing the province's growing importance as a holiday destination.

South of the Altstadt: along Maria-Theresien-Strasse towards Wilten

Heading southwards from the Altstadt, **Maria-Theresien-Strasse** cuts a swath through a grid of busy downtown streets. The sober buildings along its length are predominantly nineteenth-century apartment blocks, now occupied by run-of-the-mill boutiques and the odd restaurant. Main focus of the thoroughfare's middle section is the **Annasäule**, a column erected to commemorate the defeat of the Bavarians on St Anne's Day, July 26, 1703. It's topped by a statue of the Virgin, with St Anne herself appearing among the supporting cast of gesticulating saints at the column's base, notably a muscular St George in dragon-spearing mood. It's from the Annasäule onwards that you begin to appreciate the single most famous thing about the Maria-Theresien-Strasse: the **view** back northwards to Innsbruck's local mountain, the Nordkette, which looms majestically above the creamy-yellow town houses and trolleybus wires. A short side-trip eastwards to Wilhelm-Greil-Strasse soon brings you to the **Alpenverein-Museum** at no. 15 (on the second floor in the office of the Austrian Alpine Association, or OAV; May–Oct Mon, Tues, Thur & Fri 10am–5pm, Weds noon–7pm, Sat 10am–1pm; Nov–April same times except closed Sat; öS30/€2.19), which presents a brief overview of the history of alpinism with a display of maps, climbing equipment and models of mountain huts.

Returning to Maria-Theresien-Strasse and continuing south, the Galerie im Taxispalais at no. 45 (Tues–Sun 11am–6pm; Thurs closes 8pm; prices vary; *www.galerieimtaxispalais .at*) is the city's main venue for contemporary art shows, with exhibits filling a rather smart glass-covered central courtyard. Dominating the street's northern end, the **Triumphpforte**, or triumphal arch, was built in advance of celebrations marking the marriage of Maria Theresia's son Leopold (the future Emperor Leopold II) in 1756. The oddly stern and joyless monument (it's said that the sudden death of the empress's husband Franz caused a fundamental rethink of the arch's ornamentation), is adorned with medallions of Maria Theresia and her successor Josef II on the north side, Leopold and spouse on the south. A group of nymphs on the arch's roof add a Neoclassical touch. Beyond the arch, Leopoldstrasse continues southwards towards Wilten, 1500m distant.

Wilten

Situated in the shadow of the attractively wooded Bergisel hill, the suburb of **Wilten** offers a brace of Baroque churches and a motley collection of small museums.

Dominating the scene is the twin-towered **Wilten Basilica**, whose Rococo edifice, built in the 1750s by the Tyrolean priest-architect Franz de Paula Penz, belies the fact that it occupies a pilgrimage site of long standing. Inside, ceiling scenes by the Augsburg painter Matthäus Gündter include a particularly graphic Salome holding aloft the head of John the Baptist, and are framed by intricate mouldings, rich in leafy fronds and tendrils.

A short distance east of the basilica is the ruddy facade of **Wilten Abbey**, the entrance to which is guarded by statues of giants Thyrsus and Haymon. According to myth, itinerant dragon-slayer Haymon killed local giant Thyrsus in a dispute, and went on to found Wilten Abbey by way of penance. The seventeenth-century **abbey church** within merits a quick peek, even though it lacks the delicacy of the nearby basilica.

Next door to the abbey, the **Kaiserschützenmuseum** (May–Sept Mon–Sat 10am–4pm, Sun 9am–noon; öS30/€2.19) celebrates the imperial Tyrolean militia with displays of ceremonial uniforms and weaponry. Across the road, the tram depot contains a small **transport museum** (May–Oct Sat only; 9am–5pm; öS30/€2.19), which is little more than an engine shed containing a few locomotives, but special museum trains run from here to Igls on summer Sundays. Just down the hill from the abbey, on the corner of Leopoldstrasse and Egger-Lienz-Strasse, the Grassmayr **Glockengiesserei**, or bell foundry (Mon–Fri 9am–6pm, Sat 9am–noon; öS45/€3.29), treats visitors to a short display detailing the history of bell-casting, and a chance to peruse the offerings – models of bells, mostly – in the company's gift-shop.

Immediately to the south of the abbey complex lies the **Bergisel**, scene of the bloody battles between Andreas Hofer's rebels and Franco-Bavarian forces in 1809. At the foot of the hill stands the **Bergisel-Kaiserjägermuseum** (April–Oct daily 9am–5pm; March Tues–Sun 10am–3pm; öS25/€1.83), honouring the fighters of the Tyrolean War of Independence, and their successors in subsequent wars, in suitably reverential mode. Above the museum, paths crisscross the wooded slopes, where it's impossible to miss the take-off ramp of the **Sprungstadion**, the ski-jump arena used in the 1964 and 1976 Olympics.

Schloss Ambras

Home of Maximilian I's great-grandson Archduke Ferdinand II, **Schloss Ambras** (April–Oct daily 10am–5pm; Dec–March daily except Tues 2–5pm; öS90/€6.57) is one of the foremost Renaissance palaces in Austria, affording fascinating insight into the courtly culture of the sixteenth century. Situated 2km southeast of the Altstadt, it can be reached by taking tram #6 to the Schloss Ambras stop, or tram #3 to the end of Amraserstrasse before following paths under the autobahn and climbing for ten minutes up the wooded hillock to the Schloss.

Entering the Schloss through the western gateway, you are first directed towards the **Lower Schloss**, comprising an ensemble of outbuildings. First up, the **Rustkammer** flaunts jousting armour from the late fifteenth century, including several suits made for Archduke Ferdinand himself. The collection's most striking piece, however, is the armour worn by Ferdinand's court giant, Bartlmä Bon, at the Vienna tournament of 1560.

Ferdinand's **Kunst- und Wunderkammer** is preserved in something approaching its original form, although many of its most treasured items – including the much-admired golden salt cellar by Benvenuto Cellini – have been removed to the Kunsthistorisches Museum in Vienna (see p.107). Busts of Roman rulers from Julius Caesar to Emperor Theodosius (originally intended for the cenotaph of Maximilian in the Hofkirche) rub shoulders with games and puzzles, Far Eastern porcelain, Turkish hats and an exquisite statuette of Death carved from pearwood. More unsettling to modern eyes, the portrait gallery is filled with the freakish contemporaries who so fas-

ARCHDUKE FERDINAND II OF TYROL (1529–95)

The second son of Emperor Ferdinand I, the future Archduke Ferdinand of Tyrol looked set for a glittering imperial career. He was appointed governor of Bohemia at the age of 18, and was initially preferred by his father over his elder brother Maximilian (who was thought by many to be a closet Protestant) as heir to the throne. Yet Ferdinand disqualified himself from such a high office by falling in love with a commoner, **Philippa Welser**, daughter of an Augsburg banker. Expelled from court for not adhering to the correct breeding habits, Ferdinand was replaced by Maximilian (the future Maximilian II) in the order of succession.

Ferdinand's partial political rehabilitation came about when, according to one popular tale, Philippa travelled to Ferdinand I's court in Prague under an assumed name. There she regaled the emperor with a moving story about a wicked father who had disowned his son for falling in love with the wrong woman. Suitably humbled, the august Habsburg dropped his opposition to the relationship. Whatever the real reason for the change of heart, Ferdinand-*père* sanctioned a **morganatic marriage** between the two in 1557. Ferdinand and Philippa's sons Karl and Andreas were nevertheless given top imperial and ecclesiastical posts, with Andreas ultimately becoming a cardinal. Ferdinand himself was a devout Catholic, and Protestantism made few inroads in the Tyrol under his stewardship of the duchy.

After Welser's death in 1580, Ferdinand married the 16-year-old **Anna Gonzaga of Mantua**, producing three daughters in as many years – the youngest of whom, Anne, in true Habsburg style, married her cousin, the Emperor Matthias, in order to keep the archducal lands in the family. Anna never wholly replaced Philippa Welser in Ferdinand's affections. He built the Silberkapelle in the Hofkirche (see p.469) as a monument to Philippa, and wished to be buried there himself.

Throughout the 1580s Ferdinand increasingly threw his energies into a mania for collecting that produced the famous **Kunst- und Wunderkammer**, a museum in which works of art were displayed beside bizarre natural phenomena and trinkets from far-flung places. To educated people of the time, such juxtapositions demonstrated the infinite diversity of God's creation. The popularity of such collections survived well into the next century, as demonstrated by the Kunst- und Wunderkammer of the archbishops of Salzburg (see p.383), together with Archbishop Markus Sitticus's enthusiasm for deformed animals (see p.391). Ferdinand went a step further than many contemporaries by acquiring human exhibits with which to amaze his guests, keeping both a giant and a dwarf at Schloss Ambras in specially made quarters.

On Ferdinand's death, the Ambras collection was sold to Emperor Rudolf II – Ferdinand's great rival in the collecting of oddities. Rudolf never got round to moving the objects out of the Schloss so the collection stayed here in its entirety until 1805, when the most valuable pieces were taken to Vienna to keep them out of the hands of the Bavarians.

cinated Ferdinand: in addition to his court giant and several court dwarfs are Petrus Gonsalvus of Tenerife, the so-called "Hirsute Man", pictured here with his similarly afflicted son and daughter; and Vlad Tepesch (aka Vlad the Impaler), the fifteenth-century ruler of Transylvania who resurfaced four hundred years later as the inspiration behind Bram Stoker's *Dracula*.

Slightly further uphill, Ferdinand's **Spanische Saal** features a dazzlingly intricate wood-inlay ceiling, and walls decorated with 27 full-length portraits of the rulers of the Tyrol. From here, steps lead to the **Upper Schloss**, where an extensive **portrait gallery** holds the works of artists who are sometimes less interesting than their sitters – a vast array of European rulers and aristocrats across the centuries. The collection also offers a good crash course in Habsburg family history, starting with a portrait of Albrecht III, painted around 1430, and revealing the jutting lower lip and strong jaw that remained a family trademark thereafter. Finally, a room leading off the interior court-yard houses one of the Schloss's most enchanting artworks, an **altar of St George** carved by Sebald Bocksdorfer and painted by Sebastian Scheel about 1500, with a mar-vellous gilt relief of the saint. The wings portray Maximilian I carrying sheaves of corn – a piece of symbolism linking the knightly warrior-emperor to prosperity and the pro-tection of the harvests.

North of the Altstadt: the Hungerbergbahn and the Alpenzoo

At the northern end of the Rennweg, a large round building houses the **Rundgemälde**, or Panorama (April–Oct daily 9am–4.45pm; öS30/€2.19), a circular painting portraying the Battle of Bergisel in 1809, when Andreas Hofer's Tyrolean insurgents routed a mixed French-Bavarian force. The huge fresco was unveiled in 1896, when such panoramas were all the rage in a continental Europe fond of didactic, patriotism-induc-ing displays. Just beside the Rundgemälde, the station of the **Hungerburgbahn** funic-ular (July–Sept 8am–6pm; April–June & Oct 8.25am–5.40pm; Nov–March 8.25am–5.10pm; öS55/€4.02 return) presents the most direct route up the flanks of the **Nordkette**, ascending the affluent hillside suburb of Hungerburg before continuing by two-stage cable car to the 1905-metre **Seegrube**, site of cafe-restaurant *Seegrube*, and the 2334-metre **Hafelekar** (July–Sept 8.30am–5.30pm; April–June & Oct 8.40am–7.30pm; Nov–March 9am–6.40pm; combined return with Hungerburgbahn öS268/€19.56). The journey here will provide you with spectacular views of the city far below, as well as a broad panorama of the snow-capped Alps to the south.

Halfway up the Hungerburgbahn, you can alight at a wayside halt in order to visit the **Alpenzoo** (daily: May–Sept 9am–6pm, Oct–April 9am–5pm; öS70/€5.11), also reached by walking 800m up Wieherburggasse from the west bank of the River Inn. The zoo holds a collection of animals indigenous to Europe's mountainous regions, including bears, eagles, pine martens (largely nocturnal, so not much chance of seeing them), ibex, lynx and otter.

Eating, drinking and entertainment

Innsbruck's Altstadt is crowded with establishments offering all manner of food and drink. A constant flow of tourists ensures that not all of them are cheap, but it's extremely rare to be fobbed off with nondescript food or indifferent service wherever you are in town.

There's no shortage of daytime **snack food**, with Würstelstands on both Herzog-Friedrich-Strasse and Maria-Theresien-Strasse. The handy *Subito*, on the corner of Herzog-Friedrich-Strasse and Kiebachgasse (daily until 1am), doles out inexpensive pizza slices. A little further afield, *Prendi Pizza*, Viaduktbogen 5, and the *Ali Kebab House*, Mariahilferstrasse 12, are popular sources for quick, takeaway nosh.

For **daytime drinking**, Innsbruck has a couple of classic coffeehouses that com-pare favourably with anything Vienna has to offer. A wide range of bars are scattered throughout the centre, and the Viaduktbogen – a line of railway arches ten minutes' walk east of the Altstadt – is home to a string of varied **night-time** venues. Central bars are usually open until around 2am, although several go on for a couple of hours longer. Most drinking establishments serve snacks or substantial main meals, day and night.

Cafés

Café Central, Gilmstrasse 5. Venerable city-centre café a few steps southeast of the Altstadt. The nearest thing to a Viennese *kaffehaus* that Innsbruck possesses, with a bewildering array of coffees and mouth-watering choice of cakes. Also a great range of breakfasts, if you don't mind paying slightly above the average.

Konditorei Munding, Corner of Kiebachgasse and Schlossergasse (*www.munding.at*). Much revered traditional *konditorei* bang in the middle of the Altstadt with a gorgeous selection of pastries, cakes and own-brand sweets.

Restaurants

Al Dente, Meranerstrasse 7. Popular and youthful pasta joint in the centre of town, with a few vegetarian choices on the menu and a salad bar.

Churrasco La Mamma, Innrain 2. Big Italian place overlooking the river, serving up a wide range of not too expensive pizza and pasta fare. Outdoor terrace in summer, conservatory-style dining room with riverside views in winter.

Chili's, corner of Boznerplatz and Adamgasse. Large, brightly-decorated restaurant offering the regular range of Mexican cuisine – although it's a bit bland for real hot-food freaks.

La Cucina, Museumstrasse 26. Bright and breezy Italian restaurant with a wide range of reasonably priced pizzas, an impressive choice of pasta dishes, and more expensive Italian classics (such as *saltimbocca alla Romana*) and some excellent desserts.

Ottoburg, Herzog-Friedrich-Strasse 1 (☎0512/574652). Bustling establishment in a fifteenth-century town house, with a posh restaurant upstairs with low wooden ceilings (reservations recommended) and a more run-of-the-mill selection of Austrian standards downstairs. Closed Sun.

Philippine, Müllerstrasse 9. Eccentrically decorated restaurant with a wide choice of vegetarian dishes, usually featuring an inexpensive Tagesmenü. Closed Sun.

Prendi, Viaduktbogen. Cheapest pizzeria in town, about 10min from the Altstadt along Museumstrasse. Good place to start before embarking on a nocturnal exploration of the Viaduktbogen bars.

Sahib, Sillgasse 3. Good, slightly pricey Indian restaurant round the corner from the Landesmuseum Ferdinandeum. Main courses from around öS160/€11.68, lunchtime menus from around öS100/€7.30.

Stiegelbräu, Wilhelm-Griel-Strasse 25. A bit antiseptic despite attempts to induce a homely beer-hall atmosphere, but a good centrally located place in which to sample standard Austrian dishes, as well is inexpensive Tyrolean fare such as *Gröstl* and *Käsespätzle*. The adjoining beer bar is the place to snack on simpler fare like sausages and goulash. Closed Sun.

Stiftskeller, Stiftgasse 1. A dependable, mid-priced restaurant on the well-trodden route between the Hofkirche and Goldenes Dachl. There's always fresh trout on the menu.

Thai Li, Marktgraben 3. Plush Thai restaurant in the Altstadt with reasonably authentic fare. Main courses hover around the öS160/€11.68 mark, although there's usually a cheap lunchtime menu.

Weisses Rössl, Kiebachgasse 8. First-floor, wood-panelled restaurant above the hotel of the same name, with a good mix of tourists and locals, and wide range of Austrian food. A good place for Tyrolean specialities and inexpensive Tagesmenüs.

Bars

Elferhaus, Herzog-Friedrich-Strasse 11. Crowded, narrow, enduringly popular city-centre place with a selection of Austrian lagers and Weissbier on tap, and numerous bottled varieties from around the world. Also a popular place to eat, with a small but well-chosen menu of ribs, burgers and other pub favourites.

Hofgartencafé, Rennweg 6a (*www.hofgartencafe.at*). A pavilion in the corner of the Hofgarten park, opposite the Hofburg, with plenty of outdoor seating in the summer. Popular hangout for an affluent, dressy crowd. Open until 4am.

Innkeller, Innstrasse 1. Best of the bars on the west bank of the Inn, with youngish crowds imbibing to a predominantly alternative dance or post-rock soundtrack provided by resident DJs.

Jimmy's, Wilhelm-Greil-Strasse 17. Ultramodern and ultra-cool bar attracting hip teens and twentysomethings. Techno and alternative dance DJs play in the Blue Chip bar in the basement.

Limerick Bill's Irish Pub, Maria-Theresien-Strasse 9. Large and lively Irish pub made up of a succession of small snug rooms – including an upstairs bar. Occasional live music.

Krahvogel, Anichstrasse 12. Funky city-centre bar with a good range of Austrian and Belgian draught beers, and a big choice of snacks in the soup and sandwiches line. Outdoor seating in the courtyard at the back.

Prometheus, Hofgasse 2. Conveniently central place attracting youngish, mildly bohemian types. There's a cramped but convivial bar upstairs, which serves sandwiches and other snacks; and a sweaty cellar disco offering themed party nights – which could feature anything from salsa to Britpop.

Theresienbräu, Maria-Theresien-Strasse 51–53. Animated fun-pub serving ales brewed on the premises to a young, hedonistic crowd sucking down beer and watching pop videos on big screens.

Weli, Viaduktbogen 26. One of the less pretentious places along the Viaduktbogen, a friendly café-pub with board games, as well as good home-style cooking.

Zappa, Rechengasse 5. Stylish and friendly basement bar in the university district southwest of the centre, decorated with rock and film memorabilia and psychedelic wall paintings. Studeny clientele (it's underneath a hall of residence) and a different style of music (anything from reggae to alternative rock) every night. In-house DJs at weekends.

Entertainment

Although not in the same league as Salzburg or Graz, Innsbruck still serves up a varied cultural diet. For **high culture**, the Tiroler Landestheater, Rennweg 2 (*www.landestheater.at*), is the main venue for serious drama, opera and ballet; bigger productions sometimes make use of the Congress Centre on Rennweg. Smaller recitals occasionally take place in Schloss Ambras, site of a Festival of Early Music in August – the **Innsbrucker Festwochen der Alten Musik** – specializing in music of the Baroque and early Classical period (advance bookings can be made through the Innsbruck tourist office).

For **rock and pop**, big-name touring bands play at large multipurpose venues like the Olympiastadion or Messehalle. The best places to catch **alternative** bands, local acts, world music or **jazz** are the *Treibhaus*, Angerzellgasse 8, a cultural centre that doubles as a popular weekend drinking venue for a young arty set; or *Utopia*, Tschamlerstrasse 3, a more alternative venue 1km south of the centre which also hosts themed club nights with left-of-field DJs. Slightly further south in Wilten, *Bierstindl*, Klostergasse 6, is a cultural centre and café-bar which hosts fringe theatre and rock/jazz concerts, some of which take place in the beer garden over the summer. Innsbruck's principal **clubbing** venue, with a weekly programme of big techno nights and top-name DJs, is *Hafen*, 1500m southwest of the centre along Innrain.

Information and **tickets** for all cultural events are available from the main tourist office at Burggraben 3.

Listings

Airlines Austrian Airlines, Adamgasse 7a (☎0512/582985); Lufthansa, Südtirolerplatz 1 (☎0512/59800); Tyrolean Airways, at the airport (☎0512/2222-77).

Airport information Innsbruck (☎0512/22525); Munich (☎0049/89/9752 1313).

American Express Brixnerstrasse 3 (☎0512/582491).

Bike rental Limited choice from the train station (☎503/5385); mountain bikes from Sport Neuner, Salurnerstrasse 5 (☎0512/561501).

Books Tyrolia, Maria-Theresien-Strasse 15, has the biggest general range of English-language paperbacks. Freytag & Berndt, Wilhelm-Griel-Strasse 15 has English-language travel books and maps.

Car rental Ajax, Amraserstrasse 6 (☎0512/583232); Avis, Salurnerstrasse 15 (☎0512/571754); Budget, Leopoldstrasse 0512/580901).

Cinema Cinematograph, Museumstrasse 31 (☎0512/578500). Shows art-house films – usually subtitled rather than dubbed into German.

Consulates United Kingdom, Matthias-Schmid-Strasse 12/I (☎0512/588320; Mon–Fri 9am–noon). Other nationals should contact their embassies in Vienna.

Exchange Banks are generally open Mon–Thur 7.45am–12.30pm & 2.15–4pm, Fri 7.45am–3pm. Outside these hours, try bureaus in the train station (daily 9am–8pm); at the tourist office, Burggraben 3 (Mon–Sat 8am–7pm, Sun 9am–6pm); or the main post office (24hr), Maximilianstrasse 2.

HUT TO HUT IN THE STUBAI ALPS

The **Stubaier Höhenweg**, a circuit of the Stubaital to the southwest of Innsbruck, away from roads and villages, is arguably one of the finest multi-day tours of the Alps, and a perfect introduction to the Austrian hut system. With at least one pass to cross on each stage, the route is scenically varied, and challenging in places – several sections are laced with wire ropes to safeguard difficult or potentially dangerous steps. Trails are otherwise reasonably straightforward, if occasionally obscured by late-lying snow. Waymarking is mostly good, and each of the huts manned, with meals on offer, making heavy rucksacks unnecessary. Several stages are only about three hours long, so the circuit can feasibly be completed within five or six days by experienced mountain walkers – but the landscape is of such high quality that connoisseurs will allow at least eight.

Usually tackled in a clockwise direction, the tour starts from either Neustift or Neder, 15km south of Innsbruck, with the first day spent walking south through the green and pastoral Pinnistal as far as Karalm, before climbing over the 2380-metre Pinnisjoch to gain the *Innsbrucker Hütte* (☎05276/295) set just below the pass. Across the depths of the nearby Gschnitztal are the limestone Tribulaun peaks, while immediately above the hut to the west rises Habicht (3277m), whose summit is recommended to experienced scramblers. Yet more dramatic country lies ahead on day 2, as you make your way across a series of ridge spurs in order to reach the *Bremer Hütte* (☎0663/57545), simplest and most atmospheric of all the huts on the circuit. Heading west on day 3, the route crosses the Simmingjöchl and skirts below the Feuerstein peaks within sight of the Wilder Freiger (3418m) and its glaciers. Wilder Freiger is usually climbed from the next hut, the four-storey *Nürnberger* (☎05226/2492), while day 4 leads to the *Sulzenau Hütte* (☎05226/2432), passing immediately below it on a day of tarns, moraine ribs and alpine flowers. From Sulzenau to the *Dresdner Hütte*, on day 5, is another short stage, but with two routes to choose from: the most obvious crosses the Peiljoch, but a more challenging way – for experienced climbers with a good head for heights – crosses over the Grosser Trögler (2902m), gaining spectacular views of the region's highest peak, the Zuckerhütl. The *Dresdner Hütte* (☎05226/8112), though comfortable and with good food on offer, is set in a landscape devalued by ski machinery, with tows and cableways marching up to glacial ski-grounds. You leave this behind on day 6 with an eight-hour trek by way of the Grawagrubennieder – at 2881m, the highest crossing on the circuit and with a descent that goes down a loose stony gully – arriving at the next hut, the *Neue Regensberger Hütte* (☎05226/2520), which stands at the mouth of a marshy glen topped by the Ruderhofspitze. Little more than a morning's walk separates Neue Regensberger and the very popular *Franz Senn Hütte* (☎05226/2218) via the rocky Schrimmennieder on day 7, but it's another fine route and with a tempting glen to explore can fill a day. If you've enough time, a second night at *Franz Senn* allows a trip to the beautiful Rinnensee, a climb to the Rinnenspitze or a visit to the narrow notch of the Rinnennieder for its amazing contrasting views. The last full day of the walk (day 8) counts among the best – after an eleven-kilometre-long hillside traverse above the Oberbergtal, the trail shuffles screes at the foot of the dolomitic Kalkkogel massif before arriving at the *Starkenberger Hütte* (☎05226/2867), from where you can see a good portion of the whole Stubai circuit. Your last morning is reserved for the knee-troublingly steep descent back to Neustift.

A recommended map to take on the Stubaier Höhenweg is the *Kompass Wanderkarte* no. 83 (Stubaier Alpen Serleskamm), at 1:50,000. For more on the Austrian hut-to-hut system, see p.39.

Football FC Tirol Innsbruck play at the Tivoli Stadion on Burgenlandstrasse, southeast of the centre near the Olympiabrücke. One of Austria's better sides, they were national champions in the 1999/2000 season.

Gay organizations Homosexuelle Initiative Tirol, Innrain 100 (☎0512/562403, *www.hosi.or.at*).

Hiking tours The tourist office runs an extensive programme of guided walks – including nighttime hiking above Igls – from June to early September. They're free to anyone in possession of a *Innsbruck Club Card* (issued to anyone staying in Innsbruck – get it from the tourist office or your hotel). A hiking pass covering unlimited use of the Hungerburg funicular and the Nordkette and Patscherkofel cable cars costs öS450/€32.85 for 3 days; öS720/€52.56 for 6 days. The Österreichischer Alpenverein (Austrian Alpine Club), at Wilhelm-Griel-Strasse 15, provides hiking information and sells maps (☎0512/59547; Mon–Fri 9am–1pm, 2–5pm).

Hospital Universitätsklinik, Anichstrasse 35 (☎0512/5040).

Ice skating Indoor (open all year round) and outdoor (open mid-Nov to Feb) rinks at the Eisstadion by the Olympiabrücke (☎0512/33838). Admission öS55/€4.02, skate rental öS65/€4.75.

Internet access Café-bar Piccolo, Maria-Theresien-Strasse 16.

Laundry Bubble Point, corner of Andreas-Hofer-Strasse and Franz-Fischer-Strasse (Mon–Fri 8am–10pm, Sat & Sun 8am–8pm).

Left Luggage Lockers at the train station. Smallest locker (big enough for most packs) takes öS20 at the time of writing.

Markets Fresh fruit, veg and rural produce at the Bauernmarkt (farmers' market) in the Markthalle, at the junction of Marktgraben and Innrain. Every morning except Sun.

Motoring organizations ÖAMTC, Andechsstrasse 81 (☎0512/3320).

Pharmacies General opening hours are Mon–Fri 8am–noon & 2.30–6pm, Sat 8am–noon. Outside these hours, signs in the window of each pharmacy will indicate the location of the nearest duty pharmacy.

Police The main police station is at Kaiserjägerstrasse 8 (☎0512/5900).

Post office The main post office, at Maximilianstrasse 2, is open 24hr.

Rafting Contact the tourist office for details of rafting trips up the Inn Valley at Imst (see p.512).

Swimming pools Indoor pool at Amraserstrasse 3 (☎0512/342585); summer outdoor pool at the Tivoli sports centre, Purtschellerstrasse 1 (☎0512/342344).

Taxis ☎0512/5311; ☎0512/202070.

Tennis In summer, outdoor courts at the Eisstadion (☎0512/33838; öS120/€8.76 per hour); in winter, Indoor Tennis Courts West, near the airport at Fürstenweg 172 (☎0512/284364; from öS160/€11.68 per hour).

Train information ☎0512/1717.

Travel agents Tiroler Landesreisebüro, Wilhelm-Griel-Strasse (☎0512/59885).

Women's organizations Frauenzentrum Innsbruck, Liebeneggstrasse 15 (☎0512/580839).

EAST OF INNSBRUCK

The eastern part of the Inn Valley, known locally as the **Unterland**, includes many of the Tyrol's most absorbing historical towns – nuggets of late-Gothic culture like **Hall**, **Schwaz** and **Rattenberg**, as well as the fortress town of **Kufstein** on the border with Bavaria. All of these are good bases from which to explore a variety of neighbouring alpine villages, although for a real taste of the mountains you'd do better to plump for **Kitzbühel**, the fashionable society resort in the extreme east, or the **Zillertal**, the most breathtaking of the side-valleys feeding the River Inn from the south. Immediately north of the Zillertal is the **Achensee**, the Tyrol's biggest lake, which in summer offers a lazy waterside alternative to the more strenuous pursuits of the region.

The main autobahn and rail route to Salzburg and Vienna follows the Inn Valley eastwards, through Hall, Schwaz and Rattenberg before entering Germany just beyond Kufstein. The town of **Jenbach**, although of no particular interest in itself, is an important transport hub serving routes to the Zillertal and the Achensee. Further east, **Wörgl** commands another important junction, with road and rail routes branching off towards Kitzbühel.

Hall

At its fifteenth-century peak, **HALL** was the third largest Austrian city after Vienna and Schwaz, an important trading centre that had grown rich on the proceeds of salt mined in the mountains to the north. It was transformed into a major financial centre under Maximilian I's uncle Sigismund the Rich, who moved the Tyrolean mint here from Meran in the 1470s and began production of the *Taler*, a silver coin that became the standard unit of currency in central Europe for a time. (The place it occupied in the popular imagination is today recalled by the monetary unit named after it – the dollar.)

Modern Hall preserves one of the best ensembles of late medieval buildings in the country and is an attractive day-trip destination from Innsbruck – which is only 10km away to the west.

The Town

Hall's main attraction is the late-Gothic character of the town centre, a compact grid of medieval alleyways that zero in on a central square, the **Oberer Stadtplatz**. Immediately to the west, a short flight of steps ascends to the **Pfarrkirche St Nikolaus**, a thirteenth-century structure whose interior betrays a curious lack of symmetry, the result of an unfinished fifteenth-century programme of rebuilding that left the choir off-centre. To the left of the high altar, the **Waldaufkapelle** is named after Florian Waldauf, a peasant's son from East Tyrol who rose to become trusted sidekick of Emperor Maximilian I. Waldauf was an obsessive collector of holy relics, and in 1501 arranged delivery of the skulls of numerous minor European saints to the church in a pomp-laden procession. They now occupy the niches along the chapel's northern wall, watched over by a late-Gothic altar to the Virgin Mary, thought to be the work of Tyrolean master Michael Pacher (see p.429).

Behind the church to the east stands the **Magdalenskapelle**, an outwardly featureless grey building, which contains some excellent late-Gothic paintings, including a *Last Judgement* filled with the writhing forms of the damned. In the centre of the chapel an **altar** of 1490 displays some extraordinarily vibrant scenes on the wings, illustrating the Annunciation, Adoration of the Magi and Death of the Virgin, together with images of St Barbara and St Agnes, the latter accompanied by her symbol, the lamb.

Immediately north of the Pfarrkirche, the **Rathaus** was built in the fourteenth century by Henry, King of Bohemia and Duke of Tyrol. It was subsequently used as a hunting lodge by Maximilian I, who would set off into the mountains to indulge in the noble art of *Gamsstechen* – impaling chamoix on 4.5-metre-long pikes. Visitors can usually gain admission to the building's main ceremonial chamber, the Rathausstube, which preserves its sixteenth-century wood ceiling, although its popularity as a venue for weddings ensures that it's rarely accessible to tourists at weekends.

The **Bergbaumuseum**, or mining museum (May–Oct Mon–Sat 9am–noon & 2–5pm; öS30/€2.19), a block south of Oberer Stadtplatz on the corner of Eugenstrasse, recounts Hall's salt-mining heritage, although the attempt to recreate the atmosphere of underground galleries in the old ducal palace is less than successful. Eugenstrasse heads west from here to the **Stiftsplatz**, where a fine Baroque facade marks the location of the so-called **Damenstift**, the Carmelite convent founded in 1567 by the Archduchess Magdalena, sister of Archduke Ferdinand II of Tyrol. One of the strictest of all religious orders, Carmelites observed total silence and slept in their own coffins.

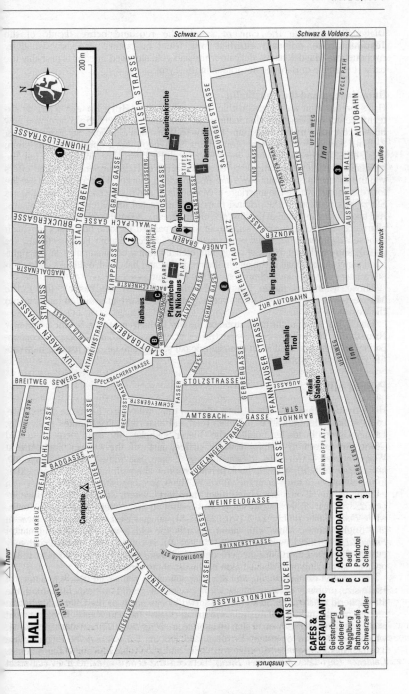

HALL

Schwaz △

Schwaz & Volders △

Innsbruck ▽

Thaur △

Innsbruck ▽

Tulfes ▷

THURNFELDSTRASSE

MILSER STRASSE

Jesuitenkirche

SALZBURGER STRASSE

Damenstift

STIFTS PLATZ

Bergbaumuseum

EUGENSTRASSE

ROSENGASSE

SCHLOSSERG

AGRAMS GASSE

WALLPACH GASSE

OBERER STADTPLATZ

STADTGRABEN

BRUCKERGASSE

MAGDALENAGT.

STRAUSS STRASSE

FUX MAGEN STRASSE

MAGDALENASTR.

KIRPPGASSE

KATHREINSTRASSE

ALTER STRASSE

KIRCHE STRASSE

BACHLECHNERSTR.

Rathaus

Pfarrkirche
St Nikolaus

PFARR PLATZ

SALVATOR GASSE

SCHMIED GASSE

LANGER GRABEN

UNTERER STADTPLATZ

MÜNZER GASSE

LEND GASSE

UNTERE LEND

FÖRSTER PARK

UFER WEG

Inn

CYCLE PATH

AUTOBAHN

AUSFAHRT N HALL

Burg Hasegg

ZUR AUTOBAHN

Kunsthalle
Tirol

FASSER GASSE

GERBERGASSE

STOLZSTRASSE

SPECKBACHERSTRASSE

RECHEJSTRASSE

SCHWEYGERSTR.

SCHEIDEN STEIN STRASSE

REIM MICHL STRASSE

BREITWEG

SEWERST

SCHILLER STR.

BADGASSE

AMTSBACH-

GASSE

KUGELANGER STRASSE

PFANNHAUSER STRASSE

BAHNHOF
STR.

AUGASSE

Train
Station

BAHNHOFPLATZ

UFERWEG

Inn

OBERE LEND

ZUR AUTOBAHN

Campsite ⚑

HEILIGKREUZ

TRIENDL STRASSE

MÖSL WEG

ZIEGELWEG

SÜDTIROLER STR.

FASSER GASSE

WEINFELDGASSE

BRIXNERSTRASSE

TRIENDLSTRASSE

INNSBRUCKER STRASSE

200 m

N

Ⓐ

ⓘ

Ⓑ

Ⓒ

Ⓓ

Ⓔ

①

②

③

Diagonally opposite the convent stands the red and ochre facade of the **Jesuitenkirche**, originally attached to a Jesuit monastery also established by Archduchess Magdalena. Its delicate white and gold stuccoed interior is probably the earliest example of Baroque decoration in the Tyrol.

Burg Hasegg and the Kunsthalle

Hall's famous mint was located within the sturdy walls of **Burg Hasegg**, a largely sixteenth-century strongpoint dominating the lower town south of the centre, and now housing the town **museum** (summer Mon–Fri 9am–noon & 2–5pm, Sat 10am–noon & 2–5pm, Sun 2–5pm; winter Mon–Thurs 9am–noon & 2–5pm, Fri 9am–noon; öS50/€3.65). The sections on local history and folklore are uninspiring, but the inevitable section on minting features a wide array of Habsburg-era coins and offers you the chance to mint your own *Taler* (for an added charge). Visitors can also see the fortress chapel, where the marriage of Maximilian I and his second wife Bianca Maria Sforza was confirmed (the original marriage, contracted for purely political reasons, had taken place in Milan in the absence of the groom). A small collection of late-Gothic altarpieces is also up for perusal, one of which, painted by local boy Marx Reichlich (whose *Adoration of the Magi* is in Innsbruck's Landesmuseum Ferdinandeum; see p.469), shows Florian Waldauf being knighted by Emperor Maximilian in the right-hand panel (Maximilian is the one in the red jacket and hat), and Waldauf's wife – herself a major donor to local churches – in the left-hand panel.

Those willing to tackle the two hundred steps of the castle's tower, the **Münzerturm**, are rewarded with sweeping views of the urban sprawl of Innsbruck to the west.

Finally, just south of the main street on the way to the train station lies the brand-new **Kunsthalle Tirol** (Tues–Sun 2–8pm; prices vary; *www.kunsthalle-tirol.at*), a contemporary art centre located in an atmospheric old salt warehouse, and hosting high-profile, challenging displays.

Practicalities

Hall's **train station** is on the eastern edges of the town centre. From the station forecourt walk straight ahead to the main road and turn right; five minutes' walk away, Langer Graben heads left uphill to the Oberer Stadtplatz, the main focus of the Old Town. An extremely helpful **tourist office**, just off the Oberer Stadtplatz at Wallpachgasse 5 (Mon–Fri 8.30am–noon & 2–6pm, Sat 9am–noon; ☎05223/56269, *hall.tirol@netway.at*), will help book **private rooms**, although most of these are either in the outskirts of town or in the village of Thaur (see opposite) 3km northeast – an enticing option if you have your own transport. *Schatz*, Innsbrucker Strasse 62 (☎05223/57994; ③), is a comfy suburban **Gasthof** on the western fringes of the town, while *Badl*, Haller Innbrücke 4 (☎05223/56784; ③), has a pleasant riverside location and bright rooms, some with views towards the old town. The more upmarket *Parkhotel*, Thurnfeldgasse 1a (☎05223/56566; ⑤), is comfortable, modern and very central. There's a **campsite** on Schiedensteinstrasse (☎05223/45464-75) next to the open-air swimming pool, about 1.5km northeast of the centre.

There aren't as many eating and drinking options as you would expect in a town of Hall's size, probably because Innsbruck is so close at hand. For inexpensive **food**, the atmospheric *Geisterburg*, Stadtgraben 18, two blocks north of the Oberer Stadtplatz, offers a popular mixture of Austrian and Italian cuisine, has a nice garden out front and is open until midnight. A small step up in price are *Nagglburg*, Ritter-Waldaufstrasse 11, which specializes in top-quality Tyrolean food, and the *Schwarzer Adler*, Eugenstrasse 3, which has a top-quality Austrian repertoire and good-value lunchtime Tagesmenüs. *Goldener Engl* (aka *Augustiner Bräu*), between the centre and the train station at

Unterer Stadtplatz 5, is another good place to try meaty Austrian favourites such as *Wiener Schnitzel* and *Zwiebelrostbraten*, as well as offering local cheapies such as *Kässpätzle*.

Best of the **drinking** venues is the *Rathauscafé*, which occupies a pair of vaulted Gothic rooms beside the town hall, and serves up a tempting range of sandwiches, lunches and cakes, as well as attracting a hip young crowd in the evenings. Otherwise, nightlife in Hall revolves around the bars on Salvatorgasse, a medieval alleyway just below the Obere Stadtplatz: the barrel-vaulted *Haller Kübel* is the best of the places here, and sometimes features live music at weekends.

Around Hall

Hall is a good base from which to explore a cluster of attractive villages clinging to the sides of the Inn Valley, among them **Thaur**, **Tulfes** and **Volders**. Popular destinations for Tyroleans, few of them receive English-speaking tourists in any great numbers. Further east, but still within striking distance, the more industrialized town of **Wattens** is home to the **Swarovski Kristallwelt**, a high-tech, multimedia exhibition built around the products of the local crystal factory.

Thaur

Three kilometres northwest of Hall, **THAUR** is an exceedingly pretty village lurking in the shadow of the Nordkette. It's known above all for preserving the kind of authentic **Tyrolean folk traditions** that have died out elsewhere. It's one of the few places that still marks **Palm Sunday** with a procession involving a life-size effigy of Jesus on a donkey, carried through the fields around the village. Originally common throughout Austria, such processions were discouraged during the reign of eighteenth-century rationalist Josef II, and most Jesus-on-a-donkey statues belonging to other villages were destroyed. Festivities in Thaur continue throughout **Holy Week**; a tableau depicting the grave of Christ is placed in the Pfarrkirche, and another procession takes place through the town on **Good Friday**.

Thaur is also an important centre for the making of Nativity scenes, or **Krippen** (see p.468). The craft is still practised by several local families, who display their *Krippen* either in the Pfarrkirche or at home between December 26 and January 15. Details of where you can see the *Krippen* are available from the tourist office in Hall – otherwise look out for signs outside private houses reading *"Weihnachtskrippe"* ("Christmas crib").

Thaur doesn't have a tourist office of its own, but **private rooms** here can be procured through the tourist office in Hall. There are also two very plush, 4-star **hotels** in the centre of the village: the *Stangl*, Kirchgasse 2 (☎05223/492828; ⑥), and the *Purner*, Dorfplatz 5 (☎05223/49149; ⑥).

Tulfes and Volders

The nearest mountain resort offering winter skiing and summer hiking is the village of **TULFES**, spread across a hillside terrace 6km to the south of Hall. Accessible by minor road, and served by buses from the Unterer Stadtplatz in Hall or from the main bus station in Innsbruck, Tulfes is the starting point for a two-stage gondola ascent to the **Tulfein Alm**, an area of alpine meadow below the area's main peak, the **Glungezer**. The Zirbenweg walk from the top of the Glungezer gondola (July–Aug & late–Dec to early April) to the top of the Patscherkofel cable car above Igls is a popular, though strenuous, three-hour hike, with great views across the valley towards the Nordkette on the opposite side.

Also on the south side of the Inn, but down on the valley floor some 4km east of Hall, is the village of **VOLDERS** (easily reached from Hall via the foot- and cyclepath that runs along the south bank of the Inn starting from the *Gasthof Badl*), site of the seventeenth-century church of **St Karl Borromäus**. A Baroque masterpiece with a striking red-and-white colour scheme, the building has been blighted by the construction of the adjacent autobahn.

Wattens and the Swarovski Kristallwelt

Eight kilometres east of Hall, and served by numerous local trains, **WATTENS** is home to one of Austria's most popular modern attractions, the **Swarovski Kristallwelt**, or "Crystal World". It was conceived as a high-profile showcase for the nearby Swarovski factory, long-standing producer of high-quality optical equipment as well as the ornamental cut-glass animals and figurines regarded as rank kitsch by some, prized collectables by others.

About twenty minutes' walk southeast of Fritzens-Wattens **train station**, the entrance to the Kristallwelt (daily 9am–6pm; öS75/€5.45; *www.swarovski-kristallwelt .com*) is itself dramatic, hidden beneath an ivy-covered hillside landscaped to form a human face – with a small waterfall emerging from the mouth. Inside, a range of sound-and-light environments created by Viennese installation artist André Heller and others (including ambient music pioneer Brian Eno) aim to induce a sense of wonder or meditative contemplation. The result is both a vastly entertaining futuristic theme park and a staggeringly vulgar monument to corporate vanity (it comes as no surprise to discover that the largest of the exhibition galleries is the gift-shop); but it's one of a kind, and kids will probably love it.

There's little else in Wattens to detain you, and you'd be wise to treat the Kristallwelt as a day-trip from Hall or Innsbruck rather than staying locally.

Schwaz and around

The bustling commercial centre of **SCHWAZ**, 20km east of Hall, bears an equally impressive historical pedigree. Until the closure of the mines some two hundred years ago, Schwaz was the the Tyrol's major producer of **silver**, a resource crucial to the upturn of Habsburg fortunes during the reign of Maximilian I. The old silver workings have been transformed into one of Austria's most popular **show-mines**, on the eastern fringes of town, near the unmissable **Haus der Völker**, an intriguing new ethnographical collection. Schwaz's town centre, by no means as pretty as those of Hall and Innsbruck, nevertheless contains a generous sprinkling of late-Gothic sights. A picturesque gorge at **Stans** and the museum at **Schloss Tratzberg** provide the main out-of-town attractions.

The Town

Schwaz's town centre spreads along the southeastern bank of the River Inn, while the main road and rail routes hug the opposite side of the valley. Bordered to the north by a few remaining portions of medieval wall, its core is marked by the **Pfarrkirche**, with its copper-shingled roof and characteristic crenellated gables. Built during the town's fifteenth-century silver-mining heyday, it was designed to cater for two separate congregations and as a consequence sports two naves: the one on the left was reserved for the burghers, the one on the right for miners. The high altar is twentieth-century neo-Gothic, but the side altar to the left is a fine piece of medieval craftsmanship dating from 1410, featuring a Madonna and Child wearing elaborately jewelled crowns. At the back of the nave near the entrance, don't miss the baptismal font of 1470, with an exquisitely carved relief of John the Baptist at the base, and the Baroque organ case high above, a cherub-and-statuette-laden affair from the 1730s.

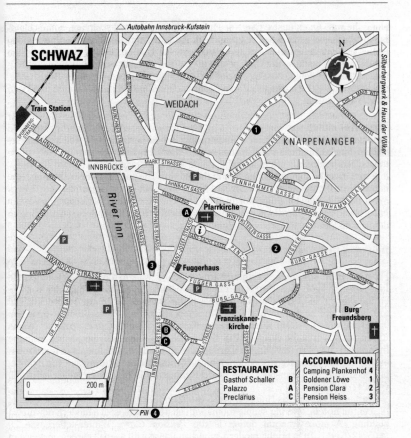

From here Franz-Josef-Strasse runs east past a sequence of town houses that betray their medieval origins, most important of which is the **Fuggerhaus**, which has traces of eighteenth-century paintings on the outside. Slightly set back from the main street is the **Franziskanerkirche**, not a source of great interest in itself, but the **cloisters** to the right contain a cycle of paintings illustrating the Passion, painted in the 1520s and currently undergoing restoration.

Burggasse leads uphill from the Franziskanerkirche towards the twelfth-century **Burg Freundsberg**, perched on a knoll about a ten-minute walk away. The small **museum** in the castle keep (mid-April to mid-Oct daily except Thur 10am–5pm; öS30/€2.19) is by no means essential viewing but includes a modest collection of nineteenth-century wooden furniture, wrought-iron crosses from local graveyards, and some late-Gothic wood panelling and wall paintings.

Haus der Völker

Husslstrasse leads northeast from the town centre towards the **Haus der Völker** (daily 10am–6pm; öS70/€5.11; www.hausdervoelker.com), about 1.5km away, a modern museum built to house the private collections of Gert Chesi, a local photojournalist who spent most of his career in Africa and Southeast Asia and collected traditional artefacts along the way. An extensive range of Thai and Burmese wood sculpture, some colourful Yoruba masks and a set-piece grouping of statuettes from Togo representing voodoo deities and fetish figures standing in a ceremonial boat are among the displays. An exhibit of flags made by the Fanti people of Ghana show images of white men crashing in aeroplanes or being eaten by crocodiles, revealing hostility towards the British colonial authorities. The museum's *Ethno-Café* sometimes has evenings devoted to African or Mexican cuisine.

The silver mine

Another kilometre further on Husslstrasse, the **Silberbergwerk** (daily May–Oct 8.30am–5pm; Christmas–April 9.30am–4pm; Nov–Christmas closed; öS150/€10.95; *www.silberbergwerk.at*) offers an exhilarating kilometre-long train ride into the mine, followed by an hour-long walking tour of the interior. The potted history of mining techniques through the ages won't appeal to everyone, but the imaginatively lit caverns make the 90-minute-long tour worthwhile. Tours are in German, although English-language headsets are provided at each stop along the way. Tours depart according to demand and are usually pretty frequent.

Practicalities

From the **train station**, a straightforward ten-minute walk to the southeast, across the Innbrücke, will get you to the centre of town. Most **buses** stop at the train station, some on the other side of the river on Andreas-Hofer-Strasse, just by the Innbrücke. The **tourist office**, in the town hall at Franz-Josef-Strasse 2 (Mon–Fri 9am–6pm, Sat 9am–1pm; ☎05242/63240, *www.tiscover.com/schwaz*), will direct you to **private rooms** (①) in Schwaz or in the village of **Pill** 4km to the west (served by hourly bus from the Innbrücke). If you're travelling in a group or with children, apartments in **farmhouses** (②) are the best bargains, although most of these are out of town, and you'll probably need your own transport. The nearest **campsite** is *Camping Plankenhof* in Pill (☎05242/64195-0).

Pension Heiss, Andreas-Hofer-Strasse 5 (☎05242/73388; ②), is one of the cheapest of the central **hotels**, offering simple rooms with shared facilities, in a modern downtown building. A more tranquil option is the *Pension Clara*, Winterstellergasse 20 (☎05242/63911; ②), a bright, modern suburban house with a small garden, just east of the tourist office. Offering slightly more comfort immediately north of the centre is the *Goldener Löwe*, Husslstrasse 4 (☎05242/62373; ④), where rooms come with TV, phone and access to an indoor pool and sauna.

The centre of town holds a wide range of **restaurants and cafés**. For a quick, cheap meal, *Palazzo*, on Franz-Josef-Strasse, is a lively pizza and pasta joint. For something more substantial, *Gasthof Schaller*, Innsbruckerstrasse 31, offers the best selection of Tyrolean food, as well as Austrian regulars, in a nice wood-panelled room, while the nearby *Preclarius*, also on Innsbruckerstrasse, specializes in South Tyrolean cuisine – that basically means Tyrolean cuisine with a few Italian recipes thrown in for good measure.

Schwaz is far enough away from Innsbruck to have a **drinking and nightlife** scene in its own right. Drawing a younger crowd are *Radio*, a narrow, crowded bar at Andreas-Hofer-Strasse 3, and *Silver City*, Franz-Josef-Strasse, a café-bar decorated in the style of a Western saloon. *Amt*, Josef-Wopfner-Strasse, and *Parterre*, by the river on Andreas-Hofer-Strasse, cater for a dressier, twenty-to-thirty-something clientele. The cosiest and most laid-back drinking hole is the *Eremitage*, Innsbruckerstrasse 14, a fashionable first-floor bar with jazz music (occasionally live) and a substantial food menu.

Around Schwaz: Stans and Schloss Tratzberg

Travelling eastwards from Schwaz, the autobahn and rail line stay close by the River Inn, while the old Schwaz–Jenbach road (served by regular buses from Schwaz) hugs the northern side of the valley, passing after 3km through the village of **STANS**. The main reason to stop off here is to visit the **Wölfsklamm** (May–Oct daily dawn–dusk; öS25/€1.83), a small but impressive stretch of gorge spanned by wooden walkways immediately north of the village centre.

Three kilometres east of Stans, an access road ascends to the left towards **Schloss Tratzberg**, another of Maximilian I's former hunting lodges, now containing a small museum which is only accessible by guided tour (April–Oct daily 10am–4pm; öS120/€8.76; *www.schloss-tratzberg.at*). On the whole, the exhibits – mostly agricultural implements and weapons – are less interesting than their surroundings, with many rooms boasting intricate Renaissance wooden ceilings. The walls of one sixteenth-century room bear frescoes depicting a genealogical tree of the Habsburg dynasty, its branches embellished with portraits of 148 family members, beginning with Rudolf I, the first of the family to don the Holy Roman crown.

The Zillertal

Backed by the impressive wall of the Zillertaler Alps and fed by a succession of deep, picturesque side-valleys (known hereabouts as the *Gründe*), the **ZILLERTAL** is the most versatile alpine vacation area east of Innsbruck. It has long been favoured by the winter package crowd, especially the British, which has led to a high degree of commercialization. Of the valley's principal centres, **Zell am Ziller** retains something of its Austrian character, while **Mayrhofen**, is solely a tourist town – full of cosmopolitan life in winter season, fairly soulless outside it. On the plus side, the scenery is as grandiose as it comes, and all the facilities required for an outdoor alpine holiday are close at hand. In summer, walking opportunities are particularly varied: the whole valley is well served by cable cars and chairlifts, most of which operate over the summer, making it easy for the most reluctant of hikers to reach high altitudes with the minimum of effort. Although the heights immediately above Mayrhofen and Zell am Ziller are the easiest ambling areas to access, there is much wilder alpine territory in the side-valleys to the south, with the **Stilluppgrund**, **Zemmgrund**, **Zamsergrund** and **Tuxertal** proving particularly rewarding. Regional **hiking maps** can be purchased at the Zell am Ziller and Mayrhofen tourist offices: the Kompas 1:50,000 *Zillertaler Alpen & Tuxer Voralpen* covers the whole valley, while the same publisher's 1:25,000 *Mayrhofen-Tuxertal-Zillergrund* map offers more detailed coverage of the region's southern end.

In **winter**, both Mayrhofen and Zell am Ziller are well-equipped ski resorts with plenty of scope for beginners and intermediates, although they're very crowded in peak periods such as late December and late January through to the end of February. Experienced skiers will probably find a bigger range of challenging pistes on the Tuxertal glacier, which is easily reached by bus from Mayrhofen and offers good skiing, with spectacular roof-of-the-alps views, all year round. The glacier is particularly popular with **snowboarders** from spring through to autumn. The village of **Hintertux**, immediately below the glacier, is a resort in its own right, but with most of the nightlife concentrated in Mayrhofen, you may prefer to base yourself down the valley.

Transport up the valley is provided by the privately owned Zillertalbahn railway, a narrow-gauge line that runs from **Jenbach** in the Inn Valley (all trains on the main Vienna–Salzburg–Innsbruck route stop here) to Mayrhofen, 30km away at the head of the Zillertal. A special steam-hauled train runs twice a day in summer, although tickets

---

ZILLERTAL SUMMER AND WINTER LIFT PASSES

For those staying any length of time in **summer** in the Zillertal, it's worth investing in a **Z-Ticket** (available early June to early Oct), which includes travel on all cable cars, gondolas and chairlifts in the Zillertal region (including the Isskogel cable car at the Gerlos Pass) together with unlimited use of open-air swimming pools and public transport in the valley. A six-day pass costs öS480/€35.04, although nine-day (öS660/€48.12) and twelve-day (öS820/€59.86) variants are also available. The pass can be purchased from tourist offices and train stations – have a passport-sized photograph ready.

Winter ski passes are many and varied: most flexible is the **Zillertaler Superskipass**, which includes all lifts in the Zillertal and Tuxertal, and includes the Tuxertal glacier (4 days öS1550/€113.15; 7 days öS2410/€175.93); although there's a cheaper version of the Zillertaler Superskipass which covers everything except the Tuxertal glacier (4 days öS1270/€92.71; 7 days öS1560/€113.88).

In addition, there are passes covering the Hintertux glacier on its own, which are available all **year round** (1 day öS450/€32.85, 3 days öS1210/€88.33, 6 days öS2130/€155.49).

---

for this service don't come cheap (a Jenbach–Mayrhofen return will set you back öS270/€19.71). From Mayrhofen, buses convey travellers into the highland valleys further south.

Zell am Ziller

Twenty kilometres south of Jenbach, the village of **ZELL AM ZILLER** is the obvious base from which to explore the mountains of the middle Ziller Valley. Cable cars to the **Gerlosstein** and the **Kreuzjoch** are within easy reach of Zell itself, while further lifts in the Gerlos Valley are only a short car or bus ride away. Comparatively free from the package tourism of Mayrhofen further up the valley, it's a quiet little place enlivened each May by a descent into alcohol-fuelled revelry known as the **Gauderfest** (see box below). The village also serves as a good spot from which to observe the **Almabtrieb** (usually the first weekend in October), when the return of the cows from the alpine pastures and end of the summer are marked by a procession and a final bout of merrymaking. In recent years, Zell has enjoyed a growing reputation as Austria's foremost **paragliding** centre.

There's little to actually see or do in the village itself, although the **Pfarrkirche** is worth a quick peek. Ceiling paintings by Franz-Anton Zeiller (another member of the prolific Zeiller brood of Reutte; see p.520) overlook the unusual circular nave, and near the door a sixteenth-century fresco of St Veronica, depicting the cloth that she used to mop Christ's brow and upon which his features subsequently appeared, is worth seeking out.

THE GAUDERFEST

Celebrated every year on the first weekend in May, the four-hundred-year-old **Gauderfest** is thought to have been invented by local brewers keen to publicize their ale, although a whole range of previously existing folk rituals have become associated with the festival over the years. Processions, various sporting contests (including wrestling on the Sunday) and the prodigious consumption of alcohol and food all serve to mark the beginning of the summer cycle of the agricultural year – the **Almabtrieb**, also a big deal in the Zillertal, marks its end. Beware the deceptively strong **Gauder beer**, brewed especially for the occasion.

ZILLERTAL ACTIVITIES

Bike rental Zell am Ziller and Mayrhofen train stations have a limited selection from öS150/€10.95 per day. Sport Hausberger, Hauptstrasse 415 (☎05285/62400), and Esso-Tankstelle Obermair, Am Marktplatz 213 (☎05285/62308), both in Mayrhofen, and SB-Markt Josef Huber, Gerlosstrasse 30, Zell am Ziller (☎05282/2220), all rent out mountain bikes from öS200/€14.60 per day. Mayrhofen tourist office also organizes guided mountain-bike tours.

Canyoning Action Club Zillertal, Hauptstrasse 458, Mayrhofen (☎05285/ 62977, *www.zillertal.com/action-club*), organize trips for those eager to abseil, swim and slide down streams and waterfalls. From öS380/€27.74 to öS900/€65.70 depending on length of trip.

Hiking Both the Mayrhofen and Zell am Ziller tourist offices organize guided walks for nonspecialists daily throughout the summer, free of charge for those with a guest card. The Alpinschule Mount Everest (see "Rock climbing") offer more challenging walks, usually involving steeper gradients and crampon-assisted walking on glaciers. Walking maps are on sale at Mayrhofen and Zell tourist offices.

Kayaking Wildwasserschule Mayrhofen, c/o Zillertaler Flugschule (☎0664/180 2483), offers courses for beginners and intermediates either on the Zemmbach immediately south of Mayrhofen, or on the Ziller downstream.

Paragliding Flugtaxi Mayrhofen, Sportplatzstrasse 300 (☎05285/63142, *www.zillertal.com/action-club*), Stocky Air, Ramsau 79a (☎05282/3786, *www.zillertal.com/stockyair*), and Zillertaler Flugschule, Hauptstrasse 476, Mayrhofen (☎0664/180 2483), all offer passenger flights, where you'll be strapped in tandem with an experienced pilot, from around öS750/€51.10. Prices do depend on where the flight starts – departures from higher altitudes obviously stay in the air longer.

Rafting Action Club Zillertal (see under "canyoning" above), arrange short trips on the River Ziller to Hippach (öS400/€29.20), or longer trips on the River Inn near Imst (öS770/€56.21).

Rock climbing Hochgebirgs and Wanderschule Tuxertal, Lanersbach-Juns 424 (☎05287/372), offer climbing courses on rocks near the Spannagelhaus beside the Hintertux Glacier, as well as climbing in ice crevasses on the glacier itself; Alpinschule Mount Everest, Hauptstrasse 458, Mayrhofen (☎05285/62829), organize day courses for intermediate climbers on the Penkenjoch above the village.

Skiing Equipment can be hired at lift stations or at sports shops throughout the valley: expect to pay daily rates of öS110–150/€8.03–10.95 for skis, öS200–350/€14.60–25.55 for snowboards, and a further öS80–130/€5.84–9.50 for boots. Discounts for longer periods are available.

Swimming Erlebnisbad Mayrhofen, Waldbadstrasse 539 (☎05285/62559), is a complex with an outdoor pool, water slides, indoor pool, sauna and solarium; Freizeitpark, Zell am Ziller, at the south end of town by the river bank (☎05282/4946), sports a large outdoor pool with water slides.

Tennis Freizeitpark, Zell am Ziller (see "Swimming" above), and Tenniscenter Mayrhofen, *Hotel Berghof*, Dursterstrasse 220 (☎05285/62254), both have outdoor and indoor courts for around öS150–250/€10.95–18.25 per hour.

Most direct route to higher altitudes, the **Kreuzjochbahn** gondola (June–Sept Oct 8.40am–4.30pm; one way öS108/€7.88, return öS165/€12.05) rises from the northeastern side of the village to a middle station at the 1039-metre **Wiesenalm** (also accessible by road), followed by a second stage to the 1760-metre **Rosenalm** in the shadow of the Kreuzjoch itself. From here, numerous hiking trails lead back down to the valley or to the various *Hütte* (which are signposted, together with an indication of walking time) offering traditional food and drink in rustic surroundings.

Practicalities

Turn right outside the train station to reach the **tourist office** in the centre of the village at Dorfplatz 3a (Mon–Fri 8.30am–12.30pm & 2.30–6pm, Sat 9am–1pm; ☎05282/2281, *www.tiscover.com/zell*), which can fix you up with **private rooms** (summer ①; winter ②), many of them in Zellbergeben, the hillside suburb west of town. Among the cheaper **hotels**, *Pension Helene*, Talstrasse 46 (☎05282/2169, *www.tiscover .com/pension.helene*; ②), 1.5km south of town on the Mayrhofen road, has plain but bright rooms, some with en-suite shower, some without. Those with their own transport might consider the *Berggasthof Enzianhof*, Gerlosberg 23 (☎05282/2237; choice of dorm beds or doubles ②), a combination of hotel and mountain hut located at the top of a winding road on the hillside east of town. Of the bigger central hotels, *Hotel Garni Maximilian*, Bahnhofstrasse 24 (☎05282/2255; summer ②; winter ③), a modern chalet-style building just south of the train station, has balconied rooms with en-suite facilities and TV, as well as the *Piccadilly Pub* on the premises if you need a bit of on-site recreation; while *Sporthotel Theresa*, Bahnhofstrasse 15 (☎05282/2286-0, *www.theresa.at*; summer ⑧; winter ⑨), is probably the swishest in town, with indoor pool, sauna and tennis. *Camping Hofer*, Gerlosstrasse 33 (☎05282/2248), is an attractive place to pitch your tent on the Gerlos Pass road 400m southeast of the centre.

For **eating**, the restaurant at *Hotel Bräu*, Dorfplatz 1, stands out above the rest, with a range of food to suit all pockets: an inexpensive choice of Tyrolean fare, more costly Austrian favourites and excellent fish. The other places on Dorfplatz, the *Tirolerhof* and the *Kirchenwirt*, also offer good-quality, mainstream Austrian fare at middle-of-the-road prices. For something a bit different, try the generous portions at *Pablo's Pizzeria* in the *Hotel Zellerhof*, near the train station at Bahnhofstrasse 3.

The road to the Gerlos Pass

Zell am Ziller is the western starting point for one of Austria's most scenic cross-mountain road routes (served by five buses a day), over the **Gerlos Pass**. The most fearsome stretch of the route is on the outskirts of Zell itself, as the road zigzags its way out of the valley onto the terrace above, where the seventeenth-century **Wallfahrtskirche Maria Rast** (a popular 45min walk out from Zell am Ziller) sits on a mountain spur overlooking the valley. A couple of hairpin bends further up the mountain lies the village of **HAINZENBERG**, site of a small **Tierpark**, where examples of the local fauna – goats, mouflon, chamois and deer – are assembled for your inspection. At the eastern end of Hainzenberg starts the Gerlossteinbahn cable car (early June to late Sept & Dec–April; one way öS67/€4.89, return öS108/€7.88), which ascends to the Gerlossteinhütte, overlooked by the rugged face of the 2166-metre **Gerlossteinwand**.

Twenty-five kilometres beyond Zell, the village of **GMUND** is linked by the Fürstalmbahn chairlift (July–Sept & Dec–April) to the higher slopes on the southern side of the valley. From here it's only 3km to the next village, **Gerlos**, on the far side of which is the Isskogelbahn chairlift (mid-June to early Oct & mid-Dec to mid-April; daily 9am–noon & 1–5pm), serving the alpine meadows above the valley to the north. A steady ten-kilometre climb from Gerlos brings you eventually to the **Durlassboden Reservoir**, where the 1531-metre summit of the Gerlos Pass marks the border between the Tyrol and Salzburg. From here the road descends to the upper reaches of the Salzach Valley and the Krimml Falls (see p.421), before continuing to the Pinzgau towns of Mittersill and Zell am See (p.414).

Mayrhofen

Ten kilometres south of Zell, **MAYRHOFEN** is one of Austria's biggest resort villages. Almost entirely dependent on package tourism, its rustic character lies buried beneath successive layers of fake alpine charm and gift-shop tawdriness. Yet, whatever its short-comings, Mayrhofen remains the ideal place from which to explore the **Gründe** that fan out to the south, as well as the range of mountains more immediately at hand. The **Penkenbahn** gondola (late May–early Oct & Dec–April; ascent öS100/€7.30, return öS165/€12.05) climbs the flanks of the Penken from a terminal at the southern end of Mayrhofen Hauptstrasse (the Finkenberger Almbahn approaches the same uplands from a different direction; see p.491), providing access to numerous **walks**. The **Ahornbahn** gondola (mid-June to early Oct & Dec–April; same prices) on the south-eastern fringes of town scales the opposite side of the valley towards the Ahornspitze, where you can enjoy yet more fine views from the terrace of the Ahornhütte at the top of the gondola, or contemplate a range of well-signposted walks. One relatively easy one-hour hike takes you to the Edelhütte to the southeast, which sits on sparse mountain grasslands close up to the 2973m Ahornspitze itself.

The main **skiing** areas are the Ahorn (with plenty of practice slopes for beginners) and the Penken (with numerous short intermediate runs). Longer intermediate runs, and more challenging black runs, are concentrated above Hintertux, 20km to the southwest (see p.491). Skiing on the Tuxertal glacier is possible all year round, making Mayrhofen one of the best places in Austria for advanced skiers to come in summer.

Practicalities

Mayrhofen's **train station** is five minutes west of the **tourist office** (Mon–Fri 8am–6pm, Sat 8am–noon & 3–6pm, Sun 10am–noon; ☎05285/6760, *www.mayrhofen.com*) in the Europahaus congress centre, which handles **private rooms** of all grades and styles. In Mayrhofen itself, expect to pay around öS250/€18.25 per person for rooms with en-suite facilities, öS200/€14.60 for rooms with shared bathrooms; rooms in the slightly more rustic hamlets of Hollenzen and Burgstall 2km north of town are slightly cheaper. Bear in mind that room prices can be thirty percent higher in winter.

Innumerable **hotels** and **pensions** offer decent-value accommodation, although many of these are block-booked by groups in winter and at the height of summer. Of the smaller pensions, *Auf der Wiese*, Schmiedwiese 170 (☎05285/64576; ②), is a nice balconied farmhouse 1km north of town (from the train station, turn left onto the main road) offering cosy rooms with en-suite facilities; *s'Hoamatl*, Dorf Haus 758 (☎05285/62749; ②), is a big suburban house at the southwestern end of town with some rooms with shared facilities, others with en-suite WC and shower; while the more central *Haus Pauline*, just east of the tourist office at Breitlahnweg 288 (☎05285/62465; summer ②), offers snug en suites with balconies. Moving up in price, *Barbara & Robert*, Dursterstrasse 254 (☎05285/62896; summer ③; winter ④), just west of the tourist office, is a modern place built in fanciful chalet style where balconied rooms come with en-suite facilities and TV, and there's a sauna and gym on site. The *Kramerwirt*, Am Marienbrunnen 346 (☎05285/6700, *www.kramerwirt.at*; ⑥), is the most characterful place in town, an old inn with modern en-suite rooms and some lovely wood-panelled breakfast and dining areas. The more modern *Sporthotel Strass*, Hauptstrasse 470 (☎05285/6705, *www.hotelstrass.com*; summer ⑦; winter ⑨), is a large chalet-style place with the kind of plush rooms that you would expect at this price, plus indoor pool, fitness centre and grassy kids' play area.

As a rule, **food** in Mayrhofen is more expensive and more mediocre than anywhere else in the Tyrol, although there are a handful of notable exceptions. *Mamma Mia* in the *Elisabeth Hotel* on Einfahrt Mitte 432, just west of the Hauptstrasse, offers a perfectly acceptable range of pizza and pasta favourites; while *Singapore*, Scheulingstrasse 371, is a dependable Chinese place with tempting öS80/€5.84 lunchtime menus, and other main courses from öS130/€9.49. Best for high-quality Tyrolean specialities and the full range of Austrian cuisine are the *Kramerwirt*, Am Marienbrunnen, a traditional Gasthof with wood-panelled rooms, and the *Wirtshaus zum Griena*, at the southern end of town at Dorf Haus 768. Consider the *Neuhaus*, Am Marktplatz (☎05285/6703), if you fancy splashing out on some excellent fish and game dishes.

Konditorei Kostner, Hauptstrasse 414, is a relaxed place in which to enjoy a daytime **drink**, as well as offering the best selection of pastries and cakes in town. The considerably funkier *Mo's*, Hauptstrasse 417, is thronged with drinkers both day and night and is also a good place to eat, with inexpensive pizza and pasta, a wide range of salads, cheap baked potatoes and take-away sandwiches. *Scotland Yard*, Scheulingstrasse 372, is an enjoyable pub with friendly staff, a wide range of Austrian ales on tap, and toasted-sandwich and french-bread-pizza snacks.

Beyond Mayrhofen

Immediately south of Mayrhofen, mountain roads provide access to the four side-valleys feeding the Zillertal: the Zillergrund, the Stilluppgrund, the Zemmgrund and the **Tuxertal**. Served by buses that depart from Mayrhofen train station, they all provide excellent walks.

Eight buses a day head up the **Zillergrund**, a narrow valley rising to the east of Mayrhofen with the **Ahornspitze** looming above it to the south. For private cars the road ends at *Gasthof Bärenbad* 15km out of Mayrhofen, while buses climb the extra 2km to the Zillergrund Reservoir. The two-hour trail to *Planauer Hütte* up above the reservoir's northern side is a popular medium-difficulty hike.

Southeast of Mayrhofen, the tranquil **Stilluppgrund** is accessible via toll road (May–Oct; öS90/€6.57 per vehicle), and is served by a couple of privately operated minibus services (June–Sept; check in the Mayrhofen tourist office for times and pick-up points). One bus goes to the *Gasthof Wasserfälle* on the banks of the **Stillupp Reservoir** 8km up the valley (also the end of the road for private cars); another goes all the way to the *Grüne-Wand-Hütte* a further 7km up. From here you can follow hiking trails that lead further up the valley, the relatively gentle 2hr ascent to the Kasseler-Hütte, squatting up on the shoulder of the high Zillertaler Alpen, being one of the most popular; or walk back to *Gasthof Wasserfälle* to pick up another bus down to Mayrhofen.

Another route into the mountains from Mayrhofen is the scenic road into the **Zemmgrund** due south of town, for much of the year only passable as far as the *Breitlahnerhütte,* 18km south of Mayrhofen. It's a popular rock-climbing area for the experienced, and the starting point for walks into the upper Zemmgrund, which veers away to the southeast. The path up the Zemmgrund is relatively easy going, the main destinations to aim for being the Alpenrosehütte, 2hr 30min away, and the Berliner Hütte another 30min further on; try and make it as far as the latter if you can – it commands excellent views of the Hormkees glacier to the south.

Southwest of the *Breitlahnerhütte*, a toll road (June–Sept only; cars öS125/€9.13, motorbikes öS60/€4.38) winds tortuously up another side-valley – the Zamsergrund – to the **Schlegeis reservoir** 6km further on. Most people end up at the *Gasthaus Dominikushütte* on the reservoir's western bank (walkable from the *Breitlahnerhütte* in about 2hrs), a convenient snack stop and a popular base for a choice of onward hiking routes. Most enticing of these is the two-hour medium-difficulty trek through the startlingly bleak landscape of the upper Zamsergrund as far as the *Pfitscherjochhaus* , bang on the Austrian-Italian border some 6km to the southwest.

The Tuxertal

Of all the valleys south of Mayrhofen, the **Tuxertal** is the most densely touristed, largely due to the popularity of the all-year skiing slopes on the **Tuxer Glacier** at the valley's head. Both the glacier and the resort villages in the valley below are well served by gondolas and chairlifts, providing a wealth of alpine itineraries.

First stop out of Mayrhofen 3km to the west is the village of **FINKENBERG**, where the Finkenberger Almbahn gondola (mid-June to mid-Oct & Dec–April; öS150/€10.95 return) serves the southern approaches to the Penken. Eight kilometres further up the valley, the village of Vorlanersbach fades imperceptibly into **LANERSBACH**, the main settlement of the Tuxertal, where you'll find the Tuxertal **tourist office** on Dorfplatz (Mon–Fri 8am–noon & 1–6pm, Sat 8am–noon; ☎05287/8506, *www.tiscover.com/tux* and *www.tux.at*). Lanersbach's **Eggalmbahn gondola** (late June to mid-Oct & Dec–April; öS95/€6.94 return) offers a direct route to the slopes of the Tuxer Alps to the west, delivering passengers to the *Eggalm* café-restaurant, in meadows just above the treeline and an excellent staging post for the wilder mountain pastures above. Most popular – and easiest – of the walks from Eggalm is the descent to the Brandalm hut just to the south (1 hr), renowned for its fine view of the white expanse of the Tuxer glacier. From the Brandalm hut you can return to Lanersbach in about an hour.

Eight kilometres further on, pressed hard against a sheer rocky slope which marks the end of the valley, the village of **HINTERTUX** is an almost exclusively 4-star hotel settlement catering for those eager to experience the all-year ski slopes on the **Tuxer Glacier** directly above. The glacier is reached by means of the **Zillertaler Gletscherbahn** (open all year round; summer öS310/€22.63 return, day pass öS350/€25.55; winter öS350/€25.55 return, day pass öS450/€32.85; *www.hintertuxergletscher.at*), a three-section gondola system which initially ascends to the 2100m **Sommerbergalm** café-restaurant, before continuing to the 2660m **Tuxer-Ferner-Haus**, which overlooks the glacier itself. After this, the state-of-the-art "Gletscherbus" (really another gondola, but with bigger cabins) speeds you onwards, providing you with a simply fantastic panorama of the surrounding mountainscape on the way up: on good days, views stretch as far as the Zugspitze in the north and the Dolomites in the south. From the top station, just below the rocky summit of the 3286-metre **Gefrorne Wand**, you can feast upon vistas of the surrounding Zillertaler Alps, and of course the glacier, which stretches out in front of you to the northwest.

If you're here in summer and you've come to do some walking, it's best to get off the Gletscherbahn at the Sommerbergeralm, from which a wide choice of potential hiking destinations are accessible. The Bichlalm, an easy ninety-minute descent to the northwest, boasts a hut serving refreshments, and is a nice spot from which to enjoy an excellent panorama of Hintertux down below. The more energetic can attempt the one-hour uphill trek from the Sommerbergeralm to the 2310-metre **Tuxerjochhaus** via the Weitental, a highland valley known for its wild flowers. You can also walk all the way up to the Tuxerjochhaus from Hintertux (2hr 30min) if you wish.

The Achensee

Framed by the Karwendel Mountains to the west and the Rofan range to the east, the **Achensee**, the Tyrol's largest lake, nestles in the **Achental**, a highland valley on the north side of the Inn. The Achensee region is famous for its **Steinöl**, a foul-smelling unguent made from the shale once mined on the shores of the lake and used as a treatment for rheumatism, arthritis, tennis elbow and skin complaints. You'll see it on sale in local pharmacies and gift-shops. There's little to choose between the resort villages edging the shore, **Maurach**, **Pertisau** and **Achenkirch** – all three have plentiful private rooms, good bathing beaches and facilities for lake sports, notably windsurfing. Maurach and Achenkirch have the better lakeside campsites.

Buses from Jenbach and Schwaz are the best way of getting to the lake from the Inn Valley. Jenbach is also the starting point for the **Achenseebahn** (*www.achenseebahn.at*), a cog railway served by steam-hauled trains that climbs up to

Maurach seven times a day between late May and late September – though ticket prices for this service are relatively high (Jenbach–Maurach return öS320/€23.36).

Maurach

Five kilometres north of Jenbach, the village of **MAURACH** occupies the high ground just short of the lake's southern end, where there are a couple of Strandbäder and a range of boat-rental outlets. The **tourist office** 100m east of the main road (Mon–Fri 8am–noon & 2–6pm, Sat 9am–noon; ☎05243/5340) will help you to find one of the numerous **private rooms** (①) and holiday apartments. A 200-bed **youth hostel** (☎05243/5239) is found on the west side of the village at Lächenwise 120a, with one **campsite** next to it, *Karwendel-Camping*, Maurach 115a (☎05243/6116), and another site, *Seecamping Wimmer*, Buchau 8 (☎05243/5217), just off the northbound Achenkirch road, next to all the lakeside amenities. **Pensions** crowd the streets winding up north from the main road through town: among them, *Haus Rofangarten*, Rofangarten 39 (☎05243/5181; ②), has large, balconied rooms with traditional furnishings.

Pertisau

Six kilometres from Maurach on the eastern side of the lake, **PERTISAU** is perhaps the most commercialized of the Achensee resorts, an agglomeration of souvenir shops and big chalet-style hotels set against the backdrop of the **Karwendel Alps**. The **tourist office**, set back from the lakefront (☎05243/5260), has a list of **private rooms** (①). *Wirthaus am See*, on the lakefront next to the landing stage (☎05243/5237; ④), is one of the Achensee's best mid-priced traditional **hotels**, featuring comfy en-suite rooms, all with balconies and some facing the water. Pertisau is the starting point for two scenic **toll roads** (both open May–Oct), heading up into the mountain valleys of the Karwendel massif; one ascends to the **Gramaialm** hut 7km to the southwest; the other to the **Gernalm**, 5km northwest of town.

Achenkirch

Unlike Pertisau, **ACHENKIRCH**, at the northern end of the lake, has preserved something of its traditional village character. The lakefront (site of beach, boat rental and windsurfing school) is about 2.5km south of the village centre, where the **tourist office** (Mon–Fri 8am–noon & 2–6pm, Sat 9am–noon; ☎05246/6270) by the church just west of the main road will direct you to the best of the **private rooms**. *Gasthof Zillertal*, Achenkirch 104 (☎05246/6396, ②), is a modern chalet-style **hotel** midway between the village centre and the lakefront; most rooms have en-suite facilities and balconies. **Campers** can choose between *Terrassencamping Schwarzenau* (☎05246/6568), on the lakefront at the southern end of town, and *Camping Achensee* (☎05246/6239), which enjoys a similar waterfront position on the other side of the Achental stream to the west. There's a small **Heimatmuseum** on the lakeside (May–Oct daily 1–6pm; öS30/€2.19), with a display of local costumes and agricultural implements. The eight-kilometre **walk** from Achenkirch to Pertisau along the traffic-free western side of the lake is a popular local excursion. North of Achenkirch, the road climbs to the German frontier 10km distant, from where there's a choice of onward routes (though no public transport) to the Bavarian towns of Tegernsee and Bad Tölz.

Rattenberg and around

East of Jenbach both railway and autobahn continue to plough along the fertile floor of the Inn Valley towards Kufstein and the German border. There are few obvious stop-offs en route save for **RATTENBERG**, a delightful small town that was an important silver-mining centre until the seventeenth century, and retains a core of historic buildings. The town also possesses a strong glass-making tradition, and the line of souvenir shops along the main street (most selling the wares of the prime producer of local glassware, Kisslinger) have made the place a popular stop-off for day-trippers. There are a couple of side-valleys near Rattenberg worth exploring, too, most notably the **Alpbachtal** and the **Wildschönau**. Neither can compare with the majesty of the Zillertal, but they're more tranquil and less touristed as a result.

The Town

Paths from Rattenberg's **train station** lead straight down to the **main square**, an extraordinarily photogenic huddle of medieval town houses resplendent in pink, yellow and greenish hues, with a ruined hilltop castle serving as a backdrop to the south. Bienerstrasse leads south from the main square towards the fifteenth-century **Pfarrkirche St Virgil**, raised on a bluff below the castle. Like the Pfarrkirche in Schwaz, the church was built with two naves, one for miners (on the right) and the other for the burghers. Heading the right-hand nave is the **St Anna altar**, whose statuary, including the touching group of angels at the base, is by Baroque sculptor Meinrad Guggenbichler, the master of Mondsee church (see p.431). At the back of the Pfarrkirche stands a shrine to **St Notburga** (1265–1313), the Rattenberg-born serving girl who became the centre of a local cult after defending the rights of servants against their rich employers. Her emblem is a sickle, a reminder of her pious refusal to work in the fields on Sundays.

North of the main square, alleyways lead down to the **Augustinermuseum** in the erstwhile Augustinian monastery (May to mid-Oct; daily 10am–5pm; öS40/€2.92), housing a collection especially rich in Gothic wood sculpture. Perhaps the most famous exhibit here, though, is a fourteenth-century gravestone depicting local worthies Johann Kummersbacher and wife, an extraordinarily delicate piece of carving for the period.

Practicalities

Rattenberg is small enough to be treated as a day-trip destination from elsewhere in the Inn Valley, although the **tourist office**, just north of the main square next to the Augustinermuseum (Mon–Fri 9am–noon & 2–4.30pm; ☎05337/63321, *www.tiscover.com/tirol-pur*), will try and fix you up with a **private room** (①) should you wish to stay. The only **hotel** in town is the *Schlosskeller*, on the corner of the square at Sparkassenplatz 13 (☎05337/62696; ③), an old-style inn with comfortable rooms – although not all are en suite. Both the *Schlosskeller* and the nearby *Platzbräu* (also on the main square) serve up traditional Austrian **food**, while *Café Lavazza*, on the way to the Pfarrkirche on Bienerstrasse, is the place to stop off for a **drink**.

Alpbach

Three kilometres west of Rattenberg, at **Brixlegg**, a minor road heads south up the **Alpbach Valley**, one of the Tyrol's most attractive rural stretches. A relatively quiet ski resort favoured by beginners and intermediates, the village of **ALPBACH** lies some 11km along this road, occupying an extremely picturesque position beneath the western flanks of the Wildschönau range. There's a **tourist office** in the village centre (Mon–Fri 9am–noon & 2–5pm; ☎05336/5211), which has details of **private rooms** in some of the village's large, timber-clad Tyrolean farmhouses, as well as information on local hiking trails. A two-stage **gondola** on the western side of the Alpbach leads up to the Hornboden, an area of mountain pasture just below the 2127-metre **Wiedersberger Horn**.

To reach Alpbach by public transport, catch a train as far as Brixlegg, where ten daily buses depart from the train station, calling at Alpbach village before ending up at Inneralpbach at the head of the valley.

The Wildschönau

Travelling northeast from Rattenberg, the next place of any significance is the industrialized town of **WÖRGL** 20km away, a dull little place with nothing to offer the tourist save for a key **railway junction** – it's here that the line to Kufstein parts company with the line to Bischofshofen, Zell am See and Kitzbühel.

A worthwhile detour from Wörgl, however, is to take the minor road that climbs out of town to the south towards the mountain villages beneath the **Wildschönau** range. The main settlements, served by eight daily buses from Wörgl and attractively situated in an alpine vale, are the resort villages of **NIEDERAU** and **OBERAU**, clusters of modern chalet-hotels that look a little sad once the winter crowds who come here to ski have retreated. Buses terminate at **AUFFACH**, 20km beyond Wörgl, where you can either take the Schatzbergbahn **gondola** (July–Aug & mid-Dec to early April; one way öS130/€9.50, return öS160/€11.68; *www.schatzbergbahn.at*) to the southern shoulder of the 1903-metre Schatzberg, or walk the remaining 3km south to **Schwarzenau**, a hamlet at the head of the valley hemmed in by a semicircle of peaks.

Kufstein and around

KUFSTEIN was a long-standing bone of contention between Bavaria and the Tyrol until Maximilian I finally brought it into the Habsburg fold in 1504. The man whose possession of modern artillery struck fear into the heart of many a Central European monarch placed a cannon nicknamed *Weckauf* ("Wake Up") on the opposite bank of the river and bombarded the defenders into submission. Nowadays the hilltop fortress draws a steady stream of visitors, although Kufstein's greatest appeal is as an ideally situated base for exploring the great outdoors. Dominating the countryside east of town are the **Kaisergebirge**, a jagged limestone massif divided into two ridges: the **Zahmer** (or "tame") **Kaiser** lie to the north, and the **Wilder Kaiser** run parallel to the south, their jagged outline providing Kufstein with an impressive backdrop. Several nearby lakes – of which the **Thiersee**, **Hechtsee** and **Hintersteinersee** are the most touristed – provide Kufstein with plenty of sites for summertime bathing; also near at hand are the skiing resorts of **Söll** and **Ellmau**, both nestling beneath the southern slopes of the Wilder Kaiser.

Cycle paths running alongside both banks of the River Inn, and numerous cycling routes towards the neighbouring hills and lakes, combine to make Kufstein and surrounds a **bike-friendly** area, too. Cycling maps can be bought from the tourist office, and bikes hired from the train station or from *Hotel zum Bären* (see below).

Arrival, information and accommodation

Kufstein's **train station** is on the west bank of the Inn; cross the bridge in front of the station forecourt to reach the Unterer Stadtplatz and the **tourist office** at no. 8 (Mon–Fri 8am–noon & 2–6pm, Sat 8am–noon; ☎05372/62207, *www.tiscover.com /kufstein*), where you can obtain a limited list of **private rooms** (①). A **campsite**, *Camping Kufstein*, Salurnerstrasse 36 (☎05372/62229-55), occupies a grassy stretch of riverbank next to the *Hotel zum Bären*.

Hotels and pensions

Gander Hof, Weissachstrasse 41 (☎05372/62432). Quiet pension in a residential area south of the centre. All rooms come with en-suite facilities. ②.

Goldener Löwe, Oberer Stadtplatz 14 (☎05372/62181). Big, centrally located hotel offering comfy en-suites with TV. Buffet breakfast included. ④.

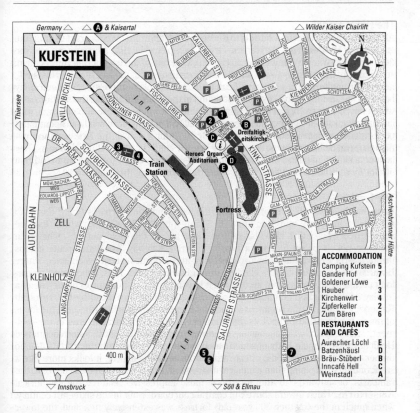

Hauber, Zellerstrasse 33 (☎05372/63539). Small pension on the western side of the train station, with small but adequate rooms with shared facilities. ①.

Kirchenwirt, Zellerstrasse 17 (☎05372/62512). Big, modern chalet-style building on the western side of the train station, offering small and basic, balconied rooms with en-suite facilities. ②.

Zipferkeller, Marktgasse 14a (☎05372/62396). Most reasonably priced of the town-centre establishments, all rooms in this modern building have en-suite facilities and TV, and there's a buffet breakfast included. ④.

Zum Bären, Salurnerstrasse 36 (☎05372/62229, *www.tiscover.com/hotelbaeren*). Comfortable suburban hotel with TV and en-suite facilities in all rooms, and featuring sauna and free bicycle rental for guests. It's 1.5km south of the centre on the banks of the River Inn (from the train station, cross the river and turn right onto the riverside footpath). ⑤.

The Town

Kufstein's modern suburbs straggle along both sides of the river, but most of what you'll want to see lies huddled below the fortress on the east bank of the Inn, around **Unterer Stadtplatz**, the picturesque main square. Raised on a bluff above the square, the facade of the **Dreifaltigkeitskirche** presents a jumble of Gothic and later architectural styles. The interior, in contrast, is pretty plain, except for a florid Rococo altar with Virgin and Child beneath a crimson canopy and floaty cherubs.

The Heldenorgel

An archway above the church leads to the open-air auditorium for concerts featuring the gargantuan **Heldenorgel**, or Heroes' Organ, completed in 1931 to commemorate the dead of World War I. With its 4307 pipes occupying one of the towers (the Burgerturm; see below) of the fortress above, and the keyboard housed at the foot of the fortress hill, next to the auditorium, it's a very difficult instrument to play – there's a 1.5-second delay between the striking of the keys and the sound of the notes. Atmospheric conditions also wreak havoc with the organ's pitch, and listening to it can be a bizarre experience, with its discordant tones blasting out across the valley. Performances (daily at noon; extra performance at 5pm in summer) cost öS10/€0.73 for a seat in the little auditorium – though it can be heard almost everywhere in town – and last about fifteen minutes. They include a couple of pieces of classical organ music (often Bach) followed by a rendition of *Alte Kamaraden*, a mawkish World War I ditty honouring the fallen.

The fortress

Immediately above the auditorium looms the pale sandstone **fortress** (daily: Easter to mid-Nov 9am–5pm; mid–Dec to Feb 11am–4pm; öS130/€9.45), which can be approached by a short funicular railway (just beside the Heldenorgel; included in entrance ticket) or on foot via a nearby covered stairway. The latter route climbs through a rock-hewn tunnel before emerging at the northwestern watchtower, where Bavarian troops using ladders climbed through a window in 1703, ushering in a year-long period of occupation. An archway just beyond leads to the **Burgerturm**, site of a display of the bright-blue tunics and ostrich-feather hats once worn by the Tyrolean Kaiserjäger, an elite rifle regiment formed by Emperor Francis I in 1815, and the focus of much local patriotism until its disbandment in 1918. One local veteran of the regiment, Max Depolo, was responsible for dreaming up the idea of the aforementioned Heldenorgel, the main body of which can be seen lurking beneath the tower's domed timber ceiling. Built for sonic effect rather than aesthetic appeal, it looks more like a stack of industrial piping than a musical instrument. From here paths lead out onto the ramparts or upwards to the fortress's most impressive feature, the cylindrical **Kaiserturm**, which towers above the central courtyard. Built in the sixteenth century, when much of the (by then 300-year-old) fortress was extensively modified, the tower is by far the most easily recognizable element of the Kufstein skyline, and has become something of a town trademark as a result. Beside the Kaiserturm is the entrance to the **Heimatmuseum**, a modest but attractively presented collection which includes the skeletons of 30,000-year-old cave bears, local furniture, antique weaponry and, perhaps most compelling, an array of eighteenth-century wooden moulds used for casting wax votive objects – in this case miniature arms and legs intended to represent those parts of the body cured after a period of prayer.

The southern end of the fortress offers plenty of opportunities for scrambling around the outer ramparts, many of which offer views of the sugarloaf-shaped **Pendling** hill on the opposite side of the valley. An open-air stage occupies the extreme southern tip of the fortress (named the Josefsburg, after Josef II, under whose reign it was extensively rebuilt), where concerts are held in summer.

Into the Wilder Kaiser

At the eastern edge of town attractive parklands merge into the wooded slopes of the **Wilder Kaiser**, a paradise for walking and mountain-biking enthusiasts. The most direct route uphill is the Wilder Kaiser chairlift (June–Sept & late Dec to early April; öS130/€9.49 return) 2km northwest of the centre, which ascends to the *Weinbergerhaus* hut and provides access to a plateau of pastureland beneath the rugged, inhospitable peaks that give the range its name. You can also take the

"Landrover taxi" (summer Tues–Sun at 10am, 11am & noon; öS65/€4.75 one way, öS100/€7.30 return), which departs from the car park at the end of Pienzenauerstrasse, 1km east of the centre, and drives up to the starting point for innumerable forest-shrouded hiking trails, the *Aschenbrenner Hütte*. Run by the family of mountaineer Peter Aschenbrenner, there's a mini-museum recalling his Himalayan expeditions of the 1930s inside.

Walks up the **Kaisertal**, a beautiful alpine valley suspended between the peaks of the Wilder Kaiser and the Zahmer Kaiser, begin at a car park 4km north of the centre at the end of Sparchnerstrasse (local Kufstein–Ebbs buses pass by). It's dubbed the "German autobahn" by locals because of its popularity with Bavarian day-trippers.

The lakes

In summer Kufsteiners head out to the string of small lakes hidden away behind the low hills northwest of the River Inn. Biggest of the lakes, and bordered by a flourishing resort that carries its name, is the **Thiersee**, 10km west of Kufstein by road and served by about nine daily buses. There are plenty of small bathing areas, a tourist office in the village centre doling out private rooms, and a campsite on the lake's western shore.

Five kilometres northwest of Kufstein, the small, forest-enclosed and altogether more modest **Hechtsee** has a Strandbad, rowing-boat rental and a popular café-restaurant. Pathways lead round the shore, through the surrounding woods and on into Germany – the border is only a few steps away from the northwestern end of the lake (it's not staffed, but take your passport in case of spot checks). Buses to the Hechtsee may run during high summer; otherwise it's easy enough to cycle there or walk from Kufstein.

Eating and drinking

There are innumerable **eating** options in central Kufstein. The Römerhofgasse in particular harbours a couple of atmospheric old inns, and there are plenty of establishments offering a good mixture of Tyrolean specialities and standard Austrian fare: *Auracher Löchl* is an atmospheric, wooden-beamed old place which boasts live folk music at weekends, while the nearby *Batzenhäusl* has cosy dining rooms adorned with hunting trophies and assorted curios. *Bräu-Stüberl*, Oberer Stadtplatz 5a, is a dependable town-centre restaurant with moderately priced Austrian regulars, and plenty of outdoor seating round the corner on Arkadenplatz. *Weinstadl*, six kilometres north of the centre on the Ebbs road, offers solid, unpretentious fare with a generous salad bar and a dining area arranged around an open fire. *Inncafé Hell*, Unterer Stadtplatz, is the main **daytime café**, with a good choice of lunchtime spaghettis and goulash-style dishes, and an outdoor terrace overlooking the river.

Plenty of lively **evening drinking** venues dot the centre; it's really a question of bar-hopping until you find the combination of music and clientele you fit in with best: *Charlie's* and *Die Gräfin* on Unterer Stadtplatz are good places to start. *Die Tenne*, Prof-Schlosser-Strasse 1, is a busy disco-bar, 25min walk north of the centre, which caters mostly to mainstream, poppy musical tastes, though with some more specialized themed nights. *Kulturfabrik*, 2km north of town at Feldgasse 12 (*www.kulturfabrik.at*), hosts jazz, rock, and alternative gigs (the tourist office will have information on what's on).

Söll and around

Southeast of Kufstein, the southern slopes of the Wilder Kaiser are home to the resort villages of **Söll**, **Scheffau** and **Ellmau**. Served by buses working the Kufstein–St

Johann and Wörgl–St Johann routes, all three have become especially popular as winter-package destinations. The pistes above the valley are linked by an extensive list system to produce a sizeable ski area – the so-called **SkiWelt Wilder Kaiser-Brixental** – which encompasses Söll, Scheffau and Ellmau as well as Hopfgarten and Brixen on the other side of the mountains to the south. The region is largely suited to beginners and intermediates, although there are a couple of black runs and some off-piste skiing on the heights above Söll. **Lift passes** covering the whole lot weigh in at öS380/€27.62 for 1 day; öS1890/€137.39 for 6 days; other permutations up to 21 days are also available.

The area is comparatively quiet in summer, although the main ski lifts open up between June and September to serve the needs of walkers. The Berg Welt walking pass (öS360/€26.28 for 7 days) covers them all.

KITZBÜHEL ACTIVITIES

Bike rental At the train station (from öS120/€8.76 per day with a valid rail ticket). Wider range of mountain bikes at Kitzsport, Jochbergerstrasse 7 (from öS220/€16.06 per day; ☎05356/62204), Stanger, Josef-Pirchl-Strasse 42 (from öS180/€13.14 per day; ☎05356/62549) and Sport Olympia, Bichlstrasse 26 (from öS220/€16.06 per day; ☎05356/71607). Biking maps of the Kitzbüheler Alpen are on sale at the tourist office, which also organizes free mountain-bike tours every Mon & Thur between June & Sept.

Golf Kitzbühel is one of Austria's big golfing centres; Golfclub Kitzbühel Schwarzee (☎05356/71645, *www.kitzbuehel-golf.com*) has an eighteen-hole course, with green fees starting at around öS650/€47.24. Between May and October there are a couple of nine-hole courses in the area, together with numerous driving ranges – contact the tourist office for details.

Hiking The tourist office provides regional hiking maps, and organizes free guided hikes in summer, and walks on snow-cleared pathways in winter (Mon–Fri at 8.45am). A Summer Holiday Pass covering all lifts in the Kitzbühel area and the Aquarena swimming pool costs öS450/€32.70 for 3 days within a 7-day period; and öS595/€43.24 for 6 days within a 10-day period.

Paragliding Hermann's Flying School, Bichlnweg 24/17 (☎05356/67138), organizes tandem flights starting at öS800/€58.14, and a range of courses.

Skiing The main skiing areas are on the Hahnenkamm to the west and the Kitzbüheler Horn to the east, both of which are crisscrossed by numerous beginners' and intermediates' runs. A few short black runs are to be found on the Hahnenkamm. In addition, the neighbouring resorts of Kirchberg (10km to the east) and Jochberg (10km south) and the Thurn Pass (20km south) provide access to more slopes suitable for beginners and intermediates. Intermediate-level skiers should try out the Kitzbühel Ski Safari, an interconnected series of lifts and runs which takes you to the Hahnenkamm, south up the valley to the Thurn Pass, from where a ski bus transports you back to Kitzbühel. There's also a large cross-country skiing area in the valley floor, and a Snowboard park including 100-metre half-pipe, table jump and quarter pie on the Horn. One-day (öS430/€31.25), six-day (öS2080/€151.16) and fourteen-day ski passes (öS3810/€276.88) are available from any of the lift stations. Each covers cable cars, lifts and buses for the whole of the Kitzbühel ski region. Equipment can be hired at lift stations or at numerous sports shops in the town centre.

Swimming Indoor pool at the Kurhaus Aquarena, Klostergasse 7 (daily 9.30am–7pm; öS90/€6.57); outdoor swimming at the municipal Strandbad at the Schwarzsee (öS40/€2.91).

Tennis Tennis Club Kitzbühel, Jochbergstrasse (☎05356/64400), from öS120/€8.76 per hour (indoor); öS150/€10.95 per hour (outdoor).

Söll

Buzzing in winter, resuming a state of rural repose in summer, **SÖLL** is a largely modern village in which newish, chalet-style apartment buildings predominate. In its **Pfarrkirche**, however, Söll possesses the most impressive Baroque monument in the western Tyrol, its riotously stuccoed and gilded interior decked out in vivid ceiling frescoes painted by Christoph Anton Mayr of Schwaz in 1768. Everything focuses on the grandiose red marble pulpit topped by a gilded swan, symbol of Christ. At the southern margins of the village there's a two-stage gondola (June–late Oct & mid-Dec to April; öS105/€7.67 return) to the 1827-metre **Hohe Salve** (calling at Hochsöll on the way), where most of the skiing activity takes place.

The **tourist office** in the village centre (Mon–Fri 8am–noon & 2.30–6pm, Sat 8am–noon; ☎05333/5216, *www.soell.com*) will help book you into **private rooms** (summer ①; winter ②). A surfeit of modern chalet-style **hotels** includes the centrally located *Feldwebel*, Dorf 73 (☎05333/5224, *feldwebel@netway.at*; summer ③; winter ⑤), which has more of a traditional Gasthof feel than some of the others, and the equally central but swankier *Postwirt*, Dorf 82 (☎05333/5081, *www.hotel-postwirt-soell.at*; summer ⑤; winter ⑦). Alternatively try *camping Franzlhof*, on the north side of the village at Dorfbichl 36 (☎05333/5117). The *Postwirt* has a good restaurant serving Tyrolean and Austrian **food** in cosy traditional rooms. One long-standing **drinking** hole that seems to survive changing fashions is the central *Whiskeymühle*, a roomy disco-bar entered through a lobby the shape of a barrel.

Scheffau and Ellmau

Apart from the cable car up the 1650-metre **Brandstadl**, there's little to detain you in **SCHEFFAU**, 5km to the east of Söll. However, a road heading north out of the village offers an inviting side-trip to the **Hintersteinersee** 4km away, a small lake picturesquely situated in the shadow of the Wilder Kaiser. A Strandbad can be found at the southern end of the lake, as well as some nice walks along the eastern shore.

Five kilometres east of Scheffau, **ELLMAU** is ideally situated for short excursions into the mountains, with the awesome Wilder Kaiser to the north, and the no-less-imposing 1555-metre **Hartkaser** to the south, the latter reached by a funicular at the western end of the village. Several chairlifts to the east, ranged between Ellmau and the next village up the valley, **Going**, provide access to the flanks of the Astberg. Beyond Ellmau, it's another 10km to **ST JOHANN IN TIROL**, a frumpy if inoffensive winter package resort which offers little incentive to linger. Luckily, there are more enticing destinations near at hand: Zell am See (see p.414) is only 40 minutes by train to the east; and Kitzbühel a mere 20 minutes to the west.

Kitzbühel and around

Centre of a winter sports area that spreads over the easternmost corner of the Tyrol, **KITZBÜHEL** began life as a medieval copper- and silver-mining town. Today, its historic core still looks, at times, like something out of a Gothic fairy tale. Squat, brightly painted town houses are set against a backdrop of pasture-laden hills that with the first snowfall promise a varied skiing terrain ideal for novices and intermediates. Main feature of the local mountainscape is the imperious ridge of the Wilder Kaiser to the north-west, which despite being almost 20km away is much more dramatic when seen from Kitzbühel than it is close up – a horizon-hogging ripple of tortured, jagged rock.

The town's development as a ski resort owes a great deal to the efforts of Franz Reisch, who imported skis from Norway in the 1890s, and made the first ski runs. The town became a magnet for film stars and Central European society figures during the inter-war years (and a recreation centre for Luftwaffe flying aces in the 1940s). Despite the onset of package tourism, Kitzbühel still retains its rich clientele and genteel air.

Those coming to Kitzbühel in search of glamour will find it at the peak of the winter season, when hotel prices are at their highest and a bejewelled *beau monde* descend on the town, but for the rest of the year, the atmosphere in Kitzbühel's restaurants and bars is reasonably egalitarian.

Kitzbühel can't really match St Anton when it comes to challenging the experienced skier. It does, however, possess one classic downhill route, the **Hahnenkamm** (it finishes up just west of the town centre, next to the golf course), which has been the scene of an annual downhill race ever since 1931. The race still features prominently in the World Cup skiing calendar – usually the last weekend in January for the men, the second to last weekend for the women. Both occasions are major society events, drawing huge hordes to the town's dainty pedestrianized centre.

THE BLITZ FROM KITZ – AND OTHER SKIING LEGENDS

Considered by many to be the birthplace of Austrian skiing, Kitzbühel is also home to the country's first genuine skiing superstar, **Toni "The Blitz from Kitz" Sailer** – the most talented skier of his generation, and arguably the greatest winter sportsman Austria has ever produced. Born in Kitzbühel in 1935, Sailer enjoyed a whirlwind career. By the age of 17 he was already the Tyrolean champion at downhill, slalom and giant slalom, and four years later snatched three gold medals (in the same disciplines) at the 1956 Winter Olympics in Cortina d'Ampezzo – an achievment unmatched before or since. Sailer's triumph had a profound effect on an Austrian public that had had little to celebrate in the years following World War II, and he was feted by mass crowds on his return from Italy. Affable, clean-cut and with pop-star good looks, Sailer was also one of Austrian sport's first mass-media celebrities. A career in singing and acting soon beckoned.

With seven world championship titles to his credit Sailer retired at the age of 22, having been warned by the International Olympic Committee that his new status as all-round ski celebrity was contrary to the spirit of amateurism that still ruled the sport. Sailer went on to star in several melodramatic piste-based adventure films, a typically Austrian genre in which he was required to do little more than play himself, although he later attended drama school in Berlin and went on to tackle stage roles. Curiously, these skiing adventures were enormously popular in Japan, and Sailer made several movies there in the 1960s. Sailer still lives in Kitzbühel, where he is president of the Rote Teufel ski school.

Sailer's successor as a focus for national sporting aspirations was **Karl "King of the Arlberg" Schranz**, a native of St Anton who was consistently rated among the world's best downhill racers throughout the late Fifties and Sixties, twice becoming overall world champion. A much more complex character than the easy-going Sailer, Schranz was notorious for his dedication to training and technique (he was the first skier to use a figure-hugging aerodynamic suit), but also prone to moments of self-doubt. Following a skiing injury in America in 1960, he sold his skis, gambled away the money in Reno, and had to take a job as a Hollywood stuntman – only returning to skiing when he heard that he'd been voted Austria's Sportsman of the Year.

Despite enjoying over a decade of success, Schranz ultimately owes his place in the Austrian pantheon to the two races he notoriously failed to win. Competing in the downhill at the 1968 Olympics in Grenoble, Schranz claimed that he'd been distracted by a policeman standing too near the course, and – in unprecedented fashion – was allowed a second run. Schranz went on to record the fastest time, edging local hero Jean-Claude Killy out of the gold medal spot, but race officials decided to disqualify Schranz after TV replays suggested that the offending policeman had in fact been a figment of the Austrian's imagination. Schranz suffered an even more humiliating rebuff at the Sapporo Olympics four years later. Three days before the games were due to start, he was disqualified by the International Olympic Committee for having been seen wearing a T-shirt advertising a well-known brand of coffee. The Austrian public was outraged: the presi-

Arrival, information and accommodation

From the **train station**, head down Bahnhofstrasse and turn left to reach the town centre, which is raised on a small hill about five minutes' walk away. The **tourist office** at Hinterstadt 18 (July–Sept & mid-Dec to mid-April Mon–Fri 8am–6pm, Sat 8am–noon & 4–6pm, Sun 10am–noon & 4–6pm; mid-April to June & Oct to mid-Dec Mon–Fri 8am–noon & 2–6pm; ☎05356/621550-0, *www.kitzbuehel.com*) has an array of English-language brochures, and – officially at least – will book rooms on your behalf. Tourist office staff have a habit of looking down on budget travellers, however, and the level of help you receive may depend on personal whim. There's a hotel information board and free telephone just outside the tourist office for those who arrive outside office hours.

dent of the Austrian Olympic Committee had his house set alight, and several IOC functionaries received death threats. In a remarkable display of popular support, an estimated 10,000 people lined the streets of Vienna to greet Schranz on his return.

Austria's bruised sporting pride was restored by the rags-to-riches story of **Franz "The Kaiser" Klammer**, born in 1953 in Mooswald, a Carinthian village some 30km away from the nearest ski lift. Klammer suddenly burst onto the scene in 1974, coming second in the downhill at the World Championships that year, and going on to win eight downhill victories in the 1974-75 World Cup series. Klammer's greatest moment came in 1976, when he bore the Austrian flag at the opening ceremony of the Innsbruck Olympics, and went on to win the downhill, sending the host nation into paroxysms of jubilation. The archetypal down-to-earth village boy made good, Klammer was popular both for his personable manner and his daredevil style, literally throwing himself down the mountains he raced on.

After finishing up as World Cup downhill champion three times in the late Seventies, Klammer's form dipped alarmingly. He failed to qualify for the Olympics in 1980, and his struggle to return to the big time became a national obsession. The Kaiser's come-back victory finally came at a World Cup race at Val d'Isère in 1981, and racing driver Niki Lauda spoke for many when he admitted to crying tears of joy on Klammer's behalf. Klammer only managed 10th place in the Sarajevo Olympics of 1984, but his place in skiing legend was by now assured.

Despite the retirement of Klammer in 1984, Austrian skiers continued to figure heavily in the world rankings, although it wasn't until the emergence of **Hermann "The Herminator" Mayer** in 1997 that the nation could once again boast a bona-fide beast of the pistes. Hailing from the ski resort of Flachau in the Salzburger Land, Mayer was overall World Cup champion in 1997/98, Austria's first overall champion since Schranz. Mayer went to the 1998 Winter Olympics in Nagano as the hot favourite for the downhill, only to fall spectacularly near the start of the course. He made up for it by winning gold in both the slalom and the super-giant slalom, and has dominated alpine skiing ever since. In 1999–2000 he headed the World Cup downhill, super-g and giant slalom standings, and became overall champion by a vast points margin – overtaking Franz Klammer's Austrian record of 27 World Cup victories in the process. Seven other Austrians made the men's overall top ten in 1999/2000, and Renate Götschl was crowned overall female champion, confirming the nation's almost total dominance of alpine skiing as the century turned.

No roundup of the superstars of Austrian snow sport would be complete without mention of one of its foremost nordic practioners, ski-jumper **Andreas "Goldi" Goldberger**. Widely considered to be the world's most promising jumper in 1997, Goldberger was caught taking cocaine in a Viennese nightclub, and was promptly suspended by the national skiing team. He briefly toyed with the idea of giving up Austrian citizenship in order to compete in the following year's Olympics under a different flag. Goldberger was soon back in the Austrian fold, although the avalanche of tedious jokes about his appetite for snow is yet to subside.

Prices for **private rooms** start from around öS230/€16.79 per person in spring and autumn, öS250/€18.25 in summer and öS300/€21.90 in winter. There's a **campsite** at the Schwarzsee, the small lake 2km north of town on the Kirchberg road (☎05356/62806, *hotel.bruggerhof@camping.netwing.at;* open all year). Regional trains (not IC or EC ones) stop at the Schwarzsee halt: turn left out of the station and the campsite is a 5-minute walk away.

Hotels and pensions

Astron Sporthotel, Schwarzseestrasse 8 (☎05356/63211-0, *www.astron-hotels.de*). Modern hotel with large, comfortable balconied rooms and an outdoor pool. ⑧.

Goldener Greif, Hinterstadt 24 (☎05356/64311, *www.tirol.com/hotel-ggreif*). Classic town-centre Gasthof in one of Kitzbühel's oldest houses, which counts film stars and European aristocrats among its guests. Modern furnishings, en-suite facilities and TV. ⑧.

Hörl, Josef-Pirchler-Strasse 60 (☎05356/63144). Conveniently placed between the train station and the centre, this is probably the cheapest place within striking distance of the action, offering cosy doubles, some with en-suite facilities. Single rooms, too, are not that expensive. ②.

Jodlhof, Aschbachweg 17 (☎05356/63004). No-frills pension in attractive chalet-style house on the east side of town near the Kitzbüheler Horn gondola station, offering rock-bottom doubles with shared facilities, and some (only slightly) more expensive rooms with en-suite facilities. ②.

Kaiser, Bahnhofstrasse 2 (☎05356/64708, *www.tiscover.com/jugendhotelkaiser*). Backpacker-friendly hotel right in front of the train station, with hostel-style 4-bed dorms as well as comfy en-suite doubles. Closes for a short period in spring and autumn. Summer ②; winter ③.

Mühlbergerhof, Schwarzseestrasse 6 (☎05356/62835). Pension in a nice suburban house ten minutes' walk northwest of the centre. All rooms have en-suite facilities. ③.

Neuhaus, Franz-Reisch-Strasse 23 (☎05356/2200). One of the cheaper options in the centre. Motorbike-friendly, ensuring a healthy influx of leather-clad guests over the summer. ③.

Rosengarten, Maurachfeld 6 (☎05356/62528-0, *rosengarten@tirol.com*). Friendly pension just west of the centre, behind the Hahnenkamm gondola station. All rooms come with en-suite shower and WC. ③.

Tennerhof, Griesenauweg 26 (☎05356/63181, *www.tiscover.com/hotel.tennerhof*). Attractive timber-clad building with flower-decked balconies, northeast of the centre on the hillside below the Kitzbüheler Horn. Comfortable rooms with TV and en-suite bathrooms, plus a wide range of amenities including sauna and both indoor and outdoor pools. ⑨.

The Town

Downtown Kitzbühel revolves around two elongated squares, **Vorderstadt** and **Hinterstadt**, each boasting a colourful ensemble of medieval merchants' houses. A twelfth-century pile at the southern end of Hinterstadt holds an engaging **Heimatmuseum** (Mon–Sat 9am–noon; öS30/€2.19), which offers a jumble of folk crafts, skiing mementos and mining artefacts – the latter revealing something of the industrial grit behind the tinseltown of present-day Kitzbühel. Between Hinterstadt and Vorderstadt stands the unassuming **Katharinenkirche**, now used as a memorial chapel honouring the dead of two world wars. Within, the small but exquisite Kupferschmidaltar was carved in 1513 by the Master of Rabenden, surrounding a relief of the Madonna and Child.

Perched on a small plateau at the northern end of Vorderstadt are two more worthwhile churches. The more obvious of the pair, the fifteenth-century **Pfarrkirche**, contains a harmonious ensemble of Baroque altars and statuary, and the Kupferschmids' family grave, a sixteenth-century slab of red marble engraved with scenes from the Passion. Immediately above, the **Liebfrauenkirche** harbours Rococo stucco-work and, in the high altar, a copy of the Cranach *Madonna and Child* from Innsbruck Cathedral (see p.467).

Into the mountains

Towering above Kitzbühel to the west, the 1655-metre Hahnenkamm can be scaled with the help of the **Hahnenkammbahn** gondola (June to mid-Oct & mid-Dec to April; öS180/€13.08 return), on the western side of town about 500m uphill from the tourist office. Before embarking on one of the many walking trails at the summit, savour the view of the Kitzbüheler Horn on the opposite side of the valley and the jagged ridge of the Wilder Kaiser to the north. The restaurant next to the cable-car station at the top contains a small **museum** (open in season when the gondola is running: daily 12.30–4pm; free), which tells the story of alpine sport in the region through an entertaining display of old photographs. The northern shoulder of the Hahnenkamm can also be approached via the **Fleckalmbahn** gondola (late June–late Sept & mid-Dec to April; öS180/€13.08 return), which commences just outside the hamlet of **Klausen**, 4km out of Kitzbühel on the Kirchberg road.

On the eastern side of town, the **Kitzbüheler Hornbahn** gondola (mid-May to late Oct & mid–Dec to April; öS180/€13.08 return) ascends to the *Adlerhütte*, where you have the choice of walking either to the 1670-metre *Alpenhaus* (also reachable by car via toll road; öS30/€2.18 per vehicle plus öS20/€1.45 per passenger) on the southeast shoulder of the Kitzbüheler Horn, or to the 2000-metre summit of the Horn itself. Either way, expect to enjoy good views of the Wilder Kaiser massif to the north, a chaos of craggy grey peaks rising suddenly out of the bottle-green lowland forests.

Eating and drinking

Most of Kitzbühel's **eating and drinking** venues are around the Hinter-stadt–Vorderstadt area, although it's worth descending to the lower lying, eastern part of the town centre to seek out a couple of the more interesting bars. You don't have to limit yourselves to the restaurants if you want to eat: a large proportion of drinking venues serve full meals, and all of them offer snacks of some kind or another.

For faster food, a couple of high-street butchers, such as J. Huber at Bichlstrasse 12, offer eat-in or takeaway *Wurst* snacks, and there's a *Prima* daytime self-service restaurant at Bichlstrasse 22.

Restaurants

Adria, Josef-Pirchl-Strasse 17. Bright, no-nonsense but relaxed pizzeria on the way into town from the station. Inexpensive, dependable pizzas and a range of other Italian eats.

Chizzo, Josef-Herold-Strasse 2. A trusty source of inexpensive Tyrolean dishes (menus change daily but almost always include a good *Gröstl*) and mid-priced Austrian regulars, in attractive wood-panelled rooms or on a pleasant outdoor terrace.

Eggerwirt, Untere Gänsbachstrasse 12. A wide range of good-quality, reasonably priced Tyrolean and Austrian food in a nice old inn. Also does good trout and a selection of game dishes. Closed Nov to mid–Dec.

Goldener Greif, Hinterstadt 24 (☎05356/64311). Top-quality Austrian and international food in refined surroundings, for those prepared to splash out a little.

Huberbräu, Vorderstadt 18. A good place to get no-nonsense Austrian fare, from Wurst-and-chips-type snacks to more substantial dishes, all at very reasonable, un-Kitzbühel-like prices.

La Fonda, Hinterstadt 13. Fairly predictable Tex-Mex food, although the lively atmosphere and piped Latin music make this a popular hangout. Also a good place to drink in the evening.

Tennerhof, Griesenauweg 26 (☎05356/63181). Posh hotel restaurant with swanky surroundings and highly regarded international gourmet cuisine. Closed Oct to mid–Dec.

Bars and cafés

Big Ben, Vorderstadt 31. A comfortable if rather staid pub-cum-café on the main street, with outdoor seating in summer. Good for a daytime coffee or a quiet evening drink. A range of snacks including toasted sandwiches and soups make this a good place for a light lunch.

Gatto Bello, Hinterstadt The most congenial of central Kitzbühel's upmarket designer bars, with lots of quirky artistic details – note the unconventional lamp shades above the ceramic-tiled bar. Atmospheric, candlelit interior, upwardly mobile clientele, and jazzy background sounds. A sheer pleasure to drink in unless you're on a tight budget.

Grieserl, Im Gries. A cosy place with a traditional Austrian feel in the small bar area, and a more elegant candlelit ambience in the covered terrace outside. Healthy mix of outsiders and locals. Toasted sandwiches, salads and a set-menu main meal available.

Highways, Im Gries 20. Roomy, raucous, good-time bar with a wide range of international beers, an even wider range of garish neon beer signs, and a youngish, hedonistic, predominantly Austrian crowd. Occasional live bands in the winter season.

The Londoner, Franz-Reisch-Strasse 4. Large, lively and enjoyable English-speaking pub which has become something of a Kitzbühel institution. Occasional live music, and a wide-ranging crowd of foreign tourists and animated young locals. Come the weekend of the Hahnenkamm race, international skiers will either be propping up the bar or serving behind it.

Olympia, Hinterstadt 6. Disco-bars in the town centre come and go, but Olympia seems to have lasted the distance. Standard selection of commercial techno played to a mixture of serious groovers and out-on-the-town tourists. Doesn't get going until after midnight.

WEST OF INNSBRUCK

West of Innsbruck, urban tourism takes much more of a back seat to the great outdoors. The attractions of the Inn Valley – the abbey at **Stams**, or small towns like **Imst** and **Landeck** – are worth a fleeting visit, but it's the deep mountain valleys that run north to south through increasingly rugged alpine terrain that merit most attention. The **Ötztal**, the **Oberinntal** and the **Paznauntal** are the main valleys to aim for, all of them offering a wide range of skiing resorts in winter and numerous hiking opportunities in summer. West of the Inn Valley, the **Arlberg** mountain range, home to **St Anton**, among the oldest of Austria's alpine resorts, marks the border between the Tyrol and the Vorarlberg. To the northwest, hard by the German border, the market town of **Reutte** and the resort village of **Ehrwald** are the two most enticing tourist targets. Nearest to Innsbruck, **Seefeld** is a beautifully situated and rather chic alpine resort, easily accessible from the Tyrolean capital.

Despite the obstacles posed by the alpine terrain, **public transport** in the area is pretty comprehensive. The A12 autobahn and main rail line forge westwards along the Inn Valley in the direction of the Vorarlberg and Switzerland, with bus routes branching off to the north and south to serve the communities in the side-valleys. Train stations such as Ötztal, Imst-Pitztal and Landeck are important nodal points, with many bus services either commencing their journeys there or passing through. Connections with the northwest, cut off from the Inn Valley by a formidable mountain barrier, are slightly more problematic. Seefeld, Reutte and Ehrwald are all served by a railway line that heads north from Innsbruck and loops through a corner of Germany before arriving back in the Tyrol. If you're approaching the area from the west, buses from Imst and Nassereith are a better bet.

Seefeld

Occupying a mountain plateau high above the northern side of the Inn Valley, **SEEFELD** is one of the most attractively situated of all Austria's alpine resorts. With low-lying,

---

SEEFELD SUMMER ACTIVITIES

Bike rental At the train station or from Sport Sailer, Dorfplatz (☎05212/2530).

Paragliding Paragleitschule Ernst Steger (☎05212/3830-0) offers tandem flights and beginners' courses, taking off from the upper slopes of the Gschwandt-kopf.

Rafting The nearest rafting centre is at Imst in the Inn Valley (see p.512). The Seefeld tourist office has details of the numerous local firms offering day-trips there.

Swimming Outdoors at Strandbad Wildsee; or indoors at Hallenbad Olympia (daily 9.30am–10pm; öS165; ☎05212/3220) just south of the centre, with water slides, whirlpool and sauna.

Tennis Tennisclub Seefeld, Mösererstrasse (☎05212/2888). Courts from öS130/hr.

Walking Twice-weekly guided walks are organized by the tourist office.

---

grassy pastures, forested slopes and rugged peaks in almost every direction, it's hard to think of a better place for an easy-going highland holiday. Seefeld's main drawback is its reputation as a slightly snooty resort for the well-heeled, reflected in accommodation prices that are among the highest in the western Tyrol. The village itself is modern and international rather than quaintly Austrian, featuring big hotels and apartment blocks, expensive boutiques, and horse-drawn fiacres ferrying tourists around the resort.

For the winter tourist, Seefeld doesn't offer the widest choice of downhill skiing terrain, although there's plenty here to keep beginners happy. It's also a good place to learn cross-country skiing. The local lift pass, the Seefeld Card, costs öS370/€26.89 for one day; and öS720/€52.32 for two days. Those staying longer would be advised to make use of the Happy Ski Card, which covers the more versatile resorts of Ehrwald (see p.519) and Lermoos as well as Seefeld. Three days cost öS1030/€74.80; seven days öS2145/€155.90. For winter walkers, several paths are cleared of snow to create an extensive network of hikes: maps are available from the tourist office

Seefeld lies on Bundesstrasse 177, which climbs laboriously out of the Inn Valley at **Zirl** 12km west of Innsbruck and heads north towards the German border. It's a route served by some **buses** from the Tyrolean capital, although **trains** are more frequent, using the rail line that links Innsbruck with Ehrwald and Reutte.

The Town

Little of real vintage survives in Seefeld save for a brace of churches, of which the **Pfarrkirche St Oswald**, dominating the central square, is a real gem. A seventeenth-century king of Northumbria, who died in battle fighting the Welsh, Oswald was canonized for his role in promoting Christianity in the English northeast, and his cult subsequently propagated in central Europe by itinerant English monks. The church has been a pilgrimage centre ever since 1384, when stories circulated of the divine punishment meted out to another Oswald – local magnate Oswald Milser – who insisted that the priest gave him a special Communion wafer traditionally reserved for the clergy. Having scoffed most of the wafer, Milser was swallowed up by a fissure that suddenly appeared in the church floor. Fragments of the wafer snatched from Milser's mouth were found to be stained with the blood of Christ and were henceforth preserved in a reliquary housed in the **Blutskapelle**, accessible by stairs on the north side of the nave. The pinnacled high altar centres on a scene showing the Madonna with St Oswald (the one with curly hair and holding a cup) standing to her right. Other paintings inside the church include scenes from the lives of Mary Magdalene and St Oswald on the north wall of the choir; the death of St Oswald, together with the fate of his namesake Oswald Milser, are the subjects of reliefs on the tympanum above the south door.

At the southeastern end of the village, the small and delightful onion-domed **Seekirche** stands on a grassy knoll against a backdrop of distant mountains – a picture-postcard setting that's more interesting than the interior of the chapel. The only other thing to do in Seefeld is take a wander around the **Wildsee**, 1km south of the centre, a small lake surrounded by rushes and rich in wildfowl. There are a pay-to-enter Strandbad and boat-rental facilities at the southernmost end of the lake.

Into the mountains

East of Seefeld's train station, the **Rosshütte funicular** (June–Sept & Dec–April; öS145/€10.59 return to Rosshütte, öS170/€12.41 return including the Seefelder Jochbahn) presents the most dramatic route into the mountains, rising to the 1760-metre Rosshütte, where there's a great view of the Zugspitze to the northwest and a choice of routes to higher altitudes. The Seefelder Jochbahn cable car (same times) ascends eastwards to the 2064-metre **Seefelder Joch**, an area of meadow beneath the 2220-metre-high **Seefelder Spitze** – to which there's a reasonably easy fifty-minute walk. Alternatively, take the Härmelkopfbahn cable car southwards from the Rosshütte to the 2050-metre **Harmelkopf**, where there's an attractive walk down to Seefeld via the **Reither Jochalm**, site of a handy refreshment hut, or a relatively easy eighty-minute uphill walk to the 2239-metre *Nördlinger Hütte*. Once here, you can choose to tackle the medium-difficulty ascent of the 2374-metre **Reither Spitze** (1hr). The Reither Spitze and the Seefelder Spitze are connected by a popular medium-difficulty trail, thereby presenting reasonably fit walkers with a tempting circuit, ascending with one cable car, and descending by the other; total time for the circuit would be about three-and-a-half hours.

Over on the southern side of town, a chairlift (June–Sept & Dec–April; öS125/€9.13 return) climbs the slopes of the **Gschwandtkopf**, where the *Ötzihütte* offers refreshments and a small display devoted to "Ötzi", the prehistoric ice man found in the Ötztaler Alps (see p.511), and a farmyard zoo for kids.

Practicalities

Heading out of the **train station**, walk straight ahead for about 200m to find the centrally located **tourist office**, at Klosterstrasse 43 (Mon–Sat 8.30am–6.00pm; ☎05212/2313, *www.seefeld-tirol.com*), where you can pick up handfuls of English-language information and book **private rooms** (summer ②; winter ③). Virtually every house in the village offers tourist accommodation of some sort, and those who arrive late in the day should be able to find a bed simply by wandering around looking for "*Zimmer Frei*" signs.

The range of **hotel** accommodation is broad enough to suit most pockets, although be aware that prices rise by anything between 25 and 50 percent in winter. At the budget end of the scale, *Stark*, Andreas-Hofer-Strasse 144 (☎05212/2104, *stark@aon.at*; ①), offers no-frills rooms with shared facilities (some more expensive ones have en-suite WC and shower) one block north of the tourist office, while *Felseneck*, Kirchwald 309 (☎05212/2540; ②), is a small and cosy house in the residential streets on the hill west of the centre, all of whose rooms are en-suite. Stepping upwards in price, *Sonneck*, Klosterstrasse 175 (☎ 05212/2387, *www.hotel-diana.at*; ④), is a small, centrally located pension just west of the Pfarrkirche. The top-of-the-range *Hotel Klosterbräu* (☎05212/2621-0, *www.klosterbraeu*; ⑨), behind the Pfarrkirche in an old sixteenth-century monastery with modern, chalet-style additions, features indoor and outdoor pools, and every conceivable comfort.

Despite its reputation as an expensive resort, **eating** out in Seefeld need not be a traumatic experience. Most of the hotels have restaurants offering cheap Tagesmenüs at lunchtime. *Putzi's Grill*, near the tourist office on Münchnerstrasse, is the place to go for Wurst and fried-chicken snacks. The *Alte Stübe* in the Karwendelhof,

Bahnhofstrasse, offers inexpensive Tyrolean specialities or more extravagant schnitzels and steaks, while *Luigi and Lois*, Innsbrückerstrasse, is a lively place with plenty of outdoor seating and a mixed Italian-Tyrolean menu. *Südtiroler Stube*, Reiterspitzstrasse 17, serves good, medium to expensive cuisine with local flavour, as well as some Italian dishes, and *Taverna Emilia Romagna*, Leutascherstrasse, has good pizzas and pasta dishes, though tables are packed in the cosy dining room.

Of the **bars**, *Café Fledermaus* on Bahnhofstrasse is a nice daytime or evening hang-out that also offers good toasted or baguette sandwiches. *Graham's Pub*, a lively Antipodean-run hangout behind the *Hotel Eden* on Münchnerstrasse, is the biggest and best of the late-night boozing venues, although the Wild West-themed *Buffalo Saloon*, on the main street, also attracts a fun-seeking crowd in the small hours, and has ribs and wings on the snack menu.

Stams

Travelling westwards along the Inn Valley from Innsbruck you'll pass by the settlements of **Zirl** and **Telfs**, pleasant enough market towns that nevertheless lack compelling attractions. If you're looking for a stop-off en route to the western Tyrol or the Vorarlberg, you'd do better to carry on as far as the village of **STAMS** 40km out of Innsbruck, site of an abbey that once served as the burial place of the *Landesfürsten*, princes of the Tyrol.

Its stocky octagonal ochre towers clearly visible across the meadows from the train station, Stams' Cistercian **abbey** was founded by Meinhard II of Tirol in the thirteenth century. The exquisite interior of the Baroque abbey **church**, its cream stucco-work and gilded altars bathed in light, is nowadays only accessible if you join a tour (July–Aug half-hourly 9–11am & 1–5pm; June & Sept at 9am, 10am, 11am, 2pm & 3pm; öS60/€4.38), which also takes in the eighteenth-century, fresco-adorned *Fürstensaal* or "princely hall" – a kind of opulent reception room. Sunken in the floor of the nave, the "Prince's Crypt" holds a succession of tombs watched over by statues of those buried here, including Sigismund the Rich's first wife – Scottish princess Eleonore Stuart – and Maximilian I's second wife, Bianca Maria Sforza. Sigismund's father, Duke Friedrich the Penniless, is buried round the corner in the monk's chancel. Visited separately from the guided tour, the **museum** on the first floor of the abbey complex (June–Sept daily except Mon 10–11.30am & 1.30–5pm; öS30/€2.19) assembles a small but remarkable collection of Gothic altarpieces. Pride of place goes to the anonymous *Grussitafel* of 1390, depicting the Coronation of the Virgin surrounded by saintly figures, and to the fairy-tale-like *Heuperger Altar* of 1426, in which a diamond-shaped central panel featuring the Virgin and Child is surrounded by twenty vivid scenes of holy men and mythical beasts.

Stams is easily digestible as a day-trip from Innsbruck, but a small **tourist office** just below the train station at the bottom of Bahnhofstrasse (Mon, Tues, Thurs & Fri 8–11.30am; ☎05263/6511) will fix you up with a **private room** should you wish to stay. The restaurant of the *Alte Schmiede*, just west of the abbey in the village centre, is a good place for a quick lunch or a more substantial evening meal, as well as being a relaxing place for a drink.

The Ötztal and around

Probably the most dramatic of the valleys feeding the Inn from the high Alps to the south, the **ÖTZTAL** is a deep, fertile vale that stretches southwards for over 50km to the rugged Ötztaler Alps, which mark Austria's border with Italy. Villages here draw plenty

---

ÖZTAL ACTIVITIES

Mountain climbing An impressive range of high alpine peaks can be tackled as one- or two-day tours in the company of local guides, who can be contacted through Bergführerstelle Vent (☎05254/8106), Bergsport und Erlebnisschule Sölden (☎05254/2546) and Ski und Hochgebirgschule Obergurgl (☎05256/305).

Paragliding Vacancia Outdoor, Hauptstrase 438, Sölden (☎05254/3100-0). Tandem flights from around öS750/€51.10.

Rafting Vacancia Outdoor, Hauptstrasse 438, Sölden (☎05254/3100-0). Rafting trips from öS490/€35.77, canyoning trips from öS850/€62.05.

Rock climbing Bergsport und Erlebnisschule Sölden, Sölden (see above under "Mountain climbing"), offer climbing courses for all abilities, and guided climbs for those with experience. There's an artificial climbing wall at Sölden's main sports centre, the Freizeitarena; and rock-climbing trails can be found at various points in the valley – Sölden tourist office will provide details.

Skiing Skiing is possible on the Rettenbach and Tiefenbach glaciers above Sölden to the west from October through to May, where there are also a couple of ski schools for beginners. The ski areas are reached via the Gletscherstrasse mountain road.

Swimming There's an indoor pool at the Freizeitarena in Sölden, on the east bank of the river (daily 11am–9pm; day ticket öS160/€11.68).

Walking Ski und Hochgebirgschule Obergurgl (see "Mountain climbing") offer a weekly programme of guided walks over the summer. Contact them or the Obergurgl tourist office (see p.510) for details.

---

of tourists, but they're not yet the inflated parodies of alpine tourism that you find elsewhere. The main skiing and hiking centres are **Sölden**, a large package resort at the head of the valley, and the three more rustic settlements that lie above it, **Untergurgl**, **Obergurgl** and **Hochgurgl**. Two glaciers above Sölden enable year-round skiing and snowboarding, while a bewildering array of trails draw hikers in summer.

All trains on the main Inn Valley rail line stop at **Bahnhof Ötztal**, the train station at the mouth of the valley, which is now a small town in its own right; about nine buses a day head up the valley from here. There's also a popular cycle path from Bahnhof Ötztal right up the valley to Obergürgl, joining the main road for short stretches but staying apart for most of the way. It's reasonably easy cycling as far as Sölden, after which the path gets considerably steeper – fit mountain bikers might enjoy the challenge.

Even if you don't have the time to explore Ötztal in depth, you should at least try and take the bus up the valley as far as Obergurgl and back down again – a wonderfully scenic ride whatever the season. For those eager to explore the region at more length, the Kompass 50:000 Ötztaler Alpen map covers hiking routes.

Sölden

A modern resort village 40km south of Bahnhof Ötztal, **SÖLDEN** straggles along both banks of the Ötztaler Ache. There's not a great deal to the place: the main street, lined with most of the shops and the bigger hotels, runs along the western side of the river, and a chalet settlement of pensions and tourist apartments spreads along the eastern side. Its popularity as a winter resort rests on the fact that it offers a range of pistes suitable for all abilities, with plenty of long, steep runs on the two main peaks – the Gaislachkogl and Giggijoch – looming over the village to the west. There's also a fair amount of off-piste skiing, and winter sports are possible in all but the summer months on the **Rettenbach glacier**, accessible from Sölden by road.

A range of **lift passes** (also including the toll for the Gletscherstrasse; see below) is available to hikers and skiers throughout the year. In **winter**, expect to pay around öS410/€29.80 for one day, öS2310/€167.87 for 6 days; in **summer** you'll pay öS310/€22.53 for 1 day; öS1590/€115.55 for 6 days.

A number of routes lead up to the heights above the western side of the valley, where you'll find a variety of hiking routes in summer. Walkers should note that there are a number of snow-cleared paths around Sölden and Vent in winter too – a map of them is available from the tourist office. **Hochsölden**, the mountain suburb located high on a ledge above the town, is accessible by road or via the Hochsölden chairlift from the northern end of Sölden (late June to late Sept & Dec–April; öS85/€6.18 return). From the top station you can pick up a number of panoramic lateral walks, or head a short way south to the *Sonnblick* café-restaurant, a popular summer and winter refreshment point with good views of the valley below. Hochsölden is also the starting point for another chairlift (same times; return öS45/€3.27; combined Hochsölden & Rotkogel return öS110/€7.99) that continues uphill to the **Rotkogel**, starting point for numerous walks. In winter, the **Giggijochbahn gondola** (Dec–April; return öS140/€10.17) connects Hochsölden with the Giggijoch, site of a new snowboard park.

At the southern end of Sölden, the Gaislachkoglbahn cable car (late June to late Sept & Dec–April; return öS235/€17.08) offers a two-stage ascent to the 3058-metre **Gaislachkogl** and access to some stupendous panoramic walks. A free brochure in English, *Cableway Hiking*, details a few of them and is available from the cable-car station.

Just beyond the cable-car station to the south, a right turn brings you onto the **Gletscherstrasse** (open May–Oct; cars öS220/€15.99, motorbikes öS65/€4.72, bus passengers öS65/€4.72), a twelve-kilometre-long road served by five daily buses from Sölden over the summer. It's more of a sightseeing trip than a route to hiking destinations, climbing steeply towards the **Rettenbach Glacier** before traversing a 1.7-kilometre tunnel beneath the Gaislacherkogl to the **Tiefenbach Glacier**. You'll find skiing pistes at both glaciers which remain open for much of the year, and a range of lifts to higher altitudes – notably the brand-new gondola from Tiefenbach to the 3309m Tiefenbachkogl. At the height of the winter season, numerous chairlifts and drag lifts link Giggijoch, Rettenbach, Gaislachkogl and Tiefenbach to each other, providing excellent conditions for exploring a wide range of pistes.

Practicalities

Buses stop in the main street, just across the river from the **tourist office**, housed in a modern sports and leisure centre known as the Freizeitarena (Mon–Sat 8am–noon & 2–6pm; ☎05254/2269, www.soelden.at). The tourist office will give you a list of vacancies in **private rooms** (summer ②; winter ③) and **hotels**, and will provide a courtesy phone from which to ring them up. In summer, a surplus of tourist beds makes finding a room rarely a problem – simply keep your eyes peeled for "Zimmer Frei" signs. Of the over 150 family-run **pensions** in the village, *Jasmin*, right next to the tourist office at Rettenbach 546 (☎05254/2571; summer ②; winter ③), *Mina*, centrally located a few steps uphill from the Hauptstrasse at Rettenbach 90 (☎05254/2146; summer ②; winter ③), and *Stefan Prantl*, 1km north of the centre at Kaisers 26 (☎05254/2525; summer ①; winter ②), are all cosy, friendly and cheap. The Hotel *Garni Granat*, Rettenbach 171 (☎05254/2246, www.hotel-granat.at; summer ③, winter ⑥), also near the tourist office, offers stylish balconied rooms with en-suite facilities and TV. At the expensive end of the scale, the top-of-the-range *Central Hotel*, Hof 418 (☎05254/2260-0, www.central-soelden.com; ⑨), has roomy apartments and indoor pool, sauna and solarium on site. *Camping Sölden*, at the southern end of town (☎05254/2627, campingsoelden@netway.at; open all year), is a terraced **campsite** overlooking the river.

As for most skiing resorts, **eating** recommendations change from season to season, and many venues close in summer. Of the places likely to be open throughout the year, there's not much to choose between the two central pizzerias: flash and loud *Gusto*, on the main street, and *Corso*, on the other side of the river, with a wider variety of Italian dishes and some Austrian, too. *Armin's Törggele Stub'n*, on the eastern side of the river, serves as a café-cum-wine bar with a good range of Tyrolean and general Austrian food. *Dorf Alm*, a building in the style of a log cabin on the main street opposite the Raiffeisenbank, is a dependable source of inexpensive Tyrolean staples.

Après-ski **drinking** kicks off at the lift stations, and continues in the numerous igloo-shaped bars scattered throughout the town. There's a strip of late-night watering holes on or around the main street: bang in the centre, *Bierhimmel* on the first floor of the Rindlhaus is a rocking, raucous alternative to the more sedate *Café-Bar Rindele* on the floor below. *Stamperl*, on the other side of the river, is a cellar-bar with neo-gothic decor that attracts a relaxed twenty-something crowd after midnight.

Above Sölden: Vent, Obergurgl and Hochgurgl

South of Sölden, the main road climbs steeply via a succession of hairpin bends to the hamlet of **ZWIESELSTEIN**, where a secondary road up to the Ventertal (served by daily buses from Sölden in summer) bears to the left. Thirteen kilometres further along is the village of **VENT**, dominated by the Tyrol's highest peak, the 3768-metre **Wildspitze**, rising to the northwest. A **tourist office** in the centre of the village (Mon–Fri 9am–noon & 2–5pm; ☎05254/8193, *www.tiscover.com/vent*) has a list of **private rooms** (② in summer, ③ in winter). Though favoured by serious climbers because of the wide choice of mountainscapes within striking distance, there are plenty of opportunities around Vent for the less ambitious, with hiking trails leading up starkly beautiful side-valleys like the **Rofental** to the southwest and the **Niedertal** due south.

The head of the Niedertal is overlooked by a high mountain pass known as the Niederjoch, across which shepherds from the Schnaltal on the Italian side of the border drive thousands of sheep every summer in search of grazing land – a practice dating back to the thirteenth century. The timing of the event depends on the weather, so contact the tourist office in Sölden for details. Just west of the Niederjoch is the Hauslabjoch, where the 5500-year-old corpse known as **Ötzi** (rendered somewhat inelegantly into English as "Frozen Fritz") was discovered by German hikers in September 1991 (see box opposite).

Obergurgl and Hochgurgl

After Zwieselstein, the main southbound road continues climbing towards the hamlet of Untergurgl, before ascending above the tree line a few kilometres further on to **OBERGURGL**, the highest village in the Tyrol, its valley girdled by glaciers and hemmed in by ridges and summits well in excess of 3000m. It's a place that revolves largely around winter sports, although a steady stream of hikers is drawn here over the summer by an unparalleled menu of alpine walks (see box on p.513). The local **tourist office** (Mon–Fri 8am–12.30pm & 2–6pm, Sat 8am–noon; ☎05256/6466, *www.obergurgl.com*) is in the centre of the village – where buses from Sölden stop – and has lists of **private rooms** in Obergurgl and Untergurgl as well as Hochgurgl higher up.

Beyond Obergurgl, the road doubles back on itself to rise to **HOCHGURGL**, the highest of the Gurgl settlements and another winter resort in its own right. From here,

ÖTZI THE ICE MAN

On September 9, 1991, German climbers Erika and Helmut Simon were walking on the Hauslabjoch on the Austrian-Italian border when they noticed a half-exposed human form protruding from the ice of the Similaun Glacier. The couple reported the find to the local police upon their arrival at the nearest alpine hut, and a helicopter was sent to investigate the following day. It took another three days for police and mountain rescue teams to free the body from the ice, during which time it became apparent that this was an extraordinary find. The world-renowned Tyrolean mountaineer Reinhold Messner, who visited the site out of curiosity because he happened to be in the area, immediately declared the corpse to be at least 3000 years old. Such an estimate was considered wildly exaggerated at the time, although it was enough to encourage Austrian state television to send a camera team to film the corpse being airlifted off the mountain – footage that was to be beamed around the world as soon as the true importance of the find became known. Archeologists from Innsbruck University were on the scene within a week to retrieve objects found alongside the corpse, although it wasn't until the body had been subjected to carbon dating that the ice man's true age – about 5500 years – was established.

Christened **Ötzi** in honour of the Ötztal above which he was found, the ice man yielded a wealth of new information about Neolithic culture in the region. Not only was the body remarkably well preserved, revealing a dark-haired, blue-eyed individual sporting charcoal tattoos, but he'd also managed to take a wide range of Stone Age artefacts to his grave. He was equipped with well-made shoes featuring separate soles and uppers, a bearskin hat, a flint knife, and a rudimentary rucksack made of skins mounted on a wooden frame. How he came to be on the Hauslabjoch remains the subject of much conjecture, although the idea that the Neolithic population on both sides of the Alps was using the high mountain passes to conduct trade remains an appealing one.

Ötzi soon became a symbol of Austrian, and more specifically Tyrolean, pride, even though it had been common knowledge in the days following Ötzi's discovery that the exact spot on which he was found lay a full 10m on the wrong side of Austria's border with Italy. Despite Ötzi's adoption by a fascinated Austrian public, he technically belonged to the Italians. Notwithstanding the strong local passions aroused, the Austrian and Italian governments just about succeeded in turning the Ötzi case into an example of internationalist co-operation rather than nationalist tub-thumping, allowing Innsbruck University to proceed with their analysis of the body on the understanding that he would ultimately be handed over to the Italians. While most Austrians were resigned to the move, the choice of the Italian city of Bolzano (which, under the name of Bozen, was part of Austria until 1918) as his final resting place rubbed salt into some Tyrolean wounds, and one shadowy group of Austrian nationalists threatened to destroy the corpse should it ever leave Austrian soil. In January 1998, however, Ötzi departed from Innsbruck complete with police escort to take up residence in Bolzano, where a £6-million museum has been built in his honour.

a **toll road** (June–Sept; öS200/€14.60 per car, öS70/€5.11 per motorbike) ascends to the 2509-metre **Timmelsjoch Pass**, which offers breathtaking panoramas before beginning a tortuous descent into the Italian South Tyrol.

The Landeck region

Beyond Bahnhof Ötztal at the mouth of the Ötztal valley, the main westbound road and rail routes continue to follow the River Inn as far as **Landeck**, where they leave the valley to begin their slow ascent of the Arlberg Pass. Provincial, workaday Landeck is of no great beauty, but it's a good base from which to visit the adjacent valleys of the

Oberinntal (or Upper Inn Valley) and the **Paznaun**, the name given to the valley of the **River Trisanna**. The Oberinntal harbours a string of small, low-key alpine resorts – **Ladis**, **Fiss**, **Serfaus**, **Pfunds** and **Nauders** are the places to aim for – while the Paznaun boasts the much ritzier skiing village **Ischgl**, an international package-holiday favourite.

Imst

Travelling west along the main rail line or motorway from Bahnhof Ötztal, you'll pass **IMST**, a small market town lying slightly to the north of the main Inn Valley, best known for its **Schemenlaufen** (or "ghost dance"), held on a Sunday in February every four or five years (the next one is due in the year 2004 or 2005). Consisting of a large procession of elaborately costumed figures, each with their own lolloping dance, the festivities are rooted in pagan rituals designed to drive away the spirit of winter.

Imst is also renowned as the most important **rafting centre** of the Inn Valley – in fact tourist offices in towns all over the western Tyrol run trips here. The biggest of the local companies offering excursions, during which you'll be challenged to negotiate fast-flowing sections of the river in a large dinghy, is Outdoor-Zentrum Haiming, Alte Bundesstrasse 27, Haiming, Imst (☎05266/87188). A short trip on the River Inn costs around öS500/€36.50, with reductions for children under 13, while a longer, more hair-raising trip on the whiter-water stretches of the river (over-13s only) costs around öS600/€43.80.

Imst-Pitztal **train station** is 3km south of town; regular buses run into the centre. Downtown Imst consists of a long main street (named Kramergasse, Johannesplatz then Pfarrgasse respectively) snaking its way from south to north. Halfway along this main strip, the **tourist office** at Johannesplatz 4 (Mon–Fri 8am–noon & 2–6pm, Sat 9am–1pm; ☎05412/6910-0) will help with accommodation. At the northern end of the main street, there's a **Pfarrkirche** with some arresting outer frescoes, notably an animated fifteenth-century scene of local miners at work. The only other reason to linger here is the **Rosengartenschlucht**, a 1.5-kilometre-long gorge accessible via a pathway just opposite the tourist office – a pleasant torrent-side walk through parkland and forest to the hillside suburb of **Hochimst** to the west.

Landeck

Originally a fortress town guarding the eastern approaches to the Arlberg Pass, **LANDECK** is today a pretty drab, semi-industrialized place, important to travellers as a source of buses into the surrounding mountains rather than as an attraction in its own right. Occupying a hillside above the River Inn to the southeast, central Landeck huddles below the fifteenth-century **Pfarrkirche St Oswald**, a beautifully proportioned late-Gothic structure built by Oswald von Schrofenstein, erstwhile lord of a (now-ruined) castle that clings to the hillside on the opposite side of the river. The high altar (the so-called *Schrofensteinaltar* of 1513) centres on a scene of the Adoration; the predella shows St Oswald, together with Oswald von Schrofenstein and his wife, kneeling in prayer. Von Schrofenstein's symbol, a rampant goat, adorns both his tomb, on the south wall of the nave, and his *Totenschild*, or memorial shield, close by the high altar.

Uphill from the church, the thirteenth-century **Schloss Landeck** houses a fairly parochial **folk museum** (daily: June–Sept 10am–5pm; öS30/€2.19), proffering the usual range of Tyrolean wooden furniture, and a room devoted to Jakob Prandtauer, the locally born architect responsible for the famous Benedictine abbey at Melk (see p.175). Period rooms upstairs include an example of the *Rauchkuche*, the open-hearthed kitchens common in Tyrolean farmhouses, and a display of the floral head-dresses worn by cows (the better the milk yield, the bigger the head-dress) at the time of the *Almabtrieb*, the mid-September descent from the high alpine pastures.

HUT TO HUT IN THE ÖTZTALER ALPS

Obergurgl and the Gurglertal

The downhill ski industry has claimed some of the slopes around **Obergurgl**, but there remain plenty of good walks amidst dramatic and unfussed mountain scenery. One of the best of these, which doesn't involve glacier crossing, is that to the *Hochwildehaus* (phone via the *Langtalereck Hütte*: ☎05256/233), a hut set fabulously on the east bank of the Gurglerferner Glacier, at the head of which rise the Hochwilde (3482m), Annakogel (3336m), Mitterkamm (3200m) and Karles-Spitze (3469m), among other peaks. The route is straightforward, takes about **four to five hours** from Obergurgl, and visits both the *Schönwies* and *Langtalereck* huts on the way. Both of these are set in idyllic locations – the first at the mouth of the Rotmoostal glen, the second with a full frontal view of the Gurglerferner's icefall.

On the west flank of the Gurglertal, opposite the Langtalereck Hütte but almost four hundred metres higher, sits the Ramolhaus, another DAV hut wardened in the summer months. A recommended walk to it along the Ötztaler Jungschützenweg takes about three and a half hours from Obergurgl, and makes an excellent introduction to the valley. There is, however, a longer traverse for fit walkers, along a trail that begins at Zwieselstein about 18km from the Ramolhaus (☎05256/223), and with a difference in altitude of 1556m. Several small tarns add sparkle to the landscape along the way, and there are a few modest summits accessible to walkers on the ridge above. The most northerly of these is the 3163-metre Nederkogel, from whose summit you can see the snowy masses of the Ötztaler Alps spread in a great arc, while to the east, across the deep Ötztal, the Stubai Alps are equally impressive.

Across the Ötztaler Alps

A reasonably tough three-day crossing of the north flank of the Ötztaler Alps, avoiding glaciers but nudging the highest peaks, gives a first-rate tour amidst outstanding alpine scenery. It starts in the Kaunertal on the district's western fringe, where the rustic *Gepatschhaus* (☎05475/215) provides overnight accommodation at the southern end of the **Gepatschspeicher reservoir** (reached by infrequent bus from Landeck via Prutz). From here a meandering trail climbs eastwards to the 3095-metre Ölgrubenjoch, a bare saddle with stunning views of the Wildspitze ahead to the east. Above to the right the Hinterer Ölgrubenspitze (3296m) is worth an hour's detour if you have the energy. From the Ölgrubenjoch you descend steeply into a glacial basin below the Sexegertenferner to gain the *Taschach Haus* (☎05413/8239), a DAV hut often used as a base for ice-climbing courses – there's an impressive icefall nearby, which provides an ideal training ground. Day 2 continues down-valley as far as the Riffelsee along the balcony path known as the Fuldaer Höhenweg; you then descend to Mittelberg before starting a demanding ascent to the *Braunschweiger Hütte* (☎05413/8236) set on the edge of a turmoil of glaciers, with the Wildspitze now to the southwest. Day 3, and the final stage of the crossing, scrambles along a ridge above the hut (there's a herd of ibex here), negotiates the Pitztaler Jöchl (2995m) and descends through the wooded Reifenbachtal to Sölden, in the upper reaches of the Ötztal.

A recommended **map** for either of the above tours is the Kompass *Wanderkarte 43* (Ötztaler Alpen), 1:50,000. For more on the Austrian hut-to-hut system, see p.39.

Practicalities

Landeck **train station** is 2km east of town, from where half-hourly local buses trundle to the **bus station** at the northern end of the main street, Malserstrasse. The **tourist office**, at the southern end of Malserstrasse (Mon–Fri 8am–noon & 2–6pm, Sat 8am–noon; ☎05442/62344), will help you with **private rooms** (①), although there are more of these in surrounding villages than in Landeck itself (you'll need your own transport). Nicest of the hotels and pensions are in **Perfuchs**, a hillside suburb overlooking the town centre on the west bank of the Inn: *Pension Thialblick*, Burschlweg (☎05442/62261; ②), and the nearby *Pension Paula* on the same road (☎05442/63371; ②); both offer good-value B&B-style accommodation. In the centre of Landeck on the east bank of the Inn, *Gasthof Greif*, Marktplatz (☎05442/62268; ③), is an old-style inn with plain, old-fashioned rooms, while *Hotel Schrofenstein*, Malserstrasse (☎05442/62395; ④), is the best of the big business hotels on the main street.

Landeck's two **campsites** are west of the centre on the road towards the Arlberg and the Paznaun: *Sport Camp Tirol*, Bruggen (☎05442/64636), 1km from the centre on the north bank of the river Sanna, organizes a range of rafting, paragliding and biking trips and tends to fill up with large school groups as a result; *Camping Riffler*, Bruggfeldstrasse 2 (☎05442/62477-4), on the south bank of the Sanna, is closer to the centre and a bit quieter.

For **eating**, the *Gasthof Greif* serves up substantial, no-nonsense schnitzel-and-chips-style meals, while the *Goldenes Fassl*, up the hill from the tourist office on Malsergasse, offers a higher standard of Tyrolean and Austrian cuisine and usually a couple of vegetarian choices. The best place in which to **drink** away the evening is *KLA4* (pronounced "Klavier") hidden behind a bank at Malserstrasse 11, a fashionable but friendly basement bar, which also does a range of hot meals.

The Oberinntal

Southwest of Landeck, the main road follows the River Inn into the **Oberinntal**, a wide vale surrounded by high Alps. Twelve kilometres out of town the village of **PRUTZ** offers a choice of routes: either straight on towards the Swiss border or uphill westwards to a terrace of highland pastures, and a sequence of three small resort villages. On the lip of the terrace is **Ladis**, a ruined castle at its centre, with excellent views across the valley towards the mountains of the Kaunertal. There's a **tourist office** (Mon–Fri 9am–noon & 2–5pm) on the main road through the village, and a Gasthof on the main road, the *Rose*, which serves good Tyrolean fare. The road continues along rolling pasturelands to **FISS**, dominated by large, modern chalet-style hotels, which again has a **tourist office** on the main road. Four kilometres further on, **SERFAUS** has been equally commercialized, although the core of the village still retains a great deal of character. It's both a resort and a working agricultural village, where chickens strut the back alleys and the smell of dung is never far away. **Buses** from Landeck stop just outside the **tourist office** in the centre (Mon–Fri 8.30am–noon & 1–5.30pm, Sat 9am–4pm; *www .serfaus-fiss-ladis.at*), which will help with accommodation. Just above the tourist office, the squat, medieval pilgrimage church of **Unsere Liebe Frau** has fragments of fifteenth-century frescoes, including a Last Judgement to the right of the entrance.

Seventeen kilometres south of Prutz, **PFUNDS** is a village that lacks extensive ski slopes of its own but nevertheless serves as a winter resort with access to pistes further up the valley around Nauders. In summer, it's also a good base for hiking. For the less active, the late-Gothic high altar in the village **Pfarrkirche** provides another reason to stop here.

Three kilometres south of Pfunds, a right fork in the road leads up the Schergenbach Valley to the small ski resort of **SAMNAUN**. Although part of Switzerland, Samnaun is only accessible from the Austrian side of the border, and enjoys special, duty-free status – thereby making it a popular day-trip destination for tourists and shoppers.

The main road south of Pfunds continues to follow the upper Inn Valley into Switzerland, where the Oberinntal becomes the Engadine. **Buses** from Landeck and Pfunds run to Scuol, where you can pick up connections to the glitzy resorts of St Moritz and Davos. Alternatively, you can take a southeast-bound road that stays on the Austrian side of the border, climbing over the Finstermünzpass to **Nauders**, another ski-resort village offering hiking opportunities in the summer.

The Paznaun

Narrow and densely wooded, with alpine pastures dotted with log-built barns covering the valley floor, it's easy to see the **Paznaun**'s rustic appeal. **Ischgl** is the valley's main centre, although **Kappl**, in the lower reaches of the valley, and **Galtür**, at the southern end of the valley, are small resorts in their own right. A summer **hiking pass** lasting six days (öS460/€33.58) is available from Ischgl tourist office, and covers the cable cars and gondolas in Kappl, Ischgl and Galtür, as well as in Samnaun over the mountains to the east.

Ischgl

Sprawled across the eastern slopes of the valley 30km southwest of Landeck, **ISCHGL** is a modern village that relies almost exclusively on the winter trade, with slopes catering for all ability ranges on the Idalp east of town, which is linked by lifts to the neighbouring ski area of Samnaun (see opposite). Main drawbacks are the package-resort artificiality of the place, and its increasingly high prices. In summer, Ischgl is relatively quiet and many of its restaurants and bars are closed, but there are plenty of possible itineraries for summer hikers, most immediate of which is to take the Silvrettabahn gondola, which ascends to the 2320m **Idalp**. There are numerous marked trails on top: one popular circuit is to walk eastwards and descend by cable car to Samnaun in the next valley, where you can return to Ischgl by bus via Landeck (check the local tourist office for times before attempting this route).

Ischgl's **tourist office**, in the centre opposite the main bus stop (Mon–Fri 8am–6pm, Sat 8am–noon & 4–6pm, Sun 8am–noon; ☎05444/5266-0, *www.ischgl.com*), will help you find a **private room** (summer ①; winter ②) or **hotel** bed.

Beyond Ischgl

Ten kilometres up the Paznaun Valley by road from Ischgl, **GALTÜR** is another small village serving the winter-package trade, though traditionally slightly cheaper than its neighbour and popular with beginners. Above Galtür, the **Silvretta Hochalpenstrasse** toll road (mid-April to mid-Dec; öS110/€8.03 per vehicle) continues southwestwards, clinging to the side of the increasingly narrow upper Trisanna Valley before arriving at the Bielerhöhe saddle and the Silvretta Reservoir, and descending into the Montafon Valley (see p.542). Buses from Landeck run as far as Bielerhöhe, where you can pick up connections to Schruns on the other side of the pass.

The Arlberg resorts

Straddling the border between the Tyrol and the Vorarlberg, the Arlberg massif is home to some of the most varied skiing terrain in the whole country, and presents both summer and winter visitors with mountainscapes of desolate beauty. The main resorts in the area are **St Anton** and St Christoph on the eastern, Tyrolean, side of the Arlberg summit, and **Zürs** and **Lech**, which fall in the province of Vorarlberg to the west and are covered in Chapter 10. You can stay at any of these resorts and make use of the facilities of the whole region, although generally St Anton and St Christoph offer the most direct access to slopes around the region's highest peak, the 2809-metre **Valluga**.

Approaching the region from Landeck, the main westbound road and rail routes follow the Rosanna Valley upstream into the Stanzertal, entering tunnels at St Anton that emerge 10km later on the Vorarlberg side of the 1793-metre **Arlberg Pass**. A minor road from St Anton winds its way over the pass itself (served by local buses working the St Anton–Lech route), passing through the chic skiing hamlet of **ST CHRISTOPH AM ARLBERG**. A small cluster of top-notch holiday dwellings, the resort began life as a fourteenth-century hospice built by local shepherd Heinrich Fidelkind von Kempten. The hospice building survived until 1957 when it was destroyed by fire, and a luxury hotel, the *Hospitz-Alm* (☎05446/26110, *www.hospiz.com*; ⑨), has now been built in its place. It's been a fairly snooty place ever since, and tourist development has been deliberately limited in an attempt to preserve its exclusivity.

Buses continue from St Christoph towards Rauzalpe, 4km beyond, where you can pick up connecting services to Zürs and Lech.

St Anton

A fashionable winter tourism centre since the 1920s, **ST ANTON** rivals Kitzbühel as the Tyrol's swishest society resort. However St Anton is much more of a magnet for the serious skier than its rival, offering a more challenging range of steep descents and off-piste opportunities than anywhere else in Austria. Possibilities for beginners do exist, but they're more limited than elsewhere, and often crowded. Indeed the popularity of St Anton ensures that there's a fair crush throughout the winter season, which usually begins slightly earlier than elsewhere in the country (the beginning of December) and can last well into April. Accommodation and restaurant prices are sky-high throughout this period, but there's no doubt that the town is an invigorating place to be, attracting a ski-hard and play-hard clientele who generate a raucous nightlife. The place can revert to a state of rural slumber over the summer, when many bars and restaurants close, and a less sybaritic crowd of hikers and mountain-sightseers moves in.

St Anton's history as a resort begins in 1901 when the Arlberg Ski Club was formed, largely on the initiative of local hotelier Carl Schuler, who was eager to stimulate winter tourism. Schuler engaged local man **Hannes Schneider** to teach the guests to ski, and the techniques developed by Schneider have formed the backbone of Austrian ski-school practice ever since. Together with British winter sports pioneer Sir Arnold Lunn, Schneider inaugurated the **Kandahar Cup** in 1928, a classic downhill race that still features in the World Cup calendar every December. St Anton's reputation for glamour was boosted by German director Arnold Fanck's decision to shoot the film *Der Weisse Rausch* (White Frenzy) here in 1931, a tale of love and adventure on the pistes which not only helped to make a star out of Hannes Schneider, but also featured future purveyor of Nazi propaganda **Leni Riefenstahl** in the female lead. Both Fanck and Riefenstahl went on to make many more snow-bound adventures for the German-speaking market, carving out a ski-film genre which is nowadays honoured in the **St Anton Film Festival** (held every September; *www.tirol.com/filmfest-st-anton*), which shows some of the old features alongside contemporary documentaries about alpine and adventure sports.

Into the mountains

St Anton itself isn't much more than a long strip of hotels, restaurants and boutiques (the central, pedestrianized portion of which is known as the Fussgängerzone), and there's little in the way of urban sights: it's the immense mountain ridges on either side that give the place its charm. If you want to just stretch your legs, it's easy enough to get up onto the lower slopes. Paths at the southwestern end of the main strip head uphill to the small **Heimatmseum** (20 June to 20 Sept daily except Weds 10am–6pm; mid-Dec to Easter Mon–Sat 3–10pm; öS30/€2.19), with a small display on traditional local crafts and the history of skiing housed in the so-called Arlberg-Kandahar Haus, a gaily painted wooden house built in 1912. Head for the crazy-golf course behind the museum to find a path which ascends (steeply in parts) alongside the **Mühltobelslucht**, a tiny wooded gorge, before emerging in the hillside suburb of Dengert. From here you can head for the *Sennhütte* café-restaurant just above; whose terrace commands invigorating views of the Rindl and Hoher Riffler peaks on the south

---

ST ANTON LIFT PASSES

The **Arlbergskipass** (valid for St Anton, St Christoph, Stuben, Lech, Zürs and Klosterle) is available from anything from half a day to the whole winter season. Sample high-season costs are öS485/€35.25 for 1 day; öS2410/€175.14 for 6 days; öS4220/€306.68 for 13 days. A 7-day pass limited to the St Anton and St Christoph lifts costs öS750/€54.50.

The equivalent summer 7-day **hiking pass** covers all St Anton lifts at a cost of öS390/€28.47 – or öS510/€37.23 with use of St Anton's indoor swimming pool thrown in.

---

side of the valley, or pick up lateral paths leading east along the hillside which offer superb, birds-eye views of St Anton.

There are numerous lifts and gondolas serving higher altitudes, creating an enormous interconnected skiing and hiking area. On the western side of town, the **Galzigbahn** (mid-July to late Sept & Dec–April; öS135/€9.86 return) rises to the 2185-metre **Galzig** (also served by a lift from St Christoph), where a two-stage cable car (same months; öS220/€16.06 return) continues upwards to the 2811m **Valluga**, passing through the 2650-metre **Vallugagrat** middle station en route. It's the extreme skiing territory on the slopes of the Valluga, especially the off-piste routes down the far side of the mountain to Zürs (see p.545), that attract the more experienced winter sportspeople. Slightly to the north of the Galzigbahn is the start of the **Gampenbahn** chairlift (early June to late Aug & Dec–April; öS125/€9.13 return) which ascends to the 1846-metre **Gampen** plateau, where there are several runs back down towards town, and a good spot for medium-altitude hikes in summer. The Gampen area is also served by the new **Nassereinbahn** gondola which departs from the eastern end of St Anton, and links up with the **Kapallbahn** chairlift to the 2330m **Kappal** (July–Sept & Dec–April; öS210/€15.33 return for the full Nassereinbahn–Kapallbahn trip), another departure point for ambitious downhill skiers. There's a snowboard funpark, with half-pipe, jumps and slides on the **Rendl**, just east of St Anton and also accessible by gondola.

Practicalities

St Anton's ultramodern **train station** (where buses also stop) is just south of the town centre, a short walk away from the **tourist office** at the western end of St Anton's Hauptstrasse (Mon–Fri 8am–noon & 2–6pm, Sat 9am–noon, Sun 10am–noon; ☎05446/22690, *www.stantonamarlberg.com*). They can point you in the right direction if you want to log on at one the several **Internet** places in town, help you find a **private room** (summer ②; winter ③) or check hotel vacancies; there's also a hotel information board and courtesy phone outside. In general, rooms are cheaper in the suburb of St Jakob which stretches for several kilometres to the east of St Anton, a much more rustic and evocative area in which to stay than the centre of town.

Among the cheaper of the **pensions** are *Tiroler Frieden*, St Anton 149 (☎05446/2247, *www.ski.arlberg.com/tiroler-frieden*; summer ①; winter ③), a simple place just east of central St Anton's Fussgängerzone with rooms sharing hall showers, and an English-speaking owner. Slightly further afield is *Haus Zauser*, St Jakob 149 (☎05446/2036, *haus-zauser@st-anton.at*; summer ②; winter ④), with cosy en-suite rooms set among fields at the far end of St Jakob, some 4km from town – although St Anton-Landeck buses (and ski-buses in season) pass nearby. Moving up in price, *Schindler*, St Anton 94 (☎05446/2207, *www.ski-arlber.com/schindler*; summer ③; winter ④) is a medium-size pension offering small en-suites with TV just west of the tourist office. The *Kaminstube am Moos*, St Anton 112 (☎05446/2681, *www.arlberg.com/kaminstube-am-moos*; summer ③; winter ⑦), is a modern **hotel** hovering above the valley in the mountain suburb of Moos, handy for après-ski venues such as the Mooserwirt and Krazy Kanguruh. Most characterful and luxurious place to stay in the centre is the 4-star *Alte Post* (☎05446/2553, *www.hotel-alte-post.at*; summer ⑧; winter ⑨).

Eating and drinking in St Anton is pretty expensive by Austrian standards, although cheaper options are never too hard to find. If you're spending a lot of time on the mountain, there are self-service restaurants and bars at the upper stations of all the main gondola routes. The *Panoramarestaurant* on the Galzig contains a reasonably priced pizza and pasta section, as well as the more expensive, à la carte *Verwallstube* in one wing. Among the more traditional mountain huts, the *Rodelalm*, just above town on the lower flanks of the Gampen, is the best place to sample traditional Tyrolean *Gröstl* dishes at prices that won't prove ruinous. Down in St Anton, both the *Arlberger Dorfbäckerei* and *Näh und Frisch*, roughly opposite each other in the Fussgängerzone, contain cheap stand-up snack bars where you can grab coffee and pastries during the daytime. Best of the sit-down **cafés** is the homely, pine-furnished *Häferl*, near the tourist office at St Anton 64a, which offers the full range of drinks as well as a tempting choice of sandwiches, soups, and strudels. The nearby *Café Schneider* in the Fussgängerzone, is more staid in style, but has the same range of food and drink at slightly cheaper prices. *Einkehr*, just east of the Fussgängerzone on the way to St Jakob, is as good a place as any to sample the standard Austrian repertoire of schnitzels and roast meats; while the more expensive *Montjola* (☎05446/2302), uphill to the west of the tourist office at St Anton 175 (signed off Alter Arlbergstrasse), attracts discerning diners with its fondue specialities.

In winter, **après-ski** begins on the upper slopes in mid-afternoon and gradually moves down to the valley below. Two semi-legendary places high above town in the mountainside suburb of Moos are *Krazy Kanguruh* and *Mooserwirt*, both of which attract a hedonistic, youngish crowd and can be relied upon to generate a party atmosphere any night of the week. Down in the centre, *Bobo's*, in the basement of the Kristall hotel at Fussgängerzone 45, is a big, raucous subterranean bar which also does decent burger-type food; while the *Piccadilly Pub*, on the Hauptstrasse, and *Underground*, a block away to the southeast, do a roaring trade in winter and are likely to be open for at least a couple of months in summer as well.

Northwestern Tyrol: Ehrwald, Reutte and around

The **northwestern Tyrol** lies cut off from the Inn Valley by the Lechtaler Alpen, and presents an alpine environment subtly different to the deep mountain valleys to the south. The lush, open vale of the **Lech Valley** around the market town of **Reutte** makes for a pleasant stop-off en route to the German border just to the north, while the Ehrwald region, a basin of pasture land presided over by the jagged grey mass of the Zugspitze, presents one of the most dramatic landscapes in the Tyrol. **Ehrwald** itself is the main centre to aim for here, the neighbouring villages of **Lermoos** and **Biberwier** being little more than its package-resort satellites.

The easiest way to get to northwestern Tyrol from the Inn Valley is by train from Innsbruck, although there's also a road over the mountains from Imst (served by buses from either Innsbruck or Imst), which passes through the village of **Nassereith** before climbing over the scenic **Fern Pass**. Nassereith itself doesn't merit a stop, and it's best to press on to **Schloss Fernsteinsee**, the local beauty spot 7km north, where there's an attractive little lake fringed by woods and mountains, a Gasthof with a good (if often busy) restaurant, and a **campsite** (May–Sept). The 1216-metre-high summit of the Fern Pass is only 2km beyond, after which it's only a short distance to the *Gasthof Zugspitzeblick*, site of another roadside restaurant and a marvellous view of the 2964m **Zugspitze**, which rears up dramatically from the valley floor like a cluster of unearthly

EHRWALD ACTIVITIES

Bike rental *Intersport*, Kirchplatz 13 (☎05673/2371), and *Zweirad Zirknitzer*, Zugspitzstrasse 16 (☎05673/3219), both offer a range of mountain bikes for around öS220–250/€16.06–18.25 per day. The tourist office organizes a range of mountain bike tours from öS400/€29.20 per person.

Hiking A selection of hiking trips with local guides (including easier walks for families with children) are organized by Ehrwald tourist office from around öS180/€13.14 per participant for easy hikes, öS250/€18.25 for more demanding ones (the latter are well worth considering if you want to attempt mountain paths that you wouldn't try on your own). They're run in conjunction with *Bergsport Total*, Kirchplatz 12 (☎05673/3461), who also provide guides for mountaineering expeditions. A couple of local guides offer llama trekking (a day-trip in the mountains with the incongruous beasts serving as baggage-carriers); contact the tourist office for details. In winter, ask the tourist office for a list of snow-cleared paths.

Paragliding Contact *Bergwanderschule Zugspitze*, Unterdorf 23, Lermoos (☎05673/3474).

Rafting *Bergsport Total* (see under "Hiking" above) or Ehrwald tourist office have details of rafting excursions (from öS550/€40.15 per trip) to either the Lech Valley to the west, or the Inn Valley to the south.

Riding *Pension Müllerhof*, Biberwier (☎05673/2344), offer a range of guided treks throughout the summer.

Rock climbing The Zugspitze region holds rock-climbing routes for all grades of ability. *Bergsport Total* (see under "Hiking" above) have details, and also offer equipment hire and guided climbs.

Swimming The indoor pool at Familienbad Ehrwald, Hauptstrasse 71 (daily 10am–8pm; öS60/€4.38; ☎05673/2718), features a children's area, water chutes, sauna and gym.

Tennis Indoor courts are available at *Zugspitz-Tennishalle*, Ehrwald (daily 8am–11pm; hourly rates start at öS120/€8.76; ☎05673/3135).

molar teeth. After a steep descent, a minor road heads off for the resort villages of Biberwier and Ehrwald, while the main road continues via tunnel to Lermoos and Reutte.

Ehrwald

Couched in the shadow of the Zugspitze and ringed by a series of similarly rugged mountains, **EHRWALD** is a resort village favoured by German and Dutch tourists, which nevertheless retains a rustic, unhurried atmosphere. It's an excellent base for a range of outdoor activities: the main skiing regions are the **Ehrwalder Alm** immediately east of Ehrwald, the **Marienberg** just above Biberwier, the **Grubigstein** above Lermoos, and the **Zugspitzplatt** below the summit of the Zugspitze – which, despite being on the German side of the border, is accessible from the Austrian side via the Tiroler Zugspitzbahn cable car and is included in some of the local **ski passes**. Best of these is the Happy Ski Pass (at the time of writing, there's no summer equivalent for hikers), which covers the Ehrwald region as well as Seefeld and the German town of Garmisch-Partenkirchen. The Pass costs öS1030/€75.19 for 3 days, öS1920/€140.16 for 6 days, and öS3230/€235.79 for 13 days – other durations are available. A one-day pass for the Zugspitze on its own weighs in at öS443/€32.34. There are good nursery slopes just outside Lermoos, a range of intermediate runs on the Zugspitzplatt, and plenty of cross-country skiing tracks in the valley floor.

One of the best times to be in Ehrwald is **Midsummer's Night** (known here as *Bergfeuer*, or "mountain fire"), when bonfires are lit on the mountains ringing the valley.

Into the mountains

Highlight of any trip to Ehrwald is the cable-car ascent of the **Zugspitze**, the inhospitable 2968-metre peak marking the Austro-German border. Buses (5–6 daily) run from Ehrwald's central Kirchplatz to the terminus of the **Tiroler Zugspitzbahn** cable car at **Obermoos**, 5km northeast of town (May–Oct & Dec–Easter; öS420/€30.66 return; *www.zugspitze.com*). Once on top you're treated to spectacular alpine views, with jagged lines of peaks arrayed to the south, and Bavarian lowlands to the north. In summer, Ehrwald tourist office organizes a guided walk up the Zugspitze (a 6hr ascent which shouldn't be tackled by the inexperienced), as well as a medium-difficulty descent of the mountain (6hr) using the route known locally as the **Gatterl**. The higher sections of the latter walk are icy throughout the year, but it's worth considering if you're reasonably fit.

Less spectacular than the Zugspitze, but providing access to a wider range of easy hikes, is the **gondola** to the **Ehrwalder Alm** (May–Oct & Dec–April; öS130/€9.49 return), which starts about 1km east of Ehrwald's Kirchplatz. There are numerous trails leading across the alpine meadows at the top, most popular of which is the one-hour walk along a gravel track to the **Seebenalm** to the southwest. Just above the Seebenalm hut is the small mountain lake, the **Seebensee**, the south end of which provides a classic view back towards the Zugspitze – the kind of vista that repeatedly crops up in alpine calendars.

Practicalities

Ehrwald's **train station** is at the northern end of the village about 1km from the centre, while **buses**, more conveniently, drop passengers on the central Kirchplatz, a few steps away from the **tourist office** at Kirchplatz 1 (Mon–Sat 8.30am–noon & 1–6pm; ☎05673/20000, *www.zugspitzarena.com*). Ask at the tourist office about booking one of the plentiful **private rooms** (summer ①; winter ②) or **pensions** (summer ②; winter ③). Of the numerous **hotels**, *Grüner Baum*, Kirchplatz (☎05673/2303, *www.tirol.com/gruener-baum*; ⑤), is comfortable and modern with smallish, balconied rooms, while the *Alpin*, Hauptstrasse 29 (☎05673/2279, *www.hotel-alpin.at*; ④), offers modern rooms, with en-suite facilities and TV, which are heated by traditional *Kachelofen* ceramic stoves.

You shouldn't need to stray too far from Kirchplatz to find decent **food**. For an inexpensive meal, *Pizzeria Al Castagno*, Kirchplatz 22, is the best of the Italians. The restaurant of the *Grüner Baum* has a good range of standard Austrian cuisine, and the *Tiroler Stub'n* in the *Hotel Sonnenspitze* on Kirchplatz has a marginally better choice of traditional Tyrolean dishes. The *Holzerstube*, just off Kirchplatz on Schulweg (☎05673/3323), is the best restaurant in town with an Austrian/international mix – reservations are advised. *Café-Bistro Rainer's* on Kirchplatz is a swanky bar-bistro offering toasted sandwiches, salads, and more pricey steaks – it's also a good place for a **drink**.

Reutte

Twenty-five kilometres northwest of Ehrwald, **REUTTE** is a pleasant enough market town, which grew rich on the profits of the salt trade between Hall in the Inn Valley and Bavaria to the north. There's not much to the town apart from one long street, which goes by the name of Untermarkt at the northern end and Obermarkt to the south. It's on Untermarkt that you'll find the most arresting edifice in town, the **Zeillerhaus**, once home to a prolific local family of painters. Paul Zeiller (1658–1738) lived there, and his son Johann-Jakob (1708–83) painted the swirling Baroque designs that adorn the outer walls. There are further reminders of the Zeiller family in the **Heimatmuseum** in the nearby Grünes Haus (May–Oct Tues–Sun 10am–noon & 2–5pm; öS40/€2.92), for the most part a very well-presented museum, even if the odd bits of weaponry and traditional wooden furniture on show fail to overwhelm. Highlight of the collection, the *Betrachtungsärgeln*, or "meditation-coffins" – 40cm high with model skeletons inside – were popular in the seventeenth and eighteenth centuries as a means of pondering the transience of earthly life. There's also a corner devoted to local man and forgotten genius **Peter Singer** (1810–82), inventor of the *Pansymphonikon*, a curious piano-type instrument with two keyboards and a wide register of sounds – although sadly, the museum doesn't possess an example.

Practicalities

Reutte's **train station** is at the northern end of town; from the main exit, walk straight ahead to reach the **tourist office** five minutes' away on the corner of Bahnhofstrasse and Untermarkt (Mon–Fri 8am–noon & 2–6pm, Sat 8am–noon; ☎05672/62336, *www.ferienregion-reutte.at*). They can fix you up with a **private room** (①), most of which are located east of the centre in the hillside suburbs of Breitenwang and Mühl. For a choice of decent **hotels,** you need look no further than Reutte's main street: the *Schwarzer Adler*, Obermarkt 75 (☎05672/62504; ③), has simple, unadorned rooms, all with en-suite facilities. Moving slightly upmarket, *Hotel-Garni Beck*, Untermarkt 11 (☎05672/62522, *www.tiscover.com/das.beck*; ③), is a nicely priced source of bright rooms with en-suite facilities, and the four-star *Gasthof zum Mohren*, Untermarkt 26 (☎05672/62345, *www.hotel-mohren.at*; ④), offers plush, comfortable quarters with en-suite facilities and TV, and some superb four-bed family rooms.

For **eating**, the restaurant of *Gasthof zum Mohren* (see above) has the best range of Tyrolean food in town, as well as more expensive schnitzels and steaks – the *Goldener Hirsch* , Mühlerstrasse 1, runs a close second. A good daytime **drinking** venue is the café of *Hotel-Garni Beck* (see above), which also serves excellent pastries in a plant-filled room on the first floor. Night-time hot spots include *Bräu Haus*, Untermarkt 7a, a roomy drinking den set back 30m from the main road, and *Jedermann Stehbeisl*, Lindenstrasse 1, a lively pub catering for a twenty-to-thirty-something crowd.

travel details

Trains

Achensee to: Jenbach (June–Sept: 7 daily; 45min; May & Oct: 3 daily; 45min).

Brixlegg to: Innsbruck (20 daily; 40min); Kufstein (18 daily; 30min).

Hall to: Fritzens-Wattens (20 daily; 8min); Innsbruck (20 daily; 8min); Schwaz (20 daily; 20min).

Innsbruck to: Bregenz (8 daily; 2hr 40min); Brixlegg (20 daily; 40min); Ehrwald (7 daily; 1hr 50min); Fritzens-Wattens (20 daily; 16min); Graz (3 daily; 6hr 15min); Hall (20 daily; 8min); Imst-Pitztal (hourly; 40min–1hr); Jenbach (every 30min; 20–35min); Kitzbühel (10 daily; 1hr 10min); Kufstein (every 30min; 45min–1hr 10min); Landeck (hourly; 45min–1hr 35min); Lermoos (7 daily; 2hr); Ötztal (hourly; 30–50min); Rattenberg (16 daily; 45min); Reutte (7 daily; 2hr 30min); St Anton (hourly; 1hr 30min); Salzburg via Bischofshofen (5 daily; 3hr 40min); Salzburg via Kufstein (7 daily; 2hr); Schwaz (20 daily; 27min); Seefeld (10 daily; 35min); Stams (hourly; 35min); Vienna via Bischofshofen (4 daily; 7hr 10min); Vienna via Kufstein (6 daily; 5hr 15min); Villach (1 daily; 4hr 10min); Wörgl (every 30min; 35–55min).

Jenbach to: Achensee (June–Sept: 7 daily; 45min; May & Oct: 3 daily; 45min); Innsbruck (every 30min; 20–35min); Mayrhofen (12 daily; 1hr); Zell am Ziller (12 daily; 45min).

Kitzbühel to: Graz (3 daily; 5hr 5min); Innsbruck (10 daily; 1hr 10min); Kirchberg in Tirol (hourly; 10min); St Johann in Tirol (hourly; 10min); Salzburg (11 daily; 2hr 30min–3hr 10min); Vienna (4 daily; 6hr); Wörgl (26 daily; 30min).

Kufstein to: Brixlegg (18 daily; 30min); Innsbruck (every 30min; 45min–1hr 10min); Rattenberg (16 daily; 25min); Salzburg (7 daily; 1hr 15min); Wörgl (20 daily; 15min).

Mayrhofen to: Jenbach (12 daily; 1hr); Zell am Ziller (12 daily; 15min).

Schwaz to: Fritzens-Wattens (20 daily; 10min); Hall (20 daily; 20min); Innsbruck (20 daily; 27min).

Wörgl to: Innsbruck (every 30min; 35–55min); Kitzbühel (26 daily; 30min); Kufstein (20 daily; 15min).

Buses

Axams to: Axamer Lizum (winter & summer only; 6 daily; 20min).

Bahnhof Ötztal to: Hochgurgl (1 daily; 1hr 50min); Obergurgl (8 daily; 1hr 25min); Sölden (9 daily; 1hr 5min); Untergurgl (8 daily; 1hr 15min); Zwieselstein (9 daily; 1hr 10min).

Brixlegg to: Alpbach (10 daily; 30min).

Ehrwald to: Innsbruck (6 daily; 1hr 50min); Lermoos (hourly; 10min); Reutte (hourly; 40min).

Hall to: Tulfes (8 daily; 20min).

Imst to: Landeck (8 daily; 30min); Nassereith (8 daily; 20min).

Innsbruck to: Axams (hourly; 25min); Ehrwald (6 daily; 1hr 50min); Igls (8 daily; 15min); Lermoos (6 daily; 2hr); Nassereith (6 daily; 1hr 15min); Patsch (8 daily; 25min); Reutte (6 daily; 2hr 30min); Tulfes (8 daily; 40min).

Jenbach to: Achenkirch (6 daily; 25min); Maurach (6 daily; 45min).

Kitzbühel to: Ellmau (4 daily; 40min); Jochberg (10 daily; 20min); Mittersill (6 daily; 50min).

Kufstein to: Ebbs (12 daily; 15min); Ellmau (8 daily; 50min); St Johann in Tirol (8 daily; 1hr 15min); Scheffau (8 daily; 40min); Söll (10 daily; 25min); Thiersee (9 daily; 15min).

Landeck to: Fiss (6 daily; 45min); Galtür (12 daily; 1hr 5min); Imst (8 daily; 30min); Ischgl (12 daily; 45min); Ladis (6 daily; 35min); Nauders (7 daily;

1hr 5min); Pfunds (7 daily; 45min); Prutz (hourly; 20min); St Anton (Mon–Fri 12 daily; Sat 9 daily; Sun 4 daily; 50min); Serfaus (6 daily; 1hr).

Mayrhofen to: Brandberg (8 daily; 15min); Gerloss Pass (5 daily; 50min); Hintertux (8 daily; 45min); Krimml (5 daily; 1hr 35min); Schlegeis Stausee (8 daily; 50min); Stillupgrund *Gasthof Wasserfälle* (5 daily; 25min); Stillupgrund *Grüne-Wand-Hütte* (3 daily; 45min); Zillergrund Stausee (4 daily; 55min).

Nassereith to: Ehrwald (6 daily; 35min); Imst (8 daily; 20min); Innsbruck (6 daily; 1hr 15min); Lermoos (6 daily; 45min); Reutte (6 daily; 1hr 15min).

Prutz to: the Weissee Glacier (2 daily; 1hr 10min).

Reutte to: Ehrwald (hourly; 40min); Elbigenalp (3 daily; 1hr); Innsbruck (6 daily; 2hr 30min); Lech (summer only: 2 daily; 2hr 10min); Lermoos (hourly; 30min); Warth (2 daily; 1hr 45min).

St Anton to: Flirsch (hourly; 20min); Landeck (hourly; 50min); Rauzalpe (7 daily; 15min); St Christoph (7 daily; 12min).

St Johann in Tirol to: Ellmau (8 daily; 25min); Kufstein (8 daily; 1hr 15min); Scheffau (8 daily; 35min); Söll (8 daily; 50min).

Schwaz to: Pill (hourly; 5min); Schloss Tratzberg (10 daily; 15min); Stans (12 daily; 10min).

Sölden to: Bahnhof Ötztal (9 daily; 1hr 5min); Hochgurgl (2 daily; 45min); Obergurgl (8 daily; 20min); Tiefenbach Glacier (4 daily; 50min); Untergurgl (8 daily; 10min); Vent (5 daily; 40min); Zwieselstein (9 daily; 5min).

Söll to: Ellmau (14 daily; 25min); Kufstein (10 daily; 25min); St Johann in Tirol (8 daily; 50min); Scheffau (14 daily; 15min); Wörgl (5 daily; 30min).

Wörgl to: Auffach (8 daily; 45min); Ellmau (4 daily; 55min); Niederau (8 daily; 25min); Oberau (8 daily; 35min); Scheffau (4 daily; 45min); Söll (5 daily; 30min).

International trains

Innsbruck to: Belgrade (1 daily; 15hr 30min); Brussels (1 daily; 14hr); Cologne (5 daily; 8hr); Florence (2 daily; 7hr 30min); Ljubljana (3 daily; 6hr 30min); Milan (2 daily; 5hr 30min); Munich–Innsbruck (8 daily; 2hr); Rome (2 daily; 8hr 30min); Venice (1 daily; 5hr); Zagreb (3 daily; 9hr); Zurich (4 daily; 4hr).

CHAPTER TEN

THE VORARLBERG

Despite falling under Habsburg control as early as the thirteenth century, Austria's westernmost province, the **Vorarlberg** (*www.vol.at/tourismus*) has always led a life slightly separate from the rest of the country. This was largely a matter of plain geography: bounded by the **Arlberg** mountain range to the east and the **Rätikon** massif to the south, communication with the rest of Austria was for centuries less than easy. Only with the construction of the Arlbergstrasse highway by Emperor Josef II in the late eighteenth century was the region properly integrated with its eastern neighbours.

Culturally and economically, the Vorarlberg has repeatedly looked towards Switzerland and southern Germany. Like the inhabitants of northern Switzerland, the Vorarlbergers are descended from the **Aleman tribes** who swept through the region during the great migrations of the sixth century AD, and to this day they speak a dialect very close to Swiss German. Indeed, in November 1918 the Vorarlbergers went so far as to declare independence from Austria, seeking union with Switzerland – a request turned down by an international community who feared that any break-up of the infant Austrian state would leave the region prone to future German expansionism. Vorarlberger separatism no longer occupies a prime place on the political agenda, but locals are still likely to view Vienna, more than 600km to the east, as a distant irrelevance. Geographically nearer cities like Munich and Zurich exert greater cultural influence on the Vorarlberg than the Austrian capital does.

Close economic ties with Switzerland and a thriving local economy have ensured that the cost of living in the Vorarlberg is higher than in the rest of Austria. Visitors will find that hotels are more **expensive** here than elsewhere, and budget choices are hard to come by, but there are still plenty of good-value private rooms to be found outside the main urban centres. Restaurants, too, are more expensive, but culinary standards are so high, and international and French-influenced cuisine so greatly valued here, that it's usually well worth paying the extra money. However, archetypal peasant dishes, such as *Kässpätzle*, a combination of cheese and pasta noodles that is very much a local staple, still feature on all restaurant menus.

Shared between Germany, Austria and Switzerland and fed by the waters of the Rhine, the **Bodensee** (**Lake Constance** in English), at the northwestern edge of the province,

ACCOMMODATION PRICE CODES

All **hotels and pensions** in this book have been coded according to the following price categories. All the codes are based on the rate for the least expensive double room during the **summer season**. In those places where winter is the high season, we've indicated both summer and winter room rates in the text.

① under öS400/€29.07
② öS400–600/€29.07–43.60
③ öS600–800/€43.60–58.14
④ öS800–1000/€58.14–72.67
⑤ öS1000–1200/€72.67–87.21

⑥ öS1200–1400/€87.21–101.74
⑦ öS1400–1600/€101.74–116.28
⑧ öS1600–1800/€116.28–130.81
⑨ over öS1800/€130.81

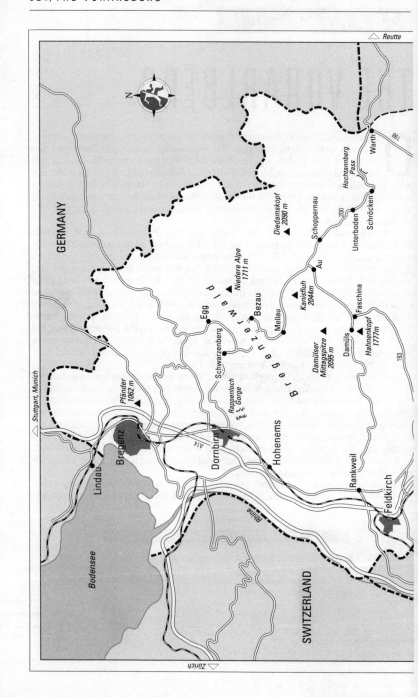

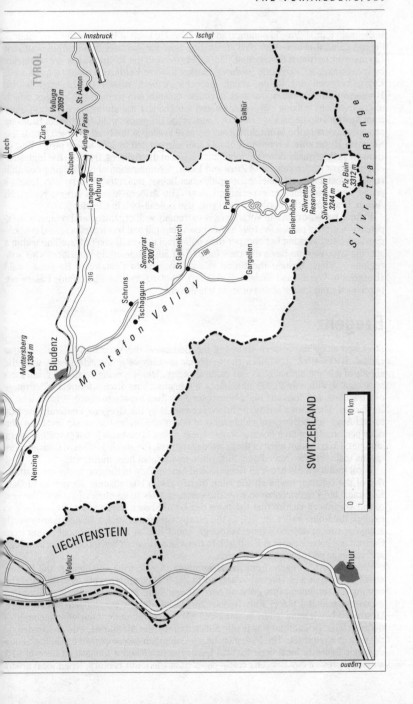

is the main tourist draw in summer, and the lakeside town of **Bregenz** the area's touristic and cultural centre – an obvious staging post for journeys to and from southern
Germany or northern Switzerland. The other towns of the **Rhine Valley** are workaday
by comparison, although the medieval market town of **Feldkirch** merits a quick visit.
Lying between the Rhine Valley and the Arlberg massif to the east is the
Bregenzerwald, an attractive area of rolling uplands and picturesque villages, which
offers excellent walking opportunities and a relaxing rural atmosphere a world away
from Austria's alpine package resorts. South of the Bregenzerwald, the town of **Bludenz**
provides access to the **Montafon**, a steeply sided valley at the head of which stands the
Silvretta Reservoir, a renowned beauty spot surrounded by lofty alpine peaks. East of
Bludenz is the equally dramatic mountain region of the **Arlberg**, home to the high-society, high-cost winter resorts of **Zürs** and **Lech**. A combination of challenging downhill
runs and extensive off-piste opportunities has helped make the Arlberg into Austria's
prime destination for the experienced skier. The Arlberg massif's largest resort, **St
Anton**, is just over the border in the Tyrol, and is dealt with in Chapter 9.

Public transport in the Vorarlberg is extremely well organized and relatively inexpensive, with day passes (öS160/€11.68) covering rail and bus travel across the whole
province often working out cheaper than individual tickets. If you're travelling within a
specific area, you can buy a day pass (öS100/€7.30) to one of the Vorarlberg's six sub-
regions – which include the Rhine valley (Bregenz to Feldkirch), Bregenzerwald
(Bregenz to Warth) and Walgau (Feldkirch, Bludenz and the Montafon). Passes are
purchased from train stations or from bus drivers.

Bregenz

Stretched along the eastern shores of the Bodensee, the Vorarlberg's administrative
capital, **BREGENZ**, combines the laid-back gentility of a lakeside resort with the
vigour of a booming business and cultural centre. Despite being relatively small for a
state capital, with only 25,000 inhabitants, it's an absorbing place offering a wider range
of attractions, activities and night-time diversions than anywhere else in Austria west of
Innsbruck. The town's artistic pedigree is ensured by the **Bregenz Festival** (late July
to late Aug), an extravagant celebration of opera and orchestral music involving outdoor performances on a floating stage, which draws in an extra 200,000 visitors every
summer. Even though most of these are day-trippers, the sudden influx of festival-goers
means that it can be exceedingly difficult to find a room here in August.

Local trains shuttle between Bregenz and Lindau 7km to the north, the most attractive of the German towns on the lake; there's also a lake-steamer service to Lindau,
Konstanz and Friedrichshaven over the summer. Good communications with the rest
of the Vorarlberg ensure that the town can be used as a touring base from which to
explore the Rhine Valley, as well as the nearby Bregenzerwald, a beautiful area worth
a day or two of anyone's time. Although about half of all international trains from
Switzerland enter Austria at Feldkirch to the south, Bregenz has its own excellent road
and rail links with Zurich and Munich.

Bregenz gets its name from the **Brigantes**, a Celtic tribe subdued by the Roman
armies of Drusus and Tiberius in around 15 BC. The conquerors placated the locals by
naming the settlement that grew up here "Brigantium" in their honour; it evolved into
a culturally mixed place, with Roman and Celtic deities worshipped side by side.
Destroyed by German tribes in about 260 AD but rebuilt under Diocletian a couple of
decades later, Brigantium was finally finished off by the **Alemanni**, who descended on
the area in around 450. The Irish missionary Columban (accompanied by Gallus, another major figure in local ecclesiastical history) established a monastery here in 610,
although present-day Bregenz really dates from the tenth century, when local aristo-

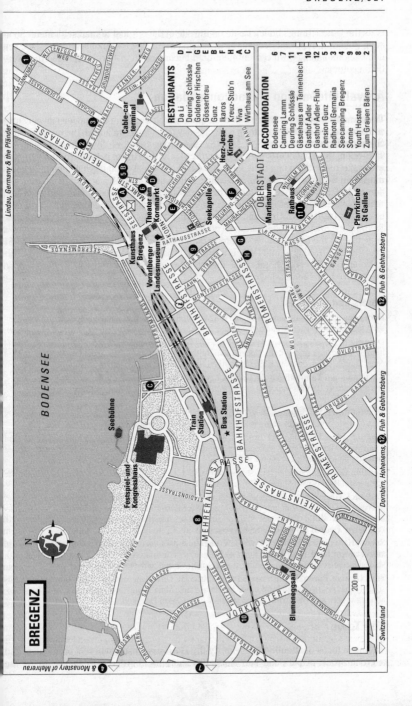

BREGENZ

BODENSEE

Lindau, Germany & the Pfänder

& Monastery of Mehrerau

Switzerland

Dornbirn, Hohenems, 12, Fluh & Gebhartsberg

12, Fluh & Gebhartsberg

N

200 m

RESTAURANTS

Da Li	D
Deuring Schlössle	I
Goldener Hirschen	G
Gösserbrau	E
Gunz	B
Ikaros	F
Kreuz-Stüb'n	H
Viva	A
Wirthaus am See	C

ACCOMMODATION

Bodensee	6
Camping Lamm	7
Deuring Schlössle	11
Gästehaus am Tannenbach	1
Gasthof Adler	10
Gasthof Adler-Fluh	12
Pension Gunz	5
Radhotel Germania	3
Seecamping Bregenz	4
Sonne	9
Youth Hostel	8
Zum Grauen Bären	2

Cable-car terminal

Herz-Jesu-Kirche

Kunsthaus Bregenz

Vorarlberger Landesmuseum

Theater am Kornmarkt

Seekapelle

OBERSTADT

Martinsturm

Rathaus

Pfarrkirche St Gallus

Seebühne

Festspiel-und Kongresshaus

Train Station

Bus Station

Blumeneggsaal

crats the Udalrichungs built a castle on the site of the original Roman settlement. Soon after, Feldkirch replaced Bregenz as the region's strategic focal point, and the place settled back into small-town contentment until becoming Vorarlberg's capital in the twentieth century.

Arrival, information and accommodation

Train and **bus stations** are next to each other on the fringes of the modern town centre at the western end of the lakefront park, an easy five-minute walk from the **tourist office** at Bahnhofstrasse 14 (July–Sept Mon–Sat 9am–7pm; Oct–June Mon–Fri 9am–6pm, Sat 9am–noon; ☎05574/4959-0, *www.bregenz.at*), which has a list of **private rooms** (②), and will make reservations for a fee of öS30/€1.46. An excellent budget choice of **accommodation** well worth reserving in advance is the **youth hostel**, just west of the train station at Mehrerauerstrasse 5 (cross to the northern side of the tracks and turn left; ☎05574/42867, *bregenz@jgh.at*), which offers en-suite singles (öS250/€18.25) and doubles (①), as well as beds in 4- and 6-person dorms. The best of Bregenz's four **campsites**, *Seecamping Bregenz*, Bodengasse 7 (☎05574/71896; mid-May to mid-Sept), occupies a large site by the lake, 3km west of town, while *Camping Lamm*, Mehrerauerstrasse 51 (☎05574/71701; May to mid-Oct), is a smaller, urban site 1.5km west of the centre.

Note: some Bregenz hotels raise their prices outrageously in the festival season, so be prepared for sudden fluctuations.

Hotels and pensions

Bodensee, Kornmarktstrasse 22 (☎05574/42300-0). Best of the mid-range choices, with TV and en-suite facilities in all rooms, and a good-value breakfast buffet. Festival season (⑧); rest of year (④).

Deuring Schlössle, Ehre-Guta-Platz 4 (☎05574/47800, *deuring@schloessle.vol.at*). Luxurious hotel housed in a former castle in the Upper Town. Atmospheric, *objet-d'art*-furnished rooms with all mod cons. Doubles from öS1850/€135.05; from öS2400/€175.20 in the festival season. (⑨)

Gästehaus am Tannenbach, Im Gehren 1 (☎05574/44174). Best of the smaller B&B-style places, in a quiet street 10min's walk east of the centre. Closed Oct–April. Rooms with shared facilities (③), en-suites (④).

Gasthof Adler, Vorklostergasse 66 (☎05574/71788). A basic, inexpensive guesthouse a 15min walk west of town. Some rooms come with en-suite shower (③), others have shared facilities. (②).

Gasthof Adler-Fluh, Fluh 11 (☎05574/44872). Country-style inn in Fluh, a hillside hamlet 4km southwest of town. A lovely place to stay if you have your own transport. Cosy rooms with shared facilities, plus some bigger rooms with en-suite bathrooms. Festival season (④); rest of year (③).

Pension Gunz, Anton-Schneider-Strasse 38 (☎05574/43657). Cheap and basic stand-by, bang in the city centre. Rooms with showers (②), rooms with showers and WC (③).

Radhotel Germania, Am Steinenbach 9 (☎05574/42766-0, *www.bregenz.at/germania*). A good international business-standard hotel with all the creature comforts. Also pitches itself as a bicycle-friendly hotel, with a cycle repair shop on site. Houses a swish restaurant with a growing gourmet reputation. Festival season (⑨); rest of year (⑥).

Sonne, Kaiserstrasse 8 (☎05574/42572, *www.bregenz.at/sonne*). Simple but comfortable pension in an apartment block right in the heart of Bregenz's pedestrianized shopping district. Rooms with shared facilities (③), or with en-suite showers (④). Closed mid–Dec to mid–April.

Zum Grauen Bären, Reichsstrasse 8 (☎05574/42823). On a main road and a bit noisy, but it's a reasonably inexpensive stand-by if other hotels are full. Most rooms are plush en-suite affairs (④), although there are a few with shared facilities (③). Closed Dec–Feb.

The Town

The main focus of attention is obviously the **Bodensee** itself, where a promenade and a green swath of parkland run along the shoreline, bordered to the south by the

Germany-bound railway line that follows the curve of the lake. Just inland from the park is the modern town centre, or **Innenstadt**, an area of mostly nineteenth- and twentieth-century construction, which holds the bulk of Bregenz's commercial and shopping activity. A more tranquil atmosphere reigns in the **Altstadt**, or **Oberstadt**, on the hill above, where much of the older architecture is concentrated.

The lakefront

The leafy parklands and well-tended flowerbeds that line the **lakefront** are frequented by promenading visitors and locals alike, who've come to savour the impressive views towards the German side of the lake. At the western end of the park stands the **Festspiel- und Kongresshaus**, built in 1980 primarily to accommodate the operatic and orchestral concerts of the Bregenz Festival, although cultural events and exhibitions are held here all year round. Moored outside the Kongresshaus is the **Seebühne**, or sea stage, a floating platform on which the festival's most prestigious performances are held. Seating for 6000 people is provided on the landward side.

West of the Kongresshaus, Strandweg continues along the lakeshore, passing summer bathing areas, open-air swimming pools and a marina before arriving, after about half an hour's walk, at the former Cistercian **monastery of Mehrerau**. The monastery buildings now serve as a school, and the church was rebuilt in 1962 in stark, angular style. Inside the church, however, a wealth of Gothic altarpieces serves as a reminder of the monastery's heyday – their vibrant colours in dramatic contrast to the grey concrete of the interior. The winged high altar alone, painted around 1500 and showing the Crucifixion and Deposition, is striking enough to make the walk here worthwhile.

The Innenstadt

Lying on the landward side of the main road and rail lines that run parallel to the shore, Bregenz's **Innenstadt** presents an unabashedly modern face to the manicured lawns of the lakefront. Guarding the entrance to the town between Seestrasse and Kornmarkt is the **Kunsthaus Bregenz** (known as "KUB" for short; Tues–Sun 10am–6pm, Thurs till 9pm; prices vary; *www.kunsthaus-bregenz.at*), a cube of green-hued glass by the Swiss master Peter Zumthor, completed in 1997 to provide a venue for high-profile contemporary art exhibitions. Expressly intended as a statement of the town's attachment to modern architecture, it's a cooly functional piece of work. Inside, undressed concrete walls and semi-opaque ceiling panels present an austere, but effective backdrop to whatever is on display.

Just behind the Kunsthaus at Kornmarkt 1, the **Vorarlberger Landesmuseum** (Tues–Sun 9am–noon & 2–5pm; öS20/€1.46; *www.vlm.at*) provides an engaging survey of the province's history and folk culture. The first floor presents a fairly routine trot through Stone, Bronze and Iron ages, but things liven up by the time you get to Roman Brigantium, the first-century settlement situated to the west of the modern town centre. There's a model of the Roman town, fragments of mosaics, and a fine sandstone relief of the Romano-Celtic goddess Epona, who, as the patron of equine stock breeding, is always depicted riding a horse. The museum's second floor concentrates on folk crafts, with a range of wooden house interiors and a selection of Vorarlberg costumes. Worth noting here is the range of different hats on display, highlighting the fact that each region within the Vorarlberg has long cultivated its own distinctive customs: women of the Grosses Walsertal swanned around in the bloated, puffball-shaped *Pelzbummera*, while Montafon ladies preferred the *Mässli*, a tall black cylinder capped by a fringe of wool.

The art collection on the third floor is particularly strong on the late-Gothic art plucked from the region's churches. Fifteenth-century Feldkirch painters **Moritz and Jörg Frosch** are represented with a series of *Totentafeln*, or memorial pictures, which usually show some deceased local bigwig kneeling in prayer below a picture of Christ or some other saintly figure, surrounded by family. Another Feldkirch luminary, **Wolf Huber**, is represented by a panel from his St Anne altar, which shows scenes from the life of Christ on the back, and St Joachim and St Anne ascending towards heaven on the front. Also on this floor is a corner devoted to local heroine **Angelika Kauffmann**, the Bregenzerwald craftsman's daughter who became a celebrated painter in late-eighteenth-century London (see p.537). Athough her portrait of the Duke of Wellington is probably the best-known work here, her taste for big narrative themes is revealed in mythological subjects, such as the atmospheric *Death of Alcestis*.

Rathausstrasse leads from the museum into the downtown shopping area, a partly pedestrianized zone grouped around the streets of Deuringstrasse, Maurachgasse and Leutbühel. At the junction of Rathausstrasse and Anton-Schneider-Strasse stands the **Seekapelle**, whose gloomy interior harbours an impressive seventeenth-century altar. A left turn from Deuringstrasse into Belruptstrasse leads to the more interesting **Herz-Jesu-Kirche**, a twentieth-century neo-Gothic affair, which features some wonderfully expressive stained glass designed in the 1950s by **Martin Häusle**. His scenes from Jesus's parables run along the north side of the nave, while Old Testament stories (such as Cain slaying Abel, Noah offering a sacrifice after surviving the Flood) are ranged along the opposite wall.

The Altstadt

Maurachgasse climbs away from the modern centre towards the **Martinstor**, a fortified gateway that once guarded the entrance to the medieval town. Just around the corner is **Martinsturm**, a medieval tower to which a bulbous wooden dome was added sometime around 1700 and has been a bit of a town landmark ever since. Inside the tower, a small **museum** displays armour and weaponry (May–Sept Tues–Sun 9am–6pm; öS30/€2.19), and there's a chance to enjoy views down towards the lake. The medieval granaries next door were converted into a chapel in the fourteenth century, and frescoes from the period include several figures of Christ and St George. Just up the street from here stands the seventeenth-century **Rathaus** (now a residential building), an imposing half-timbered construction that looks like something out of a medieval fairy tale.

Dominating a hillock 300m to the south, the **Pfarrkirche St Gallus** is believed to stand on the site of a chapel built by Irish missionaries Gallus and Columban in the seventh century. The current edifice is the usual mixture of Gothic basics (the main body of the church is fourteenth-century) and Baroque add-ons, remarkable primarily for the excesses of its stuccoed ceiling, across which cherubs vie for space with abstract patterns in pastel greens and pinks. The high altar features statues of four saints: St Gallus, the one on the extreme right, is here depicted in the company of a small bear, which, according to folklore, was the saint's companion during his wanderings.

The Pfänder and the Gebhartsberg

The most popular local excursion is to the **Pfänder**, a 1062-metre-high peak just northeast of town commanding an excellent panorama of the lake. Served by a cable car from the northern end of Belruptstrasse (daily: May–Sept 9am–7pm; Oct–April 9am–6pm; closed for at least two weeks in November; öS70/€5.11 one way; öS125/€9.13 return; *www.pfaenderbahn.at*), the Pfänder can also be reached by car by taking the Lindau road and turning right at **Lochau**, the last Austrian settlement before the German frontier. At the summit, there are four Gasthöfe within a two-hundred-metre radius offering food and drink, and a **wildlife park** (free), where Vietnamese pot-bellied pigs and

Central African goats rub shoulders with more customary denizens of central Europe such as deer, wild boar and *Mürmeltiere* (alpine marmots).

Several walks radiate outwards from the cable-car terminus, one of the most popular being the two-hour descent into Bregenz itself. Another offers a more gentle descent southwards to the attractive village of **Fluh** (1hr 30min), before heading west to the wooded ridge of the **Gebhartsberg** (40min), former site of the medieval fortress of **Hohenbregenz**. There's little to see of the castle nowadays, except for the pilgrimage chapel of St Gebhard, honouring the tenth-century nobleman's son who is thought to have been born in the fortress. Events from St Gebhard's not particularly dramatic life (relinquishing his inheritance and entering the priesthood, he rose to become bishop of Constance) feature in a cycle of nineteenth-century paintings inside the church. But most people come here to enjoy the spectacular panorama of the Bodensee and the Rhine Valley, or eat in the *Gasthof Greber* next door to the church, which serves top-quality food at fairly expensive prices, but has a good view from the terrace. Pathways descend from here to the western suburbs of Bregenz (1hr), from where you can make your own way back to the lakefront in fifteen minutes or so.

Eating and drinking

High prices in Bregenz restaurants reflect both the high local cost of living and the constant influx of well-heeled tourists, but standards here are generally outstanding, and budget choices never impossible to find. For drinking, you won't have to venture much beyond the modern town centre just inland from the lakefront.

Restaurants

Da Li, Anton-Schneider-Strasse 34. Serviceable if unexciting Chinese restaurant, though the lunchtime Mittagsmenü (usually from öS70/€5.11) is excellent value.

Deuringschlössle, Ehre-Guta-Platz 4 (☎05574/47800). Inventive mix of Austrian and international cuisine in what is one of the country's leading restaurants, with main courses exceeding öS300/€21.90. Reserve in advance.

Gasthof Adler-Fluh, Fluh 11 (☎05574/44872). Popular out-of-town restaurant in the chic village suburb of Fluh, offering expertly prepared variations on basic Austrian and Vorarlberg cuisine. Nice outdoor terrace. It's easy to get to if you have your own transport – head out of town along Römerstrasse; otherwise you'll have to take a taxi.

Goldener Hirschen, Kirchstrasse 8. An atmospheric old inn with chunky wooden furnishings, a jovial, pub-like atmosphere and stolid Austrian fare. A nice place for a drink, too.

Gösserbrau, Anton-Schneider-Strasse 1. Enduringly popular venue with something of a split personality. You can taste standard Austrian fare in the tastefully wood-panelled rooms of the main restaurant, or sup beers and munch snacks in the adjoining *rap-sak* bar, which, in contrast, looks like the set of a Sixties' sci-fi film.

Gunz, Anton-Schneider-Strasse 38. Probably the cheapest source of traditional Austrian food in town, with main courses (such as *Vorarlberger Kässpätzle*, a local variation on the noodles and cheese sauce combination) from öS90/€6.57.

Ikaros, Deuringstrasse 5. Greek restaurant with a convenient central location, informal café feel, and cheap lunchtime specials.

Kreuz-Stüb'n, Römerstrasse 5. Standard choice of Austrian food, plus local favourites like *Kässpätzle*, in the rather elegant dining room of the *Wisses Kreuz* hotel. Moderately priced.

Viva, Seestrasse 7. Excellent and popular – if slightly pricey – Mexican restaurant with the expected range of central American eats. The bar at the rear attracts a youngish crowd with its wide range of cocktails, Austrian ales and bottled Mexican beers.

Wirtshaus am See, Seepromenade. Moderately expensive Austrian and regional cuisine in a half-timbered lakeside pavilion which used to serve as the club house for local yachtsmen; large and popular beer garden outside.

Cafés and bars

Ballhaus, Quellenstrasse 49. Large, modern bar with big outdoor terrace, especially busy on summer weekends. Open till 3am.

Cuba, Bahnhofstrasse. Two-storey café-bar built around an enormous chandelier, which serves as town-centre coffee house during the day, raucous Latin bar (with in-house DJ) at night.

Erste Akt, Kornmarktstrasse 24. Popular pub-style bar with relaxing, candlelit atmosphere and a limited range of snacks. Closed Sun.

Flexibel, Rathausstrasse 27. Chic and friendly bar in the town centre catering to a relaxed crowd ranging from young drinkers to affluent thirty-somethings.

Neubeck, Anton-Schneider-Strasse 5. Smartish bar with an extensive wine list, serving food right up until 1am. Closed Sun.

S'Logo, Kirchstrasse 47 (*www.slogo.at*). Roomy, minimalist bar and Internet café midway between the Innenstadt and the Pfarrkirche St Gallus. Live bands at weekends.

Entertainment

Bregenz is well served by high culture. Most musical events take place in the Fest- und Kongresshaus, which is also the venue for two major festivals. Running from late July to late August, the **Bregenzer Festspiele** (Bregenz Festival; *www.festspiele.com*) offers a top-notch programme of opera, involving dramatic outdoor performances on the Seebühne. Usually, a populist programme of familiar favourites (recent choices have included *Fidelio*, *Porgy and Bess* and *La Bohème*) takes place on the Seebühne, while a more challenging selection of rarely performed or "difficult" operas graces the smaller auditorium indoors. The **Bregenzer Frühling**, or "Bregenz Spring", featuring ballet and orchestral performances, takes place between late March and late April.

Theater am Kornmarkt, Kornmarktstrasse, is the place for classical (German-language) **theatre**, while Blumeneggsaal, Brosswaldengasse 23 (☎05574/43955), has occasional **jazz** concerts.

Details and **bookings** for all events save the Festspiele are available from the Bregenz tourist office (see p.528). For the Festspiele, contact the festival office (Postfach 311, A-6901 Bregenz; ☎05574/407-6) as early as possible before you intend to travel. Performances are often sold out as much as nine months in advance.

Listings

Bike rental At the train station.

Car rental Herz, Immler, Am Brand 2 (☎05574/44995).

Consulates Great Britain, 2km south of the centre at Bundesstrasse 110, Lauterach (☎05574/696207). Other nationals should contact their embassy in Vienna.

Exchange Raiffeisenbank, Kornmarktstrasse 14; Sparkasse, Rathausstrasse 29; Volksbank, Bahnhofstrasse 12.

Hospital Landeskrankenhaus, C-Pedenz-Strasse 2 (☎05574/401).

Police Bahnhofstrasse 43 (☎05574/420-21).

Post office, Seestrasse 5 (Mon–Sat 7am–7pm, Sun 9am–noon).

Taxis ☎05574/1718.

The Rhine Valley: Dornbirn to Feldkirch

The Rhine marks the frontier between Austria and Switzerland for 35km, before emptying into the Bodensee just west of Bregenz. The settlements on the Austrian side of the valley form a chain of prosperous, semi-industrialized communities broken up by rich, verdant farmland, dubbed the "garden of the Vorarlberg" by overeager tourist brochures. **Feldkirch**, with its well-preserved medieval centre, is the most worthwhile of the Rhine Valley towns to visit, although **Hohenems** and **Rankweil** both possess enough of historic interest to merit a brief stop-over. The main road and rail route from Bregenz links all these towns before wheeling eastwards towards the Arlberg Pass, ensuring that one or more of them could easily be visited from Bregenz as a day-trip. Twelve kilometres south of Bregenz lies the largely modern town of **DORNBIRN**, a textile manufacturing centre from which the Vorarlberg gained much of its nineteenth-century wealth. It's an important shopping destination for Rhine valley locals, but has little of tourist appeal save for the **Rappenlochschlucht** or Rappenloch Gorge 4km southeast of the centre, where the waters of the **Dornbirner Ache** rush down from the heights of the Bregenzerwald. An impressive series of cataracts and narrow defiles accessible by wooden walkway, it can be reached via the Dornbirn–Ebnit bus (4 daily from outside Dornbirn train station), or by the more frequent municipal bus #5 from Dornbirn's Rathausplatz to the Gütlestrasse terminus – although the latter involves a 2km walk to the gorge along Gütlestrasse.

Hohenems

Seven kilometres south of Dornbirn, the small town of **HOHENEMS** sits decoratively beneath the sheer cliffs of the **Schlossberg**, upon which stands the ruined stronghold of the Ems family. Important figures to the town's destiny since the thirteenth century, the Ems brood were extraordinarily well connected in sixteenth-century Catholic circles – Wolf Dietrich von Ems was a brother-in-law of the pope – and it was as prince-archbishop of Salzburg that Wolf Dietrich's son Marcus Sitticus von Ems began construction of the Renaissance **Schloss Hohenems**, which now dominates the town's main square, the Schlossplatz. Today, the Schloss is used for exhibitions, antique fairs and classical recitals, and it's difficult to gain admission outside these events. Marcus's brother Hannibal ordered the construction of the **Pfarrkirche** next door in 1581, and a statue of the benefactor, standing in a niche, is the centrepiece of its fine Renaissance facade. Inside, Hannibal's son Kaspar von Ems is buried in a large marble sarcophagus, his effigy reclining nonchalantly on the coffin lid. Highlight of the interior is the altarpiece of pale wood which stands nearby Hannibal's grave, and which sports a series of exquisitely carved tableaux: there's a Coronation of the Virgin in the middle, with scenes of the Nativity, Annunciation and Crucifixion stacked above it in the manner of a four-storey puppet theatre. Most of the figures were carved by a local village artisan in around 1530, although several saintly statuettes were placed on either side of the Coronation a century later.

Marktstrasse heads north from the church towards Schweizer Strasse, where a **Jewish museum** (Tues–Sun 10am–5pm; öS40/€2.92), at no. 5, documents the history of the Jews who settled in Hohenems in numbers after Kaspar von Ems issued them with a Charter of Protection in 1617, making the town a relatively safe haven – although occasional pogroms were not unknown in this part of the Vorarlberg. Numbers fell dramatically after 1860, when Jews were allowed to settle anywhere in the Habsburg empire, although the local Jewish community continued to exert a strong influence on Hohenems life. One prominent local family, the Rosenthals, ran the town cotton mill, and it's in their rather sumptuous villa that the museum is housed. Original furniture and restored ceiling paintings successfully recreate the atmosphere of a nineteenth-century industrialist's house, while a wealth of photographs – notably pictures of sporting and cultural organizations in which Jews and Gentiles took part together – reveal the atmosphere of interdependence and tolerance that prevailed here. One room is dedicated to the Hohenems-born composer Salomon Sulzer (1804–1890), who contributed to the revival of nineteenth-century synagogue music. Introduced to Viennese society by Schubert, Sultzer also wrote a wide range of secular pieces, including the *Lied der Totenkopflegion* (Song of the Death's Head Legion), a tribute to those who fell in defence of the 1848 revolution. By pushing buttons in the wall, you can watch short video films about Sultzer's life, and listen to his music.

Practicalities

The **train station** is an easy ten-minute walk west of the Schlossplatz: from the station, turn left into Angelika-Kauffmann-Strasse and right into Graf-Maximilian-Strasse to get to the square. There's a **tourist office** (Mon–Fri 9am–noon & 1.30–6pm; ☎05576/42780, *wtshohenems@vol.at*) opposite the Pfarrkirche on Kirchplatz, which adjoins Schlossplatz. They can refer you to a small number of **private rooms** (②) in town. *Gasthof Hirschen*, Marktstrasse 56 (☎05576/72345; ③), is a reasonable central **hotel** offering modern rooms with en-suite facilities and TV; *Café-Konditorei Lorenz*, Bahnhofstrasse 17 (☎05576/72332; ④), is the best of the mid-range places to stay, as well as being an excellent café.

Most **eating and drinking** takes place on or around Schlossplatz. *Schloss Café*, on the main square at Schlossplatz 10, offers a comfortable setting in which to enjoy a day-time coffee or snack; *Zur alten Post*, Postplatz 1, specializes in schnitzel-style dishes and offers the odd vegetarian option; *im Palast*, occupying one side of Schloss Hohenems, is a restaurant and bar which offers similar food and has a large outdoor terrace. *Verrückt*, just beyond the Jewish museum at Schweizer Strasse 25, is the town's liveli-est drinking venue, usually open until 2–3am.

Rankweil

Very much a one-horse town, **RANKWEIL** is primarily known for the **Liebfrauenkirche** (daily: April–Sept till 8pm; Oct–March till 6pm), a pilgrimage church that surveys the town from a nearby crag. Miraculous healing properties are attributed to its thirteenth-century cross, which hangs above the main altar. Bearing a tender relief of the crucified Christ, the wooden cross was silver-plated in the eigh-teenth century to provide it with added lustre. Pilgrims are also drawn to the Baroque altar to the Virgin Mary on the left-hand side, which has a Gothic Madonna and Child as its centrepiece. A wooden parapet runs around the outside of the church, offering an excellent panorama of the Rhine Valley and the Swiss Alps, which rise to the west.

Rankweil's **train station** is on the western fringes of the centre, a short walk from the town's main thoroughfare, Ringstrasse, whence a couple of fairly obvious pathways lead up to the church. The **tourist office**, Ringstrasse 27 (Mon–Fri 9am–1pm; ☎05522/404-103), will sort out private **rooms** (②) for you. For **food**, *Restaurant schwarzer Adler*, Ringstrasse 3, offers a basic selection of grills and schnitzels and a small vegetarian menu, including such delights as vegetable strüdel; *Gasthof Mohren*, north of the centre at Stiegstrasse 17, is a much more upmarket restaurant, which draws in a good deal of business from out of town.

Feldkirch

Even though several international trains enter Austria at **FELDKIRCH**, many trav-ellers speed eastwards to Innsbruck and beyond without sampling the delights of this historic and charming market town. While tourist attractions of any real drama are rather thin on the ground, the largely pedestrianized town centre, richly endowed with a selection of late-Gothic town houses, is a pleasant place in which to amble. A medieval grid-like street plan surrounds two parallel arcaded market squares, **Neustadt** and

Marktgasse. This area is bounded to the south and west by a succession of medieval towers and gates, reminders of the original town fortifications that were last strengthened at the beginning of the sixteenth century by Emperor Maximilian I. Most impressive of these are the **Churertor**, an ornate fourteenth-century gateway guarding the southwesterly route to Chur, and the elegant, spindly **Katzenturm**, named after the lions' heads that once adorned the cannon housed here. The main attraction in the Gothic **Domkirche St Nikolaus** on the northwestern side of the centre is Wolf Huber's **Pietà** (to the right of the high altar), painted in 1521, the vestige of a much larger altarpiece honouring St Anne (another portion of which is in the Landesmuseum in Bregenz). A native of Feldkirch who spent most of his working life in the Bavarian town of Passau, Huber introduced a new sensitivity towards landscape into the religious painting of the time, visible here in the craggy hills – obviously inspired by the Rhine valley – that form the background to the scene. The church's other undoubted highlight is its stained-glass windows, completed in 1962 by local artist Martin Häusle. Abstract fields of kaleidoscopic colour blend easily with lively renditions of various saints, including a red-robed St Nicholas, patron of the church, clearly visible above the high altar.

Schlossgraben leads east from the church towards the **Schattenburg**, a hilltop strongpoint that was the seat of the counts of Montfort from the twelfth to the fourteenth centuries, although its current appearance owes much to a subsequent role as courtly residence of the imperial governors of Vorarlberg in the sixteenth century. Inside, the **Heimatmuseum** (March–Oct Sun–Tues 9am–noon & 1–5pm; öS35/€2.56) houses the usual collection of peasant crafts and furnishings.

Practicalities

Feldkirch's **train station** is a ten-minute walk north of the centre. Turn left out of the station forecourt and head down Bahnhofstrasse to reach the **tourist office**, just behind the Katzenturm at Herrengasse 12 (daily 8.30am–noon & 1.30–6pm; ☎05522/73467, *www.tiscover.com/feldkirch*). The tourist office will provide a small list of **private rooms** (②), although most are in far-flung residential suburbs like Altenstadt (3km north of town) or Tisis (2km to the south). Central hotels include *Lingg*, Kreuzgasse 10 (☎05522/72062, *lingg@eunet.at*; ④), a nice old inn overlooking the Marktgasse, although unfortunately it only has a few rooms, so you need to book ahead; and *Post*, Schlossgraben 5 (☎05522/72820; ⑤), a centrally placed establishment with TV in all rooms. The top-of-the-range *Alpenrose*, Rosengasse 4–6 (☎05522/72175, *www.tiscover.com/hotel-alpenrose*; ⑥), is a 500-year-old town house in the centre, many of whose rooms have antique furnishings. Feldkirch's **youth hostel** is in a former medieval hospital, a lovely half-timbered building 1km north of the train station at Reichsstrasse 111 (☎05522/73181; Jan–Oct; buses #1, #2 or #60 from Bahnhofstrasse) with modern dorms and doubles (①).

There's a reasonable sprinkling of **places to eat** in the town centre. Feldkirch's leading coffee-and-pastries venue is the rather swish *Café-Konditorei Zanona*, just off Marktgasse at Montfortgasse 3, which attracts a fair mixture of elderly matrons and young trendies. *Gasthof Löwen*, near the Domkirche on Neustadt, is a reliable source of Vorarlberg staples such as *Rösti* and *Kässpätzle* for around öS100/€7.30, and also offers a cheap Mittagsmenü. *Casablanca*, across the street at Neustadt 4, is another popular venue for cheap lunches, although its speciality is the Moroccan couscous dishes in the evenings, which cost around öS160/€11.68. Moving up the price scale, *Schlosswirtschaft*, Burggasse 1, inside Schloss Schattenburg, is an atmospheric place to enjoy local specialities in timber-beamed rooms; *Lingg*, Kreuzgasse, serves excellent Austrian food and offers some good-value lunchtime Tagesmenüs from öS100/€7.30. *Pancho's*, Gymnasiumgasse 5, is a Mexican restaurant that does a good range in potato skins and is also a popular place for a **drink**.

The Bregenzerwald

Although popular with Austrian, Swiss and German trippers, the rural charms of the **Bregenzerwald** remain relatively unknown to the rest of Europe. Far from being the forest that the name suggests, the region is a dense patchwork of dairy-farming villages spread across an undulating landscape of subalpine pasture. Known for its mildly tangy local *Bergkäse*, or "highland cheese", the Bregenzerwald is also famous for its architecture; here more than anywhere else in Austria, traditional wooden farmhouses are still in use, and the age-old techniques used to build them continue to inform modern construction. Using wood from local spruce trees, the typical Bregenzerwald house joins living quarters and animal stalls under a single, shallow roof. Often adorned with intricately carved eaves and balconies, they're almost always shingled – clad in tiny wooden scales that offer the best protection against the bitter winter weather.

Although the villages of the Bregenzerwald are not nearly as developed as the higher-altitude resorts further east, the hills are big enough to provide both alpine and cross-country skiing in the winter (good enough for beginners and intermediates, but there's nothing much to challenge the advanced skier), and a wealth of glorious walking opportunities all year round. The main centres are the rather humdrum Egg, and the more attractive **Bezau** and **Au**, all linked by a main road that heads southeast from Dornbirn towards Warth and the winter resorts of Lech and Zürs. The most characteristic Bregenzerwald villages, **Schwarzenberg** and **Damüls**, are only a few kilometres off this road. It's ideal territory if you're touring by car or bike, although the local bus network is quite extensive: hourly buses from Bregenz and Dornbirn ply the main route through the region, and connecting services (you'll probably have to change at Egg for Schwarzenberg, or at Au for Damüls) ensure that you're never really cut off. In addition there are less frequent buses from Damüls southwards to Bludenz (change at Thüringen; 8 daily in the winter season, 2–3 daily rest of year). Freytag & Berndt's 1:50,000 Bregenzerwald **map** is the best guide to the region's hiking and cycling routes.

Entering the region **from Bregenz or Dornbirn**, the first settlement of any size you pass through is **EGG** (pronounced "Eck"), a pleasant enough village, even if it lacks the character of the places beyond. Egg **tourist office**, on the opposite side of the square from the bus stop (☎05512/2426, *www.egg-tourismus.at*), has advice on local rooms (②) should you want to stay; although potentially more useful is the Bregenzerwald **regional tourist office** (Mon–Fri 9am–noon & 2–5pm; ☎05512/2365, *www.bregenzerwald.at*) just up the hill from here, which has a database of vacancies throughout the Bregenzerwald region. If you're stopping off in Egg for a bite to **eat** then consider the *Kässtadl* on the main street, a folksy restaurant specializing in Bregenzerwald cheese-based dishes, such as *Kässpatzle*, fondue and raclette.

BREGENZERWALD LIFT PASSES

In winter, **day passes** for skiers covering gondolas and chairlifts at a single Bregenzerwald resort usually weigh in at around öS350–400/€25.55–29.20. However for longer periods it's best to invest in the **3 valley superpass**, which covers the whole of the Bregenzerwald, as well as the neighbouring Grosses Walsertal and the Lechtal (although not the resort of Lech itself), and costs öS1100/€80.30 for 3 days; öS1800/€131.40 for 6 days; and öS3120/€227.76 for 13 days. In summer, there's usually a **Bregenzerwald summer card** which covers all the lifts in the region, although weekly prices (and what's included in the deal) change from one year to the next – local tourist offices will have details. Passes can be bought from lift stations themselves, and from some tourist offices.

ANGELIKA KAUFFMANN (1741–1807)

Born in the Swiss town of **Chur** to a family who hailed from **Schwarzenberg**, and subsequently resident in both England and Italy, **Angelika Kauffmann** has always been a cultural heroine to more than one nation. She picked up the rudiments of painting from her father Johann Josef Kauffmann, a jobbing artist from the Bregenzerwald who worked throughout Switzerland and northern Italy during Angelika's childhood. The family came home to Schwarzenberg briefly in 1757, where father and daughter worked together on the decoration of the village church, thereby giving present-day local tourist authorities sufficient reason to claim her as their own.

When the family returned to Italy, Angelika studied in Florence and Rome, and achieved some local notoriety before becoming the protégée of Lady Wentworth, the wife of the British ambassador in Venice, who took her to London in 1763. Once introduced to London society, Kauffmann went down a storm: the elements of Neoclassicism that she had picked up in Italy were very much in vogue. She certainly knew the demands of the local market, producing large, often sentimental narrative paintings of mythological and historical subjects for wealthy collectors, and dashing off appealing portraits of her high-born circle of friends.

Her private life was the cause of much society gossip, although it's fair to assume that a certain amount of this was malicious. She almost certainly had affairs with English painters Nathaniel Dance and Joshua Reynolds, the Swiss painter Fuseli, and the French revolutionary Jean-Paul Marat, before eventually concluding a disastrous marriage with a gold-digging charmer posing as the Swedish Count de Horn (sic). When he was unmasked as an impostor and bigamist, Kauffmann had to pay out the then exorbitant sum of £300 to persuade him to leave town. He died soon afterwards, leaving Kauffmann free to marry the Venetian painter Antonio Zucchi in 1781, subsequently going to live with him in Rome, where she died.

A founder member of the British Royal Academy of Art, Kauffmann's greatest achievement was to win respect as a female artist working in the male-dominated world of narrative painting. Although much of her work is in private hands, reasonable collections can be found in the Brighton Museum and Art Gallery in England, the Kunstmuseum in Chur, Switzerland, and the Vorarlberger Landesmuseum in Bregenz (see p.529).

Schwarzenberg

Ranged across grassy hillocks and surrounded by pine-clad slopes, **SCHWARZEN-BERG** represents the Bregenzerwald at its most idyllic, with many of the most important examples of the region's traditional architecture found here. It was home to artist **Angelika Kauffmann** (see box), who is remembered in a worthwhile local museum. It's also the site of two of Vorarlberg's best **restaurants**, enhancing the village's popularity amongst day-trippers from the urban centres of the Rhine Valley. Extra numbers pour into Schwarzenberg for the **Schubertiade**, a festival of Schubert-penned songs performed by top international names in the purpose-built Angelika-Kauffmann-Saal, a timber-framed concert hall on the fringes of the village. The festival is usually divided into two blocks of concerts (the first in mid-June, the second in late August–early Sept), although future years may see the event being co-hosted by both Schwarzenberg and the nearby village of Bezau. For programme details and ticket information contact Schubertiade, Villa Rosenthal, Schweizerstrasse 1, Posrfach 100, A-6845 Hohenems (☎05576/72091, *www.schubertiade.at*). An altogether more rustic slice of culture is served up at the **Alpabtrieb** of September 14–15, traditionally the time when the cows come down from the higher pastures for the winter, and nowadays the excuse for major knees-up, with folk music, cheese competitions and a big farm-produce market.

Focal point of Schwarzenberg is the **church of the Holy Trinity** (Dreifaltigkeitskirche), supposedly built over the grave of Ilga, a twelfth-century saint; her bones are concealed in a small Rococo casket inside the church on the left. The 16-year-old Angelika Kauffmann painted the medallions of the Apostles adorning the nave, and she later donated the Madonna that hangs above the main altar. The pictures of the Stations of the Cross are by her father, Johann Josef. The Kauffmann heritage can be explored further in the **Heimatmuseum** (May–Sept Tues, Thurs, Sat & Sun 2–4pm; Oct Tues & Sat 2–4pm; öS30/€2.19), in a characteristic Bregenzerwald house just up the hill from the church. The room devoted to Angelika is short on original artworks, but the prints and books on display here provide an adequate summary of her life. The museum's ethnographic collection is strong on local costumes, especially the bizarre range of women's headgear occasionally still worn on feast days: typical of this region are the *Spitzkappe*, a conical black wool hat traditionally worn on Sundays, and the *Brämenkappe* made from otter hide, a big bulbous affair rather like a Russian fur hat. Further rooms contain all manner of agricultural tools and domestic trinkets, of which the most curious are surely the *Flaschenaltäre*, or "bottle altars", which work on the same principle as a ship in a bottle, but feature tiny dolls of saints.

Practicalities

Buses pick up and set down at the crossroads by the church, whence it's a short walk 100m north to the *Gemeindeamt*, or village hall, where the **tourist office** (Mon–Fri 8am–noon; ☎05512/3570) has a list of **private rooms** (②) and holiday **apartments**. *Café Angelikahöhe* (☎05512/2985; ②), just north of the central crossroads, is a small **guesthouse** offering comfortable rooms with shared facilities, while *Gasthof Hirschen* (☎05512/2944, *www.romantikhotels.com/schwarzenberg*; ⑧), immediately next to the crossroads, is in a different league altogether, providing a wealth of creature comforts in a wonderfully restored old inn.

An inexpensive **place to eat** is *Buche* about 200m from the central crossroads on the Bezau road, which offers standard Austrian veal-and-pork cuisine alongside some cheesy Vorarlberg alternatives; their Tagesmenüs hover around the öS120/€8.76 mark. The highly regarded restaurant in the *Gasthof Hirschen* has a wood-panelled interior and a mixed international/traditional Austrian menu, with main courses starting at öS200/€14.60. Similar gourmet fare (including fresh fish from the Bodensee) at comparable prices can be found next door at the *Adler*, whose attractive, modern interior plays host to prosperous out-of-towners. The *Rumpelkeller* in the basement of the *Gasthof Hirschen* is a cosy **bar** catering for the village's younger set.

Bezau

It's relatively easy to catch buses from Schwarzenberg onwards to **BEZAU**, the next settlement of any size, 7km to the south. The unofficial capital of the Bregenzerwald, Bezau is full of the shingle-clad houses for which the area is famed, and is a convenient starting point for numerous local walks. As usual, the best way to begin exploring the highland pastures is to take the **gondola** (May–Oct & mid-Dec to mid-April daily 9am–5pm; one way öS112/€8.18, return öS156/€11.39; *www.bergbahnen-bezau.at*) from the eastern end of the village to the middle station, **Berghaus Sonderach**, or onwards to the terminus at **Baumgartenhöhe**, a ridge just below the 1711-metre-high Niedere Alpe. From either point, pathways offering panoramic views lead back down to the village.

The **tourist office** (Mon–Fri 8.30am–noon & 2–6pm; ☎05514/2295) next to the post office (where buses stop) will direct you to **private rooms** (②) or family-oriented holiday **apartments**. *Gasthof Gams*, bang in the centre near the village church

(☎05514/2220, *www.hotel-gams.at*; ⑦), is an old country inn turned into top-notch **hotel**, featuring tennis courts, outdoor pool and sauna. There's a riverside **campsite** (May–Sept) at the western end of the village, just off the main road. You'll find plenty of Gasthöfe in town offering standard Austrian **food**. For something slightly different, the central *Café-Konditorei Fröwis* has a pizzeria attached; and the *Gams* (see above) is a well-known place for traditional Vorarlberg food – although, with main courses starting at around öS200/€14.60, prices are relatively high.

Mellau

From Bezau the main Bregenz–Warth road follows the valley of the **Bregenzer Ache** through increasingly mountainous terrain, passing a succession of pleasant villages that serve as centres of low-key rural tourism throughout the year. Squatting beneath the rugged northwestern flanks of the 2044m **Kanisfluh**, the unassuming village of **MELLAU**, 3km outside of Bezau, is another excellent base for walking. There are a couple of hotels, and most of the householders in the village offer **rooms** or **apartments** to rent – there's an accommodation information board and courtesy phone in the centre of the village, where buses stop. A **gondola** at the southern end of the village (mid-June to mid-Oct & mid-Dec to mid-April daily 8.30am–4.30pm; öS110/€8.03 return) ascends to the Rossstelle, the 1400-metre-high ridge that looms above the village to the south, and the site of a small skiing area in winter. From here you can walk back down to the village in just under two hours, or take one of the trails that leads off across the highland pastures. One popular walk ascends to the **Wildguten Alpe**, one hour to the west before descending to *Gasthof Alpenfrieden*, another hour in the same direction, where you can stop for a drink or bite to eat, and then turns northeastwards back to the village; the trip takes about four hours in total. For the more ambitious, a twelve-kilometre hike (one that shouldn't be attempted without a detailed map) leads southwards to the 1882-metre **Bettler Kulm** before skirting the side of the 2095-metre **Damülser Mittagspitze** and descending to the village of Damüls (see p.540) after a total of five or six hours.

Au, Schoppernau and beyond

Nine kilometres beyond Mellau, the village of **AU** was the site of an important guild of craftsmen and builders in the eighteenth century. Relying on the indigenous aptitude for house building as a way out of rural poverty, the craftsmen of Au plied their trade throughout southern Germany, with some of them – such as Michael Beer, architect of the monastery at Kempten in Bavaria – attaining considerable fame. Aside from the usual roundup of photogenic farmhouses, there's little to see of their legacy in Au today, although this prosperous dairy village – together with the adjoining settlement of **SCHOPPERNAU** immediately to the west – is an undeniably attractive spot. If you're looking for a rural break, this is as good a place to rest up as any. The twin villages are impressively framed by mountain scenery, with the smoothly conical Üntschenspitze rising to the east, and the ubiquitous form of Kanisfluh to the west.

Midway between Au and Schoppernau, a **gondola** (July–Sept daily; June & Oct weekends only; mid-Dec to mid-April daily), ascends to the *Panorama* restaurant just below the 2090-metre summit of the **Diedamskopf**, centre of a smallish ski area (popular with beginners) in winter, and a dense network of hiking trails in summer. A brochure detailing walking routes can be obtained from the **tourist office** in the centre of Au (Mon–Fri 9am–noon & 2–5pm; ☎05515/2288), outside which local buses stop. The tourist office will also direct you to the area's plentiful **private rooms** (②) and **apartments** – many of which are in the characterful timber farmhouses of Schoppernau. Most of the **hotels** are in Au: *Gasthof Adler*, Lisse 90 (☎05515/2264; ③), is an archetypal Bregenzerwald house near the village centre, offering rooms with en-suite facilities and TV; while *Haus Alpina*, Rehmen 30 (☎05515/2365, *www.tiscover.com/hausalpina*; summer ③; winter ④), is a similarly appointed though smaller place just north of the road to Schoppernau. There's also a **campsite**, *Köbl*, Au-Neudorf 356 (☎05515/2331; May–Sept), near the gondola terminal. Most of the Gasthöfe in the two villages serve **food**: the *Alte Post* in Au's centre has traditional Vorarlberg dishes with main courses from öS150/€10.95. For **drinkers**, *S'pab* is a convivial café-bar just off the main road in Schoppernau.

Beyond Schoppernau the main road clambers towards the **Hochtannberg Pass** some 10km beyond, through an area settled by immigrants from the Swiss canton of Valais in the fourteenth century. Villages like **UNTERBODEN** and **SCHRÖCKEN** still bear the imprint of Valaisian architecture, preserving several sturdy wooden houses with painted window frames. Sometimes closed in winter due to risk of avalanche, the road that climbs above Schröcken negotiates a couple of hairpin bends before reaching the 1676-metre summit of the **Hochtannberg**, and descending towards the town of **WARTH**, a sleepy market town dunked beneath the northern foothills of the Arlberg on the other side. From here, one route (frequented in summer by four daily buses from Warth) leads east down the Lech Valley towards the Tyrol and the market town of Reutte (see p.520) 60km away, while another road (closed Dec–March) climbs south, providing low-season access to the renowned winter resorts of Lech and Zürs (see p.545), some 10 and 15km to the south respectively.

Damüls and around

A minor road heads west from Au towards **DAMÜLS**, an exceedingly pretty spot on a shelf just above the Krumbach Valley, although with a permanent population of just 330 souls, this is much more of a tourist resort than a working Bregenzerwald village. The village-centre **Pfarrkirche** boasts a series of Gothic frescoes dating from 1484, vividly evoking late-medieval piety with a lurid *Last Judgement* over the chancel arch. On the left-hand side of the nave are twenty scenes covering Christ's last days, from the entry into Jerusalem to the Crucifixion.

Damüls' proximity to higher altitudes makes it a major centre for **skiing**, with several chairlifts offering immediate access to the slopes. It doesn't feature in any of the winter package-holiday brochures, however, and is much more low-key than the Arlberg resorts further east. Nevertheless, if you're prepared to travel here independently, it's a good place for beginners, with nursery slopes just outside the village.

In summer, **walkers** can take the **chairlift** (mid-June to mid-Oct & early Dec–April daily 9am–4.45pm; öS105/€7.67 return) that runs from the valley bottom just north of the village up to **Uga**, a saddle between the peaks of **Eisenkopf** and **Mittagspitze**. The walk back into Damüls from the top of the chairlift takes about two hours. A more strenuous alternative is to head westwards beneath the Mittagspitze towards the 2051-metre-high **Ragazerblanken**, before turning south towards the **Sunsersee**, flanking the 2010-metre **Portlerhorn**, and descending back to the village. Providing access to some excellent views along the way, this particular circuit takes five to six hours.

Practicalities

Most of the houses in Damüls let out **rooms** (summer ①; winter ②): the **tourist office** (☎05510/620-0) in the village centre will provide details. Several **pensions** crowd around the Uga chairlift terminal: *Pension Johanna*, Uga 79 (☎05510/286; summer ②; winter ③), is a good budget option. *Gasthof Zimba*, Oberdamüls 202 (☎05510/379; summer ③; winter ④), west of the centre on the road to the Furka Pass, is one of the cheaper **hotels** around, but still fairly comfortable; while down in the valley, *Hotel*

Alpenblume, Uga 78 (☎05510/265, *www.tiscover.com/alpenblume*; summer ③; winter ⑤), is a large, chalet-style place with TV and phone in every room. Top of the range is the *Damülser Hof*, Oberdamüls 147 (☎05510/210, *www.tiscover.com/damuelser-hof*; summer ⑤; winter ⑧), a chalet complex with indoor swimming pools and a range of traditionally decorated rooms.

Onwards to Faschina and the Grosses Walsertal

The main road through Damüls continues by way of a tunnel to **FASCHINA**, 3km to the southeast (also accessible by a gently ascending footpath from Damüls), another mountain hamlet popular with skiers and walkers. There's a **chairlift** to the 1777-metre **Hahnenkopf**, which looks over Faschina to the west; again, the summit is a good starting point for walks back to Faschina or Damüls. From Faschina, the road descends southwards into the upper reaches of the **Grosses Walsertal**, a picturesque, steep-sided valley that runs southwestwards to **NENZING**, a town on the main road and rail route between Feldkirch and Bludenz. It's a nice trip to make by road, although recent cutbacks in rural public transport mean that bus travel may be more problematic. An occasional bus makes its way from Damüls to Fontanella, Thüringerberg or Thüringen, where there are infrequent onward connections to Bludenz and Feldkirch. It's best to check timings at the Damüls tourist office before setting out.

Bludenz, the Montafon and the Arlberg resorts

East of Feldkirch, both the main Innsbruck-bound railway line and the E60 autobahn follow the Ill Valley as far as Bludenz before ascending through the Klostertal towards the Arlberg Pass, Vorarlberg's border with the Tyrol. As the only town of any size along the route, **Bludenz** is an obvious stop-off point, although it's neither attractive nor historically interesting enough to compete with Vorarlberg's other urban centres. Bludenz does, however, stand conveniently at the entrance to the upper Ill Valley, more commonly known as the **Montafon**, which provides access to the high Alps of the **Silvretta** range. Beyond Bludenz to the east, the gradual climb to the **Arlberg** lacks nothing in terms of grandiose alpine scenery, but the settlements along the route hold too few attractions to necessitate breaking your journey. From the summit of the Arlberg, there's a choice of two routes: onwards into the Tyrol, or northwards over the Flexen Pass to the skiing villages of **Zürs** and **Lech**.

Bludenz

BLUDENZ is the obvious transport hub from which to begin exploring southeastern Vorarlberg, but if you're eager for a taste of the Alps it's probably better to change buses or trains here and press on. Bludenz's only real claim to fame is the Suchard chocolate factory across the road from the train station, and the Milka Chocolate Festival in mid-July provides an entertaining day out for kids. The town's paltry collection of sights boils down to the sixteenth-century **Pfarrkirche St Lorenz**, located on a height at the northern end of the town centre and remarkable only for its stately octagonal tower, and the adjacent **Oberer Tor,** a former city gate that now houses the town **museum** (May–Oct Mon–Sat 9am–noon & 3–5pm; öS25/€1.83), a modest collection of craft implements. Beyond the gate, rows of seventeenth-century town houses with street-level arcading add character to the main shopping area. One kilometre north of the centre, a cable car (Jan–April & Nov–March 10am–5pm; May–Oct 9am–6pm;

öS90/€6.57 return) ascends to the 1384-metre **Muttersberg**, which commands excellent views southwards to the Rätikon and Silvretta mountain ranges.

Practicalities

From the **train station** south of the centre on Bahnhofplatz, a left turn outside the station building followed by a right turn into Bahnhofstrasse will bring you to Bludenz's main street, Mutterstrasse, in about five minutes. From here, a left turn into Werdenbergerstrasse will get you to the **tourist office**, housed in the town police station at no. 42 (Mon–Fri 8am–noon & 2–5.30pm, Sat 10am–noon; ☎05552/62170, *www.bludenz.at*). There are a few **private rooms** (①) to rent in town, a list of which you can obtain from the tourist office. Best of the central **hotels** is the four-star *Schlosshotel Dörflinger*, Schlossplatz 5 (☎05552/63016; ④), which surveys the town from a hilltop behind the Pfarrkirche. Located in the hillside suburbs northwest of the centre, *Landhaus Muther*, Alemannenstrasse 4 (☎05552/65704; ③), is a smallish place offering rooms with en-suite facilities but not much else. Just west of the centre, the 45-room *Hotel-Pension Einhorn*, Alte Landstrasse 62 (☎05552/62130; ③), is an attractive modern building with TV and phone in all rooms.

For **eating**, the *Stadtbäckerei* in the train station is a convenient and popular source of cheap coffee, and eat-in or takeaway sandwiches and pastries. For something more substantial, the more central *Orangerie*, Wichnerstrasse 2a, offers a tempting range of pasta dishes, usually including a couple of vegetarian options, and cheap daily specials at lunchtimes. *Fohrenburg*, Werdenbergerstrasse 53, a beer hall-cum-restaurant attached to the Fohrenburg brewery just west of the town centre offers meaty Austrian favourites such as *Wiener Schnitzel* and *Zwiebelrostbraten*, as well as being a good place to sup the local ale. Also good for lunches is *Moccasino*, Bahnhofstrasse, a cosy café-bar and good **drinking** venue at any time of day or night.

The Montafon Valley

A narrow, high-sided valley presided over by the imperious peaks of the Rätikon and Silvretta ranges, the **MONTAFON** is one of the most dramatic stretches in the Vorarlberg. A string of picturesque villages dot the valley floor, the best of which to aim for are the twin settlements of **Schruns** and **Tschagguns**, situated about 2km apart, 15km up the valley from Bludenz, which together form the centre of a thriving winter sports scene. For much of the rest of the year, things are pretty quiet, although the valley is popular with hikers, and the **Silvretta Hochalpenstrasse** – a road that climbs to the Silvretta dam at the southeastern end of the valley before dropping down to the Paznaun Valley in the Tyrol – is one of Austria's most impressive alpine itineraries. The Freytag & Berndt 1:50,000 Montafon map is a handy guide to the valley's hiking trails. Cycling enthusiasts can take advantage of a macadamed **cycle path** that goes up the Montafon Valley from Bludenz, starting on the north side of the train station (where you can rent bicycles).

In winter the **skiing areas** on the Hochjoch above Schruns, and the Golm above Tschagguns, are particularly suitable for beginners and intermediates. There are a range of 1-day winter passes available for all the local lifts. A ski pass covering the whole valley will set you back öS1165/€85.04 for 3 days; öS2070/€151.11 for 6 days; öS3655/€266.82 for 13 days.

For those spending any length of time in the Montafon Valley, a **Montafon-Paznaun summer card** will be a worthwhile investment. The seven-day pass (available from all the region's cable-car and gondola terminals; öS515/€37.43) entitles you to free travel on all the local cable cars, gondolas and chairlifts, as well as local buses, rail travel between Schruns and Bludenz, and free entry to museums (not that there are many) and swimming pools.

Schruns and Tschagguns

Half-hourly **trains** on the narrow-gauge Montafonerbahn railway make their way from Bludenz to **SCHRUNS**, 12km up the valley. Pressed hard against the flanks of the **Hochjoch**, which rises to the southeast, the village clusters around a main square dominated by the **Pfarrkirche St Jodok**, whose elegant onion spire is more interesting than its late-nineteenth-century interior. Standing opposite the church, the **Heimatmuseum** (June to mid-Sept Tues–Sat 3–6pm, Sun 10am–noon; mid-Sept to May Tues & Fri 3–6pm; öS30/€2.19) offers a pretty thorough roundup of Montafon costumes, together with a history of the local dairy industry. At the southern end of the square stands the **Hotel Taube** (see below), where keen skier Ernest Hemingway stayed in winter 1925, dashing off a couple of chapters of *The Sun Also Rises* between trips to the pistes. Nowadays the quickest route to the heights above the town is provided by the three-stage **Hochjochbahn** cable car (mid-June to Oct & Dec–April; öS200/€14.60 return; *www.hochjochbahnen.at*), which ascends to the 2300-metre **Sennigrat**, whence you can walk back down towards the valley or embark on any number of alternative hiking trails.

Schruns **tourist office**, just south of the main square at Silvrettastrasse 6 (Mon–Fri 8am–noon & 2–6pm, Sat 9am–noon & 4–6pm; ☎05556/72166-0, *www.schruns.at* or *www.montafon.at*), has details of **private rooms** (②). Alternatively, *Pansion Bradlwarter*, 500m southwest of the train station at Auf der Litz 22 (☎05556/72123, *www.montafon.com/pension-bradlwarter*; summer ②; winter ③), has simple but comfy en-suites in a chalet-style house; while the *Hotel Taube*, bang in the centre of the village on Kirchplatz (☎05556/72384 or 72145-8, *www.tiscover.com/hotel-taube*; rooms with shared facilities ③; en suites ④), is a traditional family-run Gasthof with plenty of atmosphere. For **food**, *Bel Paese*, Im Gässle, has tasty thin-crust pizzas in the öS70–110/€5.11–8.03 range and a generous choice of pasta dishes; while the more traditional *Gasthaus zum Kreuz*, Kirchplatz 18, has the usual range of regular Austrian dishes as well as tasty and cheap fondues. The best place for an evening **drink** is *Café Einbahn* on Batloggstrasse, a cosy pub stuffed with an appealing array of junk.

About 2km west of Schruns on the opposite side of the valley is the sister settlement of **TSCHAGGUNS**, a smaller, less picturesque place, which nevertheless has its own **tourist office** in the village centre (Mon–Fri 8am–noon & 2–6pm; ☎05556/72457, *www.tschagguns.com*) doling out **private rooms** at about the same price as those in Schruns. If you want to be really pampered, then the *Montafoner Hof* hotel in the centre of the village (☎05556/7100-0, *www.montafonerhof.com*; summer ⑧; winter ⑨) is one of the best in the region, offering modern rooms in an attractive low-rise building featuring lots of timber, with covered and indoor pools on site. A minor road (served by hourly local bus) leads west from Tschagguns to the lakeside settlement of **Latschau** 4km uphill, where there's a gondola to the **Golm** (June–Sept & mid-Dec to late April), which commands an excellent panorama of the surrounding countryside.

The Silvretta Hochalpenstrasse

Between May and October, six daily buses head south from Schruns to tackle the **Silvretta Hochalpenstrasse**, a scenic mountain road that ascends to the Silvretta Reservoir and Bielerhöhe Pass at the southeastern end of the Montafon Valley. From the summit of the pass, it's possible to catch connecting services that descend into the Paznaun Valley in the Tyrol, although you should check times at Schruns tourist office before attempting the trip.

The road begins to climb in earnest just beyond the village of **Partenen**, 20km south of Schruns, rising steeply from the valley floor via a succession of hairpins. A tortuous ascent to the Vermunt Reservoir is followed by another steep climb to the larger Silvretta Reservoir and the 2036-metre summit of the Silvretta Hochalpenstrasse, the **Bielerhöhe** saddle. There you'll find a car park, a café-restaurant in the *Hotel*

HUT TO HUT IN THE SILVRETTA ALPS

The Wiesbadener Hütte

A rewarding **one-day circular walk** leaves the summit of the 2036-metre **Bielerhöhe** on the Silvretta Hochalpenstrasse. If you can't get a bed at the nearby *Madlener Haus* mountain hut (☎05558/4234), try the *Berggasthof Piz Buin* (☎05558/4231). The walk heads south alongside the Silvretta Stausee reservoir, then enters the wild-looking Ochsental, with big mountains coming into view as you progress, including Piz Buin and the glaciated peaks that form the Austro-Swiss border. After about two hours the trail reaches the *Wiesbadener Hütte* (2443m; ☎05558/4233), set on a shelf above the moraines of the Vermunt glacier. This is a good place for lunch – a hut with waitress service, which may seem a little incongruous in such a setting. Excellent views from the terrace overlook a mass of ice and snow and a bevy of attractive peaks, and walkers with alpine experience and the necessary equipment to deal with crevassed glaciers can choose to spend an extra day or two based at the hut in order to scale some of them – Piz Buin, Silvrettahorn and Dreilanderspitze are especially appealing. Walkers not so equipped or experienced should continue on the circuit by returning to the Bielerhöhe along a clear path that rises to the stony Radsattel (2652m), with an option of diverting for a half-hour's easy climb (some mild scrambling involved) to the crown of the Hohes Rad for a far-reaching, 360-degree panorama. From the Radsattel, descend to the Radsee in the Bieltal glen along a trail that spills out at the Bielerhöhe where you began.

Southwest of the Silvretta Stausee (west of the Wiesbadener Hütte) the Klostertal provides access to the uncomplicated 2751-metre Klosterpass on the frontier ridge, a traverse frequently used in a popular cross-border trek between the Saarbrücker Hütte (☎05558/4235) in Austria and Silvretta Hütte (☎083/41306) in Switzerland. East of the Wiesbadener Hütte the lengthy Jamtal digs into the mountains south of Galtür, with the Jamtal Hütte (☎05443/40814) set 10km into the glen. From this hut further routes are possible, connecting with the Heidelberger Hütte (☎05444/5418) via the Kronenjoch, for example, or with the Wiesbadener Hütte by way of the Getschnerscharte (2839m), where the Madlenerferner glacier has all but disappeared.

Silvretta Traverse

A **six-day crossing** of the Silvretta Alps can be achieved by linking a series of huts located in the parallel north-flowing glens that drain the snowbound frontier mountains. On this west to east traverse the Silvretta chain is revealed at its scenic best, while plenty of escape routes are available in case the weather turns bad – which is always possible, especially early in the summer. Start at **St Gallenkirch** in the Montafon Valley and wander south through the Gargellental to Gargellen village or, alternatively, as far as the unwardened *Madrisa Hütte* (get the key from the *Haus Wulfenia*, a Gasthof in the centre of the village) situated about 45 minutes beyond. On day 2 cross the Vergaldnerjoch, which is reached via either the Vergaldatal, or through the more challenging Wintertal and over the Valzifenzer-Joch. The route then crosses the Mittelbergjoch before dropping to the *Tübinger Hütte* (☎05556/2589). On day 3, given good conditions, you can tackle a small crevasse-free glacier below the Plattenjoch (2728m) – from which fine views show the Grosse and Kleine Seehorn – then gain the Schweizerlücke, and descend to the *Saarbrücker Hütte* before continuing to the Bielerhöhe and cutting south to the *Wiesbadener Hütte*. The traverse proceeds on day 4 to the *Jamtal Hütte* over the Radsattel and Getschnerscharte, and day 5 from the *Jamtal* to the *Heidelberger Hütte* by way of the Kronenjoch. The final stage, day 6, crosses the Ritzenjoch, followed by a descent through the Lareintal to **Galtür** – an easier alternative is to amble downstream through the Fimbertal to **Ischgl** in the Paznauntal.

The recommended **map** for the *Wiesbadener Hütte* walk and Silvretta Traverse is *Kompass Wanderkarte* no. 41 (Silvretta Verwallgruppe) at 1:50,000. For more on the Austrian hut-to-hut system, see p.39.

Silvrettasee, and stupendous views southwards across the reservoir towards the **Silvretta range**, with the 3312-metre **Piz Buin** presiding over a ridge of high Alps that marks the border between Austria and the Swiss canton of Graubünden. On the other side of the Bielerhöhe, the road descends into the Paznaun, one of the Tyrol's most attractive valleys, arriving after 20km in the skiing and hiking resort of **Ischgl** (see p.515).

Zürs and Lech

East of Bludenz, the main road and rail route climbs up the Klostertal towards the **Arlberg Pass**, some 30km distant. Near the village of **Langen**, 6km short of the summit of the pass, both railway and main road enter a fourteen-kilometre-long **tunnel**, eventually emerging at the ski resort of St Anton (see p.516) on the Tyrolean side of the Arlberg. A secondary road heads north from Langen over the **Flexen Pass** to Austria's most upmarket alpine resorts, **Zürs** and **Lech**, lying 5km apart in a beautiful highland valley formed by the Zürs and Lech streams. Both places are easy to get to by bus from Langen am Arlberg train station, where most services on the main line to Innsbruck stop. A range of **skiing** terrain varied enough to cater for all abilities has secured the region's popularity, although its reputation as a high-society playground helps to set it apart from the rest of alpine Austria. A selection of European royals habitually holiday here, and high hotel prices ensure that the hoi polloi are kept at arms length. Outside the winter season, hiking opportunities are excellent, and accommodation rates are bearable, but many of the cafés and restaurants close their doors, making the essential soullessness of the place all too apparent. If you want an authentic taste of rural Vorarlberg you'd do better to stay in one of the Bregenzerwald villages to the west.

The smaller of the two settlements, Zürs, is little more than a clump of 4-star hotels, although **LECH** still preserves a smidgeon of rural charm thanks to some attractive alpine houses, and a dainty Gothic **Pfarrkirche** which surveys the village centre from a small hillock. Inside are some faded fourteenth-century frescoes, notably on the left-hand side of the high altar, where mourners are depicted gathering around the death-bed of the Virgin Mary. Quickest routes into the mountains are provided by the cable car to the 2350-metre Rüfikopf, which towers above Lech to the east, and the cable car to the mountainside settlement of Oberlech uphill to the west. It's above Oberlech that most of the intermediate skiing terrain is located, although a well-organized lift system ensures that you can access a wide range of different runs in a single day's skiing. There are some renowned off-piste runs on the slopes of the Rüfikopf. The Arlberg Ski Pass covers, Lech, Zürs, St Christoph, St Anton and a couple of other nearby resorts, and costs öS485/€35.41 per day; öS1350/€98.55 for 3 days; öS2410/€175.93 for 6 days, or öS4220/€308.06 for 13 days.

Practicalities

Lech's **tourist office** (May, June & Sept–Nov Mon–Fri 8am–noon & 2–5pm; July & Aug Mon–Sat 8am–noon & 2–6pm, Sun 10am–noon & 2–5pm; Dec–April Mon–Fri 9am–noon & 2–6pm, Sat 9am–6pm, Sun 10am–noon & 2–5pm; ☎05583/2161-0, *www.lech.at*), easy enough to spot on your left as you enter the town from the south, will book you into a **private room** (summer ②; winter ③) or provide information on hotel vacancies. One of the few affordable **pensions** in town is the small, family-run *Haus Jehle*, Lech 242 (☎05583/2380, *haus.jehle@netway.at*; summer ②; winter ④), about 1km north of the centre on the Warth road. Of the **hotels**, the *Elizabeth*, Lech 285 (☎05583/2330, *www.hotelelisabeth.com*; summer ④; winter ⑨), a medium-sized 4-star hotel located just uphill from the main street, has comfortable en-suites and its own swimming pool; while the *Gasthof Post*, centrally located at Lech 11 (☎05583/2206-0, *www.postlech.com*; ⑨), is the top address in the village and has standards of comfort and prices to match anything in Austria – doubles start at öS7000/€511 in the high season. For **eating**, *Don Enzo* just opposite the post office offers affordable pizza and pasta dishes from öS100/€7.30 upwards, as well as more expensive Italian treats such as a decent *Saltimbocca alla Romana*. The restaurant of the nearby *Hotel Krone*, just below the church, has a reputation for top-quality Austrian and international food, although it's the restaurant of the *Gasthof Post*, unsurprisingly, that comes out on top in the gourmet stakes. Nightlife in Lech is almost non-existent in summer, and in winter fashions change pretty quickly: as a general rule, **après-ski** activity revolves around glitzy hotel bars, and there's a lack of the egalitarian fun-pubs that you'll find in other Austrian resorts.

travel details

Trains

Bregenz to: Bludenz (hourly; 1hr–1hr 20min); Dornbirn (every 30min; 12–15min); Feldkirch (every 30min; 30–45min); Hohenems (every 30min; 25min); Innsbruck (8 daily; 2hr 40min); Rankweil (every 30min; 40min).

Bludenz to: Bregenz (hourly; 1hr–1hr 20min); Innsbruck (8 daily; 1hr 40min); Schruns (every 30min; 25min); Tschagguns (every 30min; 22min).

Buses

Au to: Damüls (5 daily; 30min).

Bludenz to: Lech (6 daily; 1hr 20min); Zürs (6 daily; 1hr 10min).

Bregenz to: Bezau (hourly; 1hr); Egg (hourly; 45min).

Dornbirn to: Au (hourly; 1hr 20min); Bezau (hourly; 1hr); Egg (hourly; 50min); Lech (summer only: 3 daily; 2hr 40min); Schwarzenberg (6 daily; 40min); Warth (summer only: 3 daily; 2hr 25min).

Egg to: Schwarzenberg (hourly; 10min).

Langen to: Lech (8 daily; 30min).

Lech to: Bludenz (6 daily; 1hr 20min); Langen (8 daily; 30min); Reutte (summer only: 2 daily; 2hr 10min); Warth (summer only: 2 daily; 25min).

Schruns to: the Silvretta dam (May–Oct only: 6 daily; 35min).

Schwarzenberg to: Bezau (6 daily; 20min); Dornbirn (6 daily; 40min); Egg (hourly; 10min).

THE HISTORICAL FRAMEWORK

Austria has existed as a state with clearly defined borders only since 1918. Before that the concept of Austria – whether cultural or political – was always a vague one: an agglomeration of lands gradually accumulated and held together by representatives of two remarkable dynasties – the Babenbergs and, more notably, the Habsburgs.

THE CELTS AND THE ROMANS

Reminders of Austria's **prehistoric inhabitants** can be glimpsed in the country's museums – Vienna's Naturhistorisches Museum holds the Venus of Willendorf, a 25,000-year-old carved fertility figure, while 4000-year-old ceramics left by inhabitants of a lakeland village can be seen in the Salzkammergut town of Mondsee. However, it was only really with the arrival of the **Celts** in the first millennium BC that organized, military and industrial civilization in the Austrian lands began to take off. Initially, Celtic control of a highly lucrative **salt trade** was the key to their wealth and power. Salt mines above the modern-day village of **Hallstatt** in the Salzkammergut (see p.447) were in use from around 1000 to 500 BC. The many Bronze and Iron Age finds yielded by archeological digs in the region (and on show in Hallstatt's Heimatmusem) reveal a society that combined a

high degree of industrial organization in the mine workings themselves with a pronounced appreciation for the good things in life – as evinced by the many intricate ornaments and ceremonial daggers that have been unearthed. In the eighth century BC, Celts from Hallstatt went on to open salt mines in **Bad Dürrnberg**, above the town of Hallein (see p.402) just south of Salzburg. As at Hallstatt, there's now a popular show-mine in the old mine workings, and an important museum of Celtic culture. The other important concentration of Celtic power was in the southeast, where the kingdom of **Noricum**, centred on present-day Carinthia, established an ascendancy over neighbouring tribes in the second and first centuries BC. Celtic power here was based on the exploitation of the iron ore found deep in the Carinthian valleys around modern-day Hüttenberg. The ruined city on the **Magdalensberg** (see p.334) just north of Klagenfurt is thought to have been Noricum's capital.

Iron from Noricum was particularly valued by the **Romans**, who used it to make javelins, and the growth of trade between Rome and the Celts gradually led to the establishment of Roman economic and cultural hegemony over the region. This culminated in the establishment of Roman political control: Roman legions occupied Austria south of the Danube in 15 BC, and the area was carved up into new administrative units. Western Austria (the Vorarlberg and much of the Tyrol) became the Roman province of **Rhaetia**, most of central and southern Austria was included in a new, reconstituted **Noricum**, while the east became part of **Pannonia**, which also embraced much of present-day Hungary. For the next four centuries, the **Danube** served as the natural military frontier between the empire and the barbarian tribes beyond, with a series of fortifications, or *Limes*, built along the river's banks. Best preserved of the Roman sites in Austria today is **Carnuntum** southeast of Vienna (see p.203), an important military camp on the Danube frontier that went on to flourish as a civilian settlement. Other important centres of Roman power were **Vindobona** (Vienna), **Juvavum** (Salzburg), **Brigantium** (Bregenz), **Flavia Solva** (Leibnitz, in Styria) and **Virunum** (north of Klagenfurt), and museums in each of these places preserve good Roman-era archeological collections.

THE DARK AGES AND THE EARLY MEDIEVAL PERIOD

The Romans finally abandoned the Danube frontier in the 430s, leaving the Austrian lands open to penetration by a succession of **migrating tribes**. The two main groups were German speaking: the **Alemanni**, who settled in the Vorarlberg region as well as neighbouring Switzerland; and the **Bavarians**, who occupied Upper Austria, Lower Austria, Salzburg and the Tyrol. Biggest of the non-German groups were the **Slavs**, who moved into Carinthia and Styria, although the east of the country was periodically subjected to incursions by other races, Huns and Avars among them. Vestiges of the Celto-Roman population, still speaking a Latin dialect, retreated into the high mountain valleys on the south side of the Alps. The period from the seventh to the ninth century was marked by the **gradual Germanization** of the Austrian lands, led mostly by Bavarian warrior-aristocrats, a process that often went hand in hand with the missionary activity of the Christian church. **Salzburg** became an important ecclesiastical centre after St Virgil's establishment of a monastery there in around 700, and it was from here that ambitious proselytizing clerics set off to convert the pagan inhabitants of central and southern Austria – many of whom were linguistically and culturally Slav at this point, although they were to lose their distinctive identity as the centuries passed.

THE OSTMARK AND THE RISE OF THE BABENBERGS

A semblance of political order was imposed on central Europe by the Frankish empire of **Charlemagne**, who was crowned Holy Roman Emperor in 800. The Franks established a military colony in what is now Upper and Lower Austria in order to keep disorderly eastern European tribes at bay – carving out a territory referred to by nineteenth-century historians as the *Ostmark*, or "Eastern March". With the collapse of the Frankish empire in 888, the **Ostmark** fell under the sway of Saxon kings Otto the Great and his son Otto II, who contributed to the ongoing Germanization of the area. The Ostmark was handed over to the **Babenberg dynasty** in 976, whose job it was to protect the empire's eastern frontiers, once more marked by the Danube. The Babenbergs

ruled the territory for the next 270 years, first as margraves and later as dukes.

In their search for some kind of official birthday for their country, many twentieth-century Austrian scholars latched onto a Latin parchment from around 996, which contains the first known mention of the name *Ostarrichi*, forerunner of the modern "Österreich". However, there's little evidence to suggest that the term was in common usage at the time, and for most of the Middle Ages the region held by the Babenbergs was known as *provincia orientalis* (or "eastern province", simply a Latin version of the original "Ostmark"). The Babenberg margravate certainly didn't conform to the borders of modern-day Austria. To begin with, it was confined to a small stretch of the Danube centred most probably on Melk, but it gradually expanded eastwards as far as the River Leitha and northwards as far as the River Thaya. Successive Babenbergs founded a number of monasteries in the region, in particular **Leopold III** (1095–1136), who founded Klosterneuburg in Lower Austria (see p.160), and was later canonized for his good works, becoming the country's patron saint.

In 1156, during the reign of **Heinrich II Jasomirgott** (1141–77), the Babenbergs' margravate was at last elevated to the status of a duchy by the Holy Roman Emperor, with its new capital at Vienna. However, in 1246 the Babenberg male line came to an end with the death of Duke Friedrich II (1230–46) on the battlefield. In 1251, the future Bohemian king, **Otakar II**, took up residence in Vienna and claimed the duchy for himself, shoring up his claim by marrying Friedrich II's widow.

THE EARLY HABSBURGS

While Otakar was laying claim to the Babenbergs' inheritance, he was also putting himself forward as a candidate for the throne of the Holy Roman Empire. In the end, though, the throne was handed in 1273 to **Rudolf of Habsburg**, a little-known count whose ancestral home was the castle of Habichtsburg (hence Habsburg) above the River Reuss in modern-day Switzerland. In 1278 Otakar was defeated (and killed) by Rudolf's forces at the Battle of Marchfeld, to the east of Vienna, allowing Rudolf to lay claim to the Duchy of Austria, as Ostmark was now known. The Viennese, who had backed Otakar, were less than pleased about the outcome of the battle, and weren't easily placated by Rudolf's son, Albrecht, who had been given the duchy by his father.

The Habsburgs, though, were destined to rule over Austria for the next 640 years. At this time, "Austria" still only comprised (roughly) modern Upper Austria, Lower Austria and a southerly province acquired by Rudolf, Styria. Gradually however, the Habsburgs were able to consolidate their Austrian powerbase by annexing surrounding territories (often through marriage treaties rather than military conquest) and appointing family members to rule over them. Much of Carinthia and the Tyrol were acquired by the end of the fourteenth century, although some parts of the Tyrolean northeast remained in Bavarian hands until around 1500. One area that remained immune to Habsburg expansion at this time was the territory of Salzburg (much more than just the city of Salzburg itself, this was an area that roughly corresponds to today's Salzburger Land), which was ruled over by powerful prince-archbishops, and retained its independence until 1815.

The way in which acquired territories were shared out among members of the Habsburg family threatened to dilute the dynasty's power until the emergence of **Friedrich III** (1440–93). Despite numerous setbacks – he was besieged in the Hofburg by one of his own family in 1462 and briefly lost control of Vienna to the Hungarian king Matthias Corvinus in 1485 – Friedrich managed to unite all the Habsburg-held lands under his own control. In 1452, he became the last Holy Roman emperor to be crowned in Rome, and the following year elevated the family's dukedom to an archdukedom. The Holy Roman Empire, famously dismissed by Matthias Corvinus as "neither holy, Roman, nor an empire", was something of a fantasy, whose emperor, theoretically, ruled over all the German-speaking lands. Though this was far from reality, the position of Holy Roman emperor gave the Habsburgs enormous prestige, and they persisted with its imperial pretensions, passing the title down the male line, until its eventual dissolution in 1806 (see p.554).

MAXIMILIAN I

In the meantime, the Habsburgs continued to add to their dynastic inheritance through a series of judicious marriages by **Maximilian I** (1459–1519) and his offspring, prompting the oft-quoted maxim, adapted from Ovid: "let others wage war; you, happy Austria, marry." Building on the gains of his father Friedrich III, Maximilian did more than anyone else to turn the Habsburg family possessions into a lasting multinational empire. His 1477 marriage to Mary of Burgundy – the only child of Charles the Bold, she died while hunting in 1482 – won him a belt of territories running through modern Belgium and the Netherlands; the marriage of their son Philip the Fair to Princess Juana of Castille (daughter of Ferdinand and Isabella of Spain) ensured that a Habsburg would inherit the Spanish throne. Maximilian also consolidated Habsburg control of the Austrian heartland, driving the Bavarians out of northeastern Tyrol and defeating the Hungarians to win back Vienna – which subsequently flourished as a cultural centre under his rule. Maximilian also entered into an alliance with the Hungarian royal house, which stipulated that if the Hungarian throne fell vacant then it would pass to the Habsburg family.

Maximilian's son Philip the Fair died in 1506 (an event that drove his wife insane, and historians have since dubbed her "Juana the Mad"), and it was Maximilian's grandson Karl V who received this vast, painstakingly assembled inheritance. Crowned Holy Roman emperor in 1519, Karl ruled over an empire on which, it was said, the sun never set, with lands stretching from its Spanish possessions in South America to Vienna itself – bolstered in 1526 by the addition of the kingdoms of Bohemia and Hungary when the childless Hungarian king was killed by the Turks at the Battle of Mohács. Under Karl, Habsburg power was at its zenith, although the French – aided at various times by the north German princes and the English – prevented the Habsburgs from establishing a truly pan-European hegemony.

REFORMATION AND COUNTER-REFORMATION

Such a large territorial unit was too unwieldy to be ruled by one man, and Karl V decided to divide the imperial heritage among his successors. The Habsburgs' Spanish possessions fell to Karl's eldest son Philip II of Spain, while the core central European lands of Austria, Bohemia and Hungary passed to his younger brother

Ferdinand I (1553–64). The unity of the empire was increasingly threatened by the collapse of traditional Catholicism brought about by the **Reformation**. By the sixteenth century, the population of Austria (excluding the Tyrol) was overwhelmingly Protestant, and the Habsburg dynasty itself increasingly ambiguous in its support for the Catholic Church. Ferdinand I invited the Jesuits to Vienna in 1556 in order to shore up the decaying structures of Catholic belief, even though the atmosphere at his court was one of tolerance, attracting a wide range of European intellectuals – both Catholic and Protestant – to Vienna. The ideas of the Reformation were allowed to flourish further under Ferdinand's son and successor **Maximilian II** (1564–76), who was himself suspected of being a closet Protestant by contemporaries.

It was in the Austrian lands of the empire that the Catholic Church began its fightback. The Jesuits, now established in Vienna, were introduced to Styria in the 1580s by Maximilian II's brother the Archduke Karl, while the **Counter-Reformation** gathered momentum. Protestants became alarmed, and began to demand more and more legal rights from an imperial court that was under increasing pressure to put the full weight of its support behind one side or the other. **Rudolf II** (1576–1612), who presided over a remarkably tolerant and humanist court in the Bohemian city of Prague, tried to placate both sides, merely serving to postpone a violent religious conflict that was bound to break out sooner or later. After the brief interregnum of the Protestant-leaning **Matthias I** (1612–19), the accession to the throne of the fanatically Catholic **Ferdinand II** (1619–37) pushed the Protestant nobles of Bohemia towards armed rebellion. The conflict widened to involve neighbouring European states, and in the resulting **Thirty Years' War** the Habsburg court became increasingly identified with the Catholic ideology of the Counter-Reformation. Protestant sympathies were treated as a sign of disloyalty to the dynasty, and Protestants everywhere were subjected to a harsh crackdown. Ferdinand II's devout grandson **Leopold I** (1658–1705), who had initially trained for the priesthood, epitomized the relationship between the dynasty and Catholic piety, a relationship that increasingly relied on showmanship and spectacle – Leopold's endless rounds of praying and fasting, together with his pilgrimage journeys to cult centres like Mariazell (see p.296), were widely publicized.

THE OTTOMAN THREAT

Hardly a competent warrior-king himself, Leopold I was lucky to be on the throne at the time of one of the Habsburg Empire's greatest military victories, the defeat of the **Ottoman Turks** outside Vienna in 1683. Ottoman power had been advancing steadily across Europe from the fourteenth century onwards, and had penetrated as far as Vienna (the "city of the golden apple", as the Turks called it) once before, in 1529. On that occasion, the Turks mysteriously withdrew, despite the fact that the city had been only lightly defended. Ever since, however, the Turks had been a constant threat on the empire's southeastern borders, and the struggle against them was to provide the Habsburgs with a defining sense of historical mission. Grandiose hilltop fortresses like **Hochosterwitz** (see p.336) and **Riegersburg** (see p.292) served to keep the Ottomans at bay, while the Styrian capital **Graz** was for a time a vast armed camp from which Habsburg counter-offensives were launched. The Habsburg-Ottoman border shifted back and forth throughout the sixteenth and much of the seventeenth centuries, with the defeat of the Ottomans at the **Battle of Szentgotthàrd** (1664) finally ushering in a period of apparent stability. However, Ottoman ambitions revived a generation later, and the sudden and unexpected Ottoman advance on Vienna in 1683 led to an Austria-wide panic. At the approach of the Turks, Leopold, and anyone else who had the money, fled to the safety of Linz and Passau.

In their absence, Vienna was confronted by an army of over 200,000 men. Protected by a garrison of just 10,000 men, the Viennese were understandably ready to make peace with the grand vizier, **Kara Mustafa**. The grand vizier's crucial mistake, however, was that he was overconfident. Loath to share the booty among his army (which would be inevitable if they took the city by force), he orchestrated a two-month siege of the city. By September, however, a relief force of Poles, under their king **Jan Sobieski**, and sundry German troops under the duke of Lorraine, had come to Vienna's aid. On September 12, the papal legate Marco d'Aviano conducted a Mass on the hills above the city and, though outnumbered, the imperial forces managed to rout the Turks, in the process gaining some 20,000 buffaloes, bullocks, camels and mules, 10,000 sheep, corn and flour, sugar, oil and, most famously, coffee. Diamonds, rubies, sapphires and pearls, silver and gold, and "the most beautiful sable furs in the world", belonging to Kara Mustafa, fell into the grateful hands of King Sobieski.

Vienna was quickly followed up by further Habsburg successes, with armies led by one of the heroes of the siege, **Prince Eugène of Savoy**, penetrating deep into Ottoman territory. Victory at the **Battle of Zenta** (now in northern Yugoslavia) in 1697 was followed by the **Peace of Karlowitz**, which granted the Habsburgs control of all of the old Kingdom of Hungary, which included Transylvania and much of modern-day Croatia. Prince Eugène's capture of **Belgrade** in 1718 more or less stifled any further Ottoman dreams of expansion in Europe.

THE EIGHTEENTH CENTURY

At the same time that the Ottomans were being pushed back in the east, Austria was engaged in a long-running **war with the French**, who were contesting Habsburg control over much of the Low Countries. A string of victories between 1701 and 1714 (again, mostly presided over by Prince Eugène) re-established Austria as the prime military power on the European mainland, ushering in another (albeit short-lived) period of peace and prosperity. The main beneficiary was Leopold I's second son **Karl VI** (1711–40), a free-spending monarch under whose reign Austrian Baroque art and architecture blossomed. This was especially marked in the capital, where the disappearance of the Ottoman threat provoked a rash of building activity. Damaged churches were repaired, aristocrats built palaces in the suburbs, and Karl undertook various prestigious architectural projects – Vienna's finest Baroque church, the Karlskirche (see p.116), among them.

MARIA THERESIA (1740–80)

The area in which Karl VI singularly failed, however, was in producing a male heir to the throne. In the end, he had to accept the fact that his eldest daughter, **Maria Theresia**, was going to have to take over when he died. In an attempt to smooth her accession, Karl introduced the so-called **Pragmatic Sanction** in 1713, which allowed for female succession, and got all the states nominally within the Holy Roman Empire to promise to recognize his daughter's right to the Habsburgs' hereditary lands. Naturally enough, everyone agreed with the emperor while he was alive, and as soon as he died immediately went back on their word.

So it was that Maria Theresia found herself forced to fight the **War of the Austrian Succession** (1740–48) as soon as she took over from her father. For a while, she was even forced to hand over the imperial title to Karl of Bavaria in an attempt to pacify him, though it was eventually regained and handed to her husband, Franz Stephan of Lorraine (she herself, as a woman, could not become Holy Roman Emperor). At the end of the war in 1748, Maria Theresia was forced to cede Silesia to Prussia and, despite an attempt to win it back during the **Seven Years' War** (1756–63), it remained, for the most part, in Prussian hands.

On the domestic front, Maria Theresia's reign signalled the beginning of an **era of reform**, influenced by the ideas of the Enlightenment. The empress created a formidable centralized bureaucracy, taking power away from the provincial diets, in order to ease through her reforms. When the pope abolished the Jesuit order in 1773, Maria Theresia took the opportunity of introducing a state education system. In 1776 she abolished torture, and passed de facto abolition of the death penalty (though hard labour usually killed the convict within a year in any case). Despite her reforms, it would be wrong to get the impression that the empress was some free-thinking democrat. She believed wholeheartedly in absolutism and, as a devout Catholic, ensured Catholic supremacy within the empire with yet more anti-Protestant edicts.

JOSEF II (1780–90)

With the death of her husband in 1765, Maria Theresia appointed her eldest son, **Josef II**, as co-regent. But it wasn't until after the empress's death in 1780 that Josef's reforming zeal could come into its own. His most significant edict was the 1781 *Toleranzpatent*, which allowed freedom of worship to Lutheran, Calvinist and Greek Orthodox groups. Like his mother, Josef was himself a devout Catholic, but was even more determined to curtail church – and particularly papal – power. To this end, he dissolved four hundred contemplative or "idle" monasteries and, as many saw it, was bent on "nationalizing" the Church.

Under Josef II all religious processions (previously a daily occurrence on the streets of Vienna, and an important feature of rural life) were banned except the Corpus Christi procession. The blessed sacrament was no longer carried through the streets, causing the faithful to fall to their knees. Pope Pius VI was so concerned, he came to Vienna in person in 1782 to try to change the emperor's mind, but to no avail. With the best of intentions, Josef interfered in every aspect of his citizens' lives, causing widespread resentment. For – again like his mother – despite his enlightened policies, Josef was very much the despot. He was, above all, responsible for creating the Habsburgs' secret police force, which was to become so notorious in the nineteenth century.

THE NAPOLEONIC ERA

The Emperor Leopold II, who unenthusiastically succeeded Josef II in 1790, died suddenly of a stroke after a reign of less than two years. As a result, Leopold's eldest son became the Emperor **Franz II** (1792–1835). No great military man – his troops had been fighting the French for two years before he bothered to show himself at the front line – Franz was an unlikely candidate to become one of **Napoleon**'s great adversaries.

In his first Italian campaign, Napoleon succeeded in humiliating the Habsburg forces at Mantua, and was within 150km of Vienna when the emperor sued for peace. It was a scenario that was repeated again in 1800 when Napoleon's forces were once more marching on Vienna. By 1803, the Habsburgs had lost their possessions in the Low Countries in addition to several territories in northern Italy to the French. Napoleon added insult to injury by declaring himself emperor the following year, with the clear intention of re-establishing the Holy Roman Empire under French hegemony. In retaliation, Franz II declared himself Emperor Franz I of Austria (a hitherto non-existent title) – ironically, the gesture looked more like an admission of defeat, since Franz was already Holy Roman Emperor.

In 1805, in alliance with Russia and Britain, Austria decided to take on Napoleon again, only to suffer a crushing defeat at **Ulm**. Unable to stop the advance of the *Grande Armée*, the allies decided to regroup further east, leaving Napoleon free to **march on Vienna**, where he arrived on November 13, 1805. The imperial family had already taken flight to Hungary, carrying the contents of the Hofburg with them. Though there was no fighting, having 34,000 French troops billeted in the city put an enormous strain on the place, and supplies quickly ran short. The French stayed on until January 12, 1806, having exacted taxes and war reparations and appropriated many works of art, including four hundred paintings from the Belvedere. Four days later, Franz II returned to Vienna amid much rejoicing, though in political terms there was little to rejoice about. The **Treaty of Pressburg**, concluded after a defeat at **Austerlitz** in December 1805, had left the Habsburgs without their Italian possessions, the Tyrol and the Vorarlberg. Further humiliation followed in 1806 when Napoleon established the Confederation of the Rhine and Franz was forced to relinquish his title of Holy Roman Emperor.

For the next few years, there was no hope of the Austrians exacting any revenge. The Habsburgs applauded an **uprising in the Tyrol** (which Napoleon had awarded to his Bavarian allies) led by patriotic innkeeper **Andreas Hofer**, but shied away from offering concrete support. In the spring of 1809, however, as Napoleon encountered problems fighting Wellington in Spain, the Austrians seized the moment to reopen hostilities. Although they were once more defeated at Ratisbon, the Austrian forces under the emperor's brother, the Archduke Karl, managed to regroup to the east of Vienna. Once more Napoleon marched on Vienna. As usual, the imperial family had taken flight to Hungary, but this time the city tried to defend itself. Napoleon reached the outskirts on May 10, 1809, and sent two emissaries in to negotiate. They were promptly lynched by the Viennese; the French bombardment started the following evening. It was an uneven battle: the French fired some 1600 shells, and killed 23 civilians; in return, according to one Viennese eyewitness, "our batteries shot off a few shots; they were ineffective". The next day, the city capitulated, its 16,000-strong garrison no match for 100,000 French troops.

Napoleon's *Grande Armée* went on to suffer its first major defeat ten days later at **Aspern**, just east of Vienna. However, the Archduke Karl failed to press home his advantage, and Napoleon succeeded in holding on to Vienna, going on to defeat the Austrians decisively at nearby **Deutsch Wagram** six weeks later, when the Austrians threw in the towel. Vienna was forced to celebrate the new emperor's birthday on August 13 and, in the peace, signed on October 14, the Austrians were forced to give up Galicia and Croatia. Two days later Napoleon left Vienna, but without leaving instruction for his French engineers to blow up the city's defences. On October 29, the French held a farewell ball, and towards the end of the following month, the Emperor Franz crept back incognito into the Hofburg. Soon after Wagram, the revolt in the Tyrol finally collapsed due to lack of aid from Vienna, and Andreas Hofer was captured and shot

Clemenz **Metternich** was appointed the chief minister of Austria by Franz, and began to pursue a policy of *rapprochement*. His greatest coup in this direction was getting Napoleon to marry the Emperor Franz's 18-year-old daughter, Marie Louise, in March 1810. By 1813, with the tide turning against Napoleon, Metternich even managed to persuade his reluctant emperor to join the latest anti-French grand alliance.

THE CONGRESS OF VIENNA

Following the defeat of Napoleon at Leipzig and his exile to Elba, the victorious powers (Austria, Great Britain, Prussia and Russia) met for the **Congress of Vienna** in autumn 1814. If nothing else, the Congress was a great social success or, as one participant famously put it, *"Le congrès danse, mais il ne marche pas"*. By New Year 1815, most of the foreign delegates and their hangers-on had outstayed their welcome. The congress was costing the emperor a fortune that even he could not afford, forcing him to raise taxes, while many of the participants were living on credit notes. The congress dragged on, however, until after Napoleon escaped from Elba, finally winding itself up in May 1815, just twelve days before his final defeat at the **Battle of Waterloo**.

The congress nonetheless managed to establish a status quo in Europe. Many of the borders agreed upon in Vienna were to endure for over a century. In the peace deal, Austria won back much of north Italy and Galicia, Croatia, the Tyrol and the Vorarlberg. In addition, the city of **Salzburg** and its attendant territories were brought into Austria for the first time. On Metternich's advice, claims to the Netherlands, and other far-flung territories that would be hard to defend, were relinquished. The congress also pledged itself to further regular meetings between the heads of the victorious states – at which it was agreed that in order to maintain international peace they would combine to suppress any further revolutionary uprisings within Europe.

THE VORMÄRZ

Following the Congress, Austria enjoyed more than thirty years of peace and stability, a period known retrospectively as the **Vormärz** – literally "pre-March" – because it preceded the March 1848 revolution. In later years, the Austrians would look back on this period through rose-tinted spectacles as a time of introspective domesticity, played out to the tunes of Johann Strauss the Elder and the melodies of Franz Schubert.

This period was also, however, marked by one of the most oppressive regimes in the history of the Habsburgs. The man most closely associated with the conservative politics of *Vormärz* was Metternich. Under him, and his chief of police Count Josef Sedlnitzky, the vast machinery of the civil service that Josef II had designed to help push through reforms was now used to thwart further reforms. Censorship and the activities of the secret police and its informers did so much to stifle intellectual life that by 1848 the playwright Franz Grillparzer reflected miserably, "Despotism has destroyed my life, at least my literary life."

With the death in 1835 of the Emperor Franz I of Austria (former Franz II of the Holy Roman Empire, the title he was forced to relinquish in 1806), the Habsburgs faced something of a crisis, as the heir to the throne, **Ferdinand I** – a victim of Habsburg inbreeding – was, in the vocabulary of the day, an "imbecile", nicknamed Nandl der Trottel (Ferdy the Dotty). He was, in fact, nothing of the sort: he could be perfectly coherent, but suffered badly from epilepsy, which affected his short-term memory. To combat Ferdinand's deficiencies, a Regency Council was established, with Ferdinand as chairman – or, in his absence, his nephew the Archduke Ludwig – and his brother Franz Karl, Count Kolowrat and Metternich as permanent members. Within the council, Metternich had to struggle to maintain his influence.

THE 1848 REVOLUTION

With the deposition of the French king and the outbreak of revolution in Paris in late February 1848, a wave of **revolutionary fervour** spread throughout Europe. Austria, groaning under the weight of an oppressive bureaucracy, was no exception. On March 13, the Estates of Lower Austria, consisting of nobles and senior clergy, were due to meet in the Landhaus on Vienna's Herrengasse. They were pressing for various reforms including the freedom of the press, but top of the agenda was the removal of Metternich. In the morning a crowd gathered outside the Landhaus and, after listening to a German translation of the inflammatory speech given recently by the Hungarian revolutionary Lajos Kossuth in the Hungarian Diet, forced their way into the building. At around 1pm, a detachment of Italian grenadiers fired into the crowd, killing around thirty unarmed protesters, mostly students, and sparking a revolution.

That evening, after playing for time, Metternich finally resigned and fled from the capital (disguised as a washerwoman according to popular legend). The emperor – who, when told of the outbreak of revolution, had apparently said "But do they have permission?" – immediately made a rapid retreat, declaring, "Tell the people I agree to everything." A National Guard was formed – with Johann Strauss the Younger as *Kapellmeister* – augmented by an academic legion of armed students, with whom they were to man the city in place of the despised imperial troops. In addition a constitution was promised, and a "Responsible Ministry" of bureaucrats formed to produce it. On April 25, a **constitutional monarchy** was proposed, with two chambers elected by limited franchise based on property. This failed to quench the thirst for radical reform, and on May 15 rioting ensued in favour of a single chamber parliament elected by universal suffrage. The emperor and his entourage quickly fled to Innsbruck in a stagecoach, as barricades were erected around the city.

Elections were duly held throughout the empire (with the exception of Italy and Hungary, which were busy with their own revolutions) and the first parliament in Habsburg history met on July 22 in the unlikely surroundings of the Hofburg's Winterreitschule. The deputies were by no means revolutionaries, the majority coming from the educated middle classes, although close to a third were of peasant origin. Hampered throughout by disputes between the various nationalities, the assembly did manage to pass one lasting piece of legislation, the **emancipation of the peasantry**. By August, the court felt secure enough to return to Vienna, bolstered by General Radetzky's military victory over the rebels in Italy and the recapture of Prague by General Windischgrätz.

The spark that lit the final fuse of the Viennese revolution took place on October 6. A battalion, due to be sent to fight against Kossuth's Hungarian revolutionaries, mutinied and joined forces with radicals in the National Guard. Civil war broke out as some within the National Guard fired on the radicals. In the confusion, the war minister, General Latour, was lynched by the mob and the imperial family removed themselves once more, this time to Olomouc in Moravia. As Windischgrätz marched his troops towards the capital, the radicals among the academic legion and the National Guard erected barricades and awaited the final showdown. Their only hope lay in the possibility of a Hungarian relief force, which in the event arrived too late. After several days' bombardment and around two thousand casualties, Windischgrätz flushed out the last of the rebels on October 31.

FRANZ-JOSEF AND THE END OF THE EMPIRE

Back in Olomouc, the Emperor Ferdinand, with his brother Franz Karl, was coerced by the imperial family into renouncing the throne in favour of the latter's 18-year-old nephew, **Franz-Josef**. A new government was formed under the leadership of the arch-conservative Prince Felix Schwarzenberg, while the assembly continued to meet in nearby Moravia to try to thrash out a new constitution. Then, to the astonishment of the assembly, on February 28, 1849, Schwarzenberg announced that as the emperor had himself formulated a new constitution, their services were no longer required. Although the new constitution granted equal rights to all, it was anything but liberal, granting the emperor the power of veto over all legislation, the power to dissolve parliament and rule by decree, and the power to dismiss and appoint ministers as he saw fit. Meanwhile in Hungary, the Austrians were forced to swallow their pride and enlist the help of the Russians in order to defeat Kossuth's Hungarian revolutionaries once and for all.

THE AUSGLEICH

After ten years of relative peace, Franz-Josef suffered his first of many embarrassing military setbacks at the **Battle of Solferino** in 1859 against the French. It was not so much the resultant loss of Lombardy that was the problem, but the opportunity it gave the Hungarians to demand their independence once more. In an attempt to placate them, Franz-Josef agreed in 1861 to establish a two-chamber parliament in Vienna. The Hungarians remained unimpressed and failed to send delegates to fill any of their 85 allotted seats in the lower house.

Five years later, the empire was rocked by an even greater crisis with its army's humiliating defeat at the **Battle of Königgrätz** in the Austro-Prussian War. Not only did the Habsburgs finally lose the battle for hegemony over the rest of Germany, but they were forced to strike a deal with the Hungarians (while studiously ignoring the demands of the empire's other nationalities).

With the 1867 **Ausgleich**, or Compromise, the so-called Dual Monarchy of Austria-Hungary was established. According to this new arrangement, Franz-Josef was to be crowned king of Hungary (he was already emperor of Austria), and the Hungarians were to get their own parliament in Budapest, with autonomy over everything except defence, foreign affairs and the overall imperial budget. Everything within Hungary was to be prefaced with a *k.* for *königlich* (royal), everything in the rest of the empire was to be prefaced with the initials *k.k.* or *kaiserlich-königlich* (imperial-royal), while everything Austro-Hungarian was prefaced with *k.u.k.* or *kaiserlich-und-königlich*.

At the same time, delegates from the "Austrian" half of the empire met in Vienna's parliament. Among the delegates were Czechs, Poles, Croats, Slovenes, Italians and German-speakers from every corner of the empire, who spent most of their time arguing over language issues, and abusing each other both verbally and physically. The number of people eligible to vote increased gradually until universal male suffrage was finally introduced in 1907, but in reality, the emperor still ruled supreme since he and his ministers could pass any laws they wanted as "emergency measures", not to mention dissolve parliament and rule by decree (which they did on numerous occasions).

FIN-DE-SIÈCLE AUSTRIA

The economy suffered its worst financial crisis ever in the crash of May 1873 – the fault, it was rumoured by some, of Jewish financiers. The Jew had long been a stock Viennese scapegoat, and with the continuing influx of orthodox Jews from the rural provinces of the empire, attracted to the city by the work opportunities opened up by growing industrialization, **anti-Semitism** began to flourish. It found a spokesman in the figure of the pan-German nationalist **Georg von Schönerer**, some of whose followers used to wear the effigy of a hanged Jew on their watch chains. Schönerer's political career faltered, however, after 1888, when he was sent to prison for breaking into the offices of the Jewish-owned newspaper, the *Neues Wiener Tagblatt*.

Anti-Semitism was given a more respectable, populist twist by **Karl Lueger**. This Vienna-born politician became leader of the Christian Social Party, whose combination of Catholicism, anti-Semitism and municipal socialism went down alarmingly well with the Austrian electorate. In 1897, Lueger began a successful spell as mayor of Vienna. (The crowd that turned out for his funeral in 1910 was the largest the city had ever seen – among the mourners was the young Adolf Hitler.)

Most middle-class Jews, understandably, gravitated towards the other side of the political spectrum, dominating the upper echelons of the **Social Democratic Workers' Party** (SDAP) after it was founded in 1889. The party's chief ideologue before World War I was the Prague-born Jew **Viktor Adler**, whose peculiar brand of **Austro-Marxism** was to dominate the party's thinking for the next half-century. As far as Adler was concerned, capitalism was doomed to failure, so the party could afford to adopt a peaceful approach to politics until the time was right for revolution.

In among all the tensions between Right and Left, Jew and Gentile, rich and poor, fin-de-siècle Austria – particularly the capital Vienna – succeeded in nurturing an astonishing variety of intellectual and artistic creativity, much of it inspired by assimilated Jews. In music, **Arnold Schönberg** and his followers Alban Berg and Anton Webern changed the face of classical music with their atonal revolution. **Gustav Mahler** turned heads both as a composer and as boss of the Staatsoper. In medicine, **Sigmund Freud** coined the term "psychoanalysis", and expounded on the new discipline in his seminal *On the Interpretation of Dreams*. In 1897, the artist **Gustav Klimt** led a revolt against the artistic establishment, known as the Secession (see p.117); following in his footsteps were the likes of **Egon Schiele** and **Oskar Kokoschka**. **Otto Wagner** left the most visible legacy of this period, in the Jugendstil and early Modernist buildings that can still be seen on the streets of Vienna today.

WORLD WAR I

Ever since Prince Eugène of Savoy's great military campaigns against the Ottomans, the Austrians had been in possession of considerable territories in the northern Balkans, bringing a large number of **South Slavs** within the borders of the empire. To begin with, most of these Slovenes, Croats and Serbs were loyal to a Habsburg dynasty which seemed to offer them protection against the Turks, but the rise of **nationalism** in the nineteenth century put increasing pressure on Austria's relationship with its non-German subjects. In particular, the emergence of a **Serbian principality** (which had won independence from the Ottoman Empire in 1830) convinced those Slavs living under Habsburg rule that self-government was a realizable political goal. In 1908 Austria's annexation of the hitherto Ottoman province of **Bosnia-Herzegovina** – which contained a mixture of Serbs, Croats and Muslim Slavs – stretched Austrian-Slav relations to breaking point.

In 1914, Franz-Josef's nephew and heir **Archduke Franz-Ferdinand** committed an act of gross political folly in choosing to visit the Bosnian capital **Sarajevo** on June 28, St Vitus' day – a day sacred to the Serbs. Together with his wife Sophie, the archduke was assassinated by Gavrilo Princip, a young Bosnian Serb revolutionary who had been supplied with weapons by Serbia's chief of military intelligence. There was little genuine sadness in court circles, for, as Stefan Zweig bluntly put it, the archduke "lacked everything that counts for real popular-

ity in Austria; amiability, personal charm and easy-goingness". Even his uncle, the emperor Franz-Josef, was more relieved than anything else, as the two got on notoriously badly.

To begin with, there was also very little action by Austria on the diplomatic front, but eventually on July 23 Franz-Josef and his ministers sent an **ultimatum** to Serbia, with an impossible set of conditions and a 48-hour time limit. Serbia capitulated to almost all the conditions, but Austria-Hungary declared war anyway, without consulting its German or Italian allies. Unwilling to see any further extension of Austrian power in the Balkans, the Russians immediately mobilized, with Britain and France (Russia's allies), following suit. By August 12, the major European powers were at war.

Perhaps surprisingly, the outbreak of war brought patriotic crowds onto the streets of Vienna, and other cities around the empire, with Left and Right alike rallying round the Habsburg cause. Of course, everyone thought the war would be over by Christmas; it was only after several years of military defeats, huge casualties and food shortages that the population began to turn against the war. On October 21, 1916, Viktor Adler's son, Friedrich, took matters into his own hands and assassinated the Austrian prime minister, Count Karl Stürgkh. At his trial in May the following year, Friedrich Adler gave such a damning indictment of the war that his execution was postponed so as not to boost the antiwar cause further. On November 21, 1916, Franz-Josef died at the age of 86, leaving the throne to his 29-year-old great-nephew Karl.

The **Emperor Karl I** (see p.201) is perhaps best known for his bungled attempt at negotiating a separate peace for his empire with the western allies in March 1917. The approach was rebuffed at the time and a year later became public knowledge, causing huge embarrassment to all concerned. Only victory on the battlefield could now save the dynasty – it was not to come.

In October 1918, the empire began to crumble from within, with **national committees** taking over in the empire's regional capitals. In Vienna, the Social Democrats, who were in favour of self-determination for the empire's various nationalities, set up a provisional government under Karl Renner. On November 2, 1918, with the end of the war in sight, the Hungarian battalion guarding Schönbrunn upped and went, leaving the imperial family and their servants unguarded. The next day an armistice was signed, and eight days later the Emperor Karl I agreed to sign away his powers, withdrawing first to Eckartsau outside Vienna, and eventually, in 1919, going into exile in Switzerland.

THE FIRST REPUBLIC

The **Austrian Republic** was proclaimed from the steps of Vienna's parliament on November 12, 1918. Most of the Habsburg Empire's constituent nationalities – whether Hungarians, Czechs, Slovaks, Slovenes or Croats – had by now opted to form their own national states. What was left was a territory composed of the German-speaking parts of the empire, although even here the Austrians had to endure one particularly humiliating territorial loss – the German-speaking **South Tyrol** was given by the allies to Italy as a reward for the country's participation in the war. Few believed that the new, small-scale Austria would survive as a viable independent state, and there was precious little

enthusiasm for the new country among its people. The Christian Socials wanted a constitutional monarchy, the Pan-Germans wanted union with Germany, while the Socialists, more specifically, wanted Anschluss with a Socialist Germany. In the proclamation of November 12, the country was even described as "a constituent part of the German Republic". In the Länder, both the Tyrol and Salzburg voted overwhelmingly in favour of Anschluss with Germany (requests which were denied by the international community), while the Vorarlberg voted to join the Swiss.

In February 1919, the first national **elections** took place, creating a coalition government of the SDAP and the Christian Socials under the chancellorship of Social Democrat Karl Renner. Nevertheless, a political vacuum continued until the end of the year, with soldiers' and workers' councils threatening to follow the Soviet revolutionary example of neighbouring Bavaria, which was in the throes of Bolshevik revolution at the time, and Hungary. There were even two unsuc-

THE BREAK-UP OF THE AUSTRO-HUNGARIAN EMPIRE 1918

cessful attempts by the newly formed Austrian Communist Party (KPÖ) to stage a putsch, in April and June 1919.

The new government's foremost task, however, was to feed the population, particularly that of Vienna. Deprived of its former territories, and hampered by a bad harvest, the country managed it only with the help of the Allied Famine Relief programme. The government's next most arduous job was to negotiate the Treaty of St-Germain with the victorious allies. Many in the delegation still hoped for Anschluss with Germany, but it was not to be. The Austrians (along with the Hungarians) were branded an "enemy state", while the rest of the so-called "successor states" like Czechoslovakia were not, and were expressly forbidden ever to undertake Anschluss with Germany.

PARAMILITARY POLITICS

For most of the First Republic, the country remained split between the heavily industrialized Social Democrat-dominated capital of Vienna (nicknamed *Rotes Wien* or "Red Vienna" because of its political affiliations), where some thirty percent of the population lived, and the deeply conservative Catholic rural Länder where the Christian Socials dominated. What made this political polarization all the more dangerous was that by the mid-1920s both sides were backed up by **paramilitary organizations**. The right-wing *Heimwehr*, on the one hand, had their origins in armed groups that had defended Austria's borders in the chaotic early days of the republic. Based on individual Länder and each with their own leader, the *Heimwehr* organizations didn't share a political platform but were united in their opposition to the Left.

The Social Democrats, on the other hand, had created an ad hoc army, the *Volkswehr*, in the last weeks of the war. They continued to dominate the *Volkswehr* until it was replaced by the establishment of the official Austrian army, or *Bundeswehr*. As a result, the SDAP eventually formed its own armed division, the *Schutzbund*, in 1923. Throughout the 1920s the party mouthed the rhetoric of class war, while pursuing moderate, social-democratic policies. In 1926, the party went even further and declared itself ready to use force if necessary to protect the interests of the workers. The bourgeois press interpreted this as a call for revolu-

tion, though the slogan coined by Socialist ideologue Otto Bauer was "democratic as long as we can be; dictatorship only if we are forced to it, and insofar as we are forced". To the dismay of many on the Left, however, the SDAP proved itself much less willing to resort to violence than its right-wing foes.

AUSTRO-FASCISM

The onset of the **Great Depression** further destabilized what was already a fragile democracy. In the elections of November 1930, the *Heimwehr*, under Prince Starhemberg, won its first parliamentary seats for its newly formed political wing, the *Heimatblock*. The Social Democrats, meanwhile, emerged for the first time since 1919 as the largest single party, with 41 percent of the vote, but once more it was the Christian Socials who went on to form a series of weak coalition governments. The last of these was formed in May 1932 under the chancellorship of **Engelbert Dollfuss**, with a parliamentary majority of just one.

On March 4, 1933, in an attempt to break a tied vote in parliament, Social Democrat Karl Renner resigned as speaker in order to free himself to vote. When Renner's two deputy speakers from the Christian Social and Pan-German parties both followed suit, Dollfuss seized the opportunity to **dissolve parliament**, claiming it could no longer function properly. The same weekend, Adolf Hitler won an absolute majority in the German parliament. The onset of Nazism had a sobering effect on the majority of Austrians, particularly the SDAP, which immediately dropped its call for Anschluss.

On March 15, Dollfuss sent the police in to prevent parliament from reconvening. In response, the SDAP leadership procrastinated and held back from calling in the *Schutzbund*; two weeks later the latter was outlawed. Dollfuss was determined to combat the threat from Nazi Germany, but instead of agreeing to an anti-Nazi alliance with the SDAP the chancellor threw in his lot with Mussolini, holding the first of many meetings with the Italian dictator in April. On May 21, no doubt prompted by Mussolini, Dollfuss established the Austro-fascist Fatherland Front (VF), under the slogan "Austria Awake!"

In May the Communist Party was banned and in July the Austrian Nazi Party outlawed. A violent showdown with the Social Democrats, who still controlled municipal councils in Vienna and many other cities, followed in February 1934. The first incident took place in Linz, where the local *Schutzbund* on their own intiative opened fire on police. Three days of nationwide struggle ensued, with the bloodiest set-to in Vienna's Karl-Marx-Hof housing estate, which Dollfuss eventually ordered the army to shell into submission. The SDAP had stumbled into civil war, and it was soundly beaten. The party was swiftly outlawed, and its leaders fled abroad or were imprisoned.

Just as it appeared he had successfully established an **Austro-fascist state**, Dollfuss was assassinated on July 25, 1934, during an abortive putsch staged by Austrian Nazis, apparently without the knowledge of Hitler. His successor, **Kurt Schuschnigg**, was forced to rely ever more heavily on Mussolini for support. As a foreign policy this proved disastrous, for in 1935 Hitler and Mussolini began to patch up their differences, and suddenly Schuschnigg found himself being urged by Mussolini to come to an agreement with Hitler. Schuschnigg did just that in the Austro-German agreement of July 11, 1936. In return for Hitler's recognition of Austria's "full sovereignty", Schuschnigg agreed to an amnesty for all Nazi prisoners, and the appointment of various "prominent nationalists" – not Nazis, but authoritarian conservatives with similar leanings – to his government.

In January 1938, the Austrian police raided the apartment of Leopold Tavs, one of Schuschnigg's deputies, and discovered a plan to overthrow the government with German help. As tension between the two countries mounted, the Nazi ambassador, Franz von Papen, suggested Schuschnigg should visit Hitler at his mountain retreat at Berchtesgaden by the Austrian border. At this meeting, Hitler ranted and raved and eventually demanded, among other things, that Schuschnigg hand over yet more key governmental posts to the Austrian Nazi Party. Schuschnigg acquiesced and agreed to appoint the Nazi Dr Arthur Seyss-Inquart as interior minister.

As the Austrian Nazis increased their activities, Schuschnigg decided to chance his arm with a **plebiscite** to decide the country's future, reckoning (probably correctly) that the majority would vote against the Anschluss. Hitler was certainly not prepared to risk electoral defeat and swiftly demanded the resignation of Schuschnigg and his entire government.

Schuschnigg announced his resignation over the radio, in order to avoid "spilling German blood", and Seyss-Inquart took over the chancellorship. President Wilhelm Miklas refused to agree to the latter's appointment and resigned, and Seyss-Inquart wasted no time in inviting the German army into the country on the pretext of preventing civil war.

ANSCHLUSS AND WORLD WAR II

In the event of the Anschluss, there was no bloodshed: German troops crossed the border into Austria on March 12, 1938, and encountered no resistance whatsoever. Hitler himself began his slow and triumphant journey to the capital in the wake of his troops. First he visited his birthplace of Braunau-am-Inn, then he moved onto his "home town" of Linz, where he was received with such enthusiasm by the locals that he decided there and then to **incorporate Austria into the Greater German Reich**, rather than pursue the more conciliatory path of preserving Austrian autonomy. Eventually, on March 15, Hitler appeared on the balcony of the Hofburg before thousands of jubilant Viennese.

As a propaganda exercise, Hitler also decided to go ahead with Schuschnigg's plebiscite, which took place on April 10. The 99-percent "Yes" vote in favour of the Anschluss came as no surprise. In fact, those known to be opposed to the Nazis, including Schuschnigg and his followers, had already been arrested – some 76,000 by the time Hitler arrived in Vienna – while Jews and other "undesirables" were barred from voting. On the other hand, many whom one would expect to have opposed the Anschluss publicly declared themselves in favour, including the archbishop of Vienna, Cardinal Theodor Innitzer, and the Social Democrat Karl Renner.

Although the Treaty of St-Germain precluded any Anschluss with Germany, only the Soviet Union and Mexico lodged any formal international protest against the invasion. Meanwhile, the very name "Österreich" was wiped off the map, initially replaced by the term "*Ostmark*", but eventually simply divided into seven *Gaue*, or districts, ruled by Nazi *Gauleiter*.

THE FATE OF AUSTRIA'S JEWS

The Anschluss unleashed a "volcanic outburst of popular anti-Semitism", in the words of eyewitness George Clare. Jews were dragged out into the street, and physically assaulted and humiliated. Most anti-Semitic excesses were concentrated in Vienna, where 95 percent of Austria's 183,000 Jews lived. In one instance, in the well-to-do Viennese suburb of Währing, a group of Nazis urinated on local Jewish women as they forced them to scrub the streets in front of cheering onlookers. A large number of the city's most prominent Jews were arrested, and either sent to the camps or released with orders to leave the country.

In May 1938, without warning, 2000 Jews were arrested and shipped off to Dachau, primarily to encourage still more Jews to emigrate. On the night of November 10–11 – dubbed *Kristallnacht*, or "Crystal Night" – the majority of synagogues in the Reich were torched, and numerous Jewish premises ransacked. Another 7800 Austrian Jews were arrested that night, 4600 of whom were sent to Dachau. By the outbreak of World War II, more than half of Vienna's Jews had emigrated.

Once the Nazis had invaded Poland, their policy towards the Jews changed, with deportation to the camps favoured over forced emigration. The deportations began in earnest in February 1941, while emigration came to a complete standstill in November the same year. Of the 57,000 Jews now left in Austria, more than half had been sent to the death camps by June 1942. By the end of the war, around 200 Austrian Jews had managed to survive in hiding, with just over 2000 returning after the war.

COLLABORATION AND RESISTANCE

Although Hitler preferred to import German Nazis to many positions within Austrian Nazi hierarchy, the Austrians themselves provided more than their ten percent population ratio of concentration-camp guards. The Linz-born Nazi Adolf Eichmann, who ran Vienna's "Central Office for Jewish Emigration" and was one of the architects of the "Final Solution", is probably the most infamous, though the film *Schindler's List* has also increased the infamy of the Vienna-born camp commandant Amon Goeth. Another Linz-born Nazi, Ernst Kaltenbrunner, rose to number two in the SS to Heinrich Himmler, while the Carinthian Odilo Globocnik, with ninety other fellow Austrians on

his staff, supervised the death of some two million Jews in the extermination camps of Sobibor, Treblinka and Belzec.

Organized **resistance** to Hitler was, it has to be said, extraordinarily difficult for anti-Nazi Austrians, given the level of collaboration among their fellow citizens and the way in which the Nazis had wiped out their potential leadership. Aside from individual acts of heroism, there was very little significant non-Communist resistance within Austria. Partisan activity was restricted to a few remote alpine areas, and it wasn't until spring 1944 that an organized home resistance, codenamed O5, began to emerge.

Unlike every other Nazi-occupied country, however, the Austrians had no official government-in-exile. Exiled Austrian politicians spent their time bickering, split between an unlikely alliance between Otto von Habsburg (the son of the last emperor), the Communists and the two mainstream political parties. The most positive diplomatic step took place in November 1943, when the Allied Powers published the Moscow Declaration stating that Austria was a "victim" of Nazi aggression and that it should be re-established as a "free and democratic state".

THE LIBERATION

By April 5, 1945, the Red Army was nearing the outskirts of the Austrian capital. The O5 leadership under Major Szokoll had planned to initiate an **uprising** against the Nazis the very next day, but were betrayed by a junior officer, Lieutenant Walter Hanslick. Several of the O5 leaders were arrested, tortured and publicly hanged. The revolt had failed and it took the Russians another three days to reach Vienna's outskirts, and another five days' street fighting to finally win control of the city.

The commander in chief of the Russian troops in Austria, Marshal Tolbukhin, gave his assurances that the Soviets would liberate the country, respect the social order and refrain from appropriating any territory. In reality, Soviet troops spent much of the next few months raping Austrian women and stealing anything they could find. The actions of the Red Army during this period gave rise to the grim Viennese joke that Austria could probably survive a third world war, but it could never endure a second Liberation.

ALLIED OCCUPATION (1945-55)

On April 27, the Soviets sponsored the formation of a **provisional government** under the veteran Social Democrat Karl Renner, causing widespread alarm about Soviet intentions among the Western Allies. Although Renner's cabinet was made up, for the most part, of Socialists and members of the newly founded right-wing People's Party, or ÖVP, the Communists were given three posts, including the key positions of interior minister and education and information minister. As a form of protest at this unilateral action, the Western Allies refused to recognize the Renner government.

Meanwhile, there was continuing confusion over the occupation zones. Although the Moscow Declaration had stated that Austria was a victim of Nazi aggression, the country was nevertheless to be divided just like Germany, with Vienna, like Berlin, lying deep within the Russian sector. However, controversy over the exact zoning of Vienna helped delay

the arrival of Western troops in the capital until late August. The Russians took the opportunity of fleecing the capital and eastern Austria of all they could. Vienna, it was agreed, was to be divided between the four Allies, with the Innere Stadt preserved as an international sector, patrolled by one representative of each of the occupying powers. This comical sight on the streets of Vienna became the hallmark of the so-called "four-in-a-jeep" period – and the setting for the famous film *The Third Man* – when, as Karl Renner put it, Vienna was like a small rowing boat in which four elephants sat at the oars pulling in various directions.

ELECTIONS AND DE-NAZIFICATION

In October the Western Allies finally recognized the Renner government, and the Russians, for their part, agreed to free elections. However, whatever hopes they might have had of the Communists gaining power in Austria were dashed by the results of the **November 1945 elections**. The Communists won just 5.4 per-

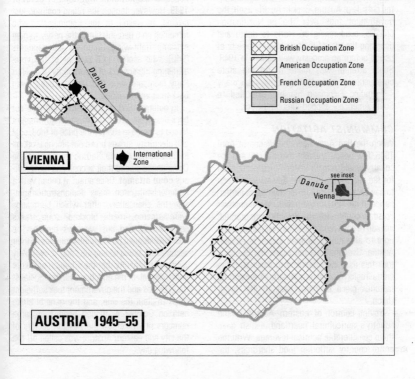

British Occupation Zone
American Occupation Zone
French Occupation Zone
Russian Occupation Zone

VIENNA

Danube

International Zone

see inset

Danube

Vienna

AUSTRIA 1945–55

cent of the vote, up from their previous high of 1.9 percent in 1932, but earning them just four seats in the 165-seat parliament, and the consolation prize of the Ministry of Electrification. In an almost exact repeat of the election results of the 1920s, the country remained split down the middle between Left and Right. Although the ÖVP won almost fifty percent of the vote, it was Renner who headed the new coalition government of the Socialist Party (SPÖ) and the ÖVP.

One of the most pressing and controversial tasks of the postwar era was the **de-Nazification process**. Initially, this was the responsibility of the Allied Powers: the Americans and the British busied themselves by handing out forms in which the respondents were invited to confess; the French, with collaborators of their own back home, were less keen to get involved; the Russians, predictably, were the most assiduous, though they were as concerned to remove political opponents as ex-Nazis. Of the half a million Austrians who were Nazi Party members, only a handful were executed at Nuremberg, mostly for crimes committed outside of Austria. Back in Austria itself, the government took over the de-Nazification process, condemning 38 Nazis to death and depriving the rest of their civil rights for a brief period before an amnesty was agreed in 1948. Some attempt was made to rid the state bureaucracy of its ex-Nazis, but inevitably many – including Eichmann himself, who fled to South America – slipped through the net.

COMMUNIST AGITATION

When the Red Army liberated Vienna in April 1945, few people thought that the city and the country would remain under Allied occupation for ten years. However, the Soviets were keen to pay back the Austrians for their mass participation in the Nazi armed forces. At the postwar Potsdam conference, the Soviets were granted, instead of cash reparations for war damage, the right to all external German assets in eastern Austria. Over the next ten years, the Russians took this as a carte blanche to asset-strip the entire region of eastern Austria, transporting factories piece by piece back to the Soviet Union.

Soviet control of eastern Austria – the country's agricultural heartland – also gave them considerable political leverage. With the entire country suffering food shortages, the Soviets deliberately hoarded supplies from their sector, supplying them direct to workers in Soviet-run industries. This won them considerable support in the eastern zone, and increased unrest in the western zones. For, despite the Communists' electoral setback, the Russians still had hopes of taking control of Austria. The winter of 1946–47 was particularly harsh, and the Communists took advantage of this by fomenting **food riots** in May 1947. The rioters besieged the Austrian chancellery and called for a national strike. In the end, the putsch failed, because the Socialist trade-union leaders refused to support the strike, and the Russians held back from using military force.

While Marshall Plan aid from the West helped ease conditions throughout Austria from the summer of 1947 onwards, the Communist coup in Czechoslovakia in February 1948 and the Berlin blockade (June 1948 to May 1949) only increased political tensions. Despite their recent setbacks, the Communists had high hopes for the **national elections of October 1949**. However, though the ruling coalition lost ground, it wasn't to the Communists, who remained on 5 percent, but to the newly formed extreme right-wing Union of Independents (VdU), who scored 11.6 percent of the vote, attracting the support of the majority of ex-Nazi Party members, who had recently been given back their voting rights.

In autumn 1950, Marshall Plan aid was cut back drastically. With the Austrian government forced to increase sharply the price of food, coal and electricity, strikes broke out among workers in cities across Austria. Seizing the moment, the Communists staged their second and most serious **coup attempt**. Once again, it began with a Communist-inspired mass demonstration outside the chancellery, after which barricades were erected, roads blocked, tram tracks cemented up and bus windows broken. The Russians stopped police reinforcements in their sector from being called up, and it was only with great difficulty that the situation was kept under control. In the end, however, the Socialist trade unions and the government took sufficient steps to stem the tide, and the general strike held on October 4, though heeded by large numbers of workers in the Russian sectors of the city and eastern Austria, was called off the following day.

THE AUSTRIAN STATE TREATY OF 1955

The **withdrawal of the four Allied Powers** from Austria in 1955 – or more specifically the Soviet withdrawal – was a unique event in the otherwise grim history of the Cold War. And something of a surprise, given the previously unscrupulous behaviour of the Soviets in Austria (and elsewhere in Europe).

For nearly ten years, negotiations over a **peace treaty** with Austria were at stalemate, with the Soviets insisting that a German peace treaty be prerequisite to an Austrian treaty. The Soviet threat over the future of Austria was used by them to try and forestall German re-armament. However, with the establishment of the Federal Republic of Germany in 1949, it was clear that this policy had failed. A struggle within the Kremlin then ensued over Soviet policy towards Austria. Following the death of Stalin, this struggle intensified and was eventually won by Khrushchev, who decided to use the Austrian State Treaty as a way of initiating a period of **détente**. Hopes of creating a Communist Austria had died with the failure of the 1950 putsch. The Soviet sector meanwhile had been bled dry and was no longer of any great economic benefit. A neutral Austria, on the other hand, created a convenient buffer that split NATO's northern and southern flanks. And so on May 15, 1955, the **Austrian State Treaty**, or *Staatsvertrag*, was signed by the four powers in Vienna's Belvedere.

CONSENSUS POLITICS: 1955-83

With the popular vote split between Left and Right, the two main parties of the ÖVP and the SPÖ formed a succession of **coalitions** which lasted until 1966. To avoid repeating the mistakes of the past, a system of *Proporz* was established, whereby the ÖVP and the SPÖ shared equally every governmental and state post. In some ways institutionalized political corruption, this process began at the top among the ministries, and continued right down to the local post office. At the same time, various special bodies or chambers representing the various interest groups – the Chamber of Trade, the Chamber of Labour and so on – were established. Like *Proporz*, these new institutions ensured that the country enjoyed an unprecedented period of political and social stability, but left the parliament without an effective opposition and created a system open to widespread abuse. Like the Germans, though, the Austrians enjoyed a period of **economic growth and prosperity**, and there were few voices of complaint.

In the elections of 1966, the People's Party at last achieved an absolute majority and formed the first **one-party government** of the postwar era. Many Austrians feared a repeat of the 1920s, but in practice little changed. The system of *Proporz* and the institutions of the corporate state continued to hand out "jobs for the boys", and only at the very top level of government were the Socialists excluded from power. However, an economic downturn in the early 1970s increased support for the SPÖ, such that they won an outright majority in the elections of 1971. Under the chancellorship of **Bruno Kreisky**, the Socialists enjoyed thirteen years of power, during which Kreisky carried the SPÖ further away from their radical Marxist past than ever before. The end came in the elections of 1983 when the SPÖ lost its overall majority and was forced into a coalition government with, of all people, the far-right Freedom Party (FPÖ).

THE WALDHEIM AFFAIR

Having struggled to make the headlines of the international press in the 1960s and 1970s, Austria was catapulted onto the world media stage in 1986 during the campaign for the Austrian presidency. The candidate for the ÖVP was **Kurt Waldheim**, a figure of some international stature who had been UN secretary-general for ten years (1972–82). However, during the campaign, Waldheim's war record was called into question. From the summer of 1942 until the end of the war, he had served as a lieutenant in the Balkans with the German army. Waldheim was never a member of the Nazi Party (one of the initial charges) and there was never any clear evidence that he was directly involved in the atrocities committed by the army in the Balkans, though he was formally charged with (but never tried for) **war crimes** by the Yugoslavs after the war. What was more difficult to believe, however, was his claim that he had no knowledge of the deportation of Greek Jews to the death camps, despite being an interpreter for the Italian army in Greece for much of the war.

To the dismay of many around the world, these charges, albeit unproven, did Waldheim's candidacy no harm at all domestically, and he was duly elected to the Austrian presidency with 54 percent of the vote. The international campaign against Waldheim began with the boycott of his swearing-in ceremony by the US ambassador, and culminated in his being put on the US Department of Justice's "Watch List". Waldheim became an international pariah, restricted in his state visits to Arab countries. At Waldheim's suggestion, a commission was set up to investigate the charges against him; however, far from exonerating him, the commission's report found him guilty of "proximity to legally incriminating acts and orders", a somewhat woolly phrase that could be applied to just about any Austrian who'd served in the German army. The British government, meanwhile, followed up the Yugoslav charge that Waldheim had been involved in war crimes against British commandos in the Balkans. The British enquiry concluded that Waldheim's rank was too junior to have had any influence over the fate of the commandos, adding that "knowledge is not itself a crime".

THE POLITICAL PRESENT

As if the Waldheim affair were not bad enough, the country has also had to contend with the rise of the FPÖ under their charismatic leader **Jörg Haider**. A strange grouping of free-market liberals and ultra-conservatives, the FPÖ was very much a fringe player in Austrian politics until the mid-1980s, when Haider began to turn it into an effective vehicle for right-wing populism. In his first stab at the polls, in 1986, Haider won nearly ten percent of the vote, frightening the two main parties back into the grand SPÖ–ÖVP coalition of the postwar years under the Socialist Franz Vranitzky. Unfortunately, this only served to play into Haider's hands, increasing popular resentment against the system of *Proporz* (from which the FPÖ is excluded) and thus boosting support for the FPÖ.

A dapper character with a sporty image (a keen skier and jogger, he's the only Austrian party leader to have attempted a bungee-jump), Haider presented himself as something new in national politics, free from the cynical power-sharing manoeuvres of the two main parties. He attended carnival celebrations dressed as Robin Hood in order to press the point home, and campaigned under the slogan "Haider: the only politician

whose handshake you can trust" in order to emphasize his disdain for the wheeling and dealing of the Viennese political elite. Both of his parents were Nazi party members who had felt sidelined by postwar Austrian society, and Haider himself deliberately courted far-right support in an attempt to gain notoriety. Elected provincial governor of Carinthia in 1990, Haider expressed enthusiasm for Nazi employment policy in a speech a year later – precipitating his fall from office, but not his fall from popularity. In 1995 he attended the annual reunion of former SS members on the Ulrichsberg near Klagenfurt, calling the assembled veterans "men of character", and he has continued to be a high-profile visitor to the mountain-top meeting ever since.

Haider's main electoral plank was to exploit the fears shared by many Austrians over the country's new wave of **immigrants**, who arrived from the former Eastern Bloc and war-torn Yugoslavia in considerable numbers in the 1990s. Nationalist frustrations were compounded by the country's entry into the European Union in 1994. Although in a referendum sixty percent voted in favour of joining, the austerity measures the country needed to implement in order to meet the criteria necessary for joining a single European currency convinced many that it had been the wrong decision.

In the national **elections in 1994 and 1995**, popular dissatisfaction was publicly registered, with Haider's FPÖ taking a staggering 22 percent of the vote, behind the ÖVP (with 28 percent) and the Socialists (on 38 percent). The biggest shock, though, was in Vienna in 1996, where the SPÖ lost its overall majority for the first time, with the FPÖ receiving 27 percent of the vote and becoming the main opposition in the Rathaus, ahead of the ÖVP.

Franz Vranitzky's successor as chancellor, **Viktor Klima**, soon established himself as a popular and trusted figure, and for a time things seemed to carry on as normal, with Klima presiding over an SPÖ/ÖVP government that included ÖVP leader **Wolfgang Schüssel** as foreign minister. However neither Klima nor Schüssel seemed capable of reversing the gradual decline of their respective parties in the polls.

OCTOBER 1999 AND AFTER

In February 1999 the FPÖ trounced both the SPÖ and the ÖVP in provincial elections in Carinthia, returning Haider to the position of provincial governor. Flushed with success, the FPÖ prepared to fight the general elections of October the same year on an openly xenophobic platform. FPÖ posters reading "Stop der Überfremdung. Österreich zuerst" ("Stop the foreign tide. Put Austria first") set the tone of the campaign. In the event the FPÖ surpassed even their own wildest dreams by squeezing into second place, beating the ÖVP into third by a margin of 415 votes (both the FPÖ and the ÖVP were awarded 52 seats in parliament). Most observers assumed that the SPÖ and the ÖVP would once again close ranks to deny Haider a role in government, but negotiations on the formation of a new coalition dragged on inconclusively, with the ÖVP demanding control of the Finance Ministry in order to force through economic austerity measures, and sitting chancellor Viktor Klima refusing to concede it. With talks between the two parties breaking down in January 2000, President Klestil had no choice but to invite the ÖVP to enter talks with the FPÖ in the hope of forming a government. Klestil – himself no big fan of Haider – knew that if he dissolved parliament and called new elections, the FPÖ would only get stronger.

Eager to fulfil his dream of becoming chancellor, ÖVP leader Schüssel put together a cabinet in which several top posts went to the FPÖ. Fearful of how the international community would react however, he succeeded in persuading Haider himself to remain in Carinthia rather than take up a ministerial job. The **new government** was sworn in by an unenthusiastic Klestil on February 2, 2000. All other EU states immediately froze bilateral relations with Austria in protest at the FPÖ's inclusion in government. In a cosmetic exercise designed to placate world opinion, Haider unexpectedly quit the FPÖ leadership in April, to be replaced by the less openly extremist Susanne Riess-Passer. The new government's programme – centred on promises to cut government spending and pave the way for tax cuts – carefully avoided any reference to the FPÖ's pre-election rhetoric, and the EU withdrew their sanctions after 6 months. Those Austrians who had voted for the ÖVP or the FPÖ were in any case resentful of the outside world's attempts to meddle in the nation's affairs. Others were deeply shamed by the FPÖ's accession to power, and launched the

Widerstand (Resistance), a rolling campaign of demonstrations and cultural events designed to show that the liberal, tolerant values of centre-left Austria were still very much alive.

Paradoxically, the ÖVP profited more from the new situation than the cocksure FPÖ. Chancellor Schüssel, together with ÖVP foreign minister Benita Ferrero-Waldner, won popular support for the way in which they appeared to defend Austria's dignity against a hostile EU. The unpopular elements of government policy – cuts in public spending and the introduction of university fees for students – tended to be blamed on their more radical coalition allies. Provincial elections in Styria in October and in Burgenland two months later saw the FPÖ vote collapse, suggesting that a large body of the Austrian electorate was happy to register a protest vote for the FPÖ when it was in opposition, but saw no further use for it now it was in power. The decision by Jörg Haider – the FPÖ's only genuinely charismatic leader – to remain in Carinthia now looked like a tactical mistake, and there was much talk of whether he would return to the national stage. As it was, Haider had his own problems: in late summer 2000 former FPÖ supporter Josef Kleindienst alleged that Haider and his circle had consistently bribed police officers to provide confidential information on FPÖ opponents. Haider countered that the police apparatus was still dominated by SPÖ appointees, who were out to smear him, but the fuse for a long-running scandal had been lit. Having consistently posed as the clean man of Austrian politics, Haider entered 2001 looking exceedingly vulnerable.

The ÖVP/FPÖ coalition may turn out to be a short-term exercise in political pragmatism rather than the opening of a new dark age, but the persistence of xenophobic attitudes in Austria – and their exploitation by the populist right – will continue to be a source of concern for both the international community and the Austrians themselves. The Waldheim Affair and the rise of the FPÖ have proved a **PR disaster** for the country, and in Austria itself there's a growing sense of bewilderment that a nation that promoted itself so successfully as the home of Lipizzaner horses and happy alpine holidays should nowadays be internationally notorious for something entirely different.

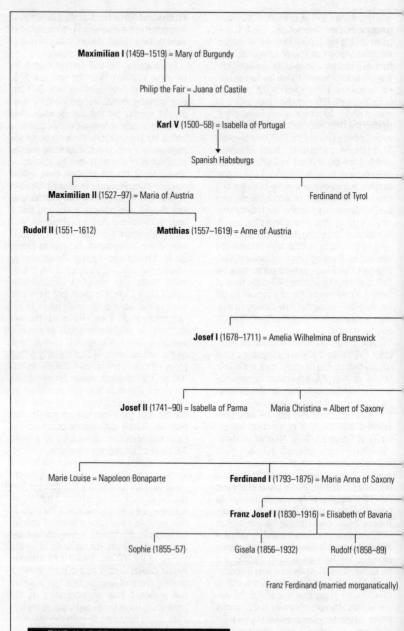

Maximilian I (1459–1519) = Mary of Burgundy

Philip the Fair = Juana of Castile

Karl V (1500–58) = Isabella of Portugal

Spanish Habsburgs

Maximilian II (1527–97) = Maria of Austria   Ferdinand of Tyrol

Rudolf II (1551–1612)   **Matthias** (1557–1619) = Anne of Austria

Josef I (1678–1711) = Amelia Wilhelmina of Brunswick

Josef II (1741–90) = Isabella of Parma   Maria Christina = Albert of Saxony

Marie Louise = Napoleon Bonaparte   **Ferdinand I** (1793–1875) = Maria Anna of Saxony

Franz Josef I (1830–1916) = Elisabeth of Bavaria

Sophie (1855–57)   Gisela (1856–1932)   Rudolf (1858–89)

Franz Ferdinand (married morganatically)

THE HABSBURG FAMILY TREE

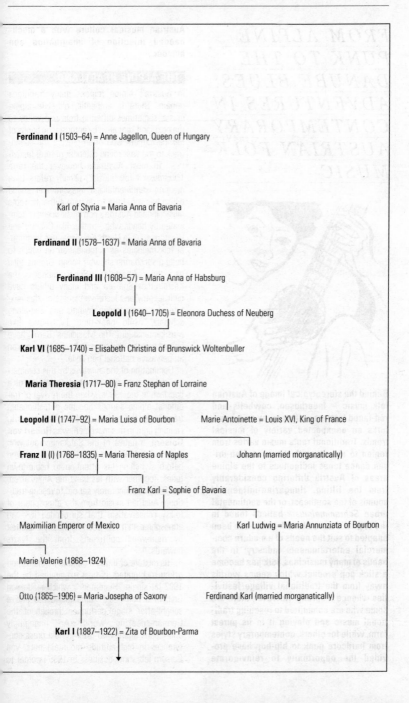

Ferdinand I (1503–64) = Anne Jagellon, Queen of Hungary

Karl of Styria = Maria Anna of Bavaria

Ferdinand II (1578–1637) = Maria Anna of Bavaria

Ferdinand III (1608–57) = Maria Anna of Habsburg

Leopold I (1640–1705) = Eleonora Duchess of Neuberg

Karl VI (1685–1740) = Elisabeth Christina of Brunswick Woltenbuller

Maria Theresia (1717–80) = Franz Stephan of Lorraine

Leopold II (1747–92) = Maria Luisa of Bourbon

Marie Antoinette = Louis XVI, King of France

Johann (married morganatically)

Franz II (I) (1768–1835) = Maria Theresia of Naples

Franz Karl = Sophie of Bavaria

Maximilian Emperor of Mexico

Karl Ludwig = Maria Annunziata of Bourbon

Marie Valerie (1868–1924)

Otto (1865–1906) = Maria Josepha of Saxony

Ferdinand Karl (married morganatically)

Karl I (1887–1922) = Zita of Bourbon-Parma

FROM ALPINE PUNK TO THE DANUBE BLUES: ADVENTURES IN CONTEMPORARY AUSTRIAN FOLK MUSIC

Behind the stereotypical image of Austrian folk music – lederhosen, cowbells and red-faced farmers puffing away on tubas – lurks an unexpected variety of musical trends. Traditional roots music varies from region to region, with the accordion-driven dance tunes indigenous to the alpine areas of Austria differing considerably from the lilting, Hungarian-influenced sounds of the southeast, or the sentimental urban *Schrammelmusik* ballads found in the capital. Above all, folk music has been adapted to suit the needs of a modern commercial entertainments industry: in the hands of many musicians, folk has become a slick pop product which seems worlds away from the traditional village festivities whence it sprung. However, there are some who are committed to rescuing traditional music and playing it in its purest form, while for others, contemporary styles from hardcore punk to hip-hop have provided the opportunity to reinvigorate

Austrian musical culture with a much-needed injection of imagination and humour.

THE ALPINE HEARTLAND

In Austria's alpine regions many traditions remain. There is authentic, old-style alpine music, sometimes differing from one valley to the next, and kept alive by enthusiastic bands of folk performers who often provide the soundtrack to the year-round calendar of rural festivities. To most Austrians however the term *Volksmusik* ("folk music") usually refers to a modern, sentimentalized, mass-market sound which has very little to do with authentic roots music. Indeed Austria's pop music scene is dominated by bands who – rather like Country and Western stars in North America – use traditional folk melodies as a foundation on which to build a saccharine showbiz sound. Groups such as the Zillertaler Schürzenjäger, the Kastelruther Spatzen and many others have built lengthy and lucrative careers on this mixture of alpine oompah-rhythms and sing-along schmalz, while peak-time TV shows like Musikantenstadl ("The Musicians' Barn") have helped turn the *Volksmusik* phenomenon into an all-pervasive national pop style.

Domination of the airwaves by this commercialized form of folk provoked something of a backlash in the 1990s, when the revival of traditional alpine sounds became a fashionable trend under the banner of **Neue Volksmusik**. Leading light in this movement was **Hubert von Goisern**, a native of the Salzkammergut who grew up listening to Hendrix and The Who before switching his attention to home-town tunes. Together with his band the Alpinkatzen, von Goisern deliberately set out to rescue traditional Austrian music from the atmosphere of folksy conservatism that surrounded it – an atmosphere that has been habitually exploited by right-wing politicians from the Nazis onwards.

His mixture of lilting mountain melodies and riffing rock guitars is best exemplified by the 1992 hit single "Hiamatadl", which made von Goisern a household name in Austria and a sought-after stage performer throughout the German-speaking world. An engagingly unorthodox figure who likes to hold press conferences in high-altitude mountain huts, von Goisern left show business in 1995 in order to travel in Tibet and Africa. He returned to Austria at the end of the decade to release "Fön", a solo album which pleasingly blends jazz, world music and folk, but which lacks the fire of old.

Emerging at the same time as von Goisern but much more radical in approach was the Linz-based duo **Attwenger**, considered by many to be Austria's answer to The Pogues, who played accordions through wah-wah pedals, and backed their songs with gunshot drum tracks and electronic hip-hop rhythms. Despite their underground gloss, Attwenger's starting point was very much the music of their home region. In their hands, traditional dance numbers like "Schleiniger", "Innviertler Ländler" and "Aberseer Ländler" (a *Ländler* is a slow folk dance in 3/4 time) became wild songs with aggressive beats. Although they enjoyed tremendous critical acclaim and were twice voted best band in Austria, they folded in 1995 due to musical exhaustion and a refusal to be part of the **Alpine New Wave** hype. Refreshed, they reunited two years later and took the public by surprise with an even more radical reduction-ist attitude. The folk elements were so diluted that they only surfaced occasionally over repeti-tive trip-hop and jungle beats.

A totally different approach is used by two highly sophisticated ensembles, who mix alpine sounds with either jazz or new classical music. **Die Knödel** (The Dumplings), formerly known as Die Verkochten Tirolerknödel (The Overcooked Tyrolean Dumplings) are an intel-lectual underground band founded in the early 1990s. Their instrumentation – using violins, viola, clarinet, bassoon, trumpet and flugelhorn – is closer to a classical music ensemble than a *Ländler* band. The four male and four female members of the octet are highly educated musi-cians who earn their living in the symphony orchestras of Austria and Germany. Though classically trained, they are not ashamed of their traditional roots or of pushing folk music into new areas. Until the summer of 1995 the Dumplings' leader, Christof Dienz wrote all their material, mixing Michael Nyman-style minimal-ism with impressionistic atmospheres to create a contemporary chamber folk music. To keep fresh they have recently commissioned pieces from composers based in their home region of Tyrol, who come from contemporary classical, jazz, rock and experimental backgrounds. The result is an exciting patchwork of alpine polkas,

waltzes and instrumental yodels, each viewed from a different angle.

While Die Knödel use classical music, Styria's **Broadlahn** uses jazz. Founded in 1982 by three school friends playing guitar, mandolin and accordion, they became a sextet in 1990 adding three experienced jazz players to their line up, on saxophone, bass and drums. Searching for the other kind of groove in tradi-tional music patterns, they have stretched the framework to the limits and occasionally beyond them. Trying to dance to their complex rhythms and complicated riffs can be disas-trous!

For information, in German, on live perfor-mances and listings, check *www.orpheum.at.*

THE VIENNESE BLUES

Schrammelmusik, the urban folk music of Austria's capital, is proof of Vienna's wistful and melancholy heart. The style was born out of the rapid industrialization of the late nineteenth century, when tens of thousands of people from all over the empire poured into the fast-growing capital, transforming it into a multicultural metropolis which soon developed its own musi-cal language. Polkas, Gypsy melodies, tunes from the Balkans, rural alpine yodels and dances mingled with Viennese waltzes, *Ländlers* and string quartets to create an excit-ing new style. The key event in the city's folk music tradition was in 1878 when Johann (1850–93) and Josef Schrammel (1852–1895) formed a trio with bass guitarist Anton Strohmayer. They called it **D'Nussdorfer** after the Viennese wine suburb where they per-formed. The two brothers became so famous that their name was given to the whole genre. *Schrammelmusik* was born. Before long, the style settled into a regular quartet form, with the addition of a small G-clarinet (played by folk-clarinettist Georg Dänzer in the Schrammels' original band), sometimes replaced by an accordion. In the 1880s and 90s, Schrammel quartets emerged all over Austria and over the border in the alpine regions of southern Germany.

Schrammelmusik's most illustrious contem-porary exponent is **Roland Neuwirth**, a dis-tinctively long-haired, bearded figure who has injected new life into what had become a half-forgotten tradition. His acoustic quintet, Die Extremschrammeln, with a traditional line-up of accordion, two violins, contra guitar and vocals, stretches *Schrammelmusik* to its limits, adding blues chords and soul grooves. Indeed Neuwirth himself originally wanted to be a blues singer, and it was only when he accepted that the Danube could never be the Mississippi that he discovered the "Viennese Blues" on his own doorstep. As he searched for his city's musical roots, he discovered similarities with the history of the blues. *Schrammelmusik* has strong links with the red light district of Old Vienna, where love songs and murder ballads were sung in taverns and brothels. Neuwirth first

mixed the Mississippi and Danube blues together but later started more radical experiments, adding electric guitars and drums to create the **Danube New Wave**.

In the 1980s he returned to the acoustic format, aiming to sound as authentic as possible, only adding new ingredients if they seemed to fit naturally. He rehearsed with two violin players for many weeks to achieve the classic Viennese timbre of slow vibrato. His accordion player Walter Soyka, who plays one of the famous squeeze boxes built in the workshop of Fritz Budowitz more than a century ago,

DISCOGRAPHY

COMPILATIONS

The Alps: Music From The Old World (World Network, Germany)
Both the old and new school of alpine folk music – although more old than new. Includes alphorn duets, exuberant yodelling from Austria's Citoller Tanzgeiger and even three rare tracks by Switzerland's legendary Appenzeller Space Schöttl, who haven't made any recordings before or since.

Oberösterreich-Salzburg – Volksmusik. Rare Schellacks 1910–1949 (Trikont, Germany)
Proving there's more to the region of Salzburg and Upper Austria than Mozart – polyphonic yodels, heavy brass and driving string music make this collection a gem.

Österreich: Musik der Regionen (Vol 1–10; (Österreichisches Volksliedwerk, Austria).
This comprehensive survey of traditional Austrian music styles is like a sound atlas. Archive and contemporary recordings from different areas. From Upper Austria around Linz and Salzburg to Lower Austria south of Vienna, you can hear the best performers play music ranging from wild yodelling and alpine horn playing to three- and four-part singing. Or take to the dance floor for

traditional waltzes, marches and *Ländler* played on accordion and fiddle or by small brass bands. There's an accompanying booklet with introductions to the regional styles (in German and English), song lyrics (in German), but hardly any information about the musicians. Distributed by Daniela Schwarz, 1230 Wien, Anton Baumgartnerstr. 44/A2/213 ☎(43) 1 6673169.

Wien: Volksmusik: Rare Schellacks 1906–1937 (Trikont, Germany)
A superb historical collection featuring the main singers and ensembles of Vienna some 70 years ago. Performing the characteristic repertoire from the *heurigen* (wine bars) which has almost disappeared. Soulful songs with passion – Danube blues!

Die besten Schrammeln Instrumental (Trikont, Germany)
Compiled by Roland Neuwirth, this is a superb collection of rare instrumentals by the great masters of the genre. In a recording from early this century you can even hear Anton Strohmayer who was guitarist in the original Schrammel Brothers trio. Real stardust!

ARTISTS

Attwenger: Most (Trikont, Germany)
Their first and best album, from 1991, features liberal radical humour and traditional dance tunes played with hip-hop drum rhythms and a head-banging Ländler-beat from the wildest of the alpine groups. Their clubby 1997 release

"Song" (Trikont) blends jungle and trip-hop hypnotics with a light flavour of traditional accordion.

Hohla-Biereder: doppelt doppelt (Fischrecords, Austria; *www.fischrecords.at*)
The brother and sister duo of Kathi Hohla and

knows the secret of achieving the right sound. To soften the tone of the instrument the old players used to put a page of newspaper inside it, but not any page would do the job. It had to be page seven of the tabloid *Die Kronenzeitung* – with the pin-up girl – as only something round and soft would guarantee the velvet tone.

For Neuwirth, the lyrics are as important as the music. He is a poet in his own right, exploring in words the cracks in modern-day life and showing the grin of death behind the charming face of Vienna. When Neuwirth and his musicians want to get away from the present day, they perform under the name of **Herzton-Schrammeln**, playing instrumentals from the repertoire of legendary ensembles such as the Original Lammer Quartett, the Butschetty Quartett and the Strohmayer Quartett playing before World War I. The aim is to recreate *Schrammelmusik* as authentically as possible. "Simply to play music the way the Schrammel Brothers did is a lifelong job", Neuwirth reflects.

Another band committed to the original, unsentimentalized Schrammel sound is the

Franz Biereder were the most amazing yodellers of the 30s and 40s with a reputation that reached far beyond the boundaries of their home area in the valley of the river Inn. Kathi Hohla ran a pub in Berndorf am Inn where she sang nearly every day making it a tourist attraction of the area.

Geschwister Simböck: Lieder & Landler aus dem Innviertel (Fischrecords, Austria)
Another strong singing duo from the Innviertel are the sisters Simböck. Their career stretched over half a century and turned the singers into an institution. Powerful, dramatic songs accompanied by accordion and fiddle. Recorded in 1987, shortly before the sisters decided to retire.

Die Knödel: Panorama (RecRec, Austria)
"Panorama" is Die Knödel's best record to date: a collection of pieces from different composers with a wonderful blend of timbres and textures. It is a welcome change from their own often somewhat overcomplicated material.

Broadlahn: Leib & Seel (BMG, Austria)
In this 1993 album, jazz improvisations emerge from folk tunes, and *Ländler* get a new look with original arrangements using everything from hand clapping to marimba. The more recent "Almrauschn im Weltempfänger" (Extraplatte, Austria) shows the band mixing the traditional folk music of Styria with sounds from every corner of the planet: Indian sitar, African marimba, even Tuvasian overtone singing - without abandoning the strong jazz vibes of the previous recordings.

Die Extremschrammeln: Essig & Öl (WEA/Warners, Austria)

The Roland Neuwirth-led outfit at the height of their art on this recording from 1994. Songs with the expressive harmony singing of Neuwirth himself and Mizzi Moravec alternate with fine instrumental dances where the schmalz of the twin violins mingles perfectly with the colours of the accordion. Not as extreme as the name of the band suggests! Just extremely good!

Hubert von Goisern und die Alpinkatzen: Omunduntn (BMG, Austria)
1994 album showing Goisern and band at their best, with Hubert's trademark gravelly vocals surfing above accordion-driven alpine beats. Features a punk-rock version of "Gott Erhalts", the pre-World War I anthem of the Habsburg Empire – a song set to the same music as "Deutschland über Alles".

Herzton-Schrammeln: Herzton-Schrammeln (Ariola, Austria)
After years of research and practice this side-project from members of the Extremschrammeln presents an array of historic Schrammelmusik tunes with the same elegance and sensitivity as the originals. More than a dozen standards (including Josef Schrammel's "Weana Gmüath" and Anton Strohmayer's "Slibowitz Tanz") played here faultlessly.

Thalia-Schrammeln: Music from Old Vienna (Naxos, Hong Kong)
Stylishly played music by the Schrammel brothers and several other composers in the genre. The piercing G-clarinet sound lends it a special character.

Thalia-Schrammeln, formed by graduates of Vienna's Musik Hochschule and featuring the traditional line-up of violins, G-clarinet and bass guitar.

Among the **restaurants** which still feature authentic live *Schrammelmusik*, the best is probably *Herrgott aus Spa*, in the Viennese sub-urb of Ottakring at Speckbacherstrasse 14 (reservations advisable; ☎0222 486 0230), where guests sitting at rustic wooden tables are regaled by different ensembles almost every night.

Christoph Wagner

BOOKS

There are quite a number of books in print about the Habsburgs and the various artistic figures in Austria's glorious past, but precious little written in English about the country in the twentieth century and not much fiction in translation – hence the rather uneven selection below. We've listed a few books that are currently out of print (o/p), but you might be able to pick them up in secondhand bookshops. For books in print, we've listed UK publishers first, then US; wherever we've cited a single publisher, it's the same publisher in both territories, unless we've specified UK or US after it. UP stands for University Press.

These days, of course, it's not so important where a book is printed, as any online bookshop can ship you a copy out in very little time. The best known one is www.amazon.co.uk (for the UK) and www.amazon.com (for North America), but if you're looking for a specific book, a book search engine like www.bookbrain.co.uk will tell you which on-line bookshop is selling it for the cheapest price.

HISTORY AND SOCIETY

Steven Beller, *Vienna and the Jews, 1867–1938* (CUP). Beller shows how the Jews played a central role in the vibrant cultural life of Vienna at the turn of the twentieth century. Thorough but rather on the dry side.

Gordon Brook-Shepherd, *The Austrians* (HarperCollins;Carroll & Graf). Readable, if a little overearnest history which attempts to trace the Austrian-ness (or lack of it) in the country's history from the Babenbergs to entry into the EU in 1994. Brook-Shepherd draws on his experience as a *Telegraph* correspondent and as someone who worked in the Allied High Commission in Vienna after World War II.

Frederic V. Grunfeld, *Prophets without Honour* (Kodansha). A useful insight into the intellectual figures of fin-de-siècle *Mitteleuropa*, including Freud, Kafka and Einstein.

William M. Johnston, *The Austrian Mind: An Intellectual and Social History 1848–1938* (University of California Press). Johnston knows his stuff, and though this is pretty academic stuff, it's a fascinating insight into fin-de-siècle Vienna.

Robert A. Kann, *History of the Habsburg Empire 1526–1918* (University of California Press). Weighty and wide-ranging 600-page account of the empire, written in the 1970s.

Robert Knight, *Contemporary Austria and the Legacy of the Third Reich 1945-95* (UCL). Highlights the failure of de-Nazification and the subsequent rise of Haider's FPÖ, the consequences of which were partly obscured by the country's postwar prosperity.

Elisabeth Lichtenberger, *Austria: Society and Regions* (Austrian Academy of Science). A scholarly account of the awkward twentieth-century history of Austria, taking the reader right up to the late 1990s.

Frederic Morton, *A Nervous Splendor: Vienna 1888/1889* (Viking); *Thunder at Twilight: Vienna 1913–1914* (P Owen). Morton has trawled through the newspapers of the time to produce two very readable dramatized accounts of two critical years in the city's history. The first centres on the Mayerling tragedy; the second, on the Sarajevo assassination.

Hella Pick, *Guilty Victim: Austria from the Holocaust to Haider* (I.B. Tauris). Probably the best book on postwar Austria, both as a political history and a meditation on the country's (often half-hearted) attempts to come to terms with the darker elements of its past.

Carl E. Schorske, *Fin-de-Siècle Vienna* (Phoenix;Random). Fascinating scholarly essays on, among other things, the impact of the building of the Ringstrasse, and of Freud, Klimt, Kokoschka and Schönberg on the city's culture.

A.J.P. Taylor, *The Habsburg Monarchy 1809–1918* (Penguin, o/p). Readable, forthright as ever and thought-provoking account of the demise of the Habsburgs.

Andrew Wheatcroft, *The Habsburgs* (Penguin). Wheatcroft's intriguing history traces the rise and fall of the Habsburgs from their modest origins in Switzerland to their demise at the head of the Austro-Hungarian empire, looking closely at individual family members, and the promotion of its dynastic image.

MEMOIRS AND TRAVEL

George Clare, *Last Waltz in Vienna; The Destruction of a Family 1842–1942* (Papermac). Incredibly moving – and far from bitter – autobiographical account of a Jewish upbringing in inter-war Vienna that ended with the Anschluss.

Edward Crankshaw, *Vienna: The Image of a Culture in Decline* (Macmillan, o/p); *Fall of the House of Habsburg* (Penguin). Part travel journal, part history, and first published in 1938, this is a nostalgic, but by no means rose-tinted, look at the city. The same author's *Fall of the House of Habsburg* is an accessible popular history of the empire's last days.

Helen Fremont, After Long Silence (Judy Piatkus Publishers). Fremont was raised as a Roman Catholic in the US only to discover as an adult that her parents were Austrian Jews who survived the Holocaust, but kept silent about it for forty years.

Patrick Leigh Fermor, *A Time of Gifts* (Penguin). The first volume of Leigh Fermor's trilogy based on his epic walk along the Rhine and Danube rivers in 1933–34. Written forty years later in dense, luscious and highly crafted prose, it's an evocative and poignant insight into the culture of *Mitteleuropa* between the wars.

Claudio Magris, *Danube* (Harvill). In this highly readable travel journal from the 1980s, Magris, a wonderfully erudite Trieste-based academic, traces the Danube, passing through Austria along the way.

Reinhard Spitzty, *How We Squandered the Reich* (Clocktower). Chilling and frank autobiographical account of a young Austrian idealist who became a member of the SS.

Simon Wiesenthal, *Sunflower* (Henry Holt;Schocken). Wiesenthal relates an instance from his time at Mathausen when an ailing SS guard called him to his bedside and asked fo forgiveness. In the second half of the book Wiesenthal asks leading intellectuals t respond to the dilemma of forgiveness.

Stefan Zweig, *The World of Yesterday* (University of Nebraska Press, o/p). Semina account of fin-de-siècle Vienna written jus before Zweig was forced by the Nazis into exile in South America, where he and his wife committed suicide.

BIOGRAPHIES

THE HABSBURGS

Steven Beller, *Franz Joseph* (Longman o/p/Addison Wesley). Shortest and mos portable of the books on Franz-Josef; more of a political than a biographical account, it's a bi short on personal history.

T.C.W. Blanning, *Joseph II* (Longman). Aimed at the general reader, this tells the story o Josef and his attempts at reform set against the background of the Austrian Enlightenment.

Jean Paul Bled, *Franz Joseph* (Blackwell, o/p) Well-rounded account of the old duffer, with a smattering of the sort of scurrilous gossip miss ing in some other biographies.

Katerina von Burg, *Elisabeth of Austria* (Windsor Publications, UK). Recent biography o the endlessly fascinating empress who was assassinated by an Italian anarchist in 1898.

Edward Crankshaw, *Maria Theresia* (Constable, UK). Readable account of the "Virgin Empress", though disappointingly shor on light touches.

Brigitte Hamann, *The Reluctant Empress* (Taschen, Cologne o/p). A surprisingly even handed account of the Empress Elisabeth's extraordinary life, warts and all. Only usually available in Vienna.

Joan Haslip, *The Emperor and the Actress* (Weidenfeld & Nicolson, o/p); *Lonely Empress Elizabeth of Austria* (Phoenix, UK). The first is a detailed, steamy account of Franz-Josef's rela tionship with his long-term mistress, the actress Katharina Schratt. Retreading some o the same material, Haslip's *Lonely Empress* is a sympathetic portrayal of the Kaiser's unhapp spouse.

Alan Palmer, *The Twilight of the Habsburgs: The Life and Times of the Emperor Francis Joseph* and *Metternich* (both Phoenix;Grove-Atlantic). The first is the latest scholarly and somewhat weighty tome on the emperor; the latter, a solid account of the arch-conservative who ruled the roost in Vienna from 1815 to 1848.

HITLER

Brigitte Hamann, *Hitler's Vienna* (OUP). A newly published account of Hitler's early youth in Vienna, which played an important part in helping form the prejudices of the Nazi leader.

MUSIC

Peter Franklin, *The life of Mahler* (CUP). A very accessible account of Mahler's life, in Cambridge UP's excellent "Musical Lives" series.

Egon Gartenberg *Johann Strauss, End of an Era* (Da Capo). The story of the waltz king and his world, originator of the Blue Danube, as well as *Die Fledermaus*

Peter Gay, *Mozart* (Penguin;Viking). A slim, easy-to-read volume which nevertheless includes a good deal of stimulating analysis. Easily the best compact Mozart biography you can get.

Malcolm Hayes, *Anton von Webern* (Phaidon). Not as well known as Schönberg, or as successful as Berg, Webern is seen by some as a progressive, and accused by others of being a Nazi sympathizer. Hayes, understandably, sits on the fence.

Alma Mahler-Werfel, *Diaries 1896–1902* (Faber). Gushingly frank diaries of a supremely attractive young woman, courted by the likes of Klimt and Zemlinsky. The period covered tracks Alma until shortly after her marriage to the composer, Gustav Mahler.

Donald Mitchell, *Gustav Mahler* (Faber; University of California Press). Mitchell's three-volume life of Mahler is a benchmark biography, as dense and wide-ranging as one of its subject's colossal symphonies.

Elizabeth Norman McKay, *Franz Schubert: A Biography* (Clarendon Press). Straightforward biography of Schubert, which does the best it can to unravel the composer's brief life from the limited source material available.

H.C. Robbins Landon, *Mozart, the Golden Years 1781–1791* (Thames & Hudson; Macmillan). Big illustrated romp through the composer's mature, Vienna years; a mixture of biography and musicology.

FREUD

Frederick C. Crews (ed), *Unauthorized Freud* (Penguin). Crews is virulently against psychoanalysis and has gathered together a whole host of Freud critics to put forward the revisionist case.

Sigmund Freud (ed. Peter Gay), *The Freud Reader* (Vintage;WW Norton). A comprehensive selection of Freud's writings on art, literature and religion as well as the usual dreams and sexuality. Spans his entire career with useful introduction.

Peter Gay, *Freud* (Papermac;WW Norton). Big tome, a healthy mixture of biography and philosophy, with a bit of spicy drama for good measure.

Michael Jacobs, *Sigmund Freud* (Sage, UK). Brief biography of the bearded one, a quick trot through his ideas and the subsequent criticisms thereof.

Ernest Jones, *Life and Work of Sigmund Freud* (Basic Books). Abridged version of the definitive three-volume biography that Jones – one of Freud's disciples – published in the 1950s just before he died.

WIESENTHAL

Alan Levy, *The Wiesenthal File* (Constable, UK). Thoroughly entertaining account of the controversial Vienna-based Nazi-hunter and the various Nazis he has helped to pursue, plus an account of the Waldheim affair.

Hella Pick, *Wiesenthal* (Phoenix; Northeastern UP). The most recent of the Wiesenthal biographies, made with the subject's co-operation. In tracking his wartime sufferings and cataloguing his postwar activities, Pick is sympathetic yet objective, and gives a rare glimpse into the octogenarian Nazi-hunter's personal life.

WITTGENSTEIN

Kimberley Cornish, *The Jew of Linz: Hitler, Wittgenstein and their Secret Battle for the*

Mind (Arrow). Utterly wacky book that in effect blames "complex, prickly" Wittgenstein for turning his schoolmate Hitler into an anti-Semite. The philosopher then recruited Kim Philby and his circle for the Russians, to make up for his role in precipitating the Holocaust. The author appears to be serious.

John Heaton & Judy Groves, *Wittgenstein for Beginners* (Icon Books). Even this accessible, irreverent series fails to shed much light on the great philosopher's complex thinking.

Ray Monk, *Ludwig Wittgenstein: The Duty of Genius* (Vintage;Viking Penguin). Exhaustive biography of the perplexing philosopher; a model of its kind, Monk's book interweaves Wittgenstein's life and thought into an inseparable entity.

AUSTRIAN FICTION AND POETRY

Ingeborg Bachmann, *Songs in Flight* (Marsilio), *The Thirtieth Year* (Holmes & Meier). An acclaimed poet, novelist and short story writer from the 1950s, Bachmann was fascinated by the impotence of language and developed a voice of her own. For a flavour of her work, try the bilingual edition of her poems, *Songs in Flight*.

Thomas Bernhard, *Cutting Timber* (Vintage;Quartet), *Wittgenstein's Nephew* (University of Chicago), *Extinction* (Penguin/University of Chicago), *Concrete* (University of Chicago) and *The Voice Imitator* (University of Chicago). Dense, stream-of-consciousness ruminations from the leading critic of the hypocrisy and mediocrity of postwar Austria. Any of the above will prove to be a good introduction to his inimitable style.

Hermann Broch, *The Death of Virgil* (Vintage); *The Guiltless* (Marlboro). With the Anschluss, Broch, who was of Jewish parentage, was briefly interned in a camp, where he began *The Death of Virgil*, which focuses on the last hours of Virgil's life and his questioning of the role his art has given him in society. *The Guiltless* is a more direct and readable examination of the dark side of mid-twentieth-century German culture.

Lilian Faschinger, *Vienna Passion* (Headline). A complex tale whose black New Yorker heroine, researching into Anna Freud in Vienna, comes across the fascinating story of Rosa

Havelka, servant to the empress and mistress to the heir to the throne at the end of the nineteenth century.

Elfriede Jelinek, *Wonderful, Wonderful Times, The Piano Teacher* and *Lust* (all Serpent's Tail). From one of the best writers to come out of Austria for some time, *The Piano Teacher* is an unsentimental look at Vienna from a woman's perspective, while *Wonderful Wonderful Times*, which takes place in the late 1950s, digs up the city's murky past. *Lust* takes a dark and disturbing look at small-town life in the Austrian provinces.

Robert Musil, *The Man Without Qualities* (Picador;Vintage); *Diaries 1899-1941* (Harper Collins;Basic Books). Often compared with Joyce and Proust's great works, Musil's 1000-page unfinished novel, *The Man Without Qualities* takes place at the twilight of the Habsburg Empire. This translation, by Sophie Wilkins includes a massive amount of material that has never appeared in English before; unfortunately the UK paperback reprint omits this text in order to squeeze the novel into a single volume – so if UK readers want to read the whole thing, they have to hunt out the two-volume hardback. Those addicted to Musil's irony-drenched, essayistic prose should also dip into his diaries.

Josef Roth, *Radetsky March* (Penguin Overlook Press). Pitifully underrated, this is Roth's finest work – a nostalgic and melancholic portrait of the moribund Vienna of Franz-Josef. Check also the secondhand stores for Roth's masterful short novels *Job, The Emperor's Tomb* and – above all – *Flight Without End*, a heartbreaking tale of dislocation and world-weariness.

Arthur Schnitzler, *Hands Around* (Dover, UK); *Dream Story* (Penguin). Schnitzler's play features ten seductions, each of which shares at least one character with the next one until the circle is complete. A classic portrayal of Viennese fin-de-siècle society, it came back to prominence in the 1950s after being filmed as *La Ronde* by Max Ophüls, and enjoyed a come back in the late 1990s on the stage in an adaptation called *The Blue Room* by David Hare. *Dream Story* was the inspiration for Stanley Kubrick's last film *Eyes Wide Shut*.

Harold B. Segel (ed), *The Vienna Coffeehouse Wits 1890–1938* (Purdue UP). A rare opportuni ty to read translated snippets of work by *Kaffeehaus* regulars such as Karl Kraus, Peter Altenberg and Felix Salten (the little-known author of *Bambi* and *The Story of a Vienna Whore*, one of which was made into a Disney cartoon).

Stefan Zweig, *The Burning Secret and Other Stories* (Penguin). Exquisitely wrought tales from fin-de-siècle Vienna, including *Letter from an Unknown Woman*, best and most poignant of Zweig's tales.

ART AND ARCHITECTURE

Alessandra Comini, *Egon Schiele* (Thames and Hudson). Contains a good selection of full colour reproductions as well as an account of his life set into its cultural context.

Gabriele Fahr-Becker, *Wiener Werkstätte 1903–1932* (Taschen) and *Hundertwasser* (Taschen). Two definitive and copiously illustrated volumes, the first showing in colour and in black and white the enormous breadth of WW's output, and the second taking a close look at Hundertwasser's later ventures into architecture.

Benedetto Gravagnolo, *Adolf Loos* (Art Data). A wonderfully illustrated book for the general reader, covering the life and works of the "father of modernism".

Peter Haiko and Roberto Schezen, *Vienna 1850–1930 Architecture* (Rizzoli). The ultimate coffee-table book on Vienna's most important works of architecture, beautifully photographed (by Schezen) and intelligently discussed.

Ingrid Helsing Almaas, *Vienna: A Guide to Recent Architecture* (Ellipsis;Könemann). Dinky illustrated pocket guide to Vienna's modern architecture of the last couple of decades, with forthright accompanying critiques and interviews.

Robert Lustenberger, *Adolf Loos* (Birkhauser o/p). One of the Studio Paperback series, cheaper than Schezen's (see below), with more text but black-and-white photos only.

Erwin Mitsch, *Egon Schiele* (Phaidon). Nicely produced, with a short introduction, then eighty colour plates and eighty more black-and-white photos.

Gilles Néret, *Klimt* (Taschen). Good-value A4-format book, with a fair sprinkling of colour and black-and-white photos, and a succinct text outlining Gustav Klimt's artistic development.

Rolf Toman (ed), *Vienna Art and Architecture* (Könemann). A huge coffee-table volume covering the city from the Middle Ages to the present day, with lots of colour illustrations, accompanied by lots of informative text.

Peter Vergo, *Art in Vienna 1898-1918* (Phaidon). Deals with the major artists of the Secession, including Klimt, Kokoscka and Schiele, and the development of the Wiener Werkstätte.

Alfred Weidinger, *Kokoschka and Alma Mahler: Testimony to a Passionate Relationship* (Prestel Verlag, available in UK). Detailed account of the artist's doomed relationship with Mahler's widow, illustrated with lots of Kokoschka's drawings and paintings from the period.

Patrick Werkner, *Austrian Expressionism: The Formative Years* (University of Washington Press). Interesting articles on Schönberg, Schiele, Kokoschka, Gerstl and Kubin; black-and-white illustrations only.

MISCELLANEOUS

Philip Blom, *The Wines of Austria* (Faber). All you need to know about regions, growers and grapes with recommendations if you can't decide which to quaff.

Cecil Davies, *Mountain Walking in Austria* (Cicerone Press, UK). Includes a description of a route to the Grossglockner's summit via the *Stüdl* and *Erzherzog-Johann* huts – for experienced and well-equipped walkers – as well as some day-walks in the neighbouring Granatspitz group.

Danube Bike Trail, (Esterbauer Verlag). A detailed guide from Passau to Vienna, covering 350 kilometres - excellent maps.

Dave Gosney, *Finding Birds in Eastern Austria* (Gostours). Precise details on where to find the feathered ones in and around the Neusiedler See in Burgenland, which is home to, among others, the great bustard.

Allan Hartley, *Hut to Hut in the Stubai Alps* (Cicerone Press, UK). Walks you through this region of the Tyrol, with magnificent glacier views along the way.

Jonathan Hurdle, *Walking Austria's Alps, Hut to Hut* (Cordee;The Mountaineers). Includes route information for a week's hut-to-hut tour of the Grossglockner, starting at Kaprun and ending at Kals am Grossglockner.

Kev Reynolds, *Walking in the Alps* (Cicerone Press;Interlink). Provides detailed route information on the Grossglockner and numerous other Austrian ranges, in clear and authoritative prose.

LANGUAGE

Although a high proportion of Austrians speak some English, any attempts at learning a few phrases of German will be heartily appreciated. That said, German is a highly complex language which you can't hope to master quickly. The biggest problem for English-speakers is that German words can be one of three genders: masculine, feminine or neuter. Each has its own ending and a corresponding ending for any attached adjectives, plus its own definite article.

PRONUNCIATION

Pronunciation (and spelling) is less of a problem, as individual syllables are generally pronounced as they're printed – the trick is learning how to place the stresses in the notoriously lengthy German words. Though Austrians speak German with a distinct accent, and each region has its own dialect, when speaking to a foreigner most folk will switch to standard German.

The following is a rundown of the basics you'll need on a short holiday to Austria. For more detail, check out the *Rough Guide German Phrasebook*, set out dictionary-style for easy access, with English–German and German–English sections, cultural tips for tricky situations and a menu reader.

VOWELS AND UMLAUTS

a as in r**a**ther

e as in g**ay**

i as in f**ee**t

o as in n**o**se

u as in b**oo**t

ä is a combination of a and e, sometimes pronounced like **e** in b**e**t (eg *Länder*) and sometimes like **ai** in p**ai**d (eg *spät*).

ö is a combination of o and e which has no real English equivalent, but is similar to the French *eu*

ü is a combination of u and e, like bl**ue**

VOWEL COMBINATIONS

ai as in wh**y**

au as in m**ou**se

ie as in tr**ee**

ei as in tr**i**al

eu as in b**oi**l

CONSONANTS

Consonants are pronounced as they are written, with no silent letters. The differences from English are:

j pronounced similar to an English y

r is given a dry throaty sound, similar to French

s pronounced similar to, but slightly softer than, an English z

v pronounced somewhere between f and v

w pronounced same way as English v

z pronounced ts

The German letter **ß** often replaces **ss** in a word: pronunciation is identical.

CONSONANT COMBINATIONS

ch is a strong back-of-the-throat sound, as in the Scottish loch

sp (at the start of a word) is pronounced shp

st (at the start of a word) is pronounced sht

GERMAN WORDS AND PHRASES

BASICS

Ja, Nein	Yes, no	*Gross, Klein*	Large, small
Bitte	Please or You're welcome	*Mehr, Weniger*	More, less
Bitte schön	A more polite form of *Bitte*	*Wenig*	A little
Danke, Danke schön	Thank you, Thank you very much	*Viel*	A lot
		Billig, Teuer	Cheap, expensive
Wo, Wann, Warum?	Where, when, why?	*Gut, Schlecht*	Good, bad
Wieviel?	How much?	*Heiss, Kalt*	Hot, cold
Hier, Da	Here, there	*Mit, Ohne*	With, without
Geöffnet, Offen, Auf	All mean "open"	*Rechts*	Right
Geschlossen, Zu	Both mean "closed"	*Links*	Left
Da drüben	Over there	*Geradeaus*	Straight ahead
Dieses	This one	*Geh weg*	Go away
Jenes	That one		

GREETINGS AND TIMES

Grüss Gott	Good day	*Übermorgen*	The day after tomorrow
Servus	Hi! or Goodbye (informal)		
Guten Morgen	Good morning	*Tag*	Day
Guten Abend	Good evening	*Nacht*	Night
Gute Nacht	Good night	*Mittag*	Midday
Auf Wiedersehen	Goodbye	*Mitternacht*	Midnight
Auf Wiederhören	Goodbye (on the telephone)	*Woche*	Week
Tschüss	Goodbye (informal)	*Wochenende*	Weekend
Wie geht es Ihnen?	How are you? (polite)	*Monat*	Month
Wie geht es dir?	How are you? (informal)	*Jahr*	Year
Heute	Today	*Am Vormittag/Vormittags*	In the morning
Gestern	Yesterday	*Am Nachmittag/Nachmittags*	In the afternoon
Morgen	Tomorrow		
Vorgestern	The day before yesterday	*Am Abend*	In the evening

DAYS, MONTHS AND DATES

Montag	Monday	*Juli*	July
Dienstag	Tuesday	*August*	August
Mittwoch	Wednesday	*September*	September
Donnerstag	Thursday	*Oktober*	October
Freitag	Friday	*November*	November
Samstag	Saturday	*Dezember*	December
Sonntag	Sunday	*Frühling*	Spring
		Sommer	Summer
Ferien	Holidays	*Herbst*	Autumn
Feiertag	Public holiday	*Winter*	Winter
Jänner	January		
Februar	February	*Montag, der erste April*	Monday, the first of April
März	March		
April	April	*Der zweite April*	The second of April
Mai	May	*Der dritte April*	The third of April
Juni	June		

SOME SIGNS

Damen/Frauen	Women's toilets	*Notausgang*	Emergency exit
Herren/Männer	Men's toilets	*Krankenhaus*	Hospital
Eingang	Entrance	*Polizei*	Police
Ausgang	Exit	*Nicht rauchen*	No smoking
Ankunft	Arrival	*Kein Eingang*	No entrance
Abfahrt	Departure	*Drücken*	Push
Ausstellung	Exhibition	*Ziehen*	Pull
Autobahn	Motorway	*Frei*	Vacant
Umleitung	Diversion	*Besetzt*	Occupied
Achtung!	Attention!	*Verboten*	Prohibited
Vorsicht!	Beware!	*Kasse*	Cash desk/ticket office
Not	Emergency		

QUESTIONS AND REQUESTS

All enquiries should start with the phrase *Entschuldigen Sie bitte* (Excuse me, please). Though strictly you should use *Sie*, the polite form of address, with everyone except close friends, young people often don't bother with it. However, the older generation and anyone official will certainly be offended if you address them with the familiar *Du*.

Sprechen Sie Englisch?	Do you speak English?	*Ist der Tisch frei?*	Is that table free?
Ich spreche kein Deutsch	I don't speak German	*Die Speisekarte bitte*	The menu please
Sprechen Sie bitte langsamer	Please speak more slowly	*Fräulein . . . !*	Waitress . . . ! (for attention)
Ich verstehe nicht	I don't understand	*Herr Ober . . . !*	Waiter . . . ! (for attention)
Ich verstehe	I understand		
Wie sagt mann das auf Deutsch?	How do you say that in German?	*Haben Sie etwas billigeres?*	Have you got something cheaper?
Können Sie mir sagen wo . . . ist?	Can you tell me where . . . is?	*Haben Sie Zimmer frei?*	Are there rooms available?
Wo ist . . . ?	Where is . . . ?	*Wo sind die Toiletten bitte?*	Where are the toilets please?
Wieviel kostet das?	How much does that cost?	*Ich hätte gern dieses*	I'd like that one
Wann fährt der nächste Zug?	When does the next train leave?	*Ich hätte gern ein Zimmer für zwei*	I'd like a room for two
Um wieviel Uhr?	At what time?	*Ich hätte gern ein Einzelzimmer*	I'd like a single room
Wieviel Uhr ist es?	What time is it?		
Sind die Plätze noch frei?	Are these seats taken?	*Hat es Dusche, Bad, Toilette?*	Does it have a shower, bath, toilet?
Die Rechnung bitte	The bill please		

NUMBERS

0	*null*	13	*dreizehn*	60	*sechzig*
1	*eins*	14	*vierzehn*	70	*siebzig*
2	*zwei*	15	*fünfzehn*	80	*achtzig*
3	*drei*	16	*sechszehn*	90	*neunzig*
4	*vier*	17	*siebzehn*	100	*hundert*
5	*fünf*	18	*achtzehn*	1000	*tausend*
6	*sechs*	19	*neunzehn*	1998	*neunzehn-hundert-acht-und-neunzig*
7	*sieben*	20	*zwanzig*		
8	*acht*	21	*ein-und-zwanzig*	1999	*neunzehn-hundert-neun-und-neunzig*
9	*neun*	22	*zwei-und-zwanzig*		
10	*zehn*	30	*dreissig*	2000	*zweitausand*
11	*elf*	40	*vierzig*	2001	*zweitausand-und-eins*
12	*zwölf*	50	*fünfzig*		

GLOSSARY

GERMAN TERMS

Abtei Abbey.

Alm High alpine pasture, meadow.

Ausstellung Exhibition.

Bach Stream.

Bad Spa, bath.

Bahnhof Station.

Bau Building.

Bauernhof Farmhouse.

Beisl Pub.

Berg Mountain, hill.

Bezirk City district.

Brücke Bridge.

Brünn Brno, capital of Moravia (Czech Republic).

Brunnen Fountain.

Burg Castle.

Buschenschank Wine-tavern (see also *Heuriger*).

Bushaltestelle Bus stop.

Denkmal Memorial.

Dom Cathedral.

Donau River Danube.

Dorf Village.

Durchgang Passageway.

Durchhaus Literally a "through-house" – a house whose ground floor is open, allowing access to a street or courtyard.

Einbahnstrasse One-way street.

Erzherzog Archduke.

Fasching Carnival.

Feiertag Holiday.

Flughafen Airport.

Freibad Outdoor swimming pool.

Friedhof Cemetery.

Fussgängerzone Pedestrian zone.

Gasse Alley.

Gehweg Footpath.

Gemälde Painting.

Gemeindeamt Local council offices.

Gemütlich Snug or cosy.

Gletscher Glacier.

Grab Grave.

Gürtel Vienna's outer ring road.

Hallenbad Indoor swimming pool.

Haltestelle Bus/tram stop.

Haus House.

Herzog Duke.

Heuriger Wine-tavern.

Hof Court, courtyard, mansion, housing complex.

Horn Peak.

Hütte Hut, mountain refuge.

Innere Stadt Inner city.

Jugendgästehaus Youth hostel.

Jugendherberge Youth hostel.

Kaffeehaus Café.

Kaiser Emperor.

Kapelle Chapel.

Kärnten Carinthia.

Kaserne Barracks.

Keller Cellar.

Kino Cinema.

Kirche Church.

Kloster Monastery, convent.

König King.

Krippe Crib, Nativity scene.

Kunst Art.

Kunst- und Wunderkammer Cabinet of curios.

Kurort Health resort.

Laibach Ljubljana, capital of Slovenia.

Land (pl *Länder*) Name given to each of the nine federal provinces of Austria.

Langlauf Cross-country skiing.

Loipe Prepared track for cross-country skiing.

Niederösterreich Lower Austria.

Not Emergency.

Oberösterreich Upper Austria.

Palast Palace.

Pfad Path.

Platz Square.

Pressburg Bratislava, capital of Slovakia.

Prinz Prince.

Prunkräume Ceremonial or state rooms in a palace or castle.

Quelle Spring.

Rathaus Town hall.

Reich Empire.

Residenz Palace.

Ring Inner-city ring road, such as the Ringstrasse in Vienna.

Ritter Knight.

Rodelbahn Toboggan run.

Rollstuhl Wheelchair.

Saal Hall.

Sammlung Collection.

Säule Column.

Schanigarten Summer terrace/back yard.

Schatzkammer Treasury.

Schloss Castle.

Schlucht Gorge.

See Lake.

Seilbahn Cable car.

Sesselbahn Chairlift.

Speicher Reservoir.

Spitze Peak.

Stadel, or **Stadl** Barn or stable.

Stadt Town.

Stau Dam.

Stausee Reservoir.

Steiermark Styria.

Stift Collegiate church.

Strand Beach, shore.

Strandbad (pl *Strandbäder*) Outdoor bathing area on a lake or river.

Strasse Street.

Streichelzoo Children's zoo (farm animals and so on).

Tal Valley.

Talsperre Dam.

Tierpark Zoo or wildlife park.

Tor Gate.

Trakt Wing (of a building).

Turm Tower.

Venedig Venice.

Viertel Quarter, district.

Volk People, folk.

Vororte The outer suburbs of Vienna which lie beyond the Gürtel: the tenth to twenty-second districts of the city.

Vorstädte The inner suburbs of Vienna which lie between the Ring and the Gürtel: the third to ninth districts of the city.

Wald Forest.

Wasserfall Waterfall.

Wien Vienna.

Zimmer Room.

POLITICAL TERMS AND ACRONYMS

Anschluss Literally a "joining together" or "union" – the euphemism coined by the Nazis for the invasion and annexation of Austria in March 1938.

Austro-fascism Term to describe the one-party state set up by Engelbert Dollfuss in 1934. Dollfuss headed the Fatherland Front (see VF), a non-Nazi clerical-fascist movement that lasted until the Anschluss in 1938.

Austro-Marxism Philosophy expounded by SDAP theorists such as Otto Bauer in the early twentieth century. While still adhering to the language of class war, its programme was essentially revisionist, arguing that the downfall of capitalism was inevitable and didn't have to be brought about by violence.

Babenbergs Dynasty who ruled over Austria from 976 to 1246.

Biedermeier The term (*Bieder* means "upright") derives from the satiric figure of Gottlieb Biedermeier, a Swabian schoolmaster created in 1850 by Ludwig Eichrocht, modelled on Eichrocht's own pious, law-abiding teacher in Baden-Baden, Samuel Sauter. It has been applied retrospectively to the period between 1815 and 1848 when Austria was under the sway of Prince Metternich. The era came to symbolize a safe, bourgeois, cosy lifestyle, and was applied to the history, art and culture of the period.

CSP (Christlichsoziale Partei) The Christian Social Party was founded in the 1890s by Karl Lueger, who later became mayor of Vienna. The Christian Socials' combination of Catholicism, municipal socialism and anti-Semitism proved popular with the Austrians. They were the main party of government in the 1920s and from their ranks rose Engelbert Dollfuss, who later introduced Austro-fascism in 1933.

FPÖ (Freiheitliche Partei Österreichs) The Austrian Freedom Party was the successor to the postwar VdU (see below). A far-right party who rose to prominence in the 1980s and scored spectacular electoral success under the charismatic and controversial leadership of Jörg Haider.

Habsburg Royal dynasty whose powerbase was Austria from 1273 to 1918. Successive generations also held the office of Holy Roman Emperor from 1452 to 1806, and by marriage, war and diplomacy acquired territories across Europe.

Heimwehr Right-wing militia whose origins lay in the local armed groups formed after the collapse of the empire in 1918. After 1927, these regional militias joined together and created a political wing, the *Heimatblock*, which supported the onset of Austro-fascism in 1933.

Holy Roman Empire Revived title of the Roman Empire first bestowed by the pope on Charlemagne in 800. The emperor was chosen by the seven electors, and the title was passed around between the Hohenstaufen, Luxembourg and Habsburg families until 1438, when the Habsburgs made it hereditary. It was dissolved on the orders of Napoleon in 1806.

Josephine Of or pertaining to the reign of Emperor Josef II (1780–1790).

KPÖ (Kommunistische Partei Österreichs) Austrian Communist Party.

Kristallnacht Literally "Crystal Night", after the broken glass that was strewn across the streets during the pogrom of November 9–10, 1938. On this one night the majority of Jewish shops and institutions in the Third Reich – and all but one of the synagogues in Vienna – were destroyed by the Nazis.

k.u.k. *kaiserlich und königlich* (imperial and royal) – a title used after 1867 to refer to everything in the Austro-Hungarian empire. Everything within Hungary was prefaced with a "k." for *königlich*, everything in the rest of the empire "k.k." (*kaiserlich-königlich*; imperial-royal).

NSDAP (National Sozialistische Deutsche Arbeiterpartei) National Socialist German Workers' Party, the official name for the German Nazi Party.

ÖVP (Österreichische Volkspartei) Austrian People's Party, the main descendant of the Christian Socials, and the principal postwar centre-right party.

Pan-German This adjective covers a whole range of far-right political parties, who advocated Anschluss with Germany, many of whom came together in the 1920s under the banner of the Greater German People's Party (Grossdeutsche Volkspartei, GDVP).

Red Vienna The period of Socialist municipal government in Vienna which lasted from 1919 to 1934.

Schutzbund SDAP militia founded in 1923.

Schütze The "Tyrolean riflemen", territorial defence units that were used in Andreas Hofer's rebellion against the Tyrol's Franco-Bavarian overlords in 1809.

SDAP (Sozial-Demokratische Arbeiterpartei) Social Democratic Workers' Party, the name given to the Socialist Party, prior to World War II.

SPÖ (Sozialistische Partei Österreichs) The postwar Austrian Socialist Party, later changed to the Sozialdemokratische Partei Österreichs, but keeping the same acronym.

Staatsvertrag The Austrian State Treaty of 1955, which signalled the withdrawal of Allied troops – American, British, French and Soviet – from Austria, in return for Austrian neutrality.

Toleranzpatent The Patent of Tolerance decreed by Josef II in 1782, which allowed freedom of religious observance to Lutherans, Jews and, to a lesser extent, Protestants.

VdU (Verband der Unabhängigen) Union of Independents. Extreme nationalist party formed in 1949 and precursor of the FPÖ.

VF (Vaterländische Front) The Fatherland Front were founded in 1934 by Engelbert Dollfuss, the Christian Social Austrian chancellor who dissolved parliament and introduced Austro-fascism in 1933. The Front was a patriotic, clerico-fascist organization aimed at preventing the Nazis from seizing power.

ART AND ARCHITECTURAL TERMS

Ambulatory Passage round the back of a church altar, in continuation of the aisles.

Art Nouveau Sinuous and stylized form of architecture and decorative arts from the 1890s, known as Secession or Jugendstil in Austria.

Atlantes Pillars in the shape of musclemen, named after the Greek god Atlas, whose job it was to hold up the world.

Baldachin A canopy over an altar, tomb, throne or otherwise.

Baroque Expansive, exuberant architectural and sculptural style of the seventeenth and eighteenth centuries, characterized by ornate decoration, complex spatial arrangement and grand vistas.

Biedermeier Simple, often Neoclassical, style of art and architecture popular from 1815 to

1848 (see under "Political terms", p.85) and in part a reaction against the excesses of the Baroque period.

Caryatid Sculptured female figure used as a column. Similar to Atlantes (see opposite).

Chancel Part of the church where the main altar is placed, usually at the east end.

Chinoiserie Decorative style drawing on Chinese art and themes.

Diapers Ornamental patterning in brickwork.

Empire Neoclassical style of architecture and decorative arts practised in the first half of the nineteenth century.

Filigree Fanciful delicate ornamental decoration in metal or stone.

Fresco Painting applied to wet plaster, so that the colours immediately soak into the wall.

Glacis Sloping ground outside the outer fortifications of a city.

Gothic Architectural style prevalent from the twelfth to the sixteenth centuries, characterized by pointed arches and ribbed vaulting.

Historicism Style of architecture which apes previous styles – ie neo-Baroque, neo-Renaissance, neo-Gothic.

Jugendstil German/Austrian version of Art Nouveau, literally "youthful style" (see also "Secession" below).

Lierne A short rib that connects the main ribs of a vaulted ceiling.

Loggia Covered area on the side of a building, usually arcaded.

Lunette An oval or semicircular opening to admit light into a dome.

Nave Main body of a church, usually stretching from the western end to the chancel.

Neoclassicism Late-eighteenth- and early-nineteenth-century style of architecture and design returning to classical Greek and Roman models as a reaction against the excess of Baroque and Rococo.

Oriel A bay window, usually projecting from an upper floor.

Quoins External cornerstones of a wall.

Ringstrasse Pompous, historicist (see above) style of architecture imitating Gothic, Renaissance, Baroque and Classical architecture, used to describe the buildings that line Vienna's Ringstrasse.

Rococo Florid, ornamental style of architecture and design, forming the last phase of Baroque.

Romanesque Solid architectural style of the late tenth to thirteenth centuries, characterized by round-headed arches and geometrical precision.

Secession Movement of artists who split (seceded – hence the term) from the city's Academy of Arts in 1897. Also used more generally as a term synonymous with Jugendstil.

Sgraffito Monochrome plaster decoration effected by means of scraping back the first white layer to reveal the black underneath.

Spandrel The surface area between two adjacent arches.

Stucco Plaster used for decorative effects.

Transepts The wings of a cruciform church, placed at right angles to the nave and chancel.

Trompe l'oeil Painting designed to fool the onlooker into thinking that it is three-dimensional.

Wiener Werkstätte (Vienna Workshops) A group of Secession artists founded in 1903.

INDEX

Stay in touch with us!

ROUGHNEWS is Rough Guides' free newsletter. In three issues a year we give you news, travel issues, music reviews, readers' letters and the latest dispatches from authors on the road.

España
THE ROUGH GUIDE TO
Andalucía
Spain
THE ROUGH GUIDE TO
Spain
Mark Ellingham and
THE ROUGH GUIDE TO
Barcelona
THE ROUGH GUIDE TO
Mallorca
Madrid
MINI ROUGH GUIDE
Simon Baskett
THE MINI ROUGH GUIDE TO
Tenerife
Christian Williams

ROUGH GUIDES: Mini Guides, Travel Specials and Phrasebooks

MINI GUIDES

Antigua
Bangkok
Barbados
Beijing
Big Island of Hawaii
Boston
Brussels
Budapest
Cape Town
Copenhagen
Dublin
Edinburgh

Florence
Honolulu
Ibiza & Formentera
Jerusalem
Las Vegas
Lisbon
London Restaurants
Madeira
Madrid
Malta & Gozo
Maui
Melbourne
Menorca

Montreal
New Orleans

Paris
Rome
Seattle
St Lucia
Sydney
Tenerife
Tokyo
Toronto
Vancouver

TRAVEL SPECIALS

First-Time Asia
First-Time Europe
Women Travel

PHRASEBOOKS

Czech
Dutch
Egyptian Arabic
European
French
German
Greek

Hindi & Urdu
Hungarian
Indonesian
Italian
Japanese
Mandarin
  Chinese
Mexican
  Spanish
Polish
Portuguese
Russian
Spanish
Swahili
Thai
Turkish
Vietnamese

ROUGH GUIDES:
Reference and Music CDs

REFERENCE

Blues:
  100 Essential CDs
Classical Music
Classical:
  100 Essential CDs
Country Music
Country:
  100 Essential CDs
Drum'n'bass
House Music
Hip Hop
Irish Music
Jazz

Music USA
Opera
Opera:
  100 Essential CDs
Reggae
Reggae:
  100 Essential CDs
Rock
Rock:
  100 Essential CDs

Soul:
  100 Essential CDs
Techno
World Music

World Music:
  100 Essential CDs
English Football
European Football
Internet
Money Online
Shopping Online
Travel Health

ROUGH GUIDE MUSIC CDs

Music of the Andes
Australian Aboriginal
Bluegrass
Brazilian Music
Cajun & Zydeco
Music of Cape Verde
Classic Jazz
Music of
  Colombia
Cuban Music
Eastern Europe

Music of Egypt
English Roots Music
Flamenco
Music of Greece
Hip Hop
India & Pakistan
Irish Music
Music of Jamaica
Music of Japan
Kenya & Tanzania
Marrabenta
  Mozambique
Native American
North African
Music of Portugal
Reggae
Salsa
Samba
Scottish Music
South African Music
Music of Spain
Sufi Music
Tango

Tex-Mex
West African Music
World Music
World Music Vol 2
Music of Zimbabwe

Kitzbuchel

1. Guest Card — how many
   - all lifts
   - other attr-ns

2. Swimming: Swartzsee
   - parking
   - fees
   - towels
   - changing rms

Salzburg

1. what's on tour
2. Parking — where
   — nicest
3. Salzburg card
   - museums

   - transport
   - other
   - near S-g ?

4 Sounds-of-Music tour
   - only f/ S-g ?
   - cost
   - times
   - is it incl. on their tour

Will you have enough stories to tell your grandchildren?

©2000 Yahoo! Inc.

Yahoo! Travel

DO YOU YAHOO!?